A
THESAURUS
OF
WORD ROOTS
OF THE
ENGLISH
LANGUAGE

Horace Gerald Danner, Ph.D.
and
Roger Noël, Ph.D.

Foreword by
Thomas J. Sienkewicz, Ph.D.
Capron Chair of Classics,
Monmouth College, Monmouth, Illinois

UNIVERSITY
PRESS OF
AMERICA

Lanham • New York • London

University Press of America®, Inc.
4720 Boston Way
Lanham, Maryland 20706

3 Henrietta Street
London WC2E 8LU England

Library of Congress Cataloging-in-Publication Data

Danner, Horace G.
A thesaurus of word roots of the English language / by Horace Gerald
Danner and Roger Noël ; foreword by Thomas J. Sienkewicz.
p.   cm.
Includes bibliographical references.
1. English language—Roots—Dictionaries.   2. English language—
Etymology—Dictionaries.   3. English language—Synonyms and
antonyms.   I. Noël, Roger, 1942–   .   II. Title.
PE1580.D36   1992   422'.03—dc20   92–9743 CIP

ISBN 0–8191–8666–X (cloth : alk. paper)

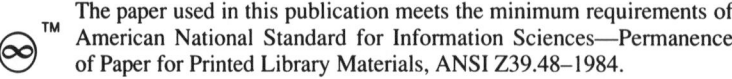

The paper used in this publication meets the minimum requirements of
American National Standard for Information Sciences—Permanence
of Paper for Printed Library Materials, ANSI Z39.48–1984.

> *Dr. Danner dedicates this book*
> *to his family*

> *Dr. Noël dedicates this book*
> *to Cookie*

iii

ACKNOWLEDGMENTS

Foremost, the authors wish to thank Craig A. Prall, who guided them in setting up the computer format of the book, and who remained in almost daily contact with Dr. Danner, giving him advice on the purchase and operation of compatible computer equipment and programs. As a computer engineer, Craig also performed each of the functions enumerated in the Colophon (see the end of book).

The authors are also grateful to Ms. Pamela Latt, Director of Student Services, Fairfax County Public Schools, Fairfax, Virginia. Ms. Latt speaks Polish as well as a number of other Slavic languages; as a linguist and as an educator, Ms. Latt made invaluable suggestions on the refinement of the book. The book is indeed a more effective educational tool because of her linguistic and pedagogical insights.*

Not only are the authors grateful to Dr. Thomas J. Sienkewicz for writing the Foreword, they are also indebted to him for suggesting improvements on the format. It was also Dr. Sienkewicz who brought the two authors together in their succession of collaborative efforts.

Appreciation is extended to Hugo De la Galvez Murillo and Herbert Rogers for editing the manuscript for readability, clarity, and for format consistency. From Bolivia, Mr. De la Galvez Murillo was one of Dr. Danner's most outstanding writing students at Montgomery College, Rockville, Maryland; Mr. Rogers, with the University Press of America, holds an M.A. in Spanish from the University of Mexico, Mexico City.

Elizabeth Wilson and Joe White, also Dr. Danner's former students, checked parts of the manuscript for readability and format consistency; their assistance in reacting to the manuscript from a student's point of view is greatly appreciated.

In addition, Frederick Klingener read the manuscript from a professional standpoint; both a linguist and an engineer, Mr. Klingener, with The MITRE Corporation, McLean, Virginia, holds an M.S. in Mechanical Engineering from Carnegie Institute of Technology, Pittsburgh, Pennsylvania.

Lastly, the authors are indebted to John O. Bell, President, Systems Services Company, Sterling, Virginia, who developed the hypertext version for IBM PCs and compatibles, and to Craig Prall, who developed the Macintosh HyperCard version. These instructional aids are available from Imprimis Publications, P. O. Box 2931, Reston, Virginia 22090.

*Ms. Latt's suggestions and assistance do not constitute an official endorsement of the book by Fairfax County Public Schools.

"Good words are worth much, and cost little."
George Herbert, *Jacula Prudentum*, 1640

This book is not a thesaurus in the common sense. Unlike the familiar collection of synonyms, this thesaurus gathers words with the same root rather than words with similar meaning. The title is appropriate, however, in an etymological sense, for *thesaurus* comes from the Greek word for "treasure chest." Just as the beautiful necklaces, rings and tiaras found inside a real treasure chest are themselves made from diamonds and sapphires and rubies, so, too, in a work of this sort, compound words are, like jewelry, shown to be manufactured from smaller gems called roots, prefixes, and suffixes.

Indeed, the focus of *A Thesaurus of Word Roots of the English Language* is not the simple, monosyllabic word, but the compound or polysyllabic word. The authors of this thesaurus have distinguished a variety of these word elements and have given them technical names, such as Simple Root, Prefixed Root, Leading Root Compound, and Trailing Root Compound. Do not be intimidated by these terms any more than you would be by different kinds of quartz or beryl or topaz. Rather learn to appraise these word elements and consider how they are joined to make different words just as a jeweler appraises and joins gems.

I first became aware of some of these gems in 1983, when I met Dr. Danner and became familiar with his little book *Words from the Romance Languages* (Manassas, Virginia: Imprimis Press, 1980). At that time, I was teaching a vocabulary-building course at Howard University in Washington, D.C., and was always searching for new ways to illustrate the use of Latin and Greek roots in English words. From the first I found Dr. Danner's method of teaching vocabulary by the use of word clusters quite effective; and I have continued to use the technique both at Howard University and, more recently, at Monmouth College in Illinois.

It was through this Monmouth connection that Dr. Danner began his successful collaboration with Dr. Roger Noël, who is professor of French and chair of the Department of Modern Foreign Languages at Monmouth College. Dr. Noël brings to this book a broad linguistic background. A native of Belgium, he is a polyglot with a solid foundation in the classical languages. These two professors bring together a breadth of linguistic experience that makes this *Thesaurus of Word Roots* an invaluable tool for all students of words.

Some of these students may want to recognize the differences between word elements such as the Latin prefix *de-*, down, from, completely, etc., and the Latin base *de*, god. Others may wish to consider more subtle features of language, such as the different meanings of *de-* in words like *deduce* (from), *declaim* (completely), *deceive* (pejorative). Indeed, even the most skilled crafter of words never ceases to marvel at words and to notice a new sheen or glimmer to a word or phrase seen many times before.

This thesaurus groups together words which, at first glance, appear to have little in common. For example, *monogamy* and *polygamy*, which have to do with "marriage," are listed with *gametangium* and *gametophyte*, which have to do with "plant reproduction." The word element uniting these words is Greek *gam*, marriage, which has been extended in scientific contexts to include various types of union and reproduction.

Certainly some of this information can be garnered from the etymologies traditionally marked by brackets in most dictionaries. A glance down the alphabetical listings of a dictionary suggests the links between words like *gametangium*, *gametophyte* and *gamophobia*, but how is one to recognize the relationship between *monogamy* and *gametangium* inasmuch as these words do not appear near each other in the dictionary? Unlike a dictionary, this thesaurus makes such links visible within a single entry.

The clustering together of words and phrases that have a common linguistic source reinforces such links between words. Thus, under the entry for *demon* (Greek) one moves from *demon* to *demoniac* to *demonolatry* to *demonophobia* to *pandemonium*; visual elements of these words enable readers to recognize verbal relationships. In other words, word morphology or form illustrates semantics or word meaning.

This emphasis on word clusters is one which the authors used with great success in their earlier book *An Introduction to an Academic Vocabulary*, (Lanham: UPA, 1990), which I recommend as a companion to this thesaurus. While the present work offers more reference features, the earlier volume is a workbook which encourages students to discover for themselves the meanings shared by various word clusters such as the following:

```
loquent
loquitor
loquacious
colloquy
colloquium
```

When words are grouped in this way, the reader readily recognizes the common root *loqu* and its meaning "to speak."

A modification of word clustering is employed in *A Thesaurus of Word Roots*. Thus, the term Leading Root Compound refers to an element which comes at the beginning of the word, while Trailing Root Compound identifies a root which follows another root. Such terminology emphasizes the location of a root within a word and leads the user of the thesaurus to think of word clusters. Thus, the Greek root *alg*, pain, feeling, appears as Leading Root Compound in words like *algedonic* and *algogenic* and as a Trailing Root Compound in words like *abdominalgia*, *adenalgia* and *neuralgia*. The following list of the derivatives of *alg* in which Leading Root Compound appears above the Trailing Root Compound illustrates such word clustering:

```
algedonic
algogenic
abdominalgia
adenalgia
neuralgia
```

There are several ways to take advantage of this book. One could start from a particular root like *dent*, tooth, and use the thesaurus to identify other words which come from this root. One could also use this thesaurus to discover the linguistic relatives of a particular word like *dentiloquy*, that is, *dent*, tooth, and *loqui*, to speak, and then glance through the entry under *dent*. Thus, one finds words such as *dental*, *denticle*, *edentate*, and *Dentyne* listed under *dent*. A standard dictionary would not provide such a broad range of references for *dentiloquy*. Thus, whether browsing through thesaurus entries or using the thesaurus as a dictionary supplement, one inevitably gains an increased awareness of words and an enlarged vocabulary.

Readers will find particularly useful several special features of *A Thesaurus of Word Roots*. Sections marked by NB help the reader avoid confusing words that look alike but which are unrelated. Thus, the entry under *dia-* cautions the reader not to link this prefix with *diamond* (actually derived from *adamant*, which means "unyielding" in Greek). Doublets or words which do not look alike but which have a common origin are also marked. Thus the entry under *dign* indicates that *dainty* and *dignity* are etymologically derived from the same word. Cross references like those among Latin *dic*, Latin *locu/loqu* and Greek *phas/phe* allow students to recognize that words like *dictation*, *locution*, and *aphasia* all have to do with "speaking." Other bonuses include the occasional addition of foreign words and phrases, such as the following under the entry for *dei*, Latin for god: *vaya con Dios* (Spanish), *adieu* (French) *adiós* (Spanish), and *actus Dei* (Latin). Other entries offer a wealth of information: under the heading for *do, dos, dot* (Greek for "gift"), one finds the proper names *Dorothy*, *Theodore*, and *Eudora*; the Greek mythical figure *Pandora*, and the placename *Eudora* in both Arkansas and Kansas.

A miser might wish to keep his vault closed, lest any small gem be lost. This treasury, however, is meant to be opened. Indeed, the more it is used, the more wealthy the user becomes. So I encourage you to take advantage of the riches the authors offer you in this thesaurus and to delve through its deepest recesses. You will be rewarded for your efforts with many good words worth much.

Thomas J. Sienkewicz
Capron Professor of Classics
Monmouth College
Monmouth, Illinois

There was a single reason for compiling this thesaurus: to provide a comprehensive, interdisciplinary list of word roots in the English language as well as examples of words from those roots. Most of the compilations of word roots already published give fewer than 100 roots; furthermore, of the roots given, usually only two or three examples of words derived from the individual roots are listed. In addition, some of these lists cover only a single discipline, for example, biology, chemistry, literature, mathematics, music, philosophy. Listing over 1,200 roots, this thesaurus is multidisciplinary, giving virtually all the major roots of all the disciplines. In addition, it lists as examples a wide range of words derived from these roots. The following paragraphs show how the thesaurus is organized for maximum benefit to the user.

Under the heading Element, the roots, as well as prefixes, are listed alphabetically; where the root has different forms, these are listed underneath the basic form. To the right of each element (whether root or prefix) in the same column, the frequency of that element is listed. This frequency is indicated by one, two, or three asterisks (* for *low*, ** for *medium*, and *** for *high*). The classifications of *low*, *medium*, and *high* are applicable for the general user. Life science and medical students may find categories that have been designated as *low* may in fact be of high frequency since the roots in this disciplines are mainly Greek, whereas the roots in the other disciplines are mainly Latin. Most authorities on linguistics agree that 75 percent of the English language consists of Latin. Since the number of medical roots is extensive, only those in general use are listed. A thesaurus of exclusively medical roots is now being prepared and will be published separately.

In the second column, From indicates the original language source of the root, i.e., Latin, Greek, Frankish, Germanic, English, Arabic, Sanskrit. Under the language source is listed the word from which the root is derived, as well as the original meaning, if it is different from the first one listed in the next column, Meaning. Also, in the From column, the Indo-European base and original meaning are listed (see discussion of the prototype Indo-European language later in this preface). In the Meaning column, the most common meanings of the root are listed, along with any extended meanings of the root as used in particular disciplines.

In the Examples column, the words from each root or prefix are categorized by linguistic forms, that is, the words of a family are categorized by Simple Root, Prefixed Root, Leading Root Compound, Trailing Root Compound, and other forms as explained in succeeding paragraphs.

The categories follow a paradigm, or model. First listed is Simple Root (the root itself together with basic suffixes); then, Prefixed Root (where the root being considered is preceded by a prefix, e.g., *prevent*, where *pre-* is the prefix and *vent*, come, is the root). Prefixes are those elements that change the meaning of the root, and are properly prepositions and adverbs in Greek or Latin. In this book, this policy has been followed; admittedly, the policy here is rather arbitrary for the sake of consistency. Some authorities regard prefixes as those elements that come invariably at the beginning of the word, for example, *auto*, self; *bi*, two; Greek *homo*, same (Latin *homo* means man); *hetero*, different. A root is variously defined: *Webster's New World Dictionary* defines a root as the fundamental element of a word or form, exclusive of all affixes (prefixes and suffixes) and inflectional phonetic changes (e.g., *-ed* of *waited*; *-er* of *prettier*). *American Heritage Dictionary* defines a root as a word or word element from which other words are formed.

In some cases, there is a category called Assimilated Prefixed Root. In linguistics, *to assimilate*, to make the same, is to change the last letter of the prefix to correspond to the first letter of the root, thus making the word easier to pronounce. For example, the word *assimilate* itself is an assimilated form. The prefix *as-* is an assimilation of *ad-*, to, toward, as in *address, adjective, administration*. In other cases, assimilations change the last letter of the prefix to a letter that is *not* the same as the first letter of the root, but to a letter that makes the word simply easier to pronounce, for example, *agnomen, ascend*. In this case, the change is more properly called a *variation*.

The next category in the paradigm is Leading Root Compound, where the root under consideration comes at the beginning of a word comprised of at least two roots, e.g., if the root under consideration is *cunei*, wedge, *cuneiform* is listed as Leading Root Compound, with *cunei* leading the compound, followed by *form*, form, shape; thus, *cuneiform* means in the shape of a wedge. Where there are different forms of the root, they are listed separately and are *italicized* at the beginning of the listing.

When necessary, there is also Prefixed Leading Root Compound, where the word consists of a prefix and two or more roots. In cases where the element under consideration is a prefix, and in cases where the number of prefixed compounds is small, the categories Prefixed Root and Prefixed Compound are combined into Prefixed Roots and Compounds.

The next category is Trailing Root Compound, where the root under consideration comes after another root, thus most likely at the end of the word. In cases where the root comes in the middle of two or more roots, the category is termed Embedded Root Compound. In this thesaurus, the embedded root is underlined.

Depending on the family, there may be additional categories. For example, there may be Elided Leading Root Compound, or Elided Trailing Root Compound; as a linguistics term, *elided* indicates the omission of beginning or ending letters. Another category is Disguised Root, indicating that the spelling of the root changed through centuries of use in locales apart from Greece and Rome. Although most words directly from Latin have remained intact or with slight modifications, many have been altered considerably as they passed into English through one of the Romance languages, in particular, French, Italian, Portuguese, and Spanish. Romanian, Catalan, and Provençal are also Romance languages, but their impact on English is minimal. Roots originally Greek were often modified as they passed into Latin, when Rome conquered Greece before the time of Christ.

There may also be Meshed Compounds, categorized as Meshed Leading Root Compound, or Meshed Trailing Root Compound; *meshed* indicates that the ending letter or letters of the prefix or leading root are the same as the first letter or letters of the next element. Most words in this category are those in which the meshed or overlapping letter is *o*.

In each of these categories, the element not under consideration as well as its meaning is listed in parentheses. For example, under the family *ped* (child), *pediatric* is listed as Leading Root Compound; consequently, *iatr* trails or follows *ped*. Therefore, after the entry *pediatric, pediatrics, pediatrician, (iatr,* healing) is listed after the entry. Only in cases where the root's meaning is obvious was the meaning not given. Different forms of the same word within a list are indicated by {curly brackets}. Not all dictionaries agree on derivative words; some dictionaries indicate those words placed within curly brackets as entries themselves.

In many examples, Synonyms of particular words are given. Where two or more sets of synonyms are applicable for the same word, these sets are numbered and separated with a semicolon, for example, **1**); **2**). There are often several synonyms for a single word; however, the authors have limited synonym listings in most cases to three items. This thesaurus does not attempt to differentiate these synonyms; that has been left to lexicographers, the makers and compilers of dictionaries.

There may also be indicated Doublets, where two words with different meanings and with different spellings were originally one word, e.g., *aptitude* and *attitude, cart* and *chart, chef* and *chief*, and *ease* and *adjacent*. The reason for their variance is that they entered English through different languages, or from the same language but at different stages of that language's development. In the thesaurus, doublets are joined by a colon, e.g., aptitude:attitude.

There may also be Cognates, where the element had a common origin with an element from a different language. It should be indicated here that English is only a small part of an extremely large prehistoric language family, which comparative linguists have called Indo-European. While there are no written records to document the existence of this common language, these linguists have been able to show this likelihood by comparing words with similar meanings and spellings in languages as diverse as English,

French, German, Greek, Irish, Latin, Russian, Spanish, and Sanskrit. For example, the cognate for English *brother* is *phrater* in Greek (although Greek has a more common term for brother--*adelphos*, as in Adelphi, Maryland; and Philadelphia, an ancient city in Lydia, as well as Philadelphia, Pennsylvania); *frater*, in Latin; *Bruder*, in German; *brat*, in Russian; *brothar*, in Gothic; *brathir*, in Old Irish; *brothir*, in Icelandic; *bhratar*, in Sanskrit; and *frère*, in French. The reader is advised to consult an encyclopedia article on Indo-European languages; *Webster's New World Dictionary* and *The American Heritage Dictionary* show the outline of the Indo-European family on the inside covers. In addition, *Webster's New World* does an excellent job of cross-referencing roots of the Indo-European family; *American Heritage* includes a treasury of Indo-European bases in its Appendix.

In many cases, Placenames have been included, e.g., there is Deovolente, Mississippi, listed under *Deo*, God, and *vol*, willing. *Deovolente* means God willing; one can only surmise the reasons for the name. Under *cur*, run, the reader will find Bon Secour, Alabama. *Secour* means literally to run under, but actually means "help"; thus, *Bon Secour* is translated Good help. Smackover, Arkansas, was named by the early French explorers *sumac covrir*, covered with sumac. Dozens of other towns in the United States have names derived ultimately from Latin, from one of the Romance languages or from Greek. In Alabama, there is a village called Onycha, Greek for fingernail; also in Alabama, there is Greek Demopolis, literally People City. In both Illinois and Missouri, there is Creve-Coeur, French for broken heart, but extended to mean "utter discouragement." In Texas, there is Corpus Christi, Latin for Body of Christ. In Ohio, there is Peninsula, almost an island; and in Maine, there is Presque Isle, French for almost an island. The reasons for these inland towns being so called are both interesting and colorful.

In some word families, there are also Latin Phrases, Latin Legal Phrases, Italian Music Terms, Greek Mythology, Roman Mythology, Constellations. There may be additional categories, peculiar to the particular word family; the reader will experience no difficulty in seeing the relationship of these categories.

In word families where a single word is used in more than one discipline, the word is listed in outline, e.g., absolute; under Interdisciplinary, the word's meanings in the different disciplines are given. This feature should prove especially beneficial to teachers in showing how words are used in disciplines other than their own. Teachers are encouraged to help their students see these relationships. It should be noted that only example words are given; there are many other words used across disciplines besides those so indicated.

The use of NB, from Latin *nota bene*, note well, indicates that the word listed, though spelled the same or similar to the root under consideration, does not belong in the family. For example, *diamond*, though beginning with the letters *dia*, is not derived from the Greek prefix *dia-*, across, through.

In cases where another root or roots have the same or a similar meaning, these are listed under Cross Reference. For example, Greek *thes*, to place, put, is cross-referenced to *pon, pos, theca*. There are also Root Notes in cases where the meaning of the root is different from the original meaning, or where there are interesting aspects to the background. For example, *aniso* is considered a root itself; however, *aniso* combines the prefix *an-*, not + *iso*, same. Consequently, the meaning of *aniso* is not the same, and can be found in *anisogamete, anisomerous, anisotropic*.

Different typefaces are used to alert the reader to certain features, e.g., *italics* are used to highlight foreign words and expressions not fully assimilated into English; narrow Helvetica is used to indicate the actual meaning of a root, as well as the translations of foreign words and phrases. In addition, narrow Helvetica is used to sequence entries within a single family; *italicized narrow Helvetica* indicates prefixes of words listed in the Examples section.

Where there are a large number of examples within a word family, these examples are separated and introduced with the beginning letters of the element, ending with the letter that is unique. The beginning have been cast in narrow Helvetica, for example, basa: basal; base: base; and basi: basic, basicity, basidium, basilar, basion, basis.

In many cases, the authors gove a short definition of the word or give explanatory notes. These definitions and notes are given for one of several reasons: to differentiate a particular word from a similar word; to give backgrounds of interesting words; or to break the simple listing of words. These definitions and explanatory notes should not be construed as comprehensive, but simply as notes of differentiations or as pointers to understanding. In no way does the thesaurus obviate the use of a dictionary; as Dr. Sienkewicz has noted in the Foreword, the thesaurus is a companion to a dictionary.

It should be stressed that this thesaurus is designed for a user to refer to when an unknown word of mainly Latin or Greek origin is encountered. By seeing other words in the same family, the user can better associate, and therefore, better remember the meaning of the root. Psychologists have indicated that when one associates an unfamiliar word with a familiar one, the learning is more permanent. The user may, however, wish to refer to Appendix B, Root Frequency List and note the high-frequency roots. The user would do well to memorize these roots and two or three illustrative words the user for each root. As an aid in memorization, users may wish to place these words on the front of an index card, listing the meaning of the root on the reverse side.

In the case of words comprised of two or more elements, users are encouraged to formulate their own definitions. To solidify the learning process, users should see if their definitions appear to fit the context of these particular words as the words are used in one's textbooks or in one's professional reading. Users may also wish to consult a dictionary to see how closely their own definitions match those of the dictionary. For some of the polysyllabic words, readers will find it necessary to consult an unabridged dictionary, such as *Webster's Third New International*. In other cases, readers will need to consult a medical, music, or law dictionary, or possibly some other specialized dictionary. All references consulted in compiling this thesaurus are listed at the end of the book under "Works Consulted."

Users are encouraged to write additional words in the blank space to the left of the word categories. The blank space can also be used for recording one's own definitions or for notes on particular words.

The thesaurus concludes with two indispensable features: the English to Roots Index (Appendix A), and the Root Frequency List (Appendix B). The Index lists each of the major meanings of a root and references them to the root in the thesaurus. For example, *good* is referenced to *bene* (Latin), *bon* (Latin), *eu* (Greek), *prob* (Latin); *water* is referenced to *aqua* (Latin), *hyd* (Greek), *lacu* (Latin), and *limn* (Latin). The advantage of this feature is that one can see the major word elements that produce a single concept in English.

By referring to the Root Frequency List, the user can locate all roots of a particular frequency in one place. This list compiles all roots in the thesaurus into three categories: High, Medium, and Low. These categories were indicated by asterisks within the thesaurus itself. Decisions as to placement of roots in a particular category are those of the authors and were based on two principles: the sheer number of words produced by a particular root, and the familiarity of the root. According to the first principle, most of the prefixes are included in the high-frequency category; according to the second principle, *foli*, leaf, for example, was included in the high-frequency category although the number of words derived from this root is comparatively small.

Users are encouraged to let the authors know of additional words that can be listed in subsequent editions of the thesaurus. Please send any comments and suggested additions or corrections to Dr. Horace G. Danner, P. O. Box 2931, Reston, Virginia 22090, or to Dr. Roger Noël, Chair, Department of Modern Foreign Languages, Georgia College, Milledgeville, Georgia 31061.

This book is being programmed for both IBM PC and Macintosh; additional information may be obtained from Imprimis Publications, P. O. Box 2931, Reston, Virginia 22090.

TABLE OF CONTENTS

A

Element	From	Meaning	Examples
a-			See *ab-* for *aversion*.
a-			See *ad-* for *abet, abeyance*.
a-			See *an-* for *atheist, atom*.
ab-,*** **abs-,** **a-**	Latin	away, off, from	PREFIXED ROOT AND COMPOUNDS:

a-: (before *m, s, v*)

man: amanuensis (one who writes for another, especially for one who is disabled) (*manus*, hand)

ment: ament (a person with a severe congenital mental deficiency; a mentally retarded person), amentia (mental retardation; compare *dementia*, under *ment* family) (from *mens*, mind)

sex: asexual (having no sex or sexual organs; sexless; designating or of reproduction without the union of male and female germ cells)

vers: aversion (see synonyms at *abhorrence*) (*vertere*, to turn)

vert: avert (literally, to turn away; **Synonyms:** prevent, preclude, obviate) (see *aversion*)

ab-:

dic: abdicate {abdication, abdicator} (*dicere*, to speak)

duc: abducent, abduct {abductor}, abduction (*ducere*, to lead)

err: aberrant {aberrance}, aberration (*errare*, to wander)

hor: (*horrere*, to shudder)

abhor (**Synonyms:** abominate, hate, detest)

abhorrence (**Synonyms:** aversion, antipathy, repugnance)

abhorrent (**Synonyms:** odious, detestable, obnoxious)

ject: abject {abjection, abjectly} (from *jacere*, to throw)

jur: abjure {abjuration, abjuratory, abjurer} (*jurare*, to swear)

lact: ablactation (the act or process of weaning) (*lact*, milk)

lat: (*lat*, past participle of *ferre*, to bear)

ablate (in *medicine*, to remove a part, especially by cutting)

ablative (the grammatical case in Latin, Sanskrit, and certain other languages expressing removal, deprivation, direction from, or manner, source, cause, agency, etc.)

[Some spacecraft use ablative shields to limit re-entry temperatures. These shields shed mass that "bears away" energy.]

lu: abluent, ablution, ablutionary (*luere*, to lave, wash)

neg: abnegate, abnegation (*negare*, to deny)

norm: abnormal, abnormity (*norma*, originally, a carpenter's square; a rule, pattern)

olish: abolish (**Synonyms:** exterminate, extirpate, eradicate) (*ab-* contrasts with *ad-*, to, toward, of *adolere*, to increase)

oma: abomasum (the fourth or digesting chamber of the stomach of a cud-chewing animal) (*omasum*, bullock's trip)

omin: abominate (to have feelings of hatred and disgust for; loathe; abhor), abomination (from *omen*)

orig: aboriginal, aborigines (the first or earliest known inhabitants of a region; natives; also, the native animals or plants of a region) (*oriri*, to arise)

1

Element	From	Meaning	Examples
ab- (cont'd)			ort: (from *oriri*, to arise)
			abort, abortive (**Synonyms:** futile, vain, fruitless)
			aborticide (destruction of the fetus in the womb; an abortifacient) (*cide*, kill)
			abortifacient (*facere*, to make, do)
			rad: abrade (to scrape or rub off; wear away by friction; erode) (*radere*, to scrape)
			ras: abrasion, abrasive (from *abrade*)
			re: abreact (in *psychoanalysis*, to relieve a repressed emotion by talking about it) (*re-*, again, prefixes *act*)
			rog: abrogate (see synonyms at *abolish*, above) {abrogable, abrogative} (*rogare*, to ask)
			rupt: (from *rumpere*, to break)
			abrupt (**Synonyms: 1)** steep, precipitous, sheer; **2)** sudden, precipitate, impetuous)
			abruption (the sudden breaking away of parts of a mass)
			scis: abscise (to separate by abscission), abscissa (see note under *sciss*), abscission (a cutting off, as by surgery; the normal separation of fruit, leaves, etc. from plants by the development of a thin layer of pithy cells at the base of their stems) (from *caedere*, to cut)
			solut: absolute (**Synonyms:** unqualified, utter, definite), absolution, absolutism, absolutist, absolutory (from *solvere*, to loosen)
			solv: absolve (**Synonyms:** acquit, exonerate, pardon) (see *absolute*)
			sorb: absorb [do not confuse with *adsorb*, "to collect (a gas, liquid, or dissolved substance) in condensed form on a surface"], absorbent, absorbed, absorbing (*sorbere*, to drink in; suck)
			sorp: absorption {absorptive, absorptivity} (from *absorb*)
			strict: abstrict, abstriction [in *botany*, the cutting off of spores from a spore-bearing branch by the formation of dividing tissues (septa), as in certain fungi] (from *stringere*, to bind, draw tight)
			surd: absurd (**Synonyms:** ludicrous, preposterous, foolish), absurdist, absurdity (*surdus*, dull, deaf, insensible)
			unda: abundant (the verb is *abound*) (**Synonyms:** plentiful, copious, profuse) (*unda*, wave)
			us: abuse (**Synonyms:** wrong, oppress, persecute), abusive (from *uti*, to use)
			abs-:
			cess: abscess, abscessed (from *cedere*, to go)
			cond: abscond (to run away and hide) (*condere*, to hide)
			senc: absence (see *absent*)
			sent: absent, absentee, absenteeism (*esse*, to be)
			tain: abstain (**Synonyms:** forbear, desist, forgo; to refrain from something by one's own choice) (see *abstention*, below) (from *tenere*, to hold)
			tem: abstemious (the roots of *abstain* and *abstemious* are not related, though the meanings of the two words are similar) (*temetum*, strong drink)

Element	From	Meaning	Examples
ab- (cont'd)			tent: abstention {abstentious} (from *tenere*, to hold)
			terg: absterge (to make clean by wiping; in *medicine*, to purge) {abstergent, abstersion} (*tergere*, to wipe)
			tin: abstinence {abstinent} (from *abstain*)
			tract: (from *trahere*, to draw)
			abstract (**Synonyms:** brief, summary, synopsis)
			abstracted (**Synonyms:** absorbed, distraught)
			abstraction (an abstracting or being abstracted; removal), abstractionism, abstractive
			trus: abstruse (hard to understand; deep; recondite, esoteric) {abstrusely, abstrusity, abstruseness) (from *trudere*, to thrust)
			LATIN PHRASES:
			ab ante (from before, in advance)
			ab extra (from without)
			ab initio [from the beginning (of the world)]
			ablocatio (a letting out to hire, or leasing for money; sometimes used in English form: *ablocation*)
			ab origine (from the origin or beginning)
			absente reo (in the absence of the defendant: abbreviated *abs. re.*)
			absit omen [may there be no (ill) omen]
			WORD NOTES: *Abbreviate* may belong in this family, or it may belong in the *ad-* family, where the *d* is assimilated to *b*, to correspond to the first letter of *brev*. *Ab-* itself is *never* assimilated.
			Advance belongs in the *ab-* family even though it begins with *ad-*. The word is derived from *ab-* + *ante-*, two prefixes.
			INTERDISCIPLINARY: absorption (in *biology*, the passing of nutrient material into the bloodstream or lymph; in *physics*, a taking in and not reflecting; partial loss in power of light or radio waves passing through a medium)
			CROSS REFERENCE: *apo-, cata-, de-, dis-, ex-, ec-, se-*
able			See *hab*.
ac-			See *ad-* for *accost*, etc.
ac***	Latin *acerbus*: bitter, morose (IE: *ak*, sharp, bitter)	sharp, bitter	SIMPLE ROOT:
			acera: acerate (in *botany*, needle-shaped) (*ceris*, a pin, needle)
			acerb: acerb (sour or astringent in taste; harsh or severe, as of temper or expression), acerbate (to make sour, bitter; to irritate, vex), acerbic, acerbity
			acero: acerose (in *botany*, shaped like a needle; having a sharp, stiff point, as a leaf)
			aceta: acetabulum (literally, vinegar cup, a cup in Roman times to hold vinegar or sauce at the table), acetal, acetate
			aceti: acetic (pertaining to, derived from, or producing vinegar or acetic acid)
			aceto: acetous (containing or producing acetic acid; sour; vinegary)
			acetu: acetum (in *pharmacy*, vinegar)
			acety: acetyl (in *chemistry*, containing the acetyl group); acetylate (also, acetylize)
			acic:
			acicula (in *biology* and *geology*, a needlelike spine, prickle, or crystal), acicular, aciculate (also, *aciculated*)
			aciculum (plural, *aciculums, acicula*; in *zoology*, a bristlelike part; seta)

Element	From	Meaning	Examples
ac (cont'd)			acid: acid {acidic, acidity}, acidulate, acidulous acr: acrid (sharp or biting to the taste or smell) acrimonious (caustic, stinging, or bitter in nature, speech, behavior, etc.), acrimony (bitterness or ill-natured animosity) PREFIXED ROOT: *ex-*: exacerbate (to make more intense or sharp; aggravate; embitter), exacerbation (*ex-*, intensive) LEADING ROOT COMPOUND: *aceti*: fy: acetify (to change into vinegar or acetic acid) (from *facere*, to make, do) *aceto*: meter: acetometer (also, *acetimeter*; an instrument used to find the amount of acetic acid present in vinegar or other solution: also *acetimeter*) (*meter*, measure) *aci*: form: aciform (needle-shaped; sharp) *acidi*: meter: acidimeter (an instrument used to find the amount or strength of acid present in a solution) DISGUISED ROOT: aglet (the metal tip at the end of a cord or lace) cute (aphetic of *acute*; clever, sharp, shrewd; pretty or attractive, especially in a lively, wholesome, or dainty way; straining for effect; artificial) eager (feeling or showing keen desire; impatient or anxious to do or get; ardent; **Synonyms: 1)** avid, keen, anxious; **2)** fervent, zealous, enthusiastic) [do not confuse *eager* with *eagre*, a high tidal wave in an estuary] ear (of corn) [*ear* of one's body is from Old English] edge (**Synonyms:** border, margin, brim) egg (with *on*; to give an edge to; to urge or incite) OLD ENGLISH COGNATE: hammer INTERDISCIPLINARY: acetabulum (in *medicine*, the cup-shaped socket in the hipbone that receives the head of the thighbone; in *zoology*, any suction disc of flukes, leeches, cephalopods, etc. used to hold a host, prey, or surface; also, the cavity into which an insect's leg fits) NOTE: *Acme* and *acne*, from *akme*, a point, top, age of maturity, are also derived from the Indo-European base of this family. These words are also found under *acro*. CROSS REFERENCE: *ox*
acantho*	Greek *akantha*: thorn (IE: *ak*, sharp, bitter)	thorny, spiny	SIMPLE ROOT: acanthaceous, acanthine, acanthous acanthus (a Mediterranean plant with lobed, often spiny leaves and long spikes of white or colored flowers; in *architecture*, a motif or conventional representation of the leaf of the acanthus plant) LEADING ROOT COMPOUND: *acanth*: oid: acanthoid (spiny; spine-shaped) (*oid*, similar to) osis: acanthosis (a benign overgrowth of the prickle-cell layer of the skin) (*osis*, condition of)

Element	From	Meaning	Examples
acantho (cont'd)			*acantho*: cephal: acanthocephalan (a parasitic, threadlike worm having a proboscis covered with thornlike hooks) (*cephal*, head) cereus: acanthocereus (a genus of weak, often trailing, cacti having noctural funnel-shaped white flowers and 3-angled spiny stems) (*cereus*, candle) cyt acanthocyte, acanthocytosis (same as *acanthrocyte*, and *acanthrocytosis*, respectively) (*cyt*, cell) pter: acanthopterygian (any of the spiny-finned fishes, as the basses, perches, etc.) (*pterygion*, a fin) NO CROSS REFERENCE
acar*	Greek *akari* (see *Root Note*)	mite, tick	ROOT NOTE: This root consists of *a-*, not + *keirein*, to cut; therefore, too short to cut. SIMPLE ROOT: acariasis (same as *acariosis*), acarid, acaridan, Acarina (an order of ectoparasites, including mites or ticks; Acarus (a genus of mites) LEADING ROOT COMPOUND: *acar*: apis: acarapis (a species of mites that invades the tracheae of honeybees causing Isle of Wight disease) (*apis*, bee) oid: acaroid (*oid*, similar to) *acaro*: logy: acarology (*logy*, study of) phob: acarophobia (*phobia*, abnormal or irrational fear of) NO CROSS REFERENCE
acou, acu*	Greek *akous*: to listen (IE: *a-* (?) + *keu*, to heed, notice, observe)	to hear	SIMPLE ROOT: acoustic {acoustical, acoustically}, acoustician acoustics (the qualities of a room, theater, etc. that have to do with how clearly sounds can be heard or transmitted; the branch of physics dealing with sound, especially with its transmission) PREFIXED ROOT: dys-: dysacousia (*dys-*, wrong, bad, abnormal) hyper-: hyperacousia (an abnormally keen sense of hearing, often with pain in the ears; same as *hyperacusia*), hyperacusia (*hyper-*, beyond) LEADING ROOT COMPOUND: *acou*: esthes: acouesthesia (*esthes*, feeling, perception) meter: acoumeter (*meter*, a device for measuring) *acouo*: phon: acouophone, acouophonia (*phone*, sound) *acousmat*: agnos: acousmatagnosis (failure to recognize sounds due to mental disorder) (*a-*, negative + *gnosis*, recognition) amn: acousmatamnesia (*amnesia*, forgetting; *amnesia* itself consists of *a-*, negative + *mnem*, memory) *acoustico*: phob: acousticophobia (morbid fear of sounds) (*phobe*, fear) *acousto*: gram: acoustogram (from *graph*, write) TRAILING ROOT COMPOUND: osteo: osteoacusis (*oste*, bone) CROSS REFERENCE: *audi, aur, oto*

Element	From	Meaning	Examples
acro***	Greek *akros* (IE: *ak*, sharp, bitter)	highest, extreme; can also designate extremities, e.g., fingers, toes	LEADING ROOT COMPOUND: *acr*: odont: acrodont (*odont*, tooth) omion: acromion (the outer extremity of the shoulder blade, or scapula) (*omos*, shoulder) onym: acronym (*onym*, name) *acro*: bat: acrobat {acrobatic} (see note under *bat*), acrobatics, as *mental acrobatics* (*bat*, walk) carp: acrocarpous (bearing fruit at the end of the stalk, as do some mosses) (*carp*, fruit) cephal: acrocephaly (same as *oxycephalic*) (*cephal*, head) drom acrodrome (running to a point; used of a form of venation in which the principal veins terminate at the leaf tip) (*drome*, run) gen: acrogen {acrogenous, or *acrogenic*} (*gen*, producing) lith: acrolith (in early Greek sculpture, a statue with stone head, hands, and feet, and a wooden trunk), acrolithic (in reference to statue, having a trunk of wood usually covered with metal or drapery and extremities of stone) (*lithos*, stone) mega: acromegaly (pathological enlargement of the bones of the hands, feet, and face, resulting from an overproduction of growth hormone that is caused, usually, by a tumor in the pituitary) {acromegalic} (*mega*, large) nic: acronical (also, *acronycal*; in *astronomy*, happening at sunset, as the rising of a star) (from *nyx*, night) nyc: acronycal (same as *acronical*) (from *nyx*, night) petal: acropetal (in *botany*, developing upward from the base toward the apex: said of certain types of inflorescence; opposed to *basipetal*) {acropetally} phob: acrophobia (morbid fear of heights) (*phobia*, fear of) polis: acropolis (literally, high city; capitalized, the high-set citadel of Athens, upon which the Parthenon was built) (*polis*, city) spir: acrospire (in *botany*, the spiral primary bud of germinating grain) Latin *spira*, coil) stic: acrostic (a verse or arrangement of words in which certain letters in each line, such as the first or last, when taken in order spell out a word, motto, etc.) (*stichos*, a line of verse) TRAILING ROOT COMPOUND: pachy: pachyacria (a condition characterized by enlargement of the soft parts of the extremities) (*pachy*, thick) DISGUISED ROOT: acme (**Synonyms**: summit, pinnacle, zenith) acne {acned} PLACENAMES: Acme (Texas, Washington, Wyoming) Akron (Alabama, Colorado, Indiana, Iowa, Kansas, New York, Ohio, Pennsylvania) CROSS REFERENCE: *alt, apic, hyps, sum*

Our writing should be *accurate*: because language expresses thought,
and if we lack the skill to speak precisely,
our thought will remain confused, ill-defined. Arthur Quiller-Couch

Element	From	Meaning	Examples

act,***
ag,
ig
	Latin
	agere
	(IE: *ag*,
	to drive,
	do)
		to act, do, move,
		conduct, drive
			SIMPLE ROOT: actor, actress
			act:
			acti:
			acting, action (**Synonyms:** battle, engagement, campaign)
			actionable (in *law*, that gives cause for an action, or lawsuit)
			activate, activator
			active (**Synonyms: 1)** energetic, vigorous, strenuous;
			  2) agile, nimble, spry), activity
			actu: actual (**Synonyms:** true, real, authentic), actualize, ac-
			  tuary, actuate
			ag:
			agen: agendum (plural, *agenda*), agency, agent
			agi:
			agile (see synonyms at *active*, above)
			agitate (**Synonyms:** upset, disturb, perturb)
			PREFIXED ROOT:
			act:
			counter-: counteract {counteractive} (*counter-*, against)
			ex-: exact (**Synonyms: 1)** demand, claim, require; **2)** explic-
			  it, precise, definite; **3)** correct, accurate), exacting, exaction,
			  exactitude (*ex-*, out)
			hyper-: hyperaction, hyperactivity (Greek *hyper-*, over, beyond)
			in-: inaction, inactivate, inactive {inactivity} (*in-*, not)
			inter-: interact {interaction}, interactant (*inter-*, between)
			re-: react, reaction, reactionary, reactor (*re-*, back, again)
			retro-: retroactive {retroactively, retroactivity} (*retro-*, back)
			trans-: transact {transactor}, transaction, transactional (*trans-*,
			  across)
			ag:
			co-: (with, together)
			coagulable, coagulant, coagulate, coagulum (from *cogere*, to
			  curdle; see *cogent*, next entry)
			cogency, cogent (forceful and to the point, as a reason or ar-
			  gument; **Synonyms:** valid, confirm, convincing) (*co-* +
			  agere)
			cogitate (**Synonyms:** think, reason, speculate), cogitative
			  (*co-* + *agitate*)
			ig:
			ex-: exigency (**Synonyms: 1)** emergency, contingency, cri-
			  sis; **2)** need, necessity, requisite) exigent, exigible, exiguous
			  {exiguity} (*ex-*, out)
			prod-: prodigal (**Synonyms:** profuse, lavish, extravagant)
			  (*pro-*, forth, away + inserted *d*)
			DOUBLE PREFIXED ROOT:
			intransigent (describing one who refuses "to transact," to com-
			  promise, or to come to agreement) (*in-*, not; *trans-*, across)
			ELIDED PREFIXED ROOT:
			amb-: (from *ambi-*, around)
			ag: ambage (a roundabout, indirect way of talking or doing
			  things) {ambagious}
			ig: ambiguous (**Synonyms:** obscure, vague, enigmatic)
			TRAILING ROOT COMPOUND:
			fum: fumigant, fumigate {fumigation} (*fumigare*, to smoke)
			fust: fustigate (to beat with a stick) (*fustis*, a stick)

Element	From	Meaning	Examples
act (cont'd)			lev: levigate (to grind to a fine powder) (*levis*, smooth)
			lit: litigable (actionable), litigant, litigate (to contest in a lawsuit; to carry on a lawsuit), litigation, litigious (given to carrying on lawsuits; quarrelsome; disputable at law) (*litis*, dispute)
			nav: navigable, navigate, navigation, navigator (*navis*, a ship)
			DISGUISED ROOT:
			purge (to cleanse or rid of impurities, foreign matter, or undesirable elements) (*purgare*, to cleanse; from *purus*, clean + *agere*, to do)
			squat (from Middle French *esquatir*; from Latin *coactus*, past participle of *cogere*, to force, compress)
			PREFIXED DISGUISED ROOT:
			as-: assay (as a *noun*, an examination or testing; as a *verb*, to test, analyze, as to *assay* gold or silver ore to determine the purity of) (*as-* assimilates *ad-*, to, toward)
			es-: essay (to test the nature or quality of; an attempt, trial; as a *noun*, pronounced ES say; in *literature*, a short composition of an analytical or interpretive kind, dealing with its subject usually from a personal view or in a limited way; as a *verb*, pronounced es SAY) (from *exagium*, a weight, weighing; further from *es-* from *ex-*, out of + *agere*, to do)
			ex-: examen, examine (**Synonyms:** scrutinize, inspect, scan), examination, examinatorial (*ex-*, out)
			FRENCH PHRASE: *agent provocateur*
			ITALIAN MUSIC TERM: *agitato*
			THEOLOGICAL TERM: actual sin (any sin committed by one's own free will, as distinguished from *original sin*)
			PLACENAME: Active, Alabama
			CROSS-REFERENCE: *agon*
actin*	Greek *aktis*, ray	rays; similar to rays; of a radiated nature	actina: actinal (of the oral region of a radiate animal, from which the rays or tentacles grow)
			actini:
			actinia (any of a genus of sea anemones) {actinian}
			actinic (actinic rays are those light rays of short wavelength, occurring in the violet and ultraviolet parts of the spectrum, that produce chemical changes, as in photography)
			actinide [actinide series: a group of radioactive chemical elements from element 89 (actinium) through element 103 (lawrencium): it resembles the lanthanide series in electronic structure]
			actinism (that property of ultraviolet light, X-rays, or other radiations, by which chemical changes are produced)
			actinium (chemical symbol: Ac)
			actino: actinon (an isotope of radon, formed by the radioactive decay of actinium; atomic weight: 217)
			LEADING ROOT COMPOUND:
			actin:
			oid: actinoid (having a radial form, as an actinozoan) (*oid*, similar to)
			actini:
			form: actiniform (in *zoology*, having radial form; rayed)
			actino:
			graph: actinograph (*graph*, write)

Element	From	Meaning	Examples
actin (cont'd)			logy: actinology (the science of light rays and their chemical effects) (*logy*, study of) meter: actinometer (in *physics*, an instrument for measuring the intensity of the sun's rays, or the actinic effect of light rays) (*meter*, measure) morph: actinomorphic (in *biology*, having radial symmetry, as a flower or a starfish) (*morph*, shape, form) myc: actinomycete, actinomycin (*myc*, fungus) scop: actinoscopy (*scope*, look) zo: actinozoan (same as *anthozoan*) (*zo*, animal) NO CROSS REFERENCE
acu			See *acou* for *osteoacusis*.
acu**	Latin *acus* (IE: *ak*, sharp, pointed)	needle	SIMPLE ROOT: acua: acuate (having a point; sharp at the end) acui: acuity (acuteness; keenness, as of thought or vision) acul: aculeate (also, *aculeated*; in *botany* and *zoology*, having an aculeus or aculei), aculeus (in *botany*, a prickle; in *zoology*, a sting) acum: acumen (keenness and quickness in understanding and dealing with a situation; shrewdness) acuminate (in *biology* and *zoology*, pointed; tapering to a point; as a *verb*, to make sharp or keen) {acuminated} acut: acutance (a measure of the steepness of an an edge in a photographic image) acute (**Synonyms**: critical, crucial), acutenaculum (needle holder) PREFIXED ROOT: *sub*-: subacute (moderately acute, as a *subacute angle*; having a tapered but not sharply pointed form, as a *subacute flower petal*; falling between acute and chronic in character; less marked in severity or duration than a corresponding acute state, as *subacute pain*) (*sub*-, under) LEADING ROOT COMPOUND: press: acupressure (compression of a bleeding vessel by inserting needles into adjacent tissue) punct: acupuncture (a traditional Chinese therapeutic technique whereby the body is punctured with fine needles) GRAMMAR TERM: acute accent [a mark (') to show the quality or length of a vowel, as in French *idée*; also, primary stress, as in *type'writer*] NO CROSS REFERENCE
ad-,*** ac-, af-, ag-, al-, an-, ap-, ar-, as-, at-, a-	Latin *ad-* (akin to English *at*)	to, at, toward	PREFIXED ROOTS: a-: (before *b*) ban: abandon (**Synonyms**: relinquish, renounce, desert), abandoned (*bannum*, a curse) bat: abate, abatement (**Synonyms**: lessening, letup, diminution) (*batuere*, to beat) bet: abet (Middle English *abetten*; from Old French *abeter*, to incite; from *a*-, to, at + *beter*, to bait; from Old Norse *beita*, bite) bey: abeyance (temporary suspension, as of an activity or function) (Old French *bayer*, to gape, wait expectantly)

9

Element	From	Meaning	Examples
ad- (cont'd)			a-: (before *sc, sp, st*)
			scend: ascend (to go up; move upward; rise; to slope or lean upward), ascendancy (or *ascendency*), ascendant (or *ascendent*), ascending (in *botany*, rising or curving upward from a trailing position, as the stems of certain vines) (from *scandere*, to climb)
			scens: ascension (the act of ascending; ascent; see *Biblical Term*, below), ascensive (see *ascend*, above)
			scrib: ascribe (**Synonyms:** attribute, impute, assign) (*scribere*, to write)
			script: ascription (from *ascribe*)
			spect: aspect (**Synonyms: 1**) appearance, semblance, guise; **2**) phase, facet, angle) (*specere*, to look)
			sper: Asperges (in the Roman Catholic Church, the sprinkling of altar, clergy, and people with holy water before High Mass; a hymn sung during this ceremony, beginning with *Asperges me*), asperse, aspersorium (a basin, font, etc. for holy water; an *aspergillum*) (from *spargere*, to sprinkle)
			spir: aspirant, aspirate (also *aspirated*), aspiration, aspirator, aspiratory, aspire, aspiring (*spirare*, to breathe)
			string: astringent {astringency} (*stringere*, to draw, pull)
			BIBLICAL TERM: The Ascension (the bodily ascent of Jesus into heaven on the fortieth day after the Resurrection; see Acts 1:9)
			ISLAND: Ascension [so named because discovered on Ascension Day (1501); located in the South Atlantic; part of the British territory of St. Helena]
			ac-: (an assimilation)
			ced: accede (**Synonyms:** consent, assent, agree) (*cedere*, to go, yield)
			cel: accelerando (in *music*, to become increasingly fast), accelerant, accelerate, acceleration, accelerative (*celerare*, to hasten)
			cent: accent, accentual [having a rhythm based on stress rather than on the length of sounds (German poetry is basically *accentual*)], accentuate (from *canere*, to sing)
			cept: accept (**Synonyms:** receive, admit, take), acceptable, acceptance, accepted, acceptor (from *capere*, to seize, take)
			cess: access, accessible, accession, accessory (in *law*, a person who, though absent, helps another to break or escape the law; accomplice) (see *accede*)
			cid: (from *cadere*, to fall)
			accidence (the part of grammar that deals with inflection of words)
			accident (in *law*, an unforeseen event that occurs without anyone's fault or negligence)
			accidental (music term; see synonyms at *adventitious*, above)
			claim: acclaim (**Synonyms:** praise, laud, extol) (see *acclamation*, next entry)
			clam: acclamation {acclamatory} (*clamare*, to cry out)
			clim: acclimate (to accustom or become accustomed to a new climate or environment), acclimatize (from Greek *klinein*, to slope)
			cliv: acclivity (an upward slope of ground; opposed to declivity), acclivous (*clivus*, hill)

10

Element	From	Meaning	Examples
ad- (cont'd)			col: accolade (literally, to the neck; an embrace formerly used in conferring knighthood; in *music*, a brace joining several staves) (*collum*, neck)
			cord: accord (**Synonyms**: agree, conform, harmonize), accordance, accordion (*cordis*, heart)
			cost: accost (*costa*, rib, side)
			count: account, accountable, accountant (from *conter*, to tell)
			coupl: accouplement (in *architecture*, the placing of columns in pairs close together) (from *copulare*, to couple)
			cred: accredit (**Synonyms**: authorize, commission, license) {accreditation} (*credere*, to trust, believe)
			cret: accrete (to grow by being added to; to grow together; adhere; in *biology*, grown together), accretion (from *crescere*, to grow)
			cru: accrual (also, *accruement*), accrue [to come as a natural growth, advantage or right (*to*); to be added periodically as an increase: said especially of interest on money] (from *accrete*, above)
			cult: acculturate, acculturation (from *colere*, to cultivate, to till)
			cumb: accumbency, accumbent (lying down; in *botany*, lying against some other part) (from *cubare*, to recline)
			cumu: accumulate, accumulation, accumulative (*cumulare*, to heap)
			cur: accuracy, accurate (having no errors; correct) (*curare*, to take care)
			cus: (from *causa*, cause)
			accusal, accusation
			accuse (**Synonyms**: charge, indict, impeach)
			accusative (explore *accusative* as a linguistics term)
			accusatory
			cust: accustom, accustomed (**Synonyms**: usual, customary, habitual)
			DOUBLE PREFIXED ROOT:
			accommodate (**Synonyms**: adapt, adjust, conform)
			accompany (**Synonyms**: attend, escort, convoy)
			accomplice (**Synonyms**: associate, colleague, companion)
			accomplish (**Synonyms**: perform, execute, effect)
			FRENCH WORDS:
			accouchement (literally, to the couch; confinement for giving birth to a child; childbirth)
			accouter (to outfit; equip, especially for military service) (a double-prefixed root: *ac*- from *ad*- + *com*-, with + *suere*, to sew)
			accouterment (also, *accoutrement*), accouterments (a personal outfit, clothes, dress; a soldier's equipment except clothes and weapons) (see *accouter*, previous entry)
			NOTE: There are other words in which *ad*- changes to *ac*-, but in which *ac*- is not an assimilation but rather a variant.
			ac-:
			quaint: acquaint (**Synonyms**: notify, inform, apprise), acquaintance (from *gnoscere*, to know)
			quie: acquiesce (**Synonyms**: consent, agree, concur), acquiescence, acquiescent (*quiescere*, to become quiet)

11

Element	From	Meaning	Examples
ad- (cont'd)			quir: acquire (**Synonyms**: get, obtain, procure), acquirement (from *quaerere*, to seek)
			quis: acquisition, acquisitive (**Synonyms**: greedy, avaricious, grasping) (from *acquire*, above)
			quit: acquit (**Synonyms**: 1) absolve, exonerate, vindicate; 2) behave, conduct, deport), acquittal, acquittance (a settlement of, or release from, debt or liability; a record of this settlement or release; receipt) (see *acquiesce*, above)
			ad-:
			apt: adapt (**Synonyms**: adjust, accommodate, conform), adapter, adaption (*apt*, fasten, attach)
			d: (from *dare*, to give)
			add (to total; to mean)
			addend, addendum (plural, *addenda*)
			dict: addict, addiction, addictive (from *dicere*, to say)
			dit: additament (a thing added; addition), addition, additive (from *add*, above)
			dress: address (**Synonyms**: speech, oration, lecture) (from *regere*, to keep straight)
			duc: (*ducere*, to lead)
			adduce (to give as a reason or proof)
			adduct (in *physiology*, to pull a part of the body toward the median axis)
			emp: ademption (from *emere*, to buy, to take)
			ept: adept (used in Medieval Latin of alchemists claiming to have arrived at the philosopher's stone; thus, highly skilled; expert) (from *apisci*, to pursue, attain)
			equa: adequacy, adequate (**Synonyms**: sufficient, enough) (from *aequus*, even, level)
			her: (from *haerere*, to stick)
			adhere (**Synonyms**: stick, cling, cleave)
			adherent (**Synonyms**: follower, disciple, partisan)
			hes: adhesion, adhesive (tending to adhere) (see *adhere*)
			hib: adhibit {adhibition} (from *habere*, to hold)
			it: adit (an approach or entrance; specifically, an almost horizontal passageway into a mine) (from *ire*, to go)
			jec: adjective [literally, thrown to (the noun or pronoun it modifies)] (from *jacere*, to throw, hurl)
			jut: adjutant (an aide; see *Doublets* below) (from *juvare*, to help)
			mini: administer (**Synonyms**: govern, rule), administration, administrator (*ministrare*, to serve)
			ren: adrenal (*renes*, kidneys)
			scit: adscititious (knowledge received from an external source; supplemental) (from *scire*, to know)
			sor: adsorb, adsorbate, adsorbent, adsorption {adsorptive} (*sorbere*, to suck in, drink)
			umbra: adumbrate {adumbration, adumbrative} (*umbra*, shade)
			vect: advection {advective} (from *vehere*, to carry)
			vent: (from *venire*, to come)
			advent (capitalized, the birth of Christ)
			adventitia (the outer covering of an organ)
			adventitious (**Synonyms**: accidental, fortuitous, incidental)

Element	From	Meaning	Examples
ad- (cont'd)			adventive (not native to the environment), adventure

adventive (not native to the environment), adventure
verb: adverb (*verbum*, word)
DOUBLETS: adjutant:aid
af-:
fab: affable (pleasant and easy to approach or talk to; friendly; gentle and kindly; **Synonyms:** amiable, obliging, genial) (from *fari*, to speak)
fair: affair, affairs (matters of business or concern) (from Middle French *a faire*, to do, the same base as in *savoir faire*, knowing how to do)
fect: (from *facere*, to do)
affect (**Synonyms: 1)** influence, impress, move; **2)** assume, pretend, feign)
affectation (**Synonyms:** pose, mannerism, airs), affected, affecting, affection, affectionate
fer: afferent (opposed to *efferent*) (*ferre*, to bear)
fian: affiance, affiant (from *fidere*, to trust)
fid: affidavit (a one-word Latin sentence: He has stated it on faith; one who makes an affidavit is an *affiant*)
fil: affiliate (**Synonyms:** related, kindred, cognate), affiliation (*filius*, son)
fin: affine, affined, affinity (*finis*, end)
fir: affirm (**Synonyms:** assert, declare, avouch), affirmation, affirmative (*firmare*, to make firm)
fix: affix, affixation, affixture (from *figure*, to fix, fasten)
fla: afflatus (from *flare*, to blow)
flict: afflict, affliction (**Synonyms: 1)** misery, woe; **2)** tribulation trouble), afflictive (from *fligere*, to strike)
flu: affluence, affluent (**Synonyms:** rich, wealthy, opulent) (*fluere*, to flow)
flux: afflux (a flow toward a point, as of blood to an organ) (from *affluence*, previous entry)
ford: afford (from Old English *forthian*, to further)
forest: afforest [to turn (land) into forest; plant many trees on]
fric: affricate {affricative}, affrication (*fricare*, to rub)
fron: affront (**Synonyms:** offend, insult, outrage) (*frons*, forehead)
fus: affusion (a pouring on, as of water in baptism) (from *fundere*, to pour)
NB: *Affray* is not in this family; it is from *ex-*, out of + Germanic *frith*, peace.
ag-
glom: agglomerate (as a *noun*, a confused or jumbled mass of things clustered together; a volcanic rock consisting of rounded and angular fragments) (*glomerare*, to form into a ball)
glut: agglutinant, agglutinate (in physiology, to cause red blood cells or microorganisms to clump together), agglutination (*gluten*, glue)
grad: aggrade [to build up the level or slope of (a river bed, valley, etc.) by the deposit or sediment] (*gradus*, step)
grand: aggrandize (to make greater, more powerful, richer, etc.; often used reflexively) {aggrandizement, aggrandizer} (*grandis*, great)

13

Element	From	Meaning	Examples
ad- (cont'd)			grav: aggravate (see *Doublets* below; **Synonyms**: intensify, heighten, enhance), aggravated, aggravation (*gravis*, heavy)
			greg: aggregate (**Synonyms**: sum, amount, total), aggregation, aggregative (*gregis*, herd, flock)
			gress: aggress, aggression, aggressive (**Synonyms**: militant, assertive), aggressor (from *aggrade*, above)
			griev: aggrieve (**Synonyms**: abuse, wrong, oppress; see *Doublets* below), aggrieved (from *aggravate*, above)
			NOTE: The following prefixes are not assimilations, but variants.
			ag-:
			nat: agnate (a relative through male descent or on the father's side) {agnation} (from *nasci*, to be born)
			nomen: agnomen [a name added to the cognomen (the last name), especially as an epithet honoring some achievement] (*nomen*, name)
			DOUBLETS: aggravate:aggrieve
			al-:
			lay: allay (**Synonyms**: relieve, assuage, mitigate) (from *alleviate*; see *Doublets* below)
			leg: *allegation, allege, allegiance* (**Synonyms**: fidelity, loyalty, fealty) (see *Note* below)
			lev: alleviate (see *Doublets* below; **Synonyms**: relieve, assuage, mitigate), alleviation (*levis*, light)
			lian: alliance (**Synonyms**: league, coalition, confederacy) (from *ally*)
			liter: alliterate, alliteration (repetition of an initial sound, usually of a consonant or cluster, in two or more words of a phrase, line of poetry, etc., e.g., "What a tale of terror now their turbulency tells!"), alliterative (*littera*, letter)
			loc: allocate (**Synonyms**: allot, assign, apportion), allocation (*locus*, place)
			low: allow (**Synonyms**: let, permit, suffer), allowable, allowance, allowedly (from *locus*, place; sense confused with *laudare*, to praise)
			lud: allude (**Synonym**: refer) (*ludere*, to play)
			lur: allure (**Synonyms**: attract, charm, fascinate), allurement, alluring (from German *Luder*, bait; not otherwise listed)
			lus: allusion, allusive (from *allude*, above)
			luv: alluvial, alluvion, alluvium (from *luere*, to wash)
			ly: ally (base of *alliance*; **Synonyms**: associate, colleague, companion) (*ligare*, to bind)
			DOUBLETS: allay:alleviate
			NOTE: Authorities are divided on whether *allege, allegation,* and *allegiance* are from this element; they may possibly come from *ex-*, out; *allegory, allele* and *allergy* are not from this prefix, coming from Greek root *allo,* other.
			an-:
			neal: anneal (from Old English *aelan*, to burn)
			nex: annex (to add on or attach, as a smaller thing to a larger one) {annexation} (from *nectere*, to bind, tie)
			nihil: annihilate (**Synonyms**: destroy, raze) (*nihil*, nothing)
			not: annotate, annotation (*notare*, to mark, note)

Element	From	Meaning	Examples
ad- (cont'd)			nounc: announce (**Synonyms:** declare, publish, proclaim), announcement (from *nuntiare*, to report)

nul: annul (**Synonyms:** abolish, rescind, revoke), annulment (*nullum*, nothing)

nunc: annunciate, annunciation, annunciator (from *announce*)

NB: Do not confuse this assimilation with the root *anni*, as in *anniversary*.

CHRISTIAN CONCEPT: The Annunciation (the angel Gabriel's announcement to Mary that she was to give birth to Jesus: Luke 1:26-38; the church festival on March 25 commemorates this event)*ap-*:

pall: appall (**Synonyms:** dismay, horrify), appalling (*pallere*, to be pale)

pan: appanage (literally, to provide with bread; a person's rightful extra gain; perquisite; adjunct) (*panis*, bread)

par: (note difference in meanings of roots)

apparatus, apparel (*parare*, to prepare)

apparent (**Synonyms:** evident, manifest, obvious), apparition (*parere*, to show)

peal: appeal (**Synonyms:** plead, sue, petition) (from *pellare*, to beat, drive)

pear: appear, appearance (**Synonyms:** look, aspect, semblance) (from *parere*, to come forth)

peas: appease (**Synonyms:** pacify, mollify, placate) (from *pax*, peace)

pell: appelant, appellate, appellation (the act of calling by a name; a name or title that describes or identifies a person or thing; designation) (see *appeal*, above)

pos: apposable, apposite (**Synonyms:** relevant, pertinent, applicable), apposition, appositive (from *ponere*, to put)

prais: appraisal, appraise (**Synonyms:** estimate, evaluate, rate) (from *apprise*, below)

prec: appreciate (**Synonyms:** value, treasure, esteem), appreciation, appreciative (from *pretium*, price)

prehen: apprehend, apprehensible, apprehension (from *pre-*, before + IE *ghed*, to grasp)

prent: apprentice (from *apprehend*)

press: appressed (pressed close to or flat against a surface: said especially of a leaf or leaf part) (from *primare*, to press)

pris: apprise (also, *apprize*; **Synonyms:** notify, inform, acquaint) (from Middle French *aprendre*, to learn, to teach)

proach: approach, approachable (from *prope*, near)

prob: approbation (official approval, sanction, or commendation) (also, *approbatory*) (from *approve*)

prop: appropriate (**Synonyms:** fit, suitable, proper), appropriation (*proprius*, one's own)

prov: approval, approve (**Synonyms:** endorse, sanction, ratify) (from *probus*, good)

prox: approximate, approximation (in *mathematics* and *physics*, a result that is not necessarily exact, but is within the limits of accuracy required) (from *prope*, near)

purt: appurtenance, appurtenant (from *appertain*)

Element	From	Meaning	Examples
ad- (cont'd)			*ar-:* raign: arraign (**Synonyms:** accuse, charge, indict) (from *ratio*, reason) rang: arrange, arrangement (from Old High German *hring*, ring) ray: array (**Synonyms:** multitude, host, legion), arrayal (from Germanic base *raid-*, to be moving) rear: arrear, arrears (unpaid and overdue debts), arrearge (from Middle English *arere*, behind; from Latin *ad retro*) rest: arrest, arresting (*restare*, to stop, to stay back; from this verb is derived the *rest* that means "remainder," as well as *restive*, meaning "balky, contrary," as *a restive horse*) riv: arrival, arrive (literally, to reach the shore) (from *ripa*, shore) rog: arrogance, arrogant (**Synonyms:** proud, haughty, insolent), arrogate (*rogare*, to ask) FRENCH EXPRESSIONS: *arrière-pensée* (literally, a backthought; a mental reservation; ulterior motive) *arriviste* (a person who has recently gained power, wealth, success, etc. and is regarded as an upstart; parvenu) (from *arrive*) ITALIAN: *arrivederci* (until we meet again; goodbye; implies a temporary parting) NB: *Arrhythmia*, from Greek *a-*, not, *rhythmos*, measure, is not in this family. *as-:* sail: assail (**Synonyms:** attack, assault, beset), assailant (from *salire*, to jump) sault: assault (see synonyms at *assail*, above) (from *assail*) sembl: assemblage, assemble, assembly (from *simul*, together) sent: assent (**Synonyms:** consent, agree, accede), assentation (*sentire*, to feel) sert: assert (**Synonyms:** declare, affirm, aver), assertion, assertive (**Synonyms:** aggressive, militant, pushing) (from *serere*, to join, bind) sess: assess (to estimate or determine the significance, importance, or value of; estimate), assessment (from *sedere*, to sit) set: asset (from Vulgar Latin *satis*, enough, filled) sever: asseverate {asseveration} (*severus*, severe, earnest) sib: assibilate (*sibilare*, to hiss) sid: assiduity, assiduous (**Synonyms:** industrious, diligent, sedulous) (from *assess*) sign: (*signare*, to sign) assign (**Synonyms: 1)** ascribe, attribute, impute; **2)** allot, apportion, allocate) assignation (something assigned; an appointment for a meeting between lovers; rendezvous) assignment simil: assimilate, assimilation (in *linguistics*, a process in which a sound tends to become like a neighboring sound in position or type of articulation) (*similis*, like) sist: assist (**Synonyms:** help, aid, succor), assistance, assistant (*sistere*, to make stand)

Element	From	Meaning	Examples
ad- (cont'd)			siz: assize (from *assess*)

soc: (*socius*, companion)

associable, associate (**Synonyms**: colleague, companion, comrade)

association {associational}, associative

[*Soccer* is derived from *association football*; so called from the British controlling body, the National Football Association]

son: assonance (a partial rhyme in which the stressed vowel sounds are alike but the consonant sounds are unlike, as in *late* and *make*) {assonant} (*sonare*, to sound)

sort: assort, assorted, assortment (from *serere*, to join together)

suag: assuage (**Synonyms**: relieve, alleviate, mitigate) (from *suavis*, sweet)

suas: assuasive (from *assuage*)

sum: assume (**Synonyms**: pretend, feign, affect), assumed, assuming (*sumere*, to take)

sur: assurance, assure, assured, assurer (from *cura*, care)

surg: assurgent (in *biology*, same as *ascending*) (*surgere*, to rise)

NB: The following words do not contain the prefix *as-*.

assassin (from Arabic *hashshashin*, hashish users)

assay (from *ex-*, out + *agere*, to transact)

at-:

tach: attach (see *Doublets* below; **Synonyms**: 1) ascribe, attribute, impute; 2) tie, bind, fasten), attaché, attachment (from IE *steig*, a point)

tack: attack (see *Doublets* below; **Synonyms**: assail, assault, beset) (from *attach*)

tain: (from *tangere*, to touch)

attain (**Synonyms**: reach, gain, achieve)

attainder (a law term)

attaint

temper: attemper (*temperare*, to control)

tempt: attempt (*temptare*, to try, urge, which yields *tempt* itself)

tend: attend (**Synonyms**: accompany, escort, convoy), attendance, attendant, attendee (*tendere*, to stretch)

tent: attention, attentive (**Synonyms**: thoughtful, considerate) (from *attend*)

tenu: attenuate (*tenuare*, to make thin or weak)

test: attest, attestation (from *testis*, witness)

tir: attire (as a *verb*, to dress, especially in fine garments; as a *noun*, clothes, especially fine or rich apparel) (*tire*, order, row, dress)

torn: attorn, attorney (**Synonyms**: lawyer, counselor, barrister) (*torner*, to turn)

tract: attract, attractant, attraction, attractive (from *trahere*, to draw, pull)

trib: attribute (**Synonyms**: 1) ascribe, impute, assign; 2) quality, property, character), attributive (*tribuere*, to assign)

trit: (from *terere*, to rub)

attrited (worn down by attrition)

Element	From	Meaning	Examples
ad- (cont'd)			attrition (a gradual diminution in number or strength due to constant stress; in *theology*, repentance that is not perfect because not prompted solely by sorrow for having offended God; compare *contrition*, under *trit*)
			DOUBLETS: attach:attack
			FRENCH: *attentat* (an attempt, especially an unsuccessful one, at an act of political violence)
			INTERDISCIPLINARY: attenuate (in *electronics*, to reduce the strength of an electrical impulse; in *microbiology*, the reduce the virulence of a bacterium or virus, usually to make a vaccine; in *botany*, an adjective; tapering gradually to a point, as the base of leaf)
			NB: *Attitude*, from *aptitude*, does not contain the assimilated prefix *ad*-.)
			PREFIX USED AS AN ENDING:
			caudad (toward the tail; opposed to *cephlad*, toward the head)
			orad (toward the mouth)
			LATIN PHRASES:
			ad astra per aspera (to the stars through difficulty)
			ad captandum vulgus (literally, to catch the crowd; to please the crowd; a logical fallacy in reasoning)
			ad hoc [to, or, for this (purpose)]
			ad hominem (literally, to the man, a form of illogical reasoning)
			ad infinitum (literally, to the endless; to infinity, endlessly, without limit)
			ad initium (literally, at the beginning)
			ad interim (literally, for the time between; in the meantime)
			ad libitum [literally, at liberty; at one's pleasure; in *music*, not so important that it cannot be omitted; opposed to *obbligato* (original meaning)]
			ad locum (at or to the place; abbreviated *ad loc.*)
			ad rem (literally, to the thing; pertinent, without digressing; in a straightforward manner)
			ad valorem (according to the worth, as *an advalorem tax*)
			a fortiori (literally, to the more powerful; for a still stronger reason; all the more)
			FRENCH: adieu; SPANISH: *adiós* (see *Note*)
			NOTE: Both the French and Spanish terms mean "goodbye," and both literally mean "to God," where the departing one is wished God's protection. Anglo-Saxon "goodbye" was originally "God be with ye."
			CROSS REFERENCE: *ob-/oc-/of-/op-/o-*
adelph*	Greek *adelphos* (see *Preface*, p. ii, for a discussion of the Indo-European cognates for *brother*)	brother	SIMPLE ROOT: adelphic (of, or relating to, a *polygynous* marriage in which the wives are sisters, or to a *polyandrous* marriage in which the husbands are brothers)
			NOTE: With addition of the adjective-forming suffix *-ous*, *adelphous* itself becomes a suffix, indicating possession of one or more groups of stamens, from *adelphus*, having the *stamens* grouped together in a brotherhood.
			TRAILING ROOT COMPOUND:
			di: diadelphous (arranged in two bundles or sets by the fusion of the filaments: said of stamens; also, having the stamens so arranged, as in the sweet pea) (*di*, two)
			is: isadelphous (*iso*, same)

Element	From	Meaning	Examples
adelph (cont'd)			mon: monadelphous (in *botany*, united by the filaments into a single tubelike group: said of stamens) (*mono*, one, alone) poly: polyadelphous (in *botany*, having stamens joined by their filaments into a number of clusters) (*poly*, many) PLACENAMES: Adelphi (Maryland, Ohio) Adelphia, New Jersey Philadelphia (literally, love of brother; City of Brotherly Love) CROSS REFERENCE: *frater*
adrenal**			See *ren*, kidney.
adjut,* adjuv	Latin *adjutare*	to help, assist	ROOT NOTE: This root consists of *ad-*, to, toward + *juvare*, to help, assist. SIMPLE ROOT: *adjut*: adjutancy, adjutant (the administrative position, or the bird; see *Doublets* below) *adjuv*: adjuvant DISGUISED ROOT: aid, aide (see *Doublets* below) (Middle English *aiden*; from Old French *aider*; from Latin *adjutare*) DOUBLETS: adjutant:aide NO CROSS REFERENCE
aeri,*** aero	Greek *aer*, air	gas, air	SIMPLE ROOT: aera: aerate (to expose to air, or cause air to circulate through), aerated, aeration, aerator aeri: aerial (in *biology*, growing in the air instead of in soil or water), aerialist, aerity LEADING ROOT COMPOUND: *aeri*: fer: aeriferous (*ferre*, to bear) fy: aerify (from *facere*, to make, do) *aero*: bat: aerobatics (from *bas*, walk) be: aerobe (an organism that requires air and free oxygen to live) (from *bios*, life) bi: aerobic, aerobium (*bios*, life) don: aerodonetics (the science of soaring in a glider) (*donein*, to shake) drom: aerodrome (chiefly British; same as *airdrome*: an airport; a landing field; an airplane hangar) (*dromo*, running) dyn: aerodyne (a heavier-than-air aircraft deriving lift from motion), aerodynamics (plural in form; used with singular verb; the dynamics of gases, especially of atmospheric interactions with moving objects) (*dyne*, power) embol: aeroembolism (*em-* prefixes *bol*, to throw) gram: aerogram (a radiogram; an airmail letter written on a standard, lightweight form that folds into the shape of an envelope and can be sent at a low postage rate) (from *graph*, write) logy: aerology (total atmospheric meteorology as opposed to surface-based study) (*logy*, study of) mechan: aeromechanics (plural in form; used with singular verb) meteor: aerometeorgraph (an aircraft instrument for simultaneously recording temperature, atmospheric pressure, and humidity) (*meteor*, lifted up + *graph*, write)

Element	From	Meaning	Examples
aeri (cont'd)			meter: aerometer (from French *aéromètre*; a device for determining the weight and density of air or other gas) (*meter*, measure)
			naut: aeronaut, aeronautics (plural in form; used with singular verb) (*naut*, ship)
			neur: aeroneurosis (also called *flying fatigue*) (*neur*, nerve + *osis*, condition)
			nom: aeronomy (the science dealing with the physics and chemistry of the upper atmosphere) (*nomos*, law)
			paus: aeropause (the region of the atmosphere above which aircraft cannot fly)
			phob: aerophobia (an abnormal fear of air, especially of drafts) (*phobia*, fear of)
			phyt: aerophyte (in *botany*, an *epiphyte*: a plant, such as certain orchids or ferns, that grows on another plant or object upon which it depends for mechanical support but not as a source of nutrients; also called "air plant") (*phyton*, plant)
			sol: aerosol (*aero* + *sol*ution)
			spher: aerosphere (the lower portion of the atmosphere in which both unmanned and manned flight is possible) (*sphere*, ball, globe)
			stat: aerostat (an aircraft, especially a balloon or dirigible, deriving its lift from the buoyancy of surrounding air rather than from aerodynamic motion), aerostatics (plural in form; used with singular verb) (*stat*, stand)
			therm: aerothermodynamics (the study of the relationship of heat and mechanical energy in gases, especially air) (*therm*, heat + *dyne*, power)
			PREFIXED LEADING ROOT COMPOUND:
			an-: anaerobe, anaerobiosis (*an-*, not + *bio*, life + *osis*, condition of)
			NB: *Aerie*, the nest of an eagle or other bird of prey that builds in a high place, is not in the family. It is probably derived from *ager*, field.
			CROSS REFERENCE: *atm*
aesthes			See *esthes*.
af-			See *ad-* for *affect*, etc.
ag-			See *ad-* for *aggrieve*, etc.
ag			See *act* for *agent*, etc.
agog**	Greek *agein*, to lead (IE: *ag-*, to drive, do)	leading	PREFIXED ROOTS AND COMPOUNDS:
			an-: anagoge (mystical interpretation, as of the Scriptures), anagogy (from *ana-*, up)
			em-: emmenagogue (a medicine that induces or hastens the menstrual flow) (*em-*, in + *men*, month)
			syn-: synagogue (literally, to bring together; an assembly of Jews for worship and religious study; also, a building or place used by Jews for worship and religious study) (*syn-*, with, together)
			TRAILING ROOT COMPOUND:
			chor: choragus (also, *choregus*; in ancient Greece, the leader of a dramatic chorus; any conductor of an intertainment or festival) (*choros*, originally, a dance; a band of dancers and singers)

Element	From	Meaning	Examples
agog (cont'd)			dem: demagogue (literally, a leader of the people; originally, a leader of the common people; now, a person who tries to stir up the people by appeals to emotion, prejudice, etc., in order to win them over quickly and gain power) (*demo*, people)
			galact: galactagogue (an agent that promotes the flow of milk) (*galact*, milk)
			hypn: hypnagogic (sleep-inducing) (*hypno*, sleep)
			myst: mystagogue (a person who interprets religious mysteries or initiates others into them)
			ped: pedagogue (literally, one who leads children; thus, a teacher; especially a pedantic, dogmatic teacher), pedagogy (the profession or function of a teacher; teaching; the art or science of teaching) (from *paed*, child)
			CROSS REFERENCE: *agon, athl, duc*
agon**	Greek *agein* (IE: *ag-*, to drive, do)	to drive, lead (originally, assembly, contest)	SIMPLE ROOT:
			agon, agonal (of or connected with death pangs)
			agonist (one who takes part in a struggle, as the main character in a drama; a muscle whose action on a joint or orifice is opposed by the action of another muscle, the antagonist)
			agonistes (designating a person engaged in a struggle: used after the word modified)
			agonistic (also, *agonistical*; striving to overcome in argument; competitive; combative; contesting; strained for effect; of or pertaining to contests)
			agonize (to be in extreme pain or suffer great anguish; as a *transitive verb*, to cause great pain in torture)
			agony (**Synonyms:** distress, suffering, anguish)
			PREFIXED ROOT:
			ant-: antagonist (literally, to struggle against; compare with *protagonist*, under *Trailing Root Compound*) (*anti-*, against)
			TRAILING ROOT COMPOUND:
			deuter: deuteragonist (in *ancient Greek drama*, the actor second in importance to the protagonist) (*deuter*, second)
			prot: protagonist (the first, or most important, actor in a Greek drama; hence any notable leader or spokesperson; compare with *antagonist*, under *Prefixed Root*) (*proto*, first)
			strat: stratagem (**Synonyms:** trick, ruse, maneuver) (*stratos*, army)
			PREFIXED DISGUISED ROOT:
			ep-: epact (the period of 11 days by which the solar year exceeds the lunar year of twelve months) (*epi-*, on, in)
			CROSS REFERENCE: *agogue, athl, duc*
agora (cont'd)	Greek *ageirein*, to assemble (IE: *ger*, to collect)	marketplace, assembly	PREFIXED ROOT:
			cat-: category (a class or division in a scheme of classification; in *logic*, any of the various basic concepts into which all knowledge can be classified; in this sense, also called predicament) (Late Latin *categoria*, accusation, predicament, category of predicables) (*cata-*, down, against)
			par-: paregoric (originally, a medicine that soothes or lessens pain; a camphorated tincture of opium, containing benzoic acid, anise oil, etc. used to relieve diarrhea) (*para-*, beside)
			LEADING ROOT COMPOUND:
			phob: agoraphobia (literally, fear of the marketplace; fear of open spaces) (*phobia*, fear of)

21

Element	From	Meaning	Examples
agora,** egor			TRAILING ROOT COMPOUND: all: allegory (a literary, dramatic, or pictorial representation, the apparent or superficial sense of which both parallels and illustrates a deeper sense just as, for example, the story of the search for the Holy Grail may illustrate an inner spiritual search) (*allos*, other) pan: panegyric [literally, (for) all the assembly; a formal eulogistic composition intended as a public compliment; elaborate praise or laudation; an encomium] (*pan*, all) CROSS REFERENCE: *greg*
agr**	Greek *ager*: a field (IE: *ag-*, to drive, do; where the cattle were driven to)	a field; wild	SIMPLE ROOT: agra: agrarian (relating to land or to the ownership of land) agre: agrestal, agrestic (rural, rustic; crude, uncouth) agri: agrimony [any plant of a genus (*Agrimonia*) in the rose family, typically having little yellow flowers on spiky stalks and bearing burlike fruits] LEADING ROOT COMPOUND: *agri*: business: agribusiness (*agriculture business*; farming and related food-processing and marketing businesses, operated as a large-scale modern industry) cult: agriculture (the science or art of cultivating land in the raising of crops; husbandry; farming) *agro*: bio: agrobiology (the quantitative science of plant life and plant nutrition) (*bio*, life) logy: agrology (the branch of soil science dealing especially with the production of crops) (*logy*, study of) mania: agromania (opposite to *agoraphobia*) (*mania*, craving) nom: agronomics, agronomy (both terms refer to the art or science of managing land or crops) (*nomos*, law) DISGUISED TRAILING ROOT COMPOUND: onager (wild ass, from *onos*, ass + *agrios*, wild) peregrine, pilgrim (see *Doublets* below; from *per-*, through + *ager*, field, country) DOUBLETS: peregrine:pilgrim BOUND COMPOUND: stavesacre (a purple-flowered larkspur of Europe and Asia, with poisonous seeds, and with emetic and cathartic properties) (Greek *staphis*, raisin + *agrios*, wild) CROSS REFERENCE: *camp* (Latin)
ailur*	Greek *ailouros*	cat	SIMPLE ROOT: ailurus LEADING ROOT COMPOUND: phil: ailurophile (also, *aelurophile*) (*phila*, love of) phob: ailurophobia (*phobia*, unreasonable fear or hatred of) pod: Ailuropoda (a genus which includes only the giant panda) (*pod*, foot) CROSS REFERENCE: *fel*
al-			See *ad-* for *allude*, etc.

Word from a literary character: gargantuan
Meaning "gigantic, enormous," the word is from Gargantua, a giant king,
noted for his size and prodigious feats and appetite.
He is the main character of Gargantua, a satire by François Rabelais.

22

Element	From	Meaning	Examples
al**	Latin *ala*: wing (IE: *aks-*, axis)	wing, armpit	ROOT NOTE: This root originally meant upper arm, and by extension, wing. The root also refers to the side parts of a specified organ or structure, e.g., aliethmoid, alinasal. SIMPLE ROOT: ala alar: alar (now, of, or like a wing; having wings; in *anatomy*, pertaining to the armpit; axillary, the original meaning of *alar*; in *botany*, pertaining to the axil), alary alat: alate alu: alula (the group of three to six small, rather stiff feathers growing on the first digit, pollex, or thumb of a bird's wing) LEADING ROOT COMPOUND: form: aliform (wing-shaped; same as *alar*, above) nas: alinasal (pertaining to the *ali nasi*, the flaring cartilaginous expansion forming the outer side of each nostril) (*nas*, nose) ped: aliped (wing-footed, as the bat) (*ped*, foot) trunk: alitrunk (the portion of the insect trunk that bears the wings) FRENCH: aileron (a movable hinged section in or near the trailing edge of an airplane wing for controlling the rolling movements of the airplane) DISGUISED ROOT: aisle (Old French *aile*, wing; originally, section of a building; *s* inserted through confusion with *isle*) CROSS REFERENCE: *axil*, *pter*
al**	Arabic	the	NOTE: The words in this family are entered as simple roots, even though they are *article + root*. SIMPLE ROOT: alca: alcaide (the commander or governor of a fortress as in Spain or Portugal) (from *quad*, to command) alcalde (the mayor or chief judicial official of a Spanish or Spanish-American town) (from *qadi*, judge) alcazar (capitalized, the palace of the Moorish kings at Seville; in lower case, a castle or fortress of the Spanish Moors) (from *qasr*, castle) alch: alchemy (see *American Heritage Dictionary*) alco: alcohol, alcoholic, alcoholism alcove (an arch, vault; a recessed section of a room, as a breakfast nook; a secluded bower in a garden; summerhouse) (Spanish *alcoba*; from Arabic *al-qubba; qubba*) ale: alembic (an apparatus formerly used for distilling) (from *anbig*, still) alf: alfalfa (literally, the best fodder) alge: algebra (literally, the rejoining of broken parts; from *jabbara*, to reunite) algo: algorism [from *al-Khowarazmi*, literally, native of Khwarazm (Khiva), mathematician of the 9th century, A.D.; the Arabic system of numerals; decimal system of counting] alid: alidade (from *al `idadah*, a rule; thus a type of surveying instrument) alif: alif (the first letter of the Arabic alphabet) alk: alkali

Element	From	Meaning	Examples
al (cont'd)			**DISGUISED ROOT:** admiral (the highest rank in the U. S. Navy) (short for *amir al bar*, leader of the sea) elixir (in full, *elixir of life*: a hypothetical substance sought for by medieval alchemists to change base metals into gold or to prolong life indefinitely; now, a supposed remedy for ailments; panacea) (*iksir*, philosopher's stone; probably from Greek *xerion*, powder for drying wounds; *xero*, dry) **PLACENAMES:** Alcatraz (the Pelican), short for Isla de Alcatraces, California Alhambra, California [Spanish; from *al hamra*, literally, the red (house); palace of the Moorish kings near Granada, Spain]. From *Alhambra* is *Alhambresque*, like the Alhambra, especially in richness of ornamentation. NOTE: There are dozens of other Arabic words in English that do not begin with *al*, e.g., apricot, assassin, azimuth, azure, burnoose, carat, cipher, cotton, elixir, gazelle, ghoul, hegira, lute, magazine, mattress, minaret, mohair, monsoon, mortise, myrrh, nadir, safari, saffron, Sahara, salaam, sequin, sheik, sherbet, sirocco, syrup, spinach, sultan, Swahili, talcum, talisman, tariff, zenith, zero. NO CROSS REFERENCE
al**	Latin *alere*; from *alescere*, to grow up (IE: *al-*, to grow, yielding English *old*)	to nourish	**SIMPLE ROOT:** alim: aliment (anything that nourishes; food; means of support; necessity; as a *verb*, to supply with aliment; nourish) alimental, alimentary, alimentary canal, alimentation alimony (literally, food, support; originally, supply of the means of living; maintenance; an allowance that a court orders paid to a person by that person's spouse or former spouse after a legal separation or divorce or while legal action on this is pending) alt: altricial [pertaining to birds that are helpless and naked, as pigeons, and which must be *fed* by parents after hatching; opposed to *precocial* (from *precocious*), pertaining to birds whose newly hatched young are covered with down and are fully active; *precocial* describes the wild birds of the Gallinae family, e.g., wild turkey, grouse, pheasant, partridge, quail] **PREFIXED ROOT:** *co*-: coalesce (literally, to grow together; join, blend, fuse, as the halves of a broken bone; to unite or merge into a single body, group, or mass; **Synonyms:** mix, mingle, blend) (*co-*, together) DISGUISED ROOT: adult, adolescent **LATIN WORDS AND PHRASES:** *alma mater* (literally, nourishing mother) *alumna* [feminine (plural, *alumnae*); *alumnus* [masculine (plural, *alumni*)] CROSS REFERENCE: *nutri, troph*

What is thinking? In what does it consist?
Thinking, in substance, is the process of getting the meanings of things.
Threshing meanings out, refining them in the mind, is done by means of the word, spoken and written.
Demiashkevich

Element	From	Meaning	Examples
alb***	Latin *albus* (IE: *albho-*, white)	white	SIMPLE ROOT: alb (from *alba vestis*, white cloak) alba: alba (Provençal, dawn) albarium (a thin, white stucco) albatross (from Spanish *alcatraz*, pelican; from Arabic *al-qadus*, water-wheel basket); probably influenced by *albus*) albe: albedo, albescent (turning white) albi: albinism, albino (a person with deficient pigmentation, exhibited by milky or translucent skin, white or colorless hair; birds and animals may also be albino) albite (a milky white variety of plagioclase, occurring in many rocks, including granite) album: album, albumen (white of an egg), albumin (white protein substance), albuminate, albuminous, albumose albus: albus LEADING ROOT COMPOUND: oid: albuminoid (*oid*, resembling, similar to) osis: albuminosis (*osis*, condition of) ur: albuminuria (the abnormal presence of albumin in the urine) (*uria*, a diseased condition of the urine) DISGUISED ROOT: abele (the white poplar tree) aubade (a piece of music composed for performance in the morning) (French; from Spanish *albada*; from Provençal *alba*, which see above) daub (*de-*, intensive + *albus*) POETIC NAME OF ENGLAND: Albion (from its *White Cliffs of Dover*) PLACENAMES: Alba (Michigan, Missouri, Texas) INTERDISCIPLINARY: albedo (in *astronomy*, the reflecting power of a planet or satellite, expressed as a ratio of reflected light to the total amount falling on the surface; in *engineering*, the reflecting ability of an object) CROSS REFERENCE: *blanc, cand, leuk*
alg**	Greek *algein*: to feel; *algos*: pain	pain, feeling	SIMPLE ROOT: algesia, algesic, algetic PREFIXED ROOT: an-: analgesia, analgesic (*an-*, not, without) hyper-: hyperalgesia, hyperalgetic, hyperalgia (*hyper-*, over, beyond) hyp-: hypalgesia, hypalgia (*hypo-*, under) LEADING ROOT COMPOUND: *alg*: gen: algogenic (*gen*, producing) edon: algedonic (pertaining to pleasure; thus *algedonic* pertains to both pleasure and pain) (*edon*, an elided form of *hedonic*, pertaining to pleasure) *algo*: lagn: algolagnia (an abnormal sexual pleasure derived from inflicting or suffering pain; masochism or sadism) (*lagneia*, lust) meter: algometer (a device for measuring sensitivity of pain produced by pressure) (*meter*, measure) phob: algophobia (*phobia*, fear of)

Element	From	Meaning	Examples
alg (cont'd)			TRAILING ROOT COMPOUND: cardi: cardialgia (same as *heartburn*; literally, heart pain: so named because mistakenly thought to be located in the heart) (*cardi*, heart) caus: causalgia (neuralgia characterized by a burning sensation) (*caus*, fever, heat) my: myalgia (pain in a muscle or muscles) (*myo*, muscle) neur: neuralgia (*neur*, nerve) nost: nostalgia (a longing to return home) (*nostos*, a return) NOTE: Do not confuse this root with *alga,* referring to seaweed; other words with similarities to this root are *algebra, algorithm* (Arabic); *algraphy* (from *al*uminum + *graphy*). CROSS REFERENCE: *dol, esthes, odyn, path, sens*
all***	Greek *allos*: other (IE: *al-*, that, yonder one; yielding English else)	other, mutually, another	SIMPLE ROOT: allele (a genetics term) PREFIXED ROOTS AND COMPOUNDS: *par-*: (from *para-*, alongside; side by side) parallax, parallel parallelepiped (a solid with six faces, each of which is a parallelogram) (*epi-*, upon + *pedon*, ground) parallelogram (*gram* from *graph*, write) LEADING ROOT COMPOUND: *all*: egor: allegory (the description of one thing under the image of another; a story in which people, things, and happenings have a hidden meanings) (from *agora*, assembly) erg: allergy (literally, other work) (*ergon*, work) onym: allonym (another name, usually historical, adopted by an author; compare *pseudonym*) (*onym*, name) *allo*: chth: allochthonous (originating elsewhere; not native to a place) (*chthon*, earth) gam: allogamy (fertilization of a flower by the pollen of another; cross-fertilization) (*gam*, marriage) graft: allograft (a graft of tissue or an organ taken from an individual of the same species as the recipient but with different hereditary factors) graph: allograph (any of the ways a unit of a writing system is formed or shaped) (*graph*, write) mer: allomerism {allomerous} (*mere*, part) metr: allometry (in *biology*, the growth of a part of an organism in relation to the growth of the whole or some other part of it) (*metry*, measurement of) morph: allomorph {allomorphic} (*morph*, shape) path: allopath, allopathy (the method of treating disease by use of agents, producing effects different from those of the disease treated; opposed to *homeopathy*) (*path*, disease) patr: allopatric (in *biology*, of or pertaining to species of organisms occurring in different but often adjacent places) (*patra*, native village; from *pater*, father) phon: allophone (*phone*, sound) plasm: alloplasm (in *biology*, a part of protoplasm that is differentiated to perform a special function, as that of the flagellum) (*plasm*, form)

Element	From	Meaning	Examples
all (cont'd)			saur: allosaurus (also, *allosaur*; a dinosaur of the Jurassic period) (*saur*, lizard) trop: allotrope (the property that certain chemical elements have of existing in two or more different forms, as carbon in charcoal, diamonds, lampblack, etc.) (*tropos*, way, manner) troph: allotrophic (rendered innutritious by the process of digestion) (*trophos*, nutrition) EMBEDDED ROOT COMPOUND: morphallaxis (*morph*, shape) CROSS REFERENCE: *alter, hetero*
alt***	Latin *altus* (IE: *al-*, to grow, nourish)	high	SIMPLE ROOT: alta: altar (from it being raised high) alti: altissimo, altitude, altitudinal alto: alto [in the Middle Ages, the highest male voice (above the tenor, which held the melody); the lowest of the three ladies' voices was *contralto*; over the centuries, the lowest ladies' part was often shortened to *alto*; consequently, that which literally refers to *high* in music actually refers to *low*] PREFIXED ROOTS AND COMPOUNDS: *contr-*: contralto (see note at *alto*, above) (*contra-*, against) *ex-*: exalt (to raise on high; elevate; lift up), exaltation, exalted (*ex-*, out) LEADING ROOT COMPOUND: *alt*: azimuth: altazimuth (from Arabic *al sumut*, the way) *alti*: graph: altigraph (*graph*, write) meter: altimeter (a device for measuring the altitude to which it is carried) (*meter*, measure) metry: altimetry (the science or practice of measuring altitudes, as with an altimeter) (*metry*, measurement of) plan: altiplano (a high plateau, as in Bolivia) (*plane*, level, even) *alto*: cumu: altocumulus (a type of cloud) (*cumulus*, pile) strat: altostratus (a type of cloud) (*stratus*, layer) tropo: altotroposphere (a portion of the atmosphere about 40 to 60 miles above the surface of the earth) (*tropo*, turn; *sphere*, ball, globe) DISGUISED ROOT: enhance (to make greater as in cost, value, attractiveness, etc.; heighten, improve, augment, etc.; as an intransitive verb, to increase, as in value or price) (from Vulgar Latin *inaltiare*, to raise high) haughty (**Synonyms**: lordly, disdainful, contemptuous) hautboy (earlier name for *oboe*; see next entry) oboe (a woodwind with a high, penetrating tone) (from French *hautbois*, high wood) SPANISH: altiplano (literally, high plane, as in Bolivia) FRENCH TERMS: *haute couture* (literally, high sewing; high fashion) *haute cuisine* (literally, high kitchen; the preparation of fine food by highly skilled chefs, or the food so prepared) *haute école* (literally, high school) *haut monde* (literally, high world; high society)

Element	From	Meaning	Examples
alt (cont'd)			*haute vulgarisation* (vulgarization on a higher level, especially as done by academics, scholars, etc.) ITALIAN: *alto-relievo* (also, *alto-rilievo*) PLACENAMES: Altadena, California Alta Loma (California, Texas) Altamont (Illinois, Kansas, Missouri, Oregon, South Dakota, Tennessee, Utah) Alta Vista (Iowa, Kansas); Altavista, Virginia Alto (Georgia, Louisiana, Michigan, New Mexico, Texas, Wisconsin); Palo Alto, California Terre Haute, Indiana (French; literally, high land, highest point on the Wabash; not the highest point in Indiana, however) CROSS REFERENCE: *acro, apic, hyps, sum*
alter,* **altr**	Latin *alter* (IE: *al-*, that, yonder one; yielding English else)	other	SIMPLE ROOT: alter: alter (**Synonyms**: change, modify, transform; not to be confused with homonym *altar*, previous family) altera: alterable, alteration, alterative (in *medicine*, gradually restoring health) alterc: altercate (to argue angrily; quarrel), altercation (**Synonyms**: quarrel, wrangle, squabble) alteri: alterity (the state or quality of being other; otherness) altern: alternant, alternate (**Synonyms**: intermittent, recurrent, periodic), alternation alternative (**Synonyms**: choice, option, preference), alternator altr: altruism (concern for the welfare of others, as opposed to egoism; selflessness), altruistic PREFIXED ROOT: *sub-*: subaltern, subalternate (following in order; successive; in *botany*, in an alternate arrangement, but tending to become opposite: said of a leaf arrangement) (*sub-*, under) *super-*: superaltern (in traditional logic, a universal proposition that is the basis for immediate interference to a corresponding subaltern) (*super-*, over, beyond) LEADING ROOT COMPOUND: quant: aliquant (in *mathematics*, designating a part of a number that does not divide the number evenly but leaves a remainder, e.g., 8 is an *aliquant* part of 36) (*quantus*, how large, how much) quot: aliquot (in *mathematics,* designating a part of a number that divides the number evenly and leaves no remainder, e.g., 8 is an *aliquot* part of 32) (*quot*, how many, or as many as) DISGUISED ROOTS: adulterate, adulterine, adulterous, adultery alias (**Synonyms**: pseudonym, nom de plume, incognito) alibi (contraction of *alius ibi*, elsewhere) alien (**Synonyms**: foreigner, stranger, emigré) aliunde (from another place; in *law*, from some other source, e.g., evidence clarifying a document but not deriving from the document itself is evidence *aliunde*) PREFIXED DISGUISED ROOT: *in-*: inalienable (that may not be taken away or transferred, as *inalienable rights* guaranteed by the Declaration of Independence) (*in-*, not)

28

Element	From	Meaning	Examples
alter (cont'd)			LATIN WORDS AND PHRASES: alter ego (literally, other I; another aspect of oneself; a very close friend or constant companion) *alter idem* (another of the same kind) *et alibi* (and elsewhere) *et alii* (and others) [*et al*. is the abbreviation for both *et alibi* and *et alii*] *inter alia* (among other things) *inter alios* (among other persons) MUSIC TERM: altered chord (a chord in which one or more tones have been chromatically altered by sharps, flats, or naturals foreign to the key) CROSS REFERENCE: *all, hetero*
alveol*	Latin from Greek *aulus*: reed (*aulus* is found in *hydraulic*, literally water tube)	trough, cavity, pit, cell	SIMPLE ROOT: alveolar, alveolate (honeycombed; full of small cavities), alveolus, alveus INTERDISCIPLINARY: alveolus (in *anatomy* and *zoology*, a small cavity or hollow, as a cell of a honeycomb, air cell or sac of a lung, tooth socket, etc.; in *dentistry*, plural *alveoli* is the ridge of the gums above and behind the upper front teeth; teethridge) NO CROSS REFERENCE
ama**	Latin *amare*	to love	SIMPLE ROOT: ama: amateur (in radio parlance, a ham, one licensed to operate radio transmitters as a hobby, for the love of it), amative, amatory amo: amorist (a person much occupied with love-making), amorous PREFIXED ROOT: en-: enamor (to fill with love and desire; captivate; usually used in the passive voice with *of* or *with*, e.g., *enamored with his job*) (en-, in) FRENCH WORDS AND PHRASES: *amour* (a love affair, especially of an illicit or secret nature; see *paramour* above) *amour propre* (self-love; love of oneself; self-esteem) PREFIXED FRENCH: para-: paramour (a lover or mistress; especially the illicit sexual partner of a married man or woman) (*para-* from *per-*, by) ITALIAN WORDS AND PHRASES: *amoretto* (an infant cupid, as in Italian art of the 16th century) (diminutive of *amore*, love) *amorino* (same as *amoretto*) *con amore* (literally, with love; tenderly; a direction to the performer in music; with enthusiasm) *inamorata* (lover; specifically, a woman in relation to the man who is her lover; sweetheart or mistress) LATIN PHRASE: *amor patriae* (literally, love of one's country; patriotism) FRENCH MEDICAL TERM: amadou (literally, lover; a fungus, originally used as a wound dressing and a hemostatic) PROPER NAME: Amadis (Spanish, love of God; name of hero in medieval romances in Spanish, French and English literatures) PLACENAMES: Amado, Arizona; Amador, California CROSS REFERENCE: *ami, eros, phil*

Element	From	Meaning	Examples
amb***	Latin *ambulare* (IE: *al*, wander)	to walk	**SIMPLE ROOT:** ambl: amble (to move at a smooth, easy gait by raising first both legs on one side, then both on the other: said of a horse, etc.; to go easily and unhurriedly; walk in a leisurely manner {ambler} ambu: ambulacrum, ambulance, ambulant, ambulate, ambulatory (as a legal term, revocable, subject to change, capable of alteration, for example, an *ambulatory disposition*) **PREFIXED ROOT:** *circum-*: circumambient (surrounding; enclosing), circumambulate (to walk around) (*circum-*, around) *per-*: perambulate, perambulator (often shortened to *pram*, a baby carriage) (*per-*, through) *pre-*: preamble (literally, walking before; an introductory statement, preface, introduction; capitalized, the introductory statement of the United States Constitution, setting forth the principles of American government and beginning with the words, "We the people of the United States, in order to form a more perfect union. . . ") (*pre-*, before) **LEADING ROOT COMPOUND:** ag: ambages (a roundabout, indirect way of talking or doing things; not to be confused with *ambiguous*, next family) ambagious (*agere*, to go) **TRAILING ROOT COMPOUND:** fun: funambulist (one who performs on a tightrope or a slack rope) (*funis*, rope) noct: noctambulate (also, *noctambulation*; walking in one's sleep; same as *somnambulism*) (*noct*, night) somn: somnambulate (to walk in one's sleep) {somnambulant, somnambulation}, somnambulism (*somn*, sleep) **DISGUISED ROOT:** alley (Middle English *aly*; from Old French *alee*, from the verb *aler*, from the French verb *aler*, to go; from Middle Latin *alare*, a contraction of *ambulare*) purlieu (originally, an outlying part of a forest, exempted from forest laws and returned to private owners; now, a place that one visits often or habitually; haunt) **PREFIXED DISGUISED ROOT:** *ex-*: exile (literally, one banished; **Synonyms:** banish, expatriate, deport) (*ex-*, out + Greek *alaomai*, I wander) **ITALIAN MUSIC TERMS:** *andante* (moderate in tempo, as though walking; as a *noun*, an andante movement or passage) *andantino* (originally, slower; now slightly faster than *andante*) **CROSS REFERENCE:** *ambi-*, *pat*, as in *peripatetic*
ambi,*** ambo, an	Latin *ambi*: *ambo* (IE: *ambhi*, around)	both, around	**SIMPLE ROOT:** amice (a cloak that is thrown around oneself) **PREFIXED ROOT:** *am-*: plex: amplexicaul (in *botany*, clasping or enveloping the stem, as the leaves of corn or of the teasels) (from *plectere*, to braid) put: amputate (to cut off an arm, leg, etc., especially by surgery) {amputation}(*putare*, to cut, to prune)

30

Element	From	Meaning	Examples
ambi (cont'd)			

amb-:

i: (from *ire*, to go)

ambiance (same as *ambience*, the preferred spelling)

ambience (an environment or its distinct atmosphere; milieu)

ambient (completely surrounding; encompassing; as *ambient noises*; circulating, as *ambient air*)

ambit (a circuit or circumference) (from same base as *ambient*)

ambition (originally, a going about seeking votes; now, a strong desire to succeed or to achieve something, as fame, power, wealth, etc.)

ambitious (**Synonyms:** aspiring, enterprising, emulous) (from same base as *ambient*)

ambitus [the exterior edge or periphery (as of a leaf, a bivalve shell, or the test (hard shell), of sea urchin)] (from *ambit*)

ig: (from *agere*, to go)

ambiguity (the state or quality of being ambiguous; **Synonyms:** vagueness, equivocation)

ambiguous (having two or more possible meanings; not clear; indefinite; uncertain; **Synonyms:** obscure, vague, enigmatic)

an-:

fract: anfractuous (full of twists, turns, and windings; roundabout; tortuous) (from *frangere*, to break)

DOUBLE PREFIXED ROOT:

circumambient (extending all around; surrounding) (*circum-*, around + *itere*, to go)

LEADING ROOT COMPOUND:

ambi:

dextr: ambidextrous (to be able to use both hands with equal ease; therefore, very skillful or versatile; also, treacherous, deceitful) (from *dexter*, right hand)

sex: ambisexual (same as *bisexual*)

syllabl: ambisyllabic (in referring to a sound or cluster of sounds, partly in the first and partly in the second or not assignable to one only of two consecutive syllables, e.g., the *n* in *cynic*)

tend: ambitendency (in *psychology*, the existence of conflicting tendencies in the same individual) (*tendere*, to stretch)

val: ambivalence (simultaneous conflicting feelings toward a person or thing, as love and hate) (*valere*, to be strong)

vers: ambiversion (in *psychology*, a condition or character trait that includes elements of both introversion and extroversion) (from *vertere*, to turn)

ambo:

cept: amboceptor (an antibody able to damage or destroy a microorganism or other cell by connecting a complement to it) [*ambo*, both + *(re)ceptor*]

DISGUISED ROOT:

ambassador (the highest-ranking diplomatic representative appointed by one country or government to represent it in another) (from *agere*, to do)

ambsace (literally, double aces, the lowest thrown at dice; misfortune; bad luck)

embassy (from *ambassador*)

Element	From	Meaning	Examples
ambi (cont'd)			GERMANIC: bivouac (a temporary military encampment in the field; originally, an encampment in which a soldier stood guard during the night) (Old High German *biwacht*, from *bi-*, by + *wacht*, guard; literally, to watch by) DUTCH: bilander (a coaster, a small, two-masted ship used on the canals and along the coast of The Netherlands) (from *bijlander*, literally, by land) CROSS REFERENCE: *amphi-, circum-, peri-*
ambo			See *ambi* for *amboceptor*.
ameb			See *amoeb*.
ami**	Latin *amare*: to love	friend	SIMPLE ROOT: amiable (**Synonyms:** affable, good-natured, obliging) amicable (see *Doublets* below) amity (peaceful relations, as between nations; friendship) PREFIXED DISGUISED ROOT: *em*: *en-*: enemy (**Synonyms:** antagonist, adversary) (*en-*, not) *im*: *in-*: inimical (like an enemy; unfriendly; in opposition; adverse; unfavorable; same derivation as *enemy*) (*in-*, not) DOUBLETS: amiable:amicable FRENCH TERM: *bon ami* (good friend; capitalized, name of a cleaning compound, a "good friend" to the cleaning person) SPANISH: *amigo* LATIN PHRASES: *amici probantur rebus adversis* (friends are proved by adversity: Cicero) *amicus Plato, sed magis amica* veritas (Plato is my friend, but a greater friend is truth) LATIN LAW TERM: *amicus curiae* (friend of the court; a disinterested party, who volunteers advice to the court) PLACENAME: Amity, Indiana NO CROSS REFERENCE
amoeb* [also spelled ameba)	Greek *ameibein*	to change	SIMPLE ROOT: *ameb*: ameba (same as *amoeba*, which is the preferred general usage) {amebic} amebiasis [infested with amoebas (or *amoebae*)] *amoeb*: amoeba (a one-celled, microscopic animal) amoebean (also, *amoebaean, amebean*; alternately answering, as in dialogue) amoebiasis (same as *amebiasis*) LEADING ROOT COMPOUND: *amoeb(o)*: oid: amoeboid (*oid*, similar to) cyt: amoebocyte (also spelled *amebocyte*: any cell capable of moving like an ameba, especially one that floats freely in the blood or other body fluids, such as a white blood corpuscle) (*cyt*, cell) CROSS REFERENCE: *camb, meta-, mut*

No writer or speaker who ignores the roots of Latin derivatives
is secure from egregious error. Stuart Sherman

Element	From	Meaning	Examples
amph***	Greek *amphi-* (IE: *ambhi,* both, around)	both sides, around	EXTENDED PREFIX: amphoteric (literally, each of two; partly one and partly the other; specifically, capable of reacting chemically either as an acid or as a base) PREFIXED ROOTS AND COMPOUNDS: amph-: eclex: ampheclexis (thus sexual selection on the part of both male and female) (*eklexis,* selection) hemer: amphemerous (circadian, or quotidian) (*hemera,* day) amphi-: bi: amphibian (any of a class of cold-blooded, scaleless vertebrates, consisting of the frogs, toads, newts, salamanders, and caecilians, that usually begin life in the water as tadpoles with gills and later develop lungs), amphibious (*bio,* life) bol: (from *ballein,* to throw) amphibole, amphibolic (having both a *catabolic* and an *anabolic* function) amphibolite (a rock consisting largely of amphibole and plagioclase) amphibology (double or doubtful meaning; ambiguity, especially from uncertain grammatical construction; also *amphiboly*) brach: amphibrach (a metrical foot in Greek and Latin verse consisting of one long syllable between two short ones, or in English, of one accented syllable between two unaccented ones, e.g., ex-PLO-sion; compare *amphimacer* below) (*brachys,* short) chro: amphichroic (in *chemistry,* exhibiting either of two colors under varying conditions, as litmus) (*chroa,* color) coel: amphicoelous (concave on both sides, as the vertebrae of fishes) (from *koilos,* hollow) mac: amphimacer (literally, long at both ends; a metrical foot in Greek and Latin verse consisting of one short syllable between two long ones, or, in English of one unaccented syllable between two accented ones, e.g., HES-i-TATE; compare *amphibrach,* above) (from *makros,* long) mix: amphimixis (in *biology,* the uniting of male and female germ cells from two individuals in reproduction; crossbreeding) (*mixis,* mixing) ox: amphioxus (the lancelet; same as *cephalochordate,* a small chordate sea animal) (*oxys,* sharp) pod: amphipod (any of several crustaceans with one set of feet for jumping or walking and another set for swimming, as the sand flea) (*pod,* foot) pro: amphiprostyle (in *architecture,* having rows of columns at the front and back, but none along the sides) (*pro-* prefixes *style,* column) styl: amphistylar (in *architecture,* having columns at both front and back, or on both sides) (*style,* column) theater: amphitheater (see note at the *the* family) thec: amphithecium (in *botany,* the outer layer of cells in the spore case of moss) (from *theke,* case) trop: amphitropous (in *botany,* having a half-inverted ovule, so that the micropyle and chalaza are at equal distances from the placenta) (*tropos,* turn)

Element	From	Meaning	Examples
amph (cont'd)			MESHED LEADING ROOT COMPOUND: amphora (in ancient Greece, a tall jar with handles that could be carried around) (from *pherein*, to bear) amphoric (pertaining to a bottle; resembling the sound made by blowing across the mouth of a bottle) (*phoreus*, bearer) amphoroloquy (the production of amphoric sounds in speaking) (*loqui*, to speak) amphorophony (an amphoric sound of the voice) (*phone*, sound) DISGUISED ROOT: ampulla (nearly round bottle with two handles, used by the ancient Greeks and Romans; in *anatomy*, a sac or dilated part of a tube or canal, as of a milk duct in a mammary gland) (diminutive of *amphora*; see above), ampullaceous (shaped like an ampulla or bladder) CROSS REFERENCE: *ambi, circum, peri*
amyg*	Greek *amygdale*: almond	almond, tonsil	ROOT NOTE: This root originally meant almond; however, it is extended to mean tonsil, because of the tonsil's shape. SIMPLE ROOT: amygdala (in *anatomy*, a tonsil) amygdalaceous (belonging to a group of shrubs and trees with soft, fleshy fruit that contains a single hard seed or stone, as the peach, almond, cherry, plum, etc.) amygdalate (of, or like almonds) amygdalin (a glucoside present in bitter almonds) amygdaline (of, or like an almond or almonds; also, having to do with the tonsils) amygdaloid (almond-shaped; also, designating or of a volcanic rock having small bubble holes filled with secondary minerals; as a *noun*, this rock) NO CROSS REFERENCE
amyl*	Greek *amylos*	starch	ROOT NOTE: This root is derived from *a-*, negative + *myle*, mill; thus, not ground at the mill. SIMPLE ROOT: amalya: amylaceous (of or like starch), amylase (an enzyme that helps change starch into sugar; it is found in saliva, pancreatic juices, etc.) amyle: amylene amylu: amylum (technical name for *starch*) LEADING ROOT COMPOUND: *amyl*: oid: amyloid (*oid*, similar to) ose: amylose (*ose*, condition of) *amylo*: gen: amylogen (the water-soluble part of the starch granule) (*gen*, producing) lys: amylolysis (the changing of starch into soluble substances) (*lysis*, loosening) psin: amylopsin (from *trypsin*, the enzyme of pancreatic juice) NO CROSS REFERENCE

Colossal, meaning "gigantic, huge, vast," and *coliseum*, an amphitheater, stadium, or large theater, are both from Colossus, a giant statue of Apollo, set at the entrance to the harbor of Rhodes circa 280 B.C., and included among the Seven Wonders of the World.

Element	From	Meaning	Examples
an-, a-***	Greek *an-*	not, without	PREFIXED ROOTS AND COMPOUNDS: a-: bas: abasia (inability to walk caused by a defect in muscular coordination) (*bas*, walk) bio: abiogenesis (same as spontaneous generation) (*bio*, life + *genesis*, producing) branch: abranchiate (without gills; as a *noun*, an animal without gills; also, *abranchial*) (*branch*, gill) bul: abulia (also spelled *aboulia*) (from *boule*, will, determination) bys: abysmal (of or like an abyss; bottomless; unfathomable; wretched to the point of despair; immeasurably bad), abyss (literally, no bottom; anything too deep for measurement; profound depth, as the abyss of time, of space, etc.; can be used figuratively, as the *abyss of despondency, shame*, etc.) carp: acarpelous (without carpels), acarpous (bearing no fruit) (*carp*, fruit) caud: acaudal, acaudate (having no tail) (*caud*, tail) caul: acaulescent (without a visible stem), acaulous (*caul*, stem) centr: acentric (having no center; not centered; placed off-center) cept: acephalous (headless; in *zoology*, having no part of the body differentiated as the head; also, having no leader, as *an acephalous organization*) (*cephal*, head) chlamyd: achlamydeous (without a cover; in *botany*, having neither sepals nor petals; without a perianth) (*chlamyd*, cloak) chlor: achlorhydria (a stomach disorder in which the stomach fails to secrete hydrochloric acid) chrom: achromatic (*chrom*, color) clinic: aclinic (also called *isoclinic*, literally, same lean, or slope (from *klinein*; Latin *clinare*, to lean) [It would appear that *aclinic* and *isoclinic* are paradoxical; however, the two words express different ways of viewing the same phenomenon: describing an imaginary line around the earth near the equator where the lines of force of the earth's magnetic field are parallel with the surface of the earth and where a magnetic needle will not *dip, slope*, or lean.] cycl: acyclic (not in cycles; in *chemistry*, having the structure of an open chain rather than a closed ring) (*cycle*, circle, ring) gnos: agnostic [a person who holds that the ultimate cause (God) and the essential nature of things are unknown and unknowable] (*gnos*, know) gon: agonic (not forming an angle) (*gon*, angle) leuk: aleukemia (*leuk*, white + *em*, from *hemo*, blood + *-ia*, condition of) ner: aneroid (as an *adjective*, not using liquid; as a *noun*, an aneroid barometer) (*neros*, liquid + *-oid*, resembling) no: anoesia, anoesis (want of understanding), anoia (mental deficiency) (*noein*, to perceive, think) nom: anomie (also, *anomy*; lack of purpose, identity, or ethical values in a person or in a society; rootlessness) (*nomos*, law)

Element	From	Meaning	Examples
an-, a- (cont'd)			ori: aorist (originally *khronos aoristos*, the indefinite tense; a past tense of Greek verbs, denoting an action without indicating whether completed, continued, or repeated, and without further limitation or implication) (from *horistos*, limited)
			path: (*pathos*, feeling)
			apathetic (**Synonyms**: impassive, stoic, stolid)
			[do not confuse with *apatetic*, in *zoology*, serving to disguise or conceal by camouflaging; imitative; as the *apatetic coloration* of certain animals]
			apathy (lack of emotion; lack of interest; listless condition; unconcern; indifference)
			polit: apolitical (not political; of no political significance; politically indifferent)
			sphalt: asphalt (also called "mineral pitch"; literally, to cause not to fall; that which bonds) (*sphallein*, to fall)
			stas: astasia (muscular incoordination in standing) (*stas*, stand)
			syn: asyndeton (to bind; therefore, without conjunctions, e.g., "Smile, shake hands, part"; "He has provided the poor with jobs, with opportunity, with self-respect." (*syn-*, together + *deton*, from *dein*, to bind)
			tara: ataraxia (also, *ataraxy*; calmness of mind and emotions; tranquillity) (*tarassein*, to disturb)
			tax: ataxia (total or partial inability to coordinate voluntary bodily movements, especially, muscular movements) (from *tassein*, to arrange)
			the: atheism, atheist (**Synonyms**: agnostic, deist, infidel) (*theos*, God)
			tom: atom (literally, that which cannot be cut further) (*tom*, cut)
			typ: atypical (not typical; not conforming to the type; irregular; abnormal)
			an-: (used before vowels)--See *Note* below.
			acanth: anacanthous (in *biology*, not having spines, without thorns) (*acanth*, thorn)
			aero: anaerobe, anaerobic (an organism, especially a bacterium that does not require air or oxygen to live; opposed to *aerobe*) (*aero*, air + *bio*, life)
			alcim: analcime (weak--from its weak electric power; a white or slightly colored zeolite) (*alkimos*, strong)
			alges: analgesia (no sense of pain) (*algesis*, sense of pain)
			alpha: analphabetic (not alphabetic; unable to read or write) (*alpha* + *beta*, the first and second letters of the Greek alphabet)
			arch: anarchism, anarchist, anarchy (*arch*, to rule)
			arthr: anarthria (inability to articulate words properly) (*arthros*, articulated)
			echo: anechoic (without an echo, as *an anechoic chamber*)
			em: anemia (in *medicine*, a condition in which there is a reduction of the number or volume of red blood corpuscles or of the total amount of hemoglobin in the bloodstream, resulting in paleness, generalized weakness, etc.; figuratively, lack of vigor or vitality; lifelessness) (from *hemo*, blood)

Element	From	Meaning	Examples
an-, a (cont'd)			erg: anergy (*erg*, work)
			esthes: anesthesia (*esthes*, feeling)
			hydr: anhydrous (*hydro*, water)
			odyn: anodyne (relieving or lessening pain; as a *noun*, any-thing that relieves pain or soothes) (*odyne*, pain)
			oma: anomalous (**Synonyms**: irregular, abnormal, unnatu-ral), anomaly (see listing under *anom* family)
			onym: anonym (an anonymous person; a pseudonym), ano-nymity, anonymous, anonymuncule (*onym*, name)
			orch: anorchous (adjective; having no testes), anorchus (noun; one without testes, or whose testes have not descended) (*orchid*, testis)
			ore: anoretic, anorexia (short for *anorexia nervosa*, lack of ap-petite for food) (*oreg*, to reach after)
			ortho: anorthopia (distorted vision in which straight lines ap-pear bent or curved) (*ortho*, straight + *opia*, vision)
			osm: anosmatic, anosmia (therefore, loss or impairment of the sense of smell) (*osme*, smell)
			DOUBLE PREFIXED ROOT:
			acatalectic (in *prosody*, having the full number of syllables, especially in the final foot) (*a-*, not + *cata-*, down)
			asynchronous (not synchronous) (*a-*, not + *syn-*, with)
			PREFIXED CLASSICAL MYTHOLOGY WORD:
			anaphrodisiac (that which lessens sexual desire, from *Aphro-dite*, the Greek goddess of love and beauty)
			NOTE: Do not confuse words with *an-* prefix + root, for ex-ample, *anarchy*, *analgesia*, with words beginning with *ana-* prefix, as in *anatomy*, where the root is *tom*, to cut.
			CROSS REFERENCE: *de-*, *dis-/di-/ dif-*, *in-/il-/im-/ir-*, *ne-*, *non-*, *un-*
ana-,*** ano-	Greek *ana*	again, over, above, anew, against, backward, reversed/reversion, throughout, up, upward; apiece also, an intensive	PREFIX NOTE: Do not confuse the elided form *ana-* with the negative prefix *an-*, the elided form of which is *a-*.
			PREFIXED ROOT:
			an-:
			agog: anagoge (literally, a leading up; mystical interpretation, as of the Scriptures; also, an uplifting of the mind to spiri-tual things) (*agein*, to lead, drive)
			od: (from *hode*, way)
			anode (in an electrolytic cell, the positively charged electrode; toward which the current flows)
			anodic (in *botany*, that half of a leaf which is turned toward the course of the generic spiral; compare *cathode*)
			odyn: anodyne (any medication that relieves pain, e.g., at-ropine, codeine, coniine, ether, hyoscine, lupulin, morphine, opium, potassium bromide) (*odyne*, pain)
			ana-:
			baen: anabaena (literally, to go up, as to the surface of the wa-ter; a fresh-water alga that contaminates reservoirs) (from *anabasis*, below)
			bapt: Anabaptist (literally, to baptize again or anew; a mem-ber of a 16th-century sect of the Reformation, originating in Switzerland, that denied the validity of infant baptism, prac-ticed baptism of only adults, and advocated religious and so-cial reforms)

37

Element	From	Meaning	Examples
ana- (cont'd)			bas: (from *bainein*, to go)
			anabas (any of a number of freshwater fishes of Africa and Southeast Asia, so named from its habit of climbing)
			anabasis (inland march; a military advance, from the retreat of Greek mercenaries in Asia Minor described in the *Anabasis* of Xenophon)
			bat: anabatic (going up; upward-moving, as *an anabatic wind*) (from *anabas*, previous entry)
			bath: anabathmos (flight of steps; "song of steps"; one of the gradual psalms in the Eastern Church) (from *bainein*, to go)
			bol: anabolism (the synthesis in living organisms of more complex substances from simpler ones; opposed to *catabolism*) (from *ballein*, to throw)
			branch: anabranch (a river branch that re-enters the main stream; a river branch that becomes absorbed by sandy ground)
			chron: anachronism (anything that is or appears to be out of its proper time in history) (*chronos*, time)
			clast: anaclastic (in *optics*, of, caused by, or causing refraction) (*clast*, break)
			clin: anaclinal (in *geology*, progressing in a direction opposite to that in which the rock strata dip, as a valley) (*clin*, lean)
			clit: anaclitic (in *psychoanalysis*, having the libido dependent upon another instinct) (*clit*, lean)
			crus: anacrusis (in *prosody*, one or more unaccented syllables added to the beginning of a line of verse which would ordinarily commence with an accented syllable) (from *krouein*, to strike)
			dem: anadem (poetic; a wreath or garland for the head) (from *dein*, to bind)
			diplo: anadiplosis (in *rhetoric*, repetition in the first part of a clause or sentence of a prominent word from the latter part of the preceding clause or sentence, usually with a change or extension of meaning) (*diplo*, double)
			drom: anadromous (going up rivers to spawn: said of salmon, shad, etc.) (*drome*, run)
			glyph: anaglyph (an ornament sculptured or embossed in low relief, as a cameo) (*glyph*, carve)
			gram: anagram (a transposition of the letters of a word or phrase to form a new word or phrase, e.g., *dear* is an anagram of *read*) (*gram*, write)
			lect: analects (collected literary excerpts or passages) (*lect*, gather)
			lemma: analemma (a scale of the sun's daily declination shown on a globe of the earth, usually in the form of an elongated 8 crossing the equator) (from *analeptic*, next entry)
			lept: analeptic (literally, to take up; in *medicine*, restorative; counteracting drowsiness or the effects of sedatives) (from *lambanein*, to take)
			logy: analogy (**Synonyms:** likeness, similarity, resemblance) (*logos*, ratio)
			ly: analysis, analytic, analytical, analytics, analyze (*lyein*, to loosen)

Element	From	Meaning	Examples
ana- (cont'd)			mne: anamnesis (to call to mind; a remembering, especially of a supposed life before this life) (*mne*, to remember) morph: (shape, form) anamorphic anamorphoscope (an optical device consisting usually of a cylindrical mirror or lens that restores to its normal proportions an image distorted by anamorphosis) (*scope*, look) anamorphosis (*osis*, condition of) nym: ananym (a pseudonym consisting of the real name written backward, as *Rennad* for *Danner*; or *Leon* for *Noel*; do not confuse with *anonym*, where the prefix is *an-*, not, without) (*onym*, name) pest: anapest (literally, struck back; so called from reversing the dactyl, a particular foot of poetry; e.g., And the SHEEN/ of their SPEARS/ was like STARS/ on the SEA; also, 'Twas the NIGHT/ before CHRIST/mas and ALL/ through the HOUSE) (from *paiein*, to strike) phas: anaphase (in *biology*, the stage or phase in mitosis following metaphase in which the divided chromosomes move away from each other to opposite ends of the cell) (*phas*, to show) phor: anaphora (literally, to bear again; a rhetorical device, in which a word or phrase is repeated at the beginning of successive clauses or sentences, for example, Dr. Martin Luther King, Jr.'s address "I Have a Dream," in which "I have a dream" is repeated in successive sentences) (*phor*, bear) phylax: anaphylaxis (in *pathology*, increased susceptibility to a foreign protein resulting from previous exposure to it, as in serum treatment) (*phylax*, guard, prevention) plast: anaplastic [in *surgery*, replacing lost tissue or parts, as by transplanting; in *pathology*, (of cells) having reverted to a more primitive form; (of tumors) having a high degree of malignancy] (*plast*, form) pty: anaptyxis [to fold up; in *linguistics*, the epenthesis, or the insertion of an extra vowel into a consonant group, usually one containing a liquid or a nasal, as in the 3-syllable pronunciation of athlete (ath uh lete)] (*ptyssein*, to fold) sarc: anasarca (in *pathology*, a pronounced, generalized dropsy) (*sarcos*, flesh) stom: anastomosis (the interconnection between blood vessels, veins in a leaf, channels of a river, etc.) (*stoma*, opening, outlet + *osis*, condition of) stroph: anastrophe (reversal of the usual parts of a sentence for rhetorical effect, e.g., *Came the dawn*, for The dawn came; *To market went she*, for She went to market) (*stroph*, turn) them: anathema (a thing or a person accursed, detested, loathed, or damned; a formal ecclesiastical curse involving excommunication) (from *tithenai*, to place) tom: anatomical, anatomist, anatomize, anatomy (the dissecting of an animal or plant in order to determine position, structure, etc. of its parts; the science of morphology or structure of animals or plants; the structure of an organism or body) (*tom*, cut)

39

Element	From	Meaning	Examples
ana- (cont'd)			*ana*: ops: an<u>oo</u>psia (in *medicine*, upward strabismus; *strabismus* is the act of squinting) (*ops*, vision) PROPER NAME: Anastasia (literally, to stand, or to rise, up; of the resurrection) CROSS REFERENCE: *re-, epi-, dia-, retro-, palin-*
ancyl			See *ankylo*.
andr**	Greek *andros* (IE: *aner, ner,* vital force)	man, male; (in *biology*, anther, stamen, the pollen- producing male organ of certain plants; as a suffix, having husbands, having stamens)	LEADING ROOT COMPOUND: *andr*: oid: android (in *science fiction*, an automaton made to resemble a human being) (*oid*, similar to) *andro*: ec: androecium (in *botany*, the stamens of a flower collectively) (from *oikos*, house) gen: androgen (a male sex hormone; in *biochemistry*, any substance that promotes masculine characteristics), androgenic, androgenous (*gen*, produce) gyn: androgyne, androgynous (*androgenous* and *androgynous* are pronounced the same) (*gyn*, woman) sphinx: androsphinx (a sphinx with the head of a man) ster: androsterone (a sex hormone usually present in male urine) (*stere*, solid) TRAILING ROOT COMPOUND: phil: philander (*phila*, love) SUFFIXED ROOT: mon: (*mono*, one) monandrous (practicing monandry; in *botany*, having only one stamen, as some flowers) monandry (the state or practice of having only male sex partner over a period of time; in *botany*, a monandrous condition) poly: polyandrous (practicing polyandry; in *botany*, having many stamens), polyandry (*poly*, many) MASCULINE NAME: Andrew (from *andreios*, manly) INTERDISCIPLINARY: polyandry (in *botany*, the presence of numerous stamens on one flower; in *zoology*, the mating of one female animal with more than one male) CROSS REFERENCE: *anthropo*, Latin *homo, masc, vir*
anem*	Greek *anemos* (IE: *an(e)*, to breathe)	wind	SIMPLE ROOT: anemone (reason for name unclear) LEADING ROOT COMPOUND: *anem*: osis: anemosis [same as *windshake* (a condition of timber in which there is separation of the concentric rings, supposedly due to strong winds during growth)] (*osis*, condition of) *anemo*: graph: anemograph (*graph*, write) logy: anemology (the study of winds) (*logy*, study of) meter: anemometer (a gauge for determining the force or speed of the wind, and sometimes its directions) (*meter*, measure) metry: anemometry (the process of determining the speed and direction of the wind with an anemometer) (*metry*, measurement of) phil: anemophilous (fertilized by the wind, as plants to which pollen is blown) (*philos*, love)

Element	From	Meaning	Examples
anem (cont'd)			scop: anemoscope (an instrument for showing or recording the direction of the wind) (*scope*, look) NOTE: Do not confuse this root with the prefixed elided root of *anemia* (*an-* + *em*, from *hemo*, blood). CROSS REFERENCE: *vent*
ang*	Greek *anchein*, to squeeze (IE: *angh*, constricted)	narrow, tight, choking	SIMPLE ROOT: anger (**Synonyms:** indignation, rage, fury) angina (*quinsy*, which see under *Disguised Root*) {anginal, or *anginous*} anguish (**Synonyms:** distress, suffering, agony) LEADING ROOT COMPOUND: *angin(o)*: oid: anginoid (resembling angina) (*oid-*, similar to, resembling) phob: anginophobia (same as *claustrophobia*) (*phobia*, fear of) DISGUISED ROOT: anxiety (**Synonyms:** care, concern, solicitude) anxious (**Synonyms:** eager, avid, keen) quinsy (an early term for *tonsillitis*; from *kyanche*, literally dog-choking; inflammation of the throat; from *kyon*, dog + *anchein*; the Spanish form is *angina tonsilar*) SPANISH: angostura (from the town Angostura, Venezuela; literally, the narrows) [A bitter tonic from the bark of the angostura tree is used as a stimulant.] GERMAN: angst (gloomy, often neurotic feeling of generalized anxiety and depression) [Since *Angst* is a German noun, it is more often capitalized.] CROSS REFERENCE: *steno*
angel*	Greek *angelos*	messenger	SIMPLE ROOT: angel (**Synonyms:** sponsor, backer) LEADING ROOT COMPOUND: logy: angelology (*logy*, study of) TRAILING ROOT COMPOUND: arch: archangel (a chief angel; angel of high rank; an angelica plant) (*arch*, first, foremost) ev: evangel (the good news; the gospel; capitalized, any of the four gospels: Matthew, Mark, Luke, John), evangelist, evangelistic, evangelize (from *eu*, good, well) PROPER NAMES: Angela, Angelica, Angelina, Angeline, Evangeline PLACENAMES: Angela, Montana; Angel City, Florida; Angeles, Texas Angeles, Pampanga Province, Luzon, The Philippines Angelica, Wisconsin; Angelus, Kansas Los Angeles, California (originally, *Nuestra Señora Reina de los Angeles*, Our Queen Lady of the Angels) Evangeline Parish, Louisiana [in Louisiana, *counties* are known as *parishes*] NOTE: Do not confuse this element with *angle*, to fish (with a hook); angle (in geometry), or the Angles (Angles of England). All these words are derived from Greek *angkos*, hook, or *angkylos*, bent. NO CROSS REFERENCE

Scarcely any of our intellectual operations could be carried on to any
considerable extent without the agency of words.
Peter Roget

Element	From	Meaning	Examples
angi*	Greek *angos*	vessel (either blood, or lymph); also, seedcase (can also mean "something contained within a vessel"	LEADING ROOT COMPOUND: *angi*: oma: angioma (a tumor composed of lymph and blood vessels) (*oma*, mass, tumor) *angio*: blast: angioblast (*blast*, shoot, sprout, embryo) card: (heart) angiocardiography (*graph*, write) angiocarditis (*itis*, inflammation) carp: angiocarpous (having fruit partially or wholly enclosed within an external covering, such as the acorn) (*carp*, fruit) gen: angiogenesis (development of blood vessels) (*gen*, producing) graph: angiography [the process of making X-ray pictures (angiograms) of blood vessels after first injecting a radiopaque substance] (*graph*, write) lith: angiolith (calcareous deposit in a wall of a blood vessel) (*lithos*, stone) logy: angiology (the study of blood and lymph vessels) (*logy*, study of) lys: angiolysis (obliteration of blood vessels as in the umbilical cord when it is tied just after birth) (*lys*, in *medicine*, destruction) sarc: angiosarcoma (a sarcoma containing many dilated blood vessels) (*sarc*, flesh + *oma*, tumor, mass) sperm: angiosperm (in *botany*, a plant having the seeds enclosed in an ovary, including monocotyledons and dicotyledons; a flowering plant; compare *gymnosperm*, under *gymn*) {angiospermous} (*sperm*, seed) tens: angiotensin (a polypeptide that is a powerful vasopressor, formed in the blood by the action of rein on a plasma protein) (from *tension*) TRAILING ROOT COMPOUND: hydr: hydrangea (literally, water vessel; any of various shrubs or trees of the genus Hydrangea, having large, flat-topped or rounded clusters of white, pink, or blue flowers; its seed pods are cup-shaped, like tiny water vessels) (*hydro*, water) spor: sporangium (in *botany*, the case or sac in which the asexual spores are produced in cryptogams and phanerogams; also called *spore case*) (*spore*, seed) EMBEDDED ROOT COMPOUND: sporangiferous (*spore*, seed + *ferre*, to bear) CROSS REFERENCE: *cell, cyt, vas*
angui*	Latin *anguis*	snake (like a snake, e.g., eel)	SIMPLE ROOT: anguine (of, pertaining to, or resembling a snake; snakelike), anguineous LEADING ROOT COMPOUND: *angui*: form: anguiform pes: anguipes (snake-footed, as in certain statues) (from *ped*, foot) *anguilli*: form: anguilliform (in the shape of an eel) CROSS REFERENCE: *herpes*

42

Element	From	Meaning	Examples
anim***	Latin *anima*: breath (IE: *an(e)*, to breathe, exhale)	life principle, breath, soul, spirit	ROOT NOTE: Many cultures link *breath* and *spirit*, believing that the spirit leaves the body with the last breath. SIMPLE ROOT: anima: anima (the passive or animal soul; an individual's true inner self reflecting archetypal ideals of conduct--used especially in contrast with *persona* in the analytic psychology of Carl Gustav Jung; also in Jungian psychology, the feminine component of a man; compare *animus*, below) animal (**Synonyms**: carnal, fleshly, sensual), animalism animate (**Synonyms**: quicken, exhilarate, stimulate) animated (**Synonyms**: 1) vivacious, sprightly; gay; 2) living, alive, vital) animi: animism {animistic} animo: animosity (**Synonyms**: enmity, hostility, antagonism) animu: animus (hostile feeling or attitude; antagonism; an animating force or underlying purpose; intention; in *Jungian psychology*, the masculine component of the unconscious of the woman; compare *anima*, above) PREFIXED ROOT: *ex*-: exanimate (lacking in animation; spiritless; lifeless, dead; also, appearing lifeless) (*ex*-, out) *in*-: inanimate (not animate; lifeless; spiritless; dull) (*in*-, not) *re*-: reanimate (*re*-, back, again) MESHED LEADING ROOT COMPOUND: animadversion (*anima* + *adversion*) (*ad*-, to, toward + *vert*, turn) animadvert (*ad*-, to, toward + *vert*, turn) TRAILING ROOT COMPOUND: equ: equanimity (**Synonyms**: composure, serenity, nonchalance) (*equa*, equal) long: longanimity (patient endurance of injuries; forbearance) magn: magnanimity, magnanimous (describing one with a noble mind, great soul, or generous spirit) (*magn*, great) pusill: pusillanimous (literally, tiny mind; timid, irresolute; **Synonyms**: cowardly, dastardly, craven) (*pusillus*, tiny; diminutive of *pusus*, little boy) un: unanimous (in complete accord) (*uni*, one) LATIN LEGAL TERMS: *animo* (with intention, disposition, design, will) *animo et corpore* (by the mind, and by the body; by the intention and by the physical act) *animus furandi* (intent to steal, or feloniously to deprive the owner permanently of his property) *animus manendi* (the intention of remaining; intention to establish residence, a point to be settled in determining the domicile or residence of a party) *animus revertendi* (the intention of returning) *animus testandi* (intention or purpose to make will; also expressed as *animo testandi*) [There are many others phrases with *animus* listed in *Black's Law Dictionary*.] PLACENAME: Las Animas, Colorado CROSS REFERENCE: *bio, spir, vit, zo*

Element	From	Meaning	Examples
aniso*	Greek *aniso* (from *an-*, not + *iso*, equal)	unequal	LEADING ROOT COMPOUND: *anis*: eiko: aniseikonia (a condition in which the image seen by one eye is larger than that seen by the other) (*eikon*, icon, image) *aniso*: gam: anisogamete (same as *heterogamete*), anisogamous (in *biology*, reproducing by the fusion of dissimilar gametes or individuals, usually differing in size) (*gam*, sexual reproduction) mer: anisomerous (in *botany*, having an unequal number of parts in the floral whorls) (*mere*, part) metr: anisometric (not isometric; with asymetrical parts) (*metr*, measure) metro: anisometropia (a condition of the eyes in which they have unequal refractive power) (*metr*, measure + *op*, eyes) trop: anisotropic (a material that has better magnetic characteristics along one axis than any other) (*trope*, turn) INTERDISCIPLINARY: anisotropic (in *botany*, having unequal responses to external stimuli; in *physics*, having properties, as conductivity, speed of transmission of lights, etc., that vary according to the direction in which they are measured) NO CROSS REFERENCE
ann,*** enn	Latin *annus* (IE: *atnos*, to go, year)	year	SIMPLE ROOT: anna: annalist, annals (a written account of events year by year in chronological order) annu: annual (for a year's time, work, etc.; lasting or living only one year or season, as some plants; also, a book, magazine, or report published once a year) {annually} annuary (yearbook, annual) annuitant, annuity (a payment of a fixed sum of money at regular intervals of time, especially yearly) PREFIXED ROOT: *ann*: *super-*: superannuate (literally, beyond the years; to set aside as, or become, old-fashioned or obsolete; to retire from service, especially with a pension, because of old age or infirmity) (*super-*, over, beyond) *enn*: *per-*: perennate, perennial (*per-*, through) LEADING ROOT COMPOUND: vers: anniversary (*vers*, turn) TRAILING ROOT COMPOUND: bi: biennial (*bi*, two) cent: centenary, centennial (*cent*, 100) dec: decennial (*dec*, ten) mill: millennium (*mill*, 1,000) oct: octennial (*oct*, eight) quad: quadrennium (*quadr*, four) sept: septennial (*sept*, seven) sext: sextennial (*sex*, six) tri: triennial (*tri*, three) vi: vicennial (*vi*, twenty)

Element	From	Meaning	Examples
ann (cont'd)			DISGUISED ROOT: solemn [from *sollennis*, yearly, annual; from *sollos*, all, entire + *annus*; from the association with annual religious festivals] LATIN PHRASES: *Anno Domini* (in the year of the Lord, e.g., 1990 A.D.) *annus mirabilis* (wondrous year) *per annum* (per year) PLACENAMES: Centenary, South Carolina; Centennial, Wyoming COLLEGE: Centenary College, Shreveport, Louisiana, celebrating the 100th year of the founding of Methodism in the United States GERMAN COGNATE: *Jahr* NO CROSS REFERENCE
annel,* annul	Latin *anus*: ring (IE: *ano*, ring)	rim, ring	SIMPLE ROOT: anne: annelid (any of a phylum of worms with a body made of joined segments or *rings*, as the earthworm, leech, etc.) annula: annular (of, like, or forming a ring, e.g., the annular growths in the trunk of tree), annulary (the third finger of the left hand: the ring finger) annulate {annulated}, annulation annule: annulet (a small ring; in *architecture*, a ringlike molding where the shaft of a column joins the capital) annulo: Annulosa (a subkingdom of animals including forms with articulate bodies and a double ventral chain of ganglia and comprising the annelid worms and the arthropods), annulose annulu: annulus (plural, *annuli*, or *annuluses*; any ring or ringlike part, mark, etc.) anu: anus (the opening at the lower end of the alimentary canal; rectum) CROSS REFERENCE: *cycl, gyr*
ano-			See *ana-*.
anom*	Greek *anom*	lawlessness	ROOT NOTE: This root consists of *an-*, not + *nomos*, law, but is extended to mean irregular, unusual (*Webster's Third*). Some authorities regard this root as coming from *an-*, not + *homo*, same (Partridge, *Origins*; *Webster's New World*; *American Heritage*) SIMPLE ROOT: anomalous (deviating from the regular arrangement, general rule, or usual method; abnormal) anomaly (in *astronomy*, a planet's angular distance from its perihelion, measured as if viewed from the sun) anomie (also, *anomy*; lack of purpose, identity, or ethical values in a person or society; rootlessness) LEADING ROOT COMPOUND: ped: anomaliped (having more or fewer of the digits united, as are the kingfisher and the kangaroo) (*ped*, foot) ASTRONOMY TERMS: anomalistic month (the mean time of the moon's revolution from perigee to perigee again, being approximately 27.554550 days) anomalistic year (the time of the earth's revolution from perihelion to perihelion again, being approximately 365 days, 6 hours, 13 minutes, 53.1 seconds) CROSS REFERENCE: *nom* (Greek)

Element	From	Meaning	Examples
ante-,*** anti-	Latin *ante* (IE: *anti*, facing, opposite, near)	before, prior to; in front of	NOTE: Though *anti-* is usually classified as a Greek prefix and *ante-*, a Latin prefix, both are derived from a single Indo-European source. In a sense, that which is before, is near, or against (*anti-*). Greek *anti-* is listed separately. EXTENDED PREFIX: anterior (comparative of *ante-*; situated in front; before in place--opposed to *posterior*; in *botany*, abaxial, inferior) PREFIXED ROOT: bell: antebellum (before the war; specifically, before the American Civil War) (*bellum*, war) ced: (*cedere*, to go) antecede (to go before in rank, place or time; precede) **antecedent** (any happening or thing prior to another; **Synonyms: 1)** cause, reason, motive; **2)** previous, prior, preceding) dat: antedate (to date before, that is, to put a date on that is earlier than the actual date, as *to antedate a check*; to make happen earlier; accelerate) diluv: antediluvian (literally, before the flood; especially, before the Biblical flood; antiquated) (*di-* from *dis-*, off + *luv*, from *luere*, to wash) fix: antefix (a small decorative fixture put at the eaves of a roof of a classic building to hide the ends of the tiles) {antefixal} (from *figere*, to fasten) meri: antemeridian [of, pertaining to, or taking place in the morning (*before* noon), as an *antemeridian* conference, or an *antemeridian* repast; not the same as *ante meridiem*, before noon, abbreviated a.m.] (from *medius*, middle) mort: antemortem (made or done just before one's death) (*mortis*, death) nat: antenatal (before birth) (*natus*, birth) nupt: antenuptial (before marriage) (from *nubere*, to marry) pend: antependium (a screen or veil hanging from the front of an altar, pulpit, etc.) (*pendere*, to hang) penult: antepenult (third from the last; the antepenult syllable of *antepenult* is te), antepenultimate (*pen*, almost + *ult*, last) typ: antetype (an earlier form; a prototype) (*type*, image) vers: anteversion (a displacing of a bodily organ, especially the uterus, in which its axis is inclined farther forward than is normal) (from *vertere*; to turn) vert: antevert (to cause anteversion of) (*vertere*, to turn) VARIANT PREFIXED ROOT: cip: anticipate (**Synonyms**: expect, hope, await) (from *capere*, to take) pasto: antipasto (an assortment, as of salted fish, marinated vegetables, meats, cheeses, and served as an appetizer; hors d'oeuvres) (from *pascere*, to feed) DISGUISED ELEMENT: ancient (**Synonyms**: old, antique, antiquated; see *Triplets* below) antic (also, *antick*; a playful, silly, or ludicrous act, trick, etc.; prank; caper; see *Triplets* below) antique (see synonyms at *ancient*; see *Triplets* below)

Element	From	Meaning	Examples
ante- (cont'd)			antlers [from Latin *ante* + *ocular* (before the eyes); *antlers* in German is *Augensprossen*, sprouts of the eyes; see *Place-names* below] rampart (an embankment of earth surmounted by a parapet and encircling a castle, fort, etc., for defense against attack; any defense or bulwark) (*re-*, again + *ante-*, before + *parare*, to prepare) WORDS BUILT ON PREFIXES: (*ab-* + *ante-*) advance (**Synonyms**: promote, forward, further), advancement (see *Doublets* below) advantage (a more favorable position; superiority) (see *Doublets* below) LATIN LEGAL TERMS: *ab ante* (before, in advance; for example, a legislature cannot agree *ab ante* to any modification or amendment to a law which a third person may make) *antea* (formerly; heretofore) *ante-factum* (done before; an act previously done) *antejuramentum* (in *Saxon law,* a preliminary or preparatory oath, required by both the accuser and the accused; the accuser swearing that he/she would prosecute the criminal, and the accused making oath that he/she was innocent of the crime with which he/she was charged) DOUBLETS: advance:advntage TRIPLETS: ancient:antic:antique UNBOUNDED COMPOUND: penny ante (a game of poker in which the ante or limit is a very small amount, as one cent; any trifling undertaking) PLACENAMES: Antler, North Dakota; Antlers, Oklahoma INTERDISCIPLINARY: antecedent (in *grammar*, the word, phrase, or clause to which a pronoun refers; in *logic*, the part of the conditional proposition that states the condition; in *mathematics*, the first term or numerator of a ratio; distinguished from *consequent*) NB: *Antenna*, from Latin *antema*, sail yard, is not in this family; neither is *antelope* in this family. CROSS REFERENCE: *antero-, pre-, pro-*
anth***	Greek *anthos* (IE: *andh,* to sprout, bloom)	flower	SIMPLE ROOT: anther: anther (the part of the flower that contains pollen), antheridium [in flowerless and seedless plants (cryptogams), the organ in which the male sex cells are developed] anthes: anthesis (the state of full bloom of a flower) antho: anthodium [plural, *anthodia*; the flower head of a composite plant, or the involucre of such a head, as in daisies and asters (*involucre*, enveloped); in *botany*, a ring of small leaves at the base of the flower, flower cluster, or fruit: *involucres* are found in all plants of the composite family] (from *anthodes*, flowerlike) PREFIXED ROOT: *ex-*: exanthem (same as *exanthema*; literally, to blossom out; a skin eruption or rash occurring in certain infectious diseases, as scarlet fever) (*ex-*, out) *peri-*: perianth (the outer envelope of a flower, including the calyx and corolla) (*peri-*, around)

Element	From	Meaning	Examples
anth (cont'd)			LEADING ROOT COMPOUND: carp: anthocarpous (literally, flower-fruit; designating or of a multiple fruit, as the pineapple or strawberry, formed from the ovaries of several blossoms) (*carp*, fruit) cyan: anthocyanin (a soluble, reddish-blue pigment in flowers and plants; also *anthocyan*) (from *kyan*, blue) log: anthology (literally, a gathering of flowers, or a collection of poems, stories, excerpts, etc., considered by the compiler as the flowers, or the best) (*log* in this particular word is derived from *legein*, to gather) phor: anthophore (from *pherein*, to bear) zo: anthozoan (any of a class of saltwater coelenterates, comprising corals, sea anemones, sea fans, etc.) (*zo*, animal) TRAILING ROOT COMPOUND: chrys: chrysanthemum (literally, golden flower) (*chrys*, gold) mon: monanthous (having only one flower, as some fruits) (*mono*, one) poly: polyanthus (literally, many flowers) (*poly*, many) CROSS REFERENCE: *flor*
anthropo***	Greek *anthropos* (IE: *andh*, to sprout, bloom)	man	LEADING ROOT COMPOUND: *anthrop*: oid: anthropoid (resembling man; manlike; especially, designating or of any of the most highly developed apes, including the chimpanzee, gorilla, orangutan, and gibbon) (*oid*, similar to) *anthropo*: centr: anthropocentric (that considers man as the central fact, or final aim, of the universe) (*centr*, center) gen: anthropogenesis, anthropogenic (*gen*, beginning) graph: anthropography (*graph*, write) logy: anthropologist, anthropology (*logy*, study of) metry: anthropometry (*metry*, measurement of) morph: anthropomorphic, anthropomorphism (the attributing of human shape or characteristics to a god, animal, or inanimate thing, as God walking and talking with Adam and Eve in the Garden of Eden), anthropomorphize, anthropomorphous (*morph*, shape) path: anthropopathy (the attributing of human feelings and passions to a god, animal, etc.) (*pathos*, feeling) phag: anthropophagi (eaters of human flesh; cannibals) {anthropophagic, anthropophagous} (*phag*, eat) TRAILING ROOT COMPOUND: cervan: cervanthropy (the delusion that one has turned into a deer) (*cervus*, deer) lyc: lycanthrope, lycanthropy (a type of mental disorder in which the person imagines himself/herself to be a wolf) (*lykos*, wolf) mis: misanthrope, misanthropy (from *miso*, hate) phil: philanthropic (**Synonyms:** humanitarian, charitable, altruistic), philanthropy (*phila*, love of) the: theanthropism (the attributing of human characteristics to God or a god; the doctrine of the union of divine and human natures in Jesus Christ) (*theos*, god)

48

Element	From	Meaning	Examples
anthropo (cont'd)			EMBEDDED ROOT COMPOUND: the: (God, god) the<u>anthropo</u>logy (*logy*, study of) the<u>anthropo</u>phagy (*phag*, eat) CROSS REFERENCE: *andr, homo* (Latin), *masc, vir*
anti-			For *anticipate* and *antipasto*, see *ante-*.
anti-***	Greek *anti* (IE: *anti*, facing, opposite)	against, opposite; facing, near	PREFIXED ROOTS AND COMPOUNDS: *ant-:* agon: antagonist (a person who opposes or competes with another; adversary; opponent; in *literature*, one who opposes the protagonist; a muscle, drug, etc. that acts in opposition to or counteracts another), antagonize (*agon*, struggle) arctic: antarctic, Antarctica (continent opposite the Arctic) helio: anthelion (*helios*, sun) onym: antonym (a word that is opposite in meaning to another word), antonymous (*onym*, name) *anti:* bary: antibaryon (an antiparticle of the baryon, as an anti-neutron, antiproton, and antihyperon) (*baryos*, heavy) bio: antibiotic (of antibiosis; destroying or inhibiting the growth of bacteria and other microorganisms) (*bio*, life) cata: anticatalyst (*cata*- prefixes *lys*, loosen) chlor: antichlor (any substance for removing excess chlorine from textiles or other substances that have been bleached) (*chlor*, green) cleric: anticlerical (opposed to the clergy or church hierarchy, especially to its influence in public affairs) climax: anticlimax (the sudden drop from the dignified or important in thought or expression to the commonplace or trivial, sometimes for humorous effect; a descent, as in a series of events, which is in ludicrous or disappointing contrast to a preceding one) (from *klinein*, to slope) clin: anticlinal (inclined in opposite directions; of or like an anticline), anticline, anticlinorium (*cline*, lean, slope) cycl: anticyclone {anticyclonic} (*cycle*, wheel, circle) dot: antidote (a remedy given to counteract a poison) (*dotos*, given) drom: antidromic (in *physiology*, conveying nerve impulses in a direction opposite to the normal) (*drom*, run) febr: antifebrile (reducing or relieving a fever) (*febr*, fever) fed: antifederalist (capitalized, a person who opposed the adoption of the U. S. Constitution) gen: antigen (an enzyme, toxin, or other substance to which the body reacts by producing antibodies) (*gen*, producer) hero: antihero (the protagonist of a novel, play, etc. who lacks the stature or virtues of a traditional hero) histam: antihistamine (any of several drugs used to minimize the action of histamine in such allergic conditions as hay fever and hives) labor: antilabor (opposed to labor unions or to the interests of workers) lith: antilithic (in *medicine*, preventing the formation or the development of calculi, as of the urinary tract) (*lithos*, stone)

49

Element	From	Meaning	Examples
anti- (cont'd)			logy: antilogy (a contradiction in ideas, statements, or terms) (*logo*, word)
			maca: antimacassar [*macassar (oil)*; an oil, originally imported from Macassar, used as a hair dressing; a small cover on the back or arms of chair, sofa, etc. to prevent soiling]
			mat: antimatter (a form of matter in which the electrical charge is the reverse of that in the usual matter of our universe)
			mer: antimere (in *zoology*, either of the corresponding parts opposite each other on both sides of an organism's axis) (*mere*, part)
			nom: antinomian (in *Christian theology*, a believer in the doctrine that faith alone, not obedience to the moral law, is necessary for salvation), antinomy (the opposition of a law, regulation, etc. to another) (*nomos*, law)
			path: antipathetic, antipathy (a strong or deep-rooted dislike; the object of such dislike; **Synonyms**: aversion, repugnance, loathing) (*pathos*, feeling)
			phon: antiphon (from which *anthem* is derived; see *Doublets* below), antiphonal, antiphonary (*phone*, sound)
			phras: antiphrasis (use of words or phrases in a sense opposite to the usual one, as for ironical effect) (*phrase*, word)
			pod: antipode (anything diametrically opposite; exact opposite) {antipodal, antipodean} (*pod*, foot)
			prot: antiproton (the antiparticle of the proton, with the same mass as the proton but a negative charge) (*protos*, first)
			pyr: antipyretic (anything that reduces fever; same as antifebrile; a febrifuge) (*pyr*, fire, fever)
			sep: antisepsis, antiseptic, antisepticize (*sepein*, to make putrid)
			stroph: antistrophe (the return movement, left to right, made by the chorus of an ancient Greek play in answering the previous strophe; other meanings) (*strophe*, turn)
			thes: antithesis (a contrast or opposition of thoughts, usually in two phrases, clauses, or sentences) (*thesis*, place)
			tox: antitoxic, antitoxin (*toxos*, poison)
			typ: antitype (the person or thing represented or foreshadowed by an earlier type or symbol; an opposite type) {anttypical, or antitypic} (*type*, image)
			DISGUISED ROOT:
			anthem (from *antiphonal*; see *Doublets* below)
			DOUBLETS: anthem:antiphone
			CROSS REFERENCE: *contra-/counter-, ob-/oc-/of-/op-/o-*
ap-			See *ad-* for *appear*, etc.
ap-			See *apo-* for *aphelion*, etc.
aper*	Latin *aperire*: to open (from *ab-*, away + *perire*, to produce)	open, uncovered	SIMPLE ROOT:
			aperient (**Synonyms**: physic, laxative, purgative)
			apéritif (an alcoholic drink taken before a meal to stimulate the appetite)
			apertura, aperture (an opening; hole; gap; the opening, or the diameter of the opening, in a camera through which light passes into the lens; in English, anglicized to *overture*; see *Disguised Root* below)
			DISGUISED ROOT:
			abri (a shelter or place of refuge, especially a dugout)

Element	From	Meaning	Examples
aper (cont'd)			overt (the opposite of *overt* is *covert*, but which does not derive from the same root as *overt*, coming instead from *cover*; *cover* is derived from *co-*, an intensive + *operire*, to hide, although Partridge states that *operire* is explicable as *ob-*, against + *aperire*) overture (English respelling of *aperture*; an introductory proposal or offer; indication of willingness to cooperate; a musical introduction to an opera or other large musical work; see *Doublets* below) pert (an elision of *aperture*, opening; thus, open, bold, impudent in speech or behavior; saucy; forward; also, chic, jaunty) DOUBLETS: aperture:overture SPANISH COGNATES: *abrir*, to open; *abierto*, open CROSS REFERENCE: *chasm, lumin, osti, stoma*
api*	Latin *apis*	bee	SIMPLE ROOT: apian, apiarian, apiarist, apiary, apis LEADING ROOT COMPOUND: *api*: cult: apiculture (the raising and care of bees) phob: apiphobia (morbid fear of bees) (*phobia*, fear of) tox: apitoxin (*toxin*, poison) vor: apivorous (feeding on bees, as some birds) (*vor*, eat) *apio*: log: apiology (*logy*, study of) therap: apiotherapy (*therap*, healing) TRAILING ROOT COMPOUND: acar: acarapis (see note at *acar* family) NO CROSS REFERENCE
apic*	Latin *apex* tip (see *apt* for derivation)	apex, tip, summit (also, tip of organ)	SIMPLE ROOT: apex (plural, *apices*; **Synonyms**: summit, peak, climax) apical (at or belonging to an apex, tip, or summit; in *linguistics*, articulated with the apex of the tongue; a sound so differentiated, as the *l, t,* or *d* in light<u>ed</u>) apiculate (in *botany*, ending abruptly in a small point, as some leaves) LEADING ROOT COMPOUND: *apici*: fix: apicifixed (attached by the apex) (from *figere*, to fasten) *apico*: ectom: apicoectomy (excision of the apical portion of a tooth root through an opening made in the overlying labial or buccal alveolar bone) (*ectom*, to remove surgically) CROSS REFERENCE: *acro*
apo-***	Greek *apo*	away from, off, from, change	PREFIXED ROOTS AND COMPOUNDS: *ap-*: helion: aphelion (the point farthest from the sun in the orbit of a planet or comet, or of a man-made satellite in orbit around the sun; opposed to *perihelion*) (*helios*, sun) heres: apheresis (also, *aphaeresis*; literally, to take away; the dropping of a letter, syllable, or phoneme at the beginning of a word, e.g., *'cause* for *because*) (*hairein*, to take) hes: aphesis (a letting go; loss of a short, unaccented vowel at the beginning of a word; thus, a form of *apheresis*, e.g., *longshore* is an aphesis of <u>along the shore</u>) (from *hienai*, to send)

Element	From	Meaning	Examples
apo- (cont'd)			hor: aphorism (a short, concise statement of a principle, e.g., *In a calm sea every man is a pilot* encapsulates the idea that the storms of life test one's mettle) (*horizein*, to limit)

apo-:

calyp: apocalypse (literally, to uncover, disclose, reveal; any of various Jewish and Christian pseudonymous writings (c. 200 B.C.--c. 300 A.D.) depicting symbolically the ultimate destruction of evil and triumph of good, and thus revealing the future; capitalized, the last book of the New Testament; the *Book of Revelation* in the Bible) (from *kalyptein*, to cover)

carp: apocarpous [in *botany*, having separate or partially joined carpels (simple pistils regarded as modified leaves)] (*carp*, fruit)

chrom: apochromatic (*chrome*, color)

cop: apocopate, apocope (*cop*, cut)

crin: apocrine (designating a type of glandular secretion in which part of the secreting cell is thrown off along with the secretion) (*crine*, separate)

cryph: apocrypha (hidden, obscure; any writings, anecdotes, etc. of doubtful authenticity or authorship; capitalized, fourteen books of the Septuagint that are rejected in Judaism and regarded by Protestants as not canonical; 11 of them are fully accepted in the Roman Catholic canon) {apocryphal} (from *kryptein*, to hide)

deic: apodeictic (also, *apodictic*; that which can be clearly shown or proven; absolutely certain; necessarily true) (from *deik*, to show)

dos: apodosis (the clause expressing the conclusion or result in a conditional sentence; opposed to *protasis*) (*dos*, to give)

gam: apogamy (the development of a plant without the union of gametes; development of a sporophyte from a gametophyte without fertilization) {apogamic, apogamous} (*gam*, marriage)

ge: (*geo*, earth)
apogee (the point farthest from the earth in the orbit of the moon or a man-made satellite)
apogeotropism (*trope*, turn)

helio: apheliotropism (*helio*, sun + *trope*, turn)

log: apologetic, apologetics, apologia (an apology; especially a formal defense of an idea, religion, etc.), apologist, apologize, apologue (a short allegorical story with a moral; fable), apology (from *logos*, word)

mict: apomict (a plant that reproduces by apomixis or that has been produced by apomixis) (see *apomixis*, next entry)

mix: apomixis (asexual reproduction of plants; espcially, the formation of seed from the tissues of the maternal parent) (from *miscere*, to mix)

neur: aponeurosis (*neur*, nerve + *osis*, condition of)

phas: apophasis (in *rhetoric*, the artful mention of something by denying that it will be mentioned, e.g., *We will not remind you of his many crimes*) (*phase*, appear)

phyg: apophyge (an architectural term; *phyg* is a cognate of Latin *fug*) (*phyg*, to flee)

Element	From	Meaning	Examples
apo- (cont'd)			phyl: apophyllite (a mineral, so named from its flaking off under the blowpipe) (*phyll*, leaf)
			phys: apophysis (from *phyein*, to grow)
			plect: apoplectic (adjective form of *apoplexy*, next entry)
			plex: apoplexy (sudden paralysis with total or partial loss of consciousness and sensation, caused by the breaking or obstruction of a blood vessel in the brain; stroke) (from *plessein*, to strike)
			sema: aposematic (in *zoology*, serving to warn off potential attackers, as the coloration of some poisonous animals; compare *sematic*: serving as a sign of danger, as the coloration of some poisonous snakes) (*sema*, sign)
			siop: aposiopsis (a sudden breaking off of a thought in the middle of a sentence as if one were unable or unwilling to continue, e.g., *The horrors I saw there--but I dare not tell them*) (*siopan*, to be silent)
			spor: apospory (the formation of a gametophyte from a sporophyte cell which has not undergone reduction division: apomixis without spora formation) (*spore*, seed)
			stas: apostasy (an abandoning of what one has believed in, as a faith, cause, principles, etc.) (*stas*, stand)
			stat: apostate, apostatize (see *apostasy*)
			stl: apostle (one who is sent) (from *stellein*, to send)
			stroph: apostrophe (to turn away from; both a grammar and a drama term) (*stroph*, turn)
			thec: apothecary, apothecium (in *botany*, an open cuplike structure containing sacs in which sexual spores are developed, as in lichens and certain fungi) (*theca*, to place, put)
			thegm: apothegm (a short, pithy saying, as Brevity is the soul of wit; epigram) (*thegm*, to cry out, utter)
			them: apothem (in *mathematics*, the perpendicular from the center of a regular polygon to any one of its sides) (*thema*, that which is placed)
			the: apotheosis (the act of raising a person to the status of a god; deification; the glorification of a person or thing; a glorified ideal) (*the*, god + *osis*, process of)
			BIBLICAL CHARACTER:
			Apollyon [destroying, ruining; the angel of the bottomless pit; the Devil; Satan (Revelation 9:11); also fictional character, an evil spirit subdued by the hero Christian, in Bunyan's *Pilgrim's Progress*] (from *apo-*, away + *lyein*, to loose)
			OLD NORSE COGNATE: awkward (turned backward; going the wrong way; **Synonyms:** clumsy, maladroit, inept)
			INTERDISCIPLINARY: apophysis (in *anatomy*, any natural outgrowth or process, especially on a vertebra or other bone; in *botany*, a swelling at the base of the capsule in some mosses)
			CROSS REFERENCE: *ab-, cata-, de-, dis-, ex-, se-*
apt,*** ept	Latin *apere* (IE: *ap*, to grasp, reach)	to grasp, reach, fasten	SIMPLE ROOT: apt (**Synonyms:** 1) fit, suitable, proper; 2) likely, liable, prone; 3) quick, prompt, ready) aptitude (**Synonyms:** talent, gift, faculty; see *Doublets* below) {aptness}

53

Element	From	Meaning	Examples
apt,*** ept			PREFIXED ROOT:
			ad-: adapt (**Synonyms:** adjust, accommodate, conform), adaptable, adaptation, adapter (or *adaptor*), adaptive (*ad-*, to, toward)
			in-: inept (**Synonyms:** awkward, clumsy), ineptitude (*in-*, not)
			DISGUISED ROOTS:
			apex (a point; a thing reached; **Synonyms:** summit, acme, zenith)
			apse (a semicircular or polygonal projection of a building, with a domed or vaulted roof)
			apsis [that point in the elliptical orbit of the moon, a planet, etc. nearest to (lower apsis) or that farthest from (higher apsis), the gravitational focus point]
			attitude (**Synonyms:** posture, stance; see *Doublets* below)
			copula (*co-*, with, together + *apere*)
			copulate (from *copula*; to have sexual intercourse), copulative (in *grammar*, connecting coordinate words, phrases, or clauses, as *a copulative conjunction*; having the nature of copula, as *a copulative verb*)
			couple (**Synonyms:** pair, yoke, span)
			lariat (a rope) (Spanish *la riata*; from Latin *re-*, again + *aptare*, to fit, tie; thus, to tie again)
			DOUBLETS: aptitude:attitude
			INTERDISCIPLINARY: copula (in *grammar*, a weakened verbal form, especially a form of *be* or any similar verb, as *seem, appear*, etc. which links a subject with a predicate complement; linking verb; in *logic*, the connecting link between the subject and predicate of a proposition)
			NB: Though the meaning of *adept* is related to that of this root, and though the spelling correlates with *inept, adept* is not in this family. *Adept* comes from *ad-*, to + *apisci*, to pursue, thus, to arrive at; originally it was used of alchemists claiming to have arrived at the philosopher's stone; thus highly skilled; expert.
			CROSS REFERENCE: *hapt, junct, zyg*
aqu***	Latin *aqua* (IE: *akwa*, water)	water	SIMPLE ROOT:
			aqua: aquarelle (a kind of painting in transparent watercolors), aquarist, aquarium (originally, a watering place for cattle; see *ewer* under *Disguised Root*), aquatic
			aque: aqueous
			PREFIXED ROOT:
			sub-: subaqueous (adapted for underwater use or existence; underwater; formed, having, or occurring under water) (*sub-*, under)
			LEADING ROOT COMPOUND:
			aqua:
			cad: aquacade (an aquatic exhibition or entertainment consisting of swimming, diving, etc., often to music) (*aqua* + cav-al*cade*)
			cult: aquaculture (the regulation and cultivation of water plants and animals for human use or consumption)
			lung: Aqualung [a trademark for a particular self-contained underwater breathing apparatus (SCUBA)]
			mar: aquamarine (from *aqua marina*, sea water) (*mar*, sea)

Element	From	Meaning	Examples
aqu (cont'd)			*aque*: duct: aqueduct (a large pipe or conduit made for bringing water from a distant source; in *anatomy*, a passage or canal) (from *ducere*, to lead) *aqui*: fer: aquifer (an underground layer of porous rock, sand, etc. containing water, into which wells can be sunk) {aquiferous} (*ferre*, to bear) DISGUISED ROOT: ewer (Old French *evier*; from Middle Latin *aquarium*, water pitcher) sewer (Middle French *esseweur*, to drain off; from Vulgar Latin *exaquare*; from Latin *ex-*, out + *aqua*) LATIN PHRASES: *aqua fortis* (strong water; nitric acid) *aqua pura* (pure water, especially distilled water) *aqua regia* (kingly water: it dissolves the "noble metals," gold and platinum; a mixture of nitric and hydrochloric acids) *aquavit* (short for *aqua vitae*, which see next entry; a Scandinavian alcoholic drink) *aqua vitae* (water of life; in *alchemy*, alcohol; brandy or other strong liquor) FRENCH WORDS AND PHRASES: *eau* (plural, *eaux*; both pronounced *oh*) *eau de Cologne* (water of Cologne: originally made at Cologne, Germany; cologne) *eau de vie* (plural *eaux de vie*; water of life; brandy, especially a clear spirit distilled from a mash of fruit other than grapes) OLD ENGLISH: island (literally, water land; in *anatomy*, a tissue or cluster of cells differing from surrounding tissue in formation) CONSTELLATION: Aquarius (this constellation supposedly outlines a man pouring water from a container in his right hand) SIGN OF THE ZODIAC: Aquarius (the water carrier) PLACENAME: Eau Claire, Wisconsin (Clear Water) CROSS REFERENCE: *hydr, hydat*
ar-			See *ad-* for *arrest*, etc.
arachn*	Greek *arachne*	spider	SIMPLE ROOT: arachnid, arachnidian LEADING ROOT COMPOUND: oid: arachnoid (*oid*, similar to) CLASSICAL MYTHOLOGY: Arachne (a girl turned into a spider by Athena for challenging the goddess to a weaving contest) INTERDISCIPLINARY: arachnoid [in *anatomy*, designating the middle of three membranes (between the dura mater and the pia mater) covering the brain and the spinal cord; in *botany*, covered with or consisting of soft, fine hairs or fibers; in *zoology*, of or like an arachnid] NO CROSS REFERENCE

Serendipity, an apparent aptitude for making fortunate discoveries accidentally, is derived from "The Princes of Serendip," a Persian fairy tale where the princes are always making fortunate discoveries quite by accident.

Element	From	Meaning	Examples
arb*	Latin *herba*: grass, herb (IE: *gher*, herb)	tree	SIMPLE ROOT: arbor (in *botany*, a tree, in contrast to a shrub; in *mechanics*, a shaft; beam; a spindle; axle; also a round bar that holds a cutting tool or an article being turned on a lathe) arbora: arboraceous (same as *arboreal*; *arborescent*) arbore: arboreal (of or like a tree); arboreous, arborescent, arboret, arboretum arbut: arbutum, arbutus LEADING ROOT COMPOUND: col: arboricole, arboricolous (tree-living) (*colere*, to inhabit) LATIN COMPOUND: arborvitae (also, *arbor vitae*; literally, tree of life) SPANISH COGNATE: *árbol* TREE PLANTING DAY: Arbor Day (observed individually by the States of the United States, usually in the spring) INTERDISCIPLINARY: arborvitae (in *anatomy*, the tree-like structure of the white substance in a longitudinal section of the cerebellum; in *botany*, any of several trees or shrubs of the cypress family, with flattened sprays of scalelike leaves) NOTE: Do not confuse *arbovirus* with this family. The word is derived from *ar*(thropod)*bo*(rne)*virus*. CROSS REFERENCE: *dendr, silv/sylv*
arbit*	Latin *arbiter*	to consider, judge	ROOT NOTE: Root is derived from *ad-*, to + *baet*, to come, go; thus, an arbiter was originally "one who went to a place to judge." SIMPLE ROOT: arbital, arbiter, arbitrable, arbitrage, arbitrageur (one who engages in arbitrage), arbitrament (arbitration; an arbitrator's verdict or award; the power to judge or right to decide), arbitrary, arbitrate, arbitration, arbitrator, arbitress (a woman arbiter) CROSS REFERENCE: *jud/jur*
arc*	Latin *arcus* (IE: *arqu*, bent, curved)	arch, bow	SIMPLE ROOT: arc, arcade, arcature, arch (another *arch* is listed under *arch*) FRENCH ARCHITECTURAL TERM: *arc-boutant* (plural, *arcs-boutants*; flying buttress) NOTE: See next family for *arcane*. NO CROSS REFERENCE
arc,* erc	Latin *arcere*: to confine (IE: *areq*, to protect, enclose)	to ward off, enclose	PREFIXED ROOT: co-: coerce (**Synonyms:** force, compel, constrain), coercion (*co-*, together) ex-: exercise (**Synonyms:** practice, drill) (*ex-*, out) DISGUISED ROOT: arcanum (shut in, hidden, elixir, secret remedy, mystery) PLACENAME: Arcanum, Ohio CROSS REFERENCE: *fend, phylac*
arch**	Greek *archein*: to be first, to rule	first, rule, chief, foremost (also, government)	SIMPLE ROOT: arch (main, chief, principal) archa: archaic (**Synonyms:** old, ancient, antique), archaism archi: archive (usually used in plural form) archo: archon (one of the nine chief magistrates of ancient Athens; a ruler) PREFIXED ROOT: an-: anarchism, anarchist, anarchy {anarchic} (*an-*, not) ex-: exarch, exarchate (*ex-*, out)

Element	From	Meaning	Examples
arch (cont'd)			LEADING ROOT COMPOUND: *arch*: anthrop: archanthropine (an extinct primate with structural characteristics intermediate between ape and man; an ape-man) (*anthropo*, man) duc: archducal, archduchess (*ducere*, to lead) duk: archduke (see previous entry) en: archenemy (*en-* prefixes *em*, from *ami*, friend) entero: archenteron (*enteron*, intestine) epi: archepiscopy (*epi-* prefixes *scopy*, a viewing) fiend: archfiend (*the* archfiend, Satan; the Devil) (Old English *feond*, devil) *arche*: gon: archegoniate, archegonium (the flask-shaped female reproductive organ in mosses, ferns, and the like) (*gon*, sexual reproduction) spor: archespore (a cell or group of cells from which the mother cells develop; also *archesporium*) (*spore*, seed) typ: archetype (**Synonyms**: model, example, paradigm) (*typos*, image, figure) *archeo*: logy: archeology (also, *archaeology*; the scientific study of the life and culture of ancient peoples, as by excavation of ancient cities, relics, artifacts, etc.) (*logy*, study of) *archi*: blast: archiblast (in *biology*, egg protoplasm; the outer of the two layers of an embryo in an early stage of development) (*blast*, shoot, sprout) carp: archicarp [in *botany*, the female reproductive organ in an ascomycetous fungus, giving rise to spore sacs (*asci*) after fertilization] (*carp*, fruit) pel: archipelago (a sea with many islands; a group or chain of many islands) (*pelagos*, sea) plasm: archiplasm (same as *archoplasm*, which see below) tect: architect, architectonic, architectonics, architecture (from *tegere*, to cover) trav: architrave (in *architecture*, the lowest part of an entablature, a beam resting directly on the tops, or capitals, of the columns; epistyle; the molding around a doorway, window, etc.) (from *trabs*, beam) *archo*: plasm: archoplasm (a specialized portion of the cytoplasm involved in the formation of the aster and spindle during mitosis) (*plasm*, form) TRAILING ROOT COMPOUND aut: (*auto*, self) autarchy [absolute rule or sovereignty; autocracy; a country under such rule; autarky (see next entry)] autarky (self-sufficiency; independence; national policy of getting along without imports) hept: heptarchy (*hepta*, seven) matri: matriarch (a woman holding a position analogous to that of a patriarch), matriarchate matriarchy (*matri*, mother)

Element	From	Meaning	Examples
arch (cont'd)			men: menarche (the first menstrual period of a girl in puberty) (*men*, month) mon: monarch, monarchal, Monarchian, Monarchianism (the doctrine of several 2d- and 3d-century Christian sects that denied the Trinity altogether or denied the equality of the three persons of the Trinity), monarchical, monarchy (*mono*, one) oli: oligarch, oligarchy (a form of government in which the ruling power belongs to a few persons) (*oligo*, small, few, scant) patri: patriarch (any of the elders or leading older male members of a community; a venerable old man), patriarchate, patriarchy (*patri*, father) phyl: phylarch (*phyl*, clan, tribe, phyle) PLACENAME: Archangel (on the White Sea of the Soviet Union; Russian name: *Arkhangelsk*) CROSS REFERENCE: *prim, proto*
ard**	Latin *arere*, to be dry (IE: *as*, to burn, glow)	to burn, be on fire	SIMPLE ROOT: ardent (**Synonyms**: passionate, impassioned) ardor (**Synonyms**: fervor, enthusiasm, zeal) DISGUISED ROOT: arid (lacking moisture; parched by heat; dry) arson (the crime of purposely setting fire to another's building or property, or to one's own, as to collect insurance) CROSS REFERENCE: *pyr*
aren*	Greek *arena*	sand	SIMPLE ROOT: arena (originally, sandy place), arenaceous (sandy; growing in sand), arenation, arenite (sandstone or other fragmental rock made up chiefly of sand grains) LEADING ROOT COMPOUND: *aren(i)*: oid: arenoid (*oid*, similar to; resembling) col: arenicolous (living or growing in sand) (*colere*, to cultivate, inhabit) NO CROSS REFERENCE
arg*	Latin *argos*: white (IE: *ar(e)g*: bright, gleaming)	silver, gleaming	SIMPLE ROOT: arge: argent, argenteous, argentic, argentine (of or like silver; silvery; as a noun, silver or any silvery substance; see *Placename* below), argentite, argentous, argentum (chemical symbol: Ag) argi: argil, argillaceous, argillite, arginase, arginine argu: argue (**Synonyms**: discuss, debate, dispute) (frequentative of *arguere*, to make clear; prove) LEADING ROOT COMPOUND: fer: argentiferous (*ferre*, to bear) TRAILING ROOT COMPOUND: hydr: hydrargyrum (silver water; mercury; chemical symbol: Hg) (*hydro*, water) lith: litharger (spume or foam of silver; an oxide of lead, PbO, used in storage batteries, ceramic cements, paints, etc.) (*lithos*, stone) pyr: pyrargyrite [a lustrous, dark-red or black mineral ($Ag_3Sb S_3$); a sulfide of silver and antimony] (*pyr*, fire) PLACENAME: Argentina (may have been so named from silver being the object of the explorers' quest) CROSS REFERENCE: *platin*

Element	From	Meaning	Examples
aristo*	Greek *aristos*	best	LEADING ROOT COMPOUND: crac: aristocracy (ruled by the best) (see *aristocrat*, next entry) crat: aristocrat {aristocratic} (from *kratos*, rule) loch: aristolochiaceous (a plant useful in childbirth; reason for term unclear) (*locheia*, childbirth) PROPER NAMES: Aristophanes (one who shows the best) Aristotle NOTE: Do not confuse with *aristology*, the art and science of dining, from *ariston*, breakfast, or lunch. CROSS REFERENCE: *optim*
arithm*	Greek *arithmein*: to count	amount, number	LEADING ROOT COMPOUND: met: arithmetic (from *metro*, measure) TRAILING ROOT COMPOUND: algo: algorithm (from Arabic *algorism* and fashioned after *arithmetic*) log: logarithm (*logos*, word, proportion, ratio) CROSS REFERENCE: *numer*
arm*	Latin *armare*: to arm (IE: *ar*, to join, fit together)	weapon, shield	SIMPLE ROOT: arm (both the part of the body, and an instrument for fighting; **Synonyms**: furnish, equip, outfit) arms, army (see *Doublets* below) arma: armada (see *Triplets* below; also *Placenames*) armadillo (any of a family of burrowing edentate mammals with an armorlike covering of bony plates; when attacked, a few of the animals roll up into a ball; see *Placenames*) armament (see *Triplets* below), armamentarium, armature (see *Triplets* below) armo: armoire (a large, usually ornate cupboard or clothespress; see *Doublets* below) armor, armorer, armorial, armory PREFIXED ROOT: *dis*-: disarmament (*dis*-, apart, away) *re*-: rearmament (*re*-, again) LEADING ROOT COMPOUND: ger: armiger (armor bearer; see *Placenames* below) (*gerere*, to bear) pot: armipotent (mighty in battle) (*potent*, power) stic: armistice (literally, a stacking of arms; see *stice*) (*stice*, standing) DISGUISED ROOT: ambry (now archaic; a cupboard, locker, or pantry; see *Doublets* below) (Middle English *almerie*; from Old French *armarie*; from Latin *armarium*, chest for tools or arms) ITALIAN: alarm (literally, to the arms) DOUBLETS: ambry:armoire; armada:army TRIPLETS: armor:armature:armament PLACENAMES: Armada, Michigan Armadillo, Mexico Armiger, Maryland NO CROSS REFERENCE

Element	From	Meaning	Examples
art**	Latin *artus*: joint (IE: *ar*, to join, fit together)	join, fit together; joint	SIMPLE ROOT: art, article articular (pertaining to a joint or joints) articulate, articulation (specialized uses in *botany, phonetics,* and *zoology*; **Synonyms:** diction, wording, vocabulary) artillery LEADING ROOT COMPOUND: fact: artifact (from *facere*, to make, do) fic: artifice (**Synonyms: 1)** art, skill, craft; **2)** stratagem, trick, ruse), artificial (from *facere*, to make, do) LATIN PHRASES: *ars longa, vita brevis* (art is long, life is short) *ars gratia artis* (art for art's sake) *ars poetica* (art of poetry) CROSS REFERENCE: *jug, zyg*
as*	Latin *asinus*	jackass, donkey	SIMPLE ROOT: ass, asinine (of, or like an ass; thus, silly, stupid, obstinate) DUTCH: easel (literally, little donkey, from its solid stance) (compare with French *chevalet*: see *caval* family) LATIN PHRASE: *ab asino lanam* (wool from an ass; blood from a stone) NO CROSS REFERENCE
as-			See *ad-* for *assent*, etc.
asper**	Latin *asper*	rough	ROOT NOTE: The root is derived from Greek *apo-* + IE *sper*, to flick away, push, thus rough. Do not confuse this root with the medical words beginning with *asper*, these being derived from *asperse*, to scatter; in addition, *aspermia* is from the prefix *a-* + *sperm*, seed, semen. SIMPLE ROOT: asperity (roughness or harshness, as of surface, sound, weather, etc. or of circumstances; harshness or sharpness of temper) PREFIXED ROOT: *ex-*: exasperate (**Synonyms:** irritate, provoke, peeve), exasperation (*ex-*, out, from) CROSS REFERENCE: *trache*
ast**	Greek *aster* (IE: *ster*, star)	star	SIMPLE ROOT: aster, asteraceous, asteriated, asterisk, asterism PREFIXED ROOT: *dis-*: disaster (literally, when the stars fall apart; **Synonyms:** calamity, catastrophe, cataclysm) (*dis-*, apart) LEADING ROOT COMPOUND: *aster*: oid: asteroid (*oid*, similar to) *astro*: bio: astrobiology (the branch of biology that investigates the existence of living organisms on planets other than Earth) (*bio*, life; *logy*, study of) cyt: astrocyte, astrocytoma (*cyt*, cell; *oma*, tumor, growth) dom: astrodome (Latin *domus*, house) dyna: astrodynamics (*dynam*, power) logy: astrology (*logy*, study of) metry: astrometry (*metry*, measurement of) naut: astronaut, astronautics (*naut*, traveler) navi: astronavigation (same as *celestial navigation*)

Element	From	Meaning	Examples
ast (cont'd)			nom: astronomical (of or having to do with astronomy; extremely large, as the numbers or quantities used in astronomy), astronomy (*nomos*, law) photo: astrophotography (*photo*, light; *graph*, write) phys: astrophysics spher: astrosphere (*spher*, ball, globe) TRAILING ROOT COMPOUND: clyp: clypeaster (a genus of large burrowing sea urchins) (*clype*, round shield) DISGUISED TRAILING ROOT COMPOUND: aspi: aspidistra (a plant of the lily family, with dark, inconspicuous flowers and large, stiff, glossy, evergreen leaves) (*aspis*, a shield + *astron*, a star) CROSS REFERENCE: *stell, sider*
at-			See *ad-* for *attend*, etc.
athl**	Greek *athlon*	a prize	SIMPLE ROOT: athlete, athletic, athletics TRAILING ROOT COMPOUND: bi: biathlete (*bi*, two) dec: decathlon (*deca*, ten) pent: pentathlon (*penta*, five) tri: triathlon (*tri*, three) CROSS REFERENCE: *agogue, agon, duc*
atmo*	Greek *atmos*	vapor	LEADING ROOT COMPOUND: meter: atmometer (an instrument for measuring the rate of evaporation of water into the atmosphere, under varying conditions) (*meter*, measure) spher: atmosphere, atmospheric, atmospherics (*spher*, ball, globe) CROSS REFERENCE: *aero*
auct			See *aug* for *auction*.
aud***	Latin *audire* (IE: *awis*, to perceive physically; grasp)	to hear	SIMPLE ROOT: audi: audible, audience, audient (in the early Christian Church, one permitted to attend the services in the narthex, or vestibule, but dismissed after the sermon), audile (in *psychology*. a person who forms in his mind auditory rather than visual or motor images), audio audit: audit, audition, auditor, auditorium, auditory PREFIXED ROOT: *in-*: inaudible (*in-*, not) *sub-*: subaudition (the act or process of understanding or mentally filling in a word or thought implied but not expressed; something thus understood or filled in) (*sub-*, under) LEADING ROOT COMPOUND: *audio*: freq: audiofrequency (of the band of audible sound frequencies or corresponding electric current frequencies, from 20 to 20,000 hertz) gram: audiogram (a graph showing the percentage of hearing loss in a particular ear, as indicated by an audiometer) (*gram* from *graph*, write) logy: audiology (*logy*, study of) meter: audiometer (an instrument for measuring the sharpness and range of hearing through the use of controlled amounts of sound) {audiometry} (*meter*, measure)

Element	From	Meaning	Examples
aud (cont'd)			phil: audiophile (a devotee of high-fidelity sound reproduction on record players, tape recorders, compact discs, etc.) (*philos*, love)
			vis: audiovisual (involving both hearing and seeing)
			DISGUISED ROOTS:
			obedience, obedient (**Synonyms:** docile, compliant, amenable) (from *obey*) (see *Triplets* below)
			obeisance (a gesture of respect or reverence, such as a bow or a curtsy; deference; from *obey*) (see *Triplets* below)
			obey (to carry out the instructions or orders of)
			oyez
			TRIPLETS: obeisence:obeisance:obedient
			LEGAL TERM: oyer and terminer (from Anglo-French *oyer et terminer*, to hear and determine)
			NB: *Audacious* and *audacity* are not in this family (see aver).
			CROSS REFERENCE: *acou, aur, oto*
aug,**** **auct,** **aux**	Latin *augere* (IE: *aug*, increase)	to increase	SIMPLE ROOT: *auct*: auction (**Synonyms:** sell, trade, vend), auctorial *aug*: augm: augment (**Synonyms:** increase, enlarge, multiply) augmentation (in *music*, variation of a theme by lengthening, usually doubling, the time value of the notes; compare *diminution*, under *mini*) augmentative (in *grammar*, increasing the force of an idea expressed by a word or denoting increased size, intensity, etc.; as a *noun*, an augmentative prefix, suffix, word, etc.; intensifier, for example, perdurable, eat up) augu: augur, augury (an omen; sign; portent; indication), august (**Synonyms:** grand, magnificent, imposing) *aux*: auxesis (in *biology*, a process in which cells grow larger but in which no cell division takes place) {auxetic}, auxiliary, auxin, auxina PREFIXED ROOT: *in*-: inaugurate (**Synonyms:** begin, commence, start) (*in*-, in) LEADING ROOT COMPOUND: chrom: auxochrome (a radical or atom group, as NH_2 or OH, needed to bond organic dyes to fabric fibers) (*chrom*, color) TRAILING ROOT COMPOUND: onych: onychauxis (overgrowth of the nails) (*onych*, nail) DISGUISED ROOTS: author (literally, an enlarger) authoritarian, authoritative (**Synonyms:** official, dogmatic) authority (**Synonyms: 1)** influence, prestige, weight; **2)** power, dominion, jurisdiction) authorization, authorize (**Synonyms:** commission, accredit, license), authorized octroi (tax on certain goods entering a town, the tax *increasing* the price of the goods) OLD ENGLISH: eke (to add to so as to make sufficient; supplement, as *to eke out a living*; to manage to make a living with difficulty) wax (as in *wax and wane*) OLD ENGLISH COMPOUND: nickname (originally, *ekename*; literally, an added name)

Element	From	Meaning	Examples
aug (cont'd)			MUSIC TERM: augmented interval (an interval that is a half step greater than the corresponding major interval, e.g., if the note in the key is *f*, that note becomes *f sharp*, indicated notationally as *#f*) CROSS REFERENCE: *creat, cresc*
aur**	Latin *auris*: ear [IE: *ous*, ear; yields English ear (of body)]	ear, to listen	SIMPLE ROOT: aural (another *aural* pertains to *aura*, air, breeze), auricle, auricula (a primrose shaped like a bear's *ear*), auricular, auriculate (having ears or earlike parts) LEADING ROOT COMPOUND: form: auriform (ear-shaped) TRAILING ROOT COMPOUND: bin: binaural (of, with, or for both ears) (*bin*, two) mon: monaural (compare *stereophonic*) (*mono*, one) RELATED WORDS: auscultate, auscultation (a listening, often with the aid of a stethoscope, to sounds in the chest, abdomen, etc. so as to determine the condition of the heart, lungs, etc.) (*aus*, base of *auris* + *cultare*, by metathesis from *clutare*, to incline) DISGUISED ROOT: ormer (from *auris maris,* ear of the sea, referring to the shape of the Channel Islands) INTERDISCIPLINARY: auricle (in *anatomy*, the external part of the ear; pinna; in *botany* and *biology*, an earlike part or organ) CROSS REFERENCE: *acou, audi, oto*
aur**	Latin *aurum* (IE: *awes*, to shine, dawn)	gold	SIMPLE ROOT: aure: aureate (of a golden color; gilded; speaking in or characterized by a florid and pompous style), aureole (halo; see *oriole* under *Disguised Root*) auri: auric (of, pertaining to, derived from, or containing gold, especially with a valence of 3) auro: auroral, aurous (of or pertaining to gold, especially with a valence of 1) auru: aurum (chemical symbol: Au) LEADING ROOT COMPOUND: *aureo*: myc: Aureomycin [a trademark for chlortetracycline, an antibiotic drug (*aureus*, golden (from its color) + *mykes*, fungus] *auri*: fer: auriferous (*ferre*, to bear, do) DISGUISED ROOT: eyrir (literally, golden; a monetary unit of Iceland) ore, oriole, ormolu, oroide orphrey, orpiment DISGUISED LEADING ROOT COMPOUND: oriflamme (the ancient royal standard of France, a red silk banner split at one end to form flame-shaped streamers) ROMAN GODDESS OF THE DAWN: Aurora (see *eo*), iden-tified with Greek *Eos* ASTRONOMICAL TERMS: *aurora australis* (aurora occurring in southern regions) (*austra*, south) aurora borealis (aurora occurring in northern regions) (Greek god Boreas, personifying the north wind)

Element	From	Meaning	Examples
aur (cont'd)			LEGENDARY PLACE: El Dorado (from *de-*, thoroughly + *aurum*) PLACENAMES: Aurelia, Iowa Aurora (Colorado, Illinois, Indiana, Iowa, Kansas, Kentucky, Minnesota, Missouri, Nebraska, New York, South Carolina, South Dakota, West Virginia) Auroraville, Wisconsin El Dorado, Arkansas NOTE: *Aurora* may be derived more directly from the Indo-European base *aues*, to shine. CROSS REFERENCE: *chrys, flav, xanth*
auto***	Greek *autos*	self	SIMPLE ROOT: autism, autistic LEADING ROOT COMPOUND: *aut*: ac: autacoid (*akos*, cure, remedy, + *oid*) arch: autarchic, autarchy (self-rule) ark: autarky (self-sufficiency) (*arkein*, to achieve, suffice) eco: autecology (from *oikos*, home, environment) hent: authentic (**Synonyms**: genuine, bona fide, veritable), authenticate, authenticity (*hentes*, prepare, achieve) op: autopsy (literally, a self-viewing) (*ops*, sight) ox: autoxidation (*auto* + *oxidation*) *auto*: bio: autobiographer, autobiography {autobiographic, autobiographical} (*bio*, life; *graph*, write) cata: autocatalysis (*cata-* prefixes *lys*, loosen) chthon: autochthon (any of the earliest known inhabitants of a place; aborigine) (*chthon*, earth) clav: autoclave (a container for sterilizing, cooking, etc. by superheated steam under pressure) (*clavis*, key) crac: autocracy (self-ruled) (*cracy*, ruled by) crat: autocrat (*crat*, ruler) didact: autodidact (a person who is self-taught) (from Avestan *didainghe*, I am taught) digest: autodigestion (*di-* from *dis-*, apart, prefixes *gest*, from *gerere*, to bear, carry) ec: autoecic (always living upon the same organism) (from *oikos*, house, home, environment) ero: autoerotism (homosexuality) {autoerotic} (*eros*, love) gam: autogamy {autogamous} (*gam*, marriage, reproduction) gen: autogenesis, autogenous (*gen*, producing) giro: autogiro (also *autogyro*) (*gyros*, circle) graph: autograph, autographic (*graph*, write) hypn: autohypnosis (*hypno*, sleep) inoc: autoinoculation (*in-* prefixes *oc*, eye) lys: autolysis (*lys*, loosen) mat: automatic, automation, automatism, automaton (from *men*, to think) mob: automobile (*mob*, move) nom: autonomic, autonomous, autonomy (independence or freedom; the right of self-government) (*nomos*, law)

64

Element	From	Meaning	Examples
auto (cont'd)			tom: autotomy (the reflex action by which a leg, claw, tail, etc., as of a lobster, starfish, or lizard, is dropped off from the body when the part is damaged or the animal is under attack) (*tom*, cut) troph: autotroph, autotrophic (making its own food by photosynthesis, as a green plant, or by chemsynthesis, as any of certain bacteria: compare heterotrophic) (*troph*, nourish) typ: autotype (any facsimile) {autotypic} (*type*, icon, image) GERMAN: *Autobahn* (contraction of *automobile* + *bahn*, a course, highway) CROSS REFERENCE: *sui*
aux			See *aug* for *auxiliary*.
aver*	Latin *avere*: to wish, desire	desire	ROOT NOTE: This element is not related to the single word *aver*, which consists of *a(d)*-, to + *ver*, truth. SIMPLE ROOT: avarice, avaricious DISGUISED ROOT: audacious (**Synonyms:** brave, courageous, valiant) audacity (**Synonyms:** temerity, effrontery, nerve) avid (**Synonyms:** eager, keen, anxious) CROSS REFERENCE: *cup, desider*
avi*	Latin *avis*	bird	SIMPLE ROOT: avian, aviary, aviate, aviator, aviatrix LEADING ROOT COMPOUND: cult: aviculture fauna: avifauna (the birds of a specified region or time) onics: avionics (*avi*ation combined with electr*onics*) DISGUISED ROOT: ocarina (a musical instrument with a fancied resemblance to a bird) osprey (literally, bone-breaker; *os*, bone + *frangere*, to break) ostrich (a swift-running bird of Africa and Southwest Asia, the only member of its order; it is the largest and most powerful of living birds, and has a long neck, very long legs with two toes on each foot, and small, useless wings) (Old French *ostrusce*; from Vulgar Latin *avistruthius*; *avis* + *strouthos*, sparrow; short for *struthiocamelus*; *camelos*, camel) DISGUISED LEADING ROOT COMPOUND: auspex (a Roman priest who found omens in the flight of birds, etc.; an augur) (contraction of *avispex*: *avis* + *spicere*, to see) auspicate, auspice (usually *auspices*), auspicial, auspicious (from the same derivation of *auspex*; a portent, omen, or augury, especially when observed in the action of birds) PLACENAME: Avis, Pennsylvania CROSS REFERENCE: *ornith*
ax*	Greek *axios* (IE: *ag*, to drive, do)	worthy	SIMPLE ROOT: axiom (a self-evident or universally recognized truth; maxim; aphorism; in *logic, mathematics*, a proposition that is assumed without proof for the safe of studying the consequences that follow from it), axiomatic LEADING ROOT COMPOUND: logy: axiology (the study of the nature of values and value judgments) (*logy*, study of) TRAILING ROOT COMPOUND: chron: chronaxy (the time interval necessary to stimulate a muscle or nerve fiber with twice the minimum current needed to elicit a threshold response) (*chron*, time)

Element	From	Meaning	Examples
ax (cont'd)			PHILOSOPHICAL TERM: *axiomata media* (literally, middle principles) CROSS REFERENCE: *dign, val*
axi**	Latin *axilla* (IE: *aks,* axis, pivot)	armpit, axle	ROOT NOTE: The meaning--armpit--is the axis or pivotal point of the arm and shoulder. SIMPLE ROOT: axia: axial (pertaining to or forming an axis; located on, around or in the direction of the axis) axil: axil (in *botany*, the angle between the upper surface of a leaf-stalk, flower stalk, branch, or similar part, and the stem or axis from which it arises) axile (in *botany*, in or of the axis) axilla (the armpit, or an analogous part) axillar (one of the feathers in the axilla of a bird's wing) **axillary** axis: **axis** (a straight line about which a body or geometrical object rotates or may be conceived to rotate; *capitalized*, the alliance of Germany and Italy (1936), later including Japan, and often with Bulgaria, Hungary, and Romania, that opposed the Allies in World War II; preceded by *The*; plural, *axes*) PREFIXED ROOT: co-: coaxial (also *coaxal*; having a common axis; designating a high-frequency mediumused for sending telephone, telegraph, television, etc., impulses) (*co-*, with, together) TRAILING ROOT COMPOUND: mon: monaxial (*mono*, one) BOUND COMPOUND: axletree (a bar, fixed crosswise under an animal-drawn vehicle, with a rounded spindle at each end upon which a wheel rotates) INTERDISCIPLINARY: **axis** [in *anatomy*, the second cervical vertebra on which the head turns; in *botany*, the main stem or central part about which organs or plant parts such as branches are arranged; in *mathematics*, an unlimited line, half-line, or line segment to orient a space or a geometrical object, especially a line about which the object is symmetrical, as the *earth's axis*] **axillary** (in *anatomy*, of, relating to, or near the axilla; in *botany*, of, pertaining to, or located in the axil: axillary buds) MIDDLE ENGLISH: axle PLACENAME: Axis, Alabama CROSS REFERENCE: *ali, pter*

Every workman in the exercise of his art should be provided with proper implements. . . . The writer as well as the speaker employs the instrumentality of words; it is in words that he clothes his thoughts; it is by means of words that he depicts his feelings. It is therefore essential that he be provided with a copious vocabulary.
Peter Roget

B

Element	From	Meaning	Examples
bacci*	Latin *bacca:* berry	berry; seed	SIMPLE ROOT: baccate (pulpy throughout like a berry; bearing berries; berry-like) LEADING ROOT COMPOUND: fer: bacciferous (bearing berries, as the holly) (*ferre*, to bear) form: bacciform (shaped like a berry) vor: baccivorous (feeding on berries: said of birds) (*vorare*, to eat) CROSS REFERENCE: *cocc, semin, sperm, spor*
bacill,* bacul	Latin *bacil:* staff (IE: *bak*, staff)	staff, rod; rod-shaped bacteria	SIMPLE ROOT: *bacill:* bacillary (rod-shaped; see *bacilliform*, below; consisting of rod-like structures; of, like, characterized by, or caused by bacilli) bacillus (any of a genus of rod-shaped bacteria which occur in chains, produce spores and are active only in the presence of oxygen; plural, *bacilli*) *bacul:* baculine (punishment administered with a rod; can also mean "pertaining to a rod"), baculum PREFIXED ROOT: *im-:* imbecile [literally, without a staff, or rod; a mentally deficient person with an intelligence quotient (IQ) ranging from 25-50, or with a mental age of three to seven years] (*im-*, a variant of *in-*, not) LEADING ROOT COMPOUND: cid: bacillicide (*cide*, kill) form: bacilliform (rod-shaped; same as *bacillary*, above) AN ANTIBIOTIC: bacitracin [from *baci*(llus) + Margaret *Trac*(y), name of an American girl from whose wounds the strain was isolated] CROSS REFERENCE: *bacteri*
bacteri**	Greek *bactron:* a staff (IE: *bak*, staff)	staff, rod (single-cell, rod-shaped microorganism)	SIMPLE ROOT: bacterium (plural *bacteria*), bacterize PREFIXED ROOT: *anti-:* antibacterial (*anti-*, against) LEADING ROOT COMPOUND: *bacteri(o):* cid: bactericide (*cide*, kill) logy: bacteriology (*logy*, study of) CROSS REFERENCE: *bacil*
bacul			See *bacill* for *baculine.*
bal,*** bol, blem	Greek *ballein* (IE: *bhel*, to swell; yields English ball)	to throw	SIMPLE ROOT: ballista, ballistics PREFIXED ROOT AND COMPOUNDS: *bal:* *anti-:* antiballistic (describing a missile intended to intercept and destroy a ballistic missile in flight; same as *guided missile*) (*anti-*, against) *blem:* *em-:* emblem (literally, to throw in; formerly, a picture with a motto or verses, allegorically suggesting some moral truth, etc.) (from *en-*, in)

Element	From	Meaning	Examples
bal (cont'd)			*peri-*: periblem (in *botany*, the meristem that produces the cortex) (*peri-*, around)

pro-: problem (literally, that which is thrown forward), problematic (**Synonyms:** doubtful, dubious) (*pro-*, forth)

bol:

amphi-: (around)

amphibole (literally, to throw around; a particular type of rock-forming materials; reason unclear)

amphibology (double or doubtful meaning; ambiguity)

ana-: anabolism (the process in a plant or animal by which food is changed into living tissue; constructive metabolism; opposite to *catabolism*, next entry) (*ana-*, again)

cata-: catabolism (opposed to *anabolism*) (*cata-*, down)

dia-: diabolic (see *devil*, under *Disguised Root*), diabolism, diabolize, diabolo (*dia-*, across)

ec-: ecbolic (literally, a throwing out; helping to bring forth the fetus in birth, or causing abortion, by contracting the uterus; said of certain drugs) (from *ex-*, out)

em-: (in)

embolism (the intercalation of a day, month, etc. into a calendar, as in leap year; in *medicine*, the obstruction of a blood vessel by an embolus too large to pass through)

embolus (literally, something thrown in; any foreign matter, as a blood clot or air bubble, carried in the bloodstream)

epi-: epiboly (*epi-*, on, upon)

hyper-: hyperbola (mathematics term), hyperbole (exaggeration for effect, not to be taken literally, e.g., *He is as strong as an ox*) (*hyper-*, over, beyond)

meta-: metabolic, metabolism (*meta-*, beyond)

para-: parabola (mathematics term), parabolic (*para-*, alongside)

sym-: symbol (literally, that which is thrown together to represent another thing) (*sym-*, with, together)

LEADING ROOT COMPOUND:

graph: bolograph (*graph*, write)

meter: bolometer (*bol* here extended to mean ray, as though "something thrown") (*meter*, measure)

TRAILING ROOT COMPOUND:

ar: ar<u>bal</u>est (*arch* + *bal*: crossbow)

disco: disco<u>bol</u>us (a discus thrower)

DISGUISED ROOT:

devil [from *diabolic*, to throw across (one's way)]

palaver (Portuguese; talk; especially, idle chatter; flattery)

parable (translates Hebrew *mashal*, a comparison; that which is thrown alongside; a short, simple story, usually of an occurrence of a familiar kind, from which a moral or religious lesson may be drawn, e.g., the Parables of Jesus) (*para-*, alongside)

parley, parliament, parlor, parole

CROSS REFERENCE: *jac/ject*

The ill and unfitting choice of words wonderfully obstructs the understanding.
Francis Bacon

Element	From	Meaning	Examples
bapt*	Greek *baptizein* (IE: *gwebh*, to dip, plunge)	to dip, immerse	SIMPLE ROOT: baptisia (a flower), baptism, baptistery (also, *baptistry*), baptize PREFIXED ROOT: *ana-*: Anabaptist (see note under *ana-*) (*ana-*, again) TRAILING ROOT COMPOUND: pedo: pedobaptism (the baptism of infants, or children before the age of accountability) (*pedo*, child) CHRISTIAN DENOMINATION: Baptist (the Protestant religious group that maintains the only form of Christian baptism is by immersion) PROPER NAME: John the Baptist, who urged that his listeners repent of their sins and be baptized NOTE: Before the Christian use of the word, *baptism* had a secular meaning, e.g., animals were baptized in a chemical solution to rid them of parasites. NO CROSS REFERENCE
bar**	Greek *baros*: weight (IE: *gwer*, heavy, mill)	heavy	SIMPLE ROOT: barite (also, *baryte*; chemical symbol: $BaSO_4$), barium (chemical symbol: Ba), barote PREFIXED ROOT: *anti-*: antibaryon (*anti-*, against) *hyper-*: hyperbaric (*hyper-*, beyond) *hypo-*: hypobaric (*hypo-*, under) LEADING ROOT COMPOUND: *bari*: ton: baritone (the range of a male voice between bass and tenor) (*tone*, stretching, tone) *baro*: gram: barogram {barograph} (from *graph*, write) meter: barometer (an instrument for measuring atmospheric pressure) (*meter*, measure) scop: baroscope (an instrument for indicating changes in atmospheric pressure) (*scope*, look) *bary*: spher: barysphere (*spher*, ball, globe) TRAILING ROOT COMPOUND: centro: centrobaric (having to do with the center of gravity) iso: isobar (*iso*, equal) CROSS REFERENCE: *grav, liber, pend, pond*
bar**	Latin *barra* (IE; *bher*, to cut with a sharp tool)	bar, impede	SIMPLE ROOT: bar (**Synonyms: 1**) hinder, obstruct, impede; **2**) shoal, bank, reef) barracks, barrage, barricade, barrier, barrister PREFIXED ROOT: *de-*: debar, debarment (*de-*, reversal) *em-*: embar, embarrass (**Synonyms:** abash, rattle, faze), embargo (*em-*, in, on) FRENCH PHRASE: *embarras de richesses* [literally, embarrassment of wealth (or, of good things); hence, too much to choose from] PLACENAME: Embarrass (Minnesota, Wisconsin) NB: *Barrator, barrater*, and *barratry*, all pertaining to cheating or fraud, are not in this family. NO CROSS REFERENCE

Element	From	Meaning	Examples
bas,*** bat, bet	Greek *bainein* (IE: *gwem*, to come)	to go, step	ROOT NOTE: The origin of these roots is from IE *gwen*, to come, to go, whence Latin *venir*, to come (see *ven*). This meaning is retained in *bat*, *bet*; however, in *bas*, the meaning is base, foundation, support. The Greek verb *bainen*, to step, to go, appears to have given rise to "a place to step upon," therefore, *base*.

SIMPLE ROOT:
basa: basal (as *basal reader*)
base: base (literally, that which can be stepped upon; **Synonyms**: basis, foundation, groundwork)
basi: basic (see *Placename* below), basicity, basidium (plural, *basidia*), basilar, basion, basis (plural, *bases*)
PREFIXED ROOT:
bai (from the verb itself):
amphi-: amphibaena (literally, one that goes in both directions; a mythological serpent having a head at each end of its body) (*amphi*-, around, both)
bas:
a-: abasia (inability to walk caused by a defect in muscular co-ordination; compare *astasia*) (*a*-, not)
ana-: anabasis (see note under *ana*-)
cata-: catabasis (variation of *katabasis*; a going or marching down or back; retreat, especially a military retreat) (*cata*-, down)
dia-: diabase, diabasic (*dia*-, through, across)
bat:
ana-: anabatic (rising; moving upward; said of air currents or winds) (*ana*-, up, again)
dia-: diabatic (literally, to cross over; in *physics*, involving the transfer of heat; opposed to *adiabatic*) (*dia*-, through, across)
bet:
dia-: diabetes (any of various diseases characterized by an excessive discharge of urine) (*dia*-, through, across)
DOUBLE PREFIXED ROOT:
adiabatic (denoting a change in volume or pressure without loss or gain of heat) (*a*-, not + *dia*-, through)
LEADING ROOT COMPOUND:
baso:
cyt: (cell)
basocyte
basocytopenia (*penia*, small, lack of, diminished)
basocytosis (same as *basophilia*) (*osis*, condition of)
phil: basophile (in *biology*, a cell or tissue that is readily stained with basic dyes: also *basophil*), basophilia (*phila*, love of)
phob: basophobia (fear of walking; also the emotional inability to stand or walk in the absence of muscle disease) (*phobia*, excessive fear of)
bato:
phob: batophobia (fear of passing close to high buildings) (*phobia*, excessive fear of)

Element	From	Meaning	Examples
bas (cont'd)			TRAILING ROOT COMPOUND: *bas*: mono: monobasic (in *chemistry*, designating an acid the molecule of which can react with only one equivalent weight of an acid, or that has one hydroxyl group capable of replacing one acid hydrogen atom) (*mono*, one) *bat*: acro: acrobat (walking on tiptoe; an expert performer of tricks on the trapeze, tightrope, etc.; skilled gymnast or tumbler), acrobatic (*acro*, top, tip) hypno: hypnobatia (same as *somnambulism*, walking in one's sleep; semantically the same as *nyctambulism*, night-walking) (*hypno*, sleep) *bate*: stereo: stereobate (a foundation, as of a building, or a solid substructure or platform of masonry) (*stereo*, solid) styl: stylobate (in *architecture*, a continuous base or coping for a row of columns) (*style*, column) PLACENAME: Basic, Mississippi NB: *Basil, basilic, basilica, basilisk* are not in this family, coming from *basileus*, king, royal. CROSS REFERENCE: *amb, cede/ceed/cess, grad/gress, it, vad, vas*
bat***	Latin *battuere* (IE: *bhat*, to strike)	to beat, strike	SIMPLE ROOT: bate: bate (to abate, lessen, lower, etc.; with bated breath) batta: battalia, battalion (can also be used as non-military term) batte: batten, batter, battery batti: batting (noun) battl: battle (see synonyms at *combat*, below) battu: battue (a beating of the underbrush and woods to drive game out toward hunters; any mass killing) [Neither *bat*, the club, nor *bat*, the flying mammal, is from this root.] PREFIXED ROOT: a-: (away) abate (**Synonyms**: wane, ebb, subside) {abator} abatement (in *law*, the termination of a suit, quashing of a nuisance, etc.) abatis (or, *abattis*: a barricade of felled trees, with branches pointed toward the enemy: now often reinforced with barbed wire) com-: (with, together) combat (**Synonyms**: battle, engagement, campaign) combatant (as an *adjective*, fighting; as a *noun*, a fighter) combative (fond of struggling or fighting; ready or eager to fight; pugnacious) de-: débat (a literary term, which see under *de-*), debatable, debate, debater (*de-*, down) re-: rebate (*re-*, again) DISGUISED ROOT: rabbet (from *rebate*) BOUND COMPOUND: battledore (from phrase *battledore and shuttlecock*)

Element	From	Meaning	Examples
bat (cont'd)			FRENCH WORDS AND PHRASES: *abattoir* (literally, a place for beating down; a slaughterhouse) *abat-voix; abat-vent; abat-jour* (architectural terms) *cheval de bataille* (literally, horse of battle; war horse) *hors de combat* (literally, out of combat; disabled) NB: *Baton*, meaning stick, is not in this family. *Baton Rouge*, Louisiana, is the French translation of Choctaw *Itu-úma*, red pole, or stick, a boundary marker. CROSS REFERENCE: *coup, cuss, fend, flict, plaud, plex/ pless*
bath,** byss	Greek *bathos* (IE: *gwadh*, plunge, to sink)	deep, depth	SIMPLE ROOT: bathos, bathyal, bathysmal PREFIXED ROOT: a-: abyss (literally, without a bottom) (*a-*, without) LEADING ROOT COMPOUND: *batho:* chrom: bathochrome [an atom or group of atoms that when introduced into a compound (as a dye) causes a visible deepening of color (as from yellow toward green)] (*chrome*, color) lith: batholith (a deep-seated rock intrusion, usually granite, often forming the base of a mountain range, and uncovered by erosion) (*lithos*, stone) meter: bathometer (an instrument for measuring depths of water) (*meter*, measure) phob: bathophobia (fear of depths) (*phobia*, excessive fear of) *bathy:* bi: bathybic (pertaining to life in the deepest parts of the oceans), bathybius (*bios*, life) chrom: bathychrome (same as *bathochrome*) (*chrom*, color) gram: bathygram (a record obtained from sonic sounding instruments) (from *graph*, write) metr: bathymetry (the measurement of depths of water in oceans, seas, and lakes: done with a bathymeter) (*metry*, measurement of) pelag: bathypelagic (distinguished from *abyssal* and *pelagic*) (*pelag*, sea) scaph: bathyscaph (from *skaphe*, boat) spher: bathysphere (a strongly built steel diving sphere used for deep-sea observation and study) (*sphere*, ball, globe) therm: bathythermograph (*therm*, heat; *graph*, write) CROSS REFERENCE: *benth*
beat*	Latin *beatus* (IE: *deu*, to venerate)	happy	SIMPLE ROOT: beatitude (perfect blessedness or happiness; a blessing; capitalized, any one of the *Beatitudes*, instructions of Jesus on how to be happy, or to live a life of contentment, from Matthew 5: 3-12) LEADING ROOT COMPOUND: fic: beatific (of, possessing, or imparting consummate bliss), beatification (from *facere*, to make, do) fy: beatify (in the *Roman Catholic Church*, to declare a deceased person to have attained the blessedness of heaven and to authorize the title of Blessed; one of the first steps toward canonization, or the declaration of a deceased person a saint) (from *facere*, to make)

Element	From	Meaning	Examples
beat (cont'd)			PROPER NAME: Beatrice LATIN TERM: *Beati possidentes* (Blessed owners; blest possessors) CROSS REFERENCE: *felic*
beau			See *bell*, beautiful.
bell**	Latin *bellus,* pretty	beautiful	SIMPLE ROOT: belle (of the ball) PREFIXED ROOT: *em-*: embellish (**Synonyms:** adorn, decorate, ornament) (*em-,* in) LEADING ROOT COMPOUND: donna: belladonna (a poisonous plant of the nightshade family; influenced by cosmetic use for dilating the eyes) (*donna,* lady) ved: belvedere (from *videre,* to see) TRAILING ROOT COMPOUND: clara: clarabella (see note under *clara*) (*clara,* clear) DISGUISED ROOT: beau (frequent and attentive male escort for a girl or woman; a dandy; fopo; plural, *beaus, beaux*) beauteous, beautician, beautification, beautiful (**Synonyms:** lovely, handsome, comely), beauty beldam (interesting paradox) DISGUISED LEADING ROOT COMPOUND: fy: beautify (from *facere,* to make, do) FRENCH PHRASES: *beau geste* (a fine or beautiful gesture; hence, an act or offer that seems fine, noble, etc. but is empty) *beau idéal* (ideal beauty; the perfect type of conception) *beau monde* (elegant world; fashionable or high society) *beaux-arts* (the fine arts) *beaux-esprits* (plural of *bel-esprit*) *belles-lettres* (beautiful letters; fine literature; literature as one of the fine arts; fiction, poetry, drama, etc., distinguished from technical and scientific writings) ITALIAN MUSIC TERM: *bel canto* (literally, beautiful song) TERM: beautiful people (often capitalized; wealthy, fashionable people of the leisure class: with *the*) PLACENAMES: Beaufort (Illinois, North Carolina, South Carolina) Beaulieu, Minnesota (beautiful place) Belleview (Florida, Kentucky, Missouri) Bellevue (Idaho, Iowa, Kentucky, Maryland, Michigan, Nebraska, Ohio, Tennessee, Texas, Washington, Wisconsin) Belvedere (California, South Carolina, Washington) Belvidere (Nebraska, New Jersey, South Dakota, Tennessee) Belle Chasse, Louisiana (good hunting) AN ENGLISHMAN: Beau Brummel (epithet for George Bryan Brummel, 1778-1840; set standards of fashion for men; now refers to an extremely well-dressed man) CROSS REFERENCE: *calli, kal*

Add 1800 more words to your vocabulary and you can graduate
from the ordinary to the superior. John H. Steadman

Element	From	Meaning	Examples
bell**	Latin *bellum* (IE: *deu*, to injure, destroy, burn)	war	PREFIXED ROOT: *ante-*: antebellum (before the war; specifically, before the American Civil War; for example, *antebellum homes*) (*ante-*, before) *post-*: postbellum (literally, after the war; occurring after the war; specifically after the American Civil War) (*post-*, after) *re-*: rebel (see *Doublets* below), rebellion (*re-*, back, again) LEADING ROOT COMPOUND: *belli*: ger: belligerence, belligerency (same as *belligerence*; state of being at war or or of being recognized as a belligerent), belligerent (**Synonyms**: bellicose, pugnacious, contentious) (*gerere*, to bear) pot: bellipotent (powerful in war) (*potis*, able) *bellic*: ose: bellicose (of a quarrelsome or hostile nature; eager for a fight or quarrel; warlike) (*ose*, condition of) DISGUISED ROOT: duel (a formal fight between two persons armed with deadly weapons; it is prearranged and witnessed by two others, called *seconds*, one for each combatant; this word is *not* derived from *duo*, two) revel (to make merry; to noisily festive; to take much pleasure (see *Doublets* below) DOUBLETS: rebel:revel LATIN TERM: *casus belli* (cause for war; an event provoking war or used as a pretext for making war) WAR GODDESS: Bellona (wife or sister of Mars, the Roman god of war) CROSS REFERENCE: *guerr*
bene***	Latin *bene*, well (IE: *deu*, to do, perform, show favor, revere)	well, good	LEADING ROOT COMPOUND: dic: (*dicere*, to say) benedicite [same base as *benediction*; Bless you! as a *noun*, the invocation of a blessing, as in asking grace at meals; *capitalized*, the canticle that begins *Benedicite, omnia opera Domini, Domino* (Bless the Lord, all ye works of the Lord)] benediction (a blessing; an invocation of divine blessings, especially at the end of a religious service; see *Doublets* below) {benedictive, benedictory} fact: (from *facere*, to make, do) benefaction (the act of doing good or helping others, especially by giving money for charitable purposes; see *Doublets* below) benefactor (a person who confers a benefit; kindly helper) {benefactress} fic: benefic, benefice, beneficence, beneficent, beneficial (in *law*, for one's own benefit; **Synonyms**: profitable, advantageous), beneficiary (*facere*, to make, do) fit: benefit (see *Doublets* below) (from *benefaction*) vol: benevolence, benevolent (*velle*, to wish) DISGUISED ROOT: benison (Middle English *benisoun*; from Old French *beneisson*; from *benediction*; see *Doublets* below)

Element	From	Meaning	Examples
bene (cont'd)			DISGUISED LEADING ROOT COMPOUND: benign (**Synonyms:** kind, kindly, benevolent), benignant (*gn* from *gen* as in *gentle*) DOUBLETS: benefit:benefaction; benison:benediction SPANISH: *bien, bueno, buenos días* LATIN PHRASE: *nota bene* [(NB), note well] ITALIAN PHRASE: *a bene placito* (at pleasure; in *music*, at the discretion of the performer; similar to *ad libitum*, at lib-erty) ROMAN CATHOLIC HYMN: Benedictus [literally, Blessed; a particular short hymn of praise used in the Mass, beginning with *Benedictus*, from Matthew 21:9; also Zacharias's hymn, sung daily at Lauds (morning services), beginning with *Benedictus*, from Luke 1:68] NB: *BENELUX*, an acronym for Belgium, the Netherlands, and Luxembourg, is the economic union of these countries. CROSS REFERENCE: *bon, eu, prob*
benth*	Greek *benthos*: depth of the sea (IE: *gwadh*, to sink)	bottom of sea	SIMPLE ROOT: benthic, benthon, benthos (all the plants and animals living on, or closely associated with, the bottom of a body of water, especially the *sea*) PREFIXED ROOT: *epi-*: epibenthos (the animals and plants living on the sea bottom between the low tide level and a depth of 100 fathoms) (*epi-*, on, upon) LEADING ROOT COMPOUND: graph: benthograph (*graph*, write) scop: benthoscope (*scope*, look) CROSS REFERENCE: *bath/byss*
bet			See *bas* for *diabetes*.
bi,*** bin, bis	Latin *bis*: twice (IE: *dwi*, from *dwo*, two)	two	ROOT NOTE: This element combines with both Latin and Greek roots. SIMPLE ROOT: binal, binary, binate PREFIXED ROOT: *com-*: combination, combine (literally, put together two by two) (*com-*, with, together) LEADING ROOT COMPOUND: *bi*: (two) ann: (note difference in root meanings) biannual (*annus*, year) biannulate (in *zoology*, having two rings or bands of color, etc.) (*anus*, ring) athl: biathlon (in the winter Olympic games, an event combining a ski run and marksmanship) (*athl*, struggle, contest) aur: biaural (same as *binaural*) camer: bicameral (literally, two-chambered, as the legislature of the United States) (*camera*, room, chamber) capsul: bicapsular (in *botany*, having two capsules or a capsule with two cells) cep: biceps (two-headed muscle) (from *caput*, head) cip: bicipital (from *biceps*) corn: bicorn (having two horns or hornlike parts) (*corn*, horn) cusp: bicuspid (*cusp*, point)

Element	From	Meaning	Examples
bi (cont'd)			cycl: (*cycle*, wheel, circle)

bicycle
bicyclic (also, *bicyclical*; of or forming two cycles, circles, etc; in *chemistry*, containing two fused rings in the molecule)
enn: biennial (from *ann*, year)
fac: bifacial (in *botany*, having two unlike opposite surfaces) (*facies*; the face; from *facere*, to make, do)
far: bifarious (twofold; in *botany*, arranged in two rows) (from *fas*, law)
fid: bifid (divided into two equal parts by a cleft, as the end of a snake's tongue; forked) (from *findere*, to cleave, divide)
fil: bifilar (having or involving the use of two threads, as certain sensitive measuring instruments) (*filum*, thread)
flag: biflagellate (in *biology*, having two whiplike parts, as certain protozoa) (*flagellum*, whip)
foc: bifocal (*focus*, originally, fireplace, hearth)
foli: bifoliate (in *botany*, having two leaves) (*foli*, leaf)
form: biform (incorporating the features of two forms)
furc: bifurcate (used as both adjective and verb), bifurcation (*furcus*, fork)
gam: bigamous, bigamy (*gamos*, marriage)
gem: bigeminy (the state of occurring in pairs, as a rhythm of the heartbeat consisting of pairs of beats) (*geminus*, twin)
gen: bigeneric (designating or of hybrids derived from two different genera) (*gen*, producing)
jug: bijugate (having two pairs of leaflets, as some pinnate leaves; also, *bijugous*) (*jugum*, yoke)
labi: bilabial, bilabiate (in *botany*, having two lips, as the corolla of the mint family) (*labium*, lip)
later: bilateral (of, having, or involving two sides, halves, factions, etc.; affecting both sides equally; reciprocally; arranged symmetrically on opposite sides of an axis) (*latus*, side)
lingu: bilingual (*lingua*, tongue)
lob: bilobate (also, *bilobated*, *bilobed*) (*lobe*, a rounded projection, usually of the ear or liver)
loc: bilocular (also, *biloculate*; in *biology*, having or divided into two cells or chambers) (*locus*, place)
man: bimanous (having two hands), bimanual (using or requiring both hands) (*manu*, hand)
mest: bimestrial (lasting two months; occurring every two months; bimonthly) (from *mensis*, month)
month: bimonthly (once every two months; also, *twice* a month; in the latter sense, *semimonthly* is the better term)
morph: (form, shape)
bimorph (in *electronics*, an assembly of two crystals cemented together and used to increase the voltage from a given stress, as in a pickup, microphone, etc.)
bimorphemic (involving or consisting of two morphemes)
nom: binomial (*nomos*, law)
par: biparous (bearing two offspring at birth; in *botany*, dividing into two branches) (*parous*, bearing)

Element	From	Meaning	Examples
bi (cont'd)			part: bipartisan, bipartite (having two parts; having two corresponding parts, one each for the two parties to a contract; in *botany*, divided in two nearly to the base, as some leaves)
			ped: biped (any two-footed animal; as an *adjective*, two-footed) (*ped*, foot)
			radi: biradial (in *biology*, having both bilateral and radial symmetry) (*radius*, rod; spoke of wheel)
			ram: biramous (having two branches, as those on the appendages of crustaceans) (*ram*, branch)
			sect: bisect (literally, to cut in two; in *geometry*, to divide into two equal parts), bisector, bisectrix (*secare*, to cut)
			serr: biserrate (a notch) (*serra*, a saw)
			sex: bisexual (of both sexes; having both male and female organs, as certain animals and plants; hermaphroditic; sexually attracted by both sexes; as a *noun*, one that is bisexual) (*sex* may be from *secare*, to cut, divide)
			sulc: bisulcate (having two grooves; in *zoology*, cloven-hoofed) (*sulcare*, to furrow)
			the: bitheism (belief in the existence of two gods, as one good and one evil) (*theo*, God)
			val: bivalence (also, *bivalency*), bivalent (*valere*, to be strong)
			valv: bivalve (also, *bivalved*) (*valva*, leaf of a folding door)
			bin: (two by two)
			ocul: binoculars (*ocul*, eye)
			bis: (twice)
			cuit: biscuit (from *coctus*, past participle of *coquere*, to cook)
			sect: bissectile [denoting the extra day (February 29) of a leap year)] (from *sextus*, sixth)
			tort: bistort (literally, twice twisted; a plant of the buckwheat family, whose twisted roots furnish an astringent) (from *torquere*, to twist)
			MESHED LEADING ROOT COMPOUND:
			bicron [*billion* + *micron*; one billionth (0.000,000,001) of a meter]
			DISGUISED ROOT:
			balance (*lance*, plural of *lanx*, dish, weighing pan; originally, a set of weighing scales)
			barouche [from Middle Latin *birotium*, two-wheeled (cart); however, the barouche is a *four-wheeled* carriage)]
			COMPUTER TERM: bit (*binary* + *digit*)
			SPECIAL USES OF *BIS*: The French use the term to indicate "Encore!" or to perform a *second* time; it is also used in music to *repeat* the passage as indicated.
			PLACENAMES: Bicycle Lake, California; Bivalve, Maryland
			INTERDISCIPLINARY:
			binomial (in *biology*, a two-word scientific name of a plant or animal; in *mathematics,* an equation or expression consisting of two terms connected by a plus or minus sign)
			biserrate (in *botany*, having notched teeth along the margin, as some leaves; doubly serrate; in *zoology*, notched on both sides, as some antennae)
			CROSS REFERENCE: *di, dicho, du, dy*

Element	From	Meaning	Examples
bib*	Latin *bibere* IE: *pi, po*, to drink; yields Greek *symposium*	to drink	SIMPLE ROOT: bib, bibacious, bibber, bibulous PREFIXED ROOT: *im-*: imbibe, imbibition (the absorption or adsorption of water by certain colloids, as in seeds, with resultant swelling of the tissues) (*in-*, in) DISGUISED ROOT: beer (originally used to distinguish this beverage from ale) beverage (any liquid for drinking, especially other than water) PREFIXED DISGUISED ROOT: *im-*: imbrue (to soak, or stain, especially with blood) (*im-*, in) NB: *Brew* is not in this family, coming instead from the same Anglo-Saxon root that yields *bread*. CROSS REFERENCE: *pot*
bibli***	Greek *biblion*	book	SIMPLE ROOT: Bible, bibliotic, bibliotics LEADING ROOT COMPOUND: graph: bibliography (*graph*, write) latry: bibliolatry (*latry*, worship of) mancy: bibliomancy (*mancy*, divination by) mania: bibliomania (a craze for collecting books, especially rare ones) (*mania*, craze) pegy: bibliopegy (the art of bookbinding) (*pegy*, to bind, to fasten) phil: bibliophile (*phila*, love of) pol: bibliopole (see note under *pol*, to sell) theca: bibliotheca (a library) (*theca*, a case) CROSS REFERENCE: *lib*
bin			See *bi* for *binocular*.
bio***	Greek *bios* (IE: *gwei*, to live)	life	SIMPLE ROOT: biota, biotic, biotin (a bacterial growth factor, $C_{10}H_{16}O_3N_2S$, one of the vitamin B group, found in liver, egg yolk, and yeast) PREFIXED ROOT AND COMPOUNDS: a-: abiogenesis (spontaneous generation) (*a-*, negative + *bio* + *genesis*) amphi-: amphibious (*amphi-*, around, both) ana-: anabiosis (a bringing back to life or consciousness; resuscitation) (*ana-*, again + *osis*, condition) anti-: antibiosis, antibiotic (*anti-*, against + *osis*, condition) cata-: catabiosis (*cata-*, down + *osis*, condition) sym-: symbiosis {symbiotic} (*sym-*, with, together + *osis*, condition) NOTE: As an ending root form, *-biosis* means "a (specified) way of living." LEADING ROOT COMPOUND: *bi*: om: biome (*oma*, mass) ops: biopsy (*ops*, vision, from *opsis*, eye) *bio*: cata: biocatalyst (*cata-* prefixes *lys*, to loosen) ceno: biocenology (the branch of biology that deals with communities of organisms and their reactions to their environment and to each other), biocenosis (*ceno*, community + *logy*, study of)

Element	From	Meaning	Examples
bio (cont'd)			chem: biochemistry (the branch of chemistry that deals with plants and animals and their life processes) cid: biocide (a poisonous chemical substance that can kill living organisms) (from *caedere*, to kill) climat: bioclimatology (the science that deals with the effects of climate on living matter) degrad: bio<u>degrad</u>able (*de-* prefixes *grade*, step) eco: bioecology (*eco*, home, environment + *logy*, study of) engin: bioengineering (a science dealing with the application of engineering science and technology to problems of biology and medicine) ethic: bioethics (the study of the ethical problems arising from scientific advances, especially in biology and medicine) (*ethos*, moral custom) gen: biogenesis (the principle that living organisms originate only from other living organisms closely similar to themselves) (*gen*, producing) geo: (earth) biogeochemical cycle (see *Webster's New World Dictionary*) biogeography (the branch of biology that deals with the geographical distribution of plants and animals) (*geo*, earth + *graph*, write) graph: biographical, biography (*graph*, write) herm: bioherm (a reeflike mass or mound of limestone built by organisms, as corals, and surrounded by rock of a different kind; compare *biostrome*) (*herma*, reef) logy: biological, biology (*logy*, study of) lumin: bioluminescence (the production of light by living organisms, as by fireflies) (*lumen*, light) lys: biolysis (the destruction of life, as by microorganisms) (*lysein*, to loosen) mass: biomass (the total mass or amount of living organisms in a particular area or volume) medi: biomedicine (the aspects of medicine that derive from, or relate to, the natural sciences, especially biology, biochemistry, and biology) metr: biometrics (that branch of biology that deals with its data statistically and by quantitative analysis), biometry (calculation of the probable human life span; in one sense, same as *biometrics*) nom: bionomics (same as *ecology*) (*nomos*, law) phys: biophysics (*phys*, growth) plasm: bioplasm (living matter; protoplasm) (*plasm*, form) scop: bioscopy (an examination to find out whether life is present) (*scopy*, a viewing) spher: biosphere (the zone of the earth, extending from its crust out into the surrounding atmosphere, which contains living organisms; all the living organisms on earth) (*sphere*, globe, ball) strom: biostrome (a thin limestone layer consisting predominantly of marine fossils, as corals; compare *bioherm*) (*stroma*, a mattress, bed, rug)

Element	From	Meaning	Examples
bio (cont'd)			syn: bio<u>syn</u>thesis (the formation of chemical compounds by the cells of living organisms, as in photosynthesis) (*syn*-prefixes *thesis*, to place, put)
			sys: biosystematics (*sys*-, a variant of *sym*-, prefixes *tem*, to set)
			tele: biotelemetry (*tele*, afar + *metry*, measurement of)
			top: biotope (*topos*, place)
			typ: biotype (*type*, image, symbol)
			TRAILING ROOT COMPOUND:
			aero: aerobe, aerobic (*aero*, air, gas)
			ceno: cenobite, cenobium (*ceno*, common, shared)
			micro: microbe (*micro*, small)
			rhizo: rhizobium (*rhizo*, root)
			sapro: saprobe (*sapro*, rotten)
			NB: *Biocellate*, from *bi*, two + *ocellate*, is not in this family; see *bi*; neither is *biotite*, after J. B. Biot (1774-1862), a French naturalist; a dark-brown or black mineral of the mica family, found in igneous and metamorphic rocks.
			EMBEDDED ROOT COMPOUND:
			auto<u>bio</u>graphy (*auto*, self + *graph*,write)
			FRATERNITY: Phi Beta Kappa (initials for the motto: *philosophia biou kubernetes*, philosophy the guide of life)
			CROSS REFERENCE: *anim, spir, vit, zo*
bis			See *bi* for *biscuit, bissectile, bistort*.
blanc**	Frankish *blanc* IE: *bhleg*, to shine)	white	ROOT NOTE: Paradoxically, *black* and *blank* are related. Originally, both words were derived from the IE root *bhleg*, to shine, as in Latin *flagrare*, flame, burn; original sense, "sooted, smoked black from flame." *Soot*, however, comes from Old English *sot*, akin to Middle Dutch *soet*, from IE *sed*, to sit, the basic sense of which is to settle.
			SIMPLE ROOT: blanch (to make white; take the color out)
			DISGUISED ROOTS: blank, blanket, bleacher
			FRENCH PHRASES:
			carte blanche (literally, white card; complete freedom to act for another in his or her absence)
			maison blanche (white house; capitalized, the name of a department store in New Orleans, Louisiana)
			CROSS REFERENCE: *alb, cand, leuk*
blast**	Greek *blastos*	shoot, sprout	SIMPLE ROOT:
			blastema (the undifferentiated embryonic tissue from which cells, tissue, and organs are developed)
			blastula (an embryo at the stage of development in which it consists of usually one layer of cells around a central cavity, forming a hollow sphere)
			PREFIXED ROOT AND COMPOUNDS:
			endo-: endoblast (same as *endoderm*) (*endo*-, within)
			epi-: epiblastic (the outer layer of cells of an embryo) (*epi*-, upon)
			hypo-: hypoblast (same as *endoderm*) (*hypo*-, under)
			LEADING ROOT COMPOUND:
			cel: blastocele (the segmentation cavity of a developing ovum or of the blastula) (*cele*, cavity)

Element	From	Meaning	Examples
blast (cont'd)			cyst: blastocyst (a blastula, which see above) (*cyst*, cell)
			derm: blastoderm {blastodermatic, blastodermic} (*derm*, skin)
			disc: blastodisc (also, *blastodisk*, the small disk of proto-plasm containing the egg nucleus)
			gen: blastogenesis (reproduction by asexual means, as by budding in corals) (*genesis*, producing)
			mer: blastomere (*mere*, part)
			por: blastopore (the opening into the gastrula cavity) (*pore*, orifice)
			spher: blastosphere (same as *blastula*, which see above) (*sphere*, ball, globe)
			zo: blastozooid (*zo*, animal + *oid*, similar to, in the shape of)
			TRAILING ROOT COMPOUND:
			erythro: erythroblast (any of the nucleated cells in bone marrow that develop into erythrocytes) (*erythro*, red)
			holo: holoblastic (compare *meroblastic*) (*holo*, whole)
			mero: meroblast (in *biology*, undergoing partial cleavage: said of an egg with a large yolk) (*mero*, part)
			meso: mesoblast (*meso*, middle)
			odont: odontoblast (a tooth cell in the outer surface of dental pulp that produces dentine) (*odont*, tooth)
			CROSS REFERENCE: *clad, germ, rhizo*
bol			See *bal* for *symbol*.
bon**	Latin *bonus* (IE: *deu*, to venerate)	good	SIMPLE ROOT:
			bonanza (Spanish; originally, fair weather; prosperity)
			bonbon, bonnie
			bonus (**Synonyms**: bounty, premium, dividend; see *Doublets* below)
			LEADING ROOT COMPOUND:
			fic: bonification (from *facere*, to make, do)
			DISGUISED ROOT:
			boon, as in *boon companion*
			bounty (see synonyms at *bonus*, above; see *Doublets* below)
			SPANISH: *bonito* (pretty, nice)
			FRENCH WORDS AND PHRASES:
			à bon marché (at a good bargain; cheap)
			bon ami (good friend; said of a man or boy)
			bon appétit [(I wish you) a hearty appetite]
			bonjour (good day; also, good morning)
			bon mot (good word; a witticism; an apt saying)
			bonsoir (good evening)
			bon vivant (literally, good living; one who enjoys good food and other pleasant things)
			bon voyage (good voyage; pleasant journey)
			bonne (good; a maidservant; a nursemaid)
			bonne amie (good friend; said of a woman or girl)
			bonne foi (good faith; honesty)
			debonair (from *débonnaire*, of good air; friendly in a cheerful way; affable; genial; easy and carefree in manner)
			embonpoint (in good condition; plumpness; corpulence)
			FRENCH EXPRESSION:
			à bon chat, bon rat (to a good cat, a good rat; tit for tat)

Element	From	Meaning	Examples
bon (cont'd)			LATIN LAW PHRASES: *bona fide* (literally, in good faith; without dishonesty, fraud, or deceit; **Synonyms:** authentic, genuine, veritable) *bona vacantia* DOUBLETS: bonus:bounty PLACENAMES: Bon Air (Tennessee, Virginia) Bonaire, Georgia; Bonanza (Colorado, Oregon, Utah) Bonhomie, Mississippi; Bon Homme Colony, South Dakota Bonifay, Florida (good faith) Bon Secour, Alabama (good help) Buenos Aires, Argentina (good air) NB: *Bonfire* is not in this family; originally, the word was 'bonefire,' from bodies being burned after a plague or a war, the only remains being that of bones. CROSS REFERENCE: *bene, eu, prob*
brachi**	Greek *brachion*: an arm (IE: *mreghu*, short)	upper arm	ROOT NOTE: Coming from *brachios*, short, *brachi* refers to the *shorter* upper arm, as opposed to the *longer* forearm. See related root, next family. SIMPLE ROOT: brachia: brachial, brachialis, brachiate (as an *adjective*, having widely spreading branches, alternately arranged; as a *verb*, to swing arm over arm from one hold to the next, as certain monkeys and apes do) brachiu: brachium (the part of the arm that extends from shoulder to elbow; in *biology*, any armlike part or process; plural, *brachia*) LEADING ROOT COMPOUND: pod: brachiopod (a member of a phylum of marine animals with hinged and upper and lower shells enclosing two arm-like parts with tentacles, used for guiding minute food particles to the mouth) (*pod*, foot) SPANISH: *bracero*, a Mexican farm laborer brought into the United States temporarily for migrant work in harvesting crops, the idea being that such a person uses his *strong arms* (from *brazo*, arm) DISGUISED ROOT: brace (**Synonyms:** pair, couple, yoke); brace and bit (carpentry tool), bracelet (literally, armlet), bracer (in *archery*, a leather guard won on the arm holding the bow) brassard (originally, armor for the arm from elbow to shoulder) brassiere (originally, arm guard) PREFIXED DISGUISED ROOT: em-: embrace (to clasp in the arms, usually as an expression of affection or desire; hug; to take up or adopt, especially eagerly or seriously, as *to embrace a new profession*) (*em-*, in) SPANISH: *brazo* (See *Placenames*) GERMAN: pretzel (originally, *brezel*, from Latin *brachium*; dough first baked in "folded arms" and given to children by priests as a reward for the children saying their prayers) PLACENAMES: Brazos (New Mexico, Texas) Brazos Island, Texas; Brazos River, Texas NO CROSS REFERENCE

Element	From	Meaning	Examples
brachy**	Greek brachys (IE: mreghu, short)	short	PREFIXED ROOT: amphi-: amphibrach (literally, short before and after; a metrical foot in Greek and Latin verse consisting of one short syllable between two long ones, e.g., HES-i-TATE) (amphi-, around, both) LEADING ROOT COMPOUND: cephal: brachycephalic (having a relatively short or broad head) (cephal, head) cran: brachycranial (broad-skulled) (crani, skull) chron: brachychronic (describing an illness of short duration) (chron, time) dactyl: brachydactylic (having short fingers or toes) (dactyl, finger) log: brachylogy (conciseness of speech) (from logos, word) pter: brachypterous (having incompletely developed or very short wings, as certain insects) (pter, wing) ur: brachyuran (also, brachyurous) (designating or of certain crabs with a short abdomen folded beneath the main body; as a noun, such a crustacean) (ur, tail) TRAILING ROOT COMPOUND: tri: tribrach [in classical poetry, a metrical foot consisting of three short syllables, two belonging to the thesis (the accented syllables) and one to the arsis (the unaccented syllable)] (tri, three) CROSS REFERENCE: brev
bract*	Latin bractea: thin metal plate	leaf, plate	SIMPLE ROOT: bract (a modified leaf, usually small and scalelike, sometimes large and brightly colored, from whose axil grows a flower or inflorescence) bracteate (having bracts) bracteolate (having bracelets) bractlet (also, bracteole) PREFIXED ROOT: e-: ebracteate (without bracts) (from ex-, out, without) CROSS REFERENCE: foli, lamin, petal, phyll
branchi*	Greek branchia	gills (of fish and others of the lower vertebrates; represented in the human fetus by the branchial arches, separated by clefts)	SIMPLE ROOT: branchia (a gill), branchiae (plural of brachion; the gills of an aquatic animasl) branchial, branchiata, branchiate (having gills) LEADING ROOT COMPOUND: branchio: bdella: branchiobdella (a genus of worms that live on the gills of crayfish) (bdella, leech) pod: branchiopod (any crustacean having gills on the feet) (pod, foot) TRAILING ROOT COMPOUND: crypto: Cryptobranchia (crypto, hidden) nudi: Nudibranchia (nudi, nude, bare) NO CROSS REFERENCE
brev***	Latin brevis	short, brief	SIMPLE ROOT: breve: breve, brevet (in military usage, a commission nominally promoting an officer to a higher honorary rank without higher pay or greater authority)

83

Element	From	Meaning	Examples
brev (cont'd)			brevi: breviary (a book containing the prayers, hymns, etc. that priests and certain other clerics of the Roman Catholic Church are required to recite daily), breviate, brevier, brevity (the quality of being brief, concise; shortness of time) PREFIXED ROOT: ab-: abbreviate (see *Doublets* below; **Synonyms**: shorten, curtail, abridge) (*ab-*, off, away, may be the true prefix, or it may be an assimilation of *ad-*, to, toward) LEADING ROOT COMPOUND: caud: brevicaudate (having a short tail) (*caud*, tail) loqu: breviloquence, breviloquent (marked by brevity of speech) (*loqui*, to speak) ped: breviped (having short legs) (*ped*, foot) rostr: brevirostrate (a beak; thus, having a short beak or bill: said of a bird) (from *rodere*, to gnaw) DISGUISED ROOT: brief (**Synonyms**: short, concise) PREFIXED DISGUISED ROOT: a-: abridge (to shorten by condensation or omission while retaining the basic contents; to reduce or lessen in duration, scope, etc.; diminish; curtail; to deprive; cut off; see *Doublets* below) (from *ad-*, to, toward) DOUBLE PREFIXED DISGUISED ROOT: unabridged (not abridged; complete; said especially of dictionaries) (Anglo-Saxon *un-*, not + *a-*, to) DOUBLETS: abridge:abbreviate LATIN PHRASE: *Ira furor brevi est* (Anger is brief madness) Horace INTERDISCIPLINARY: breve (in *law*, an initial writ; in *linguistics*, a mark put over a short vowel or short or unstressed syllable; in *music*, a note equal to two whole notes: now seldom seen in notation) CROSS REFERENCE: *brachy*
bronch*	Greek *bronchos*	windpipe	SIMPLE ROOT: bronchi: bronchial (pertaining to the bronchi or bronchioles) bronchiole (also *brochiolus*; any of the small subdivisions of the bronchi; plural, *bron-chioles*, or *bronchioli*) bronchium (plural, *bronchia*) bronchu: bronchus (any of the two main branches of the trachea, or windpipe; plural, *bronchi*) LEADING ROOT COMPOUND: *bronch*: itis: bronchitis (an inflammation of the mucous lining of the bronchial tubes) (*itis*, inflammation of) *bronchi*: ectas: bronchiectasis (an irreversible, chronic enlargement of certain bronchial tubes) (*ectasis*, a stretching out) *broncho*: cel: bronchocele (a localized dilatation of a bronchus) (from *kele*, tumor) pneu: bronchopneumonia (*pneumon*, lung) scop: bronchoscope (*scope*, view) CROSS REFERENCE: *laryng, trache*

Element	From	Meaning	Examples
bront*	Greek *bronte* (IE: *bherem*, to rustle, buzz)	thunder (extended to mean "hugeness," as in *brontosaurus*)	SIMPLE ROOT: bronteum (in *Greek drama*, a device for making the sound of thunder, usually by means of bronze jars filled with stones) LEADING ROOT COMPOUND: phob: brontophobia (fear of thunder) (*phobia*, fear of) saur: brontosaur (also, *brontosaurus*; a family of gigantic, plant-eating, four-footed dinosaurs with a long neck and tail, five-toed limbs, and a small head) (*saur*, lizard) zo: brontozoum (a genus of gigantic dinosaurs known from their 3-toed footprints (some 18 inches long, and found in the Connecticut Valley) (*zo*, animal) NO CROSS REFERENCE
bry*	Greek *bryon*: moss, lichen	moss	SIMPLE ROOT: bryales, bryonia, bryony (also, *briony*) LEADING ROOT COMPOUND: log: bryology (the branch of botany dealing with bryophytes) (*logy*, study of) phyl: bryophyllum (*phyll*, leaf) phyt: bryophyte (a group of plants comprising the true mosses and liverworts) (*phyton*, plant) NO CROSS REFERENCE
bucc*	Latin *bucca* (IE: *bheu*, to blow up, swell)	cheek, pouch, mouth	SIMPLE ROOT: bucca (the cheek; fleshy portion of side of face) buccal (pertaining to the cheek or mouth) LEADING ROOT COMPOUND: lingu: buccilingual (same as *buccolingual*) (*lingu*, tongue) PREFIXED DISGUISED ROOT: *de-*: (out) debouch (in *military* usage, to come forth from a narrow or shut-in place into open country; to come forth; emerge) debouchment (a debouching; mouth of a river; outlet) FRENCH: *débouché* (an opening for troops to debouch through; hence, an outlet, as for goods) ENGLISH COGNATES: boast (**Synonyms**: brag, vaunt, swagger) bosom (**Synonyms**: breast, bust) poach (the yolk is pocketed in the white) pock (as in the swollen pocks of chicken pox and small pox) pocket, pouch, poke (as in the expression "a pig in a poke") NB: *Buccellation*, morsel, is not in this family. CROSS REFERENCE: *ora, osc, stoma*
bul*	Greek *boulesis*: will	will power, determination	ROOT NOTE: This root is probably akin to *ballein*, to throw. SIMPLE ROOT: bule: bulesis (the will or an act of the will) buli: bulimia (hunger experienced a short time after a meal; continuous, abnormal ot morbid hunger) {bulimic} PREFIXED ROOT AND COMPOUNDS: *a-*: (without) abulia (also spelled *aboulia*; loss of will power) abulomania (a form of mental disorder characterized by abulia) (*mania*, madness) *hyper-*: hyperbulia, hyperbulesis (*hyper-*, over, beyond) NO CROSS REFERENCE

85

Element	From	Meaning	Examples
bull*	Latin *bulla*: bubble (IE: *beu*, to swell)	boil	SIMPLE ROOT: bullion PREFIXED ROOT: *e*-: ebullient (boiling or bubbling over, as with enthusiasm), ebullition (from *ex*-, out) DISGUISED ROOT: boil (from Old English *byle*; **Synonyms:** simmer, seethe, stew) PREFIXED DISGUISED ROOT: *par*-: parboil (same as *perboil*; originally, to boil completely, thoroughly; now, to boil partially) (from *per*-, through, thoroughly) FRENCH: bouillon NO CROSS REFERENCE
burs**	Greek *bursa*: hide, leather, a bag (yields English purse)	pouch, sack	SIMPLE ROOT: bursa (in *anatomy*, a sac or pouchlike cavity, especially one containing a fluid that reduces friciton); plural, *bursae*), bursal, bursala, bursar (a treasururer, especially of a college), bursary burse (also, *bourse*, which see below) PREFIXED ROOT: *dis*-: disburse (literally, out of the pocket; to pay out; expend) (*dis*-, opposite of) LEADING ROOT COMPOUND: *burs(i)*: itis: bursitis (*itis*, inflammation of) form: bursiform (in *anatomy* and *zoology*, shaped like a bursa, or sac; pouchlike) DOUBLE PREFIXED ROOT: reimburse (literally, to put back into the pocket) (*re*-, back + *im*-, a variant of *in*-, in, into) FRENCH: bourse (an exchange where securities or commodities are regularly bought and sold; Bourse, the stock exchange of Paris or of any of certain other European cities) SPANISH: bolson (big purse; in the southwestern United States, a flat desert valley surrounded by mountains and draining into a shallow lake in the center) SCOTTISH GAELIC COGNATE: sporran (a leather pouch or purse, usually covered with fur or hair, worn hanging from the front of the belt in the dress costume of Scottish Highlanders) MEDICAL PHRASE: *bursula testium* (literally, the pouch of the testicles; the scrotum) CROSS REFERENCE: *fisc*
bust			See *ure* for *combustion*.
byss			See *bath* for *abyss*.

> Particularly in science and in engineering is it true that the *best* word must be found. Mere approximation is not only inadequate, but often worse than useless. It is not sufficient that an engineer's report be written that it can be understood; it should be written so that it cannot be misunderstood. And unquestionably it is a fact that inadequate and inaccurate statement is one of the most common and serious handicaps of the average student of technological school.
> Lewis Buckley Stillwell

C

Element	From	Meaning	Examples
caco***	Greek *kakos*: bad, evil	bad, wrong, abnormal	LEADING ROOT COMPOUND: *cac(o)*: ody: cacodyl (literally, bad smell; a poisonous compound) (from *odme*, smell) demon: (evil spirit) cacodemon (an evil spirit or devil) cacodemonomania (a condition marked by delusions of being possessed by demons, or evil spirits) (*mania*, craze) eth: cacoëthes (an irresistible urge) (*ethos*, character) gen: cacogenics, cacogenesis (inability to produce hybrids that are both viable and fertile) (*gen*, producing) graph: cacography (can mean either poor handwriting or incorrect spelling) (*graph*, write) logy: cacology (substandard pronunciation or diction) (*log*, speak) phon: cacophony {cacophonous} (*phone*, sound) NB: The following words are not in this family: *cacomistle*, *cacomixle*, both of which are native Mexican for a raccoon-type animal of the southwestern United States and Mexico. CROSS REFERENCE: *dys, mal, mis*
cad,*** cas, cid	Latin *cadere*: to fall (IE: *kad*, to fall)	to cut, fall	SIMPLE ROOT: *cad*: cada: cadaver (literally, that which has fallen; a dead body, especially of a person; a corpse, as for dissection) cade: cadence (see *Doublets* below), cadent, cadenza cadu: caduca (see *Legal Terms* below) caducity (state or quality of being perishable; also senility) caducous (dropping off; fleeting; unenduring; in *botany*, falling off early, as some leaves) *cas*: cascade, casual, casually PREFIXED ROOT: *cad*: de-: decadence (the act or process of falling into an inferior conditon or state; see *Doublets* below), decadent (*de-*, from, away) *cid*: ac-: accidence, accident, accidental (**Synonyms**: fortuitous, casual, incidental) (*ac-* assimilates *ad-*, to, toward) de-: (down, away) decide (**Synonyms**: determine, conclude, resolve) decidua (a membrane lining the uterus during pregnancy, cast off at birth) deciduous (falling off at a certain season or stage of growth, as some leaves, antlers, insect wings, etc.; shedding leaves annually: opposed to *evergreen*) *ex-*: excide (to cut out) (*ex-*, out) *in-*: incidence, incident (**Synonyms**: occurrence, event, episode), incidental (see synonyms at *accidental*, above) (*in-*, in)

Element	From	Meaning	Examples
cad (cont'd)			*re-*: recidivism (literally, falling back; repeated or habitual relapse, as into crime) (*re-*, back) *oc-*: occasion (**Synonyms**: cause, chance, motive); Occident (*oc-* assimilates *ob-*, against) DOUBLE PREFIXED ROOT: co<u>in</u>cide (**Synonyms**: agree, conform, accord), coincidence, coincident, coincidental (*co-* from *com-*, with; *in-*, in, on) LEADING ROOT COMPOUND: branch: caducibranch (describing those tailed amphibians whose gills are lost in adult life) (*branch*, gills) corn: caducicorn (describing those animals which have deciduous horns) (*corn*, horn) DISGUISED ROOT: case (a container or receptacle; another *case* is derived from *capere*, to hold) chance (literally, that which falls out; see *Doublets* below; **Synonyms**: 1) occur, transpire; 2) random, haphazard, desultory) chute (Old French *cheute*, from *cheoir*, to fall) PREFIXED DISGUISED ROOT: *de-*: decay (from *decadence*; see *Doublets* below; **Synonyms**: putrefy, spoil, disintegrate) (*de-*, from, away) *es-*: escheat (in *law*, the reverting of property to the government (from *ex-*, out) *para-*: parachute (*para* from *parare*, to ward off) DOUBLETS: cadence:chance; decadence:decay LEGAL TERMS: *cadere* (to end; cease, fail) *cadit* (it falls; abates, fails, ends, ceases) *caduca* (in *civil law*, property of an inheritable quality) caducary (relating to or of the nature of escheat, forfeiture, or confiscation) MUSIC TERMS: accidental (the raising or lowering of a note within a key by a half step) incidental music (music played in connection with the presentation of a play, motion picture, poem, etc. in order to heighten the mood or effect on the audience) NB: *Caduceus* and *caducean* are not in this family; both pertain to Mercury's staff used as an emblem of the medical profession. CROSS REFERENCE: *lap; pto*
cal***	Latin *calere*: to be warm (IE: *kel*, warm)	heat, warmth	SIMPLE ROOT: *cald*: caldarium (in ancient Rome, a room for taking hot baths) caldera (a craterlike basin of a volcano), caldron (large kettle) *cale*: calenture (any fever caused by exposure to great heat) calescent (increasing in warmth, getting hotter) *calor*: calor, calorescence, caloric, caloricity, calorie, calorize PREFIXED ROOT: *de-*: decalescence {decalescent} (*de-*, down) *in-*: incalescent {incalescence} (*in-*, intensive) *re-*: recalescence {recalescent} (*re-*, again)

Element	From	Meaning	Examples
cal (cont'd)			*trans-*: transcalent (pervious to or permitting the passage of heat) (*trans-*, across)
			LEADING ROOT COMPOUND:
			cale:
			fac: calefacient (*facere*, to make, do)
			fact: calefaction, calefactory (originally, a heated room in a monastery) (*facere*, to make, do)
			calori:
			fic: calorific (*facere*, to make, do)
			meter: calorimeter {calorimetry} (*meter*, measure)
			DISGUISED ROOTS:
			camouflage (possibly from this root; its derivation is vague)
			caudle (a *warm* drink for invalids, especially a spiced and sugared gruel with wine or ale added)
			chaudron (originally, a kettle, or "hot pot"; now the color of antique red)
			chafe (from *calefacere*, to make warm; from *calere*, to be warm + *facere*, to make)
			chauffer (a small, portable stove or heater)
			chauffeur [literally, stoker (of a steam-driven car); a person hired to drive a private automobile for someone else]
			scald (from *excaldare*; literally, to wash in hot water)
			TRIPLETS: caldron:chaldron:cauldron
			FRENCH:
			chowder (*chaudière*; literally, hot pot; a thick soup made variously, but usually containing onions, potatoes, and salt pork, sometimes corn, tomatoes, or other vegetables and often, specifically clams, or fish, with milk)
			nonchalance (*noun*; **Synonyms**: equanimity, composure, serenity)
			nonchalant (*adjective*; without warmth or enthusiasm; not showing interest; showing cool lack of concern; casually indifferent)
			réchauffé (a dish of leftover food *reheated*; any used or old literary material worked up in a new form; rehash; past participle of *réchauffer*, to warm over; from *ré-*, again + *chauffer*, to warm; from Latin *ex-*, intensive + *calefacere*, to heat)
			FRENCH MEDICAL TERMS:
			chaude-pisse [a burning sensation experienced during micturition (urination)]
			chauffage (treatment with a cautery at a low heat which is passed to and fro across the tissue 1/4 inch away from it)
			PLACENAMES:
			Caliente (California; Nevada)
			Ojo Caliente, New Mexico (Hot Eye)
			CROSS REFERENCE: *caust, therm*
calc**	Latin *calcis*: lime; or Greek *chalix*, pebble)	limestone	SIMPLE ROOT:
			calca: calcar (an oven or furnace; see *calx* for another *calcar*), calcareous (or, like, or containing calcium, carbonate calcium, or lime)
			calci:
			calcic, calcimime (a white or colored liquid of whiting or zinc white, glue, and water, used as a wash for plastered surfaces)
			calcine (to change to calx or powder by heat; to burn to ashes or powder), calcite (also, *calcspar*), calcium

Element	From	Meaning	Examples
calc (cont'd)			calcu: calculable, calculate (**Synonyms:** compute, estimate, reckon), calculated (deliberately planned or intended) calculating (shrewd or cunning; scheming) calculation, calculator calculous (in *medicine*, caused by or having a calculus or calculi) calculus (originally, a small piece of limestone used in counting; any abnormal stony mass or deposit formed in the body, as in a kidney or gall bladder; in *mathematics*, a method of calculation using a special system of notation in symbols; a system of mathematical analysis using the combined methods of differential calculus and integral calculus) calx: calx (the ashy powder left after metal or mineral has been calcined) LEADING ROOT COMPOUND: col: calcicole (in *botany*, a plant that thrives in soil rich with *lime*) (*colere*, to cultivate) fer: (*ferre*, to bear) calciferol [a coalescence of *calcif(erous)* + *(ergost)erol*; vitamin D_2; it is a crystalline alcohol, $C_{28}H_{43}OH$] calciferous (of, forming, or containing calcium or calcium carbonate) fic: calcific (producing salts of lime, as in the formation of eggshells in birds and reptiles), calcification (*facere*, to make) fug: calcifuge (a plant that grows in soils low in calcareous matter) {calcifugous} (*fugere*, to flee) fy: calcify (to change into a hard, stony substance by the deposit of lime or calcium salts) (*facere*, to make) DISGUISED ROOT: chalk (a white, gray, or yellowish limestone that is soft and easily pulverized; it is composed mainly of minute sea shells) causeway (*possibly*; see note under *calx*) LATIN-GERMAN COMPOUND: calcsinter (German *kalksinter*: *kalk*, lime; from Latin *calx* + German *sinter*, slag; same as *travertine*: a light-colored, usually concretionary limestone deposited around limy springs, lakes, or streams) LATIN-ITALIAN COMPOUND: calctufa (also, *calctuff*; with tufa, a kind of porous stone, a porous lime carbonate deposited by the waters of calcareous springs; calcareous tufa) RELATED FRENCH WORD: crayon (from Latin *creta*, which also yields *cretaceous*) CROSS REFERENCE: *calx* (heel)
calc			See *calx* for *discalced*.
calli,** **kal**	Greek *kallos*: beauty	beautiful	LEADING ROOT COMPOUND: cali: sthen: calisthenics (literally, beautiful strength; simple gymnastics: exercises such as push-ups and sit-ups, to develop a strong, trim body) (*sthen*, strength) calli: graph: calligraphy (beautiful writing) (*graph*, write) op: calliope (literally, beautiful voice; a musical instrument with a series of steam whistles, played like an organ; see *Greek mythology*, below), calliopsis (*ops*, voice)

Element	From	Meaning	Examples
calli (cont'd)			pyg: callipygian (nicely formed buttocks) (*pyg*, buttocks)
			callo:
			mania: callomania (a condition marked by delusions of personal beauty) (*mania*, madness)
			kal:
			scop: kaleidoscope (an instrument for viewing beautifully formed shape) (*eido*, shape +*scope*, to view)
			DISGUISED ROOT:
			calomel (literally, beautiful black; mercurous chloride, HgCl, a white, tasteless powder, formerly used as a cathartic, for intestinal worms, etc.)
			caloyer (literally, beautiful old age; a monk of the Eastern Orthodox Church) (*yer* from *geros*, old age)
			GREEK MYTHOLOGY:
			Calliope (the Muse of eloquence and epic poetry)
			CROSS REFERENCE: *bell*
calx,* calc	Latin *calx*: heel of the foot; *calcare*: to tread	heel	SIMPLE ROOT:
			calca:
			calcaneum [plural, *calcanea*; calcaneus (plural, *calcanei*); both *calcaneum* and *calcaneus* refer to the heel bone]
			calcar (see *calc* for another *calcar*)
			calce: calceolaria (also called *slipperwort*), calceolate (in *botany*, shaped like a slipper, as the blossoms of some orchids)
			PREFIXED ROOT AND COMPOUNDS:
			de-: decalcomania (the process of transferring to glass, wood, etc. decorative pictures or designs printed on specially prepared paper) (from French *décalquer*, to trace, copy; from *de*-, down + Italian *calcare*, to press, trample + *mania*, madness for)
			dis-: discalced (barefooted, as in some religious orders) (*dis*-, without)
			re-: recalcitrant [literally, kicking back (with one's heels) at authority] (*re*-, back)
			LEADING ROOT COMPOUND:
			form: calceiform (in *botany*, slipper-shaped)
			DISGUISED ROOT:
			calk (the part of a horseshoe that projects downward to prevent slipping)
			caulk [to make (a boat, for example) watertight by filling the seams or cracks with oakum, tar, etc.; to stop up (cracks of window frames, pipes, etc.) with a filler; to make (a joint of overlapping plates) tight by hammering the edge of one plate into the side of the other]
			PREFIXED DISGUISED ROOT:
			in-: inculcate (literally, to heel in; thus, to instill strongly through repetition and urging, as to *inculcate* honesty in one's children) (*in*-, in)
			INTERDISCIPLINARY: calcar (in *botany*, a hollow projection or nectar spur, as at the base of the corolla; in *zoology*, a spur on a bird's wing or leg)
			NOTE: *Causeway* may come from *calc*, meaning limestone-- the material used to make the road; or from *calc*, heel, from its being packed down, as by walking on the passageway.
			NO CROSS REFERENCE

Element	From	Meaning	Examples
calyc*	Greek *kalyx*: cup (IE: *kel(k)*: cup)	cup, bell-shaped	**SIMPLE ROOT:** *calyc*: calycate (in *botany*, having a calyx), calyceal, calycine (also, *calycinal*), calycle, calyculate (or *caliculate*), calyculus *calyx*: calyx (plural, *calyxes*, or *calyces*; denotes cuplike outer whorl of protective floral leaves; also cuplike division of the pelvis, which itself means basin; any of various more or less cup-shaped zoological structures) **PREFIXED ROOT:** *epi-*: epicalyx [ring of small leaves (called *bracts*) at the base of certain flowers, resembling an extra outer calyx, as in the mallows; another definition: an involucre resembling the true calyx but consisting simply of a whorl of bracts (as in mallows) or resulting from the union of the sepal appendages (as in roses)] (*epi-*, upon, on, to) **LEADING ROOT COMPOUND:** oid: calycoid (like a calyx in form, color, or appearance) (*oid*, similar to) **LATIN COGNATES:** calix (same meaning as *chalice*) chalice (a cup for the consecrated wine of the Eucharist) (see *Doublets* below) (from Latin *calix*, cup, goblet) **DOUBLETS:** calix:chalice **CROSS REFERENCE:** *campan*
calyp*	Greek *kalypter*: sheath (IE: *kel*, hide, conceal; the base of Latin *conceal*)	covered	**SIMPLE ROOT:** calypter, calyptra (the remains of the female sex organ, or archegonium, of a moss, forming the caplike covering of the spore case) **PREFIXED ROOT:** *apo-*: apocalypse (literally, that which is disclosed; revelation; discovery; disclosure; capitalized, the book of Revelation, or Revelation of St. John the Divine, the last book in the New Testament) (*apo-*, away) **LEADING ROOT COMPOUND:** gen: calyptrogen (in *botany*, the layer of actively dividing cells at the tip of a root in many plants, as grasses, that produce the root cap cells) (*gen*, producing) **TRAILING ROOT COMPOUND:** eu: eucalyptus (a tree with well-covered buds) (*eu*, well) **CROSS REFERENCE:** *cel, cond, crypt, tect/teg*
camb*	Latin *cambiare*: to exchange (IE: *camb*, to bend, crook)	change	**SIMPLE ROOT:** cambist (a dealer in foreign bills of exchanges) cambium (that which changes into new layers; thus a layer of cells in the stems and roots of vascular plants that gives rise to phloem and xylem) **PREFIXED ROOT:** *pro-*: procambium (in *botany*, a layer of undifferentiated plant cells from which the vascular tissue is formed) (*pro-*, before, forward) **DISGUISED ROOT:** change (**Synonyms:** alter, vary, modify) (Middle English *changen*; from Old French *changier*; from Late Latin *cambire*) **PREFIXED DISGUISED ROOT:** *ex-*: exchange {exchangeable} (*ex-*, forth, from) **SPANISH PHRASE:** *en cambio* (on the other hand) **CROSS REFERENCE:** *amoeb, meta-, mut*

Element	From	Meaning	Examples
camera***	Latin; from Greek *kamara*: vault (IE: *kam*, to arch)	room, chamber	SIMPLE ROOT: camera, cameral, cameralist, camerata, camerate, camerlingo LEADING ROOT COMPOUND: saur: camarasaurus (a genus of American dinosaurs with the orbits and nares large and situated high on the head, suggesting adaptation to an amphibious mode of life) (*saur*, lizard) TRAILING ROOT COMPOUND: bi: bicameral (two-chambered; as the United States Congress and 49 of the 50 states) (*bi*, two) uni: unicameral (one-chambered; as the legislature of Nebraska) (*uni*, one) DISGUISED ROOT: cabaret (a restaurant serving liquor and providing entertainment, usually singing and dancing; see *Doublets* below) camber (a slight convex curve of a surface, as of a road, a ship's deck, a beam, etc.) chamber (a room in a house, especially, a bedroom; a reception room in an official residence; see *Doublets* below) chum (a shortening of *chambermate*, as pronounced in England; originally, a roommate; a close friend) comrade (from French *camarade*; see *camaraderie* below; further from Spanish *camarada*, chamber mate; a friend; close companion; capitalized, a Communist) PREFIXED DISGUISED ROOT: ante-: antechamber (*ante-*, before) FRENCH: camaraderie (comradeship, as of roommates; see *comrade* above) SPANISH: camarilla [literally, small room (a group of unofficial, often secret and usually scheming, advisers, especially of one in power (as king or premier)] DOUBLETS: cabaret:chamber LATIN PHRASES: *camera lucida* (light chamber; an apparatus containing a prism for reflecting an object on a surface so that its outline may be traced: often used with a microscope) *camera obscura* (dark chamber; a camera consisting of a dark chamber with a lens through which an image is projected in natural colors onto an opposite surface) *in camera* [in (the) chamber; secretly; in *law*, in private with a judge rather than in open court; in the chambers of a judge] GERMAN COGNATE: *Kamerad* ("I am your *comrade*"; used by German soldiers as a word of surrender in World War II) CROSS REFERENCE: *cel*
camp**	Latin *campus* (IE: *kamp*, to bend)	field, plain	ROOT NOTE: See next entry to see how the root is extended to mean "bells." SIMPLE ROOT: camp, campaign (originally, open country suited to military maneuvers; hence, military expedition; see *Doublets* below), campestral, campion, campus PREFIXED ROOT: en-: encamp, encampment (an encamping or being encamped; a camp or campsite) (*en-*, in) LEADING ROOT COMPOUND: meter: campimeter (an instrument for testing indirect or peripheral visual perception of form and color) (*meter*, measure)

Element	From	Meaning	Examples
camp (cont'd)			DISGUISED ROOT: champagne (originally, any of various wines produced in Champagne, France, located in the Ardennes plateau) champion (as a *verb*, to protect or fight for as a champion; to act as militant supporter of) (from Old French; probably from West Germanic *kampjo*, warrior; from *kamp*, battlefield; ultimately from Latin *campus*) NOTE: This word shows the influence of the early expeditions of Rome into what is now Germany. champaign [level and open country; a plain; from Latin Campania, Campagna (province in Middle Italy); see *Doublets* below] champignon (a mushroom; probably from Vulgar Latin *fungus campaniolus*, fungus growing in the fields) DOUBLETS: campaign:champaign SPANISH: *campesino* (field hand; a peasant or farm worker) *campo* (in South America, an extensive, level, grassy *plain*) *campo santo* (literally, holy field: a cemetery) LEGAL TERM: champerty (from Middle French *champart*, field rent; from *champ*, field + *part*, portion; an act of assisting the defense or the prosecution in a case, in consideration of receiving a share of the matter in the suit; the act is illegal in most states) PLACENAMES: Campaign, Tennessee; Champaign, Illinois Campobello, Colorado CROSS REFERENCE: *agri/agro*
campan*	Latin *campana*: level	bells	ROOT NOTE: This root is from *Campania* (*campus*, field), the level country about Naples, from the use of Campanian metal in making bells. SIMPLE ROOT: campana, campanula, campanulate LEADING ROOT COMPOUND: *campani*: form: campaniform (in the shape of a bell) *campano*: logy: campanology (having to do with, or the study of, bells; the art of ringing bells) ITALIAN: *campanile* (a bell tower, especially one somewhat detached from a church) SPANISH: *campanario* (same as *campanile*) *campanero* (literally, bellman; the *bellbird* of South America) *campanilla* (literally, small bell; the flower *morning glory*) NOTE: *Carillon*, though literally meaning set of four (from *quattor*, four), originally referred to a *set of four bells*; now, a set of stationary bells, each producing one tone of the chromatic scale, sounded by means of a keyboard or by a clockwork mechanism. CROSS REFERENCE: *calyc, cotyl*

It is the Word which opens the door of the treasure cave,
the Word which builds the universe and commands its power.
G. H. Bonner

Element	From	Meaning	Examples
can,** cent	Latin *cantus*: song (IE: *kan*, to sing, song)	to sing, song	SIMPLE ROOT: can: canorous (pleasing in sound; melodious; musical) cant: cant (see *Doublets* below; **Synonyms**: dialect, vernacular, jargon; another *cant* is listed under *cant*, edge) cantar: cantar, cantarist cantat: cantata (short for *musica cantata*, or *sung* music, as opposed to *sonata*), cantatrice (a female professional singer) canti: canticle, cantillate, cantillation (in *Jewish liturgy*, a chanting or reciting with certain prescribed musical phrases indicated by notations) canto: canto (any of the main divisions of certain long poems, corresponding to the chapters of a book) cantor (a church choir leader; precentor) cantu: cantus (a melody; especially, the principal part of a polyphonic work) PREFIXED ROOT: *cant*: des-: descant (literally, apart from the song; from the medieval practice of two-part singing in which there is a fixed, known melody and a subordinate melody added above) (from *dis-*, from, apart) in-: incantation (the chanting of magical words or formulas that are supposed to cast a spell or perform other magic) (*in-*, in) re-: recant (literally, to sing back; to make a formal retraction or disavowal of a statement or belief to which one has previously committed oneself) (*re-*, back) *cent*: ac-: accent, accentual (having rhythm based on stress rather than on the number of syllables or length of sounds, as some poetry), accentuate {accentuation} (*ac-* assimilates *ad-*, to, toward) in-: incentive (literally, to sing in; stimulus, encouragement) (*in-*, in, on) pre-: precentor (one who directs the church choir or the congregational singing) (*pre-*, before) DISGUISED ROOT: chant (see *Doublets* below), chanter, chantey chanticleer, or *chantecler* (originally, a rooster which had a 'clear chant,' and which appeared in Reynard the Fox tales) chantry (an endowment to pay for the saying of Masses and prayers for the soul of a specified person, often the endower) charm (**Synonyms**: attract, allure, fascinate) PREFIXED DISGUISED ROOT: en-: enchant (to cast a spell over, as by magic; bewitch; to charm greatly; delight; see synonyms at *charm*, above), enchanting, enchantment, enchantress (*en-*, in) DOUBLETS: chant:cant ITALIAN WORDS: *cantabile* (a musical direction: in an easy, flowing manner; songlike) *cantilena* (a smooth, flowing lyrical style passage or sometimes, instrumental music)

95

Element	From	Meaning	Examples
can (cont'd)			*canzone* (a lyrical poem of Provençal or early Italian trouba-dours) FRENCH WORDS AND PHRASES: *chanson* (a song) *chanson de geste* (song of heroic acts; any of the Old French epic poems of the 11th to 13th centuries, especially of the type of the *Chanson de Roland*, Song of Roland) *chanteuse* (a woman singer, especially of popular ballads) LATIN PHRASE: *cantus firmus* (literally, firm song: *plain-song*; a simple melody serving as the main theme in contra-puntal works, especially those of the Middle Ages) CROSS REFERENCE: *hymn, od* (song)
can*	Latin *canis* (IE: *kwon*, dog)	dog	SIMPLE ROOT: cana: canaglia, canaille (originally, a pack of dogs; mob; rab-ble) cani: canicular (of the Dog Days in July and August; of the Dog Star) canine (like a dog; as a noun, a dog or other canine animal, e.g., K-9 corps; a sharp-pointed tooth on either side of the upper jaw, having a long single root; in full, canine tooth) DISGUISED ROOT: kennel (from Old French *chenil*) FRENCH COGNATE: chien FRENCH: chenille (literally, hairy caterpillar; a tufted, velvety yarn used for trimming, embroidery, etc.; a fabric filled or woven with such yarn, used for rugs, bedspreads, etc.) (*canicula*, diminu-tive of *canis*; from its hairy pile) CONSTELLATION: Canicula (Sirius, the Dog Star) PLACENAMES: Isle de Chien, Florida; Prairie du Chien, Wisconsin NOTE: *Canary*, referring to the *bird*, the *dance*, the *islands*, or the *wine*, is derived ultimately from this root; see authors' *An Introduction to An Academic Vocabulary*, p. 28. CROSS REFERENCE: *cyn*
can*	Latin *canna* (IE: *gan(dh)*, container)	reed, cane, a vessel	SIMPLE ROOT: can (noun), canister cana: canal, canaliculate (adjective form of *canaliculus*), cana-liculus (in *anatomy, botany, zoology*, a very small groove, as in bone), canalization, canalize cane: cane, canella cann: canna (flower), cannon, cannonade, cannula (a tube for insertion into the body cavities or ducts, as for drainage), cannular, canon (originally, a measuring cane) cano: canonic, canonical, canonize LEADING ROOT COMPOUND: phor: canephore (a maiden bearing a reed or cane basket on her head in an early Greek religious festival) (*phore*, to bear) ITALIAN: cannelloni (plural of *cannellone*, a hollow noodle; literally, small tube; augmentative of *cannello*, a tube, joint of cane; tubular casings of boiled pasta filled with ground meat or other filling and baked in a sauce: also made of squares of boiled pasta wrapped around the filling) DOUBLETS: cañon:canyon (cañon is Spanish) PLACENAMES: Canon, Georgia; Canyon (California, Minnesota, Texas)

Element	From	Meaning	Examples
can (cont'd)			INTERDISCIPLINARY: canon (in *ecclesiology*, and often capitalized, the fundamental and essentially unvarying part of the Mass, between the Preface and the Communion, that centers on the consecration of the Host; also, a list of recognized saints as in the Roman Catholic Church; in addition, a list of the books of the Bible officially accepted by a church or religious body as genuine; in *music*, a polyphonic composition in which there are exact repetitions of a preceding part in the same or related keys) Notice that in both fields, there is a strictness of form, as though measured with a *cane*. NO CROSS REFERENCE
cand,** cend	Latin *candere*: to shine (IE: *kand*, to glow)	shining (extended to mean whiteness, openness, glowing)	SIMPLE ROOT: candle, candelle (an abrupt climb of an airplane propelled by the plane's momentum), candor (for both, see *Placenames* below) cande: candela, candelabrum (plural, *candelabrums, candelabra*), candent, candescent candi: candid, candidate (white-robed: office seekers in Rome wore white togas to signify their purity for office) PREFIXED ROOT: *cand*: *in*-: incandescent (glowing with intense heat; red-hot or, especially white-hot; very bright; shining brilliantly) {incandescence} (*in*-, intensive) *cend*: *in*-: incendiary (literally, setting on fire; having to do with willful destruction of property by fire; willfully stirring up strife, riot, rebellion, etc.) (*in*-, in, on) DISGUISED ROOT: chandelier (from Old French *chandelabra*; from Latin *candelabrum*; from *candela*, candle; a lighting fixture hanging from the ceiling, with branches for candles, light bulbs, etc.) cense (to perfume with incense; to burn incense to) censer (but not *censor*, which see under *cens*) PREFIXED DISGUISED ROOT: *in*-: incense (as a *noun*, a fragrance; as a *verb*, to make very angry; enrage) (*in*-, in) SPANISH: *candelilla* (a plant native to the Southwest and to Mexico, which yields a wax used for polishes, or for *shining*) CHURCH FEAST: Candlemas, held on February 2, commemorating the purification of the Virgin Mary; candles for sacred uses are blessed on this day BOUND COMPOUNDS: candlewood (burns with a *bright* flame) sandalwood (because of its *light-colored* wood); from Sanskrit *candrás*, shining; akin to Sanskrit *candana*, sandalwood PLACENAMES: Candle, Alaska; Candor (North Carolina, Pennsylvania) CROSS REFERENCE: *alb, blanc, leuk*

No knowledge of a science can be properly acquired until the terminology of that science is mastered, and this terminology is in the main of Greek and Latin origin.
Spencer Trotter

Element	From	Meaning	Examples
cant*	Latin *cantus*: edge; from Greek *kanthus*: corner of the eye (IE: *kantho*, corner, bend)	side; corner of the eye; angle	ROOT NOTE: Words derived from both Latin and Greek are listed without differentiation. SIMPLE ROOT: *cant*: cant (corner, edge, angle, tilt, turn; another *cant* is listed under *can*, sing) cantle (a piece, especially when cut off or out) canton [any of the political divisions of a country or territory; specifically, any of the states in the Swiss Republic; a division of an arrondissement (the largest administrative subdivision of a department) in France] cantonment (the assignment of troops to temporary quarters; the quarters assigned) *canth*: canthus (either corner of the eye; where the eyelids meet) PREFIXED ROOT: *cant*: *de-*: (from) decant [to pour off (a liquid) gently without stirring up the sediment; to pour from one container to another] decanter (a decorative glass bottle, generally with a stopper, used for serving wine, etc.) *canth*: *epi-*: epicanthus (the corner of the eye; the small fold of skin sometimes covering the inner corner of the eye, as in many Asian people) (*epi-*, upon) LEADING ROOT COMPOUND: lever: cantilever (Some authorities place this word in the *can*, dog, family; the reason for placement in either family is not clear.) NB: *Descant* is listed under the *can/cent* family. CROSS REFERENCE: *cost, hedr, lat, pleur*
cap,*** capt, cept, cip, cup, ceit, ceive [do not confuse this root with *capit*, head]	Latin *capere* (IE: *kap*, to grasp; yields English have)	to hold, seize	SIMPLE ROOT: *cap*: capab: capability (the quality of being capable; capacity; ability), capable (**Synonyms:** competent, qualified) capacio: capacious (of large capacity; able to contain or hold much; roomy; spacious) capacit: capacitance (symbol: C; the ratio of charge to potential on an electrically charged, isolated conductor; also, the ratio of the electric charge transferred from one to the other of a pair of conductors to the resulting potential difference between them) capacitate {capacitation}, capacitor (formerly called *condensor*), capacity (**Synonyms:** function, office; see *Doublets* below) capi: capias (You are to arrest: the first word of the writ; in *law*, a writ authorizing an officer to arrest the person specified therein) capiat (an instrument for removing foreign bodies from a cavity, as of the uterus) caps: capsular, capsulate (also, *capsulated*), capsule, capsulize (to enclose in a capsule; to express in concise form; condense)

Element	From	Meaning	Examples
cap (cont'd)			*capt*: capti: caption (in *law*, the part of a legal document that states the time, place, and authority of its execution) captious (**Synonyms**: critical, caviling, carping) captivate (**Synonyms**: attract, charm, fascinate) captive (see *Doublets* below) captivity capto: captor (a person who captures) captu: capture (**Synonyms**: catch, trap, ensnare) PREFIXED ROOT *ceit*: *con-*: conceit (see *Doublets* below; **Synonyms**: pride, vanity) (*con-*, with, together) *re-*: receipt (old-fashioned variation of *recipe*; a receiving or being received; a written acknowledgment that something, as goods, money, etc. has been received; see *Doublets* below) (*re-*, back) *ceiv*: *re-*: receive (see *Doublets* below; **Synonyms**: accept, admit) (*re-*, back) *cept*: *con-*: (with, together) concept (see *Doublets* below; **Synonyms**: idea, conception, thought) conceptacle (in *botany*, a sac opening outward and containing reproductive cells, found in some brown algae) conception (see synonyms at *concept*, above), conceptive, conceptual conceptualism (the doctrine, intermediate between *nominalism* and *realism*, that universals exist explicitly in the mind as concepts, and implicitly in the similarities shared by particular objects) conceptualize *contra-*: contraception, contraceptive (*contra-*, against) *de-*: deception (**Synonyms**: subterfuge, trickery, chicanery) (*de-*, from) *ex-*: except, excepting, exception, exceptionalism (*ex-*, out) *cip*: *dis-*: (apart) disciple (**Synonyms**: follower, supporter, adherent) disciplinary, discipline (**Synonyms**: punish, chastise, castigate) [Other authorities place *disciple* and its derivatives under *doc*, teach, which see.] DOUBLE PREFIXED ROOT: *ap-*: apperceive (*ap-* assimilates *ad-*, to, toward; *per-*, through) *pre-*: preoccupied (in *biology*, designating, or of, a taxonomic name already taken and hence no longer available), preoccupy (*pre-*, before; *oc-* assimilates *ob-*, against) TRAILING ROOT COMPOUND: *cap*: *mer*: mercaptan (literally, seizing mercury; any of a class of chemical compounds analogous to the alcohols, characterized by the substitution of sulphur for oxygen in the OH radical and by strong, unpleasant odors)

99

Element	From	Meaning	Examples
cap (cont'd)			*cep*: for: forceps (originally, smith's tongs; small tongs or pincers for grasping, compressing, and pulling, used especially by surgeons and dentists) (*formus*, warm) prin: prince (literally, first taken; from *prin* and *cep* are also derived *principal, principle*; see *Doublets* below) (*prin* from *primus*, first; *ce* from *cep*) *cept*: ambo: amboceptor (see note under *ambi, ambo*) *cip*: muni: municipal (of or having to do with a city, town, etc. or its local government), municipality, municipalize (*munia*, official duties, functions) parti: participant, participate, participle (in *grammar*, a verbal form having some characteristics and functions of both verb and adjective; see *Webster's New World*) {participial} (*parti*, part) prin: (from *primus*, first) principal (**Synonyms**: chief, foremost, capital) principality principium principle (**Synonyms**: theorem, postulate, proposition), principled EMBEDDED ROOT COMPOUND: emancipate (**Synonyms**: free, release, liberate) (*e*-, out + *manus*, hand) DISGUISED ROOT: cable (Middle English and Old French; from Late Latin *capulum*, a cable or rope used for securing or holding) caitiff (see *Doublets* below) case (a container, as a box, crate, chest, sheath, folder, etc.; a protective cover or covering part, as *a leather case, seedcase*; another *case* is listed under *cad/cas/cid*, which see) catch (**Synonyms**: capture, trap, snare; see *Triplets* below) chase (to follow quickly or persistently in order to catch or harm; to run after; pursue; follow; see *Triplets* below) chassé (a gliding, dance step) chassis PREFIXED DISGUISED ROOT: pur-: purchase (from *pro*-, for) re-: recover (but not *discover*, which comes from *cover*, itself coming from *co*- + *operire*, to hide) (*re*-, again) DOUBLETS: caitiff:captive; casket:caisson; concept:conceit principal:principle (see *Triplets* below) receipt:receive; recover:recuperate TRIPLETS: capture:catch:chase; principal:principle:prince FRENCH: aperçu (a glance, insight, digest) (from *apperceive*) LATIN LEGAL PHRASES: *capias ad satisfaciendum* *capias extendi facias* *capias ad respondendum* [See *Black's Law Dictionary* for an extensive treatment of these terms.] CROSS REFERENCE: *hab, ten*

Element	From	Meaning	Examples
capill*	Latin *capillus*: hair, especially of the head	hair; also, thread	ROOT NOTE: This root is possibly derived from *caput*, head (next family) + *pilus*, a hair. SIMPLE ROOT: capilla: capillaceous (having hairlike filaments; like a hair or thread; capillary) capillarity (a physics term) capillary (of, or like a hair, especially, in being very slender; having a very small bore; in or of capillaries) capilli: capillitium capillu: capillus (plural, *capilli*) PREFIXED DISGUISED ROOT: *dis-*: dishevelled (disarranged and untidy; tousled; rumpled) (*dis-*, apart, away + Old French *chevel*, hair, from *capillus*) INTERDISCIPLINARY: capillary (in *anatomy*, any of the tiny blood vessels con- necting the arteries with the veins; in *botany*, resembling hair in the manner of growth of shape; in *physics*, of or pertaining to the apparent attraction or repulsion between a liquid and a solid, observed in a capillary) CROSS REFERENCE: *trich/trix*
capit,*** cep, cip, chief	Latin *caput* (IE: *kaput*, cup-shaped)	head (also, hood that covers the head)	SIMPLE ROOT: cap (from *cappa*, cape; originally, hooded cloak) cape (one meaning: headland; a piece of land projecting into a body of water; promontory; another *cape* is derived from *cappa*, cloak; this second *cape* is listed here as well (e.g., *es-* *cape*), because of its association with *head*) capit: capital (Synonyms: chief, principal, main; see *Doublets* be- low; also see *capitol* below), capitalism, capitalization, capi- talize capitate (enlarged at the head or tip; head-shaped, as some flow- ers), capitellum capitol (refers only to the building where the legislature sits; see *capital*, above) capitulant, capitular, capitulary capitulate (Synonyms: yield, succumb, relent), capitulation capitulum (in *anatomy* and *zoology*, a knoblike part, as at the end of a bone in a joint; in *botany*, head; plural, *capitula*) capo: capo (a chieftain in a criminal organization such as the Mafia), caporal (the boss or an assistant boss of a ranch) capr: caprice (Synonyms: whim, whimsy, vagary) capt: captain (see *Doublets* below) PREFIXED ROOT: *cap*: *de-*: decapitate (to cut off the head of; behead) {decapitation} (*de-*, off, away) *re-*: recapitulate (Synonyms: repeat, iterate, reiterate) {reca- pitulation} (*re-*, again) *cape*: *es-*: (*es-*, a variant of *ex-*, out) escapade, escape (literally, to leave one's cloak or cape behind, as in breaking loose or in getting free; Synonyms: avoid, evade, elude; see *Biblical Word* below)

Element	From	Meaning	Examples
capit (cont'd)			escapement, escapism

cip:

oc-: occiput (back of the head) (*oc-* assimilates *ob-*, against)

pre-: (before) precipice (a vertical, almost vertical, or overhanging rock face; steep cliff; a greatly hazardous situation, verging on disaster) precipitant, precipitate (literally, head first; headlong; **Synonyms**: sudden, abrupt, impetuous) precipitation, precipitous (**Synonyms**: steep, abrupt, sheer)

TRAILING ROOT COMPOUND:

cep:

bi: biceps (any muscle having two heads or points of origin, especially the large muscle at the front of the upper arm that flexes the elbow joint; also, the large muscle at the back of the thigh that flexes the knee joint) (*bi*, two)

quadri: quadriceps (the large four-part extensor muscle at the front of the thigh) (*quadri*, four)

tri: triceps (a large three-headed muscle running along the back of the upper arm and serving to extend the forearm) (*tri*, three)

cip:

bi: bicipital (of the *biceps*, above) (*bi*, two)

sin: sinciput (forehead; upper half of the skull) (from *semi*, half)

DISGUISED ROOT:

cattle, chattel (see *Doublets* below)

chef (originally, *chef de cuisine*, literally, head of the kitchen), chief (see *Doublets* below)

kerchief (literally, cover the head; *ker* is the same as in *curfew*, cover the fire)

handkerchief (a kerchief that can be folded so that it can be held in the hand)

chapter (see *Doublets* below), chapiter (architectural term)

chape, chapeau, chapel, chaperon, chaplain (originally, the custodian of St. Martin's *cape, cloak*), chaplet

PREFIXED DISGUISED ROOT:

a-: achievable, achieve (**Synonyms**: 1) perform, do, execute; 2) reach, gain, attain), achievement (literally, to come to a head) (from *ad-*, to, toward)

mis-: mischief (from Old French *meschever*, to come to grief; harm, damage, or injury, especially that done by a person; a cause or source of harm, damage, or annoyance), mischievous) (Anglo-Saxon *mis-*, wrong)

FRENCH PHRASE: *cap a pie* (head to foot)

SPANISH: *caudillo* (leader; especially, a revolutonary leader)

ITALIAN MUSIC TERM: *da capo* (abbreviated *D.C.*, from the head. The term means to repeat the passage from the beginning. A similar term is *dal segno*, abbreviated *D.S.*, from the sign; repeat from the indicating sign).

LATIN PHRASE: *per capita* (literally, by heads; per person; for each person; equally to each heir)

LATIN LEGAL PHRASES:

capitale

capitis diminutio (diminution of life, or personality)

Element	From	Meaning	Examples
capit (cont'd)			[There are many other examples of Latin legal phrases using this root; see *Black's Law Dictionary*.] DOUBLETS: capital:chapter; captain:chieftain; cattle:chattel; chief:chef precipitate:precipice GERMAN: *Das Kapital* (the major work of Karl Marx, in which he described free enterprise as he saw it) BIBLICAL WORD: scapegoat [coined by William Tyndale (English translator of the Bible) to designate the goat on which the high priest of the ancient Jews confessed the sins of the people on the Day of Atonement, after which it was allowed to *escape* into the wilderness bearing those sins (see Leviticus 16:7-26)] CROSS REFERENCE: *cephal*
car*	Latin *carrum*: vehicle (from *currere*, to run) (IE: *kers*, to run)	cart, wagon	ROOT NOTE: This root is derived from Celtic *carrus*, and is related to Latin *currere*, to run, and to Middle High German *hurren*, to hurry. SIMPLE ROOT: car, career (originally, a racing course), cargo (from Spanish *cargar*, load, impose taxes) caricature (**Synonyms:** burlesque, parody, travesty) cariole, caroche carpenter (originally, one who worked on wooden carriages) carriage (**Synonyms:** bearing, demeanor, mien) carry (**Synonyms:** bear, convey, transmit) DISGUISED ROOT: charge (**Synonyms: 1)** accuse, indict, arraign; **2)** command, order, direct), charger chariot FRENCH: *chargé d'affaires* (literally, entrusted with business; a diplomatic official who temporarily takes the place of a minister or ambassador) NO CROSS REFERENCE
carcin*	Greek *karkinos*	cancer, crab	ROOT NOTE: The Indo-European relationship between *cancer* and *crab* is quite tortuous; see *Webster's New World Dictionary*. LEADING ROOT COMPOUND: *carcin*: oma: (tumor, growth) carcinoma carcinomatosis (a condition in which epithelial cancer has spread extensively throughout the body) (*osis*, diseased condition) *carcino*: gen: carcinogen {carcinogenic} (*gen*, producing) sect: carcinosectomy (inserted *s*; *ectom*, to remove surgically) DISGUISED ROOT: cancer (see *Triplets* below) canker (an ulcerlike sore, especially in the mouth) (see *Triplets* below); crab (see *Triplets* below) DISGUISED LEADING ROOT COMPOUND: oid: cancroid (like a crab; like cancer) (*oid*, similar to) TRIPLETS: cancer:canker:crab NO CROSS REFERENCE
card			See *cart, chart* for *card*.

103

Element	From	Meaning	Examples
card**	Greek *kardia* (IE: *kerd*, heart; also yields English *heart* and Latin *cord*; see *Note*)	heart	SIMPLE ROOT: cardia, cardiac (of, near, or affecting the heart; relating to the part of the stomach connected with the esophagus; see *cardialgia*, below) PREFIXED ROOT AND COMPOUNDS: *endo-*: (within) endocardium endocarditis (*itis*, inflammation) *epi-*: epicardium (the innermost layer of the pericardium) (*epi-*, around) *peri-*: (around) pericardiac (or, *pericardial*) (concerning the pericardium) pericardium pericarditis (*itis*, inflammation) LEADING ROOT COMPOUND: *card*: itis: carditis (*itis*, inflammation of) *cardi*: alg: cardialgia (a feeling of pain or discomfort in the region of the heart; same as *heartburn*, so named because mistakenly thought to be located in the heart) (*algos*, pain) oid: cardioid (in *mathematics*, a curve more or less in the shape of a heart, traced by a point on the circumference of a circle that rolls around the circumference of another equal circle) (*oid*, similar to) *cardio*: gram: cardiogram {cardiograph, cardiography} (*gram* from *graph*, write) log: cardiology {cardiologist} (*logy*, study of) myo: cardiomyopathy (*myo*, muscle; *path*, disease) pulmon: cardiopulmonary (*pulmo*, lung) tach: cardiotachometer (*tacho*, speed + *meter*, measure) vas: cardiovascular (*vas*, vessel, specifically, blood vessel) TRAILING ROOT COMPOUND: electro: electrocardiogram (EKG, where the *K* represents the Greek spelling of *cardia*: *kardia*) myo: myocardiograph, myocarditis, myocardium (*myo*, muscle; *graph*, write; *itis*, inflammation) NOTE: The Greek root refers to the *physical heart*, whereas Latin *cord* is most often used figuratively. CROSS REFERENCE: *cord*
carn***	Latin *carnis* (IE: *(s)ker*, to cut; also yields Greek *krinein*, to separate; Greek *karpos*, fruit; *English* harvest)	flesh, meat	SIMPLE ROOT: carna: carnage (**Synonyms:** slaughter, massacre, pogram) carnal (**Synonyms:** fleshly, sensual; see *Doublets* below) carnassial (designating or of the teeth of a flesh-eating animal specialized for slicing or shearing rather than tearing) carnation (a flower, originally the color of flesh) carne: carnelian (a red variety of chalcedony, used in jewelry) carni: carnival (the period of feasting and revelry just before lent; see authors' *An Introduction to an Academic Vocabulary*, p. 33) carno: carnose (like or relating to flesh; fleshy; of a fleshy consistence: used of succulent parts of plants)

Element	From	Meaning	Examples
carn (cont'd)			PREFIXED ROOT: *dis-*: discarnate (having no physical body) (*dis-*, not) *in-*: incarnadine, incarnate, Incarnate, incarnation (*in-*, in) LEADING ROOT COMPOUND: fy: carnify (to form into flesh or fleshlike tissue) (from *facere*, to make) vor: (*vorare*, to devour, eat) carnivore (any of an order of fanged, flesh-eating mammals, including the dog, wolf, cat, seal, etc.: opposed to *herbivore*; a plant that ingests small animals, especially insects) carnivorous (flesh-eating; insect-eating, as certain plants; of the carnivores) DOUBLE PREFIXED ROOT: reincarnation (rebirth of the soul in another body, as in Hindu religious belief; a new incarnation or embodiment; the doctrine that the soul reappears after death in another and different bodily form) (*re-*, again; *in-*, in) DISGUISED ROOT: carrion (the decaying flesh of a dead body, especially when regarded as food for scavenging animals; anything very disgusting or repulsive; as an *adjective*, of or like carrion; feeding on carrion) caruncle (an outgrowth of flesh, as the comb and wattles of a fowl; a swelling at or near the hilum of a seed) charnel (originally, a cemetery; a building or place where corpses or bones are deposited: in full, *charnel house*) crone (an ugly, withered old woman; hag) SPANISH: *carne de vaca* (literally, meat of the cow; beefsteak) *chili con carne* (*chili* from Nahuatl *chilli*, the dried pod of red pepper; therefore, literally, red pepper with meat; a spiced or highly seasoned dish with beef ground or in small pieces, chilies or chili powder, beans, and often tomatoes) DOUBLETS: carnal:charnel CROSS REFERENCE: *creat/cre, sarc*
carp,* cerp	Latin *carpere*: to pluck, to card (IE: *(s)ker*, to cut)	to pluck, seize	SIMPLE ROOT: carpet (originally, thick woolen cloth that had been plucked or carded) PREFIXED ROOT: *ex-*: excerpt (literally, that which has been plucked out), excerption (*ex-*, out) LEADING ROOT COMPOUND: logy: carphology (the involuntary picking at the bedclothes, seen in grave fevers and in conditions of great exhaustion) DISGUISED ROOT: scarce (originally from *excerpere*, to pick out, select; same base as *excerpt*) LATIN PHRASE: *carpe diem* (seize the day) CROSS REFERENCE: *cap, hab*
carp**	Greek *karpos* (IE: *(s)ker*, to cut, to pluck)	fruit	ROOT NOTE: This root is derived originally from the same base as the *carp* that means pluck, that is, fruit can be plucked. SIMPLE ROOT: carpel (diminutive of *karpos*; literally, little fruit; a simple pistil, regarded as a modified leaf) PREFIXED ROOT: *a-*: (without) acarpelous (also, *acarpellous*; without carpels)

105

Element	From	Meaning	Examples
carp (cont'd)			acarpous (in *botany*, bearing no fruit; sterile; barren)
			apo-: apocarp (in *botany*, a gynoecium having separate carpels)
			apocarpous (in *botany*, having separate or partially joined carpels, as the strawberry) (*apo-*, apart, away)
			endo-: endocarp (the inner layer of a ripened ovary or fruit, as the pit of a peach) (*endo-*, within, inner)
			epi-: epicarp (same as *exocarp*: the outer layer of a ripened ovary or fruit, as the skin of a plum) (*epi-*, upon)
			meso-: mesocarp (the middle layer of the wall of a ripened ovary or fruit, as the flesh of a plum) (*meso-*, middle)
			exo-: exocarp (the outer layer of a ripened ovary or fruit, as the skin of a plum) (*exo-*, outside)
			pro-: procarp (in *botany*, a female reproductive organ in certain algae) (*pro-*, before, forward)
			syn-: syncarpous (in *botany*, composed of carpels growing together) (*syn-*, with, together)
			LEADING ROOT COMPOUND:
			gon: carpogonium (the female reproductive organ in red algae) (*gon*, reproduction)
			logy: carpology (the study of the structure of fruits and seeds) (*logy*, study of)
			phag: carpophagous (fruit-eating) (*phagein*, to eat)
			phor: carpophore (from *pherein*, to bear)
			spor: carpospore (*spore*, seed)
			TRAILING ROOT COMPOUND:
			acro: acrocarpous (bearing fruit at the end of the stalk, as some mosses) (*acro*, top, extremity)
			mono: monocarp, monocarpic (also *monocarpous*; bearing fruit only once, and then dying: said of annuals, biennials, and some long-lived plants, as the bamboos and century plants) (*mono*, one)
			partheno: parthenocarpy (the development of a ripe fruit without fertilization of the ovules, as in the banana and pineapple) (*partheno*, virgin)
			poly: polycarpic (also, *polycarpous*; in *botany*, capable of flowering and fruiting an indefinite number of times, as a perennial plant; having two or more separate carpels) (*poly*, many)
			schizo: schizocarp (in *botany*, a dry fruit, as of the maple, that splits at maturity into two or more one-seeded carpels which remain closed) (*schizo*, split)
			CROSS REFERENCE: *frug/fruct, pom*
carpho			See *carp*, pluck.
cart,** chart	Greek *chartes*: leaf of paper; originally, layer of papyrus	map, chart	SIMPLE ROOT: *cart*: cartoon, cartulary (a register of charters, deeds, etc.) *chart*: chart (**Synonyms:** plan, outline, diagram) charter (**Synonyms:** hire, lease, rent) chartulary (same as *cartulary*, above) PREFIXED ROOT: dis-: discard (originally, to remove a card from the hand that has been dealt; original meaning still intact in certain card games) (*dis-*, apart, away)

Element	From	Meaning	Examples
cart (cont'd)			LEADING ROOT COMPOUND: *carto*: gram: cartogram (a map giving statistical data by means of lines, dots, shaded areas, etc.) (from *graph*, write) graph: cartograph, cartographer, cartography (*graph*, write) mancy: cartomancy (fortune-telling by means of playing cards) (*mancy*, divination) *charto*: logy: chartology (same as *cartography*) (*logy*, study of) meter: chartometer (an instrument for measuring distances on a map) (*meter*, measure) DOUBLETS: card:chart HISTORICAL DOCUMENT: *Magna Charta* (*Magna Carta*) NO CROSS REFERENCE
cas			See *cad* for *cascade*.
cast**	Latin *castus* (IE: *kes*, to cut)	clean, pure	SIMPLE ROOT: caste (originally, cut off, separated; therefore, castrated) castigate (see synonyms at *chastise*, below) castrate (to remove the testes of; emasculate) DISGUISED ROOT: chaste (not indulging in unlawful sexual activity; virtuous: said especially of women; sexually abstinent; celibate; **Synonyms**: virtuous, pure, modest) chasten (to punish in order to correct or make better; chastise; restrain from excess; subdue; make purer in style; refine) (*castus* + *agere*, to lead, drive) chastise (to punish, especially by beating; to scold or condemn sharply; **Synonyms**: punish, discipline, reprove) chastity (the quality or state of being chaste; celibacy; virginity) PREFIXED DISGUISED ROOT: *in*-: incest (literally, not clean) {incestuous} (*in*-, not) ITALIAN MUSIC TERM: castrato (formerly, especially in the 18th century, a singer castrated as a boy to preserve the soprano or contralto range of his voice) CROSS REFERENCE: *cathar, pur*
cata-***	Greek *kata*: down	down, downward, away, completely, throughout, against, backward	PREFIX NOTE: This element can also be used as an intensifier, as in *catechetical*, *catechumen*. PREFIXED ROOTS AND COMPOUNDS: *cat*-: egor: category (originally, to accuse in the assembly; a classificatory divison in a system; class; group) (*agora*, assembly) hedra: (chair) cathedra (throne of a bishop in a cathedral; the episcopal see) cathedral (originally, the chair of the bishop, or where the bishop "sits down"; thus, the largest church in the diocese) eps: cathepsin (any of several intracellular enzymes that act as catalysts in the breakdown of protein) (from *hepsein*, to boil) heter: catheter (that which is sent down; a slender tube inserted into a body passage for passing fluids) (from *heinai*, to send) hod: cathode (*hodos*, way) hol: catholic (literally, completely whole; of general scope or value; all-inclusive; universal, as catholic values), catholicity (*holos*, whole)

Element	From	Meaning	Examples
cata- (cont'd)			*cata-*:

bio: catabiosis (*bio*, life + *osis*, process or condition of)

bol: catabolism {catabolic}, catabolite (a waste product of catabolism), catabolize (from *ballein*, to throw)

caust: catacaustic (designating or of a caustic curve or surface formed by reflection; opposed to *diacaustic*) (from *kaiein*, to burn; *caustic* designates a particular curved radial surface; see *Webster's New World Dictionary*)

chres: catachresis (the incorrect use of a word, as by misapplication of terminology or by strained or mixed metaphor), catachrestic (*chresthai*, to use)

chron: catachronobiology (*chrono*, time + *bio*, life + *logy*, study of)

clast: cataclastic (of or pertaining to the deformation or fragmentation of metamorphic rock by extreme pressure) (*clast*, break)

clin: cataclinal (*clin*, lean)

clysm: cataclysm {cataclysmal, cataclysmic} (from *klyzein*, to wash)

comb: catacomb (probably from *cata tumbas*, near the tombs)

drom: catadromous (going back to or toward the sea to spawn; said of certain fresh-water fishes, such as the salmon) (*drom*, run)

falqu: catafalque (scaffold; a raised platform on which a body lies in state during an elaborate funeral) (Italian; from Latin *fala*, siege tower)

las: catalase (from *catalysis*)

lect: catalectic (in *prosody*, lacking a syllable in the last foot) (from *legein*, to leave off, cease)

leps: catalepsy (a condition in which consciousness and feeling are suddenly and temporarily lost, and the muscles become rigid: it may occur in epilepsy, schizophrenia, etc.) (from *lambanein*, to take, seize)

log: catalog (also, *catalogue*; **Synonyms**: list, inventory, register) (*logos*, word)

lys: catalysis, catalyst (*lyein*, to loosen)

lyt: catalytic (from *catalysis*)

lyz: catalyze, catalyzer (see *catalysis*)

men: catamenia (according to the month; menstruation) (*men*, month)

phor: cataphoresis (in *chemistry*, electrophoresis: the motion of charged particles, especially colloidal particles, through a relatively stationary liquid under the influence of an applied electric field provided, in general, by immersed electrodes) (*phoresis*, transmission; from *pherein*, to bear)

phyl: cataphyll (in *biology*, any rudimentary leaf, as a bud scale, preceding the true foliage) (*phyll*, leaf)

plas: cataplasia (in *biology*, a change in cells or tissues, characterized by reversion to an earlier stage), cataplasm (*plasm*, form, shape)

pult: catapult (an ancient military contrivance for throwing or shooting stones, spears, etc.) (from *pallein*, to toss, hurl)

Element	From	Meaning	Examples
cata- (cont'd)			ract: cataract (a large waterfall; any strong flood or rush of water; deluge) (from *rhegnynai*, to break)
			rrh: catarrh (inflammation of a mucous membrane, especially of the nose or throat, causing an increased flow of mucus: this term no longer in general use) (*rhein*, to flow)
			rrhin: catarrhine (long-nosed; having a slender nose with the nostrils spaced close together; as opposed to *platyrrhine*, flat-nosed) (*rhine*, nose)
			stas: catastasis (the heightened part of the action in ancient drama, leading directly to the catastrophe) (*stas*, stand)
			stroph: catastrophe (literally, to turn downward; in *Greek drama*, the culminating event of a drama, especially of a tragedy, by which the plot is resolved; denouement), catastrophic, catastrophism (*stroph*, turn)
			ton: catatonia (in *psychiatry*, a syndrome, especially of schizophrenia, marked by stupor or catalepsy, often alternating with phases of excitement) {catatonic} (*ton*, stretch)
			kata:
			bas: katabasis (same as *catabasis*)
			DOUBLE PREFIXED ROOT:
			acatalectic (incessant: in *prosody*, having the full number of syllables or metrical feet) (*a-*, not + *lect*, to stop)
			anticatalyst (*anti-*, against + *lys*, to loosen)
			anticathode (*anti-*, against + *hodos*, way)
			hypercatabolic (*hyper-* over, beyond + *bol*, to throw)
			PREFIXED DISGUISED ROOT:
			cada-: cadastre (or, *cadaster*: originally, register, list; literally, line by line; public record of the extent, value, and ownership of land within a district for purposes of taxation) (from *cata-* + *stichos*, line)
			FRENCH EXPRESSION: *catalogue raisonné* (reasoned catalog; a systematic annotated catalog, especially, a critical bibliography)
			NB: The following words are not in this family:
			catalpa (American Indian: Creek, for "head with wings," in reference to the flower of the tree)
			catamaran (Tamil, literally, to tie two logs together)
			catamite, catamount, catamountain
			CROSS REFERENCE: *ab-, apo-, de-, dis-, e-lec-lex-, se-*
caten*	Latin *catena* (IE: *kat*, to twist, twine)	chain	SIMPLE ROOT:
			catena, catenane, catenary, catenate
			catenating (forming part of a chain or complex of symptoms), catenulate
			PREFIXED ROOT:
			con-: concatenate (in *composition*, to link together, as in a chain; to connect sentences within a paragraph, and paragraphs within a composition; term has also been adopted in computer programming) (*con-*, with, together)
			ENGLISH COGNATE: chain
			INTERDISCIPLINARY: chain (in *bacteriology*, four or more cells joined end to end; in *chemistry*, a linkage of atoms in a molecule)
			NO CROSS REFERENCE

Element	From	Meaning	Examples
cathar*	Greek *katharos*	pure	SIMPLE ROOT: catharsis (purgation, especially of the bowels; term is also used in psychiatry) cathartic (**Synonyms:** physic, laxative, purgative), cathartical RELIGIOUS GROUP: Cathari (members of medieval religious sects protesting corruption in life or doctrine) CROSS REFERENCE: *cast, pur*
cau			See *cav* for *caution.*
caud*	Latin *cauda*	tail	SIMPLE ROOT: caudad (*ad-* is normally a prefix, meaning to, toward; thus, toward the tail or posterior part of the body) caudal (in *anatomy*, of, at, or near the tail or hind parts; posterior; in *zoology*, taillike), caudalis caudalward, caudate PREFIXED ROOT: *caud*: a-: acaudal (also, *acaudate*; having no tail) (*a-*, without) DISGUISED ROOT: coward (literally, with tail between the legs, as one lacking courage) coda (Italian, tail; a passage in music formally ending a composition or section; also a concluding portion of a literary or dramatic work; the finale of a classical ballet; a part added to a sonnet) cue (a variation of *queue*; not the *cue* indicating a bit of dialogue for an actor's entrance or speech; a long, tapering, tipped rod used in billiards, pool, etc. to strike the cue ball) queue (a plait of hair worn hanging from the back of the head; pigtail; a line or file of persons, vehicles, etc. waiting as to be served; a stored arrangement of computer data or programs, waiting to be processed; as a *verb*, to form in a line or file waiting to be served; often used with *up*, as *queue up*) NB: *Caudle* (see *cal*) and *caudillo* (see *capit*) are not in this family. CROSS REFERENCE: *cerc, uro*
caul*	Latin *caulis*: a stem (IE: *kaul*, *kul*, hollow, hollow stalk; yields English *hole*)	stalk, stem	SIMPLE ROOT: caulescent (in *botany*, having an obvious stem above the ground), caulicle (in *botany*, a small or rudimentary stem, as in an embryo) caulicole (also, *caulicolo*; plural, *caulicoles, caulicoli*; one of the eight stalks rising out of the leafage in a Corinthian capital and ending in leaves that support the volutes; do not confuse with *caulicolous*, under *Leading Root Compound*) (diminutive of *caul*; thus, little stalk) cauline (in *botany*, belonging to or growing on a stem; opposed to *radical*, growing on a root) caulis (in *botany*, the main stem or stalk of a plant) caulome (in *botany*, a stem structure or stem axis of a plant) PREFIXED ROOT: a-: acaulescent (in *botany*, having no stem or only a very short stem) (*a-*, without) LEADING ROOT COMPOUND: *cauli*: col: caulicolous (growing on the stems of other plants: said of certain fungi) (*colere*, to inhabit)

110

Element	From	Meaning	Examples
caul (cont'd)			*caulo:* carp: caulocarpic (having stems that bear flowers and fruit year after year) (*carp*, fruit) TRAILING ROOT COMPOUND: nudi: nudicaul (also, *nudicaulous*; in *botany*, having no leaves on the stem) (*nudi*, nude, naked) ELIDED PREFIXED TRAILING ROOT COMPOUND: am-: amplexicaul (in *botany*, having a base that clasps or encircles the stem, as some leaves do) (from *ambi-*, around + *plexi*, from *plectare*, to plait) DISGUISED ROOT: cauliflower (possibly; Partridge says *cauliflower* is derived from *cabbage*, thus cabbage flower) caudex (in *botany*, the thickened base of the stem of some perennial plants; also, a woody, trunklike stem, such as that of the tree fern; plural, *caudices, caudexes*) cole (any of a genus of plants of the crucifer family; especially, rape) coleslaw (Dutch *kool*, cabbage; akin to *cole* + *slaw* for *salade*, salad) colcannon (an Irish dish made of potatoes and greens, especially cabbage, boiled together and mashed; Irish *cal ceannan*; from *cal*, cabbage + *ceannan*, white-headed; from *ceann*, white) GERMAN: kohlrabi (from Italian *cavolo rapa*, cole rape) NB: The word *caul* itself is not in this family; neither is *caulk* or *cauldron*. NO CROSS REFERENCE
caum			See *caust, caut*.
caus,** cus	Latin *causa* (IE: *kad,* to fall)	cause, reason; judicial process; lawsuit, case	SIMPLE ROOT: causa: causable, causal, causality, causation, causative (functioning as a cause; effective; in *grammar*, designating a verb or verbal affix that expresses causation: in the phrase to fell a tree, *fell* is a causative verb) caus: cause (**Synonyms:** reason, antecedent) causerie (French; a chat; a short, informal, conversational piece of writing) PREFIXED ROOT: ac-: (assimilates *ad-*, to, toward) accusation, accusative (in *grammar*, of or pertaining to the case of a noun, pronoun, adjective, or participle; that is, the direct object of a verb or the object of certain prepositions; in *English* grammar, simply the objective case) {accusatory} accuse (**Synonyms:** charge, indict, arraign) [(the) accused: the person or persons formally charged with commission of a crime] ex-: excusable (that can be excused; pardonable; justifiable), excusatory, excuse (*ex-*, from) re-: (against) recusant (a dissenter or nonconformist) {recusancy} recuse (to disqualify or withdraw from a position of judging, as because of prejudice or personal interest)

111

Element	From	Meaning	Examples
caus (cont'd)			DOUBLE PREFIXED ROOT: inexcusable (in-, not) FRENCH LAW TERM: cause célèbre (celebrated cause; a celebrated law case, trial, or controversy) NB: Causeway is not in this family; see both calc, calx. CROSS REFERENCE: rati
caust,** caut	Greek kaiein	to burn (fever, heat)	SIMPLE ROOT: caust: caustic (Synonyms: sarcastic, satirical, sardonic) caut: cauterization, cauterize, cautery, cauterant PREFIXED ROOT: cata-: catacaustic (see note under cata-) (cata-, down) dia-: diacaustic (designating or of a caustic curve or surface formed by refraction; compare with catacaustic) (dia-, across, through) en-: encaustic (literally, burned in; painted with wax colors fixed with heat, or with any process in which colors are burned in; see ink, under Disguised Root) (en-, in) hypo-: hypocaust (a space below the floor in some ancient Roman buildings, into which hot air was piped to warm the rooms) (hypo-, under) LEADING ROOT COMPOUND: alg: causalgia (neuralgia characterized by a burning sensation) (alg, pain) TRAILING ROOT COMPOUND: holo: holocaust (burnt whole; an offering the whole of which is burned; great or total destruction of life, especially by fire; the Holocaust: the systematic destruction of over six million European Jews by the Nazis before and during World War II) (holo, whole) DISGUISED ROOT: calm (originally, a burning heat; the middle of the day, when beasts are at rest, winds fallen, the fields quiet; compare meaning of calm with siesta, short for siesta hora, the sixth hour from sunrise to noon, the hottest part of the day) ink (from encaustos, burned in; inkling, from Middle English inclen, to hint at, is not related to ink) CROSS REFERENCE: calor, therm
cav*	Latin cavus (IE: keu, a swelling, arch, cavity)	hollow, cavity	SIMPLE ROOT: cave: cave, cavern, cavernous cavi: cavity (Synonyms: hole, hollow, excavation), cavitation cavu: cavus (unusually high foot arch, as though hollow) PREFIXED ROOT: con-: concave, concavity, concavo-concave (concave on both sides, as some lenses) (con-, with, together) ex-: excavate, excavation (see synonyms at cavity, above), excavator (ex-, out) LEADING ROOT COMPOUND: corn: cavicorn (having hollow horns, as oxen, sheep, etc.) (corn, horn) ITALIAN: cavetto (in architecture, a concave molding with a curve of 90°) cavo-relievo (from cavo-rilievo, hollow relief) CROSS REFERENCE: coel/cel

Element	From	Meaning	Examples
cav,* cau	Latin *cavere*: to be on one's guard (IE: *keu*, to notice, observe; yields English *hear*)	to take heed	SIMPLE ROOT: *cau*: caution (**Synonyms**: advise, counsel, admonish), cautionary cautious (**Synonyms**: careful, meticulous, scrupulous) *cav*: caveat (let him beware, third person singular of *cavere*, take heed) PREFIXED ROOT: *pre-*: precaution, precautionary (*pre-*, before) LATIN PHRASES: *caveat emptor* (let the buyer beware) *cave canem* (beware of the dog) NB: *Caviar* is not in this family; the word is derived from Persian *khaviyar*, egg-bearing; originally, spawning fish, hence *roe*: the salted eggs of sturgeon, salmon, etc., eaten as an appetizer. CROSS REFERENCE: *para* (one meaning), *phylact*
caval*	Latin *cavallo*	horse	SIMPLE ROOT: cavalcade (originally, a procession of horsemen or carriages; any procession; a sequence or series, as of events) cavalier (originally, an armed horseman; knight; a gallant or courteous gentleman, especially as one serving as a lady's escort; as an *adjective*, free and easy; gay; also, casual or in- different toward matters of some importance; haughty; arro- gant; supercilious; see *Doublets* below) cavalry (combat troops originally mounted on horses; see *Dou- blets* below) FRENCH: chevalier (a member of the lowest rank of the French Legion of Honor; a chivalrous man; as an *adjective*, gallant, cavalier; see *Doublets* below) chivalric, chivalrous (**Synonyms**: polite, courteous, gallant), chivalry (see *Doublets* below) DOUBLETS: cavalry:chivalry chevalier:cavalier ITALIAN: *cabaletta* (literally, small horse; the bravura section of an aria or duet; reason for term uncertain) SPANISH: *caballero* (a Spanish gentleman, cavalier, or knight; in the Southwest, a horseman; a lady's escort) FRENCH TERMS: *à cheval* (literally, on horseback; astraddle; hence, straddling an issue) *cheval-de-frise* [literally, horse of Frisia (Friesland): first used by Frisians, who lacked cavalry, against Spaniards; a piece of wood with projecting spikes, formerly used to hinder en- emy horsemen; now, a row of spikes of jagged glass set into masonry on top of a wall to prevent escape or trespassing] CROSS REFERENCE: *equus, hipp*
ceit			See *cap* for *deceit*.
ceive			See *cap* for *receive*.
cel			See *coel* for *celiac*.

Knowledge of Greek and Latin roots should make the content
of science more meaningful to the student.
Dean John Pomfret

Element	From	Meaning	Examples
cel*	Latin *celare* (IE: *kel*, to conceal; yields English *hall, hell, hull*)	to hide	SIMPLE ROOT: cell cella: cella (the inner part of an ancient Greek or Roman temple, housing the statue of a god or goddess), cellar, cellarer, cellaret cellu: cellular (pertaining to or resembling a cell; consisting of or containing a cell or cells; in *telecommunications, cellular phone system* refers to the area that the system services being divided into areas or cells), cellule (a small cell) LEADING ROOT COMPOUND: itis: cellulitis (inflammation of subcutaneous tissue) (*itis*, inflammation of) oid: Celluloid (a trademark) (*oid*, similar to, resembling) ose: cellulose (*ose*, condition of) DISGUISED ROOT: clandestine (*clam*, secret + *celare*, to hide) PREFIXED DISGUISED ROOT: *con-*: conceal (**Synonyms:** hide, secrete, cache) (*con-*, with, together) ENGLISH COGNATE: color (**Synonyms:** shade, hue, tint) NORSE MYTHOLOGY: Hel, goddess of death and the underworld TERM IN CHRISTIANITY: Hell (from Hel, the underworld goddess) INTERDISCIPLINARY: cell (in *biology*, a very small, complex unit of protoplasm, usually with a nucleus, cytoplasm, and an enclosing membrane: all plants and animals are made up of one or more cells that usually combine to form various tissues; in *electricity*, a receptacle containing electrodes and an electrolyte, used either for generating electricity by chemical reactions or for decomposing compounds by electrolysis; any compartment of a storage battery) CROSS REFERENCE: *calyp, cond, cover, crypt, tech/teg*
cel*	Latin *caelum*: heaven (IE: *kel*[4], to hide, conceal, cover)	sky, heavens	SIMPLE ROOT: celesta (also, *celeste*; see *Organ Stop* below) celestial, celestine (from its blue color) celestite (chemical symbol: $SrSO_4$) DISGUISED ROOT: ceiling ORGAN STOP: celeste (also, a musical instrument having a keyboard and metal plates struck by hammers that produce bell-like tones) SOBRIQUET OF THE CHINESE EMPIRE: Celestial Empire (Latin translation of Chinese *t'ien ch'ao*, heavenly empire, from the belief that the emperors were sons of Heaven) NO CROSS REFERENCE
celeb*	Latin *celebrare*: to honor (IE: *kel*[5], to drive, incite to action)	famous	ROOT NOTE: From *celebritas*, multitude, fame, this root evolved into *celeber*, frequented, populous. SIMPLE ROOT: celebrant, celebrate (**Synonyms:** commemorate, solemnize), celebrated, celebration, celebrity PREFIXED ROOT: *con-*: concelebrate [to celebrate (the Eucharistic liturgy) jointly, the prayers being said in unison by two or more of the officiating priests] (*con-*, with, together) NO CROSS REFERENCE

114

Element	From	Meaning	Examples
celer*	Latin *celer* (IE: *kel⁵*, to drive, incite to action)	swift, fast, prompt	SIMPLE ROOT: celerity (swiftness in acting or moving; speed) PREFIXED ROOT AND COMPOUNDS: *ac-*: (assimilates *ad-*, to, toward) accelerant, accelerate {acceleration, accelerative, accelerator} accelerometer (a device for measuring acceleration, as of an aircraft, or for detecting vibrations, as in machinery) (*meter*, measure) *de-*: decelerate {deceleration, decelerator} (*de-*, reversal) MUSIC TERM: *accelerando* (with gradual quickening tempo) (*ac-* assimilates *ad-*, to, toward) CROSS REFERENCE: *tach, veloc*
cen,* coen	Greek *koinos* (IE: *com-*, with, beside)	common, shared	ROOT NOTE: The Greek spelling of this root is *koinos*, seen in the *Simple Root* below. SIMPLE ROOT: Koine (the *common* language of the Greek world), Koinea (a concept of the early Christian Church, in which the members of a congregation *shared* equally with one another) PREFIXED ROOT: *epi-*: epicene (see note under *epi-*) (*epi-*, upon) LEADING ROOT COMPOUND: *ceno*: bi: cenobite (a member of a religious order living in a monastery or convent: distinguished from *anchorite*: a person who lives alone and apart from society for religious meditation; hermit; recluse) (from *bios*, life) by: cenoby (a conventional establishment or religious community) (from *bios*, life) gon: cenogonous (oviparous at one season of the year and ovoviviparous at another: said of certain aphids) (*gon*, sexual reproduction) spec: cenospecies (separate species of organisms that are related through their capability of interbreeding, as dogs and wolves) typ: cenotype [term used in *ontogeny* (the history of the development of an individual) and in *cytology* (science of cell development)] *coen*: esthes: coenesthesia (also, *coenesthesis*; in *psychology*, the mass of undifferentiated sensations that make one aware of the body and its condition, as in the feeling of health, illness, discomfort, etc.) (*esthes*, feeling) urus: coenurus (literally, common tail; a particular tapeworm larva that attacks the brains of sheep, causing any of various diseases, as the staggers) (*ur*, tail) *coeno*: cyt: coenocyte (same as *syncytium*: in *zoology*, a mass of protoplasm containing scattered nuclei that are not separated into distinct cells, as in striated muscle fibers) (*cyt*, cell) sarc: coenosarc (the fleshy portion of the stalks and stolons of hydroids, which secretes the perisarc) (*sarkos*, flesh) NOTE: Do not confuse this root with *coenzyme*, where *co-* is an elided form of *com-*, with, together. CROSS REFERENCE: *com-, sym-*

Element	From	Meaning	Examples
cend			See *cand* for *incendiary*.
ceno,* keno	Greek *kenos*	empty	LEADING ROOT COMPOUND: *ceno*: phob: cenophobia (same as *kenophobia*: morbid fear of large open spaces; same as *agoraphobia*; *cenophobia* also means *cenotophobia*, from a completely different root; see next family) (*phobia*, fear of) taph: cenotaph (a tomb or a monument erected in honor of a person whose body is elsewhere; thus an empty tomb) (*taph*, tomb) *cenoto*: phob: cenotophobia [can mean either fear of large open places, or fear of novelty (*neophobia*); see next family] *ken*: osis: kenosis (the act of Christ in emptying himself of the form of God, taking the form of a servant, and humbling himself to the extent of suffering death; the act of voluntarily giving up personal rights and ambitions and accepting suffering as a follower of Christ) (*osis*, condition) *keno*: phob: kenophobia (same as *cenophobia*) (*phobia*, fear of) CROSS REFERENCE: *jejun, vac, van*
ceno,* caen, kain, -cene	Greek *kainos*: new (IE: *ken³*, fresh, new, young; to sprout)	new, recent	SIMPLE ROOT: kainite (a naturally occurring mineral, used in fertilizers and as a source of potassium) PREFIXED ROOT: *re-*: recent (in *geology*, of, belonging to, or designating the Holocene epoch; **Synonyms**: new, fresh, modern) (*re-*, again) LEADING ROOT COMPOUND: *ceno*: gen: cenogenesis (compare *palingenesis*) (*gen*, producing) zo: Cenozoic (designating or of the geologic era following the Mesozoic and including the present: it is characterized by the development of many varieties of mammals) (*zo*, animal) *cenoto*: phob: cenotophobia (*neophobia*; *cenotophobia* can also mean fear of large open places) (*phobia*, fear of) TRAILING ROOT COMPOUND: eo: Eocene (the oldest or earliest in time divisions) (*eo*, dawn) DISGUISED ROOT: CROSS REFERENCE: *neo, nov*
cens**	Latin *censere*: to judge (IE: *kens*, to speak solemnly)	tax, assess, judge, enrol	SIMPLE ROOT: censo: censor (not to be confused with *censer*, which see under *cand/cend*), censorial, censorious censu: censurable, censure (**Synonyms**: criticize, reprehend, blame), census PREFIXED ROOT: *re-*: recension (a revising of a text on the basis of a critical examination of sources; not to be confused with *rescind*, the noun form of which is *rescission*) (*re-*, again) CROSS REFERENCE: *arbit, jud*

The more words you know the more clearly and powerfully you will think...and the more ideas you will invite into your mind. Wilfred Funk

116

Element	From	Meaning	Examples
cent***	Latin *centum* (IE: *kmto*, hundred)	hundred; hundredth	SIMPLE ROOT: cent: cent (a monetary unit of the U.S., equal to 1/100 of a dollar) centner [in some European countries, a commercial weight roughly equal to the British *hundredweight*, specifically, 50 kg (110.23 lbs.)] centa: cental, centare (same as *centiare*) cente: centenarian, centenary, centesimal centi: centile (same as *percentile*), centime (the *hundredth* part of a franc, the Haitian gourde, the Algerian dinar, etc.) centu: centum, centurial, centurion, century LEADING ROOT COMPOUND: *cent*: enn: centennial (100 years) (from *annus*, year) *centi*: day: centiday (100th of a day: 14 minutes, 24 seconds; used especially in the study of plant growth) grad: centigrade (*gradus*, step) gram: centigram liter: centiliter meter: centimeter newton: centinewton norm: centinormal ped: centipede pois: centipoise ster: centistere *centu*: ple: centuple (from *plicare*, to fold) plic: centuplicate (from *plicare*, to fold) EMBEDDED ROOT COMPOUND: sex<u>cent</u>enary (*sex*, six) ter<u>cent</u>ennial (*ter*, third) SPANISH: centavo, centésimo, céntimo ITALIAN: centesimo LATIN COMPOUND: percent, percentile ARABIC: kantar (from Arabic *qintar*, which itself is from Latin *centenarius*; a unit of weight in Moslem countries, varying from c. 100 to c. 700 pounds) NB: *Cento*, a hodgepodge of literary or musical compositions, is not related to this root. NOTE: Do not confuse this root with *Centaur* which, in Greek mythology, was a race of monsters with a man's head, trunk, and arms, and a horse's body and legs; thus, *centaury* designates, a plant in which it was said that the centaur Chiron discovered medicinal properties. CROSS REFERENCE: *hecto, hecato*
centr***	Latin from Greek *kentron*: sharp point (IE: *kent*, to prick)	point, center	SIMPLE ROOT: centra: centrad (toward the center), central, centrale, centrality, centration centri: centric, centrical, centricity, centrist, centriole centru: centrum (in *anatomy*, the body of a vertebra) PREFIXED ROOT: a-: acentric (having no center; off center) (*a-*, without)

117

Element	From	Meaning	Examples
centr (cont'd)			*con-*: concentrate {concentration}, concentric (opposed to *eccentric*, next enttry) (*con-*, with, together)

ec-: eccentric [literally, out of center; in *mathematics*, not having the same center, as two circles inside the other; opposed to *concentric*) (*ec-* assimilates *ex-*, out)

LEADING ROOT COMPOUND:

centr:

oid: centroid (same as *center of mass*) (*oid*, similar to)

centri:

cip: centriciput (the part of the head situated between the occiput and the sinciput; therefore, the midhead) (from *caput*, head)

fug: centrifugal (fleeing from the center) centrifuge (*fugere*, to flee)

pet: centripetal (seeking the center) (*petere*, to seek)

centro:

bar: centrobaric (pertaining to the center of gravity) (*baros*, weight)

mer: centromere (*mere*, part)

som: centrosome (*soma*, body)

spher: centrosphere (*sphere*, ball, globe)

TRAILING ROOT COMPOUND:

anthro: anthropocentric (*anthropo*, man)

di: dicentra (a flower having two spurs) (*di*, two)

ego: egocentric (*ego*, self)

ethno: ethnocentric (*ethnos*, nation, people)

geo: geocentric (also, *geocentrical*; measured or viewed as from the center of the earth; having or regarding the earth as a center) (*geo*, earth)

helio: heliocentric (*helios*, sun)

poly: polycentrism (*poly*, many)

theo: theocentric (*theos*, God)

ENGLISH COGNATE: center (**Synonyms:** middle, midst)

PREFIXED ENGLISH ROOT:

con-: concenter (to bring or come to a common center; concentrate or converge) (*con-*, with, together)

epi-: epicenter (the area of the earth's surface directly above the place of origin, or focus, of an earthquake; also, *epicentrum*; plural, *epicentra*; a focal or central point) (*epi-*, upon)

hypo-: hypocenter (the focus point of an earthquake; ground zero) (*hypo-*, under)

meta-: metacenter [the intersection of the verticals through the center of buoyancy of a floating body when in equilibrium and when tilted (the point of the intersection must be above gravity for stability)] (*meta-*, between, with, after)

INTERDISCIPLINARY:

centripetal (in *botany*, developing inward toward the center, as certain flower clusters; in *physiology*, conveying toward a center; afferent)

centrosphere (in *biology*, the portion of the centrosome surrounding the centriole; central mass of an aster; in *geology*, the central part of the earth)

CROSS REFERENCE: *cente, cusp, punct/pung*

Element	From	Meaning	Examples
cep			See *capit* for *biceps, quadriceps, triceps.*
cephal***	Greek *kephal* (IE: *ghebhel*, head, beak)	head	SIMPLE ROOT: cephalad (*ad-* is the prefix, meaning to, toward; a most unusual construction--see *caudad* under *caud*), cephalic, cephalin, cephalization, cephalous PREFIXED ROOTS AND COMPOUNDS: *a-*: acephalous (headless; leaderless; in *zoology*, having no part of the body differentiated as the head) (*a-*, without) *en-*: encephalitis (prefixed with *en-*, *encephalo* is a combining form for "of the brain") (*en-*, on + *itis*, inflammation) LEADING ROOT COMPOUND: chord: cephalochordate (belonging to a subphylum which includes primitive forerunners of the vertebrates such as the lancelet) (*chord*, cord) meter: cephalometer (same as *craniometer*) {cephalometry} (*meter*, measure) pod: cephalopod (any of various mollusks, such as an octopus or nautilus, having a beaked head, an internal shell in some species, and prehensile tentacles) (*pod*, foot) thorax: cephalothorax (the head and thorax united as a single part, in certain crustaceans and arachnids) (*thorax*, chest, breastplate) TRAILING ROOT COMPOUND: acro: acrocephalic {acrocephalous, acrocephaly: same as *oxy-cephaly*, literally, sharp head} (*acro*, top) bi: bicephalous (two-headed) (*bi*, two) brachy: brachycephalic (having a relatively short or broad head) (*brachy*, short) dolicho: dolichocephalic (having a relatively long head) (*dolicho*, long) hydro: hydrocephalous, hydrocephalus {hydrocephalic} (*hydro*, water) micro: microcephaly {microcephalic} (*micro*, small) EMBEDDED ROOT COMPOUND: electroencephalogram (EEG) DISGUISED ROOT: gable NB: *Cepheid*, referring to a particular class of stars, is not related to this root, coming from the name of the constellation Cepheus. In *Greek mythology, Cepheus* is also the name of the husband of Cassiopeia and the father of Andromeda. CROSS REFERENCE: *capit*
cept			See *cap*, hold, seize, for *receptacle, reception.*
cer*	Greek *cera*	wax	SIMPLE ROOT: cera: ceraceous (waxy or waxlike), cerate (a wax plaster; a wax salve), cerated (coated with wax; possessing a *cere*, which see, next entry) cere: cere (a fleshy or waxlike swelling at the base of the upper part of the beak in certain birds, such as parrots and some birds of prey; as a *verb*, to wrap in or as if in cerecloth, as a corpse) cerement (also, *cerements*: cerecloth), cereminous cereus (a candle-shaped cactus) cero: cerotic (designating, or either of two fatty acids, esters of which are found in beeswax and other waxes and oils)

Element	From	Meaning	Examples
cer (cont'd)			ceru: cerumen (ear wax), ceruse, cerussite LEADING ROOT COMPOUND: *cer*: oma: ceroma (waxy mass) (*oma*, mass) *cere*: cloth: cerecloth (a cloth coated with wax, formerly used for wrapping the dead) *cero*: graph: cerograph, cerography (the art of making characters or designs in or with wax) (*graph*, write) mancy: ceromancy (divination from figures formed by melted wax in water) (*mancy*, divination) plast: ceroplastics (the art of modeling in wax; waxworks) (*plast*, mold) TRAILING ROOT COMPOUND: adipo: adipocere (a fatty or waxy substance produced in decaying dead bodies exposed to moisture) (*adipos*, fat) DISGUISED LEADING ROOT COMPOUND: kerogen (solid bituminous material in some shales, which yields petroleum when heated) (*keros* + *gen*, producing) kerosene (*keros* + *-ene*, suffix for an unsaturated compound) FRENCH: *ciré* (waxed; having a waxed finish; from French *cire*, wax) UNBOUND COMPOUND: *cera flava* (yellow unbleached beeswax) (*flava*, yellow) MEDICAL TERM: *cerea flexibilitas* (waxen flexibility, the capacity to maintain the limbs or other bodily parts in whatever position they have been placed (as in *catalepsy*); ceruminous gland, one of the modified sweat glands of the ear that produce earwax) NB: *Cereal* comes from *Ceres*, the Latin goddess of agriculture and grain, identified with Greek Demeter. NO CROSS REFERENCE
cera*	Greek *keras*: horn (IE: *ker*, upper part of the body)	horn, cornea	ROOT NOTE: Since horns are on the head, this root is extended to mean top of head; root also spelled with an initial *k*; see *kerato*. SIMPLE ROOT: cerastes, cereus, cernuous (with head bending down, as a flower bud) LEADING ROOT COMPOUND: *cer*: arg: cerargyrite [silver chloride (chemical symbol: AgCl), a native ore of silver; a horn silver; see *argent* for *Ag* of symbol] *cerat*: od: ceratodus (toothed; a genus of extinct lungfishes) (from *odont*, tooth) oid: ceratoid (hornlike in shape or hardness; horny) (*oid*, similar to) TRAILING ROOT COMPOUND: chel: chelicera (either of the first pair of appendages of spiders and other arachnids, used for grasping and crushing) (*cheli*, claw) clad: cladoceran (an order of crustaceans that includes the water flea) (*klados*, branch, shoot) rhino: rhinoceros (nose-horned animal) (*rhin*, nose)

120

Element	From	Meaning	Examples
cera (cont'd)			EMBEDDED ROOT COMPOUND: triceratops (a dinosaur with two large horns above the eyes, one horn on the nose, and a horny beak) (*tri*, three + *ops*, eye) DISGUISED ROOT: carat (French; from Italian *carato*; from Arabic *qirat*, pod, husk, weight of 4 grains; from Greek *keration*, little horn, carob seed) carrot (from its being shaped like a horn) CROSS REFERENCE: *corn*
cerc*	Greek *kerkos*	tail	SIMPLE ROOT: cerca: cercaria (the free-swimming larva of a parasitic trematode worm, having a forked tail) cercu: cercus (either of a pair of usually jointed, feelerlike appendages at the hind end of the abdomen of many insects) TRAILING ROOT COMPOUND: cyst: cysticercous (*cyst*, bladder, sac) diphy: diphycercal (having a tail fin in which the upper and lower lobes taper symmetrically to a point to which the spinal cord extends) (*di*, two + *phy*, produce) hetero: heterocercal (*hetero*, different) homo: homocercal (*homo*, same) iso: isocercal (*iso*, equal) CROSS REFERENCE: *caud, uro*
cerebr**	Latin *cerebrum* (IE: *ker*, top of head)	brain	SIMPLE ROOT: cerebellum (diminutive of *cerebrum*) cerebral, cerebrate (to use one's brain) LEADING ROOT COMPOUND: ide: cerebroside (any of various compounds found in the brain and other nerve tissue, yielding on decomposition a fatty acid, an unsaturated amino-alcohol, and a sugar) (*ide*, chemical compound suffix) spin: cerebrospinal (of or pertaining to the brain and the spinal cord) vas: cerebrovascular (of or pertaining to the blood vessels of the brain) (*vas*, vessel) CROSS REFERENCE: *cephal, ment, phren, psych, thym*
cern,** cert	Latin *cernere*: to sift (IE: *(s)ker*, to cut)	separate (adjective)	SIMPLE ROOT: certain (**Synonyms**: sure, confident), certainty certitude (**Synonyms**: certainty, conviction) PREFIXED ROOT: *cern*: *con*-: concern (**Synonyms**: solicitude, worry, anxiety) (*con-*, with, together) *dis*-: (apart) discern (**Synonyms**: perceive, distinguish, observe), discernible, discerning (astute, perceptive) discernment (**Synonyms**: reason, intuition, judgment) *se*-: secern (to discriminate, or distinguish) (*se-*, apart) *cert*: *as*-: ascertain (**Synonyms**: learn, determine, discover) (*as-* assimilates *ad-*) *in*-: incertitude (an uncertain state of mind; doubt; an uncertain state of affairs; insecurity) (*in-*, not)

Element	From	Meaning	Examples
cern (cont'd)			*cre*: *ex-*: excrement (waste matter from the bowels; feces) {excremental, or *excrementitious*) (*ex-*, out) *re-*: recrement (now *rare*; the worthless part of anything; dross) (*re-*, back) *cret*: *de-*: decretory (settled by decree; also, *decretive*) (*de-*, from) *dis-*: discrete (see *Doublets*), discretion, discretionary (*dis-*, apart) *se-*: secret (**Synonyms:** covert, clandestine, stealthy), secretary, secretive (*se-*, apart) LEADING ROOT COMPOUND: fic: certificate, certification, certificatory (from *facere*, to make; do) fy: certify {certified} (from *facere*, to make, do) PREFIXED DISGUISED ROOT: *de-*: decree (an official order, edict, or decision, as of a church, government, court, etc.) (*de-*, from) *dis-*: discreet (see *Doublets* below) (*dis-*, apart) DOUBLETS: discreet:discrete LATIN LEGAL TERM: *certiorari* (to be made more certain; a word in the writ; a writ to require a lower court to produce a *certified* record of a particular case tried therein) CROSS REFERENCE: *crin, priv*
cerp			See *carp* for *excerpt*.
cert			See *cern* for *certify*.
chalco*	Greek *chalkos*: copper	copper, brass	SIMPLE ROOT: chalcocite [a copper ore (chemical symbol: Cu_2S; see *cupr* for *Cu*, symbol for *copper*)] LEADING ROOT COMPOUND: graph: chalcography (*graph*, write) pyr: chalcopyrite (an important copper ore; chemical symbol: $CuFeS_2$) (*pyr*, fire) CROSS REFERENCE: *cupr*
chart			See *card/chart*.
chasm**	Greek *chasma* (IE: *ghei*, gape; probably echoic of yawning sound)	opening	ROOT NOTE: This root is related to Latin *hiare*, to gape, yawn, and is seen in *hiatus*. SIMPLE ROOT: chasm {chasmal, chasmic}, chasma (a yawning; an opening), chasmus (same as *chasma*) LEADING ROOT COMPOUND: gam: chasmogamy (in *botany*, the opening of the perianth at maturity for the purpose of fertilization, as in most flowers) (*gam*, marriage) phyt: chasmophyte (in *botany*, a plant that grows in the crevices of rocks) (*phyton*, plant) TRAILING ROOT COMPOUND: mono: monochasium (a cymose or determinate inflorescence having only a *single* main axis) (*mono*, one, single) CROSS REFERENCE: *apert, lumi, osti, stoma*
chief			See *capit*.
cheiro			See *chiro*.

Memorable sentences are memorable on account
of some single, irradiating word.   Alexander Smith

Element	From	Meaning	Examples
chel*	Greek chela (IE: ghei, gape, yawn)	claw	SIMPLE ROOT: chela [plural, chelae; a pincerlike claw of a crab, lobster, scorpion, etc.; there is another chela, from Hindi cela, boy; a follower (as of an occult philosopher or esoteric philosophy)] chelate (resembling or having chelae; as a noun, a chemical compound in which the central atom is attached to neighboring atoms) LEADING ROOT COMPOUND: cera: chelicera (see note under cera) fer: chelifer (bearing chelae) (ferre, to bear) form: cheliform (in the form of a chela, or pincerlike claw) ped: cheliped (one of the pairs of legs that bears the large chelae in decapod crustaceans) (ped, foot) NO CROSS REFERENCE
chem**	Arabic; from Greek chein: to pour	chemistry, pour	ROOT NOTE: The root is derived from Arabic al-kimiya, the art of transmutation (practiced by the Egyptians); from Greek Khemia, Black Land, or Egypt, from Egyptian Kh'mi, from khem, black. SIMPLE ROOT: chemist, chemistry LEADING ROOT COMPOUND: chem: osm: chemosmosis (chemical action between substances that are separated by a semipermeable membrane) (osmos, impulse) urg: chemurgy (see Webster's New World) (from ergon, work) chemo: auto: chemoautotrophic (producing organic matter by the use of energy obtained by oxidation of certain chemicals: said of certain bacteria) (auto, self + troph, nourish) prophyl: chemoprophylaxis (the prevention of disease by the use of chemical drugs) (pro- prefixes phylaxis, guard, protection) re: chemoreceptor (re- prefixes cept, to hold, take) spher: chemosphere (an atmospheric zone 20 to 50 miles above the earth's surface, characterized by extensive photochemical activity) (sphere, ball, globe) steril: chemosterilant (a chemical compound that can produce sterility, used especially in insect control) trop: chemotropism (the tendency of certain plants or organisms to turn or bend under the influence of chemical substances) (trope, turn) CROSS REFERENCE: fus/fund
chiasma*	Greek chi: sign of X; the Greek character X, pronounced kie, or key)	crosswise	SIMPLE ROOT: chiasma chiasmus (rhetorical device, in which the second of two parallel phrases or clauses is inverted, for example, "She went to Honolulu; to Paris went he" or "He went to the theater, but home went she") LEADING ROOT COMPOUND: typ: chiasmatypy (a twisting of homologous chromosomes about each other during one stage of meiosis, resulting in a possible interchange of genes by the chromosomes) (type, image, symbol) STATISTICAL TERM: Chi square

123

Element	From	Meaning	Examples
chiasma (cont'd)			INTERDISCIPLINARY: chiasma (in *anatomy*, a crossing or intersection of two tracts, as of nerves or ligaments; in *genetics*, a point of contact between homologous chromosomes, considered the cytological manifestation of crossing over; in *optics*, the crossing or intersection of the optic nerves on the ventral surface of the brain) NO CROSS REFERENCE
chilias**	Greek *chilias* (IE: *gheslo*, 1,000; yields Latin *kilo*)	1,000	SIMPLE ROOT: chiliad (a group of 1,000; 1,000 years) chiliasm (belief in the coming of the millennium, a period of 1,000 years) LEADING ROOT COMPOUND: arch: chiliarch (in ancient Greece, the military commander of a 1,000 men) (*archos*, leader) CROSS REFERENCE: *kilo, mil*
chil			See *cheil.*
chiro,** cheir	Greek *cheir*	hand	PREFIXED ROOT: *en-*: enchiridion (that which is small enough to be held in the hand; a handbook, manual; a *vade mecum*; see subtitle of authors' *An Introduction to An Academic Vocabulary*) (*en-*, in; with diminutive suffix *idion*) LEADING ROOT COMPOUND: *chir*: agra: chiragra (pain in the hand) (*agra*, seizure) aps: chirapsia (friction with the hands; massage) (*hapsis*, contact, touching) urg: chirurgeon (literally, one who works with his or her hands; the word yields *surgeon, surgery*, which see under *Disguised Roots*) (*urg*, a variant of *erg*, work) *chiro*: graph: chirography (*graph*, write) mancy: chiromancy (divination by reading the hands; thus, *palmistry*) (*mancy*; divination) pod: chiropodist, chiropody (*pod*, foot) pract: chiropractic (or *chiropraxis*: the practice of manipulating the joints, especially of the spine) pter: chiropteron (a bat, the flying mammal) (*pter*, wing) PREFIXED LEADING ROOT COMPOUND: *a-*: acheiropodia (a developmental anomaly characterized by absence of feet as well as hands) (*a-*, negative + *pod*, foot + *ia*, condition of) TRAILING ROOT COMPOUND: macro: macrocheiria (long-handedness) (*macro*, large) tri: tricheiria (a developmental anomaly characterized by tripling of a hand) (*tri*, three) DISGUISED ROOT: surgeon, surgery (from Old French *cirugie*, contraction of *cirugerie*; from Greek *cheirourgia*, a working with the hands (*chiro + ergein*, to work) CROSS REFERENCE: *dactyl, digit, manu/mend*
chlamyd*	Greek *chlamys*: mantle	cloak, mantle (covering, as the envelope, e.g., the perianth, sepal, and petal of a flower)	SIMPLE ROOT: chlamydate (dressed in a chlamys; in *zoology*, having a mantle or pallium, as certain mollusks) chlamydeous (in *botany*, pertaining to or having a floral envelope)

124

Element	From	Meaning	Examples
chlamyd (cont'd)			chlamydia [a widespread, gonorrhealike venereal disease caused by a bacterium (*Chlamydia trachomatis*) that also causes trachoma, etc.] chlamys (in *Greek antiquity*, a short, fine woolen mantle worn by men) PREFIXED ROOT: a-: achlamydeous (literally, without a cover; in *botany*, having neither sepals nor petals; without a perianth) (*a-*, without) meta-: metachlamydeous (*meta-*, beyond, change) LEADING ROOT COMPOUND: saur: chlamydosaurus (a genus of reptiles containing the frilled lizard of Australia) (*saur*, lizard) spor: chlamydospore (an enlarged, thick-walled cell formed between the vegetative cells of a filamentous fungus as a resistant, resting spore) (*spore*, cell) NO CROSS REFERENCE
chlor**	Greek *chloros*: greenish yellow (IE: *ghel*, to gleam, yellow, green, blue)	green (pale)	SIMPLE ROOT: chlora: chloral (even though *colorless*; chemical symbol: CCl_3-CHO; in *pharmaceutics*, $CCl_3CH(OH)_2$) chloramine (also *colorless*; chemical symbol: NH_2Cl) chlore: chlorella (any of a genus of microscopic, unicellular, green algae with spherical cells; several species are rich sources of proteins, carbohydrates, and fats) chlori: chloric, chlorine, chlorite chloro: chlorous LEADING ROOT COMPOUND: *chlor*: osis: chlorosis (an abnormal condition of plants in which the green parts lose their color turn yellow as a result of disease or lack of light) (*osis*, condition of) *chloro*: form: chloroform (chemical symbol: $CHCl_3$) (*formica*, ant) hydr: chlorohydrin (*hydro*, water) phyll: chlorophyll (*phyllon*, leaf) plast: chloroplast (an oval, chlorophyll-bearing body found in the cytoplasm in cells of green plants) (*plast*, form) PREFIXED LEADING ROOT COMPOUND: a-: achlorhydria (a stomach disorder in which the stomach fails to secrete hydrochloric acid) (*a-*, negative, opposite of) PLACENAME: Chloride, Arizona CROSS REFERENCE: *ver/vir*
chol*	Greek *chole* (IE: *ghel*, to gleam, yellow, green, blue)	gall, bile	SIMPLE ROOT: cholera, choleric, cholesteric PREFIXED ROOT: hyper-: hypercholia (*hyper-*, beyond) LEADING ROOT COMPOUND: *chol*: agog: cholagogue (inducing gall or bile) (*agogue*, leading) *chole*: ster: (solid) cholesterol (so called, because the substance was first found in the gall bladder) (*ol*, oil, fat) cholesterosis (*osis*, condition of)

Element	From	Meaning	Examples
chol (cont'd)			TRAILING ROOT COMPOUND: melan: melancholy (originally, black gall, bile; **Synonyms:** sad, sorrowful, despondent) (*melan*, black) NO CROSS REFERENCE
chondr*	Greek *chondros* (IE: *gher*, to rub away, pulverize)	grain, cartilage	SIMPLE ROOT: chondral, chondre chondri: chondric, chondrin, chondrite (a stony meteorite that contains chondrules) chondru: chondrule (a small rounded mass of various minerals, the size of a pea or smaller, contained in some stony meteorites) PREFIXED ROOT: *hypo-*: hypochondria (literally, from under the cartilage of the breastbone; abnormal anxiety over one's health, often with imaginary illnesses and severe melancholy; from the ancient belief that such feelings emanated from under the breastbone), hypochondriac, hypochondriasis (same as *hypochondria*; *hypochondriasis* is the term preferred in medicine) (*hypo-*, under) LEADING ROOT COMPOUND: oma: chondroma (a cartilaginous tumor) (*oma*, mass, tumor) NO CROSS REFERENCE
chor*	Greek *choros*: course, way	dance, chorus	ROOT NOTE: Originally *chorus* in a Greek play designated the dancers; dancers who also sang were later added to the Greek drama. SIMPLE ROOT: chora: choral, chorale chore: chorea (in *medicine*, a nervous disorder in man and dogs, characterized by ceaseless occurrence of a wide variety of rapid, jerky but well-coordinated movements, performed involuntarily; Saint Vitus' dance), choreal, choree, choreic, choreus, choreutic chori: choric, chorister choru: chorus LEADING ROOT COMPOUND: iamb: choriamb (a metrical foot consisting, in Greek and Latin verse, of two short syllables between two long ones, or, as in English verse, of two unaccented syllables between two accented ones) NO CROSS REFERENCE
chor*	Greek *choros*: clear space (IE: *ghe*, to be empty)	place (extended to mean "clear space," and is akin to *cheros*, left, bereaved, separated)	LEADING ROOT COMPOUND: chor: epi: chorepiscopus (a bishop appointed by a diocesan bishop to assist him in the exercise of his episcopal jurisdiction in a rural district) (*epi-*, over, upon + *scope*, to look) choro: graph: chorography (not to be confused with *choreography*) (*graph*, write) logy: chorology (biogeography) (*logy*, study of) CROSS REFERENCE: *loco, topo*

The quality of words, the company they keep,
their strange and sometimes unaccountable fortunes
as they journey through the centuries are rewarding fields for exploration.
J. Donald Adams

Element	From	Meaning	Examples

chord,**
cord
	Greek
	chorde
	(IE; *gher*,
	intestine)
		cord, string	SIMPLE ROOT: cord, chord
			cord: cordage, cording, cordite, cordon
			chord:
			chorda: chorda (plural, *chordae*), chordate [any of a phylum
			    (Chordata) of animals having at some stage of development a
			    notochord, gill slits, and a dorsal tubular nerve cord; the phy-
			    lum includes the vertebrates, tunicates, and lancelets]
			chorde: chordee (downward bowing of the penis as a result of a
			    congenital anomaly or a urethral infection)
			LEADING ROOT COMPOUND:
			cord: corduroy [has been thought by some to mean cord of the
			    king, *roy* being Old French for *king*; however, most authori-
			    ties claim that the word is derived from *cord duroy*, *duroy* be-
			    ing an obsolete term for a coarse woolen fabric; as a *transi-
			    tive verb*, to build (a road) of logs laid together transversely]
			TRAILING ROOT COMPOUND:
			harpsi: harpsichord (a predecessor of the piano, in the form of
			    a harp)
			mono: monochord (a musical instrument with one string) (*mo-
			    no*, one)
			noto: notochord (an elongated, rod-shaped structure composed
			    of cells, forming the primitive supporting axis of the body
			    in the lowest chordates and lying between the digestive tract
			    and the central nervous system) (*noto*, back, dorsum)
			MATHEMATICAL TERM: chord [in *geometry*, a straight
			    line, as though a *string*, joining any two points on an arc,
			    curve, or circumference (other uses of the term in *engineer-
			    ing*)]
			FRENCH PHRASES:
			cordon bleu (literally, blue ribbon; many extended meanings)
			cordon sanitaire (literally, sanitary cordon)
			NOTE: Some authorities place the music term *chord* in this
			    family, while others place it in *cord*, heart, that which pro-
			    duces harmony.
			NO CROSS REFERENCE

chrom***	Greek
	chroma
	(IE: *ghreu*,
	to rub hard
	over,
	crumble)
		color;
		originally, the
		color of skin
			SIMPLE ROOT:
			chroma: chroma, chromate, chromatic, chromatics (the scien-
			    tific study of color in reference to hues and saturation),
			    chromaticity, chromatid, chromatin
			chrome: chrome
			chromi: chromium (chemical symbol: Cr)
			chromo: chromous
			PREFIXED ROOT:
			a-: achroma, achromatic, achromatin, achromatism, achroma-
			    tize, achromatous, achromic, achromous (*a-*, without)
			apo-: apochromatic (*apo-*, away)
			hyper-: hyperchromatic, hyperchromia (*hyper-*, above, beyond)
			meta-: metachromatism, metachromatic (*meta-*, between)
			LEADING ROOT COMPOUND:
			chromo:
			gen: chromogen (*gen*, producer)
			lith: chromolithograph (*litho*, stone; *graph*, write)
			mer: chromomere (*mere*, part)
			nema: chromonema (*nema*, thread)

Element	From	Meaning	Examples
chrom (cont'd)			phil: chromophil (readily stained with dyes; as a *noun*, a chromophil cell or cell part) (*philos*, love) phor: chromophore (*phor*, to bear) plast: chromoplast (*plast*, form) som: chromosome (*some*, body) spher: chromosphere (the pinkish, glowing region around a star, especially the sun, between the hot, dense photosphere and the much hotter, tenuous corona) (*sphere*, ball, globe) *chromato*: gram: chromatogram (from *graphein*, to write) graph: chromatograph, chromatography (*graphein*, to write) lys: chromatolysis (in medicine, the disappearance of certain chromophil granules from nerve cells) (*lys*, loosen) phor: chromatophore (*phor*, to bear) TRAILING ROOT COMPOUND: auxo: auxochrome (any group of atoms that intensifies the color of a substance) (*auxo*, increase) cyto: cytochrome (*cyto*, cell) ferro: ferrochromium (also, *ferrochrome*) (*ferro*, iron) iso: isochrous (correctly spelled; same as *isochromatic*), isochromatic (in *optics*, having the same color: said of lines or curves in figures formed by interfering light waves from biaxial crystals) (*iso*, equal) mono: monochromatic (one color; also, of or producing light of one wavelength), monochrome (*mono*, one) pan: panchromatic (sensitive to all the visible colors, as *panchromatic film*) (*pan*, all) uro: urochrome (*uro*, urine) xantho: xanthochromic (*xantho*, yellow) MUSIC TERM: *chromatic scale* (an octave sequence of half steps; reason for term unclear) TRADEMARK: Kodachrome PLACENAMES: Chrome, New Jersey; Chromo, Colorado NO CROSS REFERENCE
chron***	Greek *chronos*	time	SIMPLE ROOT: chronic (lasting a long time or recurring often: said of a disease; distinguished from *acute*; **Synonyms:** inveterate, confirmed, hardened), chronicle, chronicler PREFIXED ROOT: ana-: anachronism (the representation of something as existing or occurring at other than its proper time, especially earlier) (*ana-*, against) dia-: diachronic (of or concerned with the study of changes occurring over a period of time, as in languages, mores, etc.) (*dia-*, through) para-: parachronism (a chronological error, especially one by which a date is set later than the correct one) (*para-*, alongside) syn-: synchronic, synchronicity, synchronism, synchronize, synchronous (**Synonyms:** contemporary, coeval, simultaneous) (*syn-*, with, together) DOUBLE PREFIXED ROOT: asynchronism (failure to occur at the same time) (*a-*, not; *syn-*, with)

Element	From	Meaning	Examples
chron (cont'd)			LEADING ROOT COMPOUND: *chron(o)*: axy: chronaxy (or *chronaxie*; the minimum time necessary to excite a tissue, such as that of muscle or nerve cells, with an electric current of twice the rheobase) (*axia*, value) gram: cbronogram (an inscription in which certain letters are to be read as numbers giving a date) (from *graph*, write) graph: chronograph (*graph*, write) log: chronological, chronologist, chronology (*logy*, science of) meter: chronometer {chronometric} (*meter, metry*, measure) scop: chronoscope (*scope*, look, view) TRAILING ROOT COMPOUND: geo: geosynchronous (as a *geosynchronous satellite*, "one which is *in time with the earth*") (*syn-*, with, together, prefixes *geo*, earth) EMBEDDED ROOT COMPOUND: geochronology (the branch of geology dealing with the age of the earth and its materials, the dating of evolutionary stages in plant and animal development, etc.) (*geo*, earth; *logy*, study of) geochronometry (the measurement of geologic time, as from the decay of radioactive elements) (*metry*, measurement of) DISGUISED ROOT: crony (an old friend) BOOKS OF THE BIBLE: Chronicles (two books of the Old Testament; the first book *chronicles* the reign of King David; the second, the history of the Southern Kingdom) CROSS REFERENCE: *ev, temp*
chrys**	Greek *chrysos* (originally from Hebrew and Arabic bases)	gold, yellow	SIMPLE ROOT: chrysalid (as a *noun*, same as *chrysalis*; as an *adjective*, of a chrysalis), chrysalis (the pupa of a butterfly, from its golden color) LEADING ROOT COMPOUND: *chrys*: anth: chrysanthemum (literally, golden flower) (*anthos*, flower) elephant: chryselephantine (made of, or overlaid with, gold and ivory, as some ancient Greek statues) (*elephas*, ivory) *chryso*: beryl: chrysoberyl (*beryl*, sea-green gem) lit: chrysolite (used in the names of minerals, rocks, and fossils) (*lite*, stone) pras: chrysoprase (a light-green variety of chalcedony sometimes used as a semiprecious stone) (*prason*, leek) RELIGIOUS FIGURE: Saint John Chrysostom (Golden Mouth) CROSS REFERENCE: *aur, flav, xanth*
chthon*	Greek *chthon* (IE: *ghthem*, earth, ground; yields Latin *homo*)	earth	SIMPLE ROOT: chthonian (in *Greek mythology*, designating or of the underworld of the dead and its gods or spirits) chthonic (dark, primitive, and mysterious) TRAILING ROOT COMPOUND: auto: autochthon (a person who was born where he/she lives; a native) {autochthonous} (*auto*, self) melan: melanchthon (literally, black earth; see *Historical Figure*, the name of which is a calque for the original German name) (see *calque* under *glad*) (*melan*, black)

Element	From	Meaning	Examples
chthon (cont'd)			DISGUISED ROOT: chamomile (literally, earth apple; a plant whose dried, daisylike flower heads have been used in a medicinal tea) chameleon (literally, ground lion; a particular lizard that can change its color; a changeable or fickle person) HISTORICAL FIGURE: Philip Melanchthon [1497-1560; German Protestant reformer; original name: Schwarzerd (black earth)] CROSS REFERENCE: *edaph, geo, terra, ped*
cid			See *cad* for *decide.*
cide***	Latin *caedere* (IE: *skhai,* to strike)	to kill	RAILING ROOT COMPOUND [In each of the listed words, that which is killed follows in parentheses.] acaricide (mites) bactericide (bacteria) feticide (one's offspring) filaricide (*filariae*: filamentous nematodes) filicide (one's child) fratricide [one's brother (or sister); also the act of killing relatives or fellow-countrymen, as in a civil war] fungicide (fungus) genocide (a race, as Hitler's attempt at eradicating the Jewish people) herbicide (plants, especially weeds) homocide (literally, man, although any person) insecticide (insects) matricide (one's mother) parricide (either of one's parents, or any close relative) patricide (one's father) pesticide (insects, weeds, etc.) (*pestis,* plague) regicide (king) sororicide (one's sister) suicide (oneself) uxoricide (one's wife) NO CROSS REFERENCE
cili*	Greek *cilium*: eyebrow (IE: *kel,* to hide)	eyelid, eyebrow	ROOT NOTE: This root can also designate a minute vibratile, hairlike process attached to a free surface of a cell. SIMPLE ROOT: cilia: cilia (plural of *cilium*; the eyelashes), ciliary, ciliate (also, *ciliated*; in *botany*, and *zoology*, having cilia) ciliu: cilium (plural: *cilia*) PREFIXED ROOT: *super-*: (over, beyond) superciliary (of, or near, the eyebrow) supercilious (with reference to facial expression with raised brows, indicating pride, haughtiness; thus, disdainful or contemptuous; **Synonyms:** arrogant, insolent, imperious) INTERDISCIPLINARY: cilia (in *botany*, small hairlike processes extending from certain plant cells and forming a fringe, as on the edges of some leaves; in *zoology*, short, hairlike outgrowths of certain cells, usually capable of rhythmic beating that can produce locomotion and feeding currents, as in protozoans, small worms, etc., or the movement of fluids, as in the ducts of higher forms) CROSS REFERENCE: *blephar*

Element	From	Meaning	Examples
cinct,* cing	Latin cingere (IE: kenk, to gird, encircle)	to gird, bind	SIMPLE ROOT: cinc: cinch (strong girth for securing a pack or saddle; informally, a tight grip; slang, something sure or easy) see Doublets below) cincture (something that encompasses or surrounds) cing: cingulum (in biology, a girdlelike structure, band, or marking) PREFIXED ROOT: pre-: precinct (literally, girded before) (pre-, before) suc-: succinct (to gird, to tuck up; clearly and briefly stated; terse; characterized by brevity and conciseness of speech; **Synonyms:** concise, terse, pithy) (suc- assimilates sub-, under) DISGUISED ROOT: shingles (used in Modern Latin to translate Greek zone, girdle, shingles; nontechnical name for herpes zoster; see Doublets below) DOUBLETS: cinch:shingles FRENCH: enceinte (the line of works enclosing a fortified place; the space so enclosed; another enceinte is derived from a different prefix, and means pregnant; with child) (from Latin incingere, to gird about) CROSS REFERENCE: circum-, peri-, dein
cinem,** kinem	Greek kinein: to move (IE: kei³, to set in motion)	movement	SIMPLE ROOT: cine: cinema {cinematic} kine: kinase, kinen, kinesics, kinetic, kinetics, kinetism PREFIXED ROOT: hyper-: hyperkinesia (hyper-, over, beyond) hypo-: hypokinesia (hypo-, under, below) LEADING ROOT COMPOUND: graph: cinematograph (graph, write) FRENCH: cinéaste [ciné(matographe) + (enthousi)aste, enthusiast; a person involved in motion-picture production] CROSS REFERENCE: mot, mov
ciner*	Latin cinis: ashes (IE: ken, to scratch, rub)	ashes	SIMPLE ROOT: cineraria, cinerarium, cinereous PREFIXED ROOT: in-: incinerate (to burn to ashes), incinerator (in-, in, to) DISGUISED ROOT: cinder, sinter FICTIONAL CHARACTER: Cinderella (a partial translation of German Aschenbrödel, scullion; asche, ash + brodeln, bubble up) NO CROSS REFERENCE
cing			See cinct for cingulum.
cinque*	Latin quinque (IE: penkwe, five)	five	SIMPLE ROOT: cinquain (a five-line stanza, by analogy with quatrain, a four-line stanza), cinque LEADING ROOT COMPOUND: cent: cinquecento (short for mille cinque cento, one thousand five hundred; the 16th century as a period in Italian art and literature) (cent, 100) foil: cinquefoil (in architecture, a circular design made up of five converging arcs, resembling leaves) (from foli, leaf) SPANISH COGNATE: cinco MEXICAN HOLIDAY: cinco de mayo (fifth of May) CROSS REFERENCE: penta, quin

Element	From	Meaning	Examples
cip			See *cap*, hold, seize, for *recipient*.
circum-***	Latin *circus*: circle (IE: *(s)ker*, to turn, bend)	around, round	SIMPLE ELEMENT: *circa* (usually shortened to *ca.* or *c.*), circinate, circle, circuit, circuitous, circulant, circular, circulate, circulatory, circulus, circus

PREFIXED ROOT:

circa:

dia: circadian (literally, around a day; a 24-hour period; compare *diurnal*, under *dia*) (*dia*, day)

circum:

amb: (notice difference in meanings of "amb")

circumambient (*ambient* from *ambi-*, around + *ire*, to go)

circumambulate (*ambulare*, to walk)

cis: circumcise, circumcision (*caedere*, to cut)

fer: circumference (**Synonyms**: perimeter, periphery, compass) (*ferre*, to bear)

flex: circumflex {circumflexion} (from *flectare*, to bend)

flu: circumfluent (also, *circumfluous*) (*fluere*, to flow)

fus: circumfuse {circumfusion} (from *fundere*, to pour)

loc: circumlocution {circumlocutory} (from *loqui*, to speak)

nav: circumnavigate {circumnavigation} (*navis*, ship)

nut: circumnutation (in *botany*, the irregular spiral or elliptical rotation of the apex of a growing stem, root, or shoot, caused by differences in the rate of growth of the opposite sides) (*nutare*, to nod)

pol: circumpolar (surrounding or near either pole of the earth)

rot: circumrotate (*rota*, wheel)

sciss: circumscissile (in *botany*, opening or splitting by a transverse fissure around the circumference, leaving an upper and a lower half: said of certain seed pods or capsules) (from *scindere*, to split)

scrib: circumscribe (**Synonyms**: limit, restrict, confine) (*scribere*, to write)

script: circumscription (from *circumscribe*)

spect: circumspect (**Synonyms**: careful, scrupulous, cautious) (from *specere*, to look)

stan: circumstance, circumstantial (**Synonyms**: occurrence, event, incident; see *Law Term* below) (from *stare*, to stand)

vall: circumvallate {circumvallation} (*vallum*, wall, rampart)

vent: circumvent {circumvention, circumventive} (from *venire*, to come)

volu: circumvolution (from *circumvolve*)

volv: circumvolve (*volvere*, to roll)

DISGUISED ROOT:

cirque

curb (**Synonyms**: restrain, restrict, check)

curve, curvature (in *medicine*, a curving or bending, especially an abnormal one, e.g., *curvature of the spine*), curvet

ranch, range, rank (probably through Frankish *hring*, circle, ring)

ribbon (Middle English *riban*; from Middle Dutch *ringhband*, necklace: from *ringh*, ring + band)

ringhals (a small, rough-skinned cobra of South Africa)

rink (see *rank*, above)

132

Element	From	Meaning	Examples
circum- (cont'd)			search (from Old French *cerchier*, to go around) PREFIXED DISGUISED ROOT: ar-: arrange, arrangement (*ar-* assimilates *ad-*, to, toward) de-: derange (to upset the arrangement, order, or operation of; unsettle; disorder; to make insane) {deranged, derangement} (*de-*, reversal) re-: research (**Synonyms**: investigation, inquest, inquisition) (*re-*, again) FRENCH: *recherché* (sought out with care; rare; choice; uncommon; having refinement or studied elegance; too refined; too studied) LAW TERM: circumstantial evidence CROSS REFERENCE: *ambi, amphi, peri*
cirr*	Latin *cirrus*	curl, lock	SIMPLE ROOT: cirrate, cirose (also *cirrose*), cirrus (also, *cirrhus, cirrous*) LEADING ROOT COMPOUND: *cirri*: form: cirriform (having the form of a cirrus: slender and prolonged and usually curved: used of processes, as a mollusk having a foot with a cirriform tip) ped: cirripede (or *cirriped*; literally, cirrus-footed) (*ped*, foot) *cirro*: cumul: cirrocumulus (a high-altitude cloud composed of a series of small, regularly arranged cloudlets in the form of ripples or grains) (*cumulus*, heap) neb: cirronebula (a thin cirrus veil without structure) (*nebulus*, cloud) strat: cirrostratus (a high-altitude, thin, hazy cloud, usually covering the sky and often producing a halo effect) (*stratus*, layer) INTERDISCIPLINARY: cirrus (in *biology*, a plant tendril; also, a flexible, threadlike tentacle or appendage, as the feelers of certain organisms; in *meteorology*, a formation of clouds in detached, wispy filaments, or feathery tufts, at heights above 20,000 ft.) NB: Do not confuse *cirrhosis* (literally, condition of orange tawny), a chronic disease of the liver, with this family. NO CROSS REFERENCE
cis*	Latin *cis*: nearer side (IE: *ko, ke*, this one)	on this side of	PREFIXED ROOT: alp: cisalpine [on this (the southern) side of the Alps, as viewed from Rome] atlant: cisatlantic [*on this* (the speaker's) *side* of the Atlantic] lun: cislunar (on this side of the moon, between the moon and the earth) (*luna*, moon) mont: cismontane (on this side of the mountains, especially of the Alps) PLACENAME: Cismont, Virginia (near Charlottesville; oriented from Richmond, *on this side of* the Blue Ridge Mountains) NO CROSS REFERENCE

Although the study of Greek has been for centuries an essential part of the higher education of Englishmen, the language would not have contributed greatly to the English vocabulary if had not happened to be particularly fitted to supply the need for the precise technical terms of science. Henry Bradley

Element	From	Meaning	Examples
cis***	Latin *caedere*: to cut (see **cide**)	to cut, strike	ROOT NOTE: Entered separately are other forms of this root: *cad, cas, cid.* PREFIXED ROOT: *ab-*: (away, off) abscise (to separate by abscission, which see below) abscissa (literally, cut off from; in the graph of a mathematical function, the freely variable, horizontal distance of a point from a vertical axis; compare *ordinate*) abscission (a cutting off, as by surgery; in *botany*, the normal separation of fruit, leaves, etc. from plants by the development of a thin layer of pithy cells at the base of their stems) *circum-*: circumcise [to remove the prepuce (of a male); to remove the clitoris (of a female); to purify spiritually; cleanse from sin] (*circum-*, around) *con-*: concise (**Synonyms:** terse, laconic, succinct), concision (originally, a cutting off; division; concise quality; conciseness) (*con-*, intensive) *de-*: decision, decisive (*de-*, off) *ex-*: excise (to remove a tumor, organ, etc. by cutting out or away), excision (*ex-*, out) *in-*: incise, incised, incision, incisive (**Synonyms:** trenchant, biting, caustic), incisor (a cutting tooth; any of the front teeth between the canines in either jaw) (*in-*, in) *pre-*: (before) précis (a concise abridgment; summary; abstract) precise (literally, cut off in front; shorten; **Synonyms:** 1) explicit, definite, specific; 2) correct, accurate, exact) {precisely, preciseness} precisian (a person who is strict and precise in observing rules or customs, especially of religion; specifically, a 16th- or 17th-century English Puritan) precision (the state or quality of being precise), precisionist *re-*: recision (literally, to cut down; the act of rescinding; an annulment or cancellation) (*re-*, back) DISGUISED ROOT: scissors (may come from the same root as *scission*; see **scind**) PREFIXED DISGUISED ROOT: *con-*: concinnity (a skillful arrangement of parts; harmony; elegance, especially of literary style) (*con-*, with, together) CROSS REFERENCE: *sect, scind/sciss, tail, tom*
cit,** civ	Latin *civis*: people (IE: *kei*[1], to lie, homestead)	community	SIMPLE ROOT: *cit*: citizen (**Synonyms:** national, native), city *civ*: civic, civics, civil (**Synonyms:** polite, courteous, chivalrous), civilian, civility, civilization, civilize, civilly PREFIXED ROOT: *in-*: incivility (*in-*, not) ITALIAN: citadel (a fortress on a commanding height for defense of a city; a fortified place; stronghold; a place of safety; refuge) (originally *citadella*, diminutive of *cittade*, city) LATIN LEGAL TERM: *actio civilis* (in the common law, a civil action, as distinguished from a criminal action) NAME OF UNIVERSITY: The Citadel, Charleston, South Carolina CROSS REFERENCE: *eco/oik*

Element	From	Meaning	Examples
cit**	Latin *citare*: to summon; *ciere*, to set in motion (IE: *kei³*, to set in motion)	set in motion, raise up, revive	SIMPLE ROOT: citation (a summons to appear before a court of law) cite (to summon to appear before a court of law; to quote a passage, book, speech, writer, etc.) PREFIXED ROOT: *ex-*: (out) excitable, excitant (stimulating; as a *noun*, a stimulant), exci- tation, excitative, excitatory excite (**Synonyms:** provoke, stimulate, pique), exciting excitor (same as *exciter*; also, in *physiology*, a nerve which, when stimulated, causes increased activity of the part that it supplies) *in-*: incite (**Synonyms:** instigate, arouse, foment) (*in-*, in) *re-*: (back, again) recital, recite, recitation recitative (a type of declamatory singing, with the rhythm and tempo of speech, but uttered in musical tones, used in prose parts and dialogue of operas and oratorios; *recitatives* are usu- ally followed by arias, airs or melodies) (from *recite*) TRAILING ROOT COMPOUND: os: oscitancy (drowsiness, dullness, apathy, lethargy, etc.) (*os*, mouth; *oscitare*, to yawn) soli: (from *sollus*, whole) solicit (**Synonyms:** entreat, beseech, implore), solicitous solicitor (**Synonyms:** lawyer, counsel, barrister) solicitude (**Synonyms:** care, concern, anxiety) DOUBLE PREFIXED TRAILING ROOT COMPOUND: re<u>sus</u>citate, re<u>sus</u>itator (*re-*, again; *sus-* from *sub-*, under) NO CROSS REFERENCE
civ			See *cit/civ* for *civic*, *civil*.
clad*	Greek *klados*: sprout (IE: *kel*, to strike)	branch, shoot	ROOT NOTE: This root is related to *glad*, sword, from which *gladiator* and *gladiolus* are derived. SIMPLE ROOT: cladistia, cladonia, cladoniaceous, cladus (a branch of a ramose spicule) LEADING ROOT COMPOUND: *clad*: anth: cladanthous (same as *pleurocarpous*) (*anth*, flower) od: cladode (having many sprouts), cladodus (*ode*, similar to) *clado*: carp: cladocarpous (same as *pleurocarpous*) (*carp*, fruit) cer: cladoceran [an order of crustaceans with a folded upper shell (horn) covering the body, as the water flea] (*keras*, horn) phyl: cladophyll (a flattened branch arising from the axil of a leaf) (*phyll*, leaf) CROSS REFERENCE: *blast, germ, rad, ram, rhizo*
clam,*** claim	Latin *clamare* (IE: *kel*, to cry out, yell)	to cry out	SIMPLE ROOT: *clam*: clamant (noisy; demanding attention; urgent), clamato- rial (a suborder of birds), clamor, clamorous *claim*: claim, claimable, claimant PREFIXED ROOT: *clam*: *con-*: conclamant, conclamation (*con-*, with, together) *de-*: declamation (the art of declaiming), declamatory (marked by passion or pomposity; bombastic) (*de-*, intensive)

Element	From	Meaning	Examples
clam (cont'd)			*dis-*: disclamation (an act of disclaiming; renunciation; repudiation) (*dis-*, not) *ex-*: (out) exclamation (sudden, vehement utterance; outcry; something exclaimed; exclamatory word or phrase; interjection) exclamation point (!): used after a word or sentence in writing to express surprise, strong emotion, determination, etc. exclamatory (of, containing, expressing, or using exclamation) *pro-*: proclamation (a proclaiming or being proclaimed; something that is announced officially) (*pro-*, forth) *re-*: reclamation (a reclaiming or being reclaimed; especially, the recovery of wasteland, desert, etc. by ditching, filling, or irrigating) (*re-*, back, again) *claim*: *ac-*: acclaim (**Synonyms**: praise, laud, extol), acclamation, acclamatory (*ac-* assimilates *ad-*, to, toward) *de-*: declaim (to recite a speech, poem, etc. with studied or artificial eloquence) (*de-*, intensive) *dis-*: disclaim (to give up or renounce any claim to or connection with; deny; repudiate), disclaimer (*dis-*, not) *ex-*: exclaim (literally, to cry out), exclaimer (*ex-*, out) *pro-*: proclaim (literally, to cry forth; to announce officially; announce to be; to show to be; **Synonyms**: declare, announce, publish) (*pro-*, forth) *re-*: reclaim (literally, to cry out against; **Synonyms**: recover, retrieve, recoup) {reclaimable} (*re-*, against) CROSS REFERENCE: *nunci, plor*
clar***	Latin *clarus* (IE: *kel*, to cry out, yell)	clear, bright	SIMPLE ROOT: clara: clarain, clarence (a closed, four-wheeled carriage with seats for four inside and a seat for the driver outside; from the Duke of Clarence, later William IV) clare: claret, clarety clari: clarin, clarina, clarinet, clarino, clarion, clarity (clearness or lucidity as to perception or understanding) claro: claro (light-colored and mild: said of a cigar) PREFIXED ROOT: *de-*: declarative, declaratory, declare (see synonyms at *proclaim*, previous family), declaredly (*de-*, intensive) LEADING ROOT COMPOUND: bell: clarabello (an 8-foot organ stop producing a soft, velvety tone) (*bell*, beautiful) fic: clarificant, clarificient (*facere*, to make, do) fy: clarify (*facere*, to make, do) DISGUISED LEADING ROOT COMPOUND: *clair*: aud: clairaudience (*audire*, to hear) voy: clairvoyant (from French *voir*, to see; from Latin *videre*, to see) *chiar*: chiaroscuro (literally, clear dark) (from IE *skuro*, to cover) *clere*: clerestory (literally, clear story; outside walls of rooms rising above adjoining roofs and containing high windows; an *architectural* term)

Element	From	Meaning	Examples
clar (cont'd)			ENGLISH: clear (**Synonyms:** transparent, translucent, pellucid) HISTORICAL DOCUMENT: *Declaration of Independence* FRENCH: éclair (literally, a flash, lightning) *éclaircissement* (a clarification, explanation, as of a disputed or difficult point; capitalized, the *Enlightenment*, an 18th-century European philosophical movement characterized by rationalism, an impetus toward learning, and a spirit of skepticism and empiricism in social and political thought) PROPER NAMES: Clara, Clarence, Clarice CROSS REFERENCE: *alb, cand*
clas,** clast	Greek *klasis*: breaking (IE: *kel*, to strike)	breakage, division	SIMPLE ROOT: *clas*: class (originally, one of the six divisions of the Roman people; thus, a group, set, collection, or configuration containing members having, or thought to have, at least one attribute in common) classic (of the highest rank or class), classicism, classis *clast*: clastic (designating an anatomical model with removable sections to show internal structure; in *geology*, consisting of fragments of older rocks) PREFIXED ROOT: ana-: anaclasis (in *anatomy*, a bending backward; recurvature, as a joint), anaclastic (in *anatomy*, bent backward; in *optics*, of, or caused by, or causing refraction) (*ana-*, again, backward) cata-: cataclastic (breaking down; of or pertaining to the deformation or fragmentation of metamorphic rock by extreme pressure) (*cata-*, down) LEADING ROOT COMPOUND: fic: classification, classificatory (*facere*, to do, make) fy: classify (*facere*, to do, make) TRAILING ROOT COMPOUND: eu: euclase (a silicate which is easily broken) (*eu*, good, well) icono: (*icon*, image, idol) iconoclasm (the actions or belief of an iconoclast) iconoclast (anyone opposed to the religious use of icons, or advocating the destruction of such icons; a person who attacks or ridicules traditional or venerated institutions or ideas regarded by him/her as erroneous or based on superstition) DISGUISED ROOT: clash, clone (literally, that which is broken off) FRENCH: *déclassé* (literally, to cause to lose class; as an *adjective*, having lost class; lowered in social status) CROSS REFERENCE: *frac/frag, rupt*
clav**	Latin *clavis* (IE: *kleu*, to close)	key (also, club)	SIMPLE ROOT (of words meaning "key"): clave: clave [one of a pair of small cylindrical wooden sticks used as percussion instruments by being struck together while held in cupped hands) (as an accompaniment to the rumba)] clavel (originally, the keystone of an arch; the lintel over a fireplace; mantel) clavi: claviature (the keyboard of a piano or organ; a system of fingering a keyboard instrument)

137

Element	From	Meaning	Examples
clav (cont'd)			clavicle (the collarbone, which is shaped similar to a key) {clavicular, claviculate}, clavier
			clavis (a key to words; a glossary; a key feature in the authors' *An Introduction to an Academic Vocabulary*)
			SIMPLE ROOT (of words meaning "club")
			clava (a clublike structure; See *Webster's Third* for a number of definitions), claval, clavate (in *biology*, gradually thickening near the distal end; shaped like a club)
			PREFIXED ROOT:
			con-: conclave (a room which may be locked with a key; in the Roman Catholic Church, a private meeting of the cardinals to elect a pope; any private or secret meeting; any large conference or convention) (*con-*, with, together)
			en-: enclave (literally, locked in; a territory surrounded or nearly surrounded by the territory of another country; a minority culture group living as an entity within a larger group) (*en-*, in)
			ex-: exclave (a territory of a nearby country surrounded by foreign territory: distinguished from *enclave*) (*ex-*, out)
			inter-: interclavicle (*inter-*, between)
			LEADING ROOT COMPOUND:
			chord: clavichord (a musical instrument in which the strings are struck with keys) (*chord*, string)
			TRAILING ROOT COMPOUND:
			auto: autoclave (a container for sterilizing, cooking, etc. by superheated steam under pressure) (*auto*, self)
			DISGUISED ROOT:
			clef [a symbol used in music to indicate the pitch, or the key, of the notes on the staff: there are three clefs: G (treble), F (bass), and C (tenor or alto)]
			kevel (a cleat or peg for fastening the heavy lines of a ship)
			NO CROSS REFERENCE
clemen**	Latin *clemens*	mild, gentle, calm, merciful	SIMPLE ROOT:
			clemency (*noun*; forbearance, leniency, or mercy, as toward an offender or enemy; a merciful or lenient act; mildness, as of weather)
			clement [*adjective*; forbearing; lenient; mild (as weather)]
			PREFIXED ROOT:
			in-: inclement (not mild; rough; severe; stormy; lacking mercy or leniency; harsh) {inclemency} (*in-*, not)
			PROPER NAMES: Clement, Clementine, Clementina
			CROSS REFERENCE: *leni, malac, mol*
clim,** clin, clit, cliv	Greek *klinein*; Latin: *clinare* (IE: *klei*, to lean)	to slope, lean	ROOT NOTE: Words from both Latin and Greek are listed without differentiation as to origin.
			SIMPLE ROOT:
			clim: climate, climax (**Synonyms**: summit, peak, acme)
			clin: clinamen, cline, clinic
			clit: clitoris (a small, sensitive, erectile organ at the upper end of the vulva: it corresponds to the penis in the male)
			cliv: clivus (the smooth sloping surface on the upper posterior part of the body of the sphenoid bone supporting the pons)
			PREFIXED ROOTS AND COMPOUNDS:
			clim:
			ac-: acclimate, acclimation, acclimatization, acclimatize (*ac-* assimilates *ad-*, to, toward)

Element	From	Meaning	Examples
clim (cont'd)			*clin*: a-: aclinic (see note under Greek *a*-) (*a*-, without) *ana*-: anaclinal (in *geology*, progressing in a direction opposite to that in which the rock strata dip, as a valley; compare *cataclinal*, below) (*ana*-, opposite) *anti*-: anticlinal, anticline, anticlinorium (*anti*-, against) *cata*-: cataclinal (in *geology*, descending in the same direction as the dip of the underlying rock strata, as a stream bed or valley; compare *anaclinal*, above) (*cata*-, down) *de*-: (down) declination, decline (**Synonyms**: refuse, reject, spurn) *de*-: declinometer (*meter*, measure) *in*-: inclination (**Synonyms**: leaning, propensity, proclivity), incline (*in*-, on, to) *peri*-: periclinal (in *botany*, running parallel to the surface of a plant organ or part: said of cell walls), pericline (*peri*-, around) *re*-: reclinate (in *botany*, bending downward, as a leaf or stem), recline (*re*-, down) *syn*-: synclinal (sloping downward in opposite directions so as to meet), syncline (in *geology*, a down fold in stratified rocks from whose central axis the beds rise upward and outward in opposite directions: opposed to *anticline*) (*syn*-, with, together) *clit*: *ana*-: anaclitic (in *psychoanalysis*, having the libido dependent upon another instinct) (*ana*-, back) *en*-: enclitic (literally, to lean in; to lean toward; in *grammar*, dependent on the preceding word for its stress: said as of a word that has lost its stress in combination, e.g., *man* in *layman*) (*en*-, in) *pro*-: proclitic (literally, to lean forward; in *grammar*, dependent on the following word for its stress: said as of a word that forms a phonetic unit with the following stressed word, e.g., *for* in once and *for* all) (*pro*-, forward) *cliv*: *ac*-: acclivity (opposed to *declivity*) (*ac*- assimilates *ad*-, to, toward) *de*-: declivitous, declivity (a downward slope or sloping, as of a hill: opposed to *acclivity*, which see above) (*de*-, down) *pro*-: proclivity (**Synonyms**: inclination, bent, propensity) (*pro*-, forward) LEADING ROOT COMPOUND: *andr*: clinandrium (in *botany*, a cavity or area in which the anther is situated on the column in flowers of the Orchidaceae) (*andr*, male, stamen, anther) *meter*: clinometer (an instrument for measuring angles of slope or inclination) TRAILING ROOT COMPOUND: *clin*: *iso*: isocline (*iso*, equal) *matro*: matroclinic (also, *matroclinous*; derived or inherited from the mother or maternal line) (*matro*, mother)

139

Element	From	Meaning	Examples
clim (cont'd)			mono: monoclinal (dipping in one direction: said of strata, or rock layers), monocline, monoclinic, monoclinous (in *botany*, having stamens and pistils in the same flower) (*mono*, one) patri: patriclinous (*patri*, father) *clit*: hetero: heteroclite (*hetero*, different) DISGUISED ROOT: client (originally, one leaning on another for protection), clientele PREFIXED DISGUISED ROOT: *de-*: declension, declensional (*de-*, down) CROSS REFERENCE: *clim, flect*
clit			See *clim* for *clitoris, anaclitic, enclitic*.
cliv			See *clim* for *proclivity*.
clos			See *clud/clus* for *close, disclose, eclosion*.
clud,*** clus	Latin *claudere* (IE: *kleu, klau,* close)	to close, shut; partition	SIMPLE ROOT: cluster (in *phonetics*, a group of nonsyllabic phonemes, especially a group of consecutive consonants) PREFIXED ROOT: *clud*: *con-*: conclude (**Synonyms:** 1) close, end, finish; 2) decide, determine, settle; 3) infer, deduce, judge) (*con-*, with, together) *en-*: exclude (**Synonyms:** disbar, eliminate, suspend) (*ex-*, out) *in-*: include (**Synonyms:** comprise, comprehend, involve) (*in-*, in) *oc-*: occlude, occlusion, occlusive (*oc-* assimilates *ob-*, against) *pre-*: preclude (**Synonyms:** prevent, forestall, obviate) (*pre-*, before) *se-*: seclude (to keep away or apart from others; isolate; to make private or hidden; screen) (*se-*, away) *clus*: *con-*: conclusion, conclusive (*con-*, with, together) *ex-*: exclusion, exclusionist, exclusive (*ex-*, out) *in-*: inclusion (in *biology*, a separate body, as a grain of starch, within the protoplasm of a cell), inclusive (*in-*, in) *pre-*: preclusion, preclusive (*pre-*, before) *re-*: recluse, reclusion, reclusive (*re-*, back) *se-*: seclusion, seclusive (*se-*, apart) DOUBLE PREFIXED ROOT: *mal-*: malocclusion (dental term) [depending on how used, *mal*, bad, can be considered a prefix or a root; *oc-* assimilates *ob-*, against] DISGUISED ROOT: clause FRENCH: *cloisonné* (literally, partitioned; designating or of a kind of enamel work in which the surface decoration is set in hollows formed by thin strips of wire welded to a metal plate; as a *noun*, cloisonné enamel) cloister (literally, place shut in; originally, bolt: that place of a monastery closed off to the laity) ENGLISH: close (**Synonyms:** 1) dense, compact, thick; 2) end, conclude, complete)

Element	From	Meaning	Examples
clud (cont'd)			closet, closure PREFIXED ENGLISH: *dis-*: disclose (**Synonyms**: reveal, divulge, tell), disclosure (*dis-*, opposite of) *e-*: eclosion (the emergence of an insect from its egg or from the pupal case) (from *ex-*, out) *en-*: enclose, enclosurer (*en-*, in) *ex-*: exclosure (an area protected against the entrance of animals, etc.) (*ex-*, out) INTERDISCIPLINARY: clause (in *grammar*, a group of words containing a subject and finite verb, usually forming part of a compound or complex sentence; in *law*, a particular article, stipulation, or provision in a legal document) NOTE: In Greek, *myopia*, from *myein*, to shut + *ops*, eye, is related in meaning. This root also yields *miosis, mystery, mystic.* NO CROSS REFERENCE
coc			See *coqu* for *precocial, precocious.*
coen			See *cen* for *coenesthesia, coenurus.*
cogn**	Latin *cognoscere*: to know (IE: *gen, gno*, to know, apprehend)	knowledge	ROOT NOTE: The root is a combination of *co-*, with, together + *gnoscere*, to know. SIMPLE ROOT: cognition (the mental process or faculty by which knowledge is acquired) {cognitive} cognizable (in *law*, within the jurisdiction of a court) cognizance, cognizant, cognize (to take cognizance of; notice) PREFIXED ROOT: *in-*: incognizant (*in-*, not) *pre-*: precognition {precognitive} (*pre-*, before) *re-*: recognition {recognitory or *recognitive*} recognize {recognizable} (*re-*, again) DISGUISED ROOT: quaint (pleasingly odd or unique) (from *cognitus*, known) PREFIXED DISGUISED ROOT: *ac-*: acquaint (see note under *ad-*) (*ac-* assimilates *ad-*, to) *re-*: reconnaissance, reconnoiter (*re-*, again) FRENCH: *connoisseur* (**Synonyms**: aesthete, dilettante, virtuoso) (*connaisseur*, Modern French) ITALIAN: *incognito* (**Synonyms**: pseudonym, pen name, alias) *cognoscente* (plural, *cognoscenti*; a person with special knowledge in some field, especially in the fine arts; expert) ENGLISH SIMPLES AND COMPOUNDS: know, knowing, knowledge (**Synonyms**: information, learning, erudition) note, noted (**Synonyms**: famous, renowned, celebrated) notice (**Synonyms**: discern, perceive, observe) notorious (see synonyms at *noted*, above) notify (**Synonyms**: inform, acquaint, apprise) LATIN PHRASE: *cogito, ergo sum* (I think, therefore, I am; the basic tenet of Descartes) NB: *Cogitate* and *cognomen* are not in this family; see *cogitate* under *com-* and *act*; *cognomen* under *com-* and *nomen.* CROSS REFERENCE: *gnos, scir/scis*

Element	From	Meaning	Examples
cohors*	Latin cohors (IE: gher, to enclose)	court, enclosure	ROOT NOTE: This root is combination of com-, with, together + hors, yard; hors yields hort, as in horticulture. SIMPLE ROOT: cohort (an ancient Roman military unit of 300-600 men, constituting one tenth of a legion; a band of soldiers; any group or band; an associate, colleague, or supporter; also, a conspirator or accomplice) DISGUISED ROOT: cortege (a group of attendants accompanying a person; retinue; a ceremonial procession, as at a funeral) court, courteous (see synonyms at civil, under cit, civ) courtesan (a prostitute; especially, a mistress of a king, or of a man of wealth or nobility) courtesy (excellence of manners or social conduct; polite behavior) courtier (an attendant at a royal court; a person who uses flattery to get something or to win favor) curtain, curtilage (in law, the fenced-in ground and buildings immediately surrounding a house or dwelling) curtsy (See Doublets below) DOUBLETS: courtesy:curtsy NO CROSS REFERENCE
col-			See com- for collect.
col*	Latin colare: to strain	filter, flow	SIMPLE ROOT: colander (a pan with a perforated bottom to drain off liquids, as in washing vegetables or in straining spaghetti) PREFIXED ROOT: per-: percolate [to pass (a liquid) gradually through small spaces or a porous substance; filter; permeate; to brew (coffee) in a percolator], percolator (per-, through) TRAILING ROOT COMPOUND: machi: machicolation (literally, a crushing blow; the dropping of hot liquids, heavy stones, etc., on invaders by the defenders of a castle) (macher, to crush) port: portcullis (a heavy iron grating suspended by chains and lowered between grooves to bar the gateway of a castle or fortified town) (porte, a gate) DISGUISED ROOT: coulee (a stream of molten lava, or a sheet of solidified lava; in the northwestern United States, a deep gulch or ravine, usually dry in summer) coulisse (from coulee; a grooved timber in which a sluice gate, etc. slides; also a theater term) couloir (from coulee; a deep mountain gorge or gully) cullis (in architecture, a gutter or a groove) culvert (possibly in this family) CROSS REFERENCE: flu, rrh
cole*	Greek koleos	sheath	LEADING ROOT COMPOUND: pter: coleoptera (literally, sheath-winged; an order of insects), coleopterology (pter, wing) ptil: coleoptile (the tubular protective sheath which surrounds the young shoot in the germinating grass seed) (ptilon, feather) rhiz: coleorhiza (a protective root sheath of grass seedlings through which the primary root emerges) (rhiza, root) CROSS REFERENCE: vag/vagin

142

Element	From	Meaning	Examples
coll*	Latin *collum* (IE: *kwel*, to turn)	neck	SIMPLE ROOT: col (a gap or depression between peaks in a mountain range, used as a pass; in *meteorology*, the point of lowest pressure between two anticyclones or the point of highest pressure between two cyclones) collar (anything worn or placed around the neck, as a collar of leis) collet (a collar or enclosing band; the enclosing rim within which a jewel is set; as a verb, to set a gem or other stone in a collet) PREFIXED ROOT: ac-: accolade (literally, to embrace, or to hug around the neck; in *music*, a vertical line joining two or more staves) (from *ad-*, to, toward) de-: decollate (to behead); note *décolleté*, below; decollation, decollator (*de-*, from) LEADING ROOT COMPOUND: port: colporteur (one who carries a pack swung from the neck; a person who goes from place to place distributing or selling Bibles, religious tracts, etc.) (*portare*, to carry) TRAILING ROOT COMPOUND: torti: torticollis (twisted neck; wryneck) (*tortus*, twisted) DISGUISED ROOT: cullet (from the neck of a bottle; with reference to glass debris at the neck of a bottle in blowing; scraps of waste glass than can be remelted) FRENCH PREFIXED ROOT: *décolleté* (cut low so as to bare the neck and shoulders, as some dresses; the noun is *décolletage*) CROSS REFERENCE: *cervic, trachel*
coll*	Greek *kolla*	glue	LEADING ROOT COMPOUND: *coll*: oid: colloid [term coined by Thomas Graham (1805-69), Scotch chemist; a solid, liquid, or gaseous substance made up of very small, insoluble, nondiffusible particles (as single large molecules or masses of smaller molecules) that remain in suspension in a surrounding solid, liquid, or gaseous medium of different matter] (*oid*, similar to) *collo*: typ: collotype (*type*, image, symbol) TRAILING ROOT COMPOUND: proto: protocol [originally the first leaf glued to a manuscript (describing its contents); then, an original draft or record of a document, negotiation, etc.; the customs and regulations dealing with diplomatic formality, precedence, and etiquette] (*proto*, first) FRENCH ART TERM: collage (an art form in which bits of objects are pasted together on a surface in incongruous relationship for their symbolic or suggestive effect) AMERICANISM: collodion (a highly flammable, viscous solution of nitrated cellulose; it dries quickly, forming a tough, elastic film, and is used as a protective coating for wounds, in photographic films, etc.) (*kolla*, glue + *eidos*, form) CROSS REFERENCE: *gli, glutin*

Element	From	Meaning	Examples
com-,*** col-, con-, cor-, co-	Latin com- (IE: kom, closely along, next to, with)	with, together; also used as an intensive	NOTE: *Com-* assimilates to *col-* before roots beginning with *l*; to *cor-* before *r*; *con-* appears before roots beginning with *c, d, g, j, n, q, s, t, v*; and *co-* before *h, w,* and vowels. PREFIXED ROOT: *com-*: bat: combat (**Synonyms:** battle, campaign, skirmish), combatant, combative (*battuere*, to strike, beat, fight) bin: combination, combinative, combine (**Synonyms:** join, connect, unite) (*bini*, two by two) fit: comfit (from *confect*) frey: comfrey (from *fervere*, to boil) menc: commence (**Synonyms:** begin, start, initiate), commencement (from *initiare*, to initiate, which itself is from *in-* + *ire*, to go) mensa: commensal (in *biology*, either of the organisms living in commensalism), commensalism (*mensa*, table) mensu: commensurable, commensurate (**Synonyms:** proportional, proportionate, commensurable) (*mensura*, measurement) merc: commerce (**Synonyms:** business, trade, industry), commercial, commercialism (from *merx*, merchandise) mina: commination (a threat or denunciation) (*minari*, to menace) minu: comminute (to reduce to small, fine particles) (*minuere*, to make small) miss: commissar, commissary, commission (**Synonyms:** authorize, accredit, license), commissure (from *commit*) mit: commit (**Synonyms:** entrust, confide, consign), commitment, committee (*mittere*, to send) mix: commixture (from *miscere*, to mix) mod: commode, commodious, commodity (*modus*, mode, measure) mon: common (**Synonyms:** general, ordinary, familiar), commonable, commonality, commoner, commons (IE *mei*, to barter, exchange) mot: commotion (from *movere*, to move) mov: commove (to move strongly; agitate; disturb; excite) (see *commotion*) mun: (from IE *mei*, to barter, exchange) communal, communalism, commune, community communicable, communicant, communicate, communication communion (capitalized, the Eucharist, or Holy Communion) communiqué communism, communist pact: compact (**Synonyms:** close, dense, thick), compaction (*pangere*, to fix, fasten) pan: companion (literally, one who eats bread with another; **Synonyms:** associate, colleague, comrade), companionable, companionate, company (*pan*, bread) par: comparable, comparative, compare (**Synonyms:** contrast, collate), comparison (*par*, equal) part: compart, compartment, compartmentalize (*partire*, to divide, separate)

Element	From	Meaning	Examples
com- (cont'd)			pass:

compass (**Synonyms:** range, scope, gamut) (*passum*, a step)

compassion (**Synonyms:** pity, sympathy, condolence) (*pati*, to feel)

pat: compatible (from *compassion*)

peer: compeer (from *par*, equal)

pel: compel (**Synonyms:** force, coerce, constrain) (*pellere*, to drive)

pend: compend, compendious, compendium (*pendere*, to weigh)

pens: compensable, compensate, compensation, compensator (from *pendere*, to weigh)

per: compère [originally, joint father (of the faithful)]

pet: (*petere*, to seek)

compete (**Synonyms:** rival, vie, emulate)

competence, competent (**Synonyms:** able, qualified, capable)

competition, competitive

pil: compilation, compile (*pilare*, to compress; ram down)

plain: complain, complainant, complaint (from *plangere*, to strike)

plais: complaisance, complaisant (from *complacent*)

plem: complement, complementarity, complementary (from *complete*)

plet: complete (**Synonyms:** total, whole, intact), completion (from *plere*, to fill)

plex: complex (**Synonyms:** complicated, intricate, involved), complexion (from *plectare*, to weave)

plic: complicate, complicated (see synonyms, previous entry), complication (*plicare*, to weave, fold)

plim: compliment (**Synonyms:** praise, eulogy. tribute), complimentary (from *complete*)

plot: complot (a plotting together; conspiracy; now archaic; may be seen in Shakespeare) (from *pelote*, ball)

ply: comply (from *complete*)

pon: component (**Synonyms:** element, constituent, ingredient) (*ponere*, to put)

port: comport (**Synonyms:** behave, conduct, demean), comportment (*portare*, to bring, carry)

pos: compose, composed, composer, composite, composition, compositor, compost, composure (from *ponere*, to put)

pound: compound (see *component*)

prehen: comprehend (**Synonyms:** understand, apprehend; see another set of synonyms at *comprise*, below) comprehensive (*prehendere*, to catch hold)

press: compress (**Synonyms:** contract, shrink, condense), compression, compressor (from *premere*, to press)

pris: comprise (**Synonyms:** include, comprehend, embrace) (see *prehend*)

pro: compromise (*pro-* prefixes *mise*, from *mittere*, to send)

puls: compulsion (driving force), compulsive, compulsory (from *compel*)

punct: compunction (**Synonyms: 1)** penitence, repentance, remorse; **2)** qualm, scruple) (from *pungere*, to prick)

145

Element	From	Meaning	Examples
com- (cont'd)			purg: compurgation (*purgare*, to make pure)
			put: compute (see synonyms at *calculate*, under *calc* family), computer, computation (*putare*, to reckon)
			DOUBLETS:
			complacent:complaisant; compost:compote; compute:count
			ITALIAN: *comprimario* (literally, with the first; a singer of a secondary role in an opera)
			col-:
			labor: collaborate (to work together, especially in some literary, artistic, or scientific undertaking; to cooperate with an enemy invader) {collaboration} (*laborare*, to work)
			laps: collapse (from *labi*, to fall)
			lat: collate (see synonyms at *compare*, above), collation (from *ferre*, to bear)
			later: collateral (*latus*, a side)
			leag: colleague (see synonyms at *companion*, above) (from *legare*, to appoint as deputy)
			lect: collect (**Synonyms:** gather, assemble, muster), collectanea, collected, collectible, collection, collective, collector (from *legere*, to gather)
			leg: college, collegial, collegian, collegiate (from *colleague*)
			lid: collide (from *laedere*, to strike, injure)
			lig: colligate (*ligare*, to bind)
			lim: collimate (from *linear*, to make straight)
			lis: collision (from *collide*)
			loc: collocate (to arrange or place together, especially, side by side) (*locus*, place)
			log: collogue (from *colloquy*)
			loq: colloquial, colloquy (*loqui*, to speak)
			lud: collude (to conspire) (*ludere*, to play)
			lus: collusion {collusive} (from *collude*)
			NOTE: Not all words beginning with *col* are assimilations, e.g., *collar, collard, collier, colloid, collotype.*
			con-: (before *c, d, g, j, n, q, s, t,* or *v,* or sometimes *f*)
			caten: concatenate, concatenation (a writing device as well as a computer term) (*caten*, chain link)
			cav: concave, concavity (*cavus*, hollow)
			ceal: conceal (**Synonyms:** hide, secrete, cache), concealment (from *celare*, to hide)
			ced: concede (**Synonyms:** yield, grant, acquiesce) (*cedere*, to go, yield)
			ceit: conceit (**Synonyms:** pride, vanity, vainglory), conceited (from *conceive*)
			ceiv: conceive (**Synonyms:** imagine, picture) (from *capere*, to take)
			celeb: concelebrate (*celeber*, frequented, populous)
			center: concenter (to bring or converge to a common center)
			centr: concentrate, concentration, concentrative, concentric (from *concenter*)
			cept: (see *conceive*)
			concept (**Synonyms:** idea, thought, notion)
			conceptacle (or organ or cavity enclosing reproductive bodies)
			conception (see synonyms at *concept*, previous entry)

Element	From	Meaning	Examples
com- (cont'd)			conceptus (the entire product of conception until birth, including the sac, cord, and placenta)
			cern: concern (**Synonyms:** solicitude, worry, anxiety), concerned, concerning (*cernere*, to sift)
			cert: concert, concerted, concertina, concertino (a brief concerto), concerto (*certare*, to contend, strive)
			cess: concession, concessionaire, concessionary, concessive (from *concede*)
			cinn: concinnity (a skillful arrangement of parts; harmony; elegance, especially of literary style) (from *caedere*, to cut)
			cis: concise (**Synonyms:** terse, laconic, succinct), concision (from *caedere*, to cut)
			clav: conclave (a private or secret meeting) (*clavis*, key)
			clud: conclude (**Synonyms:** 1) determine, settle, resolve; 2) close, end, terminate; 3) infer, deduce, gather) (from *claudere*, to shut)
			clus: conclusion (**Synonyms:** end, finish, outcome), conclusive (from *conclude*)
			coct: concoct {concoction, concoctive} (*coquere*, to cook)
			comit: concomitance, concomitant (accompanying, concurrent) (from *comes*, companion)
			cord: concord (agreement, harmony), concordance, concordant, concordat (*cord*, heart)
			cours: concourse (from *currere*, to run)
			cres: concrescence (in *biology*, a growing together of parts or cells) (from *crescere*, to grow)
			cret: concrete, concretion, concretionary, concretism, concretize (see *concrescence*)
			cub: concubinage, concubine (*cubare*, to lie down)
			cup: concupiscence (strong desire or appetite, especially sexual desire; lust) {concupiscent} (*cupere*, to desire)
			cur: concur (**Synonyms:** consent, agree, accede), concurrence, concurrent (*currere*, to run)
			cuss: concuss, concussion (from *quatere*, to shake)
			demn: condemn (**Synonyms:** criticize, reprehend, censure), condemnation, condemnatory (from *damnum*, loss, injury)
			dens: condensation, condense (**Synonyms:** contract, shrink, deflate), condensed, condenser (*densus*, thick)
			dign: condign (deserved; suitable: said especially of punishment for wrongdoing) (*dignus*, worth)
			dim: condiment (a seasoning or relish for food, as pepper, mustard, sauces, etc.) (from *dere*, to put, do)
			dit: condition (**Synonyms:** state, situation, status), conditional, conditioned (from *dicere*, to speak)
			dol: condole {condolatory}, condolence (see synonyms at *compassion*, above) (*dolere*, to grieve)
			dom: condominium (jointly owned) (*dominus*, master)
			don: condonation (pardon of an offense; act of condoning, especially of implying forgiveness by overlooking an offense), condone (**Synonyms:** forgive, excuse) (*donare*, to give)
			duc: conduce, conducive, conduct (**Synonyms:** direct, manage, control), conduction, conductor (*ducere*, to lead)

147

Element	From	Meaning	Examples
com- (cont'd)			fab: confabulate (to talk together in an informal way) (*fabulari*, to converse)
			fect: confect, confection, confectionary, confectioner (from *facere*, to make, do)
			fed: confederacy (**Synonyms:** comrade, ally, accomplice), confederation (from *fidere*, to trust, believe)
			fer: confer (**Synonyms:** give, grant, present), conference, conferment (*ferre*, to bear)
			fess: confess (**Synonyms:** acknowledge, admit), confessedly, confession (from *fateri*, to acknowledge)
			fid: confidant, confide (**Synonyms:** commit, entrust, relegate), confidence, confident, confidential (*fidere*, to trust)
			fig: configuration (**Synonyms:** form, figure, outline), configure (from *fingere*, to form, shape)
			fin: confine (**Synonyms:** limit, bound, restrict), confinement (*finis*, end, limit, boundary)
			firm: confirm (**Synonyms:** substantiate, corroborate, verify), confirmation, confirmed (*firmare*, to strengthen)
			fisc: confiscate (*fiscus*, money basket or chest; public treasury)
			flag: conflagrant, conflagration (a big, destructive fire) (*flagrare*, to burn)
			flat: conflate, conflation (from *flare*, to blow)
			flict: conflict (**Synonyms:** fight, contention, contest), conflicted (from *fligere*, to strike)
			flu: confluence, confluent, conflux (*fluere*, to flow)
			foc: confocal (in *mathematics*, having the same focus or foci)
			form: conform (**Synonyms:** 1) adjust, accommodate; 2) agree, accord, harmonize), conformable, conformation, conformity) (*forma*, shape, figure, image)
			found: confound (**Synonyms:** puzzle, perplex, confuse), confounded (from *fundere*, to pour)
			frat: confraternity (*frater*, brother)
			frer: confrere (a fellow member or worker; colleague or associate, as in a profession; see *confraternity*)
			front: confront {confrontation, confrontment} (*frons*, forehead)
			fus: confuse (see synonyms at *confound*), confusion (from *confound*)
			geal: congeal (from *gelare*, to freeze)
			gel: congelation (see *congeal*)
			gen: congener, congenial (**Synonyms:** friendly, genial, pleasant), congenital (**Synonyms:** innate, inborn, inbred) (from *gignere*, to produce)
			gest: congest {congestion, congestive} (from *gerere*, to carry, perform)
			glob: conglobate (also, *conglobe*) {conglobation} (*globus*, ball)
			glom: conglomerate, conglomeration (*glomus*, ball)
			glut: conglutinant, conglutinate (*gluten*, glue)
			grat: congratulate {congratulator, congratulatory}, congratulation (*gratus*, agreeable; *gratulari*, to wish joy)
			greg: congregant, congregate (to collect into a flock; gather), congregation, congregationalism (*greg*, flock, herd)

Element	From	Meaning	Examples
com- (cont'd)			gress: congress, congressional (from *gradus*, step)

gru: congruence, congruent, congruity, congruous (from IE
ghreu, to collapse, topple)

ject: conjectural, conjecture (**Synonyms**: guess, surmise)
(from *jacere*, to throw)

join: conjoin, conjoint (from *jungere*, to join)

jug: conjugal, conjugant, conjugate (*jugare*, to join)

junct: conjunct, conjunction, conjunctive (from *jungere*, to join)

jur: conjuration, conjure, conjurer (also, *conjuror*) (*jurare*, to
swear)

nat: connate, connatural (from *nasci*, to be born)

nect: connect (**Synonyms**: join, combine, unite), connection, connective (*nectere*, to fasten)

niv: (from *nictare*, to wink)
connivance, connive {conniver}
connivent (in *biology*, with the ends inclined toward each
other, as wings or anthers)

not: connotation {connotative}, connote (from *noscere*, to
know)

nub: connubial (*nubere*, to marry)

quer: conquer (**Synonyms**: vanquish, defeat, subdue) (from
quaerere, to seek, acquire)

ques: conquest (**Synonyms**: victory, triumph) (see *conquer*)

sang: consanguineous (also, *sanguine*), consanguinity (related
by blood) (*sanguis*, blood)

sci: conscience, conscientious, conscious (*scire*, to know)

script: conscript (from *scribere*, to write)

secr: consecrate (**Synonyms**: devote, dedicate, hallow), con-
secration (from *sacer*, holy)

secu: consecution, consecutive (see *consequence*)

sen: consensus, consent (**Synonyms**: assent, concur, accede),
consentaneous, consentient, consentual (*sentire*, to feel)

sequ: consequence (**Synonyms**: 1) effect, result, outcome;
2) importance, moment, weight), consequential (*sequi*, to
follow)

serv: conservancy, conservation, conservative, conservatoire,
conservator, conservatory, conserve (*servare*, to keep or hold)

sid: (*sidus*, star)

consider (**Synonyms**: study, contemplate, reflect), considerable

considerate (**Synonyms**: thoughtful, attentive), consideration,
considered, considering

sign: consign (**Synonyms**: commit, entrust, confide), con-
signee, consignment, consignor (*signare*, to sign)

sist: consist, consistency (also, *consistence*), consistent, con-
sistory (*sistere*, to stand)

soc: consociate {consociation} (*sociare*, to join)

sol: consolation, consolatory, console (**Synonyms**: comfort,
solace, relieve) (*solari*, to solace, comfort)

solid: consolidate (see synonyms at *connect*, above), consolida-
tion (*solidus*, solid)

son: consonance, consonant, consonantal (*sonus*, sound)

Element	From	Meaning	Examples
com- (cont'd)			sort: consort, consortium (*sors*, share, lot)

spect: conspectus (a general view; survey; a summary; outline; synopsis; digest) (from *specere*, to see)

spic: conspicuous (**Synonyms**: noticeable, prominent, outstanding) (see *conspect*)

spir: conspiracy (**Synonyms**: plot, intrigue, cabal), conspira-
tor, conspire (*spirare*, to breathe)

stab: constable, constabulary (*stabulum*, stable)

stan: constancy, constant (**Synonyms**: 1) faithful, loyal,
staunch, or *stanch*; 2) continual, continuous, incessant)
(from *stare*, to stand)

stell: constellation (an arbitrary configuration of stars, usually
named after some object, animal, or mythological being)
{constellatory} (*stellare*, to shine; *stella*, star)

stip: constipate, constipation (*stipare*, to cram, pack)

stit: constituency, constituent (see synonyms at *component*),
constitute, constitution, constitutional, constitutive (from
statuere, to set)

strain: constrain (**Synonyms**: force, compel, coerce) con-
strained, constraint (from *stringere*, to draw tight)

strict: constrict, constriction, constrictor (see *constrain*)

stru: construable, construe (**Synonyms**: explain, expound,
explicate) (*struere*, to pile up, build)

struct: construct (**Synonyms**: make, form, fashion), construction, constructive (from *struere*, to pile up, build)

sub: consubstantial, consubstantiation (*sub-* prefixes *stant*)

sul: consul, consulate (see *consult*)

sult: consult (literally, to call together), consultation, consul-
tative (also, *consultatory*) (from IE base *sel*, to take, seize)
[*sult* is not the same root as in *insult, desultory*; see *salt*, from
saltire, to leap]

sum: consume (**Synonyms**: 1) exhaust, expend; 2) squander,
dissipate) {consumable}, consumedly, consumer, con-
sumerism (*sumere*, to take)

summ: consummate (**Synonyms**: 1) complete, perfect, accomplish; 2) finished, supreme), consummation (*summa*,
highest)

sump: consumption, consumptive (see *consume*, above)

tact: contact, contactor (from *tangere*, to touch)

tag: contagion, contagious, contagium (from *contact*)

tain: contain (**Synonyms**: hold, accommodate), container,
containment (from *tenere*, to hold)

tam: contaminant, contaminate (**Synonyms**: taint, pollute,
defile), contamination (see *contact*)

temn: contemn (to treat with contempt, scorn, disdain;
Synonyms: despise, scorn, disdain) (*temnere*, to slight)

templ: contemplate (see synonyms at *consider*), contemplative
(**Synonyms**: pensive, reflective, meditative) (*templum*,
space in heavens marked off for augural observation)

tempo: contemporaneous (**Synonyms**: contemporary, coeval,
synchronous), contemporary (from *tempus*, time)

tend: contend {contender} (*tendere*, to extend, reach out)

Element	From	Meaning	Examples
com- (cont'd)			tent: (note difference in root meanings of *content* and *contention*)

(continued)

com- (cont'd) — Examples:

tent: (note difference in root meanings of *content* and *contention*)

content (**Synonym:** satisfy), contented (from *contain*)

contention (**Synonyms:** 1) discord, strife, dissension; 2) conflict, struggle, contest) (from *contend*)

contentious (**Synonyms:** belligerent, bellicose, pugnacious) (from *contend*)

term: conterminous (*terminus*, end)

test: contest (see synonyms at *conflict*), contestant, contestation (*testis*, a witness)

text: context, contextual, contexture (from *texere*, to weave)

tig: contiguity, contiguous (**Synonyms:** adjacent, adjoining, tangent) (from *contact*)

tin: continence (self-restraint in, especially total abstinence from, sexual activity), continent, continental (from *contain*)

ting: contingence, contingency (**Synonyms:** emergency, exigency, crisis), contingent (from *contact*)

tinu: continual (**Synonyms:** continuous, constant, incessant), continuance, continuant, continuation, continuative, continuator, continue (**Synonyms:** endure, abide, persist), continuity, continuo, continuous, continuum (from *contain*)

tort: contort (**Synonyms:** deform, warp), contortion, contortionist (from *torquere*, to twist)

tour: contour (**Synonyms:** outline, profile, silhouette) (from *tornare*, to turn)

tract: contract (see synonyms at *condense*), contraction, contractor, contractual, contracture (from *trahere*, to draw)

trib: contribute, contribution, contributory (*tribuere*, to assign)

trit: contrite, contrition (**Synonyms:** penitence, repentance, compunction) (from *terere*, to rub)

triv: contrivance, contrive (to think up; devise, scheme), contrived (from *tropus*, turn)

tum: contumacious, contumacy (stubborn refusal to submit to authority), contumely (*tumere*, to swell up)

tus: contuse, contusion (from *tundere*, to beat)

urb: conurbation (*urbs*, city)

val: convalesce, convalescence, convalescent (*valere*, to be strong)

vec: convection (from *vehere*, to carry, bear)

ven: convenance, convene (**Synonyms:** call, summon, convoke), convenience, convenient (*venire*, to come)

vent: convent (**Synonyms:** cloister, nunnery, monastery), conventicle, convention, conventional, conventual (from *venire*, to come)

verg: converge, convergence (*vergere*, to turn, bend)

vers: (see *convert*)

conversable (easy to talk to; affable; liking to talk), conversant, conversation

converse (**Synonyms:** speak, talk, discourse)

conversion

vert: convert (**Synonyms:** 1) change, alter, modify; 2) transform, transmute), converter, convertible (*vertere*, to turn)

vex: convex, convexity (from *vehere*, to bring)

Element	From	Meaning	Examples
com- (cont'd)			vey: convey (**Synonyms:** bear, transport, transmit), con-veyance, conveyor (also *conveyer*) (from *via*, way)
			vict: convict, conviction (**Synonyms: 1**) certainty, certitude, assurance; **2**) opinion, belief, sentiment), convictive (from *convince*)
			vinc: convince, convincing (*vincere*, to conquer)
			viv: convivial (having to do with a feast or festive activity; fond of eating, drinking, and good company; sociable; jovial) (*vivere*, to live)
			voc: convocation (*vocare*, to call)
			vok: convoke (see synonyms at *convene*) (see *convocation*)
			vol: convolute (rolled up in the form of a spiral with the coils falling one upon the other, as in leaves or shells; coiled), convoluted, convolution (see *convolve*)
			volv: convolve, convolvulus (*volvere*, to roll, turn)
			voy: convoy (**Synonyms:** accompany, attend, escort) (see *convey*)
			vuls: convulse, convulsion, convulsive (from *vellere*, to pluck)
			FRENCH: concierge (from *servus*, slave)
			INTERDISCIPLINARY: concretion (in *geology*, an inclu-sion in sedimentary rock, usually rounded and harder than the surrounding rock, resulting from the formation of succeeding layers of mineral matter about some nucleus, as a grain of sand; in *medicine*, a solidified mass, usually inorganic, de-posited in the body; calculus)
			cor-:
			rad: corrade {corrasion, corrasive} (*radere*, to scrape)
			rect: correct (**Synonyms:** accurate, exact, precise), correc-tion, correctitude, corrective (from *regere*, to lead straight)
			rig: corrigendum (plural, *corrigenda*), corrigible (see *correct*)
			rob: corroborant, corroborate (**Synonyms:** confirm, substan-tiate), corroborative (*robur*, strength)
			rod: corrode {corrosion, corrosive} (*rodere*, to gnaw)
			rug: corrugate, corrugation (*rugare*, to wrinkle)
			rupt: corrupt (**Synonyms:** debase, deprave, pervert), corrup-tion, corruptive (from *rumpere*, to break)
			DOUBLE PREFIXED ROOT:
			correlate, correlation, correlative (*cor-* assimilates *com-*, with, together + *re-*, back, again; *late* is from *ferre*, to bear)
			correspond (**Synonyms:** conform, accord, coincide), corre-spondence, correspondent (*cor-* assimilates *com-*, with togeth-er; *re-* prefixes *spond*)
			NOTE: Not all words beginning with *cor* are assimilations, e.g., Spanish *corrida* (a bullfighting exhibition), from same base as *corridor*; corridor, corroboree.
			co-: (before *g, gn, h,* and *vowels*)
			act: coact, coaction (from *agere*, to do)
			ad-:
			coadjutant, coadjutor (an assistant; helper) (*ad-* prefixes *jut*, from *juvare*, aid)
			coadunate (united; joined together; in *biology*, grown together) (*ad-* prefixes *unare*, to unite)

Element	From	Meaning	Examples
com- (cont'd)			ag: coagulable, coagulant, coagulase, coagulate, coagulum (*agere*, to drive)

ag: coagulable, coagulant, coagulase, coagulate, coagulum (*agere*, to drive)
alesc: (*alescere*, to grow up)
coalesce (**Synonyms**: mix, mingle, fuse)
{coalition (**Synonyms**: alliance, league, union)}
apt: coaptation (the joining or adjusting of parts to each other, as the ends of a broken bone) (*aptare*, to fit)
arct: coarctate (in *biology*, compressed or restricted) (*artare*, to press together)
ax: coaxal, coaxial (having a common axis)
effic: coefficient (*ef-*, from *ex-*, prefixes *fic*, from *facere*, to make)
enzym: coenzyme (*en-* prefixes *zym*, to ferment)
erc: coerce (**Synonyms**: force, compel, constrain), coercion, coercive (from *arcere*, to confine)
ev: coeval (see synonyms at *contemporary*) (from *aevum*, age)
ex: coexecutor [*ex-* prefixes *(s)ectut*, to follow]
gni: (*gnoscere*, to know)
cognition (the process of knowing in the broadest sense)
cognizable, cognizance, cognizant (**Synonyms**: aware, conscious, sensible), cognize
hab: cohabit (to live together as husband and wife, especially when not legally married; to live or exist together; share the same place) {cohabitation}, cohabitant (*habere*, to have, hold)
heir: coheir {coheiress}
her: (from *haerere*, to stick)
cohere (to stick together, as parts of a mass; to be united by molecular cohesion; **Synonyms**: adhere, cling, cleave)
coherence (cohesion)
coherent (sticking together; cohesion)
hes: cohesion, cohesive (see *cohere*, previous entry)
hort: cohort (enclosed company; hence, retinue, crowd) (*cohors*, enclosure; from IE base *ghrtis*, a gathering)
it: coition, coitus (both terms mean sexual intercourse) {coital} (from *ire*, to go)
WORDS WITH ALTERED ELEMENTS:
cogent (forceful and to the point, as a reason or argument; compelling; convincing) (from *agere*, to drive)
cogitate (to think deeply and seriously about) (agitare, to set in motion)
cognate (*nasci*, to be born)
cognomen (spelling influenced by association with *gnomen*, from Greek *gnoma*, mark, token; the third or family name of an ancient Roman) (*nomen*, name)
cognoscenti (Italian; from *cognition*, above; a person with special knowledge in some field, especially in the fine arts)
cognovit (short for *cognovit actionem*, he has acknowledged the action; a written acknowledgment of a debt)
VARIANT PREFIX + DISGUISED ROOT:
custom (**Synonyms**: habit, practice, wont) (*com-*, intensive + *suescere*, to become accustomed)
MUSIC TERMS:
con brio (with brilliance)

Element	From	Meaning	Examples
com- (cont'd)			*con dolore* (with sadness) *con moto* [with (animated) movement] *continuo*, a continuous bass accompaniment ITALIAN: *condottiere* (in Europe from the 14th to 16th centuries, a captain of a band of mercenaries) SPANISH: conquian (same as *cooncan*, a form of the card game rummy) (from *¿con quién?*, with whom?) conquistador (one who conquers; conqueror; see *Doublets*) ECCLESIASTICAL TERM: *confiteor* (I confess; a formal prayer, as at the beginning of a Mass, in which sins are confessed) DOUBLETS: conqueror:conquistador INTERDISCIPLINARY: conjugate (in *botany*, having two pairs of leaflets, as some pinnate leaves: bijugate; in *chemistry*, related to each other by the difference of a proton: said of acids and bases; in *grammar*, derived from the same base and, usually, related in meaning; in *mathematics*, specially related or having the same or similar properties, as two points, lines, or quantities) cohesion (in *botany*, the union of like flower parts; in *physics*, the force by which the molecules of a substance are held together: distinguished from *adhesion*) NB: The following words are not in this family: *comrade* (see *camera*), *contrast* (from *contra-*, against). CROSS REFERENCE: *syn-*
con			See *cun* for *cone*.
cond*	Latin *condere*: to hide (IE: *dhe*, to put, do)	to store, hide	PREFIXED ROOT: *abs-*: abscond (to go away hastily and secretly; run away and hide, especially in order to escape the law) (*abs-*, away) *in-*: incondite (ill-constructed; unpolished; crude (*in-*, not) *re-*: recondite (beyond the grasp of the ordinary mind or understanding; profound; abstruse; obscure and concealed) (*re-*, back) DISGUISED ROOT: sconce (a bracket attached to a wall for holding a candle, candles, or the like) (Middle English *sconse*; aphetic of Old French *esconse*, dark lantern; from *escondre*, to hide; ultimately from *abscond*) PLACENAME: Escondido, California (literally, hidden) NB: *Incondite* (from *condition*) is not in this family. CROSS REFERENCE: *calyp, cel, cover, crypt, tech/teg*
consul**	Latin *consulere*: to deliberate (IE: *sel*, to take, seize)	counsel	ROOT NOTE: The *sul* of this root should not be confused with the *sul* of the same spelling as in *insult*, *result*, and other words derived from *saltare*: *assault*, *resilient*, *somersault*; in each of these words, the root means to jump, to leap (see *salt*). SIMPLE ROOT: consul {consular}, consulate consult (to talk things over in order to decide or plan something), consultant, consultation, consultative, consulting consultor DISGUISED ROOT: counsel (Synonyms: 1) advise, caution, warn; 2) lawyer, counselor, attorney)

Element	From	Meaning	Examples
consul (cont'd)			council (a group of people called together for consultation, discussion, advice, etc.) [These two words are often confused in both form and meaning.] ALGONQUIAN WORD: caucus (*American Heritage Dictionary*; *Webster's New World Dictionary* indicates that *caucus* may be from Middle Greek *kaukos*, drinking cup) NO CROSS REFERENCE
contr-***	Latin *contra*	against, opposite, opposed to, contrary	NOTE: In *music*, this element means "lower in pitch or register," as in *contrabassoon*. EXTENDED PREFIX: contrariety (the condition or quality of being contrary; plural, anything that is contrary; inconsistency or discrepancy) contrary (**Synonyms:** opposite, antithetical, contradictory) contrast (**Synonyms:** compare, collate) PREFIXED ROOT: *contra-*: cept: contraception, contraceptive [*contra-* + *(con)ception*; *capere*, to hold, seize] dict: contradict, contradiction, contradictory (see synonyms at *contrary*, above) (*dicere*, to speak) in: contraindicate (*in-* prefixes *dic*, from *dicere*, to speak) posit: contraposition, contrapositive (from *ponere*, to place) punt: contrapuntal, contrapuntist (from *counterpoint*) (from *pungere*, to prick) vall: contravallation (*vallum*, wall, entrenchment) ven: contravene {contravention} (*venir*, to come) *contro-*: vers: controversial, controversy (from *vertere*, to turn) vert: controvert (**Synonyms:** disprove, refute, confute) (*vertere*, to turn) *contre-*: coup: contrecoup (explore *contrecoup* as a medical term) (*coup*, a blow) dans: contredanse (a folk dance in which the partners form two facing lines) temps: contretemps (an inopportune happening causing confusion or embarrassment; awkward mishap) (*temps*, time) *counter-*: (examples of) act: counteract attack: counterattack balanc: counterbalance blow: counterblow chang: counterchange (to transpose; interchange; to checker; variegate) charg: countercharge check: countercheck claim: counterclaim clock: counterclockwise cult: counterculture die: counterdie espion: counterespionage

Element	From	Meaning	Examples
contr (cont'd)			feit: counterfeit (**Synonyms: 1**) false, sham, bogus; 2) artificial, synthetic, ersatz) (*feit* from *facere*, to make, do)

feit: counterfeit (**Synonyms: 1**) false, sham, bogus; 2) artificial, synthetic, ersatz) (*feit* from *facere*, to make, do)

foil: counterfoil (the stub of a check)

forc: counterforce

intellig: counterintelligence (*intelligence* is from *intellect*, which itself is from *inter-*, between + *legere*, to gather, pick, choose)

mand: countermand (to cancel or revoke a command or order; to call back or order back by a contrary order) (*mandare*, to command)

march: countermarch

mov: countermove

offer: counteroffer (*of-* assimilates *ob-*, against)

pan: counterpane (a quilted bedspread) (from *puncta*, point)

part: counterpart

plot: counterplot

point: counterpoint (literally, pointed against; the technique of combining two or more distinct lines of music that sound simultaneously, especially with emphasis on melodic, as opposed to harmonic, progression) (from *pungere*, to prick)

pois: counterpoise (from *pendere*, to weigh)

pro: counterproductive, counterproposal

re: counterreformation (see *Religious Movement* below) counterrevolution (*re-* prefixes *volution*)

scarp: counterscarp (the outer slope or wall of a ditch or moat in a fortification) (Italian *scarpa*, scarp, slope)

shaft: countershaft (an intermediate shaft that transmits motion from the main shaft of a machine to a working part)

sink: countersink

typ: countertype (an opposite type; a parallel, or corresponding type)

vail: countervail (make up for; compensate) (from *valere*, to be strong)

ELIDED PREFIXED ROOT:

contralto (*contra + alto*)

control (from *contra- + rotulus*, roll)

PREFIX + PREFIX: encounter (**Synonyms**: battle, engagement, campaign)

DISGUISED ELEMENT:

country (directly from Old French *contree*, from Vulgar Latin *terra contrata*, region, that land which is against, as one entered or left the city)

comptroller (pronounced *controller*)

LATIN LEGAL TERM: *a contrario*

FRENCH : *au contraire* (on the contrary)

RELIGIOUS MOVEMENT: Counter-Reformation

NB: Do not confuse this prefix with *contract*, derived from *con- + tract* (to draw together).

CROSS REFERENCE: *anti-, ob-*

The terms used in the scientific world are largely, and in some sciences almost exclusively, derived from the classics.   Bernard Walker

Element	From	Meaning	Examples
cop*	Greek *koptein*: to strike (IE: *skep*, to cut)	to cut	PREFIXED ROOT: apo-: apocapate, apocope (the cutting off or dropping of the last sound or sounds of a word, e.g., *mos'* for *most*) (*apo-*, away, from) peri-: pericope (a passage, usually short, from a written work) (*peri-*, around) syn-: syncopate (to cut short; in *music*, a temporary displacement of the regular metrical accent caused typically by stressing the weak beat), syncopation, **syncope** {syncopal} (*syn-*, with, together) DISGUISED ROOT: comma (*komma*, clause in a sentence; literally, that which is cut off) INTERDISCIPLINARY: **syncope** (in *grammar*, the shortening of a word by the omission of a sound, letter, or syllable from the middle of the word; for example, *bos'n* for *boatswain*; in *medicine*, a partial or complete temporary suspension of respiration and circulation due to cerebral ischemia; *ischemia*, localized tissue anemia due to obstruction of the inflow of arterial blood) CROSS REFERENCE: *cis, scind, scis, sect, tom*
copr*	Greek *kopros*	dung, feces	LEADING ROOT COMPOUND: lal: copralalia (filthy, disgusting speech) (*lalia*, speech) *copro*: lit coprolite (fossil dung) (*lithos*, stone) log: coprology (a study of the feces; figuratively, disgusting literature) {coprological} (*logy*, study of) phag: coprophagy (the habit, especially of insects and birds, of dung-eating) (*phag*, to eat) phil: coprophilia (love of filth) (*phila*, love of) NO CROSS REFERENCE
coqu*	Latin *coquere* (IE: *pekw*, to cook)	to cook, ripen	DISGUISED ROOT: apricot [directly from Arabic *al-birquq*; from Latin *praecoquus*, early-ripened (fruit); with the exception of initial letter coming from Arabic article *al*, the, *apricot* has the same derivation as *precocious*] cook cuisine (French; now archaic when used to designate *kitchen*; style of cooking; manner of preparing food; the food prepared, as at a restaurant) (from Latin *culina*, kitchen) culinary (of the kitchen; of cooking; suitable for or used in cooking) kiln (a furnace or oven for drying, burning, or baking something, as bricks, grain, or pottery) (Middle English *kylne*; from Old English *cylne*; from Latin *culina*, cookstove) kitchen quittor [literally, the act of boiling (*Webster's Third New International*); a foot disease, especially of horses, characterized by a pus-forming fistula on the coronet] PREFIXED DISGUISED ROOT: con-: concoct (literally, to cook together; to make by combining various ingredients; compound; to devise, invent, or plan) {concoction, concoctive} (*con-*, with, together) de-: decoct (literally, to cook down; to extract the essence, flavor, etc. of by boiling), decoction (*de-*, down)

157

Element	From	Meaning	Examples
coqu (cont'd)			*pre-*: (before) precocial (pertaining to birds whose newly hatched young are covered with down and fully active; opposed to *altricial*, which see under *al*, nourish) precocious (literally, ripened beforehand; matured to a point beyond what is normal for the age, as *a precocious child*) *ri-*: ricotta (cooked, or boiled again) (*ri-* from *re-*, again) DISGUISED TRAILING ROOT COMPOUND: bis: biscuit (literally, twice-baked) (*bis*, twice) CROSS REFERENCE: *pept*
cor,** curv	Latin (from Greek *ko- rone*: anything bent (IE: *sker*, to turn, bend)	crown, curve	SIMPLE ROOT: *cor*: corona, coronation, coronary, coroner (officer of the crown, whose duty was to determine the cause of death), coronet *curv*: curvaceous, curvature (in *medicine*, the abnormal curving of a part, as *curvature of the spine*), curve (**Synonyms:** bend, twist), curvet PREFIXED ROOT: *in-*: incurvate, incurve (to curve inward) (*in-*, in) LEADING ROOT COMPOUND: lin: curvinlinear (consisting of or enclosed by a curved line or lines) ENGLISH COGNATE: crown NO CROSS REFERENCE
cord			See *chord*, string.
cord***	Latin *cordis* (IE: *kerd*, heart)	heart (figurative)	SIMPLE ROOT: cordate (in *biology*, having a heart-shaped outline: said of a leaf) cordial (**Synonyms:** amiable, affable, obliging; also an aromatic, syrupy alcoholic drink; liqueur; that which warms the heart) cordially (in a cordial manner; with sincere good will; also, with zeal; vigorously and sincerely; emphatically, as *the opponents cordially disliked each other*) cordiality PREFIXED ROOT: *ac-*: accord {according, accordingly}, accordance, accordant, accordion (*ac-* assimilates *ad-*, to, toward) *con-*: concord, concordance, concordant, concordat (literally, a meeting of the hearts; a compact; formal agreement; covenant) (*con-*, with, together) *dis-*: discord (**Synonyms:** strife, contention, dissension), discordant (*dis-*, apart, away) *ob-*: obcordate (in *botany*, heart-shaped and joined to the stem at the apex: said of certain leaves) (*ob-*, against) *re-*: record (literally, to call to mind; remember) (*re-*, again) DOUBLE PREFIXED ROOT: disaccord (*dis-*, not + *ac-* assimilates *ad-*) LEADING ROOT COMPOUND: form: cordiform (heart-shaped) TRAILING ROOT COMPOUND: miseri: misericord (literally, merciful heart; formerly, a relaxation of the strict observance of a rule or rules of a monastery)

Element	From	Meaning	Examples
cord (cont'd)			DISGUISED ROOT: core (of fruit); courage chord [in *music*, from *accord*, harmony; while the harpsichord does, in fact, produce harmony, *chord* of *harpsichord* means string; see *chord* as a root (listed separately)] PREFIXED DISGUISED ROOT: *dis-*: discourage (to dishearten; literally, to take the heart out of something) (*dis-*, opposite) *en-*: encourage (literally, to put heart into), encouragement, encouraging (giving courage, hope, or confidence) (*en-*, in) PLACENAMES: Accord, Massachusetts; Coeur d'Alene, Idaho Creve Coeur (Missouri, Illinois) [*Crève-coeur* is French for "a *heartbreaking* situation," or "utter discouragement."] CROSS REFERENCE: *card (kard)*
corn**	Latin *cornu* (IE: *ker*, upper part of the body, head; yields English horn)	horn; projecting point	SIMPLE ROOT: corn (on foot) corne: cornea, corneous, corner cornet (a brass band instrument similar to the trumpet in pitch and construction, but more compact, with a longer tube and a deeper mouthpiece) corni: cornicle, corniculate (having horns or hornlike projections) cornu: cornu (in *anatomy*, any horn-shaped structure) {cornual, cornuted} LEADING ROOT COMPOUND: *corni*: fic: cornific, cornification (from *facere*, to make, do) form: corniform (in the form of a horn) *cornu*: copia: cornucopia (horn of plenty) (*copia*, plenty) lit: cornulite (horn-shaped stone) (*lithos*, stone) TRAILING ROOT COMPOUND: bi: bicorn (having two horns or hornlike parts; crescent-shaped; also, *bicornuate*) (*bi*, two) clav: clavicorn (a group of beetle families with club-shaped antennae) (*clava*, club) longi: longicorn (literally, long-horned; having long feelers, or antennae, as some beetles) (*cornu*, horn) tri: tricorn (a three-cornered hat) (*tri*, three) uni: unicorn (a mythical horselike animal with a *single* horn growing from the center of its forehead; in the *Bible*, a *two*-horned, oxlike animal: Deuteronomy 33:17) (*uni*, one) CONSTELLATION: Capricorn (literally, goat horn; the constellation supposedly outlines a goat) PLACENAME: Unicorn, Maryland CROSS REFERENCE: *cerat (kerat)*
corp***	Latin *corpus* (IE: *krep*, body, form)	body	SIMPLE ROOT: corpora: corpora (plural of *corpus*), corporal (punishment; for military rank, see *capit*; meaning may also be influenced by this root as well) corporality, corporate, corporation, corporative, corporatory

159

Element	From	Meaning	Examples
corp (cont'd)			corpore: corporeal, corporeity
			corpos: corposant (from Portuguese *corpo santo*, holy body; from Latin *corpus sanctum*, holy body; Saint Elmo's fire)
			corps: corps, corpse (**Synonyms**: remains, carcass, cadaver)
			corpu: corpulence (also, *corpulency*), corpulent (fat and fleshy; stout; obese), corpus (plural, *corpa*), corpuscle, corpuscular
			PREFIXED ROOT:
			in-: (note difference in meanings of prefix in the following two sets of words)
			incorporeal (not consisting of matter; without material body or substance; in *law*, without physical evidence in itself but belonging as a right to a material thing or property, as a patent, copyright, etc.), incorporeity (*in*-, not)
			incorporate (*in*-, in)
			DISGUISED ROOT: corsage, corse, corselet, corset
			DOUBLETS: corpse:corps
			FRENCH EXPRESSION: *esprit de corps* [literally, spirit of the body (of persons); group spirit; sense of pride, honor, etc. shared by those in the same group or undertaking]
			SPANISH COGNATE: *cuerpo*
			LEGAL TERMS:
			corpus delicti (the body of the crime)
			habeas corpus [(that) you have the body: the first words in the Roman writ]
			PLACENAME: Corpus Christi, Texas (Body of Christ)
			CROSS REFERENCE: *soma* (not to be confused with Latin *somn*, sleep)
corr			See *cur* for *corridor*.
cosm***	Greek *kosmos*: order, universe	world, order; arrange, adorn	SIMPLE ROOT:
			cosme: cosmesis, cosmetic, cosmetician, cosmetize
			cosmi: cosmic (of the cosmos; relating to the universe exclusive of the earth; also, vast, grandiose), cosmism
			cosmo: cosmos (the universe regarded as an orderly, harmonious whole; any system regarded as ordered and whole)
			LEADING ROOT COMPOUND:
			cosmeto:
			log: cosmetologist, cosmetology (the skill or work of treating with or applying cosmetics, as in a beauty shop; beauty culture) (*logy*, study of)
			cosmo:
			drom: cosmodrome (as ending, a large field or arena; any of the sites in the Soviet Union from which artificial satellites and spacecraft are launched) (*drom*, run)
			gon: cosmogony (the astrophysical study of the origin, evolution, or generation of the universe) (*gony*, coming into being)
			graph: cosmography (the study of the constitution of the nature; a description of the world or universe) (*graph*, write)
			log: cosmology (*logy*, scientific study of)
			naut: cosmonaut (a Soviet astronaut) (*naut*, sailor)
			polis: cosmopolis (*polis*, city)
			polit: cosmopolitan (common to the whole world; at home in all parts of the earth or in many spheres of interest; in *biology*, growing or occurring in all or most parts of the earth; widely distributed), cosmopolite (see *cosmopolis*)

Element	From	Meaning	Examples
cosm (cont'd)			TRAILING ROOT COMPOUND: macro: macrocosm (the great world; the universe; any large complex entity; opposed to *microcosm*) (*marco*, large) micro: microcosm (a miniature universe; specifically, man regarded as an epitome of the world; a community regarded as a miniature or epitome of the world; in *ecology*, a small ecosystem, as a pond) (*micro*, small) FROM *COSMETIC*: cosmetologist (hairdresser) TRADEMARK: Cosmoline (an oil used in cosmetics and as a protective covering for firearms, metals, etc.) (*ol*, oil) PLACENAMES: Cosmos, Minnesota; Cosmopolis, Washington CROSS REFERENCE: *mund, tax*
cost*	Latin *costa*	rib, side	SIMPLE ROOT: costa, costard, costral PREFIXED ROOT: ac-: accost (to approach and speak to; greet first, before being greeted, especially in an intrusive way; to solicit for sexual purposes: said of a prostitute, etc.) (from *ad-*, to, toward) inter-: intercostal (between the ribs) (*inter-*, between) DISGUISED ROOT: cutlet SPANISH: *chuleta* (cutlet) ENGLISH: coast (Synonyms: shore, beach, strand) CROSS REFERENCE: *canth, hedr, lat, pleur*
cotyl*	Greek *kotyle*: cavity	cup-shaped	SIMPLE ROOT: cotyledon PREFIXED ROOT: hypo-: hypocotyl (the part of the axis, or stem, below the cotyledons in the embryo of a plant) (*hypo-*, under) TRAILING ROOT COMPOUND: di: dicotyledon (flowering plant with two seed leaves (*di*, two) mono: monocotyledon (a flowering plant having an embryo containing only one seed leaf) (*mono*, one) INTERDISCIPLINARY: cotyledon (in *anatomy*, a lobule of the placenta, especially of ruminants; in *botany*, a leaf of a plant embryo, being the first or one of the first to appear from a sprouting seed; also called *second leaf*) CROSS REFERENCE: *calyc, campan*
counter-			See *contr-*.
cour			See *cur* for *courante, courier, course.*
cout			See *sut* for *accouterment.*
cover***	French (see *Root Note*)	cover	ROOT NOTE: Root is a combination of *co-*, an intensive + Latin verb, *operire*, to hide; not related to *recover*, which see under *cap*, take, receive; also see *Prefixed Root*, under *recover*. SIMPLE ROOT: cover, coverage, coverlet covert (Synonyms: clandestine, stealthy, furtive) coverture (a covering; refuge; a concealment or disguise; in *law*, married woman) PREFIXED ROOT: dis-: (apart, away) discover [to find out, see, or know about first; Synonyms: learn, ascertain, determine; not to be confused with *invent*, to bring (something) into being which had not existed before; see *vent*]

Element	From	Meaning	Examples
cover (cont'd)			discovert (literally, not covered, hence not protected; in *law*, having no husband: said of a spinster, widow, or divorcée) discovery (in *law*, any pretrial procedures, as the taking of depositions, for compelling the disclosure of pertinent factual information) re-: re-cover (not to be confused with *recover*, doublet of *recuperate*) (*re-*, again) DISGUISED ROOT: curfew (literally, cover the fire; an order or regulation enjoining specified classes of the population to retire from the streets at a prescribed hour; from Old French *cuevrefeu*) kerchief (see note under *caput*) PLACENAME: Smackover, Arkansas (covered with sumac; named by early French explorers) CROSS REFERENCE: *teg/tect*
crac, crat***	Greek *kratos* (IE: *kar*, hard)	rule, power, form of government	TRAILING ROOT COMPOUND: aristocrat (aristocracy) (*aristos*; best, privileged) autocrat (autocracy) (*auto*, self) bureaucrat (bureaucracy) (*bureau*, administrative unit) democrat (democracy) (*demo*, people) isocrat (isocracy) (*iso*, same, equal) monocrat (monocracy) (*mono*, one) plutocrat (plutocracy) (*pluto*, wealth) theocrat (theocracy) (*theos*, god, God) pancratium (in ancient Greece and Rome, an athletic contest combining boxing and wrestling) (*pan*, all) CROSS REFERENCE: *dyn, erg, urg, pot, rect*
cras*	Greek *kerannynai*, to mix (IE: *kere*, to mix)	mixing	SIMPLE ROOT: crasis (literally, a mixture; vowel contraction in the elision of two adjacent words) PREFIXED ROOT: dys-: dyscrasia (an abnormality of some part of the body, as of the formed elements of the blood) (*dys-*, bad) TRAILING ROOT COMPOUND: idio: idiosyncrasy (literally, a private mixing or mixture; eccentricity) (*idios*, own, personal; *syn-*, with, together, prefixes *cras*) theo: theocrasy (see note under *theo*) (*theo*, god, God) DISGUISED ROOT: crater (literally, mixing bowl; mouth of a volcano) CROSS REFERENCE: *misc*
crat			See *crac* for *autocrat*, etc.
creas			See *cresc* for *increase;* *creat* for *pancreas*.
creat,* creas	Greek *kreas* (IE: *kreu*, congealed blood)	flesh, meat	SIMPLE ROOT: creatic, creatine, creatinine LEADING ROOT COMPOUND: phag: creaphagous (flesh-eating) (*phagein*, to eat) rrh: creatorrhea (the presence of undigested muscle fibers in the feces) (*rhoia*, flow) TRAILING ROOT COMPOUND: pan: pancreas (literally, all flesh; in *anatomy*, a long, soft, irregularly shaped gland lying behind the stomach, and secreting a digestive juice) (*pan*, all) NOTE: For *create*, see *cresc*. CROSS REFERENCE: *carn, sarc*

Element	From	Meaning	Examples
cred***	Latin *credere* (see *Root Note*)	to believe, trust	ROOT NOTE: This root is a combination of IE *kred*, magic power of a thing + *dhe*, to place, do. SIMPLE ROOT: crede: credence (belief, especially in the reports or testimony of another; **Synonyms:** belief, trust, confidence), credenda, credendum, credent, credentials credi: credibility, credible (**Synonyms:** plausible, specious), credit, creditor credo: credo (see *Credos* below) credu: credulity, credulous (tending to believe too readily; easily convinced; gullible) PREFIXED ROOT: *ac-*: accredit (**Synonyms:** authorize, commission, license), accreditation (*ac-* assimilates *ad-*, to, toward) *dis-*: discredit (*dis-*, reversal) *in-*: incredible, incredulous (*in-*, not) DOUBLE PREFIXED ROOT: disaccredit (*dis-*, away + *ac-* which assimilates *ad-*, to, toward) DISGUISED ROOT: creance, creant, creed (literally, to put one's heart into; see *Credos* below; from *cred* + *dhe*, to place; *cred* is related to *cord*, heart), grant PREFIXED DISGUISED ROOT: *mis-*: miscreant (an evil person; criminal; villain) (Anglo-Saxon *mis-*, wrong, bad) *re-*: recreant (literally, to give up the faith; originally, crying for mercy; cowardly, craven, disloyal, traitorous, apostate; as a *noun*, the person who manifests these characteristics) (*re-*, back, again) ITALIAN: credenza (from phrase *fare la credenza*; a buffet holding foods to be tasted before serving) CREDOS: Apostles' Creed; Nicene Creed; both begin with *Credo*: I believe CROSS REFERENCE: *fid*
crep*	Latin *crepare*: to crack (IE: *krep*, rattle, crack)	rattle, crack	SIMPLE ROOT: crepitate (to make a creaking or rattling sound; crackle) PREFIXED ROOT: *de-*: decrepit (weakened by old age, illness, or hard use; broken down; **Synonyms:** weak, feeble, infirm), decrepitate (*de-*, intensive) *dis-*: discrepancy (literally, to sound differently; lack of agreement, or an instance of this; inconsistency) (*dis-*, from) DISGUISED ROOT: craven (characterized by abject fear; **Synonyms:** cowardly, pusillanimous, dastardly; as a *noun*, a coward) crevice (a narrow crack or opening; fissure; cleft) kestrel (a bird known for its crackling cry) SPANISH: quebracho (literally, ax-breaker; a South American tree having very hard wood) NO CROSS REFERENCE

A word has power in and of itself. It comes from nothing into sound
and meaning; it gives origin to all things.
By means of words can (a person) deal with the world on equal terms.
N. Scott Momaday

Element	From	Meaning	Examples
cresc,* **** **creas,** **creat,** **cret,** **cru,** **cre**	Latin *crescere*: to grow (IE: *ker*, to grow)	to produce, grow	SIMPLE ROOT: *crea*: create, creation (The Creation: God's creating of the world) creationism (the doctrine that God creates a new soul for every human being born; opposed to *traducianism*, which see under both *trans-* and *duc*), creative, creativity, creator, creature *cres*: crescent, crescendo (Italian music term; see *decrescendo*, below), crescive PREFIXED ROOT: *cre*: *de-*: decrement (in *mathematics*, the quantity by which a variable decreases or is decreased: a negative decrement results in an increase) (*de-*, down, away) *in-*: increment (in *mathematics*, the quantity, usually small, by which a variable increases or is increased) {incremental} (*in-*, in, on) *creas*: *de-*: decrease (**Synonyms**: dwindle, lessen, reduce) (*de-*, down) *in-*: increase (**Synonyms**: enlarge, augment, multiply) (*in-*, in, on) *creat*: *pro-*: procreate (to produce young; to produce or bring into existence) {procreation} (*pro-*, forward, before) *re-*: recreate (put fresh life into) {recreative}, recreation {recreational}; re-create (to create anew) (*re-*, again) *cres*: *con-*: concrescence [in *biology*, a growing together of parts or cells, as of the lips of the blastopore along the dorsal side of the embryo during gastrulation (the process of forming an embryo)] (*con-*, with, together) *de-*: decrescendo (Italian music term; see *crescendo*, above), decrescent (decreasing; lessening; waning: said especially of the moon in its final quarter) (*de-*, opposite) *ex-*: excrescence (originally, normal outgrowth; now, an abnormal, or disfiguring outgrowth, as a bunion) (*ex-*, out) *cret*: *ac-*: accrete (to grow by being added to; in *botany*, grown together), accretion (in *law*, the addition of soil to land by gradual, natural deposits) {accretive} (*ac-* assimilates *ad-*, to, toward) *con-*: concrete (see *cern* for *discrete* and *discreet*), concretion (*con-*, with, together) DISGUISED ROOT: croissant [literally, crescent; croissants, shaped like the emblem (a crescent) of Turkey, were originated in Vienna to celebrate the defeat of the Turks by the Viennese in 1689] crew, rooky PREFIXED DISGUISED ROOT: *ac-*: accrue, accruement (*ac-* assimilates *ad-*, to, toward) *re-*: recruit (literally, to grow again) (*re-*, again) SOBRIQUET OF A CITY: New Orleans, Louisiana, is known as *Crescent City*, from its being situated along a crescent-shaped bend of the Mississippi River. CROSS REFERENCE: *aug*, *creat*

Element	From	Meaning	Examples
cret			See *cern/cert* for *discrete*.
cret			See *cresc* for *accrete*.
crim*	Latin *crimen*: accusation (IE: *skrei*, to sift, separate)	judgment	SIMPLE ROOT: crime, criminal, criminate PREFIXED ROOT: *dis-*: discriminate (to constitute a difference between; **Synonyms**: distinguish, differentiate) (*dis-*, apart) *in-*: incriminate (to charge with a crime) {incrimination} (*in-*, in) *re-*: recrimination (to answer an accuser by accusing him/her in return; reply with a counter charge) (*re-*, back, again) LEADING ROOT COMPOUND: logy: criminology (*logy*, scientific study of) FRENCH TERM: *crime passionel* (crime of passion, often personal assault or murder, incited by sexual motivations) CROSS REFERENCE: *jud, jur*
crin,* cris, crit	Greek *krinein* (IE: *skrei*, to sift, separate)	to separate, distinguish	SIMPLE ROOT: *cris*: crisis (plural, *crises*) *crit*: criterion (plural, *criteria*), critic, critical (see synonyms at *crucial*, under *cruc*) criticaster (an incompetent, inferior critic) criticize, critique (short for Greek *kritike techne*, critical art) PREFIXED ROOT: *crine*: *ec-*: eccrine, eccrinology (*ec-* assimilates *ex-*) *endo-*: endocrine (*endo-*, within) *exo-*: exocrine (*exo-*, without, outside) *cris*: *epi-*: epicrisis (*epi-*, upon) *hypo-*: hypocrisy (in *Greek drama*, the playing of a part; speaking from under the mask; consequently, pretending to be what one is not) (*hypo-*, under) *crit(e)*: *dia-*: diacritic, diacritical (serving to distinguish, as a diacritical mark) (*dia-*, across, through) *epi-*: epicritic (*epi-*, upon) *hyper-*: hypercritical (*hyper-*, over, beyond) *hypo-*: hypocrite (one who practices *hypocrisy*, which see above), hypocritical (*hypo-*, under) LEADING ROOT COMPOUND: phob: criticophobia (morbid fear of critics) (*phobia*, fear of) TRAILING ROOT COMPOUND: holo: holocrine (*holo*, whole, entire) CROSS REFERENCE: *cert*
crin*	Latin *crinis* (IE: *(s)kreis*, to shake)	hair	SIMPLE ROOT: crinal, crinet (same as *crinière*), crinion, crinite (hairy; in *botany*, having *hairy* tufts) LEADING ROOT COMPOUND: lin: crinoline (from *lino*, linen) DISGUISED ROOT: crest FRENCH: crinière (same as *crinet*, horsehair, mane; articulated armor protecting the upper surface of the neck of a medieval war horse) NB: *Crinum*, from Greek *krinon*, lily, is not in this family. CROSS REFERENCE: *capill, trich/thrix*

Element	From	Meaning	Examples
cris			See *crin* for *crisis, hypocrisy.*
crit			See *crin* for *hematocrit, hypocrit.*
cru			See *cresc* for *accrue.*
cruc,***	Latin	cross	SIMPLE ROOT:
crux	*crux*		crucial (**Synonyms**: acute, critical), cruciate, crux
	(IE: *(s)ker*,		PREFIXED ROOT:
	to turn,		*ex-*: excruciate {excruciation}, excruciating (*ex-*, out)
	bend;		LEADING ROOT COMPOUND:
	yields		fer: crucifer (a person who carries a cross, as in a church pro-
	English		cession; in *botany*, any plant of the mustard family, includ-
	cross)		ing the cabbages, cresses, etc.) {cruciferous} (*ferre*, to bear)
			fix: crucifix (the cross as a Christian symbol; a cross with the
			figure of the crucified Christ on it)
			form: cruciform (in the form of a cross; cross-shaped)
			fy: crucify (from *figere*, fix)
			FRENCH WORDS AND PHRASES:
			croix, croix de guerre (cross of war, a military decoration)
			FRENCH and SPANISH: crusade (French *croisade*; Spanish
			cruzada; both words mean "bearing the cross"; often capital-
			ized, any of the military expeditions undertaken by European
			Christians in the 11th, 12th, and 13th centuries to recover
			the Holy Land from the Moslems). Members of the expedi-
			tions sewed the symbol of the *cross of Christ* on tunics
			(outer clothing). "To take the cross" meant to become a cru-
			sader.
			PORTUGUESE: *cruzeiro*
			LATIN PHRASES:
			crux ansata (literally, cross with a handle; ankh)
			crux capitata (literally, cross having a head; same as *crux im-*
			missa)
			crux immissa (literally, cross hanging down)
			crux stellata (literally, starred cross; a cross with arms that end
			in stars)
			MUSIC TERMS:
			croisement, croisez (indication to cross the hands in piano
			playing, e.g., for the left hand to play notes in the upper reg-
			ister)
			DUTCH: cruise (orignally, to cross the sea)
			PLACENAMES:
			Las Cruces, New Mexico
			Marine on St. Croix, Minnesota
			St. Croix (the largest island of The Virgin Islands of the
			United States)
			Saint Croix Island National Monument (on the Canadian
			border in eastern Maine)
			Veracruz, California
			Veracruz, Mexico
			NO CROSS REFERENCE
crymo*	Greek	icy cold	LEADING ROOT COMPOUND:
	krymos		*crym(o)*:
	(IE: *kreu*,		odyn: crymodynia (pain caused by cold) (*odyn*, pain)
	congealed		phil: crymophilic (*philos*, love)
	blood)		phylact: crymophylactic (*phylact*, guard against)
			therap: crymotherapy
			CROSS REFERENCE: *algo, cryo, frig*

Element	From	Meaning	Examples
cryo*	Greek *cryos* (IE: *kreu*, congealed blood)	icy cold	ROOT NOTE: The root *cryo* evolved into *crystallis*, or that which appeared frosty, thus the word *crystal*. SIMPLE ROOT: cryonics, crystal (listed separately as a root) LEADING ROOT COMPOUND: *cry(o)*: alg: cryalgesia (*alges*, pain) bio: cryobiology (*bio*, life + *logy*, study of) gen: cryogen (a refrigerant), cryogenics (*gen*, producing) hydr: cryohydrate (*hydro*, water) lit cryolite (used in the names of minerals, rocks, and fossils) (*lithos*, stone) meter: cryometer (*meter*, measure) phil: cryophile, cryophilic (*philos*, love) phyt: cryophyte (a plant that grows on ice or snow, especially various algae and fungi) (*phyton*, a plant) prob: cryoprobe (a surgical instrument for conducting intense cold to small areas of body tissues in order to destroy those areas) scop: cryoscopy (the science that studies the freezing points of liquids) (*scope*, look) stat: cryostat (a regulator for maintaining a constant, low temperature) (*stat*, stand) surg: cryosurgery (surgery involving the selective destruction of tissues by freezing them, as with liquid nitrogen) therap: cryotherapy (treatment by the use of cold, as by application of ice packs or by lowering the body temperature) CROSS REFERENCE: *crymo, frig*
crypt,** krypt	Greek *kryptos*: hidden, covered (IE: *kru*, to pile up, cover)	to hide, conceal	SIMPLE ROOT: *crypt*: crypt (in *anatomy*, any of various recesses, glandular cavities, or follicles in the body) cryptic (**Synonyms**: obscure, vague, enigmatic) *krypt*: krypton (a rare gaseous chemical element present in very small quantities in air and inert to all reagents except flourine; symbol Kr: so named because of the discoverers' difficulty in isolating it) PREFIXED ROOT: *apo-*: apocrypha (any writings, anecdotes, etc., of doubtful authenticity or authorship; capitalized, the 14 books of the Septuagint that are rejected in Judaism and regarded by Protestants as not canonical; 11 of the 14 are fully accepted in the Roman Catholic Church canon) (*apo-*, away) *en-*: encrypt (to encode or encipher) (*en-*, in) *pro-*: procryptic (*pro* from *protect*; in *biology*, having a pattern or coloration adapted for natural camouflage) (*pro-*, before) LEADING ROOT COMPOUND: *crypt*: esthes: cryptesthesia (*esthes*, feeling) onym: cryptonym (*onym*, name) orchi: cryptorchism (failure of the testicles to descend into the scrotum) (*orchism*, relating to the testicles) *crypto*: bio: cryptobiosis (same as *anabiosis*) (*bio*, life + *osis*, condition of)

Element	From	Meaning	Examples
crypt (cont'd)			clast: cryptoclastic (in *mineralology*, consisting of fragments of older rocks, or microscopic grains) (*clasti*, break) gam: cryptogam {cryptogamic} (*gamo*, marriage) gram: cryptogram (from *graph*, write) graph: cryptograph, cryptographer (*graph*, write) mer: cryptomere, cryptomeria (the concealment of the seeds of the cones within bracts; the Japanese cedar) (*mere*, part) rrh: cryptorrhea (abnormal activity of an endocrine gland) (*rrh*, flow) zo: cryptzoic (relating to animals that live in hidden places, as in crevices or under leaves, rocks, etc.) (*zo*, animal) DISGUISED ROOT: grotto (a cave; a cavelike summerhouse, shrine, etc.) CROSS REFERENCE: *calyp, cell, cond*
crystal**	Greek *krymos*: icy cold (IE: *kreu*, congealed blood)	crystal	ROOT NOTE: Though the original root meant cold, icy, it evolved into that which is clear, transparent. SIMPLE ROOT: crystal, crystalline, crystallite, crystallize LEADING ROOT COMPOUND: *crystall(i, o)*: oid: crystalloid (*oid*, similar to) fer: crystalliferous (*ferous*, bearing, producing) graph: crystallography (*graph*, write) TRAILING ROOT COMPOUND: pheno: phenocryst (from *phano*, to show) DISGUISED ROOT: crude (literally, bleeding, raw, rough; from Greek *kryos*, frost and *kreas*, flesh) crust, crusty crustacean (any of a subphylum of arthropods, including shrimps, crabs, barnacles, and lobsters) crustaceous (of or like a crust; having a hard crust or shell; in *zoology*, a crustacean) INTERDISCIPLINARY: crust (in *geology*, the solid, rocky, outer portion or shell of the earth; lithosphere; in *medicine*, a dry, hard, outer layer of blood, pus, or other bodily secretion) NO CROSS REFERENCE
cten*	Greek *kteis*: comb (IE: *pek*, to pull wool or hair)	comb-like (see *Root Note*)	ROOT NOTE: The root originally meant *comb*, but evolved to mean *comblike teeth*, or *scales*. SIMPLE ROOT: ctene, ctenidial, ctenidium, ctenii LEADING ROOT COMPOUND: *cten*: oid: ctenoid (having an edge with projections like the teeth of a comb, as the posterior margin of the scales of certain fishes) (*oid*, similar to) *cteno*: cyst: ctenocyst (a characteristic sensory or balancing organ of Ctenophora situated at the aboral pole of the body) (*cyst*, sac, bladder) phor: ctenophoran, ctenophore (any of a phylum of sea animals with an oval, transparent, jelly-like body bearing eight rows of comblike plates that aid in swimming) (*phore*, bearer, producer) CROSS REFERENCE: *pectin*

Element	From	Meaning	Examples
ctet*	Greek *ktasthai*	to acquire	LEADING ROOT COMPOUND: logy: ctetology (the branch of biology that deals with the origin and development of acquired characters) (*logy*, study of) som: ctetosome (a supernumerary chromosome; a hetero-chromosome) (*som*, body) NO CROSS REFERENCE
cub,** cumb	Latin *cubare* (IE: *(k)eub*, to bend, turn)	to lie down	SIMPLE ROOT: cube, cubism cuba: cubature (the determination of cubic content; cubic content; volume) cubic: cubic (in *mathematics*, of the third power or degree; relating to the cubes of numbers or quantities) cubicle (a small sleeping compartment, as in a dormitory), cubicular cubit: cubit, cubitate, cubitus PREFIXED ROOT: *cub*: con-: concubine (literally, to lie down with) (*con-*, with, together) in-: (in, on) incubate [to sit on and hatch (eggs); to cause to develop or take form, especially gradually] incubus (a spirit or a demon thought in medieval times to lie on sleeping persons, especially on women, for the purpose of having sexual intercourse; compare *succubus*, next entry) suc-: succubus (a female demon thought in medieval times to have sexual intercourse with sleeping men; also *succuba*; plural, *succubae*; compare *incubus*, previous entry) (from *sub-*, under) *cumb*: ac-: accumbent (lying down, reclining, as *accumbent posture*; in *botany*, lying against some other part, said especially of cotyledons; a cotyledon is a leaf of the plant embryo, being the first to appear from a sprouting seed) (*ac-* assimilates *ad-*, to, toward) de-: decumbent (lying down; in *botany*, trailing on the ground and rising at the tip: said of stems) (*de-*, down) in-: incumbency, incumbent (resting, lying, leaning, or pressing upon something; holding an indicated position, role, office, etc., as *an incumbent congressman*) (*in-*, in) pro-: procumbent (lying face down; in *botany*, trailing along the ground: said of a stem) (*pro-*, forward) re-: recumbent (in *biology*, designating a part that leans or lies upon some other part or surface; **Synonyms**: prone, prostrate, supine) (*re-*, back) suc-: succumb (**Synonyms**: yield, capitulate, relent) (*suc-* assimilates *sub-*, under) LEADING ROOT COMPOUND: *cub*: oid: cuboid (in the shape of a cube; in *anatomy*, designating a cubelike bone between the instep and the heel bone) (*oid*, similar to) *cubi*: form: cubiform (in the form of a cube; cube-shaped)

Element	From	Meaning	Examples
cub (cont'd)			DISGUISED ROOT: couvade (a custom of some primitive tribes, in which the father of a child just born engages in certain rites, such as resting in bed, as if he had borne the child) covey (a small flock or brood of birds, especially partridges or quail; a small group of people or, sometimes, things) hive (of bees) PREFIXED DISGUISED ROOT: *cata*-: catacombs (which see under *cata*-) (*cata*-, down) NO CROSS REFERENCE
culp***	Latin *culpa*	blame, guilt	SIMPLE ROOT: culpa, culpable (desrving blame, as *a culpable offense*), culpability, culpatory PREFIXED ROOT: *dis*-: disculpate (same as *exculpate*) (*dis*-, apart, away) *ex*-: exculpate (to free from blame; declare or prove faultless) (*ex*-, out)
culp (cont'd)			*in*-: (note difference in meaning between the two prefixes) inculpable (not culpable; free from blame or guilt) (*in*-, not) inculpate (to blame, incriminate) {inculpatory} (*in*-, in, on) COALESCED ROOTS: culprit [short for *culpable, prit (a averer nostre bille)*, guilty, ready (to prove our case), said by the Roman prosecutor in opening the case to the jury] LATIN PHRASE: *mea culpa* (I am guilty; I am to blame; It is my fault) NO CROSS REFERENCE
cult***	Latin *colere*: to till; *cultus*, care, cultivation (IE: *kwel*, be around, dwell)	tend, care for	SIMPLE ROOT: cult culti: cultivate, cultivated, cultivation, cultivator cultu: cultural, culturati, culture, cultured, culturist LEADING ROOT COMPOUND: gen: cultigen (an organism, especially a cultivated plant, such as maize, of a kind not known to have a wild or uncultivated counterpart) (*gen*, producer) var: cultivar (a horticulturally or agriculturally derived variety of a plant, as distinguished from a natural variety) (from *cultivated + variety*) TRAILING ROOT COMPOUND: agri: agriculture (*agri*, field) horti: horticulture (*hortus*, garden) PREFIXED ROOT: *ac*-: acculturation (the process of conditioning a child to the patterns or customs of a culture) {acculturative} (*ac*- assimilates *ad*-, to, toward) GERMAN: *Kultur* [the highly systemized social organization of Hohenzollern (region of southwest West Germany, formerly a province of Prussia) or Nazi Germany; now usually ironic in application, with reference to chauvinism, militarism, terrorism, etc.] NB: *Cultrate*, knifelike, is not in this family. CROSS REFERENCE: *cur, iatr, therap*
cumb			See *cub* for *recumbent*, etc.

A word from Greek mythology: atlas, a book of maps; from the representations of the Titan Atlas upholding the heavens on his shoulders, common in 16th-century books of maps. In Greek mythology, Atlas was compelled to support forever the world on his shoulders.

Element	From	Meaning	Examples
cumu**	Latin *cumulare*: to pile up (IE: *keu*, a swelling)	heap, mass	SIMPLE ROOT: cumulative, cumulous, cumulus PREFIXED ROOT: *ac-*: accumulate (to pile up, collect, or gather together, especially over a long period of time), accumulation, accumulative (*ac-* assimilates *ad-*, to, toward) LEADING ROOT COMPOUND: form: cumuliform (designating, or having the form of, a cumulus, or especially any cloud with lofty vertical development; compare stratiform) CROSS REFERENCE: *mol, onc*
cun,* con	Greek *konos* (IE: *ka*, sharp, pointed)	cone, wedge	SIMPLE ROOT: cone *cun*: cuneal, cuneate, cuneus LEADING ROOT COMPOUND: *con*: odont: conodont (a very small, toothlike, Paleozoic fossil of uncertain zoological identification) (*odont*, tooth) oid: conoid (cone-shaped; in *geometry*, a solid described by a conic section revolving about its axis) (*oid*, form, shape) *cunei*: form: cuneiform (wedge-shaped; especially, designating the characters used in ancient Akkadian, Assyrian, Babylonian, and Persian inscriptions; as a *noun*, cuneiform characters or inscriptions) INTERDISCIPLINARY: cone (in *botany*, a reproductive structure of certain nonflowering plants, consisting of an elongated central axis upon which are borne overlapping scales, bracts, sporophylls, etc., usually in a spiral fashion, and in which are produced pollen, spores, or ovules; strobilus: cones are found in cycads, conifers, club mosses, horsetails, etc.; any similar structure, as the catkin of hops; in *zoology*, any of the flask-shaped cells in the retina of most vertebrates, sensitive to bright light and color; cone shell, any of a family of tropical marine snails, most species of which can inflict a very poisonous bite) NO CROSS REFERENCE
cup			See *cap*, hold, seize, for *recuperate*.
cup*	Latin *cupere* (IE: *kup*, to boil, smoke, be disturbed)	to desire	SIMPLE ROOT: cupid (capitalized, the Roman god of love, son of Venus: usually represented as a winged boy with bow and arrow and identified with the Greek Eros) cupidity (strong desire, especially for wealth; avarice; greed) PREFIXED ROOT: *con-*: concupiscence (strong or abnormal desire or appetite, especially sexual desire; lust) (*com-*, an intensive) DISGUISED ROOT: covet (**Synonyms**: envy, begrudge) CROSS REFERENCE: *aver*
cupr*	Latin *cuprum* (yields English copper)	copper	SIMPLE ROOT: cupreous, cupric, cuprite (chemical symbol: Cu_2O), cuprous, cuprum (chemical symbol: Cu) PREFIXED ROOT: *hyper-*: (beyond, excessive) hypercupremia (excessive amounts of copper in the blood) (*em*, short for Greek *hemo*, blood) hypercupriuria (excessive amounts of copper in the urine) (*ur*, urine)

171

Element	From	Meaning	Examples
cupr (cont'd)			LEADING ROOT COMPOUND: fer: cupriferous (bearing copper) (*ferre*, to bear) nickel: cupronickel GEOGRAPHICAL NAME: Cuivre River, in Missouri (*cuivre* is French for *copper*) CROSS REFERENCE: *chalc*
cur,*** corr, cour, curr, curs	Latin *currere* (IE: *kers*, to run, wagon)	to run	SIMPLE ROOT: *corr*: corridor (a long passageway or hall) *cour*: courante (an old, lively French dance with gliding or running steps, or the music for this; a stylized dance of this type used as a movement in a classical suite), courier, course *curr*: curre: currency (common acceptance; general use; prevalence) current (**Synonyms**: 1) prevailing, prevalent, rife; 2) tendency, drift, tenor) curri: curricle (a light, two-wheeled carriage drawn by two horses side by side), curriculum (plural, *curricula*) curru: currule *curs*: cursive, cursor, cursorial (in *zoology*, having legs or structural parts adapted for running), cursory PREFIXED ROOT: *cur(r)*: *con-*: concur (**Synonyms**: assent, accede, acquiesce), concurrence, concurrent (*con-*, with, together) *de-*: decurrent (in *botany*, extending down along the stem, as the base of some leaves) (*de-*, down) *ex-*: excurrent (to run out; project) (*ex-*, out) *in-*: (in) incur [to run in, or toward; to come into or acquire (something undesirable), as *to incur a bad reputation*; to become subject to through one's own action, as *to incur* (someone's) *wrath*], incurrence (the act of incurring) incurrent (flowing in; especially, characterized by the flowing in of water, as the *incurrent* canals of sponges) *oc-*: (from *ob-*, against) occur (**Synonyms**: happen, chance, befall) occurrence (**Synonyms**: happening, event, incident) *re-*: (back) recur (**Synonyms**: return, revert) recurrence (the act or an instance of recurring; reoccurrence, return, repetition, etc.) recurrent (in *anatomy*, turning back in the opposite direction: said of certain arteries and nerves; **Synonyms**: intermittent, periodic, alternate) *trans-*: transcurrent (running transversely) (*trans-*, across) *curs*: *dis-*: discursion (a rambling discourse), discursive (wandering from one topic to another) (*dis-*, from, apart) *ex-*: excursion (in *medicine*, the extent of movement from a central position), excursive (rambling; desultory) (*ex-*, out) *in-*: incursion (a running in or coming in, especially when undesired; inroad; a sudden, brief invasion or raid), incursive (*in-*, in)

Element	From	Meaning	Examples
cur (cont'd)			*pre-*: precursor (a forerunner; harbinger; a predecessor, as in office; a substance that precedes and is the source of another substance) (*pre-*, before)
			course:
			con-: concourse (literally, running together; a coming or flowing together; a crowd; throng; gathering) (*con-*, with, together)
			dis-: discourse (communication of ideas, information, etc., especially by talking; conversation; **Synonyms:** speak, talk, converse) (*dis-*, from, apart)
			inter-: intercourse (communication between or among people, countries, etc.; coitus; copulation: in full, sexual intercourse; see *Placenames*, below) (*inter-*, between)
			re-: recourse (literally, a running back; a turning or seeking for aid, safety, etc.) (*re-*, back)
			DISGUISED ROOT: corsair
			PREFIXED DISGUISED ROOT:
			suc-: succor (literally, to run under; thus to give assistance in time of need or distress; see *Bon Secour* under *Placenames*, below) (*suc-* assimilates *sub-*, under + *currere*)
			DOUBLETS:
			concur:concourse
			recur:recourse
			corsair:hussar (see *Slavic Cognate*)
			FRENCH EXPRESSION:
			au courant (literally, with the current, up to date; fully informed on current affairs
			FRENCH PHRASE:
			coureur de bois (woods runner: a French or French and Indian half-breed trapper, woodsman, or hunter of North America, especially Canada)
			SPANISH: corral, *corrida* (a bullfight)
			ACADEMIC RESUME: *curriculum vitae* (literally, course of life; a summary of one's personal history and professional qualifications, as that submitted by job applicant; résumé)
			PLACENAMES:
			Bon Secour, Alabama (literally, good help, from French *secours*, literally to run under, so as to give support; it has been said that Bon Secour received its name from fishermen being thankful for reaching home safely after trawling the treacherous waters of the Gulf of Mexico; consequently, they named their fishing village after *Notre Dame de Bon Secours*, Our Lady of Good Help, a cathedral in France)
			Intercourse (Alabama, Pennsylvania)
			WORD FROM A RELATED ROOT:
			curule (designating a chair like an upholstered campstool with heavy curved legs, in which only the highest civil officers of Rome were privileged to sit; privileged to sit in a currule chair; of the highest rank) (from *currus*, chariot)
			SLAVIC COGNATE: hussar (originally, a member of the light cavalry of Hungary or Croatia; a member of any European regiment of light-armed cavalry, usually with brilliant dress uniforms; see *Doublets* above) (from Hungarian *huzzar*; Serbo-Croatian *husar*)

Element	From	Meaning	Examples
cur (cont'd)			INTERDISCIPLINARY: excurrent (in *botany*, projecting beyond the tip, as the midrib of certain leaves; having an undivided projecting main stem, as fir trees; in *zoology*, of ducts, tubes, or passages whose contents flow outward) NB: Do not confuse the assimilated prefix *cor-* from *com-*, with, together, with the *cor* form of this root. CROSS REFERENCE: *drom*
cur,*** sur	Latin *cura*	care, concern (the word *care* itself, though similarly spelled, is not etymologically related to *cure*, coming instead from a Germanic root that means "grief, concern")	SIMPLE ROOT: *cur*: cura: curacy (the position, office, or work of a curate) curate (originally, any clergyman, one who has the care of souls; a clergyman who assists a vicar or rector; as a *verb*, to act as a curator for an exhibition, museum, etc.), curator curative (serving or tending to cure; of or relating to the cure of a disease) cure: cure (**Synonyms: 1**) heal, remedy; **2**) restorative, antidote), curé (in France, a parish priest) curi: curio, curiosity (a desire to learn or know; a desire to learn about things that do not properly concern one), curious (**Synonyms**: inquisitive, meddlesome, prying) *sur*: sure (from *secure*; see *Doublets* below) PREFIXED ROOT: *cur*: ac-: accuracy, accurate (**Synonyms**: correct, exact, precise) (*ac-* assimilates *ad-*, to, toward) in-: incurable, incurious (not eager to find out) (*in-*, not) pro-: (before, forward) procuration, procurator (see *Doublets* below) {procuratorial} procure (**Synonyms**: obtain, secure, acquire), procurer se-: secure (literally, away from care; see *Doublets*) (*se-*, apart, away) sine-: sinecure [literally, without care (or responsibilities), as *a sinecure position*] (*sine-*, without) *sur(e)*: as-: assurance (**Synonyms: 1**) certainty, certitude, conviction; **2**) confidence, self-possession, aplomb), assure {assured, assuredly}, assurer (*as-* assimilates *ad-*, to, toward) en-: ensure (to make sure or certain; guarantee; to make safe; protect) (*en-*, in) in-: insurance, insure {insurable}, insured, insurer (see *ensure*) TRAILING ROOT COMPOUND: mani: manicure (*mani*, hand) pedi: pedicure (*ped*, foot) DISGUISED ROOT: proctor (a contraction of procurator; see *Doublets* below) proxy (Middle English *prokecie*, contraction of *procuracie*, procuracy) DOUBLETS: procurator:proctor; sure:secure SPANISH: *curandero* (a Hispanic healer who uses magic, folk medicine, etc. to treat whatever ails the patient; feminine, *curandera*) PLACENAME: Security, Colorado NO CROSS REFERENCE

174

Element	From	Meaning	Examples
cus			See *cause* for *accuse*.
cusp*	Latin *cuspis*: spear	point	SIMPLE ROOT: cusp (a point or pointed end; apex; in *anatomy*, any of the elevations on the chewing surface of a tooth; any of the triangular flaps of a heart valve; term also used in *architecture*, *astrology*, and *astronomy*) cuspate, cuspid TRAILING ROOT COMPOUND: bi: bicuspid (any of eight adult teeth with two-pointed crowns) (*bi*, two) NB: *Cuspidor*, a spittoon, is not in this family. CROSS REFERENCE: *cente, centr, punct/pung*
cuss***	Latin *quatere*; *cutere*; *cudere* (IE: *kwet, kut,* to shake)	to shake, strike	PREFIXED ROOT: *cus*: *in-*: incus (bone in the ear, shaped like an anvil, that which is *struck*) (*in-*, in) *cuse*: *in-*: incuse (hammered or stamped in: said of the design on a coin, etc.) (*in-*, in) *cuss*: *con-*: concuss, concussion (a violent shaking; shock; agitation, as from impact; in *medicine*, a condition of impaired functioning of some organ, especially the brain, as a result of a violent blow or impact) (*con-*, with, together) *dis-*: discussant, discuss {discussable, or discussible}, discusser, discussion (*dis-*, apart) *per-*: percuss (to rap gently and firmly, as in medical diagnosis) {percussor}, percussion, percussive (*per-*, through) *suc-*: succuss (to shake forcibly) {succussion} (*suc-* assimilates *sub-*, under) DOUBLE PREFIXED ROOT: repercussion {repercussive} (*re-*, again + *per-*, thoroughly) DISGUISED ROOT: cascara, cask cashier (the verb): to dismiss from a position as though shaken from it; the noun *cashier* comes from a different root quash (to quell or suppress an uprising) squash (as a verb, to squeeze or crush; coming from a different source, the vegetable *squash* is Algonquian) CROSS REFERENCE: *bat, fend, flict, plaud, plec/pleg, pless, seism, trem*
cust			See *sues* for *custom*.
cut**	Latin *cutis* (IE: *skeut,* to cover)	skin	SIMPLE ROOT: cuta: cutaneous (of, on, or affecting the skin) cuti: cuticle, cuticula, cutin (do not confuse with *cut-in*, a motion-picture term), cutinization cutis (the vertebrate skin, including both its layers, the dermis and the epidermis; also, the dermis only; corium) PREFIXED ROOT: *per-*: percutaneous (effected or introduced through the skin, as by rubbing, injecting, etc.) (*per-*, through, thoroughly) *sub-*: subcutaneous, subcuticle, subcutis (*sub-*, under) CROSS REFERENCE: *derm, pel/pil*

Element	From	Meaning	Examples
cyan*	Greek *kyanos*: blue	blue (dark)	SIMPLE ROOT: cyana: cyanate cyani: cyanide, cyanine (chemical symbol: $C_{29}H_{35}N_2I$), cyanite PREFIXED ROOT: *hyper-*: hypercyanotic (*hyper-*, beyond) LEADING ROOT COMPOUND: *cyan*: amid: cyanamide (*amide* from *am*monia + *ide*) osis: cyanosis (a bluish coloration of the skin or mucous membranes, caused by lack of oxygen or abnormal hemoglobin in the blood) {cyanotic} (*osis*, condition of) ur: cyanurate, cyanuric (*ur*, urine) *cyano*: bacter: cyanobacteria (blue-green algae) gen: cyanogen (a colorless, poisonous, flammable gas, N:C·C:N; the radical CN, occurring in cyanides) (*gen*, producer) hydr: cyanohydrin (any of a class of organic chemical compounds containing the CN and OH radicals) (*hydro*, water) NO CROSS REFERENCE
cycl***	Greek *kykloma* (IE: *kwel*, to turn, be around, dwell)	wheel, circle	SIMPLE ROOT: cycla: cyclamate, Cyclamen [genus, from the shape of the plant's roots] cycle: cycle cycli: cyclic (also, *cyclical*), cyclist cyclo: cyclone (loosely, a windstorm with a violent, whirling movement; tornado or hurricane), cyclonite PREFIXED ROOT: *a-*: acyclic (not cyclic; not in cycles; in *chemistry*, having the structure of an open chain rather than a closed ring) (*a-*, not) *anti-*: anticyclone {anticyclonic} (*anti-*, against) *en-*: encyclical (intended for general distribution; in the Roman Catholic Church, a papal document addressed to the bishops, generally dealing with doctrinal matters) (*en-*, in) *epi-*: epicycle (in *geometry*, a circle which, by rolling around the interior of another circle, generates a hypocycloid or epicycloid, respectively) {epicyclic} (*epi-*, upon) *peri-*: pericycle (the outer layer of the stele in the root and stem of most plants) {pericyclic} (*peri-*, around) *re-*: recycle (*re-*, again) LEADING ROOT COMPOUND: *cycl*: oid: cycloid (*oid*, similar to) orama: cyclorama (see *orama*) osis: cyclosis (a regular cyclic movement of protoplasm within a cell) (*osis*, condition of) *cyclo*: meter: cyclometer (an instrument for measuring the arcs of circles) (*meter*, measure) ped: cyclopedia (same as *encyclopedia*; that which produces a well-rounded child) (from *paed*, child) pleg: cycloplegia (paralysis of those muscles of the eye responsible for visual accommodation) (*plegia*, paralysis)

Element	From	Meaning	Examples
cycl***			stom: cyclostomate (having a round mouth; of a cyclostome or the cyclostomes), cyclostome (a jawless fish) (*stoma*, mouth) thym: cyclothymia (an emotional condition characterized by alternate periods of elation and depression) (*thym*, mind) tron: cyclotron (*electron*, however, does not end with root, coming instead from *electric* + *-on*) (*tron*, instrument) PREFIXED LEADING ROOT COMPOUND: *en-*: encyclopedia (instruction to produce a well-rounded child) (*en-*, in + *ped*, child) *epi-*: epicycloid (in *geometry*, the curve traced by a point on the circumference of a circle that rolls around the outside of a fixed circle; see *hypocycloid*, next entry) (*epi-*, upon; *oid*, shape, form) *hypo-*: hypocycloid (in *geometry*, the curve traced by a point on the circumference of a circle that rolls around the inner circumference of another circle; see *epicycloid*, previous entry) (*hypo-*, under + *oid*, shape, form) TRAILING ROOT COMPOUND: bi: bicycle (*bi*, two) hemi: hemicycle (half a circle; semicircular room, wall, etc.) (*hemi*, half) hetero: heterocyclic (*hetero*, different) mono: monocyclic (n *chemistry*, containing one ring of atoms in the molecule) (*mono*, one) DISGUISED ROOT: Ku Klux [short for *Kuklos Adelphon* (literally, brothers of a circle), a Southern college fraternity (1812-1866)]; also short for *Ku Klux Klan* (the first two elements are said to be from Greek *kuklos*, circle; the word *circle* appears in names of many secret societies supporting the Confederacy, such as the Knights of the Golden Circle) GREEK MYTHOLOGY: Cyclops; *ops*, eye, literally round eye; a member of a family of giants having a *single round eye* in the middle of the forehead PLACENAME: Cyclone Peak, Montana CROSS REFERENCE: *gyro*
cyn*	Greek *kynos* (IE: *kwon*, dog, yielding English *kennel*)	dog	SIMPLE ROOT: cynic, cynicism LEADING ROOT COMPOUND: odon: cynodon (*odont*, tooth) osur: cynosure (literally, dog's tail; capitalized, an old name for the constellation Ursa Minor or for the North Star, in this constellation; in lower case, any person or thing that is a center of attention or interest; reason unclear) (*oura*, tail) PHILOSOPHICAL SECT: Cynics (probably because of their 'snarling' attitude of disbelief in the human virtues) CROSS REFERENCE: *can*

D

Element	From	Meaning	Examples
dactyl**	Greek *dactylos*: finger	finger, toe	SIMPLE ROOT: dactyl (a particular *foot* of poetry, corresponding to the three joints of the *finger*, the first beat being long followed by two short beats, e.g., "**Take** her up/**Ten**-derly") LEADING ROOT COMPOUND: gram: dactylogram (an impression made from the finger; fingerprint) (from *graph*, write) graph: dactylography (the scientific classification of *fingerprints*) (*graph*, write) logy: dactylology (sign language, that of using *fingers* and hands) (*logos*, word, speaking) scop: dactyloscopy (identification by comparison of fingerprints; also, classification of fingerprints) (*scope*, look) TRAILING ROOT COMPOUND: penta: pentadactyl (having five digits to the hand or foot, or five fingerlike parts) (*penta*, five) ptero: pterodactyl (literally, wing-finger) (*pter*, wing) DISGUISED ROOT: date (the fruit; because of it being shaped like fingers) CROSS REFERENCE: *digit*
damn,** demn	Latin *damnare*: to condemn (IE: *depno*, sacrificial beast; from *dai*, to part, divide)	harm, damage	SIMPLE ROOT: damage (**Synonyms:** injure, harm, impair) damn (**Synonyms:** curse, execrate, imprecate), damnable, damnation, damnatory, damnous PREFIXED ROOT AND COMPOUNDS: *con*-: condemn (**Synonyms:** criticize, reprehend, denounce), condemnation, condemnatory (*con-*, intensive) *in*-: indemnification, indemnify (to protect against loss, damage), indemnity (*in-*, not + *-fic*, *-fy*, from *facere*, to make) LEADING ROOT COMPOUND: fic: damnification (from *facere*, to make, do) fy: damnify (in *law*, to cause injury, damage, or loss to) (from *facere*, to make, do) LAW TERMS: damna (plural of *damnum*; damages, both inclusive and exclusive of costs) *damnum* (damage; the loss or diminution of what is a person's own, either by fraud, carelessness, or accident) *damnum absque injuria* (loss, hurt, or harm without injury; that is, without such breach of duty as is redressible by an action; a loss which does not give rise to an action for damages against the person causing it) *damnum fatale* (fatal damage; also, damage from fate; loss happening from a cause beyond human control) *damnum infectum* NOTE: There are several other law terms beginning with *damnum*; see *Black's Law Dictionary*. NO CROSS REFERENCE
dat			See *don* for *date*, *dative*.

Element	From	Meaning	Examples
de-***	Latin *dis-*: off, away	away (see note)	NOTE: Not all authorities agree on the differentiations of meanings of *de-*; furthermore, there may be overlappings of meanings. Note that some words are listed in more than one category. PREFIXED ROOT: bouch: debouch (in the *military*, to come forth from a narrow or shut-in place into open country; to come forth; emerge), débouché (an outlet, as for troops to debouch through), de-bouchment (also, *debouchure*) (from *bucca*, cheek) brid: débridement (the cutting away of dead or contaminated tissue or foreign material from a wound to prevent infection) (from Old English *bregdan*, move quickly) cad: decadence, decadent (capitalized, any of a group of late-19th-century, chiefly French writers characterized by a highly mannered style and an emphasis on the morbid and perverse) (*cadere*, to fall) cay: decay (**Synonyms**: putrefy, disintegrate, decompose) (from *decadence*) ceas: decease (**Synonyms**: die, expire), deceased (from *cedere*, to go) ced: decedent (in *law*, a deceased person) (see *decease*, previous entry) creas: decrease (**Synonyms**: dwindle, lessen, diminish) (from *crescere*, to grow) crem: decrement (from *decrease*) cres: decrescent (from *decrease*) fault: default (from *fallere*, to fail) fend: defend (*fendere*, to strike) fens: defense, defenseless, defensible, defensive (see *defend*) mand: demand (**Synonyms**: claim, require, exact) (*mandare*, to entrust) CROSS REFERENCE: *ab-, apo-, cata-, dis-, ex-, se-*
de-***	Latin	away from	PREFIXED ROOT: bauch: (Old French; beam, tree trunk) debauch (originally, to separate branches from trunk; now, to lead astray morally; **Synonyms**: debase, deprave, corrupt) debauchee (a person who indulges in debauchery) debauchery (extreme indulgence of one's appetites, especially for sensual pleasure; dissipation) falc: defalcate (literally, to cut off, as with a sickle; to steal or misuse funds entrusted to one's care; embezzle), defalcation (*falcis*, a sickle) CROSS REFERENCE: *ab-, apo-, cata-, dis-, ex-, se-*
de-***	Latin	down	PREFIXED ROOT: bas: debase (see synonyms at *debauch*, under away from) bat: (from *battuere*, to beat) débat (a type of literary composition in which two or more usually allegorical characters discuss or debate a subject; an extended discussion, debate, philosophical argument between two characters in a work of literature) debatable, debate (**Synonyms**: discuss, argue, dispute) cad: decadence (to fall down, or away, or from) (*cadere*, to fall) cal: decal (from *decalquer*, to trace, copy) (*calquer*, to copy) cid: deciduous (from *cadere*, to fall)

Element	From	Meaning	Examples
de- (cont'd)			cliv: declivitous, declivity (*clivus*, slope)
			coct: decoct, decoction (from *coquere*, to cook)
			cumb: decumbent (in *biology*, trailing on the ground on rising at the tip, as some stems) (from *cubare*, to lie down)
			curr: decurrent (in *botany*, extending down along the stem, as the base of some leaves) (*currere*, to run)
			curv: decurved (in *zoology*, curved, or bent downward)
			duc: deduce (**Synonyms**: infer, conclude, gather) (*ducere*, to lead)
			duct: deduct, deductible, deduction (see *deduce*)
			fer: defer (to give in to the wish or judgment of another), deferent (*ferre*, to bear)
			[another *defer* is from the same root, but with the prefix *dis*-]
			flex: deflexed (bent downward, as branches, leaves, or hairs) (from *deflect*, under from)
			grad: degradation, degrade (**Synonyms**: abase, humble, humiliate) (*gradus*, step)
			gree: degree (from *degrade*, previous entry)
			gress: degression (from *degrade*, above)
			ject: deject, dejecta, dejected (**Synonyms**: sad, sorrowful, melancholy), dejection (from *jacere*, to throw)
			press: depress, depressed (see synonyms at *dejected*, above), depression (from *premere*, to press)
			scend: descend (from *scandere*, to climb)
			sult: desultory (**Synonyms**: random, haphazard, casual) (from *saltire*, to leap)
			CROSS REFERENCE: *cata-*
de-***	Latin	from	PREFIXED ROOT:
			bark: debark (to unload from or leave a ship or aircraft) (from French *barque*, small boat)
			cad: decadence, decadent (*cadere*, to fall)
			cant: decant, decanter (*canthus*, edge)
			cay: decay (see synonyms at away, above) (from *decadence*, above)
			ceas: decease, deceased (from *cedere*, to go)
			ced: decedent (in *law*, a deceased person) (see *decease*, previous entry)
			ceit: deceit, deceitful (Synonyms: dishonest, lying, untruthful) (see *deceive*, next entry)
			ceiv: deceive (**Synonyms**: mislead, beguile, delude) (from *capere*, to take)
			cid: decide (**Synonyms**: determine, settle, conclude) (from *caedere*, to cut)
			clin: declination, decline (**Synonyms**: refuse, reject, repudiate) (from *climare*, to bend)
			coll: decollate, décolletage, décolleté (*collum*, neck)
			creas: decrease (see synonyms at away)
			cree: decree (any official order, edict, or decision) (from *cernare*, to sift, judge)
			crem: decrement (from *decrease*)
			cres: decrescendo, decrescent (from *decrease*)
			cret: decretal, decretory (from *decree*)

Element	From	Meaning	Examples
de- (cont'd)			

de- (cont'd)

fam: defamation (a defaming or being defamed; detraction; slander, or libel), defamatory, defame (*fama*, reputation)

feas: defeasance, defeasible (from *facere*, to do)

feat: defeat (see *Doublets* below; **Synonyms**: conquer, vanquish, overcome), defeatist (from *facere*, to make)

fec: defecate (to remove impurities from; to excrete waste matter from the bowels) (from *faex*, grounds, dregs)

fect: defect (see *Doublets* below; **Synonyms**: imperfection, blemish, flaw), defection, defective (from *facere*, to make)

fend: defend, defendant (*fendere*, to strike)

fens: defense, defensible, defensive (from *defend*)

fer: defer (to comply with) (*ferre*, to bear)

[another *defer*, a variant of *differ*, is listed under *dis-*]

fic: deficiency, deficient, deficit (from *facere*, to make)

fil: defilade, defile (*filer*, to form a line)

[another *defile* is from Old English *fylan*, foul]

fin: define, definite (**Synonyms**: explicit, exact, specific), definition, definitive (*finire*, to set a limit to, bound)

flect: deflect, deflection (*flectere*, to bend)

flex: deflex, deflexed (bent downward, as branches, leaves, or hairs) (see *deflect*)

flower: deflower (to make a woman no longer a virgin; to ravage or spoil; to remove flowers from a plant)

foli: defoliate {defoliation} (*folium*, leaf)

forc: deforce, deforciant (Old French *forcier*, to force)

form: deform (**Synonyms**: distort, contort, warp), deformation, deformity

lect: delectable, delectation (from *lacere*, to entice, to ensnare)

leg: delegacy, delegate, delegation (*legare*, to send)

let: delete (**Synonyms**: erase, expunge, efface), deletion (from *linere*, to daub)

light: delight (**Synonyms**: pleasure, joy, enjoyment), delighted, delightful (see *delectable*)

lin: delineate (describe, depict) (*linea*, line)

linq: delinquency, delinquent (*linquere*, to leave)

liqu: deliquesce (*liquescere*, to melt)

lir: delirious, delirium (**Synonyms**: mania, frenzy, hysteria) (*lira*, line, furrow)

lud: delude (see synonyms at *deceive*, above) (*ludere*, to play)

lug: deluge (from *luere*, to wash)

lus: delusion (**Synonyms**: illusion, hallucination, mirage), delusive (see *delude*)

mand: demand (**Synonyms**: claim, require, exact), demanding (*mandare*, to entrust)

marc: demarcate, demarcation (also, demarkation) (*marcar*, to mark boundaries)

mis: demise (ceasing to exist; death) (see *demit*, next entry)

mit: demit (to resign a position of office) (*mittere*, to send)

mol: demolish (**Synonyms**: destroy, raze, annihilate), demolition (*moliri*, to build)

mulc: demulcent (a medicine or ointment that soothes irritated or inflamed mucous membranes) (*mulcere*, to stroke)

Element	From	Meaning	Examples
de- (cont'd)			mur: demur (**Synonyms:** object, protest, expostulate) (*morari*, to delay)
			pil: depilate (to remove hair from a part of the body) (*pilus*, hair)
			pos: deposable, depose (to remove from office or a position of power, especially from a throne) (*poser*, to cease, lie down)
			posit: deposit (see *Doublets* below), deposition, depositor, depository (from *ponere*, to put)
			pot: depot (from *deposit*; see *Doublets* below)
			prec: (note difference in meanings of roots)
			deprecate, deprecatory (*precari*, to pray)
			depreciate (**Synonyms:** disparage, decry, minimize), depreciation (from *pretiare*, to value)
			put: deputation, depute, deputize, deputy (*putare*, to cleanse)
			riv: derivation, derivative, derive (**Synonyms:** rise, spring, originate) (*rivus*, a stream)
			rog: derogate, derogation, derogatory (*rogare*, to ask)
			scrib: describe (*scribere*, to write)
			script: description, descriptive (from *describe*, previous entry)
			sert: (from *serere*, to join)
			desert (**Synonyms:** abandon, forsake, quit)
			desert (**Synonyms:** waste, badlands, wilderness)
			[*desert*, from *deserve*, is listed under intensive]
			sign: design (**Synonyms: 1**) intend, mean, propose; **2**) plan, project, scheme), designate, designation, designing (*signare*, to sign)
			sir: desirable, desire (**Synonyms:** wish, want, crave), desirous (from *sidus*, star)
			sist: desist (**Synonyms:** stop, cease, discontinue) (*sistere*, to cause to stand)
			spic: despicable (see *despise*, next entry)
			spis: despise (**Synonyms:** scorn, disdain, contemn) (from *specere*, to look at)
			spit: despite, despiteful (from *despise*, above)
			spond: despond, despondency, despondent (**Synonyms:** hopeless, despairing, desperate) (*spondere*, to promise)
			spum: despumate (*spuma*, foam)
			sue: desuetude (*suescere*, to be accustomed)
			tail: detail (**Synonyms:** item, particular) (French *tailler*, to cut)
			tain: detain (**Synonyms:** delay, slow, retard), detainee, detainer (from *tenere*, to hold)
			tect: detect, detection, detective, detector (from *tegere*, to cover)
			tent: detent, détente, detention (see *detain*, above)
			ter: deter, deterrence, deterrent (*terrere*, to frighten)
			terg: deterge, detergency, detergent (*tergere*, to wipe, cleanse)
			termin: determinate, determine (**Synonyms: 1**) decide, settle, conclude; **2**) learn, ascertain, discover) (*terminus*, and end)
			tin: detinue (see *detain*, above)
			tract: detract, detraction (a malicious discrediting of someone's character, accomplishments, etc., as by revealing hidden faults or by slander) (from *trahere*, to draw)

Element	From	Meaning	Examples
de- (cont'd)			tri: detriment, detrimental (**Synonyms**: pernicious, baneful, noxious), detrition (from *terere*, to rub)
			via: deviate (**Synonyms**: swerve, veer, diverge), deviation (*via*, road, way)
			vot: devote (**Synonyms**: dedicate, consecrate, hallow) (from *vovere*, to vow)
			vout: devout (**Synonyms**: pious, religious, sanctimonious) (see *devote*, previous entry)
			DISGUISED ROOT: debt, debtor (*de-* + *habere*, to hold)
			DOUBLETS:
			defeat:defect
			depot:deposit
			INTERDISCIPLINARY: deliquesce (in *biology*, to melt away in the course of growth or decay, as parts of certain fungi; also, to branch into many fine divisions, as leaf veins; in *chemistry*, to become liquid by absorbing moisture from the air)
			CROSS REFERENCE: *ab-, apo-, cata-, dis-, ex-, ec-*
de-***	Latin	intensive (wholly, entirely)	PREFIXED ROOT:
			bris: debris (also, *débris*; from Old French *desbrisier*, to break apart; from Middle English *bruisen*, to smash, crush, bruise)
			claim: declaim (from *clamare*, to cry out)
			clam: declamation, declamatory (see *declaim*)
			clar: declaration, declarative, declare (**Synonyms**: announce, publish, proclaim) (*clarare*, to make clear)
			crep: decrepit (**Synonyms**: weak, feeble, enervate), decrepitate, decrepitude (*crepare*, to creak)
			cry: decry (**Synonyms**: disparage, depreciate, minimize) (from *quiritare*, to wail)
			dedi: dedicate (**Synonyms**: devote, consecrate, hallow), dedicated, dedication, dedicatory (*dicare*, to proclaim; from *dicere*, to say)
			fil: defile (**Synonyms**: contaminate, taint, pollute) (from Old English *fylan*, foul)
			flag: deflagrate {deflagration} (*flagrare*, to burn)
			lay: delay (from *laxus*, loose)
			liber: deliberate (**Synonyms**: 1) think, reason, cogitate; 2) voluntary, intentional, willful) (from *libra*, a set of scales)
			liver: deliver (**Synonyms**: rescue, redeem, ransom) (from *liber*, free)
			nomin: denominate, denomination, denominative, denominator (from *nomen*, name)
			pict: depict (**Synonyms**: sketch, draw, paint) (from *pingere*, to paint)
			port: deport (**Synonyms**: 1) banish, exile, expatriate; 2) carry, bear, convey) (*portare*, to carry)
			prav: deprave (**Synonyms**: debase, corrupt, debauch), depraved, depravity (from IE *pra*, to bend) [see reference to Indo-European in *Preface*]
			pred: depredate, depredation (from *praedari*, to plunder)
			priv: deprivation, deprive, deprived (*privare*, to separate)
			pur: depurate (*purare*, to purify)

184

Element	From	Meaning	Examples
de- (cont'd)			relict: derelict (**Synonyms:** remiss, negligent, neglectful), dereliction (*relict* itself is from *re-*, from + *linquere*, to leave) sert: desert (the fact of deserving reward or punishment) (from *deserve*, next entry) serv: deserve, deserved, deserving (*servire*, to serve) sic: desiccant, desiccate (*siccare*, to dry) sol: desolate, desolation (*solare*, to make lonely) spoil: despoil (**Synonyms:** ravage, devastate, plunder) (*spoliare*, to strip, rob) stin: destination, destine, destiny (from *stare*, to stand) ton: detonate (*tonare*, to thunder) vas: devastate (see synonyms at *despoil*, above) (*vastare*, to make empty) vour: devour (from *vorare*, to swallow whole) CROSS REFERENCE: *com-*, *en-*, *per-*
de-***	Latin	of	FRENCH: debonair (Modern French is *débonnaire*, from *de bon air*, of good air) delaine (literally, of wool) (from *lana*, wool) deluxe (of luxury) LATIN EXPRESSION: *de fide* (of faith; in the *Roman Catholic Church*, used to designate doctrines held to be revealed by God and so requiring the unconditional assent of faith by all) NO CROSS REFERENCE
de-***	Latin	off	PREFIXED ROOT: ala: dealate (having lost its wings: said of ants and other insects whose wings are shed after the mating flight) (*ala*, wing) cant: decant, decanter (*canthus*, edge) cap: decapitate (*caput*, head) cid: (from *caedere*, to cut) decide (**Synonyms:** determine, settle, conclude) deciduous (falling off or out at a certain season or stage of growth, as some leaves, antlers, insect wings, or milk teeth) hisc: dehisce (to split open along definite structural lines, as the seedpods of legumes, lilies, etc.) (*hiscere*, to gape) lug: deluge (a heavy flood; a heavy rainfall; an overwhelming, floodlike rush of anything) (from *lavare*, to lave, wash) nud: denudate, denude (*nudare*, to strip) tain: detain (to keep in custody; confine; to keep from going on; hold back) (from *tenere*, to hold) CROSS REFERENCE: *ab-*
de-***	Latin	pejorative (disparaged or made worse; from *pejor*, worse)	PREFIXED ROOT: rid: deride (**Synonyms:** ridicule, mock, taunt) (*ridere*, to laugh) ris: derision, derisive (also, *derosory*) (see *deride*) NO CROSS REFERENCE
de-***	Latin	removal	PREFIXED ROOT: bacl: debacle (**Synonyms:** disaster, calamity, catastrophe) (French *bacler*, to bar; from Latin *baculum*, rod) bar: debar (**Synonyms:** exclude, eliminate, suspend) class: déclassé (having lost class; lowered in social status, class), declassify

Element	From	Meaning	Examples
de- (cont'd)			coup: decoupage (the art of cutting out designs or illustrations from paper, foil, etc., mounting them decoratively on a surface, and applying coats of varnish or lacquer) (French *couper*, to cut) CROSS REFERENCE: *dis-*
de-***	Latin	reversal	PREFIXED ROOT: bil: debilitate (**Synonyms:** weaken, enervate, sap), debility (from IE *bel*, strong) brief: debrief (to receive information from a pilot, emissary, etc., concerning a flight or mission just completed) (from *brevis*, short) cal: decalescence (*calere*, to be warm) camp: decamp (to break or leave camp; to go away suddenly and secretly; run away) celer: decelerate {deceleration}, deceleron (an aileron used to slow down an aircraft in flight; speed brake) (*celerare*, to hasten) creas: decrease (see synonyms under away) (*crescere*, to grow) fac: deface (to spoil the appearance of; disfigure; mar) (*facies*, form, appearance) flat: deflate (**Synonyms:** contract, shrink, condense) (from *flare*, to blow) NO CROSS REFERENCE
de-***	Latin	without	PREFIXED ROOT: spair: despair (to lose or give up hope; be without hope: usually with *of*), despairing (see synonyms, next entry) (*sperare*, to hope) sper: desperate (**Synonyms:** hopeless, despondent, despairing), desperation (see *despair*) NO CROSS REFERENCE
deb**	Latin *debere*	to owe, due	SIMPLE ROOT: debit, debenture debt (in *theology*, a sin), debtor PREFIXED ROOT: *in-*: indebted (owing gratitude, as for a favaor received) (*in-*, in) DISGUISED ROOT: due (past participle of *devoir*) duty (**Synonyms:** function, office, capacity) PREFIXED DISGUISED ROOT: *en-*: endeavor (from phrase *se mettre en deveir*, to try to do) (*en-*, in) FRENCH: devoir (duty; plural, acts or expressions of due respect or courtesy as in greeting; for example, *to pay one's devoirs*; *devoir* does *not* contain the prefix *de-*) NO CROSS REFERENCE
dec*** [deci]	Latin *decem*: ten (IE: *dekm*, ten)	ten [tenth]	SIMPLE ROOT: deca: decanal (of a *dean* or *deanery*) deci: decile, decimal, decime, decimate (originally, to kill every tenth person; now, usually the obliteration of almost everyone) decum: decumen (literally, of the tenth part; has come to mean considerable, very large; as a *decumen wave*: from the notion that every tenth wave is the largest)

Element	From	Meaning	Examples
dec (cont'd)			decur: decurion (in *Roman history*, an office having charge of ten men) decus: decussate (to cross in the form of an *X*, from the Roman figure for *ten*; in *botany*, arranged in pairs growing at right angles to those above and below: said of leaves and branches) LEADING ROOT COMPOUND: *dec:* (ten) enn: decennary, decennium (from *annus*, year) *decem:* folia: decemfoliate (ten-leaved) (*foli*, leaf) *deci:* (one tenth) gram: decigram (a unit of metric weight, equal to 1/10 of a gram; 1.5432 grains, or .003527 ounce) liter: deciliter (a unit of metric volume equal to 1/10 litre; 3.39 fluid ounces or .003527 ounce) meter: decimeter (a metric unit of linear measure, equal to 1/10 meter; 3.937 inches) *decim:* vir: decemvir (ten men; in ancient Rome, a group of ten magistrates), decimvirate (*vir*, man) *decu:* ple: decuple (tenfold) (from *plicare*, to fold) TRAILING ROOT COMPOUND: duo: duodecimal, duodecimo (*duo*, two) tri: tridecime (*tri*, three) DISGUISED ROOT: dean (originally, one in charge of ten monks; later, ten soldiers; then, "many" students) (from *decanus*) dicker (originally, to haggle over the trading of hides, which came in bundles of ten) dime [from Latin *decima (pars)*, tenth (part)] doyen (French for *dean*; the senior member, or dean, as in age or rank, of a group, class, profession, etc.); doyenne (a female doyen) dozen (from *dozaine*; from Latin *duodecim*; from *duo*, two + *decem*, ten) duodenum [a section of the small intes-tine thought by ancient Romans to be the length of the breadth of twelve (*duo*, 2 + *10*) fingers] CALENDAR MONTH: December (tenth month in the Roman calendar, before March and April were added). The history of the calendar is quite tortuous. CROSS REFERENCE: *deca*
dec**	Latin *decorare:* to adorn (IE: *dek*, to receive, greet, be suitable, teach)	proper, right	ROOT NOTE: This root evolved into *dexter*, that which is *right*, and consequently designating *right-handedness*. SIMPLE ROOT: dece: decency (**Synonyms**: decorum, propriety, dignity) decent (**Synonyms**: chaste, virtuous, modest) deco: décor (or, *decor*), decorate (**Synonyms**: adorn, ornament, embellish), decoration, decorative decorous, decorum (**Synonyms**: politeness, manners, dignity)

187

Element	From	Meaning	Examples
dec (cont'd)			PREFIXED ROOT: *in-*: indecent (**Synonyms:** improper, unseemly, indelicate), indecency, indecorous (see synonyms at *indecent*), indecorum (*in-*, not) TRAILING ROOT COMPOUND: pan: pandect (an all-inclusive book; a complete body of laws; legal code; a complete or comprehensive digest); *the Pandects*, a digest of Roman civil law in fifty books, compiled for the emperor Justinian in the 6th century A.D.; the *Digest*) (*pan*, all) CROSS REFERENCE: *dext, orth, rect/reg*
deca***	Greek *deka* (IE: *dekm*, ten)	ten	SIMPLE ROOT: decade LEADING ROOT COMPOUND: *dec:* athl: decathlete, decathlon (ten athletic field events) (*athlon*, struggle, contest) *deca:* gon: decagon (a plane figure with ten sides and ten angles) {decagonal} (*gon*, angle) gram: decagram [a measure of weight equal to 10 grams (0.3527 oz.)] hedr: decahedron (a solid figure with ten plane surfaces: compare with *decagon*) (*hedra*, geometric surface) liter: decaliter [a measure of capacity, equal to ten liters (2.64 gals. liquid measure, or 9.08 qts. dry measure)] log: Decalogue (literally, ten words; the Ten Commandments) (*logos*, word) mer: (note difference in meaning of roots) Decameron [literally, ten days; a collection of a hundred tales by Boccaccio (published 1353), presented as stories told by a group of Florentines to while away ten days during a plague] (elision of *hemera*, day) decamerous (literally, ten parts; having ten parts or divisions, specifically, having the parts in tens; usually used of a flower) (*mere*, part) meter: decameter [a measure of length, equal to ten meters (32.808 ft.)] pod: decapod (a crustacean with ten legs, such as the lobster, shrimp) {decapodal} (*pod*, foot) polis: Decapolis (ten cities; in ancient Palestine, a confederacy of ten cities in the first century, B.C.) (*polis*, city) ster: decastere [a metric measure of volume, equal to 10 cubic meters (13.08 cu. yd.)] (*stere*, solid) syl: decasyllable (a line of verse having ten syllables) (*syl-* assimilates *sym-*, with, together) styl: decastyle (a temple or portico having ten columns on the front) (*style*, column) CROSS REFERENCE: *dec/deci*
dei*	Greek *deiknynai* (IE: *deik*, to point out)	to show; to give an example	SIMPLE ROOT: deictic (pointing out or proving) PREFIXED ROOT: *epi-*: epideictic (intended for display, especially rhetorical display; designed to impress) (*epi-*, upon)

188

Element	From	Meaning	Examples
dei (cont'd)			DISGUISED ROOT:
			policy (Middle French *police*; from Italian *polizza*; from Middle Latin *apodixa*; from Middle Greek *apodeixis*; from Greek from *apo-*, away + *deik*; listed also under *dict*; another *policy* is from Greek *polis*, city)
			PREFIXED DISGUISED ROOT:
			apo-: apodictic (that can be clearly shown; absolute; also *apodeictic*) (*apo-*, from)
			para-: paradigm [in *grammar*, an example of a declension (of nouns) or conjugation (of verbs), giving all the inflectional forms of a word] (*para-*, alongside)
			CROSS REFERENCE: *phan*
dei,*** div	Latin *deus* (IE: *deiwos*, god; from *dei*, to gleam, shine)	God, god, heaven	SIMPLE ROOT:
			deism (belief in the existence of a God on purely rational grounds without reliance on revelation or authority)
			deist (**Synonyms:** atheist, agnostic, infidel) {deistic}
			deity (the state of being a god; divine nature; godhood; *the Deity*: God, the invoked one)
			LEADING ROOT COMPOUND:
			dei:
			cid: deicide (the killing of a god) (*cide*, kill)
			fic: deific (deifying or making divine; godlike; divine), deification (the act of deifying; the state of being deified; a deified embodiment) (from *facere*, to make)
			fy: deify (to make a god of; to look upon or worship as a god, as *to deify money*) (from *facere*, to make)
			deo:
			dand: deodand (literally, something to be given to God; hence, forfeit to the Crown) (from *dare*, to give)
			dar: deodar (literally, tree of the gods; the Himalayan cedar) (*daru*, wood)
			EMBEDDED ROOT COMPOUND:
			eudiometer (an instrument for measuring and analyzing gases volumetrically) (*eu*, good + *meter*, measure)
			DISGUISED ROOT:
			deuce, deuced (another deuce is listed under *duo*)
			dial (originally, a sun dial)
			diva (a leading woman singer; a prima donna)
			divine (**Synonyms:** holy, sacred, hallowed)
			drat (aphetic of *God rot*)
			gossip (originally, a godparent)
			joss (Pidgin English for Latin *deus*)
			SPANISH:
			adíos (parting reply; from *a Dios*, to God; see French *adieu*, below)
			vaya con Dios (Go with God)
			días (day, as in *buenos días*; related to *Dios*)
			FRENCH: adieu (literally, to God; a parting reply; see Spanish *adios*, above)
			LATIN PHRASES:
			Dei gratia (by the grace of God; often abbreviated D.G.)
			Deo volente (God being willing; often abbreviated D.V.; see *Placename*, below)

Element	From	Meaning	Examples
dei (cont'd)			*deus ex machina* (literally, a god from a machine, a device introduced into the Greek theater for carrying a god on or off the stage, often to relieve a tangle of the plot) *Te Deum* [Thee God, an ancient hymn of thanksgiving beginning with the words *Te Deum laudamus*, We praise thee (O) God] LATIN LEGAL TERM: *actus Dei* (act of God) MOTTOES: *Dei sub numine viget* (It flourishes under the will of God) (Princeton University) *Deus nobis fiducia* (God our trust) (George Washington University) *Deus lux mea* (God my light) (Catholic University of America) *Ditat Deus* (God enriches) (State of Arizona) *Pro Deo et Patria*; For God and country (American University, Washington, D.C.) *In Deo speramus* (In God we hope) (Brown University) PLACENAME: Deovolente, Mississippi (God being willing) LITERARY WORKS: *Dei Sponsa* (The Bride of God) (Patmore) *Laus Deo* (Praise to God) (Whittier) *Lux Est Umbra Dei* (The Light Is the Shadow of God) (Symonds) CROSS REFERENCE: *theo*
dele*	Latin *delere* (*de*, from + *linere*, to line out)	erase, strike out	SIMPLE ROOT: dele, delete {deletion} PREFIXED ROOT: *in-*: indelible (incapable of being removed, erased, or washed away; permanent; enduring) (*in-*, not) LATIN PHRASE: *delenda est Carthago* (Carthage must be destroyed: the Roman view of the proper fate for a traditional enemy) NO CROSS REFERENCE
dem			See *desm* for *diadem*.
dem***	Greek *demos* (IE: *da*, to cut, divide)	people	SIMPLE ROOT: demotic (of the people; specifically; vernacular, the language of the common people; designating or of a simplified version of ancient Egyptian writing: distinguished from *hieratic*, which see under *hier*) PREFIXED ROOTS AND COMPOUNDS: *en-*: endemic (**Synonyms:** native, indigenous, aboriginal) (*en-*, in) *epi-*: (upon) epidemic (spreading rapidly and extensively among many individuals in an area: said especially of contagious diseases) epidemiology (*logy*, study of) LEADING ROOT COMPOUND: *dem*: agog: demagogue [*agog(ue)*, leader, inciter] *demi*: urg: demiurge (one who works for the people; skilled workman; creator; in *Plato's philosophy*, *Demiurge* designated the deity as creator of the material world; in *Gnostic philosophy*, a deity subordinate to the supreme deity, sometimes considered the creator of evil) (from *erg*, work) *demo*: crac: democracy (*cracy*, government, rule)

Element	From	Meaning	Examples
dem (cont'd)			crat: democrat (a person who believes in and supports government by the people), democratic, democratize (*crat*, a participant or supporter of a class or form of government) graph: demographic, demography (the statistical science dealing with the distribution of human populations) {demographer} (*graph*, write) TRAILING ROOT COMPOUND: pan: pandemic (prevalent over a whole area, country, etc.; universal; general; specifically epidemic over a large region: said of a disease) (*pan*, all) PLACENAMES: Democrat, Texas Demopolis, Alabama CROSS REFERENCE: *pleb, popul, vulg*
demi**	Latin *dimidus* (from *dis-*, apart + *med,* half)	half; also, less than usual (in size, power, etc.)	LEADING ROOT COMPOUND: god: demigod (in *mythology*, a lesser god; minor deity; offspring of a human being and a god or goddess: now, a god-like person) mond: demimondaine (French; a woman of the *demimonde*), demimonde (the class of women who have lost social standing because of sexual promiscuity; prostitutes as a group; any group whose activities are ethically questionable) (from *mundus*, world, society) semi: demisemiquaver (32nd note; half of a half of an eighth note) (*semi*, half) tass: demitasse (a small cup of or for black coffee served following dinner) (French *tasse*, cup) volt: demivolt (in *horseback riding*, a half turn with the forelegs of the horse raised) (French *volte*, a leap) EMBEDDED ROOT COMPOUND: hemidemisemiquaver (64th note; half of a 32nd note) (*hemi*, half + *quaver*, eighth note) NB: *Demijohn* is not in this family, coming instead from French *dame-jeanne*, Dame Jeanne, probably originally a fanciful name for the bottle that resembled a particularly curvaceous woman. NB: *Demiurge* is not in this family (see both *dem* and *erg*). CROSS REFERENCE: *hemi, med, meso, semi*
demn			See *damn* for *condemn*.
demon**	Greek *daemon*: spirit (IE: *da*, to cut, divide)	demon, devil	SIMPLE ROOT: *demon*: demon (a person or thing regarded as evil, cruel, etc.) {demonic}, demoniac (also, *demoniacal*), demonism, demonize *daemon*: daemon (in *Greek mythology*, any of the secondary divinities ranking between the gods and men; hence, a guardian spirit; inspiring or inner spirit; also, demon, devil) LEADING ROOT COMPOUND: latry: demonolatry (the worship of devils) (*latry*, worship) logy: demonology {demonologist} (*logy*, study of) mania: demonomania (*mania*, exaggerated desire for or pleasure in) phob: demonophobia (*phobia*, abnormal fear of) TRAILING ROOT COMPOUND: caco: cacodemon (an evil spirit or devil) (*caco*, bad)

Element	From	Meaning	Examples
demon (cont'd)			eu: eudemonia (happiness; specifically, in Aristotle's philosophy, happiness, the main universal goal, derived from a life of activity governed by reason) (*eu*, well, good) pan: pandemonium (literally, all devils; in John Milton's *Paradise Lost*, the palace built by Satan's orders as the capital of Hell; now any place or scene of wild disorder, noise, or confusion) (*pan*, all) NO CROSS REFERENCE
dendro**	Greek *dendron* IE: *deru, drewo,* firm, solid, steadfast; tree)	tree	SIMPLE ROOT: dendrite, dendron (designates a mineral, rock, and the branched part of a nerve cell) PREFIXED ROOT: *epi-*: epidendrum (a small-flowered, chiefly tropical American, epiphytic orchid) (*epi-*, upon) LEADING ROOT COMPOUND: *dendr*: oid: dendroid (treelike in form) (*oid*, similar to) *dendri*: form: dendriform (in the form of a tree; shaped like a tree) *dendro*: chron: dendrochronology (the science of dating past events or climatic changes by a comparative study of growth rings in tree trunks) (*chrono*, time + *logy*, study of) copos: dendrocopos (a particular woodpecker) (*copos*, to cut off) logy: dendrology (the scientific study of trees) (*logy*, study of) TRAILING ROOT COMPOUND: philo: philodendron (literally, loving trees) rhodo: rhododendron (literally, rose tree) DISGUISED ROOT: Druid (literally, oak-wise; a member of a Celtic religious order of priests, soothsayers, judges, poets, etc. in ancient Britain, Ireland, and France) (from IE *druwid*, oak, tree wise) ENGLISH COGNATES: betroth, tar, tray, tree, trough, true, true, trust, truth PLACENAME: Dendron, Virginia CROSS REFERENCE: *arbor, silv/sylv*
dens**	Latin *densus* (IE: *dens,* thick)	thick, crowded	SIMPLE ROOT: dense (**Synonyms: 1**) close, compact, thick; **2**) dull, slow, retarded) density PREFIXED ROOT: *con-*: condensate, condensation, condense, condenser (*con-*, with, together) LEADING ROOT COMPOUND: meter: densimeter, densitometer (*meter*, measure) NO CROSS REFERENCE
dent***	Latin *dentis* (IE: *edont,* tooth; from *ed,* to eat)	tooth	SIMPLE ROOT: dens (in medical terminology, tooth; the odontoid process of the axis) denta: dental (in *phonetics*, articulated with the tip of the tongue against or near the front teeth, as *th* in both *that* and *thin*) dentary, dentate, dentation dente: dentelate (or *dentellate*), dentelle dentic: denticle, denticulate (finely toothed; minutely dentate)

Element	From	Meaning	Examples
dent (cont'd)			dentil: dentil (in *architecture*, any of a series of small rectangular blocks projecting like teeth, as from under a cornice), dentillate dentin: dentin, dentine, dentist, dentistry, dentition dentu: dentulous, denture(s) PREFIXED ROOT: e-: edentate, edentia, edentulate, edentulous (without teeth; having lost the natural *teeth*) (from *ex-*, without) in-: indent [literally, to tooth in; one meaning of which is to set in from the margin (the first line of a paragraph, for example, as though it were bitten into)], indentured (*in-*, in) LEADING ROOT COMPOUND: form: dentiform (in the form of a tooth; tooth-shaped) fric: dentifrice (a preparation for cleaning teeth) (*fricare*, to rub) ger: dentigerous (bearing teeth) (*gerare*, to bear) lab: dentilabial (*labium*, lip) TRAILING ROOT COMPOUND: bi: bidentate (having two teeth or two toothlike processes) (*bi*, two) tri: trident [a three-pronged spear used by the retiarius (a gladiator armed with a piece of netting and a trident) in ancient gladiatorial combats; a three-pronged fish spear; in *Greek and Roman* mythology, a three-pronged spear borne as a scepter by the sea god Poseidon, or Neptune] (*tri*, three) FRENCH: dandelion (tooth of the lion, from the shape of the plant's leaf) UNBOUND COMPOUND: dent corn TRADENAME: *Dentyne* chewing gum NB: *Irredentist* (Italian for unredeemed) is not from this root; see *emp*. CROSS REFERENCE: *odont*
derm***	Greek *derma* (IE: *der*, to skin, flay)	skin	SIMPLE ROOT: derma (same as *dermis*), dermad (toward the skin; externally), dermal, dermic, dermis (the layer of skin just below the epidermis) PREFIXED ROOT: ecto-: ectoderm (the outer layer of cells an animal embryo, from which the nervous system, skin, hair, teeth, etc. are developed) (*ecto-*, outside) endo-: endoderm (*endo-*, within) epi-: epidermis {epidermal, epidermic}, epidermoid (*epi-*, upon) hypo-: hypodermic, hypodermis (*hypo-*, under) peri-: periderm (the outer bark and layer of the soft, growing tissue between the bark and the wood in plants) (*peri-*, around) LEADING ROOT COMPOUND: *derm*: alg: dermalgia (pain localized in the skin) (*alg*, pain) oid: dermoid (resembling the skin; as a noun, a demoid cyst) (*oid*, similar to) *derma*: pter: dermapteran (literally, skin wing; the earwig) (*pter*, wing) *dermat*: itis: dermatitis (*itis*, inflammation of)

193

Element	From	Meaning	Examples
derm (cont'd)			TRAILING ROOT COMPOUND: pachy: pachyderm (literally, thick-skinned, and designating the rhinoceros, hippopotamus, and the elephant; also, a thick-skinned, insensitive, stolid person) (*pachy*, thick) sclero: scleroderma (condition of hard or rigid skin) (*sclero*, hard) taxi: taxidermist (see note under *tax*) (*taxi*, arrange) xero: xeroderma (*xero*, dry) INTERDISCIPLINARY: hypodermis (in *botany*, a specialized layer of cells, as for support or water storage, lying immediately beneath the epidermis of a plant organ; in *zoology*, a layer of cells that lies beneath, and secretes, the cuticle of annelids, arthropods, etc.) CROSS REFERENCE: *cut*
des-			See *dis-* for *descry*.
desm,* deon, dem, det	Greek *dein*: to bind (IE: *de*, to bind)	ligament, band	SIMPLE ROOT: desma (plural, *desmata*); (but not *desman* and *desmarestia*), desmid, desmon, desmone PREFIXED ROOT AND COMPOUNDS: *dem*: ana-: anadem (a wreath or garland for the head; this term is classified as *old poetic*, indicating that it was never part of the everyday language, but was used chiefly in earlier poetry, or in prose where a poetic quality was desired) (*ana-*, back, up) dia-: diadem (literally, to bind on either side; a crown; an ornamental cloth headband worn as a crown; royal power, authority, or dignity) (*dia-*, across) *desm*: syn-: syndesmosis (the joining of adjacent bones as by ligaments) {syndesmotic} (*syn-*, with, together) *det*: syn-: syndetic (connecting or connected by means of conjunctions; see *asyndeton*, next entry) (*syn-*, with, together) DOUBLE PREFIXED ROOT: asyndeton (in *rhetoric*, the practice of leaving out the usual conjunctions between coordinate sentence elements, e.g., smile, shake hands, part; I came, I saw, I conquered; compare *parataxis*: regarded as a synonym of *asyndeton* by most authorities; others indicate a specific meaning: the substitution of a semicolon for a conjunction, e.g., It was cold; the snows came) (*a-*, not + *syn-*, with, together) LEADING ROOT COMPOUND: *deonto*: logy: deontology (that which is needful or binding; thus, the theory of duty or moral obligation; ethics) (*logy*, study of) *desm*: oid: desmoid (like a ligament) (*oid*, similar to) oma: desmoma (a connective tissue tumor) (*oma*, mass) NO CROSS REFERENCE

Words play an enormous part in our lives
and are therefore deserving of the closest study.
Aldous Huxley

Element	From	Meaning	Examples
deuter**	Greek *deuteros* (IE: *deu*, to move away, distance)	second; originally, farther from	SIMPLE ROOT: deuterium (chemical symbol, D), deuteron LEADING ROOT COMPOUND: *deuter*: agon: deuteragonist (in *Greek drama*, the actor second in importance to the protagonist) (*agon*, struggle) anom: deuteranomalopia (*anomalos*, irregular + *ope*, sight + *ia*; condition of) anop: deuteranope, deuteranopia [blind to the color green (apparently because of green being farther from red)] (*an-*, without + *op*, sight) *deutero*: canon: deuterocanonical (pertaining to books or sections of books in the New Testament whose authority was once contested but later accepted; compare *Apocrypha*, under both *apo-* and *crypt*) gam: deuterogamy (a marriage after the death or divorce of the first spouse; compare *bigamy* under *gam*) (*gamos*, marriage) nom: Deuteronomy (literally, second law; the book of the Old Testament in which Moses received a second set of the Ten Commandments) (*nomos*, law) plasm: deuteroplasm (food substance or yolk in the cytoplasm of an ovum or other cell) (*plasm*, form) CROSS REFERENCE: *sec/sequ*
dex			See *dic* for *index*.
dext**	Greek *dexter*: right-side (IE: *dek*, to receive, greet, be suitable)	right, well	ROOT NOTE: Extended to mean "right-handed," this root is related to *decorum* and *decent*, that which is right and proper. In ancient times, it was felt that those who were right-handed did things right or well. SIMPLE ROOT: dext: dexter [*heraldry* term: on the *right-hand* side of the shield (the left of the viewer); opposed to *sinister*], dexterity, dexterous (same as *dextrous*) dextr: dextral, dextrin, dextrose, dextron, dextrous (same as *dexterous*) LEADING ROOT COMPOUND: *dexio*: trop: dexiotropic (turning from left to right, as the whorls in most gastropod shells) (*trope*, turn) *dextro*: rota: dextrorotation, dextrorotatory (turning or circling to the right, in a clockwise direction; that turns the plane of polarized light clockwise: said of certain crystals, etc.) (Latin *rota*, turn) TRAILING ROOT COMPOUND: ambi: ambidextrous (able to use both hands with equal ease; very skillful or versatile; also, deceitful; double-dealing) {ambidexterity} (*ambi*, both) COALESCED ROOT: dextrorse (in *botany*, twining upward to the right, as the stem of the hop: opposed to *sinistrorse*) (*dexter* + *versus*, to turn) FRENCH: *destrier* (originally, to lead by the right hand; a war horse, a charger) CROSS REFERENCE: *decor, eu, orth, rect/reg*
di-			See *dis-* for *divergent*, etc.

Element	From	Meaning	Examples
di***	Greek *di*, two (IE: *dwo*, two)	two, twice	LEADING ROOT COMPOUND: gam: digamy (the second legal marriage, after the death or divorce of the first spouse) (*gamos*, marriage) gastr: digastric (designating or of a muscle that bellies out from both sides of its tendon and functions to depress the lower jaw and indirectly move the tongue) (*gaster*, belly) graph: digraph (a combination of two letters to express a simple sound, e.g., re_ad_, _sh_ow, _ph_one, gra_ph_ic) {digraphic} (*graph*, write) hedra: dihedral (having or formed by two intersecting plane faces) (*hedra*, a seat; geometric surface) lemma: dilemma (an argument necessitating a choice between equally unfavorable or disagreeable alternatives) (*lemma*, something taken or received) mer: dimerous (having two parts; specifically, having two members in each whorl: said of flowers; having two-jointed tarsi: said of insects) (*mere*, part) meter: dimeter (a line of verse containing two metrical feet or measures) (*meter*, measure) mit: dimity (a thin, strong, corded cotton cloth) (*mitos*, thread) ner: dineric (constituting, or having to do with, the surface of contact between two immiscible liquids in the same container) (*neros*, water) phthong: diphthong (a complex vowel sound made by gliding continuously from the position of one vowel to that of another within the same syllable, as *ou* in *out*, or *oi* in *oil*) (from *phtongos*, voice, sound) phyl: diphyletic (having two ancestral lines of descent) (*phyl*, tribe) phyll: diphyllous (having two leaves or sepals) (*phyll*, leaf) pno: dipnoan (a group of fish that can respire by lungs as well as gills) (from *pneu*, lung) pod: dipody (in *prosody*, a single measure consisting of two feet) (*pod*, foot) pter: dipteran, dipterous (*pter*, wing) ptych: diptych (litedrally, double-folded; originally, an ancient writing tablet having two leaves hinged together) (from *ptukhe*, a fold) stich: distich (a couplet), distichous (in *botany*, arranged in two vertical rows, as leaves on opposite sides of a stem) (*stich*, row, line, verse) syl: disyllable (a word of two syllables, e.g., *garden*, *basket*, *market*) (*syl*- assimilates *sym*-, with, together) CROSS REFERENCE: *bi/bin/bis, di, dicho, diplo, du*
dia-,*** **di-**	Greek *dia*, through (IE: *dwo*, two)	across, through, thorough, completely	PREFIXED ROOT: *di*-: oces: diocese (literally, to keep a house thoroughly; see *NB*) (*oikos*, house) op: diopsis, dioptase, diopter, dioptric (*op*, sight) orama: diorama [*di(a-)* + (pan)*orama*] orit: diorite (*dia-* + *horizon*)

Element	From	Meaning	Examples
dia- (cont'd)			ur: diuresis, diuretic (*ur*, urine)

NB: *Dioecious* (in *botany*, having male and female flowers borne on separate plants; compare *monoecious*) has the same root as *diocese*, but the beginning element is *di*, two.

dia-:

bet: diabetes (a metabolic disorder marked by excessive discharge of urine and persistent thirst), diabetic (from *bainein*, to go)

chron: diachronic, diachrony (*chronos*, time)

crit: diacritic, diacritical (from *krinein*, to separate)

dem: diadem (a crown; an ornamental cloth headband worn as a crown; royal power, authority, or dignity) (see *dein*)

drom: diadromous (*dromo*, running, moving)

gno: diagnose, diagnosis, diagnostic (*gnoscere*, to know)

gon: diagonal {diagonally} (*gon*, angle)

gram: diagram (from *graph*, write)

kin: diakinesis {diakinetic} (*kinein*, to move)

lect: dialect (**Synonyms**: vernacular, jargon, cant), dialectic (from *legein*, to tell)

log: dialogue (*logo*, word)

lys: dialysis {dialytic} (*lys*, loosen)

meter: diameter (to measure across a circle) {diametrical} (*meter*, measure)

noet: dianoetic (*noein*, to think over)

pas: diapason (through all the notes of an organ; thus, full organ) (*pason*, feminine genitive plural of *pan*, all)

ped: diapedesis (*pedan*, to leap)

phan: diaphanous (literally, to show through) (*phan*, to show)

phor: diaphoresis (perspiration, especially, when profuse), diaphoretic (producing or increasing perspiration) (*phor*, to bear)

phragm: diaphragm (literally, completely enclosed)

phys: diaphysis (the shaft of a long bone, as distinguished from the growing ends) (*phys*, growth)

rrh: diarrhea (literally, to run through) (*rrh*, run)

spora: diaspora (literally, scattering of seed; capitalized, the dispersion of the Jews) (*spore*, seed)

stas: diastase {diastatic} (from *histanai*, to cause to stand)

stem: diastem, diastema (from *histanai*, to cause to stand)

stol: diastole {diastolic} (from *stellein*, to put)

stroph: diastrophism (the process or series of processes by which the major features of the earth's crust, including continents, mountains, ocean beds, folds, and faults, are formed) {diastrophic} (*stroph*, to turn, twist)

therm: diathermancy, diathermic, diathermy (*therm*, heat)

thesis: diathesis (a predisposition to certain diseases) (*thesis*, to place)

tom: diatom {diatomaceous} (*tom*, cut)

ton: diatonic {diatonically, diatonicism} (*ton*, stretch, tone)

trib: diatribe (a bitter, abusive criticism) (from *terere*, to rub)

trop: diatropism {diatropic} (*trope*, turn)

DOUBLE PREFIXED ROOT:

adiabetic (*a-*, not + *bet*, from *bat*, to go)

Element	From	Meaning	Examples
dia- (cont'd)			adiaphoresis, adiaphoria, adiaphorous (in *medicine*, neutral, like a placebo) (*a-*, without + *phor*, to bear) adiathermancy (*a-*, without + *therm*, heat) INTERDISCIPLINARY: diadromous (in *botany*, with leaf veins radiating in a fanlike arrangement; in *zoology*, migrating between fresh and salt water: said of certain fishes) NB: *Diamond*, from *adamant*, unyielding, is not in this family; neither is *dianthus*, from *di*, two + *anthus*, flower. CROSS REFERENCE: *trans-*
dic,* dit, dex**	Latin *dicere*: to say (IE: *deik*, to point out)	to say, proclaim	SIMPLE ROOT: dicta: dictate, dictation, dictator, dictatorial (**Synonyms:** arbitrary, dogmatic, doctrinaire), dictature dicti: diction (manner of expression in words; choice of words; wording), dictionary dictu: dictum (in *law*, a judge's remark or observation on some point of law which is not essential to the case in question, hence not binding as a legal precedent) PREFIXED ROOT: *dic*: *ab-*: abdicate {abdication, abdicative, abdicator} (*ab-*, away) *de-*: dedicate (**Synonyms:** devote, consecrate, pledge), dedication, dedicative, dedicatory (*de-*, away) *in-*: indicant, indicate, indication, indicative, indicator, indicium (plural, *indicia*) (*in-*, in) *pre-*: predicable, predicament, predicant, predicate, predication, predicatory (*pre-*, before, in front of) *dict*: *ad-*: addict, addicted, addiction, addictive (*ad-*, to, toward) *contra-*: contradict (**Synonyms:** deny, gainsay, refute), contradiction, contradictory (*contra-*, against) *e-*: edict (a decree or formal declaration) (from *ex-*, out) *in-*: indict, indictment, indiction (*in-*, toward) *inter-*: interdict {interdiction, interdictive} (*inter-*, between) *pre-*: predict (**Synonyms:** augur, prognosticate, portend) {predictive}, prediction (*pre-*, before) *dit*: *con-*: condition (**Synonyms:** state, situation, status), conditional (*con-*, with, together) *in-*: indite (compare with *indict*, above) (*in-*, in) *dex*: *in-*: index (from *indicate*) (*in-*, in) TRAILING ROOT COMPOUND: *dic*: fati: fatidic (of divination or prophecy; prophetic; also *fatidical*) (*fati*, fate) juri: juridicial (of judicial proceedings) (*jurare*, to swear) vin: vindicate (**Synonyms:** absolve, acquit, exonerate; see *Disguised Roots* below) (*vindex*, claimant, avenger) *dict*: bene: benediction (see *Doublets* below) (*bene*, well, good) juris: jurisdiction (**Synonyms:** power, authority, dominion) (*juris*, right, law)

Element	From	Meaning	Examples
dic (cont'd)			male: malediction (see *Doublets* below) (*mal, male*, evil, ill, from *malus*, bad)
			vale: valediction (the act of bidding or saying farwell; something said in parting; farewell utterance), valedictorian, valedictory (*vale*, farewell)
			ver: verdict (literally, a true saying) (*ver*, true)
			DISGUISED ROOTS:
			benison (see *Doublets* below; see note under *bene*)
			ditto (the same as something said or appearing above or before; a duplicate; another of the same) [from Tuscan *detto*, said; Tuscan designates a literary dialect of Tuscany, a region of central Italy]
			ditty (literally, a thing dictated; a short, simple song) (from Old French *dité*)
			judge (literally, one who points out the right; **Synonyms:** arbiter, referee, umpire) (*jus*, law + *dicere*)
			policy (also listed under Greek *dei*)
			preach, preacher (*pre-*, before + *dicare*, to proclaim)
			revenge (**Synonym:** avenge), revengeful (**Synonyms:** vindictive, vengeful, spiteful)
			DOUBLETS:
			benison:benediction
			malison:malediction
			FRENCH WORDS AND PHRASES:
			diseuse (a woman entertainer who performs monologues, dramatic impersonations, etc.)
			voir dire (to speak truly; in *law*, an oath taken by a person to speak the truth in an examination testing his/her competence as a witness or juror; the examination itself)
			c'est-à-dire (that is to say, namely)
			LATIN PHRASE:
			ipse dixit [literally, He has said (it); a dogmatic statement]
			ENGLISH COGNATES:
			teach (**Synonyms:** instruct, educate, train)
			token (**Synonyms:** pledge, earnest, pawn)
			PLACENAMES:
			Benedicta, Maine
			Index (Kentucky, New York, North Carolina)
			Lac Indicateur, Quebec
			CROSS REFERENCE: *digit, fab/fat/fess, loqu, ora, phas/phe*
dich**	Greek *dicha* (IE: *dwo*, two)	two, asunder	SIMPLE ROOT:
			dichasium (plural, *dichasia*; in *botany*, a cyme in which two opposite branches arise below each terminal flower)
			LEADING ROOT COMPOUND:
			dich:
			opt: dichoptic (having the borders of the compound eyes separate; compare holoptic) (from *opsis*, eye, vision)
			dicho:
			gam: dichogamy (in *biology*, the maturing of pistils and stamens at different times, preventing self-pollination) (*gamo*, marriage, sexual reproduction)
			tom: dichotomize (to divide or separate into two parts), dichotomy (division into two parts, groups, or classes, especially when these are sharply distinguished or opposed) (*tom*, to cut)

Element	From	Meaning	Examples
dich (cont'd)			INTERDISCIPLINARY: dichotomy (in *astronomy*, the phase of the moon or of a planet in which just half of its surface facing the earth seems illuminated; in *biology*, *botany*, a dividing or branching into two parts, especially when repeated) CROSS REFERENCE: *bi/bin/bis, deutero, du*
didym**	Greek *didymos*	twin; testicle	SIMPLE ROOT: didymium (because of it being associated with lanthanum; chemical symbol, Di) didymous (in *biology*, growing in pairs; twin) PREFIXED ROOT: *epi-*: epididymis (a long, oval-shaped structure attached to the rear upper surface of each testicle, consisting mainly of the excretory ducts of the testicles) (*epi-*, upon) LEADING ROOT COMPOUND: itis: didymitis (*itis*, inflammation) TRAILING DISGUISED ROOT COMPOUND: tetra: tetradymite [fourfold: because it occurs in compound twin crystals; a pale, steel-gray mineral (chemical symbol: Bi_2Te_2S), consisting chiefly of tellurium and bismuth] (*tetra*, four) CROSS REFERENCE: *gemini, test*
die**	Latin *dies* (IE: *deiwos,* god; from *dei,* to gleam, shine)	day	ROOT NOTE: The base of *diurnal* (see *Simple Root*) is the basis of French *jour(nal).* SIMPLE ROOT: diurnal (opposed to *nocturnal*) PREFIXED ROOT: *circa-*: circadian (in *biology*, exhibiting approximately 24-hour periodicity) (*circa-*, around) TRAILING ROOT COMPOUND: meri: meridian (of or at noon; many other meanings) (from *medius*, middle) quoti: quotidian (daily; recurring every day; everyday; usual or ordinary; as a *noun*, anything, especially a fever, that recurs daily) (*quoti*, how many, as many) PREFIXED TRAILING ROOT COMPOUND: *ante-*: antemeridian (pertaining to the morning), ante meridiem (abbreviated a.m.) (*ante-*, before) DISGUISED ROOT: dial (from *sun dial*, that which told the time of day) diet (originally, daily food allowance; also Scottish: a day's session of an assembly) dismal (causing gloom or misery; depressing; dark and gloomy; bleak; dreary; depressed; miserable) [*mal*, bad; thus, evil days (of the medieval calendar)] SPANISH: *buenos días* (Good morning; literally, good day; even though *días* is plural; *días* is related to *deo*, God) LATIN WORDS AND PHRASES: *carpe diem* (seize the day; make the most of present opportunities) *per diem* (by the day) *post meridiem* (literally, post middle-day; abbreviated *p.m.*) *sine die* (without a day; usually used thus: Congress adjourned *sine die*, that is, adjourned without setting a day to reconvene)

200

Element	From	Meaning	Examples
die (cont'd)			INTERDISCIPLINARY: diurnal [in *botany*, opening in the daytime and closing at night: said of a flower; in *zoology*, active in the daytime; in *ecclesiology*, a service book containing prayers for the daytime canonical hours and for Compline (the last of the seven canonical hours; night prayer)] CROSS REFERENCE: *hemer, jour*
dif-			See *dis-* for *different.*
digit***	Latin *digitus*: finger (IE: *deik*, to point out)	finger, toe	ROOT NOTE: Though basically meaning finger, the root is extended to mean pointer, thus *index, indicate.* From the same IE root--*deik*--is derived *dicere*, to say (see *dic*). SIMPLE ROOT: digit (a finger or a toe; a measure of length, equal to 3/4 inch, based on the breadth of the finger; any numeral from 0 to 9: so called because originally counted on the fingers) digital (using numbers that are digits to represent all the variables involved in a calculation; using a row of digits, rather than numbers on a dial, to provide numerical information) digitalis [a flowering plant originally named *Fingerhut* (finger house, or *thimble*, thumb bell), by L. Fuchs, a German botanist, in 1542; its flowers resemble thimbles. *Dorland's Medical Dictionary* says that *digitalis* is so named because its *leaves* resemble fingers.] digitalization, digitate, digitation, digitize, digitus LEADING ROOT COMPOUND: form: digitiform (in the form of a finger; shaped like a finger) grad: digitigrade (walking on the toes with the heels not touching the ground, as cats, dogs, horses, etc.) (*gradus*, step) TRAILING ROOT COMPOUND: presti: prestidigitation (nimble fingers; sleight of hand; manual skill and dexterity in the execution of tricks) (*preste*, nimble) PREFIXED DISGUISED ROOT: *in-*: index, indicate, indication (also listed under *dic*) (*in-*, in) CROSS REFERENCE: *dactyl , dic*
dign***	Latin *dignus*: worthy (IE: *dek*, to receive, be fitting)	worth, worthy	SIMPLE ROOT: dignitary, dignatory dignity (**Synonyms**: decorum, propriety, etiquette; see *Doublets*) PREFIXED ROOT: *con-*: condign (literally, very worthy; fitting; adequate; suitable: said especially of punishment or censure for wrongdoing) {condignly} (from *com-*, an intensive) *in-*: indignant, indignation (**Synonyms**: anger, rage, fury), indignity (*in-*, not) LEADING ROOT COMPOUND: fy: dignify (to give dignity to; to make worthy of esteem; honor, exalt, or ennoble; to make seem worthy or noble, as by giving a high-sounding name to, as to *dignify* cowardice by calling it *prudence*) (from *facere*, to make, do) DISGUISED ROOT: dainty (**Synonyms**: delicate, exquisite; see *Doublets*) (from Old French *deinté*, worth, value, delicacy)

201

Element	From	Meaning	Examples
dign (cont'd)			deign (to think it not beneath one's dignity to do something, or to think it appropriate or suitable to one's dignity to do something; to condescend reluctantly to give or grant; **Synonyms**: stoop, condescend) PREFIXED DISGUISED ROOT: dis-: disdain (**Synonyms**: despise, scorn, contemn), disdainful (*dis-*, apart, away) DOUBLETS: dainty:dignity LATIN PHRASE: *infra dignitatem* (shortened to *infra dig*; colloquial for beneath one's dignity) CROSS REFERENCE: *val*
din*	Greek *deinos*: fearful, monstrous (IE: *dwei*, to fear)	terrible	LEADING ROOT COMPOUND: saur: dinosaur (literally, dreadful lizard) (*saur*, lizard) ther: dinothere (a genus of extinct elephantlike animals) (*there*, wild beast) LATIN COGNATE: dire (arousing terror or causing extreme distress; dreadful; terrible; as in *dire circumstances*) (Latin *dirus*, fearful) NO CROSS REFERENCE
diplo***	Greek *diploos*; from *di*, two + *ploos*, fold (IE: *dwo*, two + *pel*, to fold)	two-fold, twin	SIMPLE ROOT: diploë (the spongy bone between the two dense inner and outer layers of the skull bones) diploma (an official state document or historical document; charter; a certificate conferring honors, privileges, etc.) diplomacy (**Synonyms**: tact, poise, savoir-faire) diplomat, diplomatic (**Synonyms**: suave, urbane, bland) LEADING ROOT COMPOUND: *dipl*: oid: diploid (in *biology*, having twice the number of chromosomes normally occurring in a mature germ cell: most somatic cells are diploid; as a *noun*, a diploid cell) (*oid*, similar to) ont: diplont (*ont*, cell) opia: diplopia (an eye symptom in which a single object appears double; double vision) (*opia*, pertaining to sight) osis: diplosis (*osis*, condition of) *diplo*: blast: diploblastic (in *zoology*, of or pertaining to a body with only two cellular layers, the ectoderm and the endoderm) (*blast*, sprout, shoot) coccus: diplococcus (*coccus*, berry, pit) pod: diplopod (same as *millipede*) (*pod*, foot) PREFIXED LEADING ROOT COMPOUND: ana-: anadiplosis (the repetition of a key word, especially the last one, at the beginning of the next sentence, phrase, verse, or clause, usually with a change or extension of meaning, as "He gave his *life*; *life* was all he could give"; "rely on his honor; honor such as his?") (*ana-*, again) CROSS REFERENCE: *bi/bin/bis, di, dicho, du*

Word from Greek mythology: aegis (protection or worship)
Originally, Greek aigis designated a goatskin, and was the shield borne by
Zeus, and later by Athena.

Element	From	Meaning	Examples
dis-,* **dif-,** **di-** **[des-]**	Latin *dis,* apart, asunder [French]	apart, away	PREFIXED ROOT: *de-*: (*de-* from *dis-*, apart) fer: defer (to postpone) (*ferre*, to bear) *des-*: cry: descry (to catch sight of; discern distant or obscure objects; to look for and discover; detect; **Synonyms**: see, behold, view) (from *quiritare*, to wail) *di-*: (before *b, d, g, l, m, n, r, s, v*) gest: digest (**Synonyms**: abridgment, abstract, brief), digestible, digestion, digestive (from *gerere*, to bear) gress: digress (**Synonyms**: deviate, swerve, veer), digression, digressive (from *gradi*, step) lapi: dilapidate, dilapidated, dilapidation (**Synonyms**: ruin, destruction, havoc) (*lapis*, stone) lat: dilatant, dilatation, dilate (**Synonyms**: expand, swell, distend), dilation, dilator (*latus*, wide) lig: diligence, diligent (**Synonyms**: busy, industrious, assiduous) (from *legere*, to choose) lu: dilute, dilution, diluvion (*luere*, a variation of *lavare*, to wash) mens: dimension, dimensional (from *metiri*, to measure) mid: dimidiate (from *medius*, middle) rect: direct, direction, directive, director (from *regere*, to keep straight) rig: dirigible (see *direct*, previous entry) stanc: distance, distant (from *stare*, to stand) still: distill (or *distil*), distillate, distiller (*di-* from *de-*, down; *stilla*, a drop) strain: distrain, distraint (from *stringere*, to draw tight) stress: distress (**Synonyms**: suffering, agony, anguish) (see *distrain*, previous entry) strict: district (see *distress*, previous entry) vag: divagate (to wander about; stray from the subject; digress) (*vagari*, to wander) varic: divaricate, divarication, divaricator (*varicare*, to straddle) verg: diverge (see synonyms at *digress*), divergence, divergent (*vergere*, to turn) vers: divers, diverse, diversified, diversiform, diversify, diversion, diversionary, diversity (from *vertere*, to turn) vert: divert, diverticulum, divertimento (any of various light, melodic instrumental compositions in several movements), diverting (see *diverse*) vest: divest, divestiture (altered from *devest*; both prefixes are from *dis-*) (*vestire*, to clothe) vid: divide, divided, dividend, divider, dividual (from IE base *weidh*, to separate) vis: division, divisive, divisor (from *divide*) vorc: divorce (from *diverse*) vulg: divulge, divulgence (*vulgus*, the common people) vuls: divulsion (a tearing or being torn apart; violent rending or separation) (from *vellere*, to pull out)

Element	From	Meaning	Examples
dis- (cont'd)			FRENCH: *divertissement* (a diversion; amusement; a short ballet, etc., performed between the acts of play or opera; *entr' acte*; same as *divertimento*)

dis-

array: disarray (*ar-* assimilates *ad-*, to, toward)

aster: disaster (original meaning: the falling apart of the stars; thus, a calamity) (Greek *aster*, star)

burs: disburse (literally, out of the bag) (*bursa*, a bag, pouch)

calc: discalced (barefooted, as in some religious orders) (*calc*, heel)

card: discard (see *card* for background)

cern: discern (to see, recognize, or apprehend) (*cernere*, to sift, separate, perceive)

cip: disciple (**Synonyms**: follower, supporter, adherent) (from *capere*, to hold; influenced by *discere*, to learn)

claim: disclaim, disclaimer (from *clamare*, to cry out)

clam: disclamation (see *disclaim*)

clos: disclose (**Synonyms**: reveal, divulge, tell) (from *claudere*, to block up)

com: (with, together)

discomfit (*com-* prefixes *fit*, which is from *facere*, to make)

discompose (*com-* prefixes *pose*, which is from *poser*, to place)

cord: discord (**Synonyms**: strife, contention, dissension), discordant (from *cors*, heart)

count: discount (from *compute*)

cour: discourage (see *discord*)

cours: discourse (**Synonyms**: speak, talk, converse) (from *currere*, to run)

cover: (from *co-*, intensive + *operire*, to hide)

discover (**Synonyms**: learn, ascertain, determine)

discovert (in *law*, having no husband: said of a spinster, widow, or divorcée)

discovery (in *law*, any disclosure that a defendant is compelled to make, as of facts or documents)

crep: discrepancy, discrepant (*crepare*, to rattle)

creet: discreet (see *Doublets* below; **Synonyms**: circumspect, prudent, wary) (from *discern*)

cret: discrete (see *Doublets* below), discretion (from *discern*)

crim: discriminable, discriminant, discriminate, discriminating, discrimination, discriminatory (from *discern*)

curs: discursion, discursive (see *discourse*)

cuss: discuss (**Synonyms**: argue, debate, dispute), discussion (from *quatere*, to shake)

dain: disdain, disdainful (from *dignare*, to deem worthy)

eas: disease (literally, not at ease)

em: disembark (*em-* prefixes *bark*, boat)

gorg: disgorge (to bring up and expel from the throat or stomach; to vomit) (*gorge*, throat)

grac: disgrace (**Synonyms**: shame, infamy, ignominy) (from Latin *gratia*, favor)

guis: disguise (to make appear, sound, etc. different from usual so as to be unrecognizable) (*guise*, fashion, manner)

Element	From	Meaning	Examples
dis- (cont'd)			gust: disgust (**Synonyms**: sicken, nauseate, repel), disgustful, disgusting (*gustus*, taste)
			hab: dishabille (the state of being dressed only partially or in night clothes) (French *habiller*, to dress)
			inter: disinterested (*inter-* prefixes *esse*, being)
			junct: **disjunct, disjunctive** (from *jungere*, to join)
			may: dismay (**Synonyms**: appall, horrify, daunt) (from Germanic *mag*, power)
			mantl: dismantle (**Synonyms**: strip, denude, divest) (from *mantellum*, cloak, napkin, a cloth)
			miss: dismiss (**Synonyms**: eject, expel, oust), dismissal, dismissive (from *mittere*, to send)
			ob: disobedience, disobedient, disobey (**Synonyms**: violate, defy) (*ob-* prefixes *audire*, to hear)
			order: disorder (**Synonyms**: confusion, disarray, chaos)
			orient: disorient (also, *disorientate*) {disorientated} (*oriri*, to arise)
			par: (equal)
			disparage (**Synonyms**: depreciate, belittle, depreciate), disparagement
			disparate (**Synonyms**: divergent, distinct, dissimilar), disparity
			patch: dispatch (**Synonyms**: 1) haste, speed, expedition; 2) kill, murder, execute) (from *ped*, foot)
			pel: dispel (**Synonyms**: scatter, disperse, dissipate) {dispelled, dispelling} (*pellere*, to drive)
			pens: dispensable, dispensary, dispensation, dispensator, dispensatory, dispense (**Synonyms**: distribute, divide, dole) (from *pendere*, to hang, weigh)
			pers: disperse (see synonyms at *dispel*, above), dispersion, dispersive (from *spargere*, to scatter)
			play: display (**Synonyms**: show, exhibit, expose) (from *plicare*, to fold)
			plum: displume (same as *deplume*) (*pluma*, feather)
			port: disport (from which *sport* is derived) (*portare*, to carry)
			pos: disposable, dispose, disposed, disposition (**Synonyms**: temperament, character, personality) (from *ponere*, to place)
			prov: disprove (**Synonyms**: refute, confute, rebut) (from *probare*, to test)
			put: disputable, disputant, disputation, disputatious, dispute (**Synonyms**: 1) discuss; argue, debate; 2) argument, controversy), disputation (*putare*, to think)
			re: (*re-*, back, again, prefixes the root in each of the following four groups of words)
			disregard (**Synonyms**: neglect, omit, overlook)
			disrepair (state of neglect; dilapidation)
			disreputable, disrepute (see synonyms at *disgrace*, above)
			disrespect, disrespectful
			rob: disrobe (to undress)
			rupt: disrupt (to break apart; split up; render asunder) {disruption}, disruptive (from *rumpere*, to break)

Element	From	Meaning	Examples
dis- (cont'd)			**sect:** (from *secare*, to cut) dissect [to cut apart piece by piece; separate into parts, as a body for purposes of study; to examine or analyze closely; differentiated from *bisect*, to cut in two (equal lengths)] dissected (in *botany*, consisting of many lobes or segments, as some leaves; in *geology*, cut by erosion into valleys, hills) **seiz:** disseize (noun is *disseizin*, or *disseisin*) (from *sacire*, to place) **sembl:** dissemble (from *simulare*, to feign) **semin:** disseminate, disseminule (*seminare*, to sow; from *semen*, seed) **sens:** dissension (see synonyms at discord) (from *dissent*, next entry) **sent:** dissent, dissenter, dissentient, dissentious (*sentire*, to feel) **sert:** dissertation (from *serere*, to join) **sever:** dissever (from *separare*, to separate) **sid:** dissidence, dissident (literally, sitting apart; dissenting; also used as a noun: a dissenter) (*sidere*, to sit) **sil:** dissilient (springing or bursting apart, as some plant capsules or pods) (*salire*, to leap) **simil:** dissimilar (**Synonyms:** different, diverse, divergent), dissimilate, dissimilation, dissimilitude (*similis*, like) **simul:** dissimulate {dissimulation} (*simulare*, to feign) **sipat:** dissipate (see synonyms at *dispel*, above), dissipation (from *supare*, to throw) **socia:** dissociate, dissociation (*sociare*, to join) **solu:** dissoluble, dissolute, dissolution (from *dissolve*) **solv:** dissolve (**Synonyms:** 1) adjourn, prorogue, postpone, 2) melt, liquefy, thaw) (*solvere*, to loosen) **son:** dissonance, dissonant (*sonus*, a sound) **sua:** dissuade, dissuasion, dissausive (*suadere*, to persuade) **temper:** distemper (*temperare*, to mix in proportion) **tend:** distend (**Synonyms:** extend, lengthen, elongate) (*tendere*, to stretch) **tens:** distensible (from *distend*) **tinct:** distinct (see synonyms at *dissimilar*, above), distinction, distinctive (from *stinguere*, to prick) **ting:** distinguish (**Synonyms:** discriminate, differentiate), distinguished (see *distinct*, previous entry) **tort:** distort (**Synonyms:** deform, contort, warp), distortion (from *torquere*, to twist) **tract:** distract, distraction {distractive} (from *trahere*, to draw, pull) **trait:** distrait (**Synonyms:** abstracted, distraught, inattentive) (from *distract*, previous entry) **trib:** distributary, distribute (**Synonyms:** dispense, divide, dole), distributive, distributor (*tribuere*, to allot) **turb:** disturb (**Synonyms:** discompose, perturb) (*turbare*, to disorder) DISGUISED ROOT: dine, dinner (from *disjejunare*, where *jejunare* means to fast)

206

Element	From	Meaning	Examples
dis- (cont'd)			dirge [the first word of an antiphon (Psalm 5:8) in the Office for the Burial of the Dead] (from *dirigere*, to direct) DOUBLETS: discreet:discrete FRENCH: digestif (a digestive aid; especially, an after-dinner drink, as brandy) *dif-*: (before *f*): fer: (*ferre*, to bear) differ, differencia (in *logic*, a distinguishing characteristic, especially one that distinguishes one species from another of the same genus) different (**Synonyms**: inconsistency, variation, disparity) {differential, differentiation} fic: difficile, difficult (**Synonyms**: arduous, onerous, laborious), difficulty (from *facere*, to do) fid: diffidence (lack of confidence or trust in oneself; shyness), diffident (*fidere*, to trust) fract: diffract, diffraction {diffractive} (*frangere*, to break) fus: diffuse, diffusible, diffusion, diffusive (from *fundere*, to pour) DOUBLE PREFIXED ROOT: discontented (not contented; wanting something more or different) (*con-*, with, together + *tenere*, to hold) disembogue (to empty at the mouth: used of a river) (*em-* from *en-*, in; *bogue* from *bucca*, mouth) disinterested (*inter-*, between; *es* from *esse*, to be) disinfectant (*in-*, in + *fect* from *facere*, to do, make) disingenuous (not straightforward) (*in-*, in + *gen*, produce) disillusion (*il-* from *in-*, on + *lus* from *ludere*, to play) disproportionate (*pro-*, for + *portio*, a part) disapprove (*ap-* from *ad-*, to, toward + *probus*, good) disinter (to dig up or remove, as from a grave or tomb; exhume) (*in-*, in + *terra*, earth) LATIN PHRASE: *disjecta membra* (scattered parts or fragments, as of an author's writings) NB: *Distill* is not in this family, coming instead from *de-*, down, *stillare*, to drop; neither are *distinct* and *distinguish*. INTERDISCIPLINARY: dimidiate (in *biology*, having only one half developed; in *botany*, split on one side, as the calyptra of mosses) disjunct (in *music*, having to do with the use of intervals larger than a major second; in *zoology*, having the body sharply divided by deep furrows, as into head, thorax, and abdomen in most insects) disjunctive (in *grammar*, indicating a contrast or an alternative between words, clauses, etc., e.g., in the sentence John or Bob may go, but their sister may not, *or* and *but* are *disjunctive conjunctions*; in *logic*, presenting alternatives, as a *disjunctive proposition*) CROSS REFERENCE: *a-, an-, de-, in-*

Perhaps the most valuable skill to be acquired is that with words.
Max J. Herzberg

Element	From	Meaning	Examples
disc**	Greek *dikein;* akin to *deiknynai,* to show; (IE: *deik,* to point out)	to throw, to point out	SIMPLE ROOT: disc (in *biology*, any disk-shaped part or structure) disco (from *discothèque*) discus, disk (in *anatomy*, a layer of fibrous connective tissue with small masses of cartilage among the fibers) LEADING ROOT COMPOUND: *disc*: oid: discoid (also, *discoidal*; shaped like a disk; in *botany*, having disk flowers, but no ray flowers, as a composite flower head; as a *noun*, anything shaped like a disk) (*oid*, similar to) *disco*: bolus: discobolus (a discus thrower); capitalized, famous statue by Myron (from *ballein*, to throw) graph: discography (the systematic cataloging of phonograph records; a list of the recordings of a particular performer, composer, composition, etc.) (*graph*, write) phil: discophile (an expert on, or collector of, phonograph records) (*philos*, love) thequ: discotheque (from *tithenai*, to place, do) CROSS REFERENCE: *bal/bol, dict, jac/ject*
dit			See *dic* for *condition*.
dit			See *don* for *edition*.
div			See *dei* for *divine*.
do,** dos, dot	Greek *didonai:* to give (IE: *do,* to give)	gift	SIMPLE ROOT: dose PREFIXED ROOT: *dos*: apo-: apodosis (the clause expressing the conclusion or result in a conditional sentence: opposed to *prostasis*) (*apo-*, away) *dot*: anti-: antidote (literally, given against; a remedy to counteract a poison; anything that works against an evil or unwanted condition) {antidotal} (*anti-*, against) epi-: epidote {epidotic} (*epi-*, upon, over) DOUBLE PREFIXED ROOT: an-: anecdotal, anecdote (originally, a story not to be given out; **Synonyms**: story, narrative, tale) (*an-*, not + *ec-*, from *ex-*, out) LEADING ROOT COMPOUND: meter: dosimeter (a device that measures and indicates the amount of x-rays or radioactivity absorbed) (*meter*, measure) COALESCED COMPOUND: anecdotage (*anecdote + dotage*; a collection of anecdotes; senility, as characterized by the telling of rambling anecdotes: a humorous usage) GREEK MYTHOLOGY: Pandora, the first mortal woman, who in curiosity opened a box, letting out all human ills into the world (or, in a later version, letting all human blessings escape and be lost, leaving only hope) (*pan*, all) PROPER NAMES: Dorothy (*dora + theos*, God; gift of God) Eudora (*eu*, good, well; thus, good gift) Theodore (same derivation as *Dorothy*, gift of God) PLACENAME: Eudora (Arkansas, Kansas) AMERICAN AUTHORESS: Eudora Welty CROSS REFERENCE: *don/dat/dit*

Element	From	Meaning	Examples
doc**	Latin *docere* (IE: *dek*, to receive, greet, be suitable, teach)	to teach	SIMPLE ROOT: doce: docent (in some American universities, a teacher or lecturer not on the regular faculty; a tour guide and lecturer, as at a museum) doci: docile (**Synonyms:** obedient, compliant, amenable), docility docto: doctor, doctoral doctr: doctrinaire (see synonyms at *dictatorial*, under *dict*), doctrine (**Synonyms:** dogma, tenet, precept) docu: document, documentary, documentation PREFIXED ROOT: *in-*: (note difference in meanings of prefixes) indocile (not easy to teach or discipline) (*in-*, not) indoctrinate (to instruct in) (*in-*, in) NOTE: *Disciple* and *discipline* are listed in this family by *American Heritage* and by Robert Claiborne in *The Roots of English*; *Webster's New World* and *Webster's Third* list them under *cap*, to take, which see.) CROSS REFERENCE: *dogma*
dodeca*	Greek *duodeka* (*duo*, two + *deka*, ten)	twelve	LEADING ROOT COMPOUND: gon: dodecagon (a polygon with 12 sides) (*gon*, angle) hedron: dodecahedron (a polyhedron with 12 faces) (*hedron*, geometric side) phon: dodecaphonic (pertaining to, composed in, or consisting of 12-tone music) (*phone*, sound) NO CROSS REFERENCE
dogma,* dox	Greek *dokein* (IE: *dek*, to receive, greet, be suitable, teach)	to think true, to seem, opinion, judgment	SIMPLE ROOT: dogma, dogmatic, dogmatics, dogmatize PREFIXED ROOT: *para-*: paradox (a seemingly contradictory statement that may nonetheless be true) (*para-*, beyond) LEADING ROOT COMPOUND: logy: doxology (words of praise) TRAILING ROOT COMPOUND: hetero: heterodox (departing from or opposed to the usual beliefs or established doctrines, especially in religion; inclining toward heresy; unorthodox), heterodoxy (*hetero*, different) ortho: orthodox (conforming to the usual beliefs or established doctrines, as in religion, politics, etc.) (*ortho*, straight) CROSS REFERENCE: *doc*
dol**	Latin *dolere*: to feel pain; grieve (IE: *del*, *dol*, to split, cut)	sorrow, pain	SIMPLE ROOT: doleful (**Synonyms:** sad, sorrowful, melancholy), dolent, dolor, doloric, dolorous PREFIXED ROOT: *con-*: (from *com-*, with, together) condole (to express sympathy; mourn in sympathy) condolence (also, *condolement*; **Synonyms:** pity, compassion, commiseration) *in-*: indolent [literally, not to feel pain; disliking or avoiding work (as though to work would cause one pain); idle; lazy; in *medicine*, causing little or no pain, as *an indolent cyst*; slow to heal, as *an indolent ulcer*] (*in-*, not) LEADING ROOT COMPOUND: fic: dolorific (causing pain or grief) (from *facere*, to make, do) fug: dolorifuge (anything that relieves pain) (*fugere*, to flee)

Element	From	Meaning	Examples
dol**			LATIN PHRASE: *via dolorosa* (the sorrowful path that Jesus trod from the Judgment Hall to the Cross of Crucifixion) PRESCRIPTION DRUG: DOLOBID [a medication for pain to be taken *b.i.d.* (*bis in die*), or twice daily] ITALIAN MUSIC TERM: *con dolore* (with sorrow) NB: *Dole* itself is not in this family, coming from Old English *dal*, a share, parallel to. CROSS REFERENCE: *alg, esthes, odyn, path, sens*
dom***	Latin *dominus*: lord (IE: *dem*, to build)	home, master	SIMPLE ROOT: dom: domain (a territory or range of rule or control; realm; in *mathematics*, the set of possible values of an independent variable of a function; compare range) dome: dome, domestic, domesticate, domesticity domic: domicile (in *law*, one's fixed place of dwelling, where one intends to reside more or less permanently), domiciliate domin: dominance, dominant (**Synonyms**: predominant, paramount, preeminent), dominate, domination domineer, domineering (**Synonyms**: masterful, imperious, magisterial) dominical, dominie, dominion (**Synonyms**: power, authority, sway), domino (interesting relationship), dominium (law term) PREFIXED ROOT: *con*-: condominium (originally, joint rule by two or more states; in its current use, an arrangement whereby a tenant in an apartment building holds full title to his or her unit and joint ownership of the common grounds) (*con*-, with, together) *in*-: indomitable (not easily discouraged, defeated, or subdued; unyielding; unconquerable) (*in*-, not) *pre*-: predominant (see synonyms at *dominant*, above) predominate (*pre*-, before) DISGUISED ROOT: dame (capitalized, originally a title given to a woman in authority or the mistress of a household: now only in personifications; the title of a woman who has received an order of knighthood, used always with the given name) (from *domina*, lady) damoiseau (a young noble not yet made a knight) damsel (diminutive of *domina*; see *dame* above) danger (originally, absolute power of an overlord; **Synonyms**: peril, jeopardy, hazard) (Middle English *daunger*, power, domination, arrogance)· timber (originally, a building; building material) SPANISH TITLES: *Don* (equivalent to *sir* or *mister*, as *Don Pedro*) *Doña* [with tilde (~) over *n*, so that the word is pronounced approximately as DOE nyah), a title of respect equivalent to *Lady*, or *Madame*] NO CROSS REFERENCE

Word from Greek mythology: nemesis (an agent of destruction)
from Nemesis, goddess of retributive justice, or vengeance

Element	From	Meaning	Examples
don,* **dat,** **dit**	Latin *donare,* *dare* (IE: *do,* to give)	to give	SIMPLE ROOT: *dat:* data (plural of *datum,* below) dative (in *grammar,* a case that indicates the indirect object of a verb) datum (plural, *data*) *don:* donate (**Synonyms:** give, grant, bestow) donation (**Synonyms:** present, gratuity, gift) donative, donator, donee, donor PREFIXED ROOT: *dat:* *ante-:* antedate (*ante-,* before) *post-:* postdate (*post-,* after) *dit:* *e-:* editor, edition (from *ex-,* out) *per-:* perdition (literally, to give thoroughly; to give up to ruin; in *theology,* the loss of the soul; same as Hell; see *perdue* under *Prefixed Disguised Roots*) (*per-,* through) *re-:* rendition (with inserted *n*; literally, the giving back; see render) (*re-,* back) *tra-:* tradition (literally, to give over, or across; see *Doublets* below) (from *trans-,* across) *don:* *con-:* condonation, condone (to forgive, pardon, or overlook an offense) (from *com-,* with, together) *par-:* pardon {pardonable, pardoner} (from *per-,* through) DOUBLE PREFIXED ROOT extradite (**Synonyms:** banish, exile, expatriate), extradition (*ex-,* out + *tra-* from *trans-,* across) DISGUISED ROOTS: date (of month) [*date,* the fruit, comes from *dactyl,* its shape being in the form of *fingers*] dowry render (literally, to give back; see *rendition,* above) rendezvous [French; substantive use of *rendez-vous,* betake or *present yourself (yourselves)*] rent (**Synonyms:** hire, let, lease) treason (originally, the giving over of the state to its enemies; sedition; see *Doublets* below) PREFIXED DISGUISED ROOT: *ad-:* add, additament, addition, additive (*ad-,* to + *dare*) *de-:* demand (**Synonyms:** require, exact) (from *demandare,* to give in charge; from *de-,* away + *manus,* hand) *per-:* perdue [or *perdu;* from *perdition;* as an *adjective,* out of sight; in hiding; concealed, as in military ambush; as a *noun,* a contraction of *sentinelle perdue,* advanced (literally, lost) sentry, or *enfants perdus,* forlorn hope] *sur-:* surrender (to give up possession or power over; yield to another on demand or compulsion) (from *super-,* above, over, beyond) DOUBLETS: treason:tradition CROSS REFERENCE: *do, dos, dot*

Element	From	Meaning	Examples
dorm**	Latin *dormir* (IE: *dre*, to sleep)	to sleep	SIMPLE ROOT: dorma: dormant dorme: dormeuse dormi: dormition, dormitive, dormitory dormo: dormouse (a mouse that appears to be sleeping) UNBOUNDED COMPOUND: dormer window INTERDISCIPLINARY: dormant (in *botany*, temporarily inactive, as in *dormant buds*; in *geology*, inactive, quiescent, as *a dormant volcano*; in *heraldry*, lying down in a sleeping position, as a *lion dormant*) CROSS REFERENCE: *com, hypn, somn*
dors,*** **dos**	Latin *dorsum*	back (of something)	SIMPLE ROOT: *dors*: dorsad, dorsal (same as *dorsel*), dorsum *dos*: dossal (also, *dossel*) dosser (a basket for carrying things on the back) dosseret (architectural term) dossier (originally, a bundle of documents with a label attached to the back or spine) PREFIXED ROOT: *en-*: endorse (to write one's name on the back of a check, money order, or stock certificate as evidence of the legal transfer of ownership) (*en-*, in) *extra-*: extrados (in *architecture*, the outside curved surface of an arch) (*extra-*, beyond) *intra-*: intrados (in *architecture*, the inside curve or surface of an arch or vault) (*intra-*, within) *para-*: parados (an embankment of earth along the back of a trench as to protect against fire from the rear) (*para-*, alongside of) LEADING ROOT COMPOUND: *dorsi*: *ventr*: dorsiventral (same as *dorsoventral*; in *botany*, having both dorsal and ventral surfaces) (*ventr*, belly) *dorso*: *ventr*: dorsoventral (same as *dorsiventral*; in *zoology*, extending from the dorsal to the ventral side) TRAILING ROOT COMPOUND: *rere*: reredos (a screen behind the altar of a church) (Anglo-Saxon *rere*, from *rear*) DANCING TERM: *dos-à-dos* (literally, back to back, in square dancing) NOTE: Do not confuse *dossil* with this family; see *duc*. CROSS REFERENCE: *rachi*
dot			See *do* for *antidote*.
drama*	Greek *dran* (IE: *dra*, to work)	to do	SIMPLE ROOT: drama (a literary composition that tells a story, usually of human conflict, by means of dialogue and action, to be performed by actors; play; now often any play that is not a comedy) dramatic (**Synonyms:** theatrical, startling, sensational), dramatics, dramatist, dramatize LEADING ROOT COMPOUND: *urg*: dramaturgy (from *ergon*, work)

Element	From	Meaning	Examples
drama (cont'd)			TRAILING ROOT COMPOUND: melo: melodrama, melodramatic (*melos*, song) DISGUISED ROOT: drastic (acting with force; having a strong or violent effect; severe; harsh; extreme) LATIN TERM: *dramatis personnae* (literally, characters of the play; a list of the characters preceding the text of a play) NO CROSS REFERENCE
drom**	Greek *dromas*: running (IE: *der¹*, to run, walk; yields English trade, tramp, trap, tread, trip, trot)	run, course	SIMPLE ROOT: dromedary (originally, a particularly speedy camel) PREFIXED ROOT: *ana*-: anadromous (going up rivers to spawn; said of the salmon, shad, etc.; see *catadromous*) (*ana*-, up, again) *anti*-: antidromic (in *physiology*, conveying nerve impulses *running* in a direction opposite to the normal) (*anti*-, against) *cata*-: catadromous (going back to or toward the sea to spawn: said of certain freshwater fishes) (*cata*-, down) *dia*-: diadromous (*dia*-, across, through) *pro*-: prodrome (a symptom of the onset of disease), prodromous (running forward) (*pro*-, before, in front of, forth) *syn*-: syndrome (running together, as the symptoms of a particular disease) (*syn*-, with, together) TRAILING ROOT COMPOUND: acro: acrodrome (in *biology*, having veins ending at the tip of the leaf), acrodromous (*acro*, top, tip, high) aero: aerodrome (an airfield) (*aero*, air) hippo: hippodrome (in ancient Greece and Rome, a course for horse races and chariot races) (*hippo*, horse) loxo: loxodromic (having to do with sailing on rhumb lines; of oblique sailing) (*loxos*, oblique) palin: palindrome [a word or phrase that reads the same backwards as forwards, e.g., A man, a plan, Panama! (in tribute to President Theodore Roosevelt); Madam, I'm Adam (in introducing himself to Eve); name no one man] (*palin*, backward) INTERDISCIPLINARY: diadromous (in *botany*, with leaf veins radiating in a fanlike arrangement; in *zoology*, migrating between fresh and salt water: said of certain fishes) CROSS REFERENCE: *cur*
du***	Latin *duo* (IE: *dwo*, two)	two, double	SIMPLE ROOT: duet, duo dual, dualism, duality dubiety, dubious, dubiosity, dubitable LEADING ROOT COMPOUND: *du*: ple: duple (from *plicare*, to fold) plex: duplex (from *plicare*, to fold) plic: (*plicare*, to fold) duplicate (**Synonyms**: reproduction, facsimile, replica), duplication, duplicator duplicitous (characterized by duplicity; deceitful) duplicity (deceitfulness; double-dealing) *duo*: dec: duodecimal (relating to twelve or twelfths; consisting of or counting by twelves or powers of twelve), duodecimo (*dec*, ten)

Element	From	Meaning	Examples
du (cont'd)			den: duodenum [a section of the small intestine; so named because its length was approximated as the breadth of twelve (*duo*, two + *den*, a variant of *dec*, ten) fingers] logu: duologue (a conversation between two people, especially, in a dramatic performance) (*logos*, word, speech) poly: duopoly (control of a commodity or service in a given market by only two producers or suppliers) (*polein*, to sell) *duum*: vir: duumvir, duumvirate (*vir*, man) DISGUISED ROOT: deuce (another *deuce* is listed under dei) double, doubly, doublet (see *Note*) doubt (**Synonyms**: uncertainty, dubiety, skepticism) doubtful (**Synonyms**: dubious, questionable, problematic) dozen (Middle English *dozeine*; from Old French *douze*, twelve; from Latin *duo* + *decem*, ten) FRENCH: *double-entendre* (literally, double meaning; a term with two meanings, especially when one of them has a risqué or indecorous connotation; the use of such a term or terms; ambiguity) SIMPLE COMPOUND: double negative, as "I don't have no pencil." Double negatives were often used as reinforcers by Shakespeare. NOTE: In *linguistics*, a doublet is either of two words that derive ultimately from the same source but have changed in form. Doublets often have different meanings, e.g., abridge:abbreviate, royal:regal. Doublets in this list are joined by a colon, as in the preceding examples. NB: *Duel*, from Latin *bellum*, war, is not in this family. CROSS REFERENCE: *bi/bin/bis, dicho, du*
duc***	Latin *ducere* (IE: *deuk*, to pull)	to lead	SIMPLE ROOT: duc: ducal, ducat, duce duct: duct, ductile, ductility, ductule PREFIXED ROOT: *duc(e)*: ab-: abduce, abducens (medical term), abducent (opposite to *adducent*) (*ab-*, away) ad-: adduce, adducent (opposite to *abducent*), adducible (also, *adducgable*; the *silent e* is retained to preserve the *soft c*) (*ad-*, to, toward) con-: conduce, conducive (*con-*, with, together) de-: deduce (**Synonyms**: infer, conclude, gather) {deducible} (*de-*, from) e-: educe, educate, educated, education (from *ex-*, out) in-: induce (see *Doublets* below), inducement (*in-*, in) intro-: introduce {introducer} (*intro-*, inwardly) pro-: produce, producer (*pro-*, before, ahead) re-: reduce (**Synonyms**: diminish, decrease, shorten) {reducible, reducibly} (*re-*, back, again) se-: seduce (**Synonyms**: lure, entice, inveigle) (*se-*, away) tra-: traduce (to say untrue or malicious things about; defame; malign; slander; vilify; as *to traduce* someone's character; to make a mockery of; betray), traducianism (opposed to *creationism*) (from *trans-*, across)

Element	From	Meaning	Examples
duc (cont'd)			*trans-*: transducer (a device that receives energy from one system and retransmits it, often in a different form, to another) (*trans-*, across)
			duct:
			ab-: abduct {abductor}, abduction (*ab-*, away)
			ad-: adduct {adductive, adductor}, adduction (*ad-*, to, toward)
			con-: conduct (**Synonyms**: direct, manage, control), conductance, **conduction**, conductive, conductivity, conductor (*con-*, with, together)
			de-: deduct, deductible, deduction (in *logic*, the act or process of deducing; reasoning from the general to the specific, or from premises to a logically valid conclusion; also, a conclusion reached by such reasoning; distinguished from *induction*) {deductive} (*de-*, down)
			in-: induct, inductance, inductile, induction, inductive (*in-*, in)
			intro-: introduction (**Synonyms**: preface, foreword, prologue), introductory (*intro-*, inwardly)
			pro-: product, production, productive (*pro-*, before, forward)
			re-: reduction, reductionism, reductive, reductor (*re-*, back)
			se-: seduction {seductive} (*se-*, away)
			trans-: transduction (the transfer of energy from one system to another; in *genetics*, the transfer of DNA from one bacterium to another by a bacteriophage, which may lead to the acquisition of a new gene by the recipient; compare *lysogeny*) (*trans-*, across)
			TRAILING ROOT COMPOUND:
			aque: aqueduct (*aqua*, water)
			ovi: oviduct (*ovum*, egg)
			via: viaduct (*via*, road)
			DISGUISED ROOT:
			dock (from Italian *doccia*, a conduit, canal; see *douche*, below)
			doge (a chief magistrate of either of the former republics of Venice and Genoa)
			dossil (a plug, wad, or fold of cotton or cloth, as for a wound)
			douche (from Italian *doccia*, a conduit, canal; further from Italian *doccione*, water pipe; a jet of liquid applied externally or internally to some part of the body, especially as a bath or treatment)
			duchess, duchy, duke
			PREFIXED DISGUISED ROOT:
			con-: conduit (a pipe or channel for conveying fluids) (*con-*, with, together)
			en-: endue [see *Doublets* below; from *inducere*; literally, to lead in; to provide (with something); specifically, to endow with qualities, talents, etc.) (from the same elements as *induce*; related in meaning to *endow*) (*en-*, in)
			re-: redoubt (from *reductus*, literally, to lead back; thus a refuge, a stronghold; root *doubt* is not related to the single word *doubt*) (*re-*, back)
			sub-: subdue (**Synonyms**: conquer, vanquish, defeat) (*sub-*, under)
			ITALIAN:
			duce (chief, leader, a title, as in *Il Duce*, assumed by Benito Mussolini, Fascist leader of Italy from 1922 to 1943)

Element	From	Meaning	Examples
duc (cont'd)			*condottiere* (in Europe from the 14th to 16th centuries, a captain of a band of mercenaries) (from *condotto*, one hired; from Latin *conductus*, mercenary soldier; past participle of *conducere*, to hire, to lead together) DOUBLETS: endue:induce LATIN PHRASE: *reductio ad absurdum* (reduction to absurdity; in *logic*, the proof of a proposition by showing the opposite to be an obvious falsity or self-contradiction, or the disproof of a proposition by showing its consequences to be impossible or absurd) ENGLISH COGNATES: tow (**Synonyms:** pull, drag, haul), tug (see synonyms at *tow*, previous word) INTERDISCIPLINARY: conduction (in *physics*, a transmission of electricity, heat, etc., by the passage of energy from particle to particle; in *physiology*, the transmission of nerve impulses) CROSS REFERENCE: *act/ag/ig, agogue, agon*
dulc*	Latin *dulcis* (IE: *dlku*, sweet)	sweet	SIMPLE ROOT: dulcet (soothing or pleasant to hear; sweet-sounding; melodious) LEADING ROOT COMPOUND: flu: dulcifluous (*fluere*, to flow) fy: dulcify (from *facere*, to make, do) mer: dulcimer (see *mel* for background) DISGUISED ROOT: douce, douceur FRENCH TERM: *billet-doux* [literally, a sweet (love) letter] ITALIAN WORDS AND PHRASES: *dolce* *dolce far niente* [literally, it is sweet (doing nothing), or pleasant idleness] *dolce vita* [literally, (the) sweet life, or a casual way of life, characterized by dissipation and promiscuity] ORGAN STOP: dulciana PROPER NAME: Dulcinea (Don Quixote's lady love) PLACENAMES: Dulce, New Mexico Agua Dulce, Texas CROSS REFERENCE: *glyc*
dur**	Latin *durare*: to last; to harden; *durus*: hard (IE: *deru*, tree, oak)	strong, hard	SIMPLE ROOT: dura: durable, dural (of the dura mater), duramen, durance (imprisonment, especially when long continued: mainly in *durance vile*; see *Latin Phrase*, below), duration, durative dure: duress (imprisonment; the use of force or threats; compulsion) duri: during (throughout the entire time of; at some point in the entire time) duru: durum (a hard emmer wheat that yields flower and semolina used in macaroni, spaghetti, etc.) PREFIXED ROOT: en-: (from *in-*, intensive) endurable, endurance (**Synonyms:** patience, fortitude, forbearance) endure (**Synonyms: 1**) bear, suffer, tolerate; **2**) continue, last, abide), enduring in-: indurate (to make hard; harden) (*in-*, in)

Element	From	Meaning	Examples
dur**			*ob-*: obdurate (not easily moved to pity or sympathy; hard-hearted; hardened and unrepenting; impenitent; not giving in readily; stubborn; obstinate; inflexible; unyielding) (*ob-*, intensive) *per-*: perdurable, perdure (to remain in existence; continue; last) (*per-*, through) COALESCED COMPOUND: duralumin [*dur(able)* + *alumin(um)*; a strong, lightweight alloy of aluminum with copper, manganese, magnesium, and silicon] DISGUISED ROOT: dour (sullen; gloomy; forbidding; in Scottish, hard; stern; severe; also, obstinate) LATIN PHRASE: *durante vita* (during life) LATIN MEDICAL TERM: *dura mater* (literally, hard mother; the outermost, toughest, and most fibrous of the three membranes covering the brain and spinal cord) CROSS REFERENCE: *firm, rob, scler, sthen, val*
dyn*	Greek *dunasthai*: to be able	able, powerful	SIMPLE ROOT: dynamic, dynamics dynamism (the theory that force, rather than mass or motion, is the principle of all phenomena) dynast, dynasty, dyne PREFIXED ROOT: *a-*: adynamia (lack of vital force as a result of illness; debility), adynamic (*a-*, without) *hyper-*: hyperdynamia (excessive muscular activity) (*hyper-*, over, beyond) LEADING ROOT COMPOUND: electr: dynamoelectric meter: dynamometer (*meter*, measure) TRAILING ROOT COMPOUND: auto: autodyne (*auto*, self) hetero: heterodyne (*hetero*, different) thermo: thermodynamics (*therm*, heat) COINED WORD: dynamite [term coined by Alfred Nobel who discovered trinitrotoluene (TNT), and the same person who is remembered by the Nobel prizes] CROSS REFERENCE: *pot*
dys-***	Greek *dys* (IE: *dus*, bad, ill)	bad, wrong, ill, impaired, abnormal, difficult	PREFIXED ROOT: cras: dyscrasia (an abnormality of some part of the body, as of the formed elements of the blood) (*krasis*, a mixing) enter: dysentery (an intestinal inflammation characterized by abdominal pain and intense diarrhea with bloody, mucous feces) (*entera*, bowels) gen: dysgenic (causing deterioration of hereditary qualities of a stock), dysgenics (*gen*, to beget) graph: dysgraphia (impairment of the ability to write, as a result of brain dysfunction) (*graph*, write) kine: dyskinesia (impairment of body movements) (*kinem*, movement) lex: dyslexia (impairment of the ability to read, often as the result of genetic defect or brain injury) (*lex*, read) log: dyslogistic (not favorable; opprobrious; opposite to *eulogistic*) (*logos*, word)

217

Element	From	Meaning	Examples
dys- (cont'd)			menno: dysmennorrhea (painful or difficult menstruation) (from *mense*, month)
			pep: dyspepsia {dyspeptic} (*pepsis*, cooking, digestion)
			phag: dysphagia (difficulty in swallowing) (*phag*, eat)
			phas: dysphasia (impairment of the ability to speak or, sometimes, to understand language, as the result of brain injury) (*phase*, speak)
			phon: dysphonia (any difficulty in producing speech sounds) (*phone*, sound)
			phor: dysphoria (any generalized feeling of ill-being; opposed to *euphoria*) {disphoric} (*phore*, to bear)
			plas: dysplasia (a disordered growth or faulty development of various tissues or body parts) (*plasma*, form)
			pnea: dyspnea (difficult or painful breathing) (*pne*, breathing)
			top: dystopia (a hypothetical place, state, or situation in which conditions and the quality of life are dreadful) (*topos*, place)
			troph: dystrophy {dystrophic} (*trophe*, nourishment)
			ur: dysuria (difficult or painful urination) (*ur*, urine)
			CROSS REFERENCE: *mal, cac(o)*
dysi*	Greek *duein*: enter, to get into	put on, as clothing	PREFIXED ROOT:
			ec-: ecdysis (in *zoology*, the shedding of an outer layer of skin or integument, as by snakes or insects), ecdysiast (a coined word: stripteaser) (from *ex-*, out)
			NO CROSS REFERENCE

> A dictionary is merely the universe arranged in alphabetical order.
> Anatole France

E

Element	From	Meaning	Examples
ebr*	Latin *ebrius*: drunk	to drink; tipsy	ROOT NOTE: This root seems to be derived from the prefix *ex-*, out of + *bria*, winejar, thus one who has emptied the winejar. The opposite of *ebrius* is *sobrius*, from *se-*, not + *bria*, thus one who has not drunk from the winejar; thus sober. SIMPLE ROOT: ebriety, ebriosity, ebrious PREFIXED ROOT: *in-*: (intensive) inebriate (to make drunk; intoxicate; also, to excite; exhilarate; as an *adjective*, drunk, intoxicated) inebriated (**Synonyms:** drunk, tight), inebriation, inebriety CROSS REFERENCE: *bib, pot*
eccles*	Greek *ecclesia* (IE: *kel*, to call, yell)	church	ROOT NOTE: This root literally means those called out; before the Christian church was established, the term designated those chosen, or called out, to serve in public office. SIMPLE ROOT: ecclesia (in ancient Greek states, a political assembly of citizens; in *ecclesiology*, the members of a church; also, a church building; note *Spanish Cognate*, below) ecclesiastic (a clergyman or othr person in religious orders; as an *adjective*, ecclesiastical), ecclesiastical, ecclesiasticism PREFIXED ROOT: *para-*: paraclete (literally, called to the side of; one called to stand beside, or to help; capitalized, the Holy Ghost, or the Holy Spirit, as one of the Trinity in the Christian Church; the Comforter; advocate) (*para-*, beside) LEADING ROOT COMPOUND: *ecclesi(o)*: arch: ecclesiarch (in the Eastern Church, a sacristan, especially of a monastery) (*arch*, rule) latry: ecclesiolatry (excessive reverence for churchly forms and traditions) (*latry*, worship of) logy: ecclesiology (the study of ecclesiastical adornments or furnishings; the study of church doctrine) (*logy*, study of) SPANISH COGNATE: *iglesia* OLD TESTAMENT BOOK: Ecclesiastes (often termed "The Preacher"; used in the Septuagint for Hebrew *qoheleth*, he who calls together an assembly; the theme of the book is the vanity of earthly life) CATECHETICAL BOOK: Ecclesiasticus [short for *ecclesiasticus liber*, literally, church book: from its frequent use for catechetical teaching; a book of proverbs in the Old Testament Apocrypha (which see under *apo-*, and *cryph*) and the Douay Bible] [The Douay Bible is an English version of the Bible translated from the Latin Vulgate edition for the use of Roman Catholics: the New Testament was originally published at Reims (1582) and the Old Testament at Douai (1609-10).] NO CROSS REFERENCE

Element	From	Meaning	Examples
ech*	Greek *echos*	echo, sound	SIMPLE ROOT: echo, echoic, echoism PREFIXED ROOT: *an*-: anechoic (free from echoes; completely absorbing sound waves or radar signal, e.g., *an anechoic chamber*, used for special testing) (*an-*, without) *cat*-: (*cata*-, thoroughly) catechesis (oral instruction, especially of catechumens) catechetical (also, *catechetic*; consisting of, or teaching by the method of, questions and answers) catechism (a handbook of questions and answers for teaching the principles of a religion), catechize catechumen LEADING ROOT COMPOUND: lal: echolalia (automatic repetition by someone of words spoken in his/her presence, especially, as a symptom of mental illness) (*lallen*, to lull) DISGUISED ROOT: sough (pronounced either *suf*, or *sou*; as a *noun*, a soft, murmuring sound; as a *verb*, to make that sound) GREEK MYTHOLOGY: Echo (a nymph whose unrequited love for Narcissus caused her to pine away until nothing but her voice remained) CROSS REFERENCE: *phon, phthong, son*
echin*	Greek *echinos*: sea urchin (IE: *eghi*, snake)	spiny, prickly	SIMPLE ROOT: echinate, echinulate, echinus LEADING ROOT COMPOUND: *echin*: oid: echinoid (any of a class of marine animals with a water vascular system and usually with a hard, spiny skeleton, including the starfishes, sea urchins, etc.) (*oid*, similar to) *echino*: cactus: echinocactus (a very spiny cactus) cocc: echinococcus (any of a genus of tapeworms that cause disease in mammals; see *hydatid*, under *hydr*, water) (*coccus*, berry, bacteria) derm: echinoderm (see note under *derm*, skin) NO CROSS REFERENCE
eco,** ek	Greek *oikos* (IE: *weiko*, house, settlement, which also yields the *wich* and *wick* and English place-names)	home, dwelling	SIMPLE ROOT: *ec*: ecesis (the successful establishment of a plant or animal in a new locality), ecumenical, ecuminism *ek*: ekistics (the science of city and area planning) PREFIXED ROOT: *di*-: diocesan, diocese (from *dioikein*, to keep house; the district under a bishop's jurisdiction; do not confuse these two words with *dioecious*, where *di* means two; see *Trailing Root Compounds*) (*dia*-, through + *oikos*) LEADING ROOT COMPOUND: cid: ecocide (the destruction of the environment or of ecosystems, as by the use of defoliants or the emission of pollutants) (*cide*, kill) log: ecology (*logy*, scientific study of) metr: ecometrics (the use of mathematical and statistical methods in the field of economics) (*metr*, measure)

Element	From	Meaning	Examples
eco (cont'd)			nom: economic, economical (**Synonyms:** thrifty, frugal, provident), economics, economism, economize, economy (see *Placename* below) (*nomos*, law)
			phob: ecophobia (fear of home) (*phobia*, fear of; dread of)
			spec: ecospecies {ecospecific} (*specere*, to see)
			spher: ecosphere (*sphere*, ball, globe)
			ton: ecotone (the transition zone between two different plant communities, as that between forest and prairie) (*tonos*, stretching)
			typ: ecotype (a group, or race, within a species, having unique physical characteristics genetically adapted to particular environmental conditions) {ecotypic} (*typos*, a figure, model)
			TRAILING ROOT COMPOUND:
			andro: androecium (in *botany*, the stamens and the parts belonging to them, collectively; all the microsporophylls of a flower) (*andro*, male, stamen)
			auto: autoecious (in *biology*, passing the active life cycle on one host, as certain parasites do, especially rust fungi) (*auto*, self)
			di: dioecious (*di*, two)
			eur: euroky (also, *euryoky*; in *biology*, the ability of an organism to live under variable environmental conditions: opposed to *stenoky*, which see below) {eurokous, or *euryokous*) (*euro*, wide)
			hetero: heteroecious (spending alternate stages of a life cycle on different, unrelated hosts) (*hetero*, different)
			homo: homoeosis (in *biology*, an assumption by one part or structure in a series of a form characteristic of another member of the series) (*homo*, same)
			mono: monoecious (*mono*, single, alone)
			sten: stenoky (in *biology*, the ability of an organism to live only under a very narrow range of environmental conditions: opposed to *euroky*, which see above) (*steno*, narrow, small)
			tri: trioecious [having male, female, and bisexual (or, *hermaphrodite*) flowers on separate plants] (see *monoecious*, above) (*tri*, three)
			DISGUISED ROOT:
			parish, parishioner
			parochial (of, pertaining to, supported by, or located in a parish; restricted to a narrow scope; provincial)
			PLACENAME: Economy (Indiana, Pennsylvania)
			INTERDISCIPLINARY:
			dioecious (in *biology*, having the male reproductive organs in one individual and the female organs in another; having separate sexes; in *botany*, having male and female flowers on separate plants; compare *monoecious*, below)
			monoecious (in *botany*, having separate male flowers and female flowers on the same plant, as in maize; in *zoology*, having both male and female reproductive organs in the same individual; hermaphroditic; compare *dioecious*, above)
			CROSS REFERENCE: *cit/civ, dom*

Element	From	Meaning	Examples
ecto-***	Greek *ektos* (IE: *eghs*, out)	outside, external	PREFIXED ROOT: *ecto-*: blast: ectoblast (same as *epiblast*, the outer layer of cells of an embryo) (*blast*, shoot, sprout, embryo) derm: ectoderm (the outer layer of cells of an animal embryo, from which the nervous system, skin, hair, teeth, etc. are developed) {ectodermal, ectodermic} (*derm*, skin) gen: ectogenous (also, *ectogenic*; growing outside the body of the host, as certain bacteria and other parasites) (*genous*, producing) mer: ectomere {ectomeric} (*mere*, part) morph: ectomorph, ectomorphic (compare with *endomorphic, mesomorphic*) (*morph*, shape, form) plasm: ectoplasm (compare with *endoplasm*) {ectoplasmic} (*plasm*, form) proct: ectoproct (any of a phylum of minute water animals that form branching, mosslike colonies and reproduce by budding) (from *proktos*, anus) sarc: ectosarc (the ectoplasm of one-celled animals) (from *sarkos*, flesh) zo: ectozoa (parasites on the body of an animal, as lice) (*zo*, animal) DOUBLE PREFIXED ROOT: ecto<u>comm</u>ensal (a commensal living on the outer surface of the host) (*com-* prefixes *mensa*, table) ecto<u>para</u>site (any parasite living on the outer surface of an animal; opposed to *endoparasite*) (*para-* prefixes *sitos*, food) NOTE: Do not confuse this element with *ectom*, to cut out, or to surgically remove, as in *appendectomy*. NB: *Ectopia*, from *ek*, out + *topos*, place, is not in this family; it means an abnormal position of a body part or organ. CROSS REFERENCE: *exo-, extra-, juxta-, para-*
ed*	Latin *edere* (IE: *ed*, to eat, which also yields German *essen*, and English *eat*)	to eat	SIMPLE ROOT: edacious (gluttonous, voracious), edible (fit to be eaten; as a *noun*, food: usually used in plural) PREFIXED ROOT: *com-*: comedo (a glutton; plural, *comedos*, or *comedones*) (*com-*, completely) DISGUISED ROOTS: escarole [literally, pertaining to food; same as *endive*, which itself is probably from Egyptian *tybi*, January (when it is said to grow in Egypt)] esculent (as an *adjective*, fit for food; eatable; edible; as a *noun*, something fit for food, especially a vegetable) esurient (hungry, voracious, greedy) {esurience, esuriency} PREFIXED DISGUISED ROOT: *com-*: comestibles (that which can be eaten; food) (*com-*, intensive) *ob-*: obese (very fat, corpulent) {obesity} (*ob-*, completely) ENGLISH COGNATE: fret (to eat away, gnaw; to wear away by gnawing, rubbing, corroding, etc.) DUTCH COGNATE: etch (from German *etzen*, to eat) CROSS REFERENCE: *phag, vor*

222

Element	From	Meaning	Examples
edaph*	Greek *edaphos* (IE: *sed*, to sit)	bottom, ground, soil	SIMPLE ROOT: edaphic (in *ecology*, pertaining to the chemical and physical characteristics of the soil, without reference to climate; opposed to *climatic*) edaphon (the animal and plant life present in soils) LEADING ROOT COMPOUND: logy: edaphology (same as *pedology*, soil science; there is another *pedology*, from *pedo*, child, the treatment of children) (*logy*, study of) saur: edaphosauria, edaphosaurus (*saur*, lizard) SCIENTIFIC TERM: edaphic climax CROSS REFERENCE: *chth, geo, terra, ped*
edi**	Latin *aedes*: temple, house, building (IE: *ai-dh*, to burn)	build, improve	SIMPLE ROOT: aedile (in ancient Rome, a magistrate who had charge of public works, police, and the grain supply, but literally one concerned with buildings) LEADING ROOT COMPOUND: fic: (from *facere*, to make) edification (literally, act of building; instruction, especially moral or spiritual instruction, improvement, or enlightenment), edificatory edifice (**Synonyms:** building, structure, pile), edificial fy: edify (from *facere*, to make, do) CROSS REFERENCE: *struct*
ef-			See *ex-* for *effort*.
ego***	Latin *ego*	I, self	SIMPLE ROOT: ego [that portion of the psyche which possesses consciousness, maintains its identity, and recognizes and tests reality (*Dorland's*); the personality component that is conscious, most immediately controls behavior, and is most in touch with external reality (*American Heritage*)] egoism (in *ethics*, the doctrine that self-interest is the proper goal of all human actions; opposed to *altruism*), egoist, egoistic egotism (generally considered more opprobrious than *egoism*), egotist LEADING ROOT COMPOUND: centr: egocentric (self-centered; in *philosophy*, based on the belief that the world exists or can be known only in relation to the individual's mind) mania: egomania (abnormal or excessive egotism) (*mania*, craze) NB: Do not confuse this root with the *ego* in *egobronchophony*, a bleating and bronchial voice characteristic of pleuropneumonia; *ego* here is from Greek *aix*, goat; thus, literally, (to make) the sound of a goat. Another word with this root is *egophony*, a bleating quality of the voice observed in auscultation in certain cases of lung consolidation. NO CROSS REFERENCE
egor			See *agora* for *paregoric, allegory, panegyric*.
eid*	Greek *eidos* (IE: *weid*, to see)	image, form	SIMPLE ROOT: eidetic (designating or of mental images that are usually vivid and almost photographically correct) eidolon {eidolic}

Element	From	Meaning	Examples
eid (cont'd)			LEADING ROOT COMPOUND: *eid*: opto: eidoptometry (measurement of the acuteness of vision for the perception of form) (*optos*, seen + *metron*, measure) *eido*: graph: eidograph (*graph*, write) logy: eidolology (*logy*, study of) EMBEDDED ROOT COMPOUND: kaleidoscope (an instrument for viewing beautifully formed shapes) (from *calli*, beautiful; *scope*, look) DISGUISED ROOT: idol (an image of a god, used as an object of worship) idyll (or *idyl*: a short poem or prose work describing a simple, peaceful scene of rural or pastoral life), idyllic DISGUISED LEADING ROOT COMPOUND: cras: idocrase (same as *vesuvianite*) (from *krasis*, mixture) CROSS REFERENCE: *fig, form, morph, oid, plasm*
ek			See *eco* for *ekistics*.
elasm*	Greek *elasmos* (IE: *el*, to drive, move)	metal plate	LEADING ROOT COMPOUND: branch: elasmobranch (*branchia*, gills) saur: elasmosaur (*saur*, lizard) ther: elasmothere (*there*, wild beast) NO CROSS REFERENCE
elast*	Greek *elastos* (IE: *el*, to drive, move)	ductile	SIMPLE ROOT: elasti: elastic (**Synonyms**: resilient, flexible, supple), elasticity, elasticize, elastin elastr: elastration (a bloodless form of animal castration by fitting a strong rubber band about the scrotum) DISGUISED ROOT: elater (an elastic filament that scatters ripe spores, found in certain plants, as in the capsule of the liverwort), elaterite, elaterium NO CROSS REFERENCE
electr**	Greek *electrum*	shining, amber (the original meaning is uncertain)	SIMPLE ROOT: electric, electricity, electron LEADING ROOT COMPOUND: *electr*: ode: electrode (*ode*, way, path) *electro*: analys: electroanalysis (*ana-* prefixes *lys*, to loosen) card: electrocardiogram (ECG, or EKG) (from *kard*, heart) de: electrodeposit (*de-* prefixes *posit*, from *ponere*, to place) dialys: electrodialysis (*dia-* prefixes *lys*, to loosen) encephal: electroencephalogram (EEG) (*encephal*, brain) jet: electrojet (a narrow, high-velocity stream of electric energy that girdles the earth in the ionosphere above the magnetic equator) (from *jacere*, to throw) lys: electrolysis (*lys*, loosen) lyt: electrolyte (see *electrolysis*) phil: electrophilic (designating or of a chemical, ion, etc. that accepts additional electrons) (*phila*, love of) phor: electrophoresis [*electro* + *(cata)phoresis*], electrophorous (*phore*, to bear) NO CROSS REFERENCE

Element	From	Meaning	Examples
eleuthero*	Greek *eleutheros*	free	SIMPLE ROOT: eleutheria (a genus of jellyfishes) LEADING ROOT COMPOUND: dactyl: eleutherodactylus (a genus of frogs) (*dactyl*, finger) mania: eleutheromania (abnormal enthusiasm for freedom) (*mania*, craze) CROSS REFERENCE: *franc, liber, lys/lyt*
em-			*See en-* for *empathetic*, etc.
embryo**	Latin *embryon* (*en-*, in + *bryein*, to swell)	to grow (something that grows in the body)	SIMPLE ROOT: embryo (an animal in the earliest stages of its development in the uterus or egg; specifically, in humans, from conception to about the eighth week; fetus) embryonic (in an early stage; undeveloped; rudimentary) LEADING ROOT COMPOUND: *embry*: oid: embryoid (*oid*, similar to) oma: embryoma (*oma*, mass) ulc: embryulcia (an instrument for extracting a dead fetus from the uterus) (from *elkein*, to draw) *embryo*: cton: embryoctony (the artificial destruction of the living embryo, or of the unborn fetus) (from *kteinein*, to kill) gen: embryogenesis (*genesis*, producing) logy: embryology (*logy*, study of) phyt: embryophyte (a subkingdom of plants, having an enclosed embryo, as within a seed or archegonium, including bryophytes, ferns, gymnosperms, and angiosperms; compare *thallophytes*, under *phyt*) (*phyton*, plant) scop: embryoscope (*scope*, look) toc: embryotocia (same as *abortion*) (*tocia*, childbirth) tom: embryotome, embryotomy (*tom*, to cut) troph: embryotroph, embryotrophy (*troph*, nourish) CROSS REFERENCE: *aug, creat, cresc, oma, phym*
-emia**	Greek	blood disease	ROOT NOTE: The element combines *hemo*, blood, and *-ia*, condition of; therefore, a diseased condition of the blood. PREFIXED ROOT AND COMPOUNDS: a-: azotemia (the accumulation of nitrogenous substances in the blood, resulting from failure of the kidneys to remove them) (from *azote*, nitrogen; *a-*, without + *zo*, life) *an-*: anemia (*an-*, without) *hyper-*: hyperemia (*hyper-*, beyond, excessive) TRAILING ROOT COMPOUND: leuk: leukemia (*leuk*, white) tox: toxemia (*toxin*, poison) PREFIXED TRAILING ROOT COMPOUND: *hypo-*: hypoglycemia (*hypo-*, under + *glyc*, sugar) CROSS REFERENCE: *hemo, sang*
emp**	Latin *emere* (IE: *em*, to take)	to buy, take	PREFIXED ROOTS AND COMPOUNDS: *ad-*: ademption (in *law*, the extinction of a legacy by an act of the testator before his death, as by his disposal of the bequeathed property) (*ad-*, to, toward) *dir-*: diremption (see *Webster's Third New International Dictionary*) (from *dis-*, apart, away)

225

Element	From	Meaning	Examples
emp (cont'd)			*ex-*: (out) exemplary (from which is derived *example*), exempt, exemption (**Synonyms**: immunity, impunity) exemplify (to show by example; serve as an example of) (*fy* from *facere*, to make, do) *per-*: peremptory (intolerantly positive or assured; dictatorial; dogmatic; in *law*, barring further action, debate, question, etc.; final; absolute; as a general term, intolerantly positive or assured) (*per-*, intensive) *pre-*: preempt (back-formation of *preemption*), preemption (the right to purchase something, especially government-owned land, before others), preemptive (*pre-*, before) *re-*: redemption (inserted *d* for ease of pronunciation; see *Doublets* below), redemptive (also, redemptory) (*re-*, back) DISGUISED ROOT: deriment (*der-* from *dis-*; see *Webster's Third*) diriment (to interrupt; making absolutely void; nullifying) (*dis-* apart + *emere*; to take) premium (that which is taken before others; originally *praemium*, profit derived from booty; **Synonyms**: 1) bonus, bounty, dividend; 2) reward, award) (*pre-*, before) prompt (literally, to bring forth) (from *pro-*, forth + *emp*) ransom (see *Doublets* below) (from *redemption*) sample (see *Doublets* below; from *example*), sampler vintage (*vinum*, wine + *de-*, off + *emere*, to take) PREFIXED DISGUISED ROOT: *re-*: redeem (literally, to buy back; **Synonyms**: free, rescue, save), Redeemer (*re-*, back) *ex-*: example (see *Doublets* below; **Synonyms**: 1) instance, illustration; 2) model, pattern, paradigm) (*ex-*, out) *im-*: impromptu (without preparation; offhand; **Synonyms**: extemporaneous, improvised) (from *in-*, in) *ir-*: irredentist [literally, unredeemed (Italy), or those native Italians living under the authority of another government; now applied to any national under the authority of another government against his or her wishes, e.g., the displaced, nomadic Somalis in Ethiopia, Kenya, and Djibouti, when in 1960, the United Nations redrew the boundaries between those countries] (*ir-* assimilates *in-*, not + *re-*, back) DOUBLETS: ransom:redemption sample:example LATIN PHRASES: *caveat emptor* (Let the buyer beware) *exempli gratia* (abbreviated *e.g.*; Let me give an example please) SPANISH: pronto (from *prompt*) CROSS REFERENCE: *cap, prehens, rap, sum*
en-, em-**	Greek	in	PREFIXED ROOT AND COMPOUNDS: *en-*: arthr: enarthrosis (*arthr*, joint + *osis*, condition of) caen: encaenia (a festival commemorating the founding of a city, church, etc.) (*kainos*, new)

226

Element	From	Meaning	Examples
en- (cont'd)			caust: encaustic (literally, to burn in, and from which *ink* is derived; see *caust* family) (*caust*, burn)
			cephal: encephalic, encephalitis (*en-* + *cephal*, head = brain)
			chir: enchiridion (that which can be carried in one's hand; see note at *chiro*) (*chiro*, hand)
			chor: enchorial [of or used in a particular country; popular; especially, demotic (of the people)] (*chora*, country, place)
			clit: enclitic [leaning in (on the preceding word for accent); in *grammar*, dependent on its stress on the preceding word: said of a word that has lost its stress in combination (e.g., *man* in *layman*)] (from *klinein*, to lean)
			com: encomiast, encomiastic, encomium (a formal expression of high praise; eulogy; panegyric) (*komos*, a revel)
			crypt: encrypt (from *kryptein*, to hide)
			cycl: encyclical (also, encyclic), encyclopedia (see note under *cyclo*) (*cycle*, wheel, circle)
			dem: endemic (see note under *demo*) (*demos*, people)
			derm: endermic (see note under *derm*) (*derma*, skin)
			ema: enema (a liquid forced into the colon through the anus, as a purgative, medicine, etc.; clyster) (from *hienai*, to send)
			erg: energetics, energize, energumen, energy (**Synonyms:** strength, power, force) (*erg*, work)
			gram: engram (from *graphein*, to write)
			grav: engrave (from French *graver*, to incise; from Greek *graphein*, to write)
			harmon: enharmonic (*harmos*, fitting)
			phyt: enphytotic (affecting certain plants of an area at regular intervals: said of various diseases) (*phyton*, a plant)
			tasis: entasis (in *architecture*, a slight, convex swelling in the shaft of a column: it prevents the illusion of concavity produced by a perfectly straight shaft) (from *teinein*, to stretch thin)
			thus: enthusiasm (literally, having God within) (from *theos*, god, God)
			thym: enthymeme (to consider, reflect upon; in *logic*, a rhetorical argument from probabilities; that is, an argument in which one of the premises or, sometimes, the conclusion, is not expressed but implied; the following is an enthymeme in which the major premise is missing: The price of meat will go up/because of the poor corn crop) (*thymos*, mind)
			zo: enzootic (affecting animals in a certain area, climate, or season: said of diseases) (*zoion*, animal)
			zym: enzyme, enzymology (*zyme*, leaven)
			em-:
			blem: emblem, emblematic (from *ballein*, to throw)
			bol: (from *ballein*, to throw;
			embolalia (the interpolation of meaningless words into the speech) (*lal*, babble)
			embolic, embolism (intercalation, as of a day in a year; in *pathology*, the occlusion of a blood vessel by an embolus), embolus (plural, *emboli*)

227

Element	From	Meaning	Examples
en- (cont'd)			emboly (in *embryology*, the pushing or growth of one part into another, as in the formation of certain gastrulas) bry: embryo (*embryo* is listed as a family) (*bryein*, to swell) men: emmenagogue (anything used to stimulate the menstrual flow) (*men*, month + *agogue*, leading) path: empathetic, empathize, empathy (used to translate German *Einfühlung*; *ein-*, in + *fühlung*, feeling) (*pathos*, feeling) phas: emphasis {emphatic}, emphasize (*phainein*, to show) phys: emphysema (*physaein*, to blow) pir: empiric, empirical, empiricism (*peira*, a trial, experiment) por: emporium (a trading place; market) (*poros*, way) py: empyema (the accumulation of pus in a body cavity, especially in a pleural cavity) (*pyon*, pus) pyr: empyreal, empyrean (the highest heaven; specifically, among the ancients, the sphere of pure light or fire; among Christian poets, the abode of God) (*pyr*, fire) ASSIMILATED PREFIXED ROOT: *el-*: ellipse, ellipsis, ellipsoid, elliptical, ellipticity (*el-* assimilates *en-*, in; *lip* from *leipein*, to fall) PLACENAMES: Emporia (Kansas, Virginia) Emporium, Pennsylvania INTERDISCIPLINARY: engram (in *biology*, a hypothetical permanent change produced by a stimulus in the protoplasm of a tissue; in *psychology*, a permanent effect produced in the psyche by stimulation, assumed in explaining persistence of memory) NB: Enigma (inexplicable statement, or person) and *(o)enology* (the study of wine-making) are not in this family. CROSS REFERENCE: *in-* (one meaning)
en-***	Latin	in	PREFIXED ROOTS: (Some of the roots are Anglo-Saxon.) *en-*: amel: enamel (a glaze, melted substance) (Old French *amel* from Germanic *smalts*, a glaze) amor: enamor (to fill with love and desire; charm) (*amor*, love) capsul: encapsulate (also, *encapsule*; to enclose in or as if in a capsule; to put in concise form; condense) carn: encarnalize (to make incarnate; to make carnal; make sensual) (*carne*, flesh, meat) chain: enchain (to bind or hold with chains; fetter; to hold fast; captivate) chant: enchant (see *Doublets* below), enchanting, enchantment (from *incantare*, to bewitch; from *cantare*, to sing) chas: enchase (to put in a setting or serve as setting for; to ornament by engraving, embossing, or inlaying with gems, etc.) (from *case*; from *capere*, to hold) clav: enclave (a territory surrounded or nearly surrounded by the territory of another country, as the Vatican is an enclave of the city of Rome; a minority culture group living as an entity within a larger group) (*clavis*, a key) com: encompass (to shut in all around) (*com-* prefixes *pass*, a step)

Element	From	Meaning	Examples
en- (cont'd)			cour: encourage (**Synonyms:** embolden, hearten, incite), encouragement, encouraging (from *cors*, heart)
			croach: encroach (from Old French *encrochier*, to seize upon; *croach* from *croche*, a hook, as in *crochet*)
			crypt: encrypt (to encode or encipher) (*crypt*, hide)
			cult: enculturate (to cause to adapt to the prevailing cultural patterns of one's society) (*cultus*, care; from *colere*, to till)
			cumb: encumber (to burden with obligations, debt, etc.; to oppress), encumbrance (from Old French *combre*, obstruction, barrier)
			dam: endamage (to cause damage or injury to) (*damnare*, to harm)
			deav: endeavor (from *devoir*, which see under *deb*)
			dow: endow, endowment (from *dare*, to give)
			due: endue (from *ducere*, to lead)
			dur: endurable, endurance (**Synonyms:** patience, fortitude, stoicism), endure (*durare*, to harden)
			emy: enemy (literally, not a friend) (from *ami*, friend)
			feebl: enfeeble (from Old French *enfeblir*, to make feeble)
			feoff: enfeoff (in *law*, to invest with an estate held in fee) (from *fief*, property)
			fil: enfilade (a military term) (*filum*, thread)
			franch: enfranchise (originally, to free from slavery, bondage, legal obligation, etc.; to give a franchise to; specifically, to admit to citizenship, especially, the right to vote) (from *franchir*, to set free)
			gag: engage (see French *engagé*), engaged, engagement, engaging (from IE *wadh-*, a pledge)
			gen: engender (*generare*, to beget, produce)
			gin: engine, engineer (from *gignere*, to produce)
			gorg: engorge (to gorge, glut; to devour greedily; in *medicine*, to congest a blood vessel, tissue, etc. with fluid, as blood, milk, etc.) (*gorge*, throat)
			grail: engrail [to indent (an edge or rim) with concave, curved notches; to ornament the edge with such a pattern] (from Old French *gresle*, slender; from *gracilis*, scanty)
			grain: engrain (same as *ingrain*) (*granum*, seed, grain)
			gross: engross, engrossing (*grossus*, thick)
			gulf: engulf (to swallow up; overwhelm; to plunge, as into a gulf) (from Greek *kolpos*, a fold, bosom)
			hanc: enhance (**Synonyms:** intensify, aggravate, heighten) (from *altus*, high)
			jamb: enjambment (also, *enjambement*; in *prosody*, the running on of a sentence from one line or couplet to the next, with little or no pause) (Old French *jambe*, a leg, shank, pier)
			join: enjoin (from *jungere*, to bind together)
			joy: enjoy, enjoyable, enjoyment (**Synonyms:** pleasure, delight, gratification) (from *gaudere*, to be glad)
			lac: enlace (from Old French *lacer*, to tie, tangle; from Latin *laqueus*, a noose)

229

Element	From	Meaning	Examples
en- (cont'd)			light: enlighten, enlightenment; The Enlightenment (an 18th-century European philosophical movement characterized by rationalism, an impetus toward learning and a spirit of skepticism and empiricism in social and political thought)
			mity: enmity (**Synonyms:** hostility, animosity, antagonism) (from *enemy*)
			nobl: ennoble (from *nobilis*, well known)
			rapt: enrapture (also, *enravish*) (from *rapere*, to snatch, seize)
			sang: ensanguine (to stain with blood; make bloody) (*sanguis*, blood)
			scon: ensconce (from *condere*, to hide)
			semb: ensemble (in *music*, a small group of musicians playing or singing together) (from *simul*, same)
			sign: ensign (from *insignia*) (*signum*, a mark, sign)
			sil: ensilage, ensile (from *silo*)
			sue: ensue (**Synonyms:** follow, succeed, result) (from *sequi*, to follow)
			tabl: (from *tabula*, a board)
			entablature (in *architecture*, a horizontal superstructure supported by columns and composed of architrave, frieze, and cornice)
			entablement (the platform or series of platforms directly beneath a statue and on top of the dado and base)
			tail: entail (from Old French *taillier*, to cut)
			thrall: enthrall (also, *enthral*; to hold as if in a spell) (from Old English *thraell*, the constrained one)
			tic: entice (to attract by offering hope, reward or pleasure; allure; **Synonyms:** 1) lure, inveigle, beguile; 2) captivate, fascinate) (from *titio*, a burning brand)
			velop: envelop, envelope (from Old French *voloper*, to wrap)
			ven: envenom (to put venom or poison on or into; make poisonous; to fill with hate; embitter) (*venenum*, a poison)
			vi: envious (from *envy*, which see below)
			vir: environ, environment {environmental}, environmentalist, environs (*virer*, to turn)
			vis: envisage, envision (from *videre*, to see)
			voy: envoy (**Synonyms:** messenger, agent, diplomat; a postscript to a poem, essay, or book, containing a dedication, climactic summary, explanation, etc.) (from *via*, way)
			vy: envy (**Synonyms:** begrudge, covet) (from *videre*, to see)
			em-:
			balm: embalm (from Arabic *basam*, an aromatic gum resin)
			bar: embargo, embarrass (**Synonyms:** abash, discomfit, disconcert) (both terms mean literally "to bar in")
			bark: embark (from Latin *barca*, a small boat)
			bat: embattle (to provide with battlements; to prepare, array, or set in line for battle; to fortify) (*battuere*, to beat)
			bay: embay [to put or force (a boat, etc.) into a bay for protection or shelter; to shut in; enclose or surround, as in a bay]
			bell: embellish (**Synonyms:** adorn, decorate, ornament) (*bellus*, beautiful)

Element	From	Meaning	Examples
en- (cont'd)			**bezzl:** embezzle (from Old French *besillier*, to destroy) **bit:** embitter (to make bitter; make resentful or morose; to make more bitter; exacerbate; aggravate) (Old English *biter*, to bite) **blaz:** emblaze, emblazon, emblazonry (to display brilliantly; to decorate with bright colors; to spread the fame of) **blem:** emblements (in *law*, cultivated growing crops which are produced annually; also, the profits from these crops) (from Old French *blee*, grain) **bon:** embonpoint (in good condition; plumpness; a well-fed appearance) (French *en bon point*) **bosom:** embosom (to take to one's bosom; embrace; cherish; to enclose protectively; surround; shelter) **boss:** emboss (French, *bosse*, a hump; swelling) **bouch:** embouchure (literally, to put into the mouth; the mouth of a river; in *music*, the mouthpiece of a wind instrument; also, the method of applying the lips and tongue to the mouthpiece of a wind instrument) (French *bouche*, mouth; from Latin *bucca*) **brac:** embrace (**Synonyms:** include, comprise, comprehend), embracer, embracery (*brachium*, arm) **branch:** embranchment (a branching out or off, as of a river, etc.; ramification) **brang:** embrangle (to entangle; mix up; confuse; perplex) {embranglement} (may be from French *branler*, to confuse) **brasur:** embrasure (to widen an opening; an opening for a door, window, etc.) (from Old French *embraser*) **broc:** embrocate [to moisten and rub (a part of the body) with an oil, liniment, etc.] (broche, a making wet) **broid:** embroider (from an old variation of *braid*) **broil:** embroil (from Middle English *broilen*, to quarrel; from Old French *brouillier*, to dirty; the noun form of this word is Italian *imbroglio*, pronounced im BROHL yo) **bru:** embrue (same as *imbrue*) **penn:** empennage (the tail assembly of an airplane) (*penne*, feather) **per:** emperor (from *parare*, to set in order) **pir:** (notice difference in meanings of the groups of words) empire (from *emperor*) empiric, empirical, empiricism (*peira*, a trial) **ploy:** employ (**Synonyms:** use, utilize) (from *implicare*, to fold in) **press:** (notice difference in root meanings) empress (the wife of an emperor; do not confuse *empress* with *impress*) empressement (effusive regard or cordiality) (from *impress*, verb) **pris:** emprise (also, *emprize*) WORD COMPRISED OF TWO PREFIXES: encounter (**Synonyms:** battle, engagement, campaign) (*en-*, in + *contra-*, against)

231

Element	From	Meaning	Examples
en- (cont'd)			NB: *Emasculate*, from *ex-* + *masculine*, is not in this family; neither are *emaciate, emanate, emancipate, emarginate, emerge, emeritus, emigrate, eminence, emission, emollient, emotion, emulsion, emunctory*, and *enervate*. DOUBLETS: enchant:incantation SPANISH: *enchilada* (literally, to put chili into) *embarcadero* (a wharf, dock, or pier) FRENCH TERMS: *en alerte* (on the alert) *en ami* (as, or like, a friend) *en arrière* (in the rear; behind; in arrears) *en avant* (forward; onward; ahead) *en bloc* (in a block; in a mass; as a whole; all together) *en brochette* (broiled on small spits or skewers) *en brosse* (like a brush; cut short so as to stand up like brush bristles: said of hair) *en casserole* (*casserole* is a diminutive of *casse*, a small bowl) *enceinte* (not girded; the line of works enclosing a fortified place; the space so enclosed; another *enceinte* is derived from *in-*, not + *cinctus*, from *cingere*, to gird, and means pregnant; carrying an unborn child) *en croûte* [in (a) crust; wrapped in pastry and baked; said especially of meats] *en famille* [in (one's) family; with one's family; at home; in an informal way] *enfleurage* (in flower; a process of extracting perfumes by having fats absorb the exhalations of certain flowers) *engagé* (committed to, or actively supporting, a political or social cause) *en garde* (on guard; in *fencing*, the opening position from which one may either attack or defend) *en masse* (in mass; in a group; as a whole; all together) *en passant* (in passing; by the way; used as a chess term) *en prise* (in *chess*, in a position to be taken) *en rapport* (in harmony; in sympathy; in accord) *en règle* (according to rule; in order) *en route* (on the way; along the way; as *a delay en route*) *en suite* (in, or as part of, a series or set) *entente* (an understanding or agreement, as between nations; the parties to this) FRENCH PHRASE: *embarras de richesses* [embarrassment of wealth (of good things); hence, too much to choose from] INTERDISCIPLINARY: envelope (in *astronomy*, a cloudy mass surrounding the nucleus of a comet; coma; in *biology*, any enclosing membrane, skin, shell, etc.; in *mathematics*, a curve that is tangent to every one of a family of curves, or a surface that is tangent to every one of a family of surfaces) CROSS REFERENCE: *in-* (one meaning)

Word from a person's name: Machiavellian
from Niccolò Machiavelli (1469-1529), an Italian statesman and political theorist; author of *The Prince* (1513), which established Machiavelli as the father of the modern science of politics. In Elizabethan literature, there are hundreds of references that connect Machiavelli with the Devil or the Evil One.

232

Element	From	Meaning	Examples
endo-***	Greek contracts *en*-, in + *dom*, house; therefore, in the house)	within, inner	PREFIXED ROOTS AND COMPOUNDS: *end*: arch: endarch (in *botany*, having the primary xylem maturing from the center of the stem toward the outside) (*arche*, beginning) odont: endodontics (the branch of dentistry that treats disorders of the pulp; root-canal therapy) (*odonto*, tooth) osm: endosmosis (opposed to *exosmosis*) (*osm*, pushing, drive) ost: (*osteo*, bone) endosteum (the vascular connective tissue lining the marrow cavities of bones) endostosis (the formation of bone within cartilage) *endo*-: bio: endobiotic (living *within* the tissues of a host, as the malaria parasite) (*bios*, life) blast: endoblast (same as *endoderm*) (*blast*, sprout, embryo) card: (heart) endocardial (within the heart) endocarditis (inflammation of the endocardium) (*itis*, inflammation of) endocardium (the thin endothelial membrane lining the cavities of the heart) carp: endocarp (the inner layer of the wall of a ripened ovary or fruit, as the pit surrounding the seed of a plum) (*carp*, fruit) centr: endocentric (in *linguistics*, designating a construction which in its totality has the same syntactic function as one or more of its constituents, e.g., *ham and eggs* has the same syntactic function as *ham* or *eggs*) (*centr*, center) cran: endocranium (in humans, the dura mater; in insects, the processes supporting the brain in the head capsule) (*cranium*, skull) crin: endocrine, endocrinology (from *krinein*, to separate) derm: endoderm {endodermic}, endodermis (*derm*, skin) enzym: endoenzme (*en*- prefixes *zym*, fermentation) gam: endogamy (opposed to *exogamy*) (*gamos*, marriage) gen: endogenous (in *biology*, growing or developing from or on the inside), endogeny (*gen*, producing) metr: endometriosis, endometrium (*metra*, womb) mix: endomixis (a periodic reorganization of the nucleus in the cells of certain ciliates, not caused by conjugation) (*mixis*, a mixing) morph: (shape, form) endomorph (a mineral, especially a crystal, enclosed within another; compare *perimorph*) endomorphic (having a heavy body build; contrasted with ectomorphic, mesomorphic) endomorphism (a change brought about within the mass of an intrusive igneous rock) parasit: endoparasite (a parasite that inhabits the internal organs or tissues of an animal or plant; opposed to *ectoparasite*) (*sitos*, food)

233

Element	From	Meaning	Examples
endo- (cont'd)			phag: endophagous (feeding from the inside of an animal or plant: said of certain parasitic insects) (*phag*, eat) phyt: endophyte (a plant living within another plant) (*phyton*, plant) plasm: endoplasm (the inner part of the cytoplasm of a cell: distinguished from *ectoplasm*) (*plasm*, formative cell material) proct: endoproct (*proktos*, anus) scop: endoscope {endoscopic, endoscopy} (*scope*, look) skelet: endoskeleton (distinguished from *exoskeleton*) sperm: endosperm (a tissue which surrounds the developing embryo of a seed and provides food for its growth) (*sperm*, seed) spor: endospore (also, *endosporium*) (*spore*, seed) thec: endothecium (*thekion*, small case) thel: endothelium {endothelial} (*thel*, nipple) therm: endothermic (also, *endothermal*; designating, of, or produced by a chemical change in which there is an absorption of heat) (*therm*, heat) tox: endotoxin (a toxic substance found in certain disease-producing bacteria and liberated by the disintegration of the bacterial cell) (*toxi*, poison) trach: endotracheal (describing certain devices for administering anesthetic gases, etc.) (*trachea*, windpipe) DOUBLE PREFIXED ROOT: endo<u>comm</u>ensal (a commensal living within the body of the host organism) (*com-*, with, together prefixes *mensa*, table) CROSS REFERENCE: *ento-, intra-, intro-*
enigm*	Greek *ainos*	puzzle	SIMPLE ROOT: enigma (plural, *enigmas*, or *enigmata*), enigmatic, enigmatite (an *imperfectly known* mineral, which is a silicate of iron, titanium, and sodium) NOTE: Do not confuse this root with Spanish *enimagá*, of American Indian origin, and referring to the Macá people of the Gran Chaco in Paraguay and Argentina. NO CROSS REFERENCE
enn			See *ann* for *perennial*.
ennea*	Greek *ennea* (IE: *newo*, new; see *nov*)	nine	SIMPLE ROOT: ennead (a group of nine books, gods, poems, stories, etc.) {enneatic} LEADING ROOT COMPOUND: gon: enneagon (a nine-sided figure) (*gon*, angle) petal: enneapetalous (nine-petaled) CROSS REFERENCE: *nov*
ens*	Greek *ensis*	sword	SIMPLE ROOT: Ensi (a common genus of razor clams) LEADING ROOT COMPOUND: form: ensiform (as the *ensiform* shape of the gladiolus leaf) CROSS REFERENCE: *glad, xiphi*
entero**	Greek *enteron*	intestine	LEADING ROOT COMPOUND: *enter*: oide: enteroidea (intestinal fevers caused by intestional bacilli including typhoid fever) (from eidos, form) *entero*: bi: enterobiasis (infestation with pinworms) (*bio*, life)

234

Element	From	Meaning	Examples
entero (cont'd)			coc: enterococcus (a streptococcus normally present in the intestinal tract, that may be a cause of disease when found in other parts of the body) (*coccus*, bacteria) TRAILING ROOT COMPOUND lic: licentery (diarrhea characterized by the discharge of undigested or incompletely digested foods) (*leios*, smooth) NO CROSS REFERENCE
ento-**	Greek *entos*	within	PREFIXED ROOTS: *ent*: op: entoptic (do not confuse with *entopic*) (*ops*, eye) ot: entotic (*ot*, ear) *ento-*: blast: entoblast (same as *endoderm*; also *entoderm*) (*blast*, shoot, sprout, embryo) phyt: entophyte (same as *endophyte*) (*phyton*, plant) zo: entozoon (an internal animal parasite, especially a parasitic worm infesting the intestines, muscles, etc.; plural, *entozoa*) {entozoal, entozoic} (*zo*, animal) CROSS REFERENCE: *endo-, intra-*
entom**	Greek *entomon*	insect	ROOT NOTE: With *en-*, in + *tom*, cut, the element literally means cut into, as in *entom* and *entomion*, medical words. As a separate element, the element means *insect*; an *insect* is cut into segments. LEADING ROOT COMPOUND: ceci: entomocecidium (a gall caused by insects) (*ceci*, gall) fauna: entomofauna (the insects of a particular region) (*fauna*, animals) logy: entomology {entomologic, entomologist} (*logy*, scientific study of) phag: entomophagous (feeding mainly on bugs and insects) (*phag*, eat) phil: entomophilous (fertilized by insect-borne pollen: said of certain flowers) (*philein*, to love) phob: entomophobia (morbid or irrational fear of insects) NO CROSS REFERENCE
entre			See *inter-* for *entrepot, entrepreneur*, etc.
eo*	Greek *eos* (IE: *awes*, to shine)	dawn; extended to include "early time period" (in *medicine*, rose-colored, as the color of dawn)	SIMPLE ROOT: eosin (a rose-colored stain or dye; the potassium and sodium salts of tetrabromfluorescein LEADING ROOT COMPOUND: *eo*: bio: eobiont [a hypothetical precursor of living organisms in the chemical evolution preceding the occurrence of life; term coined by J. D. Bernal (1901-) F.R.S. (Fellow of the Royal Society) British physicist] (*bio*, life) cen: Eocene (designating or of the second and longest epoch of the Tertiary Period in the Cenozoic Era, during which mammals became the dominant animals) (*kainos*, new) hipp: eohippus (any of a genus of extinct progenitors of the modern horse, found in the Lower Eocene of Western United States: it was about the size of a fox and had four toes on the front feet and three on the hind) (*hippos*, horse)

Element	From	Meaning	Examples
eo (cont'd)			lith: eolith (any of the crude stone tools used in the early part of the Stone Age) {eolithic} (*lithos*, stone) phob: eosophobia (morbid fear or dread of daybreak) *eosino*: cyt: eosinocyte (same as *eosinophil*) phil: eosinophil (also *esosinophile*) (*phil*, attracted to) GREEK MYTHOLOGY: Eos, goddess of dawn; confer *Aurora* NB: **Eon**, from *aion*, an age, eternity, is not in this family. NO CROSS REFERENCE
ep*	Greek *epos* (IE: *wekw*, to speak)	word, speech	SIMPLE ROOT: epic (a long narrative poem in a dignified style about the deeds of a traditional or historical hero or heroes; examples of epics are as follows: *Iliad, Odyssey, Paradise Lost, Beowulf, Divine Comedy*), epos TRAILING ROOT COMPOUND: caco: cacoepy (bad pronunciation) (*caco*, bad, wrong) ortho: orthoepy (the study of pronunciation; phonology; the standard pronunciation of a language) (*ortho*, straight) CROSS REFERENCE: *dict, fab/fam/fat, lect/lex, logos, loqu, ora, parl, verb*
epi-***	Greek (IE: *epi, opi, near, at, toward, after*)	beside, upon, over, among, on the outside, anterior	PREFIXED ROOTS: *ep-*: act: epact [see background under *ag* (Greek root)] arch: eparch, eparchy (*archos*, ruler) hemer: (day) ephemera (ephemeral things collectively; printed matter, such as theater programs, posters, etc., meant to be of use for only a short time but preserved by collectors) ephemeral (**Synonyms**: transitory, momentary, fugitive) ephemeris (an astronomical almanac), ephemeron (the mayfly) hebe: ephebe, ephebus (see note at *hebe*) (*hebe*, young) och: epoch (the beginning of a new and important period in the history of anything) (from *echein*, to hold) ode: epode (literally, aftersong; singing or sung to music; a form of lyric poem, as of Horace, in which a short line follows a longer one) (*ode*, song) onym: eponym {eponymous}, eponymy (*onym*, name) oxy: epoxy [*epi-* + *oxy(gen)*] *epi-*: benth: epibenthos (*benthos*, sea bottom) blast: epiblast (the outer layer of cells in an embryo) (*blast*, sprout, shoot, embryo) bol: epiboly (a throwing beyond) (*ballein*, to throw) calyx: epicalyx (a ring of small bracts at the base of certain flowers, resembling an extra outer calyx, as in the mallows) (*calyx*, cup) canth: epicanthus (a small normal fold of skin from the supper eyelid sometimes covering the inner corner of the eye, as in many Asian peoples: also occurs with certain abnormal conditions, as Down's syndrome) (*canthus*, corner, edge) card: epicardium (*kardia*, heart) ced: epicedium (plural, *epicedia*; a funeral ode or hymn; dirge) (*kedos*, grief)

Element	From	Meaning	Examples
epi- (cont'd)			cen: epicene (designating a noun, as in Latin or Greek, having only one grammatical form to denote an individual of either sex; also, belonging to one sex but having characteristics of the other, or of neither; specifically, effeminate; unmanly) (*koinos*, common)
			cent: epicenter (in *geology*, a point, directly above the true center of disturbance, from which the shock waves of an earthquake apparently radiate)
			cotyl: epicotyl (in *botany*, that part of the stem of a seedling or embryo just about the cotyledons) (*cotyl*, hollow, cavit)
			cran: epicranium
			crit: epicritic (designating or of the nerve fibers in the skin that transmit the finer sensations of touch and temperature) (*krinein*, to judge)
			cycl: (*cycle*, circle, wheel)
			epicycle (in *geometry*, a circle which, by rolling around the interior or exterior of another circle, generates a hypocycloid or a eipicycloid respectively)
			epicycloid (*oid*, similar to)
			deic: epideictic (intended for display, especially rhetorical display; designed to impress) (from *deik*, show)
			dem: epidemic, epidemiology (*demos*, people)
			derm: epidermis {epidermic}, epidermoid (*derm*, skin)
			didym: epididymous (a long, oval-shaped structure attached to the rear upper surface of each testicle, consisting mainly of the sperm ducts of the testicles) (*didymoi*, double, but refers to the testicles)
			dot: epidote {epidotic} (*didonai*, to give)
			foc: epifocal (over the focus or center of disturbance of an earthquake; epicentral)
			gastr: epigastric, epigastrium (*gaster*, the stomach)
			ge(o): epigeal (also, *epigean*) (*geo*, earth)
			gen: (producing)
			epigene (in *geology*, produced or formed on or near the earth's surface, as *epigene rocks*)
			epigenesis, epigenetic
			epigenous (in *botany*, growing on the surface of a leaf or other plant part, especially on the upper surface, as some fungi)
			glott: epiglottis (*glossa*, tongue)
			gon: epigone (a descendant less gifted than his/her ancestors, or any inferior follower or imitator) (*gon*, seed, sexual reproduction)
			gram: epigram (a short poem with a witty or satirical point; any pointed statement, often antithetical, e.g., *Experience is the name one gives to his/her mistakes*), epigrammatic, epigrammaticism (from *graph*, write)
			graph: epigraph (from *epigram*), epigraphic, epigraphy (*graphein*, to write)
			gyn: epigynous {epigyny} (designating petals, sepals, and stamens that are attached to the top of the ovary; opposed to *hypogynous*) (*gyno*, female reproductive organ, ovary, pistil)
			lep: epilepsy, epileptic (from *lambanein*, to seize)

Element	From	Meaning	Examples
epi- (cont'd)			limn: epilimnion (*limne*, marshy lake)
			log: epilogue (also, *epilog*; a closing section added to a novel, play, etc., providing further comment, interpretation, or information) (from *legein*, to say)
			mer: epimere (*mere*, part)
			mys: epimysium (*mys*, muscle)
			nasty: epinasty (in *botany*, the condition in which an organ, as a leaf, turns downward because of the more rapid growth of the upper layers of cells: opposed to *hyponasty*) (from *nasein*, to press, squeeze close)
			nephr: epinephrine (*nephros*, kidney)
			neur: epineurium (a layer of connective tissue surrounding a peripheral nerve) (*neuron*, a nerve)
			phen: epiphenomenon (in *pathology*, a secondary complication arising during an illness) (from *phainein*, to show)
			phys: epiphysis (from *phyein*, to grow)
			phyt: epiphyte (see *epiphysis*) (*phyton*, plant)
			scop: episcopal (of or governed by bishops; capitalized, designating or of various churches governed by bishops, including the Protestant Episcopal and the Anglican Church) (*scope*, view, look)
			sod: episode (**Synonyms:** occurrence, event, incident), episodic (*s* of *sode* from *eis-*, into + an elided form of *hodos*, way)
			stas: epistasis (the suppression of gene expression by one or more other genes) (from *histanai*, to stand)
			stax: epistaxis (nosebleed) (from *stazein*, to fall in drops)
			stem: epistemic (of or having to do with knowledge), epistemology (from *histanai*, to stand)
			stern: episternum (*sternon*, the breastbone)
			stle: epistle, epistler (from *stellein*, to send, summon)
			stroph: epistrophe (see note under *strophe*) (*strophe*, turning)
			taph: epitaph (an inscription on tomb) (*taphos*, tomb)
			tas: epitasis (that part of play, especially in classical drama, between the prostasis, or exposition, and the catastrophe, or denouement) (from *teinein*, to stretch)
			tax: epitaxy (*taxis*, arrangement)
			thal: epithalamium (a song or poem in honor of a bride or bridegroom, or both; nuptial song) (*thalamos*, bridal chamber)
			thel: epithelioma (*thelium*, nipple + *oma*, tumor, mass)
			thet: epithet (a descriptive name, often opprobrious) (*tithenai*, to put, do)
			tom: epitome (a short statement of the main points of a book, report, incident, etc.; a person or thing that is representative or typical of the characteristics or general quality of a whole class), epitomize (from *temnein*, to cut)
			zo: epizoic, epizoon, epizootic (*zoion*, animal)
			EMBEDDED PREFIXED ROOT:
			parallelepiped (a solid with six faces, each of which is a parallelogram) (*parallel* + *ped*, foot)

Element	From	Meaning	Examples
epi- (cont'd)			CHRISTIAN FESTIVAL: Epiphany (to show forth; a festival, held January 6, commemorating the revealing of Jesus as the Christ to the Gentiles in the persons of the Magi; or, the baptism of Jesus) INTERDISCIPLINARY: epicranium (in *anatomy*, the structures covering the cranium; in *entomology*, the upper portion of the head of an insect between the frons and the neck) epigeal (in *botany*, growing on or close to the ground; directed above the ground after germination: said of cotyledons; in *zoology*, living or developing on the exposed surface of the earth or in shallow water) epigenesis (in *biology*, the theory that the germ cell is without structure and that the embryo develops as a new creation through the action of the environment on the protoplasm; in *geology*, metamorphism; in *medicine*, the appearing of secondary symptoms; a secondary symptom) CROSS REFERENCE: *ecto-, exo-, extra-, juxta-, para-*
ept			See *apt* for *inept*.
equ***	Latin *aequus*	equal	SIMPLE ROOT: equab: equable (**Synonyms:** even, uniform, regular) equal: equal (**Synonyms:** same, identical, equivalent), equalitarian (same as French *egalitarian*), equality, equalize, equalizer, equally equat: equate, equation, equator, equatorial equi: equitable, equitant (in *botany*, overlapping: said of a leaf whose base overlaps and covers partly the leaf above it, as in the iris), equity PREFIXED ROOTS AND COMPOUNDS: *ad-*: adequacy, adequate (**Synonyms:** sufficient, enough) (*ad-*; to, toward) *dis-*: disequilibrate, disequilibrium (*dis-*, apart, opposite) *in-*: (not) inequality, inequitable, inequity (do not confuse with *iniquity*, under *Prefixed Disguised Root*) inequivalve (having the two valves of the shell unequal, as an oyster) DOUBLE PREFIXED ROOT: inadequate (*in-*, not + *ad-*, to, toward) LEADING ROOT COMPOUND: *equi:* anim: equanimity (**Synonyms:** composure, serenity, nonchalance) (*animus*, the mind) *equi:* later: equilateral (having all sides equal) (*latus*, side) libr: equilibrant, equilibrate, equilibrist (one who does tricks of balancing, as a tightrope walker), equilibrium (*libra*, weight, balance) mol: equimolecular (*mol*, mass) molar: equimolar (*molar*, grinder) noc: equinoctial (relating to either of the equinoxes or to equal periods of day and night) (from *equinox*)

Element	From	Meaning	Examples
equ (cont'd)			nox: equinox (explore *vernal equinox, autumnal equinox*) (*nox*, night)
			pois: equipoise (from *pendere*, to weigh)
			poll: equipollent (equal in force, weight, or validity; equivalent in meaning or result) (*pollere*, to be strong)
			pond: equiponderant, equiponderate (*ponderare*, to weigh)
			val: equivalence, equivalent (see synonyms at *equal*) (*valere*, to be strong)
			voc: equivocal (**Synonyms**: vague, enigmatic, ambiguous), equivocate (from *vox*, voice)
			vok: equivoke (see *Doublets* below; same as French *equivoque*, which see below)
			PREFIXED DISGUISED ROOT:
			in-: iniquity (lack of righteousness or justice; wickedness) (from *iniquus*, unequal) (*in-*, not)
			FRENCH: equivoque (see *Doublets* below; same as *equivoke*: an equivocal word or phrase; equivocal)
			DOUBLETS: equivoque:equivoke
			LATIN PHRASE:
			aequo pulsat pede [(Death) knocks with equal foot] Horace
			PLACENAMES:
			Ecuador (in South America, the equator is over the countries of Ecuador, Colombia, and Brazil) (from *equator*)
			Equality (Alabama, Illinois)
			CROSS REFERENCE: *iso, par*
equ*	Latin *equus* (IE: *ekwos*, horse)	horse	SIMPLE ROOT:
			eque: equerry, equestrian, equestrienne
			equi: equine, equinia, equitation, equites
			LEADING ROOT COMPOUND:
			set: equisetum (a particular perennial plant that spreads by creeping rhizomes) (*set*, bristle, horsetail)
			CONSTELLATION: Equuleus
			CROSS REFERENCE: *caval, hippo*
erc			See *arc* for *exercise*.
erem*	Greek *eremos* (IE: *er*, loose, distant, to separate)	alone, lonely	SIMPLE ROOT: eremite (religious recluse; hermit) {eremitic}
			DISGUISED ROOT: hermit (a person who lives alone in a lonely or secluded spot, often from religious motives; recluse), hermitage (the place where a hermit lives; a place where a person can live away from other people; secluded retreat)
			CROSS REFERENCE: *mono, sol*
erg,*** urg	Greek *ergon* (IE: *werg*, to do, act)	work	SIMPLE ROOT: erg, ergon
			PREFIXED ROOT:
			an-: anergy (in *medicine*, a condition in which the body of a sensitized person fails to respond to an antigen) (*an-*, without)
			en-: (in)
			energetic (**Synonyms**: active, vigorous, strenuous)
			energid, energize, energumen
			energy (**Synonyms**: strength, power, force)
			par-: parergon (a shorter musical or literary composition that is derived from a larger work) (*para-*, alongside)
			syn-: synergism {synergistic}, synergy {synergic} (*syn-*, with)

Element	From	Meaning	Examples
erg (cont'd)			MESHED PREFIXED ROOT: *hyper-*: hypergolic [igniting spontaneously on contact with its components (said of a rocket fuel)] (*hyper-*, beyond + *erg*; from German *Hypergol*) LEADING ROOT COMPOUND: *erg*: od: ergodic (from *hodos*, way) *ergo*: graph: ergograph (an instrument for measuring and recording the amount of work that a muscle is capable or doing) (*graph*, write) latr: ergolatry (idolatrous devotion to work) (*latry*, worship of) meter: ergometer (an instrument for measuring and recording the amount of work done by a muscle or muscles over a period of time) (*meter*, measure) nom: ergonomics (the study of the problems of people in adjustment to their environment) (*nom* from *economics*) TRAILING ROOT COMPOUND: adren: adrenergic (near the kidney: *ad-*, to, near + *ren*, kidney) all: allergy (altered energy, or reaction) (*allo*, other) chem: chemurgy (see *Webster's New World*) (*chem*, chemistry) demi: demiurge (different meanings in Platonism and Gnosticism) (*demios*, belonging to the people) drama: dramaturge (a playwright; literary advisor) lit: liturgical, liturgics, liturgy (originally, public service to the gods) (*lit* ultimately from *laos*, people) metall: metallurgy (the science of metals) zym: zymurgy (the branch of chemistry dealing with fermentation, as in making wine, brewing, etc.) (*zym*, fermentation) PREFIXED TRAILING ROOT COMPOUND: *a-*: abioergy (*a-*, not + *bio*, life) DISGUISED ROOT: argon (literally, without work, and designating an inert, colorless, odorless gas constituting nearly one percent of the atmosphere) (from *a-*, not + *ergon*) georgic poem (see *Proper Name* below; a poem dealing with farming or rural life) lethargy (a condition of abnormal drowsiness or torpor; a great lack of energy) (*lethe*, forgetfulness + *a-*, not + ergon) surgery, surgeon PREFIXED DISGUISED ROOT: *in-*: inure (literally, to work in; to cause to become used to something difficult, painful, etc.) (*in-*, in + Old French *eure*, work) RELATED WORDS: bulwark (literally, bole work; *bol*, stem, trunk; see *Doublets*) boulevard (from *bulwark*; see *Doublets*) DOUBLETS: bulwark:boulevard PROPER NAME: George (literally, earthworker; from *geo*, earth + ergon) PLACENAME: Energy, Illinois CROSS REFERENCE: *labor, oper*

241

Element	From	Meaning	Examples
ero***	Greek *eros*	love (sexual)	SIMPLE ROOT: eros: eros (sexual love or desire; in *psychoanalysis*, the life instinct, based on the libido, sublimated impulses, and self-preservation) erot: erotic, erotica, eroticism (also, *erotism*), eroticize LEADING ROOT COMPOUND: *ero*: gen: erogenous (also *eratogenic*; designating or of those areas of the body, as the genital, oral, and anal zones that are particularly sensitive to sexual stimulation) (*gen*, producing) *erato*: gen: erotogenic (same as *erogenous*) (*gen*, producing) mania: erotomania (abnormally strong sexual desire) (*mania*, craving, madness) TRAILING ROOT COMPOUND: auto: autoerotism (also, *autoeroticism*) {autoerotic} (*auto*, self) ped: pederasty (the practice of loving boys as sex objects) (from *paed*, originally child, but narrowed to mean boy) GREEK MYTHOLOGY: Erato (the Muse of erotic lyric poetry and mime) Eros (god of love, son of Aphrodite: identified by the Romans with Cupid; in *lower case*, sexual love or desire; in *psychoanalysis*, libido or the psychic energy associated with it; in *theology*, a receiving love, as opposed to *agape*, a giving love) PLACENAME: Eros, Louisiana CROSS REFERENCE: *phil*
err**	Latin *errare* (IE: *er, or,* to set in motion)	to wander	SIMPLE ROOT: err (to be wrong or mistaken), erring erra: errancy, erratic, erratum (plural, *errata*) erro: erroneous, error (**Synonyms:** mistake, blunder, slip) PREFIXED ROOT: *ab-*: aberrant (deviating from what is normal), aberration (*ab-*, away) *in-*: inerrable, inerrant (both are adjectives; both mean the same: making no mistakes; infallible; unerring) (*in-*, not) NB: Though *errant* means "roving or straying from what is right or the right course," the word is from the Latin verb *itere*, to go; consequently, a *knight-errant* is one *in search of adventure*. Neither is *errand* in this family. CROSS REFERENCE: *migr, plan*; *vag*, as in *vagrant*
-escence,** (-escent)	Latin	beginning to be, becoming; giving off or reflecting light	SUFFIXED ROOT: (becoming): adolescence (adolescent) (adult) alkalescence (alkalescent) (alkaline) (giving off, reflecting light): phosphorescence (phosphorescent) (phosphorus) luminescence (luminescent) (light) PREFIXED + SUFFIXED ROOT: *con-*: convalesce, convalescence, convalescent (*con-*, with, together; *valere*, to be strong) *ob-*: obsolescence, obsolescent (*ob-*, against; *sol* from *solere*, to become accustomed) CROSS REFERENCE: *gen*

Element	From	Meaning	Examples
eschat*	Greek *eschatos*: last, farthest (IE: *egs*, out)	last things	SIMPLE ROOT: eschatocol (concluding portion of a protocol) LEADING ROOT COMPOUND: logy: eschatology (study of last things; the book of Revelation in the New Testament is regarded by Christians as a book on eschatology) (logy, study of) NO CROSS REFERENCE
eso-*	Greek *eso*	within, inside	EXTENDED PREFIX: esoteric (inner; difficult to understand; belonging to the select few; private; secret; opposed to *exoteric*) PREFIXED ROOT: trop: esotropia (to turn within, a condition in which only one eye fixes on an object while the other turns inward, producing the appearance of a cross-eye) (*trop*, turn; *ops*, eye) CROSS REFERENCE: *ento-, intra-/intro-*
esse**	Latin *esse* (IE: *es*, to be)	to be, exist	SIMPLE ROOT: esse, essence, essential (**Synonyms:** indispensable, requisite, necessary) PREFIXED ROOT: *ab-*: absence, absent (from *abesse*), absentee (*ab-*, away) *inter-*: interest, interested, interesting (*inter-*, between) *pre-*: (before, in front) present (in grammar, indicating action as now taking place, shown by adding an *s* or *es* to the third person singular verb, e.g., *she sits*; *she goes*) presentable, presentation, presentational, presentationalism presentative (in *philosophy*, immediately knowable; capable of being known without thought or reflection) presentiment (a feeling or impression or something about to happen, especially something evil; foreboding) presentive, presentment DOUBLE PREFIXED ROOT: disinterest, disinterested (lack of personal interest; not to be confused with *uninterested*) (*dis-*, opposite of) represent, representational, representative (*re-*, again + *pre-*, before) uninterested (not interested) (Anglo-Saxon prefix *un-*, not) TRAILING ROOT COMPOUND: quint: quintessence (in ancient and medieval philosophy, the fifth essence, or ultimate substance, of which the heavenly bodies were thought to be composed: distinguished from the four elements: air, fire, water, and earth; the pure, concentrated essence of anything; the most perfect manifestation of a quality or thing) {quintessential} (*quint*, five) DISGUISED ROOT: entity (being; existence; essential nature; a thing that has definite, individual existence outside or within the mind; anything real in itself) proud (**Synonyms:** arrogant, haughty, insolent) (from *pro-*, before, forward + *esse*; to be useful) PREFIXED DISGUISED ROOT: *im-*: improve (**Synonyms:** ameliorate, enhance) (*im-*, in) GERMAN TOAST: *Prosit!* (to your being--to your health) CROSS REFERENCE: *etym*

Element	From	Meaning	Examples
esthes** (also spelled, aesthes)	Greek *aisthesis*	feeling	SIMPLE ROOT: esthesia (aesthesia), esthete (aesthete), esthetic (aesthetic) PREFIXED ROOTS AND COMPOUNDS: *an-*: (not) anesthesia, anesthetic, anesthetist anesthesiologist, anesthesiology (*logy*, study of) *hyper-*: hyperesthesia (abnormal sensitivity of the skin or some sense organ) {hyperesthetic} (*hyper-*, beyond) *hypo-*: hypoesthesia (dulled sensitivity to touch) (*hypo-*, under) TRAILING ROOT COMPOUND: kine: kinesthesia (*kinema*, motion) CROSS REFERENCE: *alg, odyn, sens, pat*
estr*	Latin *oestrus*	gadfly, frenzy	ROOT NOTE: This root has been extended to refer to the sexual excitement in female mammals; often referred to as *heat*, *estrus* is comparable to *rut* of males. It is related to Lithuanian *aistra*, violent passion; to Old Norse *eisa*, to rush on; and to another Latin root, *ira*, ire. SIMPLE ROOT: estral, estrone, estrous, estruate, estrus PREFIXED ROOT: *an-*: anestrous (in the breeding cycle of many mammals, the period of sexual inactivity between two periods of estrus) (*an-*, not) LEADING ROOT COMPOUND: *estri*: ol: estriol (a female sex hormone, $C_{18}H_{24}O_2$) [*es(trus)* + *tri*, three + *-ol*, an alcohol or phenol] *estro*: gen: estrogen {estrogenic} (*gen*, producer) NO CROSS REFERENCE
eth*	Greek *ethnos*, people	custom, character	SIMPLE ROOT: ethic, ethics, ethical (**Synonyms:** moral, virtuous, righteous), ethos PREFIXED ROOT: *an-*: anethopathy (*an-*, not) LEADING ROOT COMPOUND: logy: ethology (in *biology*, the scientific study of the characteristic behavior patterns of animals) (*logy*, study of) TRAILING ROOT COMPOUND: caco: cacoëthes [literally, bad habit, or mania (an itch to do something, as in *cacoëthes scribendi*, the itch to write)] (*caco*, bad) CROSS REFERENCE: *mor*
ethn*	Greek *ethnos*: people	nation, race	SIMPLE ROOT: ethnic, ethnical, ethnicon (also, *ethnikon*; the name of a tribe, ethnic group, or people, such as Hopi, Somali, etc.) ethnos LEADING ROOT COMPOUND: centr: ethnocentrism {ethnocentric} (*centr*, center) graph: ethnography {ethnographer} (*graph*, write) log: ethnology {ethnologic, ethnological, ethnologist} (*logy*, study of) music: ethnomusicology (*music* + *logy*, study of) CROSS REFERENCE: *gen, phyl*

Element	From	Meaning	Examples
etym*	Greek *etymos*, true	true meaning	SIMPLE ROOT: etymon (literal sense of the word; the earlier form of a word, e.g., Old English *eage* is the etymon of Modern English *eye*; also, a word or morpheme from which derivatives or compounds have developed; in this book, etymons are shown in bold in the first column) LEADING ROOT COMPOUND: log: etymology (the origin and development of a word, affix, phrase, etc. to its earliest source), etymological, etymologist (*logy*, study of) CROSS REFERENCE: *esse*
eu***	Greek *eys*	good, well, normal	LEADING ROOT COMPOUND: calypt: eucalyptus (an Australian evergreen tree so named from its well-covered buds) (*calypt*, covered) char: Eucharist (giving of thanks; the celebration of the Lord's Supper, or Communion) (*charis*, favor) chrom: euchromatin (in *biology*, the portion of the chromosome containing most of the genetic material and staining less densely than the heterochromatin) (*chrome*, color) cili: euciliate (but extended to mean "hair-like process"; any of a subclass of ciliated protozoans in which cilia are present for the entire life cycle) (*cili*, eyebrow) clas: euclase (a green or blue crystalline silicate of aluminum and beryllium, used as a gem: so named from breaking easily) (from *clan*, to break) demon: eudemonia (happiness, as in Aristotle's philosophy) (*demon*, spirit) gen: eugenic (literally, well-born), eugenics (*genic*, production) log: eulogia, eulogistic, eulogy (**Synonyms:** tribute, encomium, panegyric) (from *legein*, to speak) patri: eupatrid (any of the hereditary aristocrats of ancient Athens or other Greek states) (from *pater*, father) peps: eupepsia, eupeptic (from *peptein*, to cook, digest) phem: euphemism {euphemist}, euphemize (from *phanai*, to speak) phon: euphonic (also, *euphonical*), euphonious (agreeable to the ear), euphonium, euphony (*phone*, sound) phor: euphoria (in feeling of well-being, especially an exaggerated one having no basis in truth or in reality), euphoriant (from *pherein*, to bear) phot: euphotic (*photos*, light) phu: euphuism (see note under *phy*) {euphuistic} (from *phyein*, to grow) plast: euplastic (in *physiology*, easily formed into or adapted to the formation of tissue) (from *plassein*, to form) pne: eupnea (normal breathing; opposed to *apnea*) (*pnea*, breath) than: euthanasia (*thanatos*, death) troph: eutrophic {eutrophication} (*trophe*, food) xen: euxenite (a particular mineral, so named from containing several rare elements: columbium, titanium, yttrium, erbium, cerium, and uranium) (*xenos*, stranger)

Element	From	Meaning	Examples
eu (cont'd)			VARIANT LEADING ROOT COMPOUND: angel: evangel (capitalized, any of the Four Gospels), evange- lism, evangelist (literally, good messenger), evangelize (*angel*, messenger) PROPER NAMES: Eugene, Evangeline RIVER: Euphrates (literally, easy to cross) PLACENAMES: Eudora (Arkansas, Kansas) Eugene (Missouri, Oregon) [Eufaula (Alabama, Oklahoma) is of Indian origin.] NB: *Euhemerism, Euclidian, eunuch,* and *eureka* are not in this family. *Euhemerism* is the theory of the Greek writer Euhemerus, 4th century B.C. *Euclidian* is derived from Euclid, Greek geometer of about 300 B.C.; therefore, Euclidian construction, Euclidian geometry, Euclidian space, Euclid's algorithm *Eunuch*, literally, bed-watcher, is a castrated man, employed as harem attendants in certain Oriental courts and under the Roman emperors. *Eureka* is Greek for I have found it; see note under *heur.* CROSS REFERENCE: *bene, bono*
eury*	Greek *eurys*	broad, wide, dilation	PREFIXED ROOT: an-: aneurysm (to widen throughout; a pathological blood- filled dilation of a blood vessel) (from *ana-*, throughout) LEADING ROOT COMPOUND: bath: eurybath (in *biology*, an organism that can live in a wide range of water; opposed to *stenobath*) (*bathos*, depth) halin: euryhaline (in *biology*, able to exist in waters with wide variations in their salt content; opposed to *stenohaline*) (from *hals*, salt) hygr: euryhygric (in *biology*, able to withstand·a wide range of humidity; opposed to *stenohygric*) (*hygr*, moisture) phag: euryphagous (in *biology*, eating a variety of foods; op- posed to *stenophagous*) (*phag*, eat) pyg: eurypygous (broad-rumped) (*pyg*, buttock) therm: eurytherm (an organism that can live in a wide range of temperatures; opposed to *stenotherm*) (*therm*, heat) GREEK MYTHOLOGY: Eurydice (literally, wide justice: read the story of Eurydice and Orpheus to see the irony) CROSS REFERENCE: *platy*
ev*	Latin *aevum*	age	PREFIXED ROOT: co-: coeval (of the same age or period; **Synonyms:** con- temporary, synchronous, simultaneous) (*co-*, with, together) TRAILING ROOT COMPOUND: long: longevity (a long life; great span of life; length of life; length of time spent in service, employment, etc.) med: medieval (of, like, characteristic of, or suggestive of the Middle Ages) (*med*, middle) prim: primeval (of the earliest times or ages; primal; primor- dial) (*prim*, first) CROSS REFERENCE: *chron, temp*

246

Element	From	Meaning	Examples
ex-,*** ef-, es-, e-	Latin (IE: *eghs*, out)	out of, prior, forth, from, out, beyond, away from, thoroughly, without	PREFIXED ROOT: e-: bull: ebullient (bubbling; boiling; overflowing with enthusi- asm, high spirits, etc.; exuberant), ebullition (*bullire*, to boil) duc: (*ducere*, to lead) educate (**Synonyms**: teach, instruct, train), educated, educa- tion, educational, educative educe (**Synonyms**: extract, elicit, evoke) {educible, eduction}, educt gress: egress (also, egression; the act of going out or forth; the right to go out; a way out) (from *gradi*, to step) ject: (from *jacere*, to throw) eject (**Synonyms**: evict, dismiss, oust) {ejection, ejective, ejector}, ejectment ejecta (ejected matter, as from the body, a volcano, etc.) labor: elaborate {elaboration} (*laborare*, to labor, work, toil) laps: elapse (to slip by; pass: said of time, as *an elapsed pol- icy*) (from *labi*, to glide, fall) lect: (chosen; given preference), electable, election, elective, elector, electorate (from *legere*, to pick, choose) miss: emission, emissive, emissivity (see *emit*) mit: emit (**Synonyms**: exude, expel, eject), emitter (*mittere*, to send) norm: (*norma*, rule) enormity (great wickedness; a monstrous or outrageous act; very wicked crime; enormous size or extent; vastness) enormous (out of the norm, beyond what is normal; very much exceeding the usual size, number, or degree; of great size; huge; vast; immense) ras: erase (see synonyms at *expunge*, below), eraser (from *radere*, to scrape) rect: (from *regere*, to make straight) erect (**Synonyms**: standing, vertical, upright) erectile (that can be come erect: used especially to designate tissue, as in the penis, that becomes turgid and rigid when filld with blood) erection, erector ex-: acerb: exacerbate {exacerbation} (*acerbus*, bitter) act: exact (**Synonyms**: 1) demand, claim, require; 2) ex- plicit, express, precise) (from *agere*, to do, act) alt: exalt (to raise on high; elevate; lift up; specifically, to raise in status, dignity, power, wealth, etc.) (*altus*, high) ampl: example [literally, (something) taken out; **Synonyms:** 1) instance, case, illustration; 2) model, pattern, paradigm] (from *emere*, to take) anim: exanimate (dead, inanimate) (*anima*, spirit) anth: exanthem (the term refers to a skin eruption, such as measles) (*anth*, flower) asper: exasperate (**Synonyms**: irritate, provoke, nettle), ex- asperation (*asper*, rough) ceed: exceed, exceeding, exeedingly (from *cedere*, to go)

Element	From	Meaning	Examples
ex- (cont'd)			cel: excel (**Synonyms:** surpass, transcend, outdo), excellence, excellent, excelsior (*cellere*, to rise, project)
			cept: except, excepting, exception, exceptionable, exceptional, exceptive (from *capere*, to take)
			cerpt: excerpt {excerption} (from *carpere*, to pick, pluck)
			cess: excess, excessive (**Synonyms:** exorbitant, extravagant, immoderate) (from *exceed*)
			cip: excipient (from *except*)
			cis: excisable, excise (from *caedere*, to cut)
			cit: excitable, excitant, excitation, excitative, excitatory, excite (from *ciere*, to call, summon)
			claim: exclaim (from *clamare*, to cry, shout)
			clam: exclamation, exclamatory (see *exclaim*)
			clav: exclave [from *(en)clave*] (*clavis*, key)
			clu: exclude (**Synonyms:** debar, disbar, eliminate), exclusion, exclusive, exclusivity (from *claudere*, to close)
			cog: excogitate (to think out carefully and fully) (from *co-*, with, together + *agitate*)
			cor: excoriate (to strip, scratch, or rub off the skin of; flay, abrade, chafe, etc.) (*corium*, the skin)
			crem: excrement (waste matter from the bowels) (from *excrete*).
			cres: excrescence, excrescent (*crescere*, to grow)
			cret: excreta (waste matter excreted from the body, especially sweat or urine), excrete, excretion (from *cernere*, to sift)
			cruc: excruciate, excruciating (*cruciare*, to torture, from *crux*, cross)
			culp: exculpate (to free from blame; exonerate) {exculpable, exculpation} (*culpare*, to blame)
			cur: excurrent, excursion, excursive, excursus (*currere*, to run)
			cus: excusable, excusatory, excuse (from *causa*, a charge)
			ecr: execrable, execrate (**Synonyms:** curse, imprecate, anathematize), execration (elision of *sacr/secr*, sacred)
			ecu: executant, execute (**Synonyms:** 1) slay, murder, assassinate, 2) perform, accomplish, effect), execution, executive, executor (elision of *sequi*, to follow)
			emp: exemplar, exemplary, exemplification, exemplify, exemplum, exempt, exemption (**Synonyms:** immunity, impunity) (from *example*, which see, above)
			enter: exenterate (originally, to disembowel; in *surgery*, to take out an organ) (*enteron*, bowel)
			erc: exercise (**Synonyms:** practice, drill) (from *arcere*, to enclose)
			ert: exert, exertion (**Synonyms:** effort, endeavor, pains) (from *serere*, to join, fasten together)
			foli: exfoliate {exfoliation, exfoliative} (*folium*, a leaf)
			hal: exhalant, exhalation, exhale (*halare*, to breathe)
			haust: exhaust, exhaustion, exhaustive (from *haurire*, to draw, drain)
			hib: exhibit (**Synonyms:** proof, evidence, testimony), exhibition, exhibitive (from *habere*, to hold)

Element	From	Meaning	Examples
ex- (cont'd)			hilar: exhilarant, exhilarate (**Synonyms**: animate, timulate, invigorate), exhilaration (*hilaris*, glad)
			hort: exhort (**Synonyms**: urge, press, importune), exhortation, exhortatory {exhortative} (*hortari*, to urge)
			hum: exhumation, exhume (*humus*, the ground)
			ig: exigency, exigent, exigible, exiguous (from *exact*, above)
			ile: exile (The Exile: the period in the 6th century B.C. of the Babylonian Captivity of the Jews) {exilic} (from IE *al*, to wander aimlessly)
			ist: exist, existence, existent, existential, existentialism (elision of *sistere*, to stand)
			it: exit (from *ire*, to go)
			on: exonerate (to remove the burden; to clear of blame; (**Synonyms**: absolve, acquit, pardon) (*onus*, burden)
			ora: exorable (that can be persuaded or moved by pleas) (*orare*, to speak)
			orb: exorbitance, exorbitant (see synonyms at *excessive*, above) (*orbita*, a track)
			ord: exordium (the beginning; the opening part of a speech, treatise, etc.) (*ordiri*, to lay the warp, begin)
			pand: expand (**Synonyms**: swell, distend, inflate), expanded (*pandere*, to spread, extend)
			pans: expanse, expansible, expansile, expansion, expansionism, expansive (see *expand*)
			pati: expatiate (to enlarge in discourse or writng; be copious in description or discussion) (from *spatiari*, to walk, roam)
			patri: expatriate (**Synonyms**: banish, exile, deport) (*patria*, fatherland)
			pect: (note difference in meanings of roots)
			expect (**Synonyms**: anticipate, hope, await), expectancy, expectant, expectation (an elided form of *spect*, see)
			expectorant, expectorate (from *pectus*, breast)
			ped: (*pedis*, foot)
			expediency (also, *expedience*), expedient (**Synonyms**: resource, resort, makeshift), expediential
			expedite, expedition (**Synonyms**: 1) haste, hurry, speed; 2) trip, journey, voyage), expeditious
			pel: expel (see synonyms at *eject*, above), expellant (also, *expellent*) (*pellere*, to thrust)
			pend: expend (**Synonyms**: consume, empty, spend), expendable, expenditure (*pendere*, to weigh)
			pens: expense, expensive (**Synonyms**: costly, valuable, invaluable) (see *expend*)
			per: experience, experienced, experiential, experimental (from IE *per-*, to try, risk, come over)
			pert: expert (**Synonyms**: experienced, proficient, adroit), expertise (from *experience*)
			pia: expiable, expiate (to atone for), expiatory (*piare*, to appease)
			pir: expiration, expiratory, expire, expiry (*pir* is an elided form of *spirare*, to breathe)

Element	From	Meaning	Examples
ex- (cont'd)			plain: explain (**Synonyms**: expound, explicate, elucidate) (from *planare*, to make level)
			plan: explanation, explanatory (see *explain*)
			plet: expletive (*plere*, to fill)
			plic: explicable, explicate (see synonyms at *explain*, above), explicit (**Synonyms**: express, exact, precise) (*plicare*, to fold)
			[French phrase: *explication de texte*, an intensive and exhaustive scrutiny and interpretation of a written work, often word by word]
			plod: explode (from *plaudere*, to applaud)
			ploit: exploit, exploitation, exploitative (see *explicate*)
			plor: exploration, exploratory, explore (*plorare*, to cry out)
			plos: explosion, explosive (see *explode*, above)
			pon: exponent, exponential (see *expound*, below)
			port: export, exportation (*portare*, to carry)
			pos: expose (see synonyms at *exhibit*, above) show, exposé, exposition, expositor, expository, exposure (also, *expositive*) (from *ponere*, to place)
			postul: expostulate (**Synonyms**: object, remonstrate, demur) (*postulare*, to demand)
			pound: expound (see synonyms at *explain*, above) (from *ponere*, to place)
			press: express (**Synonyms**: voice, broach, enunciate; also, see synonyms at *explicit*), expression, expressionism, expressive (same as *espresso*) (from *premere*, to press)
			propr: expropriate {expropriation} (*propius*, one's own)
			puls: expulsion {expulsive} (from *pellere*, to thrust)
			punct: expunction (an expunging or being expunged) (see next entry)
			pung: expunge (**Synonyms**: erase, efface, obliterate) (*pungere*, to prick)
			purg: expurgate {expurgation} (*purgare*, to cleanse)
			quis: exquisite (**Synonyms**: delicate, dainty) (*quaerere*, to ask)
			scind: exscind (*scindere*, to cut)
			sect: exsect {exsection} (*secare*, to cut)
			sert: exsert, exserted (projecting, as from a sheath or pod) (see *exert*)
			sic: exsiccate {exsiccation} (*siccare*, to dry)
			tant: extant (elided from *stare*, to stand)
			tem: extemporal, extemporaneous (**Synonyms**: impromptu, improvised), extempore, extemporize (*tempus*, time)
			ten: extend (**Synonyms**: lengthen, prolong, protract), extended, extender, extensible, extension, extensive, extensor, extent, extenuate, extenuation, extenuatory (*tendere*, to stretch)
			term: exterminate (**Synonyms**: extirpate, eradicate), exterminator, exterminatory (*terminus*, boundary)
			tinct: extinct (**Synonyms**: dead, deceased, defunct), extinction, extinctive (from *extinguish*)

Element	From	Meaning	Examples
ex- (cont'd)			tingu: extinguish (in *law*, to make void; nullify) (elided from *stinguere*, to extinguish)
			tirp: extirpate (to pull out by the roots; root out; destroy or remove completely; see synonyms at *exterminate*) (*stirps*, lower part of a tree)
			tol: extol (or *extoll*; to praise highly; **Synonyms:** praise, laud, acclaim) (*tollere*, to raise)
			tort: (from *torquere*, to twist)
			extort [to get (money, etc.) from someone by violence, threats, misuse of authority; exact or wrest, as though *to twist out*]
			extortion (in law, the wrongful taking of a person's money or property without his consent but by the use of threat or exaction; blackmail), extortionate, extortionist
			tract: extract (**Synonyms:** educe, elicit, evoke) (from *trahere*, to pull, draw, to draw out by effort)
			tric: extricate (*tricae*, hindrances, vexations)
			tru: extrude {extrusion}, extrusive (*trudere*, to thrust)
			uber: exuberance (also, *exuberancy*), exuberant (*uberare*, to bear abundantly)
			ud: exude (to pass out in drops, through pores, an incision, etc.; ooze; discharge; to diffuse or seem to radiate, as to exude joy) (elided from *sudare*, to sweat)
			ult: exult (to rejoice greatly) (an elision and variant of *salire*, to jump)
			ef-: (assimilates *ex*-)
			fac: efface (see synonyms at *expunge*, above) {effaceable, effacement} (*facere*, to do)
			fect: (from *facere*, to do)
			effect (**Synonyms:** consequence, result, issue).
			effective (**Synonyms:** efficacious, effectual, efficient), effectual, effectuate
			fem: effeminacy, effeminate (**Synonyms:** feminine, womanly, womanish) (*femina*, a woman)
			fer: efferent (*ferre*, to bear)
			ferv: effervesce (*fervere*, to boil)
			fet: effete (*fetus*, productive)
			fic: efficacious (see synonyms at *effective*, above), efficacy, efficiency, efficient (from *effect*)
			fig: effigy (from *fingere*, to form)
			flor: effloresce, efflorescence (*florere*, to blossom)
			flu: effluence, effluent, effluvium, efflux (*fluere*, to flow)
			fort: effort (**Synonyms:** exertion, endeavor, pains) (*fort*, strong)
			front: effrontery (**Synonyms:** temerity, audacity, nerve) (*frons*, forehead)
			fulg: effulgence {effulgent} (*fulgere*, to shine)
			fus: effuse, effusion, effusive (from *fundere*, to pour)
			DOUBLE PREFIXED ROOT:
			exaggerate [to unduly emphasize or magnify; to make (something) greater than is actually the case, as *to exaggerate the truth*] (*ex*-, out, up + *ag*-, from *ad*-, to + *agger*, pile, heap)

Element	From	Meaning	Examples
ex- (cont'd)			PREFIXED NORMAN FRENCH: cap: escape (literally, to leave one's cloak behind; **Synonyms**: avoid, evade, elude), escapement, escapism (Late Latin *cappa*, cloak) LATIN LEGAL TERM: *ex parte* (from the side, of one party) INTERDISCIPLINARY: erect (in *geometry*, to construct or draw a perpendicular, figure, etc. upon a base line; in *physiology*, to cause to become swollen and rigid by being filled with blood, as in the penis) CROSS REFERENCE: *ab-, abs-, apo-, cata-, de-, ec-*
exo-,*** ex-, ec-	Greek *exo*	out, outside, outward	EXPANDED PREFIX: exoteric, exotic, exotica PREFIXED ROOT AND COMPOUNDS: *ex-:* edra: exedra (in ancient Greece, a room, building, or outdoor area with seats, where conversations were held) (*hedra*, chair) . eges: exegesis (literally, to lead out: explanation, critical analysis, or interpretation of a word, literary passage, etc., especially of the Bible) (from *hegeisthai*, to lead, guide) odont: exodontia, exodontics (*odont*, tooth) od: exodus (from *hodus*, way) ophthalm: exophthalmous (abnormal protrusion of the eyeball) (*ophthalmos*, eye) orci: exorcise, exorcism, exorcist (*horkizein*, to make one swear) osm: exosmosis (*osmos*, impulse) ost: exostosis (an abnormal bony growth on the surface of a bone or tooth) (*osteon*, bone) *exo-:* bio: exobiology (the branch of biology investigating the possibility of extraterrestrial life and the effects of extraterrestrial life on living organism on earth) (*bio*, life; *logy*, study of) carp: exocarp (the outer layer of a ripened ovary or fruit, as the skin of plum; epicarp) (*carp*, fruit) centr: exocentric [in *linguistics*, designating or of a construction whose syntactic function is different from that of any of its constituents (e.g., *all the way* in the sentence He ran all the way); compare *endocentric*] crin: exocrine (from *krinein*, to separate) gam: exogamy (opposed to *endogamy*, both of which see under *gam*) (*gam*, marriage) gen: exogen, exogenous (*gen*, producing) spher: exosphere (the highest, least dense region of the atmosphere) (*sphere*, ball, globe) spor: exospore (in *botany*, the outer coat of a spore) (*spore*, seed) therm: exothermic (also, *exothermal*) (*therm*, heat) *ec-:* bol: ecbolic (helping to bring forth the fetus in birth, or causing abortion: said of certain drugs) (from *ballein*, to throw) centr: eccentric (not having the same center; deviating from the norm, as in conduct; out of the ordinary; odd) cles: ecclesia, ecclesiology (see *eccles*) (*logy*, study of)

252

Element	From	Meaning	Examples
exo- (cont'd)			crin: eccrine (designating or of the common sweat glands of the human body that secrete clear, watery sweat important in heat regulation; compare apocrine) (from *krinein*, to separate)
			dysi: ecdysiast [a stripteaser; coined by H. L. Mencken (1940), ecdysis (in *zoology*, the shedding of an outer layer of skin or integument, as by snakes, insects, etc.] (see *dysi*)
			lec: eclectic (selecting; choosing from various sources), eclecticism (from *legein*, to choose)
			lips: eclipse {ecliptic } (from *leipein*, to leave)
			log: (from *eclectic*)
			eclogite (a rock consisting of granular aggregate of green pyroxene and red garnet, often containing cyanite, silvery mica, quartz, and pyrite)
			eclogue (originally, a collection, especially of poems; also, a short, usually pastoral, poem, often in the form of a diaogue between two shepherds)
			stas: ecstasy (**Synonyms**; bliss, rapture, transport) (from *histanai*, to place)
			top: ectopia (see note at *top*) {ectopic} (*topos*, place)
			zem: eczema (from *zein*, to boil)
			DOUBLE PREFIXED ROOT:
			exocataphoria (the condition in which the visual axis turns downward and outward) (*cata*-, down + *phoria*, showing)
			synecdoche (see note under *syn-*) (*syn-*, with + *doche*, receive)
			EMBEDDED PREFIX: (*ectom*, to remove surgically)
			appendectomy (excision of appendix)
			masectomy (excision of female breast)
			tonsillectomy (excision of tonsils)
			NOTE: In each of the embedded prefixes, *ec*- combines with the root *tom*; together, the two elements mean to cut out surgically.
			BOOK OF THE BIBLE: Ecclesiastes (see note under *eccles*)
			SPANISH: *iglesia* (from *ecclesia*, the group that constituted "the called out ones" in the early Christian Church)
			CROSS REFERENCE: *ab-, apo-, cata-, ecto-, epi-, extra-*
extra-,*** **extro-**	Latin *exter, exterus*	outside, without	WORD BUILT ON PREFIX: extraneous (see stranger under *Disguised Root*), extreme, extremism, extremity, extremum (in *mathematics*, the maximum or minimum value of a function)
			PREFIXED ROOT:
			extra-:
			dos: extrados (in *architecture*, the outside curved surface of an arch) (from *dors*, back)
			galact: extragalactic (outside or beyond the Galaxy, or Milky Way) (Greek *galact*, milk)
			jud: extrajudicial (outside or beyond the jurisdiction of a court) (*jud*, law)
			leg: extralegal (outside of legal control or authority; not regulated by law) (*leg*, law)
			marit: extramarital (of or relating to sexual intercourse with someone other than one's spouse) (*maritus*, of marriage)

Element	From	Meaning	Examples
extra- (cont'd)			mund: extramundane (outside the physical world; not of this world) (*mundus*, world) mura: extramural (outside the walls or limits of a city, school, university, etc.; as opposed to *intramural*) (*mur*, wall) nucle: extranuclear (located or occurring outside the nucleus of a cell) (from *nux*, nut) ord: extraordinary (French, *extraordinaire*) pol: extrapolate (coined after *interpolate*, where *pol* is from *polire*, to polish) sens: extrasensory [occurring or seeming to occur apart from, or in addition to, the normal function of the usual senses, as extransensory perception (ESP)] (from *sentire*, to feel) sys: extrasystole (a disturbance of heart rhythm resulting in an extra contraction of the heart between regular beats) (*systole* from *sys-*, a variant of *syn-*, with, together + *stole*, to set up, place, send) terr: extraterrestrial, extraterritorial (*terre*, earth) uter: extrauterine (outside the uterus) vag: extravagance, extravagant (**Synonyms:** excessive, exorbitant, inordinate) (*vagari*, to wander) vas: extravasate, extravascular (*vas*, vessel) vers: extraversion (same as *extroversion*) *extro-*: vers: extroversion (see *extrovert*, next entry) vert: extrovert (*vertere*, to turn) DISGUISED ROOT: strange (**Synonyms:** peculiar, odd, quaint) stranger (**Synonyms:** foreigner, immigrant, emigré) PREFIXED DISGUISED ROOT: sic: extrinsic (**Synonyms:** extraneous, foreign, alien) (*extra-* + *secus*, following, otherwise, base of *sequi*, to follow) tror: extrorse (in *botany*, turned outward or away from the axis of growth: opposed to *introrse*) (*extra-* + *versus*, past participle of *vertere*, to turn) ITALIAN: extravaganza (a literary, musical, or dramatic fantasy characterized by a loose structure and by farce; a spectacular, elaborate theatrical production, as some musical shows; also, any elaborate, spectacular entertainment) (from *extravagance*) RELATED FORMS: exterior, external, extreme LATIN TERM: *in extremis* (at the point of death) NOTE: Do not confuse this element with the prefix *ex-*, as in *extract* (*which see* under *ex-*, Latin prefix), where the root is *trahere*, to draw, to pull, and in *extradition*; *tradition* is derived from *trans-*, across + *dare*, to give. CROSS REFERENCE: *ab-*, *apo-*, *cata-*, *ecto-*, *epi-*

F

Element	From	Meaning	Examples
fab,*** **fac,** **fam,** **fan,** **fat,** **fess**	Latin *fari* (IE: *bha-*, to speak)	to speak, to converse	SIMPLE ROOT: fab: fable (a fictitious story meant to teach a moral lesson; the characters are usually talking animals) fabled (told of in fables or legends; mythical; legendary; unreal; fictitious) fabulous (**Synonyms:** fictitious, legendary, mythical) fam: fame (the state of being well known or much talked about), famed (much talked about or widely known) famous (**Synonyms:** renowned, celebrated, noted) fata: fatal (**Synonyms:** deadly, mortal, lethal), fatalism, fatality, fatally (as determined by fate; inevitably; also, so as to cause death or disaster; mortally) fate: fate (**Synonyms:** destiny, portion, doom), fated, fateful PREFIXED ROOT: *fab*: *af*-: affable (**Synonyms:** amiable, obliging, genial) (*af*- assimilates *ad*-, to, toward) *con*-: confabulate (to talk together in an informal way; in *psychology*, to fill in gaps in the memory with detailed, but more or less unconscious, accounts of fictitious events) (*con*-, with, together) *fac*: *pre*-: preface (**Synonyms:** introduction, foreword, prologue) {prefacer} [see prefatory, the adjective form, below] (*pre*-, before) *fam*: *de*-: defamation, defamatory, defame (originally, in Latin, *diffamare*, where *dif*- assimilates *dis*-, from) *in*-: (not) ineffable (too overwhelming to be expressed or described in words; inexpressible, as *ineffable* beauty; too awesome or sacred to be spoken, as God's *ineffable* name) (*ef*- assimilates *ex*-, out) infamous (**Synonyms:** vicious, iniquitous, nefarious) infamy (**Synonyms:** disrepute, obloquy, odium) *fan*: *in*-: (not) infancy, infant (literally, not yet speaking), infantile, infantine infantry (originally, a very young person, knight's page, foot soldier; one who was not old enough to own a horse and therefore become a cavalryman) infanticide (the murder of an infant; a person guilty of this) (see *infant*, above) (*cide*, kill) *fat*: *pre*-: prefatory {prefatorial} (see *preface*) (*pre*-, before) *fess*: *con*-: confess (**Synonyms:** acknowledge, admit, own), confession, confessional, confessor (*con*-, with, together)

255

Element	From	Meaning	Examples
fab (cont'd)			*pro-*: profess, professed, profession, professional, professor, professorial, professoriate (*pro-*, before, in front of) LEADING ROOT COMPOUND: dic: fatidic (thus, of divination or prophecy; prophetic; also *fatidical*) (from *fatum*, a prophetic declaration + *dicere*, to say) PORTUGUESE AND SPANISH: *infanta* (any daughter of a king of Spain or Portugal, except the heir to the throne) *infante* (any son of a king of Spain or Portugal, except the heir to the throne) FRENCH PHRASE: *enfant terrible* (literally, terrible child; an unmanageable, mischievous child; extended to mean a person whose startlingly unconventional behavior and ideas are a source of embarrassment or dismay to a cause, group, or profession) CROSS REFERENCE: *loqu*
fabr**	Latin *fabricari*, to construct, build (IE *dhabh-* to join, fit)	to fit together, shape, form	SIMPLE ROOT: fabric, fabricate (**Synonyms:** 1) lie, prevaricate, equivocate 2) make, form, shape; see *Doublets* below) DISGUISED ROOT: forge (Middle English; from Latin *fabrica*, workshop; see *Doublets* below) DOUBLETS: fabric:forge CROSS REFERENCE: *form, plasm*
fac			See *fab* for *preface.*
fac,*** fact, fect, fic, fit, fy	Latin *facere* (IE: *dhe*, to put, set, place)	to make, do	ROOT NOTE: Some words with *-fy* may belong in other families. See *Root Note* under *fig*. SIMPLE ROOT: fact (see *Doublets* below) face: face (listed in this family and in the related *facies* family, next entry) faci: facient, facile (**Synonyms:** easy, effortless, smooth), facilitate, facility facti: facticity (the quality or state of being a fact or factual) faction (see *Doublets* below) factious (producing faction; causing dissension) factitious (not natural, genuine, or spontaneous; forced or artificial) (see *Doublets* below) factitive (in *grammar*, designating or of a verb that expresses the idea of making, calling, or thinking something to be of a certain characteristic, using a noun, pronoun, or adjective as a complement to its direct object, e.g., make the dress *short*, make the girl happy; elect him *mayor*) facto: factor (**Synonyms:** 1) element, component, ingredient; 2) agent, deputy, proxy), factorage, factorial, factorize, factory factu: factual, factualism, factuality, facture facu: facultative (in *biology*, capable of living under varying conditions, e.g., able to live independently and as a parasite or semiparasite), faculty (**Synonyms:** talent, gift, aptitude) PREFIXED ROOT: *fac*: *ef-*: efface (**Synonyms:** erase, expunge, obliterate) (*ef-* assimilates *ex-*, out)

Element	From	Meaning	Examples
fac (cont'd)			*fect*: *af-*: affect (**Synonyms** 1): assume, pretend, feign; 2) influence, impress, sway), affectionate (*af-* assimilates *ad-*, to, toward) *con-*: confect (to make up, compound, or prepare from ingredients or materials), confection (a sweet preparation of fruit or the like, as as preserve or candy), confectionary, confectioner, confectionery (*con-*, with, together) *de-*: defect (**Synonyms**: imperfection, blemish, flaw), defection, defective (*de-*, from) *ef-*: effect (**Synonyms**: consequence, result, issue) (*ef-* assimilates *ex-*, out) *in-*: infect, infection, infectious, infective (*in-*, in) *per-*: perfect (see *Doublets* below; **Synonyms**: 1) complete, entire, intact; 2) unbroken, unimpaired, undivided), perfectible, perfection, perfective (a tense of completion in Russian), perfectly (*per-*, through) *pre-*: prefect, prefecture (*pre-*, before) *re-*: refection (food or drink to be taken after a period of hunger, fasting, or fatigue; refreshment), refectory (dining hall in a monastery, convent, college, etc.) (*re-*, again) *fic*: *de-*: deficiency, deficient, deficit (see *One-word Latin Sentence*, below) (*de-*, from) *dif-*: (assimilates *dis-*) difficile, difficult (**Synonyms**: hard, arduous, laborious) difficulty (**Synonyms**: hardship, rigor, vicissitude) *ef-*: efficacious (**Synonyms**: effective, effectual, efficient), efficacy, efficiency, efficient (*ef-* assimilates *ex-*, out) *of-*: office, officer, official, officiant, officiary, officiate, officious (*of-* assimilates *ob-*, against) *pro-*: proficient {proficiency} (*pro-*, before, forward) *suf-*: suffice, sufficiency, sufficient (**Synonyms**: enough, adequate) (*suf-* assimilates *sub-*, under) *fit*: *com-*: comfit (a candy or sweetmeat; especially, a candied fruit, nut, etc.; from *confect*) (*com-*, with, together) *pro-*: profit (*pro-*, forward) DOUBLE PREFIXED ROOT: dis<u>com</u>fit, dis<u>com</u>fiture (*dis-*, reversal + *com-*, with, together) in<u>de</u>fectible (*in-*, not + *de-*, from) LEADING ROOT COMPOUND: simi: facsimile (an exact reproduction of copy; the transmission and reproduction of graphic matter by electrical means, as by radio or wire) (*similis*, similar) tot: factotum (a person hired to do all sorts of work; handyman: now a humorously formal usage) (*totus*, all, the whole) TRAILING ROOT COMPOUND: *fac*: cale: calefacient (making warm; heating; in *medicine*, a substance applied to the body to give a sensation of heat), calefaction (*cale*, heat)

257

Element	From	Meaning	Examples
fac (cont'd)			tum: tumefacient (causing or tending to cause swelling), tumefaction (*tumere*, to swell) *fact*: arti: artifact (any object made by human work, especially a simple or primitive tool, weapon, vessel, etc.) (*arte*, by skill) bene: benefaction (see *Doublets* below) benefactor (*bene*, good, well) male: malefactor (an evildoer or criminal) (*male*, bad) manu: manufacture (**Synonyms:** make, shape, fashion) (*manu*, hand) putr: putrefaction (*putris*, rotten) satis: satisfaction (in *theology*, atonement for sin) (*satis*, enough, plenty) *fic(e)*: arti: artifice (**Synonyms:** 1) art, skill, craft; 2) trick, ruse, strategem), artificial (see *artifact*) beati: beatific (*beatus*, blessed, happy) bene: benefic, benefice, beneficent, beneficial, beneficiary (*bene*, good, well) certi: certificate (from *certify*) edi: edifice (**Synonyms:** building, structure, pile) (from *edify*) male: malefic (from *malefactor*) morbi: morbific (*morbus*, a disease) muni: munificent (*munus*, a gift) poni: pontiff, pontifical, pontificate (from *pontificus*, high priest; probably from *pontis*, bridge; thus, bridge-maker) proli: prolific (producing many young or much fruit; turning out many products of the mind; **Synonyms:** fertile, fruitful, fecund) (*proles*, offspring) sacri: sacrifice (*sacri*, sacred) somni: somnific (*somnus*, sleep) *fit*: bene: benefit (see *Doublets* below) (*bene*, good, well) retro: retrofit (*retro*, backward) *fy*: ampli: amplify (possibly from Latin *amplus*, wide) beati: beatify (*beatus*, blessed; from *beare*, to make happy) certi: certify (from *certain*) digni: dignify (*dignus*, worth) edi: edify (*aedes*, a dwelling, home) forti: fortify (*fortis*, strong) fructi: fructify (*fructus*, fruit) justi: justify (*justus*, just) magni: magnify (*magnus*, great, big) modi: modify (*modus*, measure, manner) morti: mortify (to punish one's body or control one's physical desires and passions by self-denial, fasting, etc. as a means of religious or ascetic discipline) (*mors*, death) nulli: nullify (**Synonyms:** invalidate, void, negate) (*nullus*, none)

258

Element	From	Meaning	Examples
fac (cont'd)			ossi: ossify (to change or develop into bone) (*ossis*, bone)

fac (cont'd) — Examples:

ossi: ossify (to change or develop into bone) (*ossis*, bone)

petri: petrify (*petra*, stone, rock)

putr: putrefy (*putris*, rotten)

quali: qualify (to describe by giving the qualities or characteristics of; in *grammar*, to limit or modify the meaning of a word or group of words) (*qualis*, of what kind)

recti: rectify (*rectus*, straight)

satis: satisfy (**Synonym**: content) (*satis*, enough)

stupe: stupefy (*stupere*, to be stunned)

vivi: vivify (*vivus*, alive)

PREFIXED TRAILING ROOT COMPOUND:

ex-: exemplify (to show by example) (*ex-* + *emp*, buy)

DISGUISED ROOTS:

chafe (from *calefacere*, to make warm), chafing dish

fashion (see *Doublets* below; **Synonyms**: style, mode, vogue)

feasible (**Synonyms**: possible, practical, workable)

feat (an act or accomplishment showing unusual daring, skill, endurance, etc.; remarkable deed; exploit; see *Doublets* below)

feature, featured

fetish (see *Doublets* below; any thing or activity to which one is irrationally devoted; in *psychiatry*, any nonsexual object, such as a foot or a glove, that abnormally excites erotic feelings) (from French *fétiche*; from Portuguese *feitiço*, a charm, sorcery)

PREFIXED DISGUISED ROOTS:

fair:

af-: affair (*af-* assimilates *ad-*, to, toward)

fait:

par-: parfait (see *Doublets* below; French for *perfect*) (from *per-*, completely)

feas:

de-: defeasance, defeasible (from *defeat*, below)

mal-: malfeasance (wrongdoing or misconduct) (*mal-*, wrong)

mis-: misfeasance (in *law*, doing of a lawful thing in an unlawful or improper manner) (Anglo-Saxon *mis-*, wrong)

non-: nonfeasance (in *law*, failure to do what duty requires to be done; distinguished from *malfeasance, misfeasance*)

feat:

de-: defeat (**Synonyms**: conquer, vanquish, overcome), defeatism (from *dis-*, from)

feit:

counter-: counterfeit (**Synonyms**: 1) false, sham, bogus; 2) artificial, synthetic, ersatz) (from *contra-*, against)

for-: forfeit (originally, *forisfacere*, to do wrong; literally, to do beyond), forfeiture (from *foras, foris*, outside, beyond)

sur-: surfeit (**Synonyms**: satiate, cloy, glut) (from *super-*, over, beyond)

DOUBLETS:

benefaction:benefit; comfit:confect; defeat:defect

fashion:faction; feat:fact; fetish:factitious; parfait:perfect

Element	From	Meaning	Examples
fac (cont'd)			FRENCH: *savoir-faire* [literally, to know (how) to do; ready knowledge of when and how to do or say it; tact] *au fait* (literally, to the fact, well-versed, knowledgeable) *fait accompli* (literally, an accomplished fact; a thing already done, so that opposition or argument is useless) ITALIAN: confetti (from *comfit*) SPANISH: *aficionado* (related to *affection*) hacienda (originally, domestic work, landed property; from Latin *facienda*, things to be done) LATIN PHRASES: *ex post facto* [from (the thing) done afterward; done or made afterward, especially when having retroactive effect, as an *ex post facto* law] *scire facias* (literally, that you cause to know; in *law*, a writ, founded on a record, requiring the person against whom it is issued to appear and show cause why the record should not be enforced or annulled; a proceeding begun by issuing such a writ) ONE-WORD LATIN SENTENCES: *deficit* (It is lacking) *fiat* (Let it be done) CROSS REFERENCE: *act/ag/ig* for do
facies**	Latin *facies* (IE *dhe-*, to place, put)	appearance, face	ROOT NOTE: This root is related to *fac*, to make. Some words are included in both families. SIMPLE ROOT: façade (the front part of a building; the front part of anything: often used figuratively, with implications of an imposing appearance concealing something inferior) face (**Synonyms**: countenance, visage, physiognomy), facet, facial, facies PREFIXED ROOT: *fac*: de-: deface (to spoil the appearance of; disfigure; mar; to make illegible by injuring the surface of) (*de-*, reversal) sur-: surface (from *super-*, above, beyond) *fic*: super-: superficial (**Synonyms**: shallow, cursory), superficies (outer area; the outward form or aspect) (*super-*, over, beyond) DOUBLE PREFIXED ROOT: ineffaceable (impossible to wipe out or erase; indelible) (*in-*, not + *ef-*, an assimilation of *ex-*, out) LATIN LEGAL PHRASE: *prima facie* (literally, at first sight; before closer inspection) NB: *Preface* is not from this root; with the root sharing the same base as *fant* and *fab*, to talk, a *preface* is spoken before, as the *preface* of a book, or a *prefatory* remark NO CROSS REFERENCE

Clear conception leads naturally to clear and correct expression.
Nicolas Boileau-Despréaux

Element	From	Meaning	Examples
fall**	Latin *fallere* (IE *ghwel*, to bend, deviate)	to deceive, trick	SIMPLE ROOT: fallacious (containing a fallacy, as *fallacious reasoning*; misleading or deceptive; causing disappointment; delusive) fallacy PREFIXED ROOT: *in-*: infallible (incapable of error; never wrong) (*in-*, not) LEADING ROOT COMPOUND: fy: falsify (to make false) (from *facere*, to make, do) DISGUISED ROOT: fail, failing (**Synonyms:** fault, foible, vice), failure fault (see synonyms at *failing*, previous entry), faulty (having a fault, or faults; defective, blemished; imperfect, or erroneous) faucet (from Old French *faulser*, to make breach in; from Latin *falsus*, false; semantic relationship is tenuous) PREFIXED DISGUISED ROOT: *de-*: default {defaulter} (*de-*, away) FRENCH: *faux* (false; artificial, synthetic) *faux pas* (false step, a social blunder; error in etiquette; tactless act or remark) ENGLISH: false (**Synonyms:** sham, counterfeit, bogus) CROSS REFERENCE: *pseudo*
fam			See *fab* for *fame, famous.*
fan*	Latin *fanum*: sanctuary	temple	SIMPLE ROOT: fanatic (often shortened to *fan*, as a fan of a certain singer or a particular ball club), fanaticism PREFIXED ROOT: *pro-*: (before) profanation (**Synonyms:** sacrilege, desecration) profane (literally, outside the temple, hence not sacred; common) profanity (**Synonyms:** blasphemy, swearing, cursing) NO CROSS REFERENCE
fant			See *fab* for *infant.*
far*	Latin *farina* (IE *bhares*, barley)	flour	SIMPLE ROOT: farina, farinaceous, farrago PREFIXED ROOT: *con-*: confarreation (in ancient Rome, the most solemn form of marriage, marked by the offering of a cake of spelt as a sacrifice to Jupiter) (*con-*, with, together) ANGLO-SAXON COGNATE: barn, barley NO CROSS REFERENCE
farc*	Latin *farcire*	to stuff	SIMPLE ROOT: farce (early farces were used to fill interludes between acts), farcer, farceur (feminine, *farceuse*), farcical (**Synonyms:** funny, laughable, amusing) PREFIXED ROOT: *in-*: infarct (an area of dying or dead tissue resulting from obstruction of the blood vessels normally supplying the part), infarction (*in-*, in) ANGLO-SAXON: frequent (originally, crowded, filled; now, occurring often), frequentation, frequentative (in *grammar*; expressing frequent and repeated action; as a *noun*, a frequentative verb, e.g., *sparkle* is a frequentative of *spark*) NO CROSS REFERENCE

Element	From	Meaning	Examples
fasc**	Latin *fascia*	band, sash, bandage	SIMPLE ROOT: fasce: fasces (a bundle of rods bound about an ax with project-ing blade, carried before ancient Roman magistrates as a symbol of authority: later the symbol of Italian fascism; see *Political Movement*, below) fascia: fascia (plural, *fasciae*), fascial, fasciate, fasciation fascic: fascicle (a division of a book published in parts), fasci-cular, fasciculated, fasciculation, fasciculus (plural, *fasciculi*) fascin: fascine (a bundle of sticks bound together, formerly used to fill ditches, strengthen trenches, etc.) DISGUISED ROOT: fagot (a bundle of sticks, twigs, especially for use as fuel) fess (in *heraldry*, a horizontal band forming the middle third of the shield) POLITICAL MOVEMENT: Fascism [a political group bound closely together (as a band); the Fascisti, the Italian political organization, seized power and set up a fascist dictatorship (1922-43) under Benito Mussolini] INTERDISCIPLINARY: fascia (in *anatomy*, a thin layer of connective tissue covering, supporting, or connecting the muscles or inner organs of the body; in *architecture*, a flat, horizontal band, especially one of two or three making up an architrave; in *biology*, a distinct band of color) NB: *Fascinate*, from *fascinare*, to bewitch, charm, and originally denoting an amulet in the shape of a phallus, is not in this family; some authorities place *fascinate* in the *fab*, speak, family. NO CROSS REFERENCE
fat			See *fab* for *fate*.
fatu**	Latin *fatuus* (IE *bhat*, to strike)	foolish	SIMPLE ROOT: fatuity (stupidity, especially complacent stupidity) fatuous (**Synonyms:** silly, asinine, foolish) PREFIXED ROOT: *in-*: infatuate (to make foolish), infatuated, infatuation (**Syn-onyms:** love, affection, attachment) (*in-*, intensive) LATIN PHRASE: *ignis fatuus* (literally, foolish fire; a light seen at night moving over swamps or marshy places, be-lieved to be caused by the combustion of gases arising from decaying organic matter; popularly called *will-o'-the-wisp* or *jack-o'lantern*) NO CROSS REFERENCE
fe*	Germanic *fe* (IE *pek*, cattle)	cattle, property	ROOT NOTE: This root was originally Old Norse; *cattle* was considered *movable property*. The IE base of this root also yields *peculate*, to steal, *peculiar, pecuniary, impecunious*. SIMPLE ROOT: fee DISGUISED ROOTS: fellow (originally, in Old Norse *felag*, one who lays down money) feud (one meaning), fief PREFIXED DISGUISED ROOT: *in-*: infeudation (in *feudal law*, the granting of an estate in fee; enfeoffment) (*in-*, in) NO CROSS REFERENCE
fect			See *fac* for *confection, infect*.

Element	From	Meaning	Examples
fecund*	Latin *fecundus* (IE *dhe*, to suck, suckle)	fruitful	SIMPLE ROOT: fecund (**Synonyms:** fertile, fruitful, prolific) fecundate (to make fecund; to fertilize; impregnate; pollinate) {fecundation}, fecundity PREFIXED ROOT: *super-*: superfecundation (the fertilization of two ova at separate times during the same ovulation period); compare *superfetation* under *fet*, offspring (*super-*, over, beyond) NO CROSS REFERENCE
fed			See *fid* for *confederation*.
fel*	Latin *feles*	cat	SIMPLE ROOT: felid (any animal of the cat family), feline, felinity, felis (type of genus) LEADING ROOT COMPOUND: mania: felinomania (*mania*, unusual liking for) phob: felinophobia (*phobia*, irrational fear of or hatred of) GENUS: *Felidae*, a cosmopolitan family comprising the true cats--the lion, tiger, jaguar, leopard, cougar--as well as the cheetah, and extinct related forms CROSS REFERENCE: *ailur*
felic**	Latin *felix* (IE *dhe*, to suck, suckle)	happy, fertile	SIMPLE ROOT: felicitate, felicitous, felicity (happiness, bliss) PREFIXED ROOT: *in-*: infelicitous (not happy; unfortunate; sad; inappropriate; inopportune), infelicity (the quality or condition of being infelicitous; something inappropriate or unpleasing) (*in-*, not) LEADING ROOT COMPOUND: fic: felicific (producing or tending to produce happiness; now rare) (from *facere*, to do, make) SPANISH: *feliz* PROPER NAME: Felix NB: *Felo-de-se*, Anglo-Latin, literally, felon of (one)self, is not in this family; a legal term, it means suicide, or one who commits suicide. CROSS REFERENCE: *beat*
femin**	Latin *femina* (IE *dhe*, to suck, suckle; yields English female)	woman	SIMPLE ROOT: feminine (**Synonyms:** female, womanly, effeminate, feminism, feminist, feminize PREFIXED ROOT: *ef-*: effeminate (having the qualities generally attributed to women; see synonyms at *feminine*, above) (*ef-* assimilates *ex-*, out) LEADING ROOT COMPOUND: logy: feminology (*logy*, study of) phob: feminophobia (*phobia*, morbid fear of) FRENCH PHRASE: *femme fatale* (literally, fatal woman; an alluring woman, especially one who leads men to their downfall or ruin; plural, *femmes fatales*) LAW TERM: *feme covert* (a married woman) CROSS REFERENCE: *gyn*

> Life and language are alike sacred.
> Homicide and verbicide--that is, violent treatment of a word with fatal results to its legitimate meaning--are alike forbidden. Oliver Wendell Holmes

Element	From	Meaning	Examples
fend,** **fens**	Latin *fendere* (IE *gwhen*, to strike; yields English fence)	to strike	SIMPLE ROOT: fend, fender PREFIXED ROOT: *fend*: *de-*: defend {defendable}, defendant, defender (*de-*, away, from) *of-*: offend (**Synonyms:** affront, insult, outrage) (*of-* assimilates *ob-*, against) *fens*: *de-*: defense, defensible, defensive (*de-*, away, from) *of-*: offense (**Synonyms:** resentment, umbrage, pique), offensive (*of-* assimilates *ob-*, against) DOUBLE PREFIXED ROOT: in<u>de</u>fensible (*in-*, not + *de-*, from) CROSS REFERENCE: *bat, cuss, fend, fer, flict, plaud, pleg/ pless/plex*
fenestra*	Latin *fenestra*	window	SIMPLE ROOT: fenestra, fenestrated, fenestration PREFIXED ROOT: *de-*: defenestration (literally, tossing out through a window) (*de-*, from) NOTE: The words in this family are used mostly in *anatomy, architecture, biology, surgery.* NO CROSS REFERENCE
fer*	Latin *ferire* (IE *bher^2*, to cut with a sharp point; yields English bore)	to strike	PREFIXED ROOTS AND COMPOUNDS: *inter-*: (between) interfere, interference {interferential} interferon (a cellular protein produced in response to, and acting to prevent replication of, an infectious viral form within an infected cell) interferometer (*meter*, measure) CROSS REFERENCE: *bat, cuss, fend, flict, plaud, pleg/ pless/plex*
fer,*** **lat**	Latin *ferre* (IE *bher^1*, to bear)	to carry, bear	ROOT NOTE: The past participle of *ferre* is *latus*, seen in the words *ablative, collate, illate,* and *relate*; see *lat.* SIMPLE ROOT: fere: feretory (a portable reliquary; a place for keeping a reliquary) ferr: ferret (as a *verb*, to force out of hiding; search out) fert: fertile (**Synonyms:** fecund, fruitful, prolific), fertility, fertilization, fertilizer PREFIXED ROOTS: *fer*: *af-*: afferent (opposed to *efferent*, which see below) (*af-* assimilates *ad-*, to, toward) *circum-*: circumference (**Synonyms:** perimeter, periphery, circuit) (*circum-*, around) *con-*: confer (**Synonyms:** give, donate, bestow), conference, conferment (*con-*, with, together) *de-*: (down) defer (to postpone; **Synonyms:** yield, capitulate, succumb) deference (**Synonyms:** honor, homage, reverence), deferent, deferential, deferment, deferred *dif-*: differ, difference, different (**Synonyms:** diverse, divergent, distinct) (*dif-* assimilates *dis-*, apart)

Element	From	Meaning	Examples
fer (cont'd)			*ef-*: efferent (opposed to *afferent*, which see above) (*ef-* assimilates *ex-*, out)
			in-: infer (**Synonyms**: deduce, conclude, judge), inference, inferential (*in-*, in)
			of-: offer (**Synonyms**: proffer, tender, present), offering, offertory (*of-* assimilates *ob-*, against)
			pre-: prefer (to put before someone else in rank, office, etc.; promote; preferable, preference (**Synonyms**: choice, option, selection), preferential, preferment (*pre-*, before)
			pro-: proffer [to offer (usually something intangible), as *to proffer friendship*; see synonyms at *offer*] (*pro-* + *offer*)
			re-: refer (do not confuse with *allude*), referee, reference, referendum, referent, referential, referral (*re-*, back)
			suf-: suffer (**Synonyms**: 1) bear, endure, tolerate; 2) let, allow, permit) (*suf-* assimilates *sub-*, under)
			trans-: transfer, transference (*trans-*, across)
			lat:
			ab-: ablate {ablation}, ablative (*ab-*, away)
			de-: delate (to make public; to relate; to announce; now archaic) (*de-*, down)
			re-: relate, related (**Synonyms**: kindred, allied, cognate), relation, relational, relative, relativism, relativity, relator (*re-*, back)
			trans-: translate, translation (**Synonyms**: version, paraphrase, transliteration), translator (*trans-*, across)
			DOUBLE PREFIXED ROOT:
			in<u>dif</u>ference (*in-*, not; *dif-* assimilates *dis-*, away)
			TRAILING ROOT COMPOUND:
			aqui: aquifer (an underground layer of porous rock, sand, etc. containing water, into which wells can be sunk) {aquiferous} (*aqui*, water)
			auri: auriferous (bearing or yielding gold) (*auri*, gold)
			bacci: bacciferous (producing berries) (*bacci*, berry)
			coni: conifer (cone bearer, as the pine, spruce, etc.; see *Place-names* below) {coniferous} (*coni*, cone)
			cruci: crucifer (in *botany*, any plant of the mustard family, including the cabbages, cresses, etc.) {cruciferous} (*cruc*, cross)
			crystalli: crystalliferous (producing or containing crystals)
			ferri: ferriferous (*ferr*, iron)
			odori: odoriferous (giving off an odor, especially a strong or offensive odor)
			umbelli: umbelliferous (having an umbel or umbels, as plants of the umbel family; the umbel family includes celery and parsley) (from *umbra*, shade)
			voci: vociferate, vociferous (from *vox*, voice)
			DISGUISED ROOT: furtive (originally, one who carries off; a thief; now an adjective; **Synonyms**: secret, covert, clandestine)
			ENGLISH COGNATES:
			barrow, wheelbarrow
			bier (a platform or portable framework on which a coffin or corpse is placed and "carried")

Element	From	Meaning	Examples
fer (cont'd)			SCOTTISH COGNATE: bairn (literally, that which is carried; a son or daughter; a child) PLACENAMES: Conifer, Colorado Fertile (Iowa, Minnesota) NB: *Ferry* (a boat which *carries* one across a body of water, especially a river), is from Old English *ferian*, to carry. CROSS REFERENCE: *pher/phor*
ferr**	Latin *ferrum*	iron	SIMPLE ROOT: ferra: ferrate (a salt of the hypothetical ferric acid, containing the divalent negative radical FeO_4) ferre: ferreous (of, like, or containing iron) ferri: ferric, ferrite {ferritic}, ferritin ferru: ferruginated, ferruginous LEADING ROOT COMPOUND: *ferri*: cyan: ferricyanide [chemical symbol: $Cu_3[Fe(CN)_6]_2$] fer: ferriferous (*ferre*, to bear) magnet: ferrimagnetic (not the same as *ferromagnetic*, below) *ferro*: chrom: ferrochromium (also, *ferrochrome*; an alloy of iron and chromium) (*chrom*, color) cyan: ferrocyanide [chemical symbol: $Ca_2Fe(CN)_6$] (*cyan*, blue) equin: ferroequinologist (a railroad, or iron horse, fan) (*equino*, horse) gabbro: ferrogabbro [a particular igneous rock (*gabbro*) abnormally high in *iron*] magnet: ferromagnetic (not the same as *ferrimagnetic*, above) FRENCH: *fer-de-lance* (literally, iron tip of a lance; a large, poisonous pit viper, related to the rattlesnake, found in tropical America) PORTUGUESE: *ferreiro* (literally, blacksmith, but actually, a Brazilian tree frog, from its notes resembling measured beating on a copper plate) DISGUISED ROOT: farrier (a blacksmith) CHEMICAL SYMBOL: Fe (from *ferrum*) NAME OF COLLEGE: Ferrum College, Ferrum, Virginia CROSS REFERENCE: *sider*
ferv**	Latin *fervere* (IE *bher*, to boil, ferment)	to boil	SIMPLE ROOT: ferve: fervent (**Synonyms:** passionate, impassioned, ardent), fervency, fervescent fervi: fervid (**Synonyms:** eager, avid, keen) fervo: fervor (**Synonyms:** passion, enthusiasm, zeal) PREFIXED ROOT: *ef-*: effervescent {effervescence} (*ef-* assimilates *ex-*, out) DISGUISED ROOT: ferment, fermentation, fermentative ENGLISH COGNATES: barm (the yeast foam that appears on the surface of malt liquors as they ferment) bread (originally, that which was fermented) breath, breathe brew, brood CROSS REFERENCE: *bull*

266

Element	From	Meaning	Examples
fess			See *fab* for *confess.*
fest**	Latin *festus*: joyous (IE: *dhes*, gods)	festive	SIMPLE ROOT: festa: festal (of or like a joyous celebration; festive) festi: festival, festive, festivity festo: festoon (a wreath or garland of flowers, leaves, paper, etc. hanging in a loop or curve), festoonery DISGUISED ROOT: fete (see *Doublets* below) SIMPLE COMPOUND: gabfest ENGLISH: feast (see *Doublets* below), fair (festival) DOUBLETS: feast:fete SPANISH: *fiesta*; ITALIAN: *festa* GERMAN COMPOUND: *Festschrift* (*schrift*, a writing; a collection of articles by the colleagues, former students, etc., of a noted scholar, published in his or her honor) NB: *Fester* and *festination* are not in this family, each coming from different roots. NO CROSS REFERENCE
fet*	Latin *fetere* (IE *dheu*, to blow about)	to stink	SIMPLE ROOT: fetid, fetor PERSIAN TRAILING ROOT COMPOUND: asa: asafetida (a particular foul-smelling gum; derived from plants of the parsley family, *asafetida* was formerly used to treat some illnesses or, in certain folk medicines, to repel disease) (from *aza*, gum) NO CROSS REFERENCE
fet**	Latin *fetus* (IE *dhe*, to suck, suckle)	offspring	SIMPLE ROOT: fetal, fetation, fetus PREFIXED ROOT: *ef-*: effete (no longer capable of producing; spent and sterile; lacking vigor, force of character, moral stamina, etc.; decadent, soft, overrefined, etc.) (*ef-* assimilates *ex-*, out) *super-*: superfetate, superfetation (the fertilization of an ovum during a pregnancy already in existence; compare with *superfecundation*; see *fecund*) (*super-*, beyond) LEADING ROOT COMPOUND: cid: feticide (*cide*, kill) par: fetiparous (designating or of animals whose young are born incompletely developed, as marsupials) (*parous*, bearing) DISGUISED ROOT: fawn CROSS REFERENCE: *prol*
fibr*	Latin *fibra*	fiber	SIMPLE ROOT: fibril, fibrilla, fibrillation, fibrin, fibrinous LEADING ROOT COMPOUND: *fibr*: os: fibrose, fibrosis, fibrositis (*osis*, condition + *itis*, inflammation) *fibrino*: gen: fibrinogen, fibrinogenic (*gen*, produce) rrh: fibrinorrhea (*rrh*, flow) *fibro*: blast: fibroblast (*blast*, shoot, sprout) gen: fibronogen (*gen*, produce) NO CROSS REFERENCE
fic			See *fac* for *fictitious.*
fic			See *facies* for *superficial.*

Element	From	Meaning	Examples
fid,*** **fed**, **f y**	Latin *fidere* (IE *bheidr*, to urge, to be convinced)	to believe, trust; faith	SIMPLE ROOT: fide: fideism (the view that everything that can be known with certainty about God or divine things is knonwn only or primarily by faith and never by reason alone) fidelity (see *Doublets* below; **Synonyms**: allegiance, loyalty, homage) fido: Fido (man's faithful friend; at one time, a popular name for a dog) fidu: fiducial (based on firm faith; used as a standard of reference for measurement or calculation) fiduciary (designating or of a person who holds something in trust for another) PREFIXED ROOTS: *fid*: *af-*: affidavit (see *Latin Sentence*, below) (*af-* from *ad-*, to) *con-*: (with, together) confidant (feminine, *confidante*) confide (**Synonyms**: commit, entrust, consign) confidence (**Synonyms**: assurance, aplomb) confident (**Synonyms**: sure, certain, positive) confidential (**Synonyms**: familiar, intimate, close) *dif-*: diffidence, diffident (**Synonyms**: bashful, modest, demure) (*dif-* assimilates *dis-*, apart) *in-*: infidel (**Synonyms**: atheist, agnostic, deist), infidelity (*in-*, not) *per-*: (through, thoroughly) perfidious (**Synonyms**: faithless, treacherous, false) perfidy (from *per fidem decipi*, to deceive through faith; the deliberate breaking of faith; betrayal of trust; treachery) *fed*: *con-*: (with) confederate (**Synonyms**: associate, colleague, comrade) confederation (**Synonyms**: alliance, league, coalition) *fy*: *de-*: defy (to challenge the power of; resist boldly or openly; from *defy* are derived *defiance, defiant*) (*de-*, from) PREFIXED DISGUISED ROOTS: *af-*: affiance, affiant (in *law*, a person who makes an affidavit; deponent) (*af-* assimilates *ad-*, to, toward) FRENCH: fay (Old French *fei*; archaic; used in oaths, e.g., *by my fay!*; another *fay* is from Old French *feie*, from Vulgar Latin *fata*; one of the Fates; a fairy) fealty (see *Doublets* below; from Old French *feauté, fealté*; the duty and loyalty owed by a vassal or tenant to his feudal lord; also, an oath of such loyalty) fiancé (masculine), fiancée (feminine) DOUBLETS: fealty:fidelity LATIN PHRASES: *bona fide* (in good faith; without dishonesty, fraud, or deceit; **Synonyms**: authentic, genuine, veritable)

Element	From	Meaning	Examples
fid (cont'd)			*de fide* (of faith; designating those unconditional beliefs to be held by members of the Roman Catholic Church) LATIN SENTENCE: affidavit (He has stated it on faith) PORTUGUESE PHRASE: *auto-da-fé* (act of the faith: the public ceremony in which the Inquisition passed sentence on those tried as heretics; the execution by the secular power of the sentence thus passed, especially, the public burning of a heretic) PLACENAMES: Confidence, Iowa; Defiance (Iowa, Ohio) Fidelity (Illinois, Missouri) Fort Defiance (Arizona, New Mexico) Santa Fe (New Mexico, Tennessee) CROSS REFERENCE: *cred*
fid			See *fiss* for *bifid, pinnafid*.
fig,*** **fic,** **-fy**	Latin *fingere* (IE *dheigh*, to knead, form)	to form, shape, make	ROOT NOTE: Authorities are divided on whether the element *-fy* is derived from this root, or from *figere*, to fasten, or from *facere*, to make. It appears that the element belongs in all three families, depending on the root to which it is suffixed. SIMPLE ROOT: *fic*: fictile (that can be molded; plastic; formed of molded clay, earth, etc.; of pottery or ceramics), fiction, fictional, fictionalize fictitious (**Synonyms**: legendary, mythical, apocryphal), fictive (of fiction or the production of fiction; not real; imaginary) *fig*: figment, figura, figurable, figural, figurant, figurate, figuration, figurative, figure (see synonyms at *configuration*, below), figurine PREFIXED ROOT: *con*-: configuration (**Synonyms**: form, figure, shape), configurationism (same as *Gestalt psychology*) (*con*-, with, together) *dis*-: disfigure, disfigurement (*dis*-, opposite of) *ef*-: effigy (a portrait, statue, or the like, especially of a person; likeness; often a crude representation of a despised person) (*ef*- assimilates *ex*-, out) *pre*-: prefigure (to suggest beforehand) (*pre*-, before) *trans*-: (across, through) transfiguration (see *Christian Festival* below) transfigure (**Synonyms**: transform, transmute, convert) SUFFIXED ROOT: glorify (glory) nitrify (nitrogen) putrefy (*putrid*, rotten) rectify (*rect*, straight) reify (*rex*, king) DISGUISED ROOT: faint (*faint* and *feign* are both from *fig*; see *Doublets* below) feign (*feign* and *faint* are both from *fig*; see *Doublets* below) DOUBLETS: faint:feign

Element	From	Meaning	Examples
fig (cont'd)			HOMONYMS: faint, feint (both from *feign*) ANGLO-SAXON COGNATES: dairy (from *dough*; originally, a female bread maker) dough (originally, that which was formed) lady [originally, one who kneaded, or shaped, dough in bread loaves (see previous entry); compare the origin of *lord*, the keeper of the loaves] CHRISTIAN FESTIVAL: The Transfiguration [commemorating the change in the appearance of Jesus on the mountain (Matthew 17)] GREEK: paradise (from the same IE base that yields Greek *teichos*, wall; Greek *peri-*, around; park, garden, thus the Garden of Eden as a synonym for *paradise*) CROSS REFERENCE: *form, morph*
fil**	Latin *filius*, son; *filia*; daughter (IE: *dhe*, to suck, suckle)	son, or daughter	SIMPLE ROOT: filial, filiate [to affiliate; in *law*, to assign paternity to (a bastard child, for example)], filiation PREFIXED ROOT: *af-*: affiliate (**Synonyms**: related, kindred, cognate), affiliation (*af-* assimilates *ad-*, to, toward) LEADING ROOT COMPOUND: cid: filicide (the murder of one's own child) (*cide*, kill) SPANISH: *hidalgo* [Old Spanish contraction of *hijo dalgo*, son of something (that is to say, *property*)] *hijo* (literally, son; from Latin *filius*; *de-*, of; *algo*, something. The term indicates a member of the minor nobility of Spain; capitalized, it denotes a state in central Mexico.) FRENCH: *fille* (a daughter; a girl; maid; spinster) *fille de joie* (daughter of joy, a prostitute) NOTE: *Filibuster* is not in this family, coming from Spanish *filibustero*, which itself is from Dutch *vrijbuiter*, freebooter. CROSS REFERENCE: *prol*
fil**	Latin *filum* (*gwhislo*, to spin thread)	thread, line	SIMPLE ROOT: fila: filament, filamentous, filar, filaria, filature file: file (originally, *to line up* a thread; hence a line, a row or a rank, a collection of papers in chronological order) filé (pronounced fee LAY; powdered sassafras leaves, used in Creole cooking, as in *filé gumbo*) filet fill: fillet filo: filose (threadlike; having a threadlike projection) filu: filum (plural, *fila*) PREFIXED ROOT: *de-*: defilade [in the *military*, to arrange (troops, fortifications) so that the terrain will protect them, especially from gunfire against either flank], defile (see *NB*) (*de-*, from) *en-*: enfilade (in the *military*, gunfire directed from either flank along the length of a column or line of troops; also, the disposition or placement of troops that makes them vulnerable to such fire) (*en-*, in) *pro-*: profile (**Synonyms**: contour, silhouette) (*pro-*, before)

Element	From	Meaning	Examples
fil (cont'd)			LEADING ROOT COMPOUND: form: filiform (having the form of a thread or filament) gree: filigree (literally, threaded grain; delicate, lacelike orna- mental work of intertwined wire of gold, silver, etc.) pod: filopodium (a thin, narrow pseudopodium consisting primarily of ectoplasm) (*pod*, foot) TRAILING ROOT COMPOUND: bi: bifilar (having or involving the use of two threads, wires, etc. as certain sensitive measuring instruments) (*bi*, two) mono: monofilament (a single untwisted strand of synthetic material; also, *monofil*) (*mono*, one) DISGUISED ROOT: purfle (to decorate the border of; to adorn or edge with metallic thread, beads, lace, etc.; as a *noun*, an ornamental border or trimming, as the inlaid border of a vio- lin) [Middle French *pourfiler*, from *pour*, for (from Latin *pro*, before + *fil*) INTERDISCIPLINARY: defile (in the *military*, to march off, file by file; in *topography*, a narrow valley or mountain pass, through which one must walk in single file) NB: *Defile*, meaning to pollute, comes from *foul*, dirty, un- clean. NO CROSS REFERENCE
fin***	Latin *finis* (IE: *dhigw*, to stick in)	border, end	SIMPLE ROOT: fina: final (**Synonyms:** last, ultimate), finale, finalist, finality finance, financial (**Synonyms:** fiscal, monetary, pecuniary), financier fine: fine (as an *adjective*, that which is polished or finished; as a *noun*, as to pay a *fine*, *to finish* the matter; see *Music Term*, below), finery, finesse fini: finial, finical, finicky, finis, finish (**Synonyms:** close, end, conclude), finite, finitive, finitude PREFIXED ROOT: af-: affine, affinition, affinity (*af-* assimilates *ad-*, to, toward) con-: confine (**Synonyms:** limit, bound, restrict), confine- ment (*con-*, with, together) de-: (from) define (to state or set forth the meaning of a word or phrase), definite (**Synonyms:** explicit, express, exact) {definitely} definition, definitive, definitude in-: infinite, infinitesimal (in *mathematics*, a variable that ap- proaches zero as a limit), infinitude, infinitive, infinity (*in-*, not) re-: refine (to make fine or pure; to make more subtle or precise), refined, refinement, refiner, refinery, refinish (*re-*, again) trans-: transfinite (in *mathematics*, designating or of a cardinal or ordinal number that is larger than any positive integer) (*trans-*, beyond) un-: unfinished (Anglo-Saxon *un-*, not) DOUBLE PREFIXED ROOT: indefinable, indefinite (*in-*, not; *de-*, from)

Element	From	Meaning	Examples
fin (cont'd)			TRAILING ROOT COMPOUND: para: paraffin (*parum*, too little; from its chemical inertness) tre: trephine [literally, three ends; a surgical instrument for cutting out circular sections (as of bone or corneal tissue)] (*tri*, three + *phine* from *fin*) LATIN PHRASES: *ad fin* (from *ad finem*, to the end; at the end) *ad infinitum* (to infinity; endlessly; forever; without limit; often used figuratively) MUSIC TERM: fine [pronounced FEE nay; the end; the end of a repeated section, whether *da capo* (repeated from the beginning) or *dal segno* (repeated from the segno, or the *sign* indicating repeat)] CROSS REFERENCE: *term*
firm***	Latin *firmare* (IE: *dher*, to firm, harden)	to strengthen	SIMPLE ROOT: firm (**Synonyms:** hard, solid, stiff), firmament (the sky, viewed poetically as a solid arch or vault), firmamental, firmness PREFIXED ROOT: *af-*: affirm (**Synonyms:** assert, declare, aver), affirmance, affirmation, affirmative (*af-* assimilates *ad-*, to, toward) *con-*: (with, together) confirm (**Synonyms:** substantiate, corroborate, verify), confirmation, confirmatory confirmed (**Synonyms:** chronic, inveterate, hardened) *in-*: infirm (**Synonyms:** weak, feeble, frail), infirmary, infirmity (*in-*, not) ITALIAN MUSIC TERM: fermata (the holding of a tone or rest beyond its written value, at the discretion of the performer; also a printed direction, indicating such) ENGLISH FORM: farm (originally, to make a contract, thus to make firm, secure) LATIN PHRASE: *terra firma* (firm earth; solid ground) CROSS REFERENCE: *bil, fort, rob, sthen*
fisc*	Latin *fiscus* (IE: *bhidh*, pot)	purse	ROOT NOTE: This root originally designated a basket, or a pot, as for money. The root came to mean a lockable money-basket, hence, a royal or other State treasury. SIMPLE ROOT: fisc (now rare; a royal or state treasury; exchequer) fiscal (**Synonyms:** financial, monetary, pecuniary) PREFIXED ROOT: *con-*: confiscable (also, *confiscatable*), confiscate (to seize private property for the public treasury, usually as a penalty) {confiscation}, confiscatory (*con-*, together) CROSS REFERENCE: *burs*
fiss,*** **fid**	Latin *findere* (IE: *bheid-*, to split)	to split; divided into parts	SIMPLE ROOT: fissi: fissile (that can be split; fissionable: said of atoms, cells, etc.) fission (in *biology*, a form of asexual reproduction, found in various simple plants and animals, in which the parent organism divides into two or more approximately equal parts, each becoming an independent individual) {fissionable} fissu: fissura (plural, *fissurae*), fissure (a long, narrow, deep cleft or crack; a dividing or breaking into parts), fissury

Element	From	Meaning	Examples
fiss (cont'd)			LEADING ROOT COMPOUND: par: fissiparous (in *biology*, reproducing by fission) (*parous*, producing) ped: fissiped (in *zoology*, having the toes separated from each other; as a *noun*, animals such as dogs and cats with this characteristic) (*ped*, foot) rostr: fissirostral (having a broad and deeply cleft beak, as a swift or nighthawk) (*rostrum*, beak) TRAILING ROOT COMPOUND: bi: bifid (divided into two equal parts by a cleft, as the end of a snake's tongue; forked) (*bi*, two) pinnati: pinnatifid (featherlike; in *botany*, having leaves in a featherlike arrangement, with narrow lobes whose clefts extend more than halfway to the axis) (*pinna*, feather) septem: septemfid (*septem*, seven) tri: trifid (divided into three lobes or parts by deep clefts, as some leaves) (*tri*, three) ENGLISH COGNATES: beetle (the insect, not the heavy mallet) bit (as a coined word, *bit* is from *binary digit*), bite INTERDISCIPLINARY: fissure (in *anatomy*, a groove between lobes or parts of an organ, as in the liver or brain; in *medicine*, a break or ulceration where skin and mucous membrane join, especially at the anus) CROSS REFERENCE: *scind, schis/schiz*
fit			See *fac* for *benefit*.
fix,*** -fy	Latin *figere* (IE: *dhigw*, to stick in; yields English dig, dike, ditch)	to fasten, attach	NOTE: See *Root Note* for *-fy* under *fig*. SIMPLE ROOT: fix (**Synonyms**: predicament, dilemma, quandary), fixate, fixation, fixative PREFIXED ROOT: af-: affix (in *linguistics*, a prefix, suffix, or infix) {affixal}, affixation, affixture (*af-* assimilates *ad-*, to, toward) ante-: antefix (an architectural term) (*ante-*, before) in-: infix (in *linguistics*, a morpheme that is added within the base of a word, e.g., *o* in *gemology*; sometimes referred to as a *structural connective*) (*in-*, in) pre-: prefix (a syllable or group of syllables, or word joined to the beginning of another word or a base to alter its meaning or create a new word; a title, such as Dr., placed before a person's name) (*pre-*, before) suf-: suffix (an affix that follows the element to which it is added, as *-ly* in *kingly*) (*suf-* assimilates *sub-*, under) trans-: transfix (to pierce through with or as with something pointed; impale; to make motionless, as if impaled, as *transfixed with horror*) (*trans-*, through) TRAILING ROOT COMPOUND: cruci: crucifix, crucify (*cruc*, cross) DISGUISED ROOT: fibula, fichu DISGUISED TRAILING ROOT COMPOUND: micro: microfiche (*micro*, small) FRENCH PHRASE: *idée fixe* (fixed idea; an obsession) CROSS REFERENCE: *pact/pag/pex*

273

Element	From	Meaning	Examples
flag,** flam, fulg, fulm	Latin *flagrare* (IE: *bhleg,* to shine, burn)	to burn, shine	SIMPLE ROOT: *flag:* flagrancy (also, *flagrance*) flagrant (**Synonyms:** outrageous, atrocious, heinous) *flam:* flamboyant {flamboyance, or *flamboyancy*} flame (**Synonyms:** blaze, flicker, flare), flammable (term now preferred to *inflammable* in commerce, industry, etc., inasmuch as the prefix *in-* can be interpreted as meaning not, or can be used as an intensifier) *fulg:* fulge: fulgent (very bright; radiant) fulgu: fulgural, fulgurate (to give off in flashes; in *medicine*, to destroy tissue by electrical means) {fulguration}, fulgurating (also, *fulgurant*) *fulm:* fulminant, fulminate, fulminic (acid) PREFIXED ROOT: *flag:* *con-:* conflagrant, conflagration (*con-*, with, together) *de-:* deflagrate {deflagration} (*de-*, intensive) *flam:* *in-:* inflame, inflammable (see *flammable*, above), inflammation, inflammatory (*in-*, in) *fulg:* *ef-:* effulgence (great brightness; radiance; brilliance) {effulgent} (*ex-*, forth) *re-:* refulgent (shining; radiant; glowing, resplendent) {refulgence, or *refulgency*} (*re-*, back, again) FRENCH: *flambeau* (a lighted torch; a large, ornamental candlestick) LATIN LAW PHRASE: *in flagrante delicto* (also, *in flagrante;* in the very act of committing the offense; during the blazing of the crime; hence, red-handed; while engaged in sexual activity, often specifically, illicit or perverse sexual activity) NB: *Flamingo* is not in this family, though often associated with it because of the bird's flaming color. The word comes from Spanish *Flamenco*, that is, Flemish, as a jocular name because of the myth of the ruddy complexioned Flemish. CROSS REFERENCE: *cand*
flagell**	Latin *flagrum:* a scourge (IE: *bhlag,* to beat, scourge)	whip	SIMPLE ROOT: flagellant, flagellate, flagellation, flagellatory, **flagellum** LEADING ROOT COMPOUND: form: flagelliform (shaped like a flagellum) TRAILING ROOT COMPOUND: bi: biflagellate (*bi*, two) HYPHENATED SIMPLE COMPOUND: self-flagellation DISGUISED ROOT: flail (as a *noun*, a manual threshing device, consisting of a long wooden handle or a staff and a shorter, free-swinging stick attached to its end; as a *transitive verb*, to beat, thrash, or strike with or as with a flail; as an *intransitive verb*, to thresh; wave, as in arms flailing)

Element	From	Meaning	Examples
flagell (cont'd)			flog (**Synonyms:** beat, pound, pummel) INTERDISCIPLINARY: flagellum (in *biology*, a whiplike part or process of some cells, especially of certain bacteria, protozoans, etc., that is an organ of locomotion or produces a current in the surrounding fluid; in *botany*, a threadlike shoot or runner; in *zoology*, the terminal, lashlike portion of the antenna in many insects) WORD WITH POSSIBLE RELATED MEANING: flagitious (shamefully wicked; vile and scandalous, i.e., describing one who should be whipped) NO CROSS REFERENCE
flam			See *flag* for *flammable*.
flat**	Latin *flare* (IE: *bhel*, to swell, blow up)	to blow; wind	SIMPLE ROOT: flatulent, flatuous, flatuosity, flatus PREFIXED ROOTS: *af-*: afflate, afflatus (literally, to blow to, or in; an inspiration or powerful impulse, as of an artist, musician, or poet) (*af-* assimilates *ad-*, to, toward) *con-*: conflate, conflation (a combining, as of two variant readings into a single text) (*com-*, together) *de-*: deflate (**Synonyms:** contract, shrink, condense), deflation (*de-*, opposite, reversal) *in-*: inflate (**Synonyms:** expand, swell, distend), inflated, inflation, inflationary, inflationism (*in-*, in) DISGUISED ROOT: flabellum (a large fan carried by the pope's attendants on ceremonial occasions; in *zoology*, a fan-shaped organ or structure of the body) (diminutive of *flabrum*, a breeze) flavor, flavorful (full of flavor; having a pleasant odor) flute (a high-pitched woodwind instrument; in *architecture*, a long, vertical, rounded groove in the shaft of a column) FRENCH: soufflé (made light and puffy by beating; in *medicine*, and without accent, a soft, blowing sound heard on auscultation; pronounced SOO fl) (French *souffler*, to blow; from Latin *sufflare*, from *sub-*, under + *flatus*) CROSS REFERENCE: *anem, vent*
flav*	Latin *flavus* (IE: *bhlewos*, light colors)	yellow	SIMPLE ROOT: flave: flavescent (turning yellow; yellowish) flavi: flavin (a water-soluble yellow pigment, including riboflavin, found in plant and animal tissue as coenzymes of flavoprotein), flavine, flavism LEADING ROOT COMPOUND: com: flavicomous (yellow-haired) (*coma*, hair) TRAILING ROOT COMPOUND: acri: acriflavin (*acri*, sharp) ribo: riboflavin (from *ribose*; a yellow crystalline B vitamin) CROSS REFERENCE: *aur, chrys, xanth*
flect,*** flex	Latin *flectere*	to bend	SIMPLE ROOT: *flect*: flection (a bending; flexing; a bend or pent part; in *anatomy*, flexion, which see below; in *grammar*, inflection), flector *flex*: flex (to bend an arm, knee, etc.; to tense a muscle by contraction)

Element	From	Meaning	Examples
flect (cont'd)			flexi: flexible (**Synonyms:** elastic, resilient, supple), flexibility, flexile, flexion (in *anatomy*, the bending of a joint or limb by contraction of flexor muscles)
			flexo: flexor (a muscle that bends a limb or other part of the body)
			flexu: flexuous (winding or wavering), flexure (a bending, curving, or flexing, as of a heavy object under its own weight; a bend, curve, or fold)
			PREFIXED ROOT:
			flect:
			de-: deflect, deflection, deflector (*de-*, from)
			in-: inflect, inflection, inflectional (having or showing grammatical inflection, as a language in which the subject-object relation is indicated by inflection: Greek and Latin are inflectional languages, whereas English is syntactically analytical) (*in-*, in)
			re-: (back, again)
			reflect (**Synonyms:** 1) consider, study, contemplate; 2) think, reason, cogitate), reflectance, reflection
			reflective (**Synonyms:** pensive, contemplative, meditative), reflector
			flex:
			circum-: circumflex [a mark (e.g., ^, ~) used over certain vowel letters to indicate a specific sound or quality] (*circum-*, around)
			de-: deflexed (bent downward, as branches, leaves, or hairs) (*de-*, down)
			in-: (note difference in prefix meaning in each of the two words)
			inflexed (in *biology*, bent sharply downward or inward; turned toward the axis) (*in-*, in)
			inflexible (**Synonyms:** adamant, implacable, obdurate) (*in-*, not)
			re-: reflex, reflexive (in *grammar*, designating a verb having an identical subject and object, as *dressed* in the sentence *He dressed himself*; or *He talked to himself*.) (*re-*, back)
			retro-: retroflex (bent or turned backward) (*retro-*, backward)
			TRAILING ROOT COMPOUND:
			genu: genuflect (to bend the knee, as in reverence or worship; to act in a submissive or servile way) {genuflection} (*genu*, knee)
			FRENCH:
			reflet (luster or iridescence, as a metallic glaze on pottery)
			INTERDISCIPLINARY: reflex [in *linguistics*, a word, sound, or system (as writing) that is derived from a prior and especially an older (and often reconstructed) element or system (*boat* is the *reflex* of Old English *bāt*); in *mathematics*, designating an angle greater than a straight line (180 degrees); in *physiology*; designating of or an involuntary, spontaneous action, such as a sneeze, blink, or hiccup; also an involuntary response to a stimulus; in *psychology*, an unlearned or instinctive response to a stimulus]
			CROSS REFERENCE: *ancyl/ankyl, camp, vari*

Element	From	Meaning	Examples
flic**	Latin *fligere* (IE: *bhlig*, to strike)	to strike	PREFIXED ROOT: *flict*: af-: (assimilates *ad-*, to, toward) afflict (to cause pain or suffering to; distress very much) affliction (**Synonyms:** trial, tribulation, misfortune) con-: conflict (**Synonyms:** fight, struggle, contention) (*con-*, together) in-: inflict (to cause or carry out by physical assault or other aggressive action; to impose; to afflict) {inflictive}, infliction (*in-*, on, against) *flig*: pro-: profligate (literally, to strike to the ground, destroy; given over to dissipation; also, extremely wasteful; as a *noun*, a profligate person) (*pro-*, forward) CROSS REFERENCE: *bat, cuss, fend, fer, plaud, pless/plex*
flor,** flos	Latin *flos*: flower (IE: *bhlo, bhel*, to swell, sprout)	blossom	SIMPLE ROOT: *flor*: flora: flora (plural, *floras*, or *florae*), floral, floralia (an ancient Roman festival in honor of the goddess Flora and marked especially by nude dancing of courtesans) flore: flores, florescence, floret, floreted flori: floriate, floriation, florid (excessively flowery in style: ornate; tinged with red: ruddy), florin, florist, floristic floru: floruit (abbreviated *fl.*: used to indicate the period of a person's life when accurate birth and death dates are unknown), florule *flos*: floscular (diminutive of *flos*, flower), flosculous PREFIXED ROOT: de-: defloration, defloriate (*de-*, opposite of) ef-: effloresce, efflorescence (in *medicine*, an eruption of the skin; rash or other skin lesion) (*ef-* assimilates *ex-*, out) LEADING ROOT COMPOUND: bunda: floribunda (abounding in blossoms; any of a class of cultivated roses with clusters of small to medium-sized flowers produced in profusion) [with *bunda* as in Latin *moribundus*, moribund (dying away), the word actually takes on the meaning of *unda* as in *abundant*] cult: floriculture (the cultivation of flowers, especially to be cut and sold) fer: floriferous (bearing flowers; blooming abundantly) (*ferre*, to bear) gen: florigen (a plant hormone thought to stimulate the flowering of plants) (*gen*, producing) leg: florilegium (same as *anthology*) (*leg*, gather) sug: florisugent (describing those birds, such as the hummingbirds, that suck flowers) (*sugere*, to suck) TRAILING ROOT COMPOUND: *florous*: (indicates number or kind of flowers) tubuli: tubuliflorous (having flowers all or some of whose corollas are tubular: said of certain plants of the composite family) (*tubuli*, tube) uni: uniflorous (bearing a solitary flower) (*uni*, one)

277

Element	From	Meaning	Examples
flor (cont'd)			DISGUISED ROOT: ferret (a narrow ribbon of cotton, wool, silk, etc.) (from Italian *fioretti*, floss silk) flirt (originally, to move quickly from flower to flower) flour (originally, the "flower" of the wheat; the best of the wheat was ground into flour; lesser quality wheat was used as animal feed) flourish (originally, to blossom; then, to grow vigorously) flower, flowerage, flowered, floweret (same as *floret*), flowery (**Synonyms**: bombastic, grandiloquent, turgid) PREFIXED DISGUISED ROOT: *de-*: deflower (*de-*, opposite of) LATIN-ENGLISH PHRASE: flora and fauna (the flowers and wildlife of a particular region) FRENCH: floraison (flowering, blossoming, as *the floraison of popular music in the twenties*) FRENCH PHRASE: *fleur-de-lis* (flower of the lily; same as *iris*; the coat of arms of the former French royal family; in *heraldry*, an emblem resembling a lily or iris; also spelled *fleur-de-lys*) ROMAN GODDESS OF FLOWERS: Flora ISLANDS: Flores, an island in Indonesia which bounds the Flores Sea; also, westernmost island of the Azores) STATE NAME: Florida (originally *Pascua Florida*, flowery Easter, from it having been discovered on April 2, 1513, during the Easter season, and from the blooming appearance of the land) PLACENAMES: Flora, Illinois; Flora Vista, New Mexico Florence (Alabama, South Carolina); Florissant, Missouri CROSS REFERENCE: *anth*
flu,* **fluv,** **flux**	Latin *fluere* (IE: *bhleu*, to swell up, flow; yields English flood))	to flow	SIMPLE ROOT: *flu*: fluct: fluctuate (**Synonyms**: swing, sway, oscillate) flue: fluency, fluent (flowing or moving smoothly and easily; able to write or speak easily, smoothly, and expressively) fluid: fluid {fluidic, fluidity}, fluidics, fluidize fluor: fluor, fluorescence, fluoride, fluorine, fluorite *fluv*: fluvial (of, found in, or produced by a river) *flux*: **flux**, fluxion PREFIXED ROOTS: *flu*: *af-*: (assimilates *ad-*, to, toward) affluence (a flowing toward; influx; great plenty; abundance) affluent (as a *noun*, an affluent person; also, a tributary stream: opposed to *effluent*; **Synonyms**: rich, wealthy, opulent) *circum-*: circumfluent (to flow around) (*circum-*, around) *con-*: confluence (see *Placename* below), confluent (*con-*, with) *ef-*: effluence, effluent (a flowing out or forth; emanation) (*ef-* assimilates *ex-*, out) *in-*: influent, influence (**Synonyms**: authority, weight, prestige), influent, influential (*in-*, in) *re-*: refluent (flowing back, as the tide to the sea) (*re-*, back)

Element	From	Meaning	Examples
flu (cont'd)			*super-*: superfluidity, superfluity (the state or quality of being superfluous; excess; superabundance); thing not needed) superfluous (*super-*, more, beyond)

fluv:
ef-: effluvium {effluvial} (*ef-* assimilates *ex-*, out)

flux:
af-: afflux (a sudden flow toward a point, as of blood to an organ) (*af-* assimilates *ad-*, to, toward)*in-*: influx (a flowing in; inflow) (*in-*, in)
ef-: efflux (a flowing out, or emanating) (*ef-* assimilates *ex-*, out)
re-: reflux (a flowing back, as the food returning to the esophagus from the stomach; ebb) (*re-*, again, back)
LEADING ROOT COMPOUND:
fluid:
dram: fluidram (*fluid dram*; same as Greek *drachm*)
ex: fluidextract (*ex-*, out, prefixes *tract*, to pull, draw)
fluoro:
graph: fluorography (*graph*, write)
meter: fluorometer (*meter*, measure)
scop: fluoroscope (*scope*, look)
fluvi:
col: fluvicoline (that which inhabits or frequents rivers or streams) (*col*, inhabiting)
TRAILING ROOT COMPOUND:
melli: mellifluous (flowing like honey, as *a mellifluous voice*) (*mell*, honey)
DISGUISED ROOT:
fleet, flush
flume (an inclined channel that carries water from a distant source for use in irrigation, logging, placer mining, or water turbines; see *Tourist Attraction*, below)
plover (a wading and shore bird; reason for name obscure) (from *pluvia*, rain)
pluvial (literally, having to do with rain; in *geology*, formed by the action of rain)
ITALIAN: influenza, often shortened to *'flu*: literally, influence, attributed by astrologers to the *influence* of the stars
PLACENAME: Confluence, Pennsylvania
TOURIST ATTRACTION: The Flume (an 800-foot long chasm, in the Franconia Notch of the White Mountains of New Hampshire)
INTERDISCIPLINARY: flux (in *pathology*, an abnormal discharge of liquid matter from the bowels; in *chemistry*, *metallurgy*, a substance used to refine metals by combining with impurities to form a molten mixture that can be readily removed; in *physics*, a flow of matter or energy as a fluid, or regarded as a fluid)
CROSS REFERENCE: *luv, rrh, rrhag*

Element	From	Meaning	Examples
foc**	Latin *focus* (IE: *bhok*: to flame, burn)	focus (center)	ROOT NOTE: *Focus* in Latin designated the hearth or the fireplace, *where the family gathered together*. Its mathematical use was adopted by Johann Kepler (German astronomer and mathematician) in 1604 to designate the point in which rays converge (or, *gathered together at the fireplace*), or from which they seem to diverge. The root is extended to mean fire or heat (see *foyer, fuel,* and *curfew* below). SIMPLE ROOT: focus (plural, *foci*) PREFIXED ROOT: *con-*: confocal (in *mathematics*, having the same focus or foci) (*con-*, with, together) TRAILING ROOT COMPOUND: bi: bifocal, bifocals (*bi*, two) tri: trifocals (*tri*, three) DISGUISED ROOT: foyer (originally, a heated room; hence, ultimately the foyer or lobby of a theater) FRENCH: curfew (the signal in the Middle Ages to extinguish village fires and retire for the evening; modern French is *couvre-feu*) [from *covrir* (cover) + *feu* (fire)] ENGLISH COGNATE: fuel (Middle English *fewell*; from Old French *fuale, focale*; from *foca*, hearth; see *Root Note* above) NO CROSS REFERENCE
foli***	Latin *foliare*: to leaf (IE: *bhel, bhlo,* to swell, blossom)	leaf	SIMPLE ROOT: folia: foliaceous, foliage, foliaged foliar (of or like a leaf or leaves) foliate (as a *verb*, to divide into thin layers; to beat into foil; to number the leaves of a book or manuscript; as an *adjective*, having or covered with leaves; like a leaf or leaves), foliation folio: folio, foliolate (in *botany*, having or relating to leaflets), foliose, folious foliu: folium PREFIXED ROOT: *de-*: defoliate, defoliation (*de-*, from) *ex-*: exfoliate [literally, to strip of leaves; to remove (skin or bark, for example) in flakes or scales; as an intransitive verb, to come off or separate, as scales, flakes, sheets, or layers] {exfoliation, exfoliative} (*ex-*, off) *per-*: perfoliate (in *botany*, having a base surrounding the stem which bears it so that the stem seems to pass through it: said of a leaf, examples of which are the bellwort and the honeysuckle) (*per-*, through, throughout) LEADING ROOT COMPOUND: *foli:* fer: foliferous (bearing leaves) (*ferous*, bearing) *folii:* col: foliicolous (*double i* correct; growing on leaves, as certain liches, fungi, and algae) (*colere*, to inhabit) TRAILING ROOT COMPOUND: bi: bifoliate (same as *bifoliolate*) (*bi*, two) port: portfolio (*portare*, to carry) DISGUISED ROOT: foil (one meaning; another *foil* means "to frustrate")

Element	From	Meaning	Examples
foli (cont'd)			DISGUISED TRAILING ROOT COMPOUND: cinqu: cinquefoil (*cinque*, five) tre: trefoil (a three-leaved plant) (from *tri*, three) INTERDISCIPLINARY: folium (in *geology*, a thin layer of stratum, as in metamorphic rock; in *geometry*, the looping, closed part of a curve extending from a node) CROSS REFERENCE: *lam, petal, phyll*
foll**	Latin *follis* (IE: *bhel*, to blow up, swell)	windbag	SIMPLE ROOT: folly RELATED WORD: follicle (literally, little bag, from *follis*, bag, and has come to mean a husk or pod, small sac, cavity, or gland for excretion or secretion, as a *hair follicle*) INTERDISCIPLINARY: follicle (in *anatomy*, an approximately spherical group of cells containing a cavity; also, a vascular body in the ovary containing ova; in *botany*, a single-chambered fruit that splits along only one seam to release its seeds, as a milkweed pod) DISGUISED ROOT: fool, foolery, foolish (**Synonyms**: absurd, ludicrous, preposterous) PERSIAN: pul (pronounced *pool*; literally, a money bag; a coin of Afghanistan, 1/100 of the afghani) NO CROSS REFERENCE
for*	Latin *foras* (IE: *bhoros*, cut wood; from *bher*, to cut wood with a sharp tool)	outdoors; outside	ROOT NOTE: This root is derived from Latin *foras*, out-of-doors, from Old Latin *fora*, door, and which gives the English cognate *door*. SIMPLE ROOT: foreign (**Synonyms**: extrinsic, extraneous, alien) forest forensic forum (originally, an area out-of-doors, marketplace) LEADING ROOT COMPOUND: feit: forfeit (from *facere*, to make, do) DISGUISED LEADING ROOT COMPOUND: faubourg (French *bourg*, from Germanic *burg*, town; a part of a city *outside*, or once outside, the wall; suburb) foreclose (does not mean closed before, but closed out, as to *foreclose a mortgage*, meaning that the entire mortgage is payable at once, or that the collateral is forfeited, and in essence depriving the mortgagor of the right to redeem mortgaged property, as when he/she has failed in his/her payments. Through common use, *foreclose* has indeed come to mean to settle or resolve *beforehand*.) FRENCH TERMS: *hors de combat* (literally, out of combat; out of action; sidelined or disabled) *hors d'oeuvre* (literally, outside of work; outside of the ordinary meal, side dish; an appetizer or canapé served with cocktails or before a meal) NO CROSS REFERENCE

> The custom of forming compounds from Greek elements prevails in all civilized countries in Europe and America, and if a useful term of this kind is introduced in any one country, it is adopted with great promptitude into the language of all the rest.
> Henry Bradley

Element	From	Meaning	Examples
form***	Latin *forma* (IE: *mer-bh,* or *mer-gwh,* to gleam, sparkle)	form, shape, appearance, beauty	SIMPLE ROOT: form (**Synonyms:** figure, shape, profile) formal, formalism, formality, formalize, formation, formative former (one who forms; another *former,* meaning "earlier," is not from this root) formula (plural, formulas, or formulae), formulary, formulate, formulism, format PREFIXED ROOT: *con-:* (with, together) conform (**Synonyms:** agree, harmonize, coincide) conformable, conformal, conformation, conformist, conformity *de-:* deform, deformed, deformity (*de-,* opposite of) *re-:* (back, again) reform (**Synonyms:** correct, rectify, amend) reformation, reformatory, reformed GERMAN: formant (any of several frequency regions of relatively great intensity in a sound spectrum, which together determine the characteristic quality of a vowel sound) LATIN PHRASE: *pro forma* (according to form) PLACENAME: Reform, Alabama CROSS REFERENCE: *morph*
fort***	Latin *fortis* (IE: *bheregh,* high, elevated)	strong, strength	SIMPLE ROOT: fort, fortress forte: forte (when used to indicate one's strong point, pronounced *fort*; when used as a music term, meaning strong, loud, pronounced *for TAY*) forti: fortis (a consonant produced with greater articulatory tenseness and stronger expiration, e.g., \t\ in *toe,* as opposed to \d\ in *doe,* which is *lenis*) fortitude (**Synonyms:** grit, backbone, pluck) PREFIXED ROOT: *com-:* (with, together) comfort (as a *noun,* aid; encouragement; relief from distress, grief, etc.; consolation; as a *verb,* to give strength to; **Synonyms:** console, solace, relieve) comfortable (**Synonyms:** cozy, snug, restful) comforter (a person or thing that comforts; a quilted bed covering; a long woolen scarf) *The Comforter* (personification of the Messiah, as used by Isaiah; the *Holy Spirit*) *ef-:* effort (**Synonyms:** exertion, endeavor, pains), effortless (*ef-* assimilates *ex-,* out) LEADING ROOT COMPOUND: fic: fortification (the act or science of fortifying; something used in fortifying; especially, a fort or defensive earthwork, wall, etc.; a fortified place or position) (from *facere,* to do, make) fy: fortify (see *fortification*) TRAILING ROOT COMPOUND: piano: pianoforte (*piano,* soft; from *planus,* even, smooth) DISGUISED ROOT: force (**Synonyms:** compel, constrain, coerce) {forceable; same as *forcible*}, forced, forceful, forcible

Element	From	Meaning	Examples
fort (cont'd)			PREFIXED DISGUISED ROOT: *de-*: deforce [in *law*, to keep (property, etc.) from the true owner by force; to keep (a person) from rightful possession by force], deforciant (in *law*, a person who deforces another of another's property) (*de-*, from) *en-*: enforce, enforceable (notice that the *e* is retained in order to preserve the *soft c* sound), enforcement (*en-*, in) LATIN TERM: *aqua fortis* (literally, strong water: nitric acid) FRENCH TERM: *force majeure* (superior force) LATIN LAW TERM: *a fortiori* (for a stronger reason) ITALIAN MUSIC TERM: *fortissimo* (a superlative, meaning very loud) CROSS REFERENCE: *firm, rob, sthen* (cognate of *strength*)
fortu*	Latin *fortis* (IE: *bher*, to bring)	chance, fate, luck	SIMPLE ROOT: fortuitous (**Synonyms**: accidental, incidental, adventitious) fortuity (the quality or condition of being fortuitous; chance or chance occurrence) fortunate [Do not confuse the meaning of *fortuitous* and *fortunate*; see Usage Note at *fortuitous* in *American Heritage*] fortune (good luck; success; prosperity) ANGLO-SAXON PREFIXED ROOT: *mis-*: misfortune (**Synonyms**: affliction, trial, tribulation) (*mis-*, wrong, badly) *un-*: unfortunate (*un-*, not) ROMAN MYTHOLOGY: Fortuna (goddess of fortune) NO CROSS REFERENCE
foss*	Latin *fodere* (IE *bhedh*, to dig in the earth)	to dig up	SIMPLE ROOT: fossa: fossa (in *anatomy*, a cavity, pit, or hollow) {fossate} fosse: fosse (or *foss*; originally, *fossa terra*, dug earth; a ditch or moat, especially one used in fortifications), fossette (a small hollow; a dimple) fossi: fossil, fossilize fosso: fossorial (digging or adapted for digging; burrowing, as *fossorial claws*) LEADING ROOT COMPOUND: fer: fossiliferous (containing fossils) (*ferre*, to bear) ENGLISH COGNATE: bed (originally, a sleeping hollow in the ground) NO CROSS REFERENCE
found,** **fund**	Latin *fundare*: to lay the foundation of; (IE: *bhudh*, bottom; yields English bottom)	bottom, to establish	SIMPLE ROOT: *found*: found [to originate or establish (something); create; set up, as a college], foundation (**Synonyms**: base, basis, groundwork) founder (a *nautical* term, to become stuck in soft ground; as a *noun*, a person who founds or establishes, as a college or a foundation; also, a disease of horses, as if the horse had fallen to the ground) *fund*: fund, fundament (a base or foundation; the buttocks; the anus), fundamental, fundus (in *anatomy*, the base of a hollow organ, or the part farthest from the opening, as that part of the uterus farthest from the cervix) PREFIXED ROOT: *pro-*: profound, profundity (*pro-*, before, forward)

Element	From	Meaning	Examples
found (cont'd)			DISGUISED ROOT: fond (the background of a design in lace; the groundwork; foundation; basis) CROSS REFERENCE: *bath*
fract,*** **frag,** **frang,** **fring**	Latin *frangere* (IE: *bhreg,* to break)	to break	SIMPLE ROOT: *fract*: fracta: fractal (in *geometry*, an extremely irregular line or surface formed of an infinite number of similarly irregular sections) fracti: fraction, fractional, fractionate fractious (hard to manage; unruly; rebellious; refractory) fractu: fracture (**Synonyms**: break, crash, smash), fractus (a species of clouds with a ragged, shredded appearance) *frag*: fragi: fragile (see *Doublets* below; **Synonyms**: frangible, brittle, friable) fragm: fragment (**Synonyms**: part, portion, division) fragmental (in *geology*, designating or of rocks formed of the fragments of older rocks) fragmentary, fragmentate, fragmentation, fragmentize *frang*: frangible (see synonyms at *fragile*, above) PREFIXED ROOT: *fract*: *dif-*: diffract, diffraction (the bending of waves around obstacles in their path), diffractive (from *dis-*, apart) *in-*: infraction (a breaking of a law, pact, etc.; violation; infringement) (*in-*, in) *re-*: refract {refractive}, refraction, refractory (literally, to break away; thus, hard to manage) (*re-*, back) *frag*: *suf-*: suffrage, suffragette, suffragan (from *sub-*, under) *frang*: *in-*: infrangible (that cannot be broken or separated; that cannot be violated or infringed) {infrangibility} (*in-*, not) *re-*: refrangible {refrangibility} (*re-*, back) *fring*: *in-*: infringe (**Synonyms**: trespass, encroach, intrude), infringement, infringible (*in-*, in) DOUBLE PREFIXED ROOT: irrefragable (that cannot be refuted; indisputable), irrefrangible (that cannot be broken or violated; that cannot be refracted) (*ir-* assimilates *in-*, not + *re-*, back, again) MODIFIED PREFIXED ROOT: anfractuous (*an* from *ambi-fractuous*) TRAILING ROOT COMPOUND: ossi: ossifrage (literally, bone-breaker; see *Doublets* below) (*ossi*, bone) saxi: saxifrage (literally, rock-breaker; a plant, probably named from its growing in rock crevices) (*saxum*, rock) septi: septifragal (opening or dehiscing, by the breaking away of the outer walls of the carpels from the partitions) (*septi*, divider)

Element	From	Meaning	Examples
fract (cont'd)			DISGUISED ROOT: fracas (a noisy fight or loud quarrel; brawl) (a blend of *frangere* + *cassare*, to quash) frail (see *Doublets* below), frailty PREFIXED DISGUISED ROOT: *re-*: refrain (in *music*, a phrase, verse, or verses repeated at intervals in a song or poem, as after each stanza; another *refrain* is from *frenare*, to curb) (*re-*, again) DOUBLETS: frail:fragile; osprey:saxifrage ENGLISH COGNATES: breach (**Synonyms:** infraction, violation, transgression) break (see synonyms at *fracture*, above) CROSS REFERENCE: *clast, rupt*
fran*	Frankish *franc*	free (in Frankish Gaul, full freedom was the right only of the conquering people or those under their protection)	SIMPLE ROOT: franc (originally coined *Francorum rex*, the king of the French, a coin struck in 1360), franchise frank (one meaning: to send mail *free* of charge) PREFIXED ROOT: *af-*: affranchise (*af-* assimilates *ad-*, to, toward) *dis-*: disfranchise (to deprive of the rights of citizenship, especially of the right to vote) (*dis-*, reversal)
fran (cont'd)			LEADING ROOT COMPOUND: cens: frankincense (free, or pure, incense) pledge: frankpledge (literally, peace pledge) PHRASE: *lingua franca* (the language of the Franks: originally consisting basically of Italian, but containing Spanish, French, and also Greek and Arabic; it served as the common language of the Mediterranean Sea and surrounding ports; now, the term means any hybrid language) PROPER NAME: Franklin (a free man) PLACENAME: Frankfurt, Germany (from Frankfort, Ford of the Franks; from Frankfurt is derived *frankfurter*, originally known as *frankfurter sausage*) CROSS REFERENCE: *eleuther, liber, lysis, lyt, solv/solu*
frang			See *frac* for *frangible*.
frat***	Latin *frater* (IE: *bhrater*, brother; yields English brother, brotherly, brethern, "brer," as in *Brer Rabbit*)	brother	SIMPLE ROOT: frater (the eating room of a monastery, where the *brothers* ate, though this meaning is now obsolete; a brother or comrade, especially as in a fraternity), fraternal, fraternity fraternize (as the socializing of military officers with enlisted men, or vice versa) PREFIXED ROOT: *con-*: confraternity, confrere (from French *frère;* a fellow member or worker; colleague or associate, as in a profession) (*con-*, with, together) LEADING ROOT COMPOUND: cid: fratricide [the act of killing one's own brother (or sister), which is properly *sororicide*); the act of killing relatives or fellow-countrymen, as in a civil war; in the *military*, the unintentional killing of members of one's own or allied forces] (*cide*, kill) DISGUISED ROOT: friar [a member of any of various mendicant (beggar) orders, as a Franciscan or Domican]

Element	From	Meaning	Examples
frat (cont'd)			ENGLISH ROMANY (GYPSY) COGNATES: pal (from Sanskrit *bhratr*), palsy-walsy (a reduplication of *pal*) GREEK COGNATE: *phrater* (clan; later a political brotherhood, and seen in English *phratry*, a subdivision of an ancient Greek phyle; also, any of the similar units, as a group of clans, of a primitive tribe; in *anthropology*, an exogamous subdivision of the tribe, comprising two or more related clans) CROSS REFERENCE: *adelph*
fri**	Latin *fricare* (IE: *bhrei*, to cut, scrape)	to rub (extended to mean to break, as in *débris*)	SIMPLE ROOT: fria: friable (readily crumbled; brittle) frica: fricative (in *phonetics*, produced by the forcing of breath through a constricted passage) frict: friction (in *mechanics*, the resistance to motion of two moving objects or surfaces that touch), frictional friv: frivolity, frivolous PREFIXED ROOT: af-: affricate, affricative (*af-* assimilates *ad-*, to) anti-: antifriction (*anti-*, against) TRAILING ROOT COMPOUND: denti: dentifrice (*denti*, tooth) DISGUISED ROOT: fray (to make or become worn, ragged, or raveled by rubbing; to make or become weakened or strained; see NB) frazzle fry [young fish(es)] FRENCH: debris, or *débris* (the scattered remains of something broken or destroyed; ruins; rubble) NB: Another *fray* is an aphetic of *affray*, from Latin *ex-*, out + Germanic *frith*, peace; thus, a noisy brawl or quarrel; public fight or riot; breach of the peace. CROSS REFERENCE: *frag, trib, trit*
fring			See *frac, frag* for *infringe*.
fruc,** **frug**	Latin *frui*: to enjoy (IE: *bhrug*, fruit, to enjoy; yields English fruit, fruitage, fruiter, fruitful, fruition, fruity)	fruit (extended to mean "full enjoyment of")	SIMPLE ROOT: fructuary (same as *usufructuary*, which see below), fructure, fructuous LEADING ROOT COMPOUND: *fruct*: ose: fructose (a crysytalline monosaccharide found in sweet fruits and in honey; fruit sugar; levulose) (*ose*, carbohydrate) *fructi*: fer: fructiferous (bearing fruit; fruit-bearing) (*ferous*, bearing) fy: fructify (to bear fruit; become fruitful) {fructification} (from *facere*, to make, do) vor: fructivorous (fruit-eating) (*vorare*, to swallow whole) *frugi*: vor: frugivorous (fruit-eating) (*vorare*, to swallow whole) TRAILING ROOT COMPOUND: usu: (utilize) usufruct (from *usus et fructus*, use and enjoyment; in Roman and Civil Law, the right of using and enjoying all the advantages and profits of the property of another so long as the property is not damaged or altered in any way) usufructuary (a person who holds property by *usufruct*)

Element	From	Meaning	Examples
fruc (cont'd)			DISGUISED ROOT: frugal (literally, fit for food; hence, proper, appropriate, worthy; **Synonyms:** thrifty, sparing, economical) {frugality} LATIN EXPRESSION: *fructus industriales* [crops (as wheat, corn) produced by labor on the part of man; distinguished from *fructus naturales*, crops produced without any substantial assistance from man] CROSS REFERENCE: *carp, pom*
frustr*	Latin *frustra* (IE: *dhwer*, to trick)	in vain	SIMPLE ROOT: frustrate (**Synonyms:** thwart, foil, baffle); frustration, frustrative, frustratory DISGUISED ROOT: fraud (**Synonyms:** deception, subterfuge, trickery), fraudulent PREFIXED DISGUISED ROOT: *de-*: defraud (**Synonyms:** cheat, swindle, trick) (*de-*, from) NO CROSS REFERENCE
fug***	Latin *fugere* (IE: *bheug*, to flee)	to flee, run away, avoid	SIMPLE ROOT: fuga: fugacious (passing quickly away; fleeting; ephemeral; in *botany*, falling soon after blooming, as some flowers) {fugacity} fugi: fugitate (a Scots law term) fugitive (fleeing, apt to flee, or having fled, as from danger, justice, etc.; passing quickly; fleeting; evanescent; having to do with matters of temporary interest, as *fugitive essays*; roaming; shifting; as a *noun*, a person who flees or has fled from danger, justice, etc.; a fleeting or elusive thing) fugu: fugue {fuguist} PREFIXED ROOT: *re-*: (back) refuge (**Synonyms:** shelter, retreat, asylum) refugee (a person who flees from home or country to seek refuge elsewhere, as in a time of war or of political or religious persecution) refugium (a small, isolated area, as during a period of glaciation, allowing the survival of plants and animals from an earlier period; for example, in Antarctica, there is a refugium in which 33 different kinds of indigenous mosses grow) TRAILING ROOT COMPOUND: calci: calcifuge (originally, fleeing or not growing in limy soil; a plant that grows in soils low in calcareous matter) centri: centrifugal (literally, fleeing from the center) febri: febrifuge (English cognate is *feverfew*; see *English Compound*, below) (*febri*, fever) helio: heliofugal (Greek *helio*, sun) nidi: nidifugous (fleeing from the nest; describing certain birds such as the prairie grouse and shorebirds, whose young are active immediately after hatching) (*nidi*, nest) subter: subterfuge (one authority has indicated that *subter* itself means below; thus, the literal meaning of *subterfuge* is to flee under, but more generally considered to flee secretly, escape; thus any plan, action, or device used to hide one's true objective, evade a difficult or unpleasant situation, etc.; stratagem; artifice) (*subter*, secretly; akin to *sub-*, under)

Element	From	Meaning	Examples
fug (cont'd)			vermi: vermifuge (*vermin*, worms) ITALIAN MUSIC TERM: fughetta (diminutive of *fugue*; a short or condensed fugue) ENGLISH COMPOUND: feverfew (anglicized from *febrifuge*; a perennial herb thought to reduce fever) IRISH: fuidhir (from Middle Irish *fuidir*; a stranger or refugee in ancient Ireland placing himself/herself under the protection of a chief and becoming his/her tenant) PLACENAMES: Refugio, Texas Refugio Azules, Chile INTERDISCIPLINARY: centrifugal (in *botany*, developing from the center outward, as certain flower clusters; in *physiology*, conveying away from the center; efferent) fugue (in *music*, a form of composition in which a subject is announced in one voice or instrument and then developed contrapuntally in strict order by each of the other voices or instruments, as though one were *fleeing* from the other; in *psychiatry*, a state of psychological amnesia during which the subject seems to behave in a conscious and rational way, although upon return to normal consciousness the subject cannot remember the period of time nor what she/he did during it; temporary *flight* from reality) NO CROSS REFERENCE
fulg			See *flag* for *refulgent*.
fulm			See *flag* for *fulminant*.
fum**	Latin *fumus* (IE: *dheu*, to blow, smoke, be turbid)	smoke	SIMPLE ROOT: fuma: fumaric acid, fumarole (a vent in a volcanic area, from which smoke and gases arise) fume: fume, fumet (a rich, concentrated broth made from bones of fish, chicken, game birds, etc. boiled with wine, herbs, etc., used in sauces, for braising various foods, etc.) fumi: fumitory (originally *fumus terrae*, literally, smoke of the earth: so called from its smell; a plant formerly used in medicine) PREFIXED ROOT: *per*-: perfume (**Synonyms:** fragrance, bouquet, redolence) (*per*-, intensive) LEADING ROOT COMPOUND: ig: fumigant, fumigate {fumigation} (from *agere*, to do, act) NO CROSS REFERENCE
funct,** **fung**	Latin *fungi* (IE *bheug*, to enjoy)	to perform, serve	SIMPLE ROOT: *funct*: function (**Synonyms:** office, duty, capacity), functional (in *mathematics*, of, relating to, or indicating a function or functions), functionalism, functionary *fung*: fungible (interchangeable; in *law*, designating movable goods, as money or grain, any unit or part of which can replace another unit, as in discharging a debt; as a *noun*, from *res fungibilis*, a fungible thing) PREFIXED ROOT: *de*-: defunct (**Synonyms:** dead, deceased, inanimate) (*de*-, from, off)

288

Element	From	Meaning	Examples
funct (cont'd)			*dys-*: dysfunction (Greek *dys-*, impaired) *mal-*: malfunction (*mal-*, bad, badly, wrong) *per-*: perfunctory (done without care or interest or merely as a form or routine; superficial) (*per-*, intensive) CROSS REFERENCE: *act, serv*
fund			See *fus/fund* for *refund*.
fund			See *found* for *fund, fundamental*.
fung			See *funct* for *fungible*.
furc*	Latin *furca*	fork	SIMPLE ROOT: furca: furca (plural, *furcae*), furcal, furcate furcu: furcula, furculum (in *anatomy* and *zoology*, any forked part or organ, especially the wishbone) LEADING ROOT COMPOUND: cerc: furcocercous (having a forked tail) (*cerc*, tail) TRAILING ROOT COMPOUND: bi: bifurcated (having two branches or peaks; forked) (*bi*, two) PLACENAME: Belle Fourche, South Dakota (beautiful fork; *fourche* here probably refers to point of bifurcation; the city is situated on the Belle Fourche River) NO CROSS REFERENCE
fus,** fund	Latin *fundere* (IE: *gheu,* pour)	to pour	SIMPLE ROOT: fuse (**Synonyms**: mix, mingle, blend; the noun *fuse* is derived from *fuso*, a tube, cord, casing; for example, *an electrical fuse*), fusible, fusil, fusion PREFIXED ROOT: *fund:* *in-*: infundibular (also, *infundibulate*; shaped like a funnel), infundibuliform, infundibulum (in *anatomy*, any of various funnel-shaped organs or passages) (from *infuse*) (*in-*, in) *re-*: refund (literally, to pour back; to give back or restore, especially money; repay; another *refund* means "to fund again"; see *found*) (*re-*, back) *fus:* *af-*: affusion (a pouring on, as of water in baptism) (*af-* assimilates *ad-*, to, toward) *circum-*: circumfuse (to pour around; diffuse; to surround as with a fluid; suffuse) {circumfusion} (*circum-*, around) *con-*: (together) confuse (**Synonyms**: puzzle, perplex, confound) confusion (**Synonyms**: disorder, disarray, chaos) *dif-*: diffuse (**Synonyms**: wordy, verbose, prolix), diffusible, diffusion, diffusive (*dif-* assimilates *dis-*, apart) *in-*: (note difference in meanings of prefixes) infuse (literally, to pour in; instill; impart), infusion (*in-*, in) infusionism (in *theology*, the Christian doctrine that a pre-existing soul of divine origin is *infused* into the body at conception or birth; compare *creationism*, the doctrine that each human soul is a distinct and new creation by God) (*in-*, in) infusible (that cannot be fused or melted) (*in-*, not) *inter-*: interfuse (literally, to pour between) (*inter-*, between) *per-*: perfuse {perfusion, perfusive} (*per-*, through)

Element	From	Meaning	Examples
fus (cont'd)			*pro-*: profuse (**Synonyms:** lavish, extravagant, prodigal), profusion (*pro-*, forth) *re-*: refuse (both the noun, meaning "that which is thrown away," and pronounced REF yoos, or REF yooz; and the verb, meaning "reject, decline," and pronounced rih FYOOZ, are both derived from *refundere*, to pour back) (*re-*, back) *trans-*: transfuse, transfusion (*trans-*, across) DISGUISED ROOT: foison (now archaic, but originally meaning a plentiful crop; good harvest; plenty) fondant (a soft, creamy confection made of sugar, water, and cream of tartar, used as an icing, a candy, and especially a filling for other candies) fondue (or fondu; a dish made by melting cheese in wine, with a little brandy and seasoning added, used as a dip for cubes of bread; various other similar dishes) font (one meaning), found (one meaning), foundry, fount funnel futile (literally, that easily pours out; thus, untrustworthy, worthless) PREFIXED DISGUISED ROOT: *con-*: confound (literally, to pour together) (*con-*, with, together) INTERDISCIPLINARY: diffusion (in *physics*, an intermingling of molecules, ions, etc., resulting from random thermal agitation, as in the dispersion of a vapor in the air; a reflection or refraction of light or other electromagnetic radiation from an irregular surface or an erratic dispersion through a surface; scattering; in *anthropology* and *sociology*, the transmission of elements or features of one culture to another; in *speech*, wordiness, verbosity) CROSS REFERENCE: *chem*
fusc*	Latin *fuscus* (IE: *dhus*, to rage, storm, dust-colored)	cloudy, dark, somber	SIMPLE ROOT: fuscin (a brown pigment of the retinal epithelium), fuscous PREFIXED ROOT: *in-*: infuscate (darkened or tinged with brown, as the wings of an insect) (*in-*, in) *ob-*: obfuscate (to cloud over; obscure; make dark or unclear; also, to muddle, confuse, perplex) (*ob-*, against) CROSS REFERENCE: *maur*
fut*	Latin *futare* (IE: *bhau-t, bhu-t*, to strike, beat)	to strike	PREFIXED ROOT: *con-*: confute (**Synonyms:** disprove, refute, controvert) (*con-*, intensive) *re-*: refute (for *synonyms*, see *confute*, previous entry) (*re-*, again) CROSS REFERENCE: *bat, cuss, fend, fer, flict, plaud, pleg/pless/plex*
-fy			See *fac* for *magnify, rectify*, etc.

G

Element	From	Meaning	Examples
gage*	Frankish *gage* (IE: *wadh,* a pledge)	pledge	SIMPLE ROOT: gage (not related to Celtic *gauge,* to measure, from IE *gal-,* measuring rod) PREFIXED ROOT: *en-:* (in) engage (originally, to give or assign as security for a debt, etc.), engaged (pledged; especially, pledged in marriage) engagement (**Synonyms:** battle, campaign, encounter), engaging TRAILING ROOT COMPOUND: *mort:* mortgage (dead pledge) (*mort,* death) DISGUISED ROOTS: wage, wages (**Synonyms:** salary, fee, emolument), wager FRENCH: *dégagé* (pronounced day ga ZHAY; unconstrained, easy and free in manner) *engagé* (committed to supporting some aim, cause, etc.) ENGLISH: wed, wedding, wedlock (from Old English *wedlac,* literally, pledge offering) CROSS REFERENCE: *fid*
galact,** galax	Greek *galaktos:* milk (IE: *glak,* milk)	milk, galaxy	SIMPLE ROOT: *galact:* galactic (pertains both to *milk* and to the *Milky Way* or some other galaxy) *galax:* galaxy (the Milky Way of stars) PREFIXED ROOT: *inter-:* intergalactic (existing or occurring between or among galaxies) (Latin *inter-,* between) *meta-:* metagalaxy (in *astronomy,* the total assemblage of all galaxies, including all intergalactic matter; the measurable material universe) (*meta-,* between) TRAILING ROOT COMPOUND: *poly:* polygala (literally, much milk; milkwort; with Old English *wort,* plant, herb, a plant originally thought to increase the secretion of milk in nursing women) (*poly,* much) CROSS REFERENCE: *lact*
gam***	Greek *gamos* (IE: *gem,* to marry, be related)	marriage; sexual reproduction; also, joined, united	SIMPLE ROOT: *game:* gamete [a reproductive cell that is haploid and can unite with another gamete to form the cell (zygote) that develops into a new individual] {gametic} *gami:* gamic (in *biology,* that can develop only after fertilization: said of such an ovum) PREFIXED ROOTS: *a-:* agamous (producing no flowers or seeds) (*a-,* without) *apo-:* apogamy {apogamous} (the development of a plant without the union of gametes; development of a sporophyte from a gametophyte without fertilization) (*apo-,* away, away from) *endo-:* endogamy (the custom of marrying only within one's own tribes, clan, etc; cross-pollination among flowers of the same plants; opposed to *exogamy*) (*endo-,* within)

Element	From	Meaning	Examples
gam (cont'd)			*exo-:* exogamy (the custom, often inviolable, of marrying only outside one's own tribe, clan, etc.; cross-pollination among flowers of different plants; opposed to *endogamy*) {exogamous} (*exo-*, without, outside)

exo-: exogamy (the custom, often inviolable, of marrying only outside one's own tribe, clan, etc.; cross-pollination among flowers of different plants; opposed to *endogamy*) {exogamous} (*exo-*, without, outside)

LEADING ROOT COMPOUND:

gamet(o):

angi: gametangium (a cell or organ in which gametes are developed) (*ang*, vessel)

cyt: gametocyte (a parent cell, which undergoes meiosis and produces gametes) (*cyt*, cell)

gen: gametogenesis (in biology, the development of gametes) {gametogenic} (*gen*, producing)

phor: gametophore {gametophoric} (*phore*, bearing)

phyt: gametophyte (in plants, the gamete-bearing generation that is haploid and reproduces by eggs and sperms: distinguished from *sporophyte*) {gametophytic} (*phyton*, plant)

gamo:

gen: gamogenesis (reproduction by the uniting of gametes; sexual reproduction) (*genesis*, producing)

man: gamomania (a morbid desire to marry) (*mania*, craze)

petal: gamopetalous (having the petals united so as to form a tubelike corolla, as that of the morning glory)

phag: gamophagia (the disappearance of the male or female element in the conjugation of unicellular organisms) (*phag*, eat)

phob: gamophobia (morbid fear of marriage) (*phobia*, fear of)

phy: gamophyllous (having leaves or leaflike organs joined by their edges) (*phyll*, leaf)

sepal: gamosepalous (having the sepals united)

TRAILING ROOT COMPOUND:

allo: allogamy (fertilization of a flower by the pollen of another; cross-fertilization) (*allo*, other)

auto: autogamous, autogamy (*auto*, self)

bi: bigamy (the act of marrying a second time while a previous marriage is still legally in effect; compare *digamy*, below) (Latin *bi*, two)

cleis: cleistogamous (having small, unopened, self-pollinating flowers, usually in addition to the showier flowers) {cleistogamic} cleistogamy (self-pollination of certain unopened flowers) (*cleisto*, closed)

crypt: cryptogam (a plant that bears no flowers or seeds but propagates by means of spores, as algae, mosses, ferns, etc.) (*crypto*, covered, hidden)

di: digamy (a second legal marriage; marriage after the death or divorce of the first spouse; compare *bigamy*, above) (*di*, two)

dicho: dichogamous (the maturing of pistils and stamens at different times, preventing self-pollination) {dichogamous or dichogamic} (*dicho*, two, asunder)

hetero: heterogamete (opposed to *isogamete*) {heterogametic}, heterogamous {heterogamy} (*hetero*, different)

Element	From	Meaning	Examples
gam (cont'd)			holo: hologamous (having gametes essentially the same in size and form as other cells) (*holo*, whole, entire) homo: homogamy (the condition of having all flowers sexually alike; the condition of having stamens and pistils mature at the same time; inbreeding in an isolated group of individuals of the same species) {homogamous} (*homo*, same) miso: misogamist, misogamy (*miso*, hatred of) mono: monogamy (in *zoology*, the practice of having only one mate) {monogamous, or *monogamic*} (*mono*, one) poly: polygamous (in *botany*, having bisexual and unisexual flowers on the same plant or on different plants), polygamy (in *zoology*, the practice of mating with more than one of the opposite sex) {polygamist} (*poly*, many) xeno: xenogamy (fertilization by cross-pollination, especially cross-pollination between flowers on different plants) (*xeno*, stranger) DOUBLE ROOT: gamogamy (*gamogenesis*, or sexual reproduction, especially of protozoans) PREFIXED TRAILING ROOT COMPOUND: *an*-: aneugamy (literally, not well married; resulting in an abnormal number of chromosomes in the gamete) (*an*-, not + *eu*, well) CROSS REFERENCE: *nect, nod*
gar*	Germanic *warnen*: to equip oneself; yields *ward, warn, warranty*	to protect, supply	SIMPLE ROOT: garment, garnish, garnishment, garnishee, garniture, garrison DISGUISED ROOT: garret (the space just below the roof of a house; attic) guarantee, guarantor, guaranty NB: Garnet, from *pomegranate*, is not in this family. CROSS REFERENCE: *phylact, tect/teg*
gel*	Latin *gelare* (IE: *gel*, to freeze; yields English cool, chill, jelly)	freeze, set firm	SIMPLE ROOT: galantine, gelatin, gelation PREFIXED ROOT: *con*-: congelation (the process or result of congealing; see *congeal*, below) (*con*-, with, together) LEADING ROOT COMPOUND: *gel*: osis: gelosis (a hard lump which appears frozen; occurs especially in muscle tissue) (*osis*, diseased condition of) *gelo*: trip: gelotripsy (the massaging away of geloses, or indurated swellings) (*tripsis*, a rubbing) *geloto*: meter: gelotometer (an instrument for measuring the strength of jelly) (*meter*, measure) PREFIXED DISGUISED ROOT: *con*-: congeal (to change from a fluid to a solid state by, or as if by, cold; to make viscid or curled; coagulate; to make rigid, fixed, or immobile; as an intransitive verb, to become congealed; solidify) {congealment} (*con*-, with) TRADENAMES: JELLO, SURE-JEL CROSS REFERENCE: *firm, ster*

Element	From	Meaning	Examples
gel*	Greek *gelan*	to laugh	SIMPLE ROOT: gelasimus (hysterical laughter), gelastic (risible: causing laughter; laughable; funny; amusing; able or inclined to laugh; of or connected with laughter) LEADING ROOT COMPOUND: therap: gelototherapy (*therapeia*, healing) NOTE: Do not confuse this root with that of *gelatin*, coming from the Latin *gelare*, to congeal (see previous entry). NB: *Gelasian*, from Pope Gelasius (d. 496), is not in this family. CROSS REFERENCE: *rid/ris*
gen***	Greek *genus* (IE: *gen*, to produce)	race, birth, kind	ROOT NOTE: Though noted as Greek, the root was subsumed into Latin without change. The root is prefixed by both Greek and Latin elements. SIMPLE ROOT: gend: gender (in English grammar, the most familiar sets of genders are of three classes: masculine, feminine, neuter; a grammar book should be consulted on this subject) gene: gene, genesis (capitalized, book of the Bible; see below) gener: general (**Synonyms:** 1) common, ordinary, familiar; 2) universal, generic) generate, generation, generative, generator, generatrix (feminine of *generator*; in *mathematics*, a point, line, or plane whose motion generates a line, plane, figure, or solid) generi: generic (see synonyms at *general*, above; that which is not a trademark, as a *generic medicine*; in *biology*, of or characteristic of a genus) genero: generosity (**Synonyms:** munificence, magnaminity, nobleness) generous (**Synonyms:** unstinting, noble, plentiful) genet: genethliac (relating to birthdays or nativities; showing position and influence of stars at birth), genetic, genetics geni: genial (**Synonyms:** amiable, affable, obliging; another *genial* comes from Greek *genys*, chin; having to do with the chin) genic (same as *genetic*) genius (**Synonyms:** talent, gift, aptitude) genit: genital (pertaining to the reproduction or sexual organs; the term is also used in *psychoanalysis* to designate the third stage of infantile psychosexual development in which interest centers around the genital organs, the first stages being those of *anal, oral*; *genital*, therefore, designates the adult or final stage of psychosexual development in which conflicts have been resolved, libidinal drives regulated, and character structure integrated) genitival (pertaining to the genitive case in grammar), genitive (in *grammar*, a relational case, as in Latin, shown by grammatical inflection or by an analytical construction and typically expressing possession, source, or partitive concept; compare *possessive case* in English)

Element	From	Meaning	Examples
gen (cont'd)			genr: genre (a category of artistic, musical, or literary composition characterized by a particular style, form, or content) gens: gens (plural, *gentes*; originally, that belonging together by birth; in ancient Rome, a clan united by descent through the male line from a common ancestor) gent: genteel, gentile, gentility, gentle (see *Doublets* below) genu: genuine (see *Word Note* below), genus (plural *genera*) PREFIXED ROOTS: *anti-*: antigen (*anti-*, against) *con-*: congener, congenial, congenital (occurring from birth, as *a congenital disease*; **Synonyms: 1**) innate, inborn, inbred) (*con-*, with, together) *de-*: degeneracy, degenerate, degeneration, degenerative (*de-*, from) *dia-*: diagenesis (in *geology*, the physical and chemical changes occurring in sediments during and after the period of deposition up until the time of consolidation) (*dia-*, through) *en-*: engender (originally, to beget; to bring into being; bring about; cause; produce) (*en-*, in) *dys-*: dysgenic, dysgenics (plural in form, used with a singular verb; also called *cacogenics*) (*dys-*, bad, wrong, abnormal) *endo-*: endogenous, endogeny (*endo-*, within) *epi-*: (at, on, to, upon, over, besides) epigene (in *geology*, produced or formed on or near the earth's surface of the earth) epigenous (in *botany*, growing on the surface of the leaf or other plant part, especially on the upper surface, as some fungi) *exo-*: exogenous (in *biology*, of or relating to external factors, as food or light, that have an effect upon an organism) (*exo-*, outside, outer) *hypo-*: hypogenous (in *botany*, growing on the lower side of something, as spores on the underside of some fern leaves) (*hypo-*, under) *in-*: (in) ingenious (describing one showing originality; **Synonyms:** clever, cunning, shrewd) ingénue (an innocent, inexperienced, unworldly young woman) ingenuous (describing one who is naïve; **Synonyms:** naïve, artless, unsophisticated; **2**) frank, candid, outspoken) [*Ingenious* and *ingenuous* are often confused in both spelling and meaning.] *indi-*: indigene, indigenous (from *endo-*, within) *meta-*: metagenesis (in *biology*, reproduction in which there is alternation of an asexual with a sexual generation, as in many cnidarians) {metagenetic} (*meta-*, change) *palin-*: palingenesism (*palin-*, again) *para-*: paragenesis (*para-*, alongside) *pro-*: progenitive (capable of having offspring; reproductive), progenitor, progeny (*pro-*, before)

Element	From	Meaning	Examples
gen (cont'd)			LEADING ROOT COMPOUND: *genea*: log: genealogical, genealogy (a record or account of the ancestry and descent of a person) (*logy*, study of) *geno*: blast: genoblast (*blast*, shoot, bud, embryo) cid: genocide (*cide*, kill) typ: genotype (*type*, representative form, type, example) TRAILING ROOT COMPOUND: acro: acrogen (a plant, such as a fern or a moss, having a perennial stem with the growing point at the tip) {acrogenic, acrogenous} (*acro*, end, top) andro: androgen (a male sex hormone or synthetic substance that can give rise to masculine characteristics) androgenous (in *biology*, producing male offspring) (*andro*, man, male) anthropo: anthropogenesis (the study of man's origin and development) (*anthropo*, man) auto: autogenesis, autogenetic, autogenous (*auto*, self) bio: biogeny (*bio*, life) cosmo: cosmogeny (*cosmo*, world, universe) cryo: cryogenics (*cryo*, cold) cyto: cytogenics (*cyto*, cell) eu: eugenics (*eu*, good, well) hetero: heterogeneous (*hetero*, different, other) homo: homogeneity, homogeneous, homogeny (in biology, correspondence in form or structure, owing to a common origin) (*homo*, same) hydro: hydrogen (*hydro*, water) misc: miscegenation (marriage or sexual relations between a man and woman of different races) (*misc*, mixture) mono: **monogenesis**, monogenetic, monogenic, monogenism (the doctrine that all human beings are descended from a single pair of ancestors), monogeny (*mono*, one) nitro: nitrogenous (so named because niter resulted when it was sparked with oxygen in the presence of caustic potash) (*nitro*, niter) onto: ontogeny (*onto*, being, existence) oxy: oxygen (*oxy*, sharp) parthen: parthenogenesis (reproduction by the development of an unfertilized ovum, seed, or spore, as in certain insects, algae, etc.) (*partheno*, maiden) path: pathogen, pathogenesis, pathogenic (capable of causing disease, as *pathogenic bacteria*) (*patho*, disease, suffering) phot: photogenic (*photo*, light) phyl: phylogenic (*phylo*, tribe, race) BOUND COMPOUND: gentleman, gentlewoman LATIN PHRASE: *genius loci* (the guardian spirit of a place; the general atmosphere of a place)

Element	From	Meaning	Examples
gen (cont'd)			FRENCH: gendarme (formerly, a French cavalryman commanding a squad; in France, Belgium, etc., a soldier serving as an armed policeman; any policeman: a humorous usage); gendarmerie (*gendarmes* collectively) (from *gens*, people + *de-*, of + *arma*, arms) DOUBLETS: gentle:genteel PROPER NAME: Eugene (well-born) BOOK OF THE BIBLE: Genesis (the Hebrew account of the beginning of the universe, as well as the beginning of the Hebrew people, with the call of Abraham) NOTE: Partridge places *genuine* in this family; see both *Webster's New World* and *American Heritage* dictionaries for disparate accounts of the word's origin. INTERDISCIPLINARY: endogenous (in *biology*, growing or developing from or on the inside; in *biochemistry* and *physiology*, pertaining to the metabolism of nitrogenous elements of cells and tissues) monogenesis (in *biology*, the hypothetical descent of all living organisms from a single original organism or cell; in *zoology*, asexual reproduction, as by budding or spore formation) CROSS REFERENCE: *ethn, germ, gon, nat, phyl*
genu*	Latin *genu* (IE: *geneu*, knee; yields English knee)	knee	SIMPLE ROOT: geniculate (having a kneelike joint; bent sharply) LEADING ROOT COMPOUND: flect: genuflect (to bend the knee, as in reverence or worship; to act in a submissive and servile way) (*flectere*, to bend) NOTE: genuine (*American Heritage* places it in this category; *Webster's New World* places it under *gen*, birth) CROSS REFERENCE: *gon*
geo***	Greek *ge*	earth, land	SIMPLE ROOT: georgic [having to do with agriculture or husbandry; as a *noun*, a poem dealing with farming or rural life, from Virgil's *georgicum (carmen),* georgic (song)] PREFIXED ROOTS AND COMPOUNDS: apo-: apogee (away from the earth; the point farthest from the earth in the orbit of the moon or of a man-made satellite; opposed to *perigee*) (*apo-*, away) dia-: diageotropism (the tendency of the stems, branches, rhizomes, etc. of certain plants to grow in a direction horizontal to the surface of the earth) (*dia-*, through, across; *trop*, turn) epi-: epigeal (*epi-*, upon) hypo-: hypogeal (*hypo-*, under) peri-: perigee (literally, around the earth, the point nearest to the *earth* in the orbit of the moon or of a man-made satellite; opposed to *apogee*) (*peri-*, around) LEADING ROOT COMPOUND: ge: ode: geode (a globular stone having a cavity lined with inward growing crystal or layers of silica) (from *oid*, similar to) oid: geoid (the earth viewed as a hypothetical ellipsoid with the surface represented as a mean sea level) (*oid*, similar to)

Element	From	Meaning	Examples
geo (cont'd)			phyr: gephyrophobia (fear of walking on a bridge, river bank, or other structure near the water)

geo:
botany: geobotany (same as *phytogeography*) {geobotanical}
carp: geocarpic (fruit ripening beneath the ground, for example, the peanut) (*carp*, fruit)
centr: geocentric (measured or viewed as from the center of the earth; having or regarding the earth as a center)
chem: geochemistry (the branch of chemistry dealing with the chemical composition of the earth's crust and the chemical changes that occur there)
chron: (time)
geochronology (*logy*, study of)
geochronometry (*metry*, measurement of)
des: geodesic, geodesy {geodetic } (from *daiein*, to divide)
dynam: geodynamics (the study of the activity and forces inside the earth) (*dynam*, force)
gnos: geognosy (the branch of geology dealing with the composition of the earth and the distribution of its various strata and mineral deposits) (*gnos*, knowledge)
graph: geography (*graph*, write)
log: geology (*logy*, study of)
magnet: geomagnetic (pertaining to the magnetic properties of the earth)
mancy: geomancy (divination by random figures formed when a handful of earth is thrown on the ground, or as by lines drawn at random) (*mancy*, divination)
metr: geometric (of or according to geometry; characterized by straight lines, triangles, circles, or similar regular forms), geometry (originally, measurement of the earth) (*metr*, *measure*)
morph: (shape, form)
geomorphic (of, related to, or resembling the earth, its shape, or surface configuration)
geomorphology (*logy* study of)
phag: geophagy [also, *geophagia*; the eating of clay or earth, either as a psychotic symptom or to make up for lack of food, as in famine areas (do not confuse the pronunciation or meaning of this word with *geography*)] (*phagy*, eat)
phys: geophysics (the science that deals with the physics of the earth, including weather, winds, tides, earthquakes, volcanoes, etc. and their effect on the earth)
phyt: geophyte (a plant that grows in earth; especially, a perennial propagated by buds which live underground throughout the winter) (*phyton*, plant)
politic: geopolitics (the relationship between geography and politics)
pon: geoponic (of or pertaining to tillage or agriculture; agricultural), geoponics (construed as singular; the art or science of agriculture) (*pon*, to work, toil, labor)

Element	From	Meaning	Examples
geo (cont'd)			stat: geostationary (designating or of a satellite or spacecraft in an orbit above the equator, revolving at a rate of speed synchronous with that of the earth's rotation so that it always stays above the same place on the earth's surface; also called *geosynchronous*; literally, in time with the earth) (*stat*, stand) stroph: geostrophic (designating or of a force producing deflection as a result of the earth's rotation) (*stroph*, turn) syn: (with, together) geosynchronous (see *geostationary*, above) (*chron*, time) geosyncline (a very large, troughlike depression in the earth's surface containing masses of sedimentary and volcanic rocks) (*cline*, slope) tax: geotaxis (essentially the same as *geotropism*) (*taxis*, arrangement) tecton: geotectonic (having to do with the structure, distribution, shape, etc. of rock bodies, and with the structural disturbances and alterations of the earth's crust that produced them) (*tecton*, building) therm: geothermic (having to do with the heat of the earth's interior) (*therm*, heat) trop: geotropism (any positive, or negative, movement or growth of a plant or sessile animal in response to, or against, the force of gravity) {geotropic} (*trop*, turn) EMBEDDED ROOT COMPOUND: isogeotherm (an imaginary line or curved plane connecting points beneath the earth's surface that have the same average temperature) (*iso*, same; *therm*, heat) INTERDISCIPLINARY: epigeal (in *biology*, growing on or close to the ground; directed above the ground after germination: said of cotyledons; in *zoology*, living or developing on the exposed surface of the earth or in shallow water) hypogeal (in *botany*, growing or maturing underground, as peanuts, truffles, beets, turnips: said especially of cotyledons; in *zoology*, burrowing, living, or developing beneath the ground, as certain insect larvae, animals, etc.) NB: *Geoduck*, of Chinookan origin, and designating a very large edible clam, weighing over five pounds, is not in this family. CROSS REFERENCE: *chthon, edaph, terra, ped*
ger			See *ges* for *gerund, belligerent*.
ger,*** ges, gis	Latin *gerere*	to carry, do, bear	SIMPLE ROOT: ger: gerund (in English grammar, a verbal noun ending in *-ing* that has all the uses of the noun but retains certain syntactic characteristics of the verb, such as the ability to take an object or an adverbial modifier, e.g., *Playing* baseball is his passion), gerundive {gerundival} *ges*: gest: gest (or *geste*; a romantic story of daring adventures, especially a medieval tale in verse)

299

Element	From	Meaning	Examples
ger (cont'd)			**gesta:** gestate, gestation (the act or period of carrying young in the uterus from conception to birth; pregnancy; also, a development, as of a plan in the mind) **gesti:** gestic, gesticulate (to make or use gestures, especially with the hands and arms, as in adding nuances or force to one's speech, or as a substitute for speech), gesticulation **gestu:** gesture (a movement of the body to express or emphasize ideas, emotions, etc.) PREFIXED ROOT: *ger:* *con-:* congeries (a collection of things or parts massed together; heap; pile) (*con-*, with, together) *ges:* *con-:* congest, congested {congestion, congestive} (*con-*, with, together) *di-:* digest (**Synonyms:** abridgment, abstract, brief), digestion, digestive (from *dis-*, apart) *e-:* egest {egestion}, egesta (elided from *ex-*, out) *in-:* ingest (ingestion, ingestive}, ingesta (*in-*, in) *pro-:* progestation (*pro-*, before, forward) *sug-:* suggest (**Synonyms:** imply, hint, insinuate), suggestion, suggestive (*sug-* assimilates *sub-*, under) *gis:* *re-:* register (literally, to bring back; **Synonyms:** list, inventory, roster) (*re-*, back) DOUBLE PREFIXED ROOT: exaggerate (*ex-*, out; *ag-* assimilates *ad-*, to, toward) indigestion (*in-*, not; *di-* from *dis-*, apart) TRAILING ROOT COMPOUND: arm: armiger (originally, an armorbearer for a knight; squire) belli: belligerence, belligerent (**Synonyms:** bellicose, pugnacious, contentious) (*bellum*, war) DISGUISED ROOT: jest, jester FRENCH TERM: *beau geste* (plural *beaux gestes*; a fine or beautiful gesture; an act or offer that seems fine, noble, etc., but is empty) NB: Do not confuse this root with German *Gestalt*, form, shape, as in *gestalt psychology*. CROSS REFERENCE: *fer/lat, pher/phor*
ger*	Latin *geras* IE: *ger*, to grow old)	old age	SIMPLE ROOT: geratic, gerontal PREFIXED ROOT: *a-:* agerasia (an unusually youthful appearance in a person of advanced years) (*a-*, not) LEADING ROOT COMPOUND: *ger:* iatr: geriatrics (the branch of medicine that deals with the diseases and problems of old age; see *gerontology*, below) (*iatr*, heal, care) *gero:* com: gerocomia (also *gerocomy*; the care of old men; the hygiene of old age) (*com*, to care for)

300

Element	From	Meaning	Examples
ger (cont'd)			derm: geroderma (also *gerodermia*) (*derm*, skin)
			morph: geromorphism (*morph*, shape, form)
			geronto:
			cracy: gerontocracy (ruled by old men) (*cracy*, ruled by)
			logy: gerontology (the scientific study of the process of aging and of the problems of aged people; see *geriatrics*, above) (*logy*, study of)
			morph: gerontomorphosis (evolutionary development that produces extreme specialization and ultimately, extinction of a species or race, as with the dinosaurs) (*morph*, shape, form; *osis*, condition of)
			TRAILING ROOT COMPOUND:
			eri: erigeron (capitalized, a genus of herbs having flower heads resembling asters but with fewer and narrower involucral bracts; reason for name obscure) (*eri*, early)
			CROSS REFERENCE: *sen*
geran*	Greek *geranos*: crane	crane (bird)	SIMPLE ROOT: geranium (literally, small crane; sometimes called "crane's bill," because of the flower's resemblance to a crane's bill)
			TRAILING FRENCH ROOT COMPOUND:
			ped: pedigree (a list of ancestors; record of ancestry; descent; lineage; ancestry; see note under *ped*) (*ped*, foot)
			DISGUISED ROOT: crane (both the *bird* and the *machine*)
			NO CROSS REFERENCE
germ**	Latin *gignere*, to beget (IE: *gen-men*, sprig, germ, bud, sprout)	bud, shoot, fetus	SIMPLE ROOT: germ (the rudimentary form from which which a new organism is developed; any microsopic organism; origin; basis)
			german: german (closely related), germane (**Synonyms**: relevant, pertinent, apropos)
			germi: germinal, germinate {germination, germinative}
			LEADING ROOT COMPOUND:
			cid: germicide {germicidal} (*cide*, kill)
			CROSS REFERENCE: *blast, gen*
ges			See *ger* for *gestation, digest.*
giga*	Greek *gigas*	giant (extend to mean "one billion; very large)	SIMPLE ROOT: gigantean, gigantic (**Synonyms**: enormous, immense, colossal), gigantesque, gigantism
			LEADING ROOT COMPOUND:
			giga:
			cycl: gigacycle (same as *gigahertz*)
			hertz: gigahertz (a unit of frequency equal to one billion hertz) (*hertz*: a unit of frequency equal to one cycle per second; named after Heinrich Hertz, 1857-1894; German physicist]
			ton: gigaton (the explosive force of a billion tons of TNT)
			giganto:
			machy: gigantomachy (in *Greek mythology*, the struggle between the giants and the gods; now, any war between giants or superpowers)
			ENGLISH: giant (in *Greek mythology,* any of a race of huge beings of human form who war with the gods; a person or thing of great size, strength, intellect, etc.)
			CROSS REFERENCE: *mega, super-*

301

Element	From	Meaning	Examples
gis			See *ger* for *register*.
glac**	Latin *glacer*: to freeze (IE: *gel*, to freeze)	ice	SIMPLE ROOT: glace: glacé (having a smooth, glossy surface, as certain leathers or silks; candied or glazed, as fruits) glaci: glacial {glacialist}, glaciate {glaciation}, glacier, glacis [from Old French *glacier*, to slip (as on ice); a gradual slope; an embankment sloping gradually up to a fortification, so as to expose attackers to defending gunfire) LEADING ROOT COMPOUND: logy: glaciology (*logy*, study of) DISGUISED ROOT: gelid (extremely cold; frozen) glance (**Synonyms:** flash, gleam, sparkle) NO CROSS REFERENCE
glad*	Latin *gladius* (IE: *kel*, to strike)	sword	ROOT NOTE: This root is of Celtic origin and is akin to Welsh *cleddyl*, sword; it is also related to Latin *clades*, destruction; Greek *klados*, sprout, and Greek *klan*, to break; also to English *halt*. SIMPLE ROOT: gladiate (sword-shaped), gladiator, gladiolus [both the flower (from the shape of its leaves) and the bone, the *corpus sterni*, also from its shape] GERMAN CALQUE OF *GLADIOLUS* (the flower): *Schwertlilie*: sword-lily CROSS REFERENCE: *ens, xiph*
gland**	Latin *gland* (IE: *gwel*, oak, acorn)	an acorn (in the shape of)	ROOT NOTE: Root is so called from the gland being an aggregation of cells, having the texture of and shape of an *acorn*. SIMPLE ROOT: gland, glandular, glandule glanders (a disease of horses, characterized by swollen glands) glans (*glans penis*, the head or tip of the penis; *glans clitoris*, the small mass of erectile tissue at the tip of the clitoris) CROSS REFERENCE: *aden, balano*
glau*	Latin *glaucus*: gleaming; gray; originally, Greek *glaukos*	silvery gray	SIMPLE ROOT: glaucescent, glauconite (a greenish silicate of iron and potassium, found in greensand), glaucous (in *biology*, covered with a pale greenish bloom that can be rubbed off, as grapes, plums, cabbage leaves, etc.), glaucus LEADING ROOT COMPOUND: *glauc(os)*: oma: glaucoma {glaucomatous} (*oma*, mass, tumor) ur: glaucosuria [same as *indicanuria*: the presence in the urine of indicadin (a glycocide from plants that yield indigo) in excessive quantity] (*ur*, urine) CHEMICAL: glaucodot (symbol: CoFe; literally, silver-giver) CROSS REFERENCE: *arg, polio*
glob,*** **glom**	Latin *globus*; *glomus*: ball (IE: *glemb*, to make round)	ball, sphere	ROOT NOTE: The two roots are listed together, inasmuch as they are derived ultimately from the same Indo-European source. SIMPLE ROOT: globe *glob*: globa: global, globalism, globalize, globate (round like a ball) globo: globose (also, *globous*; globoid or globular)

Element	From	Meaning	Examples
glob (cont'd)			globu: globular, globule (a small spherical body), globulin, globulism, globulose, globulus (plural, *globuli*), globus *glom*: glomera: glomerate (formed into a rounded mass or ball; clustered), glomeration glomeru: glomerulate (grouped in small, dense clusters), glomerule (plural, *glomeruli*), glomerulus (plural, *glomeruli*) PREFIXED ROOT: *glob*: con-: conglobate (also, *conglobe*; to form or collect into a ball or rounded mass) (*con-*, with) *glom*: ag-: agglomerate (to collect or gather into a cluster or mass), agglomeration (*ag-* assimilates *ad-*, to) con-: conglomerate (in *geology*, made up of rock fragments or pebbles cemented together into a single mass; also, a large corporation formed by the merger or acquisition of a number of companies in unrelated, widely diversified industries), conglomeration (*con-*, with) LEADING ROOT COMPOUND: oid: globoid (*oid*, similar to) DISGUISED ROOT: clay, clip, clot, cloud, clue, glebe PLACENAME: Globe, Arizona CROSS REFERENCE: *spher*
gloss,*** **glot**	Greek *glossa*: tongue; *glochis*, point (IE: *glogh*, thorn, point)	tongue, language	SIMPLE ROOT: *glos*: gloss: gloss (words of explanation inserted between the lines of a text; another *gloss* is from Scandinavian *glosa*, to gleam, as in *glass*) glossa: glossa, glossal, glossary (a list of difficult, technical, or foreign terms with definitions or translations, glossator *glot*: glotta: glottal (also *glottic*: of or produced in or at the glottis, as a glottal sound) glotti: glottic (same as *glottal*), glottis (the opening between the vocal cords in the larynx) PREFIXED ROOT: *gloss*: hypo-: hypoglossal (*hypo-*, under) *glott*: epi-: epiglottis {epiglottal, or *epiglottic*} (*epi-*, upon) pro-: proglottid (any of the segmentlike divisions of a tapeworm's body) (*pro-*, forward) LEADING ROOT COMPOUND: *gloss*: graph: glossograph (a difficult word requiring explanation), glossographer, glossography (*graph*, write) lal: glossolalia (the speaking in tongues, a practice in certain religions) (*lal*, babble) *glott*: itis: glottitis (*itis*, inflammation of)

Element	From	Meaning	Examples
gloss (cont'd)			TRAILING ROOT COMPOUND: *gloss*: iso: isogloss (in *linguistics*, a line of demarcation between regions differing in a particular feature of language, as on a point of pronunciation, vocabulary, etc.) (*iso*, equal) tricho: trichoglossia (hairy condition of the tongue) (*trichos*, hair) *glot*: di: diglot (bilingual; also, a bilingual edition of a book) (*di*, two) mono: monoglot (speaking or writing only one language; as a noun, a monoglot person) (*mono*, one) poly: polyglot (one who speaks many languages) (*poly*, many) DISGUISED ROOT: glochidium (a diminutive of *glochis*, point) PLACENAME: Glossa, Greece INTERDISCIPLINARY: glochidium (in *botany*, a barbed hair or bristle, as on certain cacti or on the spore masses of ferns; in *zoology*, the parasitic larval stage of freshwater mussels which infests the gills, etc. of many fishes) CROSS REFERENCE: *lingu*
glut*	Latin *gluten* (IE: *glei*, to stick together)	glue	SIMPLE ROOT: glute: gluten, glutenin, glutenous gluti: glutin, glutinous PREFIXED ROOT: ag-: agglutinate, agglutination, agglutinin, agglutinogen (*ag*- assimilates *ad*-, to) con-: conglutinant (in *medicine*, promoting healing or uniting, as the edges of a wound), conglutinate (glued or stuck together; adhering) (*con*-, together) de-: deglutinate (to extract gluten from wheat, etc.) (*de*-, from) NB: *Glutitis*, from *gloutos*, buttock + *itis*, inflammation of, is not in this family. CROSS REFERENCE: *coll, gluc, gly*
glyp**	Greek *glyphein* (IE: *gleubh*, to slice)	to carve	SIMPLE ROOT: glyph (a pictograph or other symbolic character or sign, especially when cut into a surface or carved in relief; in *architecture*, a vertical channel or groove) {glyphic} glyptic (having to do with carving or engraving, especially on gems), glyptics PREFIXED ROOT: ana-: anaglyph (an ornament carved in low relief) (*ana*-, up) LEADING ROOT COMPOUND: *glypho*: graph: glyphography (*graph*, write) *glypt*: odont: glyptodont (an extinct family of edentate mammals, so called because of their fluted teeth) (*odont*, tooth) *glypto*: graph: glyptograph {glyptography} (*graph*, write)

Element	From	Meaning	Examples
glyp (cont'd)			TRAILING ROOT COMPOUND: hiero: hieroglyphics (literally, sacred carvings) (*hiero*, sacred) soleno: solenoglyph (any poisonous snake of the viper family with hollow, paired, erectile fangs) (*solen*, a channel, in reference to the snake's tubular fangs) tri: triglyph (an architectural term) (*tri*, three) NO CROSS REFERENCE
gno***	Greek *gignoskein* (IE: *gen, gno,* to know, apprehend)	to know	SIMPLE ROOT: gnom: gnome (may be related to the word meaning dwarf, inasmuch as it was felt that *gnomes* had an occult knowledge of the earth, and were so called by Paracelsus; *gnome* can also refer to a wise, pithy saying; maxim; aphorism), gnomic gnomon (can refer either to a sundial, or the part of a parallelogram remaining after a similar, smaller parallelogram has been taken away from one of its corners) gnos: gnosis, gnostic (a believer in Gnosticism, a system of belief that combines ideas derived from Greek philosophy, Oriental mysticism, and ultimately, Christianity, and stressing salvation through *gnosis*, or positive, intuitive knowledge in spiritual matters, which the Gnostics claimed to have) PREFIXED ROOT: a-: agnostic (see synonyms at *infidel*, under *fid*) (*a-*, not) dia-: diagnose, diagnosis, diagnostic (*dia-*, through) pro-: prognosis, prognostic, prognosticate (*pro-*, before) FRENCH: connoisseur (literally, a judge; one well versed; a person who has expert knowledge and keen discrimination in some field, especially in the fine arts or in matters of taste) LEADING ROOT COMPOUND: *gnomo*: log: gnomologia (a judgment; hence, a maxim or an aphorism), gnomologic *gnosio*: logy: gnosiology (the theory of knowledge) (*logy*, the study of) TRAILING ROOT COMPOUND: *gnom*: physi: physiognomy (the art or science of judging one from his/her physical appearance; the word is pronounced with or without the *g*) *gnos*: geo: geognosy (the branch of geology dealing with the composition of the earth and the distribution of its various strata and mineral deposits) (*geo*, earth) CROSS REFERENCE: *cogn, sci*
gon***	Greek *gonos*: offspring (IE: *gen,* to produce)	seed, semen	ROOT NOTE: This root is extended to include begetting or producing, and denoting mother cell or structure. SIMPLE ROOT: gona: gonad (the primary sex gland of either sex: ovary, testis), gonadal, gonadial goni: gonite, gonidium {gonidial}

Element	From	Meaning	Examples
gon (cont'd)			PREFIXED ROOT: *amphi*-: amphigony (sexual reproduction) (*amphi-*, around, both) *epi*-: epigone (a descendant less gifted than his/her ancestors, or any inferior follower or imitator) (*epi-*, upon, beyond) *hyper*-: hypergonadism (excessive secretion of the sex glands) (*hyper-*, more, beyond) LEADING ROOT COMPOUND: *gon*: acrat: gonacratia (or *spermatorrhea*) (*acratia*, incontinence) angi: gonangioectomy (*angio*, vessel + *ectomy*, surgical removal; thus, *vasectomy*) *gonad*: ectom: gonadectomy (surgical removal of an ovary or a testis) (*ectom*, to cut out) *gono*: rrh: gonorrhea (from *rhein*, to flow) TRAILING ROOT COMPOUND: arch: archegonium (the flask-shaped female reproductive organ in mosses, ferns, and the like) (*archos*, first) carp: carpogonium (the female reproductive organ in red algae) (*carpo*, fruit, seeds) cosmo: cosmogony (the origin or generation of the universe) (*cosmos*, universe) oo: oogonium (the female reproductive organ in algae and fungi) (*oo*, egg) sporo: sporogonium, sporogony (*sporo*, spore) tele: telegony (the supposed transmission of characters of one sire to offspring subsequently born to other sires by the same female) (*tele*, far off) theo: theogony (the origin or genealogy of the gods, as told in the myths) (*theo*, God, gods) MESHED LEADING ROOT COMPOUND: gonaduct (*gonad* + *duct*) CROSS REFERENCE: *gen, semin, spore, sperm*
gon***	Greek *gonia* (IE *geneu*, knee)	angle, corner	SIMPLE ROOT: gonion (the point where the bottom of the jaw curves upward toward the ear; plural, *gonia*) PREFIXED ROOT: a-: agonic (not forming an angle), agonic line (an imaginary line on the earth's surface along which true north and magnetic north are identical, and a compass needle makes no angle with the meridian) (*a-*, not) *dia*-: diagonal (literally, across or through from angle to angle; connecting two nonadjacent angles or vertices of a polygon or polyhedron, as a straight line) (*dia-*, through) LEADING ROOT COMPOUND: meter: goniometer {goniometry} (*metry*, measurement of) scop: gonioscopy (*scope*, look) TRAILING ROOT COMPOUND: ambly: amblygonite (*amblys*, dull) hexa: hexagon (*hexa*, six)

Element	From	Meaning	Examples
gon (cont'd)			octa: octagonal (*oct*, eight) ortho: orthogonal (*ortho*, straight) penta: pentagon (*penta*, five) poly: polygon (*poly*, many) tri: trigonometry (*tri*, three) NO CROSS REFERENCE
gov,** **guber**	Latin *gubernare*	to govern, guide	SIMPLE ROOT: *gov*: govern (**Synonyms**: rule, administer), governor, government *guber*: gubernatorial CROSS REFERENCE: *crac/crat*
grad,*** **gress**	Latin *gradus* (IE: *ghredh*, to strike)	step, degree	SIMPLE ROOT: *grad*: grada: gradate, gradation (in *geology*, the process of wearing away high areas of land by erosion and building up of low areas by deposition; in *linguistics*, ablaut: in full, *vowel gradation*) grade: grade, grader gradi: gradient, gradine (also, *gradin*; one of a series of steps or seats arranged in tiers; a shelf at the back of an altar, as for candlesticks) gradu: gradual, gradualism, graduate, graduation, gradus *gress*: gressorial (adapted for walking, as the feet of certain birds) PREFIXED ROOT: *grad*: *ag-*: aggrade (to build up a the level or slope of a river bed, valley, etc. by the deposit of sediment) {aggradation} (*ag-* assimilates *ad-*, to) *de-*: (down) degradation (in *geology*, the lowering of land surfaces by erosion) degrade (**Synonyms**: abase, debase, humble) degraded (disgraced, debased, depraved, etc.) degrading (that degrades; debasing) *inter-*: intergrade (to pass into another form or kind by a series of intermediate grades) (*inter-*, between) *retro-*: retrograde (*retro-*, backward) *gress*: *ag-*: aggress (to start a quarrel or be the first to attack), aggressive (**Synonyms**: militant, assertive, pushing), aggressor (a person, nation, etc. that is guilty of aggression, or makes the first unprovoked attack) (*ag-* assimilates *ad-*, to) *con-*: congress {congressional} (*con-*, with, together) *de-*: degression {degressive} (*de-*, down) *di-*: digress (**Synonyms**: deviate, swerve, veer), digression {digressive} (from *dis-*, apart, away) *e-*: egress (in *astronomy*, the emergence of a celestial body from eclipse or occultation) (*e-* assimilates *ex-*, out) *in-*: ingress (also, *ingression*), ingressive (in *grammar*, same as *inceptive*) (*in-*, into)

Element	From	Meaning	Examples
grad (cont'd)			*pro*-: progress, **progression**, progressive, progressivism (*pro*-, forward) *re*-: regress {regressor}, regression, regressive (*re*-, back) *retro*-: retrogress, retrogression (*retro*-, backward) *trans*-: transgress (to go beyond or over a limit or boundary; to break a law or commandment) (*trans*-, across) TRAILING ROOT COMPOUND: *centi*: centigrade (*cent*, 100) *planti*: plantigrade (walking on the whole foot, as a human or bear) (*plant*, sole of foot) *salti*: saltigrade (adapted for proceeding by leaping: said of certain insects and spiders) (*salti*, leap) PREFIXED DISGUISED ROOT: *de*-: degree (from *degrade*; literally, a step down) (*de*-, down) INTERDISCIPLINARY: **gradient** (in *biology*, a gradation in rate of growth, metabolism, etc. in an organism, growing part, or developing embryo; in *mathematics*, a vector pointing in the direction of the most rapid increase of a function and having coordinates that are the partial derivatives of the functions; in *physics*, the rate of change of a physical quantity, as temperature or pressure, with distance) **progression** (in *mathematics*, a sequence of numbers, each of which is obtained from its predecessor by the same rule; in *music*, the movement forward from one tone or chord to another; a succession of tones or chords) CROSS REFERENCE: *amb, cede/ceed/cess, it, vad/va*
gram,*** **graph**	Greek *gramma*: letter, drawing; *graphein*: to write (IE: *gerebh*, to carve)	to write	SIMPLE ROOT: *gram*: gram, grammar, grammarian, grammatical *graph*: grapheme, graphemics, graphic (also, *graphical*), graphics, graphite (from its use as writing material) PREFIXED ROOT: *gram*: *ana*-: anagram (see note under *ana*-) (*ana*-, again) *dia*-: diagram (*dia*-, across, through) *dia*-: epigram (**Synonyms**: maxim, adage, aphorism), epigrammatic (*epi*-, upon) *pro*-: program (*pro*-, forward) *tele*-: telegram (*tele*-, afar) *graph*: *a*-: agapha (saying ascribed to Jesus but not found in the Gospels), agraphia (the partial or total loss of the ability to write) (*a*-, not) *dys*-: dysgraphia (*dys*-, wrong, bad) *epi*-: epigraph, epigraphy (inscriptions collectively; the study that deals with deciphering, interpreting, and classifying inscriptions, especially ancient inscriptions) (*epi*-, upon) *para*-: paragraph (originally, a mark "written alongside" in the margin to indicate that a new subject is introduced) (*para*-, alongside)

Element	From	Meaning	Examples
gram (cont'd)			LEADING ROOT COMPOUND: *gramo*: phil: gramophile (a lover and collector of phonograph records) (*phil*, love of) phon: Gramophone (literally, written sound; a tradename for an early name for phonograph player) (*phone*, sound) *grapho:* logy: graphology (the study of handwriting, especially as a clue to character, aptitudes, etc.) {graphologist} (*logy*, study of) TRAILING ROOT COMPOUND: *gram*: cardio: cardiogram (*card*, heart) chrono: chronogram (an inscription in which letters, made more prominent, express a date in Roman numerals, e.g., MerCy MiXed with LoVe In hIm--MCMXLVII = 1947) (*chrono*, time) electro: electrocardiogram (ECG, or EKG, where *K* represents the initial letter of *cardio* in Greek) (*kardia*, heart) mammo: mammogram (*mammo*, breast) mono: monogram (*mono*, one) pan: pangram (a sentence that uses every letter of the alphabet, ideally only once, e.g., The quick brown fox jumps over the lazy dog) (*pan*, all) spectro: spectrogram (*spectro*, view) thermo: thermogram (*therm*, heat) *graph(y)*: allo: allograph (*allo*, other) auto: autobiography, autograph, autography (*auto*, self) bio: biography (*bio*, life) caco: cacography (*caco*, bad, wrong) calli: calligraphy (*calli*, beautiful) choreo: choreography (*choreo*, dance) chrono: chronograph (*chrono*, time) crypto: cryptograph (*crypto*, hidden) geo: geography (*geo*, earth) hetero: heterography (spelling that differs from current standard usage; spelling, as in modern English, in which the same letter does not always represent the same sound) (*hetero*, other, different) holo: holograph (*holo*, whole, entire) hypso: hypsography (*hypso*, height, high) litho: lithograph (*litho*, stone) mono: monograph (*mono*, one) phono: phonograph (*phono*, sound) photo: photograph (*photo*, light) tele: telegraph (*tele*, afar) DISGUISED ROOT: graffito (plural, *graffiti*; in *archaeology*, an ancient drawing or writing scratched on a wall or other surface)

309

Element	From	Meaning	Examples
gram (cont'd)			graft (with unhistoric -*t*, for earlier *graff*; from Middle English *graffe*, a pencil; from Greek *grapheion*, stylus, from the resemblance of the scion to a *pointed pencil*, a *writing* instrument)
			DISGUISED TRAILING ROOT COMPOUND:
			allo: allograft (*allo*, other)
			auto: autograft (tissue transplanted from one place to another on the same body) (*auto*, self)
			hetero: heterograft (same as *xenograph*: a graft of skin, bone, etc. from an individual of another species; compare *allograph*, *autograph*) (*hetero*, different)
			homo: homograft (*homo*, same)
			zeno: zenograft (*zeno*, stranger)
			CROSS REFERENCE: *scrib/script*
gramin*	Greek *gramen* (IE: *ghro*, to grow)	grass	SIMPLE ROOT:
			gramina: graminaceous, Graminales (an order of monocotyledonous plants including certain grasses and sedges)
			gramine: gramine, gramineous
			LEADING ROOT COMPOUND:
			gramini:
			fer: graminiferous (*ferre*, to bear)
			vor: graminivorous (feeding on grass; grass-eating) (*vor*, eat)
			gramino:
			logy: graminology (*logy*, study of)
			NO CROSS REFERENCE
gran**	Latin *granire*: to grain (IE: *ger*, to become ripe; yields English grain)	grain	SIMPLE ROOT:
			grana: granadilla (containing seeds; the edible fruit of certain passionflowers), granary (a building for storing grain; see *Doublets* below), grange
			grani: granita, granite
			granu: granular, granulate, granulation, granule, granulite {granulitic}, granulose
			LEADING ROOT COMPOUND:
			grani:
			vor: granivorous (feeding on grain and seeds) (*vor*, eat)
			granul:
			oma: granuloma (a firm, tumorlike granulation formed as a reaction to chronic inflammation, as from foreign bodies, bacteria, etc.) (*oma*, mass)
			granulo:
			cyt: granulocyte (*cyt*, cell)
			TRAILING ROOT COMPOUND:
			pom: pomegranate (literally, grainy apple, or an apple in which the edible portion consists of pleasantly acid flesh developed from the outer seed coat) (*pome*, apple)
			DISGUISED ROOT:
			garner (one who gathers grain; see *Doublets* below)
			garnet (from *pomegranate*, from the resemblance in color)
			gravy [originally, dish seasoned with grains (of spice)]
			grenade [originally from *pomegranate* (see previous subentry), from its shape; a small bomb detonated by a fuse and thrown by hand or fired from a rifle], grenadier

Element	From	Meaning	Examples
gran (cont'd)			TRAILING DISGUISED ROOT COMPOUND: fili: filigree (a variation of earlier *filigrain*; any delicate, lace-like ornamental work of intertwined wire of gold, silver, etc.) (*filum*, thread) PREFIXED ANGLO-FRENCH ROOT: *en*-: engrain (the same as *ingrain*) (*en*-, in) *in*-: ingrain, ingrained (*in*-, in) DOUBLETS: garner:granary GERMAN COMPOUND: einkorn (one-seeded wheat) MEDICAL TERM: *granulatio* (a granule, or granular mass) LATIN PHRASE: *cum grano salis* [(to be taken) with a grain of salt; with allowance or reservation] TRADENAME: Granolith (literally, granulated stone; used for flooring, pavement) NO CROSS REFERENCE
grand**	Latin *grandis* (IE: *gwrendh,* to swell up)	great, large	SIMPLE ROOT: grand (**Synonyms:** grandiose, magnificent, imposing) grandee, grandeur, grandiose (see synonyms at *grand*) PREFIXED ROOT: *ag*-: aggrandize (*ag*- assimilates *ad*-, to) LEADING ROOT COMPOUND: flor: grandiflora (bearing large flowers) (*flora*, flower) loqu: grandiloquent (**Synonyms:** bombastic, flowery, turgid) (*loqui*, speak) FRENCH TERMS: *grand monde* [literally, great world (fashionable society)] *grand prix* [literally, great prize (first prize, highest award in a competition)] ITALIAN MUSIC TERM: *grandioso* UNBOUNDED COMPOUNDS: grand jury grand mal (opposed to *petit mal*) ORGAN STOP: *grand jeu* (full play, full organ: diapason) CROSS REFERENCE: *macro, magni, mega*
graph			See *gram.*
grat***	Latin *gratus* IE: *gwer,* to lift up the voice)	pleasing	SIMPLE ROOT: grate: grateful grati: gratis (without charge or fee; free), gratitude gratu: gratuitous, gratuity (**Synonyms:** present, gift, donation) PREFIXED ROOT: *con*-: congratulate (to express one's pleasure), congratulation, congratulatory (from *com*-, together) *in*-: (note difference in meanings of prefix in the following words) ingratiate (from archaic *ingrate*) (*in*-, in) ingratitude (*in*-, not) LEADING ROOT COMPOUND: fic: gratification (from *facere*, to do, make) fy: gratify (to give pleasure or satisfaction; to give in to; indulge; humor) (from *facere*, to do, make)

Element	From	Meaning	Examples
grat (cont'd)			DISGUISED ROOT: grace (**Synonyms**: comeliness, kindness, condescension) gracile (gracefully slender; graceful), gracilis, graciosity, gracioso, gracious PREFIXED DISGUISED ROOT: a-: agree (**Synonyms**: conform, accord, harmonize) (from *ad-*, to) *dis*-: disgrace (public dishonor, ignominy, disrepute) {disgraceful} (*dis-*, not) LATIN PHRASES: *exempli gratia* (abbreviated *e.g.*, and meaning "Let me give you an example, please"; not to be confused with *i.e.*, abbreviation for *id est*, that is) *persona grata* (a person who is acceptable or welcome) *persona non grata* (an unwelcome person) LATIN LAW TERM: *de gratia* (by grace or favor) ITALIAN MUSIC TERMS: *con grazia* SPANISH: *gracias* (Thank you) GREEK MYTHOLOGY: Graces: the three sister goddesses who have control over pleasure, charm, and beauty in human life and in nature: Aglaia, Euphrosyne, and Thalia GAELIC AND IRISH COGNATE: bard (one who praised kings or chieftains) NO CROSS REFERENCE
grav***	Latin *gravis* (IE: *gwer*, heavy)	heavy	SIMPLE ROOT: grava: gravamen (a grievance; in *law*, the essential part of a complaint or accusation) grave: grave (*adjective*; heavy, weighty, as *grave* doubts, *grave* concern; **Synonyms**: serious, solemn, sedate) [the *noun* (place of burial) and the *verb* (to clean barnacles) come from different sources; see below for *grave* as a music term] gravid: gravid (pregnant, the idea being "heavy" with child) gravit: gravitate, gravitation, gravitative, graviton, gravity LEADING ROOT COMPOUND: meter: gravimeter (*meter*, measure) metr: gravimetric, gravimetry (*metry*, measurement of) PREFIXED ROOT: ag-: aggravate (see *Doublets* below; **Synonyms**: intensify, heighten, enhance), aggravated, aggravation (*ag-* assimilates *ad-*, to) DISGUISED ROOT: grief, grieve, grievance, grievous PREFIXED DISGUISED ROOT: ag-: aggrieve (see *Doublets* below; **Synonyms**: abuse, wrong, oppress), aggrieved (wronged; also, injured in one's legal rights) (*ag-* assimilates *ad-*, to, toward) DOUBLETS: aggrieve:aggravate MUSIC TERM: grave (pronounced grah VAE; slow and with solemnity: a direction to the performer) NB: *Margrave* and *margravate* are not in this family; neither is *gravel*. CROSS REFERENCE: *bary, liber, pend, ponder*

Element	From	Meaning	Examples
greg***	Latin *grex* (IE: *ger-*, to collect)	flock, herd	SIMPLE ROOT: gregarious (living in herds or flocks; in *botany*, growing in clusters) PREFIXED ROOT: *ag-*: aggregate (**Synonyms:** sum, amount, total), aggregation, aggregative (*ag-* assimilates *ad-*, to) *con-*: congregant, congregate (to gather into a mass or crowd; collect; assemble), congregation, congregational, congregationalism (*com-*, together) *e-*: egregious (originally, to stand out from the herd for favorable qualities; now pejorated to mean "to stand out for unfavorable qualities," as an *egregious error*) (*e-* elides *ex-*, out) *se-*: segregate (as an adjective, separate, set apart, segregated; as a verb, to separate from the main mass), segregated, segregation (*se-*, apart, away) DOUBLE PREFIXED ROOT: desegregate, desegregation (*de-*, reversal; *se-*, apart, away) PROTESTANT RELIGIOUS DENOMINATION: Congregationalism CROSS REFERENCE: *agora*
gros**	Latin *grossus,* thick	large, coarse	SIMPLE ROOT: gros (a thick fabric), gross PREFIXED ROOT: *en-*: engross (originally, to acquire in large quantity; to express formally in legal form; to take the entire attention of; thus, occupy wholly), engrossing (*en-*, in) LEADING ROOT COMPOUND: beak: grosbeak (a type of passerine bird with a thick, strong, conical bill, or beak) grain: grosgrain (see *grogram*, below) ELIDED LEADING ROOT COMPOUND: gram: grogram (formerly, a coarse fabric) (*gram*, grain) DISGUISED ROOT: grocer (originally, one who bought in large quantities), grocery DOUBLETS: grosgrain:grogram GERMAN COIN: *groschen* PLACENAMES: Grosse Pointe, Michigan; Grosse Tete, Louisiana (Big Head) CROSS REFERENCE: *magn, mega*
gru*	Latin *gruere,* to ruin (IE: *ghreu,* to collapse, topple)	to collapse, topple	PREFIXED ROOT: *con-*: congruence, congruent, congruity, congruous (*con-*, with, together) DOUBLE PREFIXED ROOT: incongruent, incongruity, incongruous (*in-*, not; *con-*, with) INTERDISCIPLINARY: congruence [also *congruency*; in *geometry*, the property of a plane or solid figure that makes it able to coincide with another plane or solid figure after a rigid transformation; in *mathematics*, the relation between two integers each of which, when divided by a third (called the *modulus*), leaves the same remainder] NO CROSS REFERENCE
guber			See *gov* for *gubernatorial*.

313

Element	From	Meaning	Examples
guerr*	Germanic *werra*, confusion, strife; yields Germanic war, warrior, warfare)	war	SPANISH: *guerrilla* FRENCH PHRASES: *c'est la guerre* (It's the war, a famous phrase during World War I, and later came into use in Great Britain and Europe during World War II to excuse any and every lapse or insufficiency or deficiency) *Croix de Guerre* (cross of war; a French military decoration for bravery in action; in World War II, the *Croix de Guerre* was awarded to those American soldiers who helped liberate France from the Nazis) *nom de guerre* (war name; formerly, a pseudonym assumed by a French soldier upon entering military service; any fictitious name taken for a particular reason) CROSS REFERENCE: *belli*
gust**	Latin *gustus* (IE: *geus*, to enjoy, taste)	taste	SIMPLE ROOT: gust (enjoyment or appreciation; in Scottish, to taste or relish), gustation, gustatory (also, *gustative*) PREFIXED ROOT: *de-*: dégustation (the act of sampling a wide variety of foods, wines, etc.; an assortment, as of foods or wines, provided for sampling) (*de-*, intensive) *dis-*: disgust {disgusting}, disgustful (*dis-*, opposite of) FRENCH WORDS: *dégoût* (distaste, loathing, disgust) *dégoûté* (feminine, *dégoûtée*; fastidious, squeamish; as a *noun*, a fastidious person) ragout (also spelled *ragoût*; literally, to revive the appetite of; a highly seasoned stew of meat and vegetables) {ragouted, ragouting} ITALIAN AND SPANISH: *gusto* LATIN PHRASE: *de gustibus non disputandum* (est) [(there is) no disputing about tastes] ENGLISH COGNATES: choice (**Synonyms:** option, alternative, preference) choose (**Synonyms:** select, elect, pick) CROSS REFERENCE *sap*
gutt*	Latin *gutta*	drop	SIMPLE ROOT: gutta, guttate, guttation, guttatim, gutter LEADING ROOT COMPOUND: fer: guttiferous (bearing or making drops) (*ferre*, to bear) form: guttiform DISGUISED ROOT: gout (a form of arthritis; originally attributed to a discharge of drops of humors) TERM USED IN PRESCRIPTION WRITING: guttatim (used drop by drop) HERALDRY TERMS: *guttée d'eau; guttée de larmes; guttée de poix* INTERDISCIPLINARY: gutta (in *architecture*, any of a series of small, droplike ornaments on a Doric entablature; in *pharmacy*, a liquid drop) NB: *Guttural* is derived from *guttur*, throat. NO CROSS REFERENCE

Element	From	Meaning	Examples
gymn**	Greek *gymnos* (IE: *nogw*, naked)	nude, naked	SIMPLE ROOT: gymnasial, gymnasiast (a student in a European Gymnasium: in Germany and in some other European countries, a secondary school for students preparing to enter a university; the curriculum stresses the classics, history, mathematics, and modern languages) gymnasium (originally, a place to exercise in the nude), gymnast, gymnastic, gymnastics LEADING ROOT COMPOUND: *gymnasi*: arch: gymnasiarch (in ancient Greece, an official who supervised athletic games, contests, and schools) (*arch*, first) *gymno*: carp: gymnocarpous (*carp*, fruit) gyn: gymnogynous (having a naked ovary) (*gyn*, woman; also, female organs, especially pistils) phob: gymnophobia (morbid aversion to the sight of the naked body) (*phobia*, fear of) scop: gymnoscopic (inclined to, or concerned with, viewing the naked body) (*scope*, view) soph: gymnosophist (a member of an ancient Hindu sect of ascetics who wore little or no clothing) (*sophos*, clever, wise) sperm: gymnosperm (*sperm*, seed, germ) CROSS REFERENCE: *nud*
gyn**	Greek *gyne* (IE: *gwena*, queen, woman)	woman	ROOT NOTE: This root can also mean female, womanish, female reproductive organs (ovaries), pistil (the ovule-bearing organ of a seed plant). SIMPLE ROOT: gynaeceum, gynaeconitis (the part of an Eastern Orthodox church reserved for women), gynesics, gynic PREFIXED ROOT: *epi*-: epigynous, epigyny (designating petals, sepals, and stamens that are attached to the top of the ovary; opposed to *hypogynous*) (*epi*-, upon) *hypo*-: hypogynous (growing attached to the receptacle, below and free from the pistil: said of the parts of some flowers; opposed to *epigynous*) (*hypo*-, under) *peri*-: perigynous (in *botany*, having the sepals, petals, and stamens attached to the rim of a cup or tube which surrounds the ovary but is not attached to it, as in the rose, spirea, etc.) (*peri*-, around) LEADING ROOT COMPOUND: *gyn*: andro: (man) gynandromorph (an abnormal organism having both male and female characteristics) (*morph*, shape, form) gynandrous (in *botany*, having the stamen, or male organ, and the pistil, or female organ, united in one column, as in the orchids) archy: gynarchy (government by a woman or women) (*archy*, government by)

Element	From	Meaning	Examples
gyn (cont'd)			iatr: gyniatrics (the branch of medicine dealing with the treatment of women's diseases) (*iatr*, healing) *gyne*: phob: gynephobia (an abnormal fear or hatred of women) (*phobia*, fear of) *gynec*: oid: gynecoid (of or characteristic of a woman or women; female) (*oid*, similar to) *gyneco*: logy: gynecology (the branch of medicine dealing with the specific functions, diseases, etc. of women) (*logy*, study of) mast: gynecomastia (the condition of overdevelopment of a *male's* breasts) (*mast*, breast) *gyno*: eci: gynoecium (the female organ or organs of a flower; pistil or pistils; the carpels, collectively) (from *oikos*, house) phor: gynophore (a stalk bearing the gynoecium above the petals and stamens) (*phore*, bearer, producer) TRAILING ROOT COMPOUNDS: andro: androgyne (an androgynous plant), androgynous (both male and female in one; hermaphroditic; in *botany*, bearing both staminate and pistillate flowers in the same inflorescence or cluster) (*andro*, man) di: digynia [an order of plants with flowers having two pistils (a pistil is the seed-bearing organ of a flower and consists of the ovary, stigma, and style)] (*di*, two) hetero: heterogynous (having two kinds of females, reproductive and nonreproductive, as ants or bees) (*hetero*, other) miso: misogynist (one who hates women) (*miso*, hate) mono: monogynous (in *botany*, having one style or pistil) (*mono*, one) poly: polygyny (the state or practice of having two or more wives or concubines at the same time) (*poly*, many) INTERDISCIPLINARY: polygyny (in *botany*, the fact of having many styles or pistils; in *zoology*, the mating of a male animal with more than one female) CROSS REFERENCE: *femin*
gyr**	Greek *gyros*, circle (IE: *guruos*, to bend, arch)	circle, spiral, ring, rotate	SIMPLE ROOT: gyra: gyral, gyrate {gyrator, gyratory}, gyration (circular or spiral motion; something gyrate, as a whorl) gyre: gyre (a circular or spiral motion; in *medicine*, a convolution; also, *gyrus*) gyro: gyro (layers of lamb or lamb and beef roasted, as on a vertical pit, and sliced) [*gyros*, circle (from rotating meat on a spit), wrongly taken as a plural] gyrose (in *botany*, marked with wavy lines or convolutions) gyru: gyrus (in *anatomy*, a convoluted ridge or fold between fissures, or sulci, especially of the cortex of the brain; plural, *gyri*)

Element	From	Meaning	Examples
gyr (cont'd)			LEADING ROOT COMPOUND: compass: gyrocompass (*com-* prefixes *pass*) magnet: gyromagnetic plan: gyroplane scop: gyroscope (*scope*, view) stat: gyrostat, gyrostatics (*stat*, stand) TRAILING ROOT COMPOUND: auto: autogyro (*auto*, self) NB: *Gyrene*, slang for a member of the Marines, is not in this family; neither are *gyrfalcon, gyron, gyronny*. CROSS REFERENCE: *cycl*

A well-educated gentleman may not know many languages, may have read very few books.
But whatever language he knows, he knows precisely; whatever word he pronounces,
he pronounces rightly; above all, he is learned in the peerage of words; knows the words of true descent and ancient blood at a glance from the words of modern canaille; remembers all their ancestry; their intermarriage; their distant relationships. John Ruskin

H

Element	From	Meaning	Examples
hab, ** **hib**	Latin *habere,* to have (IE: *ghabh,* to grasp, take; yields English have)	to hold, have	SIMPLE ROOT: habil: habile (skillful, dexterous) habiliments (clothing, dress, attire; also, furnishings or equip- ment; trappings), habilitate habit: habit (**Synonyms:** practice, custom, wont), habitable, habi- tant (also, *habitan*), habitat, habitation habitual (**Synonyms:** usual, customary, wonted), habituate, habitude, habitué, habitus PREFIXED ROOT: *hab*: *co*-: cohabit {cohabitation} (from *com*-, with, together) *dis*-: dishabille (the state of being dressed only partially or in night clothes) (*dis*-, opposite of) *in*-: inhabit, inhabitable, inhabitancy, inhabitant, inhabitation, inhabited) (*in*-, in) *re*-: rehabilitate {rehabilitation, rehabilitative} (*re*-, again) *hib*: *ad*-: adhibit, adhibition (*ad*-, to) *ex*-: exhibit (**Synonyms: 1)** proof, evidence, testimony; **2)** show, display, expose, flaunt), exhibition, exhibitioner, exhibitionism, exhibitive, exhibitor, exhibitory (*ex*-, out) *in*-: inhibit (**Synonyms:** restrain, curb, check) {inhibitive, inhibitory}, inhibition, inhibitor (*in*-, in, on) *pro*-: prohibit (**Synonyms:** forbid, interdict, proscribe), pro- hibition, prohibitionist (*pro*-, before) DISGUISED ROOT: able (Synonyms: capable, competent, qualified), ability debt, debtor (*de*-, from + *habere*) PREFIXED DISGUISED ROOT: *dis*-: disability, disable (*dis*-, opposite of) *in*-: indebted (in debt or under legal obligation to repay something received; owing gratitude, as for a favor received) (*in*-, in) *mal*-: malady [from Vulgar Latin *male habitus*, badly kept, out of condition; a disease, illness, sickness; often used figuratively] (see *Note* on *Vulgar Latin* below) LATIN LEGAL PHRASE: *habeas corpus* PREFIXED ANGLO-SAXON ROOT *be*-: behave (**Synonyms:** conduct, demean, deport) (Anglo- Saxon prefix *be*-, intensifier) NOTE: Vulgar Latin denotes the everyday speech of the Ro- man people, from which the Romance languages developed; also known as *popular Latin* as distinguished from standard or literary Latin. The major Romance languages are French, Romanian, Italian, Portuguese, Spanish, Catalan, Provençal, Rhaeto-Romanic, and Sardinian. CROSS REFERENCE: *cap, ten*

Element	From	Meaning	Examples
hagio*	Greek *hagios*: holy	sacred; also saint	LEADING ROOT COMPOUND: *hagi*: arch: hagiarchy (same as *hagiocracy*) (*archy*; that which is ruled) *hagio*: cracy: hagiocracy (rule by priests, saints, or others considered holy; theocracy) (*cracy*, rule by) graph: hagiographer, hagiographic, hagiography (*graph*, write) latry: hagiolatry (*latry*, worship of) logy: hagiology (*logy*, study of) scop: hagioscope (*scope*, view) HEBREW SCRIPTURES: Hagiographa (the third and final part of the Jewish Scriptures; those books not in the Law or the Prophets) CROSS REFERENCE: *hier, sacr, sanct*
hal*	Greek *hals*: salt	salt, sea	SIMPLE ROOT: halide, halite, halieutic LEADING ROOT COMPOUND: *hal*: oid: haloid (*oid*, similar to, shape of) *halo*: bio: halobiont (an organism living in a saline environment, as in the sea) (*biont*, living) clin: halocline (a level of marked change, especially increase, in the salinity of sea water at a certain depth) (*cline*, slope) gen: halogen {halogenous}, halogenate (*gen*, producer) meter: halometer (measures the forms of crystals in salts) (see *Note*) phil: halophile {halophilic, halophilous} (*phila*, love of) phyt: halophyte (*phyton*, plant) DISGUISED ROOT: halcyon (a bird identified with the kingfisher that was fabled to nest at sea in a floating nest about the time of the winter solstice and to calm the waves during incubation; has come to mean *peaceful* and *idyllic*) NOTE: Do not confuse this root with *halo*, originally, a threshing floor; another *halometer*, for example, measures the diffraction halo of a red blood cell. CROSS REFERENCE: *sal*
hal*	Latin *halitus*	breath	SIMPLE ROOT: halituous (covered with moisture or vapor), halitus (an exhalation; vapor; breath) LEADING ROOT COMPOUND: osis: halitosis (bad-smelling breath) (*osis*, condition of) CROSS REFERENCE: *anim, atm, spir*
haplo*	Greek *haploos* (IE: *smplos*, simple)	single, simple	ROOT NOTE: This root consists of *ha*, one + *plo*, fold) LEADING ROOT COMPOUND: *hapl*: oid: haploid (in *biology*, having the full number of chromosomes normally occurring in the mature germ cell or half the number of the usual somatic cell) (*oid*, similar to) ont: haplont (an organism in which the nuclei of the somatic cells are haploid) (*onto*, organism) osis: haplosis (in *biology*, a halving of the number of chromosomes during meiosis, through the division of a diploid cell into two haploids) (*osis*, condition of)

Element	From	Meaning	Examples
haplo (cont'd)			*haplo*: caul: haplocaulescent (in *botany*, having a simple axis) (*caul*, stem) logy: haplology (the unconscious running of two syllables into *one*, e.g., *interpretive* for *interpretative*) CROSS REFERENCE: *mono, uni*
hebe*	Greek *hebe*: youth	young (see Root Note)	ROOT NOTE: In *medicine*, this root refers to puberty, as in *hebephrenia*, or the pubes, as in *hebetomy*. In *botany*, the root refers to pubescent, or downy, as in *pubic hair*, and as in *hebeanthous*, bearing downy flowers. SIMPLE ROOT: hebetic PREFIXED ROOT: *ep*-: ephebe [literally, at age; a young man in ancient Greece between 18 and 20 years of age], ephebus (a young man undergoing physical and military training in ancient Greece) (from *epi*-, at) LEADING ROOT COMPOUND: phren: hebephrenia (a form of schizophrenia characterized by childish or silly behavior, disorganized thinking, delusions, and hallucinations, usually beginning in adolescence) (*phren*, mind) GREEK MYTHOLOGY: Hebe (the goddess of youth, daughter of Hera and Zeus: she is cupbearer to the gods) NB: *Hebetude*, mental dullness with impairment of the special senses, such as is seen in asthenic fevers, is *not* in this family. CROSS REFERENCE: *jun/juv*
hect**	Greek *hekaton*	hundred (metric)	SIMPLE ROOT: hectare LEADING ROOT COMPOUND: *hecatom*: b: hecatomb (sacrifice of 100 oxen; now, any large-scale sacrifice or slaughter) (the last letter is the truncated form of *bous*, ox) ped: hecatomped (measuring 100 feet) (*ped*, foot) styl: hecatomstylon (a 100-columned building) (*style*, column) *hecto*: cotyl: hectocotylus (one of the arms or tentacles of a male octopus, cuttlefish, or other cephalopod, which becomes modified as a sexual organ for impregnating the female) (*cotyl*, cup) gram: hectogram (a metric measure of weight equal to 100 grams, or 3.527 ounces) graph: hectograph (also, *hektograph*) (*graph*, write) liter: hectoliter (a metric measure of capacity equal to 100 liters, or 26.418 gallons) meter: hectometer (a metric unit of linear measure equal to 100 meters, or 109.36 yards) NB: *Hector*, from Greek mythology, means "holding fast." CROSS REFERENCE: *cent*
hedon*	Greek *hedone*	pleasure	SIMPLE ROOT: hedonic (having to do with pleasure), hedonics hedonism {hedonist, hedonistic}

Element	From	Meaning	Examples
hedon (cont'd)			PREFIXED ROOT: *hyp-*: hyphedonia (abnormal diminution of pleasure in acts that should normally give pleasure) (*hypo-*, under) INTERDISCIPLINARY: hedonism (in *philosophy*, the ethical doctrine that pleasure is the principal good and the proper aim of action; in *psychology*, the theory that a person always acts in such a way as to seek pleasure and avoid pain) NO CROSS REFERENCE
hedr**	Greek *hedra*: seat (IE: *sed*, sit; yields English chair)	chair, side	PREFIXED ROOT: *cat-*: cathedra, cathedral (the chair of the bishop; literally, where the bishop sits down; thus, originally, the largest church in the diocese) (*cata-*, down) PREFIXED ELIDED ROOT: *ex-*: exedra (see note under Greek *ex-*) (*ex-*, out) TRAILING ROOT COMPOUND: *di*: dihedral (having or formed by two intersecting plane faces, as a *dihedral angle*) (*di*, two) *san*: Sanhedrin (an assembly; the highest court and council in the ancient Jewish nation, having both religious and civil functions; it was abolished with the destruction of Jerusalem in 70 A.D.) (from *sym-*, with, together) LATIN TERM: *ex cathedra* (literally, to speak from the chair; when the Pope sat *in the chair*, his word was considered infallible; thus, dogmatic; often used pejoratively, as in "He is so dogmatic, speaking *ex cathedra* on every subject.") FRENCH: *chaise (longue)* (see note under *long*) NO CROSS REFERENCE
-hedron*	Greek *hedra*, seat, base (IE: *sed*, sit)	geometric figure	ROOT NOTE: The original meaning of this root is seat, yielding such words as listed under *hedr*. As a suffix, it designates a geometric figure or crystal with (a specified number of) surfaces (or bases). NOMINAL SUFFIX: *hexa*: hexahedron (*hex*, six) *holo*: holohedron (having the full number of planes required for complete symmetry: said of a crystal) (*holo*, whole, complete) *octo*: octohedron (*octo*, eight) *poly*: polyhedron (*poly*, many) *tetra*: tetrahedron (*tetra*, four) *trapezo*: trapezohedron (literally, four-footed bench) (*tra*, four + *pez*, foot) ADJECTIVAL SUFFIX: *hemi*: hemihedral (*hemi*, half) *hexa*: hexahedral (*hex*, six) *octo*: octohedral (*octo*, eight) *poly*: polyhedral (*poly*, many) NO CROSS REFERENCE
hegei*	Greek *hegemon*: leader (IE: *sag*, track down, seek)	to track down (extended to mean "leadership")	SIMPLE ROOT: hegemony (leadership or dominance, especially that of one state or nation over others) hegumen (in the Eastern Orthodox Church, the elected head of a monastery corresponding to an abbot in the Roman Catholic Church)

322

Element	From	Meaning	Examples
hegei (cont'd)			PREFIXED ROOT: *ex-*: exegesis (a critical explanation or analysis, especially of the Scriptures) {exegetic, or *exegetical*} (*ex-*, out) DOUBLE PREFIXED ROOT: ep<u>ex</u>egesis (additional explanation; further clarification) (*epi-*, upon + *ex-*, out) CROSS REFERENCE: *vestig*
helic,* **helix**	Greek *helix*: coil (IE: *wel*, to turn, twist)	spiral, snail	SIMPLE ROOT: *helic*: helical, helicon (a musical instrument resembling a bass tuba; see *Mountain Group*, below), heliconia, helictite *helix*: helix (any spiral, either lying in a single plane or, especially, moving around a cone, cylinder, etc. as a screw thread does; plural: *helices*) LEADING ROOT COMPOUND: *heli*: clin: helicline (*cline*, slope) *helic*: oid: helicoid (in *geometry*, a surface generated by the rotation of a plane or twisted curve about a fixed line so that each point of the curve traces out a circular helix with the fixed line as axis) (*oid*, similar to) *helico*: pter: helicopter (literally, spiral wing) (*pter*, wing) MOUNTAIN GROUP: Helicon (in south central Greece, on the Gulf of Corinth; in *Greek mythology*, the home of the Muses) INTERDISCIPLINARY: helix [in *anatomy*, the folded rim of cartilage around the outer ear; in *architecture*, an ornamental spiral, as a volute on a Corinthian or Ionic capital; in *mathematics*, a line so curved around a right circular cylinder that it would become a straight line if the cylinder were unfolded into a plane; in *zoology*, any of a genus (Helix) of spiral-shelled mollusks, including the common, edible European snail (*Helix pomatia*)] CROSS REFERENCE: *gyr, helminth*
helio**	Greek *helios* (IE: *swen*, sun)	sun	SIMPLE ROOT: helium (chemical symbol: He) heliacal (of or near the sun; solar; specifically, a) designating the apparent rising of a star when it is first seen again after having been invisible because of its nearness to the sun; b) designating the last setting of a star before it becomes invisible again in the sun's rays) PREFIXED ROOT: ap-: aphelion (see note under *apo-*) (*apo-*, away) par-: parhelion (a bright, sunlike optical illusion caused by sunlight passing through ice crystals in the upper atmosphere; sundog) (from *para-*, beside) peri-: perihelion (the point nearest the sun in the orbit of a planet or comet, or of a man-made satellite in orbit around the sun) (*peri-*, around) LEADING ROOT COMPOUND: *heli*: anthus: helianthus (sunflower) (*anthos*, flower)

Element	From	Meaning	Examples
helio (cont'd)			chrys: helichrysum (the marigold) (*chrysum*, gold)
			helio:
			centr: heliocentric (measured or considered as being seen from the center of the sun(*centric*, having a specified thing as its center)
			chrom: heliochrome (capitalized, a trademark; an early type of photograph in natural colors) (*chroma*, color)
			gram: heliogram (message sent by heliograph) (from *graph*, write)
			graph: heliograph (*graph*, write)
			latry: heliolatry (sun worship) (*latry*, worship of)
			meter: heliometer (so called because originally used in measuring the sun's diameter; an instrument formally used for measuring the angular distance between stars) (*meter*, measure)
			stat: heliostat (*stat*, stand)
			taxis: heliotaxis (the tendency of certain plants and animals to move or turn under the influence of sunlight) (*taxis*, arrangement)
			therap: heliotherapy (the treatment of disease by exposing the body to sunlight) (*therap*, healing, treatment)
			trop: heliotrope (a plant which turns toward the sun, as the sunflower), heliotropism (*trop*, turn)
			zo: heliozoan (interesting connection to *sun*--the radiating pseudopodia) (*zo*, animal)
			TRAILING ROOT COMPOUND:
			iso: isohel (a line on a map connecting points having equal hours of sunshine in a standard period of time) (*iso*, equal)
			GREEK MYTHOLOGY: Helios (the sun god; represented as driving across the heavens)
			ANCIENT CITY: Heliopolis, center of worship of the ancient Egyptian sun god Ra (in the Nile Delta, just north of where Cairo now stands)
			CROSS REFERENCE: *sol*
helix			See *helic* for *helix*.
helminth*	Greek *helmins* (IE: *wel*, to turn, twist)	worm	SIMPLE ROOT:
			helminth (any worm or wormlike animal, especially a worm parasite of the intestine, as the tapeworm, hookworm, or roundworm)
			helminthiasis, helminthic
			LEADING ROOT COMPOUND:
			logy: helminthology (*logy*, study of)
			TRAILING ROOT COMPOUND:
			platy: platyhelminth (*platy*, flat)
			CROSS REFERENCE: *helic, vermi*
hem***	Greek *haema* (IE: *sei*, *soi*, to drip)	blood	ROOT NOTE: The elided form of *hemo* is *em*; words indicating a diseased condition of the blood are suffixed by *emia* (listed separately).
			SIMPLE ROOT:
			hemal (having to do with blood or blood vessels), hematic (of, filled with, or colored like blood)
			hematin, hematinic (any substance that increases the amount of hemoglobin in the blood)

Element	From	Meaning	Examples
hem (cont'd)			hematite (a chemical, Fe_2O_3, which is *bloodlike*, because of its iron content)
			PREFIXED ELIDED ROOT:
			an-: anemia, anemic (*an-*, without)
			LEADING ROOT COMPOUND:
			hem:
			agg: hemagglutinate, hemagglutination (*ag-* assimilates *ad-*, to; *gluten*, glue)
			angi: hemangioma (a benign tumor, lesion, or birthmark consisting of dense clusters of blood vessels) (*angi*, vessel; *oma*, group, mass)
			hema:
			cyto: hemacytometer (a device used to count the concentration of cells in body fluids, especially the red and white cells in the blood) (*cyto*, cell)
			hemat:
			oma: hematoma (*oma*, mass, tumor)
			uria: hematuria (*uria*, diseased condition of the urine)
			hemato:
			blast: hematoblast (an immature blood cell) (*blast*, shoot, sprout)
			crit: hematocrit (*crit*, judge)
			gen: hematogenesis (same as *hematopoiesis*, below), hematogenous (forming blood; also, spread by the bloodstream, as bacteria) (*gen*, producing)
			phag: hematophagous (*phag*, eat)
			poies: hematopoiesis (*poisis*, a making)
			zo: hematozoon (*zoon*, animal, living being)
			hemo:
			cyt: hemocyte (*cyt*, cell)
			glob: hemoglobin (*globe*, rounded mass)
			phil: hemophilia, hemophilic (*philia*, loving)
			rrh: hemorrhage (*rrh*, breaking, bursting)
			rrh: hemorrhoid (*rrho*, flow; *oid*, similar to)
			stas: hemostasis (*stas*, standing, stopping)
			stat: hemostat, hemostatic (*stat*, stopping)
			CROSS REFERENCE: *emia, sang*
hemer*	Greek *hemera*	day	PREFIXED ROOT:
			ep-: (elides *epi-*, upon)
			ephemeral (literally, upon a day; lasting only a day; transitory, as *ephemeral glory; ephemeral flower; ephemeral insects*)
			ephemerid, ephemeris, ephemeron
			LEADING ROOT COMPOUND:
			hemer:
			alop: hemeralopia (day blindness) (*alaos*, blind + *ops*, eye + *ia*, condition of)
			hemero:
			bio: hemerobious (living for only a day) (*bios*, life)
			TRAILING ELIDED ROOT COMPOUND:
			hex: hexaemeron (in the Bible, an account of the six-day period of the Creation, especially that in Genesis) (*hexa*, six)
			CROSS REFERENCE: *die*

Element	From	Meaning	Examples
hemi***	Greek *hemi* (IE: *semi*, half)	half	LEADING ROOT COMPOUND: ageu: hemiageusia (loss or absence of the sense of taste on one side of the tongue) (*a-*, not + *geus*, taste) cran: hemicrania (see *migraine* under *Disguised Root*) cycl: hemicycle (a half circle; a semicircular room, wall, etc.) (*cycle*, wheel, circle) hedra: hemihedral (having half the number of faces required for complete symmetry: said of a crystal) (*hedra*, geometric surface) hydr: hemihydrate (*hydro*, water) meta: hemimetabolous (*meta-* prefixes *bol*, to throw) morph: hemimorphic, hemimorphite (*morph*, shape) ola: hemiola (a music term) (from *holo*, whole) parasit: hemiparasite (*para-* prefixes *sit*, food) pleg: hemiplegia (*plegia*, paralysis) pter: hemipteran (*pter*, wing) spher: hemisphere (*sphere*, globe, ball) stich: hemistich (half a poetic verse-line) (*stich*, verse) trop: hemitrope {hemitropic} (*trop*, turn) LEADING ROOT MASSED COMPOUND: demi: hemidemisemiquaver (a 64th note in music) (*demi*, half + *semi*, half + *quaver*, eighth note) DISGUISED LEADING ROOT COMPOUND: grain: migraine (see note under *crani*) (*hemi* + *cranium*) INTERDISCIPLINARY: hemiparasite (in *botany*, a parasitic plant, as the mistletoe, which carries on some photosynthesis but obtains a portion of its food, water, or minerals from a host plant; in *zoology*, an organism that may be either free-living or parasitic) CROSS REFERENCE: *demi, med, semi*
hen*	Greek *henos*: one (IE: *sem*, one)	one, unite	ELIDED SIMPLE ROOT: enosis (union; specifically, the proposed political union of Cyprus and Grece) LEADING ROOT COMPOUND: *hen*: osis: henosis (combination into one; in *medicine*, healing, or union) {henotic (serving to unite; in *medicine*, promoting healing; tending to heal)} (*osis*, condition of) *heno*: the: henotheism (belief in one god without asserting there is *only* one god; compared to *monotheism*, a belief in only one God) (*theo*, God) CONTRACTED PHRASE: hendiadys (a figure of speech in which two nouns joined by *and* are used instead of a noun and a modifier, e.g., *deceit and words* for *deceitful words*; *cups and gold* for *golden cups*) [contraction of *hen dia dyoin*, one (thing) by means of two] CROSS REFERENCE: *mono, uni*
hendeca*	Greek *hendeka* (*hen*, one + *deca*, ten)	eleven	LEADING ROOT COMPOUND: col: hendecacolic (in Greek and Latin prosody, made up of eleven cola) (*cola* is the plural of *colon*: a section of a prosodic period, consisting of a group of two to six feet forming a rhythmic unit with a principal accent)

326

Element	From	Meaning	Examples
hendeca (cont'd)			gon: hendecagon (a plane figure with eleven angles and eleven sides) (*gon*, angle) hedr: hendecahedron (a solid figure with eleven plane surfaces) (*hedr*, geometric side) sem: hendecasemic (containing or equivalent to eleven short syllables) (*sema*, sign) syllabl: hendecasyllable (a line of verse having eleven syllables) (*syl-* assimilates *sym-*, with) NO CROSS REFERENCE
hepa*	Greek *hepar*	liver	SIMPLE ROOT: heparin, hepatic LEADING ROOT COMPOUND: itis: hepatitis (*itis*, inflammation of) oid: hepatoid (having the structural form of the liver) (*oid*, similar to) FLOWER NAME: hepatica (a flower with liver-shaped leaves) PERSIAN: gizzard NO CROSS REFERENCE
hept*	Greek *hepta*	seven	SIMPLE ROOT: heptad, heptane LEADING ROOT COMPOUND: *hept*: arch: heptarchy (a government by seven persons) (*archy*, rule) *hepta*: gon: heptagon (*gon*, angle) hedr: heptahedron (*hedr*, geometric side) mer: Heptameron (a collection of stories, covering seven days), heptamerous (elision of *hemera*, day) meter: heptameter (a verse-line of seven feet or measures) stich: heptastich (a poem or stanza with seven lines) (*stich*, a line of verse) val: heptavalent (having a valence of seven) DISGUISED ROOT: hebdomad (seven days) {hebdomadal} OLD TESTAMENT SECTION: Heptateuch [the first seven books of the Old Testament (the Pentateuch--Genesis, Exodus, Leviticus, Numbers, Deuteronomy, usually called the Books of Law) + Joshua, and Judges] CROSS REFERENCE: *sept*
her,** heir	Latin *heres*: heir (IE: *ghe*, to be empty; leave behind)	leave behind	SIMPLE ROOT: *her*: hered: hereditament, hereditary (**Synonyms:** innate, inborn; congenital), heredity herit: heritable, heritage (**Synonyms:** inheritance, patrimony, birthright), heritance, heritor *heir*: heir PREFIXED ROOT: *in-*: inherit {inheritor; inheritress, or *inheritrix*} (*in-*, in) NO CROSS REFERENCE
her,** hes	Latin *haerere* (IE: *ghais*, to be stuck, neglect)	to stick to; to cleave	SIMPLE ROOT: hesitate PREFIXED ROOTS: *her*: *ad-*: (to) adhere (**Synonyms:** stick, cohere, cling), adherence adherent (**Synonyms:** follower, disciple, partisan)

Element	From	Meaning	Examples
her (cont'd)			*co-*: cohere (see synonyms at *adhere*, above) (*co-*, with) *in-*: inhere (to be inherent; exist as a quality, characteristic, or right; be innate), inherence (in *philosophy*, the relation of an attribute to its object), inherent (*in-*, in) *hes*: *ad-*: adhesion, adhesive (*ad-*, to) INTERDISCIPLINARY: adhesion (in *medicine*, the joining together, by fibrous tissue, of bodily parts or tissues that are normally separate; in *physics*, the force that holds together the molecules of unlike substances whose surfaces are in contact; distinguished from *cohesion*) NO CROSS REFERENCE
herpe*	Greek *herpein*: to creep (IE: *serp*, to creep)	snake	SIMPLE ROOT: herpes, herpestes (a genus which includes the mongooses), herpetic LEADING ROOT COMPOUND: log: herpetology (the study of reptiles and amphibians) (*logy*, study of) phob: herpetophobia (*phobia*, fear of) CROSS REFERENCE: *angui*
hesper*	Greek *hesperos*	evening, western	SIMPLE ROOT: Hesperian, hesperinos (a service in the Eastern Orthodox Church corresponding to vespers in the Western Church) LEADING ROOT COMPOUND: anop: hesperanopia (*an-*, not, prefixes *opia*, defective vision) ENGLISH: vesper, vesperal, vespers, vespertine EVENING STAR: Hesperus (for Venus), the most brilliant star in the solar system, second in distance from the sun; Venus is called Lucifer (light-bearer) when it appears as the morning star; Hesperus, when it appears as the evening star GREEK MYTHOLOGY: Hesperides (the nymphs who guard the golden apples given as a wedding gift by Gaea to Hera) INTERDISCIPLINARY: vespertine (in *botany*, opening or blossoming in the evening; in *zoology*, becoming active or flying in the early evening; compare *crepuscular*--active at twilight or just before sunrise) NO CROSS REFERENCE
heter***	Greek *heteros*	other, different	ROOT NOTE: This element joins with both Greek and Latin roots, for example, Latin *gen* and Greek *gon*, both pertaining to reproduction. LEADING ROOT COMPOUND: *heter*: onym: heteronym (a word with the same spelling as another but with a different meaning and pronunciation, e.g., *tear*, a drop of water from the eye, and *tear*, to rip) (*onym*, name) osis: heterosis (a phenomenon resulting from hybridization, in which offspring display greater vigor, size, resistance, etc. than the parents) (*osis*, condition of) *hetero*: cerc: heterocercal (*cerc*, tail) chrom: (*chromo*, color) heterochromatic, heterochromia heterochromosome (sex chromosome) (*soma*, body)

Element	From	Meaning	Examples
heter (cont'd)			clit: heteroclite (*clit*, bend, lean)
			cycl: heterocyclic (*cycle*, wheel, cycle)
			dox: heterodox, heterodoxy (*dox*, teaching)
			dyn: heterodyne (*dyne*, power)
			eci: heteroecious (in *biology*, living as a parasite first on one species of host and then another) (from *oikia*, house)
			gam: heterogamete (opposed to *isogamete*), heterogamous (*gam*, marriage, sexual reproduction)
			gen: heterogeneous {heterogeneity}, heterogenesis, heterogenous (*gen*, producer)
			gon: heterogony {heterogonous} (*gon*, sexual reproduction}
			graft: heterograft (same as *xenograft*) (from *graph*, write)
			graph: heterography {heterographic} (*graph*, write)
			gyn: heterogynous (having two kinds of females, reproductive and nonreproductive, as ants and bees) (*gyn*, woman; *gynous*, pertaining to female organs or pistils)
			lecith: heterolecithal (having the yolk unevenly distributed, as bird eggs; opposed to *homolecithal*) (*lekithos*, yolk of an egg)
			log: heterologous (*logo*, word, relation)
			lys: heterolysis {heterolytic} (*lys*, loosen)
			mer: heteromerous (in *botany*, having a whorl or whorls with a different number of parts from that of the other whorls) (*mere*, part)
			morph: heteromorphic (*morph*, form, shape)
			nom: heteronomous (compare *autonomous*) {heteronomy} (*nomos*, law)
			ous: Heteroousian (in *theology*, designating of, or holding the theory that God the Father and God the Son are different in substance; an adherent of this philosophy; Arian) (*ousia*, essence)
			phil: heterophil (*phila*, love of)
			phon: heterophony (the playing of a passage of music with simultaneous variations in melody or rhythm by two or more players) (*phone*, sound)
			phyll: heterophyllous (growing leaves of different forms on the same stem or plant) (*phyll*, leaf)
			phyt: heterophyte (a plant which derives its food from other plants or animals, living or dead) (*phyton*, plant)
			plast: heteroplasty (*plast*, form, shape)
			ploid: heteroploid (from *ploos*, fold)
			pter: heteropterous (same as *hemipterous*) (*pter*, wing)
			sex: heterosexual {heterosexuality}
			spher: heterosphere (the upper of two divisions of the earth's atmosphere) (*sphere*, ball, globe)
			spor: heterosporous (in *botany*, producing more than one kind of spore; especially, producing microspores and megaspores) {heterospory} (*spore*, seed)
			styl: heterostyly (the condition in which flowers on polymorphous plants have styles of different lengths, thereby encouraging cross-pollination) {heterostylous} (*styl*, column)

Element	From	Meaning	Examples
heter (cont'd)			tax: heterotaxis (an abnormal position or arrangement, as of organs of the body, rock strata, etc.) (*taxis*, arrangement)
			thall: heterothallic (*thall*, bud, shoot)
			top: heterotopia (the abnormal location of an organ, tissue, or body part; also, *heterotopy*) {heterotopic} (*topos*, place)
			troph: heterotrophic (obtaining food from organic material only; compare *autotrophic*) (*troph*, nourishment)
			typ: heterotypic (also, *heterotypical*) (*type*, image)
			zyg: heterozygote {heterozygous} (*zyg*, yoke)
			CROSS REFERENCE: *allo, alter*
heur*	Greek *heuriskein*	to find	SIMPLE ROOT: heuristic (serving to indicate or point out)
			DISGUISED ROOT: eureka [I have found it! (supposedly uttered by Archimedes when he discovered a way to determine the purity of gold by applying the principle of specific gravity)]
			PLACENAMES:
			Eureka, California; Eureka Springs, Arkansas
			NO CROSS REFERENCE
hex**	Greek *hex*	six	SIMPLE ROOT: hexad {hexadic}, hexosan, hexose
			LEADING ROOT COMPOUND:
			chloro: hexachlorophene (see *Webster's New World*)
			chord: hexachord (in medieval music, a diatonic scale of six tones, with a semitone between the third and fourth)
			emer: hexaemeron (in the Bible, the six-day period of the Creation) (from *hemera*, day)
			gon: hexagon, hexagonal (*gon*, corner, angle)
			gram: hexagram (a six-pointed star) (*gram*, something written)
			hedr: hexahedral, hexahedron (*hedra*, geometric surface)
			hydr: hexahydrate, hexahydric (*hydro*, water)
			mer: hexamerous (having six parts in each whorl: said of flowers; also written **6-merous**) (*mere*, part)
			meter: hexameter {hexametric} (*meter*, measure)
			pla: hexapla (an edition having six versions arranged in parallel columns; capitalized, Origen's edition of the Old Testament) (from *plo*, fold)
			pod: hexapod (also, *hexapodous*; having six legs, as the true insect) (*pod*, foot)
			stich: hexastich (*stich*, a line of verse)
			teuch: Hexateuch [the first six books of the Old Testament, i.e., Genesis, Exodus, Leviticus, Numbers, Deuteronomy (the five books of law) plus Joshua, the first book of history] (*euchos*, book)
			val: hexavalent (having a valence of six)
			CROSS REFERENCE: *sex*
hex*	Greek *hexis*: habit	to have, hold	LEADING ROOT COMPOUND:
			logy: hexiology (the science or study of the relations of an organism to its environment) (*logy*, study of)
			TRAILING ROOT COMPOUND:
			cac: cachexia (also, *cachexy*; a generally weakened, emaciated condition of the body, especially as associated with a chronic disease) {cachectic} (*caco*, bad)
			NB: *Cachinnation* is not related to this root.
			NO CROSS REFERENCE

Element	From	Meaning	Examples
hiat*	Greek *hiare*: to gape (IE: *ghe*, gap)	gap	SIMPLE ROOT: hiatal, hiatus, hiation DISGUISED ROOT: chasm (a deep crack in the earth's surface; abyss; narrow gorge) gape (in *zoology*, the measure of the widest possible opening of a mouth or beak), gasp, yawn PREFIXED DISGUISED ROOT: *de-*: dehisce (to burst, or split open, as a seed pod), dehiscence (a bursting or splitting open, as of a pod, anther, etc., to dis- charge its contents) (*de-*, off) NO CROSS REFERENCE
hib			See *hab* for *exhibit, inhibit.*
hibern*	Latin *hibernus*: wintry	winter	SIMPLE ROOT: hibernaculum, hibernal, hibernate {hiberna- tion, hibernator} GEOGRAPHIC NAME: Himalayas (Sanskrit; abode of the snow) NO CROSS REFERENCE
hidr*	Greek *hidros*	sweat	SIMPLE ROOT: hidrosis (perspiration; sweating, especially, excessive sweat- ing; any skin condition characterized by excessive sweating) hidrotic (having to do with sweat; causing sweat; sudorific; as a *noun*, a sudorific drug) LEADING ROOT COMPOUND: *hidr*: osis: hidrosis (perspiration; sweating, especially excessive sweating; any skin condition characterized excessive sweat- ing) (*osis*, condition of) *hidro*: mancy: hidromancy (divination by sweat) (*mancy*, divination) poie: hidropoietic (sweat-causing) (*poiein*, to make) CROSS REFERENCE: *sud*
hier**	Greek *hieros*: powerful, super- natural (IE: *eis*, to move violently, excite)	sacred, holy, powerful	SIMPLE ROOT: hieratic (of or used by priests; priestly; sac- erdotal; designating or of the abridged form of cursive hiero- glyphic writing once used by the Egyptian priests) LEADING ROOT COMPOUND: *hier*: arch: hierarch, hierarchy (government by the priests; a group of persons or things arranged in order of rank, grade, class, position, etc.) (*arch*, government by) *hiero*: crac: hierocracy (a government by priests or other clergy; a hi- erarchy; see previous entry) (*cracy*, government by) dul: hierodule (in ancient Greece, a temple slave, dedicated to the service of a god) (from *doulos*, slave) glyph: hieroglyph, hieroglyphic, hieroglyphics (literally, sa- cred carvings; hard to read or understand) (*glyph*, carve) logy: hierology (the religious lore and literature of a people) (*logy*, study of) phan: hierophant (in ancient Greece, a priest of a mystery cult; a person confidently expounding, explaining, or promoting something mysterious or obscure as though appointed to do so) (*phan*, show) CROSS REFERENCE: *hagio, sacr, sanct*

Element	From	Meaning	Examples
hipp*	Greek *hippos* (IE: *ekwos*, horse)	horse	LEADING ROOT COMPOUND: *hipp*: arch: hipparch (a Greek commander of cavalry) (*arch*, ruler) *hippo*: campus: hippocampus (in Greek and Roman mythology, a sea monster with the head and forequarters of a horse and the tail of a dolphin or fish; in *anatomy*, a ridge along the lower section of each lateral ventricle of the brain) (*campus*, sea monster) drom: hippodrome (a horse-race course) (*drome*, racecourse) pot: hippopotamus (literally, river horse) TRAILING ROOT COMPOUND: eo: eohippus (an extinct progenitor of the modern horse) (*eo*, early) CROSS REFERENCE: *caval , equus*
hod			See *od*, road, way, path.
holo***	Greek *holos* (IE: *solo*, whole; yields English holy, holiday, whole)	whole, safe	SIMPLE ROOT: holily, holiness, holism, holistic PREFIXED ROOT: cat-: catholic, catholicon (from *cata-*, down) LEADING ROOT COMPOUND: blast: holoblastic (*blast*, embryo) caust: holocaust (*caust*, burnt) crin: holocrine (*crine*, to separate) gam: hologamous (*gamous*, uniting sexually) gram: hologram (from *holograph*) graph: holograph, holographic, holography (*graph*, write) hedr: holohedral (*hedra*, geometric plane) morph: holomorphic (*morph*, shape, form) phras: holophrastic (the speaking of an entire sentence or phrase in one word, e.g., *veto*, I forbid) (*phrase*, speak) phyt: holophytic (*phyton*, plant) typ: holotype (in *taxonomy*, the single specimen chosen as the type of a new species or subspecies in the original description) (*type*, image, icon) zo: holozoic (ingesting and using complex organic material as food, as most animals) (*zo*, animal) TRAILING ROOT COMPOUND: hemi: hemiola (a music term; the ratio one and one half to one) (*hemi*, half) DISGUISED LEADING ROOT COMPOUND: but: halibut (originally eaten on holy days) (*butt*, a fish) CROSS REFERENCE: *integ; salu/salv*
hom***	Latin *homo* (IE: *ghthem*, earth, ground)	man	SIMPLE ROOT: homa: homage (**Synonyms: 1**) honor, reverence, deference; 2) allegiance, fidelity, loyalty) homi: hominid, hominize {hominization} homu: homunculus (a little man; manikin) LEADING ROOT COMPOUND: *homi*: cid: homicidal, homicide (*cide*, kill) *homin*: oid: hominoid (*oid*, similar to)

332

Element	From	Meaning	Examples
hom (cont'd)			DISGUISED ROOT: (see *hum*) human, humane, humanism, humanist humanitarian (**Synonyms:** philanthropic, charitable, altruistic), humanitarianism (the doctrine that a human being is capable of perfection with divine aid) humanities, humanity, humanize, humanly PREFIXED DISGUISED ROOT: *in-:* inhumane (*in-,* not) FRENCH: *hommage* LATIN PHRASES: *Ecce Homo* (Behold the Man; Pilate, in referring to Jesus at his trial) *Homo sapiens* (the knowledgeable man) *ad hominem* (literally, to the man; a form of illogical reasoning where argument appeals to one's prejudices, selfish interests, etc. rather than to reason; attacking one's opponent rather than dealing with the issue under discussion) SPANISH: *hombre* PLACENAMES: Humansville, Missouri; Hombre River, Honduras CROSS REFERENCE: *andr, anthropo, vir*
homo***	Greek *homos:* same	same, similar	ROOT NOTE: In medical science, the meaning of this root is extended to include a constant, unchanging state. PREFIXED ELIDED ROOT: *an-:* (not) anomalous (literally, not the same; deviating from the regular arrangement, general rule, or usual method; abnormal; **Synonyms:** irregular, abnormal, unnatural) anomaly (departure from the regular arrangement, general rule, or usual method; abnormality) LEADING ROOT COMPOUND: *hom:* erg: homergy (normal metabolism) (*erg,* work) onym: homonym (a word with the same pronunciation as another but with a different meaning, origin, and usually spelling, e.g., *boar* and *bore*), homonymous, homonymy (*onym,* name) *homeo:* morph: homeomorphism (similar in structure and form) (*morph,* shape, form) path: homeopathy (*path,* feeling) stas: homeostasis (*stasis,* standing) typ: homeotypic (*type,* image, icon) *homo:* cerc: homocercal (*cerc,* tail) chrom: homochromatic (*chroma,* color) erotic: homoeroticism (same as *homosexuality*) (*eros,* sexual love) gam: homogametic, homogamy (interbreeding) (*gam,* sexual reproduction gen: homogeneous {homogeneity}, homogenesis, homogenize, homogeny (*gen,* produce) graft: homograft (same as *allograft*) (from *graph,* write)

Element	From	Meaning	Examples
homo (cont'd)			graph: homograph (a word with the same spelling as another or others but with a different meaning and origin, and, sometimes, a different pronunciation, e.g., *bow*, the front of a ship; *bow*, to bend; *bow*, a decorative knot) (*graph*, write)
			lecit: homolecithal (having the yolk small in amount and more or less evenly distributed, as in mammal eggs; opposed to *heterolecithal*) (from *lekithos*, yolk of an egg)
			log: homologate (to approve or countenance; in *civil law*, to confirm officially), homologous, homologue, homology (*logos*, word)
			morph: homomorphic, **homomorphism**, homomorphy (*morph*, shape, form)
			ous: homoousian (also capitalized; in *theology*, of or holding the teaching that God the Father and God the Son are of the same nature; see *homoiousian*, below) (*ousia*, essence)
			phil: homophile (same as *homosexual*) (*phila*, love of)
			phob: homophobia (irrational hatred or fear of homosexuals or homosexuality) (*phobia*, fear of)
			phon: homophone (any of two or more letters or groups of letters representing the same speech sound, e.g., *c* in *civil* and *s* in *song*; *f* in *fantasy* and *ph* in *phantasy*), homophonic (same as *homonymous*; in *music*, having one melodic line at a time, the other voices or parts serving as accompaniment) (*phone*, sound)
			plast: homoplastic, homoplasty (*plast*, form, shape)
			pter: homopteran, homopterous (*pter*, wing)
			sex: homosexual {homosexuality} (from *secare*, to cut)
			spher: homosphere (*sphere*, ball, globe)
			spor: homosporous (in *botany*, producing only one kind of spore; isosporous) (*spore*, seed)
			styl: homostyly (the condition in which flowers of the same species have styles of equal length; compare with *heterostyly*) {heterostylous} (*style*, column)
			tax: homotaxis (*taxis*, arrange)
			thall: homothallic (*thallos*, young shoot)
			zyg: homozygosis, homozygote (*zyg*, pair; *osis*, condition of)
			homoio:
			ous: homoiousian (also capitalized; in *theology*, of or holding the teaching that God the Father and God the son are of a *similar* nature, not of the *same* nature; compare *homoousian*, above) (*ousia*, essence)
			homolo:
			graph: homolographic (keeping the parts in proper relative size and form) (*graphic*, a method of recording or describing)
			PREFIXED LEADING ROOT COMPOUND:
			in-: inhomogeneous (not homogeneous) (*in*-, not)
			INTERDISCIPLINARY: **homomorphism** (in *biology*, resemblance or similarity, without actual relationship, in structure and origin; in *botany*, uniformity in shape or size, as of pistils and stamens; in *zoology*, similarity between an insect's larva and its matured form)
			CROSS REFERENCE: *iso*

Element	From	Meaning	Examples

hor*	Greek
	 hora:
	 period
	 of time
	 (yields
	 English
	 year,
	 yearling,
	 yore)
		season of year;
		 extended to mean
		 "hour"
			SIMPLE ROOT: horal, horary
			 LEADING ROOT COMPOUND:
			 log: horologe (a timepiece; clock, hourglass, sundial, etc.),
			    horologic (also, *horological*), horologist, horology (from
			    legein, to say)
			 scop: horoscope {horoscopic, horoscopy} (*scope*, watch)
			 DUTCH: gherkin (an unripened cucumber; one which has not
			    reached its "season" of growth) (*kin*, a diminutive)
			 CONSTELLATION: Horologium
			 NO CROSS REFERENCE

horm*	Greek *horman*: to stir up (IE: *ser*, to stream)	to excite; impulse, attack, assault	SIMPLE ROOT: horme: horme (vital energy as an urge to purposive activity) hormi: hormic (purposively directed toward a goal) hormo: hormone, hormonize (to treat with a hormone; specifi- cally, to castrate chemically) LEADING ROOT COMPOUND: *hormo*: spor: hormospore (*spore*, seed) *hormon*: gon: hormongonium (*gonium*, reproduction) *hormono*: oid: hormonoid (*oid*, similar to) NO CROSS REFERENCE

horr*	Latin
	 horrere:
	 to bristle,
	 tremble
	 (IE: *ghers*,
	 to bristle)
		to shudder	SIMPLE ROOT:
			 horrendous, horrent
			 horrible (**Synonyms**: appalling, frightful, hideous)
			 horrid, horror (**Synonyms**: dread, dismay)
			 PREFIXED ROOT:
			 ab-: (away, from)
			 abhor (**Synonyms**: detest, despise, loathe)
			 abhorrence (**Synonyms**: aversion, repugnance, loathing)
			 LEADING ROOT COMPOUND:
			 fic: horrific (from *facere*, to make)
			 fy: horrify (**Synonyms**: dismay, appall, daunt) (see *horrific*)
			 pil: horripilate, horripilation (the erection of hair of the head or
			    body, as from fear, disease, or cold; goose flesh) (*pilus*, hair)
			 DISGUISED ROOT:
			 ordure (ultimately from *horrere*; dung, filth, manure, excre-
			    ment) (Old French *ord*, filthy)
			 NO CROSS REFERENCE

hort*	Latin
	 horiri
	 (IE: *gher*,
	 to desire)
		to urge, incite	ROOT NOTE: Root is derived from *hortari*, a frequentative of
			    horiri; in grammar, a *frequentative* expresses frequent and re-
			    peated action.
			 SIMPLE ROOT: hortation, hortatory (also, *hortative*: serving
			    to encourage or urge to good deeds; exhorting; giving advice)
			 PREFIXED ROOT:
			 ex-: exhort (**Synonyms**: urge, press, importune), exhorta-
			    tion, exhortatory (also, *exhortative*) (*ex*-, out)
			 NO CROSS REFERENCE

Word from Greek mythology: cassandra, a prophet of doom
(from Cassandra, a prophet cursed by Apollo so that her prophecies,
though they were true, were fated never to be believed)

Element	From	Meaning	Examples
hum**	Latin *humus* (IE: *ghom*, earth ground)	earth, ground	SIMPLE ROOT: huma: human, humane, humanism, humanist, humanitarian (**Synonyms**: philanthropic, charitable, altruistic), humanities, humanity humb: humble (**Synonyms**: degrade, abase, debase) humi: humiliate (see synonyms at *humble*, previous entry), humility humu: humus (a brown or black substance resulting from the partial decay of plant and animal matter) PREFIXED ROOT: *ex-*: exhume (to dig out of the earth, especially a body for forensic examination) {exhumation} (*ex-*, out) *in-*: inhume (to bury a dead body; inter) {inhumation} (*in-*, in) *super-*: superhuman (*super-*, over, beyond) *trans-*: transhumance (seasonal and alternating movement of livestock, together with the persons who tend the herds, between two regions, as lowlands and highlands) (*trans-*, across) CROSS REFERENCE: *chthon, geo, terr*
hum			See *um* for *humectant, humid, humor*.
hyal*	Greek *hyalos*	transparent, glass	SIMPLE ROOT: hyaline, hyalite LEADING ROOT COMPOUND: *hyal*: oid: hyaloid (short for *hyaloid membrane*; the delicate, pellucid, and nearly structureless membrane enclosing the vitreous humor of the eye) (*oid*, similar to) ur: hyaluronic (from *ouron*, urine) *hyalo*: gen: hyalogen (*gen*, producer) plasm: hyaloplasm (*plasm*, form) CROSS REFERENCE: *vitr*
hyd*	Greek *hydor* IE: *wed*, water)	water	SIMPLE ROOT: hydat: hydatid (watery vesicle), hydatism hydr: hydra [like the many-headed water serpent in Greek mythology (which see, below), any persistent or ever-increasing evil with many sources and causes; also small, soft-bodied freshwater polyps], hydrant, hydrase, hydrate PREFIXED ROOT: *an-*: anhydride, anhydrite, anhydrous (*an-*, without) *de-*: dehydrate, dehydration (*de-*, opposite of) LEADING ROOT COMPOUND: *hydat*: hod: hydathode (*hodos*, way) *hydr*: ang: hydrangea (a plant whose flowers resemble tiny water vessels) (*angeion*, vessel) anth: hydranth [in *zoology*, any of the feeding individuals (*zooids*) of a hydroid colony] (*anth*, flower) argyr: hydrargyrum (water silver; mercury; chemical symbol, Hg) (*argyros*, silver) aul: hydraulics (*aulos*, tube, pipe) oid: hydroid (like a hydra or polyp) (*oid*, similar to)

Element	From	Meaning	Examples
hyd (cont'd)			oxy: hydroxyl (*oxygen*) (*oxy*, sharp) *hydro*: cel: hydrocele (a collection of watery fluid in a cavity of the body, especially in the scrotum or along the spermatic cord) (*cele*, tumor) cephal: hydrocephalus (an accumulation of serous fluid within the cranium, especially in infancy), hydrocephaly (*cephal*, head) chlor: hydrochloric, hydrochloride (*chlor*, pale green) dynam: hydrodynamics (*dynam*, power) gen: hydrogen, hydrogenate (*gen*, produce) graph: hydrography (*graph*, write) kine: hydrokinetic(s) (*kinem*, movement) logy: hydrology (*logy*, study of) lys: hydrolysis (*lysis*, loosen) mancy: hydromancy (*mancy*, divination) meter: hydrometer (*meter*, measure) path: hydropathy (*pathy*, treatment) phan: hydrophane (*phan*, show) phil: hydrophilous (*phil*, love of) phob: hydrophobia (same as *rabies*, from the symptomatic inability to swallow liquids), hydrophobic (of, or having, *hydrophobia*; not capable of uniting with or absorbing *water*) (*phobia*, fear of) phon: hydrophone (*phone*, sound) plan: hydroplane (*plane*, level surface) pon: hydroponics (*ponein*, to toil) scop: hydroscope (*scope*, view) sol: hydrosol (*sol* from solution) spher: hydrosphere (all the water on the surface of the earth, including oceans, lakes, rivers, icebergs, etc.) (*sphere*, globe) stat: hydrostatics (*stat*, stand) therm: hydrothermal (*therm*, heat) zo: hydrozoan (*zo*, animal) GREEK MYTHOLOGY: Hydra (the nine-headed serpent slain by Hercules: when any one of its heads was cut off, it was replaced by two others) CONSTELLATION: Hydra (a long, irregular, Southern constellation, south of Cancer, Leo, and Virgo) RUSSIAN: vodka (diminutive of *voda*, water) IRISH: *usquebaugh* (whiskey) PLACENAME: Hydro, Oklahoma CROSS REFERENCE: *aqua*
hygi*	Greek *hygies*: sound, whole	health	ROOT NOTE: This root was derived IE *su-*, well + *gwei-*, to live, thus "living well," and is seen in the phrase *hygiene techne*, art of health. SIMPLE ROOT: hygiene, hygienic (of hygiene or health; promoting health; healthful; sanitary), hygienics, hygienist LEADING ROOT COMPOUND: latry: hygeiolatry (*latry*, worship of) GODDESS OF HEALTH: Hygeia NO CROSS REFERENCE

Element	From	Meaning	Examples
hygr*	Greek *hygros*: moist, wet	moisture	LEADING ROOT COMPOUND: graph: hygrograph (a hygrometer for continuously recording atmospheric humidity) (*graph*, write) meter: hygrometer (*meter*, measure) phyt: hygrophyte (same as *hydrophyte*) (*phyton*, plant) scop: hygroscope, hygroscopic (*scope*, view) CROSS REFERENCE: *hyd*
hylo*	Greek *hyle*: wood, forest, matter	wood, matter	SIMPLE ROOT: hyla (any of a large genus of tree frogs, as the spring peeper) LEADING ROOT COMPOUND: phag: hylophagous (feeding on wood, as do some insects) (*phag*, eat) zo: hylozoism (the doctrine that all matter is life, or that life is inseparable from *matter*) (*zo*, life) CROSS REFERENCE: *xylo*
hymen*	Greek *hymen*	membrane, caul	SIMPLE ROOT: hymen (the thin mucous membrane that closes part or sometimes all of the opening of the vagina; maidenhead) hymeneal (a wedding song) hymenium (a superficial layer of spore-producing cells in fungi) LEADING ROOT COMPOUND: pter: hymmenopteran {hymenopterous} (*pter*, wing) tom: hymenotomy (*tom*, cut) DISGUISED ROOT: hymn (originally a morning wedding song) (see next family) GREEK MYTHOLOGY: Hymen, the god of marriage CROSS REFERENCE: *can*
hymn**	Greek *hymnos*: song of praise	ode, festive song	SIMPLE ROOT: hymn (a song in praise or honor of God, a god, or gods), hymnal, hymnist LEADING ROOT COMPOUND: *hymn(o)*: od: hymnody (literally, hymn song) (*od*, song) logy: hymnology (*logy*, study of) CROSS REFERENCE: *can*
hyper-* **	Greek *hyper* (IE: *uper*, over)	excessive, more, beyond	EXTENDED PREFIX: hypera (a type of weevil) PREFIXED ROOTS AND COMPOUNDS: *hyp-*: erg: hypergolic (igniting spontaneously when mixed together, as rocket and oxidizer combinations) (*erg*, work + *ol*, oil) *hyper-*: bar: hyperbaric (*bar*, weight) bat: hyperbaton (transposition or inversion of idiomatic word order, e.g., *echoed the hills* for *the hills echoed*) bol: (throw) hyperbola (literally, to throw beyond: a mathematics term) hyperbole (exaggeration for effect and not to be taken literally, e.g., he as strong as an ox) hyperbolic (having to do with a *hyperbola* or a *hyperbole*) bor: hyperborean (beyond the north wind; very cold, frigid; a person of a far northern region; see Greek *Mythology*, below) (*boreas*, north wind)

Element	From	Meaning	Examples
hyper- (cont'd)			cata: hypercatalexia (the addition of one or more syllables in excess of the normal number in a verse or metrical line; also called *hypermeter*) (*cata-* prefixes *lex*, word) correct: hypercorrection (a nonstandard usage resulting from an overly conscious effort to avoid an error, as in the case of personal pronouns, e.g., *between you and I*, for *between you and me*) (*cor-* assimilates *com-*, with + *rect*, straight) dul: hyperdulia (special veneration of the Virgin Mary; distinguished from *dulia*: veneration given to angels and saints, and *latria*: veneration given only to God) (*dule*, a slave) em: hyperemia (an increased blood flow or congestion of blood in an organ, tissue, etc.) (*emia*, a diseased condition of the blood) esthes: hyperesthesia (an abnormal sensitivity of the skin or some sense organ) (*esthes*, feeling) gam: hypergamy (marriage with a person of a higher social class or position) (*gam*, marriage) glyc: hyperglycemia (an abnormally high concentration of sugar in the blood; opposite of *hypoglycemia*) (*glyc*, sugar; *em* from *hemo*, blood) kine: hyperkinesis (*kine*, movement) metr: hypermetropia (same as *hyperopia*) (*metr*, measurement) opia: hyperopia (abnormal vision in which the rays of light are focused behind the retina, so that distant objects are seen more clearly than near ones; farsightedness) (*op*, vision) pyr: hyperpyrexia (abnormally high fever) (*pyr*, fire, fever) son: hypersonic (designating, of, or traveling at a speed equal to about five times the speed of sound, or greater; compare *supersonic*) (*son*, sound) ton: hypertonic (having abnormally high tension or tone, especially of the muscles; having an osmotic pressure higher than that of an isotonic solution) (*ton*, stretching) trophy: hypertrophy (a considerable increase in the size of an organ or tissue, caused by enlargement of its cellular components) (*troph*, nourish) vent: hyperventilation (an extremely rapid or deep breathing that may cause dizziness, fainting, etc. as a result of a rapid loss of carbon dioxide) (*ventus*, wind) GREEK MYTHOLOGY: Hyperborean (an inhabitant of a northern region sunshine and everlasting spring, beyond the north wind) CROSS REFERENCE: *super*
hypno*	Greek *hypno* (IE: *swep*, sleep)	sleep	LEADING ROOT COMPOUND: *hypn*: osis: hypnosis {hypnotic, hypnotism} (*osis*, condition of) *hypno*: ana: hypnoanalysis (the use of hypnosis or hypnotic drugs in combination with psychoanalytic techniques) (*ana-* prefixes *lys*, loosen) bat: hypnobatia (walking in one's sleep) (*bat*, walk, step) logy: hypnology (study of sleep and hypnotism) (*logy*, study of)

Element	From	Meaning	Examples
hypno (cont'd)			EMBEDDED ROOT COMPOUND: auto<u>hypn</u>osis (*auto*, self) GREEK MYTHOLOGY: Hypnos (the Greek god of sleep, identified in Roman mythology with Somnus, the god of sleep; hence *somnolent*, sleepy, drowsy) CROSS REFERENCE: *dorm, somn, sopor*
hypo-*	Greek *hypo* (IE: *upo*, up from under)	under	PREFIXED ROOT: *hyp-*: abyss: hypabyssal (in *geology*, designating or of igneous rocks solidified at moderate depths, generally as sills or dikes) (*a-*, not, prefixes *byss*, bottom) *hypo-*: acid: hypoacidity (acidity in a lesser degree than is usual or normal, as of the gastric juice) (from *acer*, sharp) blast: hypoblast (the endoderm of a gastrula) (*blast*, embryo) caust: hypocaust (see note under *caust*) (*caust*, heat) chondr: hypochondriac, hypochondrium (*chondro*, cartilage) cor: hypocoristic (of or being a pet name; also, a diminutive or a term of endearment) (*cor*, girl) cotyl: hypocotyl (see note under *cotyl*) (*cotyl*, hollow, cavity) cris: hypocrisy (originally, play acting; a pretending to be what one is not, or to feel what one does not feel; especially, a pretense of virtue, piety, etc.) (from *krinein*, to separate) crit: hypocrite (originally, a stage actor; therefore, one who pretends to be what he or she is not) (see *hypocrisy*) cycl: hypocycloid (*cycle*, circle; *oid*, similar to) derm: hypodermic, hypodermis (*derm*, skin) gastr: hypogastric (from *gaster*, belly) ge: hypogeal (*geo*, earth) gen: hypogene, hypogenous (*gen*, produce) gloss: hypoglossal (*gloss*, tongue) glyc: hypoglycemia (*glyc*, sugar; *em* short for *hemo*, blood) gnath: hypognathous (*gnath*, jaw) gyn: hypogynous (compare *perigynous, epigynous*, under *gyn*) (*gyn*, reproduction) phys: hypophysis (the pituitary gland) (*phys*, grow) plas: hypoplasia (*plasia*, change, development) stas: hypostasis {hypostatic} (*stas*, stand) tax: hypotaxis (*taxis*, arrange) ten: hypotenuse (see note under Greek *ten*) (*ten*, stretch) thec: hypothec, hypothecate (see note under *thec*) (*thec*, a small case) therm: hypothermal (*therm*, heat) thesis: hypothesis (literally, to place under; an approved theory, proposition, supposition, etc. tentatively accepted to explain certain facts or to provide a basis for further investigation, argument, etc.) (*thesis*, place) DISGUISED PREFIX: hyphen [literally, under one; together; in one; a mark (-) used between parts of certain compound words or the syllables of a divided word, as at the end of a line] (from *hypo* + *hen*, one) CROSS REFERENCE: *infra-, sub-*

340

Element	From	Meaning	Examples
hyster*	Greek *hystera*	womb, uterus	SIMPLE ROOT: hysteria (so called because the Ancients believed that women were more excitable than men; therefore, their excitability was due to the uterus overacting; **Synonyms**: mania, frenzy, delirium) hysteric (as an adjective, hysterical; as a noun, a person subject to hysteria) hysterical (emotionally uncontrolled; extremely comical) LEADING ROOT COMPOUND: ectom: hysterectomy (*ectom*, to remove surgically) gen: hysterogenic (*genic*, causing) NOTE: *Hysteresis* is not in this family; see next family. CROSS REFERENCE: *uter*
hyster-*	Greek *hysteresis*, to be late; fall short	later	SIMPLE ROOT: hysteresis (in *physics*, the lagging of a physical effect on a body behind its cause) PREFIXED ROOT: an-: anhysteresis (not affected by hysteresis) (*an-*, not) NO CROSS REFERENCE

I

Element	From	Meaning	Examples
iat*	Greek *iatros*: physician	heal, treatment	SIMPLE ROOT: iatric, iatrical, iatreusis LEADING ROOT COMPOUND: *iath*: erg: iathergy (the state of immunity existing in an immunized organism in which the tuberculin skin sensitivity has been abolished by specific desensitization) (*ergon*, work) *iatr*: arch: iatrarchy (government by physicians) (*archy*, ruled by) TRAILING ROOT COMPOUND: *iatria*: nest: nestiatria (hunger cure; to cure by fasting) (*nestis*, fasting) *iatrics*: ger: geriatric, geriatrics, geriatrician, geriatrist (*ger*, old) ped: pediatric, pediatrician, pediatrics (from *paed*, child) *iatro*: gen: iatrogenic (induced in a patient by a physician's words or actions: said especially of imagined illnesses) (*gen*, produce) *iatry*: pod: podiatric, podiatrist, podiatry (*pod*, foot) psych: psychiatrist, psychiatry (*psyche*, mind) CROSS REFERENCE: *cur, med, therap*
ichthy*	Greek *ichthys*	fish	SIMPLE ROOT: ichthyic, ichthyism (poisoning from fish) LEADING ROOT COMPOUND: *ichthy*: oid: ichthyoid (*oid*, similar to) ornis: ichythornis (*ornis*, bird) osis: ichthyosis (a congenital, hereditary skin disease characterized by roughening and thickening of the horny layer of the skin, producing dryness and scaling) (*osis*, condition of) *ichthyo*: lit: ichthyolite (fossil of a fish or part of a fish) (*lithos*, stone) logy: ichthyology (*logy*, study of) morph: ichthyomorphic (*morph*, shape, form) phag: ichthyophagous (fish-eating, as certain birds) (*phag*, eat) saur: ichthyosaur (*saur*, lizard) CROSS REFERENCE: *pisc*
icon**	Greek *eikon* (IE: *weik*, to resemble)	image, symbol	SIMPLE ROOT: icon (an image, figure, representation), iconic LEADING ROOT COMPOUND: clasm: iconoclasm (the actions or beliefs of an iconoclast) (from *klasma*, broken thing) clast: iconoclast (anyone opposed to the religious use of images or advocating the destruction of such images; extended to mean a person who attacks or ridicules traditional or venerated institutions or ideas regarded by him/her as erroneous or based on superstition) {iconoclastic} (from *klaein*, to break) graph: iconography (same as *iconology*) (*graph*, write)

343

Element	From	Meaning	Examples
icon (cont'd)			latry: iconolatry (*latry*, worship of) logy: iconology (the study of icons, images, etc.; icons collectively; symbolic representation; symbolism) (*logy*, study of) scop: iconoscope (*scope*, look) stas: iconostasis (in the Eastern Orthodox Church, a partition or screen, decorated with icons, separating the sanctuary from the rest of the church) (*stas*, stand) NOTE: Do not confuse this root with *icos*, twenty. CROSS REFERENCE: *sema, sign*
icos*	Greek *eikos* (IE: *wikmti*, twenty)	twenty	LEADING ROOT COMPOUND: *icosa*: hedr: icosahedron, icosahedral (*hedra*, geometric face) spher: icosasphere (*sphere*, ball, globe) *icosi*: tetra: icositetrahedron (a 24-sided figure) (*tetra*, four, + *hedra*, geometric face) NO CROSS REFERENCE
icter*	Greek *ikteros*	jaundice	SIMPLE ROOT: icteric, icterine, icteritious, icterus (a genus of yellowish birds comprising the American orioles) LEADING ROOT COMPOUND: *icteri*: oid: icterioid (*oid*, similar to) *ictero*: anem: icteroanemia (*an-*, not + *emia*, disease of the blood) NOTE: Do not confuse this root with *ict*, to strike, as in *ictic*, and in *ictus*, in both their medical and music meanings. NO CROSS REFERENCE
ide**	Greek *idein*: to see (IE: *weid*, to see, know)	form, notion (as opposed to reality)	SIMPLE ROOT: idea (**Synonyms:** thought, notion, concept) ideal (**Synonyms:** model, exemplar, standard), idealist, ideation LEADING ROOT COMPOUND: crac: ideocracy (government or social *rule*, or management, based on abstract ideas, an example of which is Brook Farm, established as an experimental socialist community in 1841 near West Roxbury, Massachusetts, in an attempt by Transcendentalists to develop a union between intellectual growth and manual labor; the experiment was discontinued in 1847 because of rising debts) (*cracy*, rule by) gram: ideogram (from *graph*, write) graph: ideographic, ideography (*graph*, write) log: ideological, ideologist, ideologue, ideology (*logos*, word) meta: ideometabolic (*meta-* prefixes *bol*, to throw) mot: ideomotion, ideomotor (*mot*, move) phon: ideophone (in *linguistics*, the expression of an idea, as in many African languages, by means of a sound, often reduplicated, that creates an image of an action, object, etc.) (*phone*, sound) DISGUISED ROOT: idyll (or *idyl*; a short poem or prose work describing a simple, peaceful scene of rural or pastoral life; a scene or incident suitable for such a work; a narrative poem somewhat like a short epic, as Tennyson's *Idylls of the King*; in *music*, a simple pastoral composition) {idyllic}

Element	From	Meaning	Examples
ide (cont'd)			FRENCH: *idée* (idea) *idée fixe* (literally, fixed idea; obsession) *idée reçue* (literally, received idea; a generally accepted idea; convention; commonplace) NOTE: Do not confuse this root with *idio,* one's own. CROSS REFERENCE: *form, morph, oid* (from *eido*)
idem,* iden	Latin *idem*	same	SIMPLE ROOT: idem; identic, identical, identity LEADING ROOT COMPOUND: fic: identification (from *facere,* to make, do) fy: identify (from *facere,* to make, do) CROSS REFERENCE: *homo, iso*
idio**	Greek *idios* (IE: *suus,* his, her, one's)	one's own	SIMPLE ROOT: idiom: idiom, idiomatic idiot: idiot (literally, a private person; incapable of holding public office; extremely ignorant person), idiotism LEADING ROOT COMPOUND: blast: idioblast (*blast,* seed, embryo) gloss: idioglossia (a condition in which the affected person pronounces words so badly as to seem to speak a language of his/her own) (*glossa,* tongue, speech) lect: idiolect (in *linguistics,* the dialect of an individual) morph: idiomorphic (*morph,* shape, form) path: idiopathic {idiopathy} (designating or of a disease whose cause is unknown or uncertain) (*path,* feeling) plasm: idioplasm (*plasm,* form, shape) syn: idiosyncrasy (eccentricity) (*syn-* prefixes *cras,* mixture) FRENCH: *idiot savant* (literally, wise idiot; a mentally retarded person who possesses some remarkable special aptitude, as for memorization or rapid mental calculation, e.g., knowing the day of the week for January 19, 1920) CROSS REFERENCE: *propr*
i g			See *act* for *exigent* and *prodigal.*
ig-			See *in-* for *ignominy.*
ign**	Latin *ignis* (IE: *egnis,* of fire)	fire	SIMPLE ROOT: igne: igneous (in *geology,* produced under intense heat, as rocks of volcanic origin; pertaining to the characterisitcs of fire), ignescent ignis: ignis (medical term), ignisation (hyperthermia produced by exposure to artificial sources of heat) ignit: ignite (in *chemistry,* to heat intensely; roast), igniter, ignition PREFIXED ROOT: *pre-:* preignition (*pre-,* before) LEADING ROOT COMPOUND: fer: igniferous (*ferre,* to bear) pot: ignipotent (having power over, or mastery of, fire) (*pot,* power) COINED WORD: ignitron [*igni*(te) + (elec)*tron*] LATIN TERM: *ignis fatuus* (see explanation under *fatu*) CROSS REFERENCE: *pyr*
il-			See *in-* for *illegal, illumine.*

Element	From	Meaning	Examples
in-***	Latin (IE: *en-*, in)	in, into, on, toward, within	NOTE: The prefix is also used an an intensive, as in *instigate, infatuate.* Many of the roots or words prefixed are Anglo-Saxon, e.g., *inbeing, inbound, inbreed.*

PREFIXED ROOT:

in-:

aug: inaugurate (**Synonyms:** begin, commence, initiate) (*augere*, to grow)

cand: incandesce, incandescent (*candere*, to burn, shine)

cant: incantation (the chanting or uttering of words purporting to have magical power; repetitious wordiness; obfuscation) (from *enchant*)

carc: incarcerate (to imprison; to enclose) (*carcer*, prison)

carn: incarnadine, incarnate, incarnation (*carne*, flesh, meat)

cend: incendiary (having to do with the willful destruction of property by fire) (from *candere*, to burn, shine)

cens: incense (literally, something kindled; **Synonyms:** provoke, anger) (see *incendiary*)

cent: incentive (**Synonyms:** stimulus, spur, motive) (from *canere*, to sing)

cept: incept, inception (**Synonyms:** origin, source, beginning), inceptive (from *capere*, to hold, take)

choat: inchoate, inchoation (originally, a rural term, "to hitch up; harness"; just begun; in the early stages; incipient; rudimentary; in *law*, not yet completed or made effective), inchoative (from *cohum*, the strap from plow beam to harness)

cid: (from *cadere*, to fall)

incidence, incident (**Synonyms:** occurrence, event, episode)

incidental (**Synonyms:** accidental, fortuitous, casual), incidentally

ciner: incinerate, incinerator (from *cinis*, ashes)

cip: incipient, incipit (from *capere*, to take, hold)

cis: incise, incised, incision, incisive (**Synonyms:** trenchant, cutting, biting), incisor, incisory (from *caedere*, to cut)

cit: incite (**Synonyms:** instigate, arouse, foment), incitement (*citare*, to set in motion)

clin: inclinable, inclination (**Synonyms:** leaning, propensity, proclivity), incline, inclined, inclining (*clinare*, to lean)

clud: include (**Synonyms:** comprise, comprehend, embrace), included (in *botany*, with stamens and pistils wholly contained within the petals, sheath, etc.) (*claudere*, to close, shut)

clus: inclusion (in *biology*, a separate body, as a grain of starch, within the protoplasm of a cell), inclusive (see *include*)

corp: incorporate, incorporated, incorporation (*corp*, body)

creas: increase (**Synonyms:** enlarge, augment, multiply) (from *crescere*, to grow)

crem: increment (an addition or increase; profit; in *mathematics*, a change, positive, negative, or zero, in an independent variable) (see *increase*)

cres: increscent (increasing, growing, waxing: said especially of the moon) (see *increase*)

Element	From	Meaning	Examples
in- (cont'd)			crim: incriminate {incriminatory} (*crimen*, verdict)

cub: incubate, incubation, incubator, incubus (*cubare*, to lie down)

culc: inculcate (see note under *calc*) (from *calc*, heel)

culp: inculpate (to charge with fault; to incriminate) (*culpa*, fault)

cumb: incumbent (*cumbare*, to lie down)

cun: incunabula (extant copies of books produced before 1500; the earliest stages of anything) (*cunae*, cradle)

cur: incur (to run or fall into some consequence, usually undesirable or injurious), incurreence, incurrent (*currere*, to run)

curs: incursion (a hostile, usually sudden, entrance into or invasion of a place; raid), incursive (from *currere*, to run)

curv: incurvate, incurve (*curvus*, crooked, bent, curved)

cus: incus (in *anatomy*, the middle one of a chain of three small bones in the middle ear of man and other mammals; anvil), incuse (hammered or stamped in: said of the design on a coin; as a *noun*, such a design) (from *cudere*, to strike, hit)

dent: indent (literally, to tooth in, or bite into, as a paragraph), indentation, indention, indenture (see authors' *An Introduction to an Academic Vocabulary*) (*dent*, tooth)

dex: index (from *dicare*, to point out)

dic: indicant, indicate, (to be a sign of; betoken; imply; to point out or point to; to state or express) indication, indicative, indicator, indicia (see *index*, previous entry)

dict: indict, indiction, indictment (from *dicere*, to speak)

dit: indite (to compose or write, as a speech or poem) (from *dicere*, to speak)

duc: (*ducere*, to lead)

induce (**Synonyms**: actuate, prompt, incite), inducement induct, inductance, inductee, induction, inductive, inductor [the prefix of *inductile* means "not"]

dulg: indulge (to yield to an inclination or desire; **Synonyms**: humor, pamper, spoil), indulgence, indulgent (*dulge* of uncertain origin)

dur: indurate, induration (*durare*, to make hard)

ebri: inebriate (see note under *ebr*), inebriety (*ebr*, to drink)

fat: infatuate, infatuated, infatuation (**Synonyms**: love, affection, attachment) (*fatuus*, foolish)

fect: infect, infection, infectious (also, *infective*) (*facere*, to make, do)

fer: infer (**Synonyms**: deduce, conclude, judge), inference, inferential (*ferre*, to carry, bear) [do not confuse the use of *infer* with *imply*]

fest: infest (to overrun or inhabit in large numbers; to swarm in or over; to be parasitic in or on a host) (from IE *dhers-*, to be bold, attack)

filtr: infiltrate (fulled wool used for straining liquors), infiltration {infiltrative} (*filtrum*, felt, filter)

Element	From	Meaning	Examples
in- (cont'd)			fix: infix (in *linguistics*, used as a noun: a morpheme added within the base of a word, as the <u>underlined</u> *a* in transportation; the meaningful elements of this word are *trans-*, across + *port* from *portare*, to carry + *-tion*, the act of) (from *figere*, to fix)

fix: infix (in *linguistics*, used as a noun: a morpheme added within the base of a word, as the <u>underlined</u> *a* in transporta-tion; the meaningful elements of this word are *trans-*, across + *port* from *portare*, to carry + *-tion*, the act of) (from *figere*, to fix)

flat: inflatable, inflate (**Synonyms:** expand, swell, distend), inflated, inflation, inflationary (from *flare*, to blow)

flect: inflect, inflection, inflectional (*flectere*, to bend)

flex: inflexed (in *biology*, bent sharply downward or inward; turned toward the axis) (*in-*, in)
[see *in-*, not (next family), for *inflexible*]

flict: inflict, infliction (from *fligere*, to beat, strike)

flor: infloresence (a flowering or blossoming; in *botany*, the arrangement of flowers on the axis) (*flor*, flower, blossom)

flu: influence (**Synonyms:** authority, prestige, weight), in-fluent, influential (*fluere*, to flow)
[see *Italian*, below, for *influenza*]

flux: influx (see *influence*, previous entry)

form: inform, informant, information (**Synonyms:** data, in-telligence, advice), informative, informer (*forma*, shape, ap-pearance)

fract: infract, infraction (from *frangere*, to break)

fring: infringe (**Synonyms:** break, disobey), infringement (see *infract*, previous entry)

fund: infundibulum (in *anatomy*, a funnel-shaped organ or part) (*fundere*, to pour)

fus: infuse, infusible (the act or process of infusing; another *infusible* means "not fusible"), infusion, infusionism (the theological doctrine that the soul existed in a previous state and is infused into the body at conception or birth) (from *fundere*, to pour)

gemin: ingeminate (to repeat; reiterate) (*gemin*, twin)

gen: (*genere*, to produce)
ingenious (**Synonyms:** bright, gifted, adroit)
ingénue, ingenuity
ingenuous (**Synonyms:** candid, innocent, naive)
[*ingenious* and *ingenuous* are often confused; see differentiation under *gen*]

gest: ingest (to take into the body, as food or liquid), ingesta, ingestant (from *gerere*, to bear)

grain: ingrain, ingrained (firmly fixed)

gred: ingredient (from *gradus*, step)

gress: ingress (from *gradus*, step)

guin: inguinal (*guin*, groin)

gurg: ingurgitate (to swallow greedily or in great quantity, as food) (*gurgitare*, to flood)

hab: inhabit, inhabitant, inhabited (*habere*, to have)

hal: inhalant, inhalator, inhale, inhaler (*halare*, to breathe)

her: inhere, inherence, inherency, inherent (from *haerere*, to stick)

herit: inherit, inheritance, inherited, inheritor

Element	From	Meaning	Examples
in- (cont'd)			hib: inhibit, inhibition, inhibitor (from *habere*, to have, hold)
			hum: inhume (to bury; inter) (*humare*, to bury)
			it: (from *ire*, to go)
			initial (in *biology*, a primordial cell that determines the basic pattern of derived tissues; specifically, a meristematic cell)
			initiate (**Synonyms:** begin, commence, inaugurate), initiation, initiative, initiatory
			ject: inject, injection, injector (from *jacere*, to throw)
			junct: injunction (the act or instance of enjoining) (*jungere*, to join)
			nat: innate (**Synonyms:** natural, congenital) (*natus*, born)
			nov: innovate, innovation (*novus*, new)
			nuen: innuendo (from *nuere*, to nod)
			ocu: inoculable, inoculate (originally, to engraft a bud in another plant), inoculation, inoculum (*oculi*, eye)
			oscul: inosculate (to join together by openings at the ends: said of arteries; to intertwine: said of a vine, etc.; to join, blend, or unite intimately) (*osculari*, to kiss)
			quest: inquest (**Synonyms:** hearing, inquisition) (see *inquire*, below)
			quil: inquiline (in *zoology*, an animal living in the nest or burrow of another animal) (from *colere*, to live, dwell)
			quir: inquire (**Synonyms:** ask, query, question), inquiring, inquiry (**Synonyms:** study, scrutiny, exploration) (*quaerere*, to seek)
			quis: inquisition, inquisitive (**Synonyms:** curious, meddlesome, prying), inquisitor (see *inquire*, previous entry)
			scrib: inscribe (to write or engrave, characters, etc.) (*scribere*, to write)
			script: inscription (see *incribe*, previous entry)
			semin: inseminate (to sow; implant seed into; to inject semen into the female reproductive tract; impregnate) (*semen*, seed)
			sert: insert, inserted (in *biology*, joined by natural growth), insertion (from *serere*, to join)
			sess: insessorial (adapted for perching, as a bird's foot) (*sidere*, to settle)
			sid: insidious (**Synonyms:** artful, cunning, wily) (*sidere*, to sit)
			sign: insignia (*signum*, a mark)
			sinu: insinuate (**Synonyms:** suggest, imply, hint), insinuating, insinuation (*sinus*, curved surface, fold)
			sist: insist, insistence, insistent (from *stare*, to stand)
			sol: insolate (to expose to the sun's rays; treat by exposure to sun's rays), insolation (sun stroke) (*sol*, sun)
			spect: inspect, inspection, inspective, inspector (*specere*, to look)
			spir: inspiration, inspirational, inspiratory, inspire, inspired, inspirit (*spirare*, to breathe)
			stall: install, installation, installment (Germanic *stall*, place)
			stan: instance (**Synonyms:** case, example, illustration), instant, instantaneous, instantiate, instantly (from *stare*, stand)

Element	From	Meaning	Examples
in- (cont'd)			staur: instauration (renewal; restoration; renovation) (from *stare*, stand)
			stig: instigate (to provoke or incite to some action or course), instigation (from *stizein*, to tattoo, to prick)
			still: instill, instillation (*stillare*, to drip)
			stinct: instinct (an inborn pattern of activity), instinctive (from *stinguere*, to prick)
			stit: institute, institution, institutive (from *stare*, to stand)
			struc: (from *struere*, to pile up)
			instruct (**Synonyms: 1**) command, order, direct; **2**) teach, educate, train), instruction (**Synonyms**: tutoring, coaching, training)
			instructive, instructor
			strum: instrument (**Synonyms**: tool, implement, utensil), instrumental, instrumentalism, instrumentation (see *instruct*)
			sult: insult (**Synonyms**: offend, affront, outrage), insulting (*salire*, to leap)
			surg: insurgence, insurgency, insurgent (*surgere*, to rise)
			surr: insurrection, insurrectionary (see *insurgent*)
			teg: integument (**Synonyms**: cortex, involucre, involucrum) (see note under *teg*) (*tegere*, to cover)
			tend: intend (**Synonyms**: mean, design, propose), intendant, intended, intending, intendment (*tendere*, to stretch)
			tens: intense, intensifier, intensify (**Synonyms**: aggravate, heighten, enhance), intension, intensity, intensive (from *intend*)
			tent: intent (**Synonyms**: intention, purpose, aim), intention, intentional, intentioned (from *intend*)
			ter: inter (see note under *terr*) (*terra*, earth)
			timid: intimidate (**Synonyms**: frighten, daunt) {intimidation} (*timidus*, afraid)
			tinct: intinction (the act of dipping the Eucharistic bread into the consecrated wine, so that the communicant receives both together) (*tingere*, to dye)
			tox: intoxicant, intoxicate, intoxication (*toxicum*, poison)
			tric: intricate (**Synonyms**: complex, complicated, involved) (*tricae*, vexations)
			trig: intrigant (feminine: *intrigante*), intrigue, intriguing (from *intricate*, previous entry)
			trud: intrude (**Synonyms**: obtrude, interlope, interfere) (*trudere*, to thrust)
			trus: intrusion, intrusive (**Synonyms**: annoying, interfering, distracting) (from *intrude*, previous entry)
			tuit: intuit, intuition, intuitionism, intuitive (*tueri*, to look at)
			unda: inundant (to cover or engulf with a flood; deluge, as *to inundate with requests*), inundate (*undare*, to move in waves)
			vad: invade (**Synonyms**: trespass, infringe, intrude) (*vadere*, to come)
			vagin: invaginate, invagination (*vagina*, a sheath)
			vas: invasion, invasive (see *invade*, above)
			vect: invected, invective (from *vehere*, to carry)

Element	From	Meaning	Examples
in- (cont'd)			veigh: inveigh (see *invective*, previous entry; not related to *in-veigle*; see *ocul*)
			vent: (*venire*, to come)
			invent (**Synonyms**: devise, contrive, discover), invention, inventive, inventor
			inventory (**Synonyms**: account, catalog, register)
			vers: inverse, inversion (from *invert*, next entry)
			vert: invert (*vertere*, to turn)
			vest: invest, investitive, investiture, investment (*vestire*, to clothe)
			vestig: investigate (literally, to follow the tracks), investigation (**Synonyms**: scrutiny, exploration), investigative (*vestig*, track)
			veter: inveterate (**Synonyms**: chronic, confirmed, hardened) (*vetus*, old)
			vid: invidious (such as to excite ill will, animosity, odium, or envy) (*videre*, to see)
			vigil: invigilate (*vigilare*, to watch)
			vit: invitation, invitatory, invite (**Synonyms**: call, summon, convene), inviting (*vitare*, to strive, hasten)
			vigor: invigorate (**Synonyms**: animate, quicken, exhilarate) (*vigere*, to be strong)
			indi-: (from Old Latin *indu-*, in)
			indigene, indigenous (from *gignere*, to beget)
			indigent (from *indigere*, to be in need; *egere*, to need)
			ASSIMILATIONS AND VARIATIONS:
			il-:
			lat: illation (the act of drawing a conclusion or making an inference from premises), illative (in *grammar*, inferential; said of such words as *therefore*) (from *ferre*, to bring)
			lum: illuminant, illuminate, illumination, illuminative, illuminator, illumine, illuminism (*luminare*, to light)
			lus: illusion (**Synonyms**: delusion, hallucination, mirage), illusionary, illusionism, illusionist, illusive, illusory (from *ludere*, to play)
			lustr: (from IE *leuk*, light)
			illustrate, illustrated, illustration (**Synonyms**: instance, case, example), illustrative, illustrator
			illustrious (**Synonyms**: famous, renowned, celebrated)
			luv: illuvial, illuviate, illuviation, illuvium (not to be confused with *alluvium*) (from *lavere*, to wash)
			im-: (before *m*, *p*, and *b*)
			bib: imbibe, imbibition (see note under *bib*) (*bibere*, to drink)
			bru: imbrue (literally, to drink in; to wet, soak, or stain, especially with blood) (from *bibere*, to drink)
			bue: imbue (originally, to moisten; saturate; now, to permeate or inspire, as with principles, ideas, emotions, etc.; **Synonyms**: 1) charge, infect, fire; 2) permeate, infuse, tincture) (from *bibere*, to drink)
			man: immanent (remaining within; indwelling; inherent; compare *transcendent*) (*manere*, to remain)

351

Element	From	Meaning	Examples
in- (cont'd)			merg: immerge (*mergere*, to dip, plunge, sink)
			mers: immerse, immersed, immersible, immersion (from *immerge*, previous entry)
			migr: immigrant, immigrate, immigration (*migrare*, to change)
			min: imminence, imminent (likely to happen without delay; impending: said of danger) (*minere*, to project, threaten)
			mix: immix, immixture (from *miscere*, to mix)
			mol: immolate {immolation, immolator} (*mola*, meal)
			mur: immure (to shut up within a wall; imprison; seclude) (*murus*, wall)
			pan: impanation (see note under *pan*) (*pan*, bread)
			part: impart (to give a share or portion of; give; to make known; tell; reveal)
			peach: impeach (see under *ped*, foot)
			ped: impedance, impede, impediment (**Synonyms:** obstacle, hindrance, obstruction), impedimenta (*ped*, foot)
			pel: impel, impeller (*pellere*, to drive)
			pend: impend, impendent, impending (*pendere*, to hang)
			pet: impetuous (**Synonyms:** sudden, precipitate, abrupt), impetus (*petere*, to rush at; to seek)
			ping: impinge {impingement} (from *pangere*, to strike)
			ple: implement (**Synonyms:** tool, instrument, appliance; as a verb, to carry into effect; fulfill), impletion (*plere*, to fill)
			pli: implicate, implication, implicit, implied (*plicare*, to fold)
			port: import, importance (**Synonyms:** consequence, moment, weight), important, importation (*portare*, to carry)
			pos: impose, imposing (**Synonyms:** grand, magnificent, stately), imposition, impost (one meaning) (from *ponere*, to place)
			prec: imprecate (**Synonyms:** curse, damn, execrate) (*precari*, to pray)
			press: impress (one meaning), impressible, impression, impressionable, impressionism, impressive (*premere*, to press)
			prest: imprest (a loan or advance of money, as from government funds) (*prestare*, to lend; *prest* from pre-, before + *stare*, to stand; to become surety for)
			prim: imprimis (contraction of the phrase *in primis*, among the first; in the first place) (*primus*, first)
			prompt: impromptu (**Synonyms:** extemporaneous, extempore, improvised) (see *prompt* under *emp*)
			pugn: impugn (**Synonyms:** deny, gainsay, contradict) (*pugnare*, to fight)
			puls: impulse, impulsion, impulsive (**Synonyms:** spontaneous, instinctive, involuntary) (from *impel*, above)
			ONE-WORD LATIN SENTENCE: *imprimatur* (Let it be printed; a license or permission to publish or print a book, article, etc; any sanction or approval)
			ir:
			rad: irradiance, irradiate (to shine or throw light upon; make bright; also, to make clear; illuminate intellectually; enlighten), irradiation (*radiare*, to radiate)

Element	From	Meaning	Examples
in- (cont'd)			rig: irrigable, irrigate {irrigation, irrigative}, irriguous (*rigare*, to wash, rain)
			rupt: irrupt {irruption, irruptive} (from *rumpere*, to break)
			NOTE: *Irritate* is not in this family.
			ITALIAN:
			illuminati (people who have or profess to have special intellectual or spiritual enlightenment)
			influenza (literally, influence; the disease was attributed by astrologers to the *influence* of the stars)
			intaglio (literally, to cut into)
			ITALIAN:FRENCH DOUBLETS: imbroglio:embroil
			LATIN TERMS:
			in absentia (in absence; as though present, as "He received his college degree *in absentia*")
			in camera [in chamber (in a judge's private office rather than in open court; a closed session)]
			in cipit (from which *incipient* is derived)
			in flagrante delicto [in the very act (of committing an offense); red-handed]
			in loco parentis [in place of a parent; acting on the authority of a parent, e.g., teachers by the laws of most states are *in loco parentis* while the children they teach are under their care]
			in propria persona (in one's own person or right)
			CROSS REFERENCE: *en-, em-*
in-***	Latin	not, no, without, intensifier	NOTE: The last letter of this prefix is the initial letter of the negative particles, *ne, neg,* as in *nefarious, negate.* This prefix assimilates to *il-, ir-;* as well as to *im-* before not only *m*, but also before *b* and *p*.
			PREFIXED ROOT:
			anim: inanimate (**Synonyms:** dead, deceased, departed) (*anima*, life, soul)
			aud: inaudible (*audire*, to hear)
			cest: incest, incestuous (from *castus*, pure, chaste)
			clem: inclement (rough; severe; stormy; lacking mercy; harsh) {inclemency} (*clemens*, merciful)
			com: incompatible (*com-* prefixes *pat*, to feel)
			cond: incondite (lacking finish or refinement) (*condere*, to put together)
			cor: incorrigible (*cor-* assimilates *com-*, with; *rig* from *regere*, to lead straight)
			creat: increate (not created: said of divine beings or attributes)
			decor: indecorous (**Synonyms:** improper, unseemly, unbecoming) (*decere*, to befit)
			dol: indolent (in *medicine*, causing little or no pain; disliking or avoiding work; idle, lazy) {indolence} (*dolere*, to feel pain)
			ept: inept (**Synonyms:** awkward, clumsy, maladroit) (from *aptus*, suitable, fit)
			err: inerrable, inerrant {inerrancy} (*errer*, to rove, travel)
			ert: inert (literally, without skill or art; idle), inertia (from *ars*, skill, art)
			fer: infertile (**Synonyms:** sterile, barren, impotent) (*ferre*, to bear)

Element	From	Meaning	Examples
in- (cont'd)			fid: infidel (see synonyms at *infidel* under *fid*), infidelity (*fides*, faith)

in- (cont'd)

fid: infidel (see synonyms at *infidel* under *fid*), infidelity (*fides*, faith)

fin: infinite, infinitesimal, infinitude, infinity (*finis*, end)

firm: infirm (**Synonyms**: weak, debilitate, enervate), infirmary (*firmare*, to strengthen)

fract: infract {infractor}, infraction (from *frangere*, to break)

frang: infrangible (see *infract*, previous entry)

imi: inimical (literally, not friendly; therefore, like an enemy; adverse; unfavorable) (from *ami*, friend)

iqui: iniquitous, iniquity (lack of righteousness or justice; wickedness) (from *equi*, equal)

jur: injure (**Synonyms**: harm, damage, hurt), injurious, injury (from *jus*, right, justice)

noc: innocence, innocent, innocuous (*nocere*, to do harm)

ord: inordinate (**Synonyms**: excessive, exorbitant, extravagant) (*ordo*, straight row)

souci: insouciant {insouciance} (*soucier*, to regard, care)

term: interminable (*terminus*, end)

tract: intractable (not tractable; specifically, hard to manage) (from *trahere*, to draw, pull)

trepid: intrepid (**Synonyms**: brave, courageous, bold) (*trepidus*, alarmed, anxious)

ig-:

nobl: ignoble (**Synonyms**: abject, sordid, vile) (*nobilis*, well-known)

nom: ignominious, ignominy (*nomen*, name)

nor: (from *gnoscere*, to know)

ignore, ignorant (**Synonyms**: illiterate, unlettered, uneducated)

ignoramus [literally, We take no notice; a legal term formerly written on a bill of indictment by a grand jury that finds it to be not a true bill] [from Ignoramus, the name of a lawyer in George Ruggle's play *Ignoramus* (1615)]

SPANISH: incommunicado (in Spanish itself, *incomunicado*)

im-: (before *b*, *m*, and *p*)

bec: imbecile (literally, without a staff, without support), imbecility (from *baculus*, staff)

man: immane (cruel or brutal) (*manus*, good)

mat: immature (in *geology*, worn down only slightly by erosion, as a land surface having steeply entrenched stream valleys that lack well-developed flood plains)

med: immediacy, immediate (literally, nothing between) (*med*, middle)

medic: immedicable (that cannot be healed; incurable)

memor: immemorial (extending beyond memory or record)

mens: immense (originally, unmeasured; limitless; infinite; **Synonyms**: enormous, gigantic, colossal) (from *metiri*, to measure)

misc: immiscible (*miscere*, to mix)

mun: immune, immunity (**Synonyms**: exemption, impunity) (*munia*, duties, functions)

Element	From	Meaning	Examples
in- (cont'd)			mut: immutable (*mutare*, to change) pair: impair (see synonyms at *injure*) (from *pejor*, worse) palp: impalpable (*palpare*, to touch) pecc: impeccable, impeccant (*peccare*, to sin) pecun: impecunious (originally, without cattle; without funds; **Synonyms**: impoverished, destitute, indigent) (*pecus*, cattle) pud: impudent (**Synonyms**: impertinent, insolent, saucy) (*pudere*, to feel shame) *il-*: licit: illicit (*licere*, to be permitted) liter: illiteracy, illiterate (**Synonyms**: ignorant, unlettered, unlearned) (*liter*, letter) *ir-*: reg: irregular (**Synonyms**: abnormal, anomalous, unnatural) rever: irreverence (lack of reverence; disrespect) CROSS REFERENCE: *a-, an-, de-, dis-, ne-, non-*
inan*	Latin *inanis*	empty	SIMPLE ROOT: inane (empty; vacant; lacking sense or meaning; foolish; silly; as a noun, that which is inane, especially, the void of empty space) inanition (exhaustion from lack of food and water, or from inability to assimilate it; an absence or loss of social, moral, or intellectual vigor) inanity CROSS REFERENCE: *cen, jejun, vac, van*
infer*	Latin *inferus* (IE: *ndhos*, under; yields English under)	low, lower	SIMPLE ROOT: inferior, inferiority infernal (of the ancient mythological world of the dead; Hell) LITERARY WORK: *Inferno*, by Dante Alighieri. *Inferno* is one section of *Divine Comedy*, a long epic poem, the main theme of which is life after death, with Dante being the chief character. CROSS REFERENCE: *hypo-, infra-, sub-*
infra-**	Latin *infra* (IE: *ndhos*, under)	below	PREFIXED ROOT: lap: infralapsarian (theological term; opposed to *supralapsarian*) (*lapsus*, a fall) son: infrasonic (*sonus*, sound) struct: infrastructure (from *struere*, to build) terr: infraterritorial (*terra*, earth) DOUBLE PREFIXED ROOT: infraocclusion (*oc-* assimilated *ob-*, against + *clus*, closed) LATIN PHRASES: *infra dignatem* (often shortened to *infra dig*: colloquial for "beneath one's dignity") *ut infra* (as below) CROSS REFERENCE: *hypo, infer, neth, sub*
insul*	Latin *insula*	island	SIMPLE ROOT: insula, insular, insulate, insulin TRAILING ROOT COMPOUND: pen: peninsula (literally, almost an island, e.g., the state of Florida, bounded on three sides by water) (*pen*, almost) DISGUISED ROOT: isle, isolate, isolated

Element	From	Meaning	Examples
insul (cont'd)			NOTE: *Island* itself, however, is derived from an ancient root meaning water land. PLACENAMES: Peninsula, Ohio Presque Isle, Maine (Modern French *presqu'île*) CROSS REFERENCE: *nes*
integ*	Latin *integer* (from *in-*, not + *tangere*, to touch; thus, not touched, whole)	complete	SIMPLE ROOT: integer, integrability, integrable, integral, integrand, integrant, integrate, integration, integrative, integrity LEADING ROOT COMPOUND: *integri*: foli: integrifolious (*foli*, leaf) *integro*: differ: integro-differential DISGUISED ROOT: entire (**Synonyms**: complete, total, intact) PRINTING TERM: integral cover (self-cover; a cover of the same material as the inside pages, as of a brochure) NOTE: Some of these words are entered under the root *tang*. CROSS REFERENCE: *hol, salu/salv*
inter-***	Latin *inter*	between	NOTE: The French form of this element is *entre* (see under *French words* below). EXTENDED PREFIX: interim (the period of time between; meantime) interior, intern, internal, intrails PREFIXED ROOT: cala: intercalary, intercalate (*calare*, to call) ced: intercede (*cedere*, to go) cept: intercept, interceptor (*capere*, to take) cess: intercession, intercessor (*cedere*, to go) cost: intercostal (*costa*, rib) cours: intercourse (from *currere*, to run) cur: intercurrent (running between; intervening; occurring during another disease and modifying it) (see *intercourse*) dict: interdict (**Synonyms**: forbid, prohibit, enjoin) (from *dicere*, to speak) digit: interdigitate (to interlock the fingers) (*digit*, finger) est: interest, interested, interesting (from *esse*, to be) fac: interface, interfacial fer: interfere, interference (*ferire*, to strike) foli: interfoliate (*folium*, leaf) fus: interfuse (from *fundere*, to pour) galact: intergalactic ject: interject, interjection, interjectional (from *jacere*, to throw) lard: interlard (originally, to insert strips or pieces of fat or bacon, etc. in meat to be cooked; to intersperse; diversify) lin: interlinear (*linea*, originally, linen thread) lingu: *Interlingua* (an artificial language based largely on languages derived from Latin, for international use, especially in science) (*lingua*, tongue) locu: interlocution, interlocutor (from *loqui*, to speak)

Element	From	Meaning	Examples
inter- (cont'd)			lop: interlope (**Synonyms:** intrude, obtrude), interloper (Dutch *lopen*, to run)
			lud: interlude (*ludere*, to play)
			luna: interlunar (*luna*, moon)
			med: intermediary, intermediate (*medius*, middle)
			miss: intermission (from *intermittent*)
			mitt: intermittent (from *mittere*, to send)
			mont: intermontane (*mont*, mountain)
			nat: international (*natus*, born)
			nec: internecine (*necare*, to kill)
			oscula: interosculate (to interpenetrate; in *biology*, to have some common characteristics: said of separate species or groups) (*osculari*, to kiss)
			pell: interpellate (*pellere*, to drive, urge)
			pol: interpolate (*polire*, to polish)
			pos: interpose, interposition (from *ponere*, to place, put)
			pret: interpret, interpreter, interpretation, interpreter (from the same root as *price*, value, worth; originally from Latin *interpres*, agent between two parties)
			regn: interregnum (*regnum*, reign)
			rog: interrogate, interrogation, interrogative, interrogator, interrogatory (*rogare*, to ask)
			rupt: interrupt, interruption (from *rumpere*, to break)
			sect: intersect, intersection {intersectional} (*secare*, to cut)
			sex: intersex (in *biology*, an abnormal individual having characteristics intermediate between those of male and female), intersexual
			spers: intersperse (*spargere*, to scatter)
			stic: interstice (a small or narrow space between things or parts; crevice; chink; crack) (from *stare*, to stand)
			val:
			interval (originally, the space between palisades or walls) (*vallum*, palisade, wall)
			intervale (chiefly *New England*; low, flat land between hills or along a river or stream) (*vallis*, valley)
			ven: intervene, intervenient, intervention (*venire*, to come)
			view: interview (from *videre*, to see)
			volv: intervolve (*volvere*, to roll)
			ASSIMILATED PREFIXED ROOT:
			intel-:
			lect: intellect, intellection, intellectual (**Synonyms:** intelligent, clever) (from *legere*, to choose, pick, gather)
			leg: intelligence, intelligent (see synonyms at *intellectual*, previous entry), intelligentsia, intelligible (from *intellect*)
			PREFIXED DISGUISED ROOT:
			pris: enterprise (*pris* from IE *ghed*, to grasp)
			tain: entertain (*tain* from *tenere*, to hold)
			FRENCH WORDS:
			entre, entree (or *entrée*)
			entrecôte, entredeux, entrefer, entremets, entrepôt
			entrepreneur (same as *enterpriser* in English), *entresol*

Element	From	Meaning	Examples
inter- (cont'd)			ELEMENT USED AS BASE OF ANOTHER ELEMENT: *entero* (intestine) LATIN PHRASES: *ad interim* (in the interim; in the meantime; temporary) *inter alia* (among other things) *inter alios* (among other persons) *inter nos* [between (or among) ourselves] *inter vivos* (among living persons; between living persons; from one living person to another or others, as *inter vivos* gifts, trusts, etc.) ITALIAN MUSIC TERM: *intermezzo* (a short movement separating the major sections of a symphonic work) PLACENAMES: Intercourse (Alabama, Pennsylvania) INTERDISCIPLINARY: interval (in *mathematics*, the set containing all numbers and including one, both, or neither end point; in *music*, the difference in pitch between two tones) NAME OF COLLEGE: Virginia Intermont College, Bristol, Tennessee CROSS REFERENCE: *dia-*
intra-,*** intro-	Latin	within	SIMPLE ROOT: enter, entrance (noun) [see *entrance* (en TRANCE) as verb under *trans-*.] PREFIXED ROOT: *intra-*: coast: intracoastal (see *Geographical*, below) derm: intradermal (Greek *derm*, skin) dos: intrados (in *architecture*, the inside curve or surface of an arch or vault) (from *dorsum*, the back) mur: intramural (literally, within the walls; originally, sports played within the walls of the medieval university) (*mur*, wall) psych: intrapsychic (Greek *psyche*, mind) speci: intraspecific (within a single species) stat: intrastate (within a state, especially a state of the United States; for example, an *intrastate highway*, as opposed to an *interstate highway*) tellur: intratelluric (*telluris*, earth) uter: intrauterine (*uter*, uteris) vasat: intravasation (*vas*, vessel) ven: intravenous (*ven*, vein) *intro*: duc: introduce (*ducere*, to lead) gress: introgression (from *gradus*, step) it: introit (*itere*, to go) ject: introject (a psychoanalytic term; not to be confused with *interject*) (from *jacere*, to throw) mit: intromit (*mittere*, to send) spec: introspection (*specere*, to see) sus: introsusception (from *sub-*, under; *cep* from *capere*, to take, hold) vers: introversion (from *vertere*, to turn) vert: introvert (*vertere*, to turn)

Element	From	Meaning	Examples
intra (cont'd)			DISGUISED ROOT: denizen (from *de intus*, from within) PREFIXED DISGUISED ROOT: introrse (*intro-* + *verse*; in *botany*, facing inward, or toward the center) intrinsic (in *anatomy*, located within, or exclusivley of, a part; opposed to *extrinsic*) (*inter* + *sequent*) GEOGRAPHICAL NAME: Intracoastal Waterway (a waterway for small craft, consisting of both artificial and natural channels within the United States, from Boston, Massachusetts, to Brownsville, Texas) CROSS REFERENCE: *endo-, eso-*
ir*	Latin; (IE: *eis*, to move quickly)	anger	SIMPLE ROOT: irate (angry, wrathful, incensed), iracund (now archaic; same as irascible), irascible ire (**Synonyms:** anger, indignation, rage) NOTE: Do not confuse *irade* with *irate*; *irade* is from Arabic *iradah*, will, desire, and was formerly a decree of a Moslem ruler. NO CROSS REFERENCE
irid*	Latin *iris*: rainbow (IE: *wei*, to turn, bend)	iris (of eye)	ROOT NOTE: The word *iris* pertains both to the pupil of eye and to the flower, as well as various other related meanings. Differentiations are made as to meaning, but not to word structure. PLANTS: iris, irid, iridaceous RAINBOW: iridescent CHEMICAL: iridium [from the changing color of some of its salts (symbol: Ir)] VARIOUS: iridic (an adjective, which can refer to the chemical, the valence of four in iridium, or the iris of the eye) ALLOY: iridosmine (alloy of *iridium* and *osmium*); also spelled *iridosmium* GREEK MYTHOLOGY: Iris, goddess of the rainbow NO CROSS REFERENCE
ische*	Greek *ischein*, to hold	suppress, check	SIMPLE ROOT: ischesis LEADING ROOT COMPOUND: *isch*: emia: ischemia [a deficiency of blood in a part, due to functional constriction (*suppression*) or actual obstruction of the blood vessel] (*emia*, diseased condition of the blood) ur: ischuretic, ischuria (suppression of retention of the urine) (*ouron*, urine) *ischi*: dros: ischidrosis (suppression of the secretion of sweat) (*dros*, sweat) NB: Do not confuse with *ischium*, from *ischion*, hip, hip joint, the bone upon which the body rests when sitting. NO CROSS REFERENCE
iso***	Greek *isos*	same, equal	LEADING ROOT COMPOUND: *is*: entr: isentrope, isentropic (*en-* prefixes *trope*, turn) epi: isepiptesis (*epi-* prefixes *ptesis*, flight) *iso*: bar: isobar (*baros*, weight)

359

Element	From	Meaning	Examples
iso (cont'd)			bath: isobath (*bathos*, depth)

iso (cont'd) — Examples:

bath: isobath (*bathos*, depth)

cheim: isocheim (a line on a map connecting points of the earth's surface that have the same mean winter temperatures) (*cheima*, winter)

chor: isochor (also, *isochore*) (*chora*, a place)

chrom: isochromatic (*chrom*, color)

chron: isochronal, isochronize (*chron*, time)

chroo: isochroous (having the same color in every part) (*chroos*, color)

clin: isoclinal, isocline (*clin*, lean)

crac: isocracy (*crac*, rule)

cycl: isocyclic (*cycle*, circle, wheel)

dia: isodiametric (*dia*- prefixes *metric*, measurement)

gam: isogamete, isogamy (*gam*, marriage, sexual reproduction)

gen: isogenous (*gen*, producing)

geo: isogeotherm (*therm*, heat)

gloss: isogloss (*glossa*, tongue)

gon:
isogonic (also, *isogonal*: of or having equal angles; connecting or showing points on the earth's surface having the same magnetic declination) (*gon*, angle)
isogony (*gony*, production, generation)

gram: isogram (from *graph*, write)

hel: isohel (a line on a map connecting points having equal hours of sunshine in a standard period of time) (*helios*, sun)

hyet: isohyet (a line on a map connecting points having equal amounts of rainfall) (*hyetos*, rain)

mer: isomer, isomerism, isomerous (*mere*, part)

metr: isometrics, isometry (*metr*, measurement)

metro: isometropia (*metro*, measure + *opia*, sight)

morph: isomorph, isomorphic, isomorphism (*morph*, shape, form)

nom: isonomy (equality of laws, rights, or privileges) (*nomos*, law)

piest: isopiestic (indicating equal pressure) (*piestos*, compressible)

pleth: isopleth (*plethos*, number, quantity)

pod: isopod (also, *isopodan*) (*pod*, foot)

sceles: isosceles (designating a triangle with two equal sides) (*sceles*, leg)

seism: isoseismal (*seism*, tremor)

spor: isosporous (same as *homosporous*) (*spore*, seed)

stasy: isostasy (*stasis*, standing, still)

ther: isothere (*theros*, summer; warm)

therm: isotherm (*therm*, heat)

ton: isotone, isotonic (*tonos*, a stretching)

top: isotope (*topos*, place)

trop: isotropic (*trope*, turn)

PREFIXED LEADING ROOT COMPOUND:
an-: anisotropic (*an-*, not + *trop*, turn) (See *Note*)
NOTE: *Aniso* is considered a root itself, meaning not equal.

Element	From	Meaning	Examples
iso (cont'd)			LEADING ROOT WITH EMBEDDED PREFIXED ROOT: ag-: isoagglutination (ag- assimilates ad-; gluten, glue) anti-: (against) isoantibody (an antibody in one individual for cells or proteins of some other members of the same species) isoantigen (gen, produce) CROSS REFERENCE: equi, homo, ident, par, taut
it***	Latin ire (IE: yero, year)	to go	SIMPLE ROOT: itinerant (Synonyms: ambulatory, peripatetic, nomadic), itinerary, itinerate PREFIXED ROOT: ad-: adit (literally, to go to; an approach; entrance; an almost horizontal passageway into a mine) (ad-, to, toward) ambi-: ambit, ambition, ambitious (Synonyms: aspiring, enterprising, emulous) (ambi-, around) circu-: circuit (Synonyms: circumference, perimeter, periphery) (from circa, around) co-: coition, coitus (both terms refer to sexual intercourse) (co-, with, together) com-: comitia (in ancient Rome, an assembly of citizens for electing officials, passing laws, etc.) (com-, with, together) ex-: exit [Latin third person singular, present indicative: He (or she) leaves the stage] (ex-, out) in-: initial (in biology, a primordial cell that determines the basic pattern of derived tissues), initiate (Synonyms: begin, commence) (in-, in) intro-: introit (a psalm or hymn sung or played at the opening of a Christian worship service) (intro-, into) ob-: obit, obituary (ob-, against) pre-: preterit (also, preterite) (pre-, before) re-: reiterate, reiteration (re-, again) sed-: sedition (sed-, away) sub-: subito (Italian music term; from the same elements as sudden) (sub-, under) trans-: transient, transit, transition, transitive (in grammar, expressing an action that is thought of as passing over to and taking effect on some person or thing; taking a direct object to complete the meaning: said of certain verbs), transitory (trans-, across) DISGUISED ROOT: ambiant, ambient count (nobleman) country errant (as in knight errant, a knight of medieval romance who journeyed, wandered in search of adventure) eyre (as justices in eyre) PREFIXED DISGUISED ROOT: com-: commence (com-, with, together + initiare, to begin; initiare, from in-, in + ire, to go) is-: issue (Synonyms: 1) effect, consequence; 2) rise, derive, emanate) (is- assimilates in-, in) per-: perish (per-, through)

Element	From	Meaning	Examples
it (cont'd)			*prae-*: praetor, praetorian (capitalized, Praetorian Guard) (*prae-*, before) *sud-*: sudden (**Synonyms:** precipitate, abrupt, impetuous) (*sud-* assimilated from *sub-*, under) LATIN PHRASE: *ad initium* (at the beginning) PREFIXED GREEK COGNATE: *an-*: anion (a special application, originated by Faraday, of Greek *anion*, thing going up; the negatively charged atom or radical in an ionic compound: in electrolysis, anions move toward the anode; opposed to *cation*) (*an-*, up + *ienai*, to go) NB: *Comity*, from *co-*, with, together + IE *smei-*, to smile, and meaning civility, politeness, courtesy, is not in this family. CROSS REFERENCE: *bas/bat/bet; cede/ceed/cess; vad/vas*
ithy*	Greek *ithys* (IE: *stdh*, to go directly toward	straight, erect	LEADING ROOT COMPOUND: phall: (penis) ithyphallus (erect penis) ithyphallic (of the erect phallus, or penis; also describes a certain meter in Greek poetry; can also describe that which is obscene or lewd) CROSS REFERENCE: *ortho, rect/reg*
-itis***	Greek *ites*	inflamed	NOTE: That which is *inflamed* is shown in parentheses. SUFFIXED COMPOUND: achillobursitis (Achilles' tendon and the bursa in front of it) acroarthritis (extremities) acrobystitis (prepuce) adenitis (a gland) acrodermatitis (skin of hands and feet) adrenalitis (adrenal glands) angioleucitis (lymph vessel) angiitis (vessel, especially blood or lymph vessel) appendicitis (appendix) arthritis (any joint) balanitis (penis) bronchitis (bronchial tubes) bursitis (any bursa) cerebritis (cerebrum) encephalitis (brain) epididymitis (epididymis) gastritis (stomach) hepatitis (liver) laryngitis (larynx) meningitis (meninges, the membranes that envelop the brain and spinal cord) mesaortitis (middle coat of the aorta) mesarteritis (middle coat of an artery) nephritis (kidney) neuritis (nerve) odontitis (tooth) oophoritis (ovary) orchiditis [same as *orchitis* (testis)] osphyitis (loins) osteitis (bone) otitis (ear) ovaritis (ovary)

Element	From	Meaning	Examples
-itis (cont'd)			phallitis (penis)
			phlebitis (vein)
			rhinitis (nose)
			tonsillitis (tonsils)
			NO CROSS REFERENCE

Great leaders are great leaders because through their command of vocabulary power and culture,
they are able to make others see and feel what they see and feel.
Gain this power for yourself and you will have at your service
the greatest force ever put into the hands of mankind.
Joseph G. Brin

J

Element	From	Meaning	Examples
jac,*** ject	Latin *jactare* (IE: *ye*, to throw, do)	to throw	ROOT NOTE: Ironically, that which means to throw can also mean to lie down, probably because after an object is thrown, it *lies* (down); see *adjacent*, below. SIMPLE ROOT: jacta: jactance, jactancy, jactation jacti: jactitate, jactitation jacu: jaculation PREFIXED ROOT: *jac*: ad-: adjacent (see *Root Note*, above; **Synonyms**: adjoining, contiguous, tangent; see *Doublets* below) (*ad-*, to, toward) e-: ejaculate (to eject or discharge, especially semen; to utter suddenly and vehemently), ejaculation (ejection of semen; a sudden vehement utterance; exclamation), ejaculatory (from *ex-*, out) *super-*: superjacent (lying or resting over or beyond) (*super-*, beyond, over) *ject*: ab-: abject (**Synonyms**: base, ignoble, sordid), abjected, abjection (*ab-*, away) ad-: adjective (that which is *thrown to* the noun or pronoun it modifies) (*ad-*, to, toward) con-: conjecture (**Synonyms**: guess, surmise) (*con-*, with, together) de-: deject, dejecta, dejected (**Synonyms**: sad, sorrowful, melancholy), dejection (*de-*, down) dis-: disject (*dis-*, apart, away) e-: eject (**Synonyms**: expel, evict, dismiss), ejecta (ejected matter, as from the body, a volcano, etc.) (from *ex-*, out) in-: inject, injection, injector (*in-*, in) inter-: interject, interjection (as a part of speech, that which is thrown in without grammatical connection, e.g., Ah! Ouch! Well!) (*inter-*, between) intro-: introjection (*intro-*, within) ob-: object (**Synonyms**: protest, remonstrate, expostulate), objection, objective (*ob-*, against) pro-: project (**Synonyms**: plan, design, scheme), projector, projectile (*pro-*, forward) re-: reject (**Synonyms**: decline, refuse, repudiate) (*re-*, again) sub-: subject (**Synonyms**: theme, topic, text) (*sub-*, under) tra-: traject, trajectory (*trans-*, across) DISGUISED ROOT: ease (from *adjacent*; see *Doublets* below) jet, jetty, jettison, jetsam (compare with *flotsam*) joist FRENCH: jeton (a metal disk or counter, as for operating a pay telephone, etc.) DOUBLETS: adjacent:ease

Element	From	Meaning	Examples
jac (cont'd)			INTERDISCIPLINARY: trajectory (in *mathematics*, a curve or surface that passes through all the curves of a given family at the same angle; in *missilery*, the curved path of a projectile, especially such a path in three dimensions, from the time the projectile leaves the launching device) CROSS REFERENCE: *bal/bol, disc*
ject			See *jac* for *subject*.
jet			See *jac* for *jet, jetty, jettison*.
jour***	French; from Latin *diurnus* (IE: *dei*, to gleam, shine)	day	SIMPLE ROOT: journa: journal (a daily record of happenings, as a diary), journalese, journalism, journalist, journalistic, journalize journe: journey (**Synonyms**: trip, jaunt, expedition), journeyman (originally, one who worked by the *day*) PREFIXED ROOT: *ad*-: adjourn (**Synonyms**: prorogue, postpone, suspend), adjournment (*ad*-, to, toward) *so*-: sojourn (literally, under a day; figuratively, a temporary stay) (from *sub*-, under) FRENCH: *bonjour* (good day) *plat du jour* (dish of the day) *soupe du jour* (soup of the day) ITALIAN: *aggiornamento* CROSS REFERENCE: *die, hemera*
jud,*** jus	Latin *jus* (IE: *yewos*, fixed rule)	law, right	jus: jus (the law; the whole body of law; a particular system of law; a legal principle, right, or power) just: just (**Synonyms**: fair, impartial, unbiased), justice, justiciable, justicer, justiciar, justiciary PREFIXED ROOT: *jud*: *ad*-: adjudicate, adjudication {adjudicative}, adjudicator (*ad*-, to, toward) *in*-: injudicious (*in*-, not) *pre*-: prejudice (literally, that which is judged before; preconceived idea; **Synonyms**: bias, partiality, predilection) (*pre*-, before) *judge*: *ad*-: adjudge (*ad*-, to) *pre*-: prejudge (*pre*-, before) *just*: *ad*-: adjust (possibly; see *juxta*-) LEADING ROOT COMPOUND: *ju*: d: (from *dicere*, to say, point out) judge (**Synonyms**: arbiter, referee, umpire), judgment, judgmental judicable, judicative, judicatory; judicial, judiciary, judicious *justi*: fic: justification (from *facere*, to make, do) fy: justify {justifiable} (from *facere*, to make, do) THEOLOGICAL TERM: Judgment Day (the time of God's final judgment of all people; end of the world; doomsday)

Element	From	Meaning	Examples
jud (cont'd)			DISGUISED ROOT: hoosegow (jail; Americanism of *juzgado*, the Mexican court of justice; which meant almost automatic imprisonment for condemned North Americans) LEGAL PHRASES: *jus canonicum, jus civile, jus divinum, jus gentium* *jus naturale, jus sanguinis, jus soli* TITLE OF A MAGISTRATE: justice of the peace PLACENAMES: Justice, Illinois; Justiceburg, Texas CROSS REFERENCE: *jur, leg, nom*
jun,*** juv	Latin *juvenis* (IE: *yuwen*, young)	young	SIMPLE ROOT: *jun*: junior (contraction of *juvenior*, a comparative of *juvenis*, young), juniority *juv*: juvenal, juvenescent, juvenile, juvenilia, juvescent, juvenility PREFIXED ROOT: *re-*: rejuvenate (**Synonyms**: renew, restore, refresh), rejuvenation (*re-*, again) ENGLISH COGNATE: young (**Synonyms**: youthful, juvenile, puerile) CROSS REFERENCE: *hebe*
jur***	Latin *jurare* (IE: *yewos*, fixed rule)	to swear	SIMPLE ROOT: jurat (in *law*, a statement or certification added to an affidavit, telling when, before whom, and sometimes, where the affidavit was made) juratory, jurist, juristic, juror, jury PREFIXED ROOT: *ad-*: adjuration, adjuratory, adjure, adjurer (or *adjuror*) (*ad-*, to, toward) *ab-*: abjure (*ab-*, from, away) *ad-*: adjuration, adjuratory, adjure (*ad-*, to, toward) *con-*: conjuration, conjure, conjurer (*con-*, with, together) *in-*: injure (**Synonyms**: harm, damage, impair) (*in-*, not) *ob-*: objurgate (originally, to sue at law; to chide vehemently; upbraid sharply; rebuke; berate) (*ob-*, against) *per-*: perjure, perjury (*per-*, through) LEADING ROOT COMPOUND: consult: juriconsult (a jurist) dic: juridical, jurisdiction (**Synonyms**: authority, command, power) (*dicere*, to point out, declare) prud: jurisprudence, jurisprudent LEGAL PHRASE: *de jure* (pronounced dee JOOR ih; by right; in accordance with law; distinguished from *de facto*) CROSS REFERENCE: *jud, leg, nom*
jus			See *jud* for *justice*.
juv			See *jun* for *juvenal, rejuvenate*.
juxta-**	Latin *juxta* IE: *yug*, closely connected; *yuga*, yoke)	next to	PREFIXED ROOT: *ad-*: adjust (possibly; see *jus*) LEADING ROOT COMPOUND: pos: juxtapose, juxtaposit, juxtaposition (from *ponere*, to place) DISGUISED ROOT: joust (to combat with lances between two knights on horseback) CROSS REFERENCE: *ja/ject*

367

K

Element	From	Meaning	Examples
kain			See *ceno*, as in *recent*.
kal			See *calli* for *kaleidoscope*.
ken			See *ceno*, empty.
keto*	Greek *keto*	ketone	ROOT NOTE: The root is a back-formation of *ketone*, an arbitrary variation of *acetone*, the base of which is *aceto*, acid. SIMPLE ROOT: ketene, ketol, ketone, ketose LEADING ROOT COMPOUND: *ket*: osis: ketosis (*osis*, condition of) *keto*: gen: ketogenesis (*genesis*, producing) ster: ketosteroid (*ster*, solid; *oid*, similar to) *keton*: emia: ketonemia (*emia*, a diseased condition of the blood) ur: ketonuria (*uria*, diseased condition of the urine) NO CROSS REFERENCE
kilo**	Greek *chilioi* (IE: *gheslo*, thousand)	thousand	ROOT NOTE: This root measures individual multiples of 1,000 in metric. LEADING ROOT COMPOUND: bar: kilobar calor: kilocalorie cycl: kilocycle gram: kilogram, kilogrammeter hertz: kilohertz liter: kiloliter meter: kilometer parsec: kiloparsec ton: kiloton volt: kilovolt watt: kilowatt DISGUISED ROOT: chiliad CROSS REFERENCE: *chilias, mil*
kine			See *cinem* for *kinetic*.
klept*	Greek *kleptein* (IE: *klep*, to hide, steal)	to steal	SIMPLE ROOT: klepht (a member of the Greek patriot bands who held out in the mountains after the Turkish conquest of Greece) LEADING ROOT COMPOUND: maniac: kleptomaniac (an abnormal, persistent impulse to steal, not prompted by need) (*mania*, craze) phobia: kleptophobia TRAILING ROOT COMPOUND: biblio: biblioklept (a book thief) (*biblio*, book) NO CROSS REFERENCE
krypt			See *crypt* for *krypton*.

Words are the instruments that make thought possible. Judd

369

L

Element	From	Meaning	Examples
lab			See *lepsy* for *astrolabe*.
lab			See *lap* for *labile*.
lab**	Latin *labium* (IE: *leb*, to hang loosely)	lip	SIMPLE ROOT: labe: labellum (the lip, or lowest of the three petals forming the corolla, of an orchid, usually larger than the other two petals, and often spurred) (diminutive of *labrum*, a lip) labia: labial, labialism, labialize labiate (in *biology*, having the calyx or corolla so divided that one part overlaps the other like a lip) labiu: labium (the lower, liplike part of the corolla of certain flowers; the lower lip of an insect, formed by the fusion of the second maxillae; plural, *labia*) labr: labret (an ornament of wood, bone, etc. worn, by some South American Indians, in a hole pierced through the *lip*); labrum (a lip or liplike edge; especially, the upper or front lip of insects and other arthropods) LEADING ROOT COMPOUND: dent: labiodental (in *phonetics*, articulated with the lower lip touching the upper front teeth, as *f* or *v*) (*dent*, tooth) lingu: labiolingual (*lingua*, tongue) nas: labionasal (*nas*, nose) vel: labiovelar (soft palate) (*vel*, velum) TRAILING ROOT COMPOUND: gingivo: gingivolabial (*gingivo*, gum) NB: *Labile*, from *labilis*, to slip, fall, is not in this family. CROSS REFERENCE: *cheil/chil*
labor**	Latin *labor* (IE: *leb*, to hang loosely)	work, labor	SIMPLE ROOT: labor, laboratory, laborious PREFIXED ROOT: *e-*: elaborate (**Synonyms:** 1) perfected, painstaking; 2) ornate, intricate) (*e-* elides *ex-*, out) *col-*: collaborate {collaborative}, collaborator (*col-* assimilates *com-*, with, together) ANGLO-SAXON PREFIXED ROOT: *be-*: belabor (*be-*, intensive) MOTTO OF BROOKLYN COLLEGE: *Nil sine magno labore* (Nothing without great effort) CROSS REFERENCE: *erg, op*
lachry,* lacri	Latin *lacrima* (IE: *dakru*, tear; yields English tear)	teardrop	SIMPLE ROOT: *lachry*: lachrymal, lachrymator (a substance that irritates the eyes and produces tears, as tear gas), lachrymose *lacri*: lacrima, lacrimal (in *anatomy*, designating, of, or near the glands that secrete tears; same as *lachrymal*), lacrimalin, lacrimase, lacrimation (normal or excessive secretion or shedding of tears), lacrimator, lacrimatory A WINE: *lachryma christi* (Christ's tear; a still Italian wine produced from grapes grown near Vesuvius that are white, red, or rosé and sweet or dry) CROSS REFERENCE: *dacry*

Element	From	Meaning	Examples
lact**	Latin *lac* (IE: *glak*, milk)	milk	SIMPLE ROOT: lactic (of or obtained from milk) lacta: lactam *[lactone* + *amino]*, lactase, lactate, lactation lacte: lacteal, lactescent (becoming milky; of a milky appearance) lacto: lactol, lactone, lactose lactu: lactum lacty: lactyl PREFIXED ROOT: *ab-*: ablactation (the act or process of weaning) (*ab-*, away) *pro-*: prolactin (*pro-*, before) LEADING ROOT COMPOUND: *lacti*: fer: lactiferous (*ferre*, to bear) fic: lactific, lactification (from *facere*, to make, do) fy: lactify (from *facere*, to make, do) *lacto*: bacill: lactobacillus flav: lactoflavin (same as *riboflavin*, which see under *flav*) gen: lactogenic (capable of inducing milk secretion) (*genic*, producing) meter: lactometer (a hydrometer for determining the specific gravity, and hence the richness, of milk) (*meter*, measure) protein: lactoprotein (any of the proteins found in milk) DISGUISED ROOT: lettuce (originally, *lactuca*, from its milky juice) FRENCH TERM: *au lait* (with milk) SPANISH TERM: *con leche* (with milk) CROSS REFERENCE: *galact*
lacu*	Latin *lacuna* (IE: *lak*, accumulation of water; pond, lake; yields English lake)	lake, water	SIMPLE ROOT: lacuna (originally, a lake-like pond, as at Venice, but literally a ditch, hole, pool; has come to mean a space where something has been omitted or has come out; gap; hiatus, especially, a missing portion in a manuscript, text, etc.; in *anatomy* and *biology*, a space, cavity, or depression, specifically, any of the small cavities in bone that are filled with bone cells) lacunar (in *architecture*, a ceiling made of sunken panels) lacunose (full of lucanae) lacustrine (of, or having to do with, a lake or lakes; found or formed in lakes) DISGUISED ROOT: lagoon (from French *lagune* and Italian *laguna*) SCOTTISH COGNATE: *loch*, as in *Loch Ness* CROSS REFERENCE: *limn*
lagn*	Greek *lagneia*: lust (IE: *sleg*, to be slack, languid)	erotic desire (loose in morals)	TRAILING ROOT COMPOUND: algo: algolagnia (an abnormal sexual pleasure derived from inflicting or suffering pain; masochism or sadism) (*algo*, pain) osmo: osmolagnia (see *Note*) osphresio: osphresiolagnia {osphresiolagnic} (see *Note*) NOTE: *Osmolagnia* and *osphresiolagnia* both pertain to erotic stimulation produced by odors. NO CROSS REFERENCE

Element	From	Meaning	Examples
lal*	Greek *lalein* (IE: *la,* to mutter)	to babble, talk	SIMPLE ROOT: lallation (the substitution of the phoneme \l\ for \r\) LEADING ROOT COMPOUND: pleg: laloplegia (loss--through paralysis--of the power to speak) (*plegia*, stroke, paralysis) TRAILING ROOT COMPOUND: brady: bradylalia (*brady*, slow) echo: echolalia (the automatic repetition by someone of words spoken in his/her presence, especially, as a symptom of a mental disorder) glosso: glossolalia (the speaking in tongues, as in some religions) (*glossa*, tongue) DISGUISED ROOT: lament, lull, lullaby CROSS REFERENCE: *dict, fa/fess, loc/loqu, ora, phas/phe*
lam*	Latin *lamina* (IE: *stel,* to spread)	leaf, thin plate	ROOT NOTE: This root can also mean a layer, like a *layer cake*, not a *layer hen*; it can also mean sheets, leaves. SIMPLE ROOT: *lamell*: lamella: lamella (plural, *lamellae*) {lamellar} lamellate lamello: lamellose {lamellosity} *lamin*: lamin: lamin (an astrologer's charm consisting of a thin metal plate) lamina: lamina (plural, *laminae*) laminab: laminable laminar: laminar, laminaria, laminate, laminated, lamination lamino: laminose PREFIXED ROOT: *de-*: delaminate (to separate into layers), delamination (in *embryology*, a splitting of the blastoderm into two layers of cells) (*de-*, apart) LEADING ROOT COMPOUND: *lamelli*: branch: lamellibranch (designating or of a bivalve mollusk) (*branch*, gills) corn: lamellicorn (a beetle with plated antennae) (*cornu*, horn) form: lamelliform (having the form of a lamella; platelike or scalelike) rostr: lamellirostral (of certain waterfowl, as ducks, geese, and swans, with lamellate strainers on the inner edge of the bill) (*rostra*, beak) *lamin*: itis: laminitis (an inflammation of laminae in a horse's hoof) (*itis*, inflammation) DISGUISED ROOT: omelet (by metathesis from *lamella* to *amelette* in French) CROSS REFERENCE: *foli, petal, phyll*
lan*	Latin *lana*	wool	SIMPLE ROOT: lanner (a falcon, see *American Heritage*) lana: lanate (in *biology*, having a wooly or hairy covering or appearance) lanu: lanuginous (covered with soft, short hair; downy), lanugo (fine, soft hair)

373

Element	From	Meaning	Examples
lan (cont'd)			LEADING ROOT COMPOUND: *lan*: ol: lanolin (a fatty substance obtained from sheep wool; also *lanoline*) (*ol*, oil) ose: lanose (same as *lanate*, above) *lani*: fer: laniferous (also, *lanigerous*; bearing wool or fine hairs resembling wool; fleecy) DISGUISED ROOT: flannel, velours, velure, velvet, villus PREFIXED DISGUISED ROOT: de-: delaine [French; of, or from, wool; from *muslin de laine* (formerly, a light-weight fabric of wool or wool and cotton; now, a kind of wool, used especially in fine worsteds)] NO CROSS REFERENCE
langu*	Latin *languere*: to be weary (IE: *sleg*, loose)	faint, weary	SIMPLE ROOT: languid (without vigor or vitality; drooping; weak; without interest or spirit) languish (to lose vigor or vitality; fail in health), languishing languor (lack of vigor or vitality) DISGUISED ROOT: laches (in *law*, failure to do the required thing at the proper time, e.g., inexcusable delay in enforcing a claim) CROSS REFERENCE: *lax*
lap,** lab	Latin *labi* (IE: *leb*, *lab*, to hang down)	to fall, slide	SIMPLE ROOT: *lab*: labile (liable to change; unstable, as though likely to slip or fall; e.g., *labile* chemical compounds; in *psychiatry*, emotional instability, a tendency to show alternating states of gaiety and somberness) {lability}, labilization, labilize *lap*: lap (another *lap* is derived from *lambere*, to lick) lapse, lapsus (an error, or slip, thought to be revealing of an unconscious wish or association, e.g., *lapsus calami*, a slip of the pen; *lapsus linguae*, a slip of the tongue; *lapsus memoriae*, a lapse of the memory; in *medicine*, can also mean falling or dropping of a part; ptosis) PREFIXED ROOT: e-: elapse (to slip by; pass: said of time) (*e-* elides *ex-*, out) col-: collapse (to fall down or fall to pieces; to break down suddenly) (*col-* assimilates *com-*, with) infra-: infralapsarian (in *theology*, the predestinarian doctrine that God allowed the fall of man and elected some from the *fallen* to be saved by a redeemer; also called *sublapsarianism*; opposed to *supralapsarian*) (*infra-*, below) pro-: prolapse (in *medicine*, the falling or slipping out of place; also prolapsus; as a verb, to fall or slip out of place) (*pro-*, forward) re-: relapse (to slip or slide back into a former condition) (*re-*, back) supra-: supralapsarian (in *Calvinism*, the belief that God's plan of salvation for some people preceded the fall of man from grace, which had been predestined: opposite to *infralapsarian* and *sublapsarian*) (*supra-*, above, over, beyond) CROSS REFERENCE: *cad/cid/cas*, *pto*

374

Element	From	Meaning	Examples
lapid,* lapis	Latin *lapis*	stone	SIMPLE ROOT: lapidar: lapidarian, lapidarist (one who cuts, polishes, and engraves stones; an expert in precious stones), lapidary lapidat: lapidate (to throw stones at; to stone to death) lapil: lapillus (a small fragment of igneous rock, up to the size of a walnut, ejected from a volcano) lapi: lapis (used especially in chemistry for *stone*) PREFIXED ROOT: *di-*: dilapidated (literally, having stones thrown at; thus, run down; in a state of disrepair) (from *dis-*, apart) LEADING ROOT COMPOUND: col: lapidicolous (living under stones) (*colere*, to live) fy: lapidify (from *facere*, to make, do) LATIN TERM: *lapis lazuli* (literally, azure stone) CROSS REFERENCE: *lith, petr, sax*
lat**	Latin *latus* (IE: *stel*, to spread out)	side, wide	SIMPLE ROOT: laterad (in *anatomy*, toward the side) lateral (in *biology*; a lateral bud is one that develops in the axil between a petiole and a stem) laterality (such as *crossed laterality*), latitude latitudinarian (liberal in one's views; as a noun, one who cares little about creeds and forms) PREFIXED ROOTS AND COMPOUNDS: *col-*: collateral (situated on the side; accompanying; parallel) (*col-* assimilates *com-*, with, together) *di-*: (from *dis-*, apart, away) dilatant, dilate (to make wider or larger), dilated, dilatation, dilator (something that *dilates* an object, organ, or part) dilatometer (a device for measuring expansion caused by changes in temperature in substances) (*meter*, measure) LEADING ROOT COMPOUND: *later*: laterad (-*ad*, toward, is usually considered a prefix, but is used as a suffix in such words as *caudad*, toward the tail) *lateri*: cumb: latericumbent (lying on one's side) (from *cubare*, to lie down) flor: laterifloral (having lateral flowers) grad: laterigrade (sideways-running, as do crabs and certain spiders) (*gradus*, step) *lati*: fund: latifundium (originally, a large landed estate, especially of the ancient Romans; now, one typically owned by an absentee landlord and worked by peons, as in some Latin American countries) (*fundus*, estate; originally, bottom) TRAILING ROOT COMPOUND: bi: bilateral (having two symmetrical sides; affecting or undertaken by sides equally; binding on both parties) (*bi*, two) equi: equilateral (with all sides equal, as an *equilateral triangle*) (*equi*, equal) uni: unilateral (one-sided, as a *unilateral decision*) (*uni*, one) ventro: ventrolateral (*ventro*, belly, abdomen) CROSS REFERENCE: *canth, cost, eury, hedr, platy, pleur*

Element	From	Meaning	Examples
lat***	Latin *ferre* (IE *bher[1]*, to bear)	carry, bear	ROOT NOTE: The root is the suppletive past participle of Latin *ferre*, to carry, as in *transfer, circumference*; see *fer*. PREFIXED ROOT: *ab-*: ablate {ablation}, ablative (see note under *ab-*) (*ab-*, away) *col-*: collate, collation, collative, collator (*col-* assimilates *com-*, with, together) *di-*: dilatory (literally, carried apart; from *dilator*; tending to delay) (from *dis-*, apart, away) *e-*: elate (literally, to carry, or bring, out), elated (*e-* elides *ex-*, out) *il-*: illation (the act of drawing a conclusion or making an inference) (*il-* assimilates *in-*, in) *ob-*: oblate (in *geometry*, flattened at the poles) (*ob-*, against) *pre-*: prelate (a high-ranking ecclesiastic) (*pre-*, before) *pro-*: prolate (elongated at the poles) (*pro-*, forward) *re-*: relate, related (**Synonyms**: kindred, cognate, allied), relative (*re-*, back) *super-*: superlative (*super-*, above, beyond) *trans-*: translate, translation (**Synonyms**: version, transliteration, paraphrase) (*trans-*, across) DOUBLE PREFIXED ROOT: cor<u>re</u>late (*cor-* assimilates *com-*, with, together + *re-*, again) TRAILING ROOT COMPOUND: legis: legislate, legislation, legislator, legislature (*legis*, law) LATIN PHRASE: *prelate nullius* (a Roman Catholic prelate, usually a titular bishop, who has jurisdiction over a territory not in a diocese but subject directly to the Holy See) CROSS REFERENCE: *fer, phor/pher*
lat,* lit	Latin *latere* (IE: *laidh*, to be hidden)	to lie hidden	SIMPLE ROOT: laterbra (literally, a hiding place; a flask-shaped mass of white yolk extending from the blastodisk to the center of eggs such as those of birds) latency, latent (**Synonyms**: potential, dormant, quiescent) PREFIXED DISGUISED ROOT: *de-*: delitescent (lying hidden; not revealed) (*de-*, intensive) CROSS REFERENCE: *cond*
latr*	Greek *latreia*: worship (IE: *lei*, to possess, acquire)	worship, service	SIMPLE ROOT: latria (in *Roman Catholic theology*, the supreme worship that may be offered only to God; this word is related to *latris*, hired servant) SUFFIXED ROOT: biblio: bibliolater, bibliolatrous, bibliolatry (*biblio*, book) idol: idolatrous, idolatry (*idol*, image) mono: monolatry (the worship of one god, where several are believed to exist: distinguished from *monotheism*: a doctrine or belief that there is only one God) NO CROSS REFERENCE
laud**	Latin *laus*	praise	SIMPLE ROOT: laud, laudable, laudation, laudatory, lauditive DISGUISED ROOT: lyrate, lyre, lyre-bird (from the spread of the male's tail-feathers, as though in praise), lyric, lyrical PREFIXED DISGUISED ROOT: *al-*: allow (from both this root and *locare*, to place) (*ad-*, to)

Element	From	Meaning	Examples
laud (cont'd)			LATIN ACADEMIC PHRASES: Each of the phrases indicate above average standing at time of graduation from a university; they are listed from lowest to highest. *cum laude* (with praise) *magna cum laude* (with great praise) *summa cum laude* (with highest praise) GERMAN: *lied* [a song of praise; pronounced *leed*; (plural: *lieder*); *Liederkranz* CROSS REFERENCE: *hymn, od*
lav,*** **lot,** **lug,** **luv**	Latin *lavare* (IE: *lab*, to hang down)	to wash	SIMPLE ROOT: *lav*: lava: lava, lavage (in *medicine*, the washing out of an organ, as the stomach, intestinal tract, or sinuses), lavatic, lavation, lavatory lave: lave, lavement, lavender, lavendula, laver lavi: lavic, lavish (**Synonyms:** profuse, extravagant, prodigal) *lot*: lotic (in *ecology*, designating, of, or living in flowing water, as rivers; compare *lentic*: designating, of, or living in still water, as lakes, ponds, or marshes), lotion PREFIXED ROOT: *lu*: *ab*-: abluent, ablution, ablutionary (*ab*-, away) *di*-: diluent (a diluting substance) (from *dis*-, off, from) *lug*: *de*-: deluge (the Deluge, the great biblical flood in Noah's time: Genesis 7) (from *dis*-, off) *lut*: *di*-: dilute (to lessen the potency, strength, purity, or brilliance of by admixture), dilution (from *dis*-, off, from) *e*-: elution, elutriate, eluviate, eluvium (from *ex*-, out) *luv*: *al*-: alluvial, alluvion, alluvium (*al*- assimilates *ad*-, toward) *col*-: colluvium (*col*- assimilates *com*-, with, together) *di*-: diluvial (also, *diluvian*; of or caused by a flood; especially the Deluge; of debris left by a flood or glacier), diluvium (from *dis*-, apart, away) *il*-: illuvium (soil materials which have been leached from an upper layer of soil and deposited in a lower layer) (*il*- assimilates *in*-, in) DOUBLE PREFIXED ROOT: antediluvian (of the time before the biblical flood; thus, very old; old-fashioned or primitive; as a *noun*, an antediluvian person or thing) (*ante*-, before; *di*- from *dis*-, apart) DISGUISED ROOT: lag, lather, latrine launder, laundry loment (a legume fruit that separates at its constrictions into one-seeded segments when ripe; Roman women used it in a cosmetic wash) lye (a highly concentrated, aqueous solution of potassium hydroxide or sodium hydroxide)

Element	From	Meaning	Examples
lav (cont'd)			LATIN SENTENCE: *lavabo* [I shall wash; in the Roman Catholic Church, the ritual washing of the celebrant's hands after the offertory, accompanied by the repetition of Psalm 25:6-12 (Vulgate), beginning with *lavabo*] PLACENAME: Alluvial City, Louisiana NO CROSS REFERENCE
lax*	Latin *laxus* (IE: *sleg*, loose)	slack, loose	SIMPLE ROOT: lax (**Synonyms:** remiss, negligent, derelict), laxation laxative (**Synonyms:** aperient, purgative, cathartic) laxity (the quality or condition of being lax; looseness) PREFIXED ROOT: *re*-: relax, relaxant, relaxation (**Synonyms:** rest, repose, leisure) (*re*-, back) DISGUISED ROOT: lease (**Synonyms:** hire, charter, rent), lush (one meaning) slack (**Synonyms:** remiss, negligent, derelict), slacken PREFIXED DISGUISED ROOT: *de*-: delay (as a *verb*, to put off to a future time; postpone; to make later; slow up; detain; as a *noun*, a delaying or being delayed) (*de*-, intensifier) *re*-: (back, again) relay (originally, hounds kept as reserves at points along the course of a hunt) release (**Synonyms:** free, liberate, emancipate) FRENCH TERM: *laissez-faire* [Let the (people) do (as they please): the policy or practice of letting people act without interference or direction; specifically, the policy of letting the owners of industry and business fix the rules of competition, the conditions of labor, etc. as they please, without governmental regulation or control; also spelled *laisser faire*] TRADE NAME FOR A LAXATIVE: *Ex Lax* CROSS REFERENCE: *langu*
lect*	Greek *legein*: to pick up, gather (IE: *leg*, to gather)	to choose	PREFIXED ROOT: *ana*-: analects (selections or parts of a literary work or group of works) (*ana*-, up) *ec*-: eclectic (choosing what appears to be the best from diverse sources, systems, or styles; as a *noun*, one whose opinions and beliefs are drawn from several sources; see *Placename*, below) (from *ex*-, out) PLACENAME: Eclectic, Alabama CROSS REFERENCE: *lect* (Latin)
lect,*** leg, lex	Greek *legein*: to speak (IE: *leg*, to gather)	word, tell, read	SIMPLE ROOT: lexeme, lexical, lexicon (in *linguistics*, the stock of morphemes in a language) PREFIXED ROOT AND COMPOUNDS: *lect*: *dia*-: (through, across) dialect (**Synonyms:** vernacular, cant, jargon), dialectic, dialectical dialectology (*logy*, study of) *leg*: *pro*-: prolegomenon (a preliminary statement; often plural with singular verb: a preliminary statement or essay; foreword; a critical introduction) (*pro*-, before)

Element	From	Meaning	Examples
lect (cont'd)			*lex*: a-: alexia (a loss of the ability to read) (*a-*, without, not) dys-: dyslexia (impaired ability to read) (*dys-*, impaired) LEADING ROOT COMPOUND: *lexi(co)*: graph: lexicographer (a writer or compiler of a dictionary), lexigraphy (*graph*, write) logy: lexicology (*logy*, study of) DISGUISED ROOT: lesson NB: Do not confuse this root with another one identically spelled, but which is from Latin, and meaning law (next family). NOTE: This root is from the same base as *logos,* word, which see. CROSS REFERENCE: *ep, log, parl, verb*
leg,*** lex, lit	Latin *lex* (IE: *leg*, to gather)	law	SIMPLE ROOT: *leg*: lega: legal (see *Triplets* below; **Synonyms**: lawful, legitimate, licit), legality, legacy, legate (also listed under *leg*, charge) lege: legist legi: legis, legitimate (see synonyms at *legal*, above) *lex*: lex (plural, *leges*) LEADING ROOT COMPOUND: *leg*: lat: legislate (to make or pass a law or laws, legislation, legislative, legislature (*lat* from *ferre*, to bring) *lit*: ig: litigate, litigable, litigant, litigious (from *agere*, to drive, lead, act, do] TRAILING ROOT COMPOUND: privi: privilege, privileged (*privus*, separate, peculiar; from the same base as *private*) DISGUISED ROOT: leal (now chiefly Scottish; loyal, true; see *Triplets* below) loyal (see *Triplets* below) TRIPLETS: leal:loyal:legal LATIN PHRASES: *lex loci* (the law of the place, e.g., "When in Rome, do as the Romans do") *lex non scripta* (law not written; unwritten law; common law) *lex talionis* (law of retaliation, e.g., An eye for an eye and a tooth for a tooth) CROSS REFERENCE: *jur/jus, nom*
leg,* lit	Latin *legare*: to send as a deputy (IE: *leg*, to gather)	to charge, send	SIMPLE ROOT: legate, legatee, legation PREFIXED ROOT: al-: allege (**Synonyms**: state, aver, attest), alleged (*al-* may assimilate *ad-*, to, toward, or it may be from *ex-*, out) de-: delegate (*de-*, from) re-: relegate (**Synonyms**: commit, entrust, confide) (*re-*, away, back) CROSS REFERENCE: *miss/mitt*

Element	From	Meaning	Examples
leg,* **lect,** **lig**	Latin *legere*: to gather (IE: *leg*, to gather)	to read; speak; gather, choose	ROOT NOTE: This root is from Greek *legein*, to collect, gather, choose, speak and is related to Greek *logos*, word, reason, speech, account. Latin *leg* and Greek *leg* are probably the most difficult roots absorbed into the English language to differentiate. SIMPLE ROOT: *leg*: legend, legendary (**Synonyms:** fabulous, mythical, apocryphal) legible, legion (originally, to gather troops) legume (originally, anything that can be gathered) *lect*: lectern, lection, lector lecture (**Synonyms:** speech, address, talk) PREFIXED ROOT: *lect*: *col-*: (*col-* assimilates *com-*, with) collect (**Synonyms:** gather, assemble, muster) collectanea (a collection of writings of one or more authors; *anthology*, literary miscellany) collected (gathered together; thus, assembled; or in control of oneself; calm and self-possessed; **Synonyms:** composed, unruffled, nonchalant) collection, collectivism (same as *socialism*) *e-*: elect, election, electorate (*e-* elides *ex-*, out) *intel*: intellect (from the *lect* that means to choose rather than the *lect* that means to read; *intellect* is the ability to make choices) (from *inter-*, between, among) *neg-*: neglect (**Synonyms:** omit, overlook, disregard) (*neg-*, not) *pre-*: prelect (to lecture or discourse in public) (*pre-*, in front of, public) *se-*: select (literally, to choose out) (*se-*, apart) *leg*: *col-*: (*col-* assimilates *com-*, with) college, collegial, collegiality, collegian, collegiate collegium (a group of individuals with equal power or authority; especially, an administrative board for a Soviet commissariat) *e-*: elegant (see *Doublets* below), elegit (in *law*, a writ of execution by which a plaintiff is given possession of the defendant's goods until the plaintiff's claim is satisfied) (from *ex-*, out) *il-*: illegible (very difficult or impossible to read because badly written or printed, faded, etc.) (*il-* assimilates *in-*, not)*lig*: *di-*: diligence (a selecting out of careful effort), diligent (from *dis-*, apart) *e-*: eligible (from *ex-*, out) DOUBLE PREFIXED ROOT: ineligible (*in-*, not + *e-* which elides *ex-*, out) predilection (a preconceived liking; partiality or preference for) (*pre-*, before + *di-*, from *dis-*, apart)

380

Element	From	Meaning	Examples
leg (cont'd)			TRAILING ROOT COMPOUND: sacri: sacrilege (from *sacrilegus*, temple robber, one who gathered up sacred objects and took them away; now meaning "the act of appropriating to oneself or to secular use, or of violating, what is consecrated to God or religion"; also the intentional desecration or disrespectful treatment of a person, place, thing, or idea held sacred) (*sacri*, sacred, holy) sorti: sortilege (a divination or prophecy by casting lots; sorcery; black magic; from *sortilegus*, a fortuneteller) (from *sors*, a lot) DISGUISED ROOT: coil (literally, to gather together) (from *collect*, above) PREFIXED DISGUISED ROOT: col-: colleague (originally, one chosen along with another) (*col-* assimilates *com-*, with, together) e-: elite (also, *élite*; see *Doublets* below) (*e-* elides *ex-*, out) DOUBLETS: elite:elegant INTERDISCIPLINARY: **election** (in *theology*, the selection by God of certain people for salvation and eternal life; in *law*, a writ of execution by which a plaintiff is given possession of the defendant's goods until his/her claim is settled) CROSS REFERENCE: (for choose) *opt*; (for speak) *dict, fa/fess, loqu/loc, ora, phas/phe*
leni*	Latin *lenire*: to soften (IE: *lei*, to neglect, let go)	soft, mild	SIMPLE ROOT: lenie: lenient (not harsh or severe in disciplining, punishing, judging, etc.; mild, merciful, clement) {lenience} lenis: lenis (in *phonetics*, articulated with little muscle tension, as voiced consonants, e.g., *b, d, g, j, r, v, w, z*); opposed to *fortis*, articulated with much muscle tension, as most voiceless plosives, e.g., the sounds of *k, p,* and *t* when used initially) lenit: lenitive (softening, soothing, or mitigating, as medicines or applications), lenitude, lenity (the state of being lenient; unmerited clemency; gentleness; mercifulness) PREFIXED ROOT: re-: relent (**Synonyms**: yield, capitulate, succumb), relentless (*re-*, again) ITALIAN MUSIC TERM: *lentando* (slowly; slowing down by degrees) CROSS REFERENCE: *malac, moll, clemen*
lent,* lens	Latin *lens*	lentil, pea (lens)	SIMPLE ROOT: *lens*: lens (from its resemblance to a split lentil, pea) *lent*: lenticel (a spongy area in the bark of a woody plant, serving as a pore to permit the exchange of gases between the stem and the atmosphere) lenticle, lenticular, lenticule (any of the microscopic lenses lenticulated on a film) lentiginous, lentigo, lentil LEADING ROOT COMPOUND: form: lentiform (same as *lenticular*) NOTE: See *long* for derivation of *Lent*. NO CROSS REFERENCE

Element	From	Meaning	Examples
lep*	Greek *lepos*: husk, rind, scale (IE: *lep*, to peel off, scale)	scale	SIMPLE ROOT: leper: leper (a person having leprosy; a person to be shunned or ostracized, because of the danger of moral contamination) lepid: lepidium, lepidolite, lepidote lepr: leprose, leprosy, leprous LEADING ROOT COMPOUND: pter: lepidopteran (*pter*, wing) sarium: leprosarium (from *leprosy sanitarium*) NOTE: See *lepto*, literally, peeled, husked, but extended to mean thin, slender. NO CROSS REFERENCE: *lepto*
leps,** lept	Greek *lambanein* (IE: *(s)lagw*, to grasp, seize)	to seize, grasp (seizure)	PREFIXED ROOT: *leps*: cata-: catalepsy (a condition in which consciousness and feeling seem to be temporarily lost, and the muscles become rigid) {cataleptic} (*cata-*, down) epi-: epilepsy, epileptic (*epi-*, over, upon) pro-: prolepsis (literally, to take beforehand; in *rhetoric*, the anticipation and answering of an objection or argument before one's opponent has put it forward) (*pro-*, before) syl-: syllepsis (*syl-* assimilates *sym-*, with, together) *lept*: ana-: analeptic (see note under *ana-*) (*ana-*, up) TRAILING ROOT COMPOUND: narco: narcolepsy (*narco*, stupor) nymph: nympholepsis, nympholept (*nymph*, young wife; spring goddess) organo: organoleptic (affecting or involving an organ, especially a sense organ) DISGUISED ROOT: latch PREFIXED DISGUISED ROOT: syl-: syllable (not related to *syllabus*; see *NB* below) (*syl-* assimilates *sym-*, with, together) TRAILING DISGUISED ROOT COMPOUND: astro: astrolabe (an astronomical instrument used by the ancient Greeks for determining the positions of sun or stars) (*astro*, star) NB: *Syllabus* is not related to this family, coming from Greek *sittyba*, a parchment strip used as a label. CROSS REFERENCE: *cap, empt, prehend*
lepto*	Greek *lepein*: to peel (IE: *lep*, to peel off, scale)	fine, slender, small, thin, weak	SIMPLE ROOT: lepton (a small coin of ancient Greece; a monetary unit of modern Greece) LEADING ROOT COMPOUND: bos: leptobos (an extinct, polled bovine held to be the ancestor of domestic cattle) (*bos*, cow) cephal: leptocephalus (*cephal*, head) dactyl: leptodactylous (having thin toes, as those of birds) (*dactyl*, finger, toe) derm: leptodermous (thin-skinned) (*derm*, skin) rhin: leptorrhine (also, *leptorhine*) (*rhin*, nose) som: leptosome (*som*, body) CROSS REFERENCE: *lep, micro, petit, tenu*

Element	From	Meaning	Examples
leth*	Latin *letum* (IE: *lei*, to neglect, let go)	death	SIMPLE ROOT: lethal (**Synonyms:** fatal, deadly, mortal) LEADING ROOT COMPOUND: fer: lethiferous (death-bringing) (*ferre*, to bring) NB: *Lethargic*, from *lethe*, forgetfulness, is not in this family. CROSS REFERENCE: *mort, necro, than*
leuk,** leuc	Greek *leucos*: light (IE: *leuk*, light, brightness)	white	ROOT NOTE: Most of the words which begin with *leuk* are used in *biology* and *medicine*. SIMPLE ROOT: leucine, leucismus, leucite, leucon (same as *leukon*), leukon LEADING ROOT COMPOUND: *leuco*: pter: leucopterin (a yellowish pigment isolated from butterfly wings; symbol: $C_{10}H_{19}O_{11}N_5$) (*pter*, wing) *leuk*: em: (from *hemo*, blood) leukemia (*emia*, diseased condition of the blood) leukemogenesis (*genesis*, producing) leukemoid (*oid*, similar to) encephal: leukencephalitis (*encephal*, brain; *itis*, inflammation of) *leuko*: cyt: leukocyte (*cyt*, cell) derm: leukoderma (*derm*, skin) rrh: leukorrhea (*rrh*, flow) tom: leukotomy (*tom*, cut) TRAILING ROOT COMPOUND: mela: melaleuka (literally, black white; from the tree's black trunk and white branches: a genus of Australian and East In- dian shrubs and trees) (*mela*, black) CROSS REFERENCE: *alb, blanc*
lev,*** liev lief	Latin *levare* [IE: *legwh*, light in movement and weight; yields English light (in weight)]	to raise, lift	SIMPLE ROOT: levy leva: levade, levant, levanter, levator leve: levee, lever, leverage levi: leviable, levigate, levity, levitate PREFIXED ROOT: *lev*: al-: alleviate (see synonyms at *relieve*, previous entry), allevia- tion, alleviative, alleviator (*al*- assimilates *ad*-, to, toward) e-: elevation, elevator (*e*- elides *ex*-, out) re-: relevant (**Synonyms:** germane, pertinent, apposite) (from *relevare*, to lift up, to bear upon) (*re*-, again) *lief* (*liev*): re-: relief (*re*-, again) re-: relieve (**Synonyms:** alleviate, lighten, assuage) (*re*-, again) [*Belief* and believe, from Old English, are not in this family.] TRAILING ROOT COMPOUND: canti: cantilever (*canti* from IE *kantho*, corner, bend) DISGUISED ROOT: leaven, leavening FRENCH COMPOUND: legerdemain (literally, light of hand) FRENCH TERM: levy en masse (partial translation of French *levée en masse*; an armed rising by civilians in a territory in order to resist an approaching invader; also *levy in mass*)

Element	From	Meaning	Examples
lev (cont'd)			FRENCH AND ITALIAN ART TERMS: *bas-relief* (sculpture in which figures are carved in a flat surface so that they project only a little from the background); term derived from Italian *basso-relievo* *mezzo-relievo* (sculpture in which the figures project halfway from the background) FRENCH LEGAL TERM: *levant and couchant* (see *Webster's Third*) NB: *Leviathan* is not in this family. NO CROSS REFERENCE
lib**	Latin *liber*: fiber (IE: *leubh*, to peel off)	book	ROOT NOTE: This meaning of the root refers to the fiber between the bark of the tree and the wood itself. SIMPLE ROOT: libel: libel (any false and malicious written or printed statement, tending to expose a person to public ridicule, or to injure his/her reputation in any way) {libelee, libeler, libelous} (*libellus*, little book) libr: library LATIN WORD: *liber* (a book, especially, a book of public records, as of mortgages and deeds) LATIN PHRASE: *ex libris* (from the library of) PLACENAME: Library, Pennsylvania THE NATIONAL LIBRARY: The Library of Congress, Washington, D.C. NOTE: Do not confuse this root with *liber*, free, or with *liber*, weights, or scales (see next family). CROSS REFERENCE: *bibli*
liber**	Latin *liber* (IE: *leudh*, to grow up; rise)	free	SIMPLE ROOT: libera: liberal (**Synonyms:** progressive, advanced, left), liberalism, liberality, liberalize, liberate libert: libertarian, libertine, liberator, liberty LEADING ROOT COMPOUND: cid: liberticide (destruction of liberty; a person who destorys liberty) (*cide*, kill) PREFIXED DISGUISED ROOT: de-: deliver (**Synonyms:** rescue, redeem, ransom), deliverance, delivery (*de-*, intensive) ACADEMIC PHRASE: liberal arts (arts befitting a freeman, and included language, philosophy, history, and abstract science; comprised of the *trivium* and the *quadrivium*, required curricula in the medieval university) LATIN PHRASE: *ad libitum* (literally, at liberty; at pleasure; as one pleases; as much as one pleases; in *music*, freely: a direction to the performer) FRENCH PHRASE: *liberté, égalité, fraternité* (liberty, equality, fraternity--the motto of the French Revolution) PLACENAMES: Liberal (Kansas, Missouri) Liberty [Illinois, Indiana, Kansas, Kentucky, Maine, Mississippi, Missouri, Nebraska, New York, North Carolina, Pennsylvania (two; one in Allegheny County and one in Tioga County), South Carolina, Tennessee, Texas, Washington, Wisconsin]

Element	From	Meaning	Examples
liber (cont'd)			[There are also several counties named Liberty, as well as various towns, such as Liberty Hill, Liberty Lake, Liberty Pole, Libertyville.] Liberia (the country in Africa founded for and by freed United States slaves; the capital of Liberia is Monrovia, after President James Monroe, the U.S. president influential in helping establish Liberia) NOTE: The Anglo-Saxon base of *friend* is also free. CROSS REFERENCE: *eleuthero, franc, lysis/lyt, solv/solu*
liber**	Latin *libra*	weight, scales, balance	SIMPLE ROOT: librate (to move back and forth slowly like the beam of a balance in coming to rest; to oscillate) libration (in *astronomy*, an apparent or real oscillation of the moon's face which makes it possible to see about nine percent more of its surface other than the hemisphere which is toward the earth) PREFIXED ROOT: *de-*: deliberant, deliberate (**Synonyms: 1)** think, reason, cogitate; **2)** voluntary, willful), deliberation, deliberative (*de-*, intensive) TRAILING ROOT COMPOUND: equi: equilibrant, equilibrate (to balance equally; keep in equipose or equilibrium), equilibrium (*equi*, equal) DISGUISED ROOT: level, libra [abbreviated *lb.* (pound)] lira, livre SIGN OF THE ZODIAC: Libra (represented by a set of scales) GREEK COGNATE: liter (a pound) (see *libra*, under *Disguised Root*, above) CROSS REFERENCE: *bar, grav, pend/pond*
lic,** lect	Latin *licere*: to be permitted; *lacere*, to ensnare (IE: *leik*, to offer for sale; bargain)	to allow; ensnare, entice	SIMPLE ROOT: license (**Synonyms: 1)** freedom, liberty; **2)** authorize, commission, accredit) licentiate, licentious, licit (**Synonyms:** legal, lawful, legitimate) PREFIXED ROOT: *lic*: *de-*: delicate (**Synonyms:** dainty, exquisite), delicious (*de-*, from) *e-*: elicit (to draw forth; evoke, as to elicit an favorable response; not to be confused with *illicit*, previous entry) (*e-* elides *ex-*, out) *il-*: illicit (do not confuse with *elicit*, next entry; neither confuse the meaning of *illicit* with *illegal*) (*il-* assimilates from *in-*, not) *lect*: *de-*: delectable, delectation (*de-*, from) DISGUISED ROOT: leisure [the word for *leisure* in Greek was *school*, which eventually came to designate the *place* where Greeks spent their leisure time studying] PREFIXED DISGUISED ROOT: *de-*: delight (**Synonyms:** pleasure, joy, enjoyment) (*de-*, from)

385

Element	From	Meaning	Examples
lic (cont'd)			*di-*: dilettante (**Synonyms:** 1) amateur, neophyte, tyro; 2) aesthete, connoisseur) (from *de-*, from) LATIN CONTRACTION: *scilicet* (contraction of *scire licit*, it is permitted to know; namely; to wit; that is to say) GERMAN: delicatessen NO CROSS REFERENCE
lict			See *linq* for derelict.
lid,* lis	Latin *laedere*: to hurt	damage, to strike	PREFIXED ROOT: *lid*: *col-*: collide, collision (*col-* assimilates *com-*, with, together) *e-*: elide [literally, to strike out; thus, to leave out, suppress, omit, or ignore; to leave out, or slur over (a vowel, syllable, etc.) in pronunciation] (*e-* elides *ex-*, out) *lis*: *e-*: elision (the omission, assimilation, or slurring over of a vowel, syllable, etc. in pronunciation) (*e-* elides *ex-*, out) DISGUISED ROOT: lesion (an injury; hurt; damage) NO CROSS REFERENCE
lig,*** leg, ly	Latin *ligare* (IE: *leig*, to bind)	to bind, tie	SIMPLE ROOT: ligament (in *anatomy*, a band of tissue, usually white and fibrous, serving to connect bones, hold organs in place, etc.), ligand, ligate, ligature PREFIXED ROOT: *leg*: *al-*: allegiance (**Synonyms:** fidelity, loyalty, fealty) (*al-* assimilates *ad-*, to, toward) *lig*: *col-*: colligate (to bind together; to relate isolated facts by some reasonable explanation, especially so as to evolve a general principle) (*col-* assimilates *com-*, with, together) *ob-*: obligate (see synonyms at *oblige*), obligation, obligatory, oblige (**Synonyms:** force, compel, coerce), obligee (*ob-*, against) *re-*: religion (*re-*, back) *ly*: *al-*: ally (**Synonyms:** companion, confederate, accomplice) (*al-* assimilates *ad-*, to, toward) *re-*: rely (**Synonyms:** trust, depend, reckon) (*re-*, back) DISGUISED ROOT: furl (Old French *ferlier*, to tie up; from *firmus*, firm + *ligare*; to roll up tightly and make secure, as a flag to a staff or a sail to a spar) league (an association of states, organizations or individuals for common action; alliance; another *league* indicates a unit of distance equal to three statute miles) liege (See *Placename* below), liegeman liable (**Synonyms:** likely, apt, prone) lien (in *law*, a claim on the property of another as security for the payment of a just debt) rally [French *rallier*; from *re-*, again + *alier*, to join; see *ally* above; **Synonyms:** rouse (arouse), waken (awaken)] PREFIXED DISGUISED ROOT: *al-*: alliance (**Synonyms:** league, coalition, confederacy), alloy (*al-* assimilates *ad-*, to, toward)

386

Element	From	Meaning	Examples
lig (cont'd)			*re-*: reliable (**Synonyms**: dependable, trustworthy, authentic), reliance (*re-*, back) ITALIAN MUSIC TERMS: legato (smooth and evenly connected, with no noticeable interruption between the notes; opposite to staccato) obbligato (originally, not to be left out; indispensable: said earlier of an accompaniment essential to the proper performance of a piece, but now usually of one that can be omitted) PLACENAMES: Reliance (South Dakota, Wyoming) Liège, Belgium (in the province of Liège) CROSS REFERENCE: *cinct, sphing/sphinx, string/strict*
lign*	Latin *lignum* (IE: *leg*, to gather)	wood	ROOT NOTE: This root is derived from the same base of *collect, elect, select*, in which the common meaning is gather, or collect. This meaning evolved into collecting wood, thus the root *lign*. SIMPLE ROOT: ligneous, lignescent, lignin, lignite, lignum LEADING ROOT COMPOUND: *lig*: aloe: lignaloes (from *lignum aloës*, wood of aloes) *ligni*: fic: lignification (from *facere*, to make) form: ligniform fy: lignify (from *facere*, to make) perd: ligniperdous (that destroys wood, as a *ligniperdous* insect) (*perdere*, to destroy) NB: *Ligne*, from *linea*, line, is not in this family. CROSS REFERENCE: *xylo*
limi*	Latin *limus* [IE: *(s)lei*, slime, wet and sticky]	mud	LEADING ROOT COMPOUND: col: limicolae, limicoline (shore-inhabiting), limicolous (living in mud) (*colere*, to inhabit) vor: limivorous (*vorare*, to eat) NOTE: Do not confuse with *limin*, threshold, as in *limen*, *liminal, liminary*, and *subliminal*. NO CROSS REFERENCE
limn*	Greek *limne*: marsh	fresh water	SIMPLE ROOT: limnetic (designating, of, or living in the open waters of lakes, away from shore vegetation) PREFIXED ROOT: *epi-*: epilimnion (the upper layer of warm water in a lake, containing more oxygen than the lower layers) (*epi-*, upon) *hypo-*: hypolimnion (the lowermost, noncirculating layer of cold water in a thermally stratified lake, usually deficient in oxygen) (*hypo-*, under) LEADING ROOT COMPOUND: bio: limnobiology (*bio*, life; *logy*, study of) logy: limnology (*logy*, study of) meter: limnometer (*meter*, measure) NOTE: Henry David Thoreau is considered to be America's first limnologist. Explore *Walden's Pond*, in which Thoreau contemplates nature. NB: *Limn* itself is from *lumin*, light. CROSS REFERENCE: *lacu*

387

Element	From	Meaning	Examples
lin*	Germanic *linea*	line, cord	ROOT NOTE: Do not confuse this root with another of the same name, but being derived from Latin *linum*, flax, and from which is derived *linen*; linen was originally that which was used to line a garment, thus the garment's lining. SIMPLE ROOT: line, lineage (lineal descent from an ancestor; ancestry or extraction), lineal, lineament, linear, linearity, lineate, lineolate PREFIXED ROOT: *a-*: aline (the preferred spelling is *align*, from French *a-*, to + *ligne*, line; see *Prefixed Disguised Root*), alinement *de-*: delineate, delineation, delineative, delineator (*de-*, from) PREFIXED DISGUISED ROOT: *a-*: align, alignment (see *aline* above) *col-*: collimate (to make light rays, etc. parallel; to adjust the line of sight of a telescope, surveyor's level, etc.), collimator. These disguised roots were formed from a misreading of *collinear,* to direct in a straight line. (*col-* assimilates *com-*, with, together) EXPRESSION: *delineavit* [He (or she) drew (this): used with the artist's name on a painting, etc.] NB: *Liniment*, from *linere*, to anoint, is not in this family. NO CROSS REFERENCE
ling***	Latin *lingua*: tongue, language (IE: *dnghwa*, language)	tongue, language	SIMPLE ROOT: lingo: lingo (**Synonyms:** dialect, cant, jargon) lingu: lingua (a tongue, or an organ resembling a tongue, as the proboscis of a butterfly or moth), lingual, linguist, linguistic, linguistics, lingulate (shaped like a tongue) PREFIXED ROOT: *meta-*: metalinguistics (*meta-*, between) *sub-*: sublingual (*sub-*, under) LEADING ROOT COMPOUND: *lingua*: nas: linguanasal (*nas*, nose) *lingui*: form: linguiform (shaped like a tongue) TRAILING ROOT COMPOUND: bi: bilingual (*bi*, two) mono: monolingual (*mono*, one) ANGLICIZED: language ITALIAN: linguine [literally, little tongue; and designating a kind of pasta like spaghetti, but flat (like the tongue), and often served with seafood sauces] *lingua franca* (literally, Frankish language, a hybrid language of Italian, Spanish, French, Greek, Arabic, and Turkish elements, and which is spoken in certain Mediterranean ports) FRENCH WORDS: languet, languette FRENCH TERMS: *langue d'oc* [the language of *oc*, Provençal, yes, from Latin *hoc*, this thing, from characteristic use of *oc* for affirmation (in contrast to *langue d'oïl*); *langue d'oc* designates a group of French dialects spoken in Southern France in the Middle Ages and surviving in Provençal]

388

Element	From	Meaning	Examples
ling (cont'd)			*langue d'oïl* [the language of *oïl* (Old French *oïl*, yes), from characteristic use of *oïl* for affirmation; *langue d'oïl* designates a group of French dialects spoken in most of central and northern France in the Middle Ages; it is the Old French from which modern French is derived] CROSS REFERENCE: *gloss*
linq,* lic	Latin *linquere* (IE: *leikw*, to leave)	to leave	PREFIXED ROOT: *lic*: *de-*: delict (in *law*, an offense; misdemeanor) (*de-*, from) *re-*: relic, relict (from *relinquish*) (*re-*, away) *linq*: *de-*: delinquency, delinquent (as an *adjective*, failing or neglecting to do what duty or law requires; as a *noun*, a delinquent person, especially a juvenile delinquent) (*de-*, from) *re-*: relinquish (**Synonyms**: abandon, forgo, abdicate) (*re-*, from) DOUBLE PREFIXED ROOT: derelict (as an *adjective*, deserted by the owner; abandoned, forsaken; as a *noun*, a person or thing abandoned as worthless), dereliction (*de-*, intensive + *re-*, away) DISGUISED ROOT: loan (the act of lending; *lend*, however, is not from this root) INTERDISCIPLINARY: relict (in *ecology*, a plant or animal species living on in isolation in a small local area as a survival from an earlier period or as a remnant of an almost extinct group; in *geology*, a physical feature, mineral, structure, etc. remaining after other components have wasted away or been altered) NO CROSS REFERENCE
lip*	Greek *lipos* (IE: *leip*, to smear with grease)	fat, fatty	SIMPLE ROOT: lipa: liparis, liparous, lipase (any of a group of enzymes, especially from the pancreas, that aid in digestion by hydrolyzing fats into fatty acids and glycerol) lipi: lipid (any one of a group of fats or fatlike substances, characterized by their insolubility in water and their solubility in fat solvents such as alcohol, ether, and chloroform) LEADING ROOT COMPOUND: *lip*: ectom: lipectomy (*ectom*, to remove surgically) em: lipemia (abnormal amount of fat in the blood) (*em* short for *hemo*, blood) oid: lipoid (in *biochemistry* and *chemistry*, resembling fat) (*oid*, similar to) oma: lipoma (*oma*, tumor) *lipo*: lys: lipolysis (the decomposition of fat, as during digestion) (*lysis*, loosen) phil: lipophilic (having a strong attraction for fats) (*phila*, love) som: liposome (*soma*, body) trop: lipotropic (regulating or reducing the accumulation of fat in the body or its organs) {lipotropism} (*trop*, turn) CROSS REFERENCE: *adip*

Element	From	Meaning	Examples
lit			See *leg*, law, for *litigate*.
liter**	Latin *littera* (IE: *deph*, to stamp, which yields Greek *diphtheria*; English *letter*)	letter	SIMPLE ROOT: literacy, literal, literalism, literary, literate, literatim, literature (French, *littérature*) PREFIXED ROOT: *al-*: alliteration (the commencement of two or more stressed syllables of a word group with the same consonant sound), alliterative (*al-* assimilates *ad-*, to, toward) *il-*: illiteracy, illiterate (*il-* assimilates *in-*, not) *ob-*: obliterate (**Synonyms**: erase, expunge, efface) (*ob-*, against) *trans-*: transliterate, transliteration (*trans-*, across) TRAILING ROOT COMPOUND: bi: biliteral (*bi*, two) equi: equiliteral (*equi*, same) LATIN PHRASE: *ad litteram* (to the letter; exactly) LATIN SAYING: *vox audita perit, littera scripta manet* (The spoken word dies, the written letter remains). FRENCH TERM: *belles-lettres* [beautiful letters; fine literature; aesthetic literature; literature as one of the fine arts: fiction, poetry, drama, essays, etc., as distinguished from technical and scientific writings; the writer of such art is a *belletrist* (adjective, *belletristic*)] NO CROSS REFERENCE
lith,*** lite	Greek *lithos*	stone	SIMPLE ROOT: lithia (Li_2O), lithiasis, lithic, lithium (chemical symbol: Li) PREFIXED ROOT: *anti-*: antilithic (in *medicine*, preventing the formation or development of calculi, as of the urinary tract) (*anti-*, against) LEADING ROOT COMPOUND: *lith*: arg: litharge (chemical symbol: PbO) (*arg*, silver) oid: lithoid (having the nature of a stone; stonelike) (*oid*, similar to) *litho*: graph: lithograph, lithography (*graph*, write) logy: lithology (*logy*, study of) marg: lithomarge (a mixture of clay, sand, and limestone, that is soft and crumbly and usually contains shell fragments; a smooth, closely packed variety of kaolin) (from *marga*, marl) meteor: lithometeor (solid material, except ice, suspended in the atmosphere, as dust, smoke, or pollen) phyt: lithophyte (*phyte*, plant) pon: lithopone (a white pigment made by mixing barium sulfate with zinc sulphide, used in paints, linoleum, etc.) (*ponos*, work) spher: lithosphere (the solid, rocky part of the earth; earth's crust) (*sphere*, ball) tom: lithotomy (the surgical removal of a calculus, or mineral secretion, by cutting into the bladder) (*tom*, cut) trit: lithotrity (the process of crushing a calculus in the bladder into very small pieces so that it can be eliminated in the urine) (from *terere*, to grind, crush)

Element	From	Meaning	Examples
lith (cont'd)			TRAILING ROOT COMPOUND: *lite*: cryo: cryolite (*cryo*, cold) dendro: dendrolite (*dendro*, tree) praseo: praseolite (*pras*, leek-green) rhyo: rhyolite (*rh*, stream) sidero: siderolite (*sidero*, iron) *lith*: acro: acrolith (*acro*, topmost, extremities) angio: angiolith (*angio*, vessel) cocco: coccolith (*cocco*, berry) cyclo: cyclolith (*cyclo*, circle) eo: eolith (*eo*, early) grano: granolith (*grano*, grain) lepido: lepidolith (*lepido*, scaly) mega: megalith (*mega*, large) mono: monolithic (*mono*, one) neo: neolithic (*neo*, new) nep: nephrolith (*nephro*, kidney) oto: otolith (*oto*, ear) paleo: paleolithic (*paleo*, early, prehistoric) zo: zoolith (*zo*, animal) CROSS REFERENCE: *lap, petr, sax*
loco***	Latin *locus* (IE: *stel*, to set up, stand, location)	place	SIMPLE ROOT: local: local, locale, localism, localite, locality, localization, localize, localizer, locally locat: locate, location, locative (in *linguistics*, designating, or in the case indicating place at which or in which, as in Latin, Greek, Sanskrit, etc.; as a *noun*, the locative case; also, a word in the locative case) locul: locular (in *biology*, of, having the nature of, or consisting of loculi, or cavities), loculate (same as *locular*), locule (same as *loculus*), loculus (plural, *loculi*) locus: locus (plural, *loci*) PREFIXED ROOT: *al*-: allocate (**Synonyms:** allot, assign, apportion), allocation (*al*- assimilates *ad*-, to, toward) *co*-: co-locate [authorities are divided on this word; most prefer *collocate* (next entry) in all uses; however, it appears that both words have proper usage; use *co-locate* to indicate two military units located on the same base or post; use *collocate* to indicate two or more pieces of equipment placed next to each other, especially side by side] (*co*-, with, together) *col*-: collocate (see *co-locate* above), collocation (*col*- assimilates *com*-, with, together) *dis*-: dislocate, dislocation, dislocatory (*dis*-, apart, away) *re*-: relocate, relocation (*re*-, again) *trans*-: translocate, translocation (*trans*-, across) LEADING ROOT COMPOUND: *loco*: foco: locofoco (*foco*, fire) mot: locomotion, locomotive, locomotor (*mot*, move)

Element	From	Meaning	Examples
loco (cont'd)			*loculi:* cid: loculicidal (in *botany*, splitting open along the midribs of the carpels of which it is formed: said of a capsule) DISGUISED ROOT: couch (from *collocate*) couchant (lying down; said especially of animals; in *heraldry*, lying down or crouching, but keeping the head up, as *a lion couchant*), couching (a type of embroidery) lieu (literally, place: now used chiefly in the phrase *in lieu of*) PREFIXED DISGUISED ROOT: ac-: accouchement (literally, to put to bed, to give birth to; thus, childbirth, confinement), accoucheur (a medical man who attends childbirth; expert in obstetrics), accoucheuse (a midwife) (*ac-* assimilates *ad-*, to) al-: allow (**Synonyms:** let, permit, suffer) (from both this root and *laudare*, to praise) (*al-* assimilates *ad-*, to, toward) DISGUISED LEADING ROOT COMPOUND: ten: lieutenant (one who holds the place of one higher, e.g., a lieutenant holds the place of a captain in the US Army and US Air Force; same roots as *locum tenens*, which see below) (*ten*, hold) DISGUISED TRAILING ROOT COMPOUND: mi: milieu (surroundings; environment) (from *medius*, middle) ANGLO-SAXON-FRENCH PHRASE: *in lieu of* (in place of) LATIN PHRASES: *loca supra citato* (literally, in the place cited above; in the place before cited) *loco citato* (in the place cited or quoted: referring to a previously cited work, especially in an academic paper) *locus classicus* [literally, classical passage; most important passage (place) in a book; a passage used to clarify a point] *locus criminis* (or *delicti*) (scene of the crime) *locus in quo* (literally, place in which) *locus sigilli* (literally, place of the seal; abbreviated *L.S.*) *locum tenens* (literally, place taker; a person taking another's place for the time being; temporary substitute, as for a doctor or clergyman) LATIN LEGAL PHRASE: *in loco parentis* (in place of the parents; gives designated adults temporary custody of children not their own) LITERATURE TERM: local color (detailed representation in fiction of the setting, dialect, customs, dress, and ways of thinking, feeling, talking, or behaving characteristic of a certain region or time, introduced into a novel, short story, play, etc., to add realism. Examples of *local color* include Thomas Hardy's Essex, and Kipling's India. In the United States, Bret Harte is noted for local color of the West; Mark Twain, of the Mississippi region; George Washington Cable, of the South; E. W. Howe and Hamlin Garland, of the Midwest; Sarah Orne Jewett, of New England; as well as the stories of O. Henry and Damon Runyon about New York City) CROSS REFERENCE: *chor, top*
locut			See *loqu* for *elocution*.

Element	From	Meaning	Examples
logo***	Greek *logos* (IE: *leg*, to gather)	word, speech, reason, account	SIMPLE ROOT: logistic, Logos (sometimes lower case in expressing the Greek philosophical concept: reason thought of as constituting the controlling principle of the universe and as being manifested by speech; in *Christian theology*, capitalized: the eternal thought or word of God, made incarnate in Jesus Christ; see John 1, New Testament) PREFIXED ROOT: *ana-*: (again) analog (adjective), analogue (noun) analogous (in *biology*, similar in function but not in origin and structure) analogy (**Synonyms:** likeness, similarity, resemblance) *apo-*: apologetic, apologetics, apologia, apologize, apologue, apology (*apo-*, from) *dia-*: dialogical, dialogist, dialogue (talking together; conversation) (*dia-*, between, through) *epi-*: epilogue (a closing section added to a novel, play, etc., providing further comment, interpretation, or information) (*epi-*, upon) *para-*: paralogism (reasoning contrary to the rules of logic) (*para-*, beyond) *pro-*: prologue (**Synonyms:** introduction, preface, foreword) (*pro-*, before) *syl-*: syllogism (*syl-* assimilates *sym-*, with, together) LEADING ROOT COMPOUND: *log*: arith: logarithm (*arithmos*, number) *logo*: gram: logogram (also, *logograph*; a letter, character, or symbol used to represent an entire word, e.g., $ for *dollar*; & for *and*) (*gram*, write) graph: logography (the use of logotypes in printing) (*graph*, write) typ: logotype (*type*, representative form, example) TRAILING ROOT COMPOUND: homo: homologous (*homo*, same) horo: horologe (a timepiece, e.g., a sundial, hourglass, clock) (*horo*, hour) *logy* (scientific study of) bio: biology (*bio*, life) card: cardiology (*card*, heart) cyto: cytology (*cyto*, cell) dendro: dendrology (*dendro*, trees) dermato: dermatology (*dermato*, skin) ecclesi: ecclesiology (*eccles*, church) eco: ecology (*eco*, home, environment) onco: oncology (*onco*, tumors) paleo: paleontology (*paleo*, ancient, prehistoric) physio: physiology (*physi*, growth) rhino: rhinology (*rhino*, nose) zo: zoology (*zo*, animal) CROSS REFERENCE: *locut/loqu*

393

Element	From	Meaning	Examples
long***	Latin *longus*	long	SIMPLE ROOT: long (**Synonyms: 1)** lengthy, extensive; **2)** protracted, prolonged, extended)

longe: longe (also, *lunge*), longeron
longi: longissimus, longitude, longitudinal
PREFIXED ROOT:
al-: (*al-* assimilates *ad-*, to, toward)
allonge (literally, to make long; a slip of paper attached to a bill of exchange to provide space for additional endorsements; rider)
allongé (to extend an arm or a leg in a ballet movement; same derivation as *allonge*, previous entry)
e-: elongate (to make or become longer; stretch; in *botany*, used as an adjective: long and narrow, as certain leaves) (*e-* elides *ex-*, out)
ob-: oblong (longer one way than the other) (*ob-*, against)
pro-: prolong (**Synonyms:** extend, lengthen, protract) (*pro-*, forth)
SIMPLE COMPOUND: longshoreman (originally, one who worked along the shore; an aphetic of *alongshore*)
LEADING ROOT COMPOUND:
long:
anim: longanimity (patient endurance of injuries; forbearance) (*anim*, soul, spirit)
ev: longevity (from *aevum*, age)
longi:
corn: longicorn (having long feelers, or antennae, as some beetles) (*cornu*, horn)
DISGUISED ROOT:
Lent [refers to the lengthening of days; as a religious term, the 40-day period from Ash Wednesday (so called from the practice of putting ashes on the forehead as a sign of penitence) to Easter]
linger (**Synonyms:** stay, remain, abide)
lunge (from French *allonger*, to lengthen, thrust; a sudden thrust with a sword or other weapon; a sudden plunge forward)
PREFIXED DISGUISED ROOT:
e-: eloign [to carry away (property); in *law*, to remove private property beyond the jurisdiction of the sheriff; as a noun, a return by a sheriff stating that the goods to be seized to satisfy a just debt have been removed from the jurisdiction] (from *ex-*, out)
in-: indulge (**Synonyms:** humor, pamper, spoil) (*in-*, in)
pur-: purloin (literally, for long; thus, to steal, as in Edgar Allen Poe's "The Purloined Letter") (for *per-* from *pro-*, for)
FRENCH TERMS:
longueur (a long, boring section of a novel, musical work, etc.)
chaise longue (literally, long chair; by folk etymology, *chaise lounge*, lounge chair)
OLD ENGLISH:
lang (as in *Auld Lang Syne*, literally, Old Long Since)
belong
lumber

Element	From	Meaning	Examples
long (cont'd)			ACRONYM: LORAN [*Lo*(ng) *Ra*(nge) *N*(avigation); a system by which a ship or aircraft can determine its position by the difference in time between radio signals sent from two or more known stations] PLACENAME: Oblong, Illinois CROSS REFERENCE: *dolicho*
loqu,*** locut	Latin *loqui*	to talk, speak	SIMPLE ROOT: *locut*: locution *loqu*: loqua: loquacious (**Synonyms:** talkative, garrulous, voluble), loquacity (talkativeness, especially when excessive) loqui: loquitur (begins to speak; used as a stage direction, usually after the name of the player) PREFIXED ROOT: *locut*: *al-*: allocution (a formal address, especially one warning or advising with authority) (*al-* assimilates *ad-*, to, toward) *circum-*: circumlocution (*circum-*, around) *col-*: collocutor (a person to or with whom one speaks) (*col-* assimilates *com-*, with) *e-*: elocution (from *ex-*, out) *inter-*: interlocution, interlocutor, interlocutory (interjected, as *interlocutory wit*; in *law*, pronounced during the course of a suit, pending final decision) (*inter-*, between) *pro-*: prolocutor (a spokesman; a chairman) (*pro-*, for) *loqu*: *col-*: colloquy, colloquial, colloquialism, colloquium, colloquist (*col-* assimilates *com-*, with) *e-*: eloquence, eloquent (from *ex-*, out) *ob-*: obloquy (*ob-*, against) DOUBLE PREFIXED ROOT: ineloquent (see *eloquent*, above) (*in-*, not + *e-* from *ex-*, out) PREFIXED DISGUISED ROOT: *col-*: collogue (to confer or converse privately) (*col-* assimilates *com-*, with, together) TRAILING ROOT COMPOUND: brevi: breviloquence (*brevi*, short) grandi: grandiloquent (**Synonyms:** bombastic, flowery, turgid), grandiloquence (*grand*, full-grown, large) magni: magniloquent (*magni*, great) multi: multiloquent (*multi*, many) soli: soliloquy (*soli*, alone) ventro: ventriloquist (literally, one who speaks from the belly) (*ventro*, belly) CROSS REFERENCE: *dict, ep, fab/fam/fat, parl, verb*
lot			See *lav* for *lotion*.
lox*	Greek *loxos*	oblique	SIMPLE ROOT: loxia (same as *torticollis*), loxic (twisted), loxotic (slanting) LEADING ROOT COMPOUND: *lox*: odo: loxodograph (*hodo*, way + *graph*, write) odont: loxodont (*odont*, tooth)

Element	From	Meaning	Examples
lox*			*loxo*: cosm: loxocosm (a device to show how the inclination of earth's axis causes the day's length to vary from season to season) (*cosm*, universe) drom: loxodrome, loxodromic, loxodromics (*drom*, run) sceles: loxosceles (compare with *isosceles*) (*scel*, leg) NB: *Loxygen*, from *liquid oxygen*, is not in this family. NO CROSS REFERENCE
lubr*	Latin *lubricare*: to make smooth (IE: *sleub*, to slide, slip)	slippery	SIMPLE ROOT: lubric, lubricant, lubricate, lubricatory, lubricious, lubricity LEADING ROOT COMPOUND: *lubri*: fy: lubrify (from *facere*, to make, do) *lubrit*: orium: lubritorium (a station or room for lubricating motor vehicles) (*orium*, a place where) NO CROSS REFERENCE
luc,*** lum, lus, lux	Latin *lucere*: to shine (IE: *leuk*, to shine, bright)	light, clear	ROOT NOTE: In addition to meaning light, clear, *lum* is extended to mean the cavity or channel within a tube or tubular organ, i.e., the channel by which light passes. SIMPLE ROOT: lumen luc: lucent, lucid, lucubrate, luculent lumin: luminaire, luminal, luminance, luminary, luminescence, luminosity, luminous lus: luster, lustrate, lustring, lustrous, lustrum lux: lux (abbreviated *l$_x$*, the international system unit of illumination) PREFIXED ROOT: *luc*: e-: elucidate (**Synonyms**: explain, expound, explicate), elucidation, elucubrate (*e-* elides *ex-*, out) pel-: pellucid (very clear, easy to understand; see synonyms at *translucent*, below) (*pel-* assimilates *per-*, intensifier) re-: reluctant (reflecting light; bright) (*re-*, back) trans-: translucent (**Synonyms**: clear, transparent, pellucid) (*trans-*, across) *lum*: il-: illuminate (to give light to; to light up; also, to make clear; explain; elucidate), illumine (*il-* assimilates *in-*, in) *lus*: il-: illustrate, illustration (**Synonyms**: instance, case, example), illustrious (*il-* assimilates *in-*, in) DOUBLE PREFIXED ROOT: transilluminate (*trans-*, across + *il-* from *in-*, in) LEADING ROOT COMPOUND: *luci*: fer: Lucifer (light-bearer; the archangel cast from Heaven for leading a revolt of the angels; thus, Satan; also the planet Venus in its appearance as the morning star), luciferase, luciferin (*ferre*, to bear) *lumini*: fer: luminiferous (*ferre*, to bear)

396

Element	From	Meaning	Examples
luc (cont'd)			BRANDNAME: LUX soap bar PLACENAME: Lux, Mississippi CROSS REFERENCE: *phos, phot*
lucr*	Latin *lucrari:* to gain (IE: *lau*, to capture)	money, profit	SIMPLE ROOT: lucrative (producing wealth or profit; prof-itable; remunerative), lucre LEADING ROOT COMPOUND: fic: lucrific (from *facere*, to make, do) CROSS REFERENCE: *fe, pecu*; the single word *usury*, the act of lending money at a rate of interest that is excessively or unlawfully high, from *uti*, to use
luct*	Latin *luctare* (IE: *leug*, to bend; yields English lock)	to struggle, wrestle	PREFIXED ROOT: e-: eluctation (a bursting or struggling forth) (from *ex-*, out) re-: reluctant (**Synonyms**: disinclined, loath, averse) (*re-*, against) DOUBLE PREFIXED ROOT: ineluctable (irresistible) (*in-*, not + *e-* from *ex-*, out) CROSS REFERENCE: *act, agogue, agon, machy*
lud,*** lus	Latin *ludere* (IE: *leid*, to play, tease)	to play	SIMPLE ROOT: ludicrous (**Synonyms**: absurd, preposterous, silly) ludo (a form of pachisi played chiefly in the British Isles) PREFIXED ROOT: *lud*: al-: allude (**Synonym**: refer) (*al-* assimilates *ad-*, to) col-: collude (*col-* assimilates *com-*, with, together) de-: delude (**Synonyms**: deceive, mislead, beguile) (*de-*, from) e-: elude (**Synonyms**: escape, avoid, evade) (from *ex-*, out) il-: illude (*il-* assimilates *in-*, on) inter-: interlude (originally, a short, humorous play presented between the parts of a miracle play) (*inter-*, between) post-: postlude (*post-*, after) pre-: prelude (*pre-*, before) *lus*: al-: allusion (a brief reference in a literary work, either explicit or indirect, to a person, place, event, or another literary work or passage) (*al-* assimilates *ad-*, to) col-: collusion (*col-* assimilates *com-*, with, together) de-: delusion (**Synonyms**: illusion, hallucination, mirage), delusive, delusory (*de-*, from) e-: elusion (an eluding; escape or avoidance by quickness or cunning; evasion), elusive (from *ex-*, out) il-: illusion (see synonyms at *delusion*, above), illusive, illusory (*il-* assimilates *in-*, on) pro-: prolusion (a preliminary piece, performance, essay, etc.) (*pro-*, before) LEADING ROOT COMPOUND: fic: ludification (though now archaic, it originally meant an act of deception or mockery) NO CROSS REFERENCE
lug			See *lav* or *deluge*.
lum			See *luc* for *luminous*.

Element	From	Meaning	Examples
lumbri*	Latin *lumbricus*	worm	ROOT NOTE: This root originally meant earthworm (the genus for *earthworm* is *Lumbricus*), but is extended to mean intestinal worm. SIMPLE ROOT: lumbricalis [any of four small muscles in the palm of the hand and in the sole of the foot (from the shape of the muscles)] lumbricin (a hemolytic substance extracted from earthworms) LEADING ROOT COMPOUND: *lumbri*: cid: lumbricide (*cide*, kill) *lumbric*: oid: lumbricoid (*oid*, similar to) osis: lumbricosis (the condition of being infected with *lumbrici*) (*osis*, condition of) CROSS REFERENCE: *helminth, verm*
lun***	Latin *luna* (from *lucere*, to shine) (IE: *leuk*, to shine, bright)	moon	SIMPLE ROOT: luna: luna lunac: lunacy (**Synonyms:** insanity, dementia, psychosis) lunar: lunar, lunare [the lunate bone (*os lunatum*, moon-shaped bone)], lunarian (a supposed inhabitant of the *moon*; also, an authority on lunar astronomy; term is also used in palmistry), lunary lunat: lunate (moon-shaped, or crescentic), lunatic (a mentally deranged person, originally thought to be influenced by the *moon*; thus, the expression, "moon-struck"), lunation lune: lune, lunette lunu: lunula PREFIXED ROOT: *inter-*: interlunar (of the period of time each month when the moon cannot be seen because it is in or near conjunction with the sun) (*inter-*, between) *peri-*: perilune (*peri-*, around) *sub-*: sublunary (earthly; mundane) (*sub-*, under) TRAILING ROOT COMPOUND: demi: demilune (*demi*, half) SIMPLE COMPOUND: luna moth (because of its moonish color) FRENCH: *lundi* (*di*, day; Monday, or *Moon Day*) SPANISH: *lunes* (Monday, or *Moon Day*) AMUSEMENT PARK: Luna Park, Coney Island, Brooklyn, New York: noted for its illumination NOTE: There is another *luna*, Hawaiian, for high, above, and designating a foreman, especially of a sugar cane or pineapple plantation. NO CROSS REFERENCE
lus			See *luc* for *luster, illustrate*.
lut*	Latin *luteus*	yellow	SIMPLE ROOT: lutea: luteal lutein: lutein [an elision of *corpus lute(um)* + *in*, the chemical symbol of which is $C_{40}H_{56}O_2$, and found in green leaves, egg yolks, and in certain hormones], luteinic, luteinization, luteinize

Element	From	Meaning	Examples
lut (cont'd)			luteo: luteolin ($C_{15}H_{10}O_5$), luteous LEADING ROOT COMPOUND: oid: luteoid (*oid*, similar to) oma: luteoma (*oma*, mass, tumor) ose: luteose (*ose*, condition of) DISGUISED ROOT: lurid CROSS REFERENCE: *aur, chrys, flav, ochr, xanth*
lut, luv			See *lav* for *ablution* and *alluvion*.
lux			See *luc* for *lux*.
lymph**	Greek *lymph*: water	fluid (of the body)	ROOT NOTE: This root originally meant "spring water." SIMPLE ROOT: lymph, lymphatic (can mean sluggish: a sluggish condition was formerly thought to be due to too much lymph in the body), lymphatism PREFIXED ROOT: *endo-*: endolymph (*endo-*, within) LEADING ROOT COMPOUND: *lymph*: aden: lymphadenitis (*aden*, gland; *itis*, inflammation of) agog: lymphagogue (*agogue*, inducing) angi: (blood vessel) lymphangiitis (*itis*, inflammation of) oid: lymphoid (*oid*, similar to) *lympho*: blast: lymphoblast (*blast*, embryo) cyt: lymphocyte, lymphocytosis (*cyt*, cell; *osis*, diseased condition of) gran: lymphogranuloma (*gran*, grain; *oma*, mass, tumor) CROSS REFERENCE: *aqua, hyd, lymph*
lys,*** lyt, lyze	Greek *lyein* (IE: *leu*, to cut off, separate; yields English loose, lose)	to loosen, dissolve, free (extended to mean "to weaken," especially at the side)	SIMPLE ROOT: lysin, lysine, lysis (the process of cell destruction through the action of specific lysins; the gradual ending of disease symptoms) {lytic} PREFIXED ROOT: *lys*: *ana-*: analysis (as opposed to *synthesis*) {analytic, analytical}, analyst (*ana-*, again) *cata-*: catalysis, catalyst {catalytic} (*cata-*, down) *dia-*: dialysis {dialytic} (*dia-*, through) *para-*: paralysis (partial or complete loss, or temporary interruption, of a function, especially of voluntary motion or of sensation in some part or all of the body) {paralytic} (*para-*, alongside) *lyze*: *ana-*: analyze (*ana-*, again) *cata-*: catalyze (*cata-*, down) *para-*: paralyze (*para-*, alongside) DOUBLE PREFIXED ROOT: anticatalyst (*anti-*, against + *cata-*, down) LEADING ROOT COMPOUND: *lysi*: meter: lysimeter (a device for measuring the solubility of substances)

Element	From	Meaning	Examples
lys (cont'd)			*lyso:* gen: lysogenesis, lysogenic (*gen*, producing) som: lysosome (*som*, body) zym: lysozyme (*zym*, fermentation) TRAILING ROOT COMPOUND: acanth: acantholysis (atrophy of the prickle cell layer of the epidermis) (*acanth*, thorny) auto: autolysis, autolytic, autolyze (*auto*, self) hetero: heterolysis (*hetero*, different) hydro: hydrolysis, hydrolytic (*hydro*, water) USED AS NOUN-FORMING SUFFIX: electrolyte hydrolyte (*hydro*, water) tachylyte (a kind of basaltic volcanic glass, from its rapid decomposition in acids) (*tachy*, swift) DISGUISED ROOT: palsy (paralysis; a condition marked by loss of power to feel or to control movement in any part of the body; a weakening or debilitating influence) (from *paralysis*) TRADE PRODUCT: Lysol, a cleansing disinfectant, that *loosens* germs INTERDISCIPLINARY: analysis (in *chemistry*, the separation of compounds and mixtures into their constituent substances for purposes of determining their nature or the proportion of the constituents; in *linguistics*, the use of word order and uninflected function words rather than inflection to express syntactic relationships; in *mathematics*, a branch of mathematics, including algebra and calculus, that deals with properties of related variables, especially properties associated with limits; also, the practice of proving a mathematical proposition by assuming the result and reasoning back to the data or to already established principles) NO CROSS REFERENCE

M

Element	From	Meaning	Examples
machy*	Greek *mache*	struggle, battle	TRAILING ROOT COMPOUND: giganto: gigantomachy (in *Greek mythology*, the struggle between the giants and the gods; now, any war between giants or giant superpowers) logo: logomachy (strife or contention in words only, or an argument about words; game similar to anagrams) (*logo*, word) scia: sciamachy (a fighting with shadows or imaginary enemies) (*scia*, shadow) tauro: tauromachy (literary term for *bullfighting*) (*tauro*, bull) NB: *Macho* is not in this family; see *masc.* CROSS REFERENCE: *act, agogue, agon, luct*
macro***	Greek *makro* (IE: *mak*, long, slender)	long, large	SIMPLE ROOT: macron PREFIXED ROOT: *amphi-*: amphimacer (literally, long at both ends; a trisyllabic foot of poetry having an unaccented or short syllable between two accented or long syllables; e.g., HES-i-TATE) (*amphi-*, around, both) LEADING ROOT COMPOUND: *macr*: odont: macrodont (having very large teeth) (*odont*, tooth) *macro*: bi(o): macrobiotics (the study of prolonging life, as by special diets, etc.) {macrobiotic} (*bio*, life) cephal: macrocephaly (opposed to *microcephaly*) {macrocephalic} (*cephal*, head) clima: macroclimate (the climate over a large geographical area) cosm: macrocosm (the great world; an large complex entity; opposed to microcosm) (*cosm*, universe, world) cyst: macrocyst (*cyst*, bladder, sac) cyt: macrocyte (an abnormally large red blood corpuscle occurring especially in pernicious anemia) (*cyte*, cell) eco: macroeconomics (from *oikos*, home) evol: macroevolution (*e-* from *ex-*, which prefixes *volut*, from *volvere*, to roll) gam: macrogamete (the larger of two conjugating cells in heterogamous sexual reproduction, considered to be female) (*gam*, sexual reproduction) mer: macromere (*mere*, part) mol: macromolecule (*mol*, mass) nucl: macronucleus (*nucl*, kernel) nutr: macronutrient (any of the chemical elements required in large quantities for plant growth) (*nutrire*, to nourish) phag: macrophage (*phag*, eat) pter: macropterous (*pter*, wing) scop: macroscopic (*scope*, look) spor: macrosporangium, macrospore (*spore*, seed) CROSS REFERENCE: *long, magn, mega*

Element	From	Meaning	Examples
macu*	Latin *macula*	spot, blemish, stain	SIMPLE ROOT: macula: macula (same as *macule*; a spot, stain, blotch, etc., especially a discolored spot on the skin; also, a dark spot on the sun) maculat: maculate, maculation, maculature PREFIXED ROOT: im-: immaculate (*im-* assimilates *in-*, not) UNBOUND LATIN COMPOUND: *macula lutea* (literally, luteous spot; a small, yellowish area of especially keen vision on the retina) DISGUISED ROOT: mackle, mail (one meaning), maillot maquis (in the Mediterranean area, a dense growth of small trees and shrubs, from the the scrub bushes *dotting* a hillside) Maquis [the French underground organization that fought against German occupation forces during World War II, from the undergrowth (bushes) as a hiding place] trammel A RELIGIOUS DOCTRINE: *Immaculate* Conception (in the Roman Catholic Church, the doctrine that the Virgin Mary, though conceived naturally, was from the moment of conception free from any *stain* of original sin; sometimes confused with the *Virgin Birth:* in *Christian theology*, the doctrine that Jesus was born to Mary without violating her virginity and that she was his only human parent; in *zoology*, *virgin birth* refers to *parthenogenesis*) [*parthenos*, virgin, maiden + *genesis*, origin: reproduction by the development of an unfertilized ovum, seed, or spore, as in certain polyzoans, insects, algae, etc.] NO CROSS REFERENCE
magis**	Latin *magister* (IE: *megh*, large, much; yields English master)	master	SIMPLE ROOT: magistrate, magisterial, magistracy ECCLESIASTICAL LATIN TERM: magisterium (the authority, office, and power to teach true doctrine by divine guidance, held by the Roman Catholic Church to have been given itself alone by divine commission) GERMAN COMPOUNDS: meistergesang (songs of the *meistersingers*), meisterlied, meistersinger CROSS REFERENCE: *dom*
magn,*** maj	Latin *magnus* great (IE: *megh*, large, much)	large, great [*maj*, greater]	SIMPLE ROOT: *mag:* magn: magnate, magnitude, magnum magu: Magus (plural, *Magi*) *maj:* majo: major (see *Doublets* below), majority maju: majuscule [from *majuscula (littera)*, somewhat larger (letter); a large letter, capital or uncial, as in medieval manuscripts] LEADING ROOT COMPOUND: *magn:* anim: magnanimity, magnanimous (*anima*, soul) *magni:* fic: magnific, magnificence, magnificent (from *facere*, to make, do)

Element	From	Meaning	Examples
magn (cont'd)			fy: magnify (from *facere*, to make, do) loqu: magniloquent (*loqui*, speak) *maj*: domo: major-domo; (literally, master of the house; a man in charge of a great, royal, or noble household; chief steward; a steward or butler: humorous usage) (*domus*, house) SIMPLE COMPOUNDS: major form class (in *linguistics,* a form class that contains a relatively large number of words: in English, nouns, verbs, adjectives, and adverbs are major form classes) major general (greater than a *brigadier general*) major mode (a music term; opposed to minor mode) major premise (the first premise of a syllogism; opposed to minor premise; the major premise, the minor premise and the conclusion constitute the deductive syllogism) major scale (a music term; opposed to *minor scale*) DISGUISED ROOT: maestoso, maestro master (see *Doublets* below) mayor (see *Doublets* below) mister (see *Doublets* below), mistress mistral (from Provençal; literally, masterwind; a cold, dry north wind that blows over the Mediterranean coast of France and nearby regions) DOUBLETS: master:mister; mayor:major LATIN WORDS AND EXPRESSIONS: Magnificat (the hymn of the Virgin Mary in Luke 1:46-55, beginning with, *Magnificat anima mea Dominum,* My soul doth magnify the Lord; in lower case, any song, poem, or hymn of praise) *magnum opus* (great work, especially of art, music, or literature; masterpiece) *magna cum laude* (with great praise) ITALIAN: *magnifico* COMPARATIVES: major, majority, majuscule RELATED SANSKRIT: *maharajah, maharani, mahatma, Mahayana* HISTORICAL DOCUMENT: *Magna Charta (Magna Carta)* PLACENAME: Magna, Utah NOTE: *Magnesia* and *magnet*, as well as *magnolia*, are not in this family. CROSS REFERENCE: *grand, gros, macro, maj, mega*
magnet**	Greek *magnes*	magnet	ROOT NOTE: *Magnet* is derived from *Magnetis lithos*, or the stone of Magnesia. SIMPLE ROOT: magnet, magnetic, magnetics, magnetism, magnetize, magneto, magneton LEADING ROOT COMPOUND: electric: magnetoelectric hydro: magnetohydrodynamics (*hydro*, water; *dynam*, power) meter: magnetometer (*meter*, measure) mot: magnetomotive (*motive*, moving) spher: magnetosphere (*sphere*, ball, globe) NO CROSS REFERENCE

Element	From	Meaning	Examples
main			See *man*, hand, for *maintain, maintenance*.
maj			See *magn* for *majority*.
mal,*** male	Latin *malus*	bad, badly	NOTE: Authorities are divided on whether this element is a prefix or a root. For formatting purposes, the element is regarded in this list as a prefix. EXTENDED PREFIX: malady (**Synonyms**: disease, affection, ailment) malice (**Synonyms**: animosity, enmity, malevolnce), malicious malign (**Synonyms**: sinister, baleful), malignancy, malignant, malignity, malinger, malism, malison (now archaic; see *Doublets* below) PREFIXED ROOT: *mal*: aria: malaria (literally, bad air, and was originally thought to be caused by foul air) feas: malfeasance (from French *faire*; further from Latin *facere*, to make, do) odor: malodorous (having a bad odor; stinking) posit: malposition (faulty or abnormal position) vers: malversation (in *law*, corrupt conduct or fraudulent practices, as in public office) (*versari*, to turn) *male*: dict: malediction (see *Doublets* below) (*dicere*, to speak) fact: malefaction, malefactor (*facere*, to make, do) fic: malefic, maleficence (see *malefaction*, previous entry) vol: malevolence, malevolent (from *velle*, to wish) DOUBLE PREFIXED ROOTS AND COMPOUNDS: (*Undifferentiated as to simple prefixes, elisions and embedded assimilations*): adjust: maladjusted (*ad-* prefixes *just*) adroit: maladroit (**Synonyms**: awkward, clumsy, inept) (*mal* + French *à*, to + *droit*; from Latin *directus*, itself from *di-*, apart, from + *regere*, to keep straight) assimil: malassimilation (*as-* assimilates *ad-*, to, toward) content: malcontent (*con-* prefixes *tent*) digest: maldigestion (*di-* elides *dis-*, which prefixes *gest*, from *gerere*, to carry) erupt: maleruption (*e-* elides *ex-*, which prefixes *rupt*, from *rumpere*, to break) occlus: malocclusion (*oc-* assimilates *ob-*, which prefixes *clus*, from *claudere*, to shut) reduct: malreduction (*re-* prefixes *duct*, from *ducere*, to lead) TRAILING ROOT COMPOUND: dis: dismal (from Old French *dis mal*; further from Middle Latin *dies mali*, evil days) DOUBLETS: malison:malediction FRENCH WORDS AND EXPRESSIONS: *malaise* (a vague feeling of physical discomfort or uneasiness, as early in an illness; a vague awareness of moral or social decline) (*mal-* + *aise*, ease) *mal de mer* (seasickness) (*mer* from *mar*, sea)

Element	From	Meaning	Examples
mal (cont'd)			*malentendu* (misunderstood; poorly conceived; as a *noun*: misunderstanding) *malgré lui* (in spite of himself) LATIN PHRASES: *mala* fide (in bad faith; with intent to deceive; opposed to *bona fide*, in good faith) *malo animo* LATIN LEGAL TERMS: *malu* (wrong, evil, wicked, reprehensible) *malum in se* (a wrong in itself) *malicious mischief* (the willful destruction of another's personal property) There are many other words with this element listed in *Black's Law Dictionary*. WORD FROM FICTIONAL CHARACTER: malapropism [the exaggerated misuse of words; from Mrs. Malaprop (in Sheridan's play *The Rivals*), who makes ludicrous blunders in her use of words; from French *malapropos*, *mal à propos*, literally, not to the purpose; inappropriate] CROSS REFERENCE: *caco-, dys-, mis-* (Anglo-Saxon)
malac*	Greek *malakos* (IE: *mel*, to crush, grind)	soft; mollusks	ROOT NOTE: This root is related to Latin *molere*, to grind, and from which *meal* is derived; further, this root means "mollusks," a phylum of invertebrate animals including the chitons, oysters, clams, mussels, snails, whelks, slugs, squids, octopi, etc. SIMPLE ROOT: malacon (a brown, altered form of zircon, a mineral) LEADING ROOT COMPOUND: *mala*: pter: malapterurus (a genus consisting of the electric catfish) (*pter*, wing + *urus*, tail) *malaco*: derm: malacodermous (*derm*, skin) logy: malacology (the study of mollusks) (*logy*, study of) ost: malacostracan (of a large class of highly evolved crustaceans typically consisting of 19 segments, including the decapods, krill, and isopods) (*ostrakon*, shell) phyll: malacophyllous (*phyll*, leaf) TRAILING ROOT COMPOUND: cranio: craniomalacia (*cranium*) osteo: osteomalacia (*osteo*, bone) CROSS REFERENCE: *clemen, leni, mol*
mamm**	Latin *mamma*	breast	ROOT NOTE: The root means specifically the mother's breast; the diminutive of *mamm* is *mamilla* (usually spelled with one *m*), and means nipple, or a breast-shaped protuberance). SIMPLE ROOT: mamill: mamilla (plural, *mamillae*) {mamillary}, mamillated (having nipple-like projections), mamillation mamm: mamma (a gland for secreting milk), mammal (any of a large class of warmblooded, usually hairy vertebrates whose offspring are fed with milk secreted by the female mammary glands), mammary

Element	From	Meaning	Examples
mamm (cont'd)			LEADING ROOT COMPOUND: *mamm*: algia: mammalgia (*alg*, pain) ectom: mammectomy (*ectomy*, surgical removal) *mamma*: logy: mammalogy (the branch of zoology dealing with mammals; see *Genus* below) (*logy*, study of) plasty: mammaplasty (plastic surgery to make breasts larger or smaller) (*plasty*, forming) GENUS: Mammalia (a division of vertebrate animals, including all that possess hair and suckle, or *give milk* to their young; the study of mammals is *mammalogy*.) CROSS REFERENCE: *stern*
man,* men	Latin *manere* (IE: *men*, to remain)	to stay, remain	SIMPLE ROOT: manor, manse (the residence of a minister, especially a Presbyterian minister), mansion; ménage (a household; also housekeeping), menagerie, menial (pertaining to one retained in the mansion as a servant) PREFIXED ROOT: *m-*: immanent (living, remaining, or operating within; inherent; in *theology*, present throughout the universe; said of God; do not confuse with *imminent*, from *minere*, to project; thus, impending, likely to happen without delay; threatening: said of danger, evil, misfortune, calamity) {immanence} (*im-* assimilates *in-*, in) *per-*: permanence, permanency, permanent (**Synonyms**: stable, invariable, constant) (*per-*, through) DISGUISED ROOT: demesne [in *law*, possession (of real estate) as one's own; other meanings] [this word is not prefixed, but is a possible respelling of *domain*) remnant (see *Doublets* below) PREFIXED DISGUISED ROOT: *re-*: remain (see *Doublets* below; **Synonyms**: stay, wait, abide), remainder (*re-*, back, behind) DOUBLETS: remain:remnant FRENCH EXPRESSION: *ménage à trois* (literally, a household of three; an arrangement by which a married couple and the lover of one of them live together) NO CROSS REFERENCE
man,*** mend [main]	Latin *manus* (IE: *men²*, hand) [French]	hand	SIMPLE ROOT: mana: manacle, manage (**Synonyms**: conduct, direct, control; see *manège* below) mand: mandarin (derived from *mandate* and influenced by IE *men-*, to think), mandate (in *law*, an order from a higher court or official to a lower one; see *Latin Legal Term below*), mandatory mane: manège (or, *manege*; the art of riding and training horses; horsemanship; the paces and exercises of a training horse; a school for training horses and teaching riders; riding academy) (from *manage*) maneuver (see derivation at *manure* below; see *Doublets*) mann: manner (**Synonyms**: bearing, carriage, demeanor)

Element	From	Meaning	Examples
man (cont'd)			manu:

manual

manubrium (plural, *manubria*)

manus (the terminal part of the forelimb of a vertebrate, as the hand of a person or the forefoot of a four-legged animal; also, in Roman law, the authority of a husband over his wife)

manure (from Old French *manoeuvrer*, to work by hand, to till; *manu* + *operari*, to work) (see *Doublets* below)

PREFIXED ROOT:

man:

a-: amanuensis (an assistant who takes dictation or copies of something already written; secretary) (from *ab-*, from)

mand:

com-: command (**Synonyms**: direct, instruct) (*com-*, with)

de-: demand (**Synonyms**: claim, require, exact) (from *demandare*: *de-*, away + *dare*, to give)

mend:

com-: commend (literally, to put into the hands of another; to express approval of), commendam, commendation, commendatory (*com-*, with, together)

LEADING ROOT COMPOUND:

main:

tain: maintain (**Synonyms**: support, uphold, sustain) (from *maintenance*, next entry)

ten: maintenance (in *law*, the act of interfering unlawfully in a suit between others by helping either party) (*tenere*, to hold)

man:

cip: manciple (a steward or buyer of provisions, as for an English college, monastery, etc.) (from *capere*, to take)

sue: mansuetude (gentleness; tameness) (*suescere*, to accustom)

mani:

cur: manicure

fest: manifest (**Synonyms**: evident, apparent, obvious; see *Italian* below) (from IE *dhers*, to be bold, attack, as in *infest*)

ple: maniple (from *plere*, to fill)

pul: manipular, manipulate (**Synonyms**: handle, wield, ply), manipulation, manipulator (from *maniple*, previous entry)

manu:

fact: manufacture (**Synonyms**: make, form, shape) (from *facere*, to make, do)

miss: manumission (from *mittere*, to send)

mit: manumit (see *manumission*, previous entry)

script: manuscript (from *scribere*, to write)

TRAILING ROOT COMPOUND:

mort: mortmain (*mort*, death)

DISGUISED ROOT: mastiff (influenced by Old French *mestif*, a mongrel; from Latin *miscere*, to mix)

PREFIXED DISGUISED ROOT:

ad-: adminicle (originally, support for the hand; a thing that helps or supports; in *law*, corroborative evidence; proof that explains) (*ad-*, to, toward)

Element	From	Meaning	Examples
man (cont'd)			DOUBLETS: manage:manège; manure:maneuver FRENCH WORDS: *main* (as in *maintain, maintenance*), and *coup de main* (literally, stroke of hand; a surprise attack) manche (a heraldry term) manqué (that falls short of the goal; unsuccessful or defective; potential but unrealized; would-be; placed after the noun it modifies, e.g., *a scholar manqué*) legerdemain (originally *leger de main*; literally, slight of hand) ITALIAN WORDS: manicotti (a dish consisting of large, tubular noodles) manifesto (a public declaration of motives and intentions by a government or by a person or group regarded as having some public importance) SPANISH COGNATE: *mano* LATIN LEGAL TERM: *mandamus* (a writ commanding that a specified thing be done) U.S. DOCTRINE: *Manifest Destiny* NB: *Manifold*, from *many* + *-fold*, is not in this family; neither is *manikin*, from Dutch *manneken*, man + diminutive *ken*. CROSS REFERENCE: *chiro, dactyl*
mania***	Greek *mania* (IE: *men*, to think)	craze, madness	SIMPLE ROOT: mania (**Synonyms:** delirium, frenzy), maniac PREFIXED ROOT: hypo-: hypomania (*hypo-*, under) LEADING ROOT COMPOUND: graph: manigraphy (description of insanity in its various forms) (*graph*, write) TRAILING ROOT COMPOUND: ablutomania (a morbid desire to wash the hands) dipsomania (uncontrollable desire for alcoholic beverages) erotomania (exaggeration of sexual behavior or reaction) kleptomania (an uncontrollable impulse to steal) megalomania (delusion of grandeur; unreasonable conviction of one's extreme greatness, goodness, or power) monomania (insanity on a single subject or class of subjects) pyromania (obsessive preoccupation with fires) MEDICAL TERM: manic depressive NO CROSS REFERENCE
mar			See *masc* for *marital*.
mar**	Latin *marinus* (IE: *mori*, sea)	sea	SIMPLE ROOT: marsh mare (a sea; one of several vast, dark flat areas on the moon, Mercury, or Mars; *mare*, a mature female horse, is not from this root) marinade, marinate (see *Italian* below), marina marine, mariner, maritime PREFIXED ROOT: sub-: submarine (*sub-*, under) trans-: transmarine (crossing the sea; coming from, or being on the other side of the *sea*) (*trans-*, across) ultra-: ultramarine (*ultra-*, beyond) TRAILING ROOT COMPOUND: aqua: aquamarine (*aqua*, water)

Element	From	Meaning	Examples
mar (cont'd)			DISGUISED ROOT: cormorant (literally, sea raven) meerschaum (German, literally, sea foam) mere (one meaning), mermaid, morass ITALIAN: marinara (from *marinare*, to pickle; a tomato sauce seasoned with garlic and spices and served with pasta) FRENCH PHRASES: *bêche-de-mer* (literally, spade of the sea;, a mixed trade language, a Pidgin English spoken in the Southwest Pacific) *mal de mer* (seasickness) LATIN TERMS: *mare nostrum* (our sea: Roman name for the Mediterranean) *mare liberum* (free sea: a sea open to all nations) *mare clausum* (closed sea: a sea under the jurisdiction of one nation and not open to all others) GEOGRAPHICAL AREAS: The Maritime Provinces of Canada: Nova Scotia, New Brunswick, and Prince Edward Island Maritime Alps, the southern division of the Western Alps, along the French-Italian border PLACENAME: Miramar, Florida NAME OF POEM: "The Rime of the Ancient Mariner" by Samuel Taylor Coleridge CROSS REFERENCE: *pelag*
masc***	Latin *mas*	male	SIMPLE ROOT: masculine (**Synonyms:** male, manly, virile) PREFIXED ROOT: *e-*: emasculate (originally, to remove the testicles of, so as to deprive of power to reproduce; castrate; hence, to weaken, destroy the strength or vigor of, as the general's leadership was *emasculated* by discontent among the troops; as an *adjective*, deprived of virility, strength or vigor; effeminate) (from *ex-*, out) *com-*: commasculation (male homosexuality) (*com-*, with, together) LEADING ROOT COMPOUND: turb: masturbate [as believed by some authorities; see the root *turb*; other authorities (*Dorland's Medical Dictionary*, for example) say *mast* is a derivative of *manu*, hand] DISGUISED ROOT: male, mallard (the common wild duck, both male *and* female) marital (from *maritus*, married, husband; further from *mas*, male) SPANISH: *macho, machismo* CROSS REFERENCE: *andro, anthropo, homo* (Latin), *vir*
mater.*** matr	Latin *mater* (IE: *mater*, mother)	mother	SIMPLE ROOT: *mater*: mater (chiefly British, and often preceded by *the*) maternal, maternity *matr*: matri: matriculant (a person who has matriculated or is applying for matriculation), matriculate (to enroll, especially as student in a college or university)

Element	From	Meaning	Examples
mater (cont'd)			matrimonial (of matrimony; marital; nuptial; conjugal), matrimony (the act, rite, or sacrament of marriage; the state of being husband or wife; married life), matriotism matrix (originally, womb, public register, origin) matro: matron, matronize, matronly LEADING ROOT COMPOUND: *mater*: familia: materfamilias (the mother of a family; woman head of a household) *matri*: arch: matriarch, matriarchate, matriarchy (Greek *arch*, rule) foc: matrifocal (of a sociological group, as a household, tribe, etc., having a female as its leader) (*foc*, focus, center) cid: matricide (the act of murdering one's mother; a person who does this) (*cide*, kill) lin: matrilineal *matr*: onym: matronymic (Greek *onym*, name) PREFIXED DISGUISED ROOT: cum-: cummer (literally, with mother), meaning variously godmother, a woman companion, or a woman or girl (from *com-*, with, together) ITALIAN: *madrepore* (literally, mother pore, from its rapid production; but translated as mother stone; any of various, usually branching, stony corals which form reefs and islands in tropical seas) SPANISH COGNATE: *madre* LATIN PHRASE: *alma mater* [(our) nourishing mother; originally referred to the Roman goddesses, but now refers to the institution from which one received a degree] PLACENAMES: Sierra Madre, California *Madre de Dios* (Mother of God, a river in Peru and Bolivia) NOTE: From the same Latin base is derived *matter*, originally, the growing trunk of a tree, and from which are derived *material, matériel*. CROSS REFERENCE: *metr*
maur*	Greek *mauros*	dark, dim	PREFIXED ROOT: a-: amaurosis (partial or total blindness) {amaurotic} (*a-*, intensive + *osis*, condition of) A PEOPLE: Moor, a member of a Moslem people of mixed Arab and Berber descent living in northwest Africa A COUNTRY: Mauritania, in West Africa on the Atlantic Coast CROSS REFERENCE: *fus, mela*

Juggernaut, from Sanskrit *Jaganath*, "lord of the world,"
is an incarnation of the Hindu god Vishnu.
Because of the story that frantic devotees allowed themselves to be crushed by the Vishnu's idol
as it was being moved in procession, juggernaut has come to mean
an irresistible, overpowering, ruthless force that destroys everything in its path.
The word has been used to describe a giant battleship, a powerful football team, etc.

Element	From	Meaning	Examples

med***	Latin
	medicari
	(IE: *med*,
	to measure,
	consider,
	wise coun-
	selor,
	doctor)
		to heal,
		care for
			SIMPLE ROOT:
			medic, medicable, medical
			medicament (a healing substance; medicine; remedy)
			medicate, medication, medicatory
			medicinal, medicine, medico
			PREFIXED ROOT:
			re-: remedy (literally, health back; that which brings back
			   health; **Synonyms:** cure, heal), remediable (*re*-, back)
			DOUBLE PREFIXED ROOT:
			irremediable (*ir*- assimilates *in*-, not + *re*-, again)
			RELATED WORDS: meditant, meditate, meditation, medita-
			   tive
			CROSS REFERENCE: *cur, iatr, therap*

med***	Latin
	medius
	(IE: *me*,
	between)
		middle	SIMPLE ROOT:
			mediac: mediacy (the state or quality of being mediate)
			mediad: mediad (in *biology*, toward the median plane or axis of
			   a body or part)
			medial: medial, medialis
			median: median, mediant, medianus
			medias: mediastinum (literally, in the middle; a membranous
			   partition between two cavities of the body, especially that
			   separating the lungs or the two pleural sacs)
			mediat: mediate, mediation, mediatize (to annex a smaller state
			   to a larger one, leaving the ruler his/her title and some au-
			   thority)
			mediu: medium (plural, *media*)
			PREFIXED ROOT:
			im-: immediate (not to be in the middle) (*im*- assimilates *in*-,
			   not)
			inter-: intermediary, intermediate (*inter*-, between)
			LEADING ROOT COMPOUND:
			ev: medieval (from *aevum*, age)
			ocr: mediocre (the midpoint between high and low) (*ocris*, a
			   peak; from *acer*, sharp)
			DISGUISED ROOT:
			mean (average)
			mesne (law term), *mesne profits* (those profits accruing from
			   the time possession of land has been improperly withheld
			   from its rightful owner until his/her reinstatement in posses-
			   sion of the property; as a noun, *mesne* is the same as *mesne
			   lord*: a feudal lord holding land from a superior)
			milieu (literally, middle; environment, especially, social or cul-
			   tural setting; from Old French *mi*; from Latin *mid*, middle +
			   lieu, from *loco*, place)
			moiety (in the middle; half, either of two equal, or more or less
			   equal, parts; an indefinite share or part; in *anthropology*, any
			   of two or more primary subdivisions in some tribes)
			mullion
			PREFIXED DISGUISED ROOT:
			di-: dimidiate (considered to mean half, two, which is the true
			   meaning of *di*-; in *biology*, having only one half developed)
			   (from *dis*-, apart)

Element	From	Meaning	Examples
med (cont'd)			DISGUISED LEADING ROOT COMPOUND: di: meridian (literally, midday; of or at noon; many other meanings) (*dies*, day) LATIN PHRASE: *in medias res* (in the middle of things) ITALIAN: mezzanine, mezzo-soprano; intermezzo GEOGRAPHICAL PLACE: Mediterranean Sea (the Ancients conceived of the Mediterranean Sea as the sea in the middle of two continents) NORSE MYTHOLOGY: Midgard (also *Midgarth*; the inhabited earth, regarded as midway between heaven and hell and engirdled by a huge serpent) (from Old Norse *mithgarthr*: *mithr*, mid + *garthr*, yard) CROSS REFERENCE: *demi, meso, semi*
medull*	Latin *medulla* (IE: *smeru*, grease)	marrow	SIMPLE ROOT: **medulla** (plural, *medullas*, or *medullae*), medullated, medullation, medullization COMPOUND TERMS: medulla oblongata (literally, elongated marrow; the nervous tissue at the bottom of the brain that controls respiration, circulation, and certain other bodily functions) medullary ray (in *anatomy*, extensions of the kidney tubules into the cortical substance; in *botany*, strands of parenchymatous tissue extending from the pith to the bark) INTERDISCIPLINARY: **medulla** (in *anatomy*, the inner core of certain vertebrate body tissues, such as the marrow of bone; in *botany*, the pith or central tissue in stems of certain plants) CROSS REFERENCE: *myel*
mega***	Greek *megas* (IE: *megh*, large)	great, large (in medical terminology, abnormal enlargement)	LEADING ROOT COMPOUND: *meg*: ohm: megohm *mega*: byt: megabyte (approximately one million bytes, abbreviated *mb*) cephal: megacephalic (*cephal*, head) cycl: megacycle (one million hertz) gaea: Megagaea (*gaia*, earth) gam: megagamete (same as *macrogamete*) (*gam*, sexual reproduction) hertz: megahertz (abbreviated *MHz*) lith: megalith (*lith*, stone) phon: megaphone (*phone*, sound) pod: megapod, megapode (*pod*, foot) scop: megascopic (*scope*, look) spor: (*spore*, seed) megasporangium (*angi*, vessel; thus, *sporangium*, seed case) megasporophyll (*phyll*, leaf) theri: megatherium (an extinct genus of very large, slothlike, plant-eating animals, whose remains have been found in the Pleistocene of America) (*therion*, beast) ton: megaton *megalo*: card: megalocardia (*card*, heart)

Element	From	Meaning	Examples
mega (cont'd)			mania: megalomania (a mental disorder characterized by delusions of grandeur, wealth, power, etc; a passion for, or for doing, big things; a tendency to exaggerate) polis: megalopolis (literally, great city; an extensive, heavily populated, continuously urban area, including any number of cities) (*polis*, city) saur: megalosaur (*saur*, lizard) *megal*: ops: megalops (*ops*, eye) TRAILING ROOT COMPOUND: acro: acromegalic, acromegaly (*acro*, extremities) gastro: gastromegaly (pot belly) (*gastro*, belly) GREEK LETTER: omega [(large o) as opposed to *omicron* (small o)] CROSS REFERENCE: *long, macro, magn*
mel*	Greek *melos* (IE: *mel³*, a limb; hence, a musical member or phrase)	song, melody	SIMPLE ROOT: melic (of song or poetry, especially, early Greek lyric poetry; meant to be sung; lyric), melisma (a succession of different notes sung upon a single syllable of text, as in a Gregorian chant) LEADING ROOT COMPOUND: *mel*: ody: melody (**Synonyms:** air, tune) (*ode*, to sing) *melo*: drama: melodrama TRAILING ROOT COMPOUND: dulci: dulcimer (a stringed musical instrument with a sweet, mellow sound; in Spanish, *dulcimer* is dulcémele) (*dulci*, sweet) CROSS REFERENCE: *cant, hymn, od*
mela**	Greek *melas* (IE: *mel*, dark, dirty)	black, dark	SIMPLE ROOT: melanic, melanin, melanism, melanite, melanoid, melanous (having *black* or *dark* skin and hair) LEADING ROOT COMPOUND: *mela*: leuk: melaleuka (literally, black white; from the the tree's black trunk and white branches: a genus of Australian and East Indian shrubs and trees) (*leuk*, white) stom: melastome (literally, black mouth: so named from the stain caused by the fruit; a tropical plant) (*stoma*, mouth) *melan*: chol: melancholia, melancholy (*chol*, gall, bile) oma: melanoma (*oma*, tumor) *melano*: cyt: melanocyte (*cyte*, cell) path: melanopathy (*path*, feel) phor: melanophore (*phor*, to bear) TRAILING ROOT COMPOUND: calo: calomel (from *kalos*, beautiful) sidero: sideromelane (*sidero*, iron) GEOGRAPHICAL PLACE: Melanesia (believed named because of the dark-skinned natives; possibly because of the dark sand upon the beaches; or possibly from the appearance of the islands from the sea) CROSS REFERENCE: *maur*

Element	From	Meaning	Examples
melior*	Latin *melior* (IE: *mel⁴*, strong, big great)	better	SIMPLE ROOT: meliorable, meliorant, meliorate (opposed to *pejorate*), melioration (in *linguistics*, the process by which the meaning or connotation becomes more positive, e.g., *nice* has been ameliorated from its earlier meanings of silly, stupid, foolish), meliorism, meliority PREFIXED ROOT: a-: ameliorate (**Synonyms:** improve, better) (from *ad-*, to, toward) NO CROSS REFERENCE
mell*	Greek *mellis* (IE: *melit*, honey)	honey	LEADING ROOT COMPOUND: *meli*: lot: meliolot (sweet clover) (*lotus*, clover) phag: meliphagous (honey-eating) (*phag*, eat) *melli*: fer: melliferous (honey-bearing) (*ferre*, to bear) flu: mellifluous (literally, honey-flowing; sweetly or smoothly flowing; sweet-sounding, as *a mellifluous voice*, or *mellifluous tones* (*fluere*, to flow) TRAILING ROOT COMPOUND: hydro: hydromel (*hydro*, water) oeno: oenomel (*oeno*, wine) DISGUISED ROOT: marmalade (a jamlike preserve made by boiling the pulp, and usually the sliced-up rinds, of oranges or some other fruits with sugar) (*marmelo*, quince; from *melimelon*, sweet apple) mildew (from Old English *meledeaw*, nectar; literally, honey-dew; semantical relationship is tenuous) molasses (from Portuguese *melaço*; from Latin *mellaceus*, resembling honey) FEMININE NAME: Melissa NO CROSS REFERENCE
mem**	Latin *memor* (IE: *(s)mer*, to recall, remember)	mindful	SIMPLE ROOT: meme: memento memo: memorabilia, memorable, memorandum, memorial, memory (see *Doublets* below) PREFIXED ROOT: com-: commemorate (**Synonyms:** celebrate, solemnize, observe), commemoration, commemorative (*com-*, with) re-: remember (*re-*, back, again) DISGUISED ROOT: mean (wish, desire, intent, to have in mind; akin to German *meinen*, to have in mind) (see *mean* under *men, min*, next family) mourn [akin to Gothic *maúrnan*, to be anxious; Sanskrit *smárati* [he] remembers] FRENCH: memoir (see *Doublets* below) DOUBLETS: memoir:memory LATIN PHRASES: *in memoriam* (in memory of) *memento mori* (remember that you must die; any reminder of death) CROSS REFERENCE: *mne*

Element	From	Meaning	Examples
men,* min	Latin minari (IE: men², to project)	to threaten	SIMPLE ROOT: menace (**Synonym**: threaten), minacious (menacing, threatening) PREFIXED ROOT: men: a-: amenable (**Synonyms**: obedient, docile, tractable) (from ad-, to) pro-: promenade (literally, to drive forward) (pro-, forward) min: com-: commination (a threat or denunciation) (com-, intensive) e-: eminence, eminent (**Synonyms**: famous, celebrated, illustrious) (e- elides ex-, out) im-: imminent (describing that which is threatening, menacing; close at hand) (im- assimilates in-, on) pro-: prominence, prominent (**Synonyms**: noticeable, remarkable, outstanding) (pro-, in front) DISGUISED ROOT: mean (this word is not used singly; see next entry) PREFIXED DISGUISED ROOT: de-: demean (as to conduct oneself), demeanor (de-, from) [Note: Demean (to lower in status or character) is not related to this root.] DOUBLE PREFIXED DISGUISED ROOT: misdemeanant, misdemeanor (Anglo-Saxon, mis-, wrong + de-, from) NO CROSS REFERENCE
men,*** mes	Greek mene (IE: men, month)	moon, crescent	ROOT NOTE: See note under Latin men, mens. SIMPLE ROOT: meniscus (a crescent or crescent-shaped thing; a lens convex on one side and concave on the other; in physics, the curved upper surface of a column of liquid: as a result of capillarity, it is convex when the walls of the container are dry; concave, when they are wet) PREFIXED ROOT AND COMPOUNDS: a-: amenorrhea (abnormal absence or suppression of menstruation) (a-, not + rheein, to flow) cata-: catamenia (monthly menstrual discharge; menstruation) (cata-, according to) dys-: dysmenorrhea (painful or difficult menstruation) (dys-, abnormal, impaired, difficult + rhoia, a flowing) LEADING ROOT COMPOUND: men: arch: menarch (the beginning of menstruation; also, the first menstrual cycle of an individual) (arch, beginning) meno: logy: menology (a calendar of the months) (logy, study of) paus: menopause (the permanent cessation of menstruation) (pauein, to cease) rrhag: menorrhagia (excessive flow, excessive menstrual flow) (rrhagia, abnormal flow) rrhe: menorrhea (normal menstrual flow) (rrhea, flow, discharge) CROSS REFERENCE: Latin men, mens

Element	From	Meaning	Examples

men,***
mes
	Latin
	mensis
	(IE: *men*,
	month;
	yields
	English
	measure)
		month,
		measure
			SIMPLE ROOT:
			mensal (one meaning), menses
			menstrual, menstruate, menstruation, menstruous, menstruum
			  (plural, *menstruums*, or *menstrua*; a liquid that dissolves a
			  solid; a solvent; from an alchemistic notion of the power of
			  the menses as a solvent)
			PREFIXED ROOT:
			com-: (with, together)
			commensurable (see synonyms, next word)
			commensurate (**Synonyms:** proportional, commensurable,
			  proportionate)
			di-: dimension (in *mathematics*, a number, usually an integer,
			  representing the geometric dimensions of some physical or
			  abstract system), dimensible (from *dis*-, off, from)
			im-: immense (originally, unmeasured) (*im*- from *in*-, not)
			DOUBLE ROOT:
			in<u>com</u>mensurable (*in*-, not + *com*-, with, together)
			TRAILING ROOT COMPOUND:
			bi: bimestral (*bi*, two)
			se: semester (shortened from *cursus semestris*, literally six-
			  months course) (from *sex*, six)
			tri: trimester (*tri*, three)
			LATIN PREFIXED ENGLISH:
			im-: immeasurable (*im*- assimilates *in*-, not)
			FRENCH PHRASE:
			tous les mois (all the months; thus, every month)
			OLD ENGLISH: meal (from *mael*; originally, measure, mark,
			  appointed time; thus, time for eating)
			CROSS REFERENCE: *mod, meter, metro;* Greek *men/mes*

mend*	Latin
	mendum
	(IE: *mend*,
	a fault)
		fault	SIMPLE ROOT: mend (an aphetic of *amend*; **Synonyms:**
			  repair, patch, darn), mendacious (not truthful; lying or false),
			  mendacity, mendicant (one at fault; thus, a beggar)
			PREFIXED ROOT:
			a-: amend, amendatory, amendment, amends (as *to make
			  amends*) [*a*- is a French variant of Latin *ex*-; see next entry]
			e-: emend, emendate, emendation (from *ex*-, out)
			CROSS REFERENCE: *culp*

mening*	Greek
	meningos
		membrane	SIMPLE ROOT: meningeal, meninges (plural of *menix*; the
			  three membranes that envelop the brain and the spinal cord)
			  meningism, menix (plural, *meninges*)
			LEADING ROOT COMPOUND:
			mening:
			itis: meningitis (plural, *meningitides*) {meningitic} (*itis*, in-
			  flammation of)
			oma: meningioma (a slow-growing tumor that originates in
			  the arachnoidal tissue) (*oma*, mass, tumor)
			meningo:
			arter: meningoarteritis (inflammatory condition of the menin-
			  geal arteries) (*itis*, inflammation)
			coccus: meningococcus (the bacterium that is a common cause
			  of meningitis) (*coccus*, bacterium)
			NO CROSS REFERENCE

Element	From	Meaning	Examples
mens*	Latin *mensa*	table	SIMPLE ROOT: mensa (in *Roman Catholicism*, the top of the altar, especially, the top or central slab upon which the eucharistic elements are placed; in *dentistry*, the grinding surface of a tooth) mensal (belonging to, or used at, the table; another *mensal* pertains to *month*) PREFIXED ROOT: com-: commensal [though ending in adjectival -al, as *noun*, means a companion at meals; in *biology*, either of the organisms living in commensualism (a close association or union between two kinds of organisms, in which one is benefited by the relationship and the other is neither benefited nor harmed); as an *adjective*, designating, of, or like a commensal] (*com-*, with, together) LEGAL PHRASE: *a mensa et thoro* (from bed and board; used in divorce proceedings) AN ORGANIZATION FOR THOSE WITH HIGH IQs: Mensa Society, for those qualifying come to the common table without regard for age, race, occupation, academic degrees, or social status CONSTELLATION: Mensa (a constellation near the southern celestial pole, between Hydrus and Volans) SPANISH: mesa PLACENAMES: Mesa (Arizona, Colorado, Idaho, Washington) CROSS REFERENCE: *tab*
ment,** mind	Latin *mentis* (IE: *men*, to think)	mind	SIMPLE ROOT: mental (another *mental* pertains to the chin), mentalism, mentalist, mentality, mention, mentism PREFIXED ROOT: *ment*: a-: ament, amentia (*a-*, not) com-: comment (**Synonyms:** remark, observation, commentary), commentary, commentator (*com-*, intensive) de-: demented, dementia (**Synonyms:** insanity, lunacy, psychosis) (*de-*, out from) *min*: re-: reminisce, reminiscence, reminiscent (*re-*, again) *mind*: re-: remind (*re-*, again) LATIN PHRASE: *mens sana in corpore sano* (a healthy mind in a healthy body) MEDICAL TERM: *dementia praecox* CROSS REFERENCE: *phren, psycho, thym*
mentul*	Latin *mentula*	penis	SIMPLE ROOT: mentula, mentulate (having a large penis) LEADING ROOT COMPOUND: agra: mentulagra (literally, penis seizure; also known as *priapism*, as well as *chordee*) (*agra*, seizure) *mentulo*: mania: mentulomania (male masturbation) (*mania*, craving) CROSS REFERENCE: *aden, balano, phallo, peni*

With words we govern men. Disraeli

Element	From	Meaning	Examples
mer***	Greek *meros*	part	SIMPLE ROOT: meristem, merit PREFIXED ROOT: *anti-*: antimere (in *zoology*, either of two corresponding parts opposite each other on both sides of an organism's axis) (*anti-*, against) *ecto-*: ectomere {ectomeric} (*ecto-*, outside) *epi-*: epimere (*epi-*, upon) *meta-*: metamer, metamerism (*meta-*, between) LEADING ROOT COMPOUND: blast: meroblastic (*blast*, embyro) crin: merocrine (*crin*, separate) gen: merogenesis (*genesis*, producing) morph: meromorphic (*morph*, shape, form) plankton: meroplankton (from *planan*, to wander) TRAILING ROOT COMPOUND: allo: allomerism, allomerous (*allo*, other) arthro: arthromere (*arthro*, joint) crypto: cryptomeria (*crypto*, hidden) di: dimerous (having two parts; specifically, having two members in each whorl: said of flowers; having two-jointed tarsi: said of insects) (*di*, two) hetero: heteromerous (in *biology*, having a whorl or whorls with a different number of parts than that of the other whorls) (*hetero*, different) hexa: hexamerous (*hex*, six) homo: homomerous (*homo*, same) iso: isomer (*iso*, equal) mono: monomer, monomerous (in *botany*, having only one member, as a fruit of one carpel) (*mono*, one) penta: pentamerous (*penta*, five) poly: polymeric (*poly*, many) RELATED ROOT: merit [past participle of of Latin *merere*, to deserve, earn; from IE *smer*, to remember, care (hence, provide for, allot a share to), whence Greek *meros*, part, lot, fate] PREFIXED ROOT: demerit (*de-*, intensive) CROSS REFERENCE: *part, port*
merc*	Latin *merces*: pay wages (IE: *merk*, to seize)	to trade, buy	SIMPLE ROOT: mercenary, mercer, merchant, mercy PREFIXED ROOT: *com-*: commerce, commercial (*com-*, with, together) DISGUISED ROOT: market, mart SPANISH PROPER NAME: Mercedes (shortened from *María de Mercedes*, Mary of Mercies) ROMAN MYTHOLOGY: Mercury (*inter alia*, the god of commerce; the metallic element *mercury* is also derived from the Roman god) PLACENAME: Merced, California NO CROSS REFERENCE

Clearness is the most important factor in the use of words.
Marcus Fabius Quintilian, Roman rhetorician, A.D. c. 35--c. 95

Element	From	Meaning	Examples

merg,**
mers
	Latin
	merger
	(IE: *mezg*,
	to plunge)
		to dip,
		plunge
			SIMPLE ROOT:
			merge (**Synonyms:** mix, mingle, blend), merger
			PREFIXED ROOT:
			merg:
			e-: emerge, emergent, emergency (from *ex-*, out)
			sub-: submerge, submerse, submersion (*sub-*, under)
			mers
			de-: demerse (sink to the bottom) (*de-*, down; or intensive)
			im-: immerse, immersed (plunged into or as if into a liquid;
			   baptized by immersion), immersion (from *in-*, in)
			LEADING ROOT COMPOUND:
			anser: merganser (a large, fish-eating, diving duck) (*anser*,
			   goose)
			INTERDISCIPLINARY: immersed (in *biology*, imbedded
			   in another organ; in *botany*, growing completely under wa-
			   ter)
			CROSS REFERENCE: *bapt*

mes			See both Latin and Greek *men*/*mes*.

meso-***	Greek
	mesos
	(IE: *me*,
	between)
		middle	SIMPLE ROOT: mesial, mesic, meson
			LEADING ROOT COMPOUND:
			mes:
			arch: mesarch (*arche*, beginning)
			enceph: mesencephalon (*en-* prefixes *cephal*, head; the prefix
			   plus the root are generally considered one word--*encephalon*--
			   the mass of nerve tissue contained within the cranium)
			enchym: mesenchyme (*enchyma*, cell tissue of a specified type)
			enter: mesenteritis, mesenteron, mesentery (*enteron*, intestine)
			orchi: mesorchium (*orchis*, testis)
			meso:
			bentho: mesobenthos (all the animals and plants living on the
			   sea bottom at depths between 200 and 1,000 meters)
			   (*benthos*, bottom of the sea)
			blast: mesoblast, mesoblastic (*blast*, embryo)
			carp: mesocarp (the middle layer of the wall of a ripened ovary
			   or fruit, as the flesh of the plum) (*carp*, fruit)
			cephal: mesocephalic (*cephal*, head)
			cran: mesocranial (*cran*, cranium)
			crat: mesocratic (containing 30 to 60 percent of heavy, dark
			   minerals: said especially of igneous rocks) (*crat*, strength)
			derm: mesoderm (*derm*, skin)
			gastr: mesogastrium (*gastr*, belly)
			glea: mesoglea (*glea*, glue)
			lith: mesolithic (*lith*, stone)
			mel: mesomelic (pertaining to the midportion of the arm or
			   leg) (*mel*, limb)
			morph: mesomorph (designating the muscular or athletic type)
			   {mesomorphic}, mesomorphy (*morph*, shape, form)
			nephr: mesonephros {mesonephric} (*nephros*, kidney)
			paus: mesopause (a shortening of *meso*sphere + *pause*) (*pau-*
			   sis, a stopping)
			phyl: mesophyll (the inner part of a leaf) (*phyl-lon*, leaf)

Element	From	Meaning	Examples
meso- (cont'd)			phyt: mesophyte (*phyton*, plant) spher: mesosphere (*sphere*, ball, globe) thel: mesothelioma (*thel*, nipple; *oma*, growth, tumor) thorax: mesothorax COINED WORD: meson [from *mes(otr)on*, any of several unstable particles, first observed in cosmic rays, having a mass between that of the *electron* and the *proton*: *mesons* can exist in a variety of masses and can have a neutral, positive, or negative charge] GEOGRAPHIC PLACE: Mesopotamia (literally, in the middle of the river, but actually *between* the rivers: the Tigris and the Euphrates) GEOLOGIC ERA: Mesozoic (an era between the Paleozoic and the Cenozoic eras, i.e., between the two periods, *paleo* referring to ancient, and *ceno* referring to new) INTERDISCIPLINARY: mesarch (in *botany*, having the primary xylem maturing from the center toward both the interior and exterior of the stem, as in certain ferns; in *ecology*, beginning in a moderately moist habitat) CROSS REFERENCE: *demi, hemi, med, semi*
meta-***	Greek *meta*, along with (IE: *me*, between)	later, behind (see note)	PREFIX NOTE: This prefix can also mean after, following (*method*); between (*metope*); with, beside, situated behind, backward, reversed (*metacarpous, metathesis*); occurring later (*metazoan*); beyond, transcending (*metalinguistics, metaphysical*); changed or involving change (*metachromatism*); alternating (*metagenesis*); intensified action (*meteor*). PREFIXED ROOTS AND COMPOUNDS: *met-*: hod: (way) method (a way of doing anything; mode; procedure; process; especially, a regular, orderly, definite procedure or way of teaching, investigating, etc.), Methodist methodology (*logy*, study of) onym: metonym (see note under *onym*), metonymy (*onym*, name) *meta*: bol: metabolic, metabolism, metabolite, metabolize (from *ballein*, to throw) carp: metacarpal, metacarpus (*carpus*, wrist) center: metacenter chroma: metachromatism (*chrom*, color) galaxy: metagalaxy (the total assemblage of all galaxies, including all intergalactic matter; the measurable material universe) gen: metagenesis (*genesis*, producing) gnath: metagnathous (*gnath*, jaw) mathematics: metamathematics (the logical study of the nature and validity of mathematical reasoning and proof) mer: metamer, metamere, metamerism (*mere*, part) morph: metamorphic, metamorphism, metamorphose (*morph*, shape, form) nephro: metanephros (*nephros*, kidney)

420

Element	From	Meaning	Examples
meta- (cont'd)			or: meteor (from *eora*, a hovering in the air; akin to *aeirein*, to lift up)
			phas: metaphase (in *biology*, the stage in mitosis in which the duplicated chromosomes lie on the equatorial plane of the spindle) (*phase*, show)
			phor: metaphor (a figure of speech containing an implied comparison, in which a word or phrase ordinarily and primarily used of one thing is applied to another, e.g., *the curtain of night; the evening of life; all the world's a stage*; the hymn *"A Mighty Fortress is Our God"*; compare *simile*, where the comparison is connected by *as, like, seem*, or *appear*, as Robert Burns' line "My love's *like* a red, red rose"; changed to a metaphor, this simile would read: "My love *is* a red, red rose") (*phor*, to bear)
			phras: (diction)
			metaphrase [to translate, especially, literally; paradoxically, *to change* the phrasing or literary form of (compare *paraphrase*)]
			metaphrast (a person who translates or changes a literary work from one form to another, as prose into verse) (*phrasis*, diction)
			physi: metaphysic, metaphysical, metaphysics (*physi*, growth)
			plas: metaplasia (abnormal change of one type of adult tissue to another; conversion of one tissue into another, as of cartilage into bone), metaplasm (*plasm*, form, shape)
			psych: metapsychology (*psych*, mind; *logy*, study of)
			somat: metasomatism (*soma*, body)
			stabl: metastable (from *stare*, to stand)
			stasis: metastasis (*stasis*, stand)
			tars: metatarsal, metatarsus (*tars*, foot bones)
			thesis: metathesis (*thesis*, a placing)
			thorax: metathorax (*thorax*, chest, breastplate)
			xyl: metaxylem (*xylo*, wood)
			zo: metazoan (*zo*, animal)
			DOUBLE PREFIXED ROOT:
			metencephalon (*en-* prefixes *cephal*, head; the prefix plus the root are generally considered one word--*encephalon*--the mass of nerve tissue contained within the cranium)
			RELATED ANGLO-SAXON: midwife (literally, with wife; basic sense: woman with; woman assisting) (*wif*, woman)
			INTERDISCIPLINARY: metathesis (in *linguistics*, the transposition or interchange of letters or sounds in a word, or the result of this, e.g., *clasp* developed from Middle English *clapse* by metathesis; in *chemistry*, the interchange of elements or radicals between compounds, as when two compounds react with each other to form two new compounds)
			CROSS REFERENCE: *post/poster, mut*
metr, *** **meter**	Greek *mete* (IE: *me*, to measure)	to measure	SIMPLE ROOT: meter, metric
			PREFIXED ROOT:
			dia-: diameter [to measure across (a circle)], diametrical (also *diametral*; of, or along a diameter; designating an opposite, a contrary, a difference, etc., e.g., *diametrical opposites*) (*dia-*, across)

421

Element	From	Meaning	Examples
metr (cont'd)			*hyper-*: (beyond)

hypermeter (same as *hypercatalexis*, which see under *hyper-*)

hypermetropia (*opia*, pertaining to vision)

para-: parameter (boundary, limit) (*para-*, beside)

peri-: perimeter (measurement around a sided figure; originally, measurement around any figure) (*peri-*, around)

sym-: symmetry (*sym-*, with, together)

DOUBLE PREFIXED ROOT:

asymmetry, asymmetrical (see *symmetry*, previous entry) (*a-*, not, without + *sym-*, with, together)

LEADING ROOT COMPOUND:

metr:

echo: metrechoscopy (combined mensuration, auscultation, and inspection) (*echo*, sound + *scope*, to examine)

metro:

logy: metrology (the science of weights and measures) (*logy*, study of)

nom: metronome {metronomic} (*nomos*, law)

TRAILING ROOT COMPOUND:

meter: a device for measuring (that which is indicated in parentheses)

acoumeter (hearing)

altimeter (height)

barometer (atmospheric pressure)

chronometer (time)

cryometer (cold)

hemacytometer (blood cells)

micrometer (very small distances, angles, diameters, etc.)

odometer (distance traveled by a vehicle)

speedometer (the speed of a vehicle)

tachometer (the revolutions per minute of a revolving shaft)

telemeter (distance of an object remote from the observer)

thermometer (heat)

meter: a specified number of meters, or part of a meter

centimeter (one hundredth of a meter)

decameter (ten meters)

decimeter (one tenth of a meter)

kilometer (one thousand meters)

meter: having a specified number of metrical feet, as in *poetry*

dimeter (two feet)

hexameter (six feet)

hypermetric (having an extra syllable or syllables) (*hyper-*, beyond)

monometer (one foot)

octameter (eight feet)

pentameter (five feet)

trimeter (three feet)

metric: an adjective-forming suffix of measurement

baro: barometric (*baro*, heavy)

iso: isometric (*iso*, equal)

Element	From	Meaning	Examples
metr (cont'd)			*metry*: a noun-forming suffix meaning the process, art, or science of measuring anthropo: anthropometry (*anthropo*, man) calori: calorimetry (*calor*, heat) chrono: chronometry (*chrono*, time) geo: geometry (*geo*, earth) hygro: hygrometry (*hygro*, moisture) hypso: hypsometry (*hypso*, high, height) photo: photometry (*photo*, light) psycho: psychometry (*psych*, mind) stereo: stereometry (*stereo*, solid) tele: telemetry (*tele*, from afar) CROSS REFERENCE: *men/mes, mod*
metro**	Greek *meter* (IE: *mater*, mother)	mother	LEADING ROOT COMPOUND: *metr*: onym: metronym (same as *matronymic*; of, or derived from the name of the mother or a female ancestor) (*onyn*, name) *metro*: poli: metropolis (literally, mother city), metropolitan (*polis*, city) ALTERED LEADING ROOT COMPOUND: onym: matronymic (by its spelling, the word would appear to be placed in the Latin family *matro*) (*onyn*, name) CROSS REFERENCE: *mater*
mi,* m y	Greek *myein*	to close (extend to mean "to shut the eyes")	LEADING ROOT COMPOUND: *mi*: osis: miosis (excessive contraction of the pupil of the eye), miotic (an agent that causes contraction of the pupil of the eye; as an adjective, pertaining to or causing miosis) (*osis*, condition of) *my*: op: myope, myopia (often called *near-sightedness*) (*ops*, eye) DISGUISED ROOT: mystery (**Synonyms**: enigma, riddle, puzzle) CROSS REFERENCE: *clos*
micro***	Greek *mikros* (IE: *meik*, to flicker, blink)	small, minute	SIMPLE ROOT: micron (a unit of length equal to one millionth of a meter, or one thousandth of a millimeter) LEADING ROOT COMPOUND: *micr*: odont: microdont (having very small teeth) {microdontous, microdontism} (*odont*, tooth) *micro*: analys: microanalysis (*ana-* prefixes *lys*, loosen) bar: microbar, microbarograph (*bar*, weight; *graph*, write) be: microbe (from *bios*, life) bio: microbiology (*bio*, life; *logy*, study of) cephal: microcephaly {microcephalic} (*cephal*, head) clima: microclimatology, microclimate clin: microcline (a mineral of the feldspar group, potassium aluminum silicate, used in making porcelain) (from klinein, to lean)

Element	From	Meaning	Examples
micro (cont'd)			cocc: micrococcus (*coccus*, berry; also, a bacterium of spheri⁻cal shape, like a berry)
			cosm: microcosm (*cosm*, universe, world)
			cyt: microcyte (*cyt*, cell)
			fich: microfiche (*ficher*, to attach)
			gam: microgamete (*gam*, sexual reproduction)
			gram: microgram (one millionth of a gram)
			graph: micrograph (*graph*, write)
			lith: microlith (*lith*, stone)
			logy: micrology (*logy*, study of)
			mer: micromere (*mere*, part)
			meter: micrometer [pronounced my CROM uh ter, 1) an instrument for measuring very small distances, angles, diameters, etc., used on a telescope or microscope; 2) a micrometer caliper; 3) pronounced my crow ME ter, a micron]
			organ: microorganism
			phon: microphone (*phone*, sound)
			phyt: microphyte (*phyton*, plant)
			pyl: micropyle {micropylar} (*pyle*, gate)
			pyr: micropyrometer (*pyr*, fire, heat)
			scop: microscope (*scope*, look)
			seism: microseism (*seism*, tremor)
			spor: (*spore*, seed)
			microsporangium (*angi*, vessel)
			microspore
			microsporophyll (*phyll*, leaf)
			stom: microstomous (*stom*, mouth)
			tom: microtome, microtomy (*tom*, cut)
			DISGUISED ROOT: mica (thought by some authorities; mica that is transparent is often called *isinglass*, from the Dutch *huizenblas*, literally, sturgeon bladder)
			GREEK LETTER: omicron (small o); compare *omega* (large o)
			PLACENAME: Micronesia (one of the three major divisions of the Pacific Islands, north of the equator, east of the Philippines, and west of the International Date Line; the other two divisions are Melanesia and Polynesia. The main island groups in Micronesia are as follows: the Marianas, the Carolines; the Marshalls, the Gilberts, Wake Island, and Guam.)
			INTERDISCIPLINARY: micropyle (in *botany*, a very small opening in the outer coats of an ovule, through which the pollen tube penetrates; the corresponding opening in the developed seed; in *zoology*, a very small opening in the membrane of an ovum of some animals, through which spermatozoa can enter)
			CROSS REFERENCE: *lept, mini, petit*
migr**	Latin *migrare* (IE: *mei*, to change, exchange, wander)	to move (extended to mean "to move from place to place")	SIMPLE ROOT: migrant, migrate (**Synonyms:** emigrate, immigrate), migratory
			PREFIXED ROOT:
			e-: emigrant, emigrate (see synonyms at *migrate*, above), émigré (**Synonyms:** alien, foreigner, immigrant) (e- elides *ex-*, out)

Element	From	Meaning	Examples
migr (cont'd)			*im-*: immigrant (see synonyms at *émigré*, above), immigrate (see synonyms at *migrate*, above) (*im-* assimilates *in-*, in)
			re-: remigrant (a migrant who returns; specifically, an aphid of the winged generation that returns to its former host) (*re-*, back, again)
			trans-: transmigrant, transmigrate (to pass into another body at death: said of the soul, as in Hindu religions), transmigration (*trans-*, across)
			CROSS REFERENCE: *mob, plan, vag*
mil***	Latin *mille*	1,000	SIMPLE ROOT:
			mil: mil, mile [originally, *milia passuum* (1,000 paces); see milliary, below]
			mill: mill (the coin)
			millen: millenarian, millenary (1,000 years; or a group of a thousand units or things; see *mile* above)
			milles: millesimal
			milli: milliard (1,000 million), milliary (as an *adjective*, of the ancient Roman mile, or 1,000 paces; as a *noun*, an ancient Roman milestone), million (1,000 thousands)
			PREFIXED ROOT:
			post-: postmillenial (existing or happening after the millennium) (*post-*, after)
			pre-: premillennial, premillennialism (the belief that Christ's second coming will immediately precede the millennium) (*pre-*, before)
			LEADING ROOT COMPOUND:
			mil:
			foil: milfoil (from *folio*, leaf)
			reis: milreis (plural, *milreis*; 1,000 reis; a former Brazilian monetary unit and silver coin; superseded in 1942 by the *cruzeiro*)
			mill:
			enn: millennium (1,000 years; in *Christian theology*, the period of 1,000 years during which Christ will reign on earth; see Revelation 20:1-5) (from *ann*, year)
			milli: 1/000th:
			ampere: milliampere
			curie: millicurie
			gram: milligram
			liter: milliliter
			meter: millimeter
			micron: millimicron
			ped: millipede
			second: millisecond
			volt: millivolt
			CROSS REFERENCE: *kilo, chilias*
mim*	Greek *mimos*: imitator	to imitate	SIMPLE ROOT:
			mime:
			mime (an ancient Greek and Roman farce, in which people and events were mimicked and burlesqued)
			mimesis (in *art* and *literature*, imitation or representation), mimetic, mimetite

Element	From	Meaning	Examples
mim (cont'd)			mimi: mimic (**Synonyms:** imitate, copy, mock) mimicry (close resemblance, in color, form, or behavior, of one organism to another or to some object in its environment, as of some insects to the leaves or twigs of plants: it serves to disguise or conceal the organism from predators) mimo: mimosa (from the apparent mimicry of the sensitivity of animal life) PREFIXED ROOT: a-: amimia (loss of power to express ideas by signs or gestures) (*a-*, not) TRADENAME: Mimeograph NO CROSS REFERENCE
min			See *men/min* for *imminent, prominent.*
mind			See *ment* for *remind.*
mini***	Latin *minuere*: to lessen (IE: *mei*, to lessen)	small, less	SIMPLE ROOT: (See note on *miniature* below.) minim: minim, minimal, minimize (Synonyms: disparage, depreciate, decry), minimum (alternate plural, *minima*), minimus minis: minister, ministerial, ministrant, ministration, ministry minor: minor, minority minu: minuend, minuet (the *minuet* was written for the dance that took small steps), minus, minute, minutiae, minutiose PREFIXED ROOT: ad-: administer (**Synonyms:** govern, rule), administrate, administration, administrative, administrator, administratress, administratrix (*ad-*, to, toward) com-: comminute, comminution (*com-*, with, together) di-: diminution (in *music*, variation of a theme by shortening, usually halving, the time value of the notes; compare *augmentation* under *aug* family), diminutive, diminish (*di-* is variant of *de-*, from) LEADING ROOT COMPOUND: computer: minicomputer (*com-* prefixes *put*) fy: minify (from *facere*, to make, do) ver: miniver (a white fur worn originally by nobles and used chiefly for robes of state) (from Middle French *menu vair*, small vair, or *small fur*) DISGUISED ROOT: menu mince (to cut up or chop up meat, etc. into very small pieces; to subdivide minutely; to express or do affected elegance or daintiness; to lessen the force of; weaken, as by euphemism; often heard in the expression "to mince no words") minstrel ITALIAN MUSIC TERM: *diminuendo* NOTE ON *MINIATURE*: From Basque *minium*, red lead, the color red was used to illuminate the beginning ornate letters of manuscripts. Paradoxically, the large letters were known as "small paintings, painted with *red lead.*" *Miniature* eventually came to denote that which is *small.* CROSS REFERENCE: *lept, micro, petit*

Element	From	Meaning	Examples
mio,* mei	Greek *meion* (IE: *mei*, to lessen)	less	SIMPLE ROOT: meionite (a particular mineral), meiosis LEADING ROOT COMPOUND: *meio*: phyl: meiophylly (*phyll*, leaf) stom: meiostomatous, meiostome (*stom*, mouth) tax: meiotaxy (*taxy*, arrangement) *mio*: card: miocardia (not to be confused with *myocardia*) (*card*, heart) cene: Miocene (from *kainos*, recent) plasm: mioplasmia (*plasm*, form) prag: miopragia (decreased functional activity) therm: miothermic (*therm*, heat) CROSS REFERENCE: *mini*
mir*	Latin *mirari* (IE: *(s)mei*, to smile)	to wonder at	SIMPLE ROOT: mir, miracle, miraculous, mirador, mirage (**Synonyms**: delusion, illusion, hallucination), mirror PREFIXED ROOT: *ad*-: admirable, admirably, admiration, admire (**Synonyms**: regard, respect, esteem), admirer (*ad*-, to, toward) DISGUISED ROOT: marvel, marvelous, smile LATIN PHRASE: *mirabile dictu* (wonderful to tell) NOTE: *Thaumatology* (from Greek) is the study of miracles. NB: *Mirabelle* is not in this family. NO CROSS REFERENCE
mis-***	English (IE: *meith*, to change, exchange)	wrong, wrongly; bad, badly; no, not	PREFIXED LATIN ROOT: calc: miscalculate car: miscarriage, miscarry (*car*, originally, chariot) chanc: mischance (from *cadere*, to fall) con: misconception (*con*- prefixes *cept*) con: misconstrue (*con*- prefixes *strue*, from *struct*, build) creant: miscreant (from *credere*, to believe) demean: misdemeanor (*de*- prefixes *mean*) direct: misdirect (*di*- elides *dis*-, which prefixes *rect*) join: misjoinder (in *law*, the improper joining together of parties or of different causes of action in one lawsuit or other legal proceeding) nomer: misnomer (*nomen*, name) DOUBLE PREFIXED ROOT: (*ad*- and assimilations *al*- and *ap*-, to, toward) misadventure, misalliance, misapply, misapprehend PREFIXED ANGLO-SAXON ROOT: (examples of) misfire; misgivings; mishap; mishear; misleading; mismatch DOUBLE PREFIXED ANGLO-SAXON ROOT: misbecome, misbegotten, misbehave, misbelieve (archaic) PREFIXED FRENCH ROOT: (examples of) mischief, mischievous miscue misfeasance, misfeasor NOTE: Do not confuse this prefix with the Greek root *miso*, hate, as in *misogynist*, nor the root *misce*, mixture, as in *miscegenation* or *miscellaneous*. CROSS REFERENCE: *caco, dys*

427

Element	From	Meaning	Examples
misc,** mix	Latin *miscere*; to mix (IE: *meik*, to mix)	mixture	SIMPLE ROOT: *misc*: misc: miscellanea, miscellaneous, miscellany misci: miscible (that can be mixed) *mix*: mix (**Synonyms**: merge, blend, coalesce), mixture PREFIXED ROOT: *mict*: apo-: apomict (a plant that reproduces by apomixis) (Greek *apo-*, from) *misc*: im-: immiscible (*im-* assimilates *in-*, not) pro-: promiscuous (literally, thoroughly mixed; consisting of diverse and unrelated parts or individuals; confused; lacking standards of selection; indiscriminate) (*pro-*, intensifier) *mix*: ad-: admix, admixture (*ad-*, to, toward) amphi-: amphimixis (*amphi-*, around, both) apo-: apomixis (asexual reproduction of plants) (Greek *apo-*, from) com-: commix, commixture (*com-*, with, together) im-: immix (from *in-*, in) LEADING ROOT COMPOUND: gen: miscegenation (*gen*, producing) DISGUISED ROOT: meddle, medley (see *Doublets* below) mélange (from French *mêler*, to mix) melee (also, *mêlée*) (see *Doublets* below) mestiso (same as *mestizo:* from Ecclesiastical Latin *misticius*, of mixed race; translated from Greek *symmiktos*, commingled; a person of mixed parentage; especially in the western United States and in Latin American countries, the offspring of a Spaniard or Portuguese and an American Indian) maslin (a mixture of different sorts of grain, especially wheat and rye or their flour or meal; a bread made with such a flour or meal) mustang (from Spanish *mesteño*; from *mesta*, originally a group of grazers; from their mingling, or uncontrolled mixing; a small wild or half-wild horse of the southwest plains of the United States; though *mingle* means mixing, it comes from Greek *massein*, to massage or to knead) PREFIXED DISGUISED ROOT: apo-: apomict (in *biology*, an individual or species produced by or reproducing by *apomixis*) (*apo-*, away) REDUPLICATED ROOT: pell-mell DOUBLETS: medley:melee CROSS REFERENCE: *cras*
miser**	Latin *miser*	wretched	SIMPLE ROOT: miser, miserable miserly (**Synonyms**: stingy, niggardly, penurious) misery PREFIXED ROOT: com-: commiserate (to feel or express sorrow or sympathy for; to sympathize; condole) (*com-*, intensive)

Element	From	Meaning	Examples
miser (cont'd)			VULGATE WORD: Miserere [literally, have mercy; first word of the psalm in the Vulgate (a 4th-century Latin version of the Bible, authorized for use in the Roman Catholic Church); in the Bible, the 51st Psalm, beginning, "Have mercy upon me"] FRENCH NOVEL: *Les Misérables*, by Victor Hugo, who also wrote *The Hunchback of Notre Dame*. The two novels rank among the most popular fiction written. NO CROSS REFERENCE
miso**	Greek *mesein*: to hate; *misos*: hatred	hatred of	LEADING ROOT COMPOUND: *mis*: andry: misandry (*men*) anthropo: misanthropist (*mankind*) *miso*: cain: misocainea (*new ideas*) gam: misogamy (*marriage*) gyn: misogyny (*women*) logy: misology (*argument, reasoning,* or *enlightenment*) neism: misoneism (*something new*) ped: misopedist (*children*) soph: misosophy (*wisdom*) NOTE: Do not confuse this root with that in *misophobia* (a variant of *mysophobia*) and *mysophilia* where the root means filth or uncleanliness. CROSS REFERENCE: *odi*
miss,*** mitt	Latin *mittere*: to throw, send, put (IE: *smeit*, to throw)	to send	SIMPLE ROOT: missal (a book containing all the prayers and responses necessary for celebrating the Roman Catholic Mass throughout the year; see *Mass*, below), missile, mission, missionary, missive (a letter or written message) PREFIXED ROOT: *mise*: com-: compromise (*com-*, with, together + *pro-*, forth) de-: demise (a ceasing to exist; death; also, a law term) (*de-*, down) pre-: premise [a proposition upon which an argument is based or from which a conclusion is based; in *logic*, one of the first two propositions (*major* or *minor*) in a syllogism, from which the conclusion is drawn] (*pre-*, before) pro-: promise (*pro-*, forth) sur-: surmise (from *super-*, upon) *miss*: ad-: admissible {admissibility}, admission {admissive} (*ad-*, to, toward) com-: commissary, commission, commissure (in *anatomy*, a band of fibers joining symmetrical parts, as of the right and left sides of the brain and spinal cord) (*com-*, with, together) di-: dimissary (from *dis-*, apart, away) dis-: dismissible (*dis-*, apart, away) e-: emissary, emission (from *ex-*, out) inter-: intermission (*inter-*, between) intro-: intromission (*intro-*, within, on the inside, into) o-: omission (from *ob-*, against)

Element	From	Meaning	Examples
miss (cont'd)			*per-*: permissible, permission, permissive (*per-*, through)
			pro-: promissory, as a *promissory note* (*pro-*, forth)
			re-: remiss (**Synonyms**: negligent, derelict, slack), remission (*re-*, back, again)
			sub-: submission, submissive (*sub-*, under)
			trans-: transmissible, transmission (*trans-*, across)
			mit(t):
			ad-: admit (**Synonyms**: 1) acknoweledge, own, avow; 2) receive, accept, take), admittance (*ad-*, to, toward)
			com-: commit (**Synonyms**: entrust, confide, consign), commitment, committal, committee (*com-*, with, together)
			de-: demit (to resign a position or office) (*de-*, down)
			e-: emit, emitter (from *ex-*, out)
			inter-: intermit, intermittent (**Synonyms**: recurrent, periodic, alternate) (*inter-*, between)
			intro-: intromit (to allow to enter) (*intro-*, within, into)
			o-: omit (**Synonyms**: neglect, ignore, overlook) (from *ob-*, against)
			per-: permit (**Synonyms**: let, allow, suffer), permittivity (*per-*, through)
			re-: remit, remittal, remittance, remittent (*re-*, back)
			sub-: submit (*sub-*, under)
			trans-: transmit (**Synonyms**: carry, convey, transport), transmitter (*trans-*, across)
			TRAILING ROOT COMPOUND:
			miss:
			manu: manumission (*manu*, hand)
			mit:
			manu: manumit (*manu*, hand)
			DISGUISED ROOT:
			Mass (from *missa*, dismissal; from the words said by the priest, *ite, missa est contio, go,* the meeting is dismissed)
			mess (a small portion of food); mess hall (military term for dining area)
			message, messenger
			FRENCH TERM:
			mise en scène [(the action of) putting onto the stage (scene)]
			CROSS REFERENCE: *stol/stal, -stle*
mit*	Greek *mitos*	thread	SIMPLE ROOT: mitome (also, *mitoma*; a fine network support or framework of protoplasm in a cell)
			LEADING ROOT COMPOUND:
			mit:
			osis: mitosis (in *biology*, the indirect and more common method of nuclear division of cells) (*osis*, condition)
			mito:
			chondr: mitochondrion (*chondr*, cartilage)
			PREFIXED LEADING ROOT COMPOUND:
			a-: amitosis (direct cell division) (*a-*, not, without + *osis*, condition of)
			TRAILING ROOT COMPOUND:
			di: dimity (*di*, two)
			CROSS REFERENCE: *fil, nemat*

Element	From	Meaning	Examples
mne*	Greek *mneme* (IE: *men*, to think)	memory	SIMPLE ROOT: mnemonic, mnemonics, mnestic PREFIXED ROOT: a-: anamnesis, amnesty (to forget crimes against the state), amnesia (to forget past experiences) (*a-*, not) *hyper*-: hypermnesia (*hyper-*, beyond) LEADING ROOT COMPOUND: gen: mnemogenic (*gen*, producing) techn: mnemotechnical TRAILING ROOT COMPOUND: crypto: cryptomnesia (*crypto*, hidden) pan: panmnesia (*pan*, all) DISGUISED TRAILING ROOT COMPOUND: auto: automatic (self-memory) (*auto*, self) CROSS REFERENCE: *mem*
mob			See *mov* for *mobile*.
mod***	Latin *modus* (IE: *med*, to measure)	measure, manner	SIMPLE ROOT: moda: modal, modality mode: mode (see *Doublets* below) model (**Synonyms:** example, pattern, paradigm) moderate, moderation, moderator modern (**Synonyms:** new, fresh, novel), modernism, modernistic modest (**Synonyms: 1**) unassuming, unpretentious, unobtrusive; **2**) pure, virtuous) modi: modicum, modish modu: modular, modulate, module, modulus PREFIXED ROOT: *com*-: commode (meanings besides that of a toilet), commodity, commodious, commodity (*com-*, with, together) *im*-: immoderate, immodest (*im*- assimilates *in-*, not) DOUBLE PREFIXED ROOT: accommodate, accommodating, accommodation, accommodative (*ac*- assimilates *ad*-, to, toward + *com*-, with) incommode, incommodious, incommodity (*in*-, not + *com*-, with, together) LEADING ROOT COMPOUND: fy: modify (from *facere*, to make, do) DISGUISED ROOT: mold (a pattern, hollow form, or matrix for giving a certain form to something in a plastic or molten state) mood (see *Doublets* below; **Synonyms:** humor, temper, vein) (*mood* is ultimately from *mos*, custom) moulage (the science or practice of making a mold, as in plaster of Paris, of an object, footprint, etc., for use in crime detection) DOUBLETS: mode:mood HYBRID: *modem* (a hybrid of *mod*ulator + *dem*odulator, a coined computer term) FRENCH: *démodé* (out-of-date; old-fashioned), *modiste* ITALIAN MUSIC TERM: *moderato* (with moderation in tempo)

Element	From	Meaning	Examples
mod (cont'd)			LATIN TERMS: *modus operandi* (literally, mode of operation; a way of doing or accomplishing something) *modus vivendi* (literally, mode of living; a way of living or of getting along; a temporary agreement in a dispute pending final settlement; compromise) INTERDISCIPLINARY: mode [in *grammar*, same as *mood* (see next entry); in *music*, the selection and arrangement of tones and semitones in a scale, and indicating either one of the two forms of scale arrangement, i.e., major and minor; in *geology*, the actual mineral composition of an unaltered igneous rock; in *statistics*, the value, number, etc., that occurs most frequently in a given series) mood [in *grammar*, in many languages, a characteristic of verbs that involves the speaker's attitude toward the action expressed, indicating whether this is regarded as a fact (indicative mood), as a matter of supposition, desire, possibility, etc. (subjunctive mood), or as a command (imperative mood); also, an analytic category based on this characteristic (mood is shown by inflection, as in Latin, or analytically with auxiliaries, as English *may, might, should,* or by both); any of the forms a verb takes to indicate this characteristic; in *logic*, any of the various forms of valid syllogisms, as determined by the quantity and quality of their constituent propositions] CROSS REFERENCE: *men/mens, meter*
mol*	Latin *molos*: exertion (IE: *mo*, to strive)	mass, bulk	SIMPLE ROOT: mole: mole (a breakwater, a barrier) molec: molecular, molecule (literally, small mass; the smallest particle of an element or compound that can exist in the free state and still retain the characteristics of the element or compound) (diminutive *-cule*) moles: molest (originally, to be a burden to) PREFIXED ROOT: *de-*: demolish (**Synonyms:** destroy, raze, annihilate), demolition (*de-*, down) CROSS REFERENCE: *cumu, onc*
mol*	Latin *mollis* (IE: *mel*, to crush)	soft	SIMPLE ROOT: molle: mollescent (softening or tending to soften) mollu: mollugo, mollusc (same as mollusk), mollusk PREFIXED ROOT: *e-*: emolent, emollient (softening; soothing) (*e-* elides *ex-*, out) LEADING ROOT COMPOUND: fic: mollification (from *facere*, to make, do) fy: mollify (**Synonyms:** pacify, appease, placate) (from *facere*, to make, do) DISGUISED ROOT: moil (hard work; drudgery; confusion; turmoil) mouillé (in *phonetics*, palatalized, as the sound of Spanish *ñ* as in *cañon* or French *ll* in *fille*) mullein (a particular plant of the figwort family) CROSS REFERENCE: *clemen, leni, malac*

432

Element	From	Meaning	Examples
mol*	Latin *molere* (IE: *mel*, to crush)	to grind	ROOT NOTE: This root is extended to mean meal, grits (Spanish *mola*), that which is obtained by grinding. SIMPLE ROOT: molar, mold (loose, soft, easily worked soil, especially when rich with decayed animal or vegetable matter, and good for growing plants) PREFIXED ROOT: *e-*: emolument (literally, to grind out; gain from employment or position; payment received for work; **Synonyms:** salary, stipend, pay) (from *ex-*, out) *im-*: immolate (literally, to sprinkle a victim with sacrificial meal; thus, to sacrifice, especially, to offer or kill as a sacrifice, especially by fire, as to *immolate* oneself) (*im-* assimilates *in-*, in, on) *pre-*: premolar (*pre-*, before) TRAILING ROOT COMPOUND: *or*: ormolu (an alloy of copper and zinc used to imitate gold; gilded metal, especially brass or bronze) (*or*, gold) DISGUISED ROOT: moulin (a nearly vertical shaft through a glacier, down which a stream of surface water plunges) multure (a fee paid to the owner of a mill for the privilege of having one's grain ground there) NO CROSS REFERENCE
mon			See *mun/mon* for *common*.
mon**	Latin *monere*: to remind (IE: *men¹*, to think)	to warn, show	SIMPLE ROOT: monition (in *law*, a summons directing the recipient to appear and answer), monitor, monitory, monster, monstrance, monstrosity, monstrous (**Synonyms:** flagrant, atrocious, heinous), monument, monumental PREFIXED ROOT: *mon*: *ad-*: admonish (**Synonyms:** advise, counsel, caution), admonishment (*ad-*, to, toward) *sum-*: summon (**Synonyms:** call, convoke, convene) (*sum-* assimilates *sub-*, under, secretly) *pre-*: premonish (*pre-*, before) *monit*: *ad-*: admonition, admonitor, admonitory (*ad-*, to, toward) *pre-*: premonition (a warning in advance; a feeling that something, especially something bad, will happen; foreboding; presentiment) (*pre-*, before) *monstr*: *de-*: demonstrable, demonstrate (to show by reasoning; prove; to explain or make clear by using examples, experiments, etc.), demonstration {demonstrative} (*de-*, out, from) *re-*: (again) remonstrance (protest, complaint, or expostulation) remonstrant (capitalized, one of the Arminians in Holland who presented a *remonstrance* in 1610 setting forth their differences from strict Calvinism) remonstrate (to say or plead in protest, objection, complaint, etc.) muster (**Synonyms:** gather, collect, assemble) NO CROSS REFERENCE

Element	From	Meaning	Examples
mono***	Greek *monos* (IE: *men⁴*, single)	one, alone; extended to mean "single, unit"	ROOT NOTE: In *chemistry*, this root means "containing one atom," or "one group (of a specified element)." SIMPLE ROOT: monad, monastery, monastic, monism, monk LEADING ROOT COMPOUND: *mon*: adelph: monadelphous (see note under *adelph*) (*adelph*, brother) andr: monandrous, monandry (*andr*, man) anth: monanthous (*anth*, flower) arch: monarch, monarchianism (*arch*, rule) atom: monatomic (*atom* itself comprises *a*-, not + *tom*, cut; thus, that which cannot be cut further; same as *univalent*) aur: monaural (*aur*, hear) ax: monaxial (same as *uniaxial*) eci: monecious (a variant of *monoecious*, which see, below) ocl: monocle {monocular} (from *oculus*, eye) od: monodic, monody (literally, singing alone; a Greek ode sung by a single voice; a style of composition in which one part or melody predominates) (*ode*, song) oec: monoecious (from *oikos*, a house) opso: monopsony (a situation in *economics* in which there is only *one* buyer for a particular commodity or service) (*opson*, cooked food + *psomos*, a morsel, bit) ox: monoxide (*oxy*, sharp) *mono*: carp: monocarpellary, monocarpic {monocarpous} (*carp*, fruit) chas: monochasium (in *botany*, a cymose or determinate inflorescence having only a single main axis) (*chasis*, division) chlamyd: monochlamydeous (in *botany*, having only *one* series of perianth parts, usually designated as sepals, in a flower) (*chlamys*, cloak) chlor: monochloride (*chlor*, pale green) chord: monochord (*chord*, string) chrom: monochromat, monochrome (*chrom*, color) clin: monoclinal (dipping in one direction: said of strata, or rock layers), monocline, monoclinic (*clin*, lean) coqu: monocoque (designating a kind of construction, as of an airplane fuselage, in which the skin or outer shell bears all or most of the stresses) (*coque*, a shell) cotyl: monocotyledon (one of the two major divisions of angiosperms, characterized by a single embryonic seed leaf that appears at germination; compare *dicotyledon*) (*cotyledon*, cup-shaped) crac: monocracy (*crac*, rule) crat: monocrat (*crat*, ruled by) cyt: monocyte (*cyt*, cell) gam: monogamy (*gam*, marriage) gen: monogenesis {monogenetic, monogenic}, monogenism (*gen*, producing) glot: monoglot (*glot*, tongue, language) gram: monogram (from *graph*, write)

Element	From	Meaning	Examples
mono (cont'd)			graph: monograph (a book or long article, especially a scholarly one, on a single subject or limited aspect of a subject) (*graph*, write) gyn: monogynous, monogyny (*gyn*, woman) hydr: monohydrate {monohydric} (*hydro*, water) latr: monolatry (the worship of but one god when other gods are recognized as existing) (*latry*, worship of) lingu: monolingual (see glot, above) (*ling*, tongue, language) lith: monolith (*lith*, stone) log: monologist, monologue (also, *monolog*), monology (*log*, word) mani: monomania, monomaniacal (*mania*, craze) mer: monomer, monomerous (*mere*, part) mol: monomolecular (*mol*, mass) morph: monomorphic (*morph*, shape, form) nucl: mononuclear, mononucleosis (*nucle*, kernel) phag: monophagous (*phag*, eat) phob: monophobia (*phobia*, fear of) phon: monophonic, monophony (*phone*, sound) phthong: monophthong (a single vowel sound made while the supraglottal speech organs are in a fixed position; also, two written vowels representing a single sound; for example *oa* in *boat* is a monophthong) (*phthong*, vowel) phyl: monophyletic (*phylon*, tribe, division) phyll: monophyllous (*phyll*, leaf) pleg: monoplegia (*plegia*, stroke) pod: monopode, monopodium (*pod*, foot) poly: monopoly (from *polein*, to sell) sepal: monosepalous (same as *gamosepalous*) som: monosome (*some*, body) sperm: monospermous (*sperm*, seed) stel: monostele (*stele*, post) stich: monostich (a poem or epigram consisting of only one metrical line) (*stichos*, line, verse) stom: monostome (also, *monostomous*) (*stom*, mouth) stroph: monostrophe (*stroph*, turn) styl: monostylous (*styl*, pillar, column) syllab: monosyllabic, monosyllable (*syl*- assimilates *sym*-, with, together) the: monotheism (*theo*, God, gods) ton: monotone {monotonous} (*ton*, stretch, tone) trem: monotreme (any of the lowest order of mammals, consisting of the platypus and echidnas, which lay eggs and have a single opening for the digestive and urinary tracts and for the genital organs) (*trema*, hole) trich: monotrichous (*trich*, hair) typ: monotype {monotypic} (*type*, example, model) val: monovalent (*valor*, worth) MESHED LEADING ROOT COMPOUND: monomial (*mono* + *nomos*, law)

Element	From	Meaning	Examples
mono (cont'd)			DISGUISED ROOT: minster (not *minister*, which comes from *mini*, small, or under the authority of another; *minster* designates the church of a monastery; also, any of various large churches or cathedrals; oftened used in compounds, such as Northminster, Westminster) (see *Doublets* below) monastery (see *Doublets* below; a building or residence for monks or others who have withdrawn from the world for religious reasons; **Synonyms**: cloister, nunnery, priory) (from Greek *monazein*, to be alone) DOUBLETS: minster:monastery CHRISTIAN CONCEPT: Monarchianism (the doctrine of several Christian sects in the 2d century that the Three Persons of the Trinity are manifestations of *one* God, *single* in person) PLACENAMES: Mono, California; Monolith, California INTERDISCIPLINARY: **monad** (in the *philosophy of Leibnitz*, an *indivisible* and impenetrable unit of substance viewed as the basic constituent element of physical reality; in *biology*, any single-celled microscopic organism, especially a flagellate protozoan; in *chemistry*, an atom or radical with a valence of 1) **monoecious** (in *biology*, having both male and female organs in the *same* individual; in *botany*, having the stamens and the pistils in separate flowers on the *same* plant) CROSS REFERENCE: *erem, sol*
mont,*** **mount**	Latin *mons* (IE: *men²*, to project)	mountain	SIMPLE ROOT: *mont*: montage, montane, monte, monticule *mount*: mountain, mountaineer PREFIXED ROOT: *mont*: *inter-*: intermontane (*inter-*, between) *pro-*: promontory (a high ridge of land or rock jutting out into a sea or expanse of water; in *anatomy*, a projecting bodily part) (*pro-*, forward, forth) *trans-*: transmontane (same as *tramontane*, from Italian *tramontano*) (*trans-*, usually, across; in this case, beyond) *ultra-*: ultramontane (*ultra-*, beyond) *mount*: *a-*: amount (from *ad-*, to, toward) *de-*: demount (*de-*, reversal) *dis-*: dismount (*dis-*, removal) *par-*: paramount (literally, to the top of the mountain; thus, ranking higher than any other, as in power or importance) (from *per*, by + *a-* from *ad-*, to, toward) *re-*: remount (to mount again; as a *noun*, a fresh horse, or a supply of fresh horses, to replace another or others) (*re-*, again) *sur-*: surmount (from *supra-*, above, over) LEADING ROOT COMPOUND: bank: mountebank (originally, a person who mounted a bench and sold quack medicines; **Synonyms**: quack, charlatan, impostor)

Element	From	Meaning	Examples
mont (cont'd)			TRAILING ROOT COMPOUND: tanta: tantamount (having equal force, value, effect) (Anglo-French *tant amunter*, to amount to as much; *tant* from Latin *tantus*, so much) DISGUISED ROOT: marmot (literally, mountain mouse) ANATOMY TERM: mons (same as *mons pubis*, the fleshy, rounded elevation, covered with pubic hair, at the lower part of the adult human abdomen; also the same as *mons veneris*, mount of Venus, the *mons pubis* of the human female) PLACENAMES: Montréal (Royal Mountain); Montana (mountainous) Vermont (Green Mountains); Montenegro (dark, or black mountain) Monterey (King's Mountain); Montevallo, Alabama (mountain valley) Montevideo (Portuguese: I see a mountain), the capital of Uruguay GEOGRAPHICAL AREA: Piedmont (literally, foot of the mountain; spellings vary, e.g., *Piémont, Piemonte*) [There are various areas of Europe and the United States with this designation.] A PEOPLE: Montagnard (literally, mountaineer; a member of a people living in the hills of central Vietnam) CROSS REFERENCE: *oro*
mor**	Latin *mos* (IE: *me*, to strive strongly, be energetic)	custom, habit	SIMPLE ROOT: moral (**Synonyms:** ethical, virtuous, righteous), morale, moralism, moralist, moralistic, morality, moralize, mores PREFIXED ROOT: a-: amoral, amorality (*a-*, not) de-: demoralize (*de-*, opposite of) CROSS REFERENCE: *ethos*
mora,* **mur**	Latin *morari* (IE: *(s)mer*, to remember, care)	delay, remain	SIMPLE ROOT: mora, moratorium (a legal authorization to delay payment of money due, as by a bank or debtor nation), moratory (delaying or postponing) PREFIXED ROOT: *mora*: re-: remora (a certain fish, believed to have the ability to delay ships by attaching itself to any flat surface) (*re-*, back) *mur*: de-: demur (**Synonyms:** protest, remonstrate, expostulate), demurrage, demurral, demurrer (*de-*, from) INTERDISCIPLINARY: mora (in *linguistics*, an arbitrary unit of syllabic length; in *prosody*, the unit of metrical time, equal to the ordinary short syllable, usually indicated by a breve) NB: *Demure*, from *maturus*, mature, proper, is not in this family. NO CROSS REFERENCE

It is my experience that the short path to the simple and precise English needed by a man of science lies through the tongues of Homer, Horace, Cicero, and Vergil.
Henry Crew

Element	From	Meaning	Examples
mord,* **mors**	Latin *mordre* (IE: *mer-²*, to rub away, harm)	to bite	ROOT NOTE: The Indo-European base of this root also yields the root of *mortar* (to grind down), *morbid* (disease), Old English *murder*, *mortal* (death). SIMPLE ROOT: *mord*: mordacious, mordacity, mordant (biting, cutting, or sarcastic, as speech, wit, etc.), mordent, mordicate *mors*: morsel PREFIXED ROOT: pre-: premorse (in *biology*, abruptly truncated, as though *bitten* or broken off: said of a leaf or root) (*pre-*, before) re-: remorse (**Synonyms:** penitence, repentance, contrition) (*re-*, again) NO CROSS REFERENCE
morph***	Greek *morphe*	form, shape	SIMPLE ROOT: morpheme, morphia, morphic PREFIXED ROOTS AND COMPOUNDS: a-: amorphia, amorphism, amorphous (*a-*, without) ana-: anamorphoscope, anamorphosis (*ana-*, again) ecto-: ectomorph, ectomorphic (*ecto-*, outside) endo-: endomorph {endomorphic} (*endo-*, within) meta-: metamorphosis (*meta-*, change) peri-: perimorph (a mineral of one kind enclosing one of another kind) (*peri-*, around) LEADING ROOT COMPOUND: *morph*: all: morphallaxis (in *zoology*, the transformation of one part into another during regeneration, as in the growth of an antennule from the stump of an eye in some crustaceans) (*allo*, other) osis: morphosis (*osis*, condition) *morpho*: gen: morphogenesis (*genesis*, producing) logy: morphology (*logy*, study of) phon: morphophone, morphophonemics (*phone*, sound) TRAILING ROOT COMPOUND: allo: allomorph, allomorphic, allomorphism (*allo*, other) anthropo: anthropomorphic (*anthropo*, man) di: dimorphism (*di*, two) hemi: hemimorphic, hemimorphite (*hemi*, half) hetero: heteromorphic (*hetero*, different) holo: holomorphic (*holo*, whole) iso: isomorph (*iso*, equal) meso: mesomorph (*meso*, middle) mono: monomorphic, monomorphous (*mono*, one) neo: neomorph (*neo*, new) EMBEDDED ROOT COMPOUND: geomorphology (*geo*, earth + *logy*, study of) GREEK MYTHOLOGY: Morpheus (god of dreams; consequently, morphine) INTERDISCIPLINARY: amorphous (in *biology*, without definite or specialized structure, as some lower forms of life; in *chemistry* and *geology*, lacking a definite crystalline form)

Element	From	Meaning	Examples
morph (cont'd)			dimorphism (in *botany*, the state of having two different kinds of leaves, flowers, stamens, etc. on the same plant in the same species; in *minerology*, the property of crystallizing in two forms; in *zoology*, the occurrence of two types of individuals in the same species, distinct in coloring, size, etc.)
			monomorphic (in *chemistry*, having but one form, as one crystal form; in *zoology*, having a basic structure remaining unchanged through a series of developmental changes)
			CROSS REFERENCE: *fig, form, plasm*
mort***	Latin *mori* (IE: *mer-²*, to rub away, harm)	to die	SIMPLE ROOT:
			morta: mortal (**Synonyms:** fatal, deadly, lethal), mortalism, mortality, mortar
			morti: mortician
			mortu: mortuary
			PREFIXED ROOT:
			a-: (to)
			amort (literally, to the death; spiritless; word now archaic)
			amortise (same as *amortize*)
			amortizable, amortization, amortize (to extinguish; deaden; thus, to put money aside at intervals for gradual payment of a debt, etc.)
			ante-: antemortem (*ante-*, before)
			im-: immortal, immortalize (*im-* assimilates *in-*, not)
			post-: post-mortem (*post-*, after)
			LEADING ROOT COMPOUND:
			mort:
			gag: mortgage (literally, dead pledge) (Anglo-Saxon *gage*, pledge)
			mort: mortmain (literally, dead hand; a transfer or lands or houses to a corporate body, such as a school, church, or charitable organization, for perpetual ownership) (French *main* from *manus*, hand)
			morti:
			fic: mortification (from *facere*, to make, do)
			fy: mortify (from *facere*, to make, do)
			FRENCH: immortelle (from the feminine of *immortel*, immortal, everlasting; a plant with flowers that retain their color when dried) (*im-* assimilates *in-*, not)
			LATIN PHRASES:
			post-mortem (literally, after death; happening, done, or made after death; having to do with a post-mortem examination)
			rigor mortis (literally, stiffness of death; the progressive stiffening of the muscles that occurs several hours after death as a result of the coagulation of the blood protein)
			DISGUISED ROOT:
			morbid (of, having, or caused by disease), morbidity
			morbific (*fic* from *facere*, to make, do)
			moribund (dying; coming to an end; having little or not vital force left, as *a moribund economy*)
			murder (**Synonyms:** assassinate, execute, dispatch)
			murrain (an infectious disease of cattle)
			PLACENAME: Buttes des Mortes, Wisconsin

439

Element	From	Meaning	Examples
mort (cont'd)			NB: *Mortise*, coming from Arabic *murtazza*, joined, fixed in, is not in this family; neither is *morgue* in this family, though it is related to death. CROSS REFERENCE: *leth, necro, than*
mov,*** mot, mob	Latin *movere* (IE: *mew,* to push away)	to move	SIMPLE ROOT: *mob*: mob (see *Latin Term* below), mobile, mobility, mobilize *mot*: **motile**, motion, motive (**Synonyms**: cause, reason, antecedent), motivity, motor *mov*: move (**Synonyms**: affect, influence, impress) PREFIXED ROOT: *mob*: *im-*: immobile (*im-* assimilates *in-*, not) *mot*: *com-*: commotion (*com-*, together) *de-*: demote {demotion} (*de-*, down) *e-*: emote, emotion, emotional, emotive (*e-* elides *ex-*, out) *pro-*: promote (**Synonyms**: advance, forward, further), promoter, promotion, promotive (*pro-*, forth, forward) *re-*: remote (**Synonyms**: far, distant, removed) (*re-*, back) *mov*: *com-*: commove (to move strongly; agitate; disturb; excite) (from *commotion*) (*com-*, together) *re-*: removal, remove, removed (distant in relationship; remote; distant; disconnected), remover (*re-*, away) TRAILING ROOT COMPOUND: auto: automobile, automotive (self-moving, as opposed to being horse-drawn) (*auto*, self) loco: locomotion, locomotive (of locomotion; moving or capable of moving from one place to another; not stationary) (*loco*, place) DISGUISED ROOT: moment (**Synonyms**: importance, consequence, weight) momentarily, momentary (**Synonyms**: transitory, ephemeral, evanescent) momentous (of great moment; very important, as *a momentous decision*), momentum mutinous, mutiny FRENCH: *émeute* [pronounced approximately ae MOT; from the past participle of Old French *esmovoir* (*émouvoir*), to agitate, and is the rough equivalent of *emotion*; a popular uprising; riot] motif (translates *motive*; in *art, literature,* and *music*, a main element, feature, or theme; the inner drive, the impulse) ITALIAN MUSIC TERM: *con moto* (with animated movement: a direction to the performer) LATIN TERM: *mobile vulgus* (the fickle crowd; shortened to *mob*) PLACENAME: Remote, Oregon (Mobile, Arizona, may be related to this root; Mobile, Alabama, is not related, coming from a French proper name.) PETROLEUM COMPANY: Mobil Oil

Element	From	Meaning	Examples
mov (cont'd)			INTERDISCIPLINARY: motile (in *biology*, moving, or having the power to move spontaneously, as certain spores and microorganisms; in *psychology*, a noun: a person whose mental imagery consists chiefly of his/her own bodily motion) NB: *Momento*, an incorrect spelling of *memento*, is not in this family. CROSS REFERENCE: *cinem*
muc*	Latin *mucus* (IE: *meuk*, slippery, viscous)	moldy, sticky	SIMPLE ROOT: muci: mucilage (a sticky substance used as an adhesive), mucin muco: mucosa (the mucous membrane), mucous (adjective) mucu: mucus (noun) LEADING ROOT COMPOUND: *muc(o)*: oid: mucoid (any of a group of mucoproteins found in connective tissues, in certain types of cysts, etc.) (*oid*, similar to) protein: mucoprotein DISGUISED ROOT: meek, muck, musty ORGANIC ACID: mucic acid [$HOOC(CHOH)_4$-$COOH$], often derived from milk sugar NOTE: *Mucro*, a biology term that denotes the sharp tip of some plant and animal organs, is not related to this root; the word is Latin for sharp point; a sword's point. CROSS REFERENCE: *blenn, myx*
multi***	Latin *multus* (IE: *mel⁴*, strong, big, great)	many, much	SIMPLE ROOT: multitude (**Synonyms**: mob, host, horde), multitudinous LEADING ROOT COMPOUND: *mult*: ang: multangular (also, *multiangular*: having many angles, as certain wrist bones) *multi*: far: multifarious (having many kinds of parts or elements; of great variety; diverse; manifold) (*far*, here meaning direction, from *fas*, law) fid: multifid (cut into many divisions or lobes, as a leaf of a geranium) (*fid*, split) later: multilateral (*latus*, side) par: multipara, multiparous (of or being a multipara; in *zoology*, designating or of a species of animals that normally bears more than one offspring at birth) (*parere*, to beget) part: multipartite (same as *multilateral*) (ultimately from *parare*, to equate) ped: multiped (*ped*, foot) ple: multiple, multiplet, multiplex (*ple*, fold) plic: multiplicand, multiplicate {multiplicative}, multiplicity (*plicare*, to fold) ply: multiply (**Synonyms**: increase, enlarge, augment) (see previous entry) LATIN-GREEK HYBRID: multilith (*lith*, stone) ITALIAN: *molto* (a music term: meaning very; much, as in *molto ritardando*, much slower) CROSS REFERENCE: *poly*

Element	From	Meaning	Examples
mun*	Latin *munire*: to fortify; related to *murus*, wall (IE: *mei*, to fortify)	to protect, advise, warn	SIMPLE ROOT: munition(s), muniments (in *law*, a document or documents serving as evidence of inheritances, title to property, etc.) PREFIXED ROOT: *pre*-: praemunire, premunition (not to be confused with *premonition*) (*pre*-, before) FAULTY SEPARATION: ammunition (for French *la munition;* incorrectly represented as *l'amunition*) CROSS REFERENCE: *arm*
mun,** mon	Latin *munus*: service (IE: *mei*, to exchange)	common, public	PREFIXED ROOT: *com*-: (with, together) mon: common (**Synonyms:** general, ordinary, familiar) mun: commune, communicate, communion communism, community, communize (to subject to communal ownership and control; to cause to become communistic) *re*-: (again) mun: remunerate (**Synonyms:** reimburse, indemnify, pay) LEADING ROOT COMPOUND: cip: municipal, municipality (from *capere*, to take) fic: munificent (from *facere*, to make, do) SIMPLE COMPOUND: commonwealth (The following states of the United States use *commonwealth* as part of their official titles: Kentucky, Massachusetts, Pennsylvania, Virginia. The United States itself may properly be termed a *commonwealth*.) FRENCH: communiqué (an official communication or bulletin) POLITICAL DOCUMENT: *Communist Manifesto* (a pamphlet written in 1848 by Karl Marx and Friedrich Engels, summarizing their theory of, and program for, communism) CROSS REFERENCE: *koin, vulg*
mund*	Latin *mundus* (unknown origin)	world	SIMPLE ROOT: mundane (**Synonyms:** earthly, terrestrial; worldly) PREFIXED ROOT: *ante*-: antemundane (*ante*-, before) *trans*-: transmundane (beyond the world or worldly matters) (*trans*-, across) *ultra*-: ultramundane (being beyond the world or the limits of our solar system; beyond life) (*ultra*-, beyond) CROSS REFERENCE: *cosmo*
mur			See *mora* for *demur*.
mur**	Latin *murus*; murare, to provide with walls; (related to *munire*, to fortify) (IE: *mei*, to fortify)	wall	SIMPLE ROOT: mure (same as *immure*), mural, muralist PREFIXED ROOT: *extra*-: extramural (outside the walls of a city, school, or university, etc., as *extramural sports*) (*extra*-, outside) *im*-: immure (to shut up within walls, as in prison; confine; also, seclude or isolate oneself, as she *immured* herself in her studies) (*im*- assimilates *in*-, in) *intra*-: intramural (within the walls of a city, school, or university, etc., as *intramural sports*) (*intra*-, within) NB: Neither *demur* nor *demure* is in this family (see *mora*). CROSS REFERENCE: *mer, part, sept*

Element	From	Meaning	Examples

mus,*
mur
	Latin
	mus
	(IE: *mus*,
	mouse;
	yields
	English
	mouse;
	Sanskrit
	muscatel,
	musk)
		mouse	SIMPLE ROOT:
			mur:
			mure: murex (any of a genus of flesh-eating snails)
			muri: murid [(genus *Muris*), any of a family (*Muridae*) of ro-
			  dents, including the naked-tailed, Old World rats and mice]
			murine (of the *murids*; as a noun, a *murine rodent*)
			mus:
			musc: muscle (literally, little mouse, from the fancied resem-
			  blance of the flexing of certain muscles, as the biceps of the
			  upper arm, to the shape and movements of a mouse) (di-
			  minutive suffix -*cle*)
			muss: mussel (from its resemblance to a mouse; see previous
			  entry)
			must: musteline (a large family of fur-bearing carnivores, in-
			  cluding the weasel, marten, polecat, and mink)
			DISGUISED ROOT COMPOUND: marmot (literally, moun-
			  tain mouse; woodchuck; prairie dog)
			CROSS REFERENCE: *myo*

mut***	Latin
	mutare
	(IE: *meith*,
	to change,
	exchange)
		to change	SIMPLE ROOT:
			muta: mutability, mutable, mutant, mutantum, mutate, muta-
			  tion, mutative
			mutu: mutuum
			PREFIXED ROOT:
			com-: commute, commutate, commutation (*com-*, with, togeth-
			  er)
			im-: immutable (never changing or varying) (*im-* assimilates
			  in-, not)
			per-: permute {permutation} (*per-*, through)
			trans-: transmute {transmutation} (*trans-*, across)
			DOUBLE PREFIXED ROOT:
			incommutable (*in-*, not + *com-*, with, together)
			DISGUISED ROOT: molt
			LATIN PHRASE:
			mutatis mutandis (the necessary changes having been made)
			AMERICAN SPANISH: remuda (exchange of horses; a herd
			  of horses from which ranch hands select their mounts) (*re-*,
			  intensive + *mudar*, to change)
			CROSS REFERENCE: *amoeb, camb, meta*

myc**	Greek
	mykes
	(IE: *meuk*,
	slippery)
		fungus,
		mushroom
			SIMPLE ROOT:
			mycel: mycelium
			mycet: mycetes, mycetism (same as *mycetismus*, poisoning
			  from eating fungi, especially poisonous mushrooms)
			LEADING ROOT COMPOUND:
			myc:
			osis: mycosis (the growth of parasitic fungi on any part of the
			  body; a disease caused by such fungi) {mycotic} (*osis*, condi-
			  tion of)
			mycet:
			hemi: mycethemia (*hemo*, blood + -*ia*, condition of)
			oid: mycetoid (*oid*, similar to)
			oma: mycetoma (plural, *mycetomas*, or *mycetomata*) (*oma*,
			  mass, tumor)

Element	From	Meaning	Examples
myc (cont'd)			*myceto*: cyt: mycetocyte (*cyt*, cell) gen: mycetogenic, mycetogenous (*gen*, producing) zo: mycetozoan (*zo*, animal) *myco*: bacter: mycobacterium (plural, *mycobacteria*) lasm: mycoplasm, mycoplasma (*plasm*, form, shape) logy: mycology (the branch of botany dealing with fungi; all the fungi of a region) (*logy*, study of) protein: mycoprotein rhiz: mycorhiza (an intimate symbiotic association of the mycelium of certain fungi with the *root* cells of some vascular plants, as certain orchids, in which the hyphae often function as root hairs) (*rhiza*, root) TRAILING ROOT COMPOUND: actino: actinomycete (*actino*, rays) asco: ascomycetes (*asco*, bag, bladder) micro: micromycete (*micro*, small) phyco: phycomyces (*phyco*, seaweed) schizo: schizomycetes (*schizo*, split) strepto: streptomycin (*strepto*, twisted) NAMES OF ANTIBIOTICS DERIVED FROM ROOT: aureomycin neomycin tetramycin NOTE: An identically spelled root means mucus; the two roots are ultimately from the same base (see next entry). NO CROSS REFERENCE
myc*	Greek *mykter* (IE: *meuk*, slippery, viscous)	mucus	SIMPLE ROOT: mycteric (of or relating to the nasal cavities) LEADING ROOT COMPOUND: gastr: mycogastritis (*gastr*, belly; *itis*, inflammation of) NOTE: An identically spelled root means fungus; the two roots are ultimately from the same base (see previous entry). CROSS REFERENCE: *blenn, muc, myx*
myel**	Greek *myelos* (IE: *mus*, mouse)	marrow (extended to mean "spinal cord")	ROOT NOTE: The roots for *muscle* and *mouse* (*myo*) as well as *spinal cord* (*myelo*) are the same; all three originated from the root for mouse, *myos*. SIMPLE ROOT: myelic, myelin, myelon (the spinal cord) LEADING ROOT COMPOUND: *myel*: acephal: myelacephalous (*a-*, negative + *cephal*, head) algia: myelalgia (pain in the spinal cord) (*algia*, pain) itis: myelitis (inflammation of the spinal cord or of the bone marrow) (*itis*, inflammation) *myelo*: gram: myelogram (from *graph*, write) EMBEDDED ROOT COMPOUND: osteomyelitis (*osteo*, bone; *itis*, inflammation of) poliomyelitis (*polio*, grey; *itis*, inflammation of) CROSS REFERENCE: *medull*

How forcible are right words. Job VI, 25

444

Element	From	Meaning	Examples
myo**	Greek *mys* (IE: *mus*, mouse)	muscle	ROOT NOTE: The roots for *muscle* and *mouse* (*myo*) as well as *spinal cord* (*myelo*) are the same; all three originated from the root for mouse, *myos*. SIMPLE ROOT: myosin PREFIXED ROOT: a-: amyous (deficient in muscular tissue) (*a-*, negative) *epi*-: epimysium (the sheath of connective tissue surrounding a muscle) (*epi-*, upon) *peri*-: perimysium (connective tissue covering and binding together bundles of muscle fibers) (*peri-*, around) LEADING ROOT COMPOUND: *my*: algia: myalgia (*algia*, pain) asthen: myasthenia (*a-*, without + *sthen*, strength + *-ia*, condition of) aton: myatonia (*a-*, without + *ton*, muscle tone) atroph: myatrophy (*a-*, without + *troph*, nourish) ectom: myectomy (*ec-* from *ex-*, out; *ectom*, surgically remove) ectop: myectopia (*ec-* from *ex-*, out; *topos*, place) odyn: myodynia (*odyn*, pain) oid: myoid (*oid*, similar to) oma: myoma (a tumor consisting of muscle tissue) (*oma*, tumor) *myo*: card: (*card*, heart) myocardia, myocardium myocardiogram, myocardiograph (*gram* from *graph*, write) myocarditis (*itis*, inflammation) cel: myocele (*cele*, hernia) gen: myogenic (*gen*, producing) glob: myoglobin (*glob*, ball) graph: myograph (*graph*, write) logy: myology (*logy*, study of) neur: myoneural (*neur*, nerve) path: myopathy (*path*, disease) tom: myotome (*tom*, cut) ton: myotonia (prolonged muscle spasm, often a manifestation of certain diseases of muscles) (*ton*, stretch) NOTE: Do not confuse this root with *mi/my*, to close, as in *myopia*, literally, to close the eyes. CROSS REFERENCE: *mus*
myx*	Greek *myxa* (IE: *meuk*, slippery, viscous)	mucus, slime	LEADING ROOT COMPOUND: edema: myxedema (*edema*, swelling, tumor) emia: myxemia [*(h)em(o)*, blood; *-emia*, diseased condition of the blood] oid: myxoid (*oid*, similar to) oma: myxoma, myxomatosis (*oma*, tumor + structural *t* + *osis*, diseased condition of) CROSS REFERENCE: *blenn, muc, myc*

445

N

Element	From	Meaning	Examples
narc*	Greek *narkoun*: to benumb (IE: *(s)ner*, to twist, entwine)	stupor	SIMPLE ROOT: narcotic, narcotine, narcotism, narcotization; narcotize LEADING ROOT COMPOUND: *narc*: osis: narcosis (*osis*, condition of) *narco*: analys: narcoanalysis (*ana*- prefixes *lys*, loosen) leps: narcolepsy {narcoleptic} (*leps*, attack, fit, seizure) syn: narcosynthesis (*syn*-, with, prefixes *thesis*, place) PREFIXED TRAILING ROOT COMPOUND: a-: abionarce (inactivity due to infirmity) (*a*-, negative + *bio*, life) CROSS REFERENCE: *dorm*
nas			See *nat* for *nascent*.
nas**	Latin *nasus* (IE: *nas*, nostril)	nose	SIMPLE ROOT: nasa: nasal, nasalis (a small muscle on each side of the nose), nasality, nasalize nasi: nasion (in *craniometry*, the point in the skull at which the suture between the two nasal bones meets the suture between these and the frontal bone) nasu: nasua (a genus of mammals, consisting of the coatimundis; from Tupi *cua*, cincture + *tim*, nose + *mondi*, solitary; coatimundis have long noses; in addition, the males stay to themselves, thus their name) nasus (medical terminology for *nose*, as well as the prolongation on the front of the head of a crane fly or of certain termites) nasute (also *nasutus*, both meaning having a well-developed, or large, *proboscis*; also a member of a caste of highly modified soldier termites in which the top of the head is drawn out into a snoutlike process from which a sticky fluid can be ejected) LEADING ROOT COMPOUND: *nas*: itis: nasitis (*itis*, inflammation of) turt: nasturtium (literally, twisted nose, from the flower's acrid smell) (from *torque*, twist) *naso*: logy: nasology (the scientific study of noses) (*logy*, study of) sinus: nasosinusitis (*sinus*, a bend, fold + *itis*, inflammation of) TRAILING ROOT COMPOUND: palato: palatonasal (*palate*, roof of mouth) FRENCH MESHED COMPOUND: nasonnement (a nasal quality of the voice) (*naso* + *son*, sound) DISGUISED ROOT: *Nez Percé* (French for pierced nose; an American Indian tribe living in Idaho, Washington, and Oregon; however, there is no evidence that this tribe practiced nose-piercing)

Element	From	Meaning	Examples
nas (cont'd)			*pince-nez* (literally, nose-pincher; hence eyeglasses without temples, kept in place by a spring gripping the bridge of the nose) ENGLISH: nosegay (a bouquet of flowers pleasant to smell) NOTE: Do not not confuse this root with *nasci*, to be born, as in *nascent* (see next entry). CROSS REFERENCE: *rhin*
nat,*** nas	Latin *nasci*: to be born (IE: *gen*, to beget, produce)	birth	SIMPLE ROOT: *nas*: nascent {nascence, or *nascency*}, nasion *nat*: nata: natal (of or connected to one's birth; dating from birth; native: said of a place) nati: nation, national, native (**Synonyms**: indigenous, aboriginal, endemic), nativity (capitalized, Christmas) natu: natural, naturalism, naturalize, nature PREFIXED ROOT: *nas*: *re-*: renascence (capitalized, *Renaissance*), renascent (*re-*, again) *sub-*: subnascent (*sub-*, under) *nat*: *ad-*: adnate (in *botany* and *zoology*, congenitally joined together: said of unlike parts), adnation (*ad-*, to, toward) *ag-*: agnate (*ag-* is a variant of *ad-*, to) *ante-*: antenatal (*ante-*, before) *co-*: cognate (related by family, e.g., English *apple* and German *Apfel* are cognate *words*; *English*, *German*, and *Dutch* are cognate *languages*) (*co-*, with, together + *gnatus*, past participle of *gnasci*, older form of *nasci*, to be born) *con-*: connate, connatural (*con-*, with, together) *de-*: denationalize, denaturalize, denaturant, denature (*de-*, opposite of) *e-*: enate (elides *ex-*, out of, from) *in-*: innate (**Synonyms**: inborn, congenital, hereditary) (*in-*, in) *inter-*: international (*inter-*, between) *peri-*: perinatal (Greek *peri-*, around) *post-*: postnatal (*post-*, after) *pre-*: prenatal (*pre-*, before) *pro-*: pronatalism (any attitude or policy that encourages childbearing) [*pronate, pronation*, and *pronator*, however, are from *prone*, which itself is an extension of *pro*, before, either in place or time] (*pro-*, for) *super-*: supernatural, supernaturalism (*super-*, beyond) TRAILING ROOT COMPOUND: neo: neonatal, neonatalogist (Greek *neo*, new) DISGUISED ROOT: eigne [eldest, firstborn] [modification of Middle French *ainsné*; from Old French *ainz*, before (from Latin *ante-*) + *né*, born] naif (or *naïf*; a naive person) naissance (an original issue or growth), naissant (in *heraldry*, rising or issuing from the middle of an ordinary in the instance of an animal with only the upper part visible)

Element	From	Meaning	Examples
nat (cont'd)			naïve (**Synonyms:** ingenuous, artless, unsophisticated), naïveté (also, *naiveness*, or *naïveness*; naivety, or *naïvety*) né (also, *ne*; born; used before the original name of a man who has changed his name, e.g., George Orwell né Eric Blair) nee (also, *née*; born; used to indicate the maiden name of a married woman, as Mrs. Helen Jones, née Smith) neif (also, *naïf*, above) puisne (chiefly British; of lower rank; junior, as in appointment; as a noun, an associate justice as distinguished from chief justice; pronounced the same as *puny*; see *Doublets* below) puny (see *Doublets* below) DOUBLETS: naif:naive puisne:puny FRENCH: *au naturel* (in the natural state; hence, naked; also, prepared simply: said of food) PROPER NAME: Natalie INTELLECTUAL MOVEMENT: Renaissance (the rebirth of learning; a period of history that lasted about 300 years between the Middle Ages and modern times) FRENCH PROPER NAME: Noël (also, the French name for *Christmas*) PLACENAME: Natal, South Africa (discovered on Christmas Day, 1497, by the Portuguese navigator Vasco da Gama) CROSS REFERENCE: *gen, par*
nat*	Latin *natare* (IE: *(s)na*, to float)	to swim, float	SIMPLE ROOT: natant (swimming or floating, especially floating on the surface of the water), natation, natatorial (also, *natatory*) natatorium (an indoors swimming pool) PREFIXED ROOT: super-: supernatant (floating on the surface) (*super-*, above) NO CROSS REFERENCE
naus,* **naut**	Greek *naus*: ship (IE: *naus*, boat)	ship, sailor	SIMPLE ROOT: *naus*: nausea (originally, seasickness), nauseate, nauseous (causing nausea; specifically, sickening; disgusting) *naut*: nautical, nautilus (literally, sailor) LEADING ROOT COMPOUND: oid: nautiloid (any of a subclass of cephlapods with chambered, coiled, or straight external shells: the nautilus is the only remaining representative) TRAILING ROOT COMPOUND: aero: aeronautical (*aero*, air) astro: astronaut (*astro*, star) DISGUISED ROOT: nauplius (originally, a kind of shellfish said to sail in its shell as in a ship; the first larval stage in the development of certain crustaceans) LATIN PHRASE: *ad nauseam* (literally, to nausea; to the point of disgust; to a sickening extreme) LITERARY CHARACTER: Nausicaä (in Homer's *Odyssey*, King Alcinoüs's daughter, who discovers and secures safe passage for, the shipwrecked Odysseus) ENGLISH: noise (**Synonyms:** din, uproar, clamor) CROSS REFERENCE: *nav*

Element	From	Meaning	Examples
nav**	Latin *navis*: ship (IE: *naus*, boat)	ship, sail	SIMPLE ROOT: nave: nave (of a church), navette navic: navicular, navicula, navicella navig: navigable, navigate, navigation navy: navy {naval} PREFIXED ROOT: *circum*-: circumnavigate (*circum*-, around) DISGUISED ROOT: nacelle (a streamlined enclosure on an aircraft, especially that which houses an engine) (diminutive of *navis*) nef (French; clock in the form of a ship) NB: Do not confuse *naval* with Old English *navel*, the umbilicus. CROSS REFERENCE: *naus/naut*
ne-,*** neg-	Latin	not	EXTENDED PREFIX: negate, negation, negative PREFIXED ROOT: *ne*-: cess: (from *cedere*, to yield) necessary (**Synonyms**: essential, indispensable, requisite), necessitate, necessitous necessity (**Synonyms**: need, exigency, requisite) far: nefarious (extremely wicked; villainous; iniquitous) (*far*, law, see *fab*) sci: nescient (not knowing; ignorant) {nescience} (*scire*, to know) uter: neuter (literally, not either; neither) (*uter*, either) *neg*-: lect: neglect (**Synonyms**: omit, overlook, disregard) {neglectful; see synonyms at *negligent*, next entry} (from *legere*, to gather) lig: negligee, negligence, negligent (**Synonyms**: remiss, neglectful, derelict) (see *neglect*) oti: negotiable, negotiate {negotiatory} (*otium*, ease) DOUBLE PREFIXED ROOT: ab<u>neg</u>ate, ab<u>neg</u>ation (*ab*-, away + *aio*, I say) HYPHENATED COMPOUND: self-abnegation SPANISH: renegade, renegado (*re*-, again + *negare*, to deny) DISGUISED ROOT: nice (from *ne*- + *scire*, to know; originally, not knowing; ignorant) CROSS REFERENCE: *a-, ana-, de-, dis-, in-*
necr*	Greek *nekros* (IE: *nek*, physical death; corpse)	corpse	LEADING ROOT COMPOUND: *necr*: ops: necropsy (an examination of a dead body; post-mortem; autopsy) (*opsis*, sight, view) ose: necrosis (*osis*, condition) *necro*: bio: necrobiosis (the process of decay and death of body cells) (*bio*, life + *osis*, condition) latry: necrolatry (*latry*, worship of) logy: necrology (a list of those who have died within a certain period, as that in a newspaper; a death notice; an obituary) mancy: necromancy (*mancy*, divination)

Element	From	Meaning	Examples
necr (cont'd)			phag: necrophagia (the eating of dead bodies, especially, the practice of feeding on carrion) (*phag*, eat) phil: necrophilia (erotic attraction to corpses) (*phila*, love of) phob: necrophobia (an abnormal fear of death; an abnormal fear of dead bodies) (*phobia*, morbid fear of) polis: necropolis (a cemetery, especially one belonging to an ancient city) (*polis*, city) tom: necrotomy (the dissection of corpses; also, the surgical removal of dead bone) (*tom*, cut) RELATED WORD: nectar [literally, that which overcomes death; a drink held to confer immortality upon the gods; see further under *noc, nox, nic, nec* (Sanskrit entry)] CROSS REFERENCE: *leth, mort*
nect,*** nex	Latin *nectare* (IE: *ned*, to bind, tie; yields English net)	to tie, bind	ROOT NOTE: This root is derived from the IE root *ned*, to twist together, from which Latin *nodus*, knot, is derived, as well as French *denouement* (also, *dénouement*), and *node*. SIMPLE ROOT: nexum (a formal contract in Roman law) nexus (a bond, especially between members of a series or group; in *Roman law*, a person bound by a contract of nexum) PREFIXED ROOT: *nect*: *con*-: connect (**Synonyms:** link, associate, consolidate), connection (*con*- assimilates *com*-, with, together) *nex*: *ad*-: adnexa (accessory parts or appendages of an organ) (*ad*-, to, toward) *an*-: annex, annexion (*an*- assimilates *ad*-, to, toward) *con*-: connex, connexity (*con*- assimilates *com*-, with, together) CROSS REFERENCE: *cinct, dem, lig, strict/string*
nema*	Greek *nematos* (IE: *(s)nei*, to sew, spin)	thread	ROOT NOTE: From the genitive *nematos*, the root means that which is spun; therefore, thread; akin to *nein*, from which *needle* is derived. SIMPLE ROOT: nema (clipped form of *nematode*, which see below), nematic LEADING ROOT COMPOUND: *nemat*: helminth: nemathelminth (*helminth*, worm) ode: nematode [any of a phylum (Nematoda) of worms, often parasites of animals and plants, with long, cylindrical, unsegmented bodies and a heavy cuticle, as the hookworm, pinworm, etc.] (from *oid*, similar to) *nemato*: cyst: nematocyst (*cyst*, bladder, sac) logy: nematology (*logy*, study of) NB: Even though *nemertean*, from *Nemertes*, name of a sea nymph, refers to a phylum of marine worms, *nemertean* itself is not derived from this root, but rather from *nemertes*, unerring (reason unclear). CROSS REFERENCE: *fil*

451

Element	From	Meaning	Examples
neo***	Greek *neos* (IE: *newos,* new)	new, recent, young; in *geology,* "the chronologically last subdivision of priod)	SIMPLE ROOT: neon (a rare, colorless, and inert chemical element; symbol: Ne) neoteric (recent; new; newly invented; as a noun, a modern person; one accepting new ideas and practices) LEADING ROOT COMPOUND: anthrop: neoanthropic (*anthropo*, man) cen: Neocene (from *kainos,* also new) class: neoclassic {neoclassicism} (Latin *classis,* division) dym: neodymium [from *neo + (di)dymium,* chemical symbol, Nd] (*didymos,* twin) gaea: Neogaea (the Neotropical area of the earth, considered as one of the primary elements) (*gaia, geo,* earth) gen: neogenesis{neogenetic} (*gen,* producing) impress: neoimpressionism (*im-* prefixes *press*) latin: Neo-Latin (Modern Latin; the Latin that has come into use since the Renaissance, or about 1500 A.D., chiefly in scientific literature; Modern Latin has words formed from both Latin and Greek) lith: neolithic (*lithos,* stone) log: neologism (a new word or a new meaning for an established word), neologize, neology (*logos,* word) morph: neomorph (*morph,* shape, form) myc: neomycin (an antibiotic drug) (*myc,* fungus) nat: (*natus,* born) neonate {neonatal} neonatologist (a medical doctor specializing in the care of newborn babies) (*logy,* study of) phyt: neophyte (a convert, especially, a newly baptized member of the early Christian Church; **Synonyms:** amateur, novice, tyro) (*phyton,* plant) plas: neoplasia, neoplasm, neoplastic, neoplasticism, neoplasty (*plas,* form, shape) ten: neoteny (in *zoology,* the retention of juvenile characteristics in the adult; the development of adult features in the juvenile, as the attainment of sexual maturity in some larvae) (*ten,* stretch) zo: Neozoic (early name for Cenozoic) (*zo,* animal) TRAILING ROOT COMPOUND: miso: misoneism (hatred of innovation or change) (*miso,* hate) GEOLOGICAL PERIOD: Neocene (the period when mammals evolved to relatively modern types) (*cene,* recent) CROSS REFERENCE: *ceno, nov*
nephr*	Greek *nephros*	kidney	SIMPLE ROOT: nephridium (diminutive of *nephros*); nephrite (a semiprecious stone once worn as a supposed cure for kidney ailments), nephritic; nephron LEADING ROOT COMPOUND: itis: nephritis (inflammation of the kidneys) (*itis,* inflammation) oid: nephroid (resembling a kidney) (*oid,* similar to) oma: nephroma (tumor, or one, of renal tissue) (*oma,* tumor) CROSS REFERENCE: *ren*

Element	From	Meaning	Examples
nerv**	Latin *nervus* (IE: *(s)neu*, to twist, wind)	sinew, nerve	SIMPLE ROOT: nerva: nerval, nervate, nervature nerve: nerve (**Synonyms:** temerity, audacity, effrontery), nerved nerveless (without strength, vigor, force, or courage; weak; in-ert; unnerved; not nervous; cool; controlled; in *biology*, without nerves) nervi: nerving (in *veterinary medicine*, removal of part of a nerve trunk, as when it is chronically inflamed), nervine nervo: nervose, nervosism, nervosity, nervous (originally, strong, robust; full of nerves) nervu: nervule, nervulose, nervuration, nervure, nervus (plural, *nervi*) PREFIXED ROOT: e-: enervate (originally, to enliven; now, to debilitate (*e*- elides *ex*-, out) in-: innervate [to supply (a body part) with nerves; to stimu-late (a nerve or body part)] (*in*-, in) LEADING ROOT COMPOUND: duct: nerviduct (from *ducere*, to lead) mot: nervimotility, nervimotor (*mot*, move) CROSS REFERENCE: *neur*
nes*	Greek *nesos*	island	LEADING ROOT COMPOUND: gae: nesogaean (or, *nesogean*) (*gaea*, earth) TRAILING ROOT COMPOUND: chers: chersonese (a peninsula) (*cheros*, dry land) indo: Indonesia (Indian islands) (*indo*, India) mel: Melanesia (*mela*, black) micro: Micronesia (*micro*, small) pel: Peloponnesus (from Pelops, who in Greek mythology, is killed and served to the gods as food by his father, but later is restored to life by them; a peninsula forming the southern part of the mainland of Greece) (*pel*, dark + *ops*, face) poly: Polynesia (*poly*, many) CROSS REFERENCE: *insul*
neth*	Germanic *nether* (IE: *ni*, down)	lower	SIMPLE ROOT: nether PLACENAME: The Netherlands (which is below sea level, and was reclaimed from the sea by man-made dikes) [The Dutch are fond of saying that God made the earth but that the Hollanders made the Netherlands.] ENGLISH PREFIXED ROOT: beneath CROSS REFERENCE: *hypo, infer, infra, sub*
neur**	Greek *neuron* (IE: *(s)neu*, to twist, wind)	nerve	SIMPLE ROOT: neural, neuric, neuron PREFIXED ROOTS AND COMPOUNDS: apo-: aponeurosis (*apo*-, away + *osis*, condition of) epi-: epineurium (the layer of connective tissue surrounding a peripheral nerve) (*epi*-, upon) peri-: perineurium (*peri*-, around) sub-: subneural (*sub*-, under) LEADING ROOT COMPOUND: *neur*: osis: neurosis {neurotic) (*osis*, condition)

Element	From	Meaning	Examples
neur (cont'd)			*neuro:* logy: neurology (*logy*, study of) tom: neurotomy (*tom*, cut) CROSS REFERENCE: *nerv*
nid*	Latin *nidus* (IE: *nizdos*; nest; from *ni*, down + *sed*, sit)	nest	SIMPLE ROOT: nida: nidal, nidamental (literally, materials for a nest; relating to or producing a capsule or covering for an egg or mass of eggs) nidation, nidatory nide: nide (chiefly British; a nest or brood, especially of pheasants) nidu: nidulant (lying free in a cavity), nidularia, nidulate, nidulation, nidus (a nest for the eggs of insects, spiders, small animals; a breeding place) LEADING ROOT COMPOUND: *nidi:* col: nidicolous (reared for a time in the nest) (*cola*, inhabitant) fic: nidificant, nidificate {nidification} (from *facere*, to make) fug: nidifugous (fleeing the nest soon after hatching; describes most shore birds, the grouse, and the killdeer) (*fug*, flee) fy: nidify (from *facere*, to make, do) *nido:* log: nidologist (one who specializes in the study of birds' nests) (*logy*, study of) DISGUISED ROOT: eyas (a nestling hawk or falcon, especially one to be trained for falconry) nest (literally, to sit down) nestle (originally, to nest; to settle down comfortably and snugly; partly hidden, as a house among trees) niche (an ornamental recess, usually set in a wall, for a statue or other decoration; in *ecology*, the particular role of an individual species or organism in its community and its environment) NO CROSS REFERENCE
nihil*	Latin *nihil* (contraction of *ni*, nothing + *hilum*, thing)	nothing	SIMPLE ROOT: nil (contraction of *nihil*), nihil, nihilism, nihility PREFIXED ROOT: an-: annihilate (**Synonyms:** destroy, demolish, raze), annihilation (*an-* assimilates *ad-*, toward) LEADING ROOT COMPOUND: fy: nihilify (from *facere*, to make, do) LEGAL TERMS: *nihil debet* (he/she owes nothing) *nihil dicit* (he/she says nothing) *nihil habet* (he/she has nothing) CROSS REFERENCE: *null*
niv,* **nev**	Latin *nivus*	snow	SIMPLE ROOT: nival, nivation, niveous, niviculous STATE: Nevada MOUNTAIN RANGE: Sierra Nevada FRENCH: névé (Valais dialect; the upper part of a glacier, where the snow turns into ice; a field of snow at the head of a glacier; the granular snow typically found in such a field) NO CROSS REFERENCE

454

Element	From	Meaning	Examples

noc,***
nox
	Latin
	nox
	(IE: *nekwt,*
	nokwt,
	night)
		night	SIMPLE ROOT:
			noctui: noctuid (a large family of moths that fly at night)
			noctul: noctule (any of a genus of bats; especially, a large
			   brown species of Europe and the British Isles)
			noctur: nocturn, nocturnal (in *botany*, having blossoms that
			   open at *night*, as some flowers), nocturnality, nocturne
			LEADING ROOT COMPOUND:
			noct:
			amb: noctambulism (also, *noctambulation*; same as *somnam-*
			   bulism) (*ambulare,* to walk, move about)
			ur: nocturia (also called *nycturia*; bedwetting) (*ur,* urine)
			nocti:
			diurn: noctidiurnal (*diurnal*, pertaining to the day; from *dia,*
			   day)
			flor: noctiflorous (*flor,* flower)
			luc: noctiluca, noctilucence, noctilucent (as a *noctilucent*
			   cloud, a luminous cloud seen at night at a height of about
			   275,000 feet) (*luc,* light)
			vag: noctivagant, noctivagation (*vagare,* to wander)
			TRAILING ROOT COMPOUND:
			equi: equinox (when day and *night* are of *equal* length; the *ver-*
			   nal equinox and the *autumnal equinox,* occurring around
			   March 21 and September 21, respectively) (*equi,* equal)
			ITALIAN: *notturno* (night piece; designation for *nocturne*)
			PHRASE: nocturnal emission (an involuntary discharge of
			   semen during sleep often accompanied by an erotic dream;
			   also called *wet dream*)
			INTERDISCIPLINARY: nocturne (in *art*, a painting of a
			   night scene; also called *night piece*; in *music*, a dreamy,
			   pensive composition, especially for the piano, of a romantic
			   or dreamy character thought appropriate to night)
			CROSS REFERENCE: *nyct*

noc,**
nec,
nic,
nox
	Latin
	nocere
	(IE: *nek,*
	physical
	death;
	corpse)
		to harm,
		kill
			SIMPLE ROOT: nocuous (noxious), noxious (nocuous)
			PREFIXED ROOT:
			nec:
			inter-: internecine (mutually destructive or harmful, as *in-*
			   ternecine warfare) (*inter-,* between)
			nic:
			per-: pernicious (**Synonyms:** baneful, deleterious, detrimen-
			   tal) (*per-,* thoroughly)
			noc:
			in-: innocence, innocent (**Synonyms: 1)** sinless, virtuous;
			   2) impecaable, sptless, immaculate), innocuous (that does
			   not injure or harm; harmless; see *innoxious*) (*in-,* not)
			nox:
			in-: innoxious (not noxious; harmless; innocuous) (*in-,* not)
			ob-: obnoxious (**Synonyms:** hateful, odious, repugnant)
			   (*ob-,* against)
			LEADING ROOT COMPOUND:
			cept: nociceptive, nociceptor (of, causing, or reacting to pain)
			   (from *capere,* to take, hold)
			DISGUISED ROOT: nuisance (explore as a legal term)

Element	From	Meaning	Examples
noc (cont'd)			SANSKRIT: nectar (overcoming death, thus the drink of the gods; their food was *ambrosia*, from *a-*, not, *brotos*, mortal; thus, immortal; thus *ambrosia and nectar*, the food and the drink of the gods and immortals) (from *tarati*, he overcomes) nectarine CROSS REFERENCE: *cide*
nod*	Latin *nodus* (IE: *ned*, to twist together)	knot	SIMPLE ROOT: node: node nodi: nodical (as a *nodical month*) nodo: nodose {nodosity} nodu: nodule {nodular, nodulose, nodulous}, nodus (complication; difficulty; knotty situation, as in a play) PREFIXED ROOT: *inter-*: internode (*inter-*, between) FRENCH LITERARY TERM: denouement (also *dénouement*; literally, the "unknotting" of a plot, or the unraveling of the complication in a story) DISGUISED ROOT: lanyard, noose INTERDISCIPLINARY: node (in *anatomy*, a knotty, localized swelling; protuberance; in *astronomy*, either of the two diametrically opposite points at which the orbit of a celestial body intersects a reference plane, as the ecliptic; in *botany*, that part, or joint, of a stem from which a leaf starts to grow; in *geometry*, the point where a continuous curve crosses or meets itself; in *physics*, the point, line, or surface of a vibrating object, as a string, virtually free of vibration) internode (in *botany*, the section of a plant between two successive nodes or joints; in *zoology*, the part between two nodes, as a segment of a nerve fiber) CROSS REFERENCE: *gangli, nect/nex*
nom***	Greek *nomas* (IE: *nem*, to assign, distribute, take, arrange)	law, order, custom, portion, usage	SIMPLE ROOT: nomad, nomadic (see *Webster's New World*), nome (one meaning), nomism, nomisma PREFIXED ROOT: *anti-*: (against) antinomian (capitalized, a believer in the Christian doctrine that faith alone, not obedience to the moral law, is necessary for salvation) antinomy (a contradiction or inconsistency between two apparently reasonable principles or laws, or between conclusions drawn from them) LEADING ROOT COMPOUND: *nom*: arch: nomarch (*arch*, rule) *nomo*: graph: nomograph, nomography (*graph*, write) logy: nomology (the science of law and lawmaking) (*logy*, study of) thet: nomothetic (also, *nomothetical*) (from *thesis*, place) TRAILING ROOT COMPOUND: anthropo: anthroponomy (*anthropo*, man)

456

Element	From	Meaning	Examples
nom (cont'd)			astro: astronomer, astronomy (*astro*, star) auto: autonomic (in *botany*, resulting from internal causes), autonomist, autonomous, autonomy (*auto*, self) bi: binomial (a mathematical expression consisting of two terms connected by a plus or minus sign; also, a two-word scientific name of a plant or animal, the first capitalized and the second, lower case; the first term designates the genus; the second, the species, e.g., *Juglans regia*, royal walnut; the soft-shelled walnut; California walnut) (*bi*, two) deutero: Deuteronomy (the second iteration of the Ten Commandments; the first iteration is recorded in Exodus 20) (*deutero*, second) eco: economy (management of one's own house) (from *oiko*, house) hetero: heteronomous (*hetero*, different) metro: metronome {metronomic} (*metro*, measure) mono: monomial [*mono*, one + (*bi*)*nomial*] taxo: taxonomy (*taxo*, arrangement) DISGUISED ROOT: numismatics, nummular GREEK MYTHOLOGY: Nemesis, goddess of retributive justice, vengeance INTERDISCIPLINARY: monomial (in *algebra*, consisting of only one term; in *biology*, consisting of only one word: said of a taxonomic name) CROSS REFERENCE: *jud/jus; lex/leg*
nom***	Latin *nomen* (IE: *(o)nomn*, name; yields English name)	name	SIMPLE ROOT: nomen (the second of the three names of an ancient Roman, following the praenomen and preceding the cognomen, e.g., Marcus *Tullius* Cicero), nomial, nominal, nominalism, nominate, nominative, nominee PREFIXED ROOT: *ad-*: adnominal (in *grammar*, an adjective, especially one used as a noun, e.g., "the *lame*, the *halt*, and the *blind*," are *ad-nominals* or *adnouns* (*ad-*, to, toward) *ag-*: agnomen (*ag-*, a variant of *ad-*, to, toward) *cog-*: cognomen (*cog-*, a variant of *com-*, with, together) *de-*: denominate, denomination {denominative}, denominator (*de-*, down) *ig-*: ignominious, ignominy (loss of one's reputation; shame and dishonor; disgraceful, or contemptible behavior, quality, or act) (*ig-*, a variant of *in-*, not) *in-*: innominate (not named) (*in-*, not) *mis-*: misnomer (Middle English *mis-*, bad; wrong) *prae-*: praenomen (the first or personal name of an ancient Roman, preceding the nomen and cognomen, e.g., *Marcus* Tullius Cicero) (*prae-*, before) *pro-*: pronominal (from *pronoun*, below) (*pro-*, for) LEADING ROOT COMPOUND: clat: nomenclator (in Roman times, a servant who accompanied his master, telling him the names of the persons whom they met), nomenclature (from *calare*, to call) DISGUISED ROOT: noun (*names* places, things, persons, and concepts)

457

Element	From	Meaning	Examples
nom (cont'd)			PREFIXED DISGUISED ROOT: *ad-*: adnoun (in *grammar*, an adjective, especially one used as a noun: as "the *lame*, the *halt*, and the *blind*") (*ad-*, toward) *pro-*: pronoun (for the noun; in place of the noun) (*pro-*, for) *re-*: renown (literally, to name again; make famous) (*re-*, again) DISGUISED LEADING ROOT COMPOUND: cup: nuncupative (oral, *not written*, said especially of wills) (from *capere*, to take) LATIN PHRASE: *sine nomine* (without a name) FRENCH PHRASES: *nom de plume, nom de guerre* LATIN-ENGLISH HYBRID: surname (the family name, or last name, as distinguished from a given name; also a descriptive name or epithet added to a person's given name, e.g., Ivan the Terrible; Napoleon, the Little Corporal) (from *super-, supra-*, above, beyond, over) CROSS REFERENCE: *onoma, onym*
non***	Latin (*ne*, negative + *oinom*, one)	not, negative	NOTE: This element consists of *ne-*, negative article + *oinom*, one, and is used to give a negative force, especially to nouns and adjectives; *non-* is less emphatic than *in-* and *un-*, which often give an opposite or reverse meaning or force, e.g., *nonhuman, inhuman; non-American, un-American*. Only sample words are given, classified according to nouns or adjectives. NOUNS: chalanc: nonchalance (see adjective form below) combat: noncombatant ego: nonego entity: nonentity interven: nonintervention plus: nonplus sens: nonsense suit: nonsuit ADJECTIVES: align: nonaligned chalant: nonchalant [from obsolete French *nonchaloir*, to lack warmth (of heart); *chaloir* from Latin *calere*, to be warm] descript: nondescript (that which cannot be described) ferr: nonferrous par: nonpareil plus: nonplused (or *nonplussed*) resist: nonresistant restrict: nonrestrictive sect: nonsectarian sens: nonsensical LATIN PHRASES: *non compos mentis* (not of sound mind; mentally incapable of handling one's own affairs; often shortened to *non compos*) *non obstante* (translated notwithstanding; from use in medieval legal clauses permitting the king certain actions notwithstanding statutes to the contrary; thus, despite a law, ruling, etc.)

458

Element	From	Meaning	Examples
non- (cont'd)			*non placet* (it does not please; used in casting a negative vote)
			non possumus (we cannot, signifying the impossibility of doing a particular thing)
			non prosequitur (he/she does not prosecute; in *law*, a judgment entered against a plaintiff who fails to appear at the court proceedings of his/her suit or fails to do any other thing procedurally necessary to his/her suit; abbreviated *non pros.*)
			non sequitur (it does not follow; in *logic*, a conclusion or inference which does not follow from the premises; extended to mean a remark having no bearing on what has just been said)
			MUSIC TERM: *non troppo* (Italian; not too much; moderately: a direction to the performer, as in *allegro non troppo*, fast, but not too fast)
			CROSS REFERENCE: *a-, an-, de-, dis-/di-/dif-, in-/il-/im-/ir-, ne-, un-*
nona			See *nov* for *nonagenarian.*
noo,*	Greek	mind (thoughts)	SIMPLE ROOT:
noum,	*noos,*		*noum*: noumenon (in *Kantian philosophy*, a thing as it is in itself; unable to be known through perception but postulated as the intelligible ground of a phenomenon: opposed to *phenomenon*), noumenal, noumenism
nous	*nous*;		
	from		
	noein,		*nous*: nous (in *philosophy*, mind, understanding, reason, intellect)
	to perceive		PREFIXED ROOT:
			a-: anoesia, anoesis, anoia (*a-*, not)
			dia-: dianoetic (of or proceeding from logical reasoning rather than intuition) (*dia-*, through, across)
			para-: paranoia, paranoid (characterized by extreme suspiciousness, grandiose delusions, or delusions of persecution) (*para-*, alongside)
			LEADING ROOT COMPOUND:
			klept: nookleptia (an obsession that one's thoughts are being stolen by others) (*klept*, steal)
			logy: noology, noological (*logy*, study of)
			scop: nooscopic (*scope*, view)
			spher: noosphere (the biosphere as modified by the activities of the human mind) (*sphere*, ball, globe)
			DISGUISED ROOT: noesis {noetic}
			CROSS REFERENCE: *ment, phren, psych*
norm***	Latin	rule	SIMPLE ROOT:
	norma:		norm (**Synonyms**: average, mean, median)
	carpenter's		normal (also, *normalcy, normality*; **Synonyms**: regular, typical, natural)
	square		
	(IE: *gen,*		normalize, normative
	gno,		PREFIXED ROOT:
	to know)		*ab-*: abnormal (**Synonyms**: irregular, anomalous, unnatural), abnormity (*ab-*, away)
			e-: enormity (outrageous or heinous character; atrociousness), enormous (**Synonyms**: immense, huge, gigantic) {enormousness} (*e-* elides *ex-*, out)
			PLACENAMES: Normal (Alabama, Illinois)
			NB: *Norman* is literally north man.
			CROSS REFERENCE: *rect, reg*

Element	From	Meaning	Examples
nost*	Greek *nostos*: return home	home	LEADING ROOT COMPOUND: *nost*: algia: nostalgia (the longing, or the ache or pain to return home) (*alg*, pain) *nosto*: logy: nostology (literally, to return home; but actually refers to *gerontology*, the study of old age) (*logy*, study of) mania: nostomania CROSS REFERENCE: *dom*
not**	Latin *notare* (IE: *gen,* *gno,* to know, apprehend)	to mark, note	SIMPLE ROOT: nota: notabilia, notable, notarize, notary {notarial}, notation note: note, noted (**Synonyms:** famous, renowned, celebrated), noteless noti: notice (**Synonyms:** discern, perceive, distinguish) noticeable (**Synonyms:** remarkable, outstanding, conspicuous) notion (**Synonyms:** idea, concept, conception) notional (imaginary; in *grammar*, having full *lexical*, as distinguished from *relational*, meaning) noto: notoriety, notorious (see synonyms at *noted*, above) PREFIXED ROOT: *an*-: annotate (*an*- assimilates *ad*-, to, toward) *con*-: connote, connotation (*con*- assimilates *com*-, with) *de*-: denote {denotation, denotative} (*de*-, down) LEADING ROOT COMPOUND: fi: notifiable, notification (from *facere*, to make, do) fy: notify (**Synonyms:** inform, acquaint, apprise) (from *facere*, to make, do) TRAILING ROOT COMPOUND: protho: prothonotary (in the Roman Catholic Church, a designated person in the Vatican who records important pontifical events; also, a chief clerk in any of various law courts) (*protho* is a respelling of *proto*, first) LATIN PHRASE: *nota bene* (note well; abbreviated NB) NO CROSS REFERENCE
nounc			See *nunci* for *announce*.
nov**	Latin *novus* (IE: *newos,* new)	new	SIMPLE ROOT: nova: nova, novalia, novation (in *law*, the substitution of a new obligation or contract for an old one by the mutual agreement of all parties concerned), novative, novator, novatory nove: novel (**Synonyms:** new, modern, original), novelty novi: novice (see synonyms at *neophyte*, under *neo*), novitiate, novity PREFIXED ROOT: *in*-: innovate, innovation, innovator (*in*-, in) *re*-: renovation, renovate (**Synonyms:** renew, restore, refresh) (*re*-, again) LATIN WORDS AND PHRASES: *novum* *de novo* (anew; once more, again)

Element	From	Meaning	Examples
nov (cont'd)			*Novus ordo seculorum* (A new order of the ages, motto appearing on the United States Great Seal) FRENCH PHRASES: *nouveau riche* (newly rich; a person who has only recently become rich: often connoting tasteless ostentation, lack of culture, etc.) *nouveau roman* *nouvelle cuisine* (new cuisine; a style of French cooking that uses a minimum of fat and starch and emphasizes light sauces and the use of very fresh ingredients, often in unusual combinations prepared simply and served artistically arranged on the plate) ITALIAN: novella (a short prose narrative, usually with a moral and often satiric, as any of the tales in Boccaccio, characterized by epigrammatic terseness and point, as in *Decameron*; also, any short novel; novelette) TYPES OF STARS: nova, supernova MEDICINE TRADEMARK: Novocain (a trademark for the anesthetic *procaine hydrochloride*) PLACENAME: Nova Scotia (New Scotland) CROSS REFERENCE: *ceno, neo*
nov,* nona	Latin *novem* (IE: *newo*, new; see *Webster's* *New* *World*)	nine	SIMPLE ROOT: *nov*: November (the *ninth* month in the early Roman calendar), novena (in the Roman Catholic Church, a prayer for a particular purpose for nine days) *nona*: nonagenarian (ninety; ninety years old) nones nonillion LEADING ROOT COMPOUND: gon: nonagon (*gon*, angle) DISGUISED ROOT: noon (now 12 midday; originally, designated the *ninth* canonical hour, which was nine hours after sunrise, or 3 p.m.; the service was later changed to midday, but the name remained unchanged) none (pronounced *nohn*; the fifth of the canonical hours) CROSS REFERENCE: *ennea*
nub,* nup	Latin *nubere*: to marry a man (IE: *sneubh*, to woo)	to marry, to woo	SIMPLE ROOT: *nub*: nubile (marriageable) *nup*: nuptial (of marriage or a wedding; of or having to do with mating) PREFIXED ROOT: *nub*: con-: connubial (*con*- assimilates *com*-, with, together) *nup*: pre-: prenuptial (in *zoology*, before mating) (*pre*-, before) NOTE: Do not confuse this root with *nubilis*, from *nubes*, a cloud, thus *nubilous*. CROSS REFERENCE: *gam*

Poverty in words is a serious handicap. Through inadequate vocabulary, authority is lost.
The reader or listener loses faith in the communicator's right to treat the subject.
Joseph G. Brin

Element	From	Meaning	Examples
nucl**	Latin *nux* (IE: *kneu*, lump, nut; from *ken*, to squeeze together; yields English nut)	nut, kernel (extended to mean "a spherical body within a cell")	SIMPLE ROOT: nuclea: nuclear (of, like or forming a nucleus; of or relating to atomic nuclei, as *nuclear energy*), nucleate {nucleation} nuclei: nucleine nucleo: nucleolus (also, *nucleole*) plural, *nucleoli*) {nucleolar} nucleu: nucleus (plural, *nuclei*) PREFIXED ROOT: *pro*-: pronucleus (*pro*-, before) LEADING ROOT COMPOUND: *nucle*: oid: nucleoid (*oid*, similar to) os: nucleose, nucleosis (*ose*, *osis*, condition of) *nucleo*: fug: nucleofugal (*fugere*, to flee) petal: nucleopetal phil: nucleophile (*phile*, tendency toward) plasm: nucleoplasm (*plasm*, form, shape) protein: nucleoprotein EMBEDDED ROOT COMPOUND: mono<u>nucle</u>osis (*mono*, one; *osis*, condition of) MESHED COMPOUND: nucleon (*nucle*us + prot*on*) GERMAN COGNATE: *Nuss* DUTCH COGNATE: *noot* CROSS REFERENCE: *karyo*
nud**	Latin *nudus* (IE: *nogw*, naked)	stripped, naked	SIMPLE ROOT: nude, nudism, nudist, nudity PREFIXED ROOT: *de*-: denudate, denudation, denude (*de*-, off) LEADING ROOT COMPOUND: *nudi*: branch: nudibranch (without external gills) (*branchia*, gills) caul: nudicaul (in *botany*, having stems without leaves) (*caul*, stem) flor: nudiflorous (*flor*, flower) fy: nudify (from *facere*, to make, do) ped: nudiped (*ped*, foot) *nudo*: mania: nudomania (*mania*, craze for) phob: nudophobia (*phobia*, morbid fear of) CROSS REFERENCE: *gymn*
null**	Latin *nullus* (see **non**)	none	SIMPLE ROOT: null (see *Legal Phrase* below), nullity PREFIXED ROOT: *an*-: annul (**Synonyms**: abolish, abrogate, rescind), annulment (*an*- assimilates *ad*-, to, toward) LEADING ROOT COMPOUND: fic: nullification (in *United States history*, the refusal of a State to recognize or enforce within its territory any act of Congress held to be an infringement of its sovereignty), nullifidian (see *nullify*, next entry) fy: nullify (from *facere*, to make, do) para: nullipara (in *obstetrics*, a woman who has never given birth to a child) (*parere*, to beget) por: nullipore (*porous*, passage)

Element	From	Meaning	Examples
null (cont'd)			LEGAL PHRASE: null and void (without legal force; not binding; invalid) CROSS REFERENCE: *a-, an-, dis-, in-, ne-, neg-*
num**	Latin *numerare*: to count (IE: *nem*, to assign, distribute, take, arrange)	number	SIMPLE ROOT: number numera: numerable (that can be numbered), numerary, numer- ate, numerator (in *mathematics*, the term above or to the left of the line in a fraction, as 3 is the numerator of 3/4) numeri: numerical numero: numerous PREFIXED ROOT: *de-*: denumerable (that which can be counted) (*de-*, of) *e-*: enumerate (elided from *ex-*, out) *in-*: innumerable (that which cannot be counted) (*in-*, not) *super-*: supernumerary (*super-*, above) LEADING ROOT COMPOUND: logy: numerology (*logy*, study of) BOOK OF THE BIBLE: Numbers (the fourth book of the Old Testament, containing the two censuses of the Israelites after the Exodus) NO CROSS REFERENCE
nunci**	Latin *nuntiare*: to report (IE: *neu¹*, to shout)	to announce	PREFIXED ROOT: nuncio *an-*: annunciation, annunciator (*an-* assimilates *ad-*, to, toward) *de-*: denunciate {denunciation, denunciatory} (*de-*, down) *e-*: enunciate (**Synonyms**: utter, express, voice) (from *ex-*, out) *pro-*: pronunciation (*pro-*, forth) *re-*: renunciation {renunciative} (*re-*, back, again) PREFIXED DISGUISED ROOT: *an-*: announce (**Synonyms**: declare, publish, proclaim) (*an-* assimilates *ad-*, to, toward) *de-*: denounce (**Synonyms**: criticize, reprehend, censure) (*de-*, down) *pro-*: pronounce, pronounced (*pro-*, forth) *re-*: renounce (*re-*, again) SPANISH: *pronunciamento* (an edict announcing a *coup d'état*; any authoritarian pronouncement) CHURCH FESTIVAL: The Annunciation (March 25, com- memorating the angel Gabriel's announcement to Mary that she was to give birth to Jesus; see Luke 1:26-38) LATIN: *nuncio* (in the Roman Catholic Church, the perma- nent official representative of the Pope to a foreign govern- ment; papal ambassador) CROSS REFERENCE: *clam, plor*
nup			See *nub* for *nuptial*.
nur,** nutr	Latin *nutrire* (IE: *(s)neu*, to flow)	nourish	SIMPLE ROOT: nurture (also, *nurturance*: anything that nourishes; food; nutriment) nur: nurse (see *Doublets* below) nutr: nutrient, nutriment (see *Doublets* below), nutrition, nu- tritious, nutritive DISGUISED ROOT: nourish, nourishing, nourishment (see *Doublets* below) DOUBLETS: nourish:nurse; nourishment:nutriment CROSS REFERENCE: *al, troph*

Element	From	Meaning	Examples
nut*	Latin *nuere* (IE: *ken*, to scratch, scrape; yields English nod)	to nod, sway	SIMPLE ROOT: nutant (in *botany*, with the top bent down- ward, as though nodding; drooping; said of plants), nutation PREFIXED ROOT: circum-: circumnutation (in *botany*, the irregular spiral or el- liptical rotation of the apex of a growing stem, root, or shoot, caused by differences in the rate of growth of the op- posite sides) (*circum-*, around) DISGUISED ROOT: nudge, innuendo (originally, a law term, in which one's opinion was indicated by a nod) NO CROSS REFERENCE
nyct,* nic	Greek *nyx* (IE: *nekwt*, *nokwt*, night)	night [extended to include the genre of owls and bats (Nycteris), since they are active at night]	SIMPLE ROOT: nyctea (a genus of owls consisting of the snowy owl) nycterine (occurring at night; thus, obscure) nycteris (a genus of bats comprising the hollow-faced bats) LEADING ROOT COMPOUND: *nyct*: alg: nyctalgia (pain that occurs in sleep only, thus at night) (*alg*, pain) aphon: nyctaphonia (loss of voice during the *night*) (*a-*, not + *phone*, sound) opia: nyctalopia (night blindness) (*alaos*, blind + *ops*, eye + *ia*, condition of) emera: nyctemera (literally, night-day, but actually referring to a genus of moths of New Zealand and Australia, which have black and white spots) (*hemera*, day) ur: nycturia (also referred to as *nocturia*, or *enuresis*, bedwet- ting) (*ur*, urine) *nyctero*: hemera: nycterohemera (same as *nyctohemeral*, pertaining to both night and day) (*hemera*, day) *nycti*: trop: nyctitropism (the tendency of the leaves or petals of cer- tain plants to assume a different position at night) {nyc- titropic} (*trop*, turn) *nycto*: phil: nyctophilia (*phila*, tendency toward; love of) phob: nyctophobia (*phobia*, morbid fear of) TRAILING ROOT COMPOUND: acro: acronical (also, *acronycal*; in *astronomy*, happening at sunset, as the rising of a star) (*acro*, extremity) CROSS REFERENCE: *noc/nox*

Element	From	Meaning	Examples
ob-***	Latin (IE: *epi*, *opi*, near, at, toward, after)	against, to, toward	**PREFIXED ROOT:** *o-*: (elides *ob-*) *o-*: omit, omission [the only two words with *ob-* elision] *ob-*: con: obconic (in *botany*, conical but attached by the point; said of a leaf) cord: obcordate (in *botany*, heart-shaped, with the tapering end at the point of attachment) (*cord*, heart) dur: obdurate (hardened against good or moral influence; stubbornly impenitent; **Synonyms:** inflexible, adamant, implacable) (*durare*, to harden) edien: obedience, obedient (**Synonyms:** docile, tractable, compliant; see *obey*, below; see *Doublets* below) eisanc: obeisance (see *obey*, below; see *Doublets* below) es: obese (very fat; stout; corpulent) (from *edere*, to eat) ey: obey (to carry out or fulfill the command, order, or instruction of) (*audire*, to hear) fusc: obfuscate (to cloud over; obscure; make dark or unclear) (*fuscare*, to obscure) it: obit (to fall, die), obituary (from *ire*, to go) ject: (from *jacere*, to throw) object (**Synonyms:** remonstrate, expostulate, protest), objectify, objection, objectionable objective (**Synonyms:** impartial, unbiased, dispassionate), objectivism (compare *solipsism*) jur: objurgate (to bring a lawsuit; to scold or rebuke sharply; berate) (from *jurgare*, to sue at law; *jurgare* consists of two roots: *jur*, law + *agere*, to act, perform) lanc: oblanceolate (in *botany*, broader and rounded at the apex, and tapered at the base, as *an oblanceolate leaf*) lat: (from Latin, past participle of *obferre*, to bring to, offer) oblate [as an *adjective*, literally "carried to (the center)", and describes a particular spheroid; thus, having an equatorial diameter greater than the distance between poles; e.g., the earth is an oblate spheroid; as a *noun*, a lay person dedicated to a religious life] oblation [from Medieval Latin *ablatus*, one offered (to God)] lig: (*ligare*, to bind) obligate (as an *adjective*, used in *biology* to indicate being limited to a certain condition of life, as some parasites) obligation, oblige, obligee, obliging, obligor liqu: oblique, obliquity (*lique*, awry, slanting) liter: obliterate (**Synonyms:** erase, expunge, efface) (*liter*, letter) liv: oblivion, oblivious (probably from *levis*, smooth; from IE *lei*, slippery) long: oblong (longer than broad; elliptical; as a noun, an oblong figure)

Element	From	Meaning	Examples
ob- (cont'd)			loqu: obloquy (verbal abuse of a person or thing) (*loqui*, to speak)
			nox: obnoxious (see synonyms at *nox*) (*nox*, harm)
			ova: obovate (inversely ovate; having the shape of the longitudinal section of an egg, with the broad end at the top, as some leaves) (*ovum*, egg)
			ovo: obovoid (egg-shaped, with the broad end at the top: said of some fruits, etc.) (*ovum*, egg; *oid*, similar to)
			scen: obscene (**Synonyms**: coarse, indelicate, ribald), obscenity (from *caenum*, filth)
			op-:
			pil: oppilate (now rare; to block or obstruct the pores, bowels, etc.) (*pilare*, to ram down) [*pile*, the long, heavy timber or beam driven into the ground to support a bridge, building, dock, etc. comes from *pilum*, javelin]
			pon: opponent (**Synonyms**: antagonist, adversary, enemy) (*ponere*, to place)
			port: opportune (**Synonyms**: timely, seasonable), opportunism, opportunity (*portus*, port)
			pos: (see *opponent*)
			opposable (that can be opposed; that can be placed opposite something else, as the thumb with each finger)
			oppose (compare *appose*)
			opposite (**Synonyms**: contrary, antithetical, reverse)
			opposition
			press: oppress (**Synonyms**: wrong, persecute, aggrieve), oppression, oppressive (from *premere*, to press)
			pro: opprobrious, opprobrium (*pro-* prefixes IE *bhrom*, base of Latin *ferre*, to bear)
			pugn: oppugn, oppugnant (*pugnare*, to fight)
			os-:
			tens: ostensible [literally, to stretch before; thus, to show; apparent; seeming; professed, as *the ostensible reason* for (some particular act)], ostensive (clearly demonstrative), ostentation {ostentatious} (*ob-* + *tendere*, to stretch)
			DISGUISED ROOT: oust (literally, to stand out; or, to be stood out) (*ob-* + *stare*, to stand)
			DOUBLETS: obedience:obeisance
			LATIN WORDS AND PHRASES:
			obiit [He (or) she died]
			obiter dictum (something said incidentally, especially by a judge, and which has no bearing upon the case)
			FRENCH PHRASES:
			objet d'art (an object valued for its artistry)
			objet trouvé (found object)
			ITALIAN MUSIC TERM:
			obbligato (that part in music which originally was essential; now, that part which can be omitted)
			PLACENAMES: Opportunity (Montana, Washington)
			NB: *Obelus* and *obelisk* are not in this family; neither is *oppidan*, from *oppidum*, town.
			CROSS REFERENCE: *anti-*, *contra-/contro-*

Element	From	Meaning	Examples
oct***	Latin *octo*; Greek *okto*	eight	SIMPLE ROOT: octa: octad (a series or group of eight; in *chemistry*, an element, atom, or radical with a valence of eight) octal (of or based on the number eight) octan (occurring every eighth day, counting both days of occurrence; as a noun, an octan fever, etc.), octant octave, octavo octe: octet (also, *octette*; a group of eight) LEADING ROOT COMPOUND: *oct:* ang: octangular (angle) arch: octarchy (Greek *arch*, rule) enn: octennial (from *ann*, year) *octa:* chord: octachord (an octave of the diatonic scale; any eight-stringed musical instrument) (*chord*, string) gon: octagon (*gon*, angle) hedr: octahedrite, octahedron (*hedr*, geometric surface) mer: octamerous (often written **8-merous**) (*mere*, part) meter: octameter (a line of verse containing eight metrical feet or measures) (*meter*, measure) *octo:* deci: octodecimo (1/18 of a printer's sheet; also called *eighteenmo*, and written **18mo** or **18•**) (*deci*, tenth) gen: octogenarian (*octogeni*, eighty each) pod: octopod (*pod*, foot) pus: octopus (from *podos*, foot) syllabl: octosyllable (*syl*- assimilates *sym*-, together, with, which prefixes *lab*, to hold) *octu:* ple: octuple (from *plus*; from *plicare*, to fold) MESHED LEADING ROOT COMPOUNDS: octillion (*oct* + *million*), octoroon [*octo* + *(quad)roon*] CALENDAR MONTH: October (the eighth month in the Roman calendar, which began with March) CONSTELLATION: Octans PROPER NAMES: Octavius (masculine), Octavia (feminine) PLACENAME: Octavia (Nebraska, Oklahoma) NOTE: *Octroi*, a particular tax, and in the same family as *author* and *auction*, is not in this family. NO CROSS REFERENCE
ocul**	Latin *oculus* (IE: *okw*, to see; yields Spanish *ojo*)	eye	SIMPLE ROOT: oce: ocellate, ocellus (*ocell*, diminutive of *ocul*) ocu: ocular, ocularium, oculate, oculist, oculus (the eye of vision) PREFIXED ROOT: in-: inoculate (literally, to plant an eye into; to engraft an eye or bud from one plant to another; to immunize) (*in-*, in) TRAILING ROOT COMPOUND: bin: binocular, binoculars (*bin*, two) mon: monocle (*mono*, one)

Element	From	Meaning	Examples
ocul (cont'd)			DISGUISED ROOT: antlers (originally, *anteocular*, literally, before the eyes; see *Placenames* below; in German *Augensprossen*, eye sprouts) pinochle ullage (from Old French *eullage*, a filling up to the brim or the bunghole; the root is *ouil*, an eye; figuratively, bunghole; the amount by which a container, especially of liquid, falls short of being full) PREFIXED DISGUISED ROOT: *in-*: inveigle (from French *aveugle*, blind; originally, Latin *aboculus*; thus, to lead on by deception; entice or trick into doing or giving something, going somewhere, etc.; not related to *inveigh*; see *veh*) (*in-*, in) FRENCH ARCHITECTURAL TERM: *oeil-de-boeuf* (ox's eye; a circular or oval window) FRENCH ART TERM: *trompe l'oeil* (the so-called "fool the eye" technique) OLD NORSE COGNATE: window (*vindauga*, wind eye, or eye of the wind) PLACENAMES: Antler, North Dakota; Antlers, Oklahoma Ojo Caliente, New Mexico (Hot Eye) Ojo Feliz, New Mexico (Happy Eye) ENGLISH COGNATE: daisy (literally, day's eye) NB: *Ocelot* is not in this family. CROSS REFERENCE: *op, ophthalm*
od*	Greek *oide*: to sing (IE: *aw*, to speak)	to speak, sing	SIMPLE ROOT: ode, odeum (plural, *odea*, or *odeums*) PREFIXED ROOT: *ep-*: epode (a form of lyric poem in which a short line follows a longer one; the form was used by Horace, the Roman poet; also that part of a lyric ode which follows the strophe and the antistrophe) (from *epi-*, upon) *palin-*: palinode (originally, an ode or poem written to retract something said in a previous poem; hence, a retraction) (*palin-*, again) *par-*: parody (literally, a countersong; **Synonyms:** caricature, travesty, satire) (from *para-*, beside) *pros-*: prosody (literally, to the song, or song sung to music) (*pros-*, to) TRAILING ROOT COMPOUND: com: comedy (*com* from *komos*, banquet, festival + *aeidein*, to sing) hymn: hymnody mel: melody (**Synonyms:** air, tune) (*melos*, song) mon: monody (an ode sung by a single voice, as in an ancient Greek tragedy; lyric solo; in *music*, an early vocal style having a single voice part with continuo accompaniment, as in Baroque opera; same as *monophony*) (*mono*, one) rhaps: (from *rhaptein*, to stitch together) rhapsode (in ancient Greece, a person who recited rhapsodies, especially one who recited epic poems as a profession) rhapsodic (pertaining to a rhapsody; also extravagantly enthusiastic; ecstatic)

Element	From	Meaning	Examples
od (cont'd)			rhapsodist (a rhapsode, which see above; a person who rhapsodizes) rhapsodize (to speak or write in an extravagantly enthusiastic manner; to recite or write rhapsodies) rhapsody (in ancient Greece, a part of an epic poem suitable for a single recitation; in *music*, an instrumental composition of free, irregular form, suggesting improvisations) thren: threnody (also, *threnode*; a song of lamentation; funeral song; dirge) (*threnos*, lamentation) DISGUISED ROOT: tragedy (literally, goat song) CROSS REFERENCE: *can, hymn*
od* (hod)	Greek *hodos* (IE: *sed*, to go)	road, way, path	PREFIXED ROOTS AND COMPOUNDS: *hod*: *cat-*: cathode (*cata-*, down) *met-*: (*meta-*, between) method, methodical, Methodist, methodize methodology (*logy*, study of) *od*: *an-*: anode (in an electrolytic cell, the positively charged electrode, toward which current flows) (from *ana-*, up) *epi-*: episode (**Synonyms:** occurrence, event) (*epi-*, upon) *ex-*: exodus (see *Book of the Old Testament*, below) (*ex-*, out) *peri-*: (around) period (**Synonyms:** epoch, era, age) periodic (**Synonyms:** intermittent, recurrent, alternate) *syn-*: synod (*syn-*, with) LEADING ROOT COMPOUND: *odo*: gen: odogenesis (same as *neurocladism*: the formation of new branches by the process of a neuron) (*gen*, producing) graph: odograph (*graph*, write) meter: odometer (*meter*, measure) *hodo*: scop: hodoscope (*scope*, view) TRAILING ROOT COMPOUND: electr: electrode stom: stomodeum (*stom*, mouth) BOOK OF THE OLD TESTAMENT: Exodus [literally, the road out (of Egypt)] CROSS REFERENCE: *via*
od*	Latin *odi*: I hate (IE: *od*, hate)	hate	SIMPLE ROOT: odious (**Synonyms:** detestable, obnoxious, hateful) odium (do not confuse with *odeum*, from *ode*, song) DISGUISED ROOT: noisome (injurious to health; noxious; harmful; also, having a bad odor; foul-smelling; offensive) (from *annoy* + Anglo-Saxon suffix *-some*) PREFIXED DISGUISED ROOT: *an-*: annoy (**Synonyms:** vex, irk, bother) [from the phrase *in odio habere*, to have (or be) in hate] *en-*: ennui (weariness and dissatisfaction resulting from inactivity or lack of interest; boredom) (from *annoy*) ONE-WORD LATIN SENTENCE: *odi* (I hate) CROSS REFERENCE: *miso*

469

Element	From	Meaning	Examples
odont**	Greek *odon* (IE: *edont*, tooth; from *ed*, to eat)	tooth	SIMPLE ROOT: odontic PREFIXED ROOT: *end-*: endontics (*endo-*, within) *ex-*: exodontia (*exo-*, outside) *peri-*: periodontal, periodontics, periodontium (the tissues investing and supporting the teeth), periodontist (a dentist who specializes in periodontics) (*peri-*, around) LEADING ROOT COMPOUND: ben: odobenus (a group of walruses, from the belief that walruses use their tusks in sequence) (from *bainen*, to walk) TRAILING ROOT COMPOUND: acr: acrodont (*acro*, tip) mast: mastodon (*masto*, breast) orth: orthodontia, orthodontist (a dentist who specializes in the prevention and correction of irregularities of the teeth and malocclusion, and with associated facial problems) (*ortho*, straight) CROSS REFERENCE: *dent*
odyn**	Greek *odyne* (IE: *od*, a variation of *ed*, to eat)	pain, distress	PREFIXED ROOT: *an-*: anodyne (as an *adjective*, also *anodynic*; relieving or lessening pain; soothing; as a *noun*, anything that relieves pain) (*an-*, without) TRAILING ROOT COMPOUND: arthr: arthrodynia (*arthro*, joint) cry: cryodynia (*cryo*, cold) gastr: gastrodynia (*gastro*, belly) neur: neurodynia (*neuro*, nerve) oneir: oneirodynia (*oneiro*, dream; nightmare) CROSS REFERENCE: *alg, dolor*
oeno*	Greek *oinos*	wine	SIMPLE ROOT: oenin, oenomel LEADING ROOT COMPOUND: cyt: oenocyte (*cyt*, cell) logy: oenology (the preferred spelling is *enology*) (*logy*, study of) phil: oenophile (a person who loves wine; wine connoisseur) (*phil*, love) GREEK SAYING: en oino aletheia (translated into Latin as *in vino veritas*: In wine there is truth) CROSS REFERENCE: *vin*
oid**	Greek *eidos* (IE: *weid*, to see)	form, shape, image, resembling	SIMPLE ROOT: eidetic, eidolon EMBEDDED ROOT COMPOUND: kaleidoscope (see *Note*) ROOT AS A SUFFIX: anthro: anthropoid (*anthropo*, man) dipl: diploid (*diplo*, two) hapl: haploid (*haplo*, one) homin: hominoid (from *homo*, man) hy: hyoid (shaped like the letter *v*, upsilon; designating or of a bone or bones at the base of and supporting the tongue; U-shaped in man) (*hy*, upsilon) planet: planetoid (*oid*, similar to) spher: spheroid (sphere-like) (*oid*, similar to)

470

Element	From	Meaning	Examples
oid (cont'd)			DISGUISED ROOT: idol (an image of a god, used as an object or instrument of worship) idyll (a short poem or prose work describing a simple, pleasant, peaceful scene of rural, pastoral, or domestic life; an extended narrative poem, as "The *Idylls* of the King"; in *music*, a simple, pastoral composition) NOTE: See *eid* for the basic form of this root. CROSS REFERENCE: *form, plasm, morph*
ol*	Latin *oleum*	oil	SIMPLE ROOT: oleate, oleic, olein, oleonal [a white solid alcohol (chemical symbol: $C_{18}H_{35}OH$), from the liver oils of fish], oleosus, oleotine, oleum (plural, *olea*) LEADING ROOT COMPOUND: margar: oleomargarine meter: oleometer resin: oleoresin TRAILING ROOT COMPOUND: chol: cholesterol (*chol*, gall bladder + *ster*, solid + *ol*: cholesterol was first isolated as solid, oil particles in the gall bladder) petro: petroleum (*petro*, rock) TRADENAME: Vaseline (*Vas*, from *Wasser*, water + *el*, oil + *-ine*) NO CROSS REFERENCE
oligo*	Greek *oligos*: few (IE: *(o)leig*, wretched, illness)	elite, few	ROOT NOTE: The Indo-European precursor to this root, *leig*, meant wretched, illness, destruction, death. The idea appears to be that after a plague, only a few persons were left. LEADING ROOT COMPOUND: *olig*: arch: oligarch, oligarchy (*arch*, rule) ur: oliguria (secretion of a diminished amount of urine in relation to fluid intake) (*ur*, urine) *oligo*: chaet: oligochaete (a particular type of earthworm lacking a definite head and having relatively few body bristles) (*chaeta*, hair bristles) clas: oligoclase (*clas*, breaking) phag: oligophagous (feeding upon a limited variety of food, as certain caterpillars whose diet is restricted to a few related plants) (*phag*, eat) pol: oligopoly (control of a commodity or service in a given market by a small number of companies or suppliers) (*pol*, sell) pso: oligopsony (control of the purchase of a commodity or service in a given market by a small number of buyers) (*pson*, bread, food) troph: oligotrophic (*troph*, nourish) NO CROSS REFERENCE

The terminology of the sciences is derived almost wholly from Latin and Greek.
W. J. Holland

Element	From	Meaning	Examples
-oma**	Greek	growth, tumor	SUFFIXED ROOTS AND COMPOUND: (That which is tumorous is listed in parentheses.) adenoma (gland) astrocytoma (astrocytes: star-shaped cells) atheroma (sebaceous, or fatty cells) carcinoma (cancerous epithelial cells) cystoma (bladder) fibroma (fibrous tissue) glaucoma (the crystalline lens; from the dull gray gleam of the affected eye; *glauc*, gray) granuloma (granulation tissue) hematoma (effused blood) lymphoma (lymphoid tissue) myoma (muscle) osteochondroma (partly bone and partly cartilage) sarcoma (flesh) CROSS REFERENCE: *aug, creat, cresc, embryo, phym*
ombro*	Greek *ombros*	rain	LEADING ROOT COMPOUND: graph: ombrograph (*graph*, write) logy: ombrology (*logy*, study of) meter: ombrometer (*meter*, measure) phil: ombrophilous (*phil*, love of) phob: ombrophobe, ombrophobous (*phobia*, fear of) NO CROSS REFERENCE
omni***	Latin *omnis* (IE: *op¹*, to work)	all	SIMPLE ROOT: omneity, omnist, omnium, omnit LEADING ROOT COMPOUND: *omni*: bus: omnibus competent: omnicompetent direct: omnidirectional far: omnifarious (of all kinds, kinds, or forms) fic: omnific, omnificient (from *facere*, to make, do) pot: omnipotence, omnipotent (*potent*, power) present: omnipresent scien: omniscience, omniscient (*science*, knowledge) vor: omnivore, omnivorous (*vor*, eat) *omnium*: gather: omnium-gatherum (a miscellaneous collection of persons or things) (*um*, an apheretic variation of *them*) CROSS REFERENCE: *pan*
omphal*	Greek *omphalos*	navel, umbilicus	SIMPLE ROOT: omphalic, omphalos (navel, thus, a central point; also a rounded stone in Apollo's temple at Delphi, regarded as the center of the universe by the Ancients) LEADING ROOT COMPOUND: *omphal*: odium: omphalodium [the scar at the hilum (the point of attachment of the ovule) of a seed] *omphalo*: skep: omphaloskepsis (the act of contemplating one's navel, as an exercise for mystics) (*skep*, see, view) tom: omphalotomy (the cutting of the umbilical cord) (*tom*, cut) NO CROSS REFERENCE

472

Element	From	Meaning	Examples
on*	Latin *onus* (IE: *enos, onos,* burden, load)	burden, load	SIMPLE ROOT: onerous, onus PREFIXED ROOT: ex-: exonerate (to remove the burden from; to clear of blame or the imputation of guilt) (*ex-*, out) LATIN PHRASE: *onus probandi* (the burden of proof) NO CROSS REFERENCE
onc,* onk	Greek *onkos*	mass, tumor	LEADING ROOT COMPOUND: *onco*: gen: oncogene (*gen*, producing) logy: oncology (the branch of medicine dealing with tumors) (*logy*, study of) *onk*: ino: onkinocele (inflammation with swelling of a tendon sheath) (*ino*, fiber + *kele*, swelling) CROSS REFERENCE: *-cele, -oma*
oneir*	Greek *oneiros*	dream	SIMPLE ROOT: oneiric (of or having to do with dreams), oneirism (dreamlike hallucination in a waking state) LEADING ROOT COMPOUND: *oneir*: odyn: oneirodynia (bad, or painful, dreams; nightmares) (*odyn*, pain) ogmus: oneirogmus (emission of semen accompanying erotic dreams; same as *nocturnal emission*, or *wet dream*) *oneiro*: critic: oneirocritic (a dream interpreter) logy: oneirology (*logy*, study of) mancy: oneiromancy (*mancy*, divination) NO CROSS REFERENCE
onom*	Greek *onoma* (IE: *(o)nomn*, name)	name	SIMPLE ROOT: onomastic (in *law*, designating a signature in a handwriting different from that in the body of the instrument to which the signature is appended), onomastics (the study of the origin, form, meaning, and use of names, especially proper names), onomastican, onomastous PREFIXED ROOT: ant-: antonomasia (the substitution of another designation for a common, obvious, or normal one, *his honor* for *Judge Brown*; other uses) (from *anti-*, instead, against) LEADING ROOT COMPOUND: *ono*: mancy: onomancy (divination by names) (*mancy*, divination) *onomasio*: logy: onomasiology [the study of words and expressions having similar or associated concepts and a basis (as social, regional, occupational) for being grouped] (*logy*, study of) *onomato*: logy: onomatology (terminology) (*logy*, study of) mania: onomatomania (senseless repetition of certain words or phrases) (*mania*, madness) poeia: onomatopoeia [literally, name-making; words which represent their sounds, e.g., bobwhite, cackle, paradiddle (a pattern of beats on a snare drum executed with alternate strokes of the sticks), purr] CROSS REFERENCE: *nom, onym*

Element	From	Meaning	Examples
onto*	Greek *einai*, to be (IE: *es*, is)	being, existence	LEADING ROOT COMPOUND: gen: ontogenesis, ontogenetic, ontogeny (process by which one individual becomes dominant over others) (*gen*, produce) logy: ontologism, ontologist, ontology (*logy*, study of) TRAILING ROOT COMPOUND: dipl: diplont (*diplos*, double) CROSS REFERENCE: *esse*
onych,* onyx	Greek *onyx*	nail of the finger	SIMPLE ROOT: *onych*: onycha, onychia, onychium (same as *empodium*: a small median appendage between the claws of the tarsi of many insects and arachnids) *onyx*: onyx (an agate, the color of the fingernail; in *medicine*, a fingernail or toenail; also, pus collection between the corneal layers of the eye), onyxis PREFIXED ROOT: *an*-: anonychia (congenital absence of a nail or nails) (*an*-, without) *peri*-: perionychium (the epidermis forming the border around a fingernail or toenail) (*peri*-, around) LEADING ROOT COMPOUND: *onych*: algia: onychalgia (painful nails) (*alg*, pain) ectom: onychectomy (excision of a nail or nailbed) (*ectom*, excision) itis: onychitis (*itis*, inflammation) oma: onychoma (*oma*, tumor, mass) *onycho*: clas: onychoclasis (breaking of the nails) (*clas*, break) crypt: onychocryptosis (the ingrowing of the toenail) (*crypt*, hidden; *osis*, condition of) phag: onychophagy (the morbid habit of biting the nails) (*phag*, eat) TRAILING ROOT COMPOUND: leuk: leukonychia (*leuk*, white) PLACENAMES: Onycha, Alabama; Onyx (Arkansas, California) NO CROSS REFERENCE
onym***	Greek *onymos* (IE: *(o)nomn*, name)	name	SIMPLE ROOT: onymous (having a name; compare *anonymous*, having no name, below) PREFIXED ROOT: *an*-: anonym (an anonymous person; a pseudonym), anonymity, anonymous (*an*-, without) *ant*-: antonym (a word that is opposite in meaning to another word, e.g., *trite* is an antonym of *fresh*; opposite to *synonym*), antonymous (*anti*-, against) *ep*-: eponym {eponymic}, eponymy, eponymous (*epi*-, upon) *met*-: metonymy (the use of the name of one thing for that of another associated with or suggested by it, e.g., *the White House* for *the President*; similar to *synedoche*, a figure of speech in which a part is used for the whole, an individual for a class, a material for a thing, or the reverse of any of these) (*meta*-, along with, after)

474

Element	From	Meaning	Examples
onym (cont'd)			*par-*: paronym, paronymous (derived from the same root; cognate, as the words *attitude* and *aptitude*) (from *para-*, alongside) *syn-*: synonym (a word having the same or nearly the same meaning in one or more senses as another in the same language; opposite to *antonym*) (*syn-*, with, together) TRAILING ROOT COMPOUND: acr: acronym (*acro*, point, end, top) all: allonym (*allo*, *other*) crypt: cryptonym (*crypto*, hidden) heter: heteronym, heteronymous [pertaining to a heteronym; also, having different names, as a pair of correlatives (*son* and *daughter* are *heteronymous*)] (*hetero*, different) hom: homonym (a word with the same pronunciation as another but with a different meaning, origin, and usually spelling, e.g., *bore* and *boar*) (*homo*, same) pseud: pseudonym (*pseudo*, false) matr: matronymic (*matro*, mother) patr: patronymic (*patri*, father) CROSS REFERENCE: *onom, nom* (Latin)
onyx			See *onych*.
oo**	Greek *oon* (IE: *awi*, bird)	egg	SIMPLE ROOT: ootid (a large, haploid cell produced at the second meiotic division, that quickly becomes an egg cell) PREFIXED ROOT: *peri-*: perioothecitis (same as *perioophoritis*, inflammation of the tissues around the ovary) (*peri-*, around) LEADING ROOT COMPOUND: cyt: oocyte (in *embryology*, an egg that has not yet undergone maturation) (*cyt*, cell) gam: oogamete, oogamous (*gam*, marriage, sexual reproduction) gen: oogenesis (*genesis*, production of) gon: oogonium (*gonium*, reproductive cell) lit: oolite, oolith (*lithos*, stone) logy: oology (*logy*, study of) phyt: oophyte (*phyton*, plant) phor: oophore (*phore*, bear; ovary) sperm: oosperm (same as *zygote*) spher: oosphere (in *biology*, any of the large, spherical, nonmotile, unfertilized eggs that develop in an oogonium) (*sphere*, ball, globe) spor: oospore (in *botany*, a thick-walled, resting spore produced by the fertilization of an oosphere) (*spore*, seed) theca: ootheca (an egg case, as of certain mollusks and insects) (*theca*, case) INTERDISCIPLINARY: oogonium (in *biology*, one of the cells that form the the bulk of ovarian tissue; in *botany*, a female reproductive structure in certain fungi, containing oospores) NB: *Oolong* (a dark tea from China and Taiwan) and *oomiak* (also, *umiak*, a large, open boat, used by Eskimos) are not in this family. CROSS REFERENCE: *ov*

Element	From	Meaning	Examples
oophor**	Greek *oophoron*	ovary, ovaries	ROOT NOTE: This root consists of two roots: *oo*, egg + *phor*, to bear; together they mean bearing eggs. Both roots are entered separately in this list. LEADING ROOT COMPOUND: ectom: oophorectomy (*ectom*, to surgically remove) itis: oophoritis (*itis*, inflammation of) oma: oophoroma (*oma*, mass, tumor) CROSS REFERENCE: *ov*
op**	Greek *optikos* (IE: *okw*, to see)	eye, vision; also, opening	ROOT NOTE: When the root is suffixed with *-ia*, the meaning becomes "abnormal condition of," e.g., *amblyopia*. SIMPLE ROOT: optic, optician PREFIXED ROOT: *hyper-*: hyperopia (*hyper-*, beyond) *met-*: (*meta-*, between) metope (any of the square areas, plain or decorated, between triglyphs in a Doric frieze) metopic (literally, between the eyes, forehead; therefore, of the forehead; frontal) *syn-*: synopsis, synoptic (see *Synoptic Gospels* below) (*syn-*, with, together) LEADING ROOT COMPOUND: metry: optometry (*metry*, measurement of) TRAILING ROOT COMPOUND: ambly: amblyopia (*amblys*, dull) aut: autopsy (literally, self-viewing; inspection and dissection of a body after death, as for determination of the cause of death) (*auto*, self) dipl: diplopia (*dipl*, two) my: myopia (nearsightedness) (*myein*, to close) nyct: nyctalopia (night-blindness) (*nyct*, night; *alaos*, blind) pan: panopia, panoptic (*pan*, all) rhod: rhodopsin (*rhodo*, red) PREFIXED TRAILING ROOT COMPOUND: *a-*: ametropia (*a-*, negative; *metr*, measure, proportion) *an-*: anorthopia (distorted vision in which straight lines appear bent or curved) (*an-*, negative + *ortho*, straight) *em-*: emmetropia (correct vision) (*em-* elides *en-*, in) BIBLICAL GROUP OF BOOKS: Synoptic Gospels (the books of *Matthew, Mark, Luke*, because their authors viewed chronologically the life of Jesus from his birth to his death; *John*, who *interpreted* the events rather than *narrating* them chronologically, is so unlike the other Gospels that the book is often referred to as the *Fourth Gospel*) GREEK MYTHOLOGY: Cyclops (plural, *Cyclopes*, pronounced sie KLOH peez); any of a race of giants who had only one eye, in the middle of the forehead; therefore, cyclopean: gigantic, enormous, massive; from *Kyklops*, literally round-eyed) Pelops (the son of Tantalus; served up to the gods as food by his father and later restored to life by them; from *pellos*, dark + *ops*, face) CROSS REFERENCE: *ocul, ophthal*

Element	From	Meaning	Examples
ophi*	Greek *ophis* (IE: *ogiohi,* snake)	snake	SIMPLE ROOT: ophi: ophiasis (medical term for baldness occurring in serpentine streaks), ophic ophid: ophidian, ophidiasis (same as *ophidism*, poisoning by snake venom), ophidic, ophidism ophit: ophitic (from *ophites lithos*, snake stone, a green, mottled rock) LEADING ROOT COMPOUND: *ophi*: cleid: ophicleide (an early snake-shaped brass-wind instrument, with keys for fingering) (*cleide*, key) *ophidio*: phil: ophidiophilia (*philia*, fondness for) phob: ophidiophobia (*phobia*, morbid fear of) *ophio*: latr: ophiolatrous, ophiolatry (*latry*, worship of) logy: ophiology (*logy*, study of) phag: ophiophagous (*phag*, eat) CONSTELLATION: Ophyichus (literally, holding a serpent) CROSS REFERENCE: *angui*
ophthalm**	Greek ophthalmos (IE: *okw*, to see)	eye	SIMPLE ROOT: ophthalmia (same as *ophthalmitis*, a severe inflammation of the eyeball or conjunctiva), ophthalmic LEADING ROOT COMPOUND: *ophthalm*: iatr: ophthalmiatrics (*iatr*, healing) odyn: opthalmodynia (same as *ophthalmalgia*) (*odyn*, pain) *ophthalmo*: logy: ophthalmology (*logy*, study of) scop: ophthalmoscope (*scope*, look) TRAILING ROOT COMPOUND: megal: megalophthalmus (*megal*, large) CROSS REFERENCE: *ocul, op*
ops**	Latin *opus* (IE: *op¹*, to work, riches)	plenty, wealth; work, labor	SIMPLE ROOT: opera: opera (plural of *opus*), operand, operant, operate, operatic, operative, operatory opero: operon, operose (laborious) opul: opulent (rich, wealthy, as though the result of working; **Synonyms**: rich, wealthy, affluent) {opulence} opus: opus (plural, *opera*), opuscule (now rarely used; a minor work, as of literature) {opuscular} PREFIXED ROOT: co-: cooperate, cooperative (*co-*, with, together) DISGUISED ROOT: copious (**Synonyms**: plentiful, abundant, profuse) copy (**Synonyms**: reproduction, facsimile, duplicate) DISGUISED TRAILING ROOT COMPOUND: corn: cornucopia (horn of plenty) (*corn*, horn) FRENCH DOUBLETS: maneuver:manure FRENCH MUSIC PHRASES: *opéra bouffe* (comic, especially, farcical opera) *opéra comique* (literally, comic opera; French opera with some spoken dialogue; however, it may not be comic)

477

Element	From	Meaning	Examples
ops (cont'd)			ITALIAN WORDS AND PHRASES: *opera seria* (serious opera) operetta (diminutive of *opera*; a light, amusing opera with spoken dialogue) CROSS REFERENCE: *erg/urg, labor, plut*
opt*	Latin *optare* (IE: *op²*, to choose)	to choose	SIMPLE ROOT: opt, optative, option (**Synonyms:** choice, alternative, preference) PREFIXED ROOT: *ad-*: adopt {adoptable, adoption}, adoptive (*ad-*, to, toward) CROSS REFERENCE: *leg/lig/lect*
optim*	Latin *optimus* (IE: *op¹*, to work, riches)	best	SIMPLE ROOT: optimal (most favorable or desirable; best; optimum) optimism {optimist}, optimize optimum (in *biology*, the amount of heat, light, food, moisture, etc. most favorable for growth and reproduction) PLACENAME: Optima, Oklahoma NO CROSS REFERENCE
ora**	Latin *orare*: to recite, to speak (IE: *ous*, mouth, edge; yields English usher; French orle)	mouth, speech	SIMPLE ROOT: orac: oracle, oracular orad: orad (toward the mouth or oral region) oral: oral (**Synonym:** verbal) {orally}, oralism (the theory or practice of teaching deaf people to communicate primarily or exclusively through lip reading and speaking rather than signing) orat: orate (speak in a pompous or bombastic manner, especially one given in connection with a ceremony), oration (see *Doublets* below; **Synonyms:** speech, address, talk), orator oratorio, oratory, oratrix ori: orison (see *Doublets* below) oro: orotund (clear, strong, and deep; resonant: said of a voice; also bombastic or pompous: said of a style of speaking or writing) (from *ore rotundo*, literally, with a round mouth) PREFIXED ROOT: *ad-*: adorable, adorably, adoration, adore (**Synonyms:** revere, venerate, worship), adorer (*ad-*, to, toward) *ex-*: exorable (that can be persuaded or moved by pleas) (*ex-*, out) *in-*: inexorable (*in-*, not + *ex-*, out) *intra-*: intraoral (*intra-*, within) *per-*: peroral, perorate (to make a speech, especially a lengthy oration; to sum up or conclude a speech), peroration (*per-*, through) LEADING ROOT COMPOUND: fic: orifice (a mouth or aperture of a tube, cavity, etc.; opening) (from *facere*, to make, do) nas: orinasal (*nas*, nose) DOUBLETS: orison:oration LATIN PHRASES: *ora pro anima* [pray for the soul (of)] *ora pro nobis* (Pray for us; in the Roman Catholic liturgy, a plea to the saints) CROSS REFERENCE: *stoma*

478

Element	From	Meaning	Examples
-orama*	Greek *horama*	a view	SUFFIXED ROOT: *rama*: cin: cinerama (from *kine*, movement) *orama*: cyclo: cyclorama (*cyclo*, circle) di: diorama (*di*, two) pan: panorama (*pan*, all) CROSS REFERENCE: *scop, vid*
orb**	Latin *orbis*	circle, disk, orb	SIMPLE ROOT: orb: orb (a sphere, globe; any of the celestial spheres, as the sun, moon, etc.) orbic: orbicular, orbiculare, orbiculate, orbiculus orbit: orbit, orbita (plural, *orbitae*), orbital, orbitale, orbitalis PREFIXED ROOT: *ex-*: exorbitance, exorbitant (**Synonyms**: excessive, extravagant, inordinate) (*ex-*, out) *sub-*: suborbital (*sub-*, under) CROSS REFERENCE: *cycl*
orch*	Greek *orcheisthai*	to dance	SIMPLE ROOT: orchestra (originally, a threshing floor, and in Greek drama, designated the semicircular area in front of the stage, where the dancers performed) orchestrate, orchestration NO CROSS REFERENCE
orchid*	Greek *orchis*	testicle	SIMPLE ROOT: orchic (same as *orchidic*) orchid (because of its roots being in the shape of testicles), orchidaceous (the orchid family; also, like an orchid in showiness, beauty, etc.) orchis (same as *orchid*) LEADING ROOT COMPOUND: logy: orchidology (the study of orchids, *not* of testicles; see *orchid* under *Simple Root*) pto: orchidoptosis (the descending of the testicles) (*pto*, to fall; *osis*, condition of) tom: orchidotomy (the surgical removal of one or both testicles; castration) (*tom*, cut) TRAILING ROOT COMPOUND: crypt: cryptorchidism (*crypt*, hidden) CROSS REFERENCE: *test*
ord***	Latin *ordo*: straight row (IE: *ar*, to join, fit)	order	SIMPLE ROOT: orda: ordain (to put in order; arrange; prepare; to decree) orde: order (**Synonyms**: command, direct, instruct), orderly ordi: ordinal, ordinance (**Synonyms**: rule, statute, canon), ordinand ordinary (**Synonyms**: common, general, familiar), ordinate, ordination ordn: ordnance ordo: ordo (an annual calendar that gives directions for each day's Mass and Office) PREFIXED ROOT: *co-*: coordinate (*co-*, with, together)

Element	From	Meaning	Examples
ord (cont'd)			*extra-*: extraordinary (not according to the usual custom or regular plan; outside the regular staff) (*extra-*, beyond) *in-*: inordinate (see synonyms at *exorbitant*, see *orb*) (*in-*, not, without) *pre-*: preordain {preordination} (*pre-*, before) *sub-*: subordinate {subordinate clause, subordinating conjunction}, subordination (*sub-*, under) TRAILING ROOT COMPOUND: prim: primordial (first in time), primordium (in *embryology*, the first recognizable aggregation of cells that will form a distinct organ or part of the embryo) (*primo*, first) DISGUISED ROOT: ornery (from *ordinary*) FRENCH: ordonnance (the proper or orderly arrangement of parts, as in a painting, literary composition, etc.) PLACENAME: Orderville, California CROSS REFERENCE: *cosm, nom, tax*
orex,* orec	Greek *oregein*: to stretch out for (IE: *reg*, right)	appetite, reach for	SIMPLE ROOT: *orect*: orectic (in *philosophy*, of or characterized by appetite or desire) *orex*: orexia, orexis (the feeling and striving aspect of the mind as contrasted with the intellectual) PREFIXED ROOT: *orex*: *an-*: anorexia {anorectic} (*an-*, not) *hyper-*: hyperorexia (*hyper-*, beyond) LEADING ROOT COMPOUND: gen: orexigenic (*genic*, producing) mania: oreximania (*mania*, craving for) NO CROSS REFERENCE:
organ**	Greek *organon*	tool	SIMPLE ROOT: organ organe: organelle (a discrete structure within a cell) organi: organic, organicism, organism, organist, organization, organize organo: organon (a means of acquiring knowledge) organu: organum (a type of vocal polyphonic music in two, three, or four parts, of the 9th to the early 13th century) LEADING ROOT COMPOUND: gen: organogenesis (in *biology*, the origin and development of organs) (*gen*, producing) graph: organography (in *biology*, the descriptive study of the organs of animals and plants, especially the outer parts of plants) (*graph*, write) lept: organoleptic (*lept*, seizure) logy: organology (that branch of science dealing with the form, structure, development, and functions of plant or animal organs) (*logy*, study of) therap: organotherapy (*therap*, healing) trop: organotropic (*tropo*, turn) NB: The following words are not in this family: *organza, organzine, orgasm*. PLACENAME: Organ, New Mexico NO CROSS REFERENCE

Element	From	Meaning	Examples
ori*	Latin *oriri*	to arise, appear, begin	SIMPLE ROOT: orient: orient (the quality that determines a pearl's value; capitalized, the East, or Asia, especially the Far East), Oriental, orientation origin: origin (**Synonyms**: source, beginning, inception) original (**Synonyms**: fresh, novel, modern) originate (**Synonyms**: rise, emanate, issue) PREFIXED ROOT: *ord*: *ex*-: exordium (the opening part of a speech, etc.) (*ex*-, out) *ori*: *ab*-: aboriginal (**Synonyms**: native, indigenous, endemic), aborigine (*ab*-, away) *dis*-: disorient (to cause to lose one's way), disorientate, disoriented (*dis*-, away from) *re*-: reorient (*re*-, again) *ort*: *ab*-: abort, abortion, abortive (**Synonyms**: futile, vain, fruitless) (*ab*-, away) PREFIXED LEADING ROOT COMPOUND: cid: aborticide (*cide*, kill) fac: abortifacient (*facere*, to make, do) PLACENAMES: Orient (Iowa, Maine, South Dakota, Texas, Washington) Orienta, Oklahoma; Oriental, North Carolina NO CROSS REFERENCE
orn*	Latin *ornare* (IE: *ar*, to fit together)	to deck, furnish	SIMPLE ROOT: ornate, ornament (**Synonyms**: adorn, decorate, embellish) PREFIXED ROOT: *ad*-: (to, toward) adorn (see synonyms at *ornament*, previous entry) adornment (**Synonyms**: embellish, beautify, bedeck) *sub*-: suborn (to get or bring about by bribery or other illegal methods) (*sub*-, under) LEADING ROOT COMPOUND: fy: ornify (from *facere*, to make, do) NOTE: Do not confuse this root with *orni/ornith*, bird (see next family). NO CROSS REFERENCE
ornis,** ornith	Greek *ornis* (IE: *er*, eagle, bird)	bird	SIMPLE ROOT: *ornis*: omis (the birdlife of region) *ornith*: ornithic, ornithine LEADING ROOT COMPOUND: *orni*: scop: orniscopy (same as *ornithoscopy*: birdwatching) (*scope*, watch, observe) *ornith*: oid: ornithoid (*oid*, similar to) osis: ornithosis (*osis*, condition of) *ornithi*: phil: ornithiphilous (*philous*, inclination for) vor: ornithivorous (*vor*, eat)

Element	From	Meaning	Examples
ornis (cont'd)			*ornitho*: cephal: ornithocephalous (*cephal*, head) fauna: ornithofauna (same as ornis, under *Simple Root*; also, *avifauna*) (*fauna* designates animals of a particular region; from Faunus, the Roman god of nature) logy: ornithology (*logy*, study of) mancy: ornithomancy (*mancy*, divination) pod: ornithopod (*pod*, foot) pter: ornithopter (*pter*, wing) rhynchus: ornithorhynchus (duck-billed platypus) (*rhynchos*, bill, snout) scop: ornithoscopy (same as *orniscopy*) (*scopy*, look) DISGUISED ROOT: erne CROSS REFERENCE: *avi*
oro*	Greek *oros*	mountain	LEADING ROOT COMPOUND: *oro*: gen: orogenic, orogeny (*gen*, producing) graph: orography (*graph*, write) logy: orology (*logy*, study of) meter: orometer (*meter*, measure) *oreo*: pithecus: oreopithecus (*pith*, ape) PREFIXED LEADING ROOT COMPOUND: an-: anorogenic (in *geology*, free from mountain-making disturbance) (*an-*, not; *genic*, producing) CROSS REFERENCE: *mont*
orth***	Greek *orthos* (IE: *werdh*, to grow, climb, high)	straight, normal, right	SIMPLE ROOT: orthal, orthotics, orthotist LEADING ROOT COMPOUND: *orth*: odont: orthodontics (*odont*, tooth) ops: orthopsia (literally, straight or horizontal vision: the ability of the human eye to see better during dawn or twilight than in bright sunlight) (*ops*, vision) opt: orthoptic (*opt*, vision) *ortho*: cephal: orthocephalic (*cephal*, head) chrom: orthochromatic (*chrom*, color) clas: orthoclase (chemical symbol: $KA1Si_3O_8$) (*clas*, break) dox: orthodox, orthodoxy (*dox*, teaching) ep: orthoepy (the study of pronunciation; phonology) (*epos*, word) gen: orthogenics, orthogenesis (*gen*, producing) gnath: orthognathous (*gnathos*, jaw) gon: orthogonal (*gon*, angle) grad: orthograde (in *zoology*, walking with the body upright) (*gradus*, step) graph: orthographer, orthographic (pertaining to orthography; in *geometry*, or right angles and perpendicular lines), orthography (literally, straight writing; correct spelling) (*graph*, write) mol: orthomolecular (*mol*, mass)

Element	From	Meaning	Examples
orth (cont'd)			ped: orthopedics (also, *orthopaedics*; originally, the training of children) {orthopedic, or *orthopaedic*} (*paed*, child; originally, boy)
			pne: orthopnea (inability to breathe except in upright position) (*pnea*, breath)
			psych: orthopsychiatry (*psyche*, mind)
			pter: orthopteran (literally, straight-winged; an order of insects comprising the crickets, grasshoppers, etc.) (*pter*, wing)
			rhomb: orthorhombic (*rhomb*, turn)
			scop: orthoscope (*scope*, look)
			stat: orthostatic (*stat*, stand)
			stich: orthostichy (vertical arrangement of leaves or flowers on a stem) (*stich*, row)
			therap: orthotherapy (*therap*, treatment)
			trop: orthotropic (in *botany*, indicating vertical growth), orthotropous (*trop*, turn)
			GREEK ROOT + GERMAN ROOT COMPOUND: orthogneiss (gneiss that is derived from igneous rock)
			CROSS REFERENCE: *ithy, rect/reg*
-ory,* -orium	Latin	place where, thing for	SUFFIXED ROOT: *orium*: auditorium, sanatorium (same as *sanitarium*) *ory*: crematory, directory, dormitory, factory, lavatory, observatory, refectory, reformatory NO CROSS REFERENCE
oryct*	Greek *oryktos*: digging (IE: *reu*, to tear out, tear apart, break)	fossil	LEADING ROOT COMPOUND: *orycto*: gnos: oryctognosy (*gnos*, knowledge) logy: oryctology (*logy*, study of) *oryctero*: pus: orycteropus (an order that comprises the aardvarks) (from *pod*, foot) CROSS REFERENCE: *foss*
os**	Latin *os* (IE: *ost*, bone)	bone	SIMPLE ROOT: os: os (plural, *ossa*) ossa: ossature osse: ossein (in *biochemistry*, the organic basis for bone, the part left after the mineral matter is dissolved in dilute acids), osseous (composed of, containing, or like bone) ossi: ossicle (a small bone or bonelike structure; especially, any of the three small bones in the tympanic cavity of the ear), ossiculum (plural, *ossicula*) ossu: ossuary (a container, as an urn, vault, etc., for the bones of the dead) LEADING ROOT COMPOUND: fer: ossiferous (containing bones, as a geologic deposit) (*ferre*, to bear) frag: ossifrage (literally, rock-breaker; the osprey; see *Doublets* below) (*frag*, break) fy: ossify (from *facere*, to make, do) DISGUISED ROOT: osprey (see *Doublets* below) DOUBLETS: osprey:ossifrage CROSS REFERENCE: *ost(eo)*

Element	From	Meaning	Examples
osc**	Latin *os* (IE: *ous*, mouth, edge)	opening, mouth (extended to include "kissing")	SIMPLE ROOT: osci: oscitancy (drowsiness, dullness, apathy, etc.), oscitation oscu: osculant, oscular, osculation, osculate (to kiss; from *oscu-lum*, little mouth; in *geometry*, to touch another curve or another part of the same curve so as to have the same tangent and curvature at the point of contact) osculatory, osculum (any of the openings of a sponge through which water passes out) ost: ostiary (a porter; see *Doublets* below) PREFIXED ROOT: *in-*: inosculate (joined at the ends, rather than on an angle, or in the middle; said of arteries, ducts, etc.) (*in-*, in, on, toward) *inter-*: interosculate (to have mutual communication; interpenetrate; in *biology*, to have some common characteristics: said of separate species or groups) (*inter-*, between) DISGUISED ROOT: usher (from *ostiary*; see *Doublets* below) DOUBLETS: ostiary:usher INTERDISCIPLINARY: osculant (in *biology*, intermediate, linking, shared: said of a characteristic common to two or more groups; in *mathematics*, touching angles, as though kissing; in *zoology*, gripping or adhering together; embracing) CROSS REFERENCE: *for(is)*
-ose**	Latin	quality of	ROOT NOTE: In addition to stated meaning, this element indicates carbohydrates. SUFFIXED ROOT: *-ose* (quality of): belli: bellicose (war) clad: cladose (branch) grand: grandiose joc: jocose (joke) ram: ramose (branch) verb: verbose (word) *-ose* (carbohydrates) cell: cellulose dextr: dextrose fruct: fructose gluc: glucose lact: lactose lu: lucrose malt: maltose sucr: sucrose NO CROSS REFERENCE
-osis**	Greek	condition, action	NOTE: This element has two related meanings: that which indicates a condition, state, or action, as in *osmosis*; and that which indicates a diseased or abnormal condition, as in *neurosis* and *psychosis*. SUFFIXED ROOT: osis: hypnosis, neurosis, osmosis, psychosis otic: neurotic, psychotic, sclerotic NO CROSS REFERENCE

484

Element	From	Meaning	Examples
osm*	Greek *osmos*: impulsion (IE: *wedh*, to push, strike)	pushing	SIMPLE ROOT: osmole, osmose, osmosis, osmosity, osmotic PREFIXED ROOT: *end-*: endosmosis (*endo-*, within) *ex-*: exosmosis (*exo-*, outside) LEADING ROOT COMPOUND: gen: osmogen (*gen*, producing) logy: osmology (one meaning is the same as *osphresiology*; science of osmosis; *osmology* is also listed under *osm*, smell) phil: osmophilic (*phil*, inclination) recept: osmoreceptor (also listed under *osm*, smell) taxi: osmotaxis (*taxis*, arrangement) therap: osmotherapy (*therapy*, treatment) CROSS REFERENCE: *pel/puls*
osm*	Greek *osme* (IE: *od*, to smell, odor)	smell	SIMPLE ROOT: osma: osma, osmatic osmi: osmics, osmium (chemical symbol: OsO4; so named because of the odor of the vapor) osmy: osmyl PREFIXED ROOT: *an-*: anosmatic, anosmia (*an-*, negative) LEADING ROOT COMPOUND: *osm*: esthes: osmesthesia (*esthes*, feeling) *osmi*: dros: osmidrosis (a condition in which the sweat has an unusually strong odor) (*dros*, sweat) *osmo*: lagn: osmolagnia (*lagn*, erotic stimulation) logy: osmology (two distinct meanings; also listed under *osm*, pushing) (*logy*, study of) meter: osmometer (two meanings; also listed under *osm*, pushing) phob: osmophobia (*phobia*, fear or hate of) recept: osmoreceptor (listed also in *osm*, pushing) CHEMICAL COMPOUND: osmic acid, derived from osmium (symbol, Os) NO CROSS REFERENCE
ost**	Greek *osteon* (IE: *ost*, bone)	bone, shell	SIMPLE ROOT: osteal, ostracism, ostracize (**Synonyms:** banish, exile, expatriate) PREFIXED ROOT AND COMPOUNDS: *end-*: endosteum (the vascular connective tissue lining the marrow cavities of the bones) (*endo-*, within) *exo-*: exostosis (an abnormal bone growth on the surface of a bone or tooth) (*exo-*, out + *osis*; condition of) *hyper-*: hyperostosis (an abnormal increase in or thickening of bone tissue) (*hyper-*, over, beyond) *peri-*: (around) periosteum (the membrane of tough, fibrous connective tissue covering all bone and tissue except at the joints) periostitis (*itis*, inflammation)

Element	From	Meaning	Examples
ost (cont'd)			LEADING ROOT COMPOUND: *oste*: itis: osteitis (*itis*, inflammation of) oid: osteoid (*oid*, similar to) oma: osteoma (*oma*, growth, tumor) *osteo*: arthr: osteoarthritis (*arthr*, joint; *itis*, inflammation of) blast: osteoblast (any cell which develops into bone or secretes substances producing bony tissue) (*blast*, embryo, cell) clas: osteoclasis (the breaking down and absorption of bone tissue), osteoclast (from *klan*, to break) logy: osteology (the study of the structure and function of bones) {osteological} (*logy*, study of) malac: osteomalacia (*malac*, soft; *malacia*, softening of tissue) mye: osteomyelitis (*mye*, marrow; *itis*, inflammation of) path: osteopath, osteopathy (*pathy*, disease) phyt: osteophyte [*phyton*, growth (in medical terminology)] plast: osteoplastic (*plast*, form) por: osteoporosis (*porus*, pore; *osis*, condition of) tom: osteotome, osteotomy (*tom*, cut) CROSS REFERENCE: *oss*
oti*	Latin *otium*	ease, leisure	PREFIXED ROOT: *neg*-: negotiate (literally, not at ease; leisure; thus, to carry on business) (*neg*-, not) LEADING ROOT COMPOUND: ose: otiose (being at leisure or ease; **Synonyms**: vain, idle, hollow) (*ose*, condition of) NO CROSS REFERENCE
oto**	Greek *otos* (IE: *ous*, *aus*, ear)	ear	SIMPLE ROOT: otic PREFIXED ROOT: *par*-: parotic, parotid (situated or occurring near the ear) (*para*-, alongside) *peri*-: periotic (*peri*-, around) LEADING ROOT COMPOUND: *ot*: alg: otalgia (*alg*, pain) itis: otitis (*itis*, inflammation of) odyn: otodynia (*odynia*, pain) *oto*: cyst: otocyst (*cyst*, bladder, sac) laryng: otolaryngology (*laryng*, larynx) lith: otolith (*lith*, stone) logy: otology (*logy*, study of) scler: otosclerosis (a growth of spongy bone in the inner ear causing progressive deafness) (*scler*, hard + *osis*, condition of) scop: otoscope (an instrument for examining the ear) (*scope*, look) TRAILING ROOT COMPOUND: myos: myosotis (literally, mouse ear; the flower forget-me-not) (*myos*, mouse) CROSS REFERENCE: *acou, audi, aur*

Element	From	Meaning	Examples
ov**	Latin *ovum* (IE: *awi*, bird, egg)	egg	SIMPLE ROOT: ova: ova (plural of *ovum*), oval **ovary** ovate (egg-shaped; in *botany*, having the shape of the longitudinal section of an egg, especially with the broader end at the base) ovo: ovolo (convex molding, usually a quarter section of a circle or an ellipse) ovu: ovular, ovulate, ovulation, ovule, ovum (plural, *ova*) LEADING ROOT COMPOUND: *ov*: oid: ovoid (*oid*, similar to) *ovar*: ectom: ovarectomy (*ectom*, to remove surgically) itis: ovaritis (*itis*, inflammation of) *ovario*: tom: ovariotomy (*tom*, cut) *ovi*: duct: oviduct (from *ducere*, to lead) fer: oviferous (*ferre*, to bear) form: oviform (egg-shaped) par: oviparous (producing eggs which hatch after leaving the body of the female; opposed to *viviparous*, bearing or bringing forth living young instead of laying eggs) (*parare*, to bear) posit: oviposit, ovipositor (from *ponere*, to place) sac: ovisac (the ootheca, an egg receptacle; see both *oo* and *theca*) (*sac*, pouch) *ovo*: test: ovotestis (a single reproductive organ that produces both sperm and ova, usually at different times, as in many mollusks) (*testis*, testicle) vivi: ovoviviparous (producing eggs that are hatched within the female so that the young are born alive, as some reptiles, fishes, and snails) (*vivi*, life; *parous*, bearing) PLACENAMES: Oval, Pennsylvania; Ovalo, Texas INTERDISCIPLINARY: ovary (in *botany*, the enlarged, hollow part of the pistil or gynoecium, containing ovules; in *zoology*, the female reproductive gland producing eggs, and in the vertebrates, sex hormones) NB: Do not confuse with *ovation*, as *a standing ovation*; *ovation* comes from Greek *euai*, a cry of Bacchic joy. CROSS REFERENCE: *oo*
ox**	Greek *oxys* (IE: *ak*, sharp, bitter)	sharp, bitter, quick, acid	SIMPLE ROOT: oxa: oxalate, oxalic, oxalis oxi: oxidant, oxidation, oxide, oxime PREFIXED ROOT: *amphi-*: amphioxus (*amphi-*, around) *hyp-*: hypoxia (*hypo-*, under) *par-*: paroxysm (any sudden, violent outburst, as of action or emotion) (*para-*, alongside)

Element	From	Meaning	Examples
ox (cont'd)			LEADING ROOT COMPOUND:
			oxal (from *oxalate*):
			emia: oxalemia (*em* from *hemo*, blood; *ia*, condition of]
			oxy:
			blep: oxyblepsia (acuteness of sight) (*blepsis*, sight)
			ceph: oxycephaly (a condition in which the skull has a peaked or somewhat conical shape) (*cephal*, head)
			gen: oxygen (in German, *Sauerstoff*, sour stuff), oxygenate (*gen*, producing)
			hem: oxyhemoglobin (*hemo*, blood; *glob*, ball, sphere)
			hydr: oxyhydrogen (*hydro*, water; *gen*, producing)
			moron: oxymoron (literally, acutely silly: a figure of speech in which opposite or contradictory ideas or terms are combined, e.g., bitter sweetness, cruel kindness, laborious idleness, mournful optimist, sweet sorrow, thunderous silence, "to make haste slowly")
			osm: oxyosmia (acuteness of the sense of smell) (*osm*, smell)
			phon: oxyphonia (a sharp quality to the voice) (*phone*, sound)
			toc: (from *tokos*, childbirth)
			oxytocic (hastening the process of childbirth, as oxytocin does)
			oxytocin (a hormone of the posterior pituitary gland, serving to increase the contractions of the smooth muscle of the uterus and facilitate the secretion of milk)
			TRAILING ROOT COMPOUND:
			mon: monoxide (an oxide with one atom of oxygen in each molecule) (*mono*, one)
			CROSS REFERENCE: *ac*

The classic works of our language have become classic because of their author's command of words and undeniable power of expression. Anonymous

P

Element	From	Meaning	Examples
pac.*** **pax**	Latin *pacis*: peace; *pangere,* to strike (IE: *pak,* to fasten)	peace, binding	SIMPLE ROOT: *pac*: pact (an agreement between persons, groups, or nations; compact, covenant) *pax*: pax (a small tablet representing the Crucifixion, the Virgin, a saint, etc.: formerly kissed during the Roman Catholic Eucharistic service; the kiss of peace: a sign of Christian peace, union, and mutual love, as a handshake or embrace, given at some point in the service, especially in the Mass; see *Roman Mythology*, below) PREFIXED ROOT: *com*-: compact (**Synonyms:** close, dense, thick), compaction (*com*-, with, together) *im*-: impact (see *impinge* under *Prefixed Disguised Root*), impacted {impaction}, impactive (from *in*-, in) LEADING ROOT COMPOUND: fi: pacifier, pacifist, pacifism (from *facere,* to make, do) fic: pacific (see *Pacific* under *Ocean*, below), pacificate, pacification (from *facere,* to make, do) fy: pacify (**Synonyms:** appease, mollify, placate) (from *facere,* to make, do) DISGUISED ROOT: fang (Middle English; that which is seized) page (of book), paginal, paginate, pagination pageant, pageantry PREFIXED DISGUISED ROOT: *ap*-: appease (see synonyms at *pacify*, above) (*ap*- assimilates *ad*-, to, toward) *im*-: impinge (literally, to strike in) {impingement, impinger} (from *in*-, in) *pro*-: propaganda (see *Religious Body* below), propagate (literally, to fasten before) (*pro*-, before) LATIN TERM: *Pax Romana* (Roman peace; the terms of peace imposed by Rome on any of its dominions; any peace dictated to a subjugated people by a conquering nation) LATIN SAYINGS: *Si vis pacem, para bellum* (If you want peace, prepare for war) *Pax vobiscum* [Peace (be) with you] ROMAN CATHOLIC RELIGIOUS BODY: Propaganda (short for *Sacra Congregatio de Propaganda Fide,* Sacred Congregation for Propagating the Faith) ROMAN MYTHOLOGY: Pax (the goddess of peace, identified with the Greek goddess Irene) OCEAN: Pacific (so named by Magellan because of its tranquil, peaceful, appearance; however, the Pacific produces some of the most violent volcanoes, earthquakes, and tsunamis--popularly, but inaccurately--called tidal waves) PLACENAMES: Pacific (Missouri, Washington); Pacifica, California NO CROSS REFERENCE

Element	From	Meaning	Examples
pachy**	Greek *pachys* (IE: *bhengh*, thick, dense)	thick	SIMPLE ROOT: pachynesis, pachynsis, pachyntic LEADING ROOT COMPOUND: *pachy*: derm: pachyderm (any thick-skinned animal, such as the hippopotamus, elephant, rhinoceros) {pachydermal, or *pachydermic*}, pachydermatous, pachydermia (*derm*, skin) em: pachyemia (*em* is short for *hemo*, blood) *pachys*: andr: pachysandra (a plant with thick stamens) (*andr*, stamen) TRAILING ROOT COMPOUND: myo: myopachynsis (abnormal thickening of muscle tissue) (*myo*, muscle) CROSS REFERENCE: *platy*
pal*	Latin *palus* (IE: *pak*, to fasten)	stake (in ground)	SIMPLE ROOT: pale (a narrow, upright, pointed stake used in fences; see *NB*), palisade PREFIXED ROOT: *im-*: impale (from *in-*, in, on) DISGUISED ROOT: (from *tri-*, three + *palus*) travel (see *Doublets* below; in ancient times, transportation was so torturous that it was considered *travail*) travail (see *Doublets* below; originally an instrument of torture of three stakes) DOUBLETS: travel:travail PLACENAMES: Palos Alto, California (High Stakes) Palo Verde (Arizona, California) (Green Stake) NB: *Pale*, meaning *pallid*, *wan*, is not in this family. NO CROSS REFERENCE
pale(o)**	Greek *palaios* (IE: *kwel²*, remote)	ancient, early, prehistoric, primitive	LEADING ROOT COMPOUND: *pale*: ethn: paleethnology (*double e* correct) (*ethn*, race) onto: (being, existence) paleontography (the description of fossils) (*graph*, write) paleontology (the branch of geology that deals with prehistoric forms of life through the study of plant and animal fossils) (*logy*, study of) *paleo*: anthrop: paleoanthropic, paleoanthropology (*anthropo*, man; *logy*, study of) bio: paleobiology (*bio*, life; *logy*, study of) cen: Paleocene (the earliest epoch of the Tertiary Period in the Cenozoic Era, preceding the Eocene) (*cen*, recent) ethn: paleoethnology (the study of prehistoric races of men) (*ethn*, race) graph: paleography (*graph*, write) lith: paleolith (a Pleistocene stone tool), paleolithic (designating or of an old-world cultural period of the early Stone Age, during which man developed flint, stone, and bone tools and lived by hunting, fishing, and gathering plant foods) (*lithos*, stone) zo: Paleozoic, paleozoology (*zo*, animal; *logy*, study of) CROSS REFERENCE: *arch, prim, proto*

490

Element	From	Meaning	Examples
palin-,** palim-	Greek *palin* (IE: *kwel¹*, to turn)	again, back	EXTENDED PREFIX : palinal PREFIXED ROOT: *palim-*: pses: palimpsest (a parchment, tablet, etc. that has been written upon or inscribed two or three times, the previous text or texts having been imperfectly erased and remaining, therefore, still partly visible) (*psen*, to rub smooth) *palin-*: drom: palindrome (see examples of palindromes under *drom*), palindromia, palindromic (*drom*, run) gen: palingenesis (literally, new birth) (*gen*, producing) od: palinode (an ode or other poem written to retract something said in a previous poem; therefore, a retraction) (*ode*, song) MEDICAL TERM: *palindromic rheumatism* (an illness that clears up in reverse order of its onset; in other words, the joints which became inflamed first heal last; and those which became inflamed last, heal first) CROSS REFERENCE: *ana-*, *re-*
pan***	Greek *pas*: all, every, universal (IE: *keu*, a swelling, arch)	all, every	LEADING ROOT COMPOUND: *pan*: acea: panacea (a remedy for all diseases, evils, or difficulties; cure-all) (from *akeisthai*, to cure) chrom: panchromatic (*chrom*, color) crat: pancratium (in ancient Greece and Rome, an athletic contest combining boxing and wrestling) (*crat*, strength) creas: pancreas (literally, all flesh; the pancreas of animals, used as food, is usually called *sweetbread*) (*creas*, flesh) dect: pandect (a complete body of laws; legal code) (*dect*, contain, receive) dem: pandemic (*demo*, people) demon: pandemonium (see note under *demon*) (*demon*, devil) dora: pandora (see *Greek Mythology* under *do*; also *Place-names* below) egyr: panegyric (literally, to bring together; a formal speech or writing, praising a person or event; high or hyperbolic praise; laudation) (from *ageirein*, to bring) gen: pangenesis (*genesis*, producing) offl: pantoffle (a slipper) (from *panthophellos*, all cork, of which medieval slippers were made) opl: panoply (a full suit of armor; any protective covering; extended to mean any complete or magnificent covering or array) (from *hopla*, arms, weapon) orama: panorama (from *horama*, sight) soph: pansophy (*soph*, wisdom) the: pantheist, pantheon (*theo*, God, god) urg: panurge (see under *Literary Figures*, below) (from *erg*, work) *panto*: graph: pantograph (*graph*, write) mim: pantomime (*mimos*, mimic, actor) scop: pantoscope (*scope*, view)

491

Element	From	Meaning	Examples
pan (cont'd)			PREFIXED DISGUISED ROOT: *dia*-: diapason (through all the stops of the organ; thus, the full organ range) (*dia*-, through) LITERARY FIGURES: Panurge (literally, all work, but interpreted "ready for anything"; the gay, cowardly companion of Pantagruel in Rabelais' *Gargantua and Pantagruel*) Pangloss (literally, all tongues, in Voltaire's *Candide*) PLACENAMES: Pandora (Colorado, Ohio, Texas) NB: *Pander*, from *Pandarus*, is not in this family. [Pandarus was a leader of the Lycians in the legendary Trojan War; in medieval romances and in Boccaccio, Chaucer, and Shakespeare, Pardarus acts as the go-between for Troilus and Cressida. In modern usage, *pander* (as a *noun*) is a go-between in sexual intrigue; especially a procurer; a pimp; a person who provides the means of helping to satisfy the ignoble ambitions or desires, vices, etc. of another; as a *verb*, to act as a pander.] CROSS REFERENCE: *omni*
pan***	Latin *panis* (IE: *pat*, to feed, eat; from *pa*, to pasture cattle)	bread (extended to include *food* in general)	SIMPLE ROOT: panatela (also, *panatella*; originally, a long, narrow biscuit; a cigar of a long, narrow shape) paneity (the quality or state of being bread, as *the paneity of the eucharistic bread*) pannier (Middle French *panier*; from Latin *panarium*, breadbasket; a large basket; specifically, a wicker basket for carrying loads on the back; also, either of a pair of baskets hung across the back of a donkey, horse, etc. for carrying market produce; other meanings) pantry (originally, where fresh-baked bread was stored) PREFIXED ROOT: *ap*-: appanage (money, land, etc., given by kings and princes to their younger children as a means of support; hence, a person's rightful extra gain; perquisite; any territory governed by another country; dependency) (*ap*- assimilates *ad*-, to, toward) *com*-: (with, together) companion (originally, a bread fellow; **Synonyms**: friend, partner, acquaintance)) company (**Synonyms**: troop, troup, band) *im*-: impanation (in *theology*, the doctrine that the body and blood of Christ are present in the bread and wine of the Eucharist after consecration by the priest, with no actual change in substance; this doctrine is also called *consubstantiation*, as opposed to *transubstantiation*, in which *the bread and the wine* are believed to become the actual body and blood of Christ, as believed especially by the Roman Catholic Church) (from *in*-, in) DOUBLE PREFIXED ROOT: accompaniment, accompanist, accompany (*ac*- assimilates *ad*-, to, toward; *com*-, with, together) DISGUISED ROOT: pastern (the part of a horse's foot between the fetlock and the hoof)

Element	From	Meaning	Examples
pan (cont'd)			pastille (literally, a small loaf; a small medicated or flavored tablet; lozenge; troche; can also mean pastel, though *pastel* itself is derived from *pasta*, paste) penuche (a variation of *panocha*) SPANISH: panada (originally, a dish made of bread boiled to a pulp and flavored) panocha (from *panada*: a coarse sugar made in Mexico) RELATED ROOT: pastor (one who feeds the flock, the congregation; see *past*) LATIN PHRASE: *Panem et circenses* (shortened form of Bread and the games of the circus, the sole amusement of the plebs) (Juvenal) CROSS REFERENCE: *past*
pand,** pass	Latin *passus*: a step; *pandere*, to stretch out (IE: *pet*, to stretch out; yields English pan)	to spread out; to stretch out	SIMPLE ROOT: pas, pass, passable, passade, passado, passage, passant, passenger PREFIXED ROOT: *pand, pans*: *ex*-: expand (**Synonyms:** swell, distend, inflate), expanse, expansion, expansive (*ex*-, out) *re*-: repand (in *botany*, having a somewhat wavy margin, as *a repand leaf*) (*re*-, back) *pass*: *com*-: compass (**Synonyms:** reach, achieve, attain) {compassable} (*com*-, with, togethe) *sur*-: surpass (**Synonyms:** exceed, excel, transcend) (from *super*-, over, beyond) *tres*-: trespass (**Synonyms: 1**) encroach, infringe, intrude; **2**) invasion, infringement; **3**) transgression, fault, sin) (from Latin *trans*-, over, across) DOUBLE PREFIXED ROOT: encompass (to shut in all around; to contain; include; to bring about; achieve) (*en*-, in + *com*-, with, together) DISGUISED ROOT: fathom (originally, arms outstretched to embrace, to measure) pace (a step; literally, a stretching out of the leg; not to be confused with Latin *pace*, ablative of *pax*, peace; see *pac*) patella (originally, an ancient Roman pan or dish; a flat, triangular bone located at the front of the knee joint; also called "kneecap"; also, any dish-shaped anatomical formation) paten (a metal disk or plate, especially one of precious metal for holding the bread in a Eucharistic service) patina (in Medieval Latin, a shallow dish, pan; in Italian, originally, a mixture prepared in a bowl and used to coat calfskins; now a thin layer of corrosion that appears on copper as a result of oxidation; also called *verdigris*, green of Greece) LATIN TERM: *passim* (spread throughout, or used often; used in textual annotation to indicate that the word or passage occurs frequently in the work cited) FRENCH WORDS AND TERMS: *faux pas* (literally, false step; a social blunder) *passementerie* (trimming made of gimp, cord, beads, braid, etc.)

Element	From	Meaning	Examples
pand (cont'd)			*passe-partout* (literally, passes everywhere; that which passes or allows passage everywhere; other meanings) ITALIAN: *passacaglia* (a slow, stately Italian dance similar to the chaconne; also, a music form based on the dance, in 3/4 time and with a continuous ground bass: ground bass designates a short phrase played repeatedly against the melodies and harmonies of the upper parts) ENGLISH COMPOUNDS: passport Passover (Jewish festival; from Hebrew *pesach*, passover; see Exodus 12) NOTE: Do not confuse this root with Greek *pass*, as in *passion* and *compassion*. NO CROSS REFERENCE
pans			See *pand* for *expanse*.
par***	Latin *parare*, to equate (IE: *per(e)*, to sell, hand over in a sale; make equal)	equal	SIMPLE ROOT: par (accepted average; in *golf*, the number of strokes considered necessary to complete a hole or course in expert play) parity [another *parity* is listed under **par**, *give birth to*] parlay (not to be confused with *parley*; see *parl*) PREFIXED ROOT: *com-*: compare (**Synonyms:** contrast, collate) {comparable, comparative, comparison} (*com-*, with, together) *dis-*: (apart, away, negative) disparage (originally, to marry one of inferior rank; discredit; **Synonyms:** belittle, depreciate, decry) disparate (some authorities place this word in the *par*, equip, family, as though the meaning is *to prepare differently*; if the word is in this family, the idea is *to be unequal;* in either case, the word means the same: completely distinct or different in kind, with emphasis on incongruity or incompatibility; **Synonyms:** different, diverse, distinct) disparity (inequality or difference, as in rank, amount, quality, etc.; unlikeness; incongruity) LEADING ROOT COMPOUND: mutuel: parimutuel (a type of betting) (from *mutual*) DISGUISED ROOT: pair (**Synonyms:** couple, brace, yoke) peer {peerless} PREFIXED DISGUISED ROOT: *com-*: compeer (a person of the same rank or status; equal) (*com-*, with, together) *um-*: umpire [from Middle French *nomper*, uneven, hence an uneven number, third person; from *non-*, not + *per* (par), even] FRENCH: *au pair* (literally, an equal; designating, of, or in, an arrangement in which services are exchanged on an even basis) *nonpareil* (literally, not equal; unequaled, unrivaled, peerless) LATIN PHRASES: *ceteris paribus* (other things being equal; all else remaining the same; *ceteris* is the same as in *et cetera*, abbreviated *etc.*) *pari passu* (with equal pace; with equal speed; in equal proportion; in *law*, without preference or priority)

Element	From	Meaning	Examples
par (cont'd)			INTERDISCIPLINARY: parity (in *mathematics*, the condition existing between two integers that are both odd or even; in *physics*, a symmetry property of a wave function: expressed as +1 if no difference can be detected between the wave function and its mirror image, and as -1 if the wave function changed only in sign) NO CROSS REFERENCE
par**	Latin *parere*	show (verb), appear	PREFIXED ROOT: *ap*-: (*ap*- assimilates *ad*-, to, toward) apparent (**Synonyms**: evident, obvious, manifest) {apparently} apparition (**Synonyms**: phantom, phantasm, ghost) *trans*-: transparency, transparent (**Synonyms**: clear, translucent, pellucid) (*trans*-, across, through) PREFIXED DISGUISED ROOT: *ap*-: appear, appearance (**Synonyms**: guise, aspect, semblance) (*ap*- assimilates *ad*-, to, toward) CROSS REFERENCE: *phan/phen*
par,** per	Latin *parere*: to produce (IE: *per(e)*, to give birth to)	give birth to	SIMPLE ROOT: pare: parent, parentage (lineage; origin; derivation from a source; origin; cause) parental (in *genetics*, designating the generation from which a genetic experiment begins) pari: parity [another *parity* is listed under **par**, *equal*] part: parturient, parturition PREFIXED ROOT: *post*-: *post partum* (*post*-, after) *re*-: repertory (same as French *repertoire*; the stock of plays, operas, roles, songs, etc. that a company, actor, singer, etc. is familiar with and ready to perform) (*re*-, again) LEADING ROOT COMPOUND: fac: parturifacient (inducing or easing labor in childbirth) (*facient*, making or causing to become) TRAILING ROOT COMPOUND: bi: biparous (bearing two offspring at birth; in *botany*, dividing into two branches) (*bi*, two) feti: fetiparous (designating or of animals whose young are born incompletely developed, as marsupials) (*feti*, fetus) flori: floriparous (*flori*, flower) multi: multipara (a woman who is bearing her second child or has borne two or more children), multiparous (of or being a multipara; in *zoology*, designating or of a species of animal that normally bears more than one offspring at birth) (*multi*, many) ovi: oviparous (producing eggs which hatch after leaving the body of the female; opposed to *viviparous*) (*ov*, egg) primi: primipara (a woman who is pregnant for the first time or who has borne just one child) {primiparous} (*prim*, first) vivi: viviparous (*viv*, living) DISGUISED ROOT: viper (condensation of *vivus parere*) CROSS REFERENCE: *gen, nas/nat*

Element	From	Meaning	Examples
par,* **per,** **para-**	Latin *parare* (IE: *per(e)*, to give birth to)	to equip; to set; to place in order; to prepare; to ward off	SIMPLE ROOT: parade, pare, parry, parure (a matched set of jewelry, as earrings, bracelet, and necklace) PREFIXED ROOT: *par:* *ap-:* apparatus, apparel (clothing; garments; attire; anything that clothes or adorns) (*ap-* assimilates *ad-*, to, toward) *dis-:* disparate (**Synonyms:** separate, divergent, incommensurable; see note under *par*, equal) (*dis-*, apart) *pre-:* preparation, preparative, preparatory, prepare, preparedness (*pre-*, before) *re-:* reparable, reparation (**Synonyms:** restitution, redress, indemnification) (*re-*, again) *se-:* separate (from which *sever, several* are derived; see *Doublets* below; **Synonyms:** part, divide, sever) (*se-*, apart) *per:* *em-:* emperor (from which *empire*, below, is derived) *im-:* imperative, imperial, imperious (**Synonyms:** masterful, domineering, magisterial), imperium (from *emperor*, previous entry) LEADING ROOT COMPOUND: *par:* *flech:* parfleche (a rawhide with the hair removed by soaking it in water and lye) *para:* *chut:* parachute (see *Placename* below) (from *cadere*, to fall) *dos:* parados (an embankment of earth along the back of a trench as to protect against fire from the rear) (from *dorsum*, back) *medic:* paramedic (authorities are divided on whether *para-* in this word belongs in the family meaning alongside, in that the paramedic "works alongside" the doctor; or whether in this family, in the sense of warding off illness, or injury) *sol:* parasol (that which protects from, or wards off, the sun: an umbrella carried as a sunshade) (*sol*, sun) PREFIXED DISGUISED ROOT: *com-:* comprador (*com-*, with) *em-:* empire (supreme rule; absolute power or authority; dominion) (*em-*, in) *re-:* repair (**Synonyms:** mend, patch, darn; see *Note*) (*re-*, again) *se-:* sever (see *Doublets* below; see synonyms at *separate*, above), several [both words in this entry are from *separate*] (*se-*, apart) DOUBLE PREFIXED DISGUISED ROOT: rampart (any defense or bulwark) [*re-*, intensifier + *am-* (from *in-*, against) + *par*; thus, to prepare against] DOUBLETS: separate:sever PLACENAME: Parachute, Colorado NOTE: There is another *repair*, derived from Latin *patri*, literally, the return to one's fatherland, as to *repair* to warmer climates for the winter. NO CROSS REFERENCE

496

Element	From	Meaning	Examples
para-***	Greek (IE: *pera*, a going beyond)	alongside, resembling	PREFIXED ROOT: par-: agog: paragoge [the adding of a letter or syllable to the end of a word, either grammatically, as in *drownéd*, or unnecessarily, as in *drownéd* (DROUN did), or for ease in pronunciation, as in *amidst*] (from *agein*, to lead) agon: paragon (a model or pattern of excellence or perfection of some kind) (from *parakone*, whetstone, from *parakonan*, to sharpen against, to compare) all: parallax, parallel (lines side by side) (*allelos*, one another) anthrop: paranthropus (a type of ape-man) (*anthropo*, man) enter: parenteral (located outside the body or administered in a manner other than through the digestive track, as by intravenous or intramuscular injections) (*entero*, intestine) esis: paresis (slight or partial paralysis) (from *hienai*, to set in motion) esthes: paresthesia (abnormal or impaired skin sensation, such as burning, prickling, itching, or tingling) (*esthes*, feeling) helion: parhelion (a bright spot sometimes appearing the other side of the sun, often on a luminous ring) (*helios*, sun) od: parody (a burlesque song or poem; a humorous or satirical imitation of a serious piece of literature, musical composition, person, event, etc.) (*ode*, song) oxy: paroxytone [in *Greek grammar*, having an acute accent on the penultimate (next to last) syllable] (*oxy*, sharp) para-: bio: parabiosis (the natural or artificial fusion of two organisms, as in the development of Siamese twins or the experimental joining of animals for research) (*bio*, life) blast: parablast (in *embryology*, the nutritive yolk of a meroblastic ovum) (*blast*, embryo) ble: parable (a short, simple story, usually of an occurrence of a familiar kind, from which a moral or religious lesson may be drawn) (from *bol*, to throw) bol: parabola (a geometry term) {parabolic} (*ballein*, to throw) clet: Paraclete (an intercessor, advocate; in *Christian theology*, refers to the Third Person of the Trinity, the *Holy Spirit:* one who comes *alongside* man to be his aid; a pleader) (from *kalein*, call, invoke) digm: paradigm (a list of all the inflectional forms of a word taken as an illustrative example of the conjugation or declension to which it belongs; any example or model, as the paradigm of a paragraph) (from *deik*, show) dox: paradox (a statement that seems contradictory, unbelievable, or absurd but that may be true in fact) (*doxa*, opinion) gen: paragenesis (the order in which closely related minerals in rocks, veins, etc. have been formed) (*genesis*, producing) graph: paragraph (a practice begun in medieval times to indicate a new topic in a manuscript, by *writing alongside* in the margin), paragraphia (a form of aphasia which affects one's writing) (*graph*, write)

Element	From	Meaning	Examples
para- (cont'd)			leip: paraleipsis (a *rhetorical* device, in which a point is stressed by suggesting that it is too obvious or well-known to mention, as in the phrase "not to mention the distance involved") (*leipein*, to leave)
			log: paralogism (reasoning *contrary* to the rules of logic, especially when the reasoner is not aware of the fallacy) (*logos*, word)
			lys: paralysis (the verb is *paralyze*) {paralytic} (*lys*, loosen)
			mec: paramecium (a ciliate protozoan, usually oval and having an oral groove for feeding) (from *mekos*, length)
			meter: parameter (*meter*, measure)
			mnes: paramnesia (a distortion of memory in which fantasy and experience are confused) (*mne*, memory)
			morph: paramorphism (*morph*, shape, form)
			no: paranoia (alongside the mind; thus a certain type of madness; demented), paranoid (*nous*, mind)
			pet: parapet (a low, protective wall or railing along the edge of a roof, balcony, or similar structure) (*petta*, chest)
			phern: paraphernalia (originally, personal belongings; the articles used in some activity; equipment; gear) (*phern*, dowry)
			phras: paraphrase (**Synonyms**: translation, transliteration), paraphrastic (*phrase*, speech, word)
			phys: paraphysis (a sterile, threadlike part found with the spore-bearing organs of some ferns and mosses) (*phys*, growth)
			pleg: paraplegia (*pleg*, stroke)
			prax: parapraxis (from *prassein*, to do)
			psych: parapsychology (*psyche*, mind; *logy*, study of)
			sit: parasite (feeding upon another) (*sitos*, grain, food)
			taxi: parataxis (in *rhetorical grammar*, the placing of related clauses, etc., in a series without the use of connecting words, e.g., "I came, I saw, I conquered"; "It was cold; the snows came") (*taxi*, arrangement)
			zo: parazoan (*zo*, animal)
			DOUBLE PREFIXED ROOT:
			en-: (in)
			chyma: parenchyma (literally, to pour in beside) (from *khein*, to pour)
			thesis: parenthesis [plural, *parentheses*; literally, a putting in beside; either or both of the upright curved lines \()\ used to mark off explanatory or qualifying remarks in writing or printing; also, a mathematical term] (*thesis*, to place, put)
			syn-: (with, together)
			apsis: parasynapsis (from *haptein*, to fasten, connect)
			thesis: parasynthesis (in *linguistics*, the formation of words by adding both a derivative ending and a prefix, as in *denationalize*; also, the formation of a word by the addition of a derivational suffix to a phrase or compound, as *great-hearted*, which is *great heart*, plus *-ed*)
			PREFIXED ELIDED ROOT: paraph (from *paragraphus*; a flourish made after or below a signature, to prevent forgery)

Element	From	Meaning	Examples
para- (cont'd)			PLACENAME: Paragon, Indiana NB: The following words are not in this family: parachute (see *par*, to equip); paradise (see *peri-*) paraffin (from *parum*, too little + *affinis*, akin: from its chemical inertness) paramount (from *per-*, by + *amount*) paramour (from *par-* by + *amour*, love) paratroops (from *parachute* + *troop*) parasol (see **par**, to equip) INTERDISCIPLINARY: parenchyma (in *anatomy*, the tissue characteristic of an organ, as distinguished from connective tissue; in *botany*, tissue composed of soft, unspecialized, thin-walled cells) NO CROSS REFERENCE
parie*	Latin *paries* (IE: *(s)per*, a bar, spear)	wall of a room	SIMPLE ROOT: paries (plural, *parietes*; in *biology*, usually plural; the wall of a hollow organ, cavity, cell, etc.) parietal (dwelling within, or having authority within, the walls of buildings of a college, e.g., *parietal regulations*) INTERDISCIPLINARY: parietal (in *anatomy*, of or relating to, or forming the walls of a cavity, and especially designating either of the parietal bones, the two bones between the frontal and occipital bones; the parietal bones form part of the top and sides of the skull; in *biology*, pertaining to or forming the wall of a hollow structure; in *botany*, attached to the ovary wall: said of the ovules or placenta in certain plants) CROSS REFERENCE: *mur, sept*
parl***	French *parler* (originally from Greek *parabola*, to throw beyond)	speak	SIMPLE ROOT: parla: parlance (a style or manner of speaking or writing; language; idiom), parlando parle: parley (see note on *parlay* below) parli: parliament, parliamentary parlo: parlor (from Old French *parleoir*, room used for conversation; in medieval monasteries, a place where monks were permitted to receive occasional visitors, and where they were allowed to break their vows of silence) DISGUISED ROOT: palaver (a conference or discussion, originally between African natives and European settlers; talk, idle chatter; flattery; cajolery) (from Portuguese *palavra*, word, speech) parol, parole (possibly) ITALIAN MUSIC TERM: *parlando* (delivered or performed in an unsustained style or manner suggestive of speech) FRENCH EXPRESSIONS: *parlez-vous* (Do you speak, as in the longer phrase, *parlez-vous français?* Do you speak French?) *pourparler* (a discussion preliminary to negotiations) PLACENAMES: Lac qui Parle, Minnesota; Parlier, California NOTE: *Parlay*, from Italian *paro*, pair, an equal, is not in this family. CROSS REFERENCE: *dict, fal/fess, locu/loqu, ora, phas/phe*

Element	From	Meaning	Examples
part,*** **port**	Latin *pars,* *partis* (IE: *per(e)*, to give birth to)	part	SIMPLE ROOT: *part*: partial, partible, particle (see *Doublets* below), particular, partisan, partite, partition, partitive, partly, partner, party *port*: portion {portionable, portionless, portioner} NOTE: *Partly* and *partially* are not invariably interchangeable; see *American Heritage Dictionary*, under *partly*, **Usage**. PREFIXED ROOT: *part*: *a-*: apart, apartment (from *ad-*, to, toward) *com-*: compart {compartition, compartment} (*com-*, with) *counter-*: counterpart (from *contra-*, against) *de-*: depart, departed (**Synonyms:** defunct, extinct, inanimate) department, departure (*de-*, from) *im-*: impartial (**Synonyms:** just, objective, dispassionate), impartible (indivisible) (from *in-*, not) *re-*: repartition (distribution; a partitioning again in a different way) (*re-*, again) *port*: *ap-*: apportion (**Synonyms:** allot, assign, allocate) (*ap-* assimilates *ad-*) *dis-*: disportion (*dis-*, apart, away) *pro-*: proportion (**Synonyms:** symmetry, harmony, balance) (*pro-*, for) DOUBLE PREFIXED ROOT: disproportion, disproportionate (*dis-*, not + *pro-*, for) LEADING ROOT COMPOUND: *cip*: participant, participle, participate (**Synonyms:** share, partake) (from *capere*, to take) TRAILING ROOT COMPOUND: *bi*: bipartite (*bi*, two) DISGUISED ROOT: parcel (Middle English *parcelle*; from Vulgar Latin *particella*; from Latin *particula*, portion, particle; diminutive of *pars*; see *Doublets* below) parcener (in *law*, a coparcener: one of two persons sharing an undivided inheritance), parcenary (same as *parcener*) parse (from *pars orationis*, part of speech) PREFIXED DISGUISED ROOT: *co-*: coparcenary (in *law*, joint heirship; partnership in inheritance; also, joint partnership or ownership), coparcener (in *law*, one who shares jointly with others in an inheritance) (*co-*, with, together) DOUBLETS: parcel:particle LATIN-ANGLO-SAXON MESHED COMPOUND: partake (alteration of part taker, or one who takes part in) FRENCH: *repartee* (from *repartir*, to return quickly a thrust or a blow; thus a quick, witty reply; also, a series of such rejoinders; skill in making witty replies) AFRIKAANS: apartheid (the state of being apart) [Afrikaans, one of the official languages of South Africa, developed from 17th-century Dutch] NO CROSS REFERENCE

Element	From	Meaning	Examples
parthen*	Greek *parthenos*	maiden, virgin	LEADING ROOT COMPOUND: carp: parthenocarpy (the development of a ripe fruit without fertilization of the ovules, as in the banana and pineapple) gen: parthenogenesis (see under *gen*) CLASSICAL TEMPLE: Parthenon [the Doric temple of Athena (the goddess of wisdom, skills, and warfare) built (5th century B.C.) on the Acropolis in Athens] GREEK MYTHOLOGY: Parthenope (the siren who threw herself into the sea after her songs failed to lure Ulysses into a shipwreck) NO CROSS REFERENCE
pass			See *pand* for *compass*.
pass,** pat	Latin *pati*: to endure, suffer (IE: *pe*, to harm)	to suffer; to feel deeply, to pity	SIMPLE ROOT: *pass*: passible, passion (**Synonyms**: fervor, ardor, enthusiasm), passionate, passionless passive (inactive, but acted upon; in grammar, the passive voice), passivity *pat*: patience (**Synonyms**: endurance, fortitude, stoicism), patient PREFIXED ROOT: *pass*: com-: compassion (**Synonyms**: pity, sympathy, condolence) {compassionate} (*com-*, with, together) dis-: dispassionate (**Synonyms**: impartial, unbiased, objective) (*dis-*, not) im-: impassionate, impassioned, impassive (from *in-*, not) *pat*: com-: compatible (in computer terminology, designating or of computer components, software, etc. that can be used with a specific computer or computer system) (*com-*, with, together) im-: impatient (from *in-*, not) CHRISTIAN CELEBRATION: Passion Week [the week between Passion Sunday (the second Sunday before Easter) and Palm Sunday; however, the Passion of Christ refers to the sufferings of Christ in the period following the Last Supper and including the Crucifixion] RELATED ROOT: penury (from Latin *penuria*, want, lack) CROSS REFERENCE: *dolor, noso, path*
past**	Latin *pascere*: to feed (IE: *pat*, to feed, eat; from *pa*, to pasture cattle; yields English foster)	food, to feed, graze, protect	SIMPLE ROOT: pastor (as a Christian minister, arises from a recurrent Biblical metaphor, seen in Psalms 23:1; John 10:11 and 21:15) pastoral, pastorale (an instrumental composition with a tender melody in a moderately slow rhythm, suggestive of idyllic rural life, e.g., the "Pastorale" of Handel's *Messiah*) pasture PREFIXED ROOT: anti-: antipasto (before the meal; appetizers) (*anti-*, before) re-: repast (food and drink for a meal) (*re-*, again) NB: *Pasta, paste, pastel*, and *pastry*-are not in this family; all are derived from Greek *passein*, to sprinkle) CROSS REFERENCE: *pan* (Latin)
pat			See *pass* for *patience*.

501

Element	From	Meaning	Examples

pater,**
patri
	Latin
	pater;
	Greek
	patri
	(IE: *pater*,
	father;
	yields
	German
	Vater,
	English
	father)
		father	ROOT NOTE: The root for *father* in both Latin and Greek is
			  spelled the same in English.
			SIMPLE ROOT: patron (**Synonyms:** sponsor, backer)
			pater: pater {paternal, paternity}
			patri: patrician, patrimony, patriot {patriotism}
			PREFIXED ROOT:
			com-: compatriot (a fellow countryman; a colleague) (*com-*,
			  with)
			ex-: expatriate (**Synonyms:** banish, exile, deport) (*ex-*, out)
			im-: impetrate (to obtain by request or by entreaty; to ask for,
			  as from a *father*) (*im-*, a variant of *in-*, an intensive)
			per-: perpetrate (originally, a ritual term; probably in the
			  sense of following one's tribal leader, or father; to do or per-
			  form something evil or offensive) (*per-*, thoroughly)
			re-: repatriate (*re-*, again)
			sym-: sympatric (*sym-*, with, together)
			LEADING ROOT COMPOUND:
			pater:
			noster: paternoster (see *The Lord's Prayer*, below)
			patr:
			onym: patronymic (*onym*, name)
			patri:
			arch: patriarch, patriarchate (*arch*, rule)
			cid: patricide (*cide*, kill)
			lin: patrilineal (designating or of descent, kinship, or derivation
			  through the father instead of the mother; compare *matrilin-*
			  eal)
			TRAILING ROOT COMPOUND:
			allo: allopatric (in *biology*, of or pertaining to species of or-
			  ganisms occurring in different, but often adjacent, areas) (*al-*
			  lo, other; *patr* from *patra*, native village)
			eu: eupatrid (*eu*, good, well)
			DISGUISED ROOT: padre, papal, pattern, pope
			PREFIXED DISGUISED ROOT:
			re-: repair (to go or betake oneself to a place, as *to repair to a*
			  southern climate for the winter) (another *repair*, to mend,
			  comes from *reparare*, to put in order) (*re-*, back)
			LATIN FOR *THE LORD'S PRAYER: Paternoster* (literally
			  Our Father; the first two words of the prayer)
			LATIN PHRASE:
			ad patres [to (one's) fathers; dead]
			patriae (Father of his country: said of George Washington)
			FRENCH: *compère* (literally, joint father, but meaning *god-*
			  father; a master of ceremonies)
			HYMN FROM LATIN: *Gloria Patri* (Glory to the Father)
			SPANISH: *padre*
			PREFIXED SPANISH: compadre (literally, godfather; a close
			  friend; buddy)
			NO CROSS REFERENCE

Size of vocabulary and number of ideas are intimately related. A mastery of a large number of
words can lead to a greater range of thought. Joseph G.Brin

Element	From	Meaning	Examples
path**	Greek *pathos* (IE: *kwenth*, to suffer, endure)	feeling, disease	SIMPLE ROOT: pathetic (**Synonyms:** moving, affecting, touching) pathos (**Synonyms:** bathos, poignancy) PREFIXED ROOT: *a-*: apathy (lack of emotion; lack of interest; listless condition; indifference) {apathetic} (*a-*, not, without) *anti-*: antipathy {antipathetic} (*anti-*, against) *em-*: empathy {empathic, empathize} (*em-*, in) *exo-*: exopathic (designating a *disease* having its cause or source outside the body) (*exo-*, outside) *sym-*: sympathy (**Synonyms:** pity, compassion, condolence) {sympathetic} (*sym-*, with, together) *tele-*: telepathy (*tele-*, from afar) LEADING ROOT COMPOUND: gen: pathogen {pathogenesis, pathogenic} (*gen*, producing) log: pathology {pathological, pathologist} (*logy*, study of) TRAILING ROOT COMPOUND: allo: allopath, allopathy (*allo*, other) neuro: neuropathy (*neuro*, nerve) osteo: osteopath, osteopathy (a branch of medicine that places special emphasis on the interrelationship of the musculoskeletal system to all other body systems) (*osteo*, bone) psych: psychopathic (*psycho*, mind) PREFIXED TRAILING ROOT COMPOUND: *an-*: anethopathy (a form of psychopathic personality in which the patient apparently knows the difference between right and wrong and the consequences of transgression, yet persistently gets into trouble) (*an-*, negative + *ethos*, character) CROSS REFERENCE: *noso, pass/pat*
pax			See *pac.*
pec			See *fe* for *pecuniary, impecunious.*
pecca*	Latin *peccare*: to sin	fault, sin	SIMPLE ROOT: peccable {peccability} peccancy (sinfulness; plural, *pecancies*: a sin) peccant (sinful; sinning) PREFIXED ROOT: *im-*: impeccable (not liable to sin; incapable of wrongdoing; without defect or error; faultless), impeccant (*in-*, not) SPANISH: *peccadillo* (a minor or petty sin; slight fault; as in *innocent peccadillo*) (Spanish spelling: *pecadilo*) ITALIAN: *peccato* (sin, pity); *che peccato!* (What a pity!) LATIN SENTENCE: peccavi (I have sinned, or I have been to blame; as a *noun*, a confession of guilt) CROSS REFERENCE: *culp*
pect*	Latin *pectinare*: to comb (IE: *pag*, to fasten)	comb-like	SIMPLE ROOT: pecte: pecten (a comblike tissue around the transparent, jelly-like part of the eye in many birds and reptiles; also any comblike structure, such as of the stridulating organ of some spiders) pecti: pectinate (as *a pectinate leaf*, from its shape; also *pectinated*)

503

Element	From	Meaning	Examples
pect (cont'd)			LEADING ROOT COMPOUND: *pectinato*: pinna: pectinatopinnate (*pinna*, feather) *pectini*: fer: pectiniferous (*ferre*, to bear) form: pectiniform (resembling a scallop shell) NOTE: The stem of this root is spelled the same as the water-soluble carbohydrate *pectin*. CROSS REFERENCE: *cten*
pector*	Latin *pectus, pectoris*	breast, chest	SIMPLE ROOT: pectoral, pectoralis, pectus (one meaning: the breast of a bird) PREFIXED ROOT: *ex-*: expectorant, expectorate (to discharge from the chest; to spit) (*ex-*, out) LEADING ROOT COMPOUND: loqu: pectoriloquy (*loqui*, to speak) phon: pectorophony (*phone*, sound) DISGUISED ROOT: parapet (see note under *para-*) petronel (a carbinelike firearm of heavy caliber, used in the 15th to 17th centuries; the firearm rested against the chest in firing) LATIN PHRASES: *in petto* (literally, in the breast; secretly; said of cardinals appointed by the Pope but not named in the consistory, or the church council) *pectus est quod disertos facit* (It is the heart that makes men eloquent) Quintilian CROSS REFERENCE: *stern*
pecu*	Latin *pecus* (IE: *pek*, cattle)	money, cattle	SIMPLE ROOT: pecula: peculate (to steal or misuse money or property entrusted to one's care, especially public funds) peculi: peculiar (originally, private property, especially cattle; thus, one's own), peculium (originally, wealth in cattle) pecun: pecuniary [pertaining to money, but originally pertaining to cows; as in *pecuniary responsibility, pecuniary loss, pecuniary motives, a pecuniary offense* (one that requires payment of money)] PREFIXED ROOT: *im-*: impecunious (literally, without cattle; having no money; poor, penniless) (from *in-*, not) ANGLO-SAXON: fee, fief, feud (another *feud* is from IE *peik*, hostile) LATIN PREFIXED ANGLO-SAXON ROOT: *en-*: enfeoff (law term), infeudation (feudal law term) (*en-*, in) NO CROSS REFERENCE
ped,*** pes	Latin *pes, pedis* (IE: *ped, pod*, foot, to go)	foot	SIMPLE ROOT: *ped*: peda: pedal, pedalo (a pedal boat), pedate pede: pedestal, pedestrian pedi: pedicel (same as *pedicle*), pediment pedu: peduncle, pedunculated

Element	From	Meaning	Examples
ped (cont'd)			*pes*: pes: pes [plural, *pedes* (the terminal organ(s) of the leg, or lower limb)] PREFIXED ROOT: *dia*-: diapedesis (the migration of blood cells, especially erythrocytes, through intact capillary walls into the tissues) (*ped* is extended to mean to leap; *dia*-, across, through) *ex*-: expedient, expedite, expedition (**Synonyms: 1**) haste, hurry, speed; **2**) trip, journey, voyage) (*ex*-, out) *im*-: impedance, impede, impediment, impedimenta (*im*-, in) DOUBLE PREFIXED ROOT: in<u>ex</u>pedient (*in*-, not + *ex*-, out) LEADING ROOT COMPOUND: cur: pedicure (*cure*, care) gre: pedigree (literally, foot of the crane, and resembling the lines as in a genealogical tree; therefore, a list of ancestors; recorded or known line of descent, especially of purebred animal) (from *grus*, a crane) palp: pedipalp (either of the second pair of appendages of spiders and other arachnids, variously developed for grasping, sensing, fertilizing, etc.) (from *palpare*, to touch) TRAILING ROOT COMPOUND: *ped*: ali: aliped (having a winglike membrane connecting the toes of the feet; wing-footed, as the bat) (*ali*, wing) bi: biped (any two-footed animal) (*bi*, two) mo: moped (from *motor*) palmi: palmiped (web-footed) (*palma*, palm of hand; therefore, outstretched) sesqui: sesquipedelian (one and a half feet, as *sesquipedelian words*) (*sesqui*, one and a half) *pede*: centi: centipede (*centi*, 100) milli: millipede (*milli*, 1,000) veloci: velocipede (*veloci*, speed) DISGUISED ROOT: petiolar, petiolate, petiole pawn (**Synonyms**: pledge, earnest, token) peon (originally, foot soldier) pioneer (originally, a member of a military engineer unit trained to construct or demolish bridges, roads, trenches, etc.) PREFIXED DISGUISED ROOT: *dis*-: dispatch (**Synonyms: 1**) hurry, speed, expedition; **2**) slay, murder, assassinate) (*dis*-, apart, away) *im*-: impeach (**Synonyms**: accuse, charge, indict) (*im*-, in) DISGUISED TRAILING ROOT COMPOUND: vet: trivet (a three-legged stand for holding pots, kettles, etc. over or near a fire; see *Word Pair* below) (from Greek *tripod*) LEADING FRENCH ROOT COMPOUND: Piedmont (foot of the mountains) ENGLISH COGNATES: fetch, fetlock, fetter WORD PAIR: tripod:trivet

Element	From	Meaning	Examples
ped (cont'd)			LATIN-GREEK HYBRIDS: pedidynamometer, pedomancy, pedometer, pedopathy (any disease of the foot) HINDI: charpoy (literally, four foot; a light bedstead or cot used in India) pajamas (literally, leg, or foot garment) teapoy (literally, three-foot; a small three-legged stand; a small table for holding a tea service) MUSIC TERM: pedal point (a single continuous tone, usually in the bass, held against the changing figures or harmonies in the other parts) INTERDISCIPLINARY: pedate (in *botany*, palmately divided into three main divisions, the outer two divisions forked into smaller ones, e.g., *a pedate leaf*; in *zoology*, having a foot or feet; like a foot, footlike, e.g., *pedate appendages*) NOTE: Do not confuse this root with Greek *ped*, child (next family), as in *pediatrician, orthopedics*, nor with Latin *ped*, lice, as in *pedicular, pediculicide*. CROSS REFERENCE: *pod/pus*
ped*** (also, paed)	Greek *pais, paidos* (IE: *pou*, small, small animal, child)	child	SIMPLE ROOT: pedant (a person who lays unnecessary stress on minor or trivial points of learning, displaying a scholarship lacking in judgment or sense of proportion; a narrow-minded teacher who insists on exact adherence to a set of arbitrary rules) {pedantic, pedantry} (from *pedagogue*) PREFIXED ROOT: *pro-*: propaedeutic (providing introductory instruction) (*pro-*, for) LEADING ROOT COMPOUND: *ped*: agog: pedagogic (of or characteristic of teachers or of teaching), pedagogue (literally, one who leads children; a teacher; often specifically, a pedantic, dogmatic teacher) (*agog*, leading) erast: pederasty (literally, sexual lover of children, especially of boys) (from *eros*, love) iatr: pediatrician, pediatrics (*iatr*, heal) odont: pedodontics (a dentist specializing in children's dentistry) (*odont*, tooth) *pedo*: baptism: pedobaptism (*bapti*, to immerse) logy: pedology (the systematic study of the behavior and development of children; another *pedology* is the study of soil) (*logy*, study of) phil: pedophilia (an abnormal condition in which an adult has a sexual desire for children) (*phil*, love of) TRAILING ROOT COMPOUND: ortho: orthopedics (originally, the practice of straightening children's bones; now, the correction or prevention of skeletal deformities) (*ortho*, straight) PREFIXED TRAILING ROOT COMPOUND: *en-*: encyclopedia (originally, that which was intended to produce a well-rounded child) (*en-*, in + *cyclo*, round)

506

Element	From	Meaning	Examples
ped (cont'd)			DISGUISED ROOT: page (the person) puerile (**Synonyms:** youthful, juvenile, adolescent) puerperal (of or connected with childbirth) puerperium (the period or state of confinement during and just after childbirth) NOTE: Do not confuse with Latin *ped*, foot, or with Greek *ped*, earth. CROSS REFERENCE: *pub*
ped*	Greek *pedon* (IE: *ped*, *pod*, foot, to go)	earth, ground	SIMPLE ROOT: pedion (related to Latin *ped*, foot) LEADING ROOT COMPOUND: cal: pedocal (*calx*, lime) gen: pedogenesis (*gen*, producing) geo: pedogeography (*geo*, earth; *graph*, write) logy: pedology (another *pedology* is the study of children) (*logy*, study of) CROSS REFERENCE: *chthon, edaph, geo, terra*
pejor*	Latin *pejorare*: to become worse (IE: *ped*, *pod*, foot, to go)	worse	SIMPLE ROOT: pejoration (a worsening; depreciation; in *linguistics*, a change of meaning for the worse), pejorative (declining; becoming worse: applied to words whose basic meaning has changed for the worse, for example, *egregious*) PREFIXED DISGUISED ROOT: *im-*: impair (**Synonyms:** injure, harm, damage) (*in-*, intensive) NO CROSS REFERENCE
pel,* pil	Latin *pellis* (IE: *pel⁴*, skin, hide)	skin	SIMPLE ROOT: *pel*: pelisse, pelt (**Synonyms:** skin, hide, rind), peltry (pelts, or fur-bearing skins, collectively) *pell*: pell, pellicle (a thin skin or film, such as a thin film on the surface of a fluid; in *zoology*, a thin nonliving membrane secreted by animal cells, as the envelope covering many protozoans), pellicula (epidermis), pellicule PREFIXED ROOT: *sur-*: surplice (a white gown worn over a cassock by some clergymen; originally, worn by clergymen of northern countries over their fur coats) (from *super-*, over) [do not confuse *surplice* with its homonym *surplus*, which see under both *super-*, and *plus*] DISGUISED ROOT: palea (the upper, or inner, thin, membranous bract enclosing the flower in grasses) CROSS REFERENCE: *cut, derm*
pel,** puls	Latin *pulsare* (IE: *pel⁶*, to beat, strike)	to push, drive, beat	SIMPLE ROOT: pulsate, pulsating, pulse PREFIXED ROOT: *pel*: *ap-*: appel {appelant, appelation} (*ap-* assimilates *ad-*, to, toward) *com-*: compel (**Synonyms:** force, coerce, constrain), compellation (not to be confused with *compilation*) (*com-*, with) *dis-*: dispel (to scatter and drive away; cause to vanish; dissipate; **Synonyms:** scatter, broadcast, disperse) {dispelled, dispelling} (*dis-*, apart, away) *ex-*: expel (**Synonyms:** eject, evict, oust) (*ex-*, out)

Element	From	Meaning	Examples
pel (cont'd)			*im-*: impel, impellent, impeller (in *mechanics*, a rotor or rotor blade; a rotating device used to force a gas or fluid in a given direction under pressure), impelling (*im-*, in)
			inter-: interpellate (to question a person formally) (*inter-*, between)
			pro-: propel {propellant (also, *propellent*), propeller} (*pro-*, forth)
			re-: repel {repellent} (*re-*, back)
			puls:
			com-: compulsion {compulsive, compulsory} (*com-*, with)
			ex-: expulsion (an expelling, or forcing out) (*ex-*, out)
			in-: impulsion {impulsive} (*im-*, in)
			pro-: propulsion (*pro-*, forth)
			re-: repulsion {repulsive} (*re-*, back)
			DISGUISED ROOT:
			poussette (a country-dance figure in which a couple or couples join hands and swing around the floor)
			push (to exert pressure or force against)
			PREFIXED DISGUISED ROOT:
			ap-: appeal (**Synonyms**: plead, sue, petition) (*ap-* assimilates *ad-*, to, toward)
			re-: repeal (**Synonyms**: abolish, annul, abrogate) (*re-*, back)
			CROSS REFERENCE: *osm*
pelag*	Greek *pelagos* (IE: *plak¹*, flat)	sea, ocean	SIMPLE ROOT: pelagic (pertaining to the sea, as *pelagic animals*)
			TRAILING ROOT COMPOUND:
			archi: archipelago [a large group of islands; a sea containing a large group of islands, as the Aegean; from Italian *Arcipelago*, the Chief Sea (perhaps a misrendering of Greek *Aigaion pelagos*, the Aegean Sea)] {archipelagic} (*archi*, chief)
			CROSS REFERENCE: *mar*
pen**	Greek *pene*: almost (related to *pan*, all)	almost, need, lack	LEADING ROOT COMPOUND:
			pen:
			insul: peninsula (literally, almost an island, that is, bounded on three sides by water) (*insul*, island)
			ult: penult, penultimate (next to last, as *the penultimate syllable* of a word) (*ultima*, last)
			umbra: penumbra (literally, almost a shade: the partly lighted area surrounding the complete shadow of a body, as the moon, in full eclipse; figuratively, a vague, indefinite, or borderline area) (*umbra*, shade)
			pene:
			plain: peneplain (in *geology*, a nearly flat land surface representing an advanced stage of erosion) (from *planus*, even)
			PREFIXED LEADING ROOT COMPOUND:
			ante-: antepenult, antepenultimate (*ante-*, before)
			TRAILING ROOT COMPOUND:
			erythro: erythropenia (same as *erythrocytopenia*, a deficiency in the number of erythrocytes) (*erythro*, red)
			PLACENAME: Peninsula, Ohio
			FRENCH PLACENAME: Presque Isle, Maine
			NO CROSS REFERENCE

508

Element	From	Meaning	Examples

pen,**
pin
	Latin
	penna
	(IE: *pet*,
	to fly)
		wing, feather	SIMPLE ROOT:
			pen:
			pen: pen (from pens originally being made from quills; see
			  Note)
			penna: penna, pennant [from *pendant* (from *pendere*, to hang +
			  pennon, from *penna*, feather)], pennate (same as *pinnate*)
			penno: pennon (a long, narrow, triangular or swallow-tailed
			  flag borne on a lance as an ensign, as formerly by knights
			  and lancers; any flag or pennant; a pinion; wing)
			pin:
			pinna:
			pinna, pinnacle (**Synonyms:** summit, apex, zenith)
			pinnate (resembling a feather; in *botany*, with leaflets on each
			  side of a common axis in a featherlike arrangement)
			pinnu: pinnule (any of the smallest divisions of a leaf which is
			  doubly compound, especially in ferns)
			PREFIXED ROOT:
			em-: empennage (literally, to put feathers on an arrow; the tail
			  assembly of an airplane, consisting of vertical and horizontal
			  stabilizers, and including the fin, rudder, and elevators) (from
			  en-, in)
			LEADING ROOT COMPOUND:
			penni:
			form: penniform (in the form of a feather)
			ped: penniped (*ped*, foot)
			pinnati:
			fid: pinnatifid (having leaves in a featherlike arrangement;
			  with narrow lobes whose clefts extend more than halfway to
			  the axis) (*fid*, split)
			sect: pinnatisect (pinnatifid but with the clefts reaching to or
			  almost to the axis) (*sect*, cut)
			DISGUISED ROOT:
			panache (a plume of feathers, as on a helmet; dashing elegance;
			  carefree; spirited self-confidence; flamboyance)
			NOTE: *Pencil* is not in this family; see *peni*.
			CROSS REFERENCE: *ala, plum, pter*

pen,**
pun
	Latin
	poena:
	penalty
	(IE:
	kwoina,
	punish-
	ment;
	from *kwei*,
	to heed,
	respect,
	avenge;
	yields
	English
	pain)
		punish, pain,
		sorrow
			SIMPLE ROOT:
			pen:
			pena: penal, penalty, penance (any act of reparation, self-
			  punishment, etc. done in repentance for a sin or wrongdoing)
			  (see *Doublets* below)
			peni:
			penitence (see synonyms at *repentance*, below)
			penitent (see *Doublets* below) penitential
			penitentiary (originally designed to make one penitent)
			pun: punish (**Synonyms:** discipline, correct, chastise), puni-
			  tive (also, *punitory*)
			PREFIXED ROOT:
			pen:
			im-: impenitent (without regret, shame, or remorse; unrepen-
			  tant) (*im-*, not)
			re-: repent (see *Note* below), repentance (**Synonyms:** peni-
			  tence, contrition, compunction), repentant (*re-*, back)

Element	From	Meaning	Examples
pen (cont'd)			*pun*: *im*-: impunity (**Synonyms**: exemption, immunity) (*im*-, not) LEADING ROOT COMPOUND: logy: penology (the study of the rehabilitation of criminals and of the management of prisons) (*logy*, study of) DISGUISED ROOT: pine (to yearn; long for) PREFIXED DISGUISED ROOT: *re*-: repine (to feel or express unhappiness or discontent; complain; fret) (*re*-, again) DOUBLETS: penance:penitent LEGAL PHRASE: *subpoena* (under penalty, first words of original writ commanding that one appear in court, either as a defendant or as a witness) PLACENAME: Penitas, Texas NOTE: *Repent* (pronounced REE punt), is from *repere*, to creep; in *biology*, creeping or crawling along the ground; prostrate. CROSS REFERENCE: *alg, dolor*
pend,*** **pens,** **pond**	Latin *pendere* (IE: *(s)pen(d)*, to pull, stretch)	to hang, weigh (extended to mean "to consider," as though being weighed and evaluated; yields the frequentative *pensare*, to think)	SIMPLE ROOT: pend (to await judgment or decision) *pend*: penda: pendant pende: pendentive (in *architecture*, one of the triangular pieces of vaulting springing from the corners of a rectangular area, serving to support a rounded or polygonal dome: usually supported by a single pier) pendi: pending (not decided, determined or established) pendu: pendulosity, pendulous, pendulum *pens*: pensi: pensile, pension, pensionary, pensioner pensive (thinking deeply or seriously, often of sad or melancholy things; **Synonyms**: contemplative, meditative) *pond*: ponder, ponderable, ponderate, ponderosa pine, ponderous (**Synonyms**: weighty, massive, cumbersome) PREFIXED ROOTS AND COMPOUNDS: *pend*: *ante*-: antependium (a screen or veil hanging from the front of an altar, pulpit, etc.) (*ante*-, before) *ap*-: (assimilates *ad*-, to, toward) append, appendage, appendant, appendicle, appendicular appendix appendectomy (*ectomy*, surgical removal) appendicitis (*itis*, inflammation of) *com*-: compendious, compendium (a summary or abstract containing the essential information in a brief form) (*com*-, with, together) *de*-: depend (**Synonyms**: rely, reckon, trust) {dependable, dependence, dependency, dependent (as a *noun*, usually, dependant)} (*de*-, from) *ex*-: expend {expendable} (*ex*-, out) *im*-: impend (to be about to happen; be imminent; to threaten) {impendent}, impending (*im*-, in)

Element	From	Meaning	Examples
pend (cont'd)			*per-*: perpendicular (*per-*, intensive) *pro-*: propend (literally, to hang forward; to have propensity toward) (*pro-*, forth) *sus-*: suspend (**Synonyms: 1**) exclude, debar, disbar; **2**) adjourn, prorogue, dissolve), suspenders (from *sub-*, under) *pens*: *com-*: (with, together) compensate (**Synonyms**: remunerate, reimburse, imdemnity) compensator (any of various devices or circuits used to correct or offset some disturbing action, as speed deviations in a moving system, excessive current in a circuit, etc.) *dis-*: (out, away) dispensary (a place where something, especially medicines, is dispensed) dispensation, dispensatory, dispense (as a pharmaceutical term, abbreviated *Disp.*; **Synonyms**: distribute, divide, dole) *ex-*: expense, expensive (**Synonyms**: costly, dear, valuable) (*ex-*, out) *pre-*: prepense (planned beforehand; premeditated; compare *malice*; in *law*, evil intent; state of mind shown by intention to do, or intentionally doing of, something unlawful) (*pre-*, before) *pro-*: propensity (**Synonyms**: inclination, bent, proclivity) (*pro-*, forth) *pond*: *pre-*: preponderant (**Synonyms**: dominant, paramount, preeminent), preponderate, preponderous (*pre-*, before) DOUBLE PREFIXED ROOT: independent (*in-*, not + *de-*, down) recompense (*re-*, again + *com-*, with, together) LEADING ROOT COMPOUND: *mot*: ponderomotive (tending to produce movement of a body) *stat*: pondostatural (pertaining to weight and stature) TRAILING ROOT COMPOUND: *pend*: *sti*: stipend (**Synonyms**: wage, salary, emolument), stipendiary (*stips*, small coin or contribution made in small coin) *vili*: vilipend (to treat or regard contemptuously or slightingly; disparage; belittle) (*vili*, vile) *pond*: *equi*: equiponderant, equiponderate (*equi*, equal, same) DISGUISED ROOT: penchant (a strong liking or fondness; inclination; taste) poise (**Synonyms**: tact, diplomacy, savoir-faire) spider, spin, spindle LATIN PHRASE: *libra pondo* (a pound in weight; therefore, pound) ENGLISH: pound (see *Latin Phrase*, above) OLD FRENCH COMPOUND: avoirdupois [from Old French *aveir de peis*; *aveir*, goods; from Latin *habere*, to have + *de-*, from + *peis* (from *pensum*), weight] CROSS REFERENCE: *bar, liter, pond*

Element	From	Meaning	Examples
peni*	Latin *penis* (IE: *pes, penis,* tail)	tail, penis	SIMPLE ROOT: penic: penicillate, penicillin, penicillium penis: penis (the male organ of urination and copulation) DISGUISED ROOT: pencil (although *pencil* is in this family, *pen,* writing utensil, is not, having come from Latin *penna,* quill, feather; see *pen/pin*) PREFIXED COGNATE ROOT: pre-: prepuce [literally, before, or in front of, the penis; the fold of skin (often called *foreskin,* or *glans penis*) covering the end (*glans*) of the uncircumcised penis; also, a similar structure covering the glans of the clitoris; see *Note*] (*pre-,* before) NOTE: The root of *prepuce* is from a root other than *peni,* but is included here because of the generic meaning: Indo-European base *put,* a swelling, whence Lithuanian *pusti,* to swell, and Byelorussian *potka,* penis. CROSS REFERENCE: *caud, cerc, mentul, phall, uro*
penta***	Greek *pente* (IE: *penkwe,* five)	five	SIMPLE ROOT: pentacle (a symbol, usually a five-pointed star) pentad (the number five; a series or group of five; a five-year period; in *chemistry,* a pentavalent element or radical) LEADING ROOT COMPOUND: *pent:* ang: pentangular (having five angles) archy: pentarchy (government by five rulers) (*arch,* ruled by) athl: (from *athlos,* a contest, struggle) pentathlete (a participant in a pentathlon) pentathlon [an athletic contest in which each contestant takes part in five events (long jump, javelin throw, 200-meter dash, discus throw, and 1500-meter run); in the Olympic games, a contest of five events (5,000-meter cross-country horseback ride, 4000-meter cross-country run, 300-meter swim, foil fencing, and pistol shooting)] *penta:* chloro: pentachlorophenol (*chloro,* green + *phenol*) dactyl: pentadactyl (having five fingers or toes on each hand or foot) (*dactyl,* finger) gon: pentagon (The Pentagon, a five-sided office building housing the main offices of the Department of Defense; located in Arlington, Virginia) (*gon,* angle) gram: pentagram (same as *pentacle;* any figure of five lines) (*gram,* write) hedr: pentahedron (a solid figure with five plane surfaces) (*hedr,* geometric plane) mer: pentamerous (in *biology,* made up of five parts or divisions: also written **5-merous**) (*mere,* part) meter: pentameter (a line of verse containing five metrical feet or measures, especially English iambic pentameter, e.g., "He jests/at scars/who nev/er felt/a wound") (*meter,* measure) ploid: pentaploid (in *biology,* having five times the haploid number of chromosomes) (from *ploos,* fold) stich: pentastich (a poem or stanza of five lines) (*stich,* row)

Element	From	Meaning	Examples
penta (cont'd)			ton: pentatonic (designating or of a musical scale having only five tones) (*tonos*, stretch, tone) val: pentavalent (having a valence of five; same as *quinquevalent*) (*valere*, to be worth) FIRST FIVE BOOKS OF THE OLD TESTAMENT: Pentateuch: Genesis, Exodus, Leviticus, Numbers, Deuteronomy (*teuchos*, an implement, book) CHRISTIAN CELEBRATION: Pentecost [from *pentekoste hemera*, the fiftieth day (after Passover), the seventh Sunday after Easter, celebrating the descent of the Holy Spirit upon the Apostles; same as Whitsunday, from Old English *Hwita Sunnandaeg*, literally, White Sunday, from the white garments of candidates for baptism] PROTESTANT DENOMINATION: Pentecostal (designating or of any of various Protestant fundamentalist sects often stressing direct inspiration by the Holy Spirit, as in glossalalia, or the speaking in tongues) CROSS REFERENCE: *cinque, quin*
pep*	Greek *pessein* (IE: *pekw*, to cook)	cook, digest; ripe	SIMPLE ROOT: peps: pepsin pept: peptic, peptide, peptize, peptone PREFIXED ROOT: dys-: dyspepsia (compare *eupepsia*) (*dys-*, bad, wrong) LEADING ROOT COMPOUND: gen: peptogenic (*genic*, producing) lys: peptolysis (*lysis*, loosening) TRAILING ROOT COMPOUND: brady: bradypepsia (*brady*, slow) eu: eupeptic (of or having good digestion; also, healthy and happy; cheerful) (*eu*, well, good) DISGUISED ROOT: drupe (any fruit with a soft, fleshy part, covered by a skinlike outer layer, and surrounding an inner stone that contains the seed, such as an apricot, cherry, plum, nectarine, etc.) pumpkin (from *pepon*, literally, ripened by the sun) HINDI: pukka (literally, ripe, of full weight, cooked; good or first-rate of its kind; genuine; real) CROSS REFERENCE: *coq*
per*	Latin *periculum*: trial, danger (IE: *per*^{5}, to try, risk)	try, risk	SIMPLE ROOT: peril (**Synonyms**: danger, jeopardy, hazard), perilous (involving peril or risk; dangerous) PREFIXED ROOT: ex-: experience, experienced, experiential, experiment (**Synonyms**: trial, test), expert, expertise (*ex-*, out) im-: imperil (to put in peril; endanger) (from *in-*, in) GREEK COGNATES: empiric (a person who relies solely on practical experience rather than on scientific principles), empirical pirate (a pirate *risked* his life in his endeavors) DISGUISED ROOT: parlous (clever; shrewd; as an *adverb*, to a large extent; greatly) PLACENAME: Experiment, Georgia NO CROSS REFERENCE

Element	From	Meaning	Examples
per-***	Latin *per* (IE: *per¹*, forward, through)	through, by, thoroughly, completely; intensive	SIMPLE WORD: per (as a single word, means through, by, by means of; for each; for every, as fifty cents *per* yard)

PREFIXED ROOT AND COMPOUNDS:

amb: perambulate, perambulator (*ambulare*, to walk)

arm: disarm, disarmament, disarming (*arma*, weapons)

ceiv: perceive (**Synonyms:** discern, distinguish, observe) (from *capere*, to hold)

cent: percent, percentage, percentile (*cent*, 100)

cept: percept, perceptible (**Synonyms:** sensible, palpable, tangible), perception, perceptive, perceptual (from *capere*, to hold)

col: percolate (*colare*, to strain)

cuss: percuss {percussion, percussor} (from *quatere*, to shake)

dit: perdition (in *theology*, the loss of the soul; damnation; Hell) (from *dare*, to give)

dur: perdure {perdurable} (*durare*, to last, harden)

empt: peremptory (dictatorial; dogmatic; in *law*, precluding further debate or action) (from *emere*, to take)

enn: perennial (lasting or active throughout the whole year, as *a perennial plant*; lasting or continuing for a long time) (from *anni*, year)

fect: perfect, perfection, perfective (from *facere*, to make)

fervid: perfervid (extremely fervid; ardent) (*fervere*, to glow, boil)

fid: perfidious (**Synonyms:** faithless, false), perfidy (*fides*, faith)

fol: perfoliate {perfoliation} (*folium*, a leaf)

for: perforate {performation, perforative} (*forare*, to bore)

form: perform (**Synonyms:** execute, accomplish, achieve) {performance} (*fornir*, to accomplish)

fum: perfume {perfumer, perfumery} (*fumare*, to smoke)

funct: perfunctory (originally, to get rid of; discharge; done without care or interest) (from *fungi*, to perform)

fus: perfuse (suffuse; do not confuse with *profuse*) {perfusive} (from *fundere*, to pour)

ish: perish (literally, going to the ultimate; thus, to die) (from *ire*, to go)

jur: perjure, perjured (adjective), perjury (*jurare*, to swear)

man: permanence, permanency, permanent (*manere*, to remain)

mea: permeability, permeable, permeate (*meare*, to glide, flow, pass)

miss: permissible, permission, permissive (indulgent, lenient) (from *mittere*, to send)

mit: permit (**Synonyms:** let, allow, suffer), permittivity (*mittere*, to send)

mut: permutation, permute (*mutare*, to change)

nic: pernicious (**Synonyms:** baneful, noxious, deleterious) (from *necare*, to kill)

ora: peroral (though or around the mouth) (from *os*, mouth)

orat: perorate (the concluding part of a speech), peroration (*orare*, to pray, speak)

Element	From	Meaning	Examples
per (cont'd)			pend: perpend, perpendicular (*pendere*, to hang)
			petr: perpetrate {perpetration} (*petrare*, to accomplish)
			pet: perpetual (**Synonyms:** continual, continuous, constant), perpetuate, perpetuity (*petere*, to seek)
			plex: perplex (**Synonyms:** puzzle, confuse, bewilder) {perplexed, perplexity} (from *plectere*, to twist)
			quis: perquisite (something additional to regular profit or pay, resulting from one's position or employment, especially something customary or expected) (from *quaerere*, to seek)
			secu: persecute (**Synonyms:** wrong, oppress, aggrieve) {persecution} (*sequi*, to follow)
			sever: persevere (**Synonyms:** continue, endure, persist {perseverance, perseveration} (*severus*, difficult)
			sifl: persiflage (a light, frivolous or flippant style of writing or speaking) (*siffler*, to hiss, whistle)
			sist: persist (**Synonyms:** continue, last, abide), persistence, persistent (*sistere*, to cause to stand)
			spec: perspective (*specere*, to look)
			spic: perspicacious (**Synonyms:** shrewd, sagacious, astute), perspicuous (clearly understood; lucid) (from *specere*, to look)
			spir: perspire {perspiration, perspiratory} (*spirare*, to breathe)
			suad: persuade (**Synonyms:** induce, prevail on) {persuader} (*suadere*, to urge)
			suas: persuasion (**Synonyms:** opinion, conviction, sentiment), persuasive (from *suadere*, to urge)
			tain: pertain (to belong; be connected or associated; be a part) (from *tenere*, to hold)
			tin: pertinacious (**Synonyms:** stubborn, obstinate, dogged), pertinacity, pertinence {pertinent} (from *tenere*, to hold)
			turb: perturb (**Synonyms:** disturb, discompose, agitate) {perturbation} (*turbare*, to disturb)
			tuss: pertussis (whooping cough) {pertussal, or *pertussoid*} (*tussis*, a cough)
			us: perusal, peruse (originally, to study in detail; now, to read carefully or thoroughly; loosely, to read in a casual or leisurely way) (from *uti*, to use)
			vad: pervade {pervasion, pervasive} (*vadere*, to go)
			vers: perverse (**Synonyms:** contrary, restive, balky) {perversion} (from *vertere*, to turn)
			vert: pervert (**Synonyms:** debase, deprave, corrupt) {perverted} (*vertere*, to turn)
			vi: pervious (from *via*, way)
			DOUBLE PREFIXED ROOT:
			impervious (not capable of being penetrated) (*im-*, not)
			LATIN PHRASES:
			per annum (by the year; annually) (*annum*, year)
			per capita (literally, by heads; for each person) (*capita*, head)
			per diem (daily allowance, as for expenses) (*diem*, day)
			per mensem (by the month)
			per vias naturales (through one's natural life)

Element	From	Meaning	Examples
per- (cont'd)			INTERDISCIPLINARY: perfect (in *botany*, monoclinous: having stamens and pistils in the same flower; in *grammar*, expressing or showing a state or action completed at the time of speaking or at the time indicated; there are three perfect tenses: present perfect, past perfect, and future perfect; in *music*, designating an interval of a unison, fourth, fifth, or octave)
			NB: *Percale* and *percalin*, from Persian *pargala*, are not in this family. Neither is *person*, coming from *persona*, actor's face mask, from Etruscan *phersu*, mask.
			CROSS REFERENCE: *dia-*
peri-***	Greek *peri* (IE: *per¹*, forward, through)	around, about, near, enclosing	PREFIXED ROOT:
			anth: perianth (in *botany*, the outer envelope of a flower, consisting of the calyx and corolla, or one of these if the other is absent) (*anth*, flower)
			apt: periapt (an amulet or charm worn as protection against mischief and disease) (from *haptein*, to fasten)
			card: pericardium (*card*, heart)
			carp: pericarp (in *botany*, the wall of a ripened ovary or fruit; also called "seed vessel") (*carp*, fruit)
			chondr: perichondrium (the membrane of connective tissue covering cartilage, except at the joints) (*chondr*, cartilage)
			clin: pericline, periclinal (in *botany*, running parallel to the surface of a plant organ or part: said of cell walls) (*clin*, lean)
			cop: pericope (a passage, usually short, from a written work) (*cop*, cut)
			cran: pericranium (*cran*, skull)
			cycl: pericycle (*cycle*, circle, wheel)
			derm: periderm (in *botany*, an outer layer of tissue of plant roots and stems, consisting of the bark and the layer of growing tissue beneath the bark) (*derm*, skin)
			ge: perigee (the point nearest the earth in orbit of the moon or a satellite) (*geo*, earth)
			gyn: perigynous (in *botany*, having the sepals, petals, and stamens attached to the rim of a cup or tube which surrounds the ovary but is not attached to it, as in the rose, spiraea, etc.) (*gynous*, having female organs or pistils as specified)
			heli: perihelion (the point nearest the sun in the orbit of a planet or comet, or of a man-made satellite in orbit around the sun; opposed to *aphelion*) (*helios*, sun)
			meter: perimeter (see synonyms at *periphery*, below) (*meter*, measure)
			nephrium: perinephrium (the connective and fatty tissue surrounding the kidney) (*nephros*, kidney)
			od: period (**Synonyms:** era, age, eon) (*hodos*, way)
			odont: periodontal (of or designating the tissue and structures surrounding and supporting the teeth), periodontics (*odont*, tooth)
			pat: peripatetic (walking about from place to place; capitalized, of or pertaining to the methods of Aristotle, who conducted discussions while walking about in the Lyceum of ancient Athens) (*patein*, to tread, to walk)

Element	From	Meaning	Examples
peri- (cont'd)			pher: peripheral, peripheral vision (the area of vision just outside the line of direct sight), periphery (**Synonyms**: circumference, perimeter, circuit) (*pher*, carry) phras: (speak) periphrasis (also *paraphrase*; the use of circumlocution) periphrastic (in *grammar*, constructed by using an auxiliary word rather than an inflected form; for example, the phrases *the word of his father* and *his father did say* are *periphrastic*, while *his father's word* and *his father said* are inflected) pter: peripteral (literally, flying around; in *architecture*, built with a row of columns on all sides, e.g., the Lincoln Memorial, Washington, D.C.) (*pter*, wing) sarc: perisarc (in *zoology*, a horny external covering that encloses the polyp colonies of certain hydrozoans) (*sarc*, flesh) scop: periscope {periscopic} (*scope*, look) stom: peristome (*stom*, mouth) thec: perithecium [in certain ascomycetous fungi, a flasklike case containing the spore sacs (*asci*)] (*theca*, case, sac) DISGUISED ROOT: paradise (a place of great contentment or beauty; a place or condition of great satisfaction, happiness, or delight) (see *Webster's New World*) PLACENAMES: Paradis, Louisiana Paradise (Alaska, California, Florida, Kansas, Michigan, Montana, Nevada, Texas, Utah); Paradise Beach, Florida INTERDISCIPLINARY: peristome (in *botany*, the fringe of teeth around the opening of the spore case in mosses; in *zoology*, the area or parts surrounding the mouth or mouthlike part of various invertebrates) perimeter (in *mathematics*, a closed curve bounding a plane area; as a *military* term, a fortified strip or boundary protecting a position) CROSS REFERENCE: *amphi, circ*
pet,*** pit	Latin *petere* (IE: *pet*, to fall, fly)	to seek, demand	SIMPLE ROOT: petition (**Synonyms**: appeal, plead, sue) petulant (impatient or irritable, especially over a petty annoyance; peevish) PREFIXED ROOT: *pet*: ap-: appetency, appetite, appetizer, appetizing (*ap-* assimilates *ad-*, to, toward) com-: (with, together) compete (**Synonyms**: rival, vie, emulate) competence (**Synonyms**: ability, capacity, faculty) competent (**Synonyms**: able, capable, qualified) competition (**Synonyms**: rivalry, emulation), competitive, competitor im-: impetigo, impetuous, impetus (*im-*, a variant of *in-*, in, or possibly against) per-: perpetual (**Synonyms**: everlasting, permanent, enduring), perpetuate, perpetuity (*per-*, through)

Element	From	Meaning	Examples
pet (cont'd)			*re*-: (again) repetend (a repeated sound, word, or phrase; refrain; in *mathematics*, the digit or digits repeated indefinitely in a repeating decimal) repetition, repetitious, repetitive *pit*: *pro*-: propitiate (**Synonyms**: pacify, appease, mollify), propitious (*pro-*, before, forward) TRAILING ROOT COMPOUND: bas: basipetal (developing or moving from the apex toward the base of the stem; opposed to acropetal) centr: centripetal (literally, seeking the center; opposed to *centrifugal*, fleeing the center) PREFIXED DISGUISED ROOT: *re*-: repeat (**Synonyms**: iterate, reiterate, recapitulate) (*re-*, again) LATIN PHRASE: *petitio principii* (literally, postulation of the beginning; commonly referred to as "begging the question"; in *logic*, the fallacy of assuming in the premise of an argument that which one wishes to prove in the conclusion, e.g., *Product A* should be purchased because *Company A* makes the best products) NOTE: Do not confuse this root with *petit*, small, *which see*, nor with the Latin noun *petal*, leaf, plate (see next entry). CROSS REFERENCE: *quer*
petal***	Greek *petalon*: leaf; *petalos*: outspread (IE: *pet*, spread out)	leaf, plate	SIMPLE ROOT: petal {petalous}, petalage, petaline petalism (in ancient Greece, a type of banishment by voting with olive leaves; compare with *ostracism*) petalite [chemical symbol: LiAl(Si$_2$O$_5$)$_2$] petalon (a plate of gold fastened to the front of the Jewish high priest's miter) PREFIXED ROOT: *apo*-: apopetalous (same as *polypetalous*) (*apo-*, away) LEADING ROOT COMPOUND: *petal*: od: petalody (the conversion of stamens or other organs into petals) (*ode*, resembling) oid: petaloid (*oid*, similar to) *petali*: fer: petaliferous (bearing leaves) (*fer*, to bear) TRAILING ROOT COMPOUND: acro: acropetal (in *botany*, developing upward from the base toward the apex: said of certain types of inflorescence) [inflorescence: literally, to begin to blossom; a flowering; the arrangement of flowers on a stem or axis; flowers collectively; a single flower] (*acro*, tip) chori: choripetalous (same as *polypetalous*) (*chori*, apart, bereaved) gamo: gamopetalous (having the petals united as to form a tubelike corolla, as the morning glory) (*gam*, sexual union) mono: monopetalous (same as *gamopetalous*) (*mono*, one)

Element	From	Meaning	Examples
petal (cont'd)			poly: polypetalous (in *botany*, having separate petals) (*poly*, many) PLACENAME: Petal, Mississippi NOTE: Do not confuse this root with the Latin verb *petere*, to seek, as in *petition, appetite* (see previous entry). CROSS REFERENCE: *foli, lam, phyll*
petit*	French *petit*	small, little	SIMPLE ROOT: petit (small or of less importance; petty: now used chiefly in law; see *Black's Law Dictionary*), petite (feminine of *petit*), petty LEADING ROOT COMPOUND: to: pettitoes (pigs' feet, as an article of food; feet or toes, especially, a child's) (from *petite oye*, goose giblets; see *Webster's New World*) FRENCH TERMS: *petit four* (a small, rich tea cake, frosted and decorated) (*four*, oven) *petit mal* (literally, small illness) *petit point* (literally, small point: needlepoint done with a small stitch) *petits pois* (little peas) BOUND COMPOUND: petticoat (literally, small coat) pettyfogger (a lawyer who handles petty cases, especially one who uses unethical methods in conducting trumped up cases; a trickster; cheater; a quibbler; caviler) UNBOUND COMPOUNDS: petty cash, petty larceny FLOWER: petticoat narcissus PLACENAMES: Petit Bois Island, Jackson County, Mississippi (Small Tree) Petit Jean Mountain, Yell County, Arkansas (Little John) Petit Jean River, Yell County, Arkansas Petit Manan Point, Washington County, Maine Petty, Texas NOTE: *Petiole*, from *petiolus*, is literally small foot. However, the meaning of small is derived from the diminutive suffix *-ole*; the root *pet* is a respelling of Latin *ped*, foot. NB: *Petunia* is not in this family. CROSS REFERENCE: *lept, micro, mini*
petr**	Greek *petros*: stone; *petra*: rock	rock, stone	SIMPLE ROOT: petrosal (very hard or stony; in *anatomy*, of or located near the petrous part of the temporal bone) petrous (of or like rock; hard; designating or of that part of the temporal bone that surrounds and protects the internal ear) LEADING ROOT COMPOUND: *petr*: ol: petrol, petrolatum, petroleum (*ol*, oil) *petri*: fac: petrifaction (also *petrification*; a petrifying or being petrified; something petrified) (*facere*, to make, do) fy: petrify (literally, to make into stone; to paralyze or make numb, as with fear; stupefy; stun) (from *facere*, to make, do) *petro*: chem: petrochemistry

Element	From	Meaning	Examples
petro (cont'd)			gen: petrogenesis, petrogenetic, petrogenic (*gen*, producing) glyph: petroglyph (a rock carving) (*glyph*, carving) graph: petrography (*graph*, write) logy: petrology (*logy*, study of) DISGUISED ROOT: lamprey (from *lambere*, to lick: many lampreys cling to rocks with their mouths) parakeet, parrot, parsley perron pier (in *architecture*, a heavy column, usually square, used to support weight, as at the end of an arch; the part of a wall between windows or other openings) BOUND COMPOUND: saltpeter (from Latin *sal*, salt + *petra*; literally, salt of rock) PROPER NAMES: Peter [from Christ's statement to Simon (his former name) "Upon this rock shall I build my church," in reference to Simon's affirmation of Jesus being the Son of God] Pierre (French) (see *Placenames* below) Pedro (Spanish) PLACENAMES: Petroleum, Montana; Petrolia (California, Texas; Ontario) Petros, Tennessee; Pierre, the capital of South Dakota NB: *Petronel*, from *poitrinal*, of the chest, is a portable firearm. (Latin *pectus*, breast) CROSS REFERENCE: *lapid, -lite, lith, sax*
phag**	Greek *phagein* (IE: *bhag*, to allot)	to eat	SIMPLE ROOT: phagedena (rapidly spreading, destructive ulceration of soft tissue) PREFIXED ROOT: *a*-: aphagia (inability to swallow) (*a*-, not) *dys*-: dysphagia (difficulty in swallowing) (*dys*-, difficulty) LEADING ROOT COMPOUND: cyt: (cell) phagocyte, phagocytolytic (*lyt*, loosen) phagocytosis (*osis*, diseased condition of) TRAILING ROOT COMPOUND: aero: aerophagia (*aero*, air) anthropo: anthropophagite (literally, people-eater; a cannibal) (*anthropo*, man) bacter: bacteriophage (any virus that infects bacteria) (*bacter*-, rod) entomo: entomophagous (feeding on insects) (*entom*, insect) geo: geophagy (the eating of earth, either as a psychotic symptom or to make up for lack of food as in famine areas) (*geo*, earth) mono: monophagous (in *biology*, feeding on only one kind of food, as on a certain plant; said especially of insects) (*mono*, one) omo: omophagia (the eating of raw flesh) (*omo*, raw) sarco: sarcophagus {sarcophagous} (*sarco*, flesh) xylo: xylophagous (*xylo*, wood) CROSS REFERENCE: *ed, vor*

Element	From	Meaning	Examples
phall*	Greek *phallos* (IE: *bhel*, to swell)	penis	ROOT NOTE: The Indo-European root may be related to *bhle*, also meaning to blow, to swell up, and which yields *follis*, leather sack, giving *follicle*, *fool*, literally, windbag, bellows. SIMPLE ROOT: phallic, phallus TRAILING ROOT COMPOUND: ithy: ithyphallic [in addition to denoting the erect penis, a type of meter in Greek poetry (reason unclear)] (*ithy*, straight) CROSS REFERENCE: *aden, balano, mentul, peni*
phan,** **phas, phat, phen**	Greek *phainein* (IE: *bha*, to gleam, shine)	to show (also, to say, assert; that is, to show by saying, asserting)	SIMPLE ROOT: *phan*: phaner: phanerous (same as *phanic*) phant: phantasia, phantasm, phantasy, phantom *phen*: phenom (a shortening of *phenomenon*: a person who shows unusual ability or promise), phenomenal (in *philosophy*, known or derived through the senses, rather than through the mind), phenomenalism, phenomenon *phas*: phase (**Synonyms**: aspect, facet, angle) PREFIXED ROOTS AND COMPOUNDS: *phan*: *dia-*: diaphanous, diaphanoscopy (*dia-*, across, through) *epi-*: epiphany (see *Christian Festival*, under *epi-*) (*epi-*, upon) *phas*: *a-*: aphasia (*a-*, not, without) *ana-*: anaphase (*ana-*, again) *apo-*: apophasis (in *rhetoric*, the artful mention of something by denying that it will be mentioned, e.g., *we will not mention that he has been tardy on many occasions*) (*apo-*, away) *dys-*: dysphasia (*dys-*, wrong, bad) *em-*: emphasis, emphasize (*em-* is a variant of *en-*, in) *meta-*: metaphase (*meta-*, between) *pro-*: prophase (*pro-*, before, front) *phat*: *em-*: emphatic (in *grammar*, designating certain tenses in which a form of *do* is used as an auxiliary for emphasis, e.g., I *do* care; we *did* go) (*em-* is a variant of *en-*, in) *phec*: *pro-*: prophecy [prediction of the future under the influence of divine guidance; act or practice of a prophet; any prediction; do not confuse with *prophesy* (a verb), below] (*pro-*, before) *phen*: *epi-*: epiphenomenon (in *medicine*, a secondary or additional occurrence in the course of a disease, usually unrelated to the disease) (*epi-*, upon, after) *phes*: *pro-*: prophesy [**Synonyms**: foretell, predict, forecast; do not confuse with *prophecy* (a noun), above (*pro-*, before) *phet*: *pro-*: prophet, prophetic (*pro-*, before) LEADING ROOT COMPOUND: *phanero*: gam: phanerogam (a true seed-bearing plant) (*gam*, marriage, sexual reproduction)

Element	From	Meaning	Examples
phan (cont'd)			gen: phanerogenetic (having a known cause) (*gen*, producing) phyt: phanerophyte (in *botany*, a perennial plant with its resting buds located well above the ground and exposed to the air) (*phyton*, plant) *phantasm*: agoria: phantasmagoria (see *Webster's Third*) *pheno*: logy: phenology (the study of natural phenomena that recur periodically, as migration or blossoming, said of their relationship to climate and changes in season) (*logy*, study of) typ: phenotype (*type*, image, symbol) *phenomenon*: logy: phenomenology (*logy*, study of) TRAILING ROOT COMPOUND: *phan*: cello: cellophane (a transparent material made from cellulose) syco: sycophant (one who shows the fig, from the gesture of the fig in denouncing a criminal; hence, an informer, flatterer; now a servile self-seeker) (*syco*, fig) theo: theophany (*theo*, god, God) *phem*: blas: blaspheme, blasphemous, blasphemy (**Synonyms:** profanity, swearing, cursing) (*blas* is of unknown origin or original meaning) eu: euphemism (the use of a word or phrase that is less expressive or direct but considered less distasteful, less offensive, etc. than another, as *remains* for *corpse*) (*eu*, good, well) *phene*: phos: phosphene (a sensation of light produced by mechanical stimulation of the retina, as by pressure on the eyeball through the closed eyelid) (*phos*, light) DISGUISED ROOT: fantastic (**Synonyms:** bizarre, grotesque), fantasy pant (Middle English *panten*; from *phantasiare*, to suffer from a nightmare) CROSS REFERENCE: *dict, fal/fess, loc/loqui, ora, phon*
pher			See *phor/pher* for *periphery*.
phil*	Greek *philein*: to love	loving, love of	SIMPLE ROOT: philter (a potion thought to arouse sexual love, especially toward a certain person; any magic potion) LEADING ROOT COMPOUND: *phil*: ander: philander (used in fiction as a name for a lover; as a *verb*, to engage lightly in passing love affairs; make love insincerely: said of a man) (from *andro*, man) anthrop: philanthropic (**Synonyms:** humanitarian, charitable, altruistic), philanthropy (*anthropo*, man) atel: philately (the collection and study of postage stamps, postcards, postmarks, etc.) (*ateleia*, exemption from further tax; see *Webster's New World*) harmon: philharmonic (love of harmony) hellen: philhellene (love of Greeks or the Greek culture) (*Hellene*, a Greek)

Element	From	Meaning	Examples
phil (cont'd)			*philo*: dendr: philodendron (literally, fond of trees; a tropical American climbing plant) (*dendr*, tree) gyn: philogyny (*gyn*, woman) logy: philology (originally, the love of learning and literature; study; scholarship; the study of written records, especially literary texts, in order to determine their authenticity, meaning, etc.) (*logos*, word) pena: philopena (see *Webster's Third*) (from *poena*, penalty) pro: philoprogenitive (*pro-* prefixes *genitive*) soph: philosophy (love of knowledge) (*soph*, wisdom) TRAILING ROOT COMPOUND: aero: aerophilous (*aero*, air) biblio: bibliophile (*biblio*, book) droso: drosophila (a fruit fly) (*droso*, dew) hemo: hemophilia, hemophiliac (a person who has hemophilia) hemophilic (of or having hemophilia; growing well in a medium containing hemoglobin: said of certain bacteria) (*hemo*, blood) necro: necrophilia (*necro*, corpse) photo: photophilous (*photo*, light) sidero: siderophilous (*sidero*, iron) turo: turophile (a connoisseur of cheese) (*turo*, cheese) GREEK MYTHOLOGY: Philemon (the husband of Baucis: a poor old woman, who with Philemon, shows such hospitality to the disguised Zeus and Hermes that the grateful gods turn their humble cottage into a temple; see *Proper Names*, next entry) PROPER NAMES: Philemon (literally, affectionate; a book of the New Testament which was an epistle from the Apostle Paul to his friend Philemon; in *Greek mythology*, the husband of Baucis) Philip (literally, a horse lover) (*philos* + *hippos*, a horse) PLACENAMES: Philadelphia, Pennsylvania (often referred to as the City of Brotherly Love) (*adelph*, brother); Philo (Illinois, Ohio) NB: *Philistine*, from Hebrew *p'lishtim*, is not in this family. CROSS REFERENCE: *ama, ami, eros*
phleb*	Greek *phleps*: blood vessel (IE: *bhlegw*, to swell)	vein	LEADING ROOT COMPOUND: *phleb*: itis: phlebitis (*itis*, inflammation of) *phlebo*: logy: phlebology (*logy*, study of) tom: phlebotomy (*tom*, cut) CROSS REFERENCE: *ven, varic*
phleg,* **phlog**	Greek *phlegein*: to burn (IE: *bhel*, to gleam, white)	to burn; inflame, fever	SIMPLE ROOT: *phleg*: phlegm (as a single word, *phlegm* has come to mean body moisture); phlegmasia, phlegmatic, phlegmonous (pertaining to inflammation of subcutaneous tissues) *phlog*: phlogistic (in *medicine*, of inflammation; inflammatory), phlogiston, phlogotic PREFIXED ROOT: anti-: antiphlogistic (*anti-*, against)

Element	From	Meaning	Examples
phleg (cont'd)			GREEK MYTHOLOGY: Phlegethon, a river of fire in Hades DISGUISED ROOT: phlox (literally, flame; any of a genus of chiefly North American plants with opposite leaves and white, pink, red, or bluish flowers) LATIN COGNATE: flagrant (originally, flaming, blazing; hence, glaringly bad, notorious, outrageous) ENGLISH COGNATE: black (from that which has burned) CROSS REFERENCE: *caus, ign, -itis, pyr*
phob**	Greek *phobos*: fear, flight (IE: *bhegw*, to flee)	morbid fear of	SIMPLE ROOT: phobia, phobiac, phobic LEADING ROOT COMPOUND: NOTE: Phobias are listed in alphabetical order with the thing feared listed in parentheses or brackets. acarophobia [mites (Acarus), or of very small objects] acousticophobia (sounds) acrophobia (height, elevated places) aerophobia (air, draft) agoraphobia (market place; open places) agyiophobia (streets) aichmophobia (pointed objects) ailurophobia (cats) alcoholophobia (alcohol beverages; alcoholism) algophobia (pain) amaxophobia (vehicles) androphobia (men, males) anemophobia (wind, draft) anthropophobia (man; human beings) apiphobia (bees) aquaphobia (water) arachnophobia (spiders) astropophobia (lightning) ataxiophobia (disorder) automysophobia (being dirty, uncleanliness) autophobia (self, solitude) ballistophobia (missiles) basiphobia (walking) bathophobia (deep places) batrachophobia (frogs) belonephobia (needles) bibliophobia (books) bromidosiphobia (odors) brontophobia (thunder) cancerophobia (cancer) carcinophobia (cancer) carcinomatophobia (cancer) cardiophobia (heart disease) cenophobia (open places) cenotophobia (open places) chromatophobia (colors) chromophobia (colors) chronophobia (time) claustrophobia (confinement, closed places) climacophobia (climbing, stairs) clithrophobia (enclosed places) coitophobia (sexual intercourse) cremnophobia (precipices)

Element	From	Meaning	Examples
phob (cont'd)			criticophobia (critics) crystallophobia (glass) cynophobia (dogs) cypridophobia (sexual intercourse, for fear of contracting a venereal disease) dermaphobia (skin irritations) dextrophobia (right side) doraphobia (fur) dysmorphophobia (deforming) ecophobia (home surroundings) electrophobia (electricity) emetophobia (vomiting) entomophobia (insects) eosophobia (dawn; daybreak) eremophobia (deserted places; solitude) ereuthophobia (blushing) ergasiophobia (working) ergophobia (working) erythrophobia (the color red) febriphobia (fever) felinophobia (cats) feminophobia (women) gamophobia (marriage) gephyrophobia (crossing a bridge, river bank, or other structure near the water) glossophobia (speaking) graphophobia (writing) gymnophobia (nakedness) gynephobia (women) hadephobia (hell) hagiophobia (holy persons or things) hamaxophobia (vehicles) haphephobia (touching, or being touched) harpaxophobia (robbers) hedonophobia (pleasure) heliophobia (sun) helminthophobia (worms) hematophobia (blood; bleeding) hemophoiba (blood; bleeding) herpetophobia (snakes) hierophobia (religious or sacred objects) hodophobia (traveling) homilophobia (sermons) hyalophobia (glass) hygrophobia (dampness, moisture) hylephobia (forests) hypengyophobia (responsibility) hypnophobia (sleep) hypsophobia (high places) ideophobia (ideas) iophobia (poisoning) kenophobia (open places) keraunophobia (lightning, thunder, storms) kleptophobia (stealing)

Element	From	Meaning	Examples
phob (cont'd)			lalophobia (speaking; stuttering)
			levophobia (left side)
			lyssophobia (rabies)
			maieusiophobia (pregnancy)
			maniaphobia (insanity)
			mechanophobia (machinery)
			melissophobia (bees)
			meningitophobia (meningitis)
			merinthophobia (being bound)
			metallophobia (metal objects)
			meterophobia (meteors)
			microphobia (germs, microorganisms)
			molysmophobia (infection)
			monophobia (self, solitude)
			mysophobia (dirt, filth)
			necrophobia (corpse)
			neophobia (new things, novelty, change)
			nomatophobia (names)
			nosophobia (disease)
			nostophobia (returning home)
			nudiphobia (nudity, nakedness)
			nyctophobia (night)
			odontophobia (teeth)
			ombrophobia (rain)
			onomatophobia (names)
			ophidophobia (snakes)
			osmophobia (odors)
			osphresiophobia (odors)
			paralipophobia (neglect, or omission of some duty)
			parasitophobia (parasites)
			pathophobia (disease)
			pediculophobia (lice)
			pedophobia (children; dolls)
			peniaphobia (poverty)
			phagophobia (eating)
			pharmocophobia (drugs)
			phasmophobia (ghosts)
			phengophobia (daylight)
			phobanthropy (human beings)
			phobophobia (being afraid; fear of fears)
			phonophobia (noise or loud talking)
			photaugiaphobia (glare)
			photophobia (light)
			phthiriophobia (parasites)
			pnigophobia (choking)
			polyphobia (many things)
			ponophobia (working)
			potamophobia (rivers)
			proctophobia (rectal disease)
			psychrophobia (cold)
			rectophobia (rectal disease)
			rhabdophobia (being beaten)
			rhypophobia (dirt)
			scopophobia (being stared at, or being seen)

Element	From	Meaning	Examples
phob (cont'd)			scotophobia (night, darkness)
			siderodromophobia (trains; riding a train)
			spectrophobia (mirrors)
			spermatophobia (loss of semen)
			stasiphobia (standing upright)
			stasibasiphobia (standing and walking)
			stygiophobia (hell)
			taphophobia (being buried alive, entombed)
			teratophobia (monstrosities)
			thalassophobia (sea)
			thanatophobia (death)
			theophobia (God)
			thermophobia (heat)
			tocophobia (childbirth)
			tonitrophobia (thunder)
			topophobia (places)
			toxicophobia (poisoning)
			traumatophobia (trauma, injury)
			tremophobia (trembling)
			trichophobia (hair)
			trichopathophobia (hair)
			triskaidekaphobia (the number 13)
			vaccinophobia (vaccination)
			venerophobia (venereal disease)
			vermiphobia (worms, vermin)
			xenophobia (strangers)
			zelophobia (jealousy)
			zoophobia (animals)
			NO CROSS REFERENCE
phon***	Greek *phone* (IE: *bha*, to speak)	sound, voice	SIMPLE ROOT: phona: phonate {phonation}, phonatory phon: phone (any single speech sound), phoneme, phonemic, phonemics, phonetic, phonetics, phonetist phoni: phonic, phonics, phonism phono: phonon (a quantum of sound energy) PREFIXED ROOT: *a*-: aphonia (loss of voice due to an organic or functional disorder), aphonic (in *phonetics*, not pronounced) (*a*-, without) *anti*-: antiphon (see *Doublets* below), antiphonal, antiphonary, antiphony (*anti*-, against) *dia*-: diaphone (a group of speech sounds consisting of all the variants of a given phoneme) (*dia*-, through) *dys*-: dysphonia (*dys*-, impairment) *tele*-: telephone, telephony (*tele*-, from afar) LEADING ROOT COMPOUND: asthen: phonasthenia (weakness or hoarsness of voice) (*a*-, without + *sthen*, strength + -*ia*, condition of) gram: phonogram (from *graph*, write) graph: phonograph (*graph*, something written, drawn, or recorded) logy: phonology (*logy*, study of) meter: phonometer (*meter*, an instrument for measuring) scop: phonoscope (*scope*, look)

Element	From	Meaning	Examples
phon (cont'd)			typ: phonotype (a phonetic symbol or character, used in printing) (*type*, image, symbol) TRAILING ROOT COMPOUND: allo: allophone (*allo*, other) eu: euphony, euphonious (pleasant-sounding) (*eu*, good, well) hetero: heterophony (the playing of a passage of music with simultaneous variations in melody or rhythm by two or more performers) (*hetero*, other) ideo: ideophone (in *linguistics*, the expression of an idea, as in many African languages, by means of a sound, often reduplicated, that creates an image of an action, object, etc.) (*ideo*, idea) mono: monophonic, monophony (same as *monody*, which see under both *mono* and *od*, song) (*mono*, one) stereo: stereophonic (*stereo*, solid) DISGUISED ROOT: anthem (from *antiphonal*; thus, originally one choir singing against another choir; see *Doublets* below) DOUBLETS: antiphon:anthem ENGLISH COGNATES: ban (**Synonyms**: forbid, prohibit, proscribe) banal (**Synonyms**: insipid, vapid, flat) banish (**Synonyms**: exile, expatriate, deport) CROSS REFERENCE: *echo, son*
phor,*** **pher**	Greek *pherein* (IE: *bher*, to carry, bring)	to carry, to bear	PREFIXED ROOT: *phor*: am-: amphora (a two-handled jar with a narrow neck, used by the ancient Greeks and Romans to carry wine or oil) (from *amphi-*, around, two) ana-: anaphora, anaphorous (*ana-*, up, back) cata-: cataphoresis (same as *electrophoresis*: the migration of charged colloidal particles or of molecules through a fluid or gel subjected to an electric field) (*cata-*, down) dia-: diaphoresis (perspiration, especially when profuse), diaphoretic (*dia-*, through) dys-: dysphoria (compare *malaise*) (*dys-*, wrong, bad, ill) meta-: metaphor (a figure of speech containing an implied comparison, in which a word or phrase ordinarily and primarily used to refer to one thing is applied to another, e.g., *the curtain of night; all the world's a stage*) (*meta-*, between) *pher*: peri-: (around) peripheral (lying at the outside or away from the central part; only slightly connected with what is essential or important) periphery (**Synonyms**: circumference, perimeter, circuit) DOUBLE PREFIXED ROOT: adiaphorous (morally neutral or indifferent; neither wrong nor right; in *medicine*, neither harmful or helpful) (*a-*, not + *dia-*, through) LEADING ROOT COMPOUND: zo: phorozoon (the asexual stage in the life history of an organism) (*zo*, organism)

Element	From	Meaning	Examples
phor (cont'd)			TRAILING ROOT COMPOUND: *phor*: can: canephoros (in ancient Greece, a basket bearer) (*can*, cane, tube, reed) electro: electrophoresis (the migration of charged colloidal particles of molecules through a fluid or gel subjected to an electric field) eu: euphoria (a feeling of vigor, high spirits, and well-being) (*eu*, good, well) gono: gonophore {gonophoric, gonophorous} (*gono*, semen, seed, procreation, offspring) phos: phosphorescent (*phos*, light) sema: semaphore (any apparatus for signaling, as by an arrangement of lights, flags, and mechanical arms on railroads) (*sema*, sign) *pher*: toco: tocopherol (any of a group of closely related viscous oils that constitute vitamin E and occur chiefly in wheat-germ oil, cottonseed oil, lettuce, etc.) (*tokos*, childbirth) DISGUISED ROOT: ampulla (a diminutive of *amphora*) feretory (a portable reliquary; a place for keeping a reliquary) PROPER NAME: Christopher (Christ-bearer) INTERDISCIPLINARY: ampulla (in *anatomy*, a small dilation in a canal or duct, especially in the semicircular canal of the ear; in *ecclesiastics*, a container used in the church for wine or water at the Eucharist; also, a vessel for consecrated wine or holy oil) anaphora [in *linguistics*, the use of a word as a regular grammatical substitute for a preceding word or group of words, as the use of *it* and *do* in "I know it and he does (know it) too"; in *rhetoric*, the repetition of a word or phrase at the beginning of successive clauses or sentences] CROSS REFERENCE: *fer*
phos,** phot	Greek *phos* (IE: *bha*, to shine, gleam)	light	SIMPLE ROOT: phose (any subjective sensation, as of light or color), phosis, phosphate PREFIXED ROOTS AND COMPOUNDS: a-: aphose, aphotic region (*a-*, not, without) *tele-*: telephotography (*tele*, from afar) LEADING ROOT COMPOUND: *phos*: gen: phosgene (*gen*, producing) phen: phosphene (see note under *phen*) phor: phosphorous (*phor*, to bear) *photo*: bio: photobiotic (*bio*, life) chrom: photochromic (*chrom*, color) gen: photogenic (due to or produced by light; that looks or is likely to look attractive in photographs) (*gen*, producing) graph: photograph (*graph*, write) metry: photometry (*meter*, measure) CROSS REFERENCE: *luc, lumin*

Element	From	Meaning	Examples
phrag,* phren	Greek *phrassein* (IE: *bhrekw*, to cram together)	to fence, wall off	ROOT NOTE: This root can also refer to *nerve*, particularly those nerves that are distributed mostly over the diaphragm. Another root with the same spelling, *phren*, can refer either to the *diaphragm* or to the mind (see *phren/phron*, below). SIMPLE ROOT: phren (also refers to the *mind*); phrenic (also refers to the *mind*) PREFIXED DISGUISED ROOT: *dia-*: diaphragm (*dia-*, through) NO CROSS REFERENCE
phras**	Greek *phrazein*	to show, explain	SIMPLE ROOT: phrasal, phrase, phrasing PREFIXED ROOT: *anti-*: antiphrasis (the use of words or phrases in a sense opposite to the usual one, as for ironic effect) (*anti-*, against) *meta-*: metaphrase (a literal, word-for-word translation, as opposed to a paraphrase) {metaphrastic} (*meta-*, along with) *para-*: paraphrase (a rewording of something spoken or written, as opposed to *metaphrase*; **Synonyms**: translation, version, transliteration) (*para-*, alongside) *peri-*: periphrasis (the use of many words where one or a few would do; circumlocution) {periphrastic} (*peri-*, around) LEADING ROOT COMPOUND: gram: phraseogram (from *graph*, write) log: (*logos*, word) phraseologist (a person skilled in formulating well-turned phrases or one given to using catchy but trite phrases) phraseology (choice and pattern of words; way of speaking or writing; diction) CROSS REFERENCE: *dict, phan/phen*
phren			See *phrag/phren* for *phrenic*.
phren,** phron	Greek *phren*	mind	SIMPLE ROOT: phren: phren [this word can also refer to the *diaphragm* (see *phrag*)], phrenic (also refers to the *diaphragm*), phrenetic (same as *frenetic*; see *Triplets* below) phron: phronema (that portion of the cortex of the brain which is occupied by thought centers or association centers) TRAILING ROOT COMPOUND: brady: bradyphrenia (*brady*, slow) eu: euphrasy (same as *eyebright*, a plant formerly used in treating eye disorders) (*eu*, good, well) schizo: schizophrenia (*schizo*, split) DISGUISED ROOT: frantic (wild with anger, pain, worry, etc.; frenzied) (see *Doublets* below) frenetic (frantic, frenzied) (see *Doublets* below) frenzied, frenzy DOUBLETS: frantic:frenetic CROSS REFERENCE: *cephal, cereb, ment, thym*
phyl**	Greek *phylon*	tribe, kind	SIMPLE ROOT: phyle, phylesis, phyletism, phylic, phylum LEADING ROOT COMPOUND: *phyl*: arch: phylarch (*arch*, rule) ep: phylephebic (early manhood, youth) (*epi-*, upon + *hebe*)

Element	From	Meaning	Examples
phyl (cont'd)			*phylo*: gen: phylogeny (*gen*, producing) TRAILING ROOT COMPOUND: di: diphyletic (derived from two lines of descent) (*di*, two) mono: monophyletic (of a single stock; developed from a single ancestral type) {monophyletism} (*mono*, one) CROSS REFERENCE: *gen*
phylax,* phylact	Greek *phylax*: guard	prevention; originally, on guard	SIMPLE ROOT: *phylac*: phylactery [from *phylacterium*, safeguard, used for Hebrew *tefillah*, prayer: leather cases holding slips of Scripture passages (see Deuteronomy 6:4-9); these cases are worn by Orthodox or Conservative Jewish men during morning prayer on weekdays] *phylax*: phylaxis (inhibiting of infection by the body) PREFIXED ROOT: *ana-*: anaphylaxis {anaphylactic} (*ana-*, intensive) *pro-*: (for) prophylactic (as a *noun*, a *condom*, that which is designed to prevent sexually transmittable diseases; as an *adjective*, that which is preventative, as *prophylactic medicine*) prophylaxis (the prevention of or protective treatment for disease; in *dentistry*, *teeth cleaning* is referred to as such) DOUBLE PREFIXED ROOT: ananaphyllaxis (*an-*, not + *ana-*, intensive) CROSS REFERENCE: *cav*, *para*
phyll***	Greek *phyllon* (IE: *bhel*, to swell, sprout)	leaf	SIMPLE ROOT: phyllo (flaky pastry in very thin sheets, used especially in Greek dishes, such as baklava) phyllome (in *botany*, a leaf or analogous member) PREFIXED ROOT: *a-*: aphyllous (*a-*, without) *cata-*: cataphyll (in *botany*, any rudimentary leaf, as a bud scale, preceding the true foliage leaves) (*cata-*, down) LEADING ROOT COMPOUND: *phyll*: oid: phylloid (like a leaf; leaflike) (*oid*, similar to) *phyllo*: clad: phylloclad (also, *phylloclade*; same as *cladophyll*: a green, flattened branch arising from the axil of a leaf, with the shape and functions of a foliage leaf) (*clad*, shoot, bud) morph: phyllomorphous (*morph*, form, shape) phag: phyllophagous (*phag*, eat) pod: phyllopod (any of the subclass of primitive crustaceans with leaflike, swimming feet, as the fairy shrimp, brine shrimp, etc.) (*pod*, foot) tax: phyllotaxis (also *phyllotaxy*; in *botany*, the arrangement of leaves on a stem) (*taxis*, arrangement) xera: phylloxera (*xeros*, dry) TRAILING ROOT COMPOUND: chloro: chlorophyll (*chloro*, green) chryso: chrysophyll (*chryso*, yellow, golden) clado: cladophyll (*clados*, branch, shoot)

531

Element	From	Meaning	Examples
phyll (cont'd)			di: diphyllous (having two leaves or sepals) (*di*, two) hetero: heterophyllous (growing leaves of different forms on the same stem or plant) (*hetero*, different, other) micro: microphyll (*micro*, small) spor: sporophyll (a leaf, modified leaf, or leaflike part producing one or more sporangia) (*spore*, seed) xantho: xanthophyll {xanthophyllous} (*xanth*, yellow) DISGUISED ROOT: chervil (the last letter retains the remnant of the root; a plant of the parsley family, whose leaves are used for flavoring salads, soups, etc.; *chervil* literally means rejoicing leaf) CROSS REFERENCE: *foli, lam, petal*
physi***	Greek *physis* (IE: *bheu*, to exist, be, grow)	nature, natural, growth	SIMPLE ROOT: physic: physic, physical (**Synonyms: 1**) bodily, corporeal, corporal; **2**) material, sensible), physics, physician, physicist physiq: physique (the structure, constitution, strength, form, or appearance of the body) PREFIXED ROOT: apo-: apophysis (*apo-*, away) dia-: diaphysis (the shaft of the long bone, as distinguished from the growing ends) (*dia-*, through) epi-: epiphysics, epiphysis (*epi-*, upon) hypo-: hypophysis (literally, undergrowth; the pituitary gland of the body) (*hypo-*, under) meta-: metaphysical, metaphysics [from *ta meta ta physika*, that after the physics (in reference to location after the *Physics* in early collections of Aristotle's writings)] (*meta-*, after) LEADING ROOT COMPOUND: crat: physiocrat (a believer in the 18th-century French economic theory that land and its products are the only true sources of wealth) (*crat*, ruled by) gnomy: physiognomy (the practice of trying to judge character and mental qualities by observation of bodily, especially, facial features; the *g* may, or may not be pronounced) (*gnomon*, one who knows) graph: physiography (*graph*, write) logy: physiology (*logy*, study of) TRAILING ROOT COMPOUND: mono: Monophysite (in *theology*, a person who believes that Christ had but one nature, or a composite nature of both the human and the divine, a tenet held by members of the Coptic Church) (*mono*, one) DISGUISED ROOT: imp (from *emphytous*, literally, growth within; originally, a child; offspring; then, a devil's offspring; a young demon; a mischievous child) INTERDISCIPLINARY: apophysis (in *anatomy*, a natural outgrowth or process on a vertebra or other bone; in *botany*, a swelling at the base of the capsule in some mosses) CROSS REFERENCE: *aug, creat, cresc/cret/cru; embryo, oma, phym, phyt*

Element	From	Meaning	Examples
physo*	Greek *physa* (IE: *pu²*, to blow, swell)	gas, air, bellows	LEADING ROOT COMPOUND: cel: physocele (a tumor filled with gas or circumscribed swelling due to gas; a gas-distended hernial sac) (from *kele*, tumor) stom: physostomous (in *zoology*, having a connecting tube between the air bladder and a part of the alimentary canal, as in certain fishes) (*stom*, mouth) CROSS REFERENCE: *aer, atmo*
phyt**	Greek *phyton*: a plant (IE: *bheu*, to exist, be, grow)	a plant; bring forth	SIMPLE ROOT: phyteral, phyton PREFIXED ROOT: a-: aphytal zone (without plants; aphotic region, especially the plantless depths of the ocean floor) (*a-*, without) endo-: endophyte (in *botany*, any plant, such as certain fungi, that lives within another plant) (*endo-*, within) epi-: epiphyte, epiphytology, epiphytotic (*epi-*, upon) LEADING ROOT COMPOUND: chrom: phytochrome (*chrom*, color or coloring agent) gen: phytogenesis (*genesis*; origin) geo: phytogeography (*geo*, earth + *graph*, write) graph: phytography (*graph*, write) hormon: phytohormone (*hormos*, urging, impulse) lit: phytolite (also *phytolith*) (from *lithos*, stone) logy: phytology (earlier word for *botany*) (*logy*, study of) path: phytopathology (the study of plant diseases and their control) (*path*, disease) phag: phytophagous (the feeding on plants) (*phag*, eat) tox: phytotoxic (*toxon*, poison) TRAILING ROOT COMPOUND: auto: autophyte (*auto*, self) cryo: cryophyte (a plant that grows on ice or snow, especially various algae and fungi) (*cryo*, cold) hetero: heterophyte (a plant which obtains its food from other plants or animals, living or dead) (*hetero*, other) holo: holophytic (*holo*, whole, entire) micro: microphyte (*micro*, small) osteo: osteophyte (a small pathological bony outgrowth; spur) (*osteo*, bone) thall: thallophyte (any of a subkingdom of nonvascular plants showing no clear distinction of roots, stem, or leaves and not producing flowers or seeds: the subkingdom includes the fungi, lichens, and most algae) (*thallos*, young shoot) xero: xerophyte (*xero*, dry) DISGUISED TRAILING ROOT COMPOUND: eu: euphuism (after the character *Euphues* in two works by John Lyly; the artificial, affected, high-flown style of speaking or writing used by Lyly and his imitators, characterized by alliteration, balanced sentences, antitheses, farfetched figures of speech, etc.; not to be confused with *euphemism*) (*eu*, well) EMBEDDED ROOT COMPOUND: diphyodont (bearing two sets of teeth, as do most mammals) (*di*, two + *phy*, bear + *odont*, tooth) CROSS REFERENCE: *aug, creat/cresc/cret/cru, oma, phym*

Element	From	Meaning	Examples
pi*	Latin *pius,* devout; *piare,* to appease	devout	SIMPLE ROOT: pia: piacular (making atonement; expiatory; calling for expiation or atonement; therefore, sinful, wicked) pie: pietism, piety (see *Doublets* below; devotion to religious duties and practices) pio: pious (**Synonyms:** devout, religious, sanctimonious) pite: piteous (see synonyms at *pitiful*) piti: pitiable, pitiful (**Synonyms:** pitiable, piteous) pitiless (**Synonyms:** cruel, brutal, ruthless) pitt: pittance (originally, the small portion of food allowed a monk; any small amount or portion, especially of money) pity: pity (see *Doublets* below; **Synonyms:** commiseration, sympathy, condolence) PREFIXED ROOT: *ex-*: expiable, expiate (to make amends or reparations for wrongdoing or guilt; atone for; to pay the penalty of; suffer for) {expiation} (*ex-*, out) *im-*: impious, impiety (*im-*, a variant of *in-*, not) DOUBLE PREFIXED ROOT: ine̲x̲piable (that cannot be expiated or atoned for, as *an inexpiable sin*) (*in-*, not + *ex-*, out) DOUBLETS: pity:piety ART TERM: Pietà (a representation in painting, sculpture, etc. of Mary, the mother, grieving over the body of Jesus after the Crucifixion) CROSS REFERENCE: *vov*
pico*	Italian *piccolo*	small	ROOT NOTE: In measurements, the root has come to mean one trillionth of the unit designated by the root with which it is combined. SIMPLE ROOT: piccolo (Italian; a woodwind instrument smaller and one octave higher than a flute) LEADING ROOT COMPOUND: curie: picocurie gram: picogram meter: picometer pico: picopicogram second: picosecond CROSS REFERENCE: *micro, petit*
picro			See *pict* for *picrotoxin*.
pict**	Latin *pingere*: to paint (IE: *peig,* *peik,* colorful, sharp; yields English paint)	to paint; picture	SIMPLE ROOT: Pictor (a constellation between Carina and Dorabo), pictorial, picture, picturer, picturesque PREFIXED ROOT: *de-*: depict (to represent in a drawing, painting, etc.; portray; picture; to picture in words; describe) (*de-*, intensive) LEADING ROOT COMPOUND: *picro*: toxin: picrotoxin (a white, bitter, poisonous compound; symbol: $C_{30}H_{34}O_{13}$) (*toxin*, poison) *picto*: graph: pictograph (a picture or picturelike symbol representing an idea, as in primitive writing; hieroglyphic), pictography (*graph*, write)

Element	From	Meaning	Examples
pict (cont'd)			DISGUISED ROOT: pigment (coloring matter, usually in the form of powder, mixed with oil, water, etc. to make paints; any coloring in the cells and tissues of plants or animals; see *Doublets* below) SPANISH: pimento (see *Doublets* below), pinto PORTUGUESE: pintado (the Spanish mackerel) DOUBLETS: pimento:pigment NO CROSS REFERENCE
pil*	Latin *pilus* (IE: *pilo*, hair, especially a knot of hair)	hair	SIMPLE ROOT: pile (a soft, velvety, raised surface on a rug, fabric, etc., produced by making yarn loops on the body of the material and often, shearing them; soft, fine hair, as on wool, fur, etc.), pileous, piliation, pilose PREFIXED ROOT: *de-*: depilar, depilate (to remove hair from a part of the body), depilator (*de-*, off) TRAILING ROOT COMPOUND: caterpillar DISGUISED ROOT: pelage (the coat, or covering, of a mammal, as fur or hair) pellet (with French diminutive *et*, literally a small ball) pluck (originally, to pull out hair; **Synonyms:** fortitude, grit, backbone) plush (literally, plucked; a fabric with a soft, thick, deep pile) SPANISH COGNATES: *pelo* (hair) *pelota* (literally, ball; jai alai; reason unclear) CROSS REFERENCE: *trich*
pisc*	Latin *piscis* (IE: *pisk*, fish, yields German *Fisch*; Dutch *visch*; Modern Dutch is *vis*)	fish	SIMPLE ROOT: pisca: piscary (in *law*, the right of fishing in waters owned by another; a place for fishing), piscatorial pisci: piscina (a basin with a drain, formerly near the altar, now usually in the sacristy, for the disposal of holy water, etc.; sacrarium), piscine LEADING ROOT: *piscato*: logy: piscatology (*logy*, study of) *pisci*: cult: pisciculture vor: piscivorous (*vorare*, to eat) MESHED LEADING ROOT COMPOUND: piscidia (a plant whose leaves are poisonous to fish when the leaves contaminate the water in which the fish live) (*cid*, to kill) CLASS OF VERTEBRATES: Pisces, the superclass of vertebrates that includes all classes of fishes CONSTELLATION: Pisces (south of Andromeda) SIGN OF THE ZODIAC: Pisces (the twelfth sign, entered by the sun about February 21) NOTE: Do not confuse this root with *pisum*, pea, e.g., *pisiform*, resembling a pea in shape and size; nor with *pisse*, urine, as in *pismire*, urine + *mire*, ant (from the odor of formic acid, discharged by ants). CROSS REFERENCE: *ichthy*
pit			See *pet* for *propitiate, propitious*.

535

Element	From	Meaning	Examples
pithec*	Greek *pithekos* (IE: *bhidh*, dreadful; variation of *bhoi*, to be afraid)	ape	LEADING ROOT COMPOUND: anthrop: pithecanthropus (*Homo erectus*); literally, ape-man (*anthropo*, man) TRAILING ROOT COMPOUND: dryo: dryopithecine (of, or belonging to, a genus of fossil manlike apes) (*drys*, tree, not listed elsewhere) oreo: oreopithecus (mountain ape) (*ore*, mountain) NO CROSS REFERENCE
plac			See *platy* for *placenta*.
plac***	Latin *placere* (IE: *plak*, smooth, plain)	to please	SIMPLE ROOT: placable, placate (**Synonyms:** pacify, appease, mollify) {placatory} placid (**Synonyms:** calm, tranquil) (see *Placename* below) PREFIXED ROOT: *com-*: complacency, complacent (to be very pleasing; quiet satisfaction; contentment; specifically, self-satisfied; or smug; also, *affable*) (*com-*, intensive) *im-*: implacable (**Synonyms:** inflexible, adamant, obdurate) (*im-*, a variant of *in-*, not) DISGUISED ROOT: plea, plead (**Synonyms:** appeal, sue, petition) pleasant (**Synonyms:** pleasing, agreeable, enjoyable), pleasantry please, pleasing (see synonyms at *pleasant*), pleasurable pleasure (**Synonyms:** delight, joy, enjoyment) PREFIXED DISGUISED ROOT: *ap-*: appease (see synonyms at *placate*, above) (*ap-* assimilates *ad-*, to, toward) *dis-*: displeasure (**Synonyms:** distaste, dislike, indignation), displease (*dis-*, negative) *com-*: complaisance (a complaisant act), complaisant (inclined or disposed to please; disposition to be obliging; agreeable) (*com-*, with, together) FRENCH PHRASE: *avec plaisir* (with pleasure) LATIN SENTENCES: *placebo* (I shall please) *placet* (It pleases; a vote assent expressed by saying *placet*) PLACENAME: Lake Placid, New York RELATED MEDICAL TERM: placenta {placentate} NB: *Placard* is not in this family, coming from Dutch *placke*, piece, spot, patch. NO CROSS REFERENCE
plain			See *plang* for *complain, complaint*.
plan**	Latin *planum*, level; *planare*, to make level (IE: *plat*, broad, flat)	level, even	SIMPLE ROOT: plan (**Synonyms:** design, scheme, project), plane, planish PREFIXED ROOT: *ex-*: explanation (elucidation, clarification), explanatory (also, *explanative*) (*ex-*, out) LEADING ROOT COMPOUND: meter: planimeter (an instrument for measuring the area of a regular or irregular plane figure by tracing the perimeter of the figure) {planimetric, planimetry} (*meter*, measure)

Element	From	Meaning	Examples
plan (cont'd)			spher: planisphere (a map or chart that is the projection on a plane of the celestial sphere, usually with the North or South celestial pole as the center) (*sphere*, globe, ball) *plano*: concav: planoconcave (having one side plane and the other concave) convex: planoconvex (having one side plane and the other convex) TRAILING ROOT COMPOUND: aero: aeroplane (*aero*, air) mono: monoplane (an airplane with only one main supporting surface, or pair of wings) (*mono*, one) DISGUISED ROOT: plain, plainsong PREFIXED DISGUISED ROOT: *ex-*: explain (**Synonyms**: expound, explicate, interpret) (*ex-*, out) FRENCH: *esplanade* SPANISH: *llano* (any of the level, grassy plains covering large areas in South America; also, *plano*; see *Placenames* below) ITALIAN: piano [now meaning soft, in *music*. A pianoforte (literally, soft-loud), shortened to *piano*, and the successor to the *harpsichord*, can be played either soft or loud by a combination of touch and the use of the damper pedal.] PLACENAMES: Plains, Georgia; The Plains, Virginia; Plano (Illinois, Texas) NOTE: *Planet, planetarium, planetary*, and *plane tree* are all related to this root. The basic meaning in each of these words is spread out, wandering; the ancient astrologers claimed that unlike the stars--which were fixed--the *planets* "wandered"; *planetary*, in its general sense, means wandering, erratic, as in *planetary life*; a *plane tree* is so called from its broad, spread out leaves. NB: *Complain* and *complainant* are not in this family; see *plang*, next family. CROSS REFERENCE: *platy*
plang**	Latin *plangere* (IE: *plag*, to strike)	to lament, to strike (one's breast) in sorrow or lament	SIMPLE ROOT: plangent (striking with a deep, reverberating sound, as waves against the shore; loud and resounding, as the sound of bells; expressing sadness; plaintive) DISGUISED ROOT: plaint (an utterance of grief or sorrow; lamentation; in *law*, a statement of grievance submitted to a court as a request for redress) plaintiff (a person who brings a suit into a court of law; complainant) plaintive (expressing sorrow or melancholy; mournful; sad) PREFIXED DISGUISED ROOT: *com-*: complain (originally, to beat the chest), complainant, complaint (*com-*, intensive) NB: *Explain* is not in this family; see *plan*, previous family. CROSS REFERENCE: *clam, plor*

How long a time lies in one little word. Shakespeare

Element	From	Meaning	Examples
plas***	Greek *plassein* (IE: *plat*, flat, to smooth out)	to mold, form	SIMPLE ROOT: plasma, plaster, plastic, plastid PREFIXED ROOT: *ana-*: anaplastic, anaplasty (*ana-*, again) *cata-*: cataplasia, cataplasm (*cata-*, down) *dys-*: dysplasia, dysplasty (*dys-*, bad, wrong) *ecto-*: ectoplasm (distinguished from *endoplasm*) (*ecto-*, outside) *endo-*: endoplasm (distinguished from *ectoplasm*) (*endo-*, within) *hypo-*: hypoplasia (a conditon of decreased or arrested growth of an organ or tissue of the body) (*hypo-*, under) *meta-*: metaplasia, metaplasm (*meta-*, between) LEADING ROOT COMPOUND: *plasm*: odium: plasmodium (from *eidos*, similar to) *plasma*: gen: plasmagene (*gen*, producing) lys: plasmolysis (in *biology*, a shrinking of the protoplasm of a living cell due to loss of water by osmosis) (*lys*, loosen) pher: plasmapheresis (*pher*, to bear) TRAILING ROOT COMPOUND: *plasm*: allo: alloplasm (*allo*, other) proto: protoplasm (*proto*, first) *plast*: auto: autoplastic (*auto*, self) chromo: chromoplast (*chromo*, color) proto: protoplast (*proto*, first) *plastic*: cyto: cytoplastic (*cyto*, cell) neo: neoplastic (*neo*, new) *plasty*: auto: autoplasty (*auto*, self) cranio: cranioplasty (*cranio*, skull) hetero: heteroplasty (plastic surgery in which tissue from one individual is transferred onto another) (*hetero*, other) neo: neoplasty (*neo*, new) DISGUISED ROOT: piaster (from Italian *piastra*, thin metal plate; a coin used in Lebanon, Libya, Sudan, Syria, Turkey, and Egypt) PLACENAME: Plaster City, California INTERDISCIPLINARY: plastic (in *biology*, capable of building tissue; in *physics*, capable of undergoing continuous deformation without rupture or relaxation; in *surgery*, concerned with the remedying or restoring of malformed, injured, or lost parts) metaplasm (in *biology*, that part of the contents of a cell which consists of lifeless, nonprotoplastic matter, as certain inclusions in fatty granules or carbohydrates; in *linguistics*, a change in a word by adding, leaving out, or transposing letters or syllables) CROSS REFERENCE: *fig, form, morph*

Element	From	Meaning	Examples
platy,** plac	Greek platys (IE: plak, broad, flat; yields English place, plate)	flat, broad	SIMPLE ROOT: plac: placenta (in biology, that part of the lining of the ovary which bears the ovules), placentate, placentation plat: plate: plate, plateau, platen plati: platinous, platinum (Provençal, silver place, silver bar, silver), platitude (**Synonyms:** truism, cliché, bromide) LEADING ROOT COMPOUND: plac: oid: placoid (oid, similar to) platy: cephal: platycephalic (cephal, head) helminth: platyhelminth (helminth, worm) platy: platypus (literally, flatfooted; a monotreme mammal of Australia and Tasmania with webbed feet) (pus, foot) rhin: platyrrhine (rhin, nose) DISGUISED ROOT: plafond (a decorated ceiling) plaice (or plaise; literally, flatfish; flounder) planta (sole of foot) SPANISH: plaza; FRENCH: plateau; ITALIAN: piazza NOTE: Some of these words were listed under Latin plan; both the Latin and Greek roots have a common ancestor. NO CROSS REFERENCE
plaud,** plaus, plod, plos	Latin plaudere	clap, strike, praise	SIMPLE ROOT: plaudit (an applauding or round of applause; any expression of approval or praise) plausible (originally, deserving applause; **Synonyms:** credible, specious) PREFIXED ROOT: plaud: ap-: applaud, applause (ap- assimilates ad-, to, toward) plod: dis-: displode (same as explode) {displosion} (dis-, apart) ex-: explode {explosion} (ex-, out) im-: implode {implosion} (im-, a variant of in-, in) CROSS REFERENCE: bat, cuss, fend, flict, plec/pleg/plex
ple,* plei pleo, pleio plio	Greek pleion (IE: pelu, large amount; from pel, to pour, fill)	more	SIMPLE ROOT: pleonasm (the use of more words than are necessary for the expression of an idea; redundancy) LEADING ROOT COMPOUND: pleio: phyl: pleiophylly (an abnormal increase or excess in the number of leaves or leaflets) (phyll, leaf) taxy: pleiotaxy (an increase in the number of whorls in a flower) (taxy, arrangement) trop: pleiotropism (tropo, turn) pleo: chro: pleochroism (chroos, color) morph: pleomorphism (morph, shape, mold) plio: cen: Pliocene (cene, recent) pith: pliopithecus (pithecus, ape) CROSS REFERENCE: plen, plur, ultra

Element	From	Meaning	Examples
-ple**	Latin *plicare*, to fold (IE: *plek*, to entwine)	fold	TRAILING ROOT COMPOUND: cent: centuple (*cent*, 100) dec: decuple (*dec*, ten) du: duple (*du*, two) multi: multiple (*multi*, many) oct: octuple (*oct*, eight) quad: quadruple (*quad*, four) sept: septuple (*sept*, seven) sext: sextuple (*sex*, six) tri: triple (*tri*, three) CROSS REFERENCE: *plex/plic/ply*
pleb*	Latin *plebs*	people, masses	SIMPLE ROOT: pleb, plebe, plebeian (also spelled *plebian*), plebicular, plebs LEADING ROOT COMPOUND: scit: plebiscitary, plebiscite, plebiscitum (*scitum*, decree; from *scire*, to know) CROSS REFERENCE: *demo, popul, vulg*
plec			See *pleg* for *plectrum*.
plect			See *plex* for *complection*.
pleg,** plec, plex	Greek *plessein*: to strike (IE: *plag*, to strike)	stroke (medical), paralysis	SIMPLE ROOT: plec: plectrum (originally, a device for plucking the lyre; a thin piece of metal, bone, plastic, etc., used for plucking the strings of a guitar, mandolin, etc.) pleg: plegia (paralysis) PREFIXED ROOT: apo-: apoplectic, apoplexy (*apo-*, away) para-: paraplegia (*para-*, alongside) TRAILING ROOT COMPOUND: di: diplegia (*di*, two) hemi: hemiplegia (*hemi*, half) mono: monoplegia (*mono*, one) CROSS REFERENCE: *plex/pleg*
plen,*** plet, pli, ply	Latin *plere* (IE: *pel*, to fill)	to fill	SIMPLE ROOT: plenary, plenitude, plenitudinous, plentiful (**Synonyms**: abundant, copious, profuse), plenty, plenum PREFIXED ROOT: *plem*: com-: complement (see *Doublets* below), complementary (*com-*, with, together) im-: implement (**Synonyms**: instrument, appliance, utensil) (*im-*, a variant of *in-*, in) sup-: supplement, supply (entered here correctly, not in *ply*, from *plicare*, to fold) (*sup-* assimilates *sub-*, under) *plen*: re-: replenish {replenisher, replenishment} (*re-*, again) *plet*: com-: complete (**Synonyms**: total, whole, entire), completion (*com-*, with, together) de-: deplete (to make less by gradually using up resources, funds, strength, etc.), depletion (*de-*, from) ex-: expletive (an oath or exclamation, especially, an obscenity; term is also used in grammar) (*ex-*, out, up) re-: replete (*re-*, again)

Element	From	Meaning	Examples
plen (cont'd)			*pli*: com-: (with, together) plim: compliment (see *Doublets* below), complimentary plin: compline (also, *complin*: often capitalized; in *ecclesiology*, the last of the seven canonical hours) *ply*: com-: comply (entered here correctly, not in *ply*, from *plicare*, to fold) (*com-*, with, together) DOUBLE PREFIXED ROOT: ac<u>com</u>plish (**Synonyms: 1**) perform, execute, achieve; 2) reach, gain), accomplished, accomplishment (*ac-* assimilates *ad-*, to, toward + *com-*, with, together) LEADING ROOT COMPOUND: pot: plenipotentiary (*potis*, able) DOUBLETS: complement:compliment (both mean literally to fill up completely, as a salad or a fine wine *complements* a meal; *to compliment* someone is *to fill up* that person with respect, praise, admiration) INTERDISCIPLINARY: complement (in *grammar*, a word or group of words that, with the verb, complete the meaning and structure of the predicate; in *immunology*, any of a group of heat-sensitive proteins in the blood plasma that act with specific antibodies to destroy corresponding antigens, as bacteria or foreign proteins; in *mathematics*, the number of degrees that must be added to a given angle or arc to make it equal 90 degrees; also, the subset which must be added to any given subset to yield the original set; in *music*, the difference between a given interval and the complete octave; in *nautical usage*, the full crew of officers and men assigned to a ship) NO CROSS REFERENCE
plesios*	Greek *plesios* (IE: *pel*, to push)	near (as though pushed forward)	LEADING ROOT COMPOUND: chrono: plesiochronous (neither *synchronous* nor *asynchronous*, but in between the two) (*chron*, time) saur: plesiosaur (*saur*, lizard) syn: plesiosynchronous (*syn-*, a variant of *sym-*, with, prefixes *chron*, time) NOTE: Do not confuse this root with *plei*, more, as in *pleiophylly* (see *plei*). NO CROSS REFERENCE
plet			See *plen* for *complete*.
pleur**	Greek *pleura*	rib, side	SIMPLE ROOT: pleura: pleura (plural, *pleurae*), pleural pleuri: pleurisy, pleurite, pleuritic pleuro: pleuron (plural, *pleura*) MATHEMATICAL TERM: *pleura hypotenusa* (literally, side subtending, and shortened to *hypotenuse*; if the triangle were placed so that the hypotenuse is lying on a plane, the hypotenuse, literally stretched under, would in fact be "stretched under" the right angle) CROSS REFERENCE: *cost, hedr, later*
plex			See *pleg* for *apoplexy*.

541

Element	From	Meaning	Examples
plex,** **plic,** **ply**	Latin *plicare* (IE: *plek*, to entwine)	to fold, twist	SIMPLE ROOT: pliable (**Synonyms**: pliant, ductile, malleable), pliant (see synonyms at *pliable*) *plex*: plexor (also called *plessor*), plexus *plic*: plica, plicate (arranged in folds like those of a fan; pleated), plication, plicature *ply*: ply PREFIXED ROOTS AND COMPOUNDS: *ple*: *sup*-: supple, supplicate, supplication (*sup*- assimilates *sub*-, under) *plex*: *am*-: amplexicaul (*ambi*-, around, both + *caul*, stem) *com*-: complex, complexion (*com*-, with, together) *per*-: perplex, perplexed, perplexity (*per*-, through) *plic*: *com*-: complicate, complicity (*com*-, with, together) *ex*-: (out) explicate (**Synonyms**: explain, expound, elucidate) explicit (**Synonyms**: express, exact, precise) *im*-: implicit, implicate (*im*-, a variant of *in*-, in) *re*-: replicate (*re*-, again) *ply*: *ap*-: apply (*ap*- assimilates *ad*-, to, toward) *im*-: imply (**Synonyms**: suggest, hint, intimate) (*im*-, a variant of *in*-, in) *re*-: reply (**Synonyms**: answer, respond, retort) (*re*-, again) NB: *Comply* nor supply are not in this family; see *plen*. DOUBLE PREFIXED ROOT: acc<u>om</u>plice (*ac*- assimilates *ad*-, to, toward; *com*-, with, together) in<u>ex</u>plicable, in<u>ex</u>plicit (*in*-, not; *ex*-, out) TRAILING ROOT COMPOUND: du: duplex, duplicate (**Synonyms**: copy, reproduction, replica), duplicator, duplicity (*du*, two) multi: multiply (*multi*, many) DISGUISED ROOT: flax, flaxen plait, plash (one meaning), pleach (Old Poetic for *plait*), pleat (see *Quadruplets* below) plight (**Synonyms**: predicament, dilemma, quandary) ploy (short for *employ*) PREFIXED DISGUISED ROOT: *de*-: deploy (from *display*, next entry), deployment (from *dis*-, away) *dis*-: display (literally, to unfold for viewing) (*dis*-, away) *em*-: employ (from *imply*; **Synonyms**: use, utilize) (*em*-, in) *ex*-: exploit (from *explicate*) (*ex*-, out) BOUND COMPOUND: plywood (thin layers of wood *folded*, glued, and pressed together to give added strength) QUADRUPLETS: plait:pleat:plash:plight FRENCH: appliqué (a decoration or trimming made of one material attached, or applied, by sewing, gluing, etc. to another)

Element	From	Meaning	Examples
plex (cont'd)			INTERDISCIPLINARY: plica (in *pathology*, a matted and encrusted state of the hair, resulting from uncleanliness and vermin; in *zoology*, a fold or ridge as of skin, mucous membrane, or shell) NO CROSS REFERENCE
plod			See *plaud* for *explode*.
-ploid*	Greek *ploos* (IE: *plek*, to entwine)	fold	SUFFIXED ROOT: di: diploid (*di*, two) hetero: heteroploid (*hetero*, other) hepta: heptaploid (*hepta*, seven) hexa: hexaploid (*hexa*, six) hyper: hyperploid (*hyper-*, beyond) hypo: hypoploid (*hypo-*, under) poly: polyploid (*poly-*, many) CROSS REFERENCE: *-ple, plex/plic*
plor**	Latin *plorare*	to cry out, to wail	PREFIXED ROOT: de-: deplore {deplorable} (*de-*, intensive) ex-: explore {exploration} (*ex-*, out) im-: implore (**Synonyms:** entreat, beseech, importune) {imploration} (*im-*, a variant of *in-*, an intensive) CROSS REFERENCE: *clam, nunci, plang*
plos			See *plaud* for *explosion*.
plum*	Latin *pluma* (IE: *pleus*, to pluck out)	feather (soft)	SIMPLE ROOT: plumage (a bird's feathers, collectively) plumate (in *zoology*, resembling a feather, especially in structure), plume, plumose, plumule PREFIXED ROOT: de-: deplumation, deplume (*de-*, off) dis-: displume (same as *deplume*) (*dis-*, away, apart) LEADING ROOT COMPOUND: ped: plumiped (having feathered feet) (*ped*, foot) DISGUISED ROOT: fleece FRENCH PHRASE: nom de plume (literally, feather name; writing name, from quills being used as writing instruments) INTERDISCIPLINARY: plumule (in *botany*, the growing stem tip of the embryo of a seed, above the place of attachment of the cotyledons; in *ornithology*, a soft down feather of young birds, persisting in some adults) CROSS REFERENCE: *ali, pen, pter*
plur,** plus, plu	Latin *plus* (IE: *pel*, to fill)	many, more	SIMPLE ROOT: *plur*: plural, pluralism (in *philosophy*, the theory that reality consists of a multiplicity of beings, principles, or substances; compare *dualism*, the theory that the world is ultimately composed of, or explicable in terms of, two basic entities: mind and matter), plurality, plurel, pluries *plus*: plus (added to; increased by; in addition to) PREFIXED ROOT: non-: nonplus (literally, not more; a condition of perplexity in which one is unable to go, speak, or act further; often heard in phrases such as "I was *nonplussed* at his remark") sur-: surplus (overabundance) [not to be confused with its homonym *surplice*; see *pel, pil*] (*sur-*, a variant of *super*, above)

Element	From	Meaning	Examples
plur (cont'd)			LEADING ROOT COMPOUND: *plu*: per: pluperfect (from *plus quam perfectum*, literally, more than perfect; designating a tense in any of certain languages corresponding to the *past perfect* in English) (*per-* prefixes *fect*, from *facere*, to make, do) *pluri*: axi: pluriaxial (in *botany*, having several axes; specifically, having flowers on secondary shoots) ling: plurilingual (same as *multilingual*, speaking many languages) (*lingua*, tongue) UNBOUND COMPOUND: plus fours (originally, a tailoring term indicating an added four inches of material for overlap below the knee; now, loose knickerbockers worn, especially formerly, for active sports) LATIN PHRASE: *ne plus ultra* (no more beyond; perfection) MOTTO OF THE UNITED STATES: *E pluribus unum:* out of many, one CROSS REFERENCE: *multi, poly*
plut*	Greek *ploutos*: wealth (IE: *pel*, to fill)	wealth	LEADING ROOT COMPOUND: *plut*: arch: plutarchy (*archy*, ruled by) *pluto*: cracy: plutocracy (a government by the wealthy; a group of wealthy people who control or influence a government) (from *kratein*, to rule) crat: plutocrat {plutocratic} (from *kratein*, to rule) GREEK MYTHOLOGY: Plutus, the blind god of wealth CROSS REFERENCE: *oligo, op* (plenty, wealth)
pneu**	Greek *pneuma* (IE: *pneu*, echoic of sneeze, breathe)	breath, wind, air, spirit	SIMPLE ROOT: pneuma, pneumatic, pneumonia PREFIXED ROOT: a-: apnea (temporary stopping of breathing; asphyxia) (*a-*, not) dys-: dyspnea (difficult or painful breathing) (*dys-*, abnormal) hyper-: hyperpnea (abnormally rapid breathing; panting) (*hyper-*, beyond) LEADING ROOT COMPOUND: ectom: pneumonectomy (the surgical removal of an entire lung) (*ectom*, to cut out) itis: pneumonitis (*itis*, inflammation of) TRAILING ROOT COMPOUND: eu: eupnea (normal breathing) (*eu*, good, well) poly: polypnea (panting or rapid respiration) (*poly*, many) DISGUISED ROOT: neume (a group of notes sung, in a literal sense, while one breath lasts) CROSS REFERENCE: *aer, anem, anima*
pod,*** pus	Greek *pous* (IE: *ped*, *pod*, foot, to go)	foot, hoof	SIMPLE: podium (from *hypopodion*; literally, under the foot; originally, footstool; in *zoology*, a hand or a foot) (*hypo-*, under) PREFIXED ROOT: a-: apodal (lacking feet or legs, as snakes; lacking ventral fins) (*a-*, without) amphi-: amphipod (*amphi-*, around)

Element	From	Meaning	Examples
pod (cont'd)			*anti-*: antipodal, antipode, antipodes (*anti-*, against)

anti-: antipodal, antipode, antipodes (*anti-*, against)
em-: empodium (*em-*, in)
endo-: endopod (*endo-*, within)
sym-: sympodium (in *botany*, an apparent stem actually made up of a series of axillary branches growing one from another, giving the effect of a simple stem, as in the grape) (*sym-*, with, together)

LEADING ROOT COMPOUND:
agra: podagra (gout, especially in the big toe) (*agra*, seizure)
iatr: podiatry {podiatric, podiatrist} (*iatr*, healing)

TRAILING ROOT COMPOUND:
pod:
arthr: arthropod (the largest phylum of invertebrate animals with jointed legs, including insects, crustaceans, arachnids, and myriapods) (*arthro*, joint)
bi: bipod (a two-legged stand, as for a rifle) (*bi*, two)
cheno: chenopod (any plant of the goosefoot family, as spinach) (*cheno*, goose)
di: dipody (in *prosody*, a single measure consisting of two feet) {dipodic} (*di*, two)
mega: megapod (large-footed; as a *noun*, same as *megapode*, any of a family of large-footed, mound-building birds of Australia and the East Indies) (*mega*, large)
mono: monopode, monopodium (in *botany*, a single main stem that continues to extend at the apex in its original line of growth, giving off lateral branches or axes, as the trunk of certain pine trees) (*mono*, one, alone)
octo: octopod {octopodan, octopodous} (*octo*, eight)
pleo: pleopod (in *zoology*, any of the biramous appendages attached to the abdomen of higher crustaceans; swimmeret) (*plein*, to swim)
poly: polyp (the final letter of the word retains the first letter of the root), polypod, polypody (*poly*, many)
pseudo: pseudopodium (also, *pseudopode*) (*pseudo*, false)
pter: pteropod (*ptero*, wing)
tri: tripod, tripody (a verse or phrase of three metrical feet) (*tri*, three)
pus:
octo: octopus (*octo*, eight)
platy: platypus (literally, flat-footed) (*platy*, flat)

DISGUISED ROOT: pew (from *podium*)

TRAILING DISGUISED ROOT COMPOUND:
phalaro: phalarope (a small shorebird) [*phalaris*, coot (akin to *phalos*, white: from its white head)]

ITALIAN MUSIC TERM:
appoggiatura [literally, toward the foot (of the principal note); an auxiliary melodic note] (*ap-* from *ad-*, to, toward; *pog* from *pod*, foot)

RELATED WORD: pilot (from Italian *pedota*; from Greek *pedon*, oar blade)

PERSIAN:
pajamas (literally, leg garments)

545

Element	From	Meaning	Examples
pod (cont'd)			teapoy [literally, three-legged table or stand; extended to include a small table for use in serving tea (and usually thought to be derived from *tea*; however, *tea* is from Chinese *t'e*)] GREEK MYTHOLOGY: Oedipus (from *oidein,* to swell + *pous,* foot, literally, swollen foot: the son of Laius and Jocasta, king and queen of Thebes, who, raised by the king of Corinth, later returned to Thebes and unwittingly killed his father and married his mother; see next entry) PSYCHOANALYTIC TERM: *Oedipus complex* [the unconscious tendency of a child to be attached to the parent of the opposite sex and hostile toward the other parent (compare *Electra complex*)] CONSTELLATION: Apus (literally, footless; a southern constellation near the south celestial pole) NOTE: *Diapedesis,* from *pedan,* to leap, is derived from the Indo-European base *ped,* foot; the migration of blood cells, especially erythrocytes, through intact capillary walls into the tissues. CROSS REFERENCE: *ped* (Latin); Greek *ped* has a different meaning
poe*	Greek *poiein,* to make (IE: *kwei,* to heap up, build, make)	to make, create	SIMPLE ROOT: poem, poesy poet (**Synonyms:** bard, versifier, rhymer), poetaster, poetess, poetic, poetical, poeticism, poetics, poetize, poetry TRAILING ROOT COMPOUND: epo: epopee (an epic poem; epic poetry) (*epos,* word) hemato: hematopoiesis (the production of blood cells by the blood-forming organs) (*hemato,* blood) mytho: mythopoeic (productive of myths; myth-making) onomato: onomatopoeia [literally, name-making; words which represent their sounds, e.g., bobwhite, boom, buzz, cackle, chickadee, cuckoo, killdeer, paradiddle (a pattern of beats on a snare drum executed with alternate strokes of the sticks), purr, tinkle] (*onomato,* name) pharmaco: pharmacopoeia (a book containing an official list of medicinal drugs together with articles on their preparation and use; a collection or stock of drugs) sarco: sarcopoietic (*sarco,* flesh) PREFIXED TRAILING ROOT COMPOUND: pros-: prosopopoeia (the impersonation of an absent or imaginary speaker; personification, as of abstractions or inanimate objects) (*pros-,* before + *op,* to see: roots combined, *prosopon,* face, mask, dramatic character) CROSS REFERENCE: *fac/fic/fect/-fy*
pol*	Greek *polein*	to sell	TRAILING ROOT COMPOUND: biblio: bibliopole (a person who deals in rare books) (*biblio,* book) mono: monopoly (sole selling rights) (*mono,* one, single) oligo: oligopoly (control of a commodity or service in a given market by a small number of companies or suppliers) (*oligos,* few) CROSS REFERENCE: *ven*

Element	From	Meaning	Examples
pol*	Latin *polire*	to smooth	SIMPLE ROOT: polish (**Synonyms:** burnish, buff, shine), polite (**Synonyms:** civil, gallant, chivalrous) PREFIXED ROOT: *inter-*: interpolate [literally, to polish between; to alter, enlarge, or corrupt (a book, manuscript, etc.) by putting in new words, subject matter; in *mathematics*, to estimate a missing functional value by taking a weighted average of known functional values at neighboring points] (*inter-*, between) NO CROSS REFERENCE
polem*	Greek *polemos*: war (IE: *pel*, to shake	verbal attack	SIMPLE ROOT: polemic, polemical, polemics, polemicist NOTE: Demosthenes was known for his polemics against King Philip of Macedonia (reigned from 359-336 B.C.); these verbal denunciations came to be known as *philippics*. NO CROSS REFERENCE
poli***	Greek *polis*	city	SIMPLE ROOT: polic: police, policy [another *policy* (a written contract) is derived from *apo-*, away + *diction*] polis: polis (in ancient Greece, a city-state) polit: politic (**Synonyms:** suave, urbane, diplomatic), political, politician, polity PREFIXED ROOT: *a-*: apolitical (literally, not political; of no political significance; politically indifferent) (*a-*, not) LEADING ROOT COMPOUND: clin: policlinic (the department of a hospital where outpatients are treated; compare *polyclinic*) (*clin*, bed; from *klinein*, to recline) [do not confuse with *polyclinic*, which see under *poly*) TRAILING ROOT COMPOUND: cosmo: cosmopolitan (*cosmo*, universe) iso: isopolity (*iso*, equal) megalo: megalopolis (*megalo*, large) metro: metropolis (literally, mother city; main city; any large city or center of population, culture, etc.) (*metro*, mother) necro: necropolis (a cemetery, especially one belonging to an ancient city) (*necro*, corpse) HISTORICAL PLACENAMES: Acropolis (literally, city on a hill) Decapolis (literally, a group of ten cities) AMERICAN PLACENAMES: Annapolis (Illinois, Maryland, Missouri, Washington) Demopolis, Alabama (literally, people city) Indianapolis, Indiana SANSKRIT PLACENAME: Singapore (literally, lion city, where *pore* is from *pur*, city) CROSS REFERENCE: *civ, popul*
polio**	Greek *polios*, gray	gray (gray matter of the nervous system)	LEADING ROOT COMPOUND: mye: poliomyelitis (*mye*, marrow + *itis*, inflammation of) plasm: polioplasm (granular protoplasm) (*plasm*, form) thrix: poliothrix (greying hair) (*thrix*, hair) NO CROSS REFERENCE

Element	From	Meaning	Examples
poly***	Greek *polys*	many, diverse, much	LEADING ROOT COMPOUND: adelph: polyadelphous (in *botany*, having stamens joined by their filaments into a number of clusters) (*adelphos*, brother) andr: polyandry (*andr*, male; stamen) anthus: polyanthus (*anth*, flower) bas: polybasic, polybasite (*base*, foundation) carp: polycarpic (in *botany*, capable of flowering and fruiting an indefinite number of times) (*carp*, flower) chrom: polychromatic, polychrome, polychromy (*chrom*, color) clin: polyclinic (a clinic or hospital for the treatment of various kinds of diseases; compare *policlinic*) (*clin*, bed; from *klinein*, to recline) [do not confuse with *policlinic*, which see under *poli*) dactyl: polydactyl (*dactyl*, finger, toe) embry: polyembryony (the production of two or more embryos or individuals from a single fertilized ovum) (*embryo*, to swell) ester: polyester (*ester*, ether) gala: polygala (same as *milkwort*) (*galact*, milk) gam: polygamous (the state or practice of having two or more wives or husbands at the same time; plural marriage; compare *polygynous*; in *botany*, having bisexual and unisexual flowers on the same plant), polygamy (*gamos*, marriage) gen: polygenesis (derivation from more than one germ cell) (*gen*, producing) glot: polyglot (as an *adjective*, speaking or writing several languages; as a *noun*, one who speaks or write several languages; a book written in several languages) (*glotta*, tongue) gon: (note the different meanings in the following two words) polygon (*gon*, angle) polygonum (*gon*, knee) graph: polygraph (a lie detector) (*graph*, write) gyn: polygyny (the state or practice of having two or more wives or concubines at the same time) (*gyn*, woman) hedr: polyhedron (*hedron*, geometric plane) mer: polymer, polymeric, polymerism (*mere*, part) morph: polymorph, polymorphism, polymorphous (*morph*, shape, form) neur: polyneuritis (*neur*, nerve) nom: polynomial (*nomos*, law) p: (from *pod*, foot) polyp (literally, many feet; a tumor with a pedicle) polypary (the common base or the connecting tissue to which each member of a colony is attached) petal: polypetalous (in *botany*, having separate petals) phag: polyphagia (excessive desire for food; the eating of or subsistence on many kinds of food) (*phag*, eat) phas: polyphase (having, generating, or using alternating currents differing in phase, as *a polyphase system*) (*phas*, show) phon: polyphone, polyphonic (in *music*, having two or more voices or parts), polyphony (*phone*, sound)

Element	From	Meaning	Examples
poly- (cont'd)			phyl: polyphyletic (in *biology*, derived from more than one ancestral type) (*phyl*, race, tribe) pod: polypody (a genus of ferns with leathery pinnatifid leaves borne on creeping rootstocks) (*pod*, foot) sapro: polysaprobic (in *biology*, flourishing in a body of water having a heavy load of decomposed organic matter and almost no free oxygen) (*sapros*, rotten) sem: polysemy (the fact of having or being open to several or many meanings) {polysemous} (*sema*, sign) syl: poly<u>syl</u>labic (*syl*- assimilates *sym*-, with, together) syn: polysyndeton (in *rhetoric*, the use of conjunctions in close succession, e.g., we have ships *and* men *and* money *and* stores; here *and* there *and* everywhere; opposed to *asyndeton*, the omission of conjunctions, e.g., Smile, shake hands, part) (*syn*, with, together + *dein*, to bind) techn: polytechnic (of or providing instruction in many scientific and technical subjects) the: polytheism (belief in or worship of many gods, or more than one god; opposed to *monotheism*) (*theos*, god) troph: polytrophic (*troph*, nourish) un: poly<u>un</u>saturated (*un*-, not, prefixes *saturated*) ur: polyuria (excessive urination, as in some diseases) GREEK MYTHOLOGY: Polyhymnia (the Muse of sacred poetry) ARCHIPELAGO: Polynesia (a major division of the Pacific islands east of the international date line, and extending from the Hawaiian Islands south to New Zealand, and including the islands of the state of Hawaii; Samoa, Tonga, the Society Islands, Marquesas Islands) INTERDISCIPLINARY: polyandry (in *botany*, the presence of numerous stamens in one flower; in *zoology*, the mating of one female animal with more than one male) polygyny (in *botany*, the fact of having many styles or pistils; in *zoology*, the mating of a male animal with more than one female) CROSS REFERENCE: *multi, plur/plus/plu*
pom*	Latin *pomum*	apple, fruit	SIMPLE ROOT: poma: pomace (the crushed pulp of apples or other fruit pressed for juice), pomaceous, pomade, pomander pome: pome, pomelo (grapefruit) pomm: pommel (also, *pummel*; literally, little apple; a knob on the hilt of a sword or other weapon; the upper front part of a saddle; saddlebow; as a *verb*, to beat, pummel) LEADING ROOT COMPOUND: *pome*: gran: pomegranate (*gran*, grain) *pomi*: fer: pomiferous (bearing fruit, especially pomes) (*ferre*, to bear) *pomo*: logy: pomology (study of fruit cultivation) (*logy*, study of)

Element	From	Meaning	Examples
pom (cont'd)			ROMAN MYTHOLOGY: Pomona, goddess of fruit trees PLACENAMES: Pomona (California, Illinois, Kansas, Maryland, Missouri; also one of the Orkney Islands) CROSS REFERENCE: *carp, frug/fruct*
pon,*** pos	Latin *ponere* (IE: *paus*, to let go)	to place, to put	SIMPLE ROOT: *pon*: pone (a type of writ; not the type of cornbread in the form of small, oval loaves, which is Algonquian *äpân*) *pos*: pose (**Synonyms:** affectation, mannerism) posit, position (**Synonyms:** situation, office, post) positive (**Synonyms:** sure, certain, confident), positivism, posture PREFIXED ROOT: *pon(e)*: *com-*: component (**Synonyms:** element, constituent, ingredient) (*com-*, with, together) *de-*: deponent (to lay down, set down) (*de-*, down) *ex-*: exponent, exponential, exponible (*ex-*, out) *op-*: opponent (**Synonyms:** antagonist, adversary, enemy) (*op-* assimilates *ob-*, against) *post-*: postpone (**Synonyms:** adjourn, prorogue, dissolve), postponement (*post-*, after) *pro-*: propone, proponent (*pro-*, forth, forward) *trans-*: transponible (but not *transponder*, which is a combination of *transmitter* + re*sponder*), and not *transpontine* (where *pon* is Latin for *bridge*, as in *pontoon*) (*trans-*, across) *pos(e)/posit*: *ap-*: apposable, appose, apposite (**Synonyms:** relevant, germane, pertinent), apposition, appositive (*ap-* assimilates *ad-*, to, toward) *com-*: compose (to put together; to create; make up; constitute; to adjust or settle; reconcile, as to *compose* differences), composed, composite, composition, compositive, compositor, composure (**Synonyms:** equanimity, serenity, nonchalance) (*com-*, with) *contra-*: contraposition (*contra-*, against) *de-*: deposable, deposal, depose, deposit (see *Doublets* below), depositary, deposition, depositor, depository (*de-*, from, away) *dis-*: disposable, disposal, dispose, disposed (inclined; having a certain tendency), disposition (**Synonyms:** temperament, temper, character) (*dis-*, apart, away) *ex-*: expose (French *exposé*), exposition (not to be confused with *exhibition*), expositor, expository, expositive, exposure (*ex-*, out) *im-*: impose, imposing, imposition (*im-*, a variant of *in-*, in) *inter-*: interpose (see *Doublets* below; **Synonyms:** interfere, intervene, mediate), interposition (*inter-*, between) *juxta-*: juxtapose, juxtaposition (*juxta-*, near, beside) *op-*: opposable, opposal, oppose, opposite (**Synonyms:** contrary, antithetical, antonymous), oppositive (*op-* assimilates *ob-*, against) *post-*: postposition, postpositive (*post-*, after)

Element	From	Meaning	Examples
pon (cont'd)			*pro-*: proposal, propose (see *Doublets* below; **Synonyms:** intend, design, purpose) (*pro-*, forth)
			pre-: preposition, prepositive, prepositor (British variation of *prefect*) (*pre-*, before)
			pro-: proposition (*pro-*, forth, forward)
			pur-: purpose (see *Doublets* below; **Synonyms:** intention, intent, objective), purposive (*pur-*, a variant of *pro-*, for)
			re-: repose (the state of being at rest; dignified calmness; as a verb, to lie or beat rest), reposit, reposition, repositor, repository (*re-*, again)
			sup-: (*sup-* assimilates *sub-*, under)
			suppose, supposed (regarded as true without actual knowledge), supposition (hypothesis), supposititious
			suppositive (having the nature of, based on, or involving supposition; in *grammar*, a conjunction introducing a supposition, e.g., as if, assuming, provided, etc.)
			suppository (a small piece of medicated substance introduced into a body passage, as the vagina or rectum, where body heat causes it to melt)
			super-: superpose (in *geometry*, to make a figure coincide with another in all parts, by or as if by placing one on top of the other) (*super-*, over, above)
			trans-: transpose, transposition {transpositional} (*trans-*, across)
			post:
			com-: compost (*com-*, with, together)
			im-: impost (both meanings), impostor, imposture (*im-*, a variant of *in-*, in)
			pote:
			com-: compote (*com-*, with, together)
			DOUBLE PREFIXED ROOT:
			presuppose (**Synonyms:** presume, assume, postulate), presupposition (*pre-*, *before*; *sup-* assimilates *sub-*, under)
			superimpose (to put, lay, or stack on top of something else; to add as a dominant or unassimilated feature) (*super-*, over, beyond; *im-*, in)
			DISGUISED ROOT: pause, posture
			PREFIXED DISGUISED ROOT:
			pro-: provost [see note under *pro-* (Latin)]
			FRENCH:
			entrepôt (see *Doublets* below) (from *entreposer*; a place for storage of goods; warehouse; a distributing center for goods)
			depot (French spelling, *dépôt*; see *Doublets* below)
			DOUBLETS:
			depot:deposit; interpose:entrepôt; propose:purpose
			LEGAL TERMS:
			compos mentis (sound, or composed mind; sane)
			non compos mentis (not of sound mind; insane)
			INTERDISCIPLINARY:
			deponent (in Latin and Greek *grammar*, denoting a verb with a passive or middle voice form and an active meaning; in *law*, a person who makes an affidavit)

Element	From	Meaning	Examples
pon (cont'd)			transpose [in *mathematics*, an algebraic term: to transfer from one side of an equation to the other, reversing the plus or minus value; as a *noun*, a matrix obtained by interchanging the rows and columns of a given matrix; in *music*, to rewrite or play (a musical composition) in a different key] CROSS REFERENCE: *theca, thes/thet*
pond			See *pend/pens/pond* for *ponder, preponderant.*
popul,** publ	Latin *populus* (yields English people)	common people	SIMPLE ROOT: *popul*: popula: populace, popular (**Synonyms:** common, general, ordinary) populat: populate, population, populator populi: populist populo: populous (full of people; crowded or thickly populated) *publ*: public, publican (in ancient Rome, a collector of public revenues, tolls, etc.) publication, publish (**Synonyms:** declare, announce, proclaim), publicist PREFIXED ROOT: *de-*: depopulate, depopulation, depopulator (*de-*, negative) *re-*: repopulate (*re-*, again) TRAILING ROOT COMPOUND: re: republic, republican (the *re* in these words is *not* the prefix *re-*, again, but is from *res,* Latin for thing, affair, interest, the idea being that the public is responsible for the affairs of government. Semantically, though not etymologically, Latin *republic* is synonymous with Greek *democracy*.) SPANISH COGNATE: *pueblo* (village, people) LATIN PHRASE: *vox populi, vox Dei* (The voice of the people is the voice of God UNIVERSITY MOTTO: *Salus populi*, The welfare of the people, University of Missouri PLACENAME: Pueblo, Colorado CROSS REFERENCE: *demo, pleb, vulg*
port			See *part/port* for *portion, apportion.*
port***	Latin *portare* (IE: *per,* to come over)	to carry	SIMPLE ROOT: portable, portage, portative, portato porter, portly PREFIXED ROOT: *com-*: comport (**Synonyms:** demean, deport, acquit), comportment (*com-*, with, together) *de-*: (notice difference in meanings of prefix) deport (to behave or conduct oneself in a specified way), deportment (**Synonyms:** bearing, demeanor, mien) (*de-*, intensive) deport (to carry or send away; specifically, to force an alien to leave a country by official order; expel), deportation, deportee (*de-*, from) *dis-*: disport (literally, to carry away; the aphetic of *disport* is *sport*) (*dis-*, apart) *ex-*: export, exportation (*ex-*, out)

Element	From	Meaning	Examples
port (cont'd)			*im*-: (a variant of *in*-, in) import (to bring in; to be significant) importance (**Synonyms**: consequence, moment, weight) important (carrying a great deal of weight or value; significant) importation (the act, occupation, or business of importing) *pur*-: purport (*pur*-, a variant of *pro*-, for) *re*-: report, reportorial (*re*-, back, again) *sup*-: support (**Synonyms**: uphold, sustain, maintain) (*sup*-, an assimilation of *sub*-, under) *trans*-: transport (**Synonyms**: 1) ecstasy, bliss, rapture; 2) banish, exile, expatriate), transportation (*trans*-, across) DOUBLE PREFIXED ROOT: (*re*-, again + *ap*-, an assimilation of *ad*-, to, toward) rapport (a close or sympathetic relationship; agreement; harmony), rapporteur (a person appointed to prepare reports, studies, etc., as for a committee or conference) LEADING ROOT COMPOUND: foli: portfolio (a small briefcase for carrying loose sheets or papers) (*folium*, leaf) manteau: portmanteau (a traveling case) (from *mantle*, cloak) TRAILING ROOT COMPOUND: tele: teleportation (the theoretical transportation of matter through space by converting it into energy and then reconverting it at the terminal point) [Greek *tele* + Latin *(trans-) portation*)] DISGUISED ROOT: sport (aphetic of *disport*) MUSIC TERM: portamento (a continuous gliding from one note to another, sounding intervening tones; glide) MILITARY TERM: port arms (rifle or carbine held diagonally across the chest, in the position to be carried) CROSS REFERENCE: *fer, phor*
port**	Latin *portus*, harbor	haven, harbor, port	SIMPLE ROOT: port (a harbor; a city or town with a harbor where ships can load and unload cargo; port of entry) [There are other "ports": a *wine*, so named from Oporto, Portugal; *to carry*, as in previous family; *the left side of a ship*; *a doorway*.] PREFIXED ROOT: *im*-: (from *in*-, not) importunate (urgent or persistent in asking or demanding; insistent; refusing to be denied; annoyingly urgent or persistent) importune (**Synonyms**: 1) beg, solicit, entreat; 2) urge, exhort, press), importunity *op*-: opportune (right for the purpose; fitting in regard to circumstances: said of time, as *an opportune time* to ask for a raise; **Synonyms**: timely, seasonable), opportunism, opportunity [*op*- assimilates *ob*-, to, toward (in this use); *ob*- has other meanings that appear contradictory] DOUBLE PREFIXED ROOT: inopportune (not opportune; coming or happening at a poor time; not appropriate, as *an inopportune time* to ask for a raise) (*in*-, not + *op*-, an assimilation of *ob*-, against) NO CROSS REFERENCE

Element	From	Meaning	Examples
pos, posit			See *pon/pos* for *pose, position, deposition*.
post-***	Latin *posterus* (IE: *pos*, after; which is probably from *apo*, away)	after, later	EXTENDED PREFIX: poste: posterior, posteriority (opposed to *priority*), posterity (all of a person's descendants; opposed to *ancestry*), postern posth: posthumous (*post* is from *postumus*, superlative of *posterus*, coming after, next) posti: postiche (from *apposite*; counterfeit; artificial; superfluously decorative; as a *noun*, a substitute; pretense; hairpiece) PREFIXED ROOT: bellum: postbellum (after the war; occurring after the war, specifically the American Civil War) (*bellum*, war) diluv: postdiluvian (after the flood; of the time after the Biblical Flood; as a *noun*, a postdiluvian person or thing) hypn: posthypnotic (having to do with, or carried out in the period following a hypnotic trance, as *a hypnotic suggestion*) (*hypn*, sleep, stupor) lud: postlude (*ludere*, to play) mort: post-mortem (after death) (*mort*, death) nat: postnatal (after birth; especially, of the period immediately after birth) (*nat*, birth) nup: postnuptial (happening or done after marriage) (*nup*, marriage) ob: post-obit (after death) (*ob-*, against, prefixes *itere*, to go) orb: postorbital (in *anatomy* and *zoology*, situated behind the orbit, or eye socket; as a *noun*, a postorbital bone or scale, as in certain reptiles) (*orb*, circle) part: postpartum (the period following childbirth) (*parere*, to bear) pon: postpone (to delay until a future time; to place after in importance; subordinate) {postponement} (*ponere*, to place) posit: postposition (in *grammar*, the placing of an element after another that is related to it), postpositive (in *grammar*, placed after or added to a word) (from *ponere*, to place) prand: postprandial (after a meal; especially, after dinner) (*prand*, meal) script: postscript (abbreviated P.S.) (from *scribere*, to write) PREFIX + EXTENDED PREFIX: pre-: preposterous (originally, with the first last, and the last first; inverted; so contrary to nature, reason, or common sense as to be laughable; absurd; ridiculous) (*pre-*, before) HYBRID LATIN-ENGLISH COMPOUND: posteriomost (farthest back in time, order, or position) DISGUISED ELEMENT: puisne (literally, born later; of lower rank; junior, as in appointment; see *Doublets* below) puny (literally, born later; of inferior size, strength, or importance; weak; slight; see *Doublets* below) (*puis*, after + *ne*, from *natus*, born) DOUBLETS: puisne:puny NB: *Postulant* and *postulate*, from *poscere*, to demand, are not in this family. NO CROSS REFERENCE

Element	From	Meaning	Examples
pot*	Latin *potare* (IE: *po*, drink)	to drink	SIMPLE ROOT: pota: potable (fit to drink; drinkable), potation (the act of drinking; a drink or draft, especially of liquor), potatory poti: potion (see *Doublets* below) DISGUISED ROOT: poison (French for *drink*; came to mean "a harmful or deadly drink") (see *Doublets* below) PREFIXED DISGUISED ROOT: sym-: symposium (in ancient Greece, an entertainment characterized by drinking, music, and intellectual discussion; hence, any meeting or social gathering at which ideas are freely exchanged) (*sym-*, with, together) RUSSIAN COGNATE: pirog (feast) DOUBLETS: poison:potion CROSS REFERENCE: *bib*
pot,** pos	Latin *potis* (IE: *esti*, to be)	able, power	SIMPLE ROOT: *pos*: possibility (plural: something that is possible, e.g., "The project has possibilities") possible (**Synonyms**: practicable, feasible) possibly [in context, has two meanings: 1) by any possible means; in any case (it can't *possibly* work); 2) by some possibility; perhaps; maybe (it may *possibly* be so)] *pot*: potence, potency (**Synonyms**: strength, power, force) potent (having authority or power; convincing; effective or powerful in action, as a drug or drink; able to have an erection and therefore engage in sexual intercourse) potentate (a person having great power; ruler; monarch) potential (**Synonyms**: latent, dormant, quiescent) PREFIXED ROOT: im-: impotence, impotent (without power; lacking physical strength; unable to engage in sexual intercourse, especially because of inability to have an erection) (from *in-*, not) pre-: prepotency (in *biology*, the greater capacity of one parent to transmit certain characteristics to offspring: a concept now discredited) (*pre-*, before) LEADING ROOT COMPOUND: sess: possess (literally, to be able to sit), possessed, possession, possessive, possessory (*pos-* contraction of *potis*, able + *sedere*, to sit) TRAILING ROOT COMPOUND: des: despot (originally, *demspota*, literally, house master; absolute ruler; tyrant) omni: omnipotent (*omni*, all) pleni: plenipotentiary (*pleni*, full) DISGUISED ROOT: puissance, puissant (now archaic, but not when prefixed; see next entry) PREFIXED DISGUISED ROOT: im-: impuissant (weak, powerless) (*im-*, not) LATIN LEGAL TERM: *posse comitatus* (power of the county; usually to *posse* and held to mean "a body of persons summoned by the sheriff to assist in preserving the public peace, usually in an emergency"; other meanings)

Element	From	Meaning	Examples
pot (cont'd)			ITALIAN: podesta (mayor of a city) ENGLISH: power (**Synonyms**: dominion, jurisdiction, authority) PERSIAN: Padishah (a title of the shah of Iran; a former title of the sultan of Turkey) CROSS REFERENCE: *dynam*
pre-***	Latin *prae* (IE: *prae*, beyond)	before	PREFIXED ROOT: amb: preamble (**Synonyms**: preface, foreword, prologue) (*ambulare*, to go) axi: preaxial (in *anatomy*, situated in front of the axis of the body or a limb) (*axis*, axle) bend: prebend (things to be given; a clergyman's stipend) (from *habere*, to hold, offer) caut: precaution {precautionary} (*cavere*, to take care) ced: precede, precedence (also, *precedency*), precedent, precedential, preceding (*cedere*, to go, leave) cent: precentor (from *cantar*, to sing) cept: precept (**Synonyms**: doctrine, dogma, tenet), preceptive, preceptor, preceptory (from *capere*, to take) cess: precess, precession (not to be confused with *procession*) {precessional} (see *precede*) cinct: precinct (from *cingere*, to surround, gird) cip: precipice (a vertical, almost vertical, or overhanging rock face; steep cliff), precipitancy (also, *preciptance*), precipitant, precipitate (**Synonyms**: sudden, abrupt, impetuous) (*caput*, head) cis: précis, precise (**Synonyms**: 1) explicit, express, exact; 2) correct, accurate), precisely, precisian, precision (*caedere*, to cut) clud: preclude (**Synonyms**: prevent, forestall, obviate) (*claudere*, to close) coc: precocial (designating or of birds whose newly hatched young are covered with down and fully active; opposed to *altricial*, which see under *al*, nourish), precocious (from *coquere*, to mature, cook) cogn: precognition {precognitive} (*cognoscere*, to know) con: preconize (from which are derived *preach, preacher*) curs: precursor (**Synonyms**: forerunner, herald, harbinger) (from *currere*, to run) de: predestination (*de-* prefixes *stin*, akin to *stare*, to stand) dic: (*dicere*, to speak, say) predicable, predicament (**Synonyms**: dilemma, quandary, plight), predicant, predicate, predicatory predict (to say in advance what one believes will happen), prediction dilect: predilection (**Synonyms**: prejudice, bias, partiality) (*di-*, apart + *legere*, to choose) dom: predominant, predominate (*dominus*, master) emp: preempt, preemption, preemptive (from which *premium* is derived) (*emp*, buy) fabr: prefabricate {prefabrication} (*fabricari*, to construct, build)

556

Element	From	Meaning	Examples
pre (cont'd)			fac: preface (**Synonyms**: foreword, preamble, prologue) (from *fab*, to speak)

fat: prefatory (from *preface*)

fect: prefect, prefecture (from *facere*, to make, do)

fer: prefer, preferable, preference (**Synonyms**: choice, option, alternative), preferential, preferment (*ferre*, bear)

fig: prefiguration (a prototype), prefigure (*figurare*, to fashion)

fix: prefix {prefixal, prefixion} (from *figere*, to fix)

form: preformation (in *biology*, a former theory that every germ cell contains every part of the future organism in miniature, development being merely growth in size)

gnant: pregnant (from *gnasci*, to be born)

hens: (from IE *ghed-*, to grasp)

prehensile (adapted for holding or grasping, especially by wrapping around an object, as *a prehensile tail*, as that of the opossum)

prehension (the act of grasping or seizing)

jud: (from *judicare*, to judge)

prejudge {prejudger, prejudgment, or *prejudgement*}

prejudice (**Synonyms**: bias, partiality, predilection), prejudicial

lat: prelate, prelatism, prelature (from *ferre*, to bear)

lect: prelect (to lecture in public) {prelection} (from *legere*, to read)

lim: preliminary (*limen*, threshold)

liter: preliterate (of or belonging to a society not developed to the stage of having a written language) (*littera*, letter)

lud: prelude {preludial} (*ludere*, to play)

marit: premarital (before marriage)

maxill: premaxilla (*maxilla*, upper jaw)

med: premeditate {premeditative, premeditator} (*med*, measure)

mier: première (from *prime*)

mis: premise (in *logic*, either of the two propositions of a syllogism from which the conclusion is drawn; **Synonyms**: presume, presuppose, assume) (from *mittere*, to send)

mors: premorse (ending abruptly and unevenly, as if bitten off: said of a leaf or root) (from *mordere*, to bite)

nat: prenatal (taking place before birth) (*natus*, born)

nup: prenuptial (before a marriage or wedding; in *zoology*, before mating) (from *nubere*, to marry)

par: preparation, preparative, preparatory, prepare, preparedness (*parare*, to set in order, get ready)

pens: prepense (with malice; premeditated) (*pensare*, to think)

pon: preponderant (**Synonyms**: overpowering, major, dominant), preponderate (*pondus*, a weight)

posit: preposition (translation of Greek *prothesis*), prepositive, prepositor (from *ponere*, to place)

pos: prepossess, prepossessing (from *potis*, able + *sess* from *sedere*, to sit)

poster: preposterous (**Synonyms**: absurd, ludicrous, foolish) (*posterus*, coming after)

Element	From	Meaning	Examples
pre- (cont'd)			pot: prepotency (superiority in power, force, or influence) (*potis*, able)
			puc: prepuce [the fold of skin covering the end (glans) of the penis; foreskin; a similar fold over the end of the clitoris] (from IE *put-*, a swelling)
			[This word was listed generically under *peni*, penis.]
			re: prerequisite (*re-* prefixes *quis*)
			rog: prerogative (originally, called upon to vote first; a prior or exclusive right or privilege) (*rogare*, to ask)
			sag: presage (as a *noun*, pronounced PRES ij; as a *verb*, pri SAGE) (*sagire*, to perceive)
			scienc: prescience (apparent knowledge of things before they happen or come into being; foreknowledge) (*scire*, to know)
			scind: prescind (to detach, abstract, or isolate a meaning, one's mind, etc.) (*scindere*, to cut)
			scrib: prescribe (*scribere*, to write)
			script: prescriptible, prescription, prescriptive (from *prescribe*)
			sen: presence, present, presentable, presentation, presentative, presentiment, presentment (from *esse*, to be)
			serv: preservation, preservative, preserve (*servare*, to keep, hold)
			sid: preside, presidency, president, presidium (from *sedere*, to sit)
			stig: prestige (literally, to blindfold; originally, "illusion brought on by magic"; consequently, one who could perform tricks blindfolded was held in awe; **Synonyms**: influence, authority, weight), prestigious (from *stringere*, to bind, tighten)
			sum(pt): presume (**Synonyms**: presuppose, assume, postulate), presumption, presumptive, presumptuous (from *sumere*, to take)
			ten: pretend (**Synonyms**: assume, affect, simulate), pretense, pretention, pretentious (*tendere*, to stretch)
			text: pretext (a false reason or motive put forth to hide the real one; excuse; a cover-up; front) (*texere*, to weave)
			vail: prevail, prevailing (**Synonyms**: current, prevalent, rife) (from *valere*, to be strong)
			val: prevalent (from *prevail*; see synonyms at *prevailing*, previous entry)
			var: prevaricate (to turn aside from, or evade, the truth; to tell an untruth; lie) (*varicare*, to straddle)
			ven: prevenient, prevent (**Synonyms**: avert, preclude, obviate), prevention, preventive (*venire*, to come)
			vi: previous (**Synonyms**: prior, preceding, antecedent) (*via*, a way)
			view: preview (to view or show beforehand; receive or give a preview of) (from *videre*, to see)
			vis: previse (to inform beforehand; warn), prevision (foresight or foreknowledge; a prediction or prophecy; as a *verb*, to foresee) (from *videre*, to see)
			ALTERNATE PREFIXED ROOT: praenomen

Element	From	Meaning	Examples
pre- (cont'd)			DOUBLE PREFIXED ROOT: pre<u>de</u>cessor (*de-*, away + *cedere*, to go) pre<u>de</u>stinate (in *theology*, to foreordain by divine decree) DISGUISED ROOT: apricot (literally, "early-matured" fruit) preach (from *pre-* + *dicare*, to proclaim) SPANISH: presidio (from Latin *praesidium*, a garrison; from *praeses*, a guard; from *preside*) ITALIAN: presto (quick, nimble; from *praesto*, at hand, available; fast or at once; in *music*, in fast tempo) NOTE: *Precarious* is not in this family, being derived from prayer (see under *prec*, request); neither is *precious*, coming from *price* (see next family); nor *predacious*, from *prey*. CROSS REFERENCE: *ante-, anter-, fore-, pro-*
prec**	Latin *pretium* (IE: *per*, to sell, make equal)	price, money	SIMPLE ROOT: preciosity (great fastidiousness, over-refinement or affectation, especially in language), precious (of great price or value; costly) PREFIXED ROOT: *ap-*: appreciate (**Synonyms**: value, prize, treasure), appreciation, appreciative (*ap-* assimilates *ad-*, to, toward) *de-*: depreciate (**Synonyms**: disparage, decry, belittle) (*de-*, from) DISGUISED ROOT: praise (**Synonyms**: laud, extol, eulogize) price, priceless prize (**Synonyms**: 1) appreciate, value, treasure; 2) reward, award, premium) PREFIXED DISGUISED ROOT: *ap-*: appraise (**Synonyms**: estimate, evaluate, rate) (*ap-* assimilates *ad-*, to, toward) CROSS REFERENCE: *emp, pec*
prec*	Latin *prex;* *precari,* pray (IE: *perk*, question)	request, prayer	SIMPLE ROOT: precarious, precatory (also, *precative*) PREFIXED ROOT: *de-*: deprecate (to feel and express disapproval of; plead against), deprecatory (deprecating; apologetic or belittling) (*de-*, off, from) *im-*: imprecate (*im-*, a variant of *in-*, in, on) DISGUISED ROOT: pray (**Synonyms**: plead, petition, supplicate), prayer prithee (archaic; I pray thee; please) NO CROSS REFERENCE
prehend,*** prehens, pris	Latin *prehendere* (IE: *hend* from *ghed*, to grasp + *pre-*, before)	seize, take	SIMPLE ROOT: *prehens*: prehensile, prehension (the act of grasping or seizing; apprehension by the senses) *pris*: prison (explore *penitentiary, jail, reformatory*) PREFIXED ROOT: *prehend*: *ap-*: apprehend, apprehension, apprentice (from *apprehend*), (*ap-* assimilates *ad-*, to, toward) *com-*: comprehend (**Synonyms**: 1) include, comprise, embrace; 2) understand, appreciate) {comprehensible, comprehension, comprehensive} (*com-*, with, together)

Element	From	Meaning	Examples
prehend (cont'd)			*re-*: reprehend (**Synonyms:** criticize, blame, censure) {reprehensible, reprehension, reprehensive} (*re-*, back) *pris(e)*: *ap-*: apprise (*ap-* assimilates *ad-*, to, toward) *com-*: comprise (**Synonyms:** include, comprehend, embrace) (*com-*, with, together) *em-*: emprise (from *in-*, in) *enter-*: enterprise (an undertaking; project), enterprising (from *inter-*, in, between) *im-*: imprison (*im-*, in) *mis-*: misprision (a mistake, now especially one due to misreading, either deliberate or unintended, or to misunderstanding; scorn; contempt; in *law*, a misconduct or neglect of duty, especially by a public official; act of contempt against a government or court) (Anglo-Saxon *mis-*, wrong) *re-*: reprisal, reprise (*re-*, back, again) *sur-*: surprise (from *super-*, above, over) DOUBLE PREFIXED ROOT: incomprehensible (*in-*, not; *com-*, with, together) DISGUISED ROOT: predation, predator, predatory (from *prey*) pregnable (vulnerable to seizure or capture, as a fort) prey prize (**Synonyms:** spoil(s), pillage, booty) [another *prize* is derived from *price]* pry (one meaning) PREFIXED DISGUISED ROOT: *im-*: impregnable (not capable of being captured or entered by force) (*in-*, not) [another *impregnable* means "that can be impregnated"] FRENCH: entrepreneur (from *entreprendre*, to undertake) CROSS REFERENCE: *cap, rapt, sume/sumpt*
press***	Latin *primere*; *premere* (IE: *per*, strike)	press	SIMPLE ROOT: press (**Synonyms:** urge, exhort, importune) [another *press* means "to force into military service"), pressure PREFIXED ROOTS AND COMPOUNDS: *ap-*: appressed (pressed close to or flat against a surface) (from *ad-*, to, toward) *com-*: compress (**Synonyms:** contract, shrink, deflate), compressed, compression, compressive, compressor (*com-*, with, together) *de-*: (down) depress (**Synonyms:** dishearten, discourage, sadden), depressant, depressed (**Synonyms:** sad, melancholy, dejected), depressible, depression, depressive, depressor depressomotor *ex-*: express (**Synonyms: 1)** explicit, exact, precise; **2)** utter, broach, enunciate), expression, expressionism, expressive, expressivity (*ex-*, out) *im-*: impress, impressible, impression (**Synonyms:** idea, conception, notion), impressionable, impressionism, impressive, impressionism (*im-*, in)

560

Element	From	Meaning	Examples
press (cont'd)			*op-*: oppress (**Synonyms**: abuse, wrong, aggrieve), oppressed, oppression, oppressive (from *ob-*, against) *re-*: repress, re-press, repressed, repression, repressive (*re-*, back, again) *sup-*: suppress, suppressant, suppression (from *sub-*, under) DISGUISED ROOT: praiss (a fluid extract of tobacco) print, sprain PREFIXED DISGUISED ROOT: *im-*: imprimatur, imprint (*im-*, in) *re-*: reprimand (literally, to press back; to repress) (*re-*, back) NOTE: *Imprimis*, among the first, is not related to *imprimatur*; see *primo*. NO CROSS REFERENCE
preter*	Latin *praeter* (from *pre-*, before + *ire*, to go)	beyond, past; outside the bounds	SIMPLE ROOT: preterient (meaning transient), preterist LEADING ROOT COMPOUND: it: (from *ire*, to go) preterit (to express a past action or state, as in *grammar*) preterition (in *Calvinistic theology*, the doctrine that having elected to eternal life such as He chose, God passed over the rest leaving them to eternal death) mit: pretermit (to leave out or undone; neglect or omit; to let pass unnoticed; overlook) (*mittere*, to send) nat: preternatural (differing from or beyond what is normally found in or expected from nature; abnormal, as *preternatural* strength; same as *supernatural*) (*natus*, birth) CROSS REFERENCE: *hyper, met, super, ulter*
prim***	Latin *primus* (IE: *per*, beyond)	first	NOTE: Some of the following words are listed under the prefix *pre-*. SIMPLE ROOT: prim: prim, primp prima: primacy, primage, primal, primary, primate {primatial} prime: prime (**Synonyms**: principal, foremost, primary) primer, priming primi: primitive (explore use of *primitive* in biology, geology, linguistics, mathematics) primo: primo (in *music*, the principal or leading part, especially in a duet) primu: primula (same as *primrose*, which see below) PREFIXED ROOT: *im-*: imprimis (in the first place; among the first) (*im-*, in) LEADING ROOT COMPOUND: *prim*: ev: primeval (from *aevum*, an age) ord: primordial, primordium (*ordiri*, to begin) *primo*: gen: primogenitor, primogeniture (from *gignere*, to beget) *primato*: logy: primatology (the branch of zoology dealing with primates, especially, the apes, monkeys, and early hominids) (*logy*, study of)

Element	From	Meaning	Examples
prim (cont'd)			DISGUISED ROOT: premier (first in status or importance; chief; supreme; see French *première*) presbyterian, presbytery (see *Doublets* below) priest (originally, lead-ox) (see *Doublets* below) prince (literally, first-taken) (*prime + capere*, to take) principal, principality (same roots as *prince*) principle, principled (same roots as *prince*) pristine (characteristic of the earliest, or an earlier, period) DOUBLETS: priest:presbyterian TRIPLETS: principle:principal:prince LATIN-ENGLISH COMPOUND: primrose (literally, first rose) FRENCH: *première* (the first public presentation of a movie, play, or other performance) SPANISH: *primero* (first) LATIN PHRASE: *primus inter pares* (first among equals; said especially of the Chief Justice of the Supreme Court) LATIN LEGAL PHRASE: *prima facie* (literally, first view, and is used in the phrase, *prima facie* evidence, or that evidence adequate to establish a fact or raise a presumption of fact unless refuted) ITALIAN: *prima ballerina* (first ballerina; the principal woman dancer in a ballet company) *prima donna* (first lady; the principal woman singer in an opera or concert; colloquially, a temperamental, vain, or arrogant person) MATHEMATICAL TERM: prime number (an integer than can be evenly divided by no other number than itself and 1, as 2, 3, 5, 7, 11, 13, 17, 19; distinguished from *composite number*, an integer exactly divisible by at least one number other than itself or 1, e.g., 12, which can be divided by 2, 3, 4, 6) CROSS REFERENCE: *arch, proto*
pris			See *prehend* for *prison, reprisal.*
priv**	Latin *privus* (IE: *per*, beyond)	single, alone	SIMPLE ROOT: priva: privacy, private, privateer, privation privi: privity, privy PREFIXED ROOT: *de-*: deprivation, deprive (*de-*, intensive) LEADING ROOT COMPOUND: leg: privilege (originally, an exceptional law for or against any individual) (*legis*, a law) LEGAL TERM: privy verdict CROSS REFERENCE: *mono, uni*
pro-,*** **prod-**	Latin *pro-*	before, forward forth	EXTENDED PREFIX: pronate (from *pronare*, to bend forward) {pronation} prone (lying or leaning forward; **Synonyms**: prostrate, recumbent) [see *pronograde* below] PREFIXED ROOT: *pro-*: cambr: procambium (*cambire*, to change) ced: procedural, procedure (from *proceed*)

562

Element	From	Meaning	Examples
pro- (cont'd)			ceed: proceed, proceeding, proceeds (from *cedere*, to go)
			cess: process, procession, processional (from *proceed*)
			claim: proclaim (**Synonyms:** declare, announce, publish) (from *clamare*, to cry out)
			clam: proclamation (see *proclaim*)
			cliv: proclivity (**Synonyms:** inclination, bent, propensity) (*clivus*, a slope)
			cras: procrastinate (literally, to put forward until tomorrow; to put off doing something until a future time), procrastinator (*cras*, tomorrow)
			cumb: procumbent (from *cubare*, to lie down)
			cur: procuracy, procuration, procurator, procure (**Synonyms:** get, obtain, acquire), procurer (*cura*, a care)
			drom: prodrome (in *medicine*, a warning symptom indicating the onset of a disease) (*drom*, run)
			duc: produce (in *geometry*, to extend a line or plane), producer (*ducere*, to lead)
			duct: product, production, productive (from *produce*)
			fan: profanation, profane, profanity (*fanum*, temple)
			fess: (from *fateri*, to avow; akin to *fari*, to speak)
			profess, professed {professedly}, profession, professional, professionalism, professionalize
			professor, professoriate (also, *professoriat*; academic professors collectively; the office or position of a professor)
			fic: proficient (from *facere*, to make)
			fil: profile (**Synonyms:** outline, contour, silhouette) (*filum*, a thread)
			fit: profit (advantage; gain; benefit) (from *proficient*)
			flig: profligate (from *fligare*, akin to *fligere*, to strike)
			flu: profluent (flowing smoothly or copiously) (*fluere*, to flow)
			found: profound (from *fundus*, bottom)
			fund: profundity (see *profound*)
			fus: profuse (**Synonyms:** lavish, extravagant, prodigal), profusion (from *fundere*, to pour)
			gen: progenitive, progenitor, progeny (from *gignere*, to beget)
			gress: progress, progression, progressive (from *gradi*, a step)
			hib: prohibit (**Synonyms:** forbid, interdict, enjoin), prohibition, prohibitionist, prohibitive (from *habere*, to have)
			ject: project (**Synonyms:** plan, design, scheme), projectile, projection, projective, projector (from *jacere*, to throw)
			laps: prolapse (from *labi*, to fall)
			lix: prolix (so wordy as to be tiresome; verbose; using more words than are necessary; long-winded) (from *liquere*, to flow)
			locut: prolocutor (from *loqui*, to speak)
			long: prolong (**Synonyms:** extend, elongate, lengthen), prolonge (*longus*, long)
			men: promenade [from *minare*, to drive (animals); from *minari*, to threaten, from which *menace* is derived]
			min: prominence, prominent (**Synonyms:** noticeable, conspicuous, striking) (*minere*, to project)

Element	From	Meaning	Examples
pro- (cont'd)			misc: promiscuity, promiscuous (consisting of different elements mixed together or mingled without sorting or discrimination) (*miscere*, to mix)
			mis: promise, promising, promisor (from *mittere*, to send)
			miss: promissary (from *promise*)
			mont: promontory (may be from *mons*, mount; more likely from *prominent*)
			mot: promote (**Synonyms:** advance, forward, further), promoter, promotion, promotive (from *movere*, to move)
			mulg: promulgate (to announce to the public; to make widely known) [from *pro-* + (inserted *m*) + (*v*)*ulgate*, people]
			nom: pronominal (from *pronoun*) (*nomen*, name)
			noun: pronoun (any of a small class or relationship or signal words that assume the functions of nouns within clauses or phrases, e.g., he, it, them, her, who) (from *nomen*, name)
			nounc: pronounce (from *nuntiare*, to report)
			pel: propel, propellant, propellent, propeller (*pellere*, to drive)
			pend: propend (*pendere*, to hang)
			pens: propensity (**Synonyms:** inclination, leaning, proclivity) (from *propend*)
			pit: propitiate (**Synonyms:** pacify, appease, placate), propitious (from *petere*, to seek)
			pon: propone, proponent (a person who makes a proposal or proposition; in *law*, one who propounds something, especially, a will for probate) (from *propose*)
			port: (*portio*, a part)
			proportion (**Synonyms:** symmetry, harmony, balance)
			proportional (**Synonyms:** proportionate, commensurable, commensurate), proportionate (see synonyms at *proportional*, previous word)
			pos: (from *ponere*, to place)
			proposal, propose (**Synonyms:** intend, mean, design)
			proposition (**Synonym:** proposal) {propositional}, propositional function (a logic term; same as *sentential function*), propositus
			pound: propound (from *propone*)
			puls: propulsion (from *propel*)
			rog: prorogue (**Synonyms:** adjourn, dissolve, postpone) {prorogation} (*rogare*, to ask)
			scrib: proscribe (in ancient Rome, to publish the name of a person condemned to death, banishment, etc.; to banish, exile) (*scribere*, to write)
			script: proscription (a proscribing or being proscribed; prohibition or interdiction) (from *scribere*, to write)
			sect: prosector (a person skilled in dissection who prepares subjects for anatomical demonstration) (from *secare*, to cut)
			secut: prosecute, prosecution, prosecutor (from *sequi*, to follow)
			spect: prospect, prospective, prospectus (a statement outlining the main features of a new work or business enterprise) (from *specere*, to look)
			sper: prosper, prosperity, prosperous (from *spes*, hope)
			stit: prostitute, prostitution (from *statuere*, to cause to stand)

564

Element	From	Meaning	Examples
pro- (cont'd)			strat: prostrate (literally, to stretch out before: lying with face downward in a demonstration of great humility or abject submission; **Synonyms:** prone, supine, recumbent) [do not confuse with Greek *prostate*] (from *sternere*, to stretch out)
			tect: protect [see *protégé, Coelesced Words* below), protection, protective, protector, protectorate, protectory (from *tegere*, to cover)
			test: protest (**Synonyms:** object, remonstrate, expostulate), protestation, protestation (*testis*, a witness)
			tract: protract (**Synonyms:** extend, lengthen, elongate), protractile, protractor (from *trahere*, to draw)
			trud: protrude (to push or thrust outward) (*trudere*, to thrust)
			trus: protrusion (**Synonyms:** bulge, projection, protuberance), protrusive (obtrusive) (from *protrude*)
			tub: protuberance, protuberant, protuberate (*tuber*, a bump)
			ven: provenance, provenience (*venire*, to come)
			verb: proverb (**Synonyms:** adage, aphorism, epigram), proverbial (*verb*, word)
			vid: (*videre*, to see)
			provide, provided, providence (capitalized, God, as the guiding power of the universe)
			provident (**Synonyms:** thrifty, frugal, sparing), providential, providing
			vinc: province, provincial (root may be from Old English *frea*, lord; authorities differ on the origin of the root)
			vis: provision, provisional (**Synonyms:** temporary, ad interim, acting), proviso, provisory (from *proviso quod*, provided that), provisory (from *provide*)
			voc: provocateur (a person who provokes trouble or causes dissension) provocation, provocative (from *provoke*)
			vok: provoke (**Synonyms:** excite, stimulate, pique), provoking (from *vocare*, to call)
			vost: provost (literally, one placed at the head; a high-ranking university administrative officer) (from Old English *profost* and Old French *provost*; from Middle Latin *propositus*; *positus* from *ponere*, to put, to place)
			prod-:
			ig: prodigy, prodigious (literally, I say before; wonderful; amazing; of great power, size, etc.) (*ig* akin to *aio*, I say)
			prono-:
			grad: pronograde (in *zoology*, walking with the body parallel to the ground: most mammals except man and the higher apes are pronograde; compare *orthograde*) (*gradus*, step)
			PREFIXED DISGUISED ROOT:
			ig: prodigal (literally, to drive forth or away; see synonyms under *profuse*; see parable of Prodigal Son: Luke 15:11-32) (from *agere*, to drive)
			COALESCED WORDS:
			proffer [to offer (usually something intangible), as *to proffer* friendship] (from *pro- + offer*)
			prompt (**Synonyms:** quick, ready, apt) (from *pro-*, forth + *emere*, to take)

565

Element	From	Meaning	Examples
pro- (cont'd)			prose (ordinary speech or writing, as distinguished from *verse*; consequently, commonplace expression or quality) (from *pro- + verse*; from *vertere*, to turn)
			[*prose* is not related to *prosodic*; see next family]
			protégé (a person guided and helped, especially in the further-ance of his career, by another, more influential person) (from *protect*)
			FRENCH TERM: *procès-verbal* [literally, verbal process; an official report of proceedings or facts; minutes (of a meeting); plural: *procès-verbaux*)]
			CHRISTIAN DENOMINATION: Protestant (broadly, any Christian denomination not belonging to the Roman Catholic or Orthodox Eastern Church)
			MILITARY GROUP: Provo [by shortening and alteration of *provisional* (*wing*), name of the faction; a member of the extremist faction of the Irish Republican Army; another *provo* comes from Dutch *provokateur*; from French *provocateur*, provoker; any youth of a loosely organized anarchist movement in some European countries]
			PLACENAME: Providence, Rhode Island (named by its founder, Roger Williams, because of the *providence of God* in setting up a colony for political and religious freedom)
			NOTE: Provo, Utah, is named after Étienne Provot, an early fur trader.
			CROSS REFERENCE: *pre*
pro-,*** **pros-**	Greek *pro*	before, near	PREFIXED ROOTS AND COMPOUNDS: *pro*:
			blem: problem (a question proposed for solution or consideration; in *mathematics*, a proposition requiring solution by mathematical operations, constructions, etc.) (from *bal*, to throw)
			bosc: proboscis (a long, flexible snout or trunk, as of an elephant; a slender, tubular feeding and sucking structure of some insects and worms; a human nose, especially a prominent one, often used humorously) (*boskein*, to feed)
			carp: procarp (in *botany*, a female reproductive organ in certain algae) (*carp*, fruit)
			celeus: proceleusmatic (animating, stirring: said of a song; in *prosody*, designating a metrical foot of four short syllables) (*keleuein*, to incite)
			clit: proclitic (in *grammar*, dependent on the following word for its stress, as *for* in *once and for all*) (*klinein*, to lean)
			crypt: procryptic (in *zoology*, having protective coloration) (*crypt*, hide)
			drom: prodrome (in *medicine*, a warning symptom indicating the onset of a disease) (*dromos*, a running)
			gram: program (from *graphein*, to write)
			leg: prolegomenon (a preliminary remark; often in plural form with singular verb, a preliminary statement or essay; foreword) (*leg*, to speak)
			leps: prolepsis (from *lambanein*, to take)
			log: prologue (*logos*, a discourse)

Element	From	Meaning	Examples
pro- (cont'd)			phe: prophecy, prophesy, prophet (from *phanai*, to speak)
			phyla: prophylactic, prophylaxis (*phylax*, a guard)
			pt: proptosis (forward displacement of an organ, such as the eyeball) (from *piptein*, to fall)
			pyl: propylon (literally, front gate, or gate in front of; in *architecture*, an entrance or vestibule to a temple or group of buildings) (same as *propylaeum*; *pule*, gate)
			scen: proscenium (the apron of a stage) (*scen*, stage)
			stat: prostate (literally, one standing before; as an *adjective*, describes the gland that surrounds the urethra at the base of the bladder in most male mammals; as a *noun*, refers to the gland itself; has been understood as *stander before* the bladder) [do not confuse with Latin *prostrate*] (*stat*, stand)
			styl: prostyle (in *architecture*, having a row of columns across the front only, as in some Greek temples)
			tasis: protasis (in *Greek drama*, the opening of a play, in which the characters are introduced; in *grammar*, the clause that expresses the condition in a conditional sentence; opposed to *apodosis*) (from *teinein*, to stretch)
			thal: prothalamion (also, *prothalamium*: a song celebrating a marriage) (*thalamos*, bridal chamber)
			thall: prothallium (*thallos*, a shoot)
			thesis: prothesis (*thesis*, to place)
			thorax: prothorax (in *zoology*, that division of an insect's thorax nearest the head, and bearing the first pair of legs)
			pros-:
			elyt: proselyte (literally, to come forward; a person who has been converted from one religion to another, or from one belief, sect, party, etc. to another) (from aorist verb *erchesthai*, to come; see *aorist* under *an-, a-*)
			encephal: prosencephalon (*en-* prefix *cepha*, head)
			enchym: prosenchyma (in *botany*, a tissue of thick-walled, elongated cells without much protoplasm, found in some flowering plants) (*en-* prefixes *chyma*, literally, juice; *enchyma*, infusion)
			od: prosodic, prosody (from *oide*, song)
			op: prosopopoeia (the impersonation of an absent or imaginary speaker) (*op*, to see, + *peia*, to make)
			the: prosthesis, prosthetic, prosthetics (*thesis*, to place)
			CROSS REFERENCE: *ante-, pre-*
prob,** prov	Latin *probare*, prove; test *probus*, good (IE: *pro* + *bhu*, to grow)	to test, prove; good, proper	SIMPLE ROOT: *prob*: probabilism, probability, probable {probably} proband (same as *propositus*, which see under *pos*) probate, probation, probative (also, *probatory*: serving to test or try) probe, probity (uprightness in one's dealings) *prov*: prove, proven PREFIXED ROOT: *prob*: ap-: approbation (**Synonyms**: regard, esteem, admiration) (*ap-* assimilates *ad-*, to, toward)

Element	From	Meaning	Examples
prob (cont'd)			*re-*: reprobate (to disapprove of strongly; condemn; as a noun, an unprincipled or totally bad person; in theology, a person damned; lost soulP, reprobation (*re-*, intensive) *prov*: *ap-*: approve (**Synonyms:** endorse, sanction, certify) *re-*: reprove (to speak to in disapproval; rebuke) (*re-*, intensive) TRAILING ROOT COMPOUND: cryo: cryoprobe (*cryo*, cold) DISGUISED ROOT: proof (**Synonyms:** evidence, testimony, exhibit) (from *probe*) PREFIXED DISGUISED ROOT: *re-*: reproof (also, *reproval*) (*re-*, again) LEGAL PHRASE: probable cause (reasonable grounds for presuming guilt in someone charged with a crime) CROSS REFERENCE: *bon, eu*
prol*	Latin *proles* (from *pro-*, for + *alere*, to nourish; from IE: *al*, to grow)	offspring	SIMPLE ROOT: prolan (the gonadotrophic hormone in pregnant women's urine, used to indicate pregnancy) proletariat, proletarian (from *proletarius*, a Roman citizen of the lowest class, who serves the state only by producing off-spring), proletary LEADING ROOT COMPOUND: fer: proliferate (to bear offspring; to reproduce or produce new growth or parts rapidly and repeatedly), proliferous (*ferre*, to bear) fic: prolific (**Synonyms:** fertile, fecund, fruitful) (from *facere*, to make) LATIN PHRASE: *sine prole* (without issue; without offspring, or heirs) INTERDISCIPLINARY: proliferous (in *botany*, multiply-ing freely by means of buds, side branches, etc.; having leafy shoots growing from a flower or fruit; in *zoology*, reproduc-ing by budding, as coral) NO CROSS REFERENCE
prope			See *prox* for *approach, reproach.*
prop(ri)**	Latin *proprius*	one's own, particular	SIMPLE ROOT: *prop*: proper (**Synonyms:** fit, appropriate, suitable) property (**Synonyms:** quality, characteristic, attribute) *propri*: proprietary, proprietor, propriety (**Synonyms:** deco-rum, decency, etiquette) PREFIXED ROOT: *ap-*: appropriate (**Synonyms:** fit, suitable, proper) (*ap-* as-similates *ad-*, to, toward) *ex-*: expropriate (*ex-*, out) *im-*: improper (**Synonyms:** unseemly, unbecoming, indeco-rous), impropriate, impropriety (the quality of being im-proper; improper action or behavior) (from *in-*, not) DOUBLE PREFIXED ROOT: inappropriate (*in-*, not; *ap-* from *ad-*, to, toward) LATIN PHRASE: *in propria persona* (in one's own person or right) CROSS REFERENCE: *idio*

568

Element	From	Meaning	Examples
proto***	Greek *protos*	first, early ahead	SIMPLE ROOT: protein, protist, protium, proton, protonema LEADING ROOT COMPOUND: *prot*: agon: protagonist (the main character in a drama, novel, or story, around whom the action centers; a person who plays a leading or active part; compare *antagonist*) (*agon*, a contest) *proto*: col: protocol (originally, first leaf glued to a manuscript describing the contents) (from *kolla*, glue) hist: protohistory (the archeological history of man in the period immediately preceding recorded history) lith: protolithic (early name for *eolithic*) (*lithos*, stone) nem: protonema (in *biology*, a threadlike growth in mosses, arising from a spore and developing small buds that grow into leafy moss plants) (*nema*, thread) nota: protonotary (same as *prothonotary*) (*nota*, mark, sign) nymph: protonymph (the newly hatched form of various mites) path: protopathic (in *physiology*, designating or of certain sensory nerves having limited sensibility, that respond to heat and pain from a general area) (*pathic*, feeling, suffering) plasm: protoplasm (from *plassein*, to form) stel: protostele (*stele*, post, slab) troph: prototrophic (*troph*, nourish) typ: prototype (the first thing or being of its kind; model) (*typos*, figure, model) xyl: protoxylem (in *botany*, the first-formed xylem of a root or stem, produced by the differentiation of the procambium) zo: protozoan, protozoic (*zo*, animal) NOTE: *Proteus* is not related to this family. In *Greek mythology*, Proteus was a sea god who could change his own form or appearance at will; in lower case, *proteus* is a person who changes his/her appearance or principles easily. CROSS REFERENCE: *arch, pale(o), prim*
prov			See *prob/prov* for *prove, reprove*.
prox**	Latin *proximus* (superlative of *prope*, near)	next to, nearest	SIMPLE ROOT: proxe: proxemics (the study of the spatial needs of individuals and the environmental and cultural factors involved), proxemic proxi: proximal (in *anatomy*, situated nearest the center of the body or nearest the point of attachment of a muscle, limb, etc.) proximate, proximity (the state or quality of being near; nearness in space, time, etc.) proximo [short for *proximo mense*, old fashioned style of writing "(in the) next month"] PREFIXED ROOT: ap-: approximate (*ap-* assimilates *ad-*, to, toward) PREFIXED DISGUISED ROOT: ap-: approach (*ap-* assimilates *ad-*, to, toward) re-: reproach (*re-*, back, again) FRENCH: *rapprochement* (an establishing, or especially a restoring, of peace and harmony) NO CROSS REFERENCE

Element	From	Meaning	Examples
pseudo**	Greek *pseudein*: to lie, cheat	false	SIMPLE ROOT: pseudo LEADING ROOT COMPOUND: *pseud*: epi: Pseudepigrapha (a group of early writings not included in the Biblical canon or the Apocrypha; some were falsely ascribed to Biblical characters) (*epi-*, upon; *graph*, write) onym: pseudonym (**Synonyms**: pen name, nom de plume, alias), pseudonymous (*onym*, name) *pseudo*: carp: pseudocarp (same as *false fruit*) (*carp*, fruit) hermaphrodit: pseudohermaphrodite (a person or animal having gonads of one sex while the external genital organs and secondary sex characteristics resemble in whole or in part those of the opposite sex) (in *Greek mythology*, Hermaphroditis, was the son of Hermes and Aphrodite; while bathing, he becomes united in a single body with a nymph) morph: pseudomorph (*morph*, form) pod: pseudopodium (*pod*, foot) CROSS REFERENCE: *fall*
psych***	Greek *psyche*: to breathe, to blow, to make cold (IE: *bhes*, to blow)	mind, spirit, soul	SIMPLE ROOT: psyche (from Psyche, a maiden in Greek and Roman mythology, who personifies the soul), psychic LEADING ROOT COMPOUND: *psych*: iatr: psychiatrist, psychiatry (*iatr*, healing) odo: psychodometry (measurement of the rate of mental activity) (*odo*, way + *metry*) osis: psychosis {psychotic} (*osis*, diseased condition) *psyche*: delic: psychedelic (*delein*, to make manifest) *psycho*: ana: psychoanalysis (*ana-* prefixes *lys*, to loosen) bio: (life) psychobiography (*graph*, write) psychobiology (*logy*, study of) gen: psychogenesis, psychogenic (*gen*, producing) gram: psychogram (a subjective visualization of a mental concept) (from *graph*, write) graph: psychograph (*graph*, write) kine: psychokinesis (*kine*, movement) ling: psycholinguistics (*lingu*, tongue, language) log: psychological, psychology (*logy*, study of) metr: psychometrics, psychometry (*metr*, measurement) path: psychopath, psychopathic (*path*, disease) soma: psychosomatic (*soma*, body) therap: psychotherapy (*therapy*, treatment) tox: psychotoxic (*tox*, poison, damage) trop: psychotropic (*trop*, turn) ROMAN FOLKLORE: Psyche, a maiden who, after undergoing many hardships due to Venus' jealousy of her beauty, is reunited with Cupid and made immortal by Jupiter CROSS REFERENCE: *cephal, cerebr, ment, phren, thym*

Element	From	Meaning	Examples
psychro*	Greek *psychein*: to make cold (IE: *bhes*, to blow)	cold	LEADING ROOT COMPOUND: alg: psychroalgia (painful sensation of cold) (*alg*, pain) esthes: psychroesthesia (a sensation of cold in a part of the body, although it is warm) (*aesthes*, feeling) meter: psychrometer (*meter*, measure) phil: psychrophilic (in *biology*, growing best at low temperatures) therap: psychrotherapy (*therapy*, treatment) CROSS REFERENCE: *algo, cryo, crymo, frig*
pter**	Greek *pteron* (IE: *pet*, to fall, fly)	wing, feather; also, winglike; therefore, fins	SIMPLE ROOT: pteralium, pteretis, pteric, pterygium PREFIXED ROOT: a-: apterous (wingless), apteryx (a wingless bird, e.g., the kiwi) (*a-*, without) *peri-*: peripteral (*peri-*, around) LEADING ROOT COMPOUND: dactyl: pterodactyl (*dactyl*, finger) pod: pteropod (*pod*, foot) saur: pterosaur (*saur*, lizard) TRAILING ROOT COMPOUND: acantho: acanthopterygian (any of an order of spiny-finned fishes, as the basses, perches, etc.) (*acantho*, thorn) chiro: chiropter (literally, hand-wing; the bat) (*chiro*, hand) crosso: crossopterygian (any of a group of primitive bony fishes with rounded fins, extinct except for one species and regarded as precursors of amphibians) (*krossoi*, fringe) di: dipteran {dipterous} (*di*, two) helico: helicopter (literally, spiral wing) (*helic*, spiral) hemi: hemipteran (literally, half-wing; a true bug) (*hemi*, half) homo: homopteran, homopterous (*homo*, same) macro: macropterous (*macro*, large) ortho: orthopterous (*ortho*, straight) CROSS REFERENCE: *ali, pen, plum*
pt(o)*	Greek *piptein* (IE: *pet*, to fall, fly)	to fall	SIMPLE ROOT: ptomaine PREFIXED ROOT: *peri-*: peripeteia (a sudden change of fortune or reversal of circumstances, as in a drama) (*peri-*, around) *pro-*: proptosis (*pro-*, forward) *sym-*: symptom, symptomatic (*sym-*, with, together) DOUBLE PREFIXED ROOT: asymptote (*a-*, not; *sym-*, with, together) LEADING ROOT COMPOUND: osis: ptosis (*osis*, condition of) TRAILING ROOT COMPOUND: orchido: orchidoptosis (the descending of the testicles) (*orchid*, testicles) CROSS REFERENCE: *cad/cas/cid; lap*
pub*	Latin *puber*	adult, grown up	ROOT NOTE: Although the root means adult, it is more like becoming an adult. This root is related to *puer*, boy, thus *puerile* (see below). SIMPLE ROOT: puber: puberty, puberulent (covered with fine hairs or down)

Element	From	Meaning	Examples
pub (cont'd)			pubes: pubes (plural of *pubis*), pubescence (the soft down that covers the surface of many plants and insects), pubescent pubi: pubic (of or in the region of the pubis or the pubes, as *pubic hair*), pubis (that part of either hipbone forming, with the corresponding part of the other, the front arch of the pelvis; plural, *pubes*) RELATED ROOT: puerile (childish; silly; immature; trivial), puerilism (childishness, especially as a symptom of emotional disorder in an adult) LATIN TERM: *pubertas praecox* (precocious puberty, or puberty at an early age) CROSS REFERENCE: *hebe*, *ped* (child)
publ			See *popul/publ* for *public, publican, publication*.
pud*	Latin *pudere*	to be ashamed of	SIMPLE ROOT: pudency (modesty or prudishness) pudendum (literally, something to be ashamed of; the external genitals of the female; vula; plural, pudenda: the external genitals of either sex) {pudenda} PREFIXED ROOT: *im-*: impudent (**Synonyms**: impertinent, insolent, saucy), impudence, impudicity (from *in-*, not) NOTE: *Repudiate*, from *repudiare*, to cast off, is not in this family. NO CROSS REFERENCE
pug**	Latin *pugnare* (IE: *peug*, to punch)	to fight with fist	SIMPLE ROOT: pugilism (boxing) {pugilist, pugilistic} pugnacious (**Synonyms**: belligerent, bellicose, contentious) PREFIXED ROOT: *ex-*: expugnable (capable of being taken by storm) (*ex-*, out of) *im-*: impugn (**Synonyms**: deny, gainsay, contradict) (from *in-*, on, against) *op-*: oppugn (to oppose with argument; criticize severely; call in question; controvert) (*op-* assimilates *ob-*, against) *re-*: repugnant (**Synonyms**: odious, detestable, obnoxious) (*re-*, again) DOUBLE PREFIXED ROOT: inexpugnable (that which cannot be taken by force; unyielding) DISGUISED ROOT: poniard (a dagger) CROSS REFERENCE: *agon*
puls			See *pell* for *repulse*.
punct,*** **pung**	Latin *pungere*: to prick (IE: *peug*, to point)	point	SIMPLE ROOT: *punct*: puncta: puncta (plural of *punctum*), punctate (also, *punctated*; marked with dots or tiny spots, as certain plants and animals) {punctation} puncti: punctilio (a nice point of conduct, ceremony, etc.), punctilious (very exact; scrupulous) punctu: punctual (arriving, acting, or happening at the time or times appointed; prompt) punctuate, punctuation punctulate (marked with very small dots or holes, as certain plants and animals), punctum, punctura, puncture

Element	From	Meaning	Examples
punct (cont'd)			*pung*: pungent (producing a sharp sensation of taste or smell; sharp and piercing to the mind; poignant; painful; keenly clever) {pungency (see *Doublets* below; **Synonyms**: piquant, racy, spicy)} PREFIXED ROOT: *punct*: *com-*: compunction (**Synonyms**: penitence, repentance, contrition) (*com-*, with, together) *pung*: *ex-*: expunge (**Synonyms**: erase, efface, obliterate) (*ex-*, out) LEADING ROOT COMPOUND: form: punctiform graph: punctograph (*graph*, write) meter: punctumeter (*meter*, measure) DISGUISED ROOT: pivot (may be from this root) poignant (**Synonyms**: moving, affecting, touching) (see *Doublets* below) point, pontil (same as *punty*, which see below), pointillism pounce (one meaning) pun (probably from Italian *puntiglio*, fine point; hence, verbal quibble), puncheon (one meaning) punty (a metal rod on which the molten glass is handled in glassmaking) spontoon (a short pike carried by infantry officers in the 18th century; the *s* is from *ex-*, removal; thus to remove the point; blunted) PREFIXED DISGUISED ROOT: *ap-*: appoint (*ap-* assimilates *ad-*, to, toward) *counter-*: counterpane (a pricked quilt) (*counter-*, against) *tra-*: trapunto (quilting having a raised effect made by outlining the design with running stitches and then filling the design with cotton) (from *trans-*, through) FRENCH: *pointe* (in *ballet*, the position of being on the tip of the toe) DOUBLETS: poignant:pungent PLACENAMES: La Puente, California; Punta Gorda, Florida CROSS REFERENCE: *centr, cusp, pugn*
pung			See *punct* for *pungent*.
pur**	Latin *purus* (IE: *pu*, to purify)	clean, pure	SIMPLE ROOT: pur: pure (**Synonyms**: chaste, virtuous, modest), purée purga: purgation, purgative (**Synonyms**: physic, laxative, cathartic; that purges; purging; causing bowel movement) purgatorial, purgatory purge: purge puri: purism, purist, puritanical, purity PREFIXED ROOT: *com-*: compurgation (*com-*, with, together) *de-*: depurant, depurate, depuration (*de-*, intensive) *ex-*: expurgate, expurge (*ex-*, out) *im-*: impure (from *in-*, not)

Element	From	Meaning	Examples
pur (cont'd)			DOUBLE PREFIXED ROOT: unexpurgated (*un-*, not + *ex-*, out) LEADING ROOT COMPOUND: blind: purblind (originally, completely blind; partly blind; slow in perceiving or understanding) fic: purificator (from *facere*, to make, do) fy: purify (from *facere*, to make, do) MESHED LEADING ROOT COMPOUND: purine [*pur(us)* + *uricum*, uric acid + *in* (chemical symbol: $C_5H_4N_4$)] AN ANTIBIOTIC: puromycin BOUND COMPOUND: purebred (as an *adjective*, indicates belonging to a recognized breed with characters maintained through generations of unmixed descent; as a *noun*, indicating a purebred animal or plant) UNBOUND COMPOUNDS: pure culture (a culture medium containing only organisms of the particular species required) pure line (in *genetics*, a breed or strain of animals or plants that maintains a high degree of consistency in certain characters as a result of continued inbreeding for generations) DISGUISED ROOT: pious (also listed under *pi*; see *Webster's New World*) spurge (a family of plants, including the poinsettia, cassava, and rubber tree) (from *expurgate*, above; reason unclear) RELIGIOUS SECT: *Puritans,* those who originally sought to *purify* the Church of England. CROSS REFERENCE: *cast, pi*
pus			See *pod/pus* for *octopus*.
put*	Latin *putare* (IE: *pu*, to cleanse, to purify)	to cut, prune (extended to mean "to think over, to consider true, settle an account; reflect; consider")	SIMPLE ROOT: putamen [in *botany*, a hard or stony endocarp, as a peach stone (that which is removed in *pruning*)] putative (that in which the false has been *pruned*; therefore, commonly regarded as true; reputed; supposed) PREFIXED ROOT: *am-*: amputate (literally, to cut around) (from *ambi-*, around) *com-*: computable, computation, compute (**Synonyms:** calculate, estimate), computer, computerized (*com-*, with, together) *de-*: deputation, depute, deputy (*de-*, from) *dis-*: disputacious, disputation, dispute (**Synonyms: 1)** discuss, argue; **2)** argument, controversy) (*dis-*, apart) *im-*: imputation, impute (*im-*, in) *re-*: reputation, repute (*re-*, back, again) DISGUISED ROOT: count (see *Doublet* below) imp (originally, to engraft; child; offspring; in particular, a devil's offspring; young demon; a mischievous child) PREFIXED DISGUISED ROOT: *ac-*: account, accountability, accountable, accountant (*ac-* assimilates *ad-*, to, toward) *re-*: recount (see *Doublets* below; to tell in detail; give an account of; narrate; to tell in order or one by one) (*re-*, again)

574

Element	From	Meaning	Examples
put (cont'd)			FRENCH: raconteur (see *Doublets* below; person skilled in relating, *recounting* anecdotes; a storyteller) DOUBLETS: count:compute; recount:raconteur CROSS REFERENCE: *cise*
pyr*	Greek *pyr* (IE: *pewor*, fire)	fire, fever	SIMPLE ROOT: pyre, pyretic, pyrethrum (from the spicy taste of the root), pyretic, pyrexia, pyrite PREFIXED ROOT: *anti*-: antipyretic (*anti*-, against) *em*-: empyreal (heavenly, sublime), empyrean (*em*-, in) *hyper*-: hyperpyrexia (abnormally high fever) (*hyper*-, over, beyond) LEADING ROOT COMPOUND: *pyr*: helio: pyrheliometer (an instrument for measuring the amount of energy given off by the sun) (*helio*, sun) op: pyrope (literally, fiery-eyed; a variety of deep-red to black garnet, containing magnesium and aluminum, often used as a gem) (*ops*, eye) osis: pyrosis (heartburn) (*osis*, condition of) *pyro*: chem: pyrochemical (of chemical action at high temperatures) clast: pyroclastic (made up of rock material broken into fragments through volcanic or igneous action) (*clast*, break) con: pyrocondensation (*con*-, with, together, prefixes *dens*, thick) gen: pyrogenic (in *geology*, same as *igneous*) (*gen*, producing) gnos: pyrognostics (the characteristics of a mineral, including fusibility, flame coloration, etc., as determined by a blowpipe) (*gnosis*, recognition) graph: pyrography (the art or process of burning designs on wood or leather by the use of heated tools) (*graph*, write) lys: pyrolysis (*lysis*, loosen) mancy: pyromancy (*mancy*, divination) mania: pyromania (a persistent compulsion to start destructive fires) (*mania*, madness) phob: pyrophobia (*phobia*, fear of) phor: pyrophoric (from *pherein*, to bear) stat: pyrostat (a thermostat, especially one for high temperatures) (*stat*, stand) techn: pyrotechnic (also, *pyrotechnical*; of fireworks), pyrotechnics TRADENAME: Pyrex NOTE: *Pyriform*, in the shape of pear, is not in this family; neither is *pyramid*. CROSS REFERENCE: *febr, flag/flam, ign*

> Language is the indispensable mechanism of human life--of life such as ours that is molded, guided, enriched and made possible by the accumulation of the past experience of members of our own species.
> S. I. Hayakawa

Q

Element	From	Meaning	Examples
quadr,* **quart,** **quater,** **quatr**	Latin *quattuor:* four (IE: *kwetwor,* four)	four, fourth forty, fortieth	SIMPLE ROOT: quad (short for *quadrangle*, or *quadrat*) *quadr:* quadra: quadrant, quadrat, quadrate, quadratic, quadrature quadre: quadragesimal (lasting forty days: said of Lent; capitalized, Lenten; of or suitable for Lent; see Quadragesima, below) quadrel quadri: quadric (in *mathematics*, of the second degree: used of a function with more than two variables) quadro: quadroon quadru: quadrual *quart:* quart, quartan, quarte (in *fencing*, the fourth position); quarter, quarterage, quarter horse (known for its great sprinting speed for distances up to a quarter of a mile), quartern, quartet, quartic, quartile, quarto *quater:* quaternary, quaternion *quatr:* quatrain (a group of four lines in a stanza or poem, usually rhyming *abab*, *abba*, or *abcb*; a Shakespearean sonnet, e.g., includes four quatrains plus a rhymed couplet); quatre LEADING ROOT COMPOUND: *quadr:* angle: quadrangle enn: quadrennial, quadrennium (*enn*, year) *quadri:* cent: quadricentennial (*cent*, 100; *enn*, year) cep: quadriceps (a four-headed muscle) (*caput*, head) fid: quadrifid (divided into four parts, as a leaf or a petal) (*fid*, split, divided) ga: quadriga (n ancient Rome, a two-wheeled chariot drawn by four horses abreast) (from *jugum*, yoke) later: quadrilateral (*later*, side) ling: quadrilingual (*lingu*, tongue, language) nom: quadrinomial (compare with *binomial*) (*nomos*, law) part: quadripartite (made up or divided into four parts; shared or formulated by four persons, nations, etc., as a quadripartite pact) pleg: quadriplegia (*pleg*, stroke) sect: quadrisect (to divide into four equal parts) (*sect*, cut) val: quadrivalent (same as *tetravalent*) vi: (*via*, road) quadrivial (having or being four roads meeting in a point; also, of the *quadrivium*) quadrivium (in the Middle Ages, the higher division of the seven liberal arts, consisting of arithmetic, geometry, astronomy, and music; compare *trivium*, under *tri* and *via*) *quadru:* man: quadrumanous (in *zoology*, having all four feet adapted to functions as hands, and includes a group of primates, e.g., monkeys, baboons, apes) (*man*, hand) ped: quadruped (*ped*, foot)

Element	From	Meaning	Examples
quadr (cont'd)			ple: quadruple, quadruplet (*ple*, fold) plex: quadruplex (*plex*, fold) plic: quadruplicate (*plicare*, to fold) MESHED LEADING ROOT COMPOUND: quadrillion (*quadri* + (mi)*llion*) FRENCH: quadrille (originally, one of four groups of horse-men participating in certain exercises; from Spanish *cuadrilla*, a diminutive of *cuadro*, four-sided battle square; from Latin *quadra*, a square: a square dance of French origin, performed by four couples; music for this dance; as an *adjective*, marked with intersecting lines to form squares or rectangles) ITALIAN: quarantine (literally, a space of forty days; designating the period, originally 40 days, during which an arriving vessel suspected of carrying contagious disease is detained in port in strict isolation) DISGUISED ROOT: cahier (a book of loose leaves held together; notebook; hence, a report) (from *quire*) carillon (bells) (originally a set of four bells) catercornered (literally, four-cornered; diagonal) quire (a set of 24 or 25 sheets of paper of the same size and stock, the twentieth part of a ream) squad (originally, to form into a square; a small group of soldiers assembled for inspection, duty, etc.), squadron square (from *ex*-, out + quadrare) NAVAL TERM: quarterdeck (so called because originally, half the length of the half deck) FIRST SUNDAY OF THE FORTY DAYS OF LENT: Quadragesima; also known as Quadragesima Sunday CROSS REFERENCE: *tetra*
quer,*** **ques** **quir,** **quis**	Latin *quaerere*	to ask, seek, gain, obtain	SIMPLE ROOT: *quer*: querist, query (see synonyms at *inquire*, below) *ques*: quest, question (see synonyms at *inquire*, below), questionnaire PREFIXED ROOT: *quer*: *con*-: conquer (**Synonyms**: vanquish, defeat, overcome) (*con*-, intensive) *quest*: *con*-: conquest (**Synonyms**: victory, triumph) (*con*-, intensive) *in*-: inquest (a judicial inquiry, as a coroner's investigation of a death) (*in*-, in) *re*-: request (the act of asking or expressing a desire, for something; solicitation or petition; as a *verb*, to express a wish or desire for; **Synonyms**: entreat, petition, supplicate) (*re*-, again) *quir*: *ac*-: acquire (**Synonyms**: obtain, procure, gain) (from *ad*-, to) *in*-: inquire (**Synonyms**: ask, query, question), inquiry (*in*-, into) *re*-: require (**Synonyms**: 1) demand, claim, exact 2) lack, want, need) (*re*-, again)

Element	From	Meaning	Examples
quer (cont'd)			*quis*: *ac-*: acquisition, acquisitive (**Synonyms**: greedy, avaricious, covetous) (from *ad-*, to) *dis-*: disquisition (a formal discussion of some subject, often in writing; discourse or treatise) (*dis-*, apart) *ex-*: exquisite (**Synonyms**: delicate, dainty) (*ex-*, out) *in-*: inquisition, inquisitive (**Synonyms**: curious, meddlesome, prying) (*in-*, in) *per-*: perquisite (prerogative, right, gratuity; often referred to as *perks*) (*per-*, intensive) *re-*: requisite (**Synonyms**: 1) essential, indispensable, necessary 2) need, necessity, exigency), requisition (*re-*, again) DOUBLE-PREFIXED ROOT: prerequisite (*pre-*, before + *re-*, again) PURE LATIN FORMS: *quaere* (literally, inquire: used as a note suggesting further investigation of a point; as a noun, a query or question) *quaesitum* (the object of one's search) *quaestor* (an official of ancient Rome, with various, chiefly financial, duties) SPANISH: *conquistador* (conqueror) NB: *Querulent* and *querulous*, from *queri*, to complain, are not in this family. CROSS REFERENCE: *pet*
quie*	Latin *quietis* (IE: *kweye*, to rest)	to rest	SIMPLE ROOT: *quies*: quiescent (quiet; still; inactive; **Synonyms**: latent, potential, dormant) *quiet*: quiet (still; calm; motionless; hushed, as *a quiet motor*, or *a quiet voice*; in *law*, to make a title unassailable by freeing the fact of ownership from interference, disturbance, or question; see *Doublets* below) quietism (a mysticism based on spiritual passivity; specifically, a mysticism so minimizing or so completely rejecting human volition and effort as, often, to produce indifference to one's lot in an afterlife and to engender a sense of being incapable of any personal merit or guilt) quietude (a state of being quiet; rest; calmness) quietus (discharge or release from debt, obligation, or office) PREFIXED ROOT: *quies*: *ac-*: acquiesce (**Synonyms**: consent, assent, agree), acquiescence, acquiescent (from *ad-*, to, toward) *quit(e)*: *ac-*: acquit (**Synonyms**: 1) absolve, exonerate, pardon 2) behave, conduct, demean), acquittal (from *ad-*, to, toward) *re-*: requital, requite (**Synonyms**: 1) repay, recompense, reimburse; 2) revenge, avengue, retaliate) (*re-*, again) DISGUISED ROOT: coy (originally, quiet; silent; see *Doublets* below) quit (**Synonyms**: 1) abandon, desert, forsake; 2) stop, cease, desist)

Element	From	Meaning	Examples
quie (cont'd)			PREFIXED DISGUISED ROOT: re-: Requiem (first word of the Introit in the Mass for the Dead: *requiem aeternam donat eis*, give him eternal rest; in lower case, any dirgelike song, chant, or poem) (*re-*, back) tran-: tranquil (**Synonyms:** calm, serene, placid), tranquilize, tranquilizer, tranquillity) (from *trans-*, across) DISGUISED LEADING ROOT COMPOUND: claim: quitclaim (the release or relinquishment of a claim, action, right, or title) DOUBLETS: coy:quiet LATIN PHRASE: *requiescat in pace* (may he/she rest in peace, abbreviated *R.I.P.*) NO CROSS REFERENCE
quin**	Latin *quinque* (IE: *penkwe*, five)	five	SIMPLE ROOT: quina: quinary (consisting of five; in sets of five), quinate quint: quintain (an object supported by a crosspiece on a post, used by knights as a target in tilting), quintet, quintile LEADING ROOT COMPOUND: *quin*: dec: (ten) quindecagon (*gon*, angle) quindecennial (happening every fifteen years) (*enn*, year) quindecim (same as *quindene*, below) den: quindene (the 15th, or in modern reckoning, the 14th day after a church festival) (*den*, ten)
quin (cont'd)			*quinqu*: enn: quinquennial (happening every five years) (*enn*, year) *quinque*: foli: quinquefoliate (*foli*, leaf) val: quinquevalent (same as *pentavalent*; having a valence of five) *quintu*: ple: quintuple, quintuplet (*ple*, fold) LOGIC TERM: *quinque voces* (literally, five words; the five predicables of traditional, or Aristotelian logic; the predicables are as follows: genus, species, difference, property, and accident) CROSS REFERENCE: *cinque, penta*
quir			See *quer, ques* for *require*.
quis			See *quer, ques* for *inquisition*.
quot*	Latin *quot* (IE: *kwoti*, how many)	how many	SIMPLE ROOT: quota (short for *quota pars*, how large a part) quotable, quotation, quote, quotient LEADING ROOT COMPOUND: dia: quotidian (daily; recurring every day; commonplace; usual or ordinary) (*dia*, day) NB: *Quoth* (from Old English *cwæth*, preterite of *cwethan*, to speak, say; said: the past tense, followed by a subject in the first or third person, and usually taking a postpositive subject, as in Poe's "Quoth the raven, "Nevermore."") is not in this family. Neither is *quotha* in this family. NO CROSS REFERENCE

R

Element	From	Meaning	Examples
rac			See *rad* for *deracinate*.
rachi,* **rhachi**	Greek *rhachis* (IE: *wragh*, thorn, point)	back (of body), specifically, lower part of back; also, spine, backbone, axis	SIMPLE ROOT: rachial (or, *rachidial*), rachilla (a small or secondary rachis; specifically, the axis of a spikelet of a grass or sedge) rachion (the marginal line of a lake at which maximum wave action and undertow turmoil occur) rachis (also spelled *rhachis*) LEADING ROOT COMPOUND: alg: rachialgia (*alg*, pain) INTERDISCIPLINARY: rachis (in *botany*, the principal axis of an inflorescence or of a compound leaf; in *zoology*, the shaft of a feather, especially that part bearing the barbs) CROSS REFERENCE: *dors*
rad**	Latin *radius*: ray, beam, spoke	spoke of wheel; X-ray	SIMPLE ROOT: radial (in *anatomy*, of or near the radius or forearm) radian (a unit of angular measurement) radiance, radiant (**Synonyms:** brilliant, luminous, lustrous) radiate radiation (in *biology*, the dispersal and adaptation to new environments by a line of animals or plants, resulting in the evolution of divergent forms specialized to fit the new habitats), radiator radio radiolarian radium (a radioactive chemical element, so named because it emits rays; symbol, Ra) radius (see *Doublets* below) LEADING ROOT COMPOUND: logy: radiology (the science dealing with X-ray and other forms of radiant energy) (*logy*, study of) luc: radiolucent (*luc*, light) meter: radiometer (*meter*, measure) scop: radioscopy (*scope*, look, view) DISGUISED ROOT: ray (see *Doublets* below), rayon DOUBLETS: radius:ray INTERDISCIPLINARY: radiate (in *botany*, having ray flowers or florets; in *zoology*, having radial symmetry, as a jellyfish) NO CROSS REFERENCE
rad***	Latin *radix* (IE: *wrad*, twig, root)	root, base	SIMPLE ROOT: radical (**Synonyms:** liberal, aggressive, advanced), radicalism radicand (the number under a radical sign) radicle, radicose, radish, radicule, radix (in *mathematics*, a number made the base or root of a system of numbers) PREFIXED ROOT: e-: eradicate (**Synonyms:** exterminate, extirpate) (*e*- elides *ex*-, out)

Element	From	Meaning	Examples
rad (cont'd)			DOUBLE PREFIXED ROOT: ingradicable (*e-* from *ex-*; see previous entry) (*in-*, not + *e-*, out) DISGUISED ROOT: race (an obsolete word for tear, pluck, snatch) PREFIXED DISGUISED ROOT: *de-*: deracinate (to uproot; to extirpate) (from *dis-* from) ENGLISH: root (**Synonyms:** origin, source, beginning) INTERDISCIPLINARY: radical (in *botany*, of or coming from the root; in *mathematics*, having to do with the root or roots of a number or quantity; as a noun, the indicated root of a quantity or quantities, shown by an expression written under the radical sign; the radical sign) radicle (in *anatomy*, the rootlike beginning of a nerve, vein, etc.; in *botany*, the lower part of the axis of an embryo seedling; strictly, the root part; often, the hypocotyl, sometimes together with the root; also, a rudimentary root) CROSS REFERENCE: *rhizo*
rad, ras*	Latin *radere* (IE: *red, rod,* to scratch, gnaw)	to scrape	SIMPLE ROOT: radula (plural, *radulae*) (in most mollusks, a ribbonlike structure found in the mouth, bearing numerous rows of teeth, usually used to tear up food and take it into the mouth) *ab-*: (off, away) abrade (to rub off or away by friction; erode) abrasion, abrasive (causing abrasion; tending to provoke anger, ill will, etc.; aggressively annoying, irritating) *cor-*: corrade (to erade by the abrasive action of running water or glacial ice containing sand, pebbles, and other debris) (*cor-* assimilates *com-*, with, together) *e-*: erase (**Synonyms:** efface, expunge, obliterate) (*e-* from *ex-*, out) DOUBLE PREFIXED ROOT: inerasable (*in-*, not + *e-* from *ex-*, out) LEADING ROOT COMPOUND: form: raduliform (like a rasp; however, *rasp* itself is Germanic rather than Latin) DISGUISED ROOT: ramentum (in *botany*, any of the thin, brown scales found on fern leaves and stems) NO CROSS REFERENCE
raj,* **ran**	Sanskrit *rajati:* he rules (IE: *reg,* to put in order)	ruler	SIMPLE ROOT: raj, raja (also, *rajah*; male), rani (female) LEADING ROOT COMPOUND: raja-yoga, rajbansi, rajpramukh, rajput (or *rajpoot*) TRAILING ROOT COMPOUND: maharajah, maharani GYPSY COGNATE: rye (gentleman) CROSS REFERENCE: *arch, reg*
ram*	Latin *ramus* (IE: *wrad,* twig, root)	branch, root	SIMPLE ROOT: ramet (in *biology*, any of the members of a clone), ramose, ramous LEADING ROOT COMPOUND: fic: ramification (the arrangement of branches or offshoots) (from *facere*, to make, do) form: ramiform (branched or branchlike) fy: ramify (to divide or spread out into branches or branchlike divisions) (from *facere*, to make, do)

582

Element	From	Meaning	Examples
ram (cont'd)			ger: ramigerous (*gerere*, to bear) TRAILING ROOT COMPOUND: multi: multiramose (having many branches) (*multi*, many) CROSS REFERENCE: *clad, germ, rad, rhizo*
range			See *circum-* for *arrange, derange.*
rap,* rep	Latin *rapere* (IE: *rep*, to seize)	snatch, seize	SIMPLE ROOT: rapa: rapacious, rapacity rape: rape (the crime, *not* the plant or the refuse of grapes) rapi: rapid (**Synonyms**: fast, swift, fleet), rapine (see *Doublets* below) rapt: rapt (carried away with joy, love, etc.; enraptured), raptorial (seizing, predatorial; describing those birds of prey with a strong notched beak and sharp talons, as the eagle, hawk, owl, vulture, etc.; also, adapted for seizing prey, as *raptorial* claws) rapture (**Synonyms**: ecstasy, bliss, transport) {rapturous} PREFIXED ROOT: e-: erepsin (a mixture of peptidases in the small intestines that acts to produce amino acids) (*ex-* + *rapere* + pep*sin*) sur-: surreptitious (**Synonyms**: secret, covert, clandestine) (*sur-* assimilates *sub-*, under) DISGUISED ROOT: ravage (**Synonyms**: sack, pillage, plunder) raven (to devour greedily; to prowl hungrily; as a *noun*, an alternate spelling of *ravin*, below), ravenous ravin (see *Doublets* below) ravine (a long, deep hollow in the earth's surface; large gully; gorge) ravish (to seize and carry away forcibly; to rape a woman; to transport with joy or delight; enrapture), ravishing DOUBLETS: ravin:rapine CROSS REFERENCE: *cap, prehen*
ras			See *rad*, scrape for *erase.*
rat**	Latin *ratus* (IE: *ar*, to join, fit to- gether)	reason, reckoning	SIMPLE ROOT: rate (another *rate* comes from the same base as *repute*, to scold severely) rating, ratio (see *Doublets* below) ration, rational, rationale, rationalism, rationalization, rationalize ratiocinate (to reason out, using formal logic; Edgar Allan Poe, the inventor of the detective story, is said to be the first to use *ratiocination* in writing) LEADING ROOT COMPOUND: fy: ratify (from *facere*, to make, do) DISGUISED ROOT: reason (see *Doublets* below) PREFIXED DISGUISED ROOT: ar-: arraign (**Synonyms**: accuse, charge, indict) (*ar-* assimilates *ad-*, to, toward) de-: deraign (formerly, in *law*, to determine an issue, especially by personal combat between the litigants) (*de-*, down) DOUBLETS: reason:ratio CROSS REFERENCE: *log*

Element	From	Meaning	Examples
raz			See *rad*, scrape for *razor*.
re-***	Latin	back, again	PREFIXED ROOT:

bat: rebate (*battuere*, to beat)

bel: rebel, rebeldom, rebellion, rebellious (*bellum*, war)

bound: rebound (*bound*, to leap)

buff: rebuff (an abrupt, blunt refusal of offered advice, help, etc.) (from Old High German *biroufan*, to tussle)

buk: rebuke (to blame or scold in a sharp way; reprimand) (from Old French *buschier*, to beat from *busche*, a log) [Modern French *bûche de Noël*, traditional Christmas cake in the shape of a log]

burs: reimburse (**Synonyms:** pay, compensate, indemnify) (*im-*, in, prefixes *bursa*, bag)

cap: recapitulate {recapitulation} (*capere*, to take, hold)

ced: recede (*cedere*, to go)

ceive: receive (**Synonyms:** accept, admit, take) (from *capere*, to take)

cent: recent (*ceno*, new)

cept: receptacle, reception, receptive, receptor (from *capere*, to take)

cess: recess, recession (from *cedere*, to go)

cid: recidivism (literally, to fall back; habitual or chronic relapse, or tendency to relapse, especially into crime or anti-social behavior) {recidivist} (from *caedere*, to fall)

cip: recipe, recipience (the act of receiving), recipient (from *capere*, to take)

[NB: *Reciprocal, reciprocity* are not from the same root as *recipe* and *recipient*; see *Webster's New World*.]

cit: recital, recitation, recitative, recite (*citare*, to arouse)

claim: reclaim (see synonyms at *recover*, below) (from *clamare*, to cry out)

clin: reclinate (in *botany*, bending downward, as a leaf or stem) (*clin*, bend)

clus: recluse {reclusive}, reclusion (from *claudere*, to close)

cog: recognition, recognizance, recognize (*cognoscere*, to know)

coil: recoil (from *culus*, anus, buttocks, rump, backside) [*re-coil* (with hyphen) means "to coil again"]

concil: reconcile, reconciliation (from *council*)

cond: recondite (beyond the grasp of the ordinary mind or understanding; profound; abstruse) (*condere*, to hide)

cord: record, recorder, recording (*cordis*, mind, heart)

count: recount (to tell in detail; give an account of; narrate (from *compute*)

cours: recourse (from *currere*, to run)

cover: recover (**Synonyms:** regain, retrieve, recoup), recovery (from *recuperate*)

creant: recreant (from *credere*, to believe)

crim: recriminate (to bring a countercharge against an accuser) {recriminatory, or recriminative} (*crimin*, judge)

crud: recrudesce (to break out or become active again) (*crudus*, raw)

Element	From	Meaning	Examples
re- (cont'd)			cruit: recruit (from *crescere,* to grow)
			cumb: recumbent (in *biology,* leaning or lying upon some other part or surface; **Synonyms:** prone, supine, prostrate) (*cumbere,* to lie down)
			cup: recuperate (from *capere,* to grasp)
			cur(r): recur, recurrence, recurrent (**Synonyms:** intermittent, periodic, alternate) (*currere,* to run)
			curv: recurvate (to curve or bend back)
			cus: (from *cause*)
			recusant (a person who refuses to accept or obey established authority)
			recuse (to disqualify or withdraw from a position of judging, as because of prejudice or personal interest)
			dact: redact (to put into suitable literary form; revise; edit), redaction {redactor} (*act* + inserted *d*)
			deem: redeem (literally, to buy back; **Synonyms:** rescue, ransom, save) (from *emere,* to buy; inserted *d*)
			dempt: redemption, redemptive (from *emere,* to buy)
			doubt: redoubt (any stronghold) (from *reduce*)
			dound: redound (inserted *d*) (from *unda,* wave)
			dress: redress (to set right; rectify; **Synonyms:** reparation, restitution, indemnification) (from *di-,* apart, from + *regere,* to keep straight)
			duc: reduce (**Synonyms:** decrease, dwindle, lessen), reduction, reductive (*ducere,* to lead)
			dund: redundant (**Synonyms:** wordy, verbose, prolix) (see *redound*)
			fect: refect, refection, refectory (from *facere,* to do, make)
			fer: (*ferre,* to bear)
			refer (do not confuse use with *allude*), referee, reference
			referendum (plural, *referendums, referenda*)
			referent (in *linguistics,* the object, concept, event, etc. referred to by a term or expression)
			referential, referral
			fin: refine, refined, refinement (*finire,* to end)
			flect: (*flectere,* to bend)
			reflect (**Synonyms: 1)** think, reason, cogitate; **2)** consider, study, contemplate)
			reflectance (physics term), reflection
			reflective (**Synonyms:** pensive, contemplative, meditative)
			flex: reflex, reflexive (from *reflect;* see note under *flect/flex*)
			flu: refluent, reflux (*fluere,* to flow)
			form: reform, reformation, reformatory, reformed (*forma,* figure, shape, image)
			fract: refract, refraction, refractory (from *frangere,* to break)
			frain: (note differences in meaning of roots)
			refrain (from *frenare,* to curb, as *to refrain* from an indulgence)
			refrain (from *frangere,* to break, as a verse or phrase repeated in a song at intervals in a song or poem)
			frang: refrangible (from *refract*)
			frig: refrigerant, refrigerate (*frigus,* cold)
			fring: refringent (from *refract*)

585

Element	From	Meaning	Examples
re- (cont'd)			fug: (*fugere*, to flee) refuge (**Synonyms:** shelter, asylum, sanctuary) refugee (a person who flees from home or country to seek refuge elsewhere, as in a time of war or of political or religious persecution) refugium (a small, isolated area that has escaped the extreme changes undergone by the surrounding area) fulg: refulgent (shining; radiant) (*fulgere*, to flash, shine) fund: refund (to give back or pay back money, etc.; repay) (*fundere*, to pour) fus: refusal, refuse (**Synonyms:** decline, reject, repudiate); as a *noun*, anything thrown away (check difference in noun pronunciation) (from *refund*) fut: refutation (also, *refutal*), refute (**Synonyms:** disprove, confute, controvert) (*futare*, to strike, beat) gain: regain (**Synonyms:** recover, retrieve, recoup) gal: regale (Old French *gale*, joy, pleasure, from which *gallant* is derived) gard: regard (**Synonyms:** respect, esteem, admire) (from *guard*) gel: regelation (*gel*, set, freeze) gen: regenerate, regenerative, regenerator (*generare*, to produce) gis: register (**Synonyms:** list, catalog, inventory), registrar, registration (from *gerere*, to bear) gress: regress, regression, regressive (from *gradi*, to step, walk) gret: regret (**Synonyms:** penitence, repentance, contrition) (from Germanic *gretan*, to weep) gurg: regurgitate (to rush, surge, or flow back), regurgitation (*gurgitare*, to flood) hab: rehabilitate {rehabilitation, rehabilitative} (*habere*, to have, hold) hears: rehearsal, rehearse (from *hirpex*, a harrow) it: reiterate (**Synonyms:** repeat, recapitulate, iterate) {reiteration, reiterative} (*iterare*, to repeat) ject: reject (**Synonyms:** decline, refuse, spurn) {rejectee, rejecter/rejector, rejection, rejective} (from *jacere*, to throw) joic: rejoice (ultimately from *gaudere*, to rejoice, to be glad) join: rejoin (**Synonyms:** answer, respond, reply), rejoinder (from *jungere*, to bind) juv: rejuvenate (**Synonyms:** renew, renovate, restore) {rejuvenation, rejuvenator}, rejuvenescence (*juvenis*, young) lapse: relapse (from *labi*, to slip, fall) late: relate, related (**Synonyms:** kindred, allied, affiliate), relation, relational, relative, relativity, relator (from *refer*) lax: relax, relaxant, relaxation, relaxedly, relaxer (*laxus*, loose) leas: release (**Synonyms:** liberate, emancipate, free) (from *relax*) leg: relegate (**Synonyms:** entrust, consign, confide) (*legare*, to send) lent: relent (**Synonyms:** yield, capitulate, succumb), relentless (*lentus*, flexible, pliant, slow)

Element	From	Meaning	Examples
re- (cont'd)			lev: relevance, relevant (**Synonyms:** pertinent, apropos, apposite), relevé (a ballet movement) (*levare*, to raise) li: reliable (**Synonyms:** dependable, trustworthy, trusty) (from *rely*, below) liev: relieve (**Synonyms:** alleviate, lighten, assuage) (from *relevant*, above) linq: relinquish (**Synonyms:** abandon, waive, forgo) (*relic*, *relict* are derived from the same root as *relinquish*) lig: religion (*ligare*, to bind) luct: reluctance, reluctant (**Synonyms:** disinclined, hesitant, averse) {reluctivity} (*luctari*, to struggle) ly: rely (**Synonyms:** trust, depend, reckon) (from *ligare*, to bind) main: (from *manere*, to stay) remain (**Synonyms:** stay, tarry, linger) remainder (**Synonyms:** residue, remnant, balance) [*remnant* is also from this root] mand: remand (in *law*, to send back a case to a lower court, as for further proceedings) (*mandare*, to order) mark: remark (**Synonyms:** observation, comment) (French: *remarque*), remarkable med: remediable, remedial, remediation, remedy (**Synonyms:** cure, heal) (*mederei*, to heal) mem: remember, remembrance, remembrancer, Remembrancer (in England, any of certain officials, specifically one responsible for collecting debts to the sovereign) (*memor*, mindful) mind: remind, reminder, remindful (from *mens*, mind) minisc: reminisce, reminiscence, reminiscent (from *memini*, to remember) mis: (from *mittere*, to send) remise (in *law*, to give up a claim to; release by deed) remiss (**Synonyms:** negligent, neglectful, derelict), remissible, remission mit: remit (to forgive or pardon sins, wrongs, etc.), remittal, remittance, remittent monstr: remonstrance, remonstrate (**Synonyms:** object, protest, demur) (*monstrare*, to show) mors: remorse (**Synonyms:** penitence, repentance, compunction), remorseful (from *mordere*, to bite) mot: remote (**Synonyms:** far, distant, removed), remotion (from *remove*) mov: removable, removal, remove, removed (*movere*, to move) muner: remunerate (**Synonyms:** pay, compensate, reimburse), remuneration, remunerative (*munus*, a gift) naiss: Renaissance (from *nasci*, to be born) nas: renascence (capitalized, same as *Renaissance*), renascent (*nasci*, to be born) neg: renege (from *renegade*, see Spanish below) nitent: renitent (resisting pressure; resistant; recalcitrant) (*niti*, to struggle) nounc: renounce (from *nuntius*, messenger)

Element	From	Meaning	Examples
re- (cont'd)			nov: renovate (**Synonyms:** renew, restore, refresh) {renovation, renovative} (*novus*, new)
			nown: renown, renowned (**Synonyms:** distinguished, eminent, illustrious) (from *nomen*, name)
			nunc: renunciation (the act or an instance of renouncing) (see *renounce*, above)
			pair: (notice difference in root meanings)
			repair (**Synonyms:** mend, patch, darn) (*parare*, to get ready)
			repair (to go or betake oneself *to* a place) (from *patria*, native country)
			par: reparation (**Synonyms:** restitution, redress, indemnification), reparative (from first *repair*)
			past: repast (from *pascere*, to feed)
			patr: repatriate {repatriation} (*patria*, native country; from *pater*, father)
			peal: repeal (**Synonyms:** abolish, annul, abrogate) (from *pellere*, to drive, push)
			peat: repeat (**Synonyms:** iterate, reiterate, recapitulate) (from *petere*, to seek, demand, attack)
			pel: repel, repellant (also, *repellent*) (*pellere*, to drive, push)
			pent: repent, repentance, repentant (there is another *repent*, where the root is *repere*, to crawl, as in *reptile*; is pronounced REE punt) (*paenitere*, to repent, to feel sorry for)
			petend: repetend (from *repeat*)
			petit: repetition, repetitious, repetitive (see *repeat*)
			plead: repleader (in *law*, a second pleading; various extensions of the basic meaning)
			plen: replenish (*plenir*, to fill)
			plet: replete, repletion (from *plere*, to fill)
			plev: replevin (an action to recover personal property unlawfully taken), replevy (Old French *plevir*, to pledge)
			plic: replica (**Synonyms:** copy, reproduction, facsimile), replicate, replication (from *reply*)
			ply: reply (**Synonyms:** answer, respond, reply) (from *plicare*, to fold)
			port: report, reportage, reportedly, reporter (*portare*, to carry)
			pos: repose, reposit, repository (from *ponere*, to place)
			prehen: reprehend, reprehensible, reprehension (*prehendere*, to grasp, hold)
			press: repress, repressed, repression (from *premere*, to press)
			priev: reprieve (to postpone the punishment of) (from *reprove*)
			prim: reprimand (a severe or formal rebuke) (from *repress*)
			pris: reprisal, reprise (see *reprehend*, above)
			proach: reproach, reproachful (from *prope*, near)
			prob: reprobate, reprobation (from *reprove*)
			proof: reproof (also, *reproval*; the act of reproving or something said in reproving; censure) (from *reprove*, next entry)
			prov: reproval, reprove (to speak to in disapproval) (from *probus*, good, proper)
			pud: repudiate (**Synonyms:** decline, refuse, spurn) {repudiation, repudiator} (*pudere*, to feel shame)

Element	From	Meaning	Examples
re- (cont'd)			pugn: repugnance (**Synonyms**: aversion, antipathy, loathing), repugnant (*pugnare*, to fight)
			puls: repulse, repulsion (in *physics*, the mutual action by which bodies or particles of matter tend to repel each other; opposed to *attraction*), repulsive (from *repel*)
			put: reputable, reputation, repute, reputed (*putare*, to think)
			quest: request (**Synonyms**: entreaty, supplication, prayer) (from *require*)
			quiem: Requiem (first word of the Introit in the Latin Mass for the Dead) (from *quiet*)
			quir: require (**Synonyms**: 1) demand, claim, exact; 2) lack, want, need), requirement (from *quis*, to seek, demand)
			quis: requisite (**Synonyms**: 1) essential, indispensable, necessary; 2) need, necessity, exigency) (from *require*)
			quit: requital, requite [from *quit*; to make return or repayment for (a benefit, service, etc., or an injury, wrong, etc.)]
			scind: rescind (**Synonyms**: abolish, annul, abrogate) (*scindere*, to cut)
			sciss: rescission (from *rescind*)
			script: rescript (from *scribere*, to write)
			scu: rescue (**Synonyms**: deliver, redeem, ransom) (from Old French *escourre*, to shake, move)
			search: research (from *circare*, to go round)
			sect: resect, resection (from *secare*, to cut)
			semb: resemblance (**Synonyms**: likeness, similarity, analogy), resemble (from *simulate*)
			sent: resent, resentful, resentment (**Synonyms**: offense, umbrage, pique) (*sentir*, to feel or perceive)
			serv: reserve {reservoir}, reserved (*servare*, to keep or hold)
			sid: (from *sedere*, to sit)
			reside, residence, residency, resident, residential, residentiary
			residual, residuary, residue (for synonyms, see *remainder*, above), residuum (**Synonyms**: remainder, residue, balance)
			sign: resign (to give possession of; relinquish), resignation, resigned (*signare*, to sign)
			sil: resile, resilience (also, *resiliency*), resilient (**Synonyms**: elastic, flexible, supple) (from *salire*, to jump)
			sist: resist, resistance, resistant, resistible, resistive, resistless (*sistere*, to set)
			solu: resoluble, resolute [**Synonyms**: faithful, constant, staunch (or *stanch*)], resolution (see *resolve*, next entry)
			solv: resolvable, resolve (**Synonyms**: decide, determine, settle), resolved, resolvent (*solvere*, to loosen)
			son: resonance, resonant, resonate, resonator (*sonus*, sound)
			sort: resort (**Synonyms**: resource, expedient, makeshift) (*sortir*, to go out)
			sourc: resource (see synonyms, previous entry), resourceful (from *surgere*, which itself is from *sub-* + *regere*, straight)
			spect: respect (**Synonyms**: regard, esteem, admire), respectability, respectable, respectful, respecting, respective, respectively (from *specere*, to look)

Element	From	Meaning	Examples
re- (cont'd)			spir: respirable, respiration, respirator, respiratory, respire (*spirare*, to breathe)
			spit: respite (a delay or postponement) (from *respect*)
			splend: resplendent (this root also yields *splendid*: the only two words from this verb) (*splendere*, to shine)
			spond: respond (see synonyms at *reply*, above), respondent, responder (*spondere*, to pledge)
			spons: response (**Synonyms:** answer, reply, rejoinder), responsibility, responsible, responsive, responsory (see *respond*, previous entry)
			stit: restitution (**Synonyms:** reparation, redress, indemnification) (from *statuere*, to set up)
			staur: restaurant (see *restore*, next entry)
			stor: restoration, restorative, restore (**Synonyms:** renew, renovate, refresh) (IE *sta-*, to stand; from which *restaurant* is derived; see previous entry)
			strain: (from *stringere*, to draw tight)
			restrain (**Synonyms:** curb, check, bridle), restrained, restrainer restraint (a restraining or being restrained)
			strict: restrict (**Synonyms:** limit, bound, confine) (from *stringere*, to draw tight)
			sult: result (**Synonyms:** 1) follow, ensue, succeed; 2) effect, consequence, result), resultant (from *resile*)
			sum: resume (to take, get, or occupy or again; to summarize or make a résumé of) {résumé}, resumption (the act of resuming) (*sumere*, to take)
			sup: resupinate (in *botany*, having an upside down appearance, as the flower of an orchid; **Synonyms:** prone, prostrate, recumbent), resupine (*supine* is extended from *sub-*, under)
			surg: resurge, resurgent (from *sub-*, under + *regere*, to direct)
			tail: retail (from Old French *taillier*, to cut; yields *tailor*)
			tain: retain, retainer (from *tenere*, to hold)
			tal: retaliate (*talio*, punishment in kind)
			tard: retard, retardant, retardation, retarded, retarder (*tardare*, to make slow)
			tent: retention, retentive, retentivity (see *retain*)
			tic: reticence, reticent (from *tacere*, to be silent)
			tin: retinaculum (in *biology*, an often hooked structure, band, etc. serving to hold parts, seeds, eggs, etc. together or in place) (see *retain*)
			tir: retire (to go away, retreat, or withdraw to a private, sheltered, or secluded place), retired (*tirer*, to draw)
			tort: retort (both meanings), retortion (from *torquere*, to twist)
			tract: retract, retractile (that which can be *retracted*, or drawn back, as the claws of a cat), retraction, retractive, retractor (from *trahere*, to draw)
			treat: retreat (**Synonyms:** refuge, sanctuary, asylum) (from *retract*)
			trib: retribution {retributive, retributory} (*tribuere*, to pay)
			triev: retrieve (see synonyms at *recover*, above) (from *trouver*, to find)

Element	From	Meaning	Examples
re- (cont'd)			tus: retuse (in *botany*, having a blunt or rounded apex with a small notch, as some leaves) (from *tundere*, to strike) vanch: revanchism (the revengeful spirit moving a defeated nation to aggressively seek restoration of territories, etc.) (from *revenge*) veal: (note difference in root meanings) reveal (**Synonyms**: disclose, divulge, tell) (from *velum*, veil) reveal (a door jamb) (from *avaler*, to lower; from *vale*, valley) vel: (note difference in root meanings) revel (from *rebel*) revelation (from *reveal*) ven: (note difference in root meanings) revenant (a person who returns, as after a long absence; a ghost) (*venir*, to come) revenge (**Synonym**: avenge) (French *venger*, to take vengeance) revenue (*venir*, to come) verber: reverberant, reverberate, reverberation, reverbative, reverberatory (*verbarare*, to beat) ver: revere (**Synonyms**: reverence, venerate, worship), reverend, reverent (Latin *vereri*, to fear, feel awe) vers: revers, reversal, reverse (**Synonyms**: opposite, antithetical, antonymous), reversible, reversion (from *vertere*, to turn) vert: revert (in *biology*, to return to a former or primitive type) (see *reverse*) vest: revest (*vestire*, to clothe) vet: revet, revetment (from *revest*) view: review, reviewal, reviewer (from *videre*, to see) vil: revile (**Synonyms**: scold, upbraid, vituperate) (*vilus*, cheap, base) vis: revise, revision, revisory (from *videre*, to see) viv: revival, revive, revivify, revivescent (*vivere*, to live) voc: revocation, revocatory (*vocare*, to call) vok: revoke (see synonyms at *repeal*, above) (from *vocare*, to call) volt: revolt, revolting (from *volvere*, to roll) volu: revolute (rolled backward or downward at the tips or margins, as some leaves), revolution, revolutionary, revolutionist, revolutionize (from *revolve*, next entry) volv: revolve, revolver, revolving (*volvere*, to roll) vuls: revulsion (see synonyms at *repugnance*, above) (from *vellere*, to pull) ward: reward (**Synonyms**: prize, award, premium) (from Old French *regard*) *red*: redintegrate (*re-* + integrate; inserted *d*) *redi*: redivivus (restored to life; reborn; inserted *di*) DOUBLE-PREFIXED ROOT: (examples of) reincarnation (*carne*, meat, flesh) repercussion (from *quatere*, to shake) recollect (from *legere*, to gather)

591

Element	From	Meaning	Examples
re- (cont'd)			PREFIXED DISGUISED ROOT: render (from Latin *reddere*, to restore; from *re(d)* + *dare*, to give) rendition (from *render*) FRENCH: *réchauffé* (literally, warmed over; a dish of leftover food re-heated; any used or old literary material worked up in a new form; rehash) *recherché* (sought out with care; rare; choice; uncommon; from *research*) *réclame* (from *reclaim*, above) reconnaissance, reconnoiter (from *recognizance*) recoup (to get back an equivalent for) (*couper*, to cut, strike) rein (from *retain*) *rendezvous* [from *rendez-vous*, betake or present yourself (or yourselves)] repartee, repertoire, repertory (from *parere*, to produce, invent) *repoussé* (literally, to push back) reveille (from Latin *vigilare*, to watch) reverie (from French *rêver*, to dream) SPANISH: remuda (in the Southwest, a group of extra saddle horses kept as a supply of remounts) (from *mudar*, to change) renegade (a person who abandons one religion for another; apostate; a person who abandons a party, movement, etc. and goes over to the other side) (from *negare*, to deny) INTERDISCIPLINARY: refraction (in *astronomy*, the bending of the rays of light from a star or planet, greatest when the star or plant is low-est in the sky, so that it seems higher than it really is; in *optics*, the ability of the eye to refract light entering it, so as to form an image on the retina; the measuring of the degree of refraction of an eye) resection (in *surgery*, the removal of a part of an organ, bone, etc.; in *surveying*, a method of determining the loca-tion of a point by taking observations from its points to known locations) CROSS REFERENCE: *ab-, palin-, retro-*
rect,*** reg, rig	Latin *regere*: to rule govern (IE: *reg*, straight, stretch out, put in order; yields English right)	straight, rule right	SIMPLE ROOT: rect: rectitude (moral uprightness; rightness, as of intellectual judgment; straightness), recto, rector, rectum, rectus (plural, *recti*) rega: regal (see *Doublets* below), regalia, regality rege: regency, regent regi: regime (French, *régime*), regimen, regiment, regimenta-tion, reginal, region, regional, regionalism (in literature, the usually realistic depiction in stories, plays, etc. of a particular region of a country, especially a rural region, and of the influence of its history, customs, etc. on the lives of the characters), regius regn: regnal regu: regula, regular (**Synonyms: 1)** normal, typical, natu-ral; **2)** steady, uniform, equable), regulatory, regulate (see *Doublets* below), regulation, reguline, regulus

Element	From	Meaning	Examples
rect (cont'd)			PREFIXED ROOT: *rect*: ar-: arrect (*ar*- assimilates *ad*-, to, toward) *cor*-: correct (**Synonyms**: accurate, exact, precise), correction, correctitude, corrective, corrigendum (*cor*- assimilates *com*-, with, together) *di*-: direct, direction, directory (*de*- elides *dis*-, apart, away) *e*-: erect, erectile, erection, erector (*e*- elides *ex*-, out) *reg*: *inter*-: interregnum (*inter*-, between) DOUBLE PREFIXED ROOT: incorrigible (*in*-, not; *cor*- assimilates *com*-, with, together) insurrection (*in*-, in, upon + *sur* from *sub*-, under) resurrection (*re*-, again + *sur*- assimilates *sub*-, under) LEADING ROOT COMPOUND: *rect*: angl: rectangle *recti*: fic: rectification (from *facere*, to make, do) fy: rectify (from *facere*, to make, do) grad: rectigrade (*gradus*, step) lin: rectilinear pet: rectipetality (the tendency of growing plant organs to grow in a straight line) rostr: rectirostral (having a straight beak) (*rostra*, beak) *regi*: cid: regicide (the killing of a king) (*cide*, kill) DISGUISED ROOT: adroit (**Synonyms**: dexterous, deft, handy) (see *droit* below) dirge [from *dirige*, imperative of *dirigere*, to direct, the first word of an antiphon (Psalm 5:8) in the Office for the Burial of the Dead] dress, dressage, dresser, dressing (from Old French *drecier*, to set up, arrange) droit (a legal right; that to which one has a legal claim) ergo (therefore) realm (a kingdom; a region; sphere, area; in *ecology*, any of the primary biogeogaphic regions of the earth) reckon (**Synonyms**: 1) calculate, compute, estimate; 2) rely, trust, depend) reign rial (the basic monetary unit of Iran and Oman; same as *riyal*) rich (**Synonyms**: wealthy, affluent, opulent) right, righteous (**Synonyms**: moral, ethical, virtuous) royal (see *Doublets* below) rule (see *Doublets* below), ruler source (**Synonyms**: origin, inception, root) surge (from *surgere*, to rise straight up; from *sub*-, under + *regere*) viceroy PREFIXED DISGUISED ROOT: a-: alert (from Italian *all ' erta*, on the watch; from *alla*, at the + *erta*, a lookout; from Latin *erigere*, to erect)

593

Element	From	Meaning	Examples
rect (cont'd)			ad-: address, adroit (ad-, to, toward)
			di-: dirigible (a balloon that can be directed) (from direct)
			es-: escort (from ex-, out)
			mal-: maladroit (mal, bad + French à, to + droit; from Latin directus, itself from di-, apart, from)
			re-: redress, resource (re-, again)
			DOUBLETS: royal:regal; rule:regulate
			FRENCH:
			de règle (according to the rule or correct form)
			régisseur (a stage director)
			ASTRONOMY TERM: Regulus (a first-magnitude star, the brightest in the constellation Leo)
			PROPER NAME: Reginald (French Regnault, Renaud; German Reinhold; Italian Rinaldo; Spanish Reynaldo)
			MOTTOES:
			Regnant populi, The people rule (State of Arkansas)
			Dirigio, I direct (State of Maine)
			GERMAN: Reich, Reichsmark, Reichstag
			SANSKRIT: rajah (raja), maharajah (maharaja)
			NOTE: Register, from re-, back + gis, to bear, carry, is not in this family.
			PLACENAMES: Regal, Minnesota; Regina, Saskatchewan
			CROSS REFERENCE: ithy, ortho
reg			See rect for regular, etc.
ren**	Latin reni	kidney	SIMPLE ROOT: ren (plural, renes), renal (of or near the kidneys) reniculus (plural, reniculi), renin PREFIXED ROOT: ad-: adrenal, adrenalin (ad-, to, toward) CROSS REFERENCE: nephr
rep			See rap/rep for surreptitious.
rep*	Latin repere IE: rep, to creep, crawl)	to creep	SIMPLE ROOT: rep: repantia (a suborder of of decapod crustaceans comprising lobsters, crabs, and hermit crabs) repent (as adjective, pronounced REE punt; not related to verb, re PENT) rept: reptant (same as repent; in biology, creeping, or crawling along the ground, prostrate), reptatorial, reptile, Reptilia, reptilian PREFIXED ROOT: ob-: obreption, obreptitious (done or obtained by trickery or deceit, or by concealing the truth) (ob-, to, toward, over) NO CROSS REFERENCE
ret*	Latin rete (IE: ere, loose, separate)	net	SIMPLE ROOT: rete (in anatomy, a network or plexus, as of blood vessels or nerve fibers) retiarius (in ancient Rome, a gladiator armed with a net and a trident) retiary (of or like nets or net-making; building nets, as certain spiders; armed with a net) reticle (in optics, a network of very fine lines, wires, etc. in the focus of the eyepiece of an optical instrument), reticular

Element	From	Meaning	Examples
ret (cont'd)			reticulate (in *botany*, having the veins arranged like the threads of a net: said of leaves), reticulation, reticule **reticulum** retina (a delicate multilayer light-sensitive membrane lining the inner eyeball and connected by the optic nerve to the brain) LEADING ROOT COMPOUND: *reti*: form: retiform (having crisscrossed lines; netlike in form; reticulate) itis: retinitis (inflammation of the retina) (*itis*, inflammation) scop: retinoscope, retinoscopy (*scope*, look, view) *reticulo*: cyt: reticulocyte (*cyt*, cell) DISGUISED ROOT: réseau (a net or mesh foundation for lace) INTERDISCIPLINARY: reticulum (in *biology*, any network or netlike structure, as the weblike structure found in the protoplasm of many cells; in *zoology*, the second division of the stomach, or second stomach, of cud-chewing animals, as cows) NO CROSS REFERENCE
retro***	Latin *re-*, again + *intro-*, enter	backward, behind	LEADING ROOT COMPOUND: act: retroact, retroaction, retroactive ced: retrocede (*cedere*, to yield) choir: retrochoir (that part of a church which lies behind the choir or the main altar) flex: retroflex, retroflexion (also, *retroflection*) grad: retrograde (*gradus*, step) gress: retrogress, retrogression (see *retrograde*) spect: retrospect, retrospection, retrospective (*specere*, to look) trors: retrorse (contraction of *retroversion + e*) vers: retroversion (from *vertere*, to turn) DISGUISED ROOT: retable (see *Webster's Third*) PREFIXED DISGUISED ROOT: ar-: arrears (*ar-* assimilates *ad-*, to, toward) CROSS REFERENCE: *palin-*, *re-*
rhino*	Greek *rhis*	nose	SIMPLE ROOT: rhinal (of or pertaining to the nose; nasal) PREFIXED ROOT: *anti*-: antirhinum (a plant such as the snapdragon that has a *snoutlike* flowers) (*anti-*, against) *cata*-: catarhine (having a slender nose with the nostrils spaced close together; also, a catarhine creature, as man or certain other primates; distinguished from *platyrhine*) (*cata-*, down) LEADING ROOT COMPOUND: *rhin*: encephal: rhinencephalon (the olfactory region of the brain, in the cerebrum) (*encephal*, brain) itis: rhinitis (inflammation of the nasal mucous membranes) (*itis*, inflammation) *rhino*: ceros: rhinoceros (literally, nose-horn) (*ceros*, horn)

595

Element	From	Meaning	Examples
rhino (cont'd)			log: rhinologist (a medical doctor specializing in problems of the nose), rhinology (*logy*, study of) rrh: rhinorrhea (runny nose) (*rrh*, run) virus: rhinovirus (the chief infectious agent causing the common cold) (*virus*, poison) EMBEDDED ROOT COMPOUND: oto<u>rhino</u>laryngologist (one who specializes in the ear, nose, and throat) (*oto*, ear; *larnyx*, throat) CROSS REFERENCE: *nas*
rhizo**	Greek *rhiza* (IE: *wrad*, twig, root)	root	SIMPLE ROOT: rhizome (in *botany*, a creeping stem lying, usually horizontally, at or under the surface of the soil and differing from a root in having scale leaves, bearing leaves or aerial shoots near its tips, and producing roots from the undersurface) LEADING ROOT COMPOUND: *rhiz*: oid: rhizoid (rootlike; any of the rootlike filaments in a moss, fern, etc that attach the plant to the substratum) (*oid*, similar to) *rhizo*: bi: rhizobium (any of several bacteria found as symbiotic nitrogen fixers in nodules on the roots of the bean, clover, etc.) (*bios*, life) carp: rhizocarpous (having perennial roots but annual stems and leaves: said of perennial plants) (*carp*, fruit) cephal: rhizocephalon (*cephal*, head) cton: rhizoctonia (any of various imperfect fungi, some of which can cause various diseases of many garden vegetables and ornamental plants) (*ktonos*, murder) gen: rhizogenic {rhizogeneous, rhizogenetic} (*gen*, producing) morph: rhizomorphous (in *botany*, shaped like a root; root-shaped) (*morph*, shape, form) pod: rhizopod {rhizopodal, rhizopodous} (*pod*, foot) pus: rhizopus (*pous*, foot) spher: rhizosphere (in *ecology*, the part of the soil enclosing and influenced by the roots of a plant) (*sphere*, ball, globe) tom: rhizotomy (a surgical cutting of the spinal nerve roots, as for relieving pain) (*tom*, cut) TRAILING ROOT COMPOUND: coleo: coleorhiza (a protective root sheath of grass seedlings through which the primary root emerges) (from *koleos*, sheath) myco: mycorrhiza (*myco*, fungus) oligo: oligorhizous (*oligo*, small, few, scant, a deficiency) DISGUISED TRAILING ROOT COMPOUND: licorice CROSS REFERENCE: *blast, clad, germ, rad*
rhod**	Greek *rhodon*	rose	SIMPLE ROOT: rhodi: rhodic, rhodium (chemical symbol, Rh) rhodo: rhodora LEADING ROOT COMPOUND: *rhod*: ops: rhodopsin (*ops*, eye)

Element	From	Meaning	Examples
rhod (cont'd)			*rhodo:* chro: rhodochrosite (chemical symbol, MnCO₃) (*chros*, color) dendr: rhododendron (see *Placenames* below) (*dendro*, tree) lit: rhodolite (from *lithos*, stone) plas: rhodoplast (*plast*, form, mold) TRAILING ROOT COMPOUND: phyt: phytorhodin (*phyton*, plant) STATE: Rhode Island PLACENAME: Rhododendron, Oregon CROSS REFERENCE: *erythr*
rhomb*	Greek *rhembein*: to revolve (IE: *wer*, to turn, bend)	to spin	SIMPLE ROOT: rhombic, rhombus LEADING ROOT COMPOUND: *rhomb:* oid: rhomboid (*oid*, similar to) *rhombo:* hedr: rhombohedron (*hedron*, geometric plane) CROSS REFERENCE: *gyro, trop, vert*
rid,* **ris**	Latin *ridere*: to laugh at (IE: *wrizd*, to avert the face)	to laugh	SIMPLE ROOT: *rid:* ridicule (**Synonyms:** mock, deride, taunt) ridiculous (**Synonyms:** absurd, foolish, asinine) *ris:* risible PREFIXED ROOT: *rid:* *de-:* deride (to laugh at in contempt or scorn; make fun of; see synonyms at *ridicule*) (*de-*, intensive) *ris:* *de-:* derision (ridicule, mockery; an object of ridicule or mockery), derisive {derisory} (*de-*, intensive) DISGUISED ROOT: riant CROSS REFERENCE: *gel*
rig*	Latin *rigere*: to be stiff (IE: *(s)rig*, cold, frigid)	stiff	SIMPLE ROOT: rigi: rigid (**Synonyms: 1)** firm, unbending, inflexible; **2)** immovable; **3)** austere, stern, unyielding), rigidity rigo: rigor (**Synonyms:** difficulty, hardship, vicissitude), rigorism, rigorous LEADING ROOT COMPOUND: fy: rigidify (from *facere*, to make, do) FRENCH: *de rigueur* (strict formality) LATIN TERM: *rigor mortis* (literally, stiffness of death; the progressive stiffening of the muscles after death) NO CROSS REFERENCE
ris			See *rid/ris* for *risible, derision*.
rob**	Latin *robur*: hard oak, strength	strong, hard, tough	SIMPLE ROOT: roble (the tall oak tree of California) roborant robust (may also be related to *ruber*, red) PREFIXED ROOT: *cor-:* corroborate (literally, to make strong; **Synonyms:** confirm, substantiate, verify) (*cor-* assimilates *com-*, with, together) DISGUISED ROOT: rambunctious (formerly, *robustus*) CROSS REFERENCE: *dur, firm, fort, sthen, val*

Element	From	Meaning	Examples
rod,** **ros**	Latin *rodere* IE: *red,* *rod,* to scratch, gnaw; yields English rat)	to eat, gnaw	SIMPLE ROOT: rodent PREFIXED ROOT: *rod:* *cor-*: corrode, corrosion, corrosive (*cor-* assimilates *com-*, with, together) *e-*: erode {erodent, erodible} (from *ex-*, out) *ros:* *e-*: erosion, erosive (from *ex-*, out) GENUS: Rodentia (includes agouti, beaver, chinchilla, chip- munk, dormouse, gerbil, gopher, guinea pig, hamster, jer- boa, lemming, marmot, mouse, rat, squirrel, woodchuck; there are other, less familiar ones) CROSS REFERENCE: *phag, vor*
rog***	Latin *rogare,* to stretch out the hand (IE: akin to *reg,* straight, to stretch out)	to ask, stretch, beg	SIMPLE ROOT: rogue, rogation, rogatory PREFIXED ROOT: *ab-*: abrogate (**Synonyms:** abolish, rescind, revoke), abroga- tion, abrogator (*ab-*, away) *ar-*: arrogance, arrogant (**Synonyms:** proud, haughty, inso- lent), arrogate (*ar-* assimilates *ad-*, to, toward) *de-*: derogate, derogation, derogative, derogatory (*de-*, from) *inter-*: interrogate (**Synonyms:** query, question, catechize), interrogative, interrogatory (*inter-*, between) *pre-*: prerogative (a prior right or privilege, especially one pe- culiar to a rank, class, etc.) (*pre-*, before) *pro-*: prorogue (**Synonyms:** adjourn, dissolve, postpone) (*pro-*, for) *sub-*: subrogate (to substitute one person for another), subro- gation (*sub-*, under) *super-*: supererogation (the act of doing more than what is re- quired or expected) (*super-*, over, above, beyond) [The verb form, *supererogate*, is now obsolete.] DISGUISED ROOT: corvée (from *corrogare*, to summon to- gether, collect; thus a day of work required of a vassal by a feudal lord) CROSS REFERENCE: *elast, tend*
ros			See *rod/ros* for *erosion, corrosion*.
rot*	Latin *rota* (IE: *rota,* to run, roll; yields English roll, round)	wheel	SIMPLE ROOT: rota: rota, rotary, rotate, rotation, rotative, rotator rote: rote (may possibly be in this family; two other *rotes* have different origins) rotu: rotund, rotunda PREFIXED ROOT: *circum-*: circumrotate (to turn like a wheel) (*circum-*, around) LEADING ROOT COMPOUND: form: rotiform (shaped like a wheel) (*form*, shape) grav: rotogravure (a printing process using photogravure cylinders on a rotary press) (from French *graver*, to carve) meter: rotameter (an instrument for measuring the rate of flow of a fluid by means of a movable float inserted in a vertical tube) MESHED LEADING ROOT COMPOUND: control (from *contra-*, against + *rotulus*)

Element	From	Meaning	Examples
rot (cont'd)			DISGUISED ROOT: barouche (literally, two-wheeled, but actually a four-wheeled carriage with a collapsible hood) rowel (a small, revolving wheel with sharp projecting points, forming the end of a spur, used to spur or prick a horse) PREFIXED DISGUISED ROOT: *en-*: enroll (*en-*, in) FRENCH: roundeau [a short, lyrical poem of usually fifteen lines, with only two rhymes and with an unrhymed refrain at the end of the second and third stanzas; also, a rondo (next entry)] rondo (in *music*, a composition or movement, often the last movement of a sonata, having its principal theme stated three or more times in the same key, interposed with subordinate themes) roué (a dissipated man; debauchee; rake; one who had been "broken on the wheel"), roulette SPANISH: rodeo (literally, a going around; cattle ring) SERVICE ORGANIZATION: Rotary (originally, the club rotated from one business place to another to hold its meetings) CROSS REFERENCE: *troch*
rrh**	Greek *rhein*: to flow (IE: *sreu*, to flow)	to run, flow	PREFIXED ROOT: *cata-*: catarrh (literally, to run or flow down; inflammation of a mucous membrane, especially of the nose and throat, causing an increased flow of mucus) (*cata-*, down) *dia-*: diarrhea (*dia-*, through) LEADING ROOT COMPOUND: stat: rheostat (a device that sets the flow of electrical current; a light dimmer) (*stat*, stand) TRAILING ROOT COMPOUND: gono: gonorrhea (*gonad*, reproductive organ) hemo: hemorrhoid (*hemo*, blood; *oid*, similar to) logo: logorrhea (a ceaseless flow of words) (*logo*, word) meno: menorrhea (*meno*, moon, month) rhino: rhinorrhea (runny nose) (*rhino*, nose) CROSS REFERENCE: *flu*
rub*	Latin *rubeus* (IE: *reudh*, red; yields English rust, ruby)	red	SIMPLE ROOT: rube: rubella (German measles), rubeola (measles), rubescent rubi: rubicund, rubidium (from the red lines in its spectrum; chemical symbol: Rb), rubiginous (rust-colored; reddish-brown) rubr: rubric (originally, a law written in red), rubricate LEADING ROOT COMPOUND: fac: rubefacient (causing redness; in *medicine*, any external application, as a salve or plaster, causing redness of skin), rubefaction (*facere*, to make, do) FRENCH: rouge (a reddish powder, mainly ferric oxide, for polishing jewelry, metal, etc.; also, an old name for blusher: any of various red or reddish cosmetic powders, creams, etc. for coloring the face, especially the cheeks) PLACENAME: Baton Rouge, Louisiana CROSS REFERENCE: *erythr, rhod*

Element	From	Meaning	Examples
rud*	Latin *ruere*: to rush, fall, dig up (IE: *reud*, to tear apart; from *reu*, to tear out, dig up)	ruins, broken stones	ROOT NOTE: Though the root means broken stones, it has come to mean "primitive; uncivilized; lowly; humble; unrefined; ill-mannered." SIMPLE ROOT: rude (**Synonyms:** boorish, impolite, discourteous) ruderal (in *botany*, growing in rubbish, poor land, or waste places; can be used either as noun or adjective) rudiment (in *biology*, an imperfectly or incompletely developed organ or part), rudimentary (also, *rudimental*) PREFIXED ROOT: *e-*: erudite [literally, to take the roughness out, thus, to polish, to teach, and has come to mean deeply learned] (*e-* elides *ex-*, out) NO CROSS REFERENCE
rupt***	Latin *rumpere* (IE: *reu*, to tear out, tear apart, break)	to break	SIMPLE ROOT: rupture PREFIXED ROOT: *ab-*: abrupt (**Synonyms: 1)** steep, precipitous, sheer; **2)** sudden, precipitate, impetuous), abruption [a sudden breaking away (of parts of a mass)] (*ab-*, away) *cor-*: corrupt (**Synonyms:** debase, deprave, debauch) (*cor-* assimilates *com-*, with, together) *dis-*: disrupt (to break apart; split up; rend asunder) {disruption}, disruptive (*dis-*, apart) *e-*: erupt, eruption, eruptive (*e-* elides *ex-*, out) *inter-*: interrupt, interrupted (in *botany*, asymmetrical; irregular: said of parts not equally spaced on a stem) (*inter-*, between) *ir-*: irrupt (a bursting or breaking in; a violent invasion) {irruption, irruptive} (*ir-* assimilates *in-*, in) BOUND COMPOUND: bankrupt DISGUISED ROOT: rout (**Synonyms:** overcome, subdue, subjugate) route (literally, a broken, or beaten path), routine rut CROSS REFERENCE: *clast, fract/frag*

600

S

Element	From	Meaning	Examples
sacr,*** secr	Latin *sacer* (IE: *sak*, to sanctify, make a compact)	holy, sacred	**SIMPLE ROOT:** sacra: sacral (two meanings: of, near, or pertaining to the *sacrum*; also, pertaining to *sacred* rites or observances) sacrament (any of the seven rites of the historical Christian Church considered to have been instituted or observed by Jesus as a testament to inner grace or as a channel that mediates grace; in the liturgical churches these rites include baptism, confirmation, the Eucharist, matrimony, orders, penance, and extreme unction; capitalized, the Eucharist itself, the celebration of the Last Supper) sacre: sacred (dedicated to or set apart for the worship of a deity; made or declared holy; **Synonyms:** holy, hallowed, divine) sacri: sacrist, sacristan (a person in charge of a sacristy; see *Doublets* below), sacristy (a room in a church, usually adjoining the sanctuary, where the sacred vessels, vestments, etc. are kept; vestry) sacru: sacrum (short for *os sacrum*, translation of Greek *hieron osteron*, sacred bone, because of its use in sacrifices) **PREFIXED ROOT:** *con-*: consecrate (**Synonyms:** devote, dedicate, hallow), consecration (from *com-*, with, together) *de-*: desecrate (to take away the sacredness of; treat as not sacred; profane), desecration (**Synonyms:** sacrilege, profanation), desecrator (*de-*, reversal) *ob-*: obsecrate, obsecration (*ob-*, against) **PREFIXED ELIDED ROOT:** *ex-*: execrate (to curse; originally, to call down upon; to speak abusively or contemptuously of; denounce scathingly; to loathe; detest; abhor) (*ex-*, out) **LEADING ROOT COMPOUND:** *sacer*: dot: sacerdotal (of priests of the office of priest; priestly, as sacerdotal robes; characterized by belief in the divine authority of the priesthood), sacerdotalism (from IE *dhe-*, to do) *sacri*: fic: sacrifice (from *facere*, to make) leg: sacrilege (originally, temple robber; see synonyms at *desecration*, above) (*legere*, to gather up, rob) *sacro*: iliac: sacroiliac (of the sacrum, see above, and the ilium; especially, designating the joint between them) (from *eileos*, colic) sanct: sacrosanct (very sacred, holy, or inviolable) (*sanct*, holy) **DISGUISED ROOT:** sexton (see *Doublets* below) **DOUBLETS:** sexton:sacristan **PLACENAMES:** Sacramento (California, Kentucky) **CROSS REFERENCE:** *hagi, hier, sanct*

Element	From	Meaning	Examples
sag,** sap, sav, s i p	Latin *sapere*: to taste, perceive, be wise (IE: *sap*, to taste, perceive)	discerning, wise; to taste	SIMPLE ROOT: *sag:* sagacious (**Synonyms:** shrewd, perspicacious, astute) sagacity (penetrating intelligence and sound judgment) sage (a wise person, *not* the herb; a plant of the mint family, is derived from *salvus,* whole, and is so named from its reputed healing powers) *sap:* sap: sap (as of a tree, giving the tree its taste; as a *verb,* to undermine by digging away foundations; **Synonyms:** weaken, debilitate, enervate) sapid: sapid (having taste or flavor; palatable; agreeable to the mind), sapidity sapie: sapient (full of knowledge; sagacious; discerning; of or relating to the existing human species; **Synonyms:** wise, sage, judicious), sapiential sapo: sapor *sav:* savant, savor, savvy PREFIXED ROOT: *sag:* *pre-:* presage (to perceive beforehand) (*pre-,* before) *sip:* *in-:* insipid (without flavor, tasteless; dull, lifeless) (*in-,* not) FRENCH TERMS: *savoir-faire* [to know (how) to do; ready knowledge of when and how to do or say it; tact] *savoir-vivre* [to know (how) to live; good breeding; manner] *idiot savant* [literally, skilled idiot; a person who is generally mentally defective but who displays unusual aptitude or brilliance in some special field, e.g., knowing the day of the week for any date in recorded history) LATIN TERM: *homo sapiens* (the thinking man) ENGLISH: sake, seek, seize LATIN PREFIXED ENGLISH ROOT: *dis-:* disseize, disseizee (disseisee), disseizin (disseisin), disseizor (disseisor) (*dis-,* apart, away) NB: *Dissipate,* from *dis-,* apart, away + *supare,* to throw, is not in this family. CROSS REFERENCE: *soph*
sagitt*	Latin *sagitta*	arrow (also, straight like an arrow)	SIMPLE ROOT: sagitta (the distance from the midpoint of an arc to the midpoint of its chord) sagittal (relating to the suture between the parietal bones of the skull), sagittalis sagittate (in *botany,* describing a leaf in the shape of an arrow; that is, elongated, triangular, and having the two basal lobes prolonged downward) CONSTELLATION: Sagittarius, a large southern constellation in the brightest part of the Milky Way, beyond which lies the center of our galaxy SIGN OF THE ZODIAC: Sagittarius, the ninth sign of the zodiac, which the sun enters about November 23 NO CROSS REFERENCE

Element	From	Meaning	Examples
sal*	Latin *sal* (IE: *sal*, salt)	salt, brine	SIMPLE ROOT: sala: salad, salada, salami, salariat, salary (from Roman soldiers being paid in cakes of salt) sale: salé (in reference to speech, biting, pungent; also coarse, indelicate) sali: salina (a salt marsh, spring, pond, or lake; a land area encrusted with salt) saline, salinize sals: salse, salsilla salt: saltern, saltine LEADING ROOT COMPOUND: fer: saliferous (*fer*, to bear) fy: salify (from *facere*, to make) meter: salimeter (*meter*, measure) UNBOUND COMPOUND: salt cellar BOUND COMPOUND: saltpeter DISGUISED ROOT: sassy (variant of *saucy*; impudent; jaunty) sauce (from *salsa*, feminine of *salsus*, salted), saucer saucy (**Synonyms**: impertinent, impudent, insolent) sausage (from *salsicius*, prepared by salting) silt (probably from Scandinavian *cylte*, salt marsh) souse (originally from Old High German *sulza*, brine) LATIN PHRASE: *cum grano salis* [(to be taken) with a grain of salt] PLACENAMES: Saline, Kansas Salinas, California Salton Sea, California NB: *Salsify*, from Late Latin *saxifrica*, rock friction, is not in this family. CROSS REFERENCE: *hal*
sal*** sault, sil, sult	Latin *salire* (IE: *sel*, to jump)	to leap	SIMPLE ROOT: sala: salacious (lecherous; erotically stimulating) sali: salient (in the *military*, the part of the battle line, trench, fort, etc. which projects farthest toward the enemy) {salience} salientian (a subclass of tailless amphibians, with a broad body and well-developed hind legs: it includes frogs, toads, and tree toads) sall: sally (a sudden rushing forth, as of troops, to attack besieging forces; any sudden start into activity; a quick witticism; bright retort; quip; also, an excursion or unusual side trip; jaunt) salt: saltant (see *sauté* under *Disguised Root*) saltarello (a lively Italian dance with a hopping, skipping step; music for this dance) saltate (**Synonyms**: jump, spring, vault), saltation, saltate, saltator, saltatorial, saltatory saltier (see *next word*), saltire (in *heraldry*, a bearing like a Saint Andrew's Cross, formed by a bend and a bend sinister crossing; also, *saltier*; originally, a cross-shaped stile to keep cattle from straying, but which people could jump over)

Element	From	Meaning	Examples
sal (cont'd)			PREFIXED ROOT:

sault:

as-: assault (**Synonyms**: attack, assail, beset) (*as-* assimilates *ad-*, to, toward)

somer-: somersault (literally, to leap over; a complete reversal of opinion, sympathies, etc.) (from *super-*, over)

sil:

de-: desilient (springing or bursting apart, as some plant capsules or pods) (from *dis-*, apart)

re-: (back, again)

resile (to bounce or spring back; rebound; specifically, to come back into shape or position after being pressed or stretched: said of elastic bodies)

resilience (the ability to bounce or spring back into shape), resilient (**Synonyms**: elastic, flexible, supple)

tran-: transilient (passing abruptly or leaping from one thing, condition, etc. to another; compare *desultory*) {transilience} (*trans-*, over, across)

sult:

de-: (from)

desultor (a vaulter, one who jumps or leaps from one horse to another in the Roman circus)

desultory (passing from one thing to another in an aimless way; **Synonyms**: random, haphazard, chance)

in-: insult (literally, to jump in, or on; **Synonyms**: offend, affront, outrage) (*in-*, in, on)

re-: (back, again)

result (**Synonyms**: 1) effect, consequence, issue; 2) follow, ensue, succeed)

resultant (following as a consequence; resulting from two or more forces or agents acting together; in *physics*, a force, velocity, etc. with an effect equal to that of two or more such forces, etc. acting together)

(s)ult:

ex-: (*ex-*, out)

exult (to rejoice exceedingly; be highly elated or jubilant)

exultance, exultancy, exultant (**Synonyms**: joyful, triumphant, jubilant), exultation

LEADING ROOT COMPOUND:

grad: saltigrade (having the feet or legs adpated for leaping: said of spiders) (*gradus*, step)

DISGUISED ROOT:

salmon (the leaping fish)

sauté (to fry quickly in a pan with a little fat) (from *saltant*)

PREFIXED DISGUISED ROOT:

as-: assail (see synonyms at *assault*, above) (*as-* assimilates *ad-*, to, toward)

DOUBLETS: saltant:sauté

ITALIAN DISH: saltimbocca (literally, jump into the mouth; thin slices of veal and ham flavored with sage, rolled, and sauteed in butter)

PLACENAME: Sault Ste. Marie, Michigan

NO CROSS REFERENCE

Element	From	Meaning	Examples
salu,*** salv, san	Latin *salus*: health, safety, greeting; *salvus*, whole (IE: *solo*, whole, well-preserved)	healthy, whole	SIMPLE ROOT: *salu*: salub: salubrious (wholesome; healthful) {salubrity} salut: salutary, salutation, salutatorian (the second-highest graduate, who greets or salutes the assembled guests), salutatory, salute, salutory *salv*: salv: salvage, salvation (rescue; in *theology*, spiritual rescue from the consequences of sin; redemption), salvatory, salve, salver, salvo, salvor *san*: sane (mentally healthy; of sound mind; reasonable, rational) sanic: sanicle (a plant originally believed to have medicinal value as an astringent) sanit: sanitarian, sanitarium, sanitary, sanitation, sanity PREFIXED ROOT: *salu*: *in-*: insalubrious (not salubrious; not healthful; unwholesome) (*in-*, not) *san*: *in-*: insane, insanity (not a scientific term; used in law to indicate any form or degree of mental derangement or unsoundness of mind, permanent or temporary, that makes a person incapable of what is regarded legally as normal, rational conduct or judgment; **Synonyms**: lunacy, dementia, psychosis) (*in-*, not) DISGUISED ROOT: safe (**Synonym**: secure), save, Savior sage (the herb, from its reputed healing powers; another *sage* is listed under *sap*) solemn (*sollus*, all, whole, entire + *annus*, year; from association with annual religious festivals) solicit (*sollus*, whole + *ciere*, to set in motion), solicitor, solicitous FRENCH: *à votre santé* (to your health: a toast in drinking) *sainfoin* (from Medieval Latin *sanum faenum*, wholesome hay, and formerly used as a medicinal herb: a plant, often used for fodder) SPANISH: *a vuestra salud* (to your health: a toast in drinking) CROSS REFERENCE: *hol, integ*
sanct***	Latin *sanctus* (may be from IE: *sak*, to sanctify, make a compact)	holy	SIMPLE ROOT: sancti: sanctimonious (**Synonyms**: devout, pious, religious) sanctimony (affected piety or righteousness; hypocrisy) sanction (**Synonyms**: approve, endorse, certify), sanctity sanctu: sanctuary (**Synonyms**: asylum, refuge, haven) sanctum (a sacred place; a study or private room where one is not to be disturbed) Sanctus (an acclamation beginning "Holy, holy, holy Lord" that immediately follows the Preface as of the Mass; a musical setting for this)

Element	From	Meaning	Examples
sanct (cont'd)			LEADING ROOT COMPOUND: fy: sanctify (from *facere*, to make, do) TRAILING ROOT COMPOUND: corpo: corposant (literally, holy body; same as St. Elmo's fire) (*corpus*, body) sacro: sacrosanct (see *Reciprocal Compound*, next entry) RECIPROCAL COMPOUND: sacrosanct (both roots mean the same; one intensifies the other; very sacred, holy, or inviolable) DISGUISED ROOT: saint SPANISH: *campo santo* (literally, holy field; a cemetery) CROSS REFERENCE: *hagi, hier, sacr*
sang**	Latin *sanguis*	blood	SIMPLE ROOT: sanguinaria (the plant, bloodroot), sanguinary, sanguine, sanguineous, sanguinity, sanguinolent PREFIXED ROOT: con-: consanguinity, consanguineous (literally, of the same blood; having the same ancestor) (from *com-*, with) LEADING ROOT COMPOUND: fer: sanguiferous (*ferre*, to bear) fic: sanguification (from *facere*, to make) FRENCH TERM: *sang de boeuf* (literally, blood of the ox; oxblood: a glaze used chiefly on porcelain wares) FRENCH EXPRESSION: *de sang froid* (literally, in cold blood; heartless; as a *noun*, sang-froid: cool self-possession or composure) SPANISH: *sangría* (literally, bleeding; a Spanish fruit and wine punch; sangaree) MOUNTAIN RANGE: Sangre de Cristo Mountains (in Colorado and New Mexico; literally, blood of Christ) CROSS REFERENCE: *hemo, emia*
sans-**	French; from Latin *sine*	without	WORDS AND PHRASES: *sans* *sans-culotte* (literally, without breeches; a revolutionary; a term of contempt applied by the aristocrats to the republicans of the poorly clad French Revolutionary army, who substituted pantaloons for knee breeches) *sans doute* (without a doubt) *sans égal* (without equal) *sans peur et sans reproche* (without fear and without reproach) FRENCH-ENGLISH PHRASE: *sans-serif* (*serif* from Dutch *schreef*, stroke, line, from the verb *schrijven*, to write; from Latin *scribere*, to write) BRAND NAME: Sanka (without caffeine, the *ka* being the phonetics of the first two letters in caffeine) PLACENAME: Sans Souci, South Carolina (without a care; or carefree) HISTORICAL PLACE: Sans Souci Castle, near Berlin, built by Frederic the Great CROSS REFERENCE: *a-, an-, sine-*
sap			See *sag* for *sapient*.

Element	From	Meaning	Examples
sapr*	Greek *sapros*	rotten, decayed	LEADING ROOT COMPOUND: *sapr*: em: sapremia (blood poisoning from putrefactive microorganisms) (from *hemo*, blood + *-ia*, diseased condition of) *sapro*: be: saprobe (an organism that derives its nourishment from nonliving or decaying organic matter) {saprobic} (*bio*, life) gen: saprogenic (also, *saprogeneous*; producing decay or putrefaction) (*gen*, producing) lit: saprolite (in *geology*, completely decomposed rock lying in its original site) (*lithos*, stone) pel: sapropel (*pel*, mud) phag: saprophagous (feeding on decaying organic matter) (*phag*, eat) phyt: saprophyte (a plant that lives on and derives its nourishment from dead or decaying organic matter) (*phyton*, plant) zo: saprozoic (*zoikos*, of animals) CROSS REFERENCE: *sep*
sarc**	Greek *sarx* (IE: *twerk*, to cut)	flesh	SIMPLE ROOT: sarcasm (literally, to tear flesh like dogs; to speak bitterly), sarcastic (**Synonyms:** caustic, ironic, satirical) PREFIXED ROOT: *ana-*: anasarca (generalized edema, or dropsy) (*ana-*, throughout) *ecto-*: ectosarc (the ectoplasm of one-celled animals) (*ecto-*, outside, external) *peri-*: perisarc (the tough, nonliving, outer skeleton layer of many hydroid colonies) (*peri-*, around) LEADING ROOT COMPOUND: *sarc*: oid: sarcoidosis (a chronic condition of unknown cause, characterized by the development of lesions similar to tubercles in the lungs, bones, skin, etc.) (*oid*, similar to + *osis*, condition of) oma: sarcoma (*oma*, tumor, mass) *sarco*: carp: sarcocarp (in *botany*, the fleshy part of a stone fruit, as the plum, peach; loosely, any fleshy fruit) (*carp*, fruit) logy: sarcology (the branch of medicine that deals with the soft tissues of the body) (*logy*, study of) phag: sarcophagus (among the ancient Greeks and Romans, a limestone coffin or tomb, often inscribed and elaborately ornamented: the limestone caused rapid disintegration of the contents; any stone coffin, especially one on display, as a monumental tomb, e.g., the Tomb of the Unknown Soldier in Arlington National Cemetery) (*phag*, eat) CROSS REFERENCE: *carni, creat*

> The most important element in a human being is his thought.
> The next is the manner in which he communicates his thought.
> Thomas A. Knott

Element	From	Meaning	Examples
sat***	Latin *satis*: enough (IE: *sa*, satisfied, sated)	to fill, complete	SIMPLE ROOT: sate (**Synonyms:** satiate, surfeit, cloy) satiate (see *synonyms* at *sate*, previous entry) satiety (the state of being satiated; surfeit) satire (originally, a composite of fruits and vegetables; a medley; now a literary work filled with vices, follies, stupidities, and abuses which are held up to ridicule, derision, and contempt; **Synonyms:** caricature, burlesque, parody) (from *satura lanx*, full dish) saturable, saturant saturate (**Synonyms:** soak, drench, steep), saturated, saturation PREFIXED ROOTS AND COMPOUNDS: *dis-*: dissatisfy (*dis-*, reversal) *in-*: insatiable, insatiate (not satisfied; never satisfied; insatiable) (*in-*, not) *super-*: supersaturate (to cause a chemical solution to be more highly concentrated than is normally possible under given conditions of temperature) (*super-*, beyond) LEADING ROOT COMPOUND: fact: satisfaction (from *facere*, to make) fy: satisfy (from *facere*, to make) TRAILING ROOT COMPOUND: poly: polyunsaturated (*poly*, many, much) ANGLO-SAXON: sad (sated, full; hence, having feelings associated with satiety) ANGLO- FRENCH: asset (*assetz*, as in legal phrase *aver assetz*, to have enough; from Vulgar Latin *ad satis*, sufficient) ITALIAN MUSIC TERMS: *assai* (very: used in indicating tempo) *adagio assai* (*adagio*, slowly; thus, very slowly) *allegro assai* (*allegro*, in rapid tempo; literally, very fast; faster than allegretto but slower than presto) CROSS REFERENCE: *plen*
sault			See *sal*, to leap, for *assault*.
saur**	Greek *sauros*	lizard	SIMPLE ROOT: sauria, saurian LEADING ROOT COMPOUND: gnath: saurognathous (*gnath*, jaw) phag: saurophagous (*phag*, eat) pod: sauropod (*pod*, foot) TRAILING ROOT COMPOUND: bronto: brontosaurus (a very large, herbivorous dinosaur of the Jurassic period) (*bronto*, thunder, loud, extended to mean large) dino: dinosaur (*dino*, terrible) ichthy: ichthyosaur (also, *ichthyosaurus*; an extinct fishlike marine reptile) (*ichthy*, fish) plesio: plesiosaurus (*plesio*, near) tyranno: tyrannosaur (*tyranno*, tyrant) PLACENAME: Dinosaur, Colorado NO CROSS REFERENCE
sav			See *sag* for *savant*, *savor*.

Element	From	Meaning	Examples
sax*	Latin *saxum* (IE: *sek*, to cut)	rock, stone (broken-off piece)	SIMPLE ROOT: saxatile LEADING ROOT COMPOUND: col: (from *colere*, to dwell) saxicola [a group of Old World passerine (sparrow-type) birds, such as the whinchat, stonechat] saxicolous (in *biology* and *ecology*, inhabiting or growing among rocks) frag: saxifrage (a plant named from its growing in rock crevices) (from *frangere*, to break) CROSS REFERENCE: *lapid, lith, petr*
scal*	Latin *scalae*: stairs, ladder (IE: *skend*, to leap)	ladder	SIMPLE ROOT: scalar, scalade, scale PREFIXED ROOT: e-: escalade (the act of scaling or climbing the walls of a fortified place by ladders), escalate, escalator (*e-* elides *ex-*, out) LEADING ROOT COMPOUND: form: scalariform (resembling a ladder: having traverse bars or markings like the rounds of a ladder, e.g., *scalariform* cells of plants) CROSS REFERENCE: *scend*
scan,** scend	Latin *scandere* (IE: *skend*, to leap)	to climb	SIMPLE ROOT: scan (in *poetry*, to analyze the rising and falling rhythm in verses) scandal (closely related to previous family; thus, a ladder, and therefore a cause for stumbling; a temptation), scandalize, scandalous scandent (in *botany*, climbing by attaching itself, as a vine), scansion, scansorial scantling PREFIXED ROOT: a-: ascend, ascendancy (or *ascendency*), ascendant (or *ascendent*), ascender, ascension, ascent (from *ad-*, to, toward) de-: descend, descendant (noun), descendent (adjective), descender, descendible, descent (*de-*, down) tran-: transcend (**Synonyms**: excel, surpass, outdo), transcendent, transcendental, transcendentalism (*trans-*, across) DOUBLE PREFIXED ROOT: condescend, condescending (*con-*, with, together + *de-*, down) ISLAND: Ascension (so named because discovered on Ascension Day (1501); a small island in the South Atlantic; part of the British territory of St. Helena) CELEBRATION: Ascension Day (the fortieth day after Easter, celebrating the Ascension) PLACENAME: Ascension Parish, Louisiana (only the state of Louisiana has parishes instead of counties; from its French heritage) CROSS REFERENCE: *scal*
sch*	Greek schema (IE: *segh*, to hold fast)	form, appearance, plan	SIMPLE ROOT: schema (an outline, diagram, plan, or preliminary draft) schematic, schematism, schematize scheme (**Synonyms**: plan, design, project) scheming (given to forming schemes or plots; crafty, tricky, deceitful, etc.) CROSS REFERENCE: *form, morph, plas*

Element	From	Meaning	Examples
schis,** schiz	Greek *schizein* (IE: *skei*, to cut)	to split, cleave divide (see note at *scind*)	SIMPLE ROOT: schism, schismatic, schist LEADING ROOT COMPOUND: *schis*: oid: schizoid (similar to schizophrenia) (*oid*, similar to) ont: schizont (a large cell in many sporozoans that multiplies by schizogony, which see, below) (*onto*, organism) *schisto*: cephal: schistocephalus (*cephal*, head) cerca: schistocerca (*cerca*, tail) som: schistosome (*soma*, body) *schiz*: carp: schizocarp (in *botany*, a dry fruit, as of the maple, that splits at maturity into two or more one-seeded carpels which remain closed) (*carp*, fruit) gen: schizogenesis (in *biology*, reproduction by fission) (*gen*, producing) gon: schizogony (*gon*, sexual reproduction) myc: (fungus) schizomycete schizomycosis (*osis*, condition of) phren: schizophrenia, schizophrenic (*phren*, mind) phyt: schizophyte (*phyte*, plant) pod: schizopod (*pod*, foot) thym: schizothymia (*thym*, spirit) DISGUISED ROOT: schedule (originally, a strip of papyrus) shingle (roof covering) [*Shingles*, the nontechnical name for *herpes zoster*, is derived from *cingere*, to gird.] SPANISH: cedula (in Spanish *cédula*; any certificate or document in Spanish-speaking countries) (from *schedule*) CROSS REFERENCE: *fid* (as in *bifid*), *fiss*
scho*	Greek *schole* (IE: *segh*, to hold fast)	leisure	ROOT NOTE: The Greeks used their *leisure* time to improve their minds; the word evolved to mean the *place* where they improved their minds. SIMPLE ROOT: scholar (**Synonyms:** pupil, student) scholastic, scholasticate (a school for seminarians, especially, Jesuit seminarians), scholasticism, scholiast, scholium school (**Synonyms:** teach, instruct, educate) GERMAN: *Schule* NO CROSS REFERENCE
sci**	Latin *scire* (IE: *skei*, to cut)	to know (see note ate *scind*)	SIMPLE ROOT: scie: science, sciential, scientism {scientistic}, scientist scio: sciolism (superficial knowledge or learning) {sciolist, sciolistic}, scious PREFIXED ROOT: *ad*-: adscititious (added from an external source; supplemental) (*ad*-, to, toward) *con*-: conscience (replaced Middle English *inwit*, knowledge within), conscientious, conscious (**Synonyms:** aware, cognizant, sensible) (*con*-, with, together) *ne*-: nescient (lacking knowledge; ignorant) (*ne*-, not)

Element	From	Meaning	Examples
sci (cont'd)			*pre-*: prescience (foreknowledge, foresight) {prescient} (*pre-*, before)
			LEADING ROOT COMPOUND:
			fic: scientific (from *facere*, to make)
			TRAILING ROOT COMPOUND:
			omni: omniscient (all-knowing; one of the attributes of God) (*omni*, all)
			plebis: plebiscite (an expression of the people's will by direct ballot on a political issue) (*plebe*, common people)
			DISGUISED ROOT: nice (*ne-*, not + *scire*)
			LATIN CONTRACTION: *scilicit* (contraction of *scire licit*, it is permitted to know; namely; to wit; that is to say)
			LATIN LAW PHRASE: *scire facias* (that you cause to know; a writ, founded on a record, requiring the person against whom it is issued to appear and show cause why the record should not be enforced or annulled)
			CROSS REFERENCE: *cogn, gnos*
scind,** sciss	Latin *scindere* (IE: *skei*, to cut)	to cut, split	ROOT NOTE: The Indo-European base of this root also yields Latin *scindere*, and Greek *skhizein*, the latter yielding *schizo*, as in *schizophrenia* (see *schis* family).
			SIMPLE ROOT: scissile (capable of being cut or split easily), scissors (may also be from *cis*, as in *excise*, the *verb*, to cut out), scission (the act of cutting or splitting)
			PREFIXED ROOT:
			scind:
			ex-: exscind (to cut out; excise; extirpate) (*ex-*, out)
			pre-: prescind (literally, to cut off in front; as a *transitive* verb, to separate or divide in thought; consider individually; as an *intransitive* verb, to withdraw one's attention from) (*pre-*, in front)
			re-: rescind (**Synonyms**: abolish, annul, abrogate) (*re-*, back)
			sciss:
			ab-: abscissa (from *abscissa linea*, a line cut off; in *geometry*, the line or part of a line drawn horizontally on a graph; distinguished from *ordinate*) (*ab-*, off)
			circum-: circumscissile (in *botany*, splitting or opening along a transverse circular line, as *a circumscissile seed capsule*) (*circum-*, around)
			CROSS REFERENCE: *cis, tom*
scler*	Greek *skleros* (IE: *(s)kel*, to dry out)	hard	SIMPLE ROOT:
			sclera (the outer, tough, white, fibrous membrane covering all of the eyeball except the area covered by the cornea)
			sclerite (any of the hard plates forming the shell-like covering of arthropods)
			sclerotic (hard; sclerosed; of, characterized by, or having sclerosis)
			sclerotium {sclerotial}
			LEADING ROOT COMPOUND:
			scler:
			en: sclerenchyma (in *botany*, the plant tissue of uniformly thick-walled, dead cells, as in a stem, the shell of a nut, etc.)
			itis: scleritis (*itis*, inflammation; inflammation of the sclera) (*enchyma*, infusion; *en-*, in + *chyma*, fluid)

Element	From	Meaning	Examples
scler (cont'd)			oid: scleroid (in *biology*, hard or hardened; indurated) (*oid*, similar to)
			oma: scleroma (hardening of body tissues; tumorlike induration) (*oma*, mass)
			osis: sclerosis (*osis*, condition of)
			sclero:
			derm: scleroderma (a chronic disease in which the skin becomes hard and rigid), sclerodermatous (in *zoology*, covered with a hard outer tissue, as of horny scales or plates) (*derm*, skin)
			meter: sclerometer (an instrument for measuring the relative hardness of a substance by determining the pressure needed to cause a diamond point to scratch its polished surface)
			EMBEDDED ROOT COMPOUND: arteriosclerosis
			DISGUISED ROOT:
			shallow (**Synonyms:** superficial, cursory)
			shoal (**Synonyms:** bank, reef, bar)
			INTERDISCIPLINARY: sclerosis (in *botany*, a hardening of the cell wall of a plant, usually by an increase in lignin; in *medicine*, an abnormal hardening of body tissues or parts, especially of the nervous system or the walls of arteries; disease characterized by such hardening)
			CROSS REFERENCE: *dur, fort, rob, sthen*
scop, * scept, skept**	Greek *skopein*: to view (IE: *spek*, to peer, look carefully)	to see, watch	SIMPLE ROOT: scope
			PREFIXED ROOT:
			endo-: endoscope (an instrument for examining the inside of a hollow organ, as the bladder or rectum) (*endo*-, within)
			epi-: episcopal (*epi*-, upon)
			peri-: periscope (*peri*-, around)
			LEADING ROOT COMPOUND:
			phil: scopophilia (sexual pleasure derived from visual sources such as nudity and obscene pictures) (*phila*, love of)
			TRAILING ROOT COMPOUND:
			scope: (designating a device for viewing with the eye or examining in any way):
			cryoscope (cold)
			horoscope [literally, the hour (of one's birth)]
			kaleidoscope (literally, beautiful shapes)
			microscope (small things)
			oscilloscope (electrical waves on a fluorescent screen)
			stethoscope (hearing instrument for auscultation)
			telescope (things far away)
			scopic: (*adjective-forming suffix*):
			acroscopic (in *botany*, facing or on the side toward the apex)
			basiscopic (in *botany*, facing or on the side toward the base, e.g., the sori of most ferns are basiscopic)
			microscopic (describing that which is very small)
			nooscopic (of or relating to the examination of the mind) (from *nous*, mind)
			orthoscopic (giving an image in correct and normal proportions) (*ortho*, straight)
			telescopic (suitable for magnifying distant objects) (*tele*, afar)

Element	From	Meaning	Examples
scop (cont'd)			*scopy* (a seeing; an examination) bio: bioscopy (*bio*, life) cryo: cryoscopy (*cryo*, cold) micro: microscopy (*micro*, small) tele: telescopy (*tele*, afar) DISGUISED ROOT: skeptic, skeptical, skepticism (**Synonyms:** uncertainty, dubiety, doubt) bishop (a high-ranking Christian clergyman having authority over other clergy) (from *epi*, upon + *skopos*, look) CROSS REFERENCE: *op, -orama, spec, vid/vis*
scrib, *** **script**	Latin *scribere* (IE: *(s)ker*, to cut, incise)	to write	SIMPLE ROOT: *scrib*: scribe *script*: script, scription, scriptor, scriptory, scriptorial, scriptorium, scripture, scripturalism, scripturalist, scripturient PREFIXED ROOT: *scrib*: a-: ascribe (**Synonyms:** attribute, impute, assign) (from *ad*-, to, toward) *circum*-: circumscribe (**Synonyms:** bound, restrict, confine) (*circum*-, around) *de*-: describe (literally, to copy down) (*de*-, down) *in*-: inscribe (in *geometry*, to draw a figure inside another figure so that their boundaries touch at as many points as possible) (*in*-, in) *pre*-: prescribe (originally, to write beforehand) (*pre*-, before) *pro*-: proscribe (to banish; exile; to deprive of the protection of the law; in ancient Rome, to publish the name of a person condemned to death, banishment, etc.) (*pro*-, before, in front of) *sub*-: subscribe (originally, to sign one's name at the end of a document, etc.) (*sub*-, under) *super*-: superscribe (*super*-, beyond) *tran*-: transcribe (*trans*-, across, over) *script*: *ad*-: adscript (written after), adscription, adscriptitious (*ad*-, to) *circum*-: circumscript (*circum*-, around) *con*-: conscript (originally, to write together; enter into a list; enroll; one who is compulsorily enrolled for service in the armed forces; drafted; as a *verb*, to enroll compulsorily), conscription (*con*-, with, together) *de*-: description, descriptive (*de*-, down) *in*-: inscript, inscription (*in*-, in, on) *post*-: postscript (abbreviated *P.S.*), postscriptum (*post*-, after) *pre*-: prescript, prescriptible, prescription, prescriptive (in *law*, acquired by or based upon uninterrupted possession), prescriptorial (*pre*-, before) *pro*-: proscript {proscription} (*pro*-, before) *re*-: rescript (*re*-, again, back) *sub*-: subscription (*sub*-, under) *super*-: superscript (*super*-, above, over)

Element	From	Meaning	Examples
scrib (cont'd)			tran-: transcript, transcription (*trans-*, across) DOUBLE PREFIXED ROOT: non<u>de</u>script (hard to classify or describe) (*non-*, not + *de-*, down) TRAILING ROOT COMPOUND: manu: manuscript (originally, that which was written by hand) (*manu*, hand) DISGUISED ROOT: scarify, scribble, scrive, scrivener, serif, shear FRENCH: *escritoire* (a writing table; a secretary; Modern French is *écritoire*) FRENCH-ENGLISH: sans-serif (see listing under *sans*) ENGLISH FORMS: shrift (originally, confession to and absolution by a priest) short shrift (originally, a brief time granted a condemned person for religious confession and absolution before his/her execution; now, very little care or attention, as from lack of patience or sympathy) shrive (literally, to prescribe penance) Shrovetide (a time of penance--the three days, Shrove Sunday, Shrove Monday, Shrove Tuesday--preceding Ash Wednesday, the beginning of Lent) CROSS REFERENCE: *gram, graph*
se-,*** sed-	Latin (IE: *se,* *swe,* apart, lone)	apart, away	PREFIXED ROOT: *se-*: ced: secede (*cedere*, to go) cern: secern (to discriminate, or distinguish, as *to secern good from evil*) (*cernere*, to separate) cess: secession {secessionism} (from *secede*) clud: seclude (to keep away from others), secluded, seclusion (**Synonyms:** solitude, isolation), seclusive (from *claudere*, to shut) cret: (from *cernere*, to separate) secret (**Synonyms:** stealthy, covert, clandestine) secretary (originally, a confidential officer), secretariat secrete (two meanings; one is a back-formation from *secretion*; another, to conceal in a hiding place; cache), secretion cur: secure (see *Doublets* below), security (*cura*, care) duc: seduce (**Synonyms:** lure, entice, inveigle) (*ducere*, to lead) dul: sedulity, sedulous (**Synonyms:** busy, diligent, assiduous) (from *dolus*, trickery, guile) greg: segregate, segregated, segregation (*greg*, flock) lect: select, selection (**Synonyms:** choice, option, alternative) (from *legere*, to choose) par: separate (see *Doublets* below; **Synonyms:** divide, part, sever), separation, separatist, separative (*parare*, to make ready, arrange) *sed-*: it: sedition (**Synonym:** treason) (from *ire*, to go) DOUBLETS: sever:separate; sure:secure CROSS REFERENCE: *a-, ab-, apo-, cata-, de-, dis, e-/ec-/ ex-, for*

614

Element	From	Meaning	Examples
search			See *circum-* for *search, research.*
seb*	Latin *sebum* (IE: *seib*, to trickle, run out)	tallow (extended to mean fat, fatty, oily, or waxy material)	SIMPLE ROOT: sebaceous, sebum LEADING ROOT COMPOUND: *sebi*: fer: sebiferous (in *biology*, secreting a fatty or waxlike substance; sebaceous) (*ferre*, to bear) *sebo*: rhe: seborrhea (an excessive discharge from the sebaceous glands resulting in abnormally oily skin) (*rrh*, flow) DISGUISED ROOT: soap CROSS REFERENCE: *adipo, lipo*
sec			See *sequ* for *second.*
sec,* sic	Latin *siccus* (IE: *seikw*, to drip, pour out)	dry	SIMPLE ROOT: *sec*: secco (the art or an example of painting on dry plaster; compare *fresco*, though not listed) *sic*: siccative (a substance added to paints and some medicines to promote drying) PREFIXED ROOT: *de-*: desiccate {desiccation, desiccant} (*de-*, intensive) *ex-*: exsiccate (to dry up) (*ex-*, out) DISGUISED ROOT: sack (a dry wine) CROSS REFERENCE: *xero*
sect,*** seg	Latin *secare* (IE: *sek*, to cut)	to cut	SIMPLE ROOT: *sec*: secant (cutting, intersecting; in *geometry*, any straight line intersecting a curve at two or more points) *sect*: sectile (capable of being cut), section (**Synonyms:** part, portion, division; see *Placename* below), sectional, sectionalism, sector *seg*: segment (**Synonyms:** part, portion, piece), segmental, segmentary, segmentate PREFIXED ROOT: *dis-*: dissect (*dis-*, apart, away) *ex-*: exsect (to cut out) (*ex-*, out) *in-*: insect (literally, cut in; from its segmented bodies), insectarium (also, *insectary*), insectile (also, *insectival*) (*in-*, in) *inter-*: intersection (*inter-*, between) *re-*: resect, resection (*re-*, back, again) *sub-*: subsection (*sub-*, under) *tran-*: transect (*trans-*, across) TRAILING ROOT COMPOUND: bi: bisect (to cut into two; in *geometry*, to cut into two *equal* parts) (*bi*, two) tri: trisect (*tri*, three) DISGUISED ROOT: notch (from *an otch*, from Old French *oschier*, to notch; from Latin *absecare*, to cut off; *ab-*, off) risk (from *resecare*, to cut off; see *Doublets* below) FRENCH: sécateurs (chiefly British; shears used for pruning) risqué (from *risk*; see *Doublets* below) ENGLISH COGNATES: sail (canvas cut to catch or deflect the wind) saw (the noun)

Element	From	Meaning	Examples
sect (cont'd)			DOUBLETS: risk:risqué PLACENAME: Section, Alabama INTERDISCIPLINARY: resection (in *surgery*, the removal of part of an organ, bone, etc.; in *surveying*, a method of determining the location of a point by taking observations from it to points of known location) CROSS REFERENCE: *cise, scis, sect, tom*
secut			See *sequ* for *consecutive*.
sed-			See *se-* for *sedition*.
sed*	Latin *sedare*, to settle (IE: *sed*, to sit)	to calm	SIMPLE ROOT: sedate (**Synonyms**: serious, sober, grave) sedation (the act or process of lessening excitement, nervousness, or irritation) sedative (tending to soothe or quiet; in *medicine*, having the property of lessening excitement, nervousness, or irritation) CROSS REFERENCE: *pac/pax*
sed,*** sid, sess	Latin *sedere* (IE: *sed*, to sit)	to sit	SIMPLE ROOT: sedan (originally "sedan chair," an enclosed chair, with glass windows, carried on poles by two men, in use in Europe in the 17th and 18th centuries) *sed*: sede: sedent (sitting: said especially of a statue, as that of Lincoln in the Lincoln Memorial, Washington, D.C.) sedentary (characterized by or requiring much sitting; remaining in one area; not migratory; in *zoology*, attached to a surface and not free-moving, as a barnacle) sedi: sedilia (a set of seats, usually three, traditionally along the south side of a church, for the use of officiating clergy), sediment *sess*: sessile (of sitting, low: said of plants), session PREFIXED ROOT: *sed:* *super-*: supersede {surcease} (*super-*, beyond) *sess*: *as-*: assess (originally, to sit beside, assisting in the office of a judge; to set an estimated value on property for taxation), assessment, assessor (*as-* assimilates *ad-*, to, toward) *in-*: insessorial (adapted for perching: said of certain birds) (*in-*, in) *ob-*: obsess (to haunt or trouble in mind, especially to an abnormal degree), obsession, obsessive (*ob-*, against) *super-*: supersession (*super-*, above, beyond) *sid(e)*: *as-*: assident, assiduity, assiduous (**Synonyms**: industrious, diligent, sedulous) (*as-* assimilates *ad-*, to, toward) *dis-*: dissidence, dissident (*dis-*, apart, away) *in-*: insidiate, insidious (characterized by treachery or slyness; crafty, wily) (*in-*, in) *pre-*: preside, president, presidential, presidium (*pre-*, before) *re-*: reside, residence, resident, residential, residual, residue, residuum (**Synonyms**: remainder, remnant, balance) (*re-*, back, again)

616

Element	From	Meaning	Examples
sed (cont'd)			*sub*-: (under) subside (to sink or fall to the bottom; settle, as sediment; **Synonyms**: wane, abate, ebb) {subsidence}, subsidiary subsidy (originally, auxiliary or reserve troops), subsidize, subsidization TRAILING ROOT COMPOUND: pos: possess (literally, to sit as master), possessed, possession, possessive (from *posse*, to be able) PREFIXED TRAILING ROOT COMPOUND: *pre*-: (before) prepossess (originally, to take or occupy beforehand or before another; to prejudice or bias, especially in a favorable manner) prepossessing (that which prepossesses, or impresses favorably; pleasing; attractive) *re*-: repossess (*re*-, again) DISGUISED ROOT: séance (literally, a sitting; from French *seoir*; a meeting or session; now specifically, a meeting at which spiritualists seek or profess to communicate with the spirits of the dead) see (the official *seat*, or center of authority, of a bishop) settle (noun: a long wooden bench with a back, armrests, and sometimes a chest beneath the seat) settle (verb: **Synonyms**: decide, determine, settle) sewer (literally, to cause to sit; a medieval servant of high rank in charge of serving meals and seating guests) siege (from Old French *siege*, an aphetic of *assiege*; from Vulgar Latin *absedium*, for Latin *obsidium*; from *ob*-, against + *sedere*; thus to sit before; blockade, ambush) size (one meaning) sizar (a student receiving a scholarship allowance at Trinity College, Dublin, or at Cambridge; from *assize*, next entry) PREFIXED DISGUISED ROOT: *as*-: assize (*as*- assimilates *ad*-, to, toward) *be*-: besiege (literally, to sit before; to hem in with armed forces, especially for a sustained attack; to close in on; crowd around; to overwhelm, harass, or beset; as *besieged with debts*; *besieged with inquiries*) (Anglo-Saxon *be*-, around) SPANISH: presidio (literally, to sit in front of; thus, protect, as that of a garrison) RUSSIAN: *prezidium* (from which *presidium* is directly derived, but originally from Latin *praesidium*) ONE-WORD LATIN SENTENCE: supersedeas (you shall desist: a legal document issued to halt or delay the action of some process of law) ENGLISH COGNATES: nest (IE *ni*-, down + *sed*; literally, a place to sit down) saddle (literally, a place to sit) seat, sit soot (that which *settles*) SANSKRIT COGNATE COMPOUND: *Upanishad* [literally, secret session; any of a group of philosophical treatises contributing to the theology of ancient Hinduism, elaborating on the earlier *Vedas* (see *vid*)]

Element	From	Meaning	Examples
sed (cont'd)			WELSH COGNATE COMPOUND: eisteddfod (plural, *eisteddfods*, or *eisteddfodau*; literally, session, sitting; an annual assembly of Welsh poets and musicians, and is an ancient custom revived in the 19th century) INTERDISCIPLINARY: sessile (in *botany*, stalkless and attached directly to the base, as sessile leaves; in *zoology*, permanently attached; not free-moving) CROSS REFERENCE: *hedr*
seism*	Greek *seiein* (IE: *twei*, to excite, shake, shock)	to shake	SIMPLE ROOT: seism, seismic, seismism LEADING ROOT COMPOUND: graph: seismograph (*graph*, write) logy: seismology (*logy*, study of) meter: seismometer (a seismograph, especially one that records actual earth movements) (*meter*, measure) scop: seismoscope (an instrument indicating only the occurrence and time of earthquakes) (*scope*, look, view) CROSS REFERENCE: *cuss*
sem*	Greek *semainein*: to show (IE: *dhya*, to see, behold)	sign, symbol	SIMPLE ROOT: sema: semantic [pertaining to meaning (of signs, symbols), especially in language], semantics sematic (in *zoology*, serving as a sign of danger, as the coloration of some poisonous snakes) semi: semiotic, semiotics (in *philosophy*, the general theory of signs and symbols) PREFIXED ROOT: apo-: aposematic (serving to warn off potential attackers, as the coloration of some poisonous snakes) (*apo-*, away) LEADING ROOT COMPOUND: *sema*: phor: semaphore (any apparatus for signaling, as by an arrangement of lights, flags, and mechanical arms on railroads) (*phore*, bear) *semio*: logy: semiology (also, *semeiology*: the art or study of signs) COALESCED WORD: sememe (*semantic* + morph*eme*) CROSS REFERENCE: *sign*
sembl			See *simil* for *assemble, ensemble*.
semi***	Latin *semi* (IE: *semi*, half)	half	LEADING ROOT COMPOUND: colon: semicolon [(;) which is half a colon (:)] con: semiconductor (*con-* prefixes *duct*) dia: semidiameter (in *astronomy, half* the angular diameter of a heavenly body with a visible disk, as the moon) (*dia-* prefixes *meter*) diurn: semidiurnal (lasting only a half day; coming twice a day, as tides) (*diurnis*, day) doubl: semidouble (in *botany*, having more than the normal number of petals, ray flowers, etc., but not enough to completely conceal the stamens and pistils) liter: semiliterate (knowing how to read and write a little or knowing only how to read) (*littera*, letter) lun: semilunar (shaped like a half-moon) (*lun*, moon)

Element	From	Meaning	Examples
semi (cont'd)			ovi: semioviparous (producing living young whose natal development is incomplete, as marsupials) (*ovi*, egg + *parous*, the bearing of young) palm: semipalmate (with only a partial webbing of the anterior toes, as in some shore birds) (from IE *pele*, broad, flat) vowel: semivowel (a vowel-like sound occurring in consonantal positions in the same syllable with a true vowel, characterized by brief duration and rapid change from one position of articulation to another: the English glides *w* and *y*, as in *wall* and *yoke*, are semivowels) VARIANT MEANING: *sesqui* (one and a half), as in *sesquicentennial, sesquipedelian* CROSS REFERENCE: *hemi, demi, med, meso*
semin,* semen	Latin *semen* (IE: *se(i)* to cast, let fall; yields English seed)	seed, semen	SIMPLE ROOT: semen, seminal, seminar, seminary (originally, a seed plot or a nursery; later, a school where seeds of knowledge and truth were implanted; now, usually refers to a specialized postgraduate school for ministers, priests, rabbis), semination PREFIXED ROOT: *dis-*: disseminate (literally, to scatter seed; to scatter far and wide; spread abroad, as if by sowing) (*dis-*, apart, away) *in-*: insemination (as in *artificial insemination*) (*in-*, in) LEADING ROOT COMPOUND: fer: seminiferous (bearing seeds) (*ferre*, to bear) vor: seminivorous (eating seeds) (*vorare*, to eat) FRENCH: *semé* (in *heraldry*, having a design of many small figures; dotted, as with stars, or seeds) DISGUISED ROOT: season, seasoning CROSS REFERENCE: *sperm, spor*
semper**	Latin *semper*	always, ever	LEADING ROOT COMPOUND: vir: sempervirent (evergreen) (*virescere*, to grow green) viv: sempervivum (literally, ever-living) (*vivere*, to live) MESHED LEADING ROOT COMPOUND: sempiternal [(*semper* + *eternal*): everlasting; perpetual] MOTTO OF THE U.S. MARINE CORPS: *Semper fidelis* (always faithful) MOTTO OF THE U.S. COAST GUARD: *Semper paratus* (always prepared) MOTTO OF THE STATE OF VIRGINIA: *Sic semper tyrannis* (Thus always to tyrants) MOTTO OF THE STATE OF WEST VIRGINIA: *Montani semper liberi* (Mountaineers always free) NO CROSS REFERENCE
sen			See *sex* for *senary*.
sen***	Latin *senex* (IE: *seno*, old)	old, elder	SIMPLE ROOT: sena: senate (the house of the elders in the Roman government), senator sene: senectitude, senescent (growing old; aging) {senescence} seni: senile, senility, senior (see *Doublets* below), seniority DISGUISED ROOT: sir (see *Doublets* below), sire surly (from *sirly*, lordly, masterful; churlishy rude or bad-tempered; unfriendly or hostile; dark or dismal; menacing)

Element	From	Meaning	Examples
sen (cont'd)			DOUBLETS: sir:senior FRANKISH LEADING ROOT COMPOUND: chal: seneschal (a steward or major-domo in the household of a medieval noble) (*sini*, old + *skalk*, servant) FRENCH: *seignior, monseigneur, monsieur, seigneur* SPANISH: *señor, señora, señorita* IRISH COGNATE: sean, shanty CROSS REFERENCE: *geri*
sens,*** **sent**	Latin *sentire* (IE: *sent*, to go, find out, discover; yields English send)	feel, perceive	SIMPLE ROOT: sense (**Synonyms:** meaning, significance, acceptation) *sens:* sensa: sensate (perceived by the senses), sensation, sensational, sensatory sensi: sensibility, sensible (**Synonyms: 1**) aware, conscious, cognizant; **2**) material, physical, corporeal; **3**) perceptible, palpable, tangible; **4**) rational, reasonable), sensitive, sensitivity, sensitize senso: sensor, sensorium (the supposed seat of physical *sensation* in the gray matter of the brain), sensory sensu: sensual (**Synonyms: 1**) carnal, fleshly, animal; **2**) see other synonyms at *sensuous*), sensualism, sensuality sensuous (**Synonyms:** sensual, voluptuous, luxurious) *sent:* sente: sentence (in *grammar*, a word or group of syntactically related words that states, asks, commands, or exclaims something), sententious (expressing much in few words) senti: sentience, sentient, sentiment (**Synonyms: 1**) feeling, emotion, passion; **2**) opinion, belief, view), sentimental, sentinel (a *sentry*, next entry) sentr: sentry (a *sentinel*, previous entry) PREFIXED ROOT: *sens:* con-: consensual, consensus (opinion held by all or most; general agreement, especially in opinion) (*con-*, with, together) dis-: dissension (**Synonyms:** discord, strife, contention), dissent, dissenter, dissentient (*dis-*, apart, away) non-: nonsense {nonsensical} (*non-*, not) *sent:* as-: assent (**Synonyms:** consent, agree, concur), assentation, assenter (*as-* assimilates *ad-*, to, toward) con-: consent (**Synonyms:** assent, agree, concur), consentaneous, consentment (from *com-*, with, together) pre-: presentiment (*presentment*, however, is listed under *present*; see *NB*) (*pre-*, before) re-: resent (to feel or show displeasure and hurt or indignation at some act, remark, etc. or toward a person from a sense of being injured or offended), resentment (**Synonyms:** offense, umbrage, pique) (*re-*, intensive) LEADING ROOT COMPOUND: *sensito:* meter: sensitometer (*sensitivity* + *meter*, measure)

Element	From	Meaning	Examples
sens (cont'd)			*sensori*: motor: **sensorimotor** (from *movere*, to move) DISGUISED ROOT: scent (**Synonyms**: perfume, fragrance, bouquet, redolence) INTERDISCIPLINARY: **sensorimotor** (in *physiology*, of, pertaining to, or concerned with both the sensory and motor impulses of an organism; in *psychology*, of or pertaining to motor impulses initiated by sensory stimulation) NB: *Absent* and *present* are not in this family; see *esse*. CROSS REFERENCE: *aesth, path*
sep*	Greek *sepein*: to make putrid	to rot	SIMPLE ROOT: seps: sepsis (a poisoned state caused by the absorption of pathogenic microorganisms and their products into the bloodstream) sept: septic (causing, or resulting from, sepsis or putrefaction) PREFIXED ROOT: *anti-*: antisepsis, antiseptic (*anti-*, against) LEADING ROOT COMPOUND: emia: septicemia (blood poisoning) (*em*, short for *hemo*, blood; *-emia*, diseased condition of the blood) NB: The following words, though spelled similarly and which have related meanings, are not in this family: *sepulcher, sepulture* (see *sepul*). CROSS REFERENCE: *sapr, sepul*
sep(t)**	Latin *septum* (IE: *saip*, hedge fence)	partition, wall	SIMPLE ROOT: septa: septa (plural of *septum*), septal (of or forming a septum or septa), septarium, septate (having or divided by a septum or septa) septu: septula, septum (in *biology*, a part that separates two cavities or two masses of tissue, as in the nose, a fruit, etc.; the plural of *septum* is *septums* or *septa*) PREFIXED ROOT: *dis-*: dissepiment (in *biology*, a separating membrane or partition, as that between adjacent carpels of a compound ovary) (*dis-*, from) *tran-*: transept (the part of of a cross-shaped church at right angles to the long, main section, or nave) (*trans-*, across) LEADING ROOT COMPOUND: cid: septicidal (in *botany*, splitting along or through the septa or dissepiments in dehiscence: said of a seed capsule) frag: septifragal (in *botany*, opening, or dehiscing, by the breaking away of the outer walls of the carpels from the partitions) (from *frangere*, to break) CROSS REFERENCE: *mer, mur, part*
sept*	Latin *septem* (IE: *septm*, seven)	seven	SIMPLE ROOT: septem: September (the seventh month in the Roman calendar) septen: septenarius (a Greek or Latin verse containing seven feet), septenary (of or pertaining to the number seven; septennial; a group of set of seven; a period of seven years) septet: septet (a group of seven persons or things; in *music*, a composition for seven voices or seven instruments; the seven performers of this)

Element	From	Meaning	Examples
sept (cont'd)			septu: Septuagint [a Greek translation of the Old Testament (from Hebrew) in the third century B.C. (from *septuaginta*, seventy, "the Seventy," designation of 70 or 72 scholars who, according to an unhistorical tradition, completed the translation in 72 days on the island of Pharos)] LEADING ROOT COMPOUND: *sept*: enn: septennial (from *annus*, year) *septi*: later: septilateral (having seven sides) (*latus*, side) *septu*: ple: septuple (from *plicare*, to fold) plic: septuplicate (*plicare*, to fold) *septua*: gen: septuagenarian, Septuagesima (the third Sunday before Lent; from the 70 days extending from the third Sunday before Lent to the Saturday after Easter) CROSS REFERENCE: *hept*
sepul*	Latin *sepelire* (IE: *sep*, to honor)	to bury	NOTE: Root is a combination of *se-*, away + *pola*, shovel, that which was used for burying. SIMPLE ROOT: sepulcher (a vault for burial; grave; tomb; in the Roman Catholic Church, a small, sealed cavity, holding martyrs' relics; as a *verb*, to bury) sepulchral (of sepulchers, burial, etc.; suggestive of the grave or burial; dismal; gloomy; deep and melancholy: said of sound) sepulture (burial; interment) CROSS REFERENCE: *taph*
sequ,*** sec	Latin *sequi* (IE: *sekw*, to follow)	to follow	SIMPLE ROOT: *sec*: seco: second [the measurement of time or unit of measure, from (*pars minuta*) *secunda*, second (small part)], secondary sect: sect, sectarian, sectarianism, sectary secu: secund, secundines (same as *afterbirth*) *seq*: sequa: sequacious (tending to follow any leader; lacking individuality, as in thought; dependent; servile; compliant) sequel: sequel, sequela (in *medicine*, a diseased condition following, and usually resulting from, a previous disease) sequen: sequence (**Synonyms**: series, succession, progression), sequent, sequential seques: sequester (to set off or apart; separate; as *to sequester a jury*), sequestrant, sequestrate, sequestration, sequestrum (in *medicine*, a piece of dead bone which has become separated from the surrounding healthy bone) PREFIXED ROOT: *secu*: con-: consecution, consecutive (following in order, without interruption) (*con-*, with, together) per-: persecute (see *Triplets* below; **Synonyms**: wrong, oppress, aggrieve), persecution (*per-*, intensive)

622

Element	From	Meaning	Examples
sequ (cont'd)			*pro-*: prosecute (see *Triplets* below), prosecution, prosecutor (*pro-*, before)
			sequ:
			con-: consequence (**Synonyms:** 1) effect, result, outcome; 2) importance, moment, significance), consequent, consequential, consequently (*con-*, with, together)
			ob-: (against)
			obsequies (funeral ceremonies)
			obsequious (**Synonyms:** obedient, compliant, acquiescent)
			sub-: subsequent (*sub-*, under)
			PREFIXED ELIDED ROOT:
			ex-: (intensive)
			exequator, exequy (*sequ* is elided to *equ*)
			executant (*secut* is elided to *ecut*)
			execute (**Synonyms:** 1) kill, slay, murder; 2) perform, accomplish), execution, executioner, executive (*secut* is elided to *ecut*)
			DOUBLE PREFIXED ROOT:
			inconsequential (*in-*, not + *con-*, with, together)
			DISGUISED ROOT:
			sue (**Synonyms:** appeal, plead, petition), suer
			suit, suitable (**Synonyms:** fit, proper, appropriate), suite
			suitor (a person who requests, petitions, or entreats; a person who sues at law; a man courting or wooing a woman)
			PREFIXED DISGUISED ROOT:
			en-: ensue (**Synonyms:** follow, succeed, supplant) (*en-*, in)
			pur-: pursuant, pursue (see *Triplets* below), pursuit, pursuivant (from *pro-*, forth)
			TRIPLETS: pursue:prosecute:persecute
			LATIN TERMS:
			non sequitur (it does not follow)
			et sequens (plural, *et sequentia*; and the following)
			nolle prosequi (to be unwilling to pursue)
			ITALIAN MUSIC TERMS:
			segue (pronounced either SEG way, or SAY gway; to continue without break to or into the next part; as a noun, an immediate transition from one part to another)
			secondo (the *second* part in a concerted piece; especially, the lower part in a piano duet; one who performs a *second* part)
			PLACENAME: El Secondo, California [site of the *second* Standard Oil (now EXXON) refining site in California]
			NO CROSS REFERENCE
ser**	Latin *serere* (IE: *ser*, to line up, join)	to join, arrange	SIMPLE ROOT:
			sere (a back-formation of *series*; in *ecology*, the complete series of stages occurring in succession in communities of plants and animals until the climax is reached)
			seri: serial, seriate, seriatim, series (**Synonyms:** succession, progression, sequence)
			sert: sertularian (any family of hydroids growing in colonies made up of double-rowed branches of cupped polyps)
			PREFIXED ROOT:
			as-: assert (**Synonyms:** declare, affirm, aver), assertion, assertive {assertiveness}, assertor (*as-* assimilates *ad-*)

Element	From	Meaning	Examples
ser (cont'd)			*de-*: desert (both the verb meaning *to abandon*, as well as *barren region*; but not the *desert* derived from *deserve*, as one receiving one's *just deserts*, or punishment) (*de-*, from) *dis-*: dissertate, dissertation (*dis-*, apart, away) *in-*: insert, inserted (in *biology*, joined by natural growth), insertion (*in-*, in) PREFIXED ELIDED ROOT: *ex-*: exert {exertive}, exertion (**Synonyms**: effort, endeavor, pains) (*ex-*, out) DISGUISED ROOT: sort, sorcery, sortilege, sermon PREFIXED DISGUISED ROOT: *as-*: assort, assortment (*as-* assimilates *ad-*, to, toward) NB: *Resort* is not in this family, coming instead from *re-*, again + *sortir*, to go out, as in *sortie*. CROSS REFERENCE: *art, cosm, jug/junct, zyg*
serr*	Latin *serra* (IE: *sek*, to cut)	saw (noun)	SIMPLE ROOT: serra: serra, serranid (any of a large family of predatory percoid fishes, including the sea basses), serrate, serration serru: serrulate, serrulation SPANISH: sierra, cero (a mackerel) MOUNTAIN RANGE: Sierra Nevada [literally, snow-capped (*nevada* from *nev*, snow), saw-toothed (mountains)] INDIAN TRIBE: Serrano (Spanish for southern people; the Serranos are a Shoshonean people of southern California) CROSS REFERENCE: *sect*
serv**	Latin *servire*: to be of use; to serve	slave	SIMPLE ROOT: serve, server serva: servant servi: service, serviceable, serviette (a table napkin) servile (**Synonyms**: subservient, slavish, obsequious) servitude (**Synonyms**: slavery, bondage) PREFIXED ROOT: *de-*: deserve, deserved, deserving (*de-*, intensive) *dis-*: disservice (*dis-*, apart, away) *sub-*: subservient (*sub-*, under) LEADING ROOT COMPOUND: mechan: servomechanism DISGUISED ROOT: serf (probably of Etruscan origin) sergeant (originally one who *served* his lord in battle) PREFIXED DISGUISED ROOT: *con-*: concierge (literally, a fellow slave; a doorkeeper; a custodian or head porter, as of an apartment house or hotel) (from *com-*, with, together) *des-*: dessert (originally *dissert* or *disserve*, with the idea of clearing the table, the opposite of serving; after clearing the table or *disserving* it, the *dessert* was served).(from *dis-*, apart, away) FRENCH: sirvente (from Provençal *serviens*, a servant's song; a form of lyric verse of the Provençal troubadours satirizing political, social, or moral themes) NO CROSS REFERENCE

Element	From	Meaning	Examples
serv**	Latin *servare* (IE: *ser*, to watch over, guard)	to keep, protect	ROOT NOTE: Root is related to *servire*, to serve. PREFIXED ROOT: *con-*: conservancy, conservation, conservatism, conservative, conservatoire (same as *conservatory*), conservator, conservatory, conserve (*con-*, with, together) *ob-*: (against) observable, observance, observant, observation, observatory observe (**Synonyms: 1)** discern, perceive, notice; **2)** celebrate, commemorate, solemnize), observer *pre-*: preservation, preservative, preserve (**Synonyms:** safeguard, shield, defend) (*pre-*, before) *re-*: reservation, reserve (**Synonyms:** keep, retain, withhold), reservoir (*re-*, back) GREEK: hero CROSS REFERENCE: *arm, tect/teg*
ses			See *sex* for *sestet.*
sess			See *sed* for *session.*
sever*	Latin (see *Root Note*)	harsh, stern	ROOT NOTE: This root combines Latin *se-*, apart, away + IE base *wer-*, to be friendly; thus literally, not friendly; harsh, strict, unsparing, stern. SIMPLE ROOT: severe, severity PREFIXED ROOT: *as-*: asseverate (to state seriously or positively; aver), asseveration (*as-* assimilates *ad-*, to, toward) *per-*: perseverance (**Synonyms:** persistence, tenacity, pertinacity), persevere, perseveration, persevere (*per-*, intensive) NOTE: *Sever*, to separate, is not in this family; see *par*, to equip. NO CROSS REFERENCE
sex,*** sen, ses	Latin *sextus* (IE: *seks, sweks*, six)	six, sixth	SIMPLE ROOT: *sen*: senarius (a verse of *six* feet in Latin prosody; especially, the classical iambic trimeter) senary (of or relating to the number *six*; having six things or parts) *ses*: sestet (a stanza constituting the last six lines of a sonnet) sestina (an originally Provençal vere form consisting of six six-line stanzas and a three-line envoi, repeating the end words of the first stanza throughout according to a scheme of cruciate retrogration) *sex*: sext [often capitalized; the fourth of the canonical hours, originally set for the sixth hour of the day (counting from 6 a.m.) or noon (see *Spanish*, below] sexta: sextain (same as *sestina*, above), sextans, sextant sexte: sextet (also, *sextette*; any group of six; in *music*, a composition for six voices or six instruments) sexti: sextile (in *astrology*, the position of two heavenly bodies *sixty* degrees apart) LEADING ROOT COMPOUND: ple: sextuple (six-fold) (from *plicare*, to fold) plet: sextuplet (see *sextuple*)

Element	From	Meaning	Examples
sex (cont'd)			DISGUISED LEADING ROOT COMPOUND: semester (from *sex mensis*; originally, a period of six months) SPANISH: *siesta* (originally *siesta hora*, or sixth hour, from sunrise; thus, the hottest time of the day; see *Placename*) [*Siesta* is analogous to *calm* in Greek, where *calm* originally meant searing heat, and thus the time to close shops and seek cooler retreats.] ITALIAN: seicento (literally six hundred; an abbreviation of sixteen hundred; the 17th century; specifically, the 17th century period in the literature and art of Italy) DANISH: sextur (literally, six turn; a Danish clockwise figure dance for six couples) PLACENAME: Siesta, Florida NB: *Sexton*, a maintenance man in a church, is derived from *sacristan*, or keeper of that which is holy; see *sacr.* CROSS REFERENCE: *hexa*
sic			See *sec* for *siccative, desiccate.*
sid			See *sed* for *dissident, resident.*
sider**	Latin *sidus* (IE: *sweid,* to gleam)	star	SIMPLE ROOT: sideral (now archaic; emanating from the stars and especially those held to be malefic; baleful) sidereal (expressed in reference to the stars, as sidereal day, month, time, etc.) PREFIXED ROOT: *con-*: (with, together) consider (originally, to observe the stars for an omen; **Synonyms**: study, contemplate, weigh) considerable (worth considering; noteworthy) considerate (**Synonyms**: thoughtful, attentive) consideration *de-*: desiderate (to feel the lack of and desire for; want; miss; to long for), desiderative, desideratum (plural, *desiderata*) (*de-,* lack of, reversal) PREFIXED DISGUISED ROOT: *de-*: desirable, desire, desirous (*de-,* from) CROSS REFERENCE: *astr, stell*
sidero*	Greek *sideros*	iron	SIMPLE ROOT: siderism, siderite, sider<u>itis</u> (ironwort; *itis* not related to *itis*, inflammation) LEADING ROOT COMPOUND: osis: siderosis (any disease of the lungs caused by the inhaling of particles of iron or other metal) (*osis*, diseased condition) penia: sideropenia (iron deficiency in the blood) (*penia*, deficiency) CROSS REFERENCE: *fer*
sign***	Latin *signum* (IE: *sek,* to cut)	mark, sign, seal	SIMPLE ROOT: sign: sign (**Synonyms**: mark, token, symptom) signal: signal, signalize, signalment (a description giving distinguishing or identifying marks, as of someone wanted by the police) signar: signary, signatary (same as *signatory*), signate, signation, signatory, signature signe: signet (a seal, especially one used as a signature in marking documents as official)

626

Element	From	Meaning	Examples
sign (cont'd)			PREFIXED ROOT: as-: (as- assimilates ad-, to, toward) assign (Synonyms: 1) allot, apportion, allocate; 2) ascribe, attribute, impute) assignat (paper currency during the French Revolution with confiscated lands as the security) assignment, assignation, assignor con-: consign (Synonyms: commit, entrust, confide), consignment, consignor (con-, with, together) counter-: countersign, countersignature (counter-, opposite, against) de-: design (Synonyms: 1) intend, mean, propose; 2) plan, project, scheme), designate, designee (de-, down) en-: ensign (French; from insignia) in-: insignia (usually considered the plural of insigne; however, in modern usage, is usually considered singular) (in-, in) pre-: presignify (foreshadow) (pre-, before) re-: resign (Synonyms: abdicate, renounce, surrender), resignation, resigned (yielding and uncomplaining) (re-, back) LEADING ROOT COMPOUND: fer: signifer (a standard-bearer) (ferre, to bear) fic: (from facere, to make) significance (Synonyms: importance, consequence, moment), significant significate, signification, significative (same as significant) fy: signify (from facere, to make, do) DISGUISED ROOT: scarlet [translated from Arabic siqilat, from Latin sigillatus, adorned with little images (American Heritage Dictionary)] seal (not the animal) LATIN EXPRESSION: locus sigilli (place of the seal, and abbreviated L.S. on legal documents; often thought to stand for "legal signature") LATIN PHRASE: in hoc signo vinces (in this sign, you will conquer) ITALIAN MUSIC TERMS: segno [sign; especially the sign (S:) used at the beginning or end of a repeat] dal segno (from the sign; thus, to repeat a passage from the sign, indicated by a slanted S; see the authors' An Introduction to An Academic Vocabulary, p. 174) CROSS REFERENCE: beck, sema
sil			See sal/sault for resilient.
silv,* sylv	Latin silva (IE: (k)selwa, wood; see Root Note)	forest, trees	ROOT NOTE: This root may be derived from the same Indo-European root as is Greek xylon, wood. SIMPLE ROOT: silva: silva* (plural, silvas or silvae), silvan (also sylvan) sylvatic (of, or in, the woods; or affecting the animals in the woods, as a sylvatic plague) silvi: silvical, silvics *also spelled sylva (now archaic, but originally referred to a collection of poems, anecdotes, or literary pieces)

Element	From	Meaning	Examples
silv (cont'd)			LEADING ROOT COMPOUND: col: silvicolous (living or growing in woodlands) (*colere*, to cultivate, inhabit) cult: silviculture (the art of cultivating a forest; forestry) DISGUISED ROOT: savage (**Synonyms:** barbarian, barbaric, barbarous) (from *silvaticus*, belonging to a wood, wild) STATE OF THE UNITED STATES: Pennsylvania (Penn's Woods, from William Penn, the founder of the state) CROSS REFERENCE: *dendro, for*
simil,*** simul	Latin *similis*: like (IE: *sem*, one, together, with)	same	SIMPLE ROOT: *simil*: simila: similar, similarity (**Synonyms:** likeness, analogy, resemblance) simile: simile (a figure of speech in which one thing is likened to another dissimilar thing by the use of *like, as, seem, appear*, e.g., Robert Burns' "My love is *like* a red, red rose") simili: similitude (a person or thing resembling another) *simul*: simula: simulacrum (an image, likeness; a vague representation; sham) simulant (that which simulates) simulate (**Synonyms:** pretend, feign, affect), simulation simult: simultaneous (**Synonyms:** contemporary, synchronous) PREFIXED ROOT: *sembl*: as-: assemble (**Synonyms:** gather, collect, muster), assembly (*as-* assimilates *ad-*, to, toward) *simil*: as-: assimilable, assimilate, assimilation, assimilationism, assimilative, assimilatory (*as-* assimilates *ad-*, to, toward) dis-: dissimilar (**Synonyms:** different, diverse, disparate), dissimilate, dissimilation, dissimilitude (*dis-*, apart, away) *simul*: dis-: dissimulate [to disguise (one's true feelings, for example) under a feigned appearance] (*dis-*, apart, away) TRAILING ROOT COMPOUND: fac: facsimile (**Synonyms:** reproduction, duplicate, replicate) (from *facere*, to make) veri: verisimilar (appearing to be true or real; probable; likely), verisimilitude (*veri*, true + *simil*, same) PREFIXED DISGUISED ROOT: *sembl*: dis-: dissemble (**Synonyms:** pretend, feign, simulate) (*dis-*, apart) en-: ensemble (at the same time) (*en-*, in) re-: resemble, resemblance (**Synonyms:** likeness, similarity, analogy) (*re-*, again) RELATED WORD: simple (**Synonyms:** easy, facile, smooth) COINED MODERN COMPOUND: simulcast [*simul*(taneous) (broad)*cast*, by radio and television]

Element	From	Meaning	Examples
simil (cont'd)			NOTE: *Simian*, ape, is not related to this root, but is from *simus*, flat-nosed. CROSS REFERENCE: *homo* (Greek), *taut*
sin**	Latin *sinus*	bend, curve, hollow	ROOT NOTE: The root, meaning curving, bending, like the anatomical cavities, also designated the hanging folds of a toga, thus *sine* as a term in trigonometry (see *Simple Root*). SIMPLE ROOT: sine (in *trigonometry*, the ratio between the side opposite a given acute angle in a right triangle and the hypotenuse) sinuate, sinuous, sinuosity, sinuous sinus (a depression or cavity formed by a bending or curving) PREFIXED ROOT: *co*-: cosine (from *com*-, with) *in*-: insinuate (to introduce by windings and turnings, as though winding through hollows) (*in*-, in) LEADING ROOT COMPOUND: itis: sinusitis (*itis*, inflammation) oid: sinusoid (*oid*, similar to) INTERDISCIPLINARY: sinus (in *anatomy*, a dilated channel for the passage of chiefly venous blood; any of various air-filled cavities in the cranial bones, especially one communicating with the nostrils; in *botany*, a notch or indentation between lobes of a leaf or corolla; in *pathology*, a fistula or channel to a supporting cavity) CROSS REFERENCE: *cav*
sine**	Latin	without	PREFIX NOTE: Though *sine* with the meaning of *without* is a word, it is used only as a prefix or in phrases; see previous family for *sine*, the mathematical term). PREFIXED ROOT: cur: sinecure [from phrase *beneficium sine cura*: benefice (church office) without cure (of souls); thus, an office or position that requires little or no work and that usually provides an income], sinecurism (*cur*, care) LATIN PHRASES: *sine die* [without a day (set to reconvene) *sine nomine* (without a name) *sine prole* (without issue; without offspring; childless) *sine qua non* (without which not; an essential condition, qualification, etc.; indispensable thing; absolute prerequisite) CROSS REFERENCE: *a-, an-* (Greek), *sans*-
sip			See *sag* for *insipid*.
sist***	Latin *sistere*: to cause to stand (IE: *sta*, to stand)	to set in place	PREFIXED ROOT: *as*-: assist (**Synonyms:** help, aid, succor), assistance, assistant (*as*- assimilates *ad*-, to, toward) *con*-: consist, consistent, consistory (*con*-, with, together) *de*-: desist (**Synonyms:** stop, discontinue, cease) (*de*-, from) *in*-: insist, insistence, insistent (*in*-, in, on) *per*-: (through) persist (**Synonyms:** continue, last, endure) persistence (**Synonyms:** perseverance, tenacity, pertinacity) persistent (refusing to relent; used in both botany and zoology to indicate "remaining unchanged") v

Element	From	Meaning	Examples
sist (cont'd)			re-: resist, resistant, resistivity, resistless, resistor (re-, back) sub-: subsist, subsistance (sub-, under) tran-: transistor (*trans*fers an electrical current *across* a re*sis*tor) (*trans*-, across) PREFIXED ELIDED ROOT: ex-: exist, existential, existentialism (*ex*-, out + *sist*) CROSS REFERENCE: *stas/stat/stit*
sit**	Latin *sitos*	food, grain	PREFIXED ROOT: para-: parasite (originally, a person, as in ancient Greece, who flattered and amused his host in return for free meals; in *biology*, a plant or animal that lives on or in an organism or another species from which it derives sustenance or protection without benefiting the host and usually doing harm; **Synonyms:** sycophant, toady, leech) (*para*-, alongside) DOUBLE PREFIXED ROOT: endoparasite (see *parasite*, above; a parasite that inhabits the internal organs of its host; hookworm, tapeworm, endamoeba, etc.) (*endo*-, within) LEADING ROOT COMPOUND: logy: sitology (the study of foods, food values, nutrition, diet, etc.; dietetics) (*logy*, study of) mania: sitiomania (an abnormal craving for food) (*mania*, craving for) ster: sitosterol (any of a group of crystalline alcoholic sterols resembling cholesterol in their properties) TRAILING ROOT COMPOUND: hemi: hemiparasite (*hemi*, half; *para*-, beside, prefixes *site*) INTERDISCIPLINARY: hemiparasite [in *botany*, a parasitic plant, as the mistletoe, which carries on some photosynthesis but obtains a portion of its food, water, or minerals from a host plant; in *zoology*, an organism that may be either free-living or parasitic; facultative (capable of living under variable conditions)] CROSS REFERENCE: *gran*
soc**	Latin *socius* (IE: *sekw*, to follow)	companion, partner	SIMPLE ROOT: socia: sociability, sociable (pleasant, friendly, or affable), social, socialism, socialist, socialite, sociality, socialize socie: societal, society (**Synonyms:** circle, coterie, clique) PREFIXED ROOT: as-: (*as*- assimilates *ad*-, to, toward) associable, associate (**Synonyms:** companion, colleague, comrade) association, associational, associative con-: consociate (as a *verb*, to join together; unite in association) (*con*-, with, together) dis-: dissociate (to break the ties or connection between; sever association with), dissociation (*dis*-, apart) LEADING ROOT COMPOUND: eco: socioeconomic gram: sociogram (from *graph*, write) logy: sociology (same as *synecology*) {sociologist} (*logy*, study of)

Element	From	Meaning	Examples
soc (cont'd)			metry: sociometry (the quantitative study of group relationships) {sociometric} (*metry*, measurement of)
			path: sociopath [*socio* + *(psycho)path*; a person suffering from psychopathic personality, whose behavior is aggressively antisocial] {sociopathic} (*pathein*, to suffer, feel)
			polit: sociopolitical (from *polis*, city)
			SPORT: soccer (from *association football*, as it was originally called in England)
			CROSS REFERENCE: *sequi, sign*
sol**	Latin *sol* (IE: *swen* sun)	sun	SIMPLE ROOT: sol (the monetary unit of Peru: from the radiant sun used as a device on one side), solanine (also, *solanin*), solano, solar, solarium, solarize
			PREFIXED ROOT:
			in-: insolate (to expose to the sun so as to dry, bleach, etc.; do not confuse with *insolent* or *insulate*) (*in*-, in)
			para-: parasol (that which protects from the sun, but which can be used to protect from the rain; likewise, *umbrella*, Italian for small shade is also used to protect one from the rain; see *umbra*) (*para*-, protection against)
			LEADING ROOT COMPOUND:
			stic: solstice [literally, when the sun stands still; designates either of two points on the sun's ecliptic at which it (the ecliptic) is farthest north or farthest south of the equator, e.g., *summer solstice, winter solstice*, respectively] {solsticial} (*stice*, stand)
			TRAILING ROOT COMPOUND:
			gira: girasol (same as girandole, a revolving cluster of fireworks; also a branched candleholder) (Italian *girare*, to turn)
			DISGUISED ROOT: turnsole [originally from *tournesol* (heliotrope or sunflower); further from Latin *tornare*, to turn + *sol*; any of various plants, such as the heliotrope, that move or are believed to move, or *turn*, in response to the *sun*]
			MEDICAL TERM: *solar plexus* (with the nerve fibers, or ganglia, radiating like rays from the sun)
			ROMAN MYTHOLOGY: Sol (the sun god: identified with the Greek god Helios; the sun personified)
			CROSS REFERENCE: *heli*
sol***	Latin *solus* (IE: *s(e)wo*, apart)	alone	SIMPLE ROOT:
			sole, solitaire, solitary, solitude
			solo, solus (a stage direction)
			PREFIXED ROOT:
			de-: desolate, desolater, desolation, desolator (*de*-, intensive)
			LEADING ROOT COMPOUND:
			sol:
			ips: solipsism (the theory that the *self* can be aware of nothing but its own experiences and states; also, the theory that nothing exists or is real but the self) (*ipse*, self)
			soli:
			loqu: soliloquy (lines in a drama in which a character reveals his/her thoughts to the audience, but not to the other characters, as though *speaking only* to himself/herself) (*loqui*, speak)

Element	From	Meaning	Examples
sol (cont'd)			DISGUISED ROOT: sullen (from *solitary*, with the idea of dissociating oneself; **Synonyms:** cross, ill-natured, peevish) LAW TERMS: *sole* (unmarried) *feme sole* (literally, woman alone; in *law*, an unmarried woman; spinster; divorcée, or widow) PLACENAME: Soledad, California (solitude, loneliness) CROSS REFERENCE: *mono*
sol**	Latin *solari* (IE: *sel*, favorable, in good spirits)	to comfort	SIMPLE ROOT: solace (**Synonyms:** comfort, console, relieve) PREFIXED ROOT: *con-*: consolable, consolation, consolatory, console (both the noun and the verb) (*con-*, with, together) DOUBLE PREFIXED ROOT: disconsolate (so unhappy that nothing will comfort; inconsolable; dejected; causing or suggesting dejection; cheerless) (*dis*, not + *con-*, with, together) inconsolable (that cannot be consoled; disconsolate; broken-hearted) (*in-*, not + *con-*, with, together) DISGUISED ROOT: silly (**Synonyms:** stupid, fatuous) CROSS REFERENCE: *pac/pax*
solut,*** solv	Latin *solvere* (from *se-*, apart + *luere*, to let go, free)	to loosen	SIMPLE ROOT: *solut*: solubility, soluble, solute, solution *solv*: solvable, solvate, solve, solvent PREFIXED ROOT: *solu*: *dis-*: dissoluble (describing that which can be *dissolved*) (*dis-*, not) *solut*: *ab-*: absolute, absolution, absolutism, absolutory (*ab-*, not) *dis-*: dissolute (dissipated and immoral; profligate; debauched), dissolution (*dis-*, not) *re-*: resolute (**Synonyms:** faithful, loyal, staunch), resolution (*re-*, back, again) *solv*: *ab-*: absolve (**Synonyms:** acquit, exonerate, pardon), absolvent (*ab-*, from) *dis-*: dissolve (**Synonyms: 1)** adjourn, prorogue, postpone; **2)** melt, liquefy, thaw), dissolvent (*dis-*, away) *in-*: insolvent (not solvent; unable to pay debts as they become due; bankrupt; not enough to pay all debts, as *an insolvent inheritance*) (*in-*, not) *re-*: resolve (**Synonyms:** decide, determine, settle) (*re-*, back, again) PREFIXED DISGUISED ROOT: *as-*: assoil (from *absolve*, to set free from; thus, to atone for) (*as-* assimilates *ad-*, to, toward) ENGLISH: lose, loss OLD NORSE: loose SWISS GERMAN: loess (a fine-grained, calcareous silt or clay, thought to be a deposit of wind-blown dust)

Element	From	Meaning	Examples
solut (cont'd)			INTERDISCIPLINARY: absolute (in *grammar*, forming part of a sentence, but not in the usual relations of syntax; the use of a verb without an explicit object, as steal in "Thieves steal"; in *law*, without condition of encumbrance, as absolute ownership) CROSS REFERENCE: *lax, lys*
soma**	Greek *soma* (IE: *teu*, to swell, thick)	body	SIMPLE ROOT: soma (the body as distinct from the mind; also, all of the body cells except the germ cells; the body exclusive of the extremities), somacule, somite, somatic, somatist LEADING ROOT COMPOUND: gen: somatogenic (arising within the body in response to environment) (*gen*, producing) logy: somatology (the physiological and anatomical study of the body) (*logy*, study of) plasm: somatoplasm (the entirety of specialized protoplasm, other than germ plasm, constituting the body; the protoplasm of a somatic cell) (*plasm*, form) pleur: somatopleure (*pleura*, side, rib) typ: somatotype (the morphological type of a human body; physique, e.g., ectomorph, mesomorph, endomorph) (*type*, figure, model) TRAILING ROOT COMPOUND: *some*: auto: autosome (from *auto* + *chromosome*; any chromosome that is not a sex chromosome) (*auto*, self) chromo: chromosome (a threadlike body found in a cell nucleus and which carries genes; so called because chromosomes take on color when a cell is stained) (*chromo*, color) kary: karyosome (*karyo*, kernel) mono: monosome (an unpaired chromosome in an otherwise diploid cell; especially, an unpaired sex chromosome) (*mono*, one) *somatic*: psycho: psychosomatic (*psycho*, mind) CROSS REFERENCE: *corp*
somn**	Latin *somnus* (IE: *swep*, to sleep)	sleep	SIMPLE ROOT: somnial, somnolence (drowsiness, sleepiness), somnolent PREFIXED ROOT: *in-*: insomnia (*in-*, not) LEADING ROOT COMPOUND: *somn*: ambul: somnambulist (sleepwalker; same as *noctambulist*, literally, nightwalker), somnambulism (*ambulare*, to walk) *somni*: fac: somnifacient (tending to produce sleep; hypnotic) (*facere*, to make) fer: somniferous (inducing sleep; soporific) (*ferre*, to bring, bear) loqu: somniloquy (the act or habit of talking in one's sleep) (*loqui*, to speak) osus: somniosus (a genus of sharks which appear sleepy)

Element	From	Meaning	Examples
somn (cont'd)			*somno:* cin: somnocinematograph (a device for recording motions of those who are asleep) (*cine*, movement) ROMAN MYTHOLOGY: Somnus (god of sleep; identified with Greek god Hypnos, from which *hypnotic* is derived) TRADE NAME OF MEDICATION INDUCING SLEEP: Sominex CROSS REFERENCE: *dorm, hypno, sopor*
son***	Latin *sonus* (IE: *swen*, to sound; yields English sound)	sound	SIMPLE ROOT: sona: sonance, sonant (a voiced speech sound; a syllabic consonant; sonorant) sonar (acronym for <u>so</u>und <u>na</u>vigation and <u>r</u>anging) soni: sonic, sonicate, sonitus sonn: sonnet (from Provençal *sonet*; a poem normally fourteen lines in any of several fixed verse and rhyme schemes, typically in rhymed iambic pentameter: sonnets characteristically express a single theme or idea; explore Petrarchan sonnet, Shakespearean sonnet), sonneteer, sonnetize sono: sonorant [*sonor*(ous) + (conson)*ant*; in *phonetics*, a voiced consonant that is less sonorous than a vowel but more sonorous than an unvoiced plosive and that may occur as a syllabic (*l, m, n, r, y*, and *w* are English sonorants)], sonority, sonorous PREFIXED ROOT: as-: assonance [the repetition of identical or similar sounds in a sequence of nearby words, e.g., Thou still unravished br<u>i</u>de of qu<u>ie</u>tness/Thou foster ch<u>i</u>ld of s<u>i</u>lence and slow t<u>i</u>me (Keats' "Ode on a Grecian Urn")], assonant (having assonance) (*as-* assimilates *ad-*, to, toward) con-: consonance (harmony or agreement of elements or parts; accord; in *prosody*, a partial rhyme in which consonants in stressed syllables are repeated but vowels are not, e.g., *mocker, maker*; compare *assonance* for repetition of stressed vowels, e.g., *mate, make*), consonant {consonantal} (*con-*, with, together) dis-: dissonance (in *music*, a chord that sounds incomplete or unfulfilled until resolved to a harmonious chord), dissonant (*dis-*, apart, away) hyper-: hypersonic (of, pertaining to, or relating to speed equal to or exceeding five times the speed of sound; compare *supersonic*, below) (Greek *hyper-*, beyond) re-: resonance, resonant, resonate, resonator (*re-*, again) super-: supersonic (designating, of, or moving at a speed in a surrounding fluid greater than that of sound in the same fluid; same as *ultrasonic*) (*super-*, beyond) tran-: transonic (*tran-* elides *trans-*, across) TRAILING ROOT COMPOUND: uni: unison, unisonous (*uni*, one) FRENCH TERM: *son et lumière* (sound and light; a technique of presenting a historical spectacle, especially at night in front of a monument, etc. using special lighting effects and live or recorded narration, music, etc.)

Element	From	Meaning	Examples
son (cont'd)			ITALIAN MUSIC TERMS: sonata (originally, an instrumental composition as opposed to a cantata, literally, something sung; explore use of sonata as a composition and as a pattern of musical composition) sonatina (a short or simplified sonata) PREFIXED ENGLISH: *re-*: resound (to echo or be filled with sound; reverberate; to be celebrated; be extolled) (*re-*, again) DISGUISED ROOT: swan PLACENAME: Sonnette, Montana CROSS REFERENCE: *phon*
soph*	Greek *sophos*: skilled, clever	wisdom, skill	SIMPLE ROOT: sophism (a clever and plausible but fallacious argument or form of reasoning, whether or not intended to deceive) sophist, sophister, sophistic, sophistical (also, *sophistic*) sophisticate, sophisticated, sophistication sophistry (unsound or misleading but clever, and subtle argument or reasoning) LEADING ROOT COMPOUND: mor: sophomore (literally, wise fool; a student in the second year of college or the tenth grade at high school), sophomoric (*moros*, foolish) TRAILING ROOT COMPOUND: gymn: gymnosophist (a member of an ancient Hindu sect of ascetics who wore little or no clothing) (*gymn*, nude) pan: pansophism, pansophy (universal knowledge or wisdom), pansophies (a system or work embracing all knowledge) (*pan*, all) phil: philosopher, philosophic, philosophism, philosophize, philosophy (*philos*, loving) PERSON: Sophocles, a Greek dramatist CROSS REFERENCE: *sapi/sav/sip*
sopor*	Latin *sopor*: sleep) (IE: *swep*, to sleep)	stupor	ROOT NOTE: This root is related to *somnus*, sleep. SIMPLE ROOT: sopor, soporous LEADING ROOT COMPOUND: fer: soporiferous (compare *somniferous*) (*ferre*, to bear) fic: soporific (from *facere*, to make) ose: soporose (*ose*, condition of) CROSS REFERENCE: *somn*, *hypno*
sorb**	Latin *sorbere*, to drink in, suck (IE: *serbh*, to slurp)	to soak up	PREFIXED ROOT: *ab-*: absorb {absorbable}, absorbed, absorbent {absorbency}, absorbing, absorption {absorptive} (*ab-*, away) *ad-*: adsorb, adsorbate, adsorbent, adsorption (*ad-*, to, toward) *re-*: resorb {resorption, resorptive} (*re-*, back, again) LEADING ROOT COMPOUND: fac: sorbefacient (causing absorption) (from *facere*, to make, do) DUTCH COGNATE: slurp (from *slorpen*, to lap) NO CROSS REFERENCE

The vocabulary of science and medicine is the language of Greece and Rome.
Lack of knowledge of Greek and Latin roots hampers
the mastery of scientific terminology. Dean John Pomfet

Element	From	Meaning	Examples
soror*	Latin *soror* (IE: *sewe*, one's own)	sister	SIMPLE ROOT: sororal, sororate, sororial, sorority, sororize LEADING ROOT COMPOUND: cid: sororicide (the killing of one's sister) (*cide*, kill) PROFESSIONAL WOMEN'S CLUB: Soroptimist (combination of *sorority* and *optimism*) NO CROSS REFERENCE
sort**	Latin *sors*: sort, kind (IE: *ser*, to line up, arrange)	lot, fotune	SIMPLE ROOT: sort (**Synonyms**: type, kind, ilk), sortie PREFIXED ROOT: *as-*: assort, assorted, assortment (*as-* assimilates *ad-*, to) *con-*: consort, consortium (from *com-*, with, together) LEADING ROOT COMPOUND: leg: sortilege (the act or practice of foretelling the future by drawing lots; sorcery; witchcraft) (*leg*, to read) DISGUISED ROOT: sorcerer NO CROSS REFERENCE
spec,*** spic	Latin *specere* (IE: *spek*, to spy, watch closely)	to look	SIMPLE ROOT: speci: special (**Synonyms**: especial, specific, particular) specialize (in *biology*, to adapt parts or organs to a special condition, use, or requirement) specially, specialty, specie, species (see *Doublets* below) specimen, specious (**Synonyms**: plausible, credible) spect: spectacle, spectacled (wearing eyeglasses), spectacles (eyeglasses), spectacular, spectator, specter, spectral, spectrum (plural, *spectrums*, or *spectra*) specu: specular, speculate, speculation, speculum (a medical instrument for viewing a passage or cavity of the body) PREFIXED ROOT AND COMPOUNDS: *speci*: *con-*: conspecific (in *biology*, belonging to the same species) (*con-*, with, together) *spect*: *a-*: aspect (**Synonyms**: appearance, look, semblance) (*a-* elides *ad-*, to, toward) *circum-*: circumspect (**Synonyms**: careful, scrupulous, meticulous) {circumspection} (*circum-*, around) *con-*: conspectus (a general view; **Synonyms**: survey, summary, synopsis) (*con-*, with, together) *in-*: inspect {inspective}, inspection, inspector, inspectorate (*in-*, in) *intro-*: introspection (*intro-*, inwardly, on the inside) *per-*: perspective (*per-*, through) *pro-*: prospect, prospective (looking toward the future; expected), prospectus (*pro-*, before, in front of) *re-*: respect (**Synonyms**: regard, esteem, admire; see *Doublets* below), respectable, respective (*re-*, again) *retro-*: retrospect, retrospection (*retro-*, backward) *su-*: spect: suspect (literally, to look from under) (*su-* elides *sub-*, under) *spic*: *con-*: conspicuity, conspicuous (**Synonyms**: noticeable, remarkable, prominent) (*con-*, with, together)

Element	From	Meaning	Examples
spec (cont'd)			*de-*: despicable (*de-*, down)
			per-: perspicacity, perspicacious (**Synonyms:** shrewd, sagacious, astute), perspicuity, perspicuous (*per-*, through)
			spic: suspicion (originally, a looking up to, esteeming; later, to look up at, admire, look secretly at; mistrust, suspect), suspicious (showing or expressing suspicion)
			tran-: transpicuous (transparent; easily understood) (*trans-*, across)
			PREFIXED ELIDED ROOT:
			ex-: expect (**Synonyms:** anticipate, hope, await) (*ex-*, out)
			LEADING ROOT COMPOUND:
			speci:
			fic: specific (**Synonyms: 1)** explicit, express, exact; **2)** see *special*, above), specification (from *facere*, to make)
			fy: specify (from *facere*, to make)
			spectro:
			gram: spectrogram (from *graphein*, to write)
			graph: spectrograph (see *spectrogram*)
			helio: spectroheliogram (*helio*, sun)
			meter: spectrometer (*meter*, measure)
			scop: spectroscope (*scope*, view, look)
			DISGUISED ROOT:
			espionage, espial, espy, spy
			spice (see *Doublets* below)
			spite
			PREFIXED DISGUISED ROOT:
			de-: despise (**Synonyms:** scorn, disdain, contemn), despite, despiteful, despiteous (*de-*, down)
			re-: respite (a delay or postponement; see *Doublets*) (*re-*, back, again)
			TRAILING DISGUISED ROOT COMPOUND:
			au: auspex, auspice(s), auspicious (originally pertaining to omens based upon the flight of birds; **Synonyms:** favorable, propitious) (from *avis*, bird)
			fronti: frontispiece (originally, front of a house; then, the first page or title page of a book; later, a preface, foreword; hence, any illustration facing the first page or title page of a book or division of a book; in *architecture*, the main façade; also, a small pediment over a door, window, etc.)
			DOUBLETS: respite:respect; spice:species
			FRENCH: soupçon (literally, suspicion; a slight trace, as of a flavor; hint; suggestion)
			PLACENAME:
			Prospect (Kentucky, Maine; as well as in many other states)
			NO CROSS REFERENCE
sper*	Latin *spes* (IE: *spei*, to propser, expand)	hope	**PREFIXED ROOT:**
			de-: desperate (**Synonyms:** hopeless, despondent, despairing), desperation (*de-*, without, intensive)
			pro-: prosper (to succeed, thrive, ghrow, etc. in a vigorous way), prosperity (*pro-*, before, forward)
			PREFIXED ROOT:
			e-: esperance (*e-* elides *ex-*, out)

637

Element	From	Meaning	Examples
sper (cont'd)			PREFIXED DISGUISED ROOT: *de-*: despair (as a *verb*, to lose or give up hope; as a *noun*, loss of hope), despairing (see synonyms at *desperate*, above) (*de-*, without) SPANISH: desperado (a bold outlaw; a dangerous, reckless criminal) COINED WORD: Esperanto (literally, one who hopes, and was the pseudonym of Dr. L. L. Zamenhof, Russian physician, who invented the hoped-for universal language) MOTTO OF BROWN UNIVERSITY: *In Deo speramus*, In God we hope ENGLISH COGNATE: speed (**Synonyms**: haste, hurry, expedition) NO CROSS REFERENCE
sperm,*** **spers**	Greek *speirein*: to sow (IE: *sp(h)er(e)-*, to strew, sprinkle)	seed, sperm (literally, that which is scattered)	SIMPLE ROOT: sperm (the male generative fluid, semen) *sperm*: sperma: spermary (an organ in which male germ cells are formed; male gonad; testis), spermatic, spermatid, spermatium (plural, *spermatia*) spermi: spermine (a basic substance, $C_{10}H_{26}N_4$, found in semen, yeast, blood serum, and body tissues; it can also be prepared synthetically) *spers*: sperse (now archaic) (from *disperse*) PREFIXED ROOT: *sperm*: *endo-*: endosperm (in *botany*, the nutritive tissue of a plant seed, surrounding and absorbed by the embryo) (*endo-*, within) *spers*: *dis-*: disperse (**Synonyms**: scatter, dissipate, dispel), dispersion, dispersive (*dis-*, apart, away) *inter-*: intersperse (*inter-*, within) LEADING ROOT COMPOUND: *sperma*: ceti: spermaceti (a solid wax, at one time thought to be the congealed sperm of the whale; used in making candles, cosmetics, ointments, etc.) (*cetus*, whale) thec: spermatheca (a receptacle for storing spermatozoa in certain female invertebrates, especially insects) (*theca*, case, sheath) *spermat*: oid: spermatoid (resembling sperm) (*oid*, similar to) *spermato*: cyt: spermatocyte (*cyt*, cell) gen: spermatogenesis (*genesis*, origin, beginning) gon: spermatogonium (*gon*, cell, seed) phor: spermatophore (*phore*, bearer or producer of) phyt: spermatophyte (any seed-bearing plant) (*phyton*, plant) rrh: spermatorrhea (the too frequent involuntary discharge of semen without an orgasm) (*rrhea*, to flow) zo: spermatozoid, spermatozoon (*zo*, animal) *spermi*: cid: spermicide (*cide*, kill)

Element	From	Meaning	Examples
sperm (cont'd)			*spermio*: gen: spermiogenesis (*genesis*, beginning, origin) *spermo*: gon: spermogonium (in *botany*, any hollow structure where spermatia are formed) (*gon*, sexual reproduction) phil: spermophile (literally, seed-lover, or "fond of seed"; any of several squirrellike rodents, as the ground squirrels, that live in burrows, feed on vegetation, and sometimes damage crops) (*phil*, love of) TRAILING ROOT COMPOUND: angio: angiosperm (in *botany*, any plant characterized by having seeds enclosed in an ovary; a flowering plant) (*angio*, vessel) gymn: gymnosperm (*gymn*, naked) mono: (one) monospermous (in *botany*, having only one seed) monospermy (in *zoology*, the system in which a single sperm cell fertilizes an ovum) poly: polyspermous (*poly*, many) PREFIXED TRAILING ROOT COMPOUND: a-: azoospermia (*a-*, not + *zo*, animal) DISGUISED ROOT: spark, sparkle (**Synonyms**: flash, glance, gleam), sparkler sparse (**Synonyms**: meager, scanty, scant) sprinkle, sprinkling (a small quantity, or amount, especially one that is sprinkled, scattered, or thinly distributed) CROSS REFERENCE: *semen, spore*
sphen*	Greek *sphen* (IE: *spe*, long flat piece of wood)	wedge	SIMPLE ROOT: sphene (from the shape of its crystals; chemical symbol: $CaTiSiO_5$), sphenion spheniscus (literally, small wedge; a genus of penguins; so named for the shortness of their wings) LEADING ROOT COMPOUND: *sphen:* odon: sphenodon (the tuatara) (*odon*, tooth) oid: sphenoid (*oid*, similar to) *spheno*: cephal: sphenocephalic (*cephal*, head) gram: sphenogram (a cuneiform, or wedge-shaped, character) lith: sphenolith (*lithos*, stone) ENGLISH COGNATES: spade, spoon CROSS REFERENCE: *cunei*
spic			See *spec* for *despicable*.
spir***	Latin *spiritus*: breath, spirit (IE: *(s)peis*, to blow)	breath	SIMPLE ROOT: spiracle, spirant, spirit (see *Doublets* below) PREFIXED ROOT: a-: aspirant, aspirate, aspiration, aspire (literally, to breathe toward) (from *ad-*, to, toward) con-: conspiracy (**Synonyms**: plot, intrigue, machination), conspirator, conspiratorial, conspire (*con-*, with, together) ex-: expiration, expiratory, expire (**Synonyms**: die, decease, perish), expiry (*ex-*, out) in-: inspiration, inspirational, inspiratory, inspire (*in-*, in)

639

Element	From	Meaning	Examples
spir (cont'd)			*per-*: perspiration, perspiratory, perspire (*per-*, through)
			re-: respirable, respiration, respirator, respiratory, respire (*re-*, back, again)
			su-: suspire (from *sub-*, under)
			tran-: transpiration, transpire (**Synonyms**: happen, chance, occur) (from *trans-*, across)
			LEADING ROOT COMPOUND:
			meter: spirometer (an instrument for measuring the volume of air entering and leaving the lungs) (*meter*, measure)
			DISGUISED ROOT: sprite (see *Doublets* below), cesspool
			DOUBLETS: spirit:sprite
			FRENCH PHRASE: *esprit de corps* (literally, spirit of a body; group spirit)
			ITALIAN MUSIC PHRASE: *con spirito* (literally, with spirit; with vigor: a direction to the performer)
			NOTE: *Spire, spiral,* and *spirea,* are not in this family; neither is *acrospire*, literally ear of grain; in *botany*, the first sprout from a germinating grain seed.
			CROSS REFERENCE: *pneu*
spond,* spons**	Latin *spondere* (IE: *spend*, to bring a libation, vow)	to pledge, to make a libation	SIMPLE ROOT: spondee (originally, a solemn libation; a metrical foot of two long or accented syllables, appropriate for a solemn libation) sponsor (see *Doublets* below; **Synonyms**: patron, backer, angel)
			PREFIXED ROOT:
			de-: despond, despondence, despondent, desponding (*de-*, down)
			re-: respond, respondent, responsive (*re-*, back, again)
			DOUBLE PREFIXED ROOT:
			correspond, correspondence (*cor-* assimilates *com-*, with, together + *re-*, back, again)
			unresponsive (Anglo-Saxon *un-*, not + Latin *re-*, back, again)
			DISGUISED ROOT:
			espousal, espouse {espouser}
			spouse (see *Doublets* below)
			FRENCH: riposte (a sharp, swift response or retort; also a fencing term) (from Italian *risposta*)
			DOUBLETS: sponsor:spouse
			CROSS REFERENCE: *gage*
spor*	Greek *speirein*: to sow, strew (IE: *(s)p(h)er*, to strew, sow)	sowing seed	SIMPLE ROOT: sporadic, sporidium (plural, *sporidia*), spore
			PREFIXED ROOT:
			dia-: Diaspora (the dispersion of the Jews after the Babylonian exile), diaspore (*dia-*, across, through)
			endo-: endospore (an asexual spore formed within the cell wall of the parent cell, as in certain bacteria, fungi, and algae; the inner wall of a spore or pollen grain; intine; also called *endosporium*) (*endo-*, within)
			LEADING ROOT COMPOUND:
			spor:
			angi: sporangium (in *botany*, an organ or single cell-producing spores) (*angi*, vessel)
			ont: sporont [a sporozoan (as a zygote or pansporoblast) that engages in sporogony] (*ontos*, being)

Element	From	Meaning	Examples
spor (cont'd)			*spori*: cid: sporicidal, sporicide (*cid*, kill) fer: sporiferous (bearing spores) (*ferre*, to bear) *sporo*: blast: sporoblast (*blast*, shoot, sprout) carp: sporocarp (in *botany*, a multicellular structure in which spores of certain protozoans, e.g., red algae, lichens, are produced) (*carp*, fruit or reproductive structure) cyst: **sporocyst** (*cyst*, cell) gen: sporogenesis (in *biology*, reproduction by means of spores; the formation of spores) {sporogenic, sporogenous} (*gen*, origin) gon: sporogonium, sporogony (*gon*, reproduction) phor: sporophore (*phor*, bear) phyl: sporophyll (a leaf or leaflike organ that bears spores) (*phyll*, leaf) phyt: sporophyte (*phyton*, plant) zo: sporozoan (*zoa*, animal, organism) TRAILING ROOT COMPOUND: carpo: carposporic (*carpo*, fruit or similar reproductive structure) hetero: heterosporous (in *biology*, producing more than one kind of spore, especially, producing microspores and megaspores) (*hetero*, other) homo: homosporous (in *botany*, producing only one kind of spore; isosporous) (*homo*, same) RELATED ENGLISH WORDS: spread, sprout GERMAN: *sporenrest* INTERDISCIPLINARY: **sporocyst** (in *botany*, a resting cell giving rise to asexual spores; in *zoology*, a saclike larval stage of many trematodes which produces rediae by asexual development from germinal cells; also, a protective cyst produced by some protozoans before sporulaton, or a protozoan in such encystment) CROSS REFERENCE: *semin, sperm*
stab			See *stat* for *stability*.
stal,* **stle,** **stol**	Greek *stellein*: to set, put (IE: *stel*, to place, set up, standing, immobile; yields English still)	standing place; also, to send, as if from "a standing place"	SIMPLE ROOT: stale (another *stale* means "to urinate": said of horses and camels), stall, stallion PREFIXED ROOT: in-: install, installation, installment (or *instalment*) (*in-*, in) fore-: forestall (**Synonyms**: prevent, preclude, obviate) (English *fore-*, before) SIMPLE COMPOUND: stalemate PREFIXED ROOT: *stal*: dia-: diastalsis (the peristaltic contraction of the small intestine in digestion) (*dia-*, across, through) peri-: peristalsis (wavelike muscular contractions that propel contained matter along tubular organs, as in the alimentary canal) {peristaltic} (*peri-*, around) sy-: systaltic (*sy-*, a variant of *syn-*, with, together)

Element	From	Meaning	Examples
stal (cont'd)			*stle*:
			apo-: apostle [literally, one sent away from; capitalized, one of a group made up especially of the twelve witnesses chosen by Christ to preach the gospel (Luke 6:13-16); one of the twelve members of the Mormon administrative council] (*apo-*, away)
			epi-: epistle (a letter, message; capitalized, one of the letters written by an Apostle and included in the New Testament; a verse letter of the genre invented by Horace and imitated by poets of the 17th and 18th centuries) (*epi-*, upon)
			stol:
			dia-: diastole (*dia-*, across, through)
			GERMAN: *gestalt* as in *gestalt psychology*
			CROSS REFERENCE: to send: *miss/mitt*
			CROSS REFERENCE: to stand: *stat/stit, sist*
stan			See *stat* for *standard*.
stas,*** **stat**	Greek *histanai*: to cause to stand (IE: *sta,* to stand)	stand, place; put in order; make compact; send, set	SIMPLE ROOT:
			stas:
			stasimon (one of the regular choral odes between two episodes in a Greek tragedy possibly sung with the chorus standing in its place in the orchestra)
			stasis (a stoppage of the flow of some fluid in the body, as of blood; reduced peristalsis of the intestines resulting in the retention of feces; also, a state of equilibrium, balance, or stagnancy)
			stat:
			stata:
			statal (in *grammar*, of a passive verb form, that is, expressing a state or condition as *was closed* in "The door *was closed* all day")
			statant (of a heraldic beast: standing with all feet on the ground and seen in profile, as *a lion statant*)
			stati: statistics
			stas:
			a-: astasia (difficulty in standing because of muscular incoordination) (*a-*, not)
			apo-: apostasy (an abandoning of what one has believed in, as a faith, cause, principles, etc.) (*apo-*, away)
			cata-: catastasis (*cata-*, down)
			dia-: diastase (*dia-*, across, through)
			ec-: ecstasy (**Synonyms:** bliss, rapture, transport) (*ec-* is a variant of *ex-*, out)
			epi-: epistasis (originally, to place upon; in *genetics*, the suppression of gene expression by one or more other genes) (*epi-*, upon)
			hypo-: hypostasis {hypostatic} (*hypo-*, under)
			meta-: metastasis {metastatic} (*meta-*, with, after, between)
			stat(e):
			ana-: anastate, anastatic (*ana-*, again)
			apo-: apostate (one guilty of apostasy, which see above) (*apo-*, away)
			cata-: catastate (*cata-*, down)

Element	From	Meaning	Examples
stas (cont'd)			*hypo-*: hypostatize (*hypo-*, under)
			pro-: (before)
			prostate (literally, stands before the bladder; do not confuse with *prostrate*) (*pro-*, before)
			prostatitis (inflammation of the prostate) (*itis*, inflammation)
			stol:
			dia-: diastole (*dia-*, across, through)
			sy-: systole (*sy-*, a variant of *sym-*, with, together)
			LEADING ROOT COMPOUND:
			blast: statoblast (*blast*, bud, sprout)
			cyst: statocyst (*cyst*, cell)
			kine: statokinetic (*kine*, movement)
			scop: statoscope (*scope*, look)
			spor: statospore (*spore*, seed)
			TRAILING ROOT COMPOUND:
			stas:
			bacter: bacteriostasis (*bacter*, rod; rod-shaped microorganism)
			homeo: homeostasis (*homeo*, same)
			icon: iconostasis (*icon*, image, idol)
			iso: isostasy (*iso*, equal)
			stat:
			cryo: cryostat (*cryo*, cold)
			gyro: gyrostat (*gyro*, circle)
			hemo: hemostat (*hemo*, blood)
			hydro: hydrostat (*hydro*, water)
			rheo: rheostat (*rhe*, flow)
			sidero: siderostat (*sidero*, iron)
			thermo: thermostat (*thermo*, heat)
			PREFIXED DISGUISED ROOT:
			dia-: (across, through)
			diastem (a minor interruption in the deposition of sedimentary material)
			diastema (a marked gap between two teeth, especially of the upper jaw)
			sy-: system (from *syn-*, with, together)
			PREFIXED DISGUISED LEADING ROOT COMPOUND:
			epi-: epistemology (originally, to stand before; confront; the study or theory of the origin, nature, methods, and limits of knowledge) (*epi-*, upon + *logy*, study of)
			INTERDISCIPLINARY: hypostasis [in *medicine*, a deposit or sediment; a settling of blood in the lower parts of the body as a result of a slowing down of the blood flow; in *philosophy*, the underlying, essential nature of a thing; essence; in *Christian theology* (in full, *hypostatic union*), the unique nature of the one God; any of the three persons of the Trinity, each person having the divine nature fully and equally; the union of the wholly divine nature and of a wholly human nature in the one person of Jesus Christ]
			CROSS REFERENCE: *sist*

So is a word better than a gift.
Ecclesiasticus, *Apocrypha*

Element	From	Meaning	Examples
stat,*** stab, stan, stet, stic, stit, stor	Latin *stare* (IE: *sta*, to stand)	to stand, set	**SIMPLE ROOT:** *stab:* stabile, stability **stabile** (two general meanings: **1)** standing firm; thus, resistant to sudden change of position or condition; **2)** standing place; thus, a building for the shelter and feeding of domestic animals) *stan:* stanc: stance, stanch (also, *staunch*), stanchion stand: stand (**Synonyms:** bear, suffer, endure), standard (**Synonyms:** criterion, gauge, criterion), stanza *stat:* state: state (**Synonyms:** condition, situation, status; see *Doublets* below) {stately} stati: static (opposed to *dynamic*) station, stationary, stationer, stationery (originally describing one who sold his/her wares in one place; see *Doublets* below) statism stato: stator [a fixed part forming the pivot or housing for a revolving part (*rotor*), as in a motor, dynamo, etc.] statu: statuary, statue, statuesque stature (**Synonyms:** height, altitude, elevation) statute, statutory status (see synonyms at *state*, above) *stet:* stet (let it stand: a printer's term used to indicate that matter previously marked for deletion is to remain) *stor:* store **PREFIXED ROOT:** *stab:* *con-:* constabulary, constable (from *count*; literally, count of the stable; hence, chief groom; in the Middle Ages, the highest ranking official of a royal household, court, etc.) (*com-*, with) *e-:* establish, establishment (from *ex-*, out) *meta-:* metastable (*meta-*, after, between, among) *stanc:* *circum-:* circumstance (**Synonyms:** occurrence, event, incident) (*circum-*, around) *con-:* constancy (*con-*, with, together) *di-:* distance (from *dis-*, apart, away) *sub-:* substance (*sub-*, under) *stant:* *con-:* (with, together) constant (**Synonyms: 1)** faithful, loyal, staunch; **2)** continual, continuous, incessant) constantan [so named because of its constant temperature coefficient of resistance: any alloy of copper (c. 55%) and nickel (c. 45%), used in pyrometers and thermocouples] *dis-:* distant (**Synonyms:** far, remote, removed) (*dis-*, apart) *in-:* instant (**Synonyms:** moment, minute, second) (*in-*, upon)

Element	From	Meaning	Examples
stat (cont'd)			*stet*: *ob-*: obstetric (also, *obstetrical*; literally, to stand before; from *obstetrix*, midwife (Germanic for "she who is present"), obstetrician, obstetrics (*ob-*, against, before) *stin*: *ob-*: obstinacy, obstinate (**Synonyms**: stubborn, headstrong, pertinacious) (*ob-*, against) *stit*: *con-*: constituency, constituent, constitute, constitution, constitutional, constitutive (*con-*, with, together) *de-*: destitute (**Synonyms**: poor, indigent, impoverished), destitution (*de-*, down, away from) *in-*: institute, institution (*in-*, in) *pro-*: prostitute, prostitution (*pro-*, before) *re-*: restitute, restitution (*re-*, back, again) *sub-*: substitute, substitution (*sub-*, under) *super-*: superstition (*super-*, over, beyond) *stor*: *re-*: restoration, restore (*re-*, back, again) PREFIXED ELIDED ROOT: *ex-*: extant (**Synonyms**: living, alive) (*ex-*, out; *tant* elides *stant*) TRAILING ROOT COMPOUND: arm: armistice (literally, a stacking, or standing, of arms) (*arma*, shield, protection) DISGUISED ROOT: contrast (**Synonyms**: compare, collate) (*contra-*, against + *stare*) imprest (a loan or advance of money) (*in-*, in + *pre-*, before + stare, to stand) cost (from Middle Latin *costare*; from Latin *constare*, to stand together) oust (**Synonyms**: eject, expel, dismiss) (from Old French *ouster*; from Latin *ostare*; from *ob-*, against + *stare*, stand) press (from *pre-*, before + *stare*) rest (remainder) (from *re-*, back + *stare*) [another *rest*, peace, ease; sleep; refreshing, is from IE *ere-*, rest] restive (**Synonyms**: contrary, perverse, balky) stage, stager (one who possesses the wisdom of long experience) stapes (literally, footstand; stirrup; a small bone of the inner ear, shaped somewhat like a stirrup; from *stare* + *pes*, foot) stay (**Synonyms**: tarry, linger, sojourn; another *stay* is from Dutch *staeye*, a rope used to support a mast; a third *stay* is from Old English *staeg*, a rope) steer (both meanings: the verb, to guide; the noun, a castrated male of the cattle family) PREFIXED DISGUISED ROOT: *ar-*: arrest (literally, to stand back, to stay behind) (*ar-* assimilates *ad-*, to, toward) *ob-*: obstacle (**Synonyms**: obstruction, bar, barrier) (*ob-*, against)

Element	From	Meaning	Examples
stat (cont'd)			FRENCH: estate (see *Doublets* below)
			SPANISH: *estancia* (originally, a stopping place; a large estate, especially a cattle ranch, in Spanish America)
			DOUBLETS:
			estate:state; stationary:stationery; estate:estancia
			HISTORICAL DOCUMENT: The United States Constitution (*constituted* of seven articles and twenty-four amendments, and has been the supreme law of the nation since its adoption in 1789)
			INTERDISCIPLINARY: stable (in *chemistry*, not easily decomposed or otherwise modified chemically; in *physics*, having no known mode of decay; indefinitely long-lived: said of atomic particles)
			CROSS REFERENCE: *sist, stat* (Greek)
stell**	Latin *stella* (IE: *ster*, star)	star	SIMPLE ROOT: stella, stellar, stellate, stellula, stellular
			PREFIXED ROOT:
			con-: constellate, constellation (*con-*, with, together)
			inter-: interstellar (*inter-*, between, among)
			LEADING ROOT COMPOUND:
			ectom: stellectomy (*ectom*, to cut out surgically)
			form: stelliform (in the form of a star)
			fy: stellify (from *facere*, to make)
			DISGUISED ROOT: sterling
			PROPER NAME: Estelle, Esther
			PLACENAMES:
			Stella (Kentucky, Louisiana, Missouri, Nebraska, Tennessee)
			CROSS REFERENCE: *astr, sider*
steno**	Greek *stenos* (IE: *sten*, thin, narrow)	narrow, close, little	LEADING ROOT COMPOUND:
			graph: stenography (*graph*, write)
			phag: stenophagous (in *biology*, eating only a limited variety of food; compare *euryphagous, monophagous*) (*phag*, eat)
			therm: stenothermal (*therm*, heat)
			topic: stenotopic (in *biology*, able to withstand only a limited range in environmental conditions; opposed to *eurytopic*: able to withstand a wide range of environmental conditions) (*topos*, place)
			CROSS REFERENCE: *angi*
ster***	Greek *stereos* (IE: *ster*, rigid, stiff; yields English stare, starve, stern)	solid	SIMPLE ROOT: stere, steric, sterid
			PREFIXED ROOT:
			con-: consternate, consternation (**Synonyms:** alarm, dismay, trepidation) (*con-*, with, together)
			LEADING ROOT COMPOUND:
			ster:
			oid: steroid (*oid*, similar to)
			ol: sterol (*ol*, oil)
			ome: sterome (*ome*, mass)
			stere:
			ops: stereopsis (*ops*, sight)
			opt: stereopticon (a magic lantern, especially one made double so as to produce dissolving views) (*optic*, view)
			stereo:
			bat: stereobate (the foundation of a stone building) (from *bas*, base)

Element	From	Meaning	Examples
ster (cont'd)			chem: stereochemistry (the chemical study of spatial arrangements of atoms in molecules and of the effects of these arrangements on the molecule's properties) graph: stereograph, stereography (*graph*, write) iso: stereoisomer (*iso*, same, equal + *mere*, part) metry: stereometry {stereometric} (*metry*, measurement of) phon: stereophonic (*phone*, sound) plasm: stereoplasm (*plasm*, form) scop: stereoscope, stereoscopic (*scope*, look, view) taxis: stereotaxis {stereotactic} (*taxis*, arrange) tom: stereotomy (stonecutting) (*tom*, cut) trop: stereotropism (in *biology*, the response or motion of an organism to direct contact with a surface) (*trop*, turn) typ: stereotype, stereotypic {stereotypical} (*type*, image, symbol) TRAILING ROOT COMPOUND: andro: androsterone (*andro*, man, male) chol: cholesterol [solid fat (*sterol*) first found in gall (*chol*) bladder] deci: decistere (Latin *deci*, tenth) CROSS REFERENCE: *gel*
stet			See *stat* for *stet*.
stic			See *stat* for *armistice*.
stich*	Greek *stichos*: row, line, verse (IE: *steigh*, to step, climb)	stride, step	SIMPLE ROOT: stich (in *prosody*, a line, or verse) LEADING ROOT COMPOUND: metry: stichometry (the division of a prose piece into lines whose lengths correspond to the natural divisions of sense or to natural cadences, as in manuscripts before the adoption of punctuation) (*metry*, measurement of) myth: stichomythia (an ancient Greek arrangement of dialogue in drama, poetry, and disputation in which single lines of verse are spoken by alternate speakers) TRAILING ROOT COMPOUND: acro: acrostic (*acro*, top) di: distich (two lines of verse regarded as a unit) (*di*, two) hemi: hemistich (a half line of verse, especially when separated rhythmically from the rest of the line by a caesura; also, an incomplete or imperfect line of verse) (*hemi*, half) hepta: heptastich (*hepta*, seven) mono: monostich (one line of poetry) (*mono*, one) ortho: orthostichous (in *biology*, characterized by parallel arrangement in a vertical row) (*ortho*, straight) tele: telestich (or *telestic*: a short poem, etc. in which the last letters of the lines spell a word or words when taken in order; compare *acrostic*) (*tele*, end) tri: tristichous (*tri*, three) CROSS REFERENCE: *bas/bat, grad/gress*
stig			See *string* for *prestige*.

If you want your child to achieve success with his studies in college, look to his vocabulary. W. D. Templeton

Element	From	Meaning	Examples
stig,** stim	Latin *stitzein*: to tattoo (IE: *steig*, a point)	pricked	ROOT NOTE: The Indo-European base of these root is *steig-*, to stick; pointed; *stig* as in *stigma* is Greek but passed into Latin unchanged. SIMPLE ROOT: *stig*: stigma (in *botany*, the free upper tip of the style of a flower, on which pollen falls and develops), stigmatic, stig- matism, stigmatize *stim*: stimulant, stimulate (**Synonyms: 1)** animate, quicken, exhilarate; **2)** provoke, excite, pique) PREFIXED ROOT: *a-*: astigmatic, astigmatism (an irregularity in the curvature of a lens, including the lens of the eye, so that light rays from an object do not meet ina single focus) (*a-*, not) *ana-*: anastigmatic (*ana-*, again) *in-*: instigate (**Synonyms:** incite, arouse, foment) (*in-*, in) DISGUISED ROOT: etiquette (**Synonyms:** propriety, decorum, protocol; see *Dou- blets* below) stiletto (same as *stylet*; see *Doublets* below style (**Synonyms:** fashion, mode, vogue), stylet (a slender, pointed weapon; especially, a stiletto; in *surgery*, a slender probe; a wire inserted into a soft catheter to keep it rigid) stylus ticket (see *Doublets* below) PREFIXED DISGUISED ROOT: *stinct*: *dis-*: distinct (**Synonyms:** different, diverse, divergent), dis- tinction, distinctive (**Synonyms:** characteristic, individual) (*dis-*, apart) *in-*: instinct, instinctive (*in-*, in) *sting*: *dis-*: distinguish (**Synonyms:** discriminate, differentiate) (*dis*, apart) DOUBLETS: etiquette:ticket; stiletto:stylet FRENCH: *distingué* (having an air of distinction; distin- guished: also, sometimes *distinguée*) ENGLISH COGNATE: stick (**Synonyms:** adhere, cohere, cling) NOTE: *Extinct* and *extinguish* are not in this family. CROSS REFERENCE: *pung/punct*
stim			See *stig* for *stimulant, stimulus.*
stin			See *stat* for *obstinate.*
stit			See *stat* for *constitute, prostitute, restitution.*
stle			See *stal* for *apostle, epistle.*
stol			See *stal* for *diastole, systole.*
stom**	Greek *stoma* (IE: *stomen*, mouth)	stomach, mouth, opening	ROOT NOTE: Though the meaning of the root itself is as listed, some of the *Simple Root* words pertain to the *stom- ach* itself, the enlarged, saclike portion of the alimentary canal. SIMPLE ROOT: (*stomach*) stomach stomacher (a decorative, heavily embroidered or jeweled gar- ment formerly worn over the chest and stomach, especially by women)

Element	From	Meaning	Examples
stom (cont'd)			stomachic (also, *stomachal*: of or pertaining to the stomach; beneficial to or stimulating digestion in the stomach)
			SIMPLE ROOT: (*mouth*)
			stomatal, stomatic, stomatous (having a stoma or stomata)
			ana-: anastomosis (a connection between blood vessels, veins in a leaf, channels of a river, etc.) (*ana-*, again)
			SIMPLE ROOT: (*opening*)
			stoma (plural, *stomata*), stomal, stomian
			PREFIXED ROOT:
			peri-: **peristome** (*peri-*, around)
			LEADING ROOT COMPOUND:
			stom:
			od: stomodaeum (or, *stomodeum*; literally, on the way; the oral cavity in the digestive track of an embryo, which develops into the mouth) (from *hodios*, way, road, track)
			stomat:
			itis: stomatitis (inflammation of the oral mucosa) (*itis*, inflammation)
			stomato:
			lalia: stomatolalia [speaking through the mouth with the nares (nostrils) closed] (*lal*, babble)
			logy: stomatology (the branch of medicine dealing with the mouth and its diseases) (*logy*, study of)
			TRAILING ROOT COMPOUND:
			colo: colostomy (the surgical operation of forming an artificial anal opening in the colon)
			cyclo: cyclostome (a subclass of jawless parasitic fishes, including the lamprey and hagfish, with an eellike body and a *circular*, sucking mouth) (*cyclo*, circle)
			di: distome (a two-suckered digenetic flatfish) (*di*, two)
			INTERDISCIPLINARY:
			stoma (in *anatomy*, a small aperture in the surface of a membrane; a minute opening in the surface of the peritoneum, thought to be for the passage of fluid into the lymphatic vessels; in *botany*, one of the minute pores in the epidermis of a leaf or stem, through which gases and water vapor pass; in *zoology*, a mouthlike opening, such as the oral cavity of the nematode)
			peristome (in *botany*, the fringe of teeth around the opening of the spore case in mosses; in *zoology*, the area or parts surrounding the mouth or a mouthlike part of various invertebrates)
			CROSS REFERENCE: *ora, os*
stor			See *stat* for *store, restoration*.
strain			See *string* for *constrain*.
strait			See *string* for *strait*.
strat**	Latin *stratum*: spread, bed (IE: *ster*, to extend, stretch out)	layer	SIMPLE ROOT: stratum (plural, *stratums, strata*), stratus
			LEADING ROOT COMPOUND:
			strati:
			form: stratiform (showing stratification)
			fy: stratify (to form or arrange into layers or strata) (from *facere*, to make)

Element	From	Meaning	Examples
strat (cont'd)			graph: stratigraphy (the arrangement of rocks in layers; also, a branch of geology) (*graph*, write) *strato*: cumu: stratocumulus (a cloud type occurring in a continuous gray or whitish layer or in patches, usually with dark areas and with rounded masses) (*cumulus*, a heap, mass) spher: stratosphere (the atmospheric zone above the troposphere) (*sphere*, ball, globe) DISGUISED ROOT: street (from *strata via*, layered, or paved road) stretch, stretcher, stretchy CROSS REFERENCE: *lamin*
stress			See *string* for *distress*.
strict			See *string* for *constrict*.
string,*** strict, strain, strait, stress, strig, stig	Latin *stringere* (IE: *streig*, stiff, taut, a rope; yields Greek strangle)	to pull tight	SIMPLE ROOT: *strain*: strain, strait (see *Doublets* below; *straight* from Old English *stretch* is not related to *strait*) *strait*: strait (**Synonyms**: emergency, exigency, contingency) *stress*: stress (aphetic of *distress*, which see below) *strict*: strict (in *botany*, stiff and upright; erect; see *Doublets* below), striction, stricture *strig*: strigil, strigilate *string*: string, stringency, stringendo (in *music*, with accelerated tempo, as toward a climax), stringent PREFIXED ROOT: *stig*: pre-: prestige (originally, to blind, or to bind fast; the idea is that blindfolded jugglers impressed the spectators with their magic; thus, coveted status; **Synonyms**: influence, authority, weight) (*pre-*, in front) *strain(t)*: con-: constrain (**Synonyms**: force, compel, coerce), constraint (*con-*, with, together) dis-: (opposite of) distrain [in *law*, to seize and hold (property) as security or indemnity for a debt] distrainee (a person whose property has been distrained) distraint (in *law*, the action of distraining; seizure) re-: restrain (**Synonyms**: curb, check, bridle; see *Doublets* below), restraint (*re-*, back) *stress*: dis-: distress (originally, to constrain to do something; **Synonyms**: suffering, agony, anguish; in *law, to distrain*), distressed (one meaning: giving the appearance of being antique, as having the finish marred, as *distressed oak*), distressful (*dis-*, opposite of, away) *strict*: a-: astrict, astrictive, astriction (from *ad-*, to, toward) con-: constrict (**Synonyms**: contract, condense, compress), constriction, constrictor (*con-*, with, together) di-: district (from *distress*, the original meaning; originally, in feudal law, a territory within which a lord had jurisdiciton) (from *dis-*, apart)

Element	From	Meaning	Examples
string (cont'd)			*re-*: restrict (**Synonyms**: limit, bound, circumscribe; see *Doublets* below) (*re-*, back, again)
			string:
			a-: astringe, astringent (from *ad-*, to, toward)
			con-: constringe (to cause to contract) (*con-*, with, together)
			per-: perstringe (to find fault with; criticize) (*per-*, through)
			re-: restringent (*re-*, back, again)
			DOUBLETS: restrain:restrict; strait:strict
			ENGLISH COGNATES:
			strength (**Synonyms**: power, force, energy)
			strong (the Latin cognate is from *stringere*, to draw taut)
			CROSS REFERENCE: *ten*
stroph**	Greek *strophos*: act of turning (IE: *ster*, rigid, taut)	turn, twist	SIMPLE ROOT: strophe (in ancient Greek drama, the movement of the chorus from right to left; compare *antistrophe* under *Prefixed Root*) {strophic}
			ELIDED SIMPLE ROOT: strop (a variation of *strap*; see *Disguised Root*)
			PREFIXED ROOT:
			ana-: anastrophe (in *rhetoric*, the inversion of the usual order of words, for effect, e.g., for *The dawn came*, Came the dawn) (*ana-*, back)
			anti-: antistrophe (literally, opposite the strophe; in *ancient Greek drama*, the part that answered a previous strophe, sung by the chorus when returning from left to right) (*anti-*, opposite)
			apo-: apostrophe (literally, to turn from or away; in *Greek drama*, a turning away from the audience to address one person; in *grammar*, originally *apostrophos prosodia*, averted accent; apostrophes are used to indicate possession of nouns, e.g., Susan's teacher; the children's teacher; they are also used to indicate omitted letters in contractions, e.g., *doesn't* for *does not*) (*apo-*, away)
			cata-: catastrophe (literally, to turn down; overturn; in *Greek drama*, the culminating event, especially of a tragedy, by which the plot is resolved; denouement; a disastrous end; other meanings) (*cata-*, down)
			dia-: diastrophism (the process or series of processes by which the major features of the earth's crust, including continents, mountains, ocean beds, folds, and faults, are formed) (*dia-*, across, through)
			epi-: epistrophe (the repetition of the same word or expression at the end of successive phrases or clauses for rhetorical effect, e.g., as government *of the people, for the people*, and *by the people*; compare *anaphora*) (*epi-*, upon)
			TRAILING ROOT COMPOUND:
			bou: boustrophedon [literally, turning like an ox (while plowing); an ancient method of writing in which the lines are inscribed from right to left and from left to right] (*bous*, ox)
			DISGUISED ROOT: strap (a narrow strip or band of leather or other flexible material, often with a buckle or similar fastener at one end, for binding or securing things; dialectal form of *strop*; see *Elided Simple Root* above)
			CROSS REFERENCE: *trop, vert*

651

Element	From	Meaning	Examples
struct***	Latin *struere*: to pile up, arrange, build (IE: *ster*, to extend, stretch out, strew)	to build	SIMPLE ROOT: structural, strucuralism, structuralist, structure (**Synonyms**: building, edifice, pile) PREFIXED ROOT: *con-*: construct (**Synonyms**: make, form, shape), construction, constructive (*con-*, with, together) *de-*: destructibility, destructible, destruction (**Synonyms**: ruin, havoc, dilapidation) (*de-*, down) *in-*: instruct (**Synonyms**: 1) command, order, bid; 2) teach, educate, tutor), instruction, instructor (*in-*, in) *infra-*: infrastructure (*infra-*, below) *ob-*: obstruct (literally, to build against; **Synonyms**: hinder, block, impede), obstruction (*ob-*, against) *sub-*: substructure (*sub-*, under) *super-*: superstructure (*super-*, beyond, over) DOUBLE PREFIXED ROOT: reconstruction (*re-*, again + *con-*, with, together) PREFIXED DISGUISED ROOT: *con-*: construe (**Synonyms**: explain, expound, explicate) (*con-*, with, together) *de-*: destroy (**Synonyms**: demolish, raze) (*de-*, down) *in-*: instrument (**Synonyms**: implement, tool, appliance), instrumental, instrumentation (*in-*, in) DOUBLE PREFIXED DISGUISED ROOT: misconstrue (to construe wrongly; misinterpret; misunderstand) (Anglo-Saxon *mis-*, wrong, bad + *con-*, with) INTERDISCIPLINARY: construct [in *geometry*, a verb, to draw (a figure) so as to meet the specified requirements; in *linguistics*, a noun; a grammatical pattern consisting of two or more immediate constituents; to arrange words to form meaningful phrases, clauses, or sentences] CROSS REFERENCE: *edi*
stup*	Latin *stupere*, to be stunned, amazed) (IE: *steup*, to strike)	stunned, amazed	SIMPLE ROOT: stupendous (astonishing; overwhelming) stupid (**Synonyms**: dull, dense, slow), stupidity stupor LEADING ROOT COMPOUND: fy: stupefy (to bring into a state of stupor; stun; make dull or lethargic; to astound, bewilder) (from *facere*, to make, do) ENGLISH COGNATES: steep (**Synonyms**: abrupt, precipitous, sheer) steep (**Synonyms**: soak, saturate, drench) NO CROSS REFERENCE
styl**	Greek *stylos* (IE: *sta*, to stand)	pillar, column	SIMPLE ROOT: stylite (any of various Christian ascetics who lived on the tops of pillars) PREFIXED ROOT: *a-*: astylar (not having columns or pilasters) (*a-*, without) *amphi-*: amphistylar (in *architecture*, having columns at both front and back or on both sides) (*amphi-*, around) *epi-*: epistyle (an architrave, the lowermost part of an entablature, resting directly on top of a column in classical architecture) (*epi-*, upon)

Element	From	Meaning	Examples
styl (cont'd)			*hypo-:* hypostyle (a building having a roof or ceiling supported by rows of columns, as in ancient Egyptian architecture (*hypo-*, under) *peri-:* peristyle (a row of columns forming an enclosure or supporting a roof; any area or enclosure so formed, as a court) (*peri-*, around) *pro-:* prostyle (in *architecture*, having a row of columns across the front only, as in some Greek temples) (*pro-*, in front of; before) DOUBLE PREFIXED ROOT: amphiprostyle (with pillars in front and behind) (*amphi-*, around, on both sides + *pro-*, in front of) LEADING ROOT COMPOUND: bat: stylobate (the immediate foundation of a row of columns; also, called *stereobate*) (from *bas*, base, foundation) lite: stylolite (a small, columnlike formation in a rock deposit, usually composed of limestone with grooved or scratched sides) (*lithos*, stone) TRAILING ROOT COMPOUND: hetero: heterostyly (in *biology*, the condition in which flowers on different plants of the same species have styles of different lengths, thereby encouraging cross-pollination) (*hetero*, different) mono: monostylous (in *botany*, having one style) (*mono*, one) NB: *Style*, from Latin *stimulus*, is not related to the Greek root here. NO CROSS REFERENCE
styl**	Latin *stilus*, sharp (IE: *(s)tei*, pointed)	manner	SIMPLE ROOT: style (a slender, pointed instrument used by the ancients in writing on wax tablets; see *stylus* below; **Synonyms:** fashion, vogue, fad) stylet (see *Doublets* below) stylish, stylist, stylistic, stylistics, stylize stylus (a style or other needlelike marking device) LEADING ROOT COMPOUND: *styl:* oid: styloid (resembling a style; styliform; in *anatomy*, designating or of any of various long, slender processes, especially that at the base of the temporal bone) (*oid*, resembling) *styli:* form: styliform (shaped like a style or stylus) *stylo:* graph: stylograph, stylographic, stylography (*graph*, write) pod: stylopodium (a disk or swelling at the base of the style in plants of the umbel family) (Greek *pod*, foot) DISGUISED ROOT: stimulant (anything that stimulates) stimulate (**Synonyms: 1)** animate, quicken, exhilarate; **2)** provoke, excite, pique), stimulus ITALIAN: stiletto (a small dagger, having a slender, tapering blade; see *Doublets* below) DOUBLETS: stiletto:stylet

653

Element	From	Meaning	Examples
styl (cont'd)			INTERDISCIPLINARY: style (in *botany*, the slender, stalk-like part of a carpel between the stigma and the ovary; in *zoology*, a small, pointed projection or bristlelike process, as on some insects) CROSS REFERENCE: *mod*
suas,** suad, suag	Latin *suadere* (IE: *swad*, pleasing to the taste; yields English sweet)	advise, urge	ROOT NOTE: The Indo-European base of this root yields English *sweet*; German *süss*; Greek *hedys*; Latin *suadere*, to persuade, and *suavis*, sweet. SIMPLE ROOT: suasible, suasion, suasive, suasoria (an ancient Roman oration dealing with a problem of conscience) PREFIXED ROOT: *suad*: *dis*-: dissuade, dissuasion, dissuasive (*dis*-, reversal) *per*-: persuade (**Synonyms**: induce, convince), persuasion, persuasive (*per*-, intensive) *suag*: *as*-: assuage (**Synonyms**: relieve, allay, comfort), assuagement, assuasive (*as*- assimilates *ad*-, to, toward) FRENCH: suave, suavity ITALIAN: soave (literally, sweet, but actually a dry white Italian table wine) CROSS REFERENCE: *dulc, gluc/glyc, grat, plac*
sub-,*** suc-, suf-, sug-, sup-, sur-, sus-	Latin (IE: *upo*, up from below)	under, below, lower in rank; to a lesser degree; forming a division into smaller or less important parts; with less than the normal amount of	EXTENDED DISGUISED PREFIX: supine (**Synonyms**: prone, prostrate, recumbent) PREFIXED ROOT: *sub*-: alter: subaltern (lower in rank; secondary), subalternate (in *biology*, in an alterante arrangement, but tending to become opposite: said of leaves) (*alter*, other) aud: subaudition (*audire*, to hear) con: subcontract (*con*- prefixes *tract*, to draw, pull) du: subdue (**Synonyms**: defeat, conquer, vanquish) (from *ducere*, to lead) jac: subjacent (located beneath or below) (*jac*, throw) ject: subject (**Synonyms**: matter, topic, theme), subjective, subjectivism (from *jac*, throw) join: subjoin (to add at the end; append; annex), subjoinder (from *jungere*, to bind) jug: subjugate (to bring under dominion; conquer; subdue) (*jugum*, yoke) junct: subjunction, subjunctive (from *jungere*, to join, bind) lat: sublate (in *law*, to deny, contradict) (from *ferre*, to bear) lim: sublimate, sublimation, sublime, subliminal (*limen*, threshold) lun: sublunary (situated beneath the moon; terrestrial; earthly; mundane) (*lun*, moon) mar: submarine (*mar*, sea) med: submediant (the sixth tone of a diatonic scale) (*med*, middle) merg: submerge, submerged, submergible (*mergere*, to plunge) miss: submission (**Synonyms**: surrender, capitulation), submissive) (from *mittere*, to send)

Element	From	Meaning	Examples
sub- (cont'd)			mit: submit (**Synonyms**: relent, defer, capitulate) (*mittere*, to throw)
			ord: (from *ordo*, straight row)
			subordinate, subordination, subordinating conjunction
			subordinationism (in *theology*, the doctrine that the second and third persons of the Trinity are subordinate to the first person, God the Father; the second and third being God, the Son; and God, the Holy Spirit, respectively)
			orn: suborn (to induce a person to commit a wrong or unlawful act; to induce a person to commit perjury) (*sub-*, secretly + *ornare*, to equip)
			rept: subreption (a calculated misrepresentation through concealment of the facts; an inference drawn from such a representation) (*repere*, to creep)
			rog: (*rogare*, to ask)
			subrogate (originally, to nominate an alternative candidate; now, to substitute one person for another)
			subrogation (the substitution of one person for another, especially the legal doctrine of substituting one creditor for another)
			scrib: subscribe (**Synonyms**: assent, agree, accede) (*scribere*, to write)
			script: subscript, subscription (see *subscribe*)
			seq: subsequence, subsequent (*sequi*, to follow)
			serv: subserve, subservience, subservient (*servire*, to serve)
			sid: subside (**Synonyms**: decrease, reduce, lessen), subsidize, subsidy, subsidiary (*sidere*, to settle)
			sist: subsist, subsistence (*sistere*, to cause to stand)
			stan: substance, substandard, substantial (strong, solid, considerable, ample) substantiate (**Synonyms**: confirm, corroborate, verify), substantive (from *stare*, to stand)
			stit: substituent, substitute, substitution, substitutive (*statuere*, to cause to stand)
			strat: substrate, substratum (from *sternere*, to spread out)
			struct: substruction, substructure (from *struere*, to build)
			sum(p): subsume, subsumption (*sumere*, to take up)
			tend: subtend (*tendere*, to extend, to stretch out)
			terr: subterranean, subterrestrial (*terra*, earth)
			tract: subtract, subtraction, subtractive (see *subtrahend*)
			trahend: subtrahend (*trahere*, to draw, pull)
			DOUBLETS: subtract:subtrahend
			suc-:
			ceed: succeed (**Synonyms**: follow, supplant, ensue) (from *cedere*, to go)
			cess: success, successful, succession (**Synonyms**: series, progression, sequence), successive, successor (from *cedere*, to go)
			cinct: succinct (**Synonyms**: concise, terse, laconic) (from *cingere*, to gird)
			cor: succor (literally, to run under; help; aid) (from *currere*, to run)

Element	From	Meaning	Examples
sub- (cont'd)			cub: succubus (literally, to lie under; a female demon supposed to descend upon and have sexual intercourse with a man while he sleeps) (*cubare*, to lie)
			cumb: succumb (literally, to lie down under; to die) (*cumbere*, to lie down)
			cus: succuss, succussion (the process of shaking violently; the condition of being so shaken) (from *quatere*, to shake)
			NB: *Succory* is a doublet of *chicory*; *succulus* is from *succus*, juice.
			suf-:
			fer: suffer (literally, to bear up; **Synonyms: 1**) bear, tolerate, stand; **2**) let, allow, permit), sufferable, sufferance, suffering (*ferre*, to bear)
			fic: suffice, sufficiency, sufficient (**Synonyms:** enough, adequate) (from *facere*, to do, make)
			fix: suffix (from *figere*, to fix)
			foc: suffocate (from *fauces*, throat)
			frag: suffrage (from *fragor*, applause)
			fus: suffuse (from *fundere*, to pour)
			sug-:
			gest: suggest (**Synonyms:** imply, hint, intimate), suggestion, suggestive (that suggests ideas, especially that which is considered risqué) (from *gerere*, to bear)
			sum-:
			mon: summon (**Synonyms:** call, convoke, convene) (*monere*, to remind)
			sup-:
			plant: supplant (**Synonyms: 1**) follow, succeed, ensue; **2**) displace, supersede) (*planta*, sole of foot)
			ple: supplement, supplementary (from *supply*)
			plic: supplicant, supplicate (**Synonyms:** appeal, plead, sue), supplication (*supple* is also in this family) (*plicare*, to fold)
			ply: supply (from *plere*, to fill)
			port: support (**Synonyms:** uphold, sustain, maintain), supportable, supporter, supportive (*portare*, to carry)
			pos: suppose, supposed, supposition, suppositive, suppository (from *ponere*, to place)
			press: suppress (**Synonym:** stifle), suppression, suppressive (from *premere*, to press)
			pur: suppurate, suppuration (from *pus*, pus)
			sur-:
			rept: surreptitious (**Synonyms:** stealthy, covert, furtive) (from *rapere*, to seize)
			rog: surrogate (a deputy or substitute; in *psychiatry*, a substitute figure who replaces a father or mother in one's feelings) (see *subrogate*)
			NOTE: The non-assimilated, but rather contracted, *sur-* prefix is not in this family, but from *supra-*, over, beyond, e.g., *surmise, surmount, surname, surpass, surplice, surplus, surprise, surtax, surtout, survey, survive*, as well as the assimilated *surrender, surround*.

Element	From	Meaning	Examples
sub- (cont'd)			*sus-*:
			cept: susceptibility, susceptible, susceptive (same as suscep-tible; receptive) (from *capere*, to take)
			pect: suspect (literally, to look up at; to watch) (from *specere*, to look at)
			pend: suspend (**Synonyms: 1**) exclude, debar, disbar; **2**) adjourn, prorogue, postpone), suspenders (*pendere*, to hang)
			pens: suspense (the state of being undecided or undetermined), suspension, suspensive, suspensor, suspensory (from *suspend*)
			pic: suspicion (originally, a looking up to, as from underneath) (see *suspect*)
			tain: sustain (**Synonyms**: support, uphold, maintain) (from *tenere*, to hold)
			ten: sustenance, sustentaculum (in *anatomy*, a supporting structure), sustentation (see *sustain*)
			DOUBLE PREFIXED ROOT: subconscious
			DISGUISED PREFIXED ROOT:
			somber (see *sombrero* under *Spanish*)
			souvenir (literally, to come from under; to bring to mind) (*venir*, to come)
			FRENCH: (*sou* of *souffle* and *sobri* of *sobriquet* from French *sous*, under)
			sobriquet (a nickname; an assumed name)
			souffle, soufflé (see note under *fla*)
			soutane (French; from Italian *sottana*; from *sotto*, under; a cassock or tunic worn by Roman Catholic priests)
			SPANISH: sombrero (from *somber*, which itself is from *sub-*, + *umbra*, shade)
			LATIN PHRASES:
			subpoena (literally, under penalty, the first words in the order)
			sub rosa (literally, under the rose; secrecy, the rose being the symbol of secrecy during the Middle Ages)
			ITALIAN MUSIC TERM: *sotto voce* (literally, under the voice; in an undertone, so as not to be overheard)
			NOTE: *Subterfuge*, literally, to flee secretly, is not in this family.
			CROSS REFERENCE: *hypo, nether*
suc			See *sub-* for *succeed, succor.*
sud*	Latin *sudare*: to sweat (IE: *sweid*, to sweat)	perspire, sweat	SIMPLE ROOT:
			sudam: sudamen, sudaminal, (sudarium, sudary; see *Doublets* below)
			sudat: sudation (the act of sweating; excessive perspiration), sudatoria, sudatorium, sudatory
			PREFIXED ELIDED ROOT:
			ex-: exude (to pass out in drops through pores, an incision, etc; ooze; discharge; to diffuse or seem to radiate, as *to exude joy*), exudatory [*ex-*, out; *elided s*, because of *s* sound of *ex* (eks)]
			tran-: transudation (*trans-*, across, through)
			LEADING ROOT COMPOUND:
			fer: sudoriferous (*ferre*, to bear)

Element	From	Meaning	Examples
sud (cont'd)			fic: sudorific (from *facere*, to make) DOUBLETS: sudarium:sudary FRENCH: *sueur,* suint (the natural grease found in sheep's wool: a source of potash) PLACENAME: La Sueur, Minnesota CROSS REFERENCE: *hidr*
sues,* cust	Latin *suere* (IE: *sewe,* of oneself)	to accustom	PREFIXED ROOT: *cust*: *ac-*: accustom (*ac-* assimilates *ad-*, to, toward) *sues*: *de-*: desuetude (the state or condition of disuse) (*de-*, reversal) DOUBLE PREFIXED ROOT: disaccustom (*dis-*, apart; *ac-* assimilates *ad-*, to, toward) TRAILING ROOT COMPOUND: man: mansuetude (gentleness, tameness) (*manus,* hand) DISGUISED ROOT: mastiff (*manus,* hand, accustomed to the hand; a particular large dog of ancient breed, easily tamed) PREFIXED DISGUISED ROOT: *cos-*: costume (from *custom*, next entry) *cus-*: custom (**Synonyms:** habit, practice, wont), customable, customarily, customary, customer, customal (same as *customary*) (from *com-*, intensive + *sues*) *in-*: insolent (boldly disrespectful in speech or behavior; impertinent; impudent) (*in-*, not) NO CROSS REFERENCE
suf-			See *sub-* for *suffer*.
sug-			See *sub-* for *suggest*.
sui*	Latin *sui* (IE: *sewe,* of oneself)	oneself	LEADING ROOT COMPOUND: cid: (*cide*, kill) suicidal, suicide suicidology (the study of suicide, its causes, and its preventions, and of the behavior of those who threaten or attempt suicide) (*logy*, study of) LATIN LEGAL TERMS: *sui generis* (of one's own kind); *sui juris* (of one's own right) CROSS REFERENCE: *auto*
sult			See *sal/sault* for *insult, result*.
sum-			See *sub-* for *summary*.
sum-			See *super-* for *summit*.
sum,*** sumpt	Latin *sumere*: to take (see *Root Note*)	take, buy	ROOT NOTE: The root is a contraction of *sub-*, under + *emp*, to buy, spend or to take. SIMPLE ROOT: sumptuary (of or regulating expenses or expenditures; specifically, seeking to regulate extravagance on religious or moral grounds) sumptuous (involving great expense; costly; lavish; magnificent or splendid) PREFIXED ROOT: *sum:* *as-*: assume (**Synonyms:** pretend, feign, affect), assumed (pretended, put on, fictitious; taken for granted), assuming (*as-* assimilates *ad-*, to, toward)

Element	From	Meaning	Examples
sum (cont'd)			*con-*: consume, consumerism, consummate, consummation (*com-*, intensive)
			pre-: presume (**Synonyms:** presuppose, suppose, postulate) (*pre-*, before)
			re-: resume, résumé (*re-*, again)
			sub-: subsume (*sub-*, under)
			sump:
			as-: assumption {assumptive} (see *Placename* below)
			con-: consumption, consumptive (consuming or tending to consume; destructive; wasteful) (*con-*, with, together)
			pre-: presumption (in *law*, the inference that a fact exists, based on the proved existence of other facts), presumptive, presumptuous (from *presume*, above) (*pre-*, before)
			re-: resumption (*re-*, again)
			sub-: subsumption, subsumptive (see *subsume*) (*sub-*, under)
			LATIN: *sumpsimus* (We have taken; compare *mumpsimus*)
			LAW TERM: *assumpsit* (an agreement or promise, written, spoken, or implied, and not under seal; an action to recover damages for the non-fulfillment of such an agreement)
			FRENCH: *consommé* (a clear, highly seasoned soup made of meat or vegetable stock, or both; it is served hot or as a cold jelly; authorities are divided on whether *consommé* is from this root in which the word suggests that the meat or vegetables or both have been *consumed* in the concentration process; or whether the word is from *consummate*: to bring to completion)
			PLACENAME: Assumption Parish, Louisiana
			CROSS REFERENCE: *cap/cep, prehend, rapt*
sup-			See *sub-* for *support*.
super-***	Latin *super* (IE: *eghs*, out + *uper*, over)	beyond, over, above	NOTE: Generally regarded as a prefix because of its prepositional or adverbial usage, *super* can also be regarded as a root because of its use as an adjective, as "a super job," and from which adjectives can be formed, as those under *Simple Root*. For formatting purposes, the element is treated as a prefix in this list.
			EXTENDED PREFIX:
			super: superb (noble, grand, or majestic), superior, supernal (of, from, or as though from the heavens or the sky)
			supr: supra, supreme
			PREFIXED ROOT:
			super-:
			ann: superannuate, superannuated (**Synonyms:** old, elderly, venerable) (*annus*, year)
			cili: superciliary, supercilious (**Synonyms:** proud, arrogant, haughty) (*cilium*, eyelid)
			fecund: superfecundation (the impregnation of more than one ovum within a single menstrual cycle by separate acts of coitus, especially by different males) (*fecund*, fertile)
			feta: superfetation (*fetare*, to breed)
			fic: superficial (**Synonyms:** shallow, cursory) (*facies*, face)
			flu: superfluent, superfluid, superfluity, superfluous (*fluere*, to flow)

659

Element	From	Meaning	Examples
super- (cont'd)			galaxy: supergalaxy (from Greek *galact*, milk) jac: superjacent (*jacere*, to throw) lat: superlative (*latus*, carried) lun: superlunary (situated beyond the moon) (*luna*, moon) nat: supernatant (to swim, or float, on top of the water, as algae) (*natare*, to swim) pos: superpose (from *ponere*, to place) rog: supererogate (to pay out more than is expected; the word is now obsolete) (*e-* from *ex-*, out + *rogare*, to ask) scrib: superscribe (*scribere*, to write) sed: supersede (**Synonyms**: replace, supplant) (*sedere*, to sit) son: supersonic (*sonus*, sound) stit: superstition, superstitious (from *stare*, to stand) struct: superstructure (from *struere*, to build) ven: supervene (*venir*, to come) vis: supervise, supervision, supervisor (from *videre*, to see) *supra-:* glott: supraglottal (*glott*, tongue) laps: supralapsarian (a theology term) (*lapsus*, fall) limin: supraliminal (above the threshold of consciousness or sensation) (*limin*, threshold) mol: supramolecular (consisting of more than one molecule) (*mol*, mass) orb: supraorbital (located above the orbit of the eye) ren: suprarenal (located on or above the kidney) (*ren*, kidney) *sur-:* charg: surcharge (an additional amount added to the usual amount or cost) cingl: surcingle (French *cengle*, belt) (from Latin *cingere*, to gird) feit: surfeit (**Synonyms**: satiate, cloy, glut) (from *facere*, to do) mis: surmise (**Synonyms**: conjecture, guess, speculate) (from *mittere*, to send) mount: surmount nam: surname (a person's family name as distinguished from his/her given name) plic: surplice (originally, a fur coat) (from *pellis*, skin) plus: surplus (*plus*, more) pris: surprise (**Synonyms**: astonish, amaze, astound) (from *prendre*, to take; from *prehendere*, to seize) real: surrealism render: surrender (from *re(d)-*, back + *dare*, to give) round: surround (from *unda*, wave) tax: surtax (an extra tax on something already taxed) tout: surtout (a man's long, closefitting overcoat of the late 19th century) (from *totus*, all) veil: surveillance (from *vigilare*, to watch) vey: survey (from *videre*, to see) viv: survival, survive, survivor (*vivere*, to live)

Element	From	Meaning	Examples
super- (cont'd)			DOUBLE PREFIXED ROOT: superincumbent (lying or resting on something else; arching or overhanging) (*in-*, in + *cumbere*, to lie down) superinduce (to introduce or bring in as an addition to existent condition, effect, etc.) (*in-*, in + *ducere*, to lead) superimpose (*im-* from *in-*, in + *pos* from *ponere*, to place) superintendend, superintendent (*in-*, in + *tendere*, to stretch) PREFIXED PREFIX: insuperable (*in-*, not) DISGUISED ROOT: sum (in Roman counting, the total was placed at the top of the column) (from *summus*, highest; superlative of *super-*) summary, summation, summit (from same base as *sum*) PREFIXED DISGUISED ROOT: *con-*: consummate (from *com-*, with, together; *sum* from *supra*) FRENCH: somersault (*somer-*, over; *sault* from *saltare*, to jump) sovereign (chief; greatest, supreme), sovereignty ITALIAN: soprano (the highest singing voice of women or boys, with a range two octaves or more above middle C; also, a musical instrument with a similar range) (from *sopra*, highest) LATIN WORDS AND PHRASES: *summa cum laude* (with the greatest praise; phrase used to signify graduation with the highest honors from a college or university) *summum bonum* (the highest, or supreme, good) ECCLESIASTICAL PHRASE: *sursum corda* [Lift up (your) hearts, opening words of the Preface to the Mass; has come to mean an incitement to courage, fervor, etc.] PLACENAME: El Sobrante, California (Spanish for left over) INTERNATIONAL LAKE: Lake Superior (one of the five Great Lakes of North America; is the largest body of fresh water in the world; is also the deepest, the highest above sea level, and the farthest north and west of the Great Lakes; its area is greater than that of the state of Maine and almost that of the state of South Carolina) CROSS REFERENCE: *hyper, met, preter, ulter/ultra*
sur-			See *super-* for *surround, surtout*.
sur-			See *sub-* for *surreptitious, surrogate*.
sur			See *cur* for *insure*.
sus-			See *sub-* for *suspend*.
sut,* cout	Latin *suere* (IE: *siw*, to sew)	to sew	SIMPLE ROOT: *cout*: couture, couturier *sut*: **suture** PREFIXED ROOT: *ac-*: accouter (also spelled *accoutre*), accouterments (also spelled *accoutrements*) (*ac-* assimilates *ad-*, to, toward) DISGUISED ROOT: subulate (literally, sewing instrument; awl) SANSKRIT: sutra (literally, string, thread; collection of aphorisms and rules in both Hinduism and Buddhism)

Element	From	Meaning	Examples
sut (cont'd)			INTERDISCIPLINARY: suture (in *anatomy*, the joining together, or the irregular line of junction, of certain vertebrate bones, especially of the skull; in *botany*, a seam formed when two parts unite; a line of dehiscence along which a fruit, as a pod or capsule, splits; in *surgery*, the act or method of joining together the two edges of a wound or incision by stitching or similar means; any material, as gut, thread, wire,etc., so used; a single loop or knot of such material made in suturing) NO CROSS REFERENCE
syn-,*** sym-, syl-, sys-, sy-	Greek (*syn*; earlier *xyn*)	with, together, together with; at the same time; by means of	PREFIX NOTE: This element assimilates to *syl-* before roots beginning with *l* and to *sys-* before roots beginning with *t*; it changes to *sym-* before *m*, *p*, and *b*. PREFIXED ROOT: *sy-*: zyg: syzygy (a pair; especially a pair of opposites; in *Greek and Latin prosody*, a group of two feet, as a dipody; see *zyg*) (*zygon*, yoke) *sy-*: stal: systaltic (from *stellein*, to send) stol: systole (from *stellein*, to draw, to pull) *syl-*: lab: syllabary, syllabicate, syllable (literally, that which holds together) (from *lambanein*, to hold) leps: syllepsis (from *syllable*, previous entry) log: syllogism (*logos*, word) NB: *Syllabus* is not in this family. *sym-*: (before the bilabial consonants *b*, *m*, and *p*) bio: symbiosis, symbiotic, symbiont (*bio*, life) bol: symbol, symbology (*bol*, to throw) metr: symmetrical (that which is not symmetrical is *asymmetrical*), symmetry path: sympathy (*pathos*, feeling) patri: sympatric (in *ecology*, of or pertaining to closely related species of organisms occurring in the same geographic area) (*patri*, father) petal: sympetalous (same as *gamopetalous*) phon: symphonic, symphony (literally, harmony of sounds; short for symphony orchestra) (*phone*, sound) phys: symphysics, symphysis (*phys*, growth) pod: sympodium (in *botany*, an apparent stem actually made up of a series of axillary branches growing one from another, giving the effect of a single stem, as in the grape) (*pod*, foot) pos: symposiac, symposiarch, symposium (literally, a drinking together; originally, a drinking party where talk flowed freely) (*posis*, a drinking) pto: symptom (literally, that which falls together) (*pto*, to fall) DOUBLE PREFIXED ROOT: (*a-*, not, without) asymbiotic (*bio*, life) asyndeton (see example under *dein*) asymmetrical (*meter*, measure)

Element	From	Meaning	Examples
syn- (cont'd)			*syn-*:

syn-:

agog: synagogue (literally, a bringing together) (*agog*, leading)

aleph: synalepha (the contraction into one syllable of two adjacent vowels, usually by elision, e.g., *th' eagle* for *the eagle*)

aps: synapse, synapsis (from *haptein*, to join)

arthr: synarthrosis (*arthro*, joint)

carp: syncarp, syncarpous (*carp*, fruit)

chrom: synchromesh, synchronize, synchronous (That which is *not synchronous* is *asynchronous*) (*chron*, time)

clast: synclastic (*clast*, break)

clin: synclinal (*clin*, lean)

cop: syncopate, syncopation (in *music*, a shifting of the accent), syncope (*cop*, cut)

cret: syncretism, syncretize (from *Cretan*; to join together in the manner of the Cretan cities against a common enemy)

dactyl: syndactyl, syndactylalism (*dactyl*, finger)

dic: syndic, syndicate (**Synonyms:** monopoly, corner, cartel) (IE *deik*, to point out)

drom: syndrome (that which runs together, as the symptoms of a disease) (*drome*, run)

ere: syneresis (the contraction of two consecutive vowels or syllables into one syllable, so as to form a diphthong, as *oi* as in *oil*) (*er* is a shortening of *hairein*, to take)

erg: synergetic, synergism, synergy (*erg*, work)

ese: synesis (a grammatical construction which conforms to the meaning rather than to strict syntactic agreement or reference, e.g., Has *everyone* washed *their* hands?) (*hienai*, to set in motion)

ize: synizesis (the contraction of two adjacent vowels into a single syllable, without the formation of a diphthong; in *biology*, the massing of the chromatin in meiosis during synapsis) (*hizein*, to sit)

kary: synkaryon (the nucleus resulting from the fusion of male and female nuclei during fertilization) (*karyon*, nut, kernel, nucleus)

od: synod, synodical (from *hodos*, way)

oe: synoecious (in *botany*, having male and female flowers in the same inflorescence; having both antheridia and archegonia in the same cluster) (from *oikos*, house)

onym: synonym (a word that means the same or nearly the same as another in the same language), synonymous, synonymy (*onym*, name)

ops: synopsis (**Synonyms:** abridgment, abstract, brief) (*opsis*, view)

opt: synoptic (e.g., the Synoptic Gospels, Matthew, Mark, and Luke, the authors of which *view* the life of Jesus from his birth to his death, as opposed to John, who *interprets* the life of Jesus) (from *opsis*, view)

ov: (coined by Paracelsus; origin unknown) synovia (lubricating fluid secreted by the membranes of joint cavities, tendon sheaths, etc.)

Element	From	Meaning	Examples
syn- (cont'd)			synovitis (inflammation of a synovial membrane) (*itis*, inflammation)
			tax: syntax (*tax*, arrange)
			thes: synthesis {synthetic} (*thesis*, to place)
			DOUBLE PREFIXED ROOT:
			syn<u>ec</u>doche (a figure of speech in which a part is used for a whole, an individual for a class, a material for a thing, or the reverse of any of these, e.g., *bread* for *food*; *the army* for *a soldier*; *copper* for *a penny, a Croesus* for *a rich man,* or *the law* for *a policeman*) (*ec-* from *ex-*, from + *dechesthai*, to receive)
			sys-:
			tem: system, systematic, systemic (from *histanai*, to set)
			NOTE: An unusual combination is *geosynchronous*, in which a root precedes a prefix; with *geo*, earth, a geosynchronous satellite is "in time *with* the earth."
			CROSS REFERENCE: *com-*

Words have the power to mold men's thinking, to direct their willing and acting.
Aldous Huxley

T

Element	From	Meaning	Examples
tab**	Latin *tabula* (IE: *tel*, flat, a board)	board, plank	SIMPLE ROOT: tabe: tabernacle [see *Doublets* below; originally, a temporary dwelling, as a tent or hut; in Judaism, the portable sanctuary used by the Jews from the time of their post-Exodus wanderings in the wilderness to the building of Solomon's Temple (Exodus 25-27)] tabla: tablature table: table, tablet tabu: tabular, tabulate, tabulator, tabular LEADING ROOT COMPOUND: oid: tabloid (from *Tabloid*, a trademark for a tablet of condensed medicine; a newspaper of small format giving the news in condensed form, usually with illustrated, often sensational material) (*oid*, similar to) DISGUISED ROOT: tavern (originally spelled *tabern*, which is also the base of *tabernacle*; see *Doublets* below) DOUBLETS: tabernacle:tavern FRENCH: tableau (a striking, dramatic scene or picture; plural *tableaux*, or *tableaus*) FRENCH EXPRESSIONS: *tableau vivant* (living tableau; a representation of a scene, picture, etc. by a person or group in costume, posing silently without moving) *table d'hôte* (table of the host; a complete meal, served at a restaurant or hotel for a set price: distinguished from *à la carte*, by the card, or a set amount for individual items on the menu) LATIN PHRASE: *tabula rasa* (literally, erased tablet; the mind before it receives the impressions gained from experience; especially, in the philosophy of Locke, the unformed, featureless mind; also, a need or opportunity to start from the beginning; a clean slate) DUTCH: rijstafel (or *rijstafel*; literally, rice table; an Indonesian meal in which rice is served with a wide variety of foods and sauces in side dishes) CROSS REFERENCE: *mens*
tac, tic*	Latin *tacere*: to be silent (IE: *take*, to be silent)	silent, quiet	SIMPLE ROOT: tacet [in *music*, It is silent: a direction to be *silent* for (the indicated time)], tacit, taciturn PREFIXED ROOT: re-: reticent (habitually silent or uncommunicative; taciturn; reserved) {reticence} (*re-*, again) NO CROSS REFERENCE
tach*	Greek *tachos*: speed (IE: *dhengh*, to reach, strong, fast)	speed, swift	ROOT NOTE: *Tacho* refers to speed; *tachy*, swift; *tachisto*, a superlative of *tachy*, i.e., swiftest. SIMPLE ROOT: tachina (fly; a type of fly in which the larvae live as parasites within the bodies of other insects) LEADING ROOT COMPOUND: *tacho*: meter: tachometer (an instrument used to determine speed, especially the rotational speed of a shaft) (*meter*, measure)

Element	From	Meaning	Examples
tach (cont'd)			*tachisto*: scop: tachistoscope (an apparatus that projects transient images onto a screen to test visual perception) (*scope*, look) *tachy*: card: tachycardia (*card*, heart) graph: tachygraphy (the art or practice of rapid writing or shorthand; especially, the stenography of the ancient Greeks and Romans) (*graph*, write) lyt: tachylyte (a rock that decomposes quickly in acids; a kind of basaltic volcanic glass) (from *luein*, to dissolve) meter: tachymeter (a surveying instrument used for the rapid measurement of distances, elevations, and bearings) (*meter*, measure) CROSS REFERENCE: *celer, veloc*
tact			See *tax/tact* for *tactical*.
tact,*** tang	Latin *tangere* (IE: *tag*, to touch, grasp)	to touch, feel, perceive	SIMPLE ROOT: *tact*: tact (**Synonyms**: poise, diplomacy, savoir-faire), tactful tactile (that can be perceived by the touch; tangible; of, having, or related to the sense of touch) {tactility}, taction, tactless *tang*: tangent, tangential, tangible (**Synonyms**: perceptible, sensible, palpable) PREFIXED ROOT: *tact*: *con-*: contact, contactor (in *electronics*, a device for repeatedly making and breaking a circuit, usually automatically) (*con-*, with, together) *in-*: intact (literally, untouched; not impaired in any way; having all parts; whole) {intactness} (*in-*, not) *tang*: *co-*: cotangent (the tangent of the complement of a directed angle or arc) {cotangential} (*co-*, with, together) *in-*: intangible (not capable of being perceived, precisely defined, or identified; elusive; as a *noun*, something intangible; especially, an asset that cannot be perceived by the senses) (*in-*, not) DISGUISED ROOT: taint (see synonyms at *contaminate*, below), tainted task (**Synonyms**: job, obligation, assignment; see *Doublets* below) taste, tasteful, tasteless, tasty tax (see *Doublets* below) PREFIXED DISGUISED ROOT: *tag*: *con-*: contagion, contagious, contagium (*con-*, with, together) *tain*: *at-*: (assimilates *ad-*, to, toward) attain (literally, to touch to; **Synonyms**: reach, achieve, gain) attainder (from same base as *attain*, but meaning loss of civil rights, inheritance, property, etc. of a person sentenced to death or outlawed) attaint (to convict of a crime punishable by attainder) attainture (attainder, dishonor, disgrace)

Element	From	Meaning	Examples
tact (cont'd)			*tam*: *con-*: contaminant, contaminate (**Synonyms**: taint, pollute, defile), contamination (*con-*, with, together) *tax*: *sur-*: surtax (an extra tax) (from *super-*, over, beyond) *teg*: *in-*: integer (see *Doublets* below), integrable, integral, integrand (in *mathematics*, the function or expression to be integrated), integrant, integrate, integration, integrator, integrity (**Synonyms**: honesty, sincerity, probity) (*in-*, not) *tig*: *con-*: contiguous (**Synonyms**: bordering, adjoining, adjacent), contiguity (*con-*, with, together) *ting*: *con-*: (with, together) contingence, contingency [**Synonyms**: emergency, crisis, strait(s)] **contingent** (**Synonyms**: accidental, incidental, adventitious) *tire*: *en-*: entire (literally, not touched; **Synonyms**: complete, total, whole; see *Doublets*, below), entirety (Old French; from Latin *integrum*, accusative of *integer*) (*en-*, not) DOUBLETS: entire:integer; task:tax LATIN PHRASE: *noli me tangere* (touch me not) PLACENAMES: Tangent, Oregon; Tangent Point, Alaska INTERDISCIPLINARY: contingent (in *logic*, true only under certain conditions or in certain contexts; not always or necessarily true; in *philosophy*, not subject to determinism) CROSS REFERENCE: *hapt*
tail*	French *taillier*: to cut (IE: *tal*, to grow, sprout)	cut, decide	SIMPLE ROOT: tail (only as a legal term, as *estate in tail*), taillage (same as *tallage*, under *Disguised Root*), tailor *de-*: detail (**Synonyms**: item, particular) (*de-*, intensive) *en-*: entail (to cause or involve by necessity or as a consequence, as *a loss entailing no regret*; in *law*, to limit the passage of a landed estate to a specified line of heirs) (*en-*, in) DISGUISED ROOT: tallage (a piece cut out of the whole; see *Black's Law Dictionary*) ITALIAN: intaglio (literally, to cut in) CROSS REFERENCE: *cide/cis, sect, tom*
tain			See *ten*, Latin, for *maintain*.
tang			See *tact* for *tangent*.
taph*	Greek *thaptein*: to bury, to inter	tomb	PREFIXED ROOT: *epi-*: epitaph (literally, over a tomb; originally, a funeral oration; an inscription on a tombstone or monument in memory of the one or ones buried there) (*epi-*, upon, over) LEADING ROOT COMPOUND: phob: taphephobia (fear of being buried alive) (*phobia*, fear of) TRAILING ROOT COMPOUND: ceno: cenotaph (a monument erected in honor of a dead person whose remains lie elsewhere) (*ceno*, empty) CROSS REFERENCE: *sepul*

Element	From	Meaning	Examples
tas			See *ten/tas* for *epitasis, protasis*.
taur*	Latin *tauros* (IE: *teu,* to swell)	bull (also, bovine)	SIMPLE ROOT: Taurus (second sign of the zodiac), tauric, taurine LEADING ROOT COMPOUND: *taur*: odont: taurodont (*odont*, tooth) *tauro*: bol: taurobolium (in primitive Mediterranean regions, a ceremony in which participants were baptized with the blood of a sacrificed bull) (*bol*, throw) chol: taurocholic acid (crystalline acid occurring as a constituent of bile; from it being being first obtained from ox bile) (*chol*, bile) machy: tauromachy (in Spanish, *tauromaquia*) (Greek *machy*, battle, contest) morph: tauromorphic (in the shape of bull) (*morph*, shape, form) trag: taurotragus (a genus of large African antelopes consisting of the elands) (*tragus*, he-goat) DISGUISED ROOT: bittern (bird that bellows like a bull) SPANISH: *toro, torero, toreador* NO CROSS REFERENCE
tax, tact**	Greek *taktikos*: of order; *tassein*, to arrange (IE: *tag,* to set aright)	arrangement	SIMPLE ROOT: *tact*: tactic, tactical, tactician, tactics (**Synonym**: strategy; in *military usage*, a distinction is made between these two words; *strategy* is the utilization of all of a nation's forces, through large-scale, long-range planning and development, to ensure security or victory; *tactics* deals with the use and deployment of troops in combat) *tax*: taxeme, taxis PREFIXED ROOT: a-: ataxia (literally, disorderly; total or partial inability to coordinate voluntary bodily movements, especially muscular movements) (*a-*, not) epi-: epitaxy (see *Webster's Third*) (*epi-*, over, upon) hypo-: hypotaxis (the dependent or subordinate construction or relationship of clauses with connectives; for example, in the sentence *I shall despair if you don't come*, "if you don't come" is the *hypotaxis*; compare *parataxis*, next entry, as well as *asyndeton*, under *syn-* and *dein*) (*hypo-*, under) para-: parataxis (the coordination of grammatical elements such as phrases or clauses, without the use of coordinating elements such as conjunctions, as *It was cold; the snows came*; the semicolon in the sentence takes the place of a coordinate conjunction) (*para-*, alongside, beside) syn-: syntax (literally, to arrange in order; to put together; in *grammar*, the way in which words are put together to form phrases and sentences) (*syn-*, with, together) LEADING ROOT COMPOUND: *taxi*: derm: taxidermy (the art or operation of preparing, stuffing, and mounting the skins of dead animals for exhibition in a lifelike state) (*derm*, skin)

Element	From	Meaning	Examples
tax (cont'd)			*taxo*: nom: taxonomy (the science, laws, or principles of classification; in *biology*, the theory, principles, and process of classifying organisms in established categories) (*nomos*, law, guiding principles) TRAILING ROOT COMPOUND: *taxis*: geo: geotaxis (in *biology*, the movement of an organism in response to the forces of gravity) {geotactic} (*geo*, earth) hetero: heterotaxis (an abnormal position or arrangement, as of organs of the body, rock strata, etc.) (*hetero*, other, different) homo: homotaxis (in *geology*, a similarity of layers, or in the fossil content, between strata of different regions not necessarily formed at the same time) (*homo*, same) photo: phototaxis (the movement of an organism in response to stimulus of light) (*photo*, light) phyll: phyllotaxis (in *botany*, the arrangement of leaves on a stem; the principles of such arrangement; also, *phyllotaxy*) {phyllotactic} (*phyllo*, leaf) *taxy*: chemo: chemotaxis (the response of certain living cells and organisms to a chemical) (*chemo*, chemical) eu: eutaxy (a well-ordered arrangement) (*eu*, good, well) INTERDISCIPLINARY: taxis (in *biology*, the movement of a free-moving cell or organism toward or away from some external stimulus; in *surgery*, the replacement by hand of some displaced part without cutting any tissue) NB: *Tax*, from Latin *taxare*, to assess, compute, and from *tangere*, to feel, to touch, is not in this family; neither is *taxi*, from *taximeter*, an instrument for computing fares in a taxicab, in this family (see *tact, tang*). CROSS REFERENCE: *cosm, nom, ord, tang*
tax			See *tact, tang* for *tax, taxation*.
techn**	Greek *tekhne*: art, skill (IE: *tekth*, to weave, build, join)	cover	ROOT NOTE: Eric Partridge says that the interrelationships between this root and the Latin roots *tect, teg, tex* are not entirely clear. Since Latin and Greek are both in the Indo-European family of languages, taken together, the commonality appears to be that of a builder, or one who covers. SIMPLE ROOT: technic, technical, technicality, technician, technique technitium (a chemical derived from the irradiation of molybdenum with deutrons and in the fission of uranium; symbol, Tc) tectonic (of or having to do with building; constructional; architectural; designating, of, or pertaining to changes in the structure of the earth's crust, the forces responsible for such deformation, or the external forms produced), tectonics tectonism (same as *diastrophism*: the process by which the earth's surface is reshaped through rock movements and displacements) LEADING ROOT COMPOUND: cracy: technocracy (*cracy*, ruled by)

Element	From	Meaning	Examples
techn (cont'd)			graph: technography (*graph*, write) log: technological, technology (*logy*, study of) TRAILING ROOT COMPOUND: archi: architect (literally, master builder) (*archi*, first) pyro: pyrotechnic (*pyro*, fire) CROSS REFERENCE: *tect,/teg*
tect,*** **teg**	Latin (see *Root Note* under **techn**) (IE: *(s)teg*, to cover)	to cover (see *Root Note* under *techn*)	SIMPLE ROOT: *tect*: tectr: tectrix (a wing covert of a bird; *covert*, hidden, concealed, here, refers to the small feathers covering the bases of the larger feathers of a bird's wing and tail) tectu: tectum (in *anatomy* and *zoology*, a rooflike structure or covering) *teg*: tegmen, tegular, tegument PREFIXED ROOT: *tect*: de-: detect (to catch or discover, as in a misdeed; to discover or manage to perceive something hidden or not easily noticed, as *to detect a flaw in an argument*), detectable (or *detectible*), detective, detector (*de-*, intensive) ob-: obtect (also, *obtected*; in *entomology*, enclosed or covered by a hardened secretion) (*ob-*, intensive) pro-: protect (**Synonyms**: defend, guard, preserve), protection (see *Placename* below), protective (*pro-*, in front of) *teg*: in-: integument (an outer covering or coat, such as the skin of an animal, the coat of a seed, or the membrane enclosing an organ) (*in-*, on) DISGUISED ROOT: test (**Synonyms**: trial, experiment) testaceous (of, like, or from shells; having a hard shell; in *biology*, of the color of unglazed earthenware) tile (see *Doublets* below) toga (a Roman citizen's formal outer garment, or *cover*) tuille [Old French; from which is derived English *tile* (previous entry); also, see *Doublets*, below; a steel plate used in medieval armor for protecting the thigh] DOUBLETS: tile:tuille FRENCH: protégé/protégée (one who is *protected*: a person guided and helped, especially in the furtherance of his/her career, by another, more influential person) ENGLISH COGNATES: tog (a coat), togs (outer garments, clothes) thatch (as *a thatched hut*) IRISH: shanty PERSIAN: *taj* (as in *Taj Mahal*, literally Crowned Place) PLACENAME: Protection, Kansas CROSS REFERENCE: *calyp, cover, cel, cond*

Phylactery, from Greek *phylax*, watchman, is used for Hebrew *tefillah*, prayer, or that which guards one from evil. From *phylax* is derived *prophylactic*, preventive, protective, as *prophylactic medicine*; as a noun, a condom, also *prophylaxis*, a dental term for "professional teeth cleaning," or that which guards against tooth decay.

Element	From	Meaning	Examples
tel*	Greek *telos,* final, completion of a cycle (IE: *kwel¹*, to revolve, move, around)	the end, completion	SIMPLE ROOT: telic (directed or tending toward a goal or purpose; purposeful) telium (a pustulelike structure formed on the tissue of a plant infected by a rust fungus), telson PREFIXED ROOT: *dys-:* dystelelogy (the doctrine of purposelessness in nature, compare *teleology,* below) (*dys-,* faulty, bad) *en-:* entelechy (from Aristotelian philosophy) (*en-,* in) LEADING ROOT COMPOUND: *tel*: anthrop: Telanthropus (a genus of southern African fossil hominids held to comprise forms intermediate in some respects between the australopithecus and true man) (*anthropo,* man) *tele*: logy: teleology (the philosophical study of manifestations of design or purpose in natural processes or occurrences; compare *dystelelogy,* above) (*logy,* study of) *teleuto*: spor: teleutospore (same as *teliospore,* below) (*spore,* seed) *telo*: phas: telophase (in *biology,* the final stage, or phase, of mitosis, in which the parent cell becomes completely divided into two cells, each having a reorganized nucleus) *telio*: spor: teliospore (in *biology,* a thick-walled, blackish resting spore of rusts and smuts, from which the basidium arises) (*spore,* seed) DISGUISED ROOT: talisman (an object marked with magical signs and believed to confer on its bearer unnatural powers or protection) CROSS REFERENCE: *eschat*
tele-***	Greek *tele* (IE: *kwel²*, distant, remote)	from afar, far off	PREFIXED ROOT: *tele*: cast: telecast (*tele*vision + broad*cast*; to broadcast by television; as a *noun,* a television broadcast) gony: telegony (the supposed influence of one sire on offspring sired by subsequent males on the same female) (*gony,* production of) gram: telegram (from *graph,* write) graph: telegraph {telegraphic} (*graph,* write) kine: telekinesis {telekinetic} (*kinesis,* movement) meter: telemeter (*meter,* measure) metry: telemetry (*metry,* process of measuring) path: telepathy {telepathic, telepathist} (*path,* feel, perceive) phon: telephone, telephonic, telephony (*phone,* sound) phot: telephoto, telephotograph (*photo,* light + *graph,* write) scop: telescope, telescopic, telescopy (*scope,* look) vis: television (from *videre,* to see) *telo*: dynam: telodynamic (of or for the transmission of mechanical power to a distance by cables and pulleys) (*dynam,* power) PLACENAME: Telegraph, Texas

Element	From	Meaning	Examples
tele- (cont'd)			AN ACRONYM: teleran [*tele(vision) r(adar) a(ir) n(avigation)*]: an electronic aid to aerial navigation by which data received by radar, maps of the terrain, etc. are transmitted to aircraft by television] NOTE: Do not confuse this root with the *tele* that means the end (see previous family). NO CROSS REFERENCE
temn*	Latin *temnere*: to slight, despise	to hate, despise	PREFIXED ROOT: *con*-: (with, together) contemn (**Synonyms**: despise, scorn, disdain), contemner (also, *contemnor*) contempt (the feeling or actions of a person toward someone or something considered low, worthless, or beneath notice) POSSIBLY AKIN TO: contumacy, contumacious, contumely, contumelious (see under *tum*) NB: This root is not related to *tempt* (see *tend*, stretch). CROSS REFERENCE: *miso, odi*
temp***	Latin *tempus*, time; *temperare*, to observe proper measure (IE: *temp*, to pull; from *ten*, to stretch)	time; to observe proper measure	SIMPLE ROOT: tempe: temper (**Synonyms**: 1) disposition, temperament, character; 2) mood, humor, vein) temperament (see synonyms at *temper*, previous entry), tempest (original meaning related to *time*) tempo: tempo, temporal, temporary (**Synonyms**: provisional, acting), temporize PREFIXED ROOT: *con*-: (with, together) contemplate (**Synonyms**: consider, study, weigh) contemporaneous, contemporary (**Synonyms**: coeval, synchronous, simultaneous), contemporize *contre*-: contretemps (an inopportune or embarrassing occurrence; a mishap) (from *contra*-, against) *dis*-: (notice difference in meanings of prefix in each of the identically spelled words) distemper (to upset or unbalance the functions of; derange; disorder (*dis*-, apart) distemper (to mix colors or pigments with water and glue, size, or some other binding material) (*dis*-, intensive) *ex*-: extemporal, extemporaneous (**Synonyms**: impromptu, extempore, improvised), extemporary, extempore, extemporize (*ex*-, out) DISGUISED ROOT: tense (as used in grammar; another *tense* is listed under Latin *ten*, to stretch out) LATIN PHRASES: *pro tempore* [for the time (being); usually shortened to *pro tem*, as *chairman pro tem*] *tempus fugit* (time flies) CROSS REFERENCE: *chron, ev*, as in *medieval*
ten,*** tent, tain, tin	Latin *tenere* (IE: *ten*, to pull, stretch)	to hold	SIMPLE ROOT: tenab: tenable (that can be held, defended, or maintained) tenac: tenace (from Spanish *tenaza*, tongs, pincers; a bridge term) tenacious, tenacity

Element	From	Meaning	Examples
ten (cont'd)			tenaculum (in *surgery*, a pointed, hooked instrument for lifting and holding parts, as blood vessels)
			tenan: tenant (a person who pays rent to occupy or use land, a building, etc.; a person who possesses lands, etc. by any kind of title)
			tene: tenement, tenet (**Synonyms:** doctrine, dogma, precept), tennis (from Anglo-French *tenetz*, receive; a cry by the server before play)
			teno: tenon, tenor (during the Middle Ages, in 6-part harmony, the tenor held the melody; **Synonyms:** tendency, trend, inclination)
			tenu: tenure, tenuto
			PREFIXED ROOT:
			tain:
			ab-: abstain (**Synonyms:** refrain, forbear) {abstainer} (*abs-*, away)
			con-: contain (**Synonyms:** hold, accommodate), container, containment (*con-*, with, together)
			de-: detain {detainment}, detainer (*de-*, away)
			enter-: entertain (**Synonyms:** amuse, divert, beguile), entertainer, entertaining, entertainment (*enter-*, between)
			ob-: obtain (**Synonyms:** procure, acquire, gain) {obtainable, obtainer, obtainment} (*ob-*, against)
			per-: pertain (to relate to) (*per-*, through)
			re-: retain, retainer (*re-*, back, again)
			sus-: sustain (**Synonyms:** support, uphold, maintain) (*sus-*, a variant of *sub-*, under)
			ten:
			sus-: sustenance (*sus-*, a variant of *sub-*, under)
			un-: untenable (Anglo-Saxon *un-*, not)
			tent:
			ab-: abstention (*abs-*, away)
			con-: content (**Synonym:** satisfy) (*con-*, with, together)
			de-: detention (*de-*, away)
			re-: retention, retentive, retentivity (*re-*, back, again)
			sus-: sustentaculum (in *anatomy*, a supporting structure) (*sus-*, a variant of *sub-*, under)
			tin:
			ab-: abstinence (*abs-*, away)
			con-: (with, together)
			continence, continent, continental
			continual (**Synonyms:** continuous, constant, incessant), continuance, continuant, continuation
			continue (**Synonyms:** last, endure, abide), continuity, continuous, continuum
			de-: detinue (in *law*, the unlawful detention of personal property; an action or writ for the recovery of property unlawfully detained) (*de-*, away)
			per-: pertinacious (**Synonyms:** stubborn, obstinate, dogged), pertinacity, pertinence, pertinent (*per-*, through)
			re-: retinue (the retainers accompanying a person of rank) (from *retain*)

Element	From	Meaning	Examples
ten (cont'd)			DOUBLE PREFIXED ROOT: impertinence, impertinent (impudent, presumptuous, rude) (from *in-*, not + *per-*, through) [appertain (to belong properly as a function, part, etc.; relate) (see *Note*) appurtenance (anything that appertains) (from *appertain*, previous entry)] (*ap-* assimilates *ad-*, to, toward; *per-*, *pur-*, through) TRAILING ROOT COMPOUND: *tain*: main: maintain (see synonyms at *sustain*), maintenance (French *main*; from Latin *manus*, hand) *ten*: lieu: lieutenant (French *lieu*; from Latin *loco*, place; hence, one who holds the place of) LATIN TERM: *locum tenens* (literally, place taker; a person taking another's place for the time being; temporary substitute, as for a doctor or clergyman; this phrase corresponds root by root with French *lieutenant*) ITALIAN MUSIC TERMS: continuo (a continuous bass accompaniment, indicated by a shorthand method in notation, and played on a harpsichord or organ, especially in baroque music) sostenuto (in a sustained or prolonged manner) (from *sustain*) ECONOMIC UNION: *Conseil de l'Entente* [Council of the Entente: formed in 1959 of the French African colonies of Ivory Coast, Upper Volta (now *Burkina Faso*), Benin, and Niger, having special agreements with France] NOTE: *Attain* is under *tang*. CROSS REFERENCE: *cap, hab*
ten, tas**	Greek *teinein*: to stretch, strain (IE: *ten*, to pull, stretch)	to stretch, intensify	SIMPLE ROOT: tenesmus (a painful and distressing but ineffectual urge to evacuate the rectum or urinary bladder) PREFIXED ROOT: *tas*: epi-: epitasis (that part of a play, especially in classical drama, between the protasis, or exposition, and the catastrophe or dénouement) (*epi-*, upon) pro-: protasis (in *drama*, the opening of a play, in which the characters are introduced; in *grammar*, the clause that expresses the condition in a conditional sentence; opposed to *apodosis*; see *epistasis*) (*pro-*, before) *ten*: hypo-: hypotenuse (originally *pleura hypotenuse*, a side subtending, or "stretched under" the right angle) (*hypo-*, under) *ton*: peri-: peritoneum (literally, stretched around, across; the membrane lining the walls of the abdominal cavity and enclosing the viscera) (*peri-*, around) TRAILING ROOT COMPOUND: bronchi: bronchiectasis (chronic dilation of the bronchial tubes, with cough and formation of mucupurulent matter) (*bronchi*, windpipe)

Element	From	Meaning	Examples
ten (cont'd)			tele: telangiectasis (a chronic dilation of groups of capillaries of the blood vascular system causing dark-red blotches on the skins, as birthmarks) (*tele-*, end + *angi*, blood vessel + *ectasis*, dilatation, extension)
			DISGUISED ROOT:
			tetanus (a spasm of stretched muscles)
			tone (stretching a string; thus producing a sound)
			CROSS REFERENCE: *string, ton*
ten,*** **tens, tent**	Latin *tendere* (IE: *ten*, to pull, stretch; yields English thin)	to stretch out	SIMPLE ROOT:
			tend:
			tend (to move or extend in a certain direction; to have an inclination, tendency, bias, etc. to do something; incline)
			tendency (**Synonyms**: trend, current, drift), tendentious
			tender (both adjective and verb), tendon
			tens: tense (**Synonyms**: tight, taut), tensile (of, undergoing, or exerting tension; capable of being stretched), tensive
			tent: tent, tentacle, tenter
			tenu: tenuity, tenuous (very thin, as a fiber; rare, as air at high altitudes)
			PREFIXED ROOTS AND COMPOUNDS:
			ten:
			at-: attenuate, attenuation (assimilates *ad-*, to, toward)
			ex-: extenuate (literally, to make thin; to lessen or attempt to lessen the magnitude of an offense or guilt by providing partial excuses), extenuating (as in *extenuating circumstances*), extenuation (*ex-*, out)
			tend:
			at-: attend (**Synonyms**: accompany, escort, convoy), attendance (*at-* assimilates *ad-*, to, toward)
			con-: contend (**Synonyms**: discuss, argue, debate), contender (*con-*, with, together)
			dis-: distend (or *distension*; to stretch out; to expand, as by pressure from within; make or become swollen) (*dis-*, apart, away)
			ex-: extend (**Synonyms**: lengthen, elongate, prolong), extended, extender (*ex-*, out)
			in-: intend (to stretch out for; aim at; **Synonyms**: mean, design, propose), intendance, intendant, intendment (legal term) (*in-*, in, at)
			os-: ostend, ostensible (apparent; seeming; professed), ostension, ostensive, ostensory, ostentation {ostentatious} (from *ob-*, against)
			por-: portend (to stretch forth) (*por-* from *pro-*, forth)
			pre-: pretend (**Synonyms**: assume, feign, simulate), pretended, pretender (*pre-*, before)
			sub-: subtend (to extend under or be in opposite to in position; in *botany*, to enclose in an angle, as between a leaf and a stem) (*sub-*, under)
			tens:
			at-: attensity (*at-* assimilates *ad-*, to, toward)
			dis-: distensible, distension (or, *distention*) (*dis-*, apart, away)
			ex-: extension, extensity, extensive, extensor (*ex-*, out)

675

Element	From	Meaning	Examples
ten (cont'd)			*in-*: (in, at) intense, intension, intensity, intensive intensifier, intensify (**Synonyms**: aggravate, heighten, enhance) (*fy* from *facere*, to make, do) *pre-*: pretense, pretension (*pre-*, before) *tent*: *at-*: attention, attentive (**Synonyms**: thoughtful, considerate) (*at-* assimilates *ad-*, to, toward) *con-*: contention (**Synonyms**: conflict, fight, struggle), contentious (*con-*, with, together) *de-*: (from *dis-*, apart) detent (in *mechanics*, a part that stops or releases a movement, as a catch for controlling the striking of a clock) détente (or *detente*), a lessening of tension or hostility, especially, between nations, as through treaties, trade agreements, etc. [Note: *Detention* is under *ten*, to hold.] *ex-*: extent (*ex-*, out) *in-*: (in) intent, intention (**Synonyms**: purpose, aim, goal) intentional (**Synonyms**: voluntary, deliberate, willful) *por-*: portent, portentous (**Synonyms**: foreboding, ominous, fateful) (*por-*, akin to *per-*, through) *pre-*: pretentious (*pre-*, before) DOUBLE PREFIXED ROOT: superintend, superintendent (*super-*, over, beyond + *in-*, in) LEADING ROOT COMPOUND: meter: tensimeter (*tension* + *meter*; an instrument that measures small changes in gas or vapor pressure) DISGUISED ROOT: temper, tempt BOUND LATIN-ANGLO-SAXON COMPOUND: tenterhook (any of the hooked nails that hold cloth stretched on a tenter; on tenterhooks: in suspense, filled with anxiety) FRENCH PHRASES: *double-entendre* (pronounced DOO blahn TAHN druh; literally, double meaning; a term with two meanings, especially, when one of them has a risqué or indecorous connotation) *entente cordiale* (literally, a friendly understanding, especially between governments) *malentendu* (a misunderstanding) LATIN TERM: *in extenso* (at full length; without abridgment) INTERDISCIPLINARY: tentacle (in *botany*, one of the hairs on the leaves of insectivorous plants, such as the sundew; in *zoology*, an elongated, flexible, unsegmented protrusion, such as one of those surrounding the mouth or oral cavity of the hydra, sea anemone, or squid) CROSS REFERENCE: *elas, lepto/lepid*
ter*	Latin *tertius*	third	SIMPLE ROOT: terc: terce (or, *tierce*), tercel, tercet tern: ternar (or, *terner*; a university student assigned to the third and lowest rank and required to pay the lowest fees; compare *seconder*) tert: tertiary, tertian (as *tertian harmony*, the common form of harmony in music as opposed to, e.g., *quartal harmony*)

Element	From	Meaning	Examples
ter (cont'd)			DISGUISED ELEMENT: tierce (third) tiercel (in *falconry*, a male hawk, especially the male peregrine; so named because it was believed that every third bird in a nest is a male) LATIN: *Ter Sanctus* (Thrice Holy: Holy, Holy, Holy: used in reference to *Sanctus, Sanctus, Sanctus*, of the Trishagion of the Mass or of the *Te Deum*) ITALIAN: terzetto (a vocal piece for three voices) GERMAN: *Terz, Terzett* (a vocal piece for three voices) INTERDISCIPLINARY: tierce (in *ecclesiology*, the third of the seven canonical hours; in *measurements*, a former measure of liquid capacity, equal to a third of a pipe, or 42 gallons; in *card games*, a sequence of three cards of the same suit; in *fencing*, the third position from which a parry or thrust can be made; in *music*, an interval of a third) NO CROSS REFERENCE
terg*	Latin *tergere*: to rub off (IE: *ter²*, to rub, turn)	wipe clean	PREFIXED ROOT: *abs-*: absterge, abstergent, abstersion, abstersive (*abs-*, away) *de-*: deterge, detergence, detergent, detersion (*de-*, from, off) DISGUISED ROOT: terse (*wiped clean* of excess words; **Synonyms:** concise, laconic, succinct) CROSS REFERENCE:
term***	Latin *terminus* (IE: *ter¹*, to get over, break through)	end, boundary	SIMPLE ROOT: term, termer, terminable, terminal, terminate, termination, terminator, terminus (plural, *termini*) PREFIXED ROOT: *con-*: conterminous (having a common boundary; contained within the same boundaries or limits, as the *conterminous* United States includes all the States except Alaska and Hawaii) (*con-*, with, together) *de-*: (from) determinant, determinate, determination, determinative determine (**Synonyms:** learn, ascertain, discover), determined *ex-*: exterminate (**Synonyms:** abolish, extinguish, extirpate), extermination, exterminator (*ex-*, out) LEADING ROOT COMPOUND: *logy*: terminology (nomenclature; study of terms) (*logy*, study of) COINED WORD: termone [short for *de(term)ining horm(one)*: sex-determining hormone] LATIN PHRASES: *terminus ad quem* (end toward which; end, conclusion) *terminus a quo* (end from which; starting point, origin, beginning) CROSS REFERENCE: *fin*
terr***	Latin *terra* (IE: *ters*, to dry)	earth	SIMPLE ROOT: terra: terrace, terrain, terrane, terrarium, terrazzo terre: terrene, terrestrial (in *zoology*, living on the ground; not aquatic, arboreal, or aerial; **Synonyms:** earthly, worldly, mundane), terrier, terrine terri: territorial, territorialism, territoriality, territorialize, territoriality, territory

Element	From	Meaning	Examples
terr (cont'd)			PREFIXED ROOT: *in-*: inter (to put a dead body into a grave or tomb; bury), interment (*in-*, in) *sub-*: subterranean (lying beneath the earth's surface; underground; also, secret, hidden; as a *noun*, one who lives underground) (*sub-*, under) DOUBLE PREFIXED ROOT: dis<u>in</u>ter (*dis-*, reversal + *in-*, in) LEADING ROOT COMPOUND: *terr*: aque: terraqueous (*aqua*, water) *terra*: myc: Terramycin (literally, earth fungus; trademark for oxytetracycline) (*myc*, fungus) *terri*: col: terricolous (literally, land dweller; in *biology* and *zoology*, living in or on the ground) (*colere*, to dwell) gen: terrigenous (earthborn, or born of the earth; also, produced by the earth; in *geology*, designating or of sea-bottom sediment derived from erosion of land) (*gignere*, to be born) TRAILING ROOT COMPOUND: medi: mediterranean (as an *adjective*, surrounded nearly or completely by dry land: said of large bodies of water, as lakes or seas; capitalized, the Mediterranean Sea; a collective designation for the languages of that area) (*medius*, middle) DISGUISED ROOT: tureen [literally, earthen (vessel); a broad, deep dish with a cover used for serving soups, stews, and the like] LATIN PHRASES: *terra alba* (literally, white earth) *terra cotta* (literally, cooked earth) *terra firma* (literally, firm land; solid ground; dry land) *terra incognita* (literally, unknown land; unexplored territory; an unknown or unexplored field of knowledge) CROSS REFERENCE: *adeph, chthon, geo, ped*
tessa			See *tetra* for *diatessaron*.
test**	Latin *testis* (IE: *trei*, three)	witness	ROOT NOTE: The association between this root and the original meaning of *three* is quite interesting. See Eric Partridge's *Origins: A Short Etymological Dictionary of Modern English*. In addition, there are stories of one swearing by his testes in giving his testimony in the Roman court. *Webster's Third* presents interesting aspects under *testament*, *testis*. SIMPLE: testa: testament (originally, a covenant, especially one between God and man) testate (having made and left a valid will), testation, testator teste: testes (plural of *testis*, testicle) testi: testimonial, testimony, testis (plural, *testes*), testicle PREFIXED ROOT: *at-*: attest (*at-* assimilates *ad-*, to, toward) *con-*: contest (**Synonyms:** conflict, fight, struggle), contestant, contestation (*con-*, with, together)

Element	From	Meaning	Examples
test (cont'd)			*de-*: detest (originally, to curse by calling on the gods to witness; **Synonyms**: hate, despise, abhor), detestability, detestable, detestation (*de-*, down)
			in-: intestacy, intestate (having made no will; not disposed of by a will; as a noun, a person who has died intestate) (*in-*, not)
			ob-: obtest (to beg for; beseech; supplicate; to call to witness) {obtestation} (*ob-*, against)
			pro-: protest (**Synonyms**: object, remonstrate, expostulate), protestant (of Protestants or Protestant beliefs, practices, etc.) (*pro-*, forth)
			LEADING ROOT COMPOUND:
			fy: testify (from *facere*, to make, do)
			DIVISIONS OF THE BIBLE: *Old Testament, New Testament*
			CROSS REFERENCE: *orchid*
tetra,*** tess	Greek *tetras*: four; *tessara*: square (IE: *kwetwer*, four)	four, square	SIMPLE ROOT:
			tess: tessa, tesselate, tessalation, tessera
			tetra: tetra (clipping of *tetragonum*, square; a tropical fish); tetrad
			PREFIXED ROOT:
			dia-: diatessaron (literally, through the four; the four Gospels--Matthew, Mark, Luke, John--combined into a single account) (*dia-*, through)
			LEADING ROOT COMPOUND:
			tetr:
			arch: tetrarch (in the ancient Roman Empire, the ruler of a fourth part of a province; subordinate prince, governor, etc.), tetrarchy (*arch*, ruler)
			atom: tetratomic (*a-*, not + *tom*, to cut)
			tetra:
			bas: tetrabasic (designating or of an acid having four replaceable hydrogen atoms per molecule)
			brach: tetrabrach (in *Greek and Latin prosody*, a word or foot containing four short syllables) (*brachy*, short)
			chord: tetrachord (literally, four-stringed, in *music*, a series of four tones comprising a total interval of a perfect fourth, e.g., from C to F; half an octave) (*chord*; string)
			evangel: tetraevangelium (the Four Gospels, the first four books of the New Testament: Matthew, Mark, Luke, John; see *diatessaron*, above) (*evangel*; good news)
			hedron: tetrahedron (a solid figure with four triangular faces) (*hedron*, geometric plane)
			logy: tetralogy (a series of four dramas, three tragic and one satiric, performed together at the ancient Athenian festival of Dionysus) (from *logos*, word)
			mer: tetramerous (in *biology*, made up of four parts or divisions; in multiples of four; also written **4-merous**) (*mere*, part)
			meter: tetrameter (a line of verse consisting of four metrical feet or measures)
			ploid: tetraploid (in *biology*, having four times the haploid number of chromosomes) (*ploid*, fold)

Element	From	Meaning	Examples
tetra (cont'd)			pod: tetrapod (any vertebrate having four legs or limbs, including the mammals, birds, reptiles, etc.) (*pod*, foot) pter: tetrapterous (in *zoology*, having four wings) (*pter*, wing) spor: tetrasporangium (in *botany*, a sporangium containing four asexual spores), tetraspore (*spore*, reproductive body) stich: tetrastich (a poem or stanza of four lines), tetrastichous (in *biology*, in four vertical rows, as the flowers on some spikes) (*stich*, line) val: tetravalent (having a valence of four; same as *quadrivalent*) ELIDED LEADING ROOT COMPOUND: ode: tetrode [an electron tube having four electrodes (a cathode, control grid, anode, and, usually, a screen grid): used to generate, amplify, modulate, or demodulate electrical signals] (*hodos*, way; from IE *sed*, to go) CONTRACTION: tetryl [*tetr*(anitrometh)*yl* (aniline)] CROSS REFERENCE: *quad, quat*
tex*	Latin *texere* (IE: *tekth*, to weave, build, join)	to weave, build	NOTE: See *Root Note* under *technic*. SIMPLE ROOT: text (**Synonyms**: subject, theme, topic), textile, textual, textualism, textuary, texture, texturized PREFIXED ROOT: con-: context, contextual, contexture (*con-*, with, together) pre-: pretext (an ostensible or professed purpose; pretense; excuse; as a *verb*, to allege as an excuse) (*pre-*, before) DISGUISED ROOT: tissue, toga ITALIAN MUSIC TERM: tessitura (literally, texture; the average level of pitch of a specific vocal composition, operatic role, etc.) FRENCH TERM: *tête-à-tête* (literally, head to head; an intimate conversation) may be related to this root. CROSS REFERENCE: *struct, tech*
thall*	Greek *thallein*: to sprout (IE: *dhal*, to blossom)	flourish, bloom	SIMPLE ROOT: thalli: thallic, thalline, thallium (chemical symbol, Ti) thallu: thallus (in *botany*, the undifferentiated stemless, rootless, leafless plant body characteristic of thallophytes) LEADING ROOT COMPOUND: *thall*: oid: thalloid (of, resembling, or constituting a thallus) (*oid*, similar to) *thalli*: fer: thalliferous (containing or yielding thallium) (*ferous*, bearing) form: thalliform (having the form of a thallus) *thallo*: gen: thallogen (a plant in which growth is not restricted to an apical growing point; compare *acrogen*) (*gen*, origin) phyt: thallophyte (any plant or plantlike organism which includes the algae, fungi, and bacteria) (*phyton*, plant) spor: thallospore (*spore*, seed) TRAILING ROOT COMPOUND: hetero: heterothallic (producing male gametangia in one structure or plant and female gametangia in a different structure or plant, as in some algae and fungi) (*hetero*, different)

Element	From	Meaning	Examples
thall (cont'd)			homo: homothallic (having male and female reproductive structures in the same thallus, as in some algae and fungi) (*homo*, same) GREEK MYTHOLOGY: Thalia [literally, the blooming one; the Muse of comedy and pastoral poetry; Bloom, one of the three Graces: Aglaia (Brilliance), Euphrosyne (Joy), and Thalia (Bloom), the three sister goddesses who have control over pleasure, charm, and beauty in human life and in nature] CROSS REFERENCE: *anth, flor*
thanat*	Greek *thanatos* (IE: *dheu*, to be smoky, stormy)	death	LEADING ROOT COMPOUND: *thanat*: ops: "Thanatopsis," [a poem by William Cullen Bryant (who coined the word), in which the poet viewed or mused upon death. An often-quoted passage of this poem reads as follows: "...sustained and soothed/By an unfaltering trust, approach thy grave/Like one that wraps the drapery of his couch/About him and lies down to pleasant dreams." This passage may be a paraphrase from Lucretius (99-55 B.C.): Why dost thou not retire like a guest sated with the banquet of life, and with calm mind embrace, thou fool, a rest that knows no care? *De Rerum Natura,* On the Nature of Things, Book I, l., I (Introduction)]; or from Horace (Quintus Horatius Flaccus), *Satires,* book I] (*opsis*, a seeing) *thanato*: phob: thanatophobia (morbid fear of death) (*phobia*, fear of) TRAILING ROOT COMPOUND: eu: euthanasia (literally, pleasant death) (*eu*, good) DISGUISED ROOT: tansy GREEK MYTHOLOGY: Thanatos (death personified) CROSS REFERENCE: *let, mort, necro*
the**	Greek *theasthai*: to see (IE: *dhau*, to see)	viewing	SIMPLE ROOT: theater, theorem, theoretical [or, pertaining to, or consisting of theory; not practical (as distinguished from *applied*)], theorem (in *mathematics* and *physics*, a proposition embodying something to be proved), theoretical, theoretician, theoretics, theorize, theory (**Synonyms:** hypothesis, law) PREFIXED ROOT: amphi-: amphitheater (an oval or round structure having tiers of seats rising gradually outward from an open space or arena at the center) (*amphi-*, around) INTERDISCIPLINARY: theorem (in *logic*, a proposition that can be deduced from the premises or assumptions of a system; in *mathematics*, a theoretical proposition, statement, or formula embodying something to be proved from other propositions or formulas) CROSS REFERENCE: *ops, scop, vid/vis*
theca*	Greek *thekion*: case, cover (IE: *dhe*, to place, put)	case, sheath	SIMPLE ROOT: theca, thecate, thecial, thecium PREFIXED ROOT: amphi-: amphithecium (in *botany*, the outer layer of cells of the spore-containing capsule of a moss) (*amphi-*, around) apo-: (away) apothecary (literally, to put away; to store; a pharmacist; a drugstore)

Element	From	Meaning	Examples
theca (cont'd)			apothecium (literally, storehouse; an open disk-shaped or cup-shaped fruiting body in certain fungi, lined with a spore-bearing layer) *endo-*: endothecium (in *botany*, the inner tissue of an anther or a moss capsule) (*endo-*, within, inside) *hypo-*: hypothec (literally, something put under pledge; security; in *law*, security or right given to a creditor over a debtor's property without transfer of possession or title), hypothecate (*hypo-*, under) *peri-*: perithecium (in *botany*, a small fruiting body in certain fungi, containing ascospores) (*peri-*, around) TRAILING ROOT COMPOUND: *biblio*: bibliotheca (a library) (*biblio*, book) *myxo*: myxotheca (the horny sheath at the end of bird's lower mandible) (*myxo*, mucus) *oo*: ootheca (an egg receptacle; same as *ovisac*) (*oo*, egg) DISGUISED ROOT: tick (covering for a pillow or mattress) INTERDISCIPLINARY: **theca** (in *botany*, a spore case or capsule; in *anatomy* and *zoology*, any sac enclosing an organ or a whole organism, as the covering of an insect pupa) CROSS REFERENCE: *pon/pos, thes/thet*
theo***	Greek *theos* (IE: *dhewes*, to storm, breathe)	God	SIMPLE ROOT: theist, theistic, theism (belief in one God, as opposed to *pantheism, polytheism*; also, belief in one God who is creator and ruler of the universe and known by revelation) PREFIXED ROOT AND COMPOUNDS: *a-*: atheist (hence, one who denies the existence of God or gods; **Synonyms**: agnostic, infidel) (*a-*, not) *apo-*: apotheosis (the exaltation of a person to the rank of a god), apotheosize (*apo-*, away; *osis*, condition of) LEADING ROOT COMPOUND: *the*: *od*: theody (a hymn praising God) (*ode*, song) *theo*: *centr*: theocentric (centering on God as the prime concern, as *a theocentric cosmology*) *crac*: theocracy (government by a god regarded as the ruling power or by priests or officials claiming divine sanction) (*cracy*, ruled by) *cras*: theocrasy (the process whereby two or more originally distinct deities are thought of, or worshiped as, a single deity) (*cras*, mix) *dic*: theodicy (a system of natural theology aimed at seeking to vindicate divine justice in allowing evil to exist) (*dic*, judgment) *gon*: theogony (a recitation of the origin and genealogy of the gods, especially as in ancient epic poetry) (*gony*, production of) *log*: theological, theologism, theology (the study of the nature of God and religious truth; rational inquiry into religious questions, especially those posed by Christianity) (*logy*, the study of)

Element	From	Meaning	Examples
theo (cont'd)			machy: theomachy (a battle against the gods; strife among the gods) (*machy*, struggle) morph: theomorphism (the depiction or conception of man as having the form of a god) (*morph*, shape, form) phan: theophanic, theophany (in *mythology* and *theology*, the visible appearance of a god or God to man) (*phan*, to show) phob: theophobia (a fear of the wrath of God) (*phobia*, fear of) TRAILING ROOT COMPOUND: heno: henotheism (belief in one god without asserting there is only one god; compared to *monotheism*, a belief in *only* one God) (*heno*, one) mono: monotheism (the doctrine or belief that there is only one God), monotheist (*mono*, one) pan: pantheism, pantheist, pantheon (a temple dedicated to all the gods; see *Note*) (*pan*, all) PREFIXED DISGUISED ROOT: *en-*: enthusiasm (literally, God within; **Synonyms**: passion, fervor, zeal) (*en-*, in) PROPER NAMES: Theobald (literally, brave god) Theodore, Theodora (literally, gift of God) NOTE: Capitalized, *Pantheon* is a building in which the famous dead persons of a nation are entombed or commemorated, as Westminster Abbey in England or the church of Sainte-Geneviève in Paris. NB: *Theodolite*, a surveying instrument, is not in this family. CROSS REFERENCE: *dei*
thera**	Greek *theraps*: attendant	treatment	SIMPLE ROOT: therapeusis, therapeutic, therapeutics (the branch of medicine concerned with the remedial treatment of disease), therapy TRAILING ROOT COMPOUND: cryo: cryotherapy (*cryo*, cold) hyro: hydrotherapy (*hydro*, water) CROSS REFERENCE: *iatri*
therm***	Greek *therme*: heat (IE: *gwher*, hot)	heat	SIMPLE ROOT: thermal, thermic, thermion, Thermos PREFIXED ROOT: *dia-*: diathermy (the therapeutic generation of local heat in body tissues by high-frequency electromagnetic waves) (*dia-*, across, by transmission) ecto-: ectotherm, ectothermic (opposed to *endothermic*) (*ecto-*, outside, external) endo-: endotherm, endothermic (opposed to *ectothermic*) (*endo*, within) exo-: exothermic (*exo-*, outside, external) hyper-: hyperthermia (unusually high fever) (*hyper-*, beyond) hypo-: hypothermal, hypothermia (*hypo-*, under) DOUBLE PREFIXED ROOT: adiathermancy (the quality of being impervious to heat waves) (*a-*, not + *dia-*, through) LEADING ROOT COMPOUND: *therm*: ist: thermistor (coalescence of *therm*al res*istor*)

Element	From	Meaning	Examples
therm (cont'd)			*thermo:* chem: thermochemistry (the chemistry of heat and heat-associated chemical phenomena) dynam: thermodynamics (the physics of the relationship between heat and other forms of energy) (*dyna*, power) graph: thermography, thermography (*graph*, write) meter: thermometer (*meter*, measure) phil: thermophilic (in *biology*, requiring high temperatures for normal development, as certain bacteria) (*phila*, love of) pile: thermopile (*pile*, heap, series) spher: thermosphere (the outermost shell of the atmosphere, between the mesosphere and outer space) (*spher*, ball, globe) stat: thermostat (*stat*, to set) TRAILING ROOT COMPOUND: homoio: homoiothermous (maintaining a relatively constant and warm body temperature that is independent of environmental temperature; warm-blooded) (*homoio*, same, similar) iso: (equal) isobathytherm (*bathy*, deep); isogeotherm (*geo*, earth) poikilo: poikilotherm, poikilothermous (in *zoology*, having a body temperature that *varies* with the external environment; compare *homoiothermous*, above) (*poikilos*, various) CROSS REFERENCE: *cal*
thes,* thet**	Greek *thesis*: act of placing down (IE: *dhe*, to put, place, set)	to place, put	SIMPLE ROOT: thesis PREFIXED ROOT: *thes:* anti-: antithesis (a contrast or opposition of thoughts, usually in two phrases, clauses, or sentences, e.g., *You are going; I am staying*; the second part of such an expression) (*anti-*, against) dia-: diathesis (but meaning "in different directions" in this word; a predisposition to certain diseases) (*dia-*, through) hypo-: hypothesis (literally, to place under; an unproved theory, proposition, supposition, etc. tentatively accepted to explain certain facts or to provide a basis for further investigation, argument, etc.) (*hypo-*, under) meta-: metathesis (a transposition; term used in linguistics and chemistry) (*meta-*, over) pro-: prothesis (in *grammar*, the addition of a letter, syllable, or phoneme to the beginning of a word) (*pro-*, before) pros-: prosthesis (the replacement of a missing part of the body by an artificial substitute) (*pros-*, to) syn-: synthesis (the putting together of parts so as to form a whole) (*syn-*, with, together) *thet:* anti-: antithetical (**Synonyms:** opposite, contrary, reverse) (*anti-*, against) epi-: epithet (literally, that which is added to; an adjective, noun, or phrase used to characterize some person or thing, such as *America the Beautiful*, the *Little Corporal* for Napoleon) (*epi-*, upon)

Element	From	Meaning	Examples
thes (cont'd)			*hypo-*: hypothetical (of or based on a hypothesis; suppositional; conjectural; uncertain; conditional) (*hypo-*, under) *pros-*: prosthetics (from *prosthesis*; plural in form; used with a singular verb; prosthetic surgery) (*pros-*, to) *syn-*: synthetic (**Synonyms:** artificial, counterfeit, spurious) (*syn-*, with, together) DOUBLE PREFIXED ROOT: ep*en*thesis (a phonetic change which involves the insertion of an unhistorical sound or syllable in a word, as the extra syllable in the pronunciation, e.g., *ath uh lete* for *athlete*) (*epi-*, upon + *en-*, in) par*en*thesis (plural, *parentheses*) (*para-*, alongside + *en-*, in) DISGUISED ROOTS: thematic (of or constituting a theme or themes; in *linguistics*, of or relating to the stem of a word or to a vowel ending a stem that precedes an inflectional ending) theme (**Synonyms:** subject, topic, text) INTERDISCIPLINARY: thesis (in *logic*, an unproved statement assumed as a premise; distinguished from *hypothesis*; in *prosody*, the unstressed part of a foot; however, in *classical prosody*, designated the unaccented section of a measure, the difference in usage due to a misunderstanding of the original Greek word; in *music*, the accented section of a measure; the downbeat) CROSS REFERENCE: *pon, pos, theca*
thrix			See *tricho* for *leptothrix*.
thym*	Greek *thymos* (IE: *dheu,* to blow)	soul, spirit, mind	SIMPLE ROOT: thymic (of the mind) PREFIXED ROOT: *en-*: enthymeme (literally, to have in mind; in *logic*, an argument in which one of the premises or, sometimes, the conclusion is not expressed but implied) (*en-*, in) TRAILING ROOT COMPOUND: schizo: schizothymia (schizoid behavior that resembles schizophrenia) (*schizo*, split) CROSS REFERENCE: *cerebr, ment, phren, psych*
tic			See *tac/tic* for *reticent*.
tin			See *ten*, Latin, for *continent, retinue.*
tom***	Greek *temnein* (IE: *tem,* to cut)	to cut	ROOT NOTE: The root is often joined with *ec-*, from *ex-*, out, to form *ectom*, to surgically remove; and with *en-* to form *entom*, insect, which is cut into segments (see *entomology*, below) SIMPLE ROOT: tome (literally, a piece cut off; hence, part of a book, volume; originally, any volume of a work of several volumes; a book, especially a large, scholarly or ponderous one) PREFIXED ROOT: *a-*: atom (literally, that which cannot be cut further; the smallest component of an element) (*a-*, not) *ana-*: anatomy (literally, to cut up) (*ana-*, up, again) *dia-*: diatom (literally, to cut through; any of various unicellular or colonial algae, having siliceous cell walls consisting of two overlapping, symmetrical parts) (*dia-*, through)

685

Element	From	Meaning	Examples
tom (cont'd)			*en-*: entomology (literally, the study of that which is cut, or divided, into sections; study of insects and bugs; see *entom*, which is itself a family) (*en-*, in)
			epi-: epitome (literally, to cut short; a short statement of the main points of a book, report, incident, etc.; abstract; summary; a person or thing that is representative or typical of the characteristics or general quality of a whole class, as *the epitome of honesty*) (*epi-*, upon)
			LEADING ROOT COMPOUND:
			graph: tomography [a technique for making x-ray pictures of a predetermined plane section of a solid object by blurring out the images of other planes; often called CAT (computer-assisted tomography) scan] (*graph*, write)
			TRAILING ROOT COMPOUND:
			auto: autotomy (reflex separation of a part or limb from the body; also, the division of the whole into two or more pieces, as in crustaceans, echinoderms, or worms) (*auto*, self)
			dicho: dichotomize, dichotomous, dichotomy (division into two usually contradictory parts or opinions; schism) (*dicho*, two)
			episio: episiotomy (an incision of the perineum, often performed during childbirth to prevent injury to the vagina) (*epision*, pubic region)
			gastr: gastrotomy (an incision into the stomach) (*gastro*, stomach, belly)
			xylo: xylotomy (the preparation of sections of wood for microscopic study) (*xylo*, wood)
			PREFIXED TRAILING ROOT COMPOUND:
			ap-: appendectomy (the surgical removal of the appendix) (*ap-* assimilates *ad-*, to, toward + *pendere*, to hang)
			DISGUISED ROOT:
			tmesis (the separation of the parts of a compound word by one or more intervening words, e.g., *where I go ever* instead of *wherever I go*)
			tonsorial (of a barber or barbering: often used humorously)
			tonsure (a clipping off or shaving off of part or all of the hair of the head, done especially, formerly, as a signal of entrance into the clerical or monastic state)
			INTERDISCIPLINARY: dichotomy (in *astronomy*, the phase of the moon or an inferior planet in which half its disk appears illuminated; in *botany*, branching characterized by successive forking into two approximately equal divisions; in *logic*, the division or subdivision of a class into two mutually exclusive parts)
			CROSS REFERENCE: *cis, sect, scis*

It is fatal to the highest success to have command
of a noble language and to have nothing to say in it;
it is equally fatal to have noble thoughts and to lack
the power of giving them expression.
Hamilton Wright Mabie

Element	From	Meaning	Examples
ton**	Greek *tonos*: stretching (IE: *tenu*, thin; from *ten*, stretch)	stretching, tone, sound	SIMPLE ROOT: tonal, tonality, tone, tonic, tonicity PREFIXED ROOT: *hyper-*: hypertonia (also, *hypertonicity*), hypertonic (opposite of *hypotonic*, below) (*hyper-*, beyond, over) *hypo-*: hypotonic (the opposite of *hypertonic*, which see, above) (*hypo-*, under) TRAILING ROOT COMPOUND: mono: monotone, monotonous, monotony (lack of variation or variety; tiresome sameness or uniformity) (*mono*, one) INTERDISCIPLINARY: tone (in *music*, the interval of a major second; a whole step; also the characteristic quality or timbre of a particular instrument or voice; in *physiology*, the tension in resting muscles; normal firmness of tissue) hypertonic (in *chemistry*, having the higher osmotic pressure of two solutions; in *pathology*, having extreme muscular or arterial tension) monotone (in *mathematics*, designating sequences the successive numbers of which either consistently increase or decrease but do not oscillate in relative value; in *music*, a single tone repeated with different words or time values, as in plainsong) CROSS REFERENCE: *phon, son, ten*
top***	Greek *topos* (IE: *top*, to arrive, goal)	place	SIMPLE ROOT: topiary (designating or of the art of trimming and training shrubs or trees into unusual, ornamental shapes) topic (**Synonyms:** subject, theme, text), topical (of a particular place; in *medicine*, of, for a particular part of the body) PREFIXED ROOT: utopia [literally, not a place, a term coined by Sir Thomas More (1516) to describe a perfect society; see More's book *Utopia*] (*u-* from *ou-*, not) LEADING ROOT COMPOUND: *top*: onym: toponym, toponymy (also spelled *toponomy*, where *nom* is Latin for "name") (*onym*, name) *topo*: graph: topographer, topography (literally, the description of a place; the detailed and accurate description of a place or region) (*graph*, write) log: topological, topology (the topographical study of a given place in relation to its history; in *mathematics*, the study of properties of geometric configurations invariant under transformation by continuous mappings) (*logy*, study of) TRAILING ROOT COMPOUND: hetero: heterotopia (the displacement of an organ or part in the body) (*hetero*, other, different) GRAMMATICAL TERM: topic sentence (the placement of the sentence that expresses the main or central thought of the paragraph, and usually is at or near the beginning of the paragraph) WORK BY ARISTOTLE: *Topika* (from the material being divided into topics) CROSS REFERENCE: *chor, loco*

Element	From	Meaning	Examples
torn,* **tour**	Latin *tornare*: to turn in a lathe (IE: *ter*², to rub, rub with a turning motion)	to turn	SIMPLE ROOT: *torn*: tornado (probably from Spanish *tornar*, to turn, yielding *tronada*, thunder, thunderstorm), tornal, tornaria *tour*: tour, tourney (to take part in a tournament), tournament, tourniquet PREFIXED ROOT: *torn*: *at*-: attorn, attorney (one who *turns to* his client) (*at*- assimilates *ad*-, to, toward) *con*-: contour (in *agriculture*, the making of furrows along the natural contour lines so as to avoid erosion, as on a hillside, often called *contour rows*, or *contour farming*) (*con*-, with) *tour*: *de*-: detour (*de*-, away) DISGUISED ROOT: terret, turnip PREFIXED DISGUISED ROOT: *re*-: return, returnable (*re*-, back) FRENCH: *tournedos* (a small, found beefsteak cut from the tenderloin, often with a strip of bacon, suet, etc. tied around it) (*tourner*, to turn + *dos*, back) FRENCH PHRASES: *tour de force* (literally, feat of strength; a feat of strength or virtuosity) *tour d' horizon* (literally, tour of the horizon; a brief but comprehensive review) SPANISH: tornillo (literally, screw; diminutive of *torno*, winch, spindle, wheel; the screw bean) ENGLISH COGNATE: turn (**Synonyms**: curve, bend, twist) CROSS REFERENCE: *vert*
tort,** **torq**, **tors**	Latin *torquere* (IE: *terk*, to turn; from *ter*², to rub)	to twist	SIMPLE ROOT: *torq*: torque, torques (twisted necklace: a ring of hair, feathers, or modified skin around the neck of an animal or bird, of a distinctive color or form) *tors*: torsa: torsade (a twisted cord used in drapery) torsi: torsibility, torsion, torsional (also, *tortional*) torso: torso (a twisted column; *torso*, referring to the trunk of the human body, is Italian from Latin *thyrsus*, stalk, stem) *tort*: tort: tort (a wrongful act, injury, or damage, not involving a breach of contract, for which a civil action can be brought) torte: torte [literally, twisted (bread); a rich cake made of eggs, finely chopped nuts, and crumbs or a little flour] torti: tortile, tortional (also, *torsional*), tortious (legal term) torto: tortoise tortu: tortuosity, tortuous (full of twists, turns, curves, or windings; winding; crooked; not straightforward; devious; specifically, deceitful or tricky) torture (the inflicting of severe pain to force information or confession, get revenge, etc.) torturous (causing, marked, or accompanied by torture) [Note difference between *tortuous* and *torturous*.]

Element	From	Meaning	Examples
tort (cont'd)			PREFIXED ROOT: *con-*: contort (see synonyms at *distort*, next entry), contortion, contortive (*con-*, with, together) *dis-*: distort (**Synonyms:** twist, deform, contort), distortion (*dis-*, apart, aside) *ex-*: extort, extortion, extortive (*ex-*, out) *re-*: retort (**Synonyms:** answer, respond, reply; as a *noun*, a closed laboratory vessel with an outlet tube, used for distillation, sublimation, or decomposition by heat) (*re-*, back) LEADING ROOT COMPOUND: collis: torticollis (a contracted state of the neck muscles producing an unnatural position of the head) (*collum*, neck) TRAILING ROOT COMPOUND: bis: bistort (literally, twice-twisted; a certain type of plant having pointed clusters of small, pinkish flowers) (*bis*, twice) DISGUISED ROOTS: tart (a twisted pie; also, a loose woman or prostitute) torch (originally made with twisted straw dipped in wax) torment (**Synonyms:** bait, badger, hound), tormentil **truss** DISGUISED TRAILING ROOT COMPOUND: nas: nasturtium (literally, nose twister, because of its acrid smell; however, the smell of the *American* nasturtium is not acrid) (*nas*, nose) ITALIAN: tortellini (a pasta in tiny ring-shaped or round pieces, filled with meat, vegetables, etc. and served with a sauce or in a broth) SPANISH: tortilla FRENCH LEGAL TERM: tort-feasor (a person who commits or is guilty of a tort) (from *faiseur*, one who does; from *facere*, to do, make) OLD HIGH GERMAN: queer (**Synonyms:** peculiar, odd, quaint) OLD NORSE: thwart (**Synonyms:** frustrate, foil, baffle) INTERDISCIPLINARY: truss (in *architecture*, a bracket; in *engineering*, a framework of wooden beams or metal bars, often arranged in triangles, to support a roof, bridge, or similar structure; in *medicine*, a supportive device worn to prevent enlargement of a hernia or the return of a reduced hernia) NO CROSS REFERENCE
tour			See *torn/tour* for *tour, tourniquet.*
tox**	Greek *toxikon* (originally, poison in which arrows were dipped)	poison	SIMPLE ROOT: toxic, toxicant, toxicity, toxin PREFIXED ROOT: *anti-*: antitoxic, antitoxin (*anti-*, against) *endo-*: endotoxin (a toxin produced within a microorganism and released upon destruction of the cell in which it is produced) (*endo-*, within) *exo-*: exotoxic (*exo-*, without) *in-*: intoxicate (literally, to smear poison in; to excite to a point beyond self-control; make wild with excitement and happiness) (*in-*, in)

Element	From	Meaning	Examples
tox (cont'd)			LEADING ROOT COMPOUND: *tox:* alb: toxalbumin (any of various toxic proteins) (*alb*, white) emia: toxemia (a condition in which poisonous substances are spread throughout the body by the bloodstream, especially toxins produced by pathogenic bacteria or by cells of the body; also spelled *toxsemia*) (*emia*, diseased condition of the blood) en: tox<u>en</u>zyme (*en-* prefixes *zym*, leaven, yeast) oid: toxoid (*oid*, similar to) *toxic:* osis: toxicosis (any pathological condition resulting from poisoning) (*osis*, condition of) *toxico:* gen: toxicogenic (*genic*, producing) logy: toxicology (the study of the nature, effects, and detection of poisons and the treatment of poisoning) (*logy*, study of) LEADING ROOT PREFIXED TRAILING ROOT: *anti-:* <u>toxin</u>anti<u>toxin</u> (a mixture of a toxin, as from diphtheria, and its antitoxin with a slight excess of toxin, formerly used as a vaccine) (*anti-*, against) TRAILING ROOT COMPOUND: auto: autotoxin (a poison that acts on the organism in which it is generated; do not confuse with *autoxidation*) (*auto* + *oxidation*) (*auto*, self) CROSS REFERENCE: *vir(us)*
trach*	Greek *trachys*, rough	rough; windpipe	ROOT NOTE: This root is from the Greek phrase *tracheia arteria*, rough windpipe; it has come to mean "windpipe." In *botany*, the word has other uses. SIMPLE ROOT: trachea, tracheal, tracheate, tracheid, tracheole trachyte (literally, rough stone; a light-colored igneous rock consisting essentially of alkalic feldspar) LEADING ROOT COMPOUND: *trach:* oma: trachoma (a contagious viral disease of the conjunctiva of the eye characterized by inflammation, hypertrophy, and granules of adenoid tissue) (*oma*, mass) *trache:* algia: trachealgia (pain in the trachea) (*algia*, pain) itis: tracheitis (inflammation of the trachea) (*itis*, inflammation) *tracheo:* scop: tracheoscopy (the inspection of the interior of the trachea) (*scope*, look) tom: tracheotomy (incision of the trachea) (*tom*, cut) INTERDISCIPLINARY: trachea (in *anatomy*, a thin-walled tube of cartilaginous and membranous tissue descending from the larynx to the bronchi and carrying air to the lungs; in *botany*, one of the tubular conductive vessels in the xylem of plants; in *zoology*, one of the internal respiratory tubes of insects and some other terrestrial arthropods) CROSS REFERENCE: *bronch, laryng*

690

Element	From	Meaning	Examples
tract***	Latin *trahere* (IE: *dheragh,* to pull, draw along)	to pull, drag, draw	SIMPLE ROOT: tract (see *Doublets* below), tractor tracta: tractable (**Synonyms:** obedient, compliant, acquiescent) tractate (a treatise or dissertation) tracti: tractile (capable of being drawn out in length, as certain metals; ductile), traction, tractive (used for pulling or drawing) PREFIXED ROOT: *tract:* *abs-:* abstract (**Synonyms:** abridgment, brief, summary), abstracted [removed or separated (from something); hence, withdrawn in mind; preoccupied] (*abs-*, away, away from) *at-:* attract, attraction, attractive (*at-* assimilates *ad-*, to, toward) *con-:* (with, together) contract (**Synonyms:** shrink, condense, compress), contractile contraction (in *grammar*, the shortening of a word or phrase by the omission of one of more sounds or letters; a word form resulting from this, e.g., *doesn't* for *does not*) contractor, contractual, contracture *de-:* detract, detraction {detractive} (*de-*, away) *dis-:* distract, distracted, distraction (*dis-*, apart, away) *ex-:* extract (**Synonyms:** educe, elicit, evoke), extraction, extractive, extractor (*ex-*, out) *in-:* intractable (**Synonyms:** unruly, refractory, recalcitrant) (*in-*, not) *pro-:* protract (**Synonyms:** prolong, extend), protractile, protraction, protractor (*pro-*, forward) *re-:* retract (see *Doublets* below), retractile (capable of being drawn back or in, as the *retractile claws* of cats), retraction, retractive, retractor (*re-*, back, again) *sub-:* subtract, subtraction, subtractive (*sub-*, under) *trahend:* *sub-:* subtrahend (a quantity or number to be subtracted from another) (*sub-*, under) DISGUISED ROOT: trace, tracer trail, trailer train (**Synonyms:** teach, educate, instruct) trait (**Synonyms:** quality, property, character; see *Doublets* below), treat, treaty trawl (from Middle Dutch *tragel,* dragnet; from Latin *trahere*) treatise (a formal account in writing treating systematically some subject, especially a discussion of facts, evidence, or principles and the conclusions based on these) PREFIXED DISGUISED ROOT: *dis-:* distrait (from *distract;* absent-minded; inattentive), distraught (a variation of *distrait*) (*dis-*, apart, away) *en-:* entreat (**Synonyms:** beg, beseech, importune) (*en-*, in) *mis-:* mistreat (Anglo-Saxon *mis-*, wrong, badly) *por-:* portrait, portray (to make a picture of portrait of; depict; delineate; to play the part of as in a play) (from *pro-*, forth)

Element	From	Meaning	Examples
tract (cont'd)			re-: retreat (see *Doublets* below; **Synonyms**: shelter, refuge, asylum) (*re-*, back, again) DOUBLETS: tract:trait; retract:retreat NO CROSS REFERENCE
trans-***	Latin *trans* (IE: *ter²*, to rub, turn)	across	EXTENDED PREFIX: transeunt (in *philosophy*, productive of effects outside the mind) transom (literally, that which is across; see *Doublets*) PREFIXED ROOT: tra-: (before *d, j, l, m, n, v*) dit: tradition (the passing down of elements of a culture from generation to generation, especially by oral communication), traditional (from *tradere*, to hand over; *dare*, to give) duc: traduce (to say untrue or malicious things about; as *to traduce* someone's character; to make a mockery of; betray; **Synonyms**: defame, malign, slander), traducianism (the theological doctrine that the human soul is propagated along with the body; opposed to *creationism*, which see under *cresc*) (*ducere*, to lead) ject: traject, trajectory (*jacere*, to throw) vers: traverse (from *vertere*, to turn) vest: travesty (**Synonyms**: caricature, burlesque, parody) (*vestire*, to dress; see *transvestite*, below) tran-: scend: transcend (**Synonyms**: excel, surpass, outdo), transcendent, transcendental, transcendentalism (from *scandere*, to climb) scrib: transcribe (*scribere*, to write) script: transcript, transcription (see *transcribe*) (see *transcribe*) sect: transect (to divide by cutting transversely) (*secare*, to cut) sept: transept (the part of a cross-shaped church at right angles to the long, main section, or nave) (*septum*, enclosure) sil: transilient (from *salire*, to jump, leap) sist: transistor (a device that *trans*fers an electrical current across a re*sistor*) (*trans- + sistor*) spic: transpicuous (from *specere*, to look) spir: transpiration, transpire (*spirare*, to breathe) spond: transponder (*trans*mitter + re*sponder*) sud: transudation, transude (*sudare*, to sweat) *trans*: act: transact {transactor}, transaction (from *agere*, to drive, do) ceiv: transceiver [a module consisting of a radio receiver and transmitter: *trans(mitter) + (re)ceiver*] (from *capere*, to hold) duc: transducer, transduction (*ducere*, to lead) fer: transfer (**Synonyms**: convey, carry, transport), transferal (or *transferral*), transference (*ferre*, to bear) fig: (from *fingere*, to form) transfiguration (a radical transformation of figure or appearance; metamorphosis; see *Biblical Concept* below) transfigure (**Synonyms**: transform, convert, metamorphose) fin: transfinite (beyond the finite) (*finire*, to end)

Element	From	Meaning	Examples
trans- (cont'd)			fix: transfix (to pierce through with or as if with a pointed weapon; to fix fast; impale; to render motionless, as with terror, amazement, or awe) {transfixion} (*figere*, to pierce, fix)
			form: transform (**Synonyms**: change, alter, vary), transformer, transformation (*formare*, to form)
			fus: transfuse, transfusion (from *fundere*, to pour)
			gress: transgress, transgression (**Synonyms**: breach, infraction, violation), transgressor (from *gradi*, to walk)
			human: transhumance (seasonal and alternating movement of livestock, together with the humans who tend the herds, between two regions, as lowland and highlands) (*humus*, earth)
			i: transience, transient (**Synonyms**: ephemeral, fleeting, fugitive), transitory (from *itere*, to go)
			it: transit, transition, transitive (*itere*, to go)
			lat: translate (in theology, to convey directly to heaven without death), translation (**Synonyms**: version, paraphrase, transliteration), translator (from *transfer*, above)
			liter: transliterate (*littera*, letter)
			loc: translocate, translocation (*locus*, place)
			luc: translucent (transmitting light but causing sufficient diffusion to eliminate perception of distinct images; **Synonyms**: clear, transparent) (*lucere*, to shine)
			mar: transmarine (crossing the sea; being beyond or coming from across the sea) (*mar*, sea)
			migr: transmigrate, transmigration (*migrare*, go, move)
			miss: transmissible, transmission (see *transmit*)
			mit: transmit (**Synonyms**: carry, bear, convey), transmittal, transmittance, transmitter (*mittere*, to send)
			mont: transmontane (located beyond a mountain or mountain range) (*mont*, mountain)
			mund: transmundane (beyond the world or worldly affairs) (*mundus*, world)
			mut: transmutation, transmute (**Synonyms**: vary, modify, convert) (*mutare*, to change)
			par: transparency, transparent (see synonyms at *translucent*, above) (*parere*, to show)
			port: transport (**Synonyms**: ecstasy, rapture, euphoria), transportation (*portare*, to carry)
			pos: transpose (**Synonyms**: reverse, invert), transposition (*poser*, to place)
			sex: transsexual (a person with an overwhelming desire to become the other sex)
			sub: transsubstantiate (to change one substance into another; transmute; transform; in *theology*, to change the substance of the Eucharistic bread or wine into the true presence of Christ), transsubstantiation (compare *consubstantiation*; see *stan* family) (*sub-* prefixes *stant*, stand)
			vers: transversal (in *geometry*, a line that intersects a system of lines), transverse (athwart; crosswise) (*vertere*, to turn)
			vest: transvestism (also, *transvestitism*: the abnormal desire to dress in the clothing of the opposite sex) (*vestire*, to dress)

693

Element	From	Meaning	Examples
trans- (cont'd)			**DOUBLE PREFIXED ROOT:** transcon̲d̲u̲c̲tance (*con-*, with, together + *ducere*, to lead) intran̲s̲igent (the negative of verb *transact*; therefore, describing one who refuses *to transact*, to compromise, or to come to agreement) (*in-*, not + *ig* from *agere*, to do, act) **DISGUISED ELEMENTS:** traffic (**Synonyms**: business, industry, commerce) traitor (not related to *trait*; see previous family) trance [Middle English *traunce*; from Old French *transe*; from *transir*, "to pass (from life to death)"; from Latin *transire*, the same roots as *transit*] tranquil (**Synonyms**: 1) calm, placid, halcyon; 2) still, silent, noiseless), tranquilizer treason (from the same roots as *tradition*, above) trespass (literally, to step across; see synonyms at *transgression*) (*tres-* from *trans-*; *pass* from *passum*, step) trestle (see *Doublets*) **PREFIXED DISGUISED ELEMENT:** *en-*: entrance (stress on second syllable, meaning "to put into a *trance*") [*Entrance*, with stress on first syllable, EN trance, the act of entering, is derived from Latin *intra*, within.] **INTERDISCIPLINARY:** transcendental (in *mathematics*, not capable of being determined by any combination of a finite number of equations with rational integral coefficients; not expressible as an integer or quotient of integers: said of numbers, especially nonrepeating infinite decimals; in *philosophy*, concerned with the a priori basis of knowledge; minimizing the importance or denying the reality of sense experience) transformation (in *linguistics*, the process of converting a syntactic construction into a semantically equivalent construction according to the rules shown to generate the syntax of the language; in *mathematics*, the replacement of the variables in an algebraic expression by their values in terms of another set of variables; a mapping of one space onto another or onto itself) transitive [in *grammar*, expressing an action that is carried from the subject to the object; requiring a direct object to complete its meaning: said of a verb or verb construction; in *mathematics*, designating a relation having the property that, whenever a first element bears a particular relation to a second that in turn bears this same relation to a third, the first element bears this relation to the third (*identity* and *equality* are transitive relations)] translocation (in *botany*, the transport of organic food materials in solution through tissues from one part of a plant to another; in *genetics*, the transfer of a portion of a chromosome to a new location in the chromosome or into another chromosome) **DOUBLETS:** transon:trestle **A BIBLICAL CONCEPT:** The Transfiguration (the sudden emanation of radiance from Jesus' person that occurred on the mountain; see Matthew 17:2; Mark 9:2) **CROSS REFERENCE:** *dia-*

Element	From	Meaning	Examples
trauma**	Greek *trauma* (IE: *ter²*, to rub, turn)	wound, hurt	SIMPLE ROOT: trauma {traumatic}, traumatize INTERDISCIPLINARY: trauma (in *pathology*, a wound, especially one produced by sudden physical injury; in *psychiatry*, an emotional shock that creates substantial and lasting damage to the psychological development of the individual, generally leading to neurosis) NO CROSS REFERENCE
tri***	Greek *tri* (IE: *trei*, three)	three	ROOT NOTE: *Tritos*, derived from *tri*, means third; see *tritanopia*, below LEADING ROOT COMPOUND: *tri*: arch: triarchy (government by three persons; triumvirate) (*archy*, ruled by) atom: triatomic (containing three atoms per molecule) brach: tribrach (a foot of poetry with three short or unstressed syllables, two belonging to the thesis and one to the arsis) (*brach*, short) chrom: trichromatic (*chrom*, color) crot: tricrotic (in *medicine*, having three waves or elevations to one beat of the pulse) (*crot*, beat) dactyl: tridactyl (in *zoology*, having three toes, claws, or similar parts) (*dactyl*, finger) er: trierarch (the commander of a trireme, an ancient Greek or Roman galley, usually a warship, with three banks of oars on each side) (*eres*, to row + *archos*, leader) glyph: triglyph (*glyph*, carving) gon: trigon, trigonal, trigonometry (*gon*, angle + *metry*, measurement of) hedr: trihedral, trihedron (a figure formed by the intersection of three non-coplanar lines) (*hedron*, geometric figure) phyl: triphylite (a phosphate containing lithium, iron, and manganese) (*phylum*, tribe) pod: tripod, tripody (a verse or phrase of three metrical feet) (*pod*, foot) *trit*: anop: tritanopia (a rare and obscure type of defective color vision, formerly called *blue blindness*) (*trit*, a third + *an-*, not + *opia*, sight) CROSS REFERENCE: *test, tri* (Latin)
tri***	Latin *tri* (IE: *trei*, three)	three	SIMPLE ROOT: triad (a group of three persons, things, ideas, etc.; trinity; a musical chord of three tones, especially one consisting of a root tone and its third and fifth) tribe (one of the *three* groups into which Romans were originally divided), trio LEADING ROOT COMPOUND: angl: triangle cent: tricentennial (happening once in 300 years; as a *noun*, a 300th anniversary or its celebration) (*cent*, 100 + *enn*, year) cep: triceps (literally, three-headed muscle; the large muscle at the back of the upper arm that extends the forearm when contracted) (from *caput*, head)

Element	From	Meaning	Examples
tri (cont'd)			dent: trident (a three-pronged spear used in ancient Roman gladiatorial combats; in *Greek and Roman mythology*, a three-pronged spear borne as a scepter by the sea god Poseidon, or Neptune) (*dent*, tooth)
			enn: triennial, triennium (from *ann*, year)
			furc: trifurcate (having three forks or branches) (*furca*, a fork)
			later: trilateral (pertaining to three lines) (*later*, side)
			lingu: trilingual (of or in three languages) (*lingua*, tongue)
			liter: triliteral (consisting of three letters, especially three consonants) (*littera*, letter)
			lob: trilobate (having three lobes, as some leaves; also, *trilobated, trilobed*)
			loc: trilocular (having three chambers, cells, or cavities) (*locus*, place; extended to mean cavity)
			mer: trimerous (having the parts in sets of three: said of a flower; also written **3-merous**) (*mere*, part)
			mes: trimester (a period or term of three months) (from *mensis*, month)
			plic: triplicate (three-fold) (*plicare*, to fold)
			reme: trireme (see *trierarch*)
			via: (road)
			trivial (originally where three roads meet, and thus the place for common talk)
			trivium (in the Middle Ages, the lower division of the seven liberal arts; specifically, the *three* arts of grammar, logic, and rhetoric; compare *quadrivium*, under *quad* and *via*)
			DISGUISED AND MESHED ELEMENTS:
			travail, travel (originally, an instrument of torture composed of three stakes; see *Doublets* below) (*tri + palus*, stake)
			treble (originally, the third highest female voice in musical harmony, when the total number of parts was six; see *Doublets* below)
			trellis
			trephine (a type of small crown saw used in surgery to remove a circular section, as of bone from the skull) (*tri + phin* from *fines*, ends)
			trey (a playing card with three spots, or a throw of dice totaling three)
			trillion [*three* x (m)illion]
			triple (see *Doublets* below), triplet
			DOUBLETS: travail:travel; treble:triple
			GEOLOGICAL PERIOD: Triassic (because divided into *three* groups)
			COUNTRY: Trinidad (see story in authors' *An Introduction to an Academic Vocabulary*)
			NB: *Triage*, from French *trier*, from which *try* and *trial* are derived, is not in this family; triage (pronounced TREE ahzh) designates a system of assigning priorities of medical treatment to battlefield casualties on the basis of urgency, chance for survival, etc.
			NOTE: The Latin root *trib*, from which *tribe* and *tribute* are derived, is from this root (see next family).
			CROSS REFERENCE: *tri* (Greek)

Element	From	Meaning	Examples
trib**	Latin *tribus* (combines *tri*, three + IE *bha*, *bheu*, to grow, flourish)	allot, give, pay	SIMPLE ROOT: triba: tribal, tribalism tribe: tribe (one third of the Roman people) tribu: tribune, tributary, tribute (**Synonyms:** encomium, eulogy, panegyric) PREFIXED ROOT: *at-*: attribute (**Synonyms:** 1) ascribe, impute, assign; 2) quality, property, trait) (*at-* assimilates *ad-*, to) *con-*: contribute, contribution, contributory, as *contributory negligence* (*con-*, with, together) *dis-*: distributary, distribute (**Synonyms:** dispense, divide, dole), distribution, distributive, distributor (*dis-*, apart) *re-*: retribution {retributive, retributory} (*re-*, back, again) INTERDISCIPLINARY: distributive (in *grammar*, referring to each member of a group regarded individually, e.g., *each* and *either* are distributive words; in *logic*, distributed in a given proposition: said of a term; in *mathematics*, the principle in multiplication that allows the multiplier to be used separately with each term of the multiplicand) CROSS REFERENCE: *do/dos/dot; don/dat/dit*
trib*	Latin *tribulare* (IE: *ter*[2], to rub, turn)	to oppress, afflict	SIMPLE ROOT: triba: tribade (literally, one who rubs; a lesbian) tribadism (homosexuality between women; lesbianism) tribu: tribulation (**Synonyms:** affliction, trial, misfortune) PREFIXED ROOT: *trib*: *dia-*: diatribe (literally, to rub through; a bitter and abusive criticism or denunciation; invective) (*dia-*, through) LEADING ROOT COMPOUND: electric: triboelectricity (an electric charge developed upon the surface of material, as by rubbing silk upon glass) logy: tribology (the study of friction between interacting parts, such as gears, and ways of reducing it) (*logy*, study of) lumin: triboluminescence (*lumin*, light) CROSS REFERENCE: *fric*
tric*	Latin *tricae*: trifles, perplexities (IE: *ter*[2], to rub, turn)	hindrance	PREFIXED ROOT: *ex-*: extricate (to release from an entanglement; disengage; to cause to be liberated or emitted) (*ex-*, out) *in-*: intricate (having many complexly arranged elements; **Synonyms:** complex, complicated, involved) (*in-*, in) DOUBLE PREFIXED ROOT: inextricable (incapable of being disentangled or untied; too intricate or complicated to solve; firmly resisting one's attempts at escape or resolution) (*in-*, not + *ex-*, out) PREFIXED DISGUISED ROOT: *in-*: intrigue (**Synonyms:** conspiracy, machination, cabal) (*in-*, in) ENGLISH COGNATE: trick (**Synonyms:** ruse, stratagem, maneuver) NO CROSS REFERENCE:

Element	From	Meaning	Examples
tricho,* thrix	Greek *thrix*	hair	**SIMPLE ROOT:** trichina (literally, hairy; a parasitic nematode worm, infesting the intestines of various mammals) {trichinous} trichite (a small needle-shaped filament or crystal) trichome (a hairlike or bristlelike outgrowth, as from the epidermis of a plant) **PREFIXED ROOT:** *amphi-*: amphitrichous (having a flagellum or flagella at both ends, as certain microorganisms) (*amphi-*, around) *peri-*: peritrichous (*peri-*, around) **LEADING ROOT COMPOUND:** *trich*: iasis: trichiasis (a condition of ingrowing hairs about an orifice, especially of ingrowing eyelashes) (*iasis*, pathological condition of) oid: trichoid (resembling hair; hairlike) (*oid*, similar to) *trichin*: osis: trichinosis (a disease caused by eating inadequately cooked pork containing trichinae) (*osis*, diseased condition of) *tricho*: cyst: trichocyst (*cyst*, sac, pouch) gyn: trichogyne (a receptive filament of the female reproductive structure of certain fungi and algae) (*gyne*, female reproductive process) **TRAILING ROOT COMPOUND:** *trich*: mono: monotrichous (having one flagellum at only one pole or end of certain bacteria) (*mono*, one) oligo: oligotrichia (congenital thinness of the growth of hair) (*oligo*, few, little) ulo: ulotrichous (having short woolly hair, characteristic of some races) (*ulo*, woolly) *thrix*: (used only as a terminal word element) lepto: leptothrix (capitalized, a genus of microorganisms with a thin sheath) (*lepto*, thin, slender) monil: monilethrix (a disease condition in which the hairs exhibit beadlike enlargements and become brittle) (*monile*, necklace) **INTERDISCIPLINARY:** peritrichous (in *botany*, having flagella evenly distributed over the entire surface of the cell: said of bacteria; in *zoology*, having a wreath of cilia around the mouth: said of protozoans) NOTE: Do not confuse this root with certain words beginning with *trich*, where *tri* forms the root for three, as in *tricheira*, a combination of *tri*, three + *chiro*, hand. CROSS REFERENCE: *crini*

... Naturally I am biased in favor of boys learning English;
I would make them all learn English;
and then I would let the clever ones learn Latin
as an honor, and Greek as a treat.
Winston Churchill

Element	From	Meaning	Examples
trit,* **trim**	Latin *terere*: to rub (IE: *ter²*, to rub, turn)	to rub away, wear out	SIMPLE ROOT: trite (**Synonyms:** hackneyed, stereotyped, commonplace) triturant, triturate (to rub, crush, or grind into very fine particles of powder; pulverize), trituration (in *pharmacy*, a mixture of a medicinal substance with sugar of milk) PREFIXED ROOT: *trim:* *de-:* (off) detriment (damage, injury, harm; anything that causes damage or harm) detrimental (**Synonyms:** pernicious, baneful) *trit:* *at-:* attrition (a rubbing away by friction; a gradual diminution in number or strength due to constant stress; in *theology*, repentance for sin motivated by fear of punishment rather than for love of God) (*at-* assimilates *ad-*, to, toward, against) *con-:* (with, together) contrite (feeling deep sorrow or remorse for having sinned or done wrong; penitent) contrition (**Synonyms:** penitence, repentance, compunction) *de-:* detrition, detritus (fragments of rock produced by disintegration or wearing away; any accumulation of disintegrated material, or debris) {detrital} (*de-*, off, from) NO CROSS REFERENCE
troch*	Greek *trechein*: to run (IE: *dhregh*, to run; yields English truck)	wheel; running	SIMPLE ROOT: trochaic (of, pertaining to, or consisting of trochees; as a *noun*, a trochaic foot, line, or verse) trochal (in *zoology*, resembling a wheel) troche (a medicinal lozenge) trochee (in Greek, *trokhaios* (*pous*), running (foot); a metrical foot of two syllables, the first accented and the other unaccented, as in English verse, or the first long and the other short, as in Latin verse, e.g., "**Peter,/ Peter,/ pumpkin/ eater**") trochlea (an anatomical structure felt to resemble a wheel) trochlear (in *botany*, shaped liked a pulley) LEADING ROOT COMPOUND: oid: trochoid (literally, similar to a wheel; capable of or exhibiting rotation about a central axis) (*oid*, similar to) MESHED LEADING ROOT COMPOUND: trochelminth (*helminth*, worm) CROSS REFERENCE: *rot*
trop***	Greek *tropos* (IE: *trep*, to turn)	turn, way, manner	SIMPLE ROOT: trope (the figurative use of a word or expression; a figure of speech; a word or phrase interpolated as an embellishment in the sung parts of certain medieval liturgies) tropic (literally, solstice point at which the sun "turns" back and moves toward the earth), tropical tropism (in *biology*, the responsive growth or movement of an organism toward or away from an external stimulus) PREFIXED ROOT: *amphi-:* amphitropous (in *biology*, partly inverted, so that the point of attachment is near the middle: said of an ovule or seed) (*amphi-*, around)

Element	From	Meaning	Examples
trop (cont'd)			

ana-: anatropous (in *biology*, inverted, so that the micropyle is next to the hilum, and the embryonic root is at the other end: said of an ovule) (*ana-*, up, back)

dia-: diatropism (in *botany*, the tendency of some plant parts to place themselves crosswise to the line of force of a stimulus) (*dia-*, across)

en-: entropy (a measure of the capacity of a system to undergo spontaneous change; the formula is $dS = dQ/T$) (*en-*, in)

eso-: esotropia (a condition in which only one eye fixes on an object while the other turns inward, producing the appearance of cross-eye) (*eso-*, within)

LEADING ROOT COMPOUND:

logy: tropology (the use of tropes or figurative language; a method interpreting Scripture in a figurative, moralistic way rather than in a literal sense) (*logy*, speaking)

pause: tropopause (a combination of _troposphere_ + *pause*; a transition zone between the troposphere and the stratosphere, at which the drop in temperature with increasing height increases)

phil: tropophilous (in *botany*, able to adjust to conditions of heat or cold, dryness or moisture, etc., as in seasonal changes: said of plants) (*phil*, love of)

phyt: tropophyte (any tropophilous plant, as a deciduous tree) (*phyton*, plant)

spher: troposphere (the atmosphere from the earth's surface to the *tropopause*, which see above) (*sphere*, ball, globe)

TRAILING ROOT COMPOUND:

allo: allotrope, allotropy (the existence of two or more crystalline or molecular structural forms of an element) (*allo*, other, divergence)

chrom: chromotropic (turning to or attracting color or pigment) (*chrome*, color)

geo: geotropism (any movement or growth of a living organism in response to the force of gravity: movement toward the center of the earth) (*geo*, earth)

helio: heliotrope, heliotropism (the tendency of certain plants or other organisms to turn or bend under the influence of light, especially sunlight) (*helios*, sun)

hemi: hemitrope (also, *hemitropic*) (*hemi*, half)

iso: isotropic (also, *isotropous*) (having physical properties, such as conductivity, elasticity, etc., that are the same regardless of the direction of measurements) (*iso*, same)

neuro: neurotropic (having an affinity for nervous tissue, as certain viruses and poisons) (*neuro*, nerve)

photo: phototropism (in *botany*, the movement of a part of a plant toward or away from light sources; see *heliotropism*, above) {phototropic} (*photo*, light)

rheo: rheotropism (the tendency of an organism, especially a plant, to respond to the stimulus of a current of water by some change in the direction of growth) (*rheo*, to flow)

sito: sitotropism (response of living cells to the presence of nutritive elements) (*sito*, food)

Element	From	Meaning	Examples
trop (cont'd)			thixo: thixotropy (the property exhibited by some gels of liquefying when stirred or shaken or of returning to the hardened state upon standing) (*thixo*, touching)
			PREFIXED TRAILING ROOT COMPOUND:
			an-: anisotropic (*an-*, not + *iso*, same; *aniso*, not the same)
			COINED WORD: entropy (a term coined by German physicist R.J.E. Clausius, 182288, to designate a thermodynamic measure of the amount of energy unavailable for useful work in a system undergoing change; other modern meanings) (*en* is from <u>energy</u> "turned" toward)
			MYTHOLOGY: Atropos (one of the three Fates, thus inexorable, inflexible; *a-*, not + *tropos*)
			DISGUISED ROOT:
			trophy (from Greek *tropaion*, a token of an enemy's defeat)
			CROSS REFERENCE: *stroph, vert*
troph***	Greek *trephein* (IE: *dherebh*, to coagulate)	to nourish nutrition	SIMPLE ROOT:
			trophic (of nutrition; having to do with the processes of nutrition)
			trophicity, trophism
			PREFIXED ROOT:
			a-: atrophy (a wasting away, especially of body tissue, an organ, etc. or the failure of an organ part to grow or develop, because of insufficient nutrition) (*a-*, not)
			dys-: dystrophy (faulty nutrition; faulty development, or degeneration, e.g., *muscular dystrophy*) (*dys-*, bad, abnormal, impaired)
			hyper-: hypertrophy (a considerable increase in the size of an organ or tissue, caused by enlargement of its cellular components) (*hyper-*, beyond)
			hypo-: hypotrophy (progressive degeneration and functional loss of cells and tissues; **Synonyms:** abiotrophy, atrophy) (*hypo-*, under)
			LEADING ROOT COMPOUND:
			troph:
			all: trophallaxis (the exchange of regurgitated food, glandular secretions, etc., among members of a colony of social insects) (*allo*, other)
			tropho:
			blast: trophoblast (a layer of nutritive ectoderm outside the blastoderm, by which the fertilized ovum is attached to the uterine wall and the developing embryo receives its nourishment) (*blast*, shoot, sprout)
			plasm: trophoplasm (the nutritive or vegetative substance of an organic cell, as fat or yolk granules; compare *idioplasm*) (*plasm*, form)
			zo: trophozoite (a protozoan, especially of certain parasitic species, during the active feeding and growing stage in contrast with reproductive and infective stages) (*zo*, animal)
			TRAILING ROOT COMPOUND:
			auto: autotrophic (making its food by photosynthesis, as a green plant, or by chemosynthesis, as any of certain bacteria) (*auto*, self)

701

Element	From	Meaning	Examples
troph (cont'd)			eu: eutrophic (designating or of a lake, pond, etc., rich in plant nutrient minerals and organisms but often deficient in oxygen in midsummer) (*eu*, good, well) hetero: heterotrophic (obtaining food from organic material only; unable to use inorganic matter to form proteins and carbohydrates) (*hetero*, other) lipo: lipotrophic (regulating or reducing the accumulation of fat in the body or its organs) (*lipos*, fat) mono: monotrophic (requiring only one kind of food; that is, *monophagous*, where *phag* means eat) (*mono*, one) poly: polytrophic (obtaining nourishment from more than one kind of organic material, as many pathogenic bacteria) (*poly*, many) CROSS REFERENCE: *al, nutr*
trud,** **trus**	Latin *trudere*: to thrust out (IE: *treud*, to squeeze, push)	to thrust	PREFIXED ROOT: *trude*: *de-*: detrude (literally, to thrust down; force down; to thrust away or out) {detrusion} (*de-*, down) *ex-*: extrude [to push or thrust out; to shape (metal or plastic, for example) by forcing through a die] (*ex-*, out) *in-*: intrude [**Synonyms:** obtrude, interlope; in *geology*, to thrust (molten rock) into a stratum] (*in-*, in) *ob-*: obtrude (see synonyms at *intrude*, above) (*ob-*, against) *pro-*: protrude (to jut out, project) (*pro-*, forth) *trus*: *ab-*: abstruse (literally, pushed away; difficult to understand; **Synonyms: 1)** ambiguous, equivocal, obscure; **2)** mysterious, esoteric, occult) (*ab-*, away) *ex-*: extrusion (see *extrude*) *in-*: intrusion, intrusive (see *intrude*; besides being a general term, it is used in both *geology* and *linguistics*) (*in-*, in) *ob-*: obtruse, obtrusion, obstrusive (brash, intrusive, undesirably noticeable; unattractively showy) (*ob-*, against) *pro-*: protrusion, protrusive (see *protrude*) (*pro-*, forth) ENGLISH COGNATES: threat, threaten, thrust CROSS REFERENCE: *ject, pel/puls*
tub*	Latin *tuber*: lump, swelling (IE: *teu*, to swell)	to swell up	SIMPLE ROOT: tuber, tubercle tuberular, tuberculate tuberculous, tuberose (tuberous), tuberosity NOTE: The *tube* + *rose* (flower) is a tuberose (tuberous) plant. Though pronounced *tube rose* (with equal accents), the tuberose is not in the rose family. PREFIXED ROOT: *pro-*: protuberance (that which protrudes; a bulge or knob), protuberant, protuberate (*pro-*, forth, outward) LEADING ROOT COMPOUND: oid: tuberculoid (resembling tuberculosis; resembling a tubercle) (*oid*, similar to) osis: tuberculosis (*osis*, diseased condition of) DISGUISED ROOT: truffle CROSS REFERENCE: *edema, tum*

Element	From	Meaning	Examples
tuit,* tut	Latin *tueri*: to look at	to guard; to look at	SIMPLE ROOT: tuition, tutelage, tutor (**Synonyms**: teach, instruct, educate) PREFIXED ROOT: *in-*: intuit, intuition (**Synonyms**: reason, discernment, judgment), intuitive, intuitivism (*in-*, in, on) CROSS REFERENCE: *phalact, scop, vid*
tum*	Latin *tumere*: to swell (IE: *teu*, to swell, increase)	to swell up, increase	SIMPLE ROOT: tume: tumescence, tumescent tumi: tumid (swollen; bulging; inflated or pompous) {tumidity, or *tumidness*} tumo: tumor (a swelling on some part of the body; a mass of new tissue growth independent of its surrounding structures) tumu: tumular, tumulous, tumult, tumultuous, tumulus (an artificial burial mound, especially, an ancient burial mound) PREFIXED ROOT: *con-*: (with, together) contumacious (obstinately disobedient or rebellious; insubordinate) contumacy, contumelious contumely (*noun*, even though ending in *-ly*; the adjectival form is *contumelious*, haughtily and contemptuously) *de-*: detumescence (contraction following expansion, especially restoration of a swollen organ or part to normal size) (*de-*, reversal) *in-*: intumesce (to swell or expand; enlarge) (*in-*, intensive) LEADING ROOT COMPOUND: fac: tumefacient, tumefaction (*facere*, to make) fy: tumefy (*facere*, to make) ENGLISH: thumb CROSS REFERENCE: *edema, tub*
tund,* tus	Latin *tundere* IE: *steu*, to strike)	to beat, strike, thrust	PREFIXED ROOT: *tund*: *ob-*: obtund (to dull or deaden; make less intense) (*ob-*, against) *tuse*: *con-*: contuse (to injure without breaking the skin; bruise), contusion (*con-*, intensive) *ob-*: obtuse (not sharp, acute, or pointed; rounded at the extremity: said of a leaf, petal; dull in perception, feeling, or intellect) (*ob-*, against) *re-*: retuse (literally, beaten back; having a rounded or blunt apex with a shallow notch: said chiefly of leaves) (*re-*, back) DISGUISED ROOT: pierce (from *per-*, through + *tundere*) ENGLISH COGNATES: steep (**Synonyms**: abrupt, precipitous, sheer) steep (**Synonyms**: soak, saturate, impregnate) CROSS REFERENCE: *bat, cuss, fend, flict, plaud, plex/ pless*

Expression from Roman mythology: Janus-faced (two-faced; hypocritical)
The god who was the guardian of the portals and the patron of beginnings and endings.
He is shown as having two faces, one in the front of his head, and the other in the back.
January, coming at the beginning of the year, is named after Janus.

Element	From	Meaning	Examples
turb**	Greek *turba*: turmoil, uproar (IE: *twer*, to stir up)	to agitate; tumult, turmoil	SIMPLE ROOT: turbo turbi: turbid, turbinate (shaped like a top; spinning like a top), turbine turbu: turbulence, turbulent PREFIXED ROOT: dis-: disturb (**Synonyms**: discompose, perturb, agitate), disturbance (*dis-*, intensive) per-: perturb (see synonyms at *disturb*, previous entry), perturbation (*per-*, intensive) TRAILING ROOT COMPOUND: mas: masturbate (possibly; *mas* is thought by some authorities to come from *manus*, hand; other authorities think it *may* be derived from *masc*, male) DISGUISED ROOT: trouble INTERDISCIPLINARY: turbinate (in *anatomy*, designating a small curved bone that extends horizontally along the lateral wall of the nasal passage; in *zoology*, spiral and decreasing sharply in diameter from base to apex: said of shells) CROSS REFERENCE: *act/ag/ig*
turg*	Latin *turgere*	to swell	SIMPLE ROOT: turgescent (becoming swollen; swelling) turgid (**Synonyms**: bombastic, grandiloquent, euphuistic) turgor (the normal distention or rigidity of plant cells) CROSS REFERENCE: *edema, tuber, tum*
tus			See *tund* for *contusion*.
tut			See *tuit* for *tutor*.
typ**	Greek *typos* (IE: *(s)teup*, to strike)	mold, die	SIMPLE ROOT: type, typical PREFIXED ROOT: a-: atypical (not typical; varying from the type) (*a-*, not) ante-: antetype (an earlier form of something; prototype) (Latin *ante-*, before) anti-: antitype (that which is foreshadowed by or identified with an earlier symbol or type, such as a figure in the New Testament who has a counterpart in the Old Testament) (*anti-*, opposite) proto-: prototype (in the first form; original) (*proto-*, first) LEADING ROOT COMPOUND: *typi*: fy: typify (to serve as a typical example of; to represent by an image, form, or model; symbolize; prefigure) (from *facere*, to make) *typo*: graph: typographer, typographic, typography (*graph*, write) logy: typology (*logy*, study of) TRAILING ROOT COMPOUND: arche: archetype (an original model; **Synonyms**: ideal, model, exemplar) (*arche*, first) mono: monotype (in *biology*, the sole member of its group, such as a species that also constitutes a genus) (*mono*, one) stereo: stereotype, stereotyped, stereotypy (*ster*, solid, hard) CROSS REFERENCE: *plasm/plast*

Element	From	Meaning	Examples
tyro*	Greek *tyros*	cheese, caseous	LEADING ROOT COMPOUND: oid: tyroid (*oid*, resembling) oma: tyroma (a caseous tumor; a new growth or nodule of cheesy material) (*oma*, mass) osis: tyrosis (cheesy degeneration or caseation) (*osis*, diseased condition) NB: As a single word, *tyro*, from *tiro*, young soldier, is not in this family. NO CROSS REFERENCE

U

Element	From	Meaning	Examples
uber*	Latin *uber* (IE: *udh*, udder)	fruitful, fertile	SIMPLE ROOT: uberous, uberity PREFIXED ROOT: *ex-*: exuberance (also, *exuberancy*), exuberant (growing profusely; luxuriant or prolific; characterized by good health and high spirits; full of life; uninhibited), exuberate (*ex-*, out) LATIN PHRASE: *uberrima fides* (most abundant faith) ENGLISH: udder (a baglike mammary organ containing two or more glands, each with a separate teat, as in cows) CROSS REFERENCE: *carp, fecund, fruct, pom*
ulter-,*** ultra-	Latin *ulter* (IE: *al*, beyond)	beyond; last	EXTENDED PREFIX: *ulter*: ulterior *ulti*: ultima, ultimate, ultimatum, ultimo *ultra*: ultra (going beyond the usual limit; excessive; extreme, especially in opinions), ultraism, ultraist LEADING ROOTS AND COMPOUND: *ultimo*: gen: ultimogeniture (*gen*, to begin) *ultra*: centri: ultracentrifuge (*centri*, center + *fugere*, to flee) con: ultraconservative (*con-* prefixes *servare*, to keep, guard) high: ultrahigh frequency (abbreviated UHF) mar: ultramarine (*mar*, sea) micro: ultramicroscopic (*micro*, small + *scope*, look) mont: ultramontane (literally, beyond the mountains; of or pertaining to the area south of the Alps, especially Italy) (*mont*, mountain) mund: ultramundane (*mundus*, world) nat: ultranationalism red: ultrared son: ultrasonic (*sonus*, sound) violet: ultraviolet virus: ultravirus TRAILING ROOT COMPOUND: pen: penult, penultimate (almost the last; next to last, as the penultimate syllable of *penultimate* is *ti*) (*pen*, almost) DISGUISED ROOTS: else outrage (an extremely vicious or violent act; a deep insult or offense; great anger, indignation, etc.) outrageous (**Synonyms**: flagrant, atrocious, heinous) FRENCH: *outrance* (the extreme limit; utmost extremity) *outré* (exaggerated; eccentric; bizarre) LATIN PHRASES: *ultima Thule* (literally, farthest Thule; the northernmost region of the habitable world as thought by ancient geographers; now, any remote goal or ideal) *ultra vires* (beyond the legal power or authority of a person, corporation, etc.) CROSS REFERENCE: *hyper, meta, preter, super*

Element	From	Meaning	Examples
um*	Latin *umere*: to be moist; *umectus*, moist (IE: *wegw*, moist, moisten)	moist	SIMPLE ROOT: hume: humectant (substance that clears nasal passages) humi: humid (**Synonyms**: damp, dank, moist), humidor humo: humor (in *medieval physiology*, one of the four fluids of the body: blood, phlegm, choler, and black bile, the dominant of which was thought to determine the character and general health of a person; **Synonyms**: 1) indulge, pamper, spoil; 2) mood, temper, vein; 3) wit, irony, satire), humoral humoresque, humorist, humorous (**Synonyms**: witty, facetious, jocose) LEADING ROOT COMPOUND: fy: humidify (from *facere*, to make, do) CROSS REFERENCE: *hygr*
umb*	Latin *umbra*: shade	shade, shadow	SIMPLE ROOT: umbe: umbel, umbellate (also, *umbellated*), umbellule, umber umbra: umbra (in *physics*, a perfect or complete shadow, in which no direct light is received from the source of illumination) umbrage (**Synonyms**: offense, resentment, pique), umbrageous (giving shade; shady; easily offended) umbre: umbrella (Italian; literally, small shade; any comprehensive, protective organization, alliance, strategy, or device) umbro: umbrous (shady; shadowed) PREFIXED ROOT: *ad-*: adumbral, adumbrant, adumbrate (*ad-*, to, toward) *in-*: inumbrate (literally, to put in shadow) (*in-*, in) LEADING ROOT COMPOUND: fer: umbelliferous (bearing an umbel or umbels, as plants of the umbel family) (*ferre*, to bear) TRAILING ROOT COMPOUND: pen: penumbra (literally, almost a shadow) (*pen*, almost) DISGUISED ROOT: somber (dark and gloomy or dull, as though *under the shade*; mentally depressed or depressing; melancholy; see especially *umbrella* and *sombrero*, below) (from *sub-*, under + *umbra*) FRENCH: umbrette (the hammerkop: a bird intermediate in some respects between storks and herons; see *Webster's Third New International*) SPANISH: *sombrero* (literally, under the shade; actually, that which provides a shade; a wide-brimmed hat) (*som-* from *sub-*, under) NOTE: *Squirrel* is from Greek *ski*, shadow + *ouros*, tail; see *ur.* NO CROSS REFERENCE
unct,* ung	Latin *unguere*: to anoint with oil (IE: *ongw*, ointment, salve)	oil, ointment	SIMPLE ROOT: *unct*: unction, unctuous (when used to describe soil, soft and rich) {unctuosity} *ung*: unguent (a salve or ointment) PREFIXED ROOT: *in-*: inunction (the act of rubbing ointment into the skin) (*in-*, in) DISGUISED ROOT: ointment

Element	From	Meaning	Examples
unct (cont'd)			PREFIXED DISGUISED ROOT: *an-*: anoint (from Old French *enoindre*; from Latin *inungere*, where prefix *in-* means in) CROSS REFERENCE: *ol/ole*
und*	Latin *unda* (IE: *wed*, to wet)	wave	SIMPLE ROOT: unda, undine, undulant, undulate, undulation PREFIXED ROOT: *ab-*: abundance, abundant (**Synonyms**: plentiful, copious, profuse) (*ab-*, away) *in-*: inundate, inundation (*in-*, in) *red-*: redundancy, redundant (exceeding what is necessary or natural) (*red-*, intensive) DOUBLE PREFIXED ROOT: superabundant (*super-*, over, beyond + *ab-*, away) DISGUISED ROOT: sound [to measure the depth or depths of water (or a body of water, especially, with a weighted line] (from *sub-*, under + *unda*) PREFIXED DISGUISED ROOT: *ab-*: abound (literally, to overflow; to be plentiful; to exist in large numbers or amounts) (*ab-*, away) *red-*: redound [to overflow; to have a result or effect on (the credit or discredit) of someone or something] (*red-*, intensive) *sur-*: surround (from *super-*, over, beyond) DOUBLE PREFIXED DISGUISED ROOT: superabound (*super-*, beyond + *ab-*, away) ORGAN STOP: *unda maris* (literally, wave of the sea; an 8-foot stop that produces undulations) NO CROSS REFERENCE
ung			See *unct* for *ungent*.
uni***	Latin *unus* (IE: *oinos*, the, this, this one)	one, single	SIMPLE ROOT: Uniate (also, *Uniat*; from Russian *uniya*, the union establishing the church: a member of any Eastern Christian Church in union with the Roman Catholic Church but with its own rites, customs, etc.) union (**Synonyms**: 1) alliance, league, confederacy; 2) unity, solidarity) unique [one and only; single; sole; having no like or equal; (highly unusual; extraordinary; rare, etc.: a common usage still objected to by some)] unit, unitage, unitarian, unitary, unite (**Synonyms**: join, combine, connect), unity (see synonyms at *union*) DOUBLE PREFIXED ROOT: coadunate (*co-*, with, together + *ad-*, to, toward) LEADING ROOT COMPOUND: *un*: anim: unanimous (literally, of one mind) (*anim*, life, soul, spirit) *uni*: axi: uniaxial camera: unicameral (only the state of Nebraska has a unicameral legislature; the other 49 states and the United States Government have bicameral legislatures) (*camera*, room, chamber) cep: uniceps (a single-headed muscle) (from *caput*, head) corn: unicorn (*corn*, horn)

Element	From	Meaning	Examples
uni (cont'd)			cost: unicostate (having only one costa, rib, or ridge; in *botany*, having only one main rib: said of a leaf) (*cost*, rib)
			cycl: unicycle (*cycle*, circle, wheel)
			di: unidirectional (*di-*, from *dis-*, apart, prefixes *rect*, straight)
			foli: unifoliate (same as *unifoliolate*, having only one leaf although one leaf compound in structure, as a leaf of the orange) (*folium*, leaf)
			form: uniform, uniformitarianism, uniformity
			fy: unify {unifiable, unifier} (from *facere*, to make)
			jug: unijugate (in *botany*, having only one pair of leaflets: said of a pinnate leaf) (*jug*, join)
			later: unilateral (in *biology*, arranged or produced on one side of an axis) (*latus*, side)
			lin: unilineal (showing descent through only one line of the family, either that of the father or that of the mother), unilinear
			loc: unilocular (in *botany* and *zoology*, having, or made up of, only one loculus, compartment, cell, or chamber) (*locus*, place; cavity)
			ov: uniovular (*ovum*, egg)
			par: uniparental, uniparous (*parere*, to give birth to)
			pot: unipotent, unipotential (from *posse*, to be able)
			ram: uniramous (*ramus*, branch)
			sex: unisexual [of only one sex; in *botany*, diclinous (having the stamens and pistils in separate flowers); in *zoology*, producing either eggs or sperm, not both; dioecious]
			son: unison, unisonous (*sonus*, sound)
			val: univalent (*valere*, to be strong)
			valv: univalve (also, *univalved*)
			vers:
			universal (**Synonyms:** general, generic), universalism (capitalized, the theological doctrine that all souls will eventually find salvation in the grace of God)
			universe (**Synonyms:** earth, world), university (from *vertere*, to turn)
			voc: univocal (having a single, sharply defined sense of nature; unambiguous) (*vocare*, to call)
			TRAILING ROOT COMPOUND:
			tri: triune (*tri*, three)
			DISGUISED ROOT: inch , onion, ounce, uncial
			GERMANIC: alone, anon, atone (*at + one*), none, once, eleven (literally, one left over--after counting to ten on fingers or toes)
			RELIGIOUS DENOMINATION: Unitarian, the belief in the *unity* of God rather in the doctrine of the Trinity as found in the creeds of the Christian Church, the Trinity being that of the Father, the Son, and the Holy Spirit
			PLACENAMES:
			Unicorn, Maryland
			Unity (Maine, Oregon)
			Unityville, Pennsylvania
			CROSS REFERENCE: *mono, priv, sol*

Element	From	Meaning	Examples
ur*	Greek *oura* (IE: *orsos*, a variation of *ers*, the buttocks, tail)	tail, buttocks	**LEADING ROOT COMPOUND:** chord: urochord (in *zoology*, a notochord limited to the caudal region, as in tunicates) (*chord*, cord) pod: uropod (*pod*, foot) pyg: uropygial gland (an oil-secreting gland at the base of a bird's tail), uropygium (the posterior part of a bird's body, from which the tail feathers grow; rump) (*pyg*, rump) **TRAILING ROOT COMPOUND:** macr: macruran (literally, large tail; a suborder of crustaceans with large abdomens, including the lobsters, shrimps, etc.) (*macro*, large) xipho: xiphosuron (*xipho*, sword) **DISGUISED ROOT:** squirrel (*ski*, shadow, literally, shadow tail) **ANGLO-SAXON:** arse (used by Shakespeare for the buttocks) **CROSS REFERENCE:** *caud, cerc*
ur**	Greek *ouron* (IE: *wed*, to wet)	urine	**SIMPLE ROOT:** ura: urate, uraturia ure: urea, urease, ureter, uretic, urethra uri: uric, urinal, urinant, urinary, urinate, urine, urinous **PREFIXED ROOT:** di-: diuresis, diuretic (from *dia-*, through) en-: enuresis (involuntary urination) (*en-*, in) dys-: dysuria (painful or difficult urination) (*dys-*, bad, difficult) **LEADING ROOT COMPOUND:** *ur:* agog: uragogue (inducing urmination) (*agog*, leading, inducing) ana: uranalysis (*ana-* prefixes *lys*, loosen) emia: uremia (*emia*, diseased condition of the blood) *urethr:* itis: urethritis (inflammation of the urethra) (*itis*, inflammation of) *urethro:* scop: urethroscope (an instrument for examining the interior of the urethra) (*scope*, look) *urino:* genital: urinogenital (variation of *urogenital*) *uro:* chrom: urochrome (the pigment responsible for the normal yellow color of urine) (*chrom*, color) genital: urogenital (of, pertaining to, or involving both the urinary and genital functions) lith: urolith (*lith*, stone) logy: urology (the medical study of the physiology and pathology of the urogenital tract) (*logy*, study of) scop: uroscopy (*scope*, look) **MESHED LEADING ROOT COMPOUND:** urinalysis (*ana-*, apart + *lysis*, loosening; same as *uranalysis*) **TRAILING ROOT COMPOUND:** brady: bradyuria (slowness in passing urine) (*brady*, slow) noct: nocturia (Latin *noct*, night)

Element	From	Meaning	Examples
ur (cont'd)			nyct: nycturia (Greek *nyct*, night) [Both *nocturia* and *nycturia* mean the same: bedwetting.] pyr: pyuria (abnormal condition of pus in the urine) (*py*, pus) strang: strangury (literally, urination by drops; slow and painful urination) (*stranx*, a drop) NO CROSS REFERENCE
urb**	Latin *urbs*	city	SIMPLE ROOT: urban, urbane (**Synonyms:** suave, diplomatic, politic), urbanism, urbanite, urbanity, urbanize PREFIXED ROOT: *con-*: conurbation (*con-*, with, together) *ex-*: exurb (a region, generally semirural, beyond the suburbs of a city, inhabited largely by persons of the upper-income group) (*ex-*, out) *sub-*: suburb, suburban, suburbia (*sub-*, under) LATIN PHRASE: *ab urbe condita* (from the founding of the city; Rome, founded circa 753 B.C.) CROSS REFERENCE: *cit, civ, metro, polis*
ure*	Latin *urere* (IE: *eus*, to burn)	to burn	SIMPLE ROOT: uredinium, uredo (same as *urticaria*: an allergic skin condition characterized by itching, burning, stinging, and the formation of smooth patches, or wheals, usually red) LEADING ROOT COMPOUND: spor: uredospore (a reddish spore that is produced in the uredinium of a rust fungus) (*spore*, seed) DISGUISED ROOT: bust (interesting relationship: see *American Heritage Dictionary*) PREFIXED DISGUISED ROOT: *com-*: combust, combustion, combustible (*com-*, with, together) CROSS REFERENCE: *cal, caust, therm*
urg			See *erg* for *chemurgy* and *liturgy*.
us,** ut	Latin *uti*	to use, employ	SIMPLE ROOT: *us*: usa: usable, usage (**Synonyms:** practice, custom, wont) use: use (**Synonyms:** employ, utilize) useless (**Synonyms:** futile, abortive, vain) usu: usual (**Synonyms:** customary, habitual, wonted), usurer, usurious, usury *ut*: ute: utensil (**Synonyms:** implement, tool, instrument) uti: utilitarian, utility, utilize (see synonyms at *use*) PREFIXED ROOT: *us*: *ab-*: abuse (**Synonyms:** oppress, persecute, aggrieve), abusive (*ab-*, away) *dis-*: disuse (*dis-*, apart, away) *mis-*: misuse (Anglo-Saxon *mis-*, wrong) *per-*: peruse (literally, to use up; originally, to examine in detail; scrutinize) (*per-*, through, thoroughly) *util*: *dis-*: disutility (*dis-*, apart, away)

Element	From	Meaning	Examples
us (cont'd)			LEADING ROOT COMPOUND: urp: usurp (to take or assume power, a position, property, rights, etc. and hold in possession by force or without right), usurpation (from *rapere*, to seize) NO CROSS REFERENCE
uter*	Latin *uterus*	uterus, womb	SIMPLE ROOT: uterine (pertaining to the *uterus*; also, having the same mother but a different father, as *uterine* sisters), utero, uterus PREFIXED ROOT: *intra-*: intrauterine (within the uterus, as *an intrauterine device*) (*intra-*, within) CROSS REFERENCE: *hyster*
uxor*	Latin *uxor*	wife	SIMPLE: uxorial (pertaining to, characteristic of, or befitting a wife), uxorious (excessive or irrationally submissive or devoted to one's wife) LEADING ROOT COMPOUND: cid: uxoricide (*cide*, to kill) loc: uxorilocal (same as *matrilocal*) (*locus*, place) NO CROSS REFERENCE

> Words, like glasses, obscure everything which they do not make clear.
> Joseph Joubert

713

V

Element	From	Meaning	Examples
vac**	Latin *vacare*: to be empty, be free	empty	**SIMPLE ROOT:** vacan: vacancy (empty space; the state of being empty in mind; lack of intelligence, interest, or thought), vacant (**Synonyms**: empty, void, vacuous) vacat: vacate (in *law*, to make void; annul), vacation vacu: vacual, vacuity, vacuole, vacuous (see synonyms at *vacant*, previous entry), vacuum **PREFIXED ROOT:** e-: evacuate (to make empty; remove the contents of; to withdraw from), evacuation (an evacuating or being evacuated; something evacuated, specifically, feces) evacuee (*e-* elides *ex*, out) **DISGUISED ROOT:** void (see synonyms at *vacant*, above) **PREFIXED DISGUISED ROOT:** a-: avoid (**Synonyms**: escape, evade, elude) (from *ex-*, out) de-: devoid (completely without; empty or destitute of) (from *dis-*, apart) CROSS REFERENCE: *cen, inan, jejun, van*
vacc*	Latin *vacca*	cow	**SIMPLE ROOT:** vaccinal, vaccinate, vaccination vaccine (originally, lymph, or a preparation of this, from a cowpox vesicle, containing the causative virus and used in vaccination against cowpox or smallpox), vaccinia (cowpox) SPANISH: *vaquero* (a man who herds cattle; cowboy) GULLAH: buckaroo (altered after *vaquero*) NOTE: *Gullah* is the language of a tribal group in Liberia; also refers to Blacks living on the South Carolina or Georgia coast or nearby islands. CROSS REFERENCE: *taur*
vad,* vas	Latin *vadere*: to go (IE: *wadh*, to go, stride forward; yields English wade)	to go, step	**PREFIXED ROOT:** vad: e-: evade (see synonyms at *avoid*, vac family) {evadable, evader} (from *ex-*, out) in-: invade (**Synonyms**: trespass, encroach, infringe) (*in-*, in) per-: pervade (to be prevalent throughout) (*per-*, through) vas: e-: evasion, evasive (from *ex-*, out) in-: invasion (*in-*, in) per-: pervasion, pervasive (tending to pervade or spread throughout) (*per-*, through) AMERICAN SPANISH: *vamoose* (from Spanish *vamos*, let us go; to leave quickly or hurriedly) LATIN PHRASE: *vade mecum* (literally, go with me; a handbook, a part of the title of authors' book: *An Introduction to An Academic Vocabulary*: A *Vade Mecum* for the Serious Student) SPANISH PHRASE: *Vaya con Dios* (Go with God) TITLE OF NOVEL: *Quo Vadis?* (Where Are You Going?) CROSS REFERENCE: *bas/bat, ced, grad, it*

Element	From	Meaning	Examples
vag**	Latin *vagus*	wandering (nerve)	SIMPLE ROOT: vaga: vagabond (see synonyms at *vagrant*, below), vagal, vagary (**Synonyms:** caprice, whim, crotchet) vagi: vagile, vagility (the capacity or tendency of an organism to become widely dispersed) vagr: vagrancy, vagrant (**Synonyms:** vagabond, bum, tramp) vagu: vague (**Synonyms:** obscure, enigmatic, cryptic) vagus (designating the tenth cranial nerve, often called the *wandering nerve*) PREFIXED ROOT: *extra-*: (more than, outside) extravagance (excessive expenditure or outlay of money; unrestrained or fantastic excess, as of actions, opinions, etc.; profusion) extravagant (**Synonyms: 1**) excessive, exorbitant, immoderate; **2**) profuse, prodigal, luxuriant) extravagaza LEADING ROOT COMPOUND: *vag*: itis: vagitis (inflammation of the *vagus*, *not* of the *vagina*, which is *vaginitis*) (see next family) *vago*: tom: vagotomy (*tom*, cut) ton: vagotonia (a disorder resulting from overstimulation of the vagus nerve, causing a slowing of the heart rate, fainting, etc.) {vagatonic} (*ton*, stretching) trop: vagotropic (affecting, or acting upon, the vagus nerve) (*trop*, turn) CROSS REFERENCE: *err, migr, plan*
vagin*	Latin *vagina*	sheath; cover, pod	SIMPLE ROOT: vagina, vaginal, vaginant, vaginate, vaginula, vaginismus, vagitus PREFIXED ROOT: *e-*: evaginate (literally, to unsheath; to turn inside out; to cause to protrude by turning inside out) {evagination} (*e-* elides *ex-*, out) *in-*: invaginate (to place or receive into a sheath; same as *intussuscept*) (*in-*, in) LEADING ROOT COMPOUND: ectom: vaginectomy (*ectom*, to cut out surgically) itis: vaginitis (*itis*, inflammation of) odyn: vaginodynia (*odyn*, pain) DISGUISED ROOT: vanilla (from its sheathlike capsules) MEDICAL TERM: *vagina synovialis* (synovial sheath; same as *vagina tendinis*, tendinous sheath, the synovial sheath of a tendon, especially of the hand or foot) INTERDISCIPLINARY: vagina (in *biology* and *zoology*, the passage leading from the external genital orifice to the uterus in female animals; in *botany*, a sheathlike structure, such as that formed by the base of a leaf enclosing a stem) CROSS REFERENCE: *cole*

Element	From	Meaning	Examples
val**	Latin *valere*: to be strong (IE: *wal*, strong)	strong, worth	SIMPLE ROOT: vale: valence, valetudinarian (paradoxically, designates one in *poor* health) vali: valiant (**Synonyms**: brave, valorous, dauntless) valid (**Synonyms**: sound, cogent, convincing), validate, validity valo: valor (**Synonyms**: courage, bravery, bravado) valu: value (**Synonyms**: appreciate, prize, treasure), valued PREFIXED ROOT: *ambi-*: ambivalence (simultaneous conflicting feelings toward a person or thing), ambivalent (*ambi-*, around, both) *con-*: convalesce, convalescence (*con-*, with, together) *de-*: devaluation, devalue (*de-*, reversal) *e-*: evaluate (**Synonyms**: estimate, appraise, rate) (*e-* elides *ex-*, out) *in-*: invalid [either *noun* or *adjective* (as a *noun*, stressed on first syllable; as an *adjective*, on the second)], invalidate (*in-*, not) *pre-*: prevalence, prevalent (**Synonyms**: prevailing, current, rife) (*pre-*, before) *trans-*: transvalue (to evaluate a new principle, especially one rejecting conventional or accepted standards) (*trans-*, across) LEADING ROOT COMPOUND: dict: valediction, valedictorian [from *vale*, farewell (imperative of *valere*, to be well, strong; at a graduation ceremony, the valedictorian is the student with the highest standing and is the last to speak, while the salutatorian--the student with the second-highest academic standing--salutes or greets the assembly, and is the first to speak)] (from *dicere*, to speak) TRAILING ROOT COMPOUND: equi: equivalent (**Synonyms**: same, identical, equal) (*equi*, equal, same) mono: monovalent (in *bacteriology*, capable of resisting one strain of a given species of disease-producing organism because the right antibodies or antigens are present) (*mono*, one) PREFIXED DISGUISED ROOT: *vail*: *a-*: avail [to be of use or advantage to; to assist; to help; as a *noun*, use, benefit, or advantage; now used chiefly in the phrase *to* (or *of*) *no avail*], availability, available (*a-*, intensive) *counter-*: countervail (to make up for; compensate; to counteract; be successful against; avail against) (*counter-*, against) *pre-*: prevail, prevailing (**Synonyms**: current, prevalent, rife) (*pre-*, before) LATIN PHRASE: *ad valorem* (literally, according to the value; describing the tax based upon the worth of an object, such as a car) ENGLISH: wield (**Synonyms**: handle, manipulate, ply) CROSS REFERENCE: *firm, fort, rob, sthen*

717

Element	From	Meaning	Examples
val*	Latin *vallatus* (IE: *wel*, to turn)	wall, palisade	SIMPLE ROOT: vallation (a defense wall or earthwork) PREFIXED ROOT: circum-: circumvallate (to surround with a rampart or other defensive barrier; as an adjective, surrounded by or as if by a rampart) (*circum-*, around) inter-: interval [originally, the space between the ramparts (*walls*) of a castle; in *music*, the space between pitches as indicated by notes on a staff] (*inter-*, between) DISGUISED ROOT: wall (Middle English *walle*; Old English *weall*, from Latin *vallum*, palisade, wall, from *vallus*, stake) CROSS REFERENCE: *mer, mur, part, sept*
valv*	Latin *valva*: leaf of folding door; akin to *volvere*, to roll (IE: *wel*, to turn, roll)	folding door	SIMPLE ROOT: valve valva: valvate (in *botany*, meeting without overlapping, as the petals of some flower buds; opening by valves, as a pea pod) valvu: valvular, valvule (a small valve) LEADING ROOT COMPOUND: itis: valvulitis (inflammation of a valve, especially of the heart) (*itis*, inflammation of) TRAILING ROOT COMPOUND: bi: bivalve (a particular type of mollusk with two valves or shells hinged together, as a mussel, clam, oyster, etc.) (*bi*, two) tri: trivalve (having three valves, as a shell, or a speculum, a medical instrument) {trivalvular} (*tri*, three) uni: univalve (a mollusk, especially a gastropod, having a single shell; the shell of such a mollusk; as an *adjective*, pertaining to or having such a shell; see note under *uni*) (*uni*, one) INTERDISCIPLINARY: valve [in *anatomy*, a membranous fold or structure which permits body fluids to flow in one direction only, or opens and closes a tube, chamber, etc.; in *botany*, any of the segments into which a pod or capsule separates when it bursts open; a lidlike part in some anthers, through which pollen is discharged; either of the boxlike halves forming the cell walls of a diatom; in *mechanics*, any device in a pipe or tube that permits a flow in one direction only, or regulates the flow of whatever is in the pipe, by means of a flap, lid, plug, etc. acting to open or block the passage; in *music*, a device in certain brass instruments, as the trumpet, that opens (or closes) an auxiliary to the main tube, lengthening (or shortening) the air column and lowering (raising) the pitch; in *zoology*, each separate part making up the shell of a mollusk, barnacle, etc; any of the parts forming the sheath of an ovipositor in certain insects] NO CROSS REFERENCE
van*	Latin *vanus*: empty, idle (IE: *(e)wa*, to lack)	vain, empty	SIMPLE ROOT: vanish (Synonyms: disappear, fade) vanity (Synonyms: pride, conceit, vainglory) PREFIXED ROOT: e-: (e- elides *ex-*, out) evanesce (to fade from sight like mist or smoke; disappear; vanish), evanescence evanescent (Synonyms: transient, transitory, ephemeral)

Element	From	Meaning	Examples
van (cont'd)			DISGUISED ROOT: vain (**Synonyms:** idle, hollow, otiose) vaunt (**Synonyms:** boast, swagger, crow) NB: Although *inane* is not in this family, the word itself means vain, empty. From this word are also *inanition, inanity.* CROSS REFERENCE: *cen, inan, jejun, vac*
vap**	Latin *vapor* (IE: *wep,* to give off vapors)	steam, cloud	SIMPLE ROOT: vapi: vapid (tasteless; flavorless; uninteresting; lifeless; dull; boring; **Synonyms:** insipid, flat, banal) vapo: vapor, vaporization, vaporizer, vaporous PREFIXED ROOT: e-: evaporable, evaporate (e- elides *ex-*, out) LEADING ROOT COMPOUND: meter: vaporimeter (*meter*, measure) ITALIAN: vaporetto (short for *bateau à vapeur*, calque of English *steamboat*) [see *Linguistics Note*] NEOLOGISM: evapotranspiration (the total water loss of the soil, including that by direct *evaporation* and that by *transpiration* from the surface of plants) LINGUISTICS NOTE: *Calque*, from *calcare*, to press, trample, designates a linguistics borrowing by which a specialized meaning of a word or phrase in one language is transferred to another language by a literal translation, e.g., *masterpiece* is a calque of German *Meisterstück.* CROSS REFERENCE: *atmo*
var**	Latin *variare*: to change, to vary (IE: *wa,* to turn, bend)	to vary, bend	SIMPLE ROOT: vara (literally, a forked pole; in Spain and Portugal, a unit of linear measure, varying from 31 to 33 inches) varus (an abnormally bent or curved condition, especially of the foot) varia: **variable**, variance (**Synonyms:** discord, strife, contention), variant, variate, **variation**, variator varic: varicella (diminutive of *variola*; chickenpox), varicellate (in *zoology*, marked with small or indistinct ridges: said of certain shells) varie: varied (**Synonyms:** miscellaneous, heterogeneous, motley), variegate, variegated, varier (a person who varies), varietal, variety vario: variola (any of a group of virus diseases characterized by pustular eruptions, including smallpox, cowpox, and horsepox) variolar (same as *variolous*) variole (a tiny pit or depression, as on some parts of an insect; any of the whitish spherules in variolite, which see below) variolous (of or relating to variola, or smallpox) variorum (an edition or text, as of a literary work, containing notes by various editors, scholars, etc.) various (**Synonyms:** different, diverse, divergent) varis: varistor [contraction of *var(ious) (res)istor*, a semi-conductor resistor whose resistance varies with the voltage applied] vary: vary (**Synonyms:** change, alter, modify)

719

Element	From	Meaning	Examples
var (cont'd)			**PREFIXED ROOT:** *pre-*: prevaricate (literally, to walk crookedly; to turn aside or from, or evade, the truth; **Synonyms:** lie, equivocate, fabricate) (*pre-*, before) **LEADING ROOT COMPOUND:** *vari*: color: varicolored (of several or many colored; motley) form: variform (varied in form; having various forms) *vario*: lite: variolite (a basaltic or andesite rock in which whitish spherules of feldspar are embedded) (from *lith*, rock) meter: variometer (any of various devices designed to measure or record small variations in some quantity) (*meter*, measure) *variol*: oid: varioloid (a mild form of variola occurring in a person who has had a previous attack or who has been vaccinated) (*variola + oid*, in the form of) **DISGUISED ROOT:** verandah (an open porch or portico; originally, a forked stick for spreading out nets) miniver (literally, small vair; *vair* is a variegated fur for trimming garments, especially ceremonial robes, as of royalty) **INTERDISCIPLINARY** variable (in *astronomy*, short for *variable star*; in *biology*, tending to deviate in some way from the type; aberrant; in *mathematics*, having no fixed value; in *mathematics* and *physics*, a part of a mathematics expression that may assume any value in a specific, related set of values; a symbol for such a part: opposed to *constant*) variation (in *astronomy*, a change in or deviation from the mean motion or orbit of a planet, satellite, etc.; in *ballet*, a solo dance; in *biology*, a deviation from the usual or parental type in structure or form; an organism showing such deviation; in *mathematics*, the manner in which two or more quantities change relative to one another; in *music*, the repetition of a theme or musical idea with changes or embellishments in harmony, rhythm, key, etc., especially any of a series of such repetitions developing a single theme) CROSS REFERENCE: *ankylo/ancy, flect*
varic,* varix	Latin *varix*: dilated vein (IE: *wer*, a raised area)	vein (enlarged)	**SIMPLE ROOT:** varicellate (in *zoology*, marked with small or indistinct ridges: said of certain shells) varicose (enlarged veins) **varix** **LEADING ROOT COMPOUND:** *varic*: osis: varicosis {varicosity} *varico*: cele: varicocele (a varicose condition of the veins of the spermatic cord in the scrotum) (*cele*, rupture, tumor) tom: varicotomy (the surgical excision of a varix, especially of a varicose vein) (*tom*, cut; *ectom*, to cut out) ENGLISH COGNATE: wart (literally, a raised place)

Element	From	Meaning	Examples
varic (cont'd)			INTERDISCIPLINARY: **varix** (in *medicine*, a permanently and irregularly swollen or dilated blood or lymph vessel, especially a vein; varicose vein; in *zoology*, a prominent ridge across the whorls of various univalve shells, showing an earlier position of the outer lip) CROSS REFERENCE: *phleb, ven*
vas			See *vad* for *evasion*.
vas**	Latin *vas*	vessel, duct	SIMPLE ROOT: vas (in *anatomy* and *biology*, a vessel or duct), vase **vascular** (see *Biology Term* below), vasculose vasculum (a covered metal case, often cylindrical, used by botanists for carrying specimens) PREFIXED ROOT: *extra-*: extravasate (to allow or force blood, etc. to flow from its normal vessels into the surrounding body tissues) (*extra-*, more than, outside) LEADING ROOT COMPOUND: *vas*: ectom: vasectomy (*ectom*, to remove surgically) *vaso*: con: vasoconstriction, vasoconstrictor (*con-* prefixes *strict*, to bind) di: vasodilator (from *dis-*, prefixes *latus*, wide) mot: vasomotor TRAILING ROOT COMPOUND: cardio: cardiovascular (*cardio*, heart) DISGUISED ROOT: **vessel** (a utensil for holding something, as a vase, bowl, pot, kettle, etc.) ANATOMY TERM: *vas deferens* [literally, the vessel that carries down (see *deference*); the highly convoluted duct that conveys sperm from the testicle to the ejaculatory duct of the penis] RUSSIAN COGNATE: bas (pronounced *vahs*) BIOLOGY TERM: vascular bundle INTERDISCIPLINARY: **vascular** (in *anatomy* and *zoology*, designating or of the vessels, or system of vessels, for conveying blood or lymph; in *botany*, of or pertaining to the specialized conducting cells, xylem and phloem, that convey water and food in plants) **vessel** (in the *Bible*, a person thought of as being the receiver or repository of some spirit or influence; in *anatomy* and *zoology*, a tube or duct containing or circulating a body fluid; in *botany*, a continuous, water-conducting tube in the xylem, composed of a vertical row of single-cell segments whose end walls have disappeared) NB: *Vaseline*, from German *Wasser*, water + Greek *elaion*, oil, is not in this family. CROSS REFERENCE: *angi, cyt*

It is obvious that we cannot begin to be citizens in a democracy if we are only partly capable of understanding our own language, if we cannot distinguish between truth and falsehood, between sense and nonsense, if we do not realize that language and the word are still more powerful than the atom bomb, that like a weapon it can be used for or against us. Victor Grove

721

Element	From	Meaning	Examples
vect,*** veh, vex	Latin *vehere* (IE: *wegh*, to go)	to carry	**SIMPLE ROOT:** *vect*: **vector** *veh*: vehe: vehement (acting or moving with great force; violent; impetuous; having or characterized by intense feeling or strong passion; fervent, impassioned, etc.) vehi: vehicle, vehicular **PREFIXED ROOT:** *vect*: *ad*-: advect, advection (*ad*-, to, toward) *con*-: convection (from *com*-, with, together) *e*-: evection (a periodical variation in the motion of the moon in its orbit, caused by the attraction of the sun) (*e*- elides *ex*-, out) *in*-: invective (literally, a carrying in; an attack; as a *noun*, a denunciatory or abusive expression; vehement denunciation; vituperation; as an *adjective*, characterized by abuse and insult) (*in*-, in) *vex*: *con*-: convex, convexity (from *com*-, with, together) **DISGUISED ROOT:** vein (**Synonyms**: mood, humor, temper), veined, veinlet, veinule veiny (having or showing veins; full of veins, as flesh, leaves, or marble) weigh (**Synonyms**: consider, study, contemplate) wagon **PREFIXED DISGUISED ROOT:** *in*-: inveigh (to carry in; to make a violent verbal attack; talk or write bitterly; rail) (*in*-, in) **INTERDISCIPLINARY: vector** (in *biology*, an animal, as an insect, that transmits a disease-producing organism from one host to another; in *mathematics*, a physical quantity with both magnitude and direction, such as a force or velocity; other meanings) CROSS REFERENCE: *fer, ger/ges, lat, pher/phor*
veloc*	Latin *velox*: quick (IE: *wegh*, to go)	speed	**SIMPLE ROOT:** veli: velitation (a hostile encounter; skirmish or dispute) velo: veloce, velocity *velo*: drom: velodrome (an indoor arena with a track banked for bicycle races) (*dromos*, run) *veloci*: ped: velocipede (*ped*, foot) **DISGUISED ROOT:** velites (in ancient Rome, lightly armed foot soldiers) (*velox*, swift + *vehere*, to carry) CROSS REFERENCE: *celer, tach*

> The knowledge of a word varies from a vague acquaintance
> with it to a complete accuracy of understanding it.
> Anonymous

Element	From	Meaning	Examples
ven*	Latin *venum*: sale (IE: *wesno*, price)	to sell	SIMPLE ROOT: vena: venal, venality (state, quality, or instance of being venal; willingness to be bribed or bought off, or to prostitute one's talents for mercenary considerations) vend: vend (shortened from *venum dare*, to offer for sale), vendable (see *vendible*), vendee (the person to whom a thing is sold; buyer), vendible (capable of being sold), vendition, vendor FRENCH: vendue (public auction, sale) CROSS REFERENCE: *pol*
ven*	Latin *vena*	vein	SIMPLE ROOT: vena: venation (an arrangement or system of veins, as in an animal part, an insect's wing, or a leaf; such veins collectively) veno: venose (veined, or veiny, as an insect's wing), venosity (the state or quality of being *venose* or *venous*), venous venu: venule PREFIXED ROOT: *intra-*: intravenous (in or directly into, a vein or veins, as *an intravenous injection*) {intravenously} (*intra-*, within) LEADING ROOT COMPOUND: *vene*: sect: venesection (same as *venisection*) *vini*: punct: vinipuncture (from *pungere*, to prick) LATIN MEDICAL TERM: vena cava (hollow vein; in *anatomy*, either of two large veins conveying blood to the right atrium of the heart) INTERDISCIPLINARY: venous (in *biology*, of a vein or veins; having veins or full of veins; veiny; in *physiology*, designating blood being carried in the veins back to the heart and lungs) CROSS REFERENCE: *phleb, varic*
ven,*** vent	Latin *venire* (IE: *gwa*, to go, come)	to come	SIMPLE ROOT: venture, venue PREFIXED ROOT: *ven(e)*: a-: avenue (*a-* elides *ad-*, to, toward) *ad-*: advene (*ad-*, to, toward) *co-*: covenant (from *com-*, with, together) *con-*: convenance, convene (**Synonyms**: call, summon, convoke), convenience, convenient (*con-*, with, together) *contra-*: contravene (*contra-*, against) *e-*: event (**Synonyms**: occurrence, incident, episode) eventual, eventuality, eventuate (from *ex-*, out) *inter-*: intervene, intervenient (*inter-*, between) *pro-*: provenance (the place of origin; derivation) (*pro-*, forth) *re-*: (back) revenant (one who returns after an absence; one who returns after death; ghost) revenue (literally, that which comes back) *super-*: supervene (to come or happen as something additional or to the normal course of events) (*super-*, beyond)

Element	From	Meaning	Examples
ven (cont'd)			*vent*:
			a-: aventurine (also, *aventurin*; a glass resembling the mineral *avventurina*, *avventurina* itself being named because of its rarity) (from *ad-*, to, toward)
			ad-: (to, toward)
			advent (capitalized, the four weeks preceding, or coming before, Christmas)
			Adventism (the belief that Christ's second coming to earth and the Last Judgment will soon occur), Adventist
			adventitious (acquired by accident; added by chance; not inherent; in *biology*, appearing in an unusual place or in an irregular or sporadic manner, as *adventitious leaves*)
			adventive (in *botany*, as an *adjective*, not native to the environment; as a *noun*, a plant not native to the environment)
			adventure, adventurer, adventuresome, adventuress, adventurism, adventurous
			con-: convent (**Synonyms**: cloister, abbey, priory), conventicle, convention, conventional, conventual, conventuality (from *com-*, with, together)
			in-: (in)
			invent (**Synonyms**: devise, contrive, discover), invention (in *music*, a short composition, usually for a keyboard instrument, developing a single short motif in counterpoint), inventive
			inventor, inventory (**Synonyms**: list, catalog, register)
			inter-: intervention, interventionist (*inter-*, between)
			ob-: obvention (*ob-*, against)
			pre-: prevent (**Synonyms**: forestall, preclude, obviate), prevention, preventive (*pre-*, before)
			super-: supervention (*super-*, over, beyond)
			DOUBLE-PREFIXED ROOT:
			inconvenient, inconvenience (*in-*, not + *con-*, with, together)
			reconvene (*re-*, again + *con-*, with, together)
			FRENCH PREFIXED ROOT:
			par-: parvenu (a person who has suddenly acquired wealth or power, especially one who is not fully accepted socially by the class into which he/she has risen; upstart; *nouveau riche*, newly rich) (from *per-*, through)
			sou-: souvenir (from Latin *subvenire*, to come to mind) (from *sub-*, under)
			NO CROSS REFERENCE
vent*	Latin *ventus* (IE: *wentos*, wind)	wind	SIMPLE ROOT: vent
			venta: ventage, ventail (the lower front part of a medieval helmet, fitting over the neck)
			venti: ventilate, ventilation, ventilator, ventilatory (in *medicine*, of, pertaining to or involved in breathing and the oxygenation of blood)
			PREFIXED ROOT:
			hyper-: hyperventilate (*hyper-*, over, excessive)
			LEADING ROOT COMPOUND:
			fact: ventifact (any stone shaped by the abrasion of wind-blown sand) [vent + (arti)fact]
			CROSS REFERENCE: *anem*

Element	From	Meaning	Examples
ventr**	Latin *venter* (IE: *udero*, belly)	belly, abdomen	SIMPLE ROOT: **venter** ventra: **ventral**, ventralis ventri: ventricle (in *anatomy* and *zoology*, any of various cavities or hollow organs; specifically, a) either of the two lower chambers of the heart which receive blood from the atria and pump it into the arteries; b) any of the four small continuous cavities within the brain) ventricular, ventriculus (in *zoology*, that part of the alimentary tract of an insect where digestion takes place) LEADING ROOT COMPOUND: *ventri*: loqui: ventriloquial, ventriloquism, ventriloquist (literally, one who speaks from the belly), ventriloquize (*loqui*, speak) *ventric*: ose: ventricose (large-bellied; in *biology*, swelling out on one side) (*ose*, condition of) *ventro*: dors: ventrodorsal (of or involving both the ventral and dorsal surfaces) (*dors*, back) later: ventrolateral (of or involving both the ventral and lateral surfaces) (*later*, side) INTERDISCIPLINARY: **venter** (in *anatomy* and *zoology*, the abdomen, or belly; the uterus; the wide swelling portion, as though a belly, of the muscle; in *biology*, a similar swollen structure or joint; in *law*, the womb as the source of offspring, as *children of the first venter*, meaning "children of the first wife") **ventral** (in *anatomy* and *zoology*, of, near, on, or toward the belly or the side of the body where the belly is located: in humans the front, or anterior, side but in most other animals the lower, or inferior, side; in *botany*, of or belonging to the inner or lower surface) CROSS REFERENCE. *cel*
ver***	Latin *verus* (IE: *weros*, true)	true	SIMPLE ROOT: very (**Synonyms**: same, identical, equal) vera: veracious (habitually truthful; honest; true; accurate) veracity (**Synonyms**: truth, verity, verisimilitude) veri: verily, verism (realism or naturalism in the arts) veritable, verity (see synonyms at *veracity*, above) PREFIXED ROOT: a-: aver (**Synonyms**: assert, declare, affirm) (from *ad-*, to, toward) LEADING ROOT COMPOUND: *ver*: dict: verdict (to render a true saying; in law, the formal finding of a judge or jury on a matter submitted to them in a trial) (from *dicere*, to speak) *veri*: dic: veridical (expressing the truth; accurate; veracious) (*dicere*, to speak)

Element	From	Meaning	Examples
ver (cont'd)			fi: verifiable (from *facere*, to make, do)
			fic: verification (in *law*, a short formulaic oath concluding a pleading and affirming that the pleader is ready to prove his/her allegations) (from *facere*, to make)
			fy: verify (**Synonyms:** confirm, corroborate, substantiate) (from *facere*, to make, do)
			simil: verisimilitude (the appearance of being true or real; something having the mere appearance of being true or real; see synonyms at *veracity*) (*simil*, same)
			FRENCH: *voir dire* [literally, to speak the truth (see *verdict*); in *law*, a preliminary examination concerning the competence of a prospective witness or juror]
			ITALIAN: *verismo* (*verism*, which see above; also, a style of opera dealing with the lives of common people and usually characterized by violent or tragic situations and highly dramatic performance)
			UNIVERSITY MOTTOES:
			Gratia et Veritas, Grace and Truth (Goucher)
			Lux et veritas, Light and Truth (Yale)
			Veritas: Christo et Ecclesiae, Truth: For Christ and the Church (Harvard)
			Veritas et Virtus, Truth and Virtue (Pittsburgh)
			Veritas liberabit vos, The truth shall make you free. (Southern Methodist)
			Veritas vos liberabit, The truth shall make you free. (Johns Hopkins)
			Veritatem cognoscetis et veritas vos liberabit, You shall know the truth and the truth shall make you free. John 8:32 (Tennessee)
			CROSS REFERENCE: *etym*
ver,*** vir	Latin verd; green virere, to be green	green	SIMPLE ROOT:
			ver:
			verda: verdant (green with vegetation; covered with green growth; inexperienced, immature, or unsophisticated)
			verde: verderer (in medieval England, a judicial officer who maintained law and order in the king's forests)
			verdu: verdure (the fresh-green color of growing things; greenness; green growing plants and trees: green vegetation)
			vir:
			vireo: vireo (greenfinch; any of a family of small, insect-eating, American songbirds, with olive-green or gray plumage)
			vires: virescence (the condition of becoming green; specifically, in *botany*, the turning green of petals, or other parts that are not normally so, due to the abnormal presence of chlorophyll), virescent (turning or becoming green; greenish)
			vir: virid (bright green with or as if by vegetation; verdant)
			LEADING ROOT COMPOUND:
			gris: verdigris (from *vert de Greece*, literally, green of Greece; same as *patina*, which see under *pand/pas*)
			ter: verditer (from Old French *verd de terre*, literally, green of the earth; either of two basic carbonates of copper, used as a blue or green pigment)
			juice: verjuice (the sour, acid juice of green or unripe fruit, as of crab apples, grapes, etc.; sourness of temper, looks, etc.)

726

Element	From	Meaning	Examples
ver (cont'd)			TRAILING ROOT COMPOUND: bili: bilivirdin (a green compound occurring in the bile, sometimes caused by oxidation of bilirubin) (Swedish *bili*; from Latin *bilis*, bile) FRENCH PHRASE: *terre-verte* (literally, green earth; any of several green earths or clays containing iron siliates used as a green pigment by artists) DISGUISED ROOT: farthingale [a hoop or circular pad worn about the hips by women in the 16th and 17th centuries; from Old French *verdugalle*; from Spanish *verdugado*, provided with hoops (made from young shoots of trees)] STATE: Vermont (Green Mountain; there is also the Green Mountain range in Vermont) RIVER: Verdigris (rises in east-central Kansas and flows generally south to the Arkansas River in northeastern Oklahoma) CROSS REFERENCE: *chlor*
verb**	Latin *verbum*	word	ROOT NOTE: This root translates Greek *rhema*, verb, and is related to the following Greek words: *irony, rhematic, rhetor, rhetoric*. SIMPLE ROOT: verb (any of a class of words expressing action, existence, or occurrence, or used as an auxiliary or copula, and usually constituting the main element of a predicate) verbal (**Synonym**: oral), verbalism, verbalist, verbalize, verbatim, verbiage, verbose PREFIXED ROOT: *ad-*: adverb (in grammar, a word that functions , adverbial, adverbializer (*ad-*, to, toward) *pro-*: proverb (**Synonyms**: adage, aphorism, epigram) (*pro-*, before, forward) DISGUISED ROOT: verve (vigor and energy in ideas or expression of them) LATIN WORDS AND PHRASES: *ad verbum* (to a word; word for word; verbatim) *verbatim et literatim* (word for word and letter for letter) *verbum sapienti sat est* (a word to the wise is sufficient; usually shortened to *verbum sap*) CROSS REFERENCE: *ep, lect/lex, log, parl*
verm**	Latin *vermis* (IE: *wer*, to turn, bend)	worm, parasite	SIMPLE ROOT: vermic: vermicelli (literally, little worms), vermicular, vermiculate, vermiculite vermil: vermilion (the color of red earthworms) vermin: vermin, vermination, verminous vermis: vermis (plural, *vermes*) LEADING ROOT COMPOUND: form: vermiform (in the form of a worm, as the appendix, the medical name for which is *vermiform appendix*) fug: vermifuge (*fugere*, to flee) DISGUISED ROOT: verbena (a particular garden flower) vervain (a family of verbenas) FRENCH: vermeil (the color of vermilion)

Element	From	Meaning	Examples
verm (cont'd)			vermouth (from *vermout*; from German *Vermuth*, literally, wormwood; a fortified wine flavored with wormwood) PLACENAMES: [Note differences in spelling.] Vermilion, Ohio Vermillion, Indiana, Kansas, South Dakota) CROSS REFERENCE: *helic, helminth*
vert,*** vers	Latin *vertere*, to turn (IE: *wert*, to turn)	to turn, bend	SIMPLE ROOT: *vers*: versa: versant (the slope of a mountain or a mountain chain; the general slope, or declination, of a region), versatile verse: verse, versed, versicle (a short verse or verse part, usually of a Psalm, used especially in antiphonal prayer) versi: version (**Synonyms**: translation, paraphrase, transliteration) *vert*: verte: vertebra (plual, *vertebrae*), vertebrate, vertex verti: **vertical**, verticil (in *botany*, a circular arrangement of leaves or flowers around a stem; whorl), vertiginous, vertigo PREFIXED ROOTS AND COMPOUNDS: *vers(e)*: *a-*: (from *ab-*, away) averse (**Synonyms**: reluctant, disinclined, hesitant) aversion (**Synonyms**: antipathy, repugnance, loathing) *ad-*: (to, toward) adversary (**Synonyms**: opponent, antagonist, enemy) adversative (in *grammar*, expressing opposition or antithesis, as the words *but, yet, however, nonetheless*) adverse (**Synonyms**: contrary, balky, stubborn), adversity *con-*: (with, together) conversable, conversant, conversation, conversational 1) converse (verb; **Synonyms**: speak, talk, discourse) 2) converse (adjective; reversed in position, order, action, etc.; opposite, contrary, turned about; in *logic*, a proposition obtained from another proposition by conversion) *contro-*: controversial, controversy (**Synonyms**: argument, dispute, wrangling) (*contro-*, against) *di-*: (from *dis-*, apart, away) divers, diverse (**Synonyms**: different, divergent, distinct) diversion, diversionary, diversionist, diversity diversification, diversified, diversify (*fic, fi* and *fy* from *facere*, to do, make) diverticulitis (*itis*, inflammation of) diverticulosis (*osis*, an abnormal condition) *extro-*: extroversion (in *medicine*, same as *exstrophy*) (*extro-*, outside) *ob-*: obversion, obversive (*ob-*, against) *per-*: perverse (see synonyms at *adverse*, above), perversion, perversity, perversive (*per-*, through) *re-*: (back, again) revers (the reverse side of a fabric turned to show the facing, like the lapel) reverse (**Synonyms**: opposite, antithetical, antonymous)

Element	From	Meaning	Examples
vert (cont'd)			*sub-*: subversion, subversive (*sub-*, under)

trans-: transverse (in *geometry*, designating the axis that passes through the foci of a hyperbola, or the part of the axis between the vertices) (*trans-*, across)

vert:

a-: avert (**Synonyms**: prevent, forestall, preclude) (from *ab-*, from, away)

ad-: (to, toward)

advert [allude; to remark or comment about or in relation to (usually followed by *to*)], advertent {advertence, advertency} advertise (also, *advertize*), advertisement, advertising)

con-: convert, converter, convertible (from *com-*, with, together)

contro-: controvert (**Synonyms**: disprove, refute, confute) (*contro-*, against)

di-: divert (**Synonyms**: amuse, entertain, beguile), diverticulum (in *anatomy*, a normal or abnormal pouch or sac opening out from a tubular organ or main cavity), diverting (from *dis-*, apart, away)

extro-: extrovert (opposite of *introvert*), extroverted (*extro-*, outside)

intro-: introvert (opposite of *extrovert*), introverted (*intro-*, inside)

ob-: obvert (in *logic*, to state the obverse of a proposition) (*ob-*, against)

per-: pervert (**Synonyms**: debase, deprave, corrupt), perverted (*per-*, through)

re-: revert (*re-*, again, back)

retro-: retroversion (a turning back; a turning or tilting backward of an organ or part, especially of the uterus) (*retro-*, backward)

sub-: subvert (*sub-*, under)

DOUBLE-PREFIXED ROOT:

inadvertent (*in-*, not + *ad-*, to, toward)

LEADING ROOT COMPOUND:

fi: versification, versifier, versify (*fic, fi*, and *fy* from *facere*, to make, do)

aster: verticillaster (in *botany*, an almost circular flower arrangement formed by a pair of dichasia facing each other on the stem, as in some mints) (Greek *aster*, star)

TRAILING ROOT COMPOUND:

anni: anniversary (*anni*, year)

uni: universe, university (*uni*, one)

MESHED TRAILING ROOT COMPOUND:

dextrorse (in *botany*, twining, or *turning*, upward to the right, as the stem of the hop) (from *dexter* + *verse*)

introrse (opposite of *dextrorse*)

retrorse (in *biology*, bent or turned backward or downward) (*retro* + *vertere*)

UNBOUND LATIN COMPOUND: *vice versa* (the order or relation being reversed; conversely)

Element	From	Meaning	Examples
vert (cont'd)			DISGUISED ROOT: prose (ordinary speech or writing, as distinguished from verse; therefore, commonplace expression or quality) (from *pro-*, before, forward + *vertere*) varsity (from 18th century British pronunciation of *university*) divorce FRENCH: *divertissement* (a diversion; a short ballet, etc., performed between the acts of a play or opera) *vers de société* (verse of society; witty, polished light verse) ITALIAN: *conversazione* (conversation; a social gathering for conversation about literature, the arts, etc.) *divertimento* (any of various light, melodic instrumental compositions in several movements) PLACENAME: Traverse, Minnesota INTERDISCIPLINARY: **versatile** (in *botany*, turning about freely on the filament to which it is attached, as an anther; in *zoology*; moving forward or backward, as the toes of a bird; movable in any direction, as the antenna of an insect) **vertex** (in *anatomy* and *zoology*, the top or crown of the head; in *geometry*, the point of intersection of the two sides of an angle; a corner point of a triangle, square, cube, parallelepiped, or other geometric figure bounded by lines, planes, or lines and planes; in *optics*, the point at the center of a lens at which the axis of symmetry intersects the curve of the lens) **vertical** (in *anatomy* and *zoology*, of the vertex of the head; in *biology*, in the direction in which the axis lies; lengthwise) **revert** (in *biology*, to return to a former or primitive type; show ancestral characteristics normally no longer present in the species; in *law*, to go back to a former owner or the heirs of such owner) CROSS REFERENCE: *flect, stroph/strep, torn/tour, trop*
vesic*	Latin *vesica*	bladder, blister	ROOT NOTE: The original meaning of this root is bladder; from this meaning is derived blister, from it being shaped like a bladder. SIMPLE ROOT: **vesicle** vesica: vesica (same as *bladder*), vesical, vesicant (causing blisters), vesicate (to blister), vesicatory vesicu: vesicula, vesicular, vesiculate LATIN PHRASE: *vesica piscis* (literally, fish bladder; a pointed oval figure typically composed of two intersecting arcs) INTERDISCIPLINARY: **vesicle** (in *anatomy, zoology, medicine*, a small cavity or sac filled with fluid, especially, a small, round elevation of the skin containing a serous fluid; blister; in *botany*, a small, bladderlike sac filled with air; in *geology*, a small, spherical cavity in volcanic rock, produced by bubbles of air or gas in the molten rock) CROSS REFERENCE: *asco, cyst*

Element	From	Meaning	Examples
vest**	Latin *vestire*: to dress (IE: *wes*, to clothe)	to clothe	SIMPLE ROOT: vest, vested (as *vested interest*), vestee vesti: vestiary (a supply room for clothing, as in a monastery), vesting vestm: vestment (a garment; robe; gown; especially, an official robe or gown) vestr: vestry (a room in a church where the clergy put on their vestments and where the sacred vessels are kept; sacristy) vestu: vesture (in *law*, everything growing on land except trees, as grass or grain) PREFIXED ROOT: *de-*: devest (originally, to undress; strip; in *law*, to take away a right, property, etc.) (from *dis-*, from) *di-*: divest, divestiture (from *dis-*, apart, away) *in-*: invest (to clothe; array; adorn), investitive, investiture, investment (*in-*, in) *re-*: revest (see *Doublets* below) (*re-*, again) *tra-*: travesty [disguised; a grotesque or farcical imitation for purposes of ridicule; burlesque; a crude, distorted, or ridiculous representation (of something), as a trial that was a travesty of justice] (*trans-*, across) *trans-*: transvestite (*trans-*, across) PREFIXED DISGUISED ROOT: *re-*: revet (see *Doublets* below), revetment (*re-*, again) DOUBLETS: revest:revet NB: The following words are not in this family: vestibule (from *vestibulum*, entrance hall) investigate (from *vestigare*, to track, from *vestigium*, footprint; see next family) CROSS REFERENCE: *dysi*
vestig*	Latin *vestigium*	footprint, trace	SIMPLE ROOT: vestige (in *biology*, a degenerate, atrophied, or rudimentary organ or part, more fully developed or functional in an earlier stage of development of an individual or species) {vestigial} PREFIXED ROOT: *in-*: investigate (literally, to follow in the tracks of; to search into so as to learn the facts; inquire in systematically) (*in-*, in) CROSS REFERENCE: *hegei*
vex			See *vect* for convex.
vey			See *vi* for convey.
vi,*** via, vey, voy	Latin *via* (IE: *wei*, to go, strive toward)	way, road	SIMPLE ROOT: via: via (by way of) viaticum (in ancient Rome, money or supplies provided as traveling expenses to an officer on an official mission; capitalized, the Eucharist as given to a dying person or to one in danger of death) voy: voyage (**Synonyms**: trip, journey, expedition) PREFIXED ROOT: vey: *con-*: convey (**Synonyms**: carry, bear, transport), conveyance (from *com-*, with, together)

Element	From	Meaning	Examples
vi (cont'd)			*vi*: *de-*: deviate (**Synonyms:** swerve, veer, diverge), deviation, deviator, devious (literally, off the main road) (*de-*, off) *ob-*: (against) obviate (literally, to meet in the way; **Synonyms:** prevent, preclude, forestall) obvious (**Synonyms:** evident, apparent, manifest) *per-*: pervious (open to passage or entrance; permeable; open to arguments, ideas, or change) (*per-*, through) *pre-*: previous (literally, leading the way; going before; **Synonyms:** prior, preceding, antecedent) (*pre-*, before) *voy*: *con-*: convoy (as a *verb*, to accompany on the way for protection, either by sea or land; to escort; **Synonyms:** accompany, attend) (*con-*, with, together) *en-*: (in) envoy (a messenger, agent; a diplomat) envoy (a postscript to a poem, essay, or book, containing a dedication, climactic summary, explanation, etc.) DOUBLE-PREFIXED ROOT: impervious (*im-*, a variant of *in-*, not + *per-*, through) LEADING ROOT COMPOUND: duct: viaduct (a long bridge usually to carry a road or railroad over a valley, gorge, etc.) (from *ducere*, to lead) TRAILING ROOT COMPOUND: tri: trivial (literally, pertaining to three roads; may have developed from the small talk at the crossroads) (*tri*, three) PREFIXED DISGUISED ROOT: *in-*: invoice (from *envoy*: literally, the way in: an itemized list of goods sold) (*in-*, in) FRENCH TERM: *bon voyage* (literally, good voyage; pleasant journey: a farewell to the traveler) LATIN TERMS: trivium (see note under *tri*; compare with *quadrivium*; also see authors' *An Introduction to an Academic Vocabulary*) *via media* (a middle way; course between two extremes) *viaticum* (in ancient Rome, money or supplies provided as traveling expenses to an officer on an official mission; capitalized, Viaticum refers to the Eucharist as given to a dying person or one in danger of death) CROSS REFERENCE: *od*
vibr*	Latin *vibrare* (IE: *weip*, to turn, vacillate)	to shake	SIMPLE ROOT: vibrac: vibracular, vibraculum (in *zoology*, any of the specially modified zooids in a colony of bryozoans, with a whiplike, movable form) vibran: vibrant (quivering or vibrating, especially in such a way as to produce sound; throbbing with life and activity; lively; vigorous, energetic, radiant, sparkling, vivacious) vibrat: vibrate (**Synonyms:** oscillate, fluctuate, undulate) vibratile, vibration, vibrative, vibratory, vibrator vibri: vibrio, vibrissa (in *anatomy* and *zoology*, any of the stiff hairs growing in or near nostrils of certain animals)

Element	From	Meaning	Examples
vibr (cont'd)			ITALIAN MUSIC TERM: vibrato (a pulsating effect, less than extreme than a tremolo, produced by a rapid alternation of a given tone with a barely perceptible variation in pitch) CROSS REFERENCE: *cuss*
vic*	Latin *vicis*: change (IE: *weik*[4], to bend, change)	substitute	SIMPLE ROOT: vica: vicar, vicarage, vicarial, vicariate, vicarious (taking the place of another thing or person as the deputy of another) vice: vice (one meaning; another *vice* is from Latin *vitium*, blemish, offense, as in *vice squad*) vici: vicissitude (**Synonyms**: difficulty, hardship, rigor) LEADING ROOT COMPOUND: roy: viceroy (French *roy*; from Latin *rex*, king) DISGUISED LEADING ROOT COMPOUND: viscount SIMPLE COMPOUND: vice-president LATIN TERM: *vice versa* (the order or relation being reversed; conversely) NO CROSS REFERENCE
vict,** vinc	Latin *vincere* (IE: *weik*[5], to conquer)	to conquer	SIMPLE ROOT: *vict*: victor, victorious, victory (**Synonyms**: conquest, triumph) *vinc*: vincible (capable of being overcome or defeated; now rare; see the commonly used negative, *invincible*, below) PREFIXED ROOT: *vict*: *con-*: convict, conviction (**Synonyms**: 1) certainty, certitude, assurance; 2) opinion, belief, view), convictive (*con-*, with, together) *e-*: evict (**Synonyms**: eject, expel, dismiss) (from *ex-*, out) *vince*: *con-*: convince, convincing (*con-*, with, together) *e-*: evince (from *ex-*, out) *in-*: invincible (that cannot be overcome; unconquerable (*in-*, not) DISGUISED ROOT: vanquish (**Synonyms**: conquer, defeat, subdue) NB: *Victim* is not in this family. NO CROSS REFERENCE
vid,*** vis, v y	Latin *videre* to see (IE: *weid*, to see)	to see, to examine	SIMPLE ROOT: *vid*: video (coined to correspond with *audio*) *vis*: visa: visa (an endorsement on a passport showing that it has been examined by the proper officials of a country and granting the bearer entry into or passage through that country) visage (**Synonyms**: face, countenance, physiognomy) visi: visibility, visible, vision, visional, visionary, visit, visitable visitant (a visitor, especially one from a strange or foreign place; a supernatural being, as supposedly perceived by a person; ghost; in *zoology*, a migratory bird in any of its temporary resting places) visitation, visitatorial, visitor (**Synonyms**: visitant, guest, caller)

Element	From	Meaning	Examples
vid (cont'd)			viso: visor (Middle English *visere*; from Anglo-French *viser*; from Old French *visiere*; from *vis*, a face; from Latin *visus*, a look, a seeing)
			vist: vista (Italian; a view or outlook, especially one seen through a long passage, as between rows of houses or trees)
			visu: visual, visualize
			PREFIXED ROOT:
			vic: advice (noun; see *advise*, below)
			vid:
			in-: invidious (such as to excite ill will, odium, or envy; giving offense; giving offense by discriminating unfairly, as *invidious comparisons*) (*in-*, in, upon)
			vide:
			e-: (from *ex-*, out)
			evidence (**Synonyms**: proof, testimony, exhibit)
			evident (**Synonyms**: apparent, manifest, obvious)
			pro-: (before)
			provide (see *Doublets* below)
			Providence (referring to God, the guiding power of the universe; the One who sees ahead; see *Placenames* below)
			provident (**Synonyms**: thrifty, frugal, sparing; see *Doublets* below)
			vis(e):
			ad-: (to, toward)
			advisable {advisability}
			advise (verb; see *advice* above; **Synonyms**: counsel, admonish, caution), advisement, advisor, advisory
			en-: envisage (visualize, imagine), envision (*en-*, in)
			in-: invisible (the Invisible, God) (*in-*, not)
			pre-: previse (to foresee; to notify in advance) (*pre-*, before)
			pro-: provision, provisional (**Synonyms**: temporary, ad interim, acting), proviso (*pro-*, before)
			re-: revise, revision, revisionist, revisory (*re-*, again)
			super-: supervise {supervision}, supervisor (*super-*, over)
			tele-: television (Greek *tele-*, afar; Greek-Latin hybrid)
			vy:
			en-: envy (**Synonyms**: begrudge, covet) (*en-*, in)
			DOUBLE PREFIXED ROOT:
			improvident, improvisation, improvise (*im-* from *in-*, not + *pro-*, before)
			DISGUISED ROOT:
			prudent (wise in handling practical matters; exercising good judgment or common sense; careful about one's conduct; circumspect; discreet; from *provident*; see *Doublets* below), prudential
			vizard (a mask for disguise or protection)
			voyeur, voyeurism (a perversion in which sexual gratification is obtained by looking at sexual objects or scenes; from French *voir*, to see)
			PREFIXED DISGUISED ROOT:
			im-: imprudent (from *in-*, not)
			TRAILING DISGUISED ROOT COMPOUND:
			bel: belvedere (literally, beautiful view) (*bel*, beautiful)

Element	From	Meaning	Examples
vid (cont'd)			clair: clairvoyance, clairvoyant (literally, seeing clearly) (from *clarus*, clear) ANGLO-FRENCH: view PREFIXED ANGLO-FRENCH: *inter-*: interview (*inter-*, between) *pre-*: preview (*pre-*, before) *re-*: review (*re-*, again) ANGLO-FRENCH PREFIXED ENGLISH-FRENCH: *pur-*: purvey (see *Doublets* below; to furnish or supply, especially food or provisions) {purveyor} (from *per-*, through) *sur-*: survey (from *super-*, over, beyond) DOUBLETS: prudent:provident; purvey:provide FRENCH TERMS: *arriviste* (a parvenu; nouveau riche) (from *arrive*) *déjà vu* (literally, already seen; in *psychology*, the illusion that one has previously had an experience that is actually new to one) *au revoir* [until we meet again; from *au*, to the + *revoir*, seeing again; goodbye (*revoir* from *re-*, again + French form of *videre*)] *vis-à-vis* (face to face with; opposite) *voilà* (literally, see there; behold, there it is!; often used as an interjection) LATIN TERMS: *inter vivos* (between living persons; from one living person to another, as *inter vivos* gifts, trusts, etc.) *quod vide* (which see, and abbreviated *q.v.*) *videlicit* (It is permitted to see; namely; that is) SPANISH WORDS AND PHRASES: aviso (advice, information, notification; also, a dispatch boat *hasta la vista* (translated, "*See* you later.") GREEK: idea, ideal, idealist, ideate ENGLISH: wise, guise PREFIXED ENGLISH: disguise (*dis-*, apart, away) SANSKRIT: *Veda* (any of four ancient sacred books of Hinduism) PLACENAMES: Providence, Rhode Island (named by Roger Williams, its founder) Flora Vista, New Mexico CROSS REFERENCE: *op, -orama, scop, spec*
vig*	Latin *vigilare*: to watch, to be alert; from *vegere*, to arouse (IE: *weg*, to be awake)	watchful	SIMPLE ROOT: vigil, vigilance (state or quality of being vigilant; watchfulness) vigilant (**Synonyms:** watchful, alert, wide-awake) vigilantism (see *vigilante*, under *Spanish*, below) PREFIXED ROOT: *in-*: invigilate (to keep a watch on) (*in-*, in, on) DISGUISED ROOT: vedette [formerly, a mounted sentinel posted in advance of the outposts of an army; also, a small scouting boat used to observe and report on an opposing naval force; a well-known personality, especially of the entertainment world]

Element	From	Meaning	Examples
vig (cont'd)			PREFIXED DISGUISED ROOT: *re-*: reveille (*re-*, again) *sur-*: surveillance, surveillant (from *super-*, over, beyond) SPANISH: vigilante ITALIAN MUSIC TERM: *vigoroso* TERM: vigilance committee (a group organized outside of legal authority to keep order and punish crime because the usual law enforcement agencies do not exist or are alleged to be inefficient) CROSS REFERENCE: *phylact*
vin*	Latin *vinum* (yields English wine)	wine	SIMPLE ROOT: vinyl vina: vinaceous (of or like wine or grapes; wine-colored; red) vine: vine {vinic}, vinery, vineyard vino: vinous {vinosity} vint: vintage (from *vindemia*, grape-gathering; from *vinum* + *demere*, to take off; *demere* is derived from *de-*, off + *emere*, to take), vintager, vintner LEADING ROOT COMPOUND: *vine*: gar: vinegar (from French *vinaigre*: *vin* + *aigre*, sour; *aigre* is from Latin *acris*, from which *acrid*, sharp, pointed, as well as *eager* and *edge*, is derived; see *ac*, sharp) *vini*: cult: viniculture fer: vinifera, viniferous (wine-producing) (*ferre*, to bear) fic: vinification (from *facere*, to make, do) fy: vinify (from *facere*, to make, do) ITALIAN AND SPANISH: *vino* FRENCH: *vin ordinaire* (literally, ordinary wine, inexpensive non-vintage table wine) *vin rosé* (literally, pink wine; rosé) CROSS REFERENCE: *oeno*
vin*	Latin *vim*: force	vigor, strength	LEADING ROOT COMPOUND: dic: (*dicere*, to speak) vindicate (to clear of accusation, blame, suspicion or doubt with supporting arguments or proof: **Synonyms**: absolve, acquit, pardon), vindication, vindicatory vindictive (**Synonyms**: vengeful, revengeful, spiteful) DISGUISED ROOT: vengeance (the return of one injury for another, in punishment or retribution; revenge; the desire to make such a return) vengeful (see synonyms at *vindictive*, above) vim PREFIXED DISGUISED ROOT: a-: avenge (see synonyms at *revenge*, below) (*e-* elides *ad-*, to) *re-*: revenge (**Synonym**: avenge) (*re-*, again) ITALIAN: vendetta (a feud in which the relatives of a murdered or wronged person seek vengeance on the wrongdoer or members of his/her family; any bitter quarrel or feud) NO CROSS REFERENCE
vinc			See *vict* for *convince*.

Element	From	Meaning	Examples
vio*	Latin *violare*: to show force	strength, force	SIMPLE ROOT: violate, violation (**Synonyms:** breach, infraction, transgression) violence, violent PREFIXED ROOT: *in-*: (not) inviolable (safe or secured against violation or profanation; kept sacred) inviolate (not violated; kept sacred or unbroken) LAW TERMS: *violent presumption* (from *violenta praesumptio aliquando est plena probatio*: Violent presumption is sometimes full proof; in the law of evidence, proof of a fact by the proof of circumstances which necessarily attend to it) *vis major* (literally, greater force; Act of God) SCOTS LAW TERM: violent profits (see *Webster's Third New International Dictionary*) CROSS REFERENCE: *firm, fort, rob, sthen, val*
vir			See *ver/vir* for *vireo, virescence*.
vir**	Latin *virtus* (IE: *wiros*, man)	man	SIMPLE ROOT: vira: virago (ironically, refers to a noisy, domineering *woman*; a scold) viri: virile (**Synonyms:** male, masculine, manly) virilism (in *medicine*, the development of secondary male sex characteristics in a woman) virt: virtual (in computer terminology, designating or of a kind of memory that makes use of disk space to supplment main memory while large programs are being executed), virtually virtue (originally, the qualities of a man: capacity, strength) {virtuosity} virtuoso (**Synonyms:** aesthete, dilettante, connoisseur) virtuous (**Synonyms:** 1) chaste, pure, modest; 2) moral, ethical, righteous) TRAILING ROOT COMPOUND: decem: decemvir (a member of a council of ten magistrates in ancient Rome: in 451-450 B.C. this body drew up the first Roman code of laws) (*decem*, ten) duum: duumvir, duumvirate (*duum*, two) tri: triumvir (*tri*, three) CROSS REFERENCE: *anthropo, homo, masc*
vir**	Latin *virus*, poison, slime (IE: *weis*, to flow)	poison, virus	SIMPLE ROOT: viro: virose, virosis viru: virulence (also, *virulency*) virulent [in *medicine*, violent and rapid in its course; highly malignant (said of a disease); able to overcome natural defenses of the host; highly infectious (said of microorganisms)] virus (originally, venom, as of a snake; anything that corrupts or poisons the mind or character; evil or harmful influence)

737

Element	From	Meaning	Examples
vir (cont'd)			PREFIXED ROOT: a-: avirulent (not virulent or no longer virulent, as certain bacteria) (a-, not) LEADING ROOT COMPOUND: vir: oid: viroid (oid, resembling) viri: fic: virific (from facere, to make) viru: cide: virucide (cide, to kill) CROSS REFERENCE: tox
vis			See vid for vision.
vit,*** viv	Latin vita: life; vivere: to live (IE: gwei, to live)	life, living	SIMPLE ROOT: vit: vita (a biography or autobiography, often a brief one; also, short for curriculum vitae) vital (**Synonyms**: living, alive, animate), vitalism, vitality vitalize (**Synonyms**: animate, quicken, exhilarate) vitals (short for vital signs: indicators of the efficient functioning of the body; especially, pulse, temperature, and respiration), vitamin viv: vivacious, vivacity, vivarium, viveur, vivid PREFIXED ROOT: vit: de-: devitalize (de-, reversal) viv: con-: convivial (having to do with a feast or festive activity; sociable; jovial) {conviviality} (con-, with, together) re-: revival, revive (re-, back, again) sur-: survive, survivor (from supra-, above, over, beyond) LEADING ROOT COMPOUND: fy: vivify (to give life to; animate) (from facere, to make) par: viviparous (bearing live young) (parere, to bear) sect: vivisection (medical research consisting of surgical operations or other experiments performed on living animals) (sect, cut) DISGUISED ROOT: viable (capable of living, for example, as a newborn infant or fetus reaching a stage of development that will permit it to survive and develop under normal conditions; **Synonyms**: possible, practical, feasible) viand (an article of food; plural: food of various kinds; especially of choice dishes) victual PREFIXED DISGUISED ROOT: in-: inviable (unable to live and develop normally) (in-, not) FRENCH TERMS: bon vivant (a person who enjoys good food and drink and other luxuries) savoir-vivre [literally, to know (how) to live; good breeding; manners] vive [(long) live (someone or something specified)!: an exclamation of acclaim]

Element	From	Meaning	Examples
vit (cont'd)			ITALIAN AND SPANISH: *viva* [(long) live (someone or something specified)!: an exclamation of acclaim] LATIN TERMS: *vive valeque* (Live and keep well: used at the end of letters) *viva voce* (with living voice; by word of mouth; orally) MUSIC TERM: *vivace* (in a lively, spirited manner) ACADEMIC TERM: *curriculum vitae* (literally, the course of one's life) TRADENAME FOR MEN'S HAIR CONDITIONER: Vitalis CROSS REFERENCE: *anim, bio*
vitr*	Latin *vitrum*	glass	ROOT NOTE: Though basically meaning *glass*, the root has evolved to include biting, caustic, sharp, thus vitriolic. SIMPLE ROOT: vitre: vitreous, vitrescent vitri: vitric, vitrine, vitriol (from its glassy appearance), vitri-olic LEADING ROOT COMPOUND: form: vitriform fy: vitrify (from *facere*, to make) PREFIXED LEADING ROOT COMPOUND: *de-*: devitrify (to take away or destroy the glassy qualities of; also, to make glass, etc., for example, opaque, hard, and crystalline, as by prolonged heating) (*de-*, away, from) LATIN TERM: *in vitro* (in a test tube) CROSS REFERENCE: *hyal*
v i v			See *vit* for *vivacious*.
voc,*** vok	Latin *vocare*: to call (IE: *wekw*, voice)	call, voice	SIMPLE ROOT: vocab: vocable (a word or term, especially one regarded as unit of sounds or letters rather than as a unit of meaning), vocabulary vocal: vocal (having a voice; capable of speaking or making oral sounds; expressing or inclined to express oneself in speech; speaking freely or vociferously), vocalic, vocalise, vocalism, vocalist, vocalize vocat: vocation (one's calling), vocational vocative (in *grammar*, designating, of, or in the case of nouns, pronouns, or adjectives used in direct address to indicate the person or things addressed) PREFIXED ROOT: *voc*: *a-*: avocation (literally, called away from one's vocation; thus, a hobby), avocatory (*a-* elides *ab-*, away) *ad-*: advocate (**Synonyms**: support, advocation, uphold) advocatory (*ad-*, to, toward) *con-*: convocation (the act of convoking; a group that has been convoked, especially an ecclesiastical or academic assembly) (*con-*, with, together) *de-*: devocalize [in *phonetics*, to make (a voiced sound) voice-less] (*de-*, reversal) *e-*: evoke (**Synonyms**: educe, elicit, extort), evocation, evocative (*e-* elides *ex-*, out)

Element	From	Meaning	Examples
voc (cont'd)			*in-*: invocation (the act of calling upon God, a god, a saint, the Muses, etc. for a blessing, help, inspiration, support, or the like; a formal prayer used in invoking, as at the beginning of a church service) {invocational, invocatory} (*in-*, in)
			pro-: provocation, provocative (*pro-*, before)
			re-: revocable, revocation, revocatory (*re-*, again, back)
			vok:
			con-: convoke (**Synonyms:** call, summon, convene) (*con-*, with, together)
			in-: invoke (to ask solemnly for; implore; entreat; to resort to or put into use a law, ruling, penalty, etc. as pertinent) {invoker} (*in-*, in)
			pro-: provoke (**Synonyms:** excite, stimulate, pique) {provoker}, provoking (*pro-*, before)
			re-: revoke (**Synonyms:** abolish, abrogate, annul) (*re-*, again, back)
			DOUBLE PREFIXED ROOT:
			irrevocable (that cannot be revoked, recalled, or undone; unalterable) (*ir-* assimilates *in-*, not + *re-*, again)
			LEADING ROOT COMPOUND:
			fer: vociferant, vociferate, vociferous (**Synonyms:** clamorous, strident, obstreperous) (*ferre*, to bear)
			TRAILING ROOT COMPOUND:
			equi: equivocal, equivocation, equivoque (*equi*, equal, same)
			uni: univocal (*uni*, one)
			DISGUISED ROOT: vouch, voucher, vowel
			PREFIXED DISGUISED ROOT:
			a-: (from *ad-*, to, toward)
			avouch (**Synonyms:** assert, declare, affirm)
			avow (**Synonyms:** acknowledge, admit, confess), avowal, avowed {avowedly}
			ad-: advowson (in *English law*, the right to name the holder of a church benefice) (*ad-*, to, toward)
			ENGLISH: voice (**Synonyms:** utter, express, broach)
			LATIN TERM: *advocatus diaboli* (devil's advocate)
			ITALIAN MUSIC TERM: *sotto voce* (literally, under the voice)
			NO CROSS REFERENCE
vol*	Latin *velle* (IE: *wel*, to wish, choose)	to wish	SIMPLE ROOT:
			voli:
			volition (**Synonym:** will; see *English Cognate*, below)
			volitive (of or arising from the will; in *grammar*, expressing a wish, as a verb, mood, etc.)
			volu:
			voluntary (**Synonyms:** intentional, deliberate), volunteer
			voluptuous (**Synonyms:** sensuous, luxurious, epicurean)
			TRAILING ROOT COMPOUND:
			bene: benevolence, benevolent (**Synonyms:** kind, kindly, benign) (*bene*, good, well)
			male:
			malevolence (noun; the quality or state of being malevolent; malice; spitefulness; ill-will)

Element	From	Meaning	Examples
vol (cont'd)			malevolent (adjective; wishing evil or harm to others; having or showing ill will; malicious) (*male*, ill, bad) DISGUISED ROOT: velleity (the weakest kind of desire or volition; a mere wish, one that does not lead to the slightest action; a faint or vague desire or tendency) LATIN LEGAL PHRASE: *nolle prosequi* (I am not willing to prosecute) ENGLISH COGNATE: will (volition) PLACENAME: Deovolente, Mississippi (God willing) NO CROSS REFERENCE
vol**	Latin *volare*	to fly	SIMPLE ROOT: volan: volant (capable of *flying*; moving quickly or nimbly; in *heraldry*, depicted with the wings extended as in flying) volat: volatile (originally, flying or able to fly; likely to shift quickly and unpredictably; unstable; explosive; as a computer term, designating or of memory that does not retain stored data when the power supply is disconnected) volatilize (to make volatile; cause to pass off as vapor) vole: vole (one derivation: in old card games, the winning of all the tricks in a deal) voli: volitant (flying, flitting, or constantly in motion; capable of flight), volitation (the act of flying; flight; the ability to fly) voll: volley; volley ball (the purpose of which is to keep the ball *flying*) FRENCH DISH: *vol-au-vent* (literally, flight in the wind: a baked pastry shell of puff paste, filled with a stew of chicken, game, fish, etc.) LATIN TERM: *muscae volitantes* (literally, flying flies: specks that appear to float before the eyes, caused by defects or impurities in the vitreous humor) NB: *Volar*, from *vola*, palm, sole, pertains to the sole of the foot, or the palm of the hand. NO CROSS REFERENCE
vol***	Latin *volvere* (IE: *wel*, to turn, roll)	to roll	SIMPLE ROOT: volu: voluble, volume (originally, a roll of parchment), voluminous, volute volv: Volvox (a genus of green algae flagellates that form spherical colonies), volvulus (a twisting of the intestine upon itself, causing obstruction) PREFIXED ROOT: *vol*: *e-*: evolute, evolution (*e-* elides *ex-*, out) *volt*: *re-*: (back, again) revolt (a rising up against the government; rebellion; insurrection; any refusal to submit to or accept authority, custom, etc.) revolting (engaged in revolt; rebellious; causing revulsion; disgusting; repulsive; offensive; loathsome) *voluc*: *in-*: involucel (a secondary involucre), involucre (*in-*, in)

Element	From	Meaning	Examples
vol (cont'd)			*volut*

circum-: circumvolution (the act of rolling or turning around a center or axis; a fold, twist, or spiral; a circuitious course or form) (*circum-*, around)

con-: convolute (rolled up in the form of a spiral with the coils falling one upon the other, as in leaves or shells), convoluted, convolution (*con-*, with, together)

de-: devolution (in *biology*, evolution of structures toward greater simplicity or disappearance; degeneration) (*de-*, down)

in-: involute (intricate; involved; rolled up or curled in a spiral; in *botany*, rolled inward at the edges, as involute leaves; also a mathematics term), involution (*in-*, in)

ob-: obvolute (having overlapping margins: said of leaves or petals; also obvolutive) {obvolution} (*ob-*, against, around)

re-: revolute (rolled backward or downward at the tips or margins, as some leaves), revolution, revolutionary (*re-*, back)

volv:

circum-: circumvolve (*circum-*, around)

con-: convolve (to roll, coil, or twist together) (*con-*, with, together)

de-: devolve {devolvement} (*de-*, down)

e-: evolve (to develop by gradual changes) (*e-* elides *ex-*, out)

in-: (in)

involve (**Synonyms**: comprise, comprehend, embrace)

involved (**Synonyms**: complex, complicated, intricate)

inter-: intervolve (*inter-*, between)

re-: revolve (**Synonyms: 1)** turn, rotate, spin; **2)** orbit, circle; **3)** ponder, study), revolver, revolving (*re-*, back, again)

volvu:

con-: convolvulus (*con-*, with, together)

DISGUISED ROOT:

vault (intensive of *volvere*)

voussoir (in *architecture*, any of the wedge-shaped stones of which an arch or vault is built)

NOTE: Do not confuse this root with the *vol* in *volition, voluntary, volunteer.*

INTERDISCIPLINARY:

involucre (in *anatomy*, a membranous covering or envelope; in *botany*, a ring of small leaves or bracts, at the base of the flower, flower cluster, or fruit; involucres are found in all plants of the composite family)

involution (in *anatomy*, a part formed by rolling or curling inward, as in the formation of a gastrula; in *biology*, a retrograde or degenerative change; in *grammar*, an involved construction, especially one created by a clause separating a subject from its predicate; in *mathematics*, the raising of a quantity to any given power; in *medicine*, the return of an organ to its normal size after distention, as of the womb after childbirth; also, a decline in the normal functions of the human body, or of an organ, that occurs with age, as the changes taking place at the menopause)

NO CROSS REFERENCE

Element	From	Meaning	Examples
vor**	Latin *vorare* (IE: *gwer*, to devour, gorge; yielding gorge)	to eat, devour	SIMPLE ROOT: voracious, voracity, vorago, vorant [*heraldry term*, to show the act of devouring (one's enemies)] TRAILING ROOT COMPOUND: api: apivorous (*api*, bee) bacci: baccivorous (*bacci*, berry) carni: carnivorous (*carni*, meat, flesh) herbi: herbivorous (*herb*, herbs, grass) insecti: insectivorous (*insect*, insects) omni: omnivorous (describing that which eats all things; can be used figuratively, as an *omnivorous reader*) (*omni*, all) pisci: piscivorous (*pisci*, fish) PREFIXED DISGUISED ROOT: de-: devour (*de-*, intensive) HERALDRY: vorant (shown in the act of *devouring*) CROSS REFERENCE: *ed, phag, rod/ros*
vot*	Latin *vovere*: to vow; yields English vow	to speak solemnly	SIMPLE ROOT: votary (**Synonyms**: devotee, habitué, fan) votable, vote votive (designed to accomplish or fulfill a special intention, promise, etc., or to express thanks or devotion, as *a votive offering*) PREFIXED ROOT: de-: devote (**Synonyms**: dedicate, consecrate, hallow), devoted, devotion, devotional (*de-*, from) PREFIXED DISGUISED ROOT: de-: devout (**Synonyms**: pious, religious, sanctimonious) (*de-*, from) CROSS REFERENCE: *dic, loqu/locut*
voy			See *vi* for *convoy*.
vulg*	Latin *vulgus* (IE: *wel*, to crowd, throng)	common people	SIMPLE ROOT: vulgar (of, characteristic of, or common to the great mass of people in general; common; popular; **Synonyms**: 1) coarse, gross, ribald; 2) common, general, ordinary), vulgarity, vulgarism Vulgate (a Latin version of the Bible prepared by St. Jerome in the 4th century, authorized as the official biblical text of the Roman Catholic Church; in lower case, any text or version in common acceptance; the vernacular or common speech; as an adjective, commonly accepted; popular) vulgus PREFIXED ROOT: di-: divulge (**Synonyms**: reveal, disclose, tell) (from *dis-*, apart) pro-: promulgate (*m* substituted for *v* for easier pronunciation) (*pro-*, before, forth) LATIN PHRASE: *ad captandum vulgus* (to catch, or please, the crowd), a logical fallacy CROSS REFERENCE: *demo, pleb, popul*

It is certain that he who cannot express in words what he means
does not himself know exactly what it is.
Demiaschkevich

Element	From	Meaning	Examples
vuls**	Latin *vellere*: to pull, pluck (IE: *wel⁴*, to tear, pull, wound)	to tear apart	**PREFIXED ROOT:** *a*-: avulsion (in *law*, the sudden transference of a piece of land from one person's estate to another's without change in ownership, as by a change in the course of a stream) (*a*-, from) *con*-: convulse (to shake or disturb violently; agitate; to cause convulsions, or spasms, in; to cause to shake with laughter, rage, or grief), convulsion, convulsive (*con*-, with, together) *di*-: divulsion (a violent rending, or tearing, apart; not to be confused with *divulge*, to proclaim publicly) (from *dis*-, apart, away) *e*-: evulsion (*e*- elides *ex*-, out) *re*-: revulsion (*re*-, back, again) **DISGUISED ROOT:** svelte (literally, to tear out until thin) vellicate (to twitch, pluck, etc.; now rarely used) NO CROSS REFERENCE
v y			See *vid* for *envy*.

> Poets that lasting marble seek
> Must come in Latin or in Greek.
> *Of English Verse*, Edmund Waller

X

Element	From	Meaning	Examples
xanth*	Greek *xanthos*	yellow	SIMPLE ROOT: xantha: xanthate xanthe: xanthein, xanthene xanthi: xanthic, xanthine xantho: xanthone, xanthous LEADING ROOT COMPOUND: *xanth*: oma: xanthoma (a small tumor, especially of the skin, formed by a deposit of lipids, often in a soft, rounded, yellowish mass) (*oma*, mass) *xantho*: cephal: xanthocephalous (literally, yellow-headed; the yellow-headed blackbird) (*cephal*, head) croid: xanthocroid (having light-colored hair and complexion) (*cro*, color; *oid*, similar to) phyll: xanthophyll (a yellow, crystalline pigment found in plants; it is related to carotene and is the basis of the yellow seen in autumn leaves) (*phyll*, leaf) CROSS REFERENCE: *aur, chrys, flav*
xeno**	Greek *xenos*	stranger	SIMPLE ROOT: xenon (chemical symbol: Xe) PREFIXED ROOT: a-: axenic (used especially of animals isolated from all other living things or of their environment) (*a-*, without) LEADING ROOT COMPOUND: *xen*: orex: xenorexia (an appetite disorder leading to the repeated swallowing of foreign bodies not ordinarily digested) (*orex*, appetite) *xeno*: bio: xenobiotic (designating or of a chemical substance that is foreign, and usually harmful, to living organisms; as a *noun*, such a substance) (*bio*, life) gam: xenogamy (cross-pollination between flowers on different plants) (*gam*, marriage, reproduction) gen: xenogenesis (the supposed production of an individual completely different from either of its parents) (*genesis*, beginning) graft: xenograft (a graft of skin, bone, etc., from an individual of another species) (from *graph*, stylus) lith: xenolith (in *geology*, a rock fragment different in kind from the igneous rock in which it is embedded) (*lithos*, rock) mania: xenomania (an inordinate attachment to foreign things, customs, institutions, manners, etc.) (*mania*, craving for) phil: xenophilia (attraction to or admiration of strangers or foreigners or of anything foreign or strange; compare *xenomania*, above) {xenophile, xenophilic} (*philas*, love of) phob: xenophobe, xenophobia (fear or hatred of strangers or of anything foreign or strange) (*phobia*, fear of)

Element	From	Meaning	Examples
xeno (cont'd)			TRAILING ROOT COMPOUND: eu: euxenite (literally, good stranger; or hospitable; a mineral containing several rare elements) (*eu*, good, well) pyro: pyroxene (any of a group of monoclinic or orthorhombic ferromagnesian minerals that do not contain the hydroxyl radical; they are common in igneous, and some metamorphic, rocks: so called from the mistaken belief that pyroxene was foreign or a stranger to igneous rocks) (*pyr*, fire) CROSS REFERENCE: *allo, hetero*
xero**	Greek *xeros* (IE: *ksero*, dry)	dry	LEADING ROOT COMPOUND: *xer*: opthalm: xerophthalmia (a form of conjunctivitis characterized by a dry and lusterless condition of the eyeball and caused by a deficiency of vitamin A) {xerophthalmic} (*ophthalmia*, abnormal condition of the eye) osis: xerosis (abnormal dryness, as of the skin or eyeball) (*osis*, condition of) *xero*: cheil: xerocheilia (dryness of the lips) (*cheil*, lip) derm: (skin) xeroderma (literally, yellow skin; same as *ichthyosis*) xerodermosteosis (*oste*, bone + *osis*, diseased condition of) graph: xerography (see *Tradename*, below) (*graph*, write) phag: xerophagy (the eating of only dry foods and water, as the strictest type of fast, observed in the Eastern Churches during Lent and especially during Holy Week) (*phag*, eat) phil: xerophilous (capable of thriving in a hot, dry climate, as certain plants and animals) {xerophily} (*phila*, love of) phyt: xerophyte (a plant structurally adapted to growing under very dry or desert conditions) (*phyton*, plant) sere: xerosere (a sere beginning in a dry area) (*sere*, the complete series of stages occurring in succession in communities of plants and animals until the climax is reached) TRAILING ROOT COMPOUND: phyll: phylloxera (literally, dry leaf; any of a family of homopteran insects that attack the leaves and roots of certain plants, including the grapevine) (*phyll*, leaf) DISGUISED ROOT: elixir (see note under Arabic *al*) LATIN COGNATE: serene (**Synonyms**: calm, placid, tranquil) serenity (**Synonyms**: equanimity, composure, nonchalance) TRADENAME: Xerox (manufacturer of dry copiers; the word should not be used generically) NO CROSS REFERENCE
xiph*	Greek *xiphos*	sword	SIMPLE ROOT: Xiphias (a genus comprising the swordfish) LEADING ROOT COMPOUND: *xiph*: oid: xiphoid (in *anatomy* and *zoology*, shaped like a sword; ensiform) (*oid*, similar to) *xiphi*: stern: xiphisternum (in *anatomy* and *zoology*, the cartilaginous process at the lowermost end of the sternum)

746

Element	From	Meaning	Examples
xiph (cont'd)			*xipho*: cost: xiphocostal (*costa*, ribs) phyll: xiphophyllous (a leaf in the shape of a *sword*) (*phyll*, leaf) *xiphos*: ur: ziphosuran (any of an order of arthropods made up of the horseshoe crabs and related extinct forms) (*ur*, tail) CROSS REFERENCE: *ens, glad*
xylo*	Greek *xylon*	wood	SIMPLE ROOT: xylan, xylem, xylene, xylidine LEADING ROOT COMPOUND: *xyl*: ose: xylose (a white crystalline aldose sugar, used in dyeing, tanning, and in diabetic diets; also called *wood sugar*) *xylo*: graph: xylograph, xylography (wood engraving, especially of an earlier period; the art of printing texts or illustrations, sometimes with color, from wood blocks, as distinct from *typography*) (*graph*, write) phag: xylophagous (feeding on woods, as certain insects) (*phag*, eat) phon: xylophone (a musical percussion instrument consisting of a mounted row of wooden bars graduated in length to sound a chromatic scale, played with two mallets) (*phone*, sound) tom: xylotomy (the preparation of sections of wood for microscopic study) (*tomy*, cutting) CROSS REFERENCE: *hylo*

747

Z

Element	From	Meaning	Examples
zo***	Greek zoion	animal	SIMPLE ROOT: zodia, zodiac, zoea, zoic, zoism, zoo (short for *zoological garden*), zoon

SIMPLE ROOT: zodia, zodiac, zoea, zoic, zoism, zoo (short for *zoological garden*), zoon

PREFIXED ROOTS AND COMPOUNDS:

a-: (not, without)

azote (nitrogen, because the gas does not support life)

azotemia (*emia*, diseased condition of the blood)

epi-: (on, upon)

epizoic (living on or attached to the external surface of an animal, but not parasitic)

epizoon (a parasite or commensal living on the outside of an animal's body)

epizootic (epidemic among animals; as a *noun*, an *epizootic disease*)

epizootiology (the study of epidemic animal diseases)

meta-: metazoan (any of a large subkingdom made up of all animals whose bodies, originating from a single cell, are composed of many differentiated cells arranged into definite organs) (*meta-*, between)

LEADING ROOT COMPOUND:

zo:

oid: zooid (*oid*, similar to)

zoo:

gam: zoogamete (in *biology*, a motile gamete) (*gam*, sexual reproduction)

gen: zoogenic (caused by or starting in animals, as a disease) (*genic*, origin)

geo: zoogeography (the science dealing with the geographical distribution of animals) (*geo*, earth + *graph*, write)

graph: zoography (the branch of zoology concerned with the description of animals, their habits, etc.) (*graph*, write)

latry: zoolatry (*latry*, worship of)

log: zoological, zoologist, zoology (the science, a branch of biology, that deals with animals, their life, structure, growth, classification, etc.; the animal life of an area; fauna; the characteristics or properties of an animal or animal group) (*logy*, study of)

morph: zoomorphic, zoomorphism (*morph*, shape, form)

nos: zoonosis (a disease that can be transmitted to man by vertebrate animals) {zoonotic} (*noso*, disease)

para: zooparasite (a parasitic animal; see *parasite* under *sito*)

phag: zoophagous (same as *carnivorous*, which see under *carni*) (*phag*, eat)

phil: zoophilous (extreme love for animals; specifically, abnormal sexual attraction for animals) (*phila*, love)

phob: zoophobia (an abnormal fear of animals) (*phobia*, fear of)

phyt: zoophyte (any animal, as coral, sponge, etc., having somewhat the appearance and character of a plant) (*phyton*, plant)

Element	From	Meaning	Examples
zo (cont'd)			spor: zoosporangium (in *botany*, a sporangium in certain fungi and algae, producing zoospores) {zoosporangial} (*spore*, reproductive body + *angi*, vessel) TRAILING ROOT COMPOUND: cyto: cytozoic (*cyto*, cell) holo: holozoic (*holo*, whole) meso: Mesozoic (*meso*, middle) micro: microzoaria (*micro*, small) proto: protozoa (*proto*, first) CROSS REFERENCE: *anim, bio, spir, vit*
zyg*	Greek *zygon* (IE: *yugo*, yoke)	yoke, pair, united	SIMPLE ROOT: zygoma, zygon, zygomatic, zygosis (plural, *zygoses*), zygote (a cell formed by the union of male and female gametes; fertilized egg cell before cleavage), zygous PREFIXED ROOT: a-: azygous (unmatched; not one of a pair; having no mate; odd; as, an *azygous* muscle) (*a-*, not) sy-: syzygy (*sy-* elides *syn-*, together) LEADING ROOT COMPOUND: *zyg*: oid: zygoid (*oid*, similar to) osis: zygosis (*osis*, condition of) *zygo*: dactyl: zygodactyl (but extended to include toe; having the toes arranged in two opposed pairs, two in front and two in the rear; as a *noun*, a zygodactyl bird, as the parrot) (*dactyl*, finger) gen: zygogenesis (in *biology*, reproduction in which male and female gametes and nuclei fuse) (*genesis*, origin) morph: zygomorphic (in *biology*, bilaterally symmetrical) (*morph*, form) phyt: zygophyte (*phyton*, plant) pter: zygoptera (*pter*, wing) spor: zygospore (in *botany*, a thick-walled, resting spore formed by conjugation of two isogametes) (*spore*, seed) TRAILING ROOT COMPOUND: hetero: (different) heterozygosis (the condition of being a heterozygote; the production of a heterozygote by the union of unlike gametes) (*osis*, condition of) heterozygote, heterozygous homo: homozygous (*homo*, same) DISGUISED ROOT: zeugma (a rhetorical figure of speech in which a single word, usually a verb or adjective, is syntactically related to two or more words, with only one of which it seems logically connected, e.g., The room was not light, but his fingers were; to wage war on peace; The businessman left in high spirits and a Cadillac; she opened the door and her heart to the homeless boy) CROSS REFERENCE: *jug/junct*

To be a power one must know how to use language; and how can you place words together unless you know their derivation and their real meaning. Henry Kraemen

Element	From	Meaning	Examples
zym*	Greek *zume*	ferment, leaven	SIMPLE ROOT: zymase (an enzyme present in yeast), zyme PREFIXED ROOT: *en-*: enzyme (*en-*, in) LEADING ROOT COMPOUND: *zym*: oid: zymoid (*oid*, similar to) urg: zymurgy (the branch of chemistry dealing with fermentation, as applied in wine making, brewing, etc.) (from *erg*, work; therefore, -*urgy* is the science, technique, or process of working with or by means of) *zymo*: gen: zymogen, zymogenesis, zymogenic (*gen*, origin) logy: zymology (the study of fermentation) (*logy*, the study) lys: zymolysis {zymolytic} (*lys*, loosen) meter: zymometer (an instrument used to measure the degree of fermentation) (*meter*, measure) DOUBLE PREFIXED COMPOUNDS: endoenzyme (an enzyme that functions within the cell) (*endo-*, within + *en-*, in) hyperazotemia [*hyper-*, excess + *a-*, not + *zot* (from *zoion*, animal) + *em* (from *hemo*, blood) + -*ia*, diseased condition of] TRAILING ROOT COMPOUND: lyso: lysozyme (a particle found in egg whites, tears, saliva, etc. that can kill certain bacteria by dissolving the cell walls) (*lys*, loosen) NO CROSS REFERENCE

The Latin element in modern English is so great that there would be
no difficulty in writing hundreds of consecutive pages in which the proportion
of words of native English and French etymology...would not
exceed five percent of the whole.
Henry Bradley

APPENDIX A
ENGLISH TO ROOTS INDEX

Where there are multiple forms of a root, only the first is given; see the listed family for additional forms.
Infinitives (e.g., to run, to leap), are shown without the infinitive identifier "to";
where there might be confusion between parts of speech, the part of speech is listed in
parentheses after the entry word.

A

abdomen: *ventr*
able: *dyn, pot*
abnormal: *caco-,
    dys-*
about: *peri-*
above: *ana-, super-*
account: *logo*
accustom: *sues*
acid: *ox*
acorn: *gland*
acquire: *ctet*
across: *dia-, trans-*
act: *act*
action: *-osis*
adorn: *cosm*
adult: *pub*
advise: *mun, suas*
afar: *tele*
afflict: *trib*
after: *meta-, post-*
again: *ana-, palin-,
    re-*
against: *ana-, anti-,
    cata-, contr-, ob-*
age: *ev*
agitate: *turb*
ahead: *proto*
air: *physo, pneu*
aircraft: *aeri*
all: *omni, pan*
allot: *trib*
allow: *lic*
almond: *amyg*
almost: *pen*
alone: *erem, mono,
    priv, sol*
alongside: *para-*
alternated: *meta-*
always: *semper*
amber: *electr*
among: *epi-*
amount: *arithm*
ancient: *paleo*
anew: *ana-*
anger: *ir*
angle: *cant, gon*
animal: *zo*

announce: *nunci*
anterior: *epi-*
anther: *andr*
apart: *dis-, se-*
ape: *pithec*
apex: *apic*
appear: *ori, par*
appearance: *facies,
    form, sch*
appetite: *orex*
apple: *pom*
arch: *arc*
arise: *ori*
arm (upper): *brachi*
armpit: *al, axi*
around: *ambi-,
    amph-, circum-,
    peri-*
arrange: *cosm, ser*
arrangement: *tax*
arrow: *sagitt*
ash: *ciner*
ashamed of (to be):
    pud
ask: *quer, rog*
assault: *horm*
assembly: *agora*
assess: *cens*
assist: *adjut*
asunder: *dich*
at: *ad-*
attach: *fix*
attack: *horm*
avoid: *fug*
away: *ab-, cata-,
    de-, dis-, se-*
away from: *apo-,
    de-, ex-*
axis: *rachi*

B

babble: *lal*
back (noun): *dors,
    rachi*
back: *palin-, re-*
backbone: *rachi*
backward: *ana-,
    cata-, retro*

bad: *caco-, dys-,
    mal-, mis-*
badly: *mal-*
balance: *liber*
ball: *glob*
band: *desm, fasc*
bandage: *fasc*
bar: *bar*
base: *rad*
battle: *machy*
bear (verb): *ger,
    fer, lat, phor*
beat (verb): *bat,
    pel, tund*
beautiful: *bell,
    calli*
beauty: *form*
becoming: *-esce*
bee: *api*
before: *ante-, pre-,
    pro-* (both Greek
    and Latin)
beg: *rog*
begin: *ori*
beginning: *-esce*
behind: *meta-,
    retro-*
being: *onto*
believe: *cred, fid*
bell: *campan*
bell-shaped: *calyc*
bellows: *physo*
belly: *ventr*
below: *infra-, sub-*
bend : *flect, sin,
    var, vert*
berry: *bacci*
beside: *epi-, meta-*
best: *aristo, opt*
better: *melior*
between: *inter-*
beyond: *ex-,
    hyper-, meta-,
    preter, super-,
    ulter-*
bile: *chol*
bind (verb): *lig,
    cinct, nect*
binding: *pac*

bird: *avi, ornis*
birth: *gen, nat*
birth to (give): *nat,
    par*
bite (verb): *mord*
bitter: *ac, ox*
black: *mela*
bladder: *vesic*
blame: *culp*
blemish: *macu*
blister: *vesic*
blood disease:
    -emia
blood: *hem, sang*
bloom: *thall*
blossom: *flor*
blow (verb): *flat*
blue (dark): *cyan*
board: *tab*
body: *corp, soma*
boil: *bull, ferv*
bone: *os, ost*
book: *bibli, lib*
border: *fin*
both: *ambi*
both sides: *amph*
bottom: *edaph,
    found*
bottom (of sea):
    benth
boundary: *term*
bovine: *taur*
bow: *arc*
brain: *cerebr*
branch: *clad, ram*
brass: *chalco*
bread: *pan*
break: *frac, rupt*
breakage: *clas*
breast: *mamm,
    pector*
breath: *anim, hal,
    pneu*
breathe: *spir*
brief: *brev*
bright: *clar*
brine: *sal*
bring forth: *phyt*
broad: *eury, platy*

broken stones: *rud*
broken-off piece: *sax*
brother: *adelp, frat*
bud: *germ*
building: *edi*
build (verb): *struct, tex*
bulk: *mol*
bull: *taur*
burden: *on*
burn (verb): *caust, flag, phleg, ure*
bury: *sepul*
buy (verb): *emp, merc, sum*
by: *per-*

C

call: *voc*
calm: *clemen, sed*
cancer: *carcin*
cane: *can*
care: *cur*
care for: *cult, med*
carry: *fer, ger, lat, phor, port, vect*
cart: *car*
cartilage: *chondr*
carve: *glyp*
case: *theca*
caseous: *tyro*
cat: *ailur, fel*
cattle: *fe, pecu*
caul: *hymen*
cause: *caus*
cavity: *alveol, cav*
cell: *alveol*
center: *centr*
chain: *caten*
chair: *hedr*
chamber: *camera*
chance: *fortu*
change: *amoeba, apo-, camb, mut*
changed: *meta-*
character: *ethos*
charge: *leg*
chart: *cart*
check (verb): *ische*
cheek: *bucc*
cheese: *tyro*
chemistry: *chemo*
chest: *pector*
child: *ped*
choking: *ang*

choose: *lect, leg, opt*
chorus: *chor*
church: *eccles*
circle: *cycl, gyr, orb*
city: *poli, urb*
clap: *plaud*
claw: *chel*
clean: *cast, pur*
clear: *clar, luc*
cleave: *her*
climb: *scan*
cloak: *chlamyd*
close (adjective): *steno*
close (verb): *clud, mi*
clothe: *vest*
cloud: *vap*
cloudy: *fusc*
club: *clav*
coarse: *gros*
cold: *psychro*
collapse: *gru*
color: *chrom*
column: *styl*
comb-like: *cten, pectin*
come: *ven*
comfort: *sol*
common: *cen, mun*
common people: *popul, vulg*
community: *cit*
compact (make): *stas*
companion: *soc*
complete: *integ, sat*
completely: *cata-, dia-, per-*
completion: *tel*
conceal: *crypt*
concern: *cur*
condition: *-osis*
conduct: *act*
conquer: *vict*
consider: *arbit*
contrary: *contr-*
converse: *fab*
cook (verb): *coqu, pep*
copper: *chalco, cupr*
cord: *chord, lin*
cornea: *cera*
corner of eye: *cant*

corpse: *necr*
counsel: *consul*
course: *drom*
court: *cohors*
cover: *cover, techn, vagin*
cover (verb): *tect*
covered: *calyp*
covering: *chlamyd*
cow: *vacca*
crab: *carcin*
crack: *crep*
crane (bird): *geran*
craze: *mania*
create: *poe*
creep: *rep*
crescent: *men*
cross: *cruc*
crosswise: *chiasma*
crowded: *dens*
crown: *cor*
cry out: *clam, plor*
crystal: *crystal*
cup: *calyc*
cup-shaped: *cotyl*
curl: *cirr*
curve: *sin*
custom: *ethos, mor, nom*
cut (verb): *cad, cis, cop, put, scind, sect, tail, tom*

D

damage: *damn, lid*
dance: *chor, orch*
dark: *fusc, maur, mela*
daughter: *fil*
dawn: *eo*
day: *die, hemer, jour*
death: *leth, thanat*
decayed: *sapr*
deceive: *fall*
decide: *tail*
deck (verb): *orn*
deep: *bath*
degree: *grad*
delay: *mora*
demand: *pet*
demon: *demon*
depth: *bath*
desire (verb): *aver, cup*
despise: *temn*
devil: *demon*

devour: *vor*
devout: *pi*
die (noun): *typ*
die (verb): *mort*
different: *heter*
difficult: *dys-*
dig up: *foss*
digest: *pep*
dilation: *eury*
dim: *maur*
dip (verb): *bapt, merg*
discerning: *sag*
disease: *path*
disk: *orb*
dissolve: *lys*
distinguish: *crin*
distress: *odyn*
diverse: *poly*
divide: *schis*
divided into parts: *fiss*
division: *clas*
do: *act, drama, fac, ger*
dog: *can, cyn*
donkey: *ass*
door (folding): *valv*
double: *du*
down: *cata-, de-*
downward: *cata-*
drag: *tract*
draw: *tract*
dream: *oneir*
drink: *bib, ebr, pot*
drive: *act, agon, pel*
drop: *gutt*
dry: *sec, xero*
ductile: *elast*
dung: *copr*
dwelling: *eco*

E

ear: *aur, oto*
early: *paleo, proto*
early time period: *eo*
earth: *chthon, edaph, geo, hum, ped, terra*
ease: *oti, scho*
eat: *ed, phag, rod, vor*
echo: *echo*
egg: *oo, ov*
eight: *oct*

elder: *sen*
eleven: *hendeca*
elite: *oligo*
employ: *us*
empty: *ceno, inan,*
vac, van
enclose: *arc*
enclosing: *peri-*
enclosure: *cohors*
end: *fin, tel, term*
enjoyment of: *fruc*
enroll: *cens*
ensnare: *lic*
entice: *lic*
envelope: *chlamyd*
equal: *equi, iso, par*
equip: *par*
erase: *dele*
erect: *ithy*
erotic desire: *eros,*
lagn
establish: *found*
even: *plan*
evening: *hesper*
ever: *semper*
every: *pan*
examine: *vid*
example of: *dei*
excessive: *hyper-*
excite: *horm*
exist: *esse*
existence: *onto*
explain: *phras*
external: *ecto-*
extreme: *acro*
extremities: *acro*
eye: *ocul, op,*
ophth
eyebrow: *cili*
eyelid: *cili*

F

face: *facies*
facing: *anti-*
faint: *langu*
faith: *fid*
fall (verb): *cad, lap,*
pto
false: *pseudo*
famous: *celeb*
far off: *tele*
farther from: *deuter*
fast: *celer*
fasten: *apt, fix*
fat: *lip, sebi*
fate: *fortu*
father: *pater*

fatty: *lip, sebi*
fault: *mend, pecca*
fear of: *phob*
feather: *pen, plum,*
pter
feces: *copr*
feed (verb): *past*
feel: *pass, sens,*
tact
feeling: *alg, esthes,*
path
fence (verb): *phrag*
ferment: *zym*
fertile: *felic, uber*
festive: *fest*
festive song: *hymn*
fetus: *germ*
fever: *caust, phleg,*
pyr
few: *oligo*
fiber: *fibr*
field: *agr, camp*
fight with the fist:
pug
fill: *plen, sat*
filter: *col*
find: *heur*
fine: *lepto*
finger: *dactyl, digit*
fire: *ign, pyr*
first: *arch, prim,*
proto
fish: *ichthy, pisc*
fit together: *art,*
fabr
five: *cinque, penta*
flat: *platy*
flee: *fug*
flesh: *carn, creat,*
sarc
float: *nat*
flock: *greg*
flour: *far*
flourish: *thall*
flow: *col, flu, rh*
flower: *anth*
fluid (of body):
lymph
fly (verb): *vol*
focus: *foc*
fold: *plex, -ple,*
-ploid
folding door: *valv*
follow: *sequ*
food: *past, sit*
foolish: *fatu*
foot: *ped, pod*
footprint: *vestig*

force: *vio*
foremost: *arch*
forest: *silv*
fork: *furc*
form: *eid, fabr, fig,*
form, ide,
morph, oid,
plas, sch
forth: *pro-*
fortune: *sort*
forty: *quadr*
forward: *pro-*
fossil: *oryct*
four: *quadr, tetra*
free: *eleuthero,*
fran, liber, lys
freeze: *gel*
frenzy: *estr*
fresh water: *limn*
friend: *ami*
from: *ab-, apo-, de-*
from afar: *tele*
front of: *ante-*
fruit: *carp, fruc,*
pom
fruitful: *fecund,*
uber
fungus: *myc*
furnish: *orn*

G

gadfly: *estr*
gain: *quer*
galaxy: *galact*
gall: *chol*
gap: *hiat*
gas: *aeri, physo*
gather: *leg*
gentle: *clemen*
geometric figure:
-hedron
giant: *giga*
gills: *branchi*
gird: *cinct*
give: *do, don, trib*
give birth to: *nat,*
par
glass: *hyal, vitr*
glowing: *cand*
glue: *coll, glut*
gnaw: *rod*
go: *bas, it, vad*
God, god: *dei, theo*
gold: *aur, chrys*
good: *bene, bon,*
eu, prob
govern: *gov*

government: *arch*
grain: *chondr, gran,*
sit
grasp: *apt, leps*
grass: *gramin*
gray: *polio*
graze: *past*
great: *grand, magn,*
mega
green: *chlor, ver*
grind: *mol*
ground: *edaph, geo,*
hum, ped, terra
grow: *cresc,*
embryo
grown up: *pub*
growth: *physi*
growth (tumor):
-oma
guard (verb): *tuit*
guard (on): *phylax*
guide: *gov*
guilt: *culp*

H

habit: *mor*
hair: *capill, crin,*
pil, trich
half: *demi, hemi,*
semi
hand: *chiro, man*
hang: *pend*
happy: *beat, felic*
harbor: *port*
hard: *dur, rob,*
sclero
harm: *damn, noc*
harsh: *sever*
hate: *od, temn*
hatred of: *miso*
have: *hab, hex*
haven: *port*
head: *capit, cephal*
heal: *iat, med*
health: *hygi*
healthy: *salu*
heap: *cumu*
hear: *acou, aud*
heart: *card, cord*
heat: *cal, caus,*
therm
heaven: *dei*
heavens: *cel*
heavy: *bar, grav*
heed (take): *cav*
heel: *calx*
help: *adjut*

herd: *greg*
hidden: *lat*
hide (verb): *cel,*
   cond, crypt
high: *alt*
highest: *acro*
hindrance: *tric*
hold (verb): *hab,*
   cap, hex, ten
hollow: *alveol,*
   cav, sin
holy: *hier, sacr,*
   sanct
home: *dom, eco,*
   nost
honey: *mell*
hoof: *pod*
hope: *sper*
horn: *cera, corn*
horse: *caval, equus,*
   hipp
how many: *quot*
hundred: *cent, hect*
hurt: *trauma*
husband: *andr*

I

ice: *glac*
icy cold: *crymo,*
   cryo
ill: *dys-*
image: *eid, icon,*
   oid
imitate: *mim*
immerse: *bapt*
impaired: *dys-*
impede: *bar*
improve: *edi*
impulse: *horm*
in: *en-, in-*
incite: *hort*
increase: *aug*
inflame: *phleg*
inflamed: *-itis*
inner: *endo-*
insect: *entom*
inside: *eso-*
intensify: *ten*
intensive: *ana-,*
   com-, de-, per-,
   peri-
intestine: *entero*
into: *in-*
iris: *irid*
iron: *ferr, sider*
island: *insul, nes*

J

jackass: *as*
jaundice: *icter*
join: *art, ser*
joined: *gam*
judge: *arbit, cens*
judgment: *crim,*
   dogma
judicial process:
   caus

K

keep: *serv*
kernel: *nucl*
ketone: *keto*
key: *clav*
kidney: *nephr,*
   adren, ren
kill: *cide, noc*
kind: *gen, phyl*
kissing: *osc*
knee: *genu*
knot: *nod*
know: *gno, sci*
knowledge: *cogn*

L

labor: *ops*
lack: *pen*
ladder: *scal*
lake: *lacu*
lament: *plang*
land: *geo*
language: *gloss,*
   ling
large: *grand, gros,*
   macro, magn,
   mega
last things: *eschat*
last: *ulter-*
later: *hyster-,*
   meta-, post-
laugh: *gel, rid*
law: *jud, leg, nom*
lawlessness: *anom*
lawsuit: *caus*
layer: *strat*
lead (verb): *duc,*
   agon
leadership: *hegei*
leading: *agog*
leaf: *bract, foli,*
   lam, petal, phyll
lean (verb): *clim*

leap: *sal*
leave: *linq*
leave behind: *her*
leaven: *zym*
leisure: *oti, scho*
lens: *lent*
lentil: *lent*
less: *mini, mio*
lesser: *sub-*
less than usual:
   demi
letter: *liter*
level: *plan*
lie down: *cub*
lie hidden: *lat*
life: *bio, vit*
life principle: *anim*
lift: *lev*
ligament: *desm*
light: *luc, phos*
limestone: *calc*
line: *fil, lin*
lip: *lab*
listen: *aur*
little: *petit, steno*
living: *vir*
lizard: *saur*
load: *on*
lock (of hair): *cirr*
lonely: *erem*
long: *long, macro*
look: *spec*
look at: *tuit*
loose: *lax*
loosen: *lys, solut*
lot: *sort*
love: *ama*
love (sexual): *ero,*
   lagn
love of: *philo*
loving: *philo*
low: *infer*
lower: *infer, neth*

M

madness: *mania*
magnet: *magnet*
maiden: *parthen*
make: *fac, poe*
male: *andr, masc*
man: *andr,*
   anthropo, hom,
   vir
manner: *mod, styl*
mantle: *chlamyd*
many: *multi, plur,*
   poly

map: *cart*
mark: *sign*
mark (verb): *not*
marketplace: *agora*
marriage: *gam*
marrow: *medull,*
   myel
marry: *nub*
mass: *cumu, mol,*
   onc
masses: *pleb*
master: *dom,*
   magis
matter: *hylo*
measure: *men,*
   metr, mod
meat: *carn*
membrane: *hymen,*
   mening
memory: *mne*
merciful: *clemen*
messenger: *ang*
metal plate: *elasm*
middle: *med, meso-*
mild: *clemen, leni*
milk: *galact, lact*
mind: *ment, noo,*
   phren, psych,
   thym
mindful: *mem*
minute: *micro*
mite: *acar*
mixing: *cras*
mixture: *misc*
moist: *um*
moisture: *hygr*
mold: *typ*
mold (verb): *plas*
moldy: *muc*
mollusks: *malac*
money: *lucr, pecu,*
   prec
month: *men*
moon: *lun, men*
more: *hyper-, ple,*
   plur
moss: *bry*
mother: *mater,*
   metro
mountain: *mont,*
   oro
mouse: *mus*
mouth: *bucc, ora,*
   osc, stoma
move: *act, migr,*
   mov
movement: *cinem*
much: *multi, poly*

mucus: *myc, myx*
mud: *limi*
muscle: *myo*
mushroom: *myc*
mutually: *all*

N

nail (of finger):
  onych
naked: *gymn, nud*
name: *nom, onom,*
  onym
narrow: *ang, steno*
nation: *ethno*
natural: *physi*
nature: *physi*
navel: *omphal*
near: *anti-, peri-,*
  plesios, pro-
nearest: *prox*
neck: *coll*
need: *pen*
needle: *acu*
negative: *non-*
nerve: *nerv, neur*
nest: *nid*
net: *ret*
new: *ceno, neo,*
  nov
next to: *prox*
night: *noc, nyct*
nine: *ennea, nov*
nod: *nut*
none: *null*
normal: *eu, orth*
nose: *nas, rhino*
not: *an-, in-, mis-,*
  ne-, non-
not having: *ex-*
note: *not*
nothing: *nihil*
notion: *ide*
nourish: *al, nur,*
  troph
nude: *gymn*
number: *arithm,*
  num
nut: *nucl*
nutrition: *troph*

O

oblique: *lox*
observe: *temp*
obtain: *quer*
ocean: *pelag*
ode: *hymn*

of: *de-*
off: *ab-, apo-, de-*
offspring: *fet, prol*
oil: *ol, unct*
oily: *sebi*
ointment: *unct*
old: *sen*
old age: *ger*
on: *in-*
one: *hen, mono,*
  uni
one's own: *idio,*
  propr
oneself: *sui*
open: *aper*
opening: *chasm,*
  op, osc, stoma
openness: *cand*
opinion: *dogma*
opposed to: *contr-*
opposite: *anti-,*
  contr-
oppress: *trib*
orb: *orb*
order: *cosm, nom,*
  ord
other: *all, alter,*
  heter
out: *ex-, exo-*
out of: *ex-*
outdoors: *for*
outside: *ecto-,*
  epi-, exo-, extra-
outside the bounds:
  preter
outward: *exo-*
ovary: *oophor*
over: *ana-, epi-,*
  super-
owe: *deb*

P

pain: *alg, dol,*
  odyn, pen
paint (verb): *pict*
pair: *zyg*
palisade: *val*
paralysis: *pleg*
parasite: *verm*
part: *mer, part*
particular: *propr*
partition: *sep(t)*
partner: *soc*
past: *preter*
path: *od*
pay: *trib*
pea: *lent*

peace: *pac*
pejorative: *de-*
penis: *mentul,*
  peni, phall
people: *dem*
people (common):
  pleb, vulg
perceive: *sens, tact*
perform: *funct*
perianth: *chlamyd*
perspire: *sud*
petal: *chlamyd*
picture: *pict*
pillar: *styl*
pit: *alveol*
place: *chor, loco,*
  stas, top
place (verb): *pon,*
  thes
place in order: *par*
place where: *-ory*
plain: *camp*
plan: *sch*
plank: *tab*
plant (noun): *phyt*
plate: *bract, lam,*
  petal
play: *lud*
please: *plac*
pleasing: *grat*
pleasure: *hedon*
pledge: *gage, spond*
plenty: *ops*
pluck: *carp*
plunge (verb):
  merg
pod: *vagin*
point: *centr, cusp,*
  punct
point out: *disc*
poison: *tox, vir*
port: *port*
portion: *nom*
pouch: *burs*
pour: *chemo, fus*
power: *crac, pot*
powerful: *dyn, hier*
praise: *laud, plaud*
prayer: *prec*
prehistoric: *paleo*
prepare: *par*
press: *press*
prevention: *phylax*
price: *prec*
pricked: *stig*
prickly: *echino*
primitive: *paleo*
prior to: *ante-, ex-*

prize: *athl*
proclaim (verb): *dic*
produce (verb):
  cresc
profit: *lucr*
projecting point:
  corn
prompt: *celer*
proper: *dec, prob*
proper measure:
  temp
property: *fe, propr*
protect: *gar, mun,*
  past, serv
prove: *prob*
prune (verb): *put*
public: *mun*
pull: *tract*
pull tight: *string*
punish: *pen*
pure: *cast, cathar,*
  pur
purse: *fisc*
push: *pel*
pushing: *osm*
put: *pon, thes*
put on (as
  clothing): *dysi*
puzzle: *enigm*

Q

quality of: *-ose*
quick: *ox*
quiet: *tac*

R

race: *ethno, gen*
rain: *ombro*
raise: *lev*
raise up: *cit*
rattle: *crep*
rays: *actin*
reach: *apt*
reach for: *orex*
read: *lect, leg*
reason: *caus, logo,*
  rati
recent: *ceno, neo*
red: *rub*
reed: *can*
reflecting light:
  -esce
remain: *man, mora*
removal: *de-*
request: *prec*

resembling: *oid,*
 para-
rest: *quie*
reversal: *de-*
reversed: *ana-,*
 meta-
revive: *cit*
rib: *cost, pleur*
right: *dec, dext,*
 jud, orth, rect
rim: *annel*
ring: *annel, gyr*
ripe: *pep*
ripen: *coqu*
risk: *per*
road: *od, vi*
rock: *petro, sax*
rod: *bacill, bacteri*
roll (verb): *vol*
room: *camera*
root: *rad, ram,*
 rhizo
rose: *rhod*
rot: *sep*
rotate: *gyr*
rotten: *sapr*
rough: *asper, trach*
round: *circum-*
rub: *fri*
rub away: *trit*
ruins: *rud*
rule: *arch, crac,*
 norm, rect
ruler: *crac, raj*
run: *cur, drom, rrh*
run away: *fug*
running: *troch*

S

sack: *burs*
sacred: *hagio, hier,*
 sacr
safe: *hol*
sail: *nav*
sailor: *naus*
saint: *hagio*
salt: *hal, sal*
same: *homo, idem,*
 iso, simil
sand: *aren*
sash: *fasc*
saw (noun): *serr*
say: *dic*
scale: *lep*
scales: *liber*
scrape: *rad*
sea: *hal, mar, pelag*

seal: *sign*
season of year: *hor*
second: *deuter*
see: *scop, vid*
seed: *bacci, gon,*
 semin, sperm
seedcase: *angi*
seek: *pet, quer*
seem: *dogma*
seize: *cap, carp,*
 leps, prehend,
 rap
seizure: *leps*
self: *auto*
sell: *pol, ven*
semen: *gon, semen*
send: *leg, miss,*
 stas, stle
sepal: *chlamyd*
separate (verb):
 cern, crin
serve: *funct*
service: *latr*
set (verb): *par,*
 stas, stat
set firm: *gel*
set in motion: *cit*
set in place: *sist*
seven: *hept, sept*
sew: *sut*
sexual reproduction:
 gam
shade: *umbra*
shadow: *umbra*
shake: *cuss, seism,*
 vibr
shape: *fabr, fig,*
 form, morph,
 oid
shared: *cen*
sharp: *ac, ox*
sheath: *cole, theca,*
 vagin
shell: *ost*
shield: *arm*
shine: *flag*
shining: *cand,*
 electr
ship: *naus, nav*
shoot (noun):
 blast, clad, germ
short: *brachy, brev*
show (verb): *dei,*
 mon, par, phan,
 phras
shudder: *horr*
shut (verb): *clud*

side: *cant, cost,*
 hedr, lat, pleur
sign: *sem, sign*
silent: *tac*
silver: *arg*
silvery gray: *glau*
similar: *homo*
simple: *haplo*
sin: *pecca*
sinew: *nerv*
sing: *can, od*
single: *haplo, priv,*
 uni
sister: *soror*
sit: *sed*
six: *hex, sex*
sixth: *sex*
skill: *soph*
skin: *cut, derm, pel*
sky: *cel*
slack: *lax*
slave: *serv*
sleep: *dorm,*
 hypno, somn
slender: *lepto*
slide: *lap*
slime: *myx*
slippery: *lubr*
slope: *clim*
small: *lepto,*
 micro, mini,
 petit, pico
smell: *osm*
smoke: *fum*
smooth: *pol*
snail: *helic*
snake: *angui,*
 herpe, ophi
snatch: *rap*
snow: *niv*
soak up: *sorb*
soft: *leni, malac,*
 mol
soil: *edaph*
solid: *ster*
somber: *fusc*
son: *fil*
song: *can, mel*
sorrow: *dol, pen*
soul: *anim, psych,*
 thym
sound: *echo, phon,*
 son, ton
sowing seed: *spor*
speak: *fab, leg,*
 loqu, od, parl
speak solemnly:
 vot

speech: *ep, logo,*
 ora
speed: *tach, veloc*
sperm: *semen,*
 sperm
sphere: *glob*
spherical body:
 nucl
spider: *arachn*
spin: *rhomb*
spine: *rachi*
spiny: *acantho,*
 echino
spiral: *gyr, helic*
spirit: *anim, pneu,*
 psych, thym
split: *fiss, scind,*
 schis
spoke of wheel: *rad*
spot: *macu*
spread out: *pand*
sprout: *blast*
square: *tetra*
staff: *bacill, bacteri*
stain: *macu*
stake (in ground):
 pal
stalk: *caul*
stamen: *andr*
stand: *stas, stat*
standing place: *stal*
star: *ast, sider, stell*
starch: *amyl*
stay: *man*
steal: *klept*
steam: *vap*
stem: *caul*
step: *bas, grad,*
 stich, vad
stern: *sever*
stick to: *her*
sticky: *muc*
stiff: *rig*
stink: *fet*
stone: *lapid, lith,*
 petro, sax
store (verb): *cond*
straight: *ithy, orth,*
 rect, sagitt
stranger: *xeno*
strength: *fort, vin,*
 vio
strengthen: *firm*
stretch: *rog, ten,*
 ton
stride: *stich*
strike: *bat, cis,*
 cuss, fend, fend,

*flic, fut, lid,
plang, plaud,
tund*
strike out: *dele*
string: *chord*
stripped: *nud*
stroke (medical):
pleg
strong: *dur, fort,
rob, val*
struggle: *luct,
machy*
stuff (verb): *farc*
stupor: *narc, sopor*
substitute: *vic*
suffer: *pass*
summit: *apic*
sun: *helio, sol*
supply: *gar*
suppress: *ische*
sway: *nut*
swear: *jur*
sweat: *hidr, sud*
sweet: *dulc*
swell (verb): *turg,
tub, tum*
swift: *celer, tach*
swim: *nat*
sword: *ens, glad,
xiph*
symbol: *icon, sem*

T

table: *mens*
tail: *caud, cerc,
peni, ur*
take: *emp, prehend,
sum*
talk: *lal, loqu*
tallow: *sebi*
taste: *gust, sag*
tax: *cens*
teach: *doc*
tear apart: *vuls*
teardrop: *lachry*
tell: *lect*
temple: *fan*
ten: *dec, deca*
tend: *cult*
terrible: *din*
test (verb): *prob*
testicle: *didym,
orchid*
the (Arabic): *al*
thick: *dens, pachy*
thin: *lepto*
think true: *dogma*

third: *ter*
this side of: *cis-*
thorny: *acantho*
thorough: *dia-*
thoroughly: *ex-,
per-*
thoughts: *noo*
thousand: *chilias,
kilo, mil*
thread: *capill, fil,
mit, nema*
threaten: *men*
three: *tri* (both
Greek and Latin)
through: *dia-, per-*
throughout: *ana-,
cata-*
throw: *bal, disc,
jac*
thrust: *trud, tund*
thunder: *bront*
tick: *acar*
tie (verb): *lig, nect*
tight: *ang, steno*
time: *chron, temp*
tip: *apic*
to: *ad-, ob-*
to be: *esse*
toe: *dactyl, digit*
together: *com-,
syn-*
tomb: *taph*
tone: *ton*
tongue: *gloss, ling*
tonsil: *amyg*
tool: *organ*
tooth: *dens, odont*
topple: *gru*
touch: *tact*
tough: *rob*
toward: *ad-, in-,
ob-*
trace (noun): *vestig*
track down: *hegei*
trade (verb): *merc*
transparent: *hyal*
treatment: *iat, thera*
tree: *arbol, dendro*
trees: *silv*
tribe: *phyl*
trick: *fall*
trough: *alveol*
true: *ver*
true meaning: *etym*
trust: *cred, fid*
try: *per*
tumor: *-oma, onc*
tumult: *turb*

turmoil: *turb*
turn: *torn, stroph,
trop, vert*
twelve: *dodeca*
twenty: *icos*
twice: *bi, di*
twin: *didym, diplo*
twist: *plex, stroph,
tort*
two-fold: *diplo*
two: *bi, di, dich,
du*

U

umbilicus: *omphal*
uncovered: *aper*
under: *hypo-, sub-*
unequal: *aniso*
unite: *hen*
united: *gam, zyg*
up: *ana-*
upon: *epi-*
upward: *ana-*
urge: *hort, suas*
urine: *ur*
usage: *nom*
use (verb): *us*
uterus: *hyster, uter*

V

vain (in): *frustr*
vain: *van*
vapor: *atmo*
vary: *var*
vein: *phleb, varic,
ven*
verbal attack:
polem
vessel: *angi, can*
view: *-orama*
viewing: *the*
vigor: *vin*
virgin: *parthen*
vision: *op*
voice: *phon, voc*

W

wagon: *car*
wail: *plor*
walk: *amb*
wall: *sep(t), val*
wall (of a room):
mur, parie
wall off: *phrag*

wander: *err*
wandering: *vag*
war: *bell, guerr*
ward off: *arc, par*
warmth: *cal*
warn: *mon, mun*
wash (verb): *lav*
watch: *scop*
watchful: *vig*
water: *aqu, hyd,
lacu, limn*
wave: *und*
wax: *cer*
waxy: *sebi*
way: *od, vi*
weak: *lepto*
weaken: *lys*
wealth: *ops, plut*
weapon: *arm*
wear out: *trit*
weary: *langu*
weave: *tex*
wedge: *cune, sphen*
weigh: *pend*
weight: *liber, pond*
well: *bene, dext, eu*
western: *hesper*
wheel: *cycl, rot,
troch*
whip: *flagell*
white: *alb, blanc,
leuk*
whiteness: *cand*
whole: *hol, salu*
wide: *eury, lat*
wife: *uxor*
wild: *agr*
will power: *bul*
wind: *anem, flat,
pneu, vent*
windbag: *foll*
window: *fenestra*
windpipe: *bronch,
trach*
wine: *oeno, vin*
wing: *al, pen, pter*
winglike: *pter*
winter: *hibern*
wipe clean: *terg*
wisdom: *soph*
wise: *sag*
wish: *vol*
with: *com-, syn-*
within: *endo-,
ento-, eso-, in-,
intra-*

without: *an-, ex-,
    extra-, sans-,
    sine*
witness: *test*
woman: *femin,
    gyn*
womb: *hyster, uter*
wonder at: *mir*
woo: *nub*
wood: *hylo, lign,
    xylo*
wool: *lan*
word: *ep, erg, lect,
    logo, verb*
work: *labor, ops*
world: *cosm, mund*
worm: *helminth,
    lumbri, verm*
worse: *pejor*
worship: *latr*
worth: *dign, val*
worthy: *ax, dign*
wound: *trauma*
wrestle: *luct*
wretched: *miser*
write: *gram, scrib*
wrong: *caco-, dys-,
    mis-*

X

X-ray: *rad*

Y

year: *ann*
yellow: *chrys, flav,
    lut, xanth*
yoke: *zyg*
young: *hebe, jun,
    neo*

Appendix B
Root Frequency List

Where there are multiple forms of a root, only the first is given; see the listed family for additional forms.
Decisions as to placement into a particular category are those of the authors.
The reader is advised to commit these roots and their meanings to memory.

HIGH FREQUENCY

ab- (away)
ac (sharp)
acro (high)
act (to do, move)
ad- (to, toward)
aeri (air)
alb (white)
all (other)
alt (high)
alter (other)
amb (walk)
ambi (around, both)
amph (around, both sides)
an- (not)
ana- (again)
anim (breath, spirit)
ann (year)
ante- (before)
anth (flower)
anthropo (man)
anti- (against)
apo- (away)
apt (to grasp)
aqu (water)
arm (to shield)
aud (hear)
aug (increase)
auto (self)

bal (throw)
bas (step)
bat (strike, beat)
bene (good, well)
bi (two)
bibli (book)
bio (life)
brev (short)

caco (bad)
cad (fall)
cal (heat)
camera (room)
cap (to hold, seize)
capit (head)
carn (meat)
cata- (down)

cent (hundred)
centr (point, center)
cephal (head)
chrom (color)
chron (time)
cide (kill)
circum- (around)
cis (kill)
clam (shout)
clar (clear)
clud (close)
com- (with, together)
contr- (against)
cord (heart)
corp (body)
cosm (world)
cover (cover)
crac (rule, power)
cred (believe)
cresc (increase)
cruc (cross)
culp (guilt, blame)
cult (tend, care for)
cur (to run)
cur (to tend, concern)
cuss (to strike)
cycl (circle, wheel)

de- (away, down)
dec (ten)
deca (ten)
dei (God; god)
dem (people)
dent (tooth)
derm (skin)
di (two)
dia- (across, through)
dic (to speak)
digit (finger, toe)
dign (worth)
diplo (two-fold)
dis- (apart, away)
dom (master)
don (give)

dors (back of)
du (two)
duc (to lead)
dys- (abnormal, wrong)

ecto- (outside)
ego (self; I)
en- (Greek; in)
en- (Latin; in)
endo- (within)
epi- (upon)
equ (equal)
erg (work)
ero (sexual love)
eu (good, well)
ex- (out)
exo- (outside)
extra- (beyond)

fab (to speak)
fac (to make, do)
fer (to carry)
fid (to trust, believe)
fig (to form)
fin (to end)
firm (firm)
fiss (to split)
fix (to attach)
flect (to bend)
flu (to flow)
foli (leaf)
form (shape)
fort (strong)
frac (to break)
frat (brother)
fug (to flee)

gam (marriage)
gen (birth, nation, race)
geo (earth)
ger (to carry, bear)
glob (ball, sphere)
gloss (tongue)
gno (to know

gon (angle)
gon (seed, semen)
grad (step)
gram (write)
grat (please)
grav (heavy)
greg (flock)

hem (blood)
hemi (half)
heter (other)
hol (whole)
hom (man)
homo (same)
hyd (water)
hyper- (over, beyond)
hypo- (under)

in- (in)
in- (not)
inter- (between)
intra- (within)
iso (same)
it (to go)
-itis (inflammation of)

jac (to throw)
jour (day)
jud (to judge)
jun (young)
jur (to swear)

lav (to wash)
lat (to carry, bear)
lect (word)
leg (read)
leg (law)
lev (to lift, raise)
lig (to bind, tie)
ling (tongue)
lith (stone)
loco (place)
logo (word)
long (long)
loqu (to speak)

761

luc (light, clear)
lud (to play)
lun (moon)
lys (to loosen)

macro (large)
magn (large)
mal (bad, badly)
man (hand)
mania (craze, madness)
masc (male)
mater (mother)
med (heal, care for)
med (middle)
mega (large)
men (Greek; moon, crescent)
men (Latin; month, measure)
mer (part)
meso- (middle)
meta- (later)
metr (measure)
micro (small)
mil (thousand)
mini (small)
mis- (wrong, badly)
miss (to send)
mod (mode, measure)
mono (single, alone)
mont (mountain)
morph (shape, form)
mort (death)
mov (to move)
multi (many)
mut (to change)

nat (birth)
ne-, (not)
nect (tie, bind)
neo (new)
noc (night)
nom (Greek; law)
nom (Latin; name)
non- (not)
norm (rule)

ob- (against)
oct (eight)
omni (all)
onym (name)
ord (order)
orth (straight)

pac (peace)
pan (all)
pan (bread)
par (equal)
par (equip)
para- (alongside)
parl (talk)
part (part)
ped (foot)
ped (child)
pend (hang)
penta (five)
per- (through)
peri- (around)
pet (seek)
petal (leaf, plate)
phil (love of)
phob (fear)
phon (sound)
phor (to bear)
phyll (leaf)
physi (nature, life)
plac (to please)
plas (to mold)
plen (full)
pod (foot)
poli (city)
poly (many)
pon (to place)
port (to carry)
post- (after)
pre- (before)
prehend (seize, grasp)
press (press)
prim (first)
pro- (Latin; before)
pro- (Greek; before)
proto (first)
psych (mind)
punct (point)

quadr (four)
quer (to seek)

rad (root)
re- (again)
rect (straight)
retro- (backward)
rog (ask)
rupt (break)

sacr (holy)
sal (leap)
salu (healthy, whole)
sanct (holy)
sat (filled)

scop (view)
scrib (to write)
se- (apart, away)
sect (to cut)
sed (to sit)
semi (half)
sen (old)
sens (feeling)
sequ (to follow)
sex (six)
sign (sign)
simil (same)
sist (to stand)
sol (alone)
solut (loosen)
son (sound)
spec (to see)
sperm (seed)
spir (to breathe)
spond (to pledge)
spor (seed)
stas (stand, place)
stat (to stand, set)
ster (solid)
string (to pull tight)
struct (to build)
sub- (under)
sum (to take)
super- (over, beyond)
syn- (with, together)

tact (to touch)
tect (to cover)
tele- (from afar)
temp (time)
ten (Latin; hold)
ten (Greek; stretch)
ten (Latin; stretch)
term (end, boundary)
terr (earth)
tetra (four)
theo (God)
therm (heat)
thes (place)
tom (to cut)
top (place)
tract (to pull, draw)
trans- (across)
tri (Greek; three)
tri (Latin; three)
trop (to turn)
troph (to nourish)

ulter- (beyond, last)
uni (one)

vect (to carry)
ven (to come)
ver (green)
ver (truth)
vert (turn)
vi (road)
vid (to see)
vit (life, living)
voc (to call)
vol (to roll)

zo (animal, life)

acu (needle)
adrenal (kidneys)
agog (leading)
agon (to drive)
agora (marketplace)
agr (field)
al (wing, armpit)
al (Arabic *the*)
al (nourish)
alg (pain, feeling)
ama (love)
ami (friend)
andr (man)
arch (first, rule)
ard (tree)
art (to join)
asper (rough)
ast (star)
athl (prize)
aur (ear)
aur (gold)
axi (armpit, axle)

bacteri (rod-shaped
  microorganism)
bar (heavy)
bar (impede)
bath (deep)
bell (beautiful)
bell (war)
blanc (white, blank)
blast (shoot, sprout)
bon (good)
brachi (upper arm)
brachy (short)
burs (pouch, bag)

calc (limestone)
calli (beautiful)
camp (field, plain)
can (to sing)
cand (white,
  shining)
card (heart)
carp (fruit)
cart (chart, map)
cast (clean, pure)
caus (cause, reason)
caust (to burn)
cens (to tax, assess)
cephal (head)
cerebr (brain)
cern (to separate)
chasm (opening)

chem (chemistry; to
  pour)
chilias (thousand)
chiro (hand)
chlor (green)
chord (cord)
chrys (golden)
cinem (movement)
cit (community)
cit (set in motion)
clas (breakage,
  division)
clav (key)
clemen (mild)
clim (slope, lean)
cogn (knowledge)
consul (counsel)
cor (crown, curve)
crypt (hidden)
crystal (crystal)
cub (to lie down)
cumu (heap, mass)
cut (skin)

dactyl (finger)
damn (harm,
  damage)
deb (to owe)
dec (proper)
demi (half)
demon (devil)
dendro (tree)
dens (thick,
  crowded)
deuter (second)
dext (right)
dich (two, asunder)
didym (twin;
  testicle)
die (day)
disc (to throw)
do (to give)
doc (to teach)
dol (pain)
dorm (to sleep)
drom (run, course)
dur (strong, hard)

eco (home,
  environment)
edi (to build,
  improve)
electr (shining)
embryo (growing)

-emia (diseased
  blood condition)
emp (to buy)
entero (intestine)
ento- (within)
entom (insect)
err (to wander)
-escence (becoming)
esse (being)
esthes (feeling)

fabr (to fit together)
facies (appearance)
fall (to trick,
  deceive)
fasc (band, sash)
fatu (foolish)
felic (happy, fertile)
femin (woman)
fend (to strike)
ferr (iron)
ferv (to boil)
fest (festive)
fet (to stink)
fil (son, daughter)
fil (thread)
flag (to burn)
flagell (whip)
flat (to flow)
flic (to strike)
flor (to blossom)
foc (focus)
foll (windbag)
found (bottom)
fri (to rub)
fruc (fruit)
fum (smoke)
funct (to perform)
fus (to pour)

galact (milk)
germ (bud, shoot,
  fetus)
glac (ice)
gland (acorn)
glyp (to carve)
gov (to govern,
  guide)
gran (grain)
grand (great, large)
gros (large)
gust (taste)
gymn (nude, naked)
gyn (woman)
gyr (circle, wheel)

hab (to hold, have)
hect (hundred)
hedr (chair)
helio (sun)
her (to leave behind)
her (to stick to)
hex (six)
hier (holy)
hum (earth)
hymn (ode)
hyster (womb)

icon (image)
ide (form)
idio (one's own)
ign (fire)
infra- (below)
integ (whole, entire)

juxta- (next to)

kilo (thousand)

lab (lip)
labor (to work)
lact (milk)
lap (to fall)
lat (wide, side)
laud (praise)
leps (seize)
leuk (white)
lib (book)
liber (free)
liber (scales)
lic (allow)
liter (letter)
lymph (fluid)

magis (master)
magnet (magnet)
mamm (breast)
mar (sea)
mela (black, dark)
mem (mindful)
ment (mind)
merg (to dip,
  plunge)
metro (mother)
migr (to move)
misc (mixture)
miser (wretched)
miso (hate)
mon (warn)
mor (custom)

mun (common, public)
mur (wall)
myc (fungus)
myel (marrow)
myo (muscle)

nas (nose)
nav (ship)
nerv (nerve)
neur (nerve)
noc (harm)
not (mark, note)
nov (new)
nub (marry)
nucl (kernel)
nud (naked, stripped)
null (none)
num (number)
nunci (announce)
nur (nourish)

ocul (eye)
odont (tooth)
odyn (pain)
oid (similar to)
-oma (tumor, mass)
oo (egg)
oophor (ovary)
op (eye, vision)
ops (plenty, wealth)
ophthalm (eye)
ora (mouth, speech)
orb (circle, disk, orb)
organ (tool)
ornis (bird)
os (bone)
osc (opening)
-ose (quality of)
-osis (condition of)
ost (bone, shell)
oto (ear)
ov (egg)
ox (sharp)

pachy (thick)
pale(o) (ancient)
palin- (backward)
pand (spread out)
par (to show)
pass (suffer)
past (feed)
pater (father)
path (feeling, disease)
pel (push)

pen (almost)
pen (wing)
pen (punish)
petro (rock)
phag (to eat)
phan (to show)
phos (light)
phras (to show)
phren (mind)
phyl (tribe)
phyt (plant)
pict (to paint)
plan (level)
plang (to lament)
platy (flat)
plaud (to clap)
-ple (fold)
pleg (stroke)
pleur (side)
plex (fold)
plor (to cry out)
plur (many, more)
pneu (breath)
polio (gray)
popul (people)
port (haven)
pot (power)
prec (price)
prec (prayer)
priv (alone, single)
prob (to test)
prop(ri) (one's own)
prox (next to)
pseudo (false)
pter (wing, feather)
pug (to fight)
pur (to cleanse)

quin (five)

rad (spoke of wheel)
rat (reason, ratio)
ren (kidney)
rhizo (root)
rhod (red)
rob (strong, hard)
rod (to eat, gnaw)
rrh (to flow)

sag (wise)
sang (blood)
sans- (without)
sarc (flesh)
saur (lizard)
scan (to climb)
schis (to split)
sci (to know)
scind (to cut, split)

semper (always)
sep(t) (partition)
ser (to join, arrange)
serv (slave)
serv (protect)
sider (star)
sin (bend, curve)
sine (without)
sit (food)
soc (companion)
sol (comfort)
sol (sun)
soma (body)
somn (sleep)
sorb (to suck in)
sort (lot, fortune)
stell (star)
steno (narrow)
stig (pricked)
stl (to send)
stom (mouth)
strat (layer)
stroph (twisted, turn)
styl (column)
styl (manner)
suas (advise, urge)

tab (board)
tax (arrange)
techn (cover)
test (witness)
the (viewing)
ton (to stretch, tone)
tort (to twist)
tox (poison)
trauma (hurt, wound)
trib (allot)
trud (to thrust)
turb (to agitate)
typ (mold, die)

ur (urine)
urb (city)
us (to use, utilize)

vac (empty)
vag (wandering)
val (worth, strong)
vap (steam, cloud)
var (to vary, bend)
vas (vessel)
ventr (belly)
verb (word)
verm (worm)
vest (to clothe)

vict (to conquer)
vir (man)
vol (to wish)
vor (to eat)
vuls (to tear apart)

xeno (stranger)
xero (dry)

acantho (thorny, spiny)
acar (mite, tick)
acou (hear)
actin (rays)
adelph (brother)
adjut (to help, assist)
ailur (cat)
alveol (trough, pit)
amoeba (change)
amyg (almond; tonsil)
amyl (starch)
anem (wind)
ang (narrow)
angel (messenger)
angi (vessel)
angui (snake)
aniso (unequal)
annel (rim, ring)
anom (lawlessness)
aper (opne)
api (bee)
apic (apex)
arachn (spider)
arb (tree)
arbit (to consider, judge)
arc (arch, bow)
arc (ward off)
aren (sand)
arg (silver)
aristo (best)
arithm (amount, numbers)
as (ass, donkey)
atmo (vapor)
aver (desire)
avi (bird)
ax (worthy)

bacci (berry, seed)
bacill (rod; bacteria)
bapt (to immerse)
beat (happy)
benth (bottom of sea)
bib (to drink)
bract (leaf, plate)
branchi (gills)
bronch (windpipe)
bront (thunder)
bry (moss)
bucc (cheek)

bul (will power)
bull (to boil)

calx (heel)
calyc (cup)
calyp (covered)
camb (change)
campan (bells)
can (dog)
can (reed)
cant (side)
capill (hair, thread)
car (cart, wagon)
carcin (cancer, crab)
carp (pluck, seize)
caten (chain)
cathar (pure)
caud (tail)
caul (stalk, stem)
cav (hollow)
cav (take heed)
caval (horse)
cel (hide)
cel (sky)
celeb (famous)
celer (swift)
cen (common)
ceno (empty)
ceno (new, recent)
cer (wax)
cera (horn, cornea)
cerc (tail)
chalco (copper, brass)
chel (claw)
chiasma (crosswise)
chlamyd (cloak, mantle)
chol (gall)
chondr (cartilage)
chor (dance)
chor (place)
chthon (earth)
cili (eyebrow)
cinct (to gird)
ciner (ashes)
cinque (five)
cirr (lock, curl)
cis (on this side of)
clad (shoot, sprout)
cohors (court)
col (filter, flow)
cole (sheath)
coll (neck)
coll (glue)

cond (to hide)
cop (to cut)
copr (dung, feces)
coqu (to cook)
corn (horn)
cost (side)
cotyl (cup-shaped)
cras (mixing)
creat (meat, flesh)
crep (to crackle)
crim (judgment)
crin (separate)
crin (hair)
crymo (cold)
cryo (cold)
cten (comb-like)
ctet (to acquire)
cun (cone, wedge)
cup (desire)
cupr (copper)
cusp (point)
cyan (blue)
cyn (dog)

dei (to show)
dele (to erase)
desm (ligament, band)
din (terrible)
dodeca (twelve)
dogma (to think true)
drama (to work, to do)
dulc (sweet)
dyn (powerful)
dysi (to put on, as clothing)

ebr (to drink)
eccles (church)
ech (echo)
echin (spiny, prickly)
ed (to eat)
edaph (ground, bottom)
eid (form)
elasm (plate)
elast (ductile)
eleuthero (free)
enigm (puzzle)
ennea (nine)
ens (sword)
eo (dawn)

ep (word, speech)
equ (horse)
erem (alone)
eschat (last things)
eso- (within)
estr (gadfly)
eth (custom)
ethn (nation)
etym (true meaning)
eury (broad, wide)
ev (age)

fan (temple)
far (flour)
farc (to stuff)
fe (cattle, fee)
fecund (fruitful)
fel (cat)
fenestra (window)
fer (to strike)
fet (to stink)
fibr (fiber)
fisc (purse)
flav (yellow)
for (outdoors)
fortu (lot, chance)
foss (to dig)
fran (free)
frustr (in vain)
furc (fork)
fusc (dark, cloudy)
fut (to strike)

gage (pledge)
gar (to protect)
gel (freeze)
gel (laugh)
genu (knee)
ger (old age)
geran (crane)
giga (giant)
glad (sword)
glau (silvery gray)
glut (glue)
gramin (grass)
gru (to collapse)
guerr (war)
gutt (drop)

hagio (sacred)
hal (salt)
hal (breath)
haplo (single)
hebe (young)
hedon (pleasure)

-hedron (geometric plane)
hegei (to track down)
helic (spiral)
helminth (worm)
hemer (day)
hen (one, unite)
hendeca (eleven)
hepa (liver)
hept (seven)
herpe (snake)
hesper (evening)
heur (to find)
hex (have, hold)
hiat (gap)
hibern (winter)
hidr (sweat)
hipp (horse)
hor (season of year)
horm (to excite)
horr (to shudder)
hort (to urge, incite)
hyal (glass, transparent)
hygi (health)
hygr (moisture)
hylo (wood, matter)
hymen (membrane)
hypno (sleep)
hyster- (later)

iat (healing)
ichthy (fish)
icos (twenty)
icter (jaundice)
idem (same)
inan (empty)
infer (low)
insul (island)
ir (anger)
irid (iris)
ische (suppress, check)
ithy (straight)

keto (ketone)
klept (to steal)

lachry (teardrop)
lacu (lake)
lagn (erotic desire)
lal (to babble)
lam (leaf)
lan (wool)
langu (faint, weary)
lapid (stone)
lat (lie hidden)

latr (worship of)
lax (loose)
lect (choose)
leg (charge, send)
leni (mild)
lent (pea)
lep (scales, scaly)
lepto (thin, slender)
leth (death)
lid (damage)
lign (wood)
limi (mud)
limn (fresh water)
lin (line, cord)
linq (to leave)
lip (fat)
lox (oblique)
lubr (slippery)
lucr (money, profit)
luct (struggle)
lumbri (worm)
lut (yellow)

machy (struggle)
macu (blemish, spot)
malac (soft, mollusk)
maur (dark, dim)
medull (marrow)
mel (song, melody)
melior (better)
mell (honey)
man (to stay, remain)
men (to threaten)
mend (fault)
mening (membrane)
mens (table)
mentul (penis)
merc (buy, trade)
mi (to close)
mim (imitate)
mio (less)
mir (to wander at)
mit (thread)
mne (memory)
mol (mass, bulk)
mol (soft)
mol (grind)
mora (delay, remain)
mord (bite)
muc (moldy)
mun (protect)
mund (world)
mus (mouse)
myc (mucus)

myx (mucus, slime)

narc (stupor)
nat (swim)
naus (ship)
necr (corpse)
nema (thread)
nephr (kidney)
nes (island)
neth (under)
nid (nest)
nihil (nothing)
niv (snow)
nod (knot)
noo (mind)
nost (home)
nov (nine)
nub (marry)
nut (nod)
nyct (night)

od (sing)
od (road)
od (hate)
oeno (wine)
ol (oil)
oligo (few)
ombro (rain)
omphal (navel)
on (burden)
oneir (dream)
onom (name)
onto (being)
onych (fingernail)
ophi (snake)
opt (choice)
optim (best)
-orama (a view)
orch (dance)
orchid (testicle)
orex (appetite)
ori (to arise)
orn (to deck)
oro (mountain)
-ory (place where)
oryct (fossil)
osm (pushing)
osm (smell)
oti (ease, leisure)
ox (sharp)

pal (stake in ground)
par (give birth to)
parie (wall of a room)
parthen (virgin)
pecca (sin)

pect (comb-like)
pector (chest, breast)
pecu (cattle, money)
ped (ground, earth)
pejor (worse)
pel (skin)
pelag (sea)
pep (to cook, ripen)
per (to try, risk)
petit (small)
phall (penis)
phleb (vein)
phleg (to burn, fever)
phrag (to wall off)
phylax (guard, prevention)
physo (air, gas)
pi (devout)
pico (small)
pil (hair)
pisc (fish)
pithec (ape)
ple (more)
pleb (people, masses)
plesios (near)
-ploid (fold)
plum (feather)
plut (riches)
poe (to make, create)
pol (to sell)
pol (to polish)
polem (verbal attack)
pom (apple, fruit)
pot (to drink)
preter (beyond)
prol (offspring)
psychro (cold)
pt(o) (to fall)
pud (to be ashamed)
put (to cut)
pyr (fire)

quie (to rest)
quot (how many)

rachi (back of body)
rad (scrape)
ram (branch, root)
raj (ruler)
rap (to snatch)
rep (to creep)
ret (net)
rhino (nose)

rhomb (to spin)
rid (laugh)
rig (stiff)
rot (wheel)
rub (red)
rud (ruins)

sagitt (arrow)
sal (salt)
sapr (rotten)
sax (rock)
scal (ladder)
sch (form, appearance)
scho (leisure)
scler (hard)
seb (tallow)
sec (dry)
sed (calm)
seism (shake)
sem (sign, symbol)
semin (seed, semen)
sep (rot)
sept (seven)
sepul (to bury)
serr (saw, noun)
sever (harsh, stern)
sider (iron)
silv (forest, trees)
soph (wisdom)
sopor (stupor)

soror (sister)
sper (hope)
sphen (wedge)
stal (standing place)
stich (stride, step)
stle (to send)
stup (stunned)
sud (perspire, sweat)
sues (to accustom)
sui (oneself)
sut (to sew)

tac (silent)
tach (speed)
tail (to cut)
taph (tomb)
taur (bull)
tel (end)
temn (to hate)
ter (third)
terg (to wipe clean)
tex (to weave)
thall (flourish, bloom)
thanat (death)
theca (case)
thera (treatment)
thym (mind)
torn (turn)
trach (windpipe)
trib (oppress)

tric (hindrance)
tricho (hair)
trit (to rub)
troch (wheel, running)
tub (to swell up)
tuit (to watch)
tum (to swell)
tund (to strike)
turg (to swell)
tyro (cheese)

uber (fruitful)
um (moist)
umb (shade, shadow)
unct (oil, ointment)
und (wave)
ur (tail)
ure (to burn)
uter (uterus)
uxor (wife)

vacca (cow)
vad (to go, step)
vagin (sheath)
val (wall)
valv (hinged door)
van (empty)
varic (enlarged vein)
veloc (speed)

ven (to sell)
ven (vein)
vent (wind)
vesic (bladder, blister)
vestig (track, trace)
vibr (to shake)
vic (substitute)
vig (watchful)
vin (wine)
vin (strength)
vio (strength)
vir (poison)
vitr (glass)
vol (to fly)
vol (to wish)
vot (to speak solemnly)
vulg (common people)

xanth (yellow)
xiph (sword)
xylo (wood)

zyg (to join)
zym (to ferment)

WORKS CONSULTED

Abrams, M. H., *A Glossary of Literary Terms*, 3rd Edition. New York: Holt, Rinehart and Winston, Inc., 1985.

Alexander, Henry, *The Story of Our Language*. Garden City, New York: Dolphin Books (Doubleday & Company, Inc.), 1962.

American Heritage Dictionary of the English Language, The, William Morris, Editor. Boston: Houghton Mifflin Company, 1975.

American Heritage Dictionary of Indo-European Roots (revised and edited by Calvert Watson). Boston: Houghton Mifflin Co., 1985.

Ayers, Donald M., *English Words from Latin and Greek Elements*. Tucson: The University of Arizona Press, 1965.

Bartlett, John, *Familiar Quotations*. Boston: Little, Brown and Company, 1980.

Black, Henry Campbell, *Black's Law Dictionary*. St. Paul: West Publishing Co., 1979.

Borror, Donald J., *Dictionary of Word Roots and Combining Forms*. Palo Alto: Mayfield Publishing Company, 1960.

Castillo, Carlos, and Otto F. Bond, *Spanish Dictionary*. Chicago: The University of Chicago Press, 1972.

Claiborne, Robert, *The Roots of English*. New York: Times Books, 1989.

Funk, Wilfred, *Word Origins and Their Romantic Stories*. New York: Bell Publishing Company, 1978.

Gamkrelidze, Thomas V. and V. V. Ivanov, "The Early History of Indo-European Languages," *Scientific American*, March 1990.

Greene, Amsel, *Word Clues*. New York: Barnes & Noble, Inc., 1967.

Harvard Dictionary of Music, Willi Apel, Editor. Cambridge, Mass.: Harvard University Press, 1965.

Jespersen, Otto, *Growth and Structure of the English Language*. New York: The Free Press, 1968.

Johnson, Edwin Lee, *Latin Words of Common English*. New York: D. C. Heath and Company, 1931.

Mawson, C. O. Sylvester, *Dictionary of Foreign Terms*, Second Edition. New York: Crowell Publishers, 1975.

New Cassell's German Dictionary, The, Henry T. Betteridge, Editor. New York: Funk & Wagnalls, 1962.

Partridge, Eric, *Origins: A Short Etymological Dictionary of Modern English*. New York: The Macmillan Company, 1961.

Random House Dictionary of the English Language, The, College Edition, Laurence Urdang, Editor-in-Chief. New York: Random House, 1968.

Robertson, Stuart, and Frederic G. Cassidy, *The Development of Modern English*, 2nd Edition. Englewood Cliffs, N.J.: Prentice-Hall, 1954.

Shevoroshkin, Vitaly, "The Mother Tongue: How Linguists Have Constructed the Ancestor of All Living Languages," *The Sciences*, May/June 1990.

Smith, Robert W. L., *Dictionary of English Word Roots*. Totawa, New Jersey: Littlefield, Adams & Co., 1966.

Taber's Cyclopedic Medical Dictionary, Edition 14, Clayton L. Thomas, Editor. Philadelphia: F. A. Davis Company, 1981.

Thrall, William Flint, and Addison Hibbard, *A Handbook to Literature*. Indianapolis: The Odyssey Press, 1972.

Webster's New World Dictionary of the English Language, Third College Edition, Victoria Neufeldt, Editor in Chief. New York: Webster's New World, 1988.

Webster's Third New International Dictionary, Unabridged, Philip Babcock Cove, Editor. Springfield, Massachusetts: G & C Merriam Company, Publishers, 1976.

Word Mysteries & Histories. Boston: Houghton Mifflin co., 1986.

ABOUT THE AUTHORS

Horace Gerald Danner

Dr. Danner is from Elamville, Alabama. He attended Troy State University, Troy, Alabama; he graduated with a B.A. in Social Sciences from the University of the Philippines, Quezon City.

He holds a Bachelor of Music and a Master of Education from New Orleans Baptist Theological Seminary, New Orleans, Louisiana. He has done additional graduate work at the following universities: University of Virginia, Charlottesville; James Madison University, Harrisonburg, Virginia; George Washington University, Washington, D.C.; and George Mason University, Fairfax, Virginia.

He received the Ph.D. in Education from The American University, Washington, D.C.

Together with Dr. Noël, Dr. Danner co-authored *An Introduction to an Academic Vocabulary* (Lanham: UPA, 1990).

He divides his time between writing educational materials and speaking at various educational activities.

Dr. Danner has three children and four grandchildren: Nathan, Alissa, Margaret Anne, and Donna Jean.

Roger Noël

Dr. Noël was born in Wallonia, the French-speaking part of Belgium. He received a *Licence en Philosophie et Lettres* (Dutch, German, English) from the University of Liège, Belgium; a Master's in French from the University of Missouri in Columbia, Missouri; and a Ph.D. in French Language and Literature from Washington University in St. Louis, Missouri.

Dr. Noël taught French and Italian for several years at the University of Missouri in St. Louis. During the writing of this book, he was chair of the Department of Modern Foreign Languages at Monmouth College, Monmouth, Illinois; he is now chair of the Department of Modern Foreign Languages at Georgia College, Milledgeville, Georgia.

He is the author of *Joufroi de Poitiers: Traduction Critique* (New York: Peter Lang, 1987); he is also co-author of *An Introduction to an Academic Vocabulary* (Lanham: UPA, 1990). In addition, he is co-editor of the *Journal of Baltic Studies*, 1991-1996. He is currently working on an English translation of Gian Enrico Rusconi's *La teoria critica della società*.

On August 6, 1991, the French government bestowed upon Dr. Noël the decoration *Chevalier dans l'ordre des Palmes Académiques*.

In addition to teaching, writing, and making scholarly translations, he is also a commercial translator, most recently translating into French the *Official Guide to the 1988 Seoul Olympic Games*, and Burger King Corporation manuals.

Dr. Noël and his wife Cookie have two daughters.

COLOPHON

From Greek *Kolophon* (κολοφων), **summit,** or **final touch.**
Or perhaps, *colophon* is from Greek *kolophos* (κολοφωξ),
which was the name of the very last island in the Greek chain of islands;
hence, the last page of a Greek document was called *colophon.*

The roots of this book were first garnered from a number of sources, and then entered into a database using an IBM PC XT with the program dBase III; as words from these roots were located, they were entered into the program. Even with the aid of dBase III, it took the authors approximately three years simply to enter the words and to categorize them.

It took an additional two years to refine the data and to have the thesaurus checked by the authors, editors, and professional readers.

Craig Prall then transferred the file from the PC to a Macintosh using TOPS networking software. The book was then converted from the dBase format to a text file. Finally, the text file was read into Microsoft Word and placed into tables. The authors continued to add to the reservoir of words and to further refine the format. The final product was formatted on an Apple Macintosh IIsi™ with a Radius Pivot™ monitor and Key Tronic extended keyboard. The camera-ready copy was printed on a Texas Instruments microLaser™ PS35 PostScript™ laser printer.